Richard Holmes

is the author of *Footsteps: Adventures of a Romantic Biographer* (1985), described by Michael Holroyd as 'a modern master-piece', *Coleridge: Early Visions*, winner of the 1989 Whitbread Book of the Year Prize, and *Dr Johnson & Mr Savage*, winner of the 1993 James Tait Black Prize. *Shelley: The Pursuit*, which won the Somerset Maugham Prize in 1974 when it was originally published, was Richard Holmes's extraordinary first book. Now, after twenty years, it has established itself as a classic account of one of the great rebels of Romantic literature. 'It is an attempt,' reflects Holmes in his new Preface, 'to write biography as a form of modern epic, in which speed of action, colour and move-ment, travel and the sense of poetic adventure, predominate over everything else.' He is a Fellow of the Royal Society of Literature and in 1992 was made an OBE. He lives in London and Norwich, with the novelist Rose Tremain.

SHELLEY

THE PURSUIT

RICHARD HOLMES

Flamingo
An Imprint of HarperCollinsPublishers

To Helen Rogan and Margaret Amaral

Flamingo
An Imprint of HarperCollins*Publishers*
77–85 Fulham Palace Road,
Hammersmith, London W6 8JB

Published by Flamingo 1995
9 8 7 6 5 4 3 2 1

First published in Great Britain by
Weidenfeld and Nicolson 1974
Second hardback edition published by HarperCollins 1994

Author photograph by Irmeli Jung

ISBN 0 00 638671 7

Set in Bembo

Printed in Great Britain by
HarperCollinsManufacturing Glasgow

Contents

Contents

Illustrations

Photographs not attributed have been taken by the author.

Preface to
the New Edition (1994)

This is a young man's book. I completed it at the age of 29, the same age at which Shelley drowned in the Gulf of Spezia. It shares something of the recklessness of its subject, the pursuer and the pursued. I think it should remain like that. It is an attempt to write literary biography as a form of modern epic, in which speed of action, colour and movement, travel and the sense of poetic adventure, predominate over everything else. 'I always go on until I am stopped,' said Shelley, 'and I never am stopped.' I still think this is the essential truth about his remarkable life, which continues so vividly into the present day, a restless and demanding presence for each younger generation to encounter.

Looking back after twenty years, I see more clearly the partialities and enthusiasms in what I researched and wrote, angrily rejecting much of the critical tradition, returning to original sources, and following Shelley everywhere over his own ground through England, Ireland, France and Italy. I have described the intense, dreamlike obsession of this work – a process of trial and error and self-education – in my later book, *Footsteps*. I have made some corrections and reparations (especially to Mary Shelley) there. But I believe the political and philosophical focus of the biography, the sense of Shelley's energy and intellectual power, his impetuous physical impact on all those around him, still holds good. So I am content, on reflection, to let the book stand as a true history of my time in Shelley's company. Others wiser and more scholarly than myself will continue to correct it, and to that end I have included a New Select Bibliography of more recent studies, many critical of aspects of my own work, which I urge the reader to consult. But above all I urge the re-reading of Shelley's poetry and essays, especially after 1816: no other Romantic writer *learned*, and changed, and developed his art so swiftly.

The open-ended nature of biography is one of its mysterious attractions. No *Life* is ever definitive: it draws or rejects from past work, it reflects often unconsciously the concerns and questions of its own age, and it passes on something hidden to the future. Every serious attempt at an historic portrait of the dead will subtly absorb the *milieu* and temperament of its living author, however objective he or she sets out to be. This is precisely the strength, rather than the weakness, of its subjectivity. It is the vital element that Hippolyte Taine, the first great European theorist of biography, curiously overlooked in his efforts to define a 'scientific' genre of Life Studies, as a sort of human botany. Biography is only scientific in the sense that it is experimental: it tests one version of the facts. But all good biography must do more, must risk more, if it is to live for any time in the imagination. It must finally transcend facts and documentation, and risk an artistic style and form appropriate to its age.

It is now evident to me that this biography, as I put it in *Footsteps*, was written by 'a child of the English 1960s'. Nevertheless that happened to be a particularly fruitful moment to rediscover Shelley's story, with its special explosive mixture of fantasy, poetry and radical ideas, so close to the passionate hopes and aspirations of that time. If the present age of the *fin-de-siècle* is a darker and less certain one, Shelley's peculiar energy and idealism may stand out even more forcefully, a sharp flame against the shadows. What makes him cruel, and even absurd, may also gather a particular and poignant resonance. He, in the end, was a child of the European Enlightenment, and believed that the world could be revolutionized by language, and that fire was the element of imagination.

Much has changed in Shelley studies since I wrote. The Victorian penumbra has dissolved, the shade of Dr Leavis has retreated, and Shelley is again popular with students, though his extra-curricular attractions remain – thankfully – high. A brilliant effort of textual refinement and republication has continued in America, under the scholarly leadership of Donald H. Reiman with the resources of the Carl H. Pforzheimer Library in New York and the Bodleian Library in Oxford. Following K.N. Cameron's pioneering work, much has been clarified in Shelley's socio-political background. A new generation of literary critics has championed Shelley's intellectual gifts, his 'sceptical idealism', and the glimmering metaphorical subtleties of his poetic language. Both deconstructionist and feminist critics have been drawn to his work, with often dazzling results. A notable, and properly maverick, group of British writers and scholars including William St Clair, Paul Foot, Howard Brenton, Claire Tomalin, Angela Leighton, Timothy Webb and P. M. Dawson have explored much that is new and controversial. There have been Shelley novels, Shelley plays, and Shelley films. A valuable scholarly survey and listing of much of this work is available in *The New Shelley: Later*

Twentieth Century Views, edited by G. Kim Blank (St Martin's Press, New York, 1991); and I have included a careful choice from the whole field in my New Select Bibliography.

Some things do not change. André Maurois's charming 'Shelley Romance', famously entitled *Ariel* (the first Penguin biography of 1925), was dashingly re-issued for Shelley's bicentenary. It was a book that I mockingly referred to in my original Introduction, as the cause of much mischief in Shelley's after-life. I found myself in the ironic position of being asked to write a brief panegyric for the back-cover of the new edition (Pimlico, 1991). My feelings about *Ariel* had not changed, but I had come to respect Maurois as an embattled pioneer of French biography, especially in his Lives of *Victor Hugo* (1954), *The Three Dumas* (1957), and above all *Balzac* (1965), which have still not received proper recognition in French criticism. Disguised in the hectic persona of a blurb-writer, I therefore tried to fit Maurois's early and influential experiment with the 'romanced' form into the larger development of Shelley's twentieth-century biography. I reprint here what I finally wrote – after much misgiving – for it bears on the whole complicated question of how biographies grow 'out of date', and yet may still retain a significant literary presence.

This remarkable little book almost succeeded in destroying Shelley's reputation as a serious writer and poet for 50 years. Written in France in the 1920s, it is a sort of Jazz Age biography of the 'bright young things' of Shelley's circle, narrated in a clipped, flippant, risqué style of unparalleled brilliance. Syncopating between fact and fiction, inventing dialogue, sentimentalising love-scenes, colouring-up landscapes, it traces the fiery and unforgettable young poet's disastrous flight-path through a galaxy of 'flapper' girls, the two Harriets, Mary, Eliza, Cornelia, Claire, Emilia, and Jane, until finally quenched in the Gulf of Spezia. The great central period of Shelley's creative work between 1817 and 1821 skims by in a score of effortless pages. Instead, he emerges as the enchanting Ariel-figure, a sexy spark arcing between the philosophic Godwin and the diabolic Byron, half man and half meteorite.

André Maurois later said ruefully that he had written the book to 'exorcise' his own youthful romanticism, but instead had inadvertently canonised it for an entire generation. So *Ariel* is now an historic landmark in modern literary biography, as fine as any miniature produced by Lytton Strachey or Harold Nicolson, a classic reminder of both the power and the perils of the form.

In a way my biography set out to destroy everything that Maurois's stood for. But I now see that it was simply part of a much larger and continuing biographic process of bringing the present to bear imaginatively on the past. One day perhaps a new Taine will define a discipline, if not exactly a science, of Comparative Biography in which we will all have played a part.

My own personal connections with Shelley hauntingly remain. In 1991 I was wrecked in a 28-foot sailing boat in the North Sea, but was pulled to safety with my two companions by an Airsea Rescue helicopter. Thinking again about the mystery of his last days on the Tuscan coast, when he saw visions and wrote the unfinished 'Triumph of Life', I briefly abandoned biography and tried another form of exploration, a radio-drama entitled 'To the Tempest Given'. In 1992 I celebrated his 200th birthday by a more peaceful crossing of the bay of Lerici, in a small fishing boat out of Porto Venere, accompanied by my English rose.

Talking with a younger generation of readers, I see how Shelley has become increasingly a European figure, a Dante among English poets, and an image of Faustian daring, whose writing and travels still inspire that primary spirit of adventure into a wider world of ideal possibilities. Nothing is so moving to the biographer as finding an old copy of his book in a stranger's hands, battered and wine-stained from its voyages, its margins scrawled, its poetry underlined, its pages bent with maps and postcards, its cover bleached with sun and sea. I hope this new edition has such luck.

RICHARD HOLMES, *Paris, July 1994*

Introduction

There will always be Shelley lovers, but this book is not for them. The angel they seek can be found in the golden reminiscences of Trelawny, or the charming romance by André Maurois, or within those innumerable slim selections of Shelley's lyrics whose contents have remained virtually unaltered since the first anthology of 1829, a French edition in an olive cover. That fluttering apparition is not to be found here, where a darker and more earthly, crueller and more capable figure moves with swift pace through a bizarre though sometimes astonishingly beautiful landscape.

Of all the English Romantic poets, Shelley was the most determinedly professional writer. Many years after his death, Wordsworth called him 'one of the best *artists* of us all; I mean in workmanship of style'. By the end of his life Shelley had mastered and translated from Italian, Spanish, German, Latin and Greek, and had rendered several fragments from Arabic. From the very start he was a writer who interested himself in political and philosophic ideas, rather than purely aesthetic ones. In contrast with his younger contemporary John Keats, who cordially disliked him, Shelley's letters and essays are rarely concerned with the subject of Poetry as such, and with the possible exception of Robert Browning, Edward Thomas and perhaps Allen Ginsberg, he has never been a poet's poet in the true sense.

Those celebrated late Italian lyrics – 'To a Skylark', 'The Cloud', 'To Jane', 'When the Lamp is Shattered' – which subsequently established his reputation among a sentimental Victorian reading public, and among generation after generation of schoolchildren, were never of serious concern to Shelley. For the most part they were products of periods of depression and inactivity, haphazard acts of inattention when the main work could not be pushed forward. Throughout his life, Shelley's major creative effort was concentrated on producing a series of long poems and poetic dramas aimed at the main political and spiritual problems of his age and society. He accompanied these with a brilliant but little known series of speculative essays on more practical aspects of the same problems, sometimes witty and original, but always learned and controversial. One can speak of Shelley as a writer in the most comprehensive sense: poet, essayist,

dramatist, pamphleteer, translator, reviewer and correspondent. He was moreover a writer who moved everywhere with a sense of ulterior motive, a sense
of greater design, an acute feeling for the historical moment and an overwhelming consciousness of his duty as an *artist* in the immense and fiery process of
social change of which he knew himself to be a part. Shelley's lyrics were
mere sparks in this comet's trail.

From the age of nineteen, Shelley passed through a series of personal crises,
dictated partly by chance but increasingly by choice, which had the cumulative
effect of forcing him further and further away from the family, class and cultural background into which he had been born. By the time his life was cut
short, one month before his thirtieth birthday, he was a complete exile, both
geographically and spiritually. The encroaching condition of exile plays a
highly significant part in his story. At the time of his death his reputation was
almost literally unspeakable in England, an object to be torn apart between the
conservative and radical reviews, but not on the whole to be mentioned in polite
London society. In this he was quite unlike his aristocratic friend and rival Lord
Byron who, though similarly exiled, always had a tremendous popular following in England, and who by sailing to Greece instantly canonized himself on the
altars of English liberalism. Moreover, while Byron had achieved perhaps the
greatest international readership of the age, Shelley had achieved almost
none. Thus while exile had brought Byron fame and the kind of notoriety that
is quickly transmuted into fashionable glamour, it brought to Shelley both
literary obscurity and personal disrepute. A few days after Shelley's death,
Byron wrote to Tom Moore in London, 'there is thus another man gone about
whom the world was ill-naturedly, and ignorantly, and brutally mistaken' – but
it was a mistake which his Lordship himself had frequently helped to
compound.

Shelley's exile, his defection from his class and the disreputability of his beliefs and behaviour, had a tremendous effect on the carefully partisan handling of
his biography by the survivors of his own circle and generation, and even more
so by that of his son's. In the first, the generation of his family and friends,
fear of the moral and social stigma attached to many incidents in Shelley's
career prevented the publication or even the writing of biographical material
until those who were in possession of it, like Hogg, Peacock and Trelawny,
were respectable Victorians in their sixties, who were fully prepared to forget,
to smudge and to conceal. With one exception, almost no significant biographical material appeared until more than thirty years after his death. Shelley's
second wife, Mary, was the key to his biography both in her own experiences
and in her access to papers. Yet Mary Shelley was actually prevented from writing anything fuller than the brief introduction to Galignani's edition of the

Posthumous Poems in 1824, and the editorial 'Notes' to the first *Complete Works* of 1839–40. She was prevented partly by the same considerations of propriety as Shelley's friends, but even more by the fact that Shelley's father, Sir Timothy Shelley of Field Place, specifically forbade any such publications until after his own death, on pain of the removal of the annuity, Mary's only regular source of income, with which she was just able to support herself and her son – Sir Timothy's grandson and heir – Percy Florence Shelley. Sir Timothy did not hesitate to remind Mary of this interdiction through his solicitor Whittan, and made the ban singularly effective by outliving his detested son by twenty-two years, and dying at the age of 90 in 1844. Mary, who had contented herself with enshrining the remembered image of her husband in a series of noble and emasculated figures in her fiction, especially *The Last Man* (1826) and *Lodore* (1835), died without further revelations only seven years later in 1851.

In the second generation, control of the Shelley papers passed to Boscombe Manor and Sir Percy Florence's wife, Lady Jane Shelley, who made it her life work to establish an unimpeachable feminine and Victorian idealization of the poet. The main obstacles were the irregularities of Shelley's love-life, the radicalism of his political views and the philosophic difficulty of much of his major work. She substituted for them the image of the gentle, suffering lyric poet, a misunderstood man more sinned against than sinning, whose reputation and social standing were gradually rehabilitated. Suppression, alteration and even destruction of certain journals, letters and papers here began in earnest; though to be fair these were not much worse than those already carried out by friends like Hogg. But the cumulative distortion became large. Moreover, the vetting and control which Lady Jane exercised over the chosen scholars who were allowed into the sanctuary, notably Richard Garnett and Edward Dowden, a professor at Trinity College Dublin, was strict and to some degree ruthless. This is witnessed most particularly by the entirely unscrupulous handling of the Harriet Shelley material; but there are many other places where the record was intentionally falsified, and details of the more significant ones are discussed in the course of my narrative for they frequently throw much light. They may also be gathered from the Garnett, Dowden, Rossetti correspondence which has been published, and a wild but spirited polemical attack by Robert Metcalf Smith in *The Shelley Legend* (1945). This crucial period of Shelley studies was crowned by Edward Dowden's two-volume standard *Life* (1886), whose damaging influence is still powerfully at work in popular estimates of Shelley's writing and character.

The decisive modern reinterpretation of Shelley began in America. It may be said to date from the biographical work of Newman Ivey White, and the textual scholarship of F.L. Jones. Together with a third American scholar, Kenneth Neill Cameron, who became the first editor of the Shelley Collection in the Pforzheimer Library in New York, these men began a movement which has started a complete transformation of the assessment of Shelley's life and work. Their monuments are White's two-volume *Shelley* of 1940, and Jones' two-volume *Letters* of 1964; full details of the rest of their work appear in my references. They returned everywhere to original manuscript sources and contemporary material, meticulously comparing printed versions and frequently having recourse to infra-red equipment, and launching a new younger generation of researchers. Any modern English biography must be profoundly indebted to this scholarship, and for me it has been both the indispensable foundation of this book, and an inspiring example.

While the biographic material of Shelley's life has taken more than a hundred years to begin its re-emergence from the penumbra of Victorian proprieties, many of Shelley's actual writings have suffered from an equivalent languishing fate. This too has led to a great distortion in the literary estimate of Shelley's importance. The publishing history of many of Shelley's major poems is a curious one, while the last reasonably complete edition of his prose in England was in 1880. His most important political essay was first published in a limited private edition one hundred years after it was composed, while several of his best poems have only been authoritively edited and printed in the last decade. With the exception of Carl Grabo's *The Magic Plant* (1936), and an essay by W.B.Yeats, there is virtually no literary criticism or critical commentary which is worth reading before 1945. Again, details of the history of Shelley publication occur in the body of my narrative where they throw light on Shelley's reputation, as in the extraordinary case of *Queen Mab*. Probably the most faithful, effective and discriminating of Shelley's earliest publishers were the band of radical pirate printers who fought the battle for a free press in the 1820s, and later the battle for Chartism.

In a field across which immense troops of scholars are now constantly being deployed, one hesitates to claim originality. The reader who asks what is literally 'new' partly misunderstands the nature of this kind of biographical research. It is more the case that perspectives change, 'old' facts and events and documents take on new significance and relations, while fresh local research puts events and experiences in a new setting, drawing in elements that before had not been given proper consideration. What is constantly new is not the past itself, but the way we look back on it. My book will be found to be different from previous biographies in several ways, apart from the original local research upon which it is based. I have used both Mary's and Claire's Journals more fully than previous writers, and for the first time I think Claire is given her full and proper place in Shelley's life. I have offered fully documented reinterpretations of the two great biographical mysteries in Shelley's career – the 'assassination' attempt in Wales in 1813, and the problematical 'Neapolitan' child born in the winter of 1818. I have made constant reference to Shelley's manuscript working notebooks in the Bodleian Library, Oxford, in an attempt to show more clearly how Shelley's great poetic themes were gradually conceived and progressively executed. Finally, I have redrawn the critical estimate of both Shelley's major poetry and his prose, and attempted to set it as vividly as possible in its immediate physical setting, and against the disturbed and excited political period which brought it into being, and which flashes up through the years towards our own. This last is a comparison that I have never presumed to mention, since that has not been my task. But it stands there for anyone who has eyes to see, ears to hear, or heart to feel, sometimes so close that Shelley's life seems more a haunting than a history.

1
A Fire-Raiser

His bedroom window looked west, towards the setting sun. There was a wide lawn, with a shallow bank to roll down, and then a cluster of enormous trees, elms with rooks in, cedars, American redwoods brought back to England by his grandfather, and further and darker, rhododendrons and fir trees. Through the trees was the lake. Then there was the orchard and the south meadow, and beyond an even bigger lake which was called Warnham Pond. It was two lakes really, joined by a stone bridge. His father kept the boat there, and the fishing lines. His father stood among the reeds and shot the wild duck, with their bottle-green feathers, and the snipe. In Warnham Pond there lived the Great Tortoise. Sometimes at night it rose out of the depth of the water and came trundling over the lawns. In the woods there was another monster, the Great Snake. He talked to his nurse about it. She said it lived in St Leonard's Forest and was at least three hundred years old. His nurse came from Horsham, and talked with a soft Sussex burr. Sometimes he told his sister Elizabeth about the Great Tortoise and the Great Snake, and she was very frightened. But she was only two.[1]

The house was called Field Place. There was a tall oak staircase, which shone in the candlelight when he went to bed. Field Place had once been a Tudor farmhouse, and it still had a great stone-floored kitchen, and many little cupboard rooms and locked doors and attics with cobwebbed beams. The new part was Georgian, a stately symmetrical façade, with high windows, and two wings enclosing a central portico, that looked out over the lawn. At the back were the new stables built by his grandfather. The carriages were kept here, and the horses. The groom pretended to play cards with him: 'Be I to play trumps, Master Bysshe?'[2] His mother loved riding. She was very beautiful, and everyone admired her in the village when she rode through on her horse. She gave money to the poor people. She told him that he must learn to ride a horse, and fish, and shoot game in the woods.[3] He had his own pony. The steward Lucas helped him to learn things. Lucas sometimes lent him money to give to the poor people.

When his father Timothy came down from Parliament he sat in his study. He was very tall, and fair-haired, and dressed very carefully. On one wall of his study was a picture of Christ crucified, and on the other an Italian print of Vesuvius erupting.[4] His father made all the family and the servants go to church, but he prefered not to talk about God. The servants liked him because he was kind. Timothy had a long nose, and very fair arched eyebrows. Every day he sent a messenger about grandfather's health. Grandfather Bysshe lived in Horsham in a little cottage by the river Arun. When Timothy went to see him, old Bysshe shouted curses and oaths. Old Bysshe was very rich and stuffed bank-notes behind the sofa. Timothy was frightened of him.

When he was six years old his father sent him to the little day school run by the vicar of Warnham church, the Reverend Edwards, a Welshman. He went each morning down the lane to the vicarage carrying a bundle of books under his arm, and he learnt the rudiments of Latin and Greek. His father liked him to learn passages of Latin poetry, and he would recite them by heart in the drawing-room after tea, acting out the meaning with his arms. His sisters Elizabeth and Mary watched Bysshe in silent admiration, amazed not only that he could remember so many words but that he could show by the expressions on his face and the waving of his arms that he knew what they meant.[5] His mother liked him to recite the comic mock-melancholy of Gray's lines on The Cat and the Goldfish. To Elizabeth and Mary, and even little Hellen who was born when Bysshe was seven, he seemed infinitely wise and full of mysterious knowledge, like a kind of magician.

He told them stories, made up from his explorations in the garden, and in the woods, and round the lake, and in the old part of the house. Sometimes he came to their nursery, and sometimes in the evening he gathered them into a corner of one of the main rooms. A long time afterwards his sister Hellen recalled: 'The tales to which we have sat and listened evening after evening, seated on his knee, when we came to the dining-room for dessert, were anticipated with that pleasing dread, which so excites the minds of children, and fastens so strongly and indelibly on the memory. There was a spacious garret under the roof of Field Place, and a room, which had been closed for years, excepting an entrance made by the removal of a board in the garret floor. This unknown land was made the fancied habitation of an Alchemist, old and grey, with a long beard. Books and a lamp, with all the attributes of a picturesque fancy, were poured into our listening ears. We were to go and see him "some day"; but we were content to wait, and a cave was to be dug in the orchard for the better accommodation of this Cornelius Agrippa. Another favourite theme was the "Great Tortoise" that lived in Warnham Pond; and any unwonted noise was accounted for by the presence of this great beast. . . .'[6]

Elizabeth, who was only two years younger than Bysshe, sometimes contributed to these magical and monstrous creations, but it was Bysshe who was always the leader, who alone had access to the arcane knowledge brought back from his lessons at the vicarage, from his moonlight rides around the woods, from the shadow-land of locked rooms, and from his store of mysterious books. Long after, a battered copy of M.G.Lewis's *Tales of Terror* was found in the children's library at Field Place, its margins annotated with grotesque children's sketches which Bysshe had made of devils, horned monsters and spirits.[7] As a mature man, Bysshe's working notebooks were to be annotated with the same ghastly homunculi. His sisters adored him, and they feared him. Bysshe, the favourite of the servants, and secure in his position as tribal chief, ran riot at Field Place. Even to the grown-ups he seemed full of 'pranks' and 'mischief' and driven by his 'wonderfully exuberant imagination'.

Hellen could remember only *incidents*, 'but nothing that either preceded or followed them, connectedly'.[8] Bysshe had a way of disappearing for hours on end, and then coming back with marvellous adventures to relate, which usually had some strange twist. Hellen remembered 'on one occasion he gave the most minute details of a visit he paid to some ladies, with whom he was acquainted at our village: he described their reception of him, their occupations, and the wandering in their pretty garden. . . . There must have been something peculiar in this little event, for I have often heard it mentioned as a singular fact, and it was ascertained almost immediately, that the boy had never been to the house.' No explanation was forthcoming; it was regarded as peculiar by his parents, but not punished.[9] On another occasion, he became obsessed with the idea of finding the secret hiding-place of one of his apparitions in the upper floors of Field Place, and it was found that he had taken a long stick and driven it repeatedly through the ceiling of a little low back passage of the house in an effort to plumb the secret chamber. The damage was extensive, and he was rebuked.[10]

He was fascinated by moonlight and candlelight, and fire very soon entered into his rituals as a storyteller, ghost-raiser and alchemist. His sisters – there were now four of them, since little Margaret had been born when Bysshe was eight and a half – were more and more drawn into his world of magic and supernatural horror. ' . . . we dressed ourselves in strange costumes to personate spirits or fiends, and Bysshe would take a fire-stove and fill it with some inflammable liquid and carry it flaming into the kitchen and to the back door; but discovery of this dangerous amusement soon put a stop to many repetitions.'[11] On another occasion, perhaps in retaliation for the ban, he was rumoured to have set fire to the rotund form of the butler, Mr Laker. Timothy, an easy-going man, but a father concerned with proprieties, decided that he must think of sending his son away to school. There were consultations in the family: Timothy wanted to send Bysshe to Eton, but he was still too young for that, and first the boy's classics would need a wider grounding. His mother talked to her sisters in Horsham, one of whom was married to Timothy's legal agent in the district, T.C.Medwin. Their son Tom was at a preparatory school near London, where the headmaster was a Scotsman and a classical scholar. This seemed to promise well both for Bysshe's character discipline and his academic education. At the age of ten, he was sent away from Field Place and the adoring society of his sisters, and entered at Syon House Academy, Isleworth, just south of the Thames near Brentford.

The only boy whom Bysshe vaguely knew at the school was his cousin Tom Medwin, four years his senior. Medwin later summed up his experience simply: 'Sion House was indeed a perfect hell to him.'[12] It was a sombre brick building, standing back from the Brentford road, and its gloomy walls were entered by a forbidding gate. In the seventeenth century it had belonged to a Bishop of London, and the dark-panelled, echoing, freezing banquet hall now formed the main schoolroom. The food was sparse, and the washing facilities consisted of a cold plunge. On Saturdays the great school treat was a stew made up from all the nutritious leftovers of the previous week. There were about sixty boys in all, but they ranged in age from 8 to 18, and nearly all of them were sons of London merchants and shopkeepers and successful traders. None of them had Bysshe's county background, or his rural upbringing. The focus of school life was an outside play-yard, surrounded on four sides by high stone walls and a paling fence, with a battered elm tree in the middle. The tree was not like those at Field Place: it carried the school bell, which summoned them to the cold plunge, the refectory, the classroom, and the dormitory. The Bell Tree ruled their lives with a harsh clang that even Medwin could not remember years later without flinching at the sound of its 'odious din' jarring in his ears. In this playground, with its prison walls, and its roar of voices, shouting, calling, laughing and yelling, the bullying took place.

Percy Bysshe Shelley found himself in a new and hostile world. For the first time he was conscious of his own appearance, and his own physical limitations. At Syon House he was remembered as a tall, thin, awkward boy, somehow both large and slight. He had a long face, with the marked Shelley nose and brow, and a ruddy, freckled country-child complexion. His eyes were large, blue, staring. His hair was longer than most of the London boys wore it, and curled and tangled round his face in natural profusion.[13] His hands and features were fine, with that characteristic girlish delicacy of bone structure belonging to English upper-class children. In the tribal universe of a lower-middle-class preparatory school, with its brute system of physical loyalties and rigid conformism, Shelley was almost completely without recourse. Medwin, who obeyed the schoolboy code, and did not interfere – 'we all had to pass through this ordeal' – recalled the early days and weeks. 'All tormented him with questionings. There was no end to their mockery, when they found that he was ignorant of pegtop or marbles, or leap-frog, or hopscotch, much more of fives or cricket. One wanted him to spar, another to run a race with him. He was a tyro in both these accomplishments, and the only welcome of the Neophyte was a general shout of derision.'[14] When he was alone, Medwin observed Shelley crying quietly.

In the schoolroom, Shelley watched Dr Greenlaw construe Homer and take snuff and make jokes about farting like 'the winds in the Cave of Aeolus'.[15] He was a small, red-faced man, with a sharp Scottish accent, and a gift for extracting schoolboy humour out of Greek and Latin texts, calling them *facetiae*. He carried his spectacles perched, with faintly mocking intent, on the top of his eyebrows, except when he grew angry, and lowered them with silent menace onto his broad rubicund nose with its snuff-taking nostrils. His clouts were aimed over the side of the head, and could knock a schoolboy from his desk.[16] Shelley found time to sketch the trees of Field Place in his exercise books, and gaze out of the schoolroom window to watch the swallows gathering for their autumnal migration.[17] His Sussex childhood seemed very far away. Only two things offered themselves as possible resources to be drawn on: one was his imaginary world of monsters and demons and apparitions. The other was an unexpected discovery – he found he had inherited something of his grandfather's character, and had a violent and absolutely ungovernable temper once he grew angry.

'Poor Shelley,' exclaimed Medwin of the bullying, 'he was always the martyr.' Yet Shelley was frequently a fighter as well, and was soon renowned for his paroxysms of fury. Tom Medwin preferred to give only a hint of this in his *Life*, for he wanted to present an angelic childhood: 'he was naturally calm, but when he heard or read of some flagrant act of injustice, oppression or cruelty, then indeed the sharpest marks of horror and indignation were visible in his countenance'. But other pupils remembered Shelley's temper with more distinctness. 'The least circumstance that thwarted him produced the most violent paroxysms of rage; and when irritated by other boys, which they, knowing his infirmity, frequently did by way of teasing him, he would take up anything, or even any little boy near him, to throw at his tormentors.'[18] Another recalled that when he had been flogged, he would roll on the floor, not from pain, but overcome with frustration and indignity. When he hit out, it was frequently without control, 'like a girl in Boys' clothes', lashing out with open hands. All his life, Shelley was to detest violence and the various forms of 'tyranny' which it produced. Yet the exceptional violence in his own character, the viciousness with which he reacted to opposition, was something he found difficult to accept about himself. Much later, his passionate belief in a philosophy of freedom was to be weakened and contradicted by problems of political violence and active resistance which he found it hard to resolve.

The shock of the school experience also darkened and distorted the monsters and romantic demons of Field Place. Isolated and at bay, his mind became increasingly unsettled, and while his days were full of persecutions, his nights now seemed no less tormented. The occurrences recorded half-jocularly by Tom Medwin and others have a counterpart in many a boy's childhood. But with Shelley they were different, for they hung on beyond boyhood; they hung on all his life.

He was subject to strange, and sometimes frightful dreams, and was haunted by apparitions that bore all the semblance of reality. We did not sleep in the same dormitory, but I shall never forget one moonlight night seeing Shelley walk into my room. He was in a state of somnambulism. His eyes were open, and he advanced with slow steps to the window, which, it being the height of summer, was open. I got out of bed, seized him with my arm, and waked him – I was not then aware of the danger of suddenly rousing the sleep walker. He was excessively agitated, and after leading him back with some difficulty to his couch, I sat by him for some time, a witness to severe erethism of his nerves, which the sudden shock produced.[19]

The visions and sleepwalking recorded by Mary Shelley in the last weeks of Shelley's life – he was then aged 29 – correspond to these earliest ones. Medwin's mention of 'erethism of the nerves' – abnormal excitement of them – is also the first record of the mysterious complaint, part constitutional and part psychosomatic, which becomes a permanent feature of Shelley's life from the age of 20.

Shelley's experiences at Syon House Academy might not in themselves have been important if they had not been so strongly reinforced by the events and experiences of later life. But looking back, it seemed to him that the first ten years of his life at Field Place had been a magic circle of freedom and love, a pre-Lapsarian Paradise, and the entry into school, which was the first part of his entry into the outside world, was like the Fall. As a man, he was very rarely to refer to Field Place explicitly in his writing, for the sense of betrayal was overwhelmingly strong and bitter. But in a notebook of 1816, there is a fragment which he wrote in Switzerland at the age of 24:

Dear Home, thou scene of earliest hopes and joys,
The least of which wronged Memory ever makes
Bitterer than all thine unremembered tears.[20]

At the very end of his life, in a mood of more distant reminiscence, he scrawled in one of his Italian notebooks a rough string of visionary verses that recall this first decade in terms of the garden world of a lost Eden:

A schoolboy lay near a pond in a copse
Blackberries just were out of bloom
And the golden bloom of the sunny broom . . .
The pine cones they fell like thunder drops
When the lazy noon breathed so hard in its trance
That it wakened the sleeping fir-tree tops.
Under a branch all leafless & bare
He was watching the motes in their mimic dance
Rolling like worlds through the dewy air
And he closed his eyes at last to see
The network of darkness woven inside
Till the fire-tailed stars of the night of his brain
Like birds round a pond did flutter & glide
And then he would open them wide again.[21]

These first ten years of Shelley's life had been extremely sheltered. Yet they were also the last years of the eighteenth century, and a time of exceptional disturbance in the affairs of men, 'the times that try men's souls'. Events that had occurred far beyond the narrow circle of his knowledge were henceforth to effect the whole tenor of his career.

Shelley had been born in 1792. It was the year in which Tom Paine published his *Rights of Man*, and the year in which the French Revolutionary forces declared war on Europe. It was the beginning of a decade of unprecedented upheaval which affected most of Europe and had repercussions not only in politics but also in literature and science. England, which was to stand firm against the French Revolutionary pressures from without, was shaken and transformed by the forces of change acting within. The nineties in England saw the first meetings of the Radical London Corresponding Society, and the formation of the early tenuous network of Working Men's Associations across the major industrial cities of the north. It saw an unprecedented increase in the national production of cotton and metal goods with a corresponding shift of the population into the manufacturing centres and the undermining of the old rural patterns of life which were so accurately studied and lamented by William Cobbett in his travel essays and polemic journalism.

The nineties saw the circulation of the revolutionary political works of William Godwin, Mary Wollstonecraft, Tom Paine and Horne Tooke, beside a flood of subversive pamphleteering. From the Continent, a wave of new ideas arrived in popular translations of Condorcet, d'Holbach, Voltaire, Volney and Laplace, together with reports of transactions in the Revolutionary Conventions. The transformation of the solid, eighteenth-century English sensibility, with its Johnsonian cast of insular common sense, was marked most strikingly and simply by the transformation in subject matter which now attracted English writers and artists. Robert Southey, a future poet-laureate, wrote a verse play about the agrarian leader Wat Tyler, and his friend Coleridge composed a powerful drama *The Fall of Robespierre*. William Blake produced his first prophetic books, *The French Revolution* and *America: A Prophesy*. William Wordsworth, who had himself witnessed some of the early stages of the revolution in Paris, turned to stories of poverty, low rural life, insanity and the supernatural in the most representative book of the period, *Lyrical Ballads*. The first genuinely popular reading market developed in response to the glut of lurid gothic tales and romances published in cheap editions, tales of horror by M.G.Lewis – who soon earned the sobriquet 'Monk', after his best-selling title – and novels of pursuit and haunting by Ann Radcliffe, Charlotte Dacre, Joanna Baillie, and even by the philosopher Godwin in his book *Caleb Williams*, a story of obsessional pursuit, pointedly subtitled, *Things as They Are*.

In painting, the macabre work of Henry Fuseli, himself a frequenter of the Godwin circle, and the demoniac vision of Blake, characteristically achieved through a brilliant series of technical innovations in printing method, quickly dominated the visual frontiers. The old order of Joshua Reynolds faltered and gave way, and the young Turner first exhibited his oils in the Royal Academy.

In science, the first experimental work on electricity, gases and combustion was beginning to yield striking and hitherto unexpected results. In Manchester, John Dalton was preparing his theories on the absorption of gases; in Clifton, the young superintendent of the Pneumatic Institution, Humphry Davy, was completing his early researches into nitrous oxide, voltaic batteries and the elements of chemical composition. The first sociological study of major importance was published by Thomas Malthus in 1798, *An Essay on Population*.

The decade saw revolutionary activities as diverse as the idealism of Bristol Pantisocracy, illicit leveller associations like the Spencean Society, and the LCS working movement for popular education and democratic rights which led to the Treason Trials of Hardy, Tooke and Thelwall. The newspapers and the taverns throughout the land were full of talk of French informers and bloodthirsty Jacobins who wished to destroy the whole fabric of society, and the cartoonists drew huge guillotines dripping with gore and grotesque figures with mad eyes and red caps of liberty. For the first time in English history, an institution at Whitehall called the Home Office began to develop a nationwide network of surveillance, and throughout the nineties there was a steady extension of judicial controls and civilian spy systems among the ordinary people. Directed first by William Pitt, and later by his successor to the premiership Lord Liverpool, there was an increasingly rigid imposition of political and religious censorship in the courts: the two great instruments of the Lord Chancellor in this respect being the twin laws of Seditious and Blasphemous Libel.

It was, finally, a decade of war: at first only a distant war, fought largely at sea; but later a war that came to every man's doorstep in the form of conscription, high prices, food shortages bordering on famine, garrisoned soldiery, social unrest among the manufacturing classes, and a proliferation of agents from the Customs, Excise, Post Office and Home Office. Above all it came in the ceaseless, swelling, uncontrollable agitation – to a degree never before known in this island – of new *ideas*: a great wind of restless, contradictory, ill-defined ideas, but ideas none the less that blew open new doors and windows in men's minds and changed their lives for ever. War had always accelerated both social and economic trends in England, and this war was to last for the best part of eighteen years.

Shelley was born into an age of upheaval. Yet it might be assumed that Horsham, Sussex, still slumbering in its traditional eighteenth-century pattern of seasonal labour, sheep markets, village festivals, and still dominated by squire and parson, was in reality very little affected by these distant commotions and rumblings among politicians, intellectuals and city-dwellers. But the social crust was no longer as solid as it seemed. This particularly applied to the family that occupied the squire's house at Field Place, with its long drive, its plantations of oaks and cedars, its pond and eccentric 'American Garden' of redwoods and semi-tropical plants. In that part of southern England, 'Shelley' was indeed an ancient name in the county aristocracy, and the original family of the Shelley-Michelgroves had an impeccable pedigree and a baronetage bestowed by James I. But Shelley's own family did not derive directly from this respected stock: his was a junior and inferior branch, descended by a long trellis of younger brothers and obscure marriages, and settling uneasily at the beginning of the eighteenth century on Fen Place, near Worth in Sussex.[22] Here John Shelley, Shelley's great-great-grandfather lived, and from here Shelley's direct ancestry can be traced through the restless, indigent and rather murky history of two opportunist younger sons. It was to be an important factor in Shelley's later life that at the time of his birth, the family at Field Place was socially *arriviste*. Its subsequently vaunted blood-connection with the literary Shelley-Sidneys of Penshurst Place was as tenuous as the most liberal laws of cousinage will allow.

Shelley's great-grandfather, Timothy Shelley, the third of five sons, was forced to emigrate to America to make his living in the reign of George I. There it appears that he became a merchant, married a New York miller's widow, lost his money and turned into a quack doctor.[23] During this period Bysshe Shelley, the second son and Shelley's grandfather, was born in Newark, New Jersey in 1731. Some years later, Timothy's fortune was saved by the death of one elder brother and the insanity of another, and he was able to bring his colonial family back to England, including his son Bysshe.

Bysshe Shelley, Shelley's grandfather, was a determined and individualistic man whose initiative and disregard for social proprieties was not squirearchical, but wholly of the New World. He was a tall, striking figure, with the long Shelley nose, cold eyes and a thin, purposeful lip. His drive and nonconformity brought him worldly success, together with the unpopularity of those descendants who benefited from him. In 1752 he instigated a family tradition by eloping with a 16-year-old girl, the daughter of a wealthy clergyman, and marrying her in Mayfair. The girl died nine years later, and Bysshe inherited the estates. In 1769 he repeated the process, with even greater success, this time eloping with a daughter of the aristocratic Sidney Perry family who owned estates in Sussex, Kent and Gloucester. This brought him social *cachet* rather than money. Bysshe inherited Field Place and the Fen Place estates in 1790, became a baronet in 1806, and died in 1815 leaving a fortune of £200,000. He spent much of his time in building a new ancestral home in the shape of Castle Goring by the sea in Sussex, but at the end of his life he preferred to live in his small cottage near the Horsham tavern, a crotchety eccentric feared by his children both legitimate and otherwise. £12,816 in loose banknotes was found dispersed among his furniture and books in the Horsham cottage at his death.[24]

Shelley's father, Timothy – named after the American 'apothecary' – was born of Bysshe's first marriage to Miss Mary Catherine Michell, the clergyman's daughter, in 1753. In him, Bysshe's wildness and self-assertion were temporarily subdued. As befitted the son of a self-made man, he quietly conformed to the new social surroundings and awaited the descent of the baronetcy from the father who always despised him. He attended University College, Oxford, and presented it with silver candlesticks; he then made the Grand Tour and entered Lincoln's Inn. He became mildly interested in politics, and attached himself to Norfolk's wing of the Foxite Whigs. But he was always in spirit an easy-going place-man, and a conformist. He did what was expected of him. Norfolk was fighting a local county battle against his Tory rival Lady Irwin, and bought up the Horsham electorate. He managed to get Timothy nominated as Member for the town for the 1790–2 parliamentary session. But finally Lady Irwin succeeded in a petition against the election, and Timothy was deprived of his seat, having to be re-elected for New Shoreham, another of the Duke's extensive political properties.

Meanwhile, Timothy had married Elizabeth Pilfold of nearby Warnham in

October 1791. He installed his new bride in Field Place, as old Bysshe was busy building at Goring. Their first child, a son christened Percy Bysshe, was born ten months later on 4 August 1792. Timothy was aged 40, and his new wife aged 29.

Perhaps the most remarkable single fact of Shelley's childhood is that while both parents comfortably outlived him, neither left a single word of reminiscence about his early boyhood.* We know nothing directly of his relationship with his mother during his first fifteen years, and Shelley rarely mentioned her in later life. From a few stray remarks in letters from Oxford, and from passing references by his cousin Tom Medwin and his undergraduate friend T.J.Hogg, we can gather that the feelings between mother and son were exceptionally close and warm up to the time that Shelley went to school. After this Shelley seems to have found his mother increasingly distant and unresponsive, and there are indications that he felt deeply rejected. Shelley's sense of betrayal was finally to erupt in an extraordinary accusation of adultery which he made at the age of 19. But apart from this, his feelings were shrouded in mystery.

The marriage was not one which old Bysshe would have regarded as a favourable *coup*, although the Pilfolds had some standing locally in the ranks of the Sussex squirearchy. Elizabeth was a large, handsome woman, with bold features, a mass of light brown curling hair and a strong mouth which seemed to curl with a suggestion of disdain. Timothy Shelley was proud enough of her to have both their portraits painted by George Romney. She had a reputation for being a determined woman, a good letter writer but not interested in literature. Her main love was for horses and the countryside, and she much enjoyed her popularity among the common people of Warnham and Horsham. As a child she had lost her own mother when young, and had been brought up in the family of Lord and Lady Ferdinand Pool, whose main distinction was in the field of racehorse breeding.[25] There is a hint of a somewhat masculine character, and it was rumoured that she could be domineering and even violent within her marriage, but this is not certain.[26] She had seven children in all, two sons and five daughters, one of whom died in infancy. Her second son John (who eventually inherited the baronetcy) was, however, not born until 1806, when Shelley was 14 and already at Eton, and his presence never really impinged on Shelley himself either in boyhood or adolescence, though the sense of maternal betrayal may have been emphasized by a transfer of attention from the elder son to the

---

* Timothy, as noted in the Introduction, forbade all biography, and the only substantial eye-witness accounts of Shelley's early years at Field Place depend on two sources: a series of ten letters written by his younger sister Hellen between 1856 and 1857 when she was an ageing lady of 57; and the reminiscences of his cousin Tom Medwin first published in 1847, when also in his fifties. The one person who really understood Shelley's childhood from the inside was his closest sister, Elizabeth. She died early, having remained under the paternal influence, and never broke her silence.

younger. For Shelley, the pre-Lapsarian land of Field Place was constructed from a society of sisters, and this was to have a marked affect on his later life in which the 'sisterly' ideal played a conscious part. His closest sister and greatest childhood friend was Elizabeth, born in May 1794, and it was with her that his first literary attempt was to be published. She was 8 when he first went to Syon House Academy. His other sisters were Mary, born in 1797, Hellen in 1799 and Margaret in 1801. It is again suggestive of the maternal influence that though they were all acknowledged to be markedly good-looking, only one of them eventually married.

If he was strangely silent about his mother, Shelley was always outspoken about his relationship with his father Timothy. Timothy was to play a major part in the upheavals of Shelley's life between the ages of 18 and 23, and from that time on Shelley always dramatized him as the worst kind of tyrant and hypocrite. Subsequently he also interpreted his early childhood as a time of extreme oppression, with his father in the role of persecutor, and he was later to develop a story that he suffered continually from illness, while on one occasion his father Timothy tried to have him certified and taken away secretly to a madhouse. Quite apart from having no evidence from Timothy himself on these matters, there is every reason to treat these melodramatic accounts with great caution. At another level they are extremely suggestive, for they show the earliest development of that mythopoeic faculty which was to become one of the major elements in Shelley's creative power and originality.

Shelley's reaction against his family was also to develop a strong moral and political character. Writing from Shelley's own point of view, this interpretation was to be put most thoughtfully by his Hampstead friend, the liberal editor Leigh Hunt, in an essay of 1828, long before the other memoirs and reminiscences of his boyhood had been collated or published.

The family connexions of Mr Shelley belonged to a small party in the House of Commons, itself belonging to another party. They were Whig Aristocrats . . . to a man of genius, endowed with a metaphysical acuteness to discern truth and falsehood, and a strong sensibility to give way to his sense of it, such an origin, however respectable in the ordinary point of view, was not the very luckiest that could have happened for the purpose of keeping him within ordinary bounds. With what feelings is truth to open its eyes upon this world among the most respectable of our mere party gentry? Among licensed contradictions of all sorts? Among the Christian doctrines and worldly practices? Among foxhunters and their chaplains? Among beneficed loungers, noli-episcopalian bishops, rakish old gentlemen, and more startling young ones who are old in the folly of *knowingness*? In short, among all those professed demands of what is right and noble, mixed with real inculcations of what is wrong and full of hypocrisy. ... Mr Shelley began to think at a very early age, and to think too of these anomalies. He saw that at every step in life some compromise was expected between a truth which he was expected not to violate, and a colouring and double meaning of it which forced him upon the violation.

Hunt went on to indict the class in more general terms, concluding: 'Whenever a character like Mr Shelley's appears in society, it must be considered with reference to these systems.'[27]

This is very much how Shelley expressed his own case in later life. At root it was a political case, but broadened out into a general claim for moral righteousness set over against the corruption of society.

It was during the two years spent at Syon House, between 1802 and 1804, that Shelley first came to feel that in some sense society as a whole was a hostile force and something to be combated. Besides his rages and his nightmares, he found other weapons close at hand in the games and magic of Field Place: horror books, alchemy, ghost-raising, chemical and electrical experiments, astronomy and the delights of outrageous speculation all served their turn. With these he found he could make his own kind of freedom within the stone walls of the Syon House playground, and also, as with his sisters, he found he could exert certain kinds of power and respect among his fellow-pupils, even a kind of hidden fear. One contemporary subsequently wrote:

> During the time that I was there the most remarkable scholar was ... Percy Bysshe Shelley, who was then about twelve or thirteen (as far as I can remember), and even at that early age exhibited considerable poetical talent, accompanied by a violent and extremely excitable temper, which manifested itself in all kinds of eccentricities. ... His imagination was always roving upon something romantic and extraordinary, such as spirits, fairies, fighting, volcanoes, etc., and he not unfrequently astonished his schoolfellows by blowing up the boundary palings of the playground with gunpowder, also the lid of his desk in the middle of schooltime, to the great surprise of Dr Greenlaw himself and the whole school.[28]

Tom Medwin recalled him taking up his favourite position by the southern wall, day after day in the playground, pacing backwards and forwards like a caged animal, with his weird, impetuous movements and animated face: 'I think I see him now – along the southern wall, indulging in various vague and undefined ideas, the chaotic elements, if I may say so, of what afterwards produced so beautiful a world.'[29]

One escape was simply to break bounds and go into Brentford. There was a brisk trade in battered dictionaries and old books which were sold by the weight to a local grocer in return for cheese, bread and fruit.[30] Shelley's great discovery was a cheap bookseller who stocked Minerva Press editions, in their distinctive blue paper covers, each priced sixpence. Minerva Press, which was perhaps the greatest of the contemporary popular publishing houses, operating from a narrow shop in Leadenhall Street, printed most of the best horror novels and gothic romances of the period. Tom Medwin saw his cousin purchase at Norbury's dark shop in the High Street Ann Radcliffe's *The Italian*, a wild and sinister romance called *Zofloya, or the Moor*, Matthew Lewis's *The Monk* and many other promising titles. They made for him an alternative world of 'haunted castles, bandits, murderers and other grim personages', a world which never entirely left him, as his later friend, Thomas Love Peacock, was vividly to testify. This world was no longer so innocent as it has been at Field Place: the devil had entered in. Moreover, it was no longer a happily shared fantasy, but a secretive, isolated, one; a world of sleepwalking and bad dreams.

Apart from Tom Medwin, Shelley found little companionship at Syon House, except for one romantic friendship, a 'devoted attachment' which he recalled gratefully many years after when analysing his own emotional development. 'The object of these sentiments was a boy about my own age, of a character eminently grave, generous and gentle. . . . There was a delicacy and simplicity in his manner, inexpressibly attractive. . . . The tones of his voice were so soft and winning that every word pierced into my heart, and their pathos was so deep that in listening to him the tears often have involuntarily gushed from my eyes.' Shelley was so moved by this friendship that he wrote a long and enthusiastic letter to his mother at Field Place explaining the warmth of his feelings.

I suppose she thought me out of my wits, for she returned no answer to my letter. I remember we used to walk the whole play-hours up and down by some moss-covered palings, pouring out our hearts in youthful talk. We used to speak of the ladies with whom we were in love, and I remember that our usual practice was to confirm each other in the everlasting fidelity, in which we had bound ourselves towards them and towards each other. I recollect thinking my friendship exquisitely beautiful. Every night, when we parted to go to bed, I remember we kissed each other.[31]

The failure of his mother to respond on this occasion was one of the small indications to Shelley that her sympathy and affection was steadily being withdrawn. She merely thought he was a bit mad. Yet at Oxford, Hogg was to notice how he still loved to talk of his feelings for his mother and his sisters; especially his sister Elizabeth.

The patterns of male love and friendship were to be very important in

Shelley's life, and he again reverted to this first close attachment outside the circle of Field Place, in his description of the statue of Bacchus and Ampelus in the Uffizi Gallery, which he saw at Florence when he was 27: 'One arm of Bacchus rests on the shoulder of Ampelus . . . just as you may have seen (yet how seldom from their disseevering and tyrannical institutions do you see) a younger and an elder boy walking in some remote grassy spot of their playground with that tender friendship towards each other which has so much of love. The countenance of Bacchus is sublimely sweet and lovely, taking a shade of gentle and playful tenderness from the arch looks of Ampelus, whose cheerful face turned towards him, expresses the suggestions of some droll and merry device.'[32] By this time, it was self-evident to him that school was just one of many tyrannical and perverse institutions.

In his early twenties, Shelley deliberately attempted to establish a specific moment of revolt at Syon House, which he wrote about as having the quality and intensity of something like a religious conversion. Passages in 'Hymn to Intellectual Beauty' (1816) and in the Dedication to *The Revolt of Islam* (1817) have become famous memorials of this, although the thin, high-pitched egotism of their tone largely vitiates them as poetry.

> Thoughts of great deeds were mine, dear Friend, when first
>   The clouds which wrap this world from youth did pass.
> I do remember well the hour which burst
>   My spirit's sleep: a fresh May-dawn it was,
>   When I walked forth upon the glittering grass,
> And wept, I knew not why; until there rose
>   From the near schoolroom, voices, that, alas!
> Were but one echo from a world of woes –
> The harsh and grating strife of tyrants and of foes.
>
> And then I clasped my hands and looked around –
>   – But none was near to mock my streaming eyes,
> Which poured their warm drops on the sunny ground –
>   So, without shame, I spake: – 'I will be wise,
>   And just, and free, and mild, if in me lies
> Such power, for I grow weary to behold
>   The selfish and the strong still tyrannise
>   Without reproach or check.' I then controlled
> My tears, my heart grew calm, and I was meek and bold.[33]

That this moment ever had a definite historical existence during Shelley's time at Syon House is doubtful. Yet it records faithfully enough the shock that the school experience had on him, and in Shelley's elaborate private myth of his own childhood it forms one of the most significant parts.

One teacher alone had any lasting positive effect on Shelley at Syon House, or made any real contact with his inner imaginative world. This was an itinerant, eccentric lecturer, Dr Adam Walker - a 'mad doctor' in the best eighteenth-century tradition of Priestley and Erasmus Darwin – who frequently made teaching tours of schools such as Winchester, Eton and their preparatory off-spring. Walker was primarily an inventor and astronomer, who had made his name with a popular scientific textbook published in 1779, *Familar Philosophy*.* He lectured on the stars and the zodiac, on the planets of the solar system, on magnetism and electricity, on the possibilities of extra-terrestial life or the 'plurality of worlds', and above all on the practical use of the telescope and the solar microscope. These subjects grafted perfectly on to Shelley's already thriving occult interests, and vastly enlarged his field for practical experiments, devices and fantastic speculation. Tom Medwin recalled his breathless curiosity as he gazed through one of Walker's telescopes at Saturn, 'its atmosphere seeming to him an irrefragable proof of its being inhabited like our globe'; and after another lecture, peering spellbound through a microscope at mites seething in cheese, the wing of a fly, 'the vermicular *animalculae* in vinegar' and other invisible forms of biological life. Later these revelations would form the subject for endless conversations, back and forth by the southern wall of the detested playground.[34]

Shelley's attitude to science was never to be 'scientific' in the empirical sense, but speculative and imaginative. Chemistry, electricity, astronomy fused easily with alchemy, fire-worship, explosives and psychical investigations. At Oxford, Hogg was to describe Shelley in his rooms as 'the chemist in his laboratory, the alchemist in his study, the wizard in his cave'.[35] His later adherence to Necessity shows the continuing desire for such a magical key to invisible laws, such as an alchemical formula of life. Yet Shelley was to be much more naturally inclined to the field of social sciences – sociology, psychology, even para-psychology – than the physical ones.

At Syon House Adam Walker's lectures fascinated Shelley above all with the ideas of new sources of power: steam power, electrical power, free flight and air power, chemical power controlling agriculture and the climate. Hogg records many of Shelley's diatribes on these subjects at Oxford. It was Adam Walker's assistant who sold Shelley – or helped him to build – his more advanced forms of electrical generators. Walker also procured Shelley his most precious

* Dr Adam Walker, 1731–1821, was also the inventor of the patent empyreal air-stove, the patent celistina harpsichord, and the eidouranion or transparent orrery, a device for projecting an illuminated model of the solar system and the stars.

piece of 'philosophic' equipment, the solar microscope in its rugged mahogany travelling box, which was to go with him on many of his subsequent voyagings.[36]

The disruptive and in many ways traumatic effect of Shelley's two years at Syon House gradually made itself felt during his holidays at Field Place. The house and garden still retained its paradisiac aura. He could still return temporarily to the old warmth and security and freedom, and his sisters were if anything more adoring and compliant companions and followers than before. But Shelley's natural mischievousness had become more uncontrollable, his games and experiments more violent, and his authority over his sisters more domineering. Gunpowder devices and fire balloons were constructed in distant parts of the orchard, and his own and his sisters' clothes were constantly stained and burnt by acids and caustics. Elizabeth alone was an entirely willing co-partner in these escapades; the other children were frequently terrified by their wild elder brother. Hellen wrote: 'When my brother commenced his studies in chemistry, and practised electricity upon us, I confess my pleasure in it was entirely negatived by terror at its effects. Whenever he came to me with his piece of folded brown packing-paper under his arm and a bit of wire and a bottle (if I remember right), my heart would sink with fear at his approach; but shame kept me silent, and, with as many others as he could collect, we were placed hand-in-hand round the nursery table to be electrified.'[37] Finally Shelley suggested that he would be able to cure their chilblains by this method of electrification, but his sister's 'terror overwhelmed all other feelings' and she complained to their parents. Shelley was required to desist. A similar episode was recorded some six years later at Oxford by Hogg. Shelley kept his scout's small simpleton son James under half-comic threats of sudden electrocution, so that James 'roared aloud with ludicrous and stupid terror, whenever Shelley affected to bring by stealth any part of his philosophical apparatus near to him'.[38]

Another victim of Shelley's experiments at Field Place was a local tom-cat, which appears to have been wired up to what Tom Medwin called an 'electrical kite' flying in a thunderstorm overhead. The result of this test was not recorded.[39] It was perhaps this cat that Shelley celebrated in his earliest recorded piece of juvenile verse, five stanzas about 'a cat in distress' written on a sheet of paper with a small cat painted on the top, probably by Elizabeth. The cat in question is suffering simply from hunger, but even at the age of eleven, Shelley gives its sufferings a characteristic supernatural twist:

> You would not easily guess
> All the modes of distress
> Which torture the tenants of earth;

> And the various evils,
> Which like so many devils,
> Attend the poor souls from their birth.

The doggerel also contains a sly cross-reference to the relationship between Shelley's father Timothy and old Bysshe, which shows the quickness with which he had seized on the nature of the feelings between father and son:

> Some a living require,
> And others desire
> An old fellow out of the way;
> And which is the best
> I leave to be guessed,
> For I cannot pretend to say.[40]

A similar kind of humorous self-assurance, which verges on the cynicism of a spoilt child, was shown in his first known letter dating from the summer before he went to Eton. He invites a girl-friend, a certain Miss Kate of Horsham, to a picnic expedition boating on Warnham Pond. The letter is franked 'free', as if it had been posted by his father under parliamentary privilege, though it was actually carried by Tom Medwin. The letter ends: 'Mama depends on you bringing Tom over tomorrow, and if you don't we shall be very much disappointed. Tell the bearer not to forget to bring me a fairing, which is some gingerbread, sweetmeat, hunting-nuts, and a pocket book. Now I end. I am not, Your obedient servant, P B Shelley.'[41] Yet underneath the confident façade, the nightmares and the anxiety continued, and the sense of betrayal. It was first noticed at this time that Shelley began taking his pony out for long periods, or going on mysterious night-time expeditions. The old servant of the family was sent to follow him at a discreet distance, but he returned to report with a puzzled shake of his grey head: 'Master Bysshe only took a walk and came back again.'

In 1804, Shelley left Syon House Academy and the protective friendship of Tom Medwin; and in September of that year, one month after his twelfth birthday, he was sent to Eton College. On the morning of his departure, a fire was discovered in the washroom at Field Place, started by one of Shelley's 'chemical preparations' ignited in the fire grate with the chimney valve closed. It seems to have been timed to coincide with his leave-taking. His sisters remembered that 'much was made of this incident'.[42]

Shelley was at Eton for six years, one of 400 Oppidans and some seventy scholars. The latter lived in College, had their fees paid, and were distinguished by their black academic gowns. The former, of which Shelley was one, were fee-paying, and lived in various school houses and lodgings. The years were divided into 'elections', with a strict and brutally enforced system of social hierarchies, and it was traditional that the junior election always 'fagged' – acting as menial servants for senior boys. At the time of Shelley's election, the Lower School were ruled by the notorious, squat, roaring figure of Dr Keate, soon to become the headmaster of the whole College when he earned his sobriquet 'Flogger'. He was both a feared and a ridiculed figure, with a grimacing bulldog face glaring out beneath a large tricorn hat, whose harsh military régime set the tone for barbaric behaviour among the boys until they reached the relative civilization of the Remove and the Sixth Form in their last two years.

Shelley lodged during his first years in the house of Mr Hexter, the writing master; and latterly in the liberal sanctum of the classics master, Dr Bethel. A fragment of a letter which has survived to his father, ends characteristically: 'PS. I can equivocally promise (a good) account from Mr Hexter. . . .'[43] He was quickly recognized as an exceptional Latin scholar, and a remarkable non-conformist, and the bullying from fellow-pupils was extremely severe. He refused to valet for his fagmaster Matthews, and thus forfeited the traditional right of protection which senior boys exercised when bullying in a junior election had become too severe. He was consequently disliked by his senior year[*] and was tormented by his peers. In his second and third years, he even found that the junior elections mocked him for his 'wild and marked peculiarity', and the best account of the bullying and Shelley-hunting was left by a boy one year below.

He was known as 'Mad Shelley'; – and many a cruel torture was practised upon him for his moody and singular exclusiveness. Shelley was my senior; and I, in common with others, deemed him as one ranging between madness and folly. . . . Conscious of his own superiority – of being the reverse of what the many deemed him – stung by the injustice of imputed madness, by the cruelty, if he were mad, of taunting the afflicted, his rage became boundless. Like Tasso's jailer, his heartless tyrants all but raised up the demon which they said was in him. I have seen him surrounded, hooted, baited like a maddened bull, – and at this distance of time I seem to hear ringing in my ears the cry which Shelley was wont to utter in his paroxysms of revengeful anger.

---

[*] Among Shelley's senior election was John Taylor Coleridge, who later savaged his character and poetry in an anonymous review in the *Quarterly* for April 1819. Taylor did not forget the upstart fag: '[Mr Shelley] speaks of his school as "a world of woes", of his masters as "tyrants", of his school-fellows as "enemies", – alas! what is this, but to bear evidence against himself? every one who knows what a public school ordinarily must be, will only trace in these lines the language of an insubordinate, a vain, a mortified spirit.'

The madness which Shelley subsequently wrote into his own childhood probably had its root here. On winter evenings, while waiting in the cloisters to go
into the upper school for supper, there was a particular game called 'nailing' in
which a muddy football was kicked through the crowd and shot as hard as
possible at one agreed target. Frequently this was Shelley.

There were other diversions of the mob.

The particular name of some particular boy would be sounded by one,
taken up by another and another, until hundreds echoed and echoed the name.
. . . The Shelley! Shelley! Shelley! which was thundered in the cloisters was
but too often accompanied by practical jokes, – such as knocking his books
from under his arm, seizing them as he stooped to recover them, pulling and
tearing his clothes, or pointing with the finger, as one Neapolitan maddens
another. The result was, as stated, a paroxysm of anger which made his eyes
flash like a tiger's, his cheeks grow pale as death, his limbs quiver, and his hair
stand on end.[44]

Shelley remembered these first years at Eton with an intensity of loathing that
affected many of his later attitudes towards organized authority and social conformism. To Thomas Love Peacock, a close friend of later years, he recounted
them with feelings of abhorrence which Peacock never heard him express on any
other subject except the Chancellor Eldon.[45] He told Peacock that he had been
provoked once into striking a penknife through the hand of one of his tormentors
and pinning it to the desk; the incident reappeared in one of his poems written
at the age of 25.[46] Mary Shelley recalled in 1825: 'I have often heard our Shelley
relate the story of stabbing an upper boy with a fork. . . . He always described it,
in my hearing, as an almost involuntary act, done on the spur of anguish, and
that he made the stab as the boy was going out of the room.'[47] Such sudden
outbreaks of violence were to recur.

The bullying at Eton, after it had entered Shelley's own adult mythography,
was later passed on to admirers and biographers as a glowing part of Shelley
hagiography. By 1839, Mary Shelley was to put the matter on the plane of
divine heroism and angelic self-sacrifice:

Inspired with ardour for the acquisition of knowledge, endowed with the
keenest sensibility and with the fortitude of a martyr, Shelley came among his
fellow-creatures, congregated for the purposes of education, like a spirit from
another sphere. . . . To a devoted attachment to those he loved he added a
determined resistance to oppression. Refusing to fag at Eton, he was treated
with revolting cruelty by masters and boys: this roused instead of taming his

spirit, and he rejected the duty of obedience when it was enforced by menaces and punishment.[48]*

But Mary Shelley, as an imaginative writer, was also deeply interested in the realities of Shelley's mind and upbringing. Prevented from anything more than superficial biography, she was to turn to fiction, in order to unravel further the real nature of Shelley's conflict with school authorities and fellow-pupils. In her fourth novel, *Lodore* (1835), which follows the career of a vaguely Byronic hero called Fitzhenry, there is an early passage about his unhappiness at school which represents much of her own reflections on Shelley's childhood.

Many individual details recall the Field Place upbringing and the school in the novel is stated to be Eton. But Mary's portrait is not quite straightforward. She seems deliberately to split Shelley's characteristics between two personae: Fitz-henry and his schoolfriend Derham, and the friendship itself recalls the ones that Shelley referred to at Syon House. The device of splitting Shelley's character-istics between two personae is one she used in other novels. *Lodore* is now obscure and difficult to obtain, and it is worth quoting it here at length.

The distinction that Lord Lodore's title and residence bestowed upon Longfield, made his son and heir a demigod among the villagers. As he rode through it on his pony, every one smiled on him and bowed to him; and the habit of regarding himself superior to all the world became too much a habit to afford triumph. . . . He would not wantonly have inflicted a pang upon a human being; yet he exerted any power he might possess to quell the smallest resistance to his desires. . . . Any poor family visited by rough adversity, any unfortunate child enduring unjust oppression, he assisted earnestly and with all his heart. He was as courageous as a lion, and, upon occasion, soft-hearted and pitiful; but once roused to anger by opposition, his eyes darted fire, his little form swelled, his boyish voice grew big, nor could he be satisfied except by the most entire submission on the part of his antagonist. Unfortunately for him, submission usually followed any stand against his authority. . . .

At the age of thirteen he went to Eton, and here everything wore an altered and unpleasing aspect. Here were no servile menials nor humble friends. He stood one among many – equals, superiors, inferiors, all full of a sense of their own rights, their own powers; he desired to lead, and he had no followers; he wished to stand aloof, and his dignity, even his privacy, was continually

---

* This may be taken as a premonition of the mid-Victorian attitude to Shelley's life which was glowingly propagated by Lady Jane Shelley in her *Shelley Memorials: From Authentic Sources* (1859), and much subsequent sentimentalizing scholarship down to Maurois's *Ariel* (1924) which was originally intended as an 'exorcism'. Its finest visual flower may be seen in Shelley's marble monument at University College, Oxford: the recumbent statue, with bronze sea nymphs weeping below the plinth, is by E. Onslow Ford, 1894.

invaded. His school fellows soon discovered his weakness – it became a bye-word among them, and was the object of such practical jokes, as seemed to the self-idolizing boy, at once frightful and disgusting. . . . He fixed his large dark eyes on them, and he curled his lips in scorn, trying to awe them by haughtiness and frowns, and shouts of laughter replied to the concentrated passion of his soul. He poured forth invective, and hootings were the answer. He had one other resource, and that in the end proved successful: – a pitch battle or two elevated him in the eyes of his fellows, and as they began to respect him, so he grew in better humour with them and himself. . . . He resented injustice wherever he encountered or fancied it; he equally spurned it when practised on himself, or defended others when they were its object – freedom was the watchword of his heart.[49]

The character here drawn is deliberately made too extroverted and dignified for Shelley as he was; but the general outline is strongly reminiscent of him, and it is interesting to see Mary locate part of the fault in his own background and character, rather than purely in the savagery of the school. To compensate the portrait, Mary drew in Fitzhenry's friend Derham, an extreme version of the other side of Shelley's nature, the introverted one. Derham, whom the older boy befriends and protects, is small, beautiful, 'effeminate' and strangely foolish, being totally unable to learn in class.

The boy was unlike the rest; he had wild fancies and strange inexplicable ideas. . . . He seemed incapable of feeling the motives and impulses of other boys: when they jeered at him he would answer gravely with some story of a ghastly spectre, and tell wild legends of weird beings, who roamed through the dark fields by night, or sat wailing by the banks of streams: he was struck, he smiled and turned away; he would not fag; he never refused to learn, but could not; he was the scoff, and butt, and victim, of the whole school.[50]

Somewhere between these two fictional creations, in a combination of their aggressive egotism and their wild private fantasies, Mary Shelley's final view of Shelley as a child seems to lie.

Of the damage that the early Eton experience did to him, repeating and reinforcing the Syon House pattern and reaction, there can be little doubt. Fear of society *en masse*, fear of enforced solitude, fear of the violence within himself and from others, fear of withdrawal of love and acceptance, all these were implanted at the centre of his personality so that it became fundamentally unstable and highly volatile. Here too seem to lie the sources of his compensatory qualities: his daring, his exhibitionism, his flamboyant generosity, his instinctive and demonstrative hatred of authority.

Shelley's changing conduct in the vacations at Field Place bears out the profoundly disturbing effect of school upon him between the ages of 12 and 16. There are stories of him wandering about the garden in disguise, of spending whole nights locked in Warnham Church, and of applying to the local Horsham lawyer for work as a gamekeeper's boy, wearing ragged clothes and speaking in heavy Sussex dialect.

When the Shelleys went to pay a summer visit to their cousins the Groves at Fern House in Wiltshire, Shelley's presence was largely remembered for the expedition he led into the private plantation where he chopped down several young fir trees, much to Mr Grove's displeasure.[51] This was also the first time he met his beautiful cousin Harriet Grove, one year his senior. They hardly spoke to each other.

During another summer at Field Place, Shelley took all four of his sisters on a secret and illicit expedition to Strood, travelling cross-country. They made their way by sunken fences and stiles, but where there was a wall Shelley eschewed the gate and made everyone clamber over the stonework. Hellen remembered that she was 'big enough to be pulled over', but little Margaret – who was then about five – was unable to manage so she was 'gently thrown across' on to the grass. On the way back she was so tired Shelley carried her in his arms, telling her to 'be careful to hold her feet' so that his trousers did not get damaged. They all arrived back in the evening sadly soiled, as Hellen remembered, and Shelley's escapade met with frowns. But it was repeated in various forms whenever, as his sister put it, 'he could steal away with us'.[52] The curious parental fear that Shelley was in some way trying to make off with his sisters was to become a definite alarm from the time he entered Oxford onwards. He was rebuked for playing too roughly with the baby John, and crashing his push-carriage in a strawberry bed. It was not thought amusing either that the first word he taught him to speak was 'devil', which came out 'debbee'.[53]

Shelley was still closest to Elizabeth, and it was at this period that he wrote his first play with her, which they sent to Matthews the comedian in London. It has not survived, but one of his contemporaries at Eton remembered Shelley's attempts to put on plays at school during his third or fourth year. 'The boys often invited him to rehearse these productions with a mock interest, and then, just when he thought the audience were thoroughly enraptured, burst out into fits of laughter.'[54] So the counterpoint between school and home continued. A temporary alliance was formed between Shelley and his grandfather – now Sir Bysshe – and he was encouraged to put some of his own and his sisters' poems into print in a private edition published by a local bookseller, the bill paid by the baronet. Shelley urged all his sisters to work on macabre themes, and he especially praised Hellen for producing the line, 'an old woman in her bony gown'.[55] It seems that old Bysshe had the pleasure of watching his grandson shock his son, for once one of these publications was discovered by the authorities at Field Place it was instantly bought up and destroyed.

In 1806 or 1807, he was sent home from Eton for several weeks with a feverish illness, and was nursed at Field Place. Shelley was later to describe this as an expulsion, and said that his father in a fury tried to put him in a madhouse. There is no independent evidence for either this or the expulsion, but the illness certainly occurred. Little Margaret vividly remembered seeing him walking round the garden by himself during his convalescence, and coming to find her at the dining-room window. But he had been forbidden to talk to her, and she remembered him somehow trapped outside, his nose and lips pressed against the glass in a kiss.[56]

By 1808, Shelley's fourth year at Eton, he finally began to rise out of the miseries of the lower elections, and establish something of his own freedom and identity. He had now moved to Dr Bethel's house, in a room directly above the Doctor's study, and he began to make himself felt with his experiments, on one occasion electrifying his housemaster who inadvertently put his hand on a wired-up doorknob, and on another being discovered in a circle of blue spirit flame apparently trying to raise the devil. He blew up an old tree stump near his lodgings with an advanced gunpowder device, and later had his whole library of chemical books banned by Bethel and sent back to Field Place.[57] His co-fag and one friend of the early days, Andrew Amos, was alienated by these brushes with authority, and he was rather bitterly taunted by Shelley as 'Amos Apyrist' – the man who hates or fears fire.

His interest in the occult remained part of the developing world of scientific magic. Another friend, Walter Halliday, recalled: 'We used to wander for hours about Clewer, Frogmore, the Park at Windsor, the Terrace; and I was a delighted and willing listener to his marvellous stories of fairyland, and apparitions, and spirits, and haunted ground; and his speculations were then, (for his mind was far more developed than mine), of the world beyond the grave.'[58]

Hogg gave a detailed summary of Shelley's pursuits in this direction when he first described them at Oxford, two years later:

He was passionately attached to the study of what used to be called the occult sciences, conjointly with that of the new wonders, which chemistry and natural philosophy have displayed to us. His pocket money was spent in the purchase of books relative to these darling pursuits – of chemical apparatus and materials. The books consisted of treatises on magic and witchcraft, as well as those more modern ones detailing the miracles of electricity and galvanism. Sometimes he watched the livelong nights for ghosts. At his father's house, where his influence was, of course, great among the dependents, he even planned how he might get admission to the vault, or charnel-house, at Warnham Church, and might sit there all night, harrowed by fear, yet trembling with expectation, to see one of the spiritualized owners of the bones piled around him.[59]

Peacock, who always understood this side of Shelley better than Hogg and was prepared to write about it more carefully, says that in after-life Shelley himself laughed over many of these incidents, yet 'he often spoke of them to me'. Peacock felt it was worth putting on record the fact that 'if he had ever any faith in the possible success of his incantations, he had lost it before I knew him'.[60] Peacock was cautious, for he knew that Shelley's cast of mind was deeply affected by these adolescent interests, which were not so much abandoned as developed, intellectualized, refined and further sophisticated. Many curious incidents in later life can be traced to this root.

Hogg's narration of one of Shelley's solitary devil-raising sessions reflects certain descriptions and scenes in Shelley's later poetry:

> He consulted his books, how to raise a ghost; and once, at midnight, – he was then at Eton – he stole from his Dame's house, and quitting the town, crossed the fields towards a running stream. As he walked along the pathway amidst the long grass, he heard it rustle behind him; he dared not look back; he felt convinced that the devil followed him; he walked fast, and held tight the skull, the prescribed assistant of his incantations. When he had crossed the field he felt less fearful, for the grass no longer rustled, so the devil no longer followed him.[61]

In this little piece of comic macabre is the first appearance of one of those ghostly 'following figures' which were to haunt Shelley both in his life and his writing throughout his remaining years. The first occasion on which Shelley consciously admitted this obsession to himself was in the poem, 'Oh! There are spirits of the air', written when he was 23.[62]

The one adult figure of importance in Shelley's life at Eton was Dr James Lind. Lind had been at one time physician to the Royal Household, and was now retired, living at Windsor, and teaching part-time at the college. He was a mild, silver-haired, professorial and somewhat eccentric figure. He had been a scholar and a traveller. His journeys had taken him to Iceland, India and China, and his collection of stones and curios was extensive. He was fascinated by typography and set up and printed his own little pamphlets. He had a wide knowledge of mythological and philosophical writings, both Greek and Oriental, and had published three papers for the Royal Society.[63] He was interested in hermetic writings, and it was rumoured that he was an amateur demonologist.[64] Shelley found in him both an intellectual guide and an emotional father-figure, and in this respect he was to be the precursor of William Godwin.

During Shelley's last two years at Eton he was taken under the Doctor's wing, and was frequently invited to Lind's house in Windsor for tea, which was served in a variegated selection of teacups by the Doctor's niece. Lind encouraged Shelley to be systematic in his reading and speculation, discussing with him the philosophical limitations of Pliny's natural history, and recommending his first liberal and radical texts, the works of Benjamin Franklin, Condorcet the materialist and Voltaire the sceptic. Shelley's interest in Lucretius as a sound, classical authority for an anti-religious and scientific-materialist philosophy was also probably fostered by Lind; and there is some evidence that Shelley's first contact with Godwin's writing was a glimpse of Lind's copy of *Political Justice*.[65] Lind's interest in pamphleteering encouraged Shelley in his own printing schemes, and Lind also taught him the value of the postal debate.

Shelley's strategy, adopted from the Doctor, was to write to well-known authorities on religious or philosophical questions, posing as a distressed spinster, puzzled curate or other intellectual innocent. Having once hooked a reply the innocent correspondence would step up the level of the debate, until suddenly the unwary Doctor of Divinity found himself having to argue for his life. Shelley delighted in this form of intellectual ambush, and Hogg recorded that in 1810 Shelley had several postal debates in progress simultaneously. Shelley's favourite pseudonym was the harmless-sounding 'Reverend Merton', and his most distinguished catch was no less than the Dean of St Paul's.[66] Hogg also said, less reliably, that Dr Lind was amused to hear of old Bysshe's capacity for cursing, and that he taught Shelley a formal Rite of Damnation to be pronounced against political enemies.

It was Dr Lind who first read Plato – still regarded both in schools and universities as a subversive and corrupting author – with Shelley and drew his attention to the *Phaedrus* and the *Symposium*. This was an introduction which was to bear fruit in a masterly translation when Shelley was 26. Shelley commemorated Dr Lind in two of his poems of 1817, *The Revolt of Islam* and 'Prince Athanase', in which he was transformed, like Godwin, into a mythical personage: the sage, the rescuer, the healer. Shelley celebrated this in his description of the education of Prince Athanase by the magus Zonoras, the 'one beloved friend' with eyes 'whose arrowy light shone like the reflex of a thousand minds'. The platonic teaching was presented by Shelley in retrospect as something intellectually and emotionally sacred:

Thus through his age, dark, cold, and tempest-tossed,
Shone truth upon Zonoras; and he filled
From fountains pure, nigh overgrown and lost,

The spirit of Prince Athanase, a child,
With soul sustaining songs of ancient lore
And philosophic wisdom, clear and mild,

And sweet and subtle talk they evermore,
The pupil and the master, shared . . . .[67]

The adolescent idea of learning as a kind of alchemy which provided the
secret key to wisdom was gradually to become transformed into a more mature
and political conception. Learning became the private and secret weapon against
public tyranny, passed on by the aged philosopher to the youthful activist. It
was almost the idea of the 'conspiracy of the intellect'. Shelley expounded this
view of his education in the mouth of another Lind-like sage and father-figure
in the other poem of 1817, *The Revolt of Islam*.

'Yes, from the records of my youthful state,
    And from the lore of bards and sages old,
From whatsoe'er my wakened thoughts create
    Out of the hopes of thine aspirings bold,
    Have I collected language to unfold
Truth to my countrymen; from shore to shore
    Doctrines of human power my words have told,
They have been heard, and men aspire to more
Than they have ever gained or ever lost of yore.

'In secret chambers parents read, and weep,
    My writings to their babes, no longer blind;
And young men gather when their tyrants sleep,
    And vows of faith each to the other bind. . . .

'The tyrants of the Golden City tremble
    At the voices which are heard about the streets,
The ministers of fraud can scarce dissemble
    The lies of their own heart; but when one meets
    Another at the shrine, he inly weets,
Though he says nothing, that the truth is known;
    Murderers are pale upon the judgement-seats,
And gold grows vile even to the wealthy crone,
And laughter fills the Fane, and curses shake the Throne. . . .'[68]

If Dr Lind had gradually inherited over the years the position of spiritual father and guide, Timothy, by contrast, was to be transformed into the type of false father, betrayer and tyrant.

According to Shelley it was Dr Lind who came to Field Place to prevent his beloved pupil from being committed to the asylum by the tyrant father Timothy during his fever. Lind's contrast with Timothy was overt in Shelley's mind. 'This man . . . is exactly what an old man ought to be. Free, calm-spirited, full of benevolence, and even of youthful ardour; his eye seemed to burn with supernatural spirit beneath his brow, shaded by his venerable white locks; he was tall, vigorous, and healthy in his body; tempered, as it had ever been, by his amiable mind. I owe that man far, ah! far more than I owe to my father; he loved me, and I shall never forget our long talks where he breathed the spirit of the kindest tolerance and the purest wisdom.'[69] So he told Mary Shelley, on the night in 1814 when he declared his love for her.

By 1809, when Shelley was 17, the friendship with Lind had brought out the first clear marks of dawning intellectual maturity, and Eton had begun to smooth some of its expensive social polish over the disturbed and volatile personality beneath. His sisters remembered their 'silent, though excessive' admiration as their elder brother stood in beautifully fitting silk pantaloons warming his coat-tails in front of the massive fire at Field Place. To an Eton friend he wrote nonchalantly of shooting at thousands of wild ducks and geese 'in our River and Lake' all day, and reading novels and romances all night. Tom Medwin saw him down three snipe in three successive shots at the end of the pond. In another letter he issued an invitation in the Eton style of the day: 'I hope we shall have the Pleasure of your Company at Field Place at Easter, & that you will conjointly with Il Padre & myself esclipse the Beau's & Belles of the Horsham Ball. . . . O how I wish you were here to enliven our Provincial Stupidity & how I regret the Frost – I am your affectionate friend.'[70] It is notable that his father is still referred to in a markedly amiable light.

A new attraction who entered briefly but intensely into his life in 1809 was his beautiful cousin, Harriet Grove, who came to stay with the rest of her family at Field Place during the spring. His new-found appetite for postal debates had led him to write to his cousin as well, and in her diary between January and April 1809 she recorded the receipt of weekly letters. The friendship began on paper before it began in fact, and it was to retain a novelettish quality throughout the next eighteen months. Shelley first properly met Harriet in April, at a time when he described himself immersed in solitude at Field Place, having 'no Employment, except writing Novels & Letters'. His youngest sisters were now themselves away at school. The descent of the Grove family for several days cheered him up and excited him: an inseparable romantic foursome was formed of Shelley, Harriet, her closest brother Charles, and Elizabeth Shelley. There were moonlit walks to Strood – Shelley's old favourite – and twilit rambles round St Irving's, a beautiful Elizabethan manor house near Horsham with gardens and fountains laid out by Capability Brown. Shelley, Harriet and Elizabeth planned poems and novels together, and when the Groves moved up to Town to stay at John Grove's house in Lincoln's Inn Fields, Shelley, Elizabeth and Mrs Shelley rapidly joined them. Shelley wrote pointedly to an Eton friend: 'I shall be in London on the 16th at the Opera on Tuesday – observe *who* I am with, & I will ask your opinion at some future period.'[71]

In London, they all went to see Hellen and Margaret Shelley at their school in Clapham, and Hellen was much impressed by Harriet's prettiness as Tom Medwin had been at Field Place – 'like some Madonna of Raphael'. She remembered that Shelley was very full of himself and showing off, and much to everyone's embarrassment spilt a glass of port wine on the headmistress's table-cloth. Then they all went into the garden and 'there was much ado to calm the spirits of the wild boy'.[72] The curious thing was that the two cousins looked very much alike, and Shelley seemed to revel in this sense of twinship. In May, the Groves returned to Wiltshire and Shelley went back to Eton for his last year. Charles Grove remembered that 'Bysshe was full of life and spirits, and very well pleased with his successful devotion to my sister.'[73] Harriet tacitly agreed to act as his Muse, and the friendship brought him both kudos and self-confidence. He continued to write to her regularly in Wiltshire, but his letters instead of being full of romantic declarations, were packed out with Shelley's strange mixture of grim, gothic fantasies and poems, and lumps of ill-digested Condorcet and Lucretius. By September, Harriet had grown both alarmed and slightly bored with the correspondence, and she showed some of it to her parents who advised her to break it off. Shelley was piqued rather than upset by this develop-ment, but he continued to address her as a convenient Muse in the poems which he was writing with Elizabeth, and in the following spring he met her again at Field Place. Neither Shelley's nor Harriet's parents regarded this in any way as ill-advised. Harriet had some arguments with her brother Charles about a gothic novel Shelley had written, which she was prepared to patronize: 'I think it makes him [Charles] appear very illnatured to criticise so *very* much.'[74] Shelley himself was sulking, and she found his behaviour strange and odd, but they walked again at St Irving's and Strood, and had 'a long conversation', in which nothing very constructive seemed to emerge. They had little in common, and it was only in her absence that Shelley could feel very strongly about her.

For her part Harriet certainly did not take the matter very seriously, and by the end of the year she had announced her formal engagement to a local gentleman farmer, William Helyer. Shelley by this time was at Oxford, and it was only during the winter vacation of 1810, when he first heard the news, that he reacted with melodramatic despair, and Elizabeth spoke of watching him very carefully when he went out for walks with his gun. But by this time, quite other forces were at work, and Harriet's 'betrayal' provided a natural *mise en scène*. It was an affair, like the other myths of his childhood, that flourished in retrospect and in his angry memories of persecution and love withdrawn.

Shelley was 18 in 1810, and in his last term at Eton he finally established himself as a notable classical scholar, a tolerated eccentric with strange philosophical views and, something rather smarter, a popular author. In April, the gothic novel upon which he had been working both at Eton and Field Place for some eighteen months, appeared under the announcement in *The British Critic*: 'Zastrozzi; a Romance. By P.B.S. 5s.' Shelley earned the remarkable sum of £40 for this work, printed by J.Robinson, and circulated in time to bring him considerable admiration and notoriety in his leaving term at Eton. The £40 was spent on a farewell dinner, which suggests that he had established not merely a niche but an active following by the time he left. Hogg records that he was dignified by the title 'the Eton Atheist', a title reserved for those who had successfully opposed the school authorities. The implication was sociological rather than theological; but it implied recognition.

On Election Day, 30 July 1810, Shelley delivered one of Cicero's speeches against Catiline as his contribution to the leaving ceremony, and it was generally understood that the tall, thin, strangely animated figure who would be going up to Oxford in the autumn had recently completed a translation of the first fifteen books of Pliny's *Historia Naturalis*. Tom Medwin added that at this time Shelley's favourite among contemporary poets was Robert Southey, and that he knew Southey's massive oriental verse narrative *Thalaba* almost by heart. Shelley liked to chant the demonic formula from Southey's *Curse of Kehama* while fixing his eye on his companion –

And water shall see thee
And fear thee, and fly thee
The waves shall not touch thee
As they pass by thee!

He had also developed the eccentricity of muttering bits of *Macbeth* and Coleridge's *Ancient Mariner* under his breath, which he added to the natural peculiarity of his high, sharp laughter at unexpected moments. The 'eccentric' style, perhaps partly imitated from Dr Lind, was a deliberate piece of character creation, and revealed that the slightly spoilt arrogance of the eldest child had survived the long infernal trial of his schooldays. At this time he wrote to

Edward Graham, the young music master who taught Shelley's sisters at Clapham and lived at the fashionable address of 29 Vine Street, Piccadilly: 'It is never my custom to make new friends whom I cannot own to my old ones.... . I act unlike every mortal enough in all conscience, without seeking for more Quixotish adventures.'[75] Graham actually became a close friend during this summer of 1810, and helped Shelley with his literary schemes, while sharing with him and Elizabeth in the wilder weavings of their horror fantasies.

The months before Oxford saw a burst of literary publications, which suggests that Timothy had granted Shelley an allowance to indulge in this more adult form of 'pranking'. There were four completed works, apart from a lost horror tale called *The Nightmare*, which it appears Shelley wanted Henry Fuseli to illustrate.[76] Besides *Zastrozzi*, which came out in the spring, Shelley completed a book of poems with Elizabeth; a verse melodrama *The Wandering Jew*, which was partly written by Tom Medwin; and *St Irvyne, or The Rosicrucian*, a second romance in the style of *Zastrozzi*, concerning alchemy and free love and unspeakable crimes of passion. *St Irvyne* was duly published during Shelley's first term at Oxford, but the verses of *The Wandering Jew* stuck at Ballantyne's office and did not appear in book form until the Shelley Society solemnly brought it forth in 1887. The book of poems appeared in September. All the works were lurid in the extreme, a grand vindication of the educational powers of the Minerva Press.

The most interesting, *Zastrozzi*, is a work of pure pastiche, and draws continually – even down to names – on the novels and stories of Lewis, Mrs Radcliffe and the *Zofloya* of Charlotte Dacre. The protagonists are the standard cardboard figures of the genre: Verezzi the suffering hero and Zastrozzi the persecuting villain: Julia the blonde virginal heroine (Verezzi's true love) and Mathilda the hot-blooded scarlet woman (raven-haired and Zastrozzi's accomplice in crime). It has however provided perfect raw material for a modern psychoanalytic study which yields the succinct interpretation that Shelley was 'an introspective schizoid type with arrested sexual development at an undifferentiated stage, showing itself in elements of narcissism, homosexuality, and immature heterosexuality'.[77] Certain unusual qualities in Shelley's juvenile work *do* show up through the psychoanalytic screen; and certain significant repetitions of structure and theme do relate to later developments – not so much directly in Shelley's life, but rather more in his work.

Throughout the tale, Verezzi, like the best heroes of the type, is pursued or tortured or seduced, or all three simultaneously. But the way this occurs is on at least one occasion less typical. At the beginning of the tale he is immured in a cave, chained to a rock, starved and driven mad. This is clearly an early rendition of the 'asylum' incident at Field Place: it recurs in *The Revolt of Islam* (1817) and *Prometheus Unbound* (1820).

Mathilda and Julia are standard types again, but Verezzi's agonized inability to choose between them, for he falls in love with both, one sexually and the other platonically, is more original. At the height of the imaginative and sexual excitement he is confronted by both at once in the same room: his reaction is traumatic – first he swoons and loses consciousness, then he awakes and stabs himself to death in a kind of ecstasy. The two contrasting women, and the suicidal or self-immolating third alternative are recurrent in Shelley's work; they are to be found in *Alastor* (1815), *Prometheus Unbound* (1819) and in *Epipsychidion* (1821). They are also in Peacock's brilliant comic variation on the Shelleyan theme, *Nightmare Abbey* (1818).

Finally, in the character of Zastrozzi, the towering irrepressible villain, we have an early draft of the Satanic outcast, the damned atheist, who confronts his judges and remains unmoved in the final scenario, gaining, at the last, a heroic stature by default.[78] This figure became enormously important to Shelley, and sophisticated variations on him appear in nearly all the longer poems: *Queen Mab* (1813), *The Revolt of Islam*, *Prometheus Unbound* and *The Cenci* (1819) – as well as in many of the shorter ones.

The question of violence, first encountered in Shelley's reaction to school, now occurred for the first time as a literary peculiarity. The violence in *Zastrozzi* is striking; it is physical violence and often presented with blatant satisfaction. Here, for example, the scarlet woman ends the career of the virginal blonde:

> 'Die, detested wretch,' exclaimed Mathilda, in a paroxysm of rage, as she violently attempted to bathe the stiletto in the life-blood of her rival; but Julia starting aside, the weapon slightly wounded her neck, and the ensanguined stream stained her alabaster bosom. She fell on the floor, but suddenly starting up, attempted to escape her bloodthirsty persecutor. Nerved anew by this futile attempt to escape her vengeance, the ferocious Mathilda seized Julia's floating hair, and holding her back with fiend-like strength, stabbed her in a thousand places; and, with exulting pleasure, again and again buried the dagger to the hilt in her body, even after all remains of life were annihilated. At last the passions of Mathilda, exhausted by their own violence, sank into a deadly calm; she threw the dagger violently from her, and contemplated the terrific scene before her with a sullen gaze.[79]

There is a sense in which all this, too, can be dismissed – and perhaps should be – as cheerful plagiarism. Nevertheless the skill and relish with which the action is drawn out is remarkable; and more so is the fact that the basic rhythm of the action, its frantic climax and torpid decline, reflects not so much an act of ordinary assault, as the specific act of rape.*

The intoxicating sense of freedom which Shelley felt in his departure from Eton allowed many of his darker and solitary preoccupations (witnessed in *Zastrozzi*) to bubble up again more lightly in the camaraderie between himself, Elizabeth and Edward Graham. A letter informing Graham that the Shelley family were coming to Town, and would meet him in Clapham, contained the following macabre instructions:

> Stalk along the road towards them – & mind & keep concealed as my mother brings a blood stained stiletto which she purposes to make you bathe in the lifeblood of her enemy. Never mind the Death-demons, & skeletons dripping with the putrefaction of the grave, that occasionally may blast your straining eyeball – Persevere even though Hell & destruction should yawn beneath your feet – 'Think of all this at the frightful hour of midnight, when the Hell Demon leans over your sleeping form, & inspires those thoughts which eventually will lead you to the gates of destruction'. . . .[80]

A note by Elizabeth added, with suitable Rosicrucian cyphers, that the Hell Demon was to be honoured with the title of 'HD'. This demon proved to be a useful all-purpose persona, for it featured prominently in more serious, melodramatic form in the collection of poetry by Shelley and Elizabeth, published anonymously and entitled *Original Poetry by Victor and Cazire*. The book appeared in September 1810, the month before Shelley went to Oxford.

This was Shelley's first poetical production: an entirely third-rate collection of bad gothic verses, sixteen pieces and a fragment in all. Among these were two verse epistles by Elizabeth; some half a dozen sentimental 'Songs' addressed by Shelley to Harriet Grove; translations from German and Italian material; a revolutionary declamation about Ireland; and Shelley's imitation of Chatterton, 'Ghasta; or the Avenging Demon!!!' There was also a straight plagiarism from a horror-poem by Monk Lewis which led to the whole edition being pulped before the end of the year. No less than 1,500 copies of the book were printed in Worthing, and published in Pall Mall by John James Stockdale. It was again financed, according to Hogg, by Shelley's grandfather, old Bysshe. The contents and style give a fair indication of Shelley's imaginative development at the age of 18: he could not be called precocious. But the collection gave him a new

---

* Dr Eustace Chesser's analytic summary of the novel, though dogmatic and infected by some of Shelley's own melodrama, is none the less worth bearing in mind. 'Some introverts are cold and withdrawn, but Shelley is not of this type. His emotions are exceptionally violent. His hatred is passionate, almost murderous; his love is of unbearable intensity. . . . Shelley's aggression is personified by his persecutor. Since both Zastrozzi and Verezzi are different aspects of Shelley, he is his own tormentor.'

sense of achieved identity, and he filled his letters to Graham with hard-headed professional remarks about 'pouching' the reviewers. Amazingly, two periodicals did actually notice it.*

The longish ballad poem 'Ghasta; or the Avenging Demon!!!' contains many suggestive elements. In it Shelley first introduced the figure of the Wandering Jew, the cursed exile who is damned to eternal wandering over the earth. The exile figure already fascinated Shelley: the Jewishness seemed insignificant in itself, though the Jewish conception of God – the Jehovah figure – was already abhorrent to him. He was to write to his friend Hogg during a frantic exchange of letters over the winter vacation of 1810/11: 'For the immoral "never to be able to die, never to escape from some shrine as chilling as the clay-formed dungeon which now it inhabits" is the future punishment I believe in.' This was Shelley's first conception of 'the damned'. He also immediately clarified in the same letter what was the opposite, his conception of 'the saved': it was love. 'Love, love *infinite in extent*, eternal in duration, yet (allowing your theory in that point) perfectible should be the reward.'[81] The exile, the damned, is withdrawn from the central warmth of love into eternal and icy orbit; the saved, the justified, is for ever enclosed in its perfect stable glowing heart. It was the lesson of Field Place.

'Ghasta' also contained Shelley's first poetical presentation of one of the 'following figures' who had appeared in the little anecdote retold by Hogg. The scene is a misty castle in a drear wilderness, a nightmare vision of Field Place. Along the 'terrace' a Hell Demon begins to accumulate:

> Light the cloud as summer fog,
>   Which transient shuns the morning beam;
> Fleeting as the cloud on bog,
>   That hangs or on the mountain stream. –
>
> Horror seized my shuddering brain,
>   Horror dimmed my starting eye,
> In vain I tried to speak, – In vain
>   My limbs essayed the spot to fly –
>
> At last the thin and shadowy form,
>   With noiseless, trackless footsteps came, –
> Its light robe floated on the storm,
>   Its head was bound with lambent flame.

* *The British Critic* assumed the author was a lady, and left it at that. *The Literary Panorama*, October 1810, noted sympathetically: 'Surely modern poets are the most unhappy of men! Their imaginations are perpetually haunted with terrors. ... Can anything possibly be finer – that is, more terrific – that is – ahem! – than the following?'

In chilling voice drear as the breeze
   Which sweeps along th' autumnal ground,
Which wanders thro' the leafless trees,
   Or the mandrake's groan which floats around.

'Thou art mine and I am thine,
   'Till the sinking of the world,
I am thine and thou are mine,
   'Till in ruin death is hurled —

Shelley's passion for the rhythmic chanting alchemical formula shows well in the last verse. The Demon dissolves at dawn, but daylight gives the poet little peace, 'melancholy seized my brain', and when night returns, so does the horror:

At last came night, ah! horrid hour,
   Ah! chilling time that wakes the dead,
When demons ride the clouds that lower,
   — The phantom sat upon my bed.[82]

This final picture may well account for the fact that Shelley wrote to Graham concerning the painter Henry Fuseli. Fuseli's bedside vision of the 'Nightmare' is one of the signatures of the horror art of the period.

Victor and Cazire demonstrated how the horror genre could be developed in different directions. Shelley's Demons were never to prove intractable or rigid: on the contrary they adapted themselves to his interests and assimilated his intellectual developments with an almost sinister ease. In 'The Irishman's Song', they showed signs of a dawning political dimension born of crude revolutionary sentiment:

Our foes ride in triumph throughout our domains,
And our mightiest heroes lie stretched on the plains.
. . . the yelling ghosts ride on the blast that sweeps by,
And 'my countrymen! vengeance!' incessantly cry.[83]

These are nothing less than the primitive ancestors of the fiends of *Prometheus Unbound*.

Shelley enrolled for the Michaelmas term at University College, Oxford, in October 1810. Before he set out, his father Timothy gave him some worldly advice in the study with its pictures of Christ crucified and Vesuvius erupting. Tom Medwin happened to be present, and recorded: 'He would provide for as many natural children as [Bysshe] chose to get, but that he would never forgive him for making a *mésalliance*.'[84] Shelley, the romantic author of *Zastrozzi*, the demon-raiser and the Eton atheist, stared at his father with silent scorn. Father and son took the Oxford coach together, and when they arrived, Timothy made a special point of taking Shelley round to the leading bookseller, Slatter's in the High. 'My son here,' said Timothy Shelley, 'has a literary turn; he is already an author, and do pray indulge him in his printing freaks.'[85]

2
Oxford: 1810–11

The bookshop of Slatter and Munday, with its wide bow display window, stood on one side of the Oxford High; nearly opposite on the other side of the street stood the gatehouse of University College. The college was one of Oxford's most venerable foundations, dating from 1249, though its buildings – the first quadrangle, the hall and the chapel – all dated from the mid-seventeenth century. Walking under the vaulted gatehouse beneath the solicitous eyes of the lodge porter, and turning to his rooms in the south-west corner of the quad, Shelley was overwhelmed by the impression of entering the inner temple of an ecclesiastical institution, some grim Jacobean seminary for ancient clerics. His rooms, on the first floor, overlooked the trim green walks of Fellows' Garden to the west, and on the other side the chapel across the quad to the east. The Master had recently spent several thousand pounds renovating the latter building, and it now boasted an extravagant gothic façade of buttresses, looming battlements and sportif pinnacles.[1]

Into this stronghold of royalist tradition and prejudice, Shelley unloaded trunkloads of French philosophy, German horror novels, his solar microscope and several crates of chemical and electrical equipment, including a system of Voltaic batteries and a hand-cranked generator. A long battle instantly began with his scout, whose job it was to clean the apartment and to bring Shelley whatever light meals and domestic requirements he might need. But by the end of November it was clear that Shelley had permanently established his chaos of tangled 'philosophic' apparatus, broken crockery, expensive clothes flung in heaps, acid-burnt carpets, and across all available surfaces, including the floor, a permanent cascade of calf-bound quarto and folio volumes interspersed with the occasional blue-paper cover of the Minerva Press.

The first impression of his undergraduate friend Hogg was never forgotten:

Books, boots, papers, shoes, philosophical instruments, clothes, pistols, linen, crockery, ammunition, and phials innumerable, with money, stockings,

prints, crucibles, bags, and boxes, were scattered on the floor in every place.
. . . The tables, and especially the carpet, were already stained with large spots
of various hues, which frequently proclaimed the agency of fire. An electrical
machine, an air-pump, the galvanic trough, a solar microscope, and large
glass jars and receivers, were conspicuous amidst the mass of matter. Upon the
table by his side were some books lying open, several letters, a bundle of new
pens, and a bottle of japan ink, that served as an ink stand; a piece of deal,
lately part of the lid of a box, with many chips, and a handsome razor that had
been used as a knife.[2]

The only factor that kept this swelling pandemonium in bounds was not
Shelley's scout but the college system of double doors or 'oaks' which sealed off
each set of rooms, both visibly and audibly, from the staircase and the outside
world. Shelley recounted that on his second morning, after the scout had left
and, according to custom, 'sported the oak' of the outer door, he had later run
hurriedly out to the bookshop and precipitantly flinging open his first door in
the dark, had bounded headlong into the second. Shelley observed acidly that
the oak was the tree of knowledge.[3]

The Michaelmas term of winter 1810 soon convinced Shelley that his first
impressions of Oxford were representative. The Master and Fellows of his
college were, of course, all clergymen, and the only intellectual distinction it
could claim from past history was that Dr Johnson regularly used to spend the
evening there with Sir Robert Chambers, Vinerian Professor of English Law,
and Sir William Jones the orientalist, on which occasions he would personally
consume three bottles of port. The undergraduates at University College still
only numbered some 200 in Shelley's time, and the total number in all three
years at Oxford was well under 5,000, so it was a close-knit and somewhat
claustrophobic society. Oxford had no Faculties of Science, and Shelley's main
requirements seem to have been to attend Chapel daily each morning, deliver a
translation into Latin of an article from the *Spectator* once a week, and visit his
tutor once a term. Personal academic supervision was minimal, and undergraduates, especially those from county backgrounds, were expected to do a
good deal of private entertaining, take an active part in the drinking, sporting
and whoring life of the city, and to do a little light general reading among the
Greek and Latin classics. Particularly during the years of the Napoleonic Wars,
and more than a decade before the growth of such remarkable institutions as
'The Apostles' at Cambridge, where young writers such as Tennyson and
Richard Monckton Milnes could gather, the intellectual life of the universities
was virtually dormant. Hogg remembered Shelley returning mournfully from
one of his early tutorials:

They are very dull people here. . . . A little man sent for me this morning, and told me in an almost inaudible whisper that I must read; 'you must read' he said many times in his small voice. I answered that I had no objection. He persisted. . . . 'Must I read Euclid?' I asked sorrowfully. 'Yes, certainly; and when you have read the Greek works I have mentioned, you must begin Aristotle's Ethics; and then you may go on to his other treatises. It is of the utmost importance to be well acquainted with Aristotle.' This he repeated so often that I was quite tired, and at last I said 'Must I care about Aristotle? What if I do not mind Aristotle?' I then left him, for he seemed to be in great perplexity.[4]

For Shelley, intoxicated by the freedom which the university gave in comparison to Eton, and yet suffocated by the atmosphere of entrenched, comfortable, and venal clerical *auctoritas*, Oxford rapidly took shape in his mind as a personal challenge, a fortress of superstition and mediocrity, which required above all rousing from its antiquated slumbers; it had to be outraged by sheer excess of behaviour, and taken by a dazzling intellectual storm. It was a Bastille of the spirit, and he had arrived in person to open its gates.

Shelley was not much affected by the official life of the college, for he swiftly organized his own, making a point of keeping an outlandish timetable, frequently reading sixteen hours a day, and often sleeping between 6 and 10 in the evening curled up like an animal on his hearthrug in front of the fire, then getting up to talk and conduct chemical experiments throughout the night. It was also noted that the talking would sometimes take place in his sleep 'incoherently for a long while'.[5] Very occasionally he held informal parties, and a note has survived inviting a fellow-undergraduate, James Roe, to 'wine & poetry in my room'.[6] He detested dining in evening Hall, and missed it (by oversleeping) as often as possible. He pushed out of the very few lectures he attended before they were over; and had a trick of leaping up the moment morning chapel was finished, so that he was demonstrably the first out, effecting 'a ludicrously precipitate retreat to his rooms'.[7] To complete the public image of a brilliant young heretic, Shelley grew his hair long at a time when the cab-man crew-cut was fashionable, and purchased from his 'Oxford Taylor's Messers Dry', one 'superfine olive coat with Gilt buttons' and a set of memorable striped marcela waistcoats.[8]

The one institution at Oxford which Shelley was disposed to take seriously was Slatter and Munday's, and having introduced the proprietors to *Zastrozzi*, he was soon planning a whole series of new publications. To start with there was his second gothic romance *St Irvyne, or The Rosicrucian*. It had been printed by Stockdale, but December saw it prominently displayed on Slatter's shelves under the anonymous authorship of 'A Gentleman of the University of Oxford'. Besides the lurid horror and violence of the previous book, it contained dashes of erotic melodrama and flickerings of progressive social theory from Condorcet, Paine and Godwin. Ginotti, its sinister Italianate protagonist, had a double identity and was also cursed with the secret of Eternal Life, another Wandering Jew, and in his long, raving monologues, one can recognize the mental features of his undergraduate creator:

> From my earliest youth, before it was quenched by complete satiation, *curiosity*, and a desire of unveiling the latent mysterious of nature, was the passion by which all the other emotions of my mind were intellectually organised. . . . Love I cared not for, and wondered why men perversely sought to ally themselves to weakness. Natural philosophy [*i.e. physical science*] at last became the peculiar science to which I directed my eager enquiries; thence I was led into a train of labyrinthine meditations. I thought of *death.* . . .[9]

Copies were distributed to his Oxford acquaintances, to various relations in Sussex, anonymously to a number of university Fellows and to his small circle of admirers at his sisters' school in Clapham – including the beautiful girl who had been nominated to enact Venus in the *Fête Champêtre*[10] and whose name he later learnt was Harriet Westbrook. But it took sterner stuff to shake Bodley's dome.

It was through fierce argument about the relative merits of Italian and German gothic writers that Shelley made his one close friend at Oxford. Shelley first met Thomas Jefferson Hogg at one of the detested dinners in Hall early in November; and started a discussion which led back to his rooms, where Hogg was duly impressed and stayed on until dawn. Visits were reciprocated, and Hogg soon learnt to recognize the familiar sound of Shelley's footsteps 'running through the quiet quadrangle in the still night'.[11] A shared feeling of ridicule for the college authorities, and a mutual enthusiasm for speculative opinions and heretical tastes rapidly drew the two young men together, and the friendship became by far in a way the most important influence on Shelley at Oxford; while Hogg was later to call Shelley 'a whole university in himself to me'. Hogg was Shelley's first real intimacy outside the world of Field Place, and the friendship was to grow into a passionate attachment, so that far more truly than Harriet Grove, one can say that T. J. Hogg was Shelley's first love affair.

At the time of their meeting, Hogg was aged 18 like Shelley, but had already spent a summer term at University College. He was a broad, stocky figure beside Shelley's tall elegant outline, and a silhouette of him wearing the academical tasselled cap shows a curling, rather supercilious lip, and a fine, prominent

Roman nose, with his head tilted in a sharply inquisitorial manner. His background was very different from Shelley's, coming from solid professional middle-class stock in northern England, where his father, John Hogg, was a lawyer and administrator with respectable connections with the clergy of Durham Cathedral. The large family lived at Norton Durham, and young Hogg was intended for the Law. Shelley was attracted by his wide reading in contemporary literature and political philosophy, and his acutely logical mind which frequently produced savage humour at the expense of opponents, and also of the college authorities. At the same time there was something curiously gullible and bovine about Hogg's temperament, which made him both a loyal admirer of Shelley's extravagance, and the perfect, tireless audience for Shelley's nocturnal fantasies and speculative monologues. Hogg would listen to these entranced, egging Shelley on with his own suggestions and ironic asides, and years later in *The Life of Shelley** he recorded them with immense gusto as if he could remember every word:

The galvanic battery is a new engine; it has been used hitherto to an insignificant extent, yet has it wrought wonders already; what will not an extraordinary combination of troughs, of colossal magnitude, a well arranged system of hundreds of metallic plates, effect? The balloon has not yet received the perfection of which it is surely capable. . . . Why are we still so ignorant of the interior of Africa? – why do we not despatch intrepid aeronauts to cross it in every direction, and to survey the whole peninsula in a few weeks? The shadow of the first balloon, which a vertical sun would project precisely underneath it, as it glided silently over that hitherto unhappy country, would virtually emancipate every slave, and would annihilate slavery for ever. . . . 'What do you say of metaphysics?' I continued. . . . 'Ay, metaphysics,' he said, in a solemn tone, and with a mysterious air, 'that is a noble study indeed! If it were possible to make any discoveries there, they would be more valuable than anything the chemists have done, or could do; they would disclose the

---

* Hogg first contributed a long article to the *New Monthly Magazine* in 1832 entitled 'Reminiscences of Shelley at Oxford'; later he was allowed access to Shelley papers kept at Field Place and wrote the first two volumes of *The Life of Shelley* covering the poet's career until 1814. It was published in 1858, after which permission to use the Shelley papers was withdrawn. Hogg's presentation of Shelley is brilliantly anecdotal, but consistently humorous and facetious, with a great deal of his own autobiography intermixed. He altered the text of Shelley's letters, to soften their radicalism, and characteristically 'Atheist' is always printed as 'Deist', and 'atheistical' as 'philosophical'. Pronouns were also changed to disguise his emotional involvement in Shelley's life. Hogg has been harshly viewed by later scholars, but his own life was crippled partially by his connection with Shelley: disaster at Oxford, disinheritance and failure to achieve high distinction at the Bar. He wrote sadly: 'It is difficult to view [Shelley] with the mind which I then bore – with a young mind; to lay aside the seriousness of old age; for twenty years of assiduous study have induced, if not in the body, at least within, something of premature old age.'

analysis of the mind, and not of mere matter!' Then rising from his chair, he paced slowly about the room, with prodigious strides, and discoursed of souls with still greater animation and vehemence than he had displayed in treating of gases – of a future state – and especially of a former state – of pre-existence, obscured for a time through the suspension of consciousness – of personal identity, and also of ethical philosophy ... until he suddenly remarked that the fire was nearly out, and the candles glimmering in their sockets, when he hastily apologised for remaining so long.[12]

Shelley and Hogg would frequently study in each other's rooms, and work on chosen authors simultaneously. Hogg casually revealed that he too had written a romance, provisionally entitled *Leonora*, and Shelley eagerly read the manuscript, relishing the atheistical undertones. He promised to send it instantly to the obliging Mr Stockdale. When Shelley slept on the hearth rug, Hogg would read on quietly at the table, and he was always amazed by the way Shelley would abruptly awake after a few hours, rubbing his hair wildly and launching without pause into a rapid and highly involved discussion of some abstruse problem.

In the afternoons they usually walked out together in the countryside round Oxford, encountering various bizarre adventures, which Hogg liked to recall as episodes out of Cervantes with himself as the solid Sancho Panza and Shelley as the amiably lunatic Don Quixote. Once there was a boy beating a donkey; then a gipsy waif begging for milk; a dog in a farmyard that bit off Shelley's coat-tail; and a secret garden into which Shelley trespassed, overcome by the enchantment, and then fled precipitantly away through a hedge. Then there were Shelley's strange pastimes, playing endless ducks-and-drakes on the mere below Shotover Hill; sailing paper boats on every available pond and puddle until Hogg turned blue with cold and irritation in the winter air; and the inevitable half hour of shooting practice with a fine pair of duelling pistols which Shelley tucked into his topcoat, the favourite target being the round parliamentary franking on letters sent from Field Place pinned up against a tree.[13]

The fascination with fire-arms was one of many elements in Shelley's character which Hogg, a very down-to-earth personality despite all his masterly sarcasms, could never really account for. Another was Shelley's almost maniac disregard, on certain occasions, for the commonplace decencies of normal public behaviour, as the time when he seized a baby out of its mother's arms while crossing Magdalen Bridge and began earnestly to question it about the nature of its Platonic pre-existence so that he might prove a point in an argument he was having with Hogg concerning metempsychosis. A third, and even more significant facet, which Hogg all his life tended to discount as mere comic 'fancy', was Shelley's natural and sometimes overwhelming sense of the macabre. Hogg remembered with surprise Shelley's reaction to one of his own heavy-humoured remarks about reading too much, without really appreciating its significance. ' "If I were to read as long as you read, Shelley, my hair and teeth would be strewed about on the floor, and my eyes would slip down my cheeks . . . or at least I should become so weary and nervous that I should not know whether it were so or not." [Shelley] began to scrape the carpet with his feet, as if teeth were actually lying upon it, and he look fixedly at my face, and his lively fancy represented the empty sockets; his imagination was excited. . . .'[14] Four years later Shelley was to induce violent hysteria in a girl by exactly the same piece of quaint 'fancy'.

But in the ripening friendship of Shelley and Hogg, these were mere details. Their real identity of purpose and outlook was formed in the furnace of political discussion, and although Hogg chose not to recall the fact in after years, it would seem that the young legal-minded egalitarian from Durham was highly influential in introducing Shelley to new texts and doctrines. From Shelley's few letters of the period, and his expression of political views, their intellectual diet seems to have been a richer and richer one of sceptics and radicals: David Hume and Gibbon, Voltaire and Condorcet, Paine and Franklin, Rousseau, Godwin and even the political economist Adam Smith.[15] Shelley also began to fasten on all the political news he could gather; he became familiar with Leigh Hunt's *Examiner*, William Cobbett's plebeian troubleshooter the *Political Register*, and he followed the struggles of Sir Francis Burdett, the radical MP for Westminster, and the trial of Peter Finnerty, an Irish journalist who had reported scathingly on the military expedition to Walcheren in the Low Countries.[16] The Whig alignment that he had inherited from his Sussex background of Sir Bysshe and Timothy and the Duke of Norfolk, gradually fell away in the heat of their night-long discussions, and he moved towards the extra-parliamentary groups of intellectuals and French-inspired revolutionary activists. Hogg described an undergraduate 'stranger', knowing only of Shelley through his political disputations and the 'short argumentative essays which he composed as voluntary exercises', imagining that he had become totally possessed by the spirit of Hume, ' "or rather, he represents one of the enthusiastic and animated materialists of the French school, whom revolutionary violence lately intercepted at an early age in his philosophical career" '.[17] Gradually Shelley realized that his next appearance on Slatter and Munday's shelves would have to be in a more radical cause, aiming openly at public authority.

Yet there was far more growing between Shelley and Hogg than simply political sympathy. Hogg found Shelley remarkably frank about his own private feelings and affairs, and he talked for hours about Field Place, and his concept of the ideal woman which he would discuss with 'a curious fastidiousness'. He talked of the differences between physical and extra-physical passion, and in long, thoughtful self-examinations, which Hogg also apparently remembered in detail, Shelley tactfully introduced the presence of his sisters:

'The love of the sexes, however pure, still retains some taint of earthly grossness; we must not admit it within the sanctuary.' He was silent for several minutes, and his anxiety visibly increased. 'The love of a mother for a child is more refined; it is more disinterested, more spiritual; but,' he added, after some reflection, 'the very existence of the child still connects it with the passion which we have discarded,' and here lapsed into his former musings. 'The love a sister bears towards a sister,' he exclaimed abruptly, and with an air of triumph, 'is unexceptionable.'[18]

Offering to lend Hogg money, Shelley was to write at about this time: 'Tell me then if you want cash, as I have nearly drained you, & all delicacy, like sisters stripping before each other is out of the question.'[19]

By the end of their first term together, Shelley had convinced Hogg that he ought to fall in love with his sister Elizabeth, and for that purpose it was arranged that Hogg would write regularly to Field Place during the vacation, both to declare his feelings to the girl, and also to keep Shelley intimately informed of the progress of his emotions. This somewhat curious agreement was to provide Shelley – if not his sister – with fine material for a passionate exchange of letters between the two friends, during December and January.

For Hogg, the sudden friendship swept him off his feet, and for all his studious ironies and hard-headed argumentation, a new and fantastic world of possibilities and adventures burst over him. The favourite memory that Hogg seemed to take away with him for the vacation was that of Shelley enthroned in the primal chaos of his room, wildly enraptured with one of his alarming experiments, ceaselessly discoursing on future achievements, and in the meantime transforming himself into a kind of electrical daemon, an 'unearthly' spirit of pure creative force, a fiery visionary:

He then proceeded, with much eagerness and enthusiasm, to show me the various instruments, especially the electrical apparatus; turning round the handle very rapidly, so that the fierce, crackling sparks flew forth; and presently standing upon the stool with glass feet, he begged me to work the machine until he was filled with the fluid, so that his long, wild locks bristled and stood on end. Afterwards he charged a powerful battery of several large jars; labouring with vast energy, and discoursing with increasing vehemence of the marvellous powers of electricity, of thunder and lightning; describing an electrical kite that he had made at home, and projecting another and an enormous one, or rather a combination of many kites, that would draw down from the sky an immense volume of electricity, the whole ammunition of a mighty thunderstorm; and this being directed to some point would there produce the most stupendous results.[20] *

At Field Place the winter vacation of 1810–11 began with a crisis. Shelley's publisher, Stockdale, had grown suspicious of the influence that Hogg was having over Timothy Shelley's son, and on reading the manuscript of Hogg's ideological novel *Leonora*, his worst fears were confirmed. He talked with Timothy privately when he was in London, shortly before Christmas, and warned him that a fellow-undergraduate was corrupting his son's religious principles and leading him into lawless speculations.[21] Timothy took up the matter with Shelley at Field Place, cautioning him against bad influences. Shelley immediately wrote to Hogg on 20 December:

> There is now need for all my art, I must resort to deception – My Father called on Stockdale in London who has converted him to an Xtian, he mentioned your name as a supporter of Deistical Principles. My father wrote to me & I am now surrounded, environed by dangers to which compared the Devils who besieged St Anthony all were inefficient. – They attack me for my detestable principles, I am reckoned an outcast, yet defy them & laugh at their inefficient efforts.[22]

Shelley posed to Hogg as a hero in one of their own romances, and it is difficult to tell how serious the matter was. It seems however, that Timothy was genuinely alarmed; 'My father wished to withdraw me from College, I *would* not consent to it. – There lowers a terrific tempest, but I stand as it were on a Pharos, & smile exultingly at the vain beating of the billows below.'

This at any rate was a promising beginning to their correspondence, and during the next five weeks Shelley and Hogg wrote steadily to each other by return of post, Shelley's thick wads of missive leaving Field Place two or three times a week with the 'post-free' stamp of his father's franking. Elizabeth was soon informed of her admirer's talents, but disappointingly she seemed reluctant to involve herself. Shelley wrote on Boxing Day: 'I read most of your letters to my sister; she frequently enquires after you, and we talk of you often. I do not

---

* It is one of the instructive ironies of literary history that it was precisely this image which William Hazlitt used to attack the irresponsibility of Shelley's wild radicalism in a celebrated essay ten years later, 'On Paradox and Commonplace': 'It would seem that [Mr Shelley] wanted not so much to convince or inform, as to shock the public by the tenor of his productions, but I suspect he is more intent upon startling himself with his electrical experiments in morals and philosophy; and though they may scorch other people, they are to him harmless amusements, the coruscations of an Aurora Borealis, that play around the head, but do not reach the heart! Still I could wish he would put a stop to the incessant, alarming whirl of his Voltaic battery.'

wish to awaken her intellect too powerfully; this must be my apology for not communicating all my speculations to her. Thanks, *truly* thanks for opening your heart to me, for telling me your feelings towards [her]. Dare I do the same to you? I dare not to myself, how can I to another, perfect as he may be . . .?'[23]

However, while the passion between his friend and his favourite sister seemed reluctant to ignite, Shelley soon found in the not unexpected news of Harriet Grove's engagement in Wiltshire sufficient material for more heated self-revelations. He told Hogg that his cousin had abandoned him on account of his anti-religious opinions, and Hogg apparently wrote back concerning the heroism necessary in the pursuit of the atheistical principles in a prejudiced society. Shelley picked up his cue, and transformed himself into one of the cursing outcasts of Romance, furious for revenge:

> Oh! I burn with impatience for the moment of Xtianity's dissolution, it has injured me; I swear on the altar of perjured love to revenge myself on the hated cause of the effect which *even now* I can scarcely help deploring. – Indeed I think it is to the benefit of society to destroy the opinions which *can* annihilate the dearest of its ties. Inconveniences would now result from my *owning* the novel which I have in preparation for the press. I give out therefore that I will publish no more; every one here, but the select few who enter into its schemes believed my assertion – I will stab the wretch in secret. – Let us hope that the wound which we inflict tho' the dagger be concealed, will rankle in the heart of our adversary.[24]

The perjured love was of course Harriet Grove's, and the 'novel' was an unknown production, now of atheistical tendencies, which Shelley in the event never had time to publish. The letter ended with a fighting motto: 'Adieu – Ecrasez l'infame ecrasez l'impie.' This, as appeared later during the following term at Oxford, was not merely the motto of Voltaire's elegant critique of revealed Christianity; it was also something far more sinister, the watchword of the international revolutionary Jacobins of the 1790s, known as the Illuminists.

Shelley's ragings against Christianity seemed to take place in a strange kind of twilight world, a world essentially adolescent, in which the actions and emotions of his private fantasies – the world of HD and Zastrozzi – had partially crossed over into the public world of real relationships, of Field Place, of the Groves, of Oxford, of theological debate. This invasion of fact by fiction would be regarded in a mature adult as a kind of insanity, a paranoia. But Shelley was not mature, he acted out the fiction with the intensity of childhood.

With the coming of the New Year 1811, Shelley indulged himself at Field Place in a series of tortuous scenarios which he recounted in detail for Hogg's benefit. One night he had gone to bed with 'a loaded pistol and some poison' by his side – but 'did not die'.[25] On another occasion he wrote that he had spent most of the night 'pacing a churchyard'.[26] His passion against Christianity increased in violence, and became more purely melodramatic: 'Yet here I swear, and as I break my oath may Infinity Eternity blast me, here I swear that never will I forgive Christianity! . . . Oh how I wish I *were* the Antichrist, that it were *mine* to crush the Demon, to hurl him to his native Hell never to rise again – I expect to gratify some of this insatiable feeling in Poetry.'[27] The last consideration was obviously the most important one, and in his next letter five stanzas about 'long visions of soul racking pain' were enclosed. Shelley was aware of the disturbing violence in his letters, and in the adult and public side of his personality he tried to 'place' and distance it for Hogg. Thus all his more frantic missives contain little notes of marginal comment, either wry or whimsical. In one letter he observed suddenly: 'How can you fancy that I can think you mad; am I not the wildest, most delirious of enthusiasm's offspring?'[28] In another: 'I have wandered in the snow for I am cold wet & mad – Pardon me, pardon my delirious egotism, this really shall be the last. . . .'[29] By mid-January his explanations were more matter-of-fact: 'My head is rather dizzy today on account of not taking rest, & a slight attack of Typhus.'[30] 'Excuse my mad arguments, they are none at all, for I am rather confused, & fear in consequence of a fever they will not allow me to come on the 26 [January], but I will. Adieu.'[31]

With the approach of the Easter term, Timothy Shelley, who had been observing his elder son's strange behaviour with many misgivings, decided that he should attempt to exert a calming paternal influence. He spent some time in his study trying to debate with Shelley on religious issues, an unusual experience for both of them which Shelley duly reported back to Hogg. 'I attempted to Deistify my father; mirabile dictu! he for a time listened to my arguments. . . .' But when it came down to Shelley's flushed and triumphant conclusion that Christianity could be logically disproved, Timothy brushed aside the undergraduate dialectics, and silenced Shelley with an 'equine argument – in effect these words "I believe because I do believe." '[32] Both Timothy and Mrs Shelley were only too aware of the social and political stigma attached to anything that smacked of – dread word – 'atheism', especially in an intensely conservative and wholly theological institution like Oxford. Atheism implied immorality, social inferiority and unpatriotic behaviour all in one sweep; during a time of war against the revolutionary forces in Europe, it also implied treachery, revolutionism and foreign degeneracy. At Field Place in that January of 1811, it caused the deepest anxiety: 'My mother fancies me in the High road to Pandemonium, she fancies I want to make a deistical coterie of all my little sisters.'[33] Mrs Elizabeth Shelley, who knew of old her son's wild leadership of the other children, and his instinct for proselytizing, was perfectly correct.

In the third week of January, Hogg came sweeping to his beleaguered friend's rescue. He had been putting his legalistic talents to work, and had extracted from Locke's *Essay concerning Human Understanding* the basis for a waterproof brief against not merely Christianity but also the idea of God itself. He sent it to Shelley, who was delighted, and wrote back enthusiastically: 'Your systematic cudgel for Xtianity is excellent, I tried it again with my Father who told me that 30 years ago he had read Locke but this made no impression.'[34] This 'systematic cudgel' was the basis of the little pamphlet which, with certain Humean additions by Shelley, became the notorious Oxford pamphlet *The Necessity of Atheism*.

By the end of the vacation, Timothy had changed his tack. After making enquiries of the Hogg family at Durham, and discovering that Hogg's grandfather had made the family fortune as agent for the Dean and Chapter of Durham Cathedral, he felt the situation was not as dangerous as it had first looked. He told Shelley that he approved of the friendship, and asked him to invite Hogg to Field Place for the Easter vacation.

Shelley's letters to Timothy at the beginning of the next term also suggest that his father had come to an arrangement concerning Shelley's theology. Shelley could believe what he liked in private or among friends, but he must not circulate his views publicly in the university. Shelley seemed to react rationally enough to this compromise. In February he continued to debate questions with his father in private correspondence in a confidential, if slightly mocking, manner. At the end of a long discussion of the Deistical tradition, Shelley wrote: 'At some leisure moment may I request to hear your objections, (if any yet remain) to my private sentiments – "Religion fetters a reasoning mind with the very bonds which restrain the unthinking one from mischief" – this is my great objection to it.'[35] He was on strong ground here, and he knew it.

In addition Shelley agreed to turn his publishing freaks to the more orthodox business of composing a prize-winning poem on the subject of the Parthenon. Timothy went to considerable trouble to get Shelley background material on this from a learned cleric, the Reverend Edward Dalloway.[36] Shelley specifically reassured his father that he would keep his views private as far as the university authorities were concerned.

But Timothy had not fully appreciated the powerful forces which the friendship with Hogg, and the mutual love letters concerning Elizabeth and Harriet Grove, had released in Shelley. The two undergraduate friends had been brought together at the most intense level of emotional revelation. Love – frustrated, ideal or profaned – became their common topic, the conspiratorial philosophy which drew them together in the 'duties of friendship'. In their artificial paradise of misery and passion, their own relationship could reach a molten intimacy without hesitations or embarrassments. Atheism, love, philosophical discussions of idealism, were all fuel for the communicating flame:

> The question is, What do I love? it is almost unnecessary to answer. Do I love the person, the embodied identity, (if I may be allowed the expression)? No! I love what is superior, what is excellent, or what I conceive to be so, and wish, ardently wish to be convinced of the existence of a God that so superior a spirit should derive happiness from my exertions – for Love is Heaven, and Heaven is Love. Oh! that it were. You think so too, – yet you disbelieve the existence of an eternal omnipresent spirit. Am I not mad? alas I am, but I pour my ravings into the ear of a friend who will pardon them.[37]

One thinks of poor Timothy Shelley trying to cool his son with the idea of a prize-winning poem on the Parthenon. The invitation to Hogg for the Easter vacation was a wiser thought, but it came into effect far too late. When Shelley went back to Oxford for his second term in the last week of January 1811, he was going back to wage a secret war in a conspiracy of sacred friendship in which his main target was the theological authorities of the university. Fiction had become fact.

Shelley and Hogg were not now in the mood to be content with theoretical and private speculations, in politics, or poetry, or in theology. They embarked instead on a cleverly conceived and planned campaign to publicize their ideas within Oxford through the medium of Slatter and Munday's bookshop. The first fruits of this had been a decoratively printed and assiduously circulated edition of the supposed *Posthumous Poems of Margaret Nicholson*, a collection of pastiches in the *Victor and Cazire* style, but with altered subject matter. Romantic and demoniac themes gave way to poems attacking warfare, monarchy, poverty and political oppression. One piece also gained a certain local notoriety for its apparent eroticism.* The whole, with its expensive binding and grotesque gothic type set, became something of a *succès de scandale*, and the subject of much university gossip in February.

But Shelley was out for bigger game, and he now turned his attention to the 'cudgel against Christianity', which Hogg had produced during the vacation. He edited and polished it, fitted it with introductory and concluding material, and sent it secretly to be printed in Sussex, under the mildly provocative title

---

* Shelley wrote to Graham at the end of November 1810: 'The part of the Epithalamium which you mention [i.e. from the end of Satan's triumph] is the production of a friend's *mistress* . . . [it] will make it sell like wildfire.' Mrs Nicholson had regrettably attempted to assassinate King George III in 1786; she was subsequently committed to a Bedlam. King George escaped both fates. Shelley posed as her nephew, anxious to publish a 'more copious collection of my unfortunate Aunt's Poems', if the first had any success.

The Necessity of Atheism. Under Shelley's hand the pamphlet became a neat and effective piece of theological polemic, about 1,000 words long, beginning with a tag from Bacon on the value of clarity of thought and logical demonstration. Its introduction set a tone of conscious innocence and integrity which was perfectly calculated to enrage a prejudiced reader. 'As love of truth is the only motive which actuates the Author of this little tract, he earnestly entreats that those of his readers who may discover any deficiency in his reasonings, or may be in possession of proofs which his mind could never obtain, would offer them, together with their objections to the Public, as briefly, as methodically, as plainly as he has taken the liberty of doing. Thro' deficiency of proof, An Atheist.'

The pamphlet then examines the proofs of a Deity available in three ways: through personal evidence of the senses, through reasoning as to the Prime Cause, and through the testimony of others. Each of these is in turn proved, syllogistically, to be inadequate. The pamphlet then demurely observes that 'it is also evident that as belief is a passion of the mind, no degree of criminality can be attached to disbelief'. It concludes reassuringly: 'It is almost unnecessary to observe, that the general knowledge of the deficiency of such a proof, cannot be prejudicial to society: Truth has always been found to promote the best interests of mankind. – Every reflecting mind must allow that there is no proof of the existence of a Deity. Q.E.D.'

Hogg remarks that Shelley was particularly pleased with the mathematical effect of the 'potent characters' Q.E.D. at the end, like a kind of charm, especially designed for 'their efficacy in rousing antagonists'.[38] It has been noted that this is almost the first known open avowal of atheism in print in England.[39]

Copies of *The Necessity of Atheism* arrived from the Worthing printers on or just before St Valentine's Day. Shelley and Hogg immediately began the process of distributing and mailing, taking great care to remain anonymous. A few days later the Oxford booksellers agreed to display copies in their bow window overlooking the High, apparently not having glanced beyond the title page. Seizing the opportunity, Shelley scattered copies throughout the shop, pricing them at sixpence. This was a dramatic chance for Shelley, but in the event also a fatal one. After only twenty minutes the Reverend Jocelyn Walker, a fellow of New College, walked in and read the little tract, immediately ordering all copies to be burnt at the back of the shop. Horrified, the booksellers complied. One copy was retained as evidence for the university authorities.

Munday, sensing trouble, wrote to Phillips the Worthing printer, and advised him to destroy all copies and type-sets immediately as it looked as if a prosecution for Blasphemous Libel was afoot.[40]

On 17 February, Shelley wrote to his father from Oxford with cheery reassurance:

It is needless to observe that in the Schools Colleges &c which are all on the principle of Inquisisatorial [sic] Orthodoxy with respect to matters of belief I shall perfectly coincide with the opinions of the learned doctors, although by the very rules of reasoning which their *own systems* of logic teach me I could refute their errors. – I shall not therefore publically come under the act 'de heretico comburendo'.[41]

Yet here arises one of Shelley's extremely characteristic pieces of calculating duplicity. For the very same day, 17 February, he wrote to his friend Edward Graham, who was acting as a kind of literary agent for him in London with Stockdale, that he had completed sending copies of *The Necessity of Atheism* to all the bishops, and heads of colleges, and that they must now consider plans for advertising and publishing the tract in London.[42] By this date also, the pamphlet had been advertised in the *Oxford University and City Herald*, and exposed for sale in Slatter and Munday's window.[43] Shelley was coolly playing his own double game. 'I intended to have come to London on Saturday, but if I left Oxford so abruptly I shd. be suspected as the Author of the tract,' he apprised Graham.

It is doubtful if the mere twenty minutes of sale at Munday's would itself have led to Shelley's arraignment and expulsion. There were, after all, alternative penalties: for example, he could have been rusticated for a term. It was Shelley's deliberately inflammatory tactic of mailing the pamphlet to all the bishops and all the heads of colleges which put the matter into a wider and more dangerous arena. This he perhaps intended; but he could not have foreseen the party-political antagonisms which he inflamed.

This was further exacerbated on 9 March when he advertised *A Poetical Essay on the Existing State of Things** to be sold price two shillings, 'by a Gentleman of the University of Oxford'. This was the openly political side of Shelley's campaign with Hogg against the authorities, and the declared intention of the sale of the poem was that of 'assisting to maintain in Prison Mr Peter Finnerty, imprisoned for libel'.[44] On 7 February Peter Finnerty the Irish journalist had finally been sentenced to eighteen months' imprisonment for his protests against the government's disastrous military policies. Finnerty had written for the Whig *Morning Chronicle* and the Walcheren fiasco was the result of Tory policy. Finnerty's case was taken up at once in London by the left ginger group of the new Whigs, notably Sir Francis Burdett, and by the *Examiner* group of liberals who always fought with considerable daring on free

---

* Of the poem itself we know nothing, but what appears to be a later version occurs in the Esdaile MS Notebook, a collection of works written between 1810 and 1814; it is his first short piece of recognizable poetic qualities, though obviously influenced by Wordsworth.

speech issues. Meetings were held at the traditional centre of reform politics, The Crown and Anchor, and Shelley read the accounts avidly. In Oxford, the *Herald* opened a public subscription for Finnerty, and on 2 March four courageous names had appeared with one-guinea donations. One of these was 'Mr P.B. Shelley'.[45] On the same day, Shelley wrote a private letter to Leigh Hunt, the 27-year-old editor of the *Examiner*. His ostensible motive was to congratulate Hunt on his recent acquittal in a libel action.* Shelley introduced himself as follows: 'My father is in Parliament, and on attaining 21 I shall, in all probability, fill his vacant seat.' This apparently indicated that he was considering a political career within the auspices of the left wing of the Whigs.

But Shelley's real reason for writing was that he had concocted in discussions with Hogg a plan for uniting the many dislocated reform groups which had remained splintered and ineffective virtually since the nineties, when Pitt took the nation into war with the French, calling for national unity and suppression of agitators and radical groups. Shelley's plan was that a meeting should be called of all reform elements, and from this there should be constructed a 'form of methodical society which should be organized so as to resist the coalition of the enemies of liberty which at present renders any expression of opinions on matters of policy dangerous to individuals'.[46] It has been pointed out that this suggestion preceded the formation of just such a 'methodical organization' in the Hampden Clubs of Major Cartwright which brought together both solid parliamentary Whigs and popular reformers, in the final months of the Napoleonic War.[47] But Shelley's suggestion for an extra-parliamentary political reform organization went further than this. As his letter to Hunt shows, he had a particular historical model in mind:

> It has been for want of societies of this nature that corruption has attained the height at which we now behold it, nor can any of us bear in mind the very great influence, which some years since was gained by *Illuminism*, without considering that a society of equal extent might establish *rational liberty* on as firm a basis as that which would have supported the visionary schemes of a completely-equalized community.[48]

The comparison with Illuminism must have shaken Hunt when he read it. The Illuminists were the secret international Jacobin society, dedicated to worldwide revolutionary conspiracy, founded by Dr Adam Weishaupt, in Ingolstadt in May 1776. Their doctrine was one of militant egalitarianism, the destruction of private property, religion and 'superstitious' social forms such as marriage.

* The *Examiner* had carried an article against military flogging entitled 'One Thousand Lashes'; Henry Brougham brilliantly defended the case under the jaundiced eye of Lord Ellenborough who never usually missed a chance to put a publisher in the stocks.

Their methods were essentially conspiratorial, based on the Masonic type of secret lodges, and with a tradition of antinomian underground movement dating back to a medieval Spanish sect of the same name. In England their work was known exclusively through the rabid witch-hunting four-volume treatise on their infamies by the French emigré the Abbé Augustin Barruel: *Histoire du Jacobinisme* (1797). This book had come into Shelley's hands, possibly through Hogg, in his first term at Oxford; and it was the Illuminists' watchword that he had quoted in his letters of the Christmas vacation. There was no reply to Shelley's letter from Hunt, but the idea of that visionary 'completely-equalized community' as the basis for movements of political liberty remained an active ideal for Shelley for the next two years; and in modified form throughout his life.*

By this time in mid-March of 1811, Shelley's views and publications had become widely known among the small circle of Fellows and undergraduates, and the notoriety that he had deliberately set out to court had been at least partially achieved. If he had not yet exactly stormed the stronghold, he had succeeded in arousing its distasteful interest.

Charles Kilpatrick Sharpe, an MA of Christ Church College, wrote to his patron Lord Bury, with what he took to be an amusing piece of undergraduate scandal:

> Talking of books, we have lately had a literary sun shine forth upon us here, before whom our former luminaries must hide their undiminished heads – a Mr Shelley, of University College, who lives upon arsenic, aquafortis, half-an-hours sleep in the night, and is desperately in love with the memory of Margaret Nicolson. He hath published what he terms [her] Posthumous Poems, printed for the benefit of Mr Peter Finnerty, which, I am grieved to say, though stuffed full of treason, is extremely dull; but the author is a great genius, and if he be not clapped up in Bedlam or hanged, will certainly prove one of the sweetest swans on the tuneful margin of the Cherwell.

Sharpe, who was preparing for his later career as an anonymous Tory writer on the authoritarian *Quarterly Review*, completed his survey with genial disapproval.

> Our Apollo next came out with a prose pamphlet in praise of Atheism, which I have not as yet seen, and there appeared a monstrous Romance in one volume, called St. Irvyne or The Rosicrucian. . . . All the heroes are confirmed robbers and causeless murderers, while the heroines glide *en chemise* through

* For the most lively contemporary account of the Illuminist movement, see John Robison, *Proofs of a Conspiracy Against all the Religions and Governments of Europe*. London, 1798. Shelley's treasured edition of the Abbé Barruel's polemic study was the exhaustive *Memoirs Illustrating the History of Jacobinism*, trans. the Hon. Robert Clifford, 4 vols, London, 1798.

the streets of Geneva, tap at the palazzo doors of their sweethearts, and on being denied admittance leave no card, but run home to their warm beds, and kill themselves.[49]

The University authorities were at this moment considering Shelley's case, and certainly took the untimely advertisements, together with the previous public subscription for Finnerty in the *Herald*, as strong evidence that Mr Shelley of University College was at the centre of a Whig agitation movement. It is known, from the previous election of Lord Grenville, that University College especially had the most staunch Tory prejudices; and Hogg firmly implies that the expulsion now became 'an affair of party'.[50] Medwin, with different sources, raises the same suspicion.[51] Moreover, there was now little doubt in the authorities' mind that the author of *Posthumous Poems*, of the Finnerty publicity, and of the scabrous tract *The Necessity of Atheism* were one and the same undergraduate, and a singularly dispensable troublemaker. Of Hogg's co-partnership they were probably still uncertain.

On the morning of 25 March, Shelley was summoned to a meeting of the Master and Fellows of University College. When he entered the room, Shelley saw that they had a copy of *The Necessity of Atheism* in front of them. Precisely what happened next has always been disputed, for Hogg published a heroic and fictionalized version, and Shelley himself apparently had printed the 'text' of a speech he made in an Oxford newspaper. Peacock says that Shelley, long after, talked as if he had debated with the dons in some large public assembly.

One salient point is clear. Shelley refused to acknowledge the authorship of the pamphlet on the grounds that it had been published anonymously, and the assembled authority therefore had no legal right to ask him a leading question.[52] Hogg makes a great deal of this in Shelley's words to the Master: 'Such proceedings would become a court of inquisitors, but not free men in a free country. . . . I have experienced tyranny and injustice before, and I well know what vulgar violence is. . . .'

The fact is that Shelley must have either lost his temper or his nerve in choosing to defend himself in this oblique way. The pamphlet stood on the proposition that 'disbelief' could not be criminal; and that the whole object of the argument was to seek a serious intellectual rebuttal. The authorship of the pamphlet was clearly known. If, then, Shelley had freely admitted that he (with Hogg) was the author, and that he had never claimed to make an outright statement of atheism, but merely demanded a proper intellectual inquiry into the matter on the logical principles of Hume and Locke (both academically respectable), his position would have been very strong indeed. He could not have been accused of actual atheism; he could only have been convicted of debating unpalatable arguments in public. Even at Oxford in 1811, it would not have been altogether easy to expel a man merely for showing academic initiative. Shelley's case was in reality very sound, but he abandoned it by deliberately inflammatory tactics and a tendentious defence. The result was that he was expelled, according to the bureaucratic formula, for 'contumacy in refusing to answer certain questions put to (him)'.[53] This was of course extremely convenient for the college, for the expulsion did not turn upon anything so embarrassing as a question of belief, of political allegiance, or of the right of intellectual inquiry. It was a simple flouting of college discipline.

Shelley was, for the instant, appalled. He rushed to Hogg's room and 'sat on the sofa, repeating with convulsive vehemence, the words, "Expelled! Expelled!" his head shaking with emotion and his whole frame quivering'.[54] Medwin was to observe similar emotion when Shelley burst into his rooms in the Temple, two days later, at 4 in the morning: ' "Medwin, let me in, I am expelled:" here followed a sort of loud, half-hysterical laugh, and a repetition of the words – "I am expelled", with the addition of "for Atheism" '.[55]

Meanwhile, Hogg, the sacred friend and co-author of the tract, rapidly presented himself at the Master's meeting to protest, as he subsequently wrote, at the injustice of the proceedings. But his protestations were useless, and he fell into the same trap as Shelley, refusing to admit the authorship.[56] He too was expelled immediately, with a signed and sealed document that he claims was already prepared on the Master's desk. They were flamboyant to the last, as C. J. Ridley, a member and later a Fellow of the College recalled. 'Towards afternoon a large paper bearing the College seal, and signed by the Master and Dean, was affixed to the hall door, declaring that the two offenders were publically expelled. ... The aforesaid two made themselves as conspicuous as possible by great singularity of dress, and by walking up and down the centre of the quadrangle as if proud of their anticipated fate.'[57]

Ridley summed up the general feeling about Shelley and Hogg together when they came to leave the university, in the following measured terms. 'I believe no one regretted their departure for there were but few, if any, who were not afraid of Shelley's strange and fantastic pranks, and the still stranger opinions he was known to entertain; but all acknowledged him to have been very goodhumoured and of a kind disposition. T. J. Hogg had intellectual powers to a great extent, but unfortunately, misdirected. He was not popular.'[58]

The following bleak March morning, after hectic dreamlike hours of packing and bidding a few bravado farewells, they caught the 8 o'clock mail to London. Shelley had been round to Munday's shop and thoughtfully borrowed £20 from John Slatter.[59] Almost twelve years later, in January 1823, Slatter was still trying to collect the debt.

In London, Shelley visited the Groves and took tea, then went to his friend Graham and put up for a couple of nights. Later he saw Medwin. He was testing all their reactions and the degree of their sympathy; he was also steeling himself for the real confrontation: with his father. The exchange of letters which took place in the next fifteen days was one of the most decisive of his career. They reflect on all that had gone before in the relationship, and in Shelley's childhood; and also set the pattern for much of what subsequently occurred.

The evidence of the newspaper editor Joseph Merle in his reminiscences is important at this point, as to Shelley's state of mind. Merle, who had met Shelley at Graham's and was of the same age, recalled in 1841 the period immediately after Shelley had quitted Oxford:

> On all other subjects he was one of the mildest and most modest youths I have ever known; but once let religion be mentioned, and he became alternately scornful and furious. If his opinions were contradicted, he contented himself in the first instance with jeers on the weakness of the person who dissented from his views. If the contradiction was kept up, and his adversary became animated in defence of revealed religion, his countenance underwent a fearful change, and his eye became one of fire.[60]

That fearful change in countenance is to be met with more than once. Merle even suggested that Shelley at times showed definite unbalance. 'Overstudy had made him mad on religious subjects; and as on all others, his mind was fresh and vigorous, he was in the condition of a monomaniac who is incurable, because his insanity is concentrated in one faculty.' Looking back, Merle was to conclude that Shelley, with his intelligence, his social standing and his 'pecuniary means' had become with such a temperament and such principles 'a dangerous member of society'.[61]

These views are to be borne in mind in the general impression Shelley made during the crucial exchange between himself and Timothy. Three days after his expulsion Shelley wrote to his father from Edward Graham's address. The letter is worth quoting very fully; it has both an innocence and a kind of mocking worldly wisdom:

> My dear Father, you have doubtless heard of my misfortune and that of my friend Mr Hogg. ... The case was this, ... we found to our surprise that (strange as it may appear) the proofs of an existing Deity were as far as we had observed, defective. We therefore embodied our doubts on the subject, & arranged them methodically in the form of 'The Necessity of Atheism', thinking thereby to obtain a satisfactory, or unsatisfactory answer from men who had made Divinity the study of their lives. – How then were we treated?

not as our fair, open, candid conduct might demand, no argument was publickly brought forward to disprove our reasoning, & it at once demonstrated the weakness of their cause, & their inveteracy on discovering it, when they publickly expelled myself & my friend. . . . I know too well that your feeling mind will sympathise too deeply in my misfortunes. I hope it will alleviate your sorrow to know that for *myself* I am perfectly indifferent to the late tyrannical violent proceedings of Oxford. Will you present my affectionate duty to my mother, my love to Elizabeth. . . . May I turn your attention to the advertisement, which surely deserved an *answer*, not expulsion. Believe me, my dear Father, ever most affectionately dutifully yours, Percy B. Shelley.[62]

On his copy of the pamphlet at Field Place, Timothy scrawled the single word 'Impious'.

It must be recalled that Shelley was not yet 19 when he had to face this crisis, and he had no real idea of its implications, or the scale on which his father was disappointed in him. Even so, the letter is a curious mixture: a bold, not to say supercilious self-defence, coupled with a rather naïve distortion of the true facts ('our open, fair, candid conduct'). Most curious of all, there is about the general tone of the letter a kind of self-satisfaction.

While Shelley was awaiting his father's reaction, he took rooms at 15 Poland Street with Hogg. It was a dark little back sitting-room on the first floor, with trellised vines on the wallpaper. Timothy, shocked and dismayed, hurried to London and put up at Miller's Hotel, his usual Town residence, just over Westminster Bridge. It was here, on Sunday, 7 April, that the famous meeting between Timothy and the two young men took place. Edward Graham's father was also present. As far as we can gather from Hogg, Shelley tried to brazen it out, putting on his wildest manner, and was soon involved in bitter recriminations with his father. Hogg plays the scene as follows:

> Mr Timothy Shelley received me kindly; but he presently began to talk in an odd, unconnected manner; scolding, crying, swearing, and then weeping again: no doubt he went on strangely. . . . Shelley was sitting at that moment, as he often used to sit, quite on the edge of his chair. Not only did he laugh aloud, with a wild, demoniacal burst of laughter, but he slipped from his seat, and fell on his back at full length on the floor. 'What is the matter, Bysshe? Are you ill? are you dead? are you mad? Why do you laugh?' It was not easy to return a satisfactory answer to his father, or to Mr Graham. . . .[63]

Hogg's account is certainly stylized, and he was careful at the same time to show how he, Hogg, quickly struck up an understanding with the 'poor old governor'.

Nevertheless it tallies in general outline with the impression that Merle, quite independently, gave of Timothy's clumsy anxiety and Shelley's maddening, and sometimes frightening irrepressibility at this time. Merle saw Timothy at Field Place, where Timothy 'had a long conversation, in the course of which he almost shed tears when alluding to the doctrines which his son professed, and took a pleasure in promulgating'.[64] Merle later saw Shelley at Horsham, and remonstrated with him:

> As I proceeded he became angry; indeed almost furious. 'Do not,' said he, 'talk such stuff to me; I hear enough of it at home. There is my father, who with a painting of that imposter Christ, hanging up in his library, is sometimes vain enough to suppose that he can bring reason prostrate before absurdity. I have too many of these follies before my eyes: they drive me mad!' And mad, indeed, he was. I think I see him still. His eyes flashed fire; his words rolled forth with the impetuosity of a mountain-torrent; and even [sic] attitude aided the manifestation of passion.[65]

This interview of Merle's with Shelley ended in Shelley storming out of the tavern. Hogg is guarded on the point, but something similar probably occurred at Miller's Hotel.

This is implied in Timothy's subsequent letter to his son, apparently written on the next day, then corrected and sent off more calmly on Tuesday morning, 9 April. Timothy was still determined to reason with Shelley, and the letter, though grave and severe, is not by any means completely hostile. He began by refusing to accept Shelley's intransigence:

> I am unwilling to receive and act on the information you gave me on Sunday, as the ultimate determination of your mind. The disgrace which hangs over you is most serious, and though I have felt as a father, and sympathized in the misfortune which your criminal and improper acts have begot: yet, you must know, that I have a duty to perform to my own character, as well as to your younger brother and sisters. Above all, my feelings as a Christian require from me a decided and firm conduct towards you.

Timothy then laid down two proposals; that Shelley should go at once to Field Place and should be placed under the care of such tutors as Timothy felt were suitable. This was to be the basis of a reconciliation between them. Otherwise, Timothy wrote sternly: 'I am resolved to withdraw myself from you, and leave you to the punishment and misery that belongs to the wicked pursuit of an opinion so diabolical and wicked as that which you have dared to declare, if you shall not accept the proposals I shall go home on Thursday – I am, your affectionate and most afflicted father, T. Shelley.'[66]

Shelley's reaction to this letter was bitterly contemptuous. He instantly wrote a note in which he dismissed Timothy's peace formula: 'I feel it my Duty altho' it gives me pain to wound the Sense of Duty to your own character to that of your family & your feelings as a Christian decidedly to refuse my assent to both the Proposals in your letter. . . .'[67] The flippancy of this reply, and the deliberately insulting sarcasm tell us a good deal about Shelley's state of mind. Undoubtedly he was deeply wounded by Timothy's threat to 'withdraw' himself – a threat far more disturbing for him than any persecution – and reacted with blind desire to hurt in return. Though he wrote in the language of one gentleman coolly insulting another, his feelings were those of a child betrayed. He was quite deaf to the note of entreaty in his father's painful defence of his own motives.

But most damaging of all, Shelley was too young and too self-absorbed to realize that Timothy's letter was the product of a man desperately unsure of himself. It was partly personal uncertainty, torn between anger and disappointment for his son; but much more it was social uncertainty. Timothy was fearful of the social effects of such a disgrace. At the centre of Timothy's feelings lay the terror of the social *arriviste* who dreads compromising his standing in the society of his peers and his overlords. The emphasis on Duty, especially the duty to his family, the duty as a *respectable* Christian, all indicate the presence of this pressure. But Shelley could see no more than theological hypocrisy and paternal treachery; while Timothy could see no more than a spoilt and over-confident son dragging the whole family into social disgrace. So they were content to wound each other in the dark.

Four days later, Shelley, marginally calmed by the reasonableness of Hogg's father's reaction, allowed himself to be talked into submitting his own set of 'peace proposals' to Timothy. These included an immediate return to Field Place, and a promise to make certain apologies and refrain from further publications. But he boldly insisted on 'unrestrained correspondence', and announced that 'Mr P.B. Shelley may be permitted to select the situation in life, which may be consonant with his intentions, to which he may judge his abilities adequate.'[68]

The deliberate condescension in the tone only infuriated Timothy further, and hid from him Shelley's attempt at a gesture of goodwill. He had by this time learnt from his solicitor Whitton that a public prosecution of *The Necessity of Atheism* was possible and even likely, for blasphemous libel, and his fear of the social stigma now carried the day. He made the fatal mistake of putting all further communications with Shelley through the intermediary of the solicitor, 'to guard my character and honour in case of any prosecutions in the courts'.[69] Whitton was a sentencious high Tory, narrowly legalistic in outlook, easily offended and totally unable to comprehend how Shelley's mind worked.

Timothy's appointment of him as intermediary thus put a hopeless barrier between father and son, preparing for an endless fund of misunderstanding and mutual recrimination to be built up. It was a fatal mistake, and one made primarily from fear.

Shelley reacted to this news, on 17 April, with renewed violence. He now felt utterly betrayed by his father, and struck back with an overwhelming desire to cause pain in return. Hogg had agreed to return to his own paternal roof, and left London the same day, thus leaving Shelley unsupported and unrestrained. He dashed off a note to Whitton from his Poland Street sitting-room, announcing that he intended to resign his claim to the family inheritance of Sir Bysshe Shelley's property, and accept a £2,000 annuity if the remainder should be broken up 'equally with my sisters and my mother'.[70] When the news reached his father on 22 April – Whitton had attempted to forestall it – Timothy wrote back to his solicitor with profound dismay. 'I never felt such a shock in my life, infinitely more than when I heard of his expulsion.'[71] Shelley had instinctively struck at his father's most sensitive point: the ambition, inherited from grandfather to father, to secure the family name in the undivided and orderly inheritance from generation to generation of a solid body of English landed estates.

This marked, more really than the expulsion from Oxford, Shelley's first significant step in the process of self-exile which came to dominate much of his life. Perhaps characteristically, the gesture had at its core a gratuitous violence; for such a renunciation was of course legally quite empty until Shelley had attained the age of 21. Still, it accorded with his egalitarian principles, and besides those he had little else left.

3
Wales and Limbo: 1811

Shelley now found himself existing in a kind of limbo. He kept on his sitting-room at Poland Street, but it was lonely without Hogg, and he was running out of money. He complained of solitude and made a virtue of having nothing but an ill-kept overcoat to wear. He read, wrote letters and retired to bed at 8 to make the days pass. Until he decided to stay with relatives in Wales at the beginning of July, his life was to be unsettled and shapeless. The correspondence with Hogg continued, and Shelley kept up his contacts with the Medwins, John Grove and Edward Graham in London. But in Sussex both Timothy and Sir Bysshe sealed themselves away from him.

At the end of April, Shelley crossed paths with his father, who had come up to Town to consult with Whitton, and they bumped into each other in Grove's corridor: 'I met my father in the passage, and politely enquired after his health, he looked as black as a thunder cloud & said "Your most humble Servant!" I made a low bow & wishing him a very good morning passed on. He is very irate about my proposals. I cannot resign anything till I am 21, I cannot do anything, therefore I have 3 more years to consider the matter you mentioned.'[1]

A possible ally appeared in the form of Captain Pilfold, one of Shelley's uncles on his mother's side. Pilfold was a retired naval officer, a veteran of Trafalgar, crusty and good-humoured by all accounts, and he felt Timothy had acted precipitately towards his eldest son. He was prepared to sympathize with Shelley and help him. Pilfold had a house at Cuckfield near Horsham, and it was from this welcome base that Shelley eventually renewed his siege of Timothy on Friday, 10 May. Timothy had announced that he would not have Shelley back at Field Place, except on his own terms. Shelley nevertheless threatened to come, at which Timothy retaliated with – 'Oh then I shall take his sister away, before he comes.'[2] The position was now curiously reversed, with Timothy at bay, and Shelley barking at his heels. We learn from a letter to Hogg that the Shelley family had rallied round Timothy during the crisis rather than his son: Elizabeth, for example, refused to have 'an Atheist correspond with her. She talks of Duty to her Father.'[3]

Shelley was still writing fiercely to Hogg of the 'cold Prejudice and selfish fear' of which religion was the child, and appealed to Hogg for his constant support: '. . . I appeal to your own heart to your own feelings. At that tribunal I feel that I am secure, I once could *tolerate* Christ – he then merely injured me – he merely deprived me of all that I cared for, touching myself, on Earth – but now he has done more and I cannot forgive.' The strange, mythical transformation of his feelings into theological terms continued, half suggesting a kind of mental breakdown. For the rest, he was confused, demoralized, vainly attempting to get a grip of his situation. 'I don't know where I am, where I will be. – Future present past is all a mist, it seems as if I had begun existence anew under auspices so unfavourable. – Yet no, that is stupid.'[4]

Harriet Grove's elder brother John, then aged 26 and training in London as a surgeon, attempted to intervene on his young cousin's behalf, 'flattering like a courtier', and at one visit Timothy agreed to supply Shelley with £200 per annum 'and leave [him] to misery'. But on return to Field Place he cancelled the offer.[5] Shelley was not without family allies, as this shows, and by 29 April his immediate financial worries were being dealt with, probably by Pilfold or Grove, and he felt sure enough to offer aid to Hogg who was at York.[6] His passion against Timothy was not abated though it matured on reflection as the days went by. He sent off to Hogg a 'mad effusion', in which his father plays the role of a hunting lion or tiger or blood-sucking monster, and Shelley himself becomes the pursued llama, the fleeting hind, sinking in 'a trance of despair'. The poem was later adapted for the Esdaile Notebook and entitled 'Dares the Lama'. Its final lines generalize Shelley's picture of himself heroically matched against the pursuing horror of religion, unrepentent to the bitter end:

> For in vain from the grasp of Religion I flee
> The most tenderly loved of my soul
> Are slaves to its hated control
> It pursues me, it blasts me! oh where shall I fly
> What remains but to curse it, to curse it & die.[7]

The 'tenderly loved' are Elizabeth Shelley, and perhaps Harriet Grove.

In prose, however, Shelley's feelings were rather less meek and he developed a practical strategy. He was certain that he had complete hereditary power over the estate which would fall to him legally at 21, and he felt confident of forcing Timothy to terms: 'The estate is *entirely* entailed on me, totally out of the power of the enemy, he is yet angry beyond measure; pacification is remote; but I *will*

be at peace vi et armis; I will enter his domains preserving a quaker-like carelessness of opposition, I shall manage a l'Amerique & seat myself quietly in his
mansion turning a deaf ear to any declamatory objections.'[8] Meekness, in
personal relations, now seemed to him a decidedly *religious* kind of fault, so that
he could write of a certain Revd Faber, whom he had offended with his atheism:
'Poor fool! His Christian mildness, his consistent forgiveness of injuries amuses
me; he is *le vrai esprit de Christianisme*, which Helvetius talks of . . .'[9] Of all
Shelley's London supporters, Captain Pilfold alone, 'a very hearty fellow',
seemed sufficiently fierce. Shelley delightedly told Hogg that he had 'illuminated' Pilfold on religious matters in return for his noble aid, and the Captain had
responded well. 'A physician named Dr J—— dined with us last night, who is a
redhot saint; the captain attacked him, warm from "The Necessity", and the
doctor went away very much shocked.'[10] It looked like his first proselytizing
success; but it was not a permanent one.

Another ideological landmark during this unsettled interim period was
Shelley's first visit to the editor of the *Examiner*, Leigh Hunt, to whom he had
written from Oxford in March. Hunt invited him to a Sunday breakfast at
Hampstead.

Shelley's impression of the Hunts, given for Hogg's benefit, characteristically
lacked all human or physical elements. He judged them as a pair of potentially
interesting theories, but rather less enlightened than himself. 'Hunt is a man of
cultivated mind, & certainly exalted notions; – I do not entirely despair of
rescuing him out of this damnable heresy from Reason – Mrs Hunt is a most
sensible woman, she is by no means a Xtian, & rather atheistically given; – It is a
curious fact that they were married when they were both Wesleyan Methodists
& subsequently converted each other.'[11] There was, probably, a certain ironic
bravado intended in all this, though one is reminded of Merle's comments
concerning religious monomania. Hunt in his turn remembered Shelley as an
intense, self-conscious, elegant but rather immature figure: 'a youth, not come to
his full growth, very gentlemanly, earnestly gazing at every object that interested him, and quoting the Greek dramatists'.[12] Greek quotation appeared as
part of the running debate he was having about the role of individual virtue
within the process of political reform. Was Antigone immoral, he wondered.
'Did she wrong when she acted in direct in noble violation of the laws of a
prejudiced society?' Hardly, he concluded, since 'political affairs are quite
distinct from morality'.[13]

At this date his idea of the enlightened and the virtuous still contained the
strong Methodistical element of the 'elect', the spiritually chosen. He remained
far from William Godwin's idea of a public and *political* standard of virtue, upon
which general reform might be based. 'What constitutes real virtue, motive or

consequence? surely the former. . . . I have left the proof to Aristotle – shall we take Godwin's criterion, expediency – oh surely not. Any very satisfactory general reform is I fear impracticable, human nature taken in the mass. . . .'[14] The most immediate consequence of this highly selective and meritocratic form of moral dogma, was, it appeared, that for 'men of honour' marriage was detestable, and 'antimatrimonialism' was to be recommended. A friendship with Hunt did not develop at this time.

In Poland Street, in that rather dark back sitting-room, Shelley was becoming aware of his own solitary identity, divorced for the first time from the society of Field Place or Oxford, and cut off from the impassioned discussions with Elizabeth or Harriet Grove or Hogg. This kind of solitude, not merely a physical one but also a social and spiritual one, was his first taste of an experience that was to become terribly familiar. Now there were only the four walls with the vine trellis wallpaper, and the maid coming up with the meals, or going down with the post. After two weeks it began to press upon him with real horror and he wrote about it to Hogg.

> Solitude is most horrible; in despite of the αφιλαυτια* which perhaps vanity has a great share in, but certainly not with my own good will I cannot endure the horror the evil which comes to *self* in solitude . . . what strange being I am, how inconsistent, in spite of all my boasted hatred of self – this moment thinking I could so far overcome Nature's law as to exist in complete seclusion; the next shrinking from a moment of solitude, starting from my own company *as it were that of a fiend*, seeking anything rather than a continued communion with *self* – Unravel this mystery – but no. I tell you to find the clue which even the bewildered explorer of the cavern cannot reach. . . .[15]

At this unguarded moment, Shelley here touched on one of the great themes and images of his later poetry, and one of the great difficulties of his personal life. He was both fascinated and terrified by the workings of his own mind viewed in solitude. Though his work almost never became realistically auto-biographical in the sense of Wordsworth's *Prelude,* or studiously self-analytic in the mode of Coleridge's poems, nevertheless the secret workings of his own personality and the half-hidden movements of his mind at a subconscious level, were for him an ever-deepening source of imagery, and poetic myth-making. The accent was always on fear, on mystery and on hidden terror.

Passages from his letters written at Poland Street strikingly predict much later

---

* Literally, 'the lack of self-love'. Shelley was much concerned by the possibility, or impossibility, of disinterested love at this time. Somewhat obscure evidence, revealed much later in his Italian writing, suggests that these weeks in Poland Street, Soho, witnessed his first sexual experiences. See Chapter 26.

work: his second long poem was to be called 'Alastor, or the Spirit of Solitude'; the image of the pursuing fiend which had already appeared during Shelley's school period, was to become a central motif in many individual works; while the notion of the mind as an unexplored cave, a bewildering labyrinth through which the explorer must risk his search for a personal identity, was to fill his poems, his notebook and his prose speculations. For him, 'inquiry' came to mean in essence travelling, movement outwards or inwards, rather than analysis, the accumulation of different categories at a single stable point. The image of the journey, especially the subterranean journey, constantly recurs in this respect.

In his battle with solitude, Shelley tried to divert himself with his cousin Medwin's company on brisk walks, especially around the Serpentine and through Regent's Park. It was always a relief to revert to childhood games, and Medwin found Shelley mixing intense discussion of dreams with energetic bouts of ducks-and-drakes, the number of bounds called out loud 'with the utmost glee'. Then there were silent moments of paper-boat-building followed by anxious launching rituals.* In the discussion of dreams, it transpired that Shelley had been keeping a dream journal. Perhaps this accounted for his early evenings.

> At this time Shelley was ever in a dreamy state, and he told me he was in the habit of noting down his dreams. The first day he said, they amounted to a page, the next to two, the third to several, till at last they constituted the greater part of his existence. . . . One morning he told me he was satisfied of the existence of two sorts of dreams, the Phrenic and the Psychic; and that he had witnessed a singular phenomenon, proving that the mind and soul were separate and different entities – that it had more than once happened to him to have a dream, which the mind was pleasantly and actively developing; in the midst of which, it was broken off by *a dream within a dream* – a dream of the soul, to which the mind was not privy; but that from the effect it produced – the start of horror with which he waked – must have been terrific.[16]

These were already familiar concerns. The sense of a doubleness in the mind, the psychic dreams ever ready to invade the phrenic one, just as the self is waited on by its own 'fiend'; and more explicit even, the realization that the psychic dream – the dream *within* the dream – is something uncontrollable, alien, fearful and horrifying. They remained permanent interests with Shelley in his lifelong exploration of psychic and parapsychic phenomena, conducted with the ever-present mixture of fascination and revulsion.

* Both Hogg and Peacock suffered from this eccentricity for years of their acquaintance with Shelley; Hogg's accounts include the launching of large-denomination banknotes on the Serpentine. In 1814 Shelley graduated to fire-boats launched on Hampstead ponds.

Medwin says that the habit of 'systematizing of dreams' revived Shelley's somnambulism and he used to wander about at night in a trance. On one occasion he even got so far as to leave Poland Street altogether. Medwin says he was crossing Leicester Square at 5 in the morning when his attention was caught by a group of urchins gathered round a hunched shape under one of the railings; the shape turned out to be Shelley, fully dressed and curled up fast asleep. Medwin woke him up, and found that Shelley was as surprised as he at the discovery.[17] The story might sound unlikely, except that it is matched by several recorded incidents of a similar type at various stages of Shelley's life.*

One of the side-effects of Shelley's loneliness was that from mid-April he began to rely on the company of the Westbrook sisters. Shelley had first met the youngest, Harriet, through his own sisters Elizabeth and Hellen, at their school at Clapham. The Westbrooks were the daughters of a retired merchant and coffee-house proprietor, John Westbrook, colloquially known by some contemporaries as 'Jew' Westbrook. Mr Westbrook's establishment had been the Mount Street Coffee House in Grosvenor Square, respectable and very prosperous. On his death, he left an estate of £60,000.[18] Westbrook was, in effect, achieving that most difficult piece of English social navigation: moving from the lower middle class to the upper middle class. In the process his wife seems to have been reduced to an almost invisible nonentity, and his daughters split by a kind of cultural lag: the elder, Eliza (who was 29) being sharply self-educated and consciously refined; while the younger, Harriet, (then 16) was an almost perfectly natural middle-class creation, very neat in her dress and manners and writing, and exceedingly pretty. She was also immature for her age, and had come to rely upon her elder sister, both emotionally and morally, as a second and much more influential mother. Hogg always tended to ridicule the social pretensions of the Westbrooks, but he had his own reasons for this. Medwin refers to Harriet admiringly as 'a handsome blonde', but remarks that it was, socially, an ill-judged friendship. Eliza was taller, sallow, with long jet-black hair which she spent much time in combing.[19]

Shelley, whose letters to Hogg are full of the Westbrook sisters from 18 April on, compared them thoughtfully: Harriet was 'the more noble, yet not so cultivated as the elder – a larger diamond, yet not so highly polished'.[20] As the visits between Westbrook's house at 23 Chapel Street and Shelley's lodgings developed, he found Eliza consciously appealing to his speculative interests, and discussing what she referred to elegantly as 'Voltaire's Philosophique Diction-naire'. Harriet, less consciously perhaps, appealed to other feelings. Shelley's

---

* No record of the 'dream journal' survives, but there are several fragments of prose, probably dating from 1815, in which dreams and related psychological phenomena of memory symbolism are discussed: Bod. MS Shelley adds. c. 4, Folder 22–23. See Chapter 12.

gently ironic description of one of his visits showed that he was well aware of the female strategy: 'My poor little friend [Harriet] has been ill, her sister sent for me the other night. I found her on a couch pale; – Her father is civil to me, very strangely, the sister is too civil by half. – She began talking about *l'amour*; I philosophised, & the youngest said she had such a headache that she could not bear conversation. – Her sister then went away & I staid till half past twelve. Her father had a large party below – he invited me – I refused.' Shelley for his own part was already considering the Westbrooks as candidates for his own future plans. His comment on this evening's *tête à tête* was: 'Yes! the fiend the wretch shall fall. Harriet will do for one of the crushers, & the eldest (Eliza) with some taming will do too. They are both very clever, & the youngest (my friend) is amiable.'[21] Shelley used the word in its root meaning: worthy of passionate love.

Shelley established a characteristic hold over Harriet's mind, inspiring her with atheistic ideas, encouraging her to think for herself and challenge her surroundings, forcing her especially to question the polite drawing-room assumptions of the schooling she was receiving, like Shelley's sisters, at Clapham. They agreed to call this prison, and, more slowly, to identify her father as yet another paternal tyrant.

Harriet recorded her own reactions to Shelley's explosive entry into her adolescent life, in a letter to an Irish friend, written one year later. She describes the shelteredness of her upbringing, the way her father kept her out of 'places of fashionable resort and amusement', and how she was taught to respect standards of self-sufficiency, economy and hard work so that she thought to herself 'twas better even to be a beggar or to be obliged to gain my bread with my needle than to be the inhabitant of those great houses when misery and famine howl around'. She records how thoroughly the Christian religion was inculcated, so that apart from the occasional dream of a handsome Redcoat, she assumed that if she married anyone it would be a clergyman.[22]

There was much in this to attract Shelley: the simple moral earnestness set off by physical beauty, and the selflessness which resonated perfectly with Shelley's current plans for disinheriting himself from his family and his class. But even more attractive was the sisterly horror, the spinal shiver, with which she reacted to his atheism. 'You may conceive with what horror I first heard that Percy was an Atheist; at least so it was given out at Clapham; at first I did not comprehend the meaning of the word; therefore when it was explained I was truly petrified. I wondered how he could live a moment professing such principles. . . . I would listen to none of his arguments, so afraid was I that he should shake my belief: at the same time I believed in eternal punishment, and was dreadfully afraid of his supreme Majesty the Devil. I thought I should see him if I listened to his arguments. I often dreamed of him & felt such terror when I heard his name mentioned.'[23] It is not coincidental that in the final comment about her dreams, it is difficult to tell if she is referring to His Supreme Majesty or Shelley. Almost the last thing she ever wrote about him was that he was a vampire.

All in all there was a wonderfully attractive *simplicity* about Harriet, that irradiated both her personality and her person. Peacock, one of her great defenders, has recalled this well:

> She had a good figure, light, active and graceful. Her features were regular and well proportioned. Her hair was light brown, and dressed with taste and simplicity. In her dress she was truly *simplex munditiis*. Her complexion was beautifully transparent; the tint of the blush rose shining through the lily. The tone of her voice was pleasant; her speech the essence of frankness and cordiality; her spirits always cheerful; her laugh spontaneous, hearty, and joyous. She was well educated. . . . Her manners were good . . . to be once in her company was to know her thoroughly.[24]

There was, however, in Harriet's make-up a certain kind of passive fatalism, a slightly doll-like quality, which made her over-dependent on her family, and especially upon her elder sister Eliza. This led her to resign herself too easily to the difficulties of circumstance. In extreme form this weakness brought her to thoughts of suicide, which she contemplated with a calm gravity. Hogg, among others, remarked on her willingness to discuss suicide, and the regularity with which the subject came up in her conversations with Shelley. This flaw in her transparency was probably the result of being brought up as the showpiece of the family. She had always been prevented from asserting herself, expressing herself, or thinking for herself. She was, as she herself realized, surrounded by fears, inhibitions and devils. Shelley realized this too. Harriet would do for 'one of the crushers' of 'the fiend' – which one can take as an amalgam of Christianity, Superstition and Parental Authority.

From all these things Shelley longed to liberate Harriet. As he put it to Hogg at the beginning of May, in terms of a problem that they both faced (Shelley with Harriet, Hogg with Elizabeth):

> I almost despair – you have not only to conquer all the hateful prejudices of religion, not only to conquer duty to father, *duty* indeed of all kind – but I see in the background a monster more terrific. Have you forgotten the tremendous Gregory: the opinion of the world, its myriads of hateful champions, its ten thousand of votaries who deserved a better fate, yet compulsatorily were plunged into this – I tremble when I think of it. Yet *marriage* is hateful detestable – a kind of ineffable sickening disgust seizes my mind when I think of this most despotic most unrequired fetter which prejudice has forged to confine its energies. Yet this is Xtianity – & Xt *must* perish before this can fall.[25]

This in a sense is one of Shelley's earliest statements of a radical politics. What was at first only a theological or moral position now took on a social extension as he fell in love with Harriet. In attacking marriage as it was formulated at the beginning of the nineteenth century, without legal protection for women and without provision for divorce, Shelley was attacking a nexus of fundamental social values: inheritance, property, possession and legal representation.

Yet Shelley was largely mistaken in reading his own personal problems into Harriet's life. It is difficult to see that before his advent, either the Clapham school or Mr Westbrook were genuine sources of 'tyranny'. The upbringing was strict and conventional, but it fitted with Shelley's own puritanism in many respects. What was a real source of tyranny for Harriet, and one which Shelley signally failed to appreciate or act against, was the damagingly over-dependent relationship with Eliza. It was this, and possibly this alone, which gave Harriet her immaturity, her doll-like fatalism and her world of superstitious devils, the kind that governesses traditionally create to obtain mental control over their charges. Shelley acknowledged the dominating side of Eliza, as his remark about 'taming' her makes clear. But it transpired that Shelley himself came to depend on such a secondary female figure, and was not prepared to dispense with her until too late.

An oblique light can be thrown on how Shelley intended to liberate Harriet, by a reminiscence of Merle's which dates from about the summer of this year. Shelley wrote to Merle to ask his aid in mounting an educational experiment of a somewhat unusual kind. He wished to create an educational situation which would 'shut out enquiry on subjects of religious or social government'. For this purpose, Shelley wrote, 'I wish to find two young persons of not more than four or five years of age; and should prefer females, as they are usually more precocious than males. . . . I will withdraw from the world with my charge, and in some sequestered spot direct their education. They shall know nothing of men or manners until their minds shall have been sufficiently matured to enable me to ascertain, when brought into play, what the impressions of the world are upon the mind when it has been veiled from human prejudice.' Merle's response was, he says, one of scandalized disbelief. 'The idea of a youth of twenty shutting himself from the world with two females until an age when, without religious instruction, they would have no other guarantee for their chastity than the reason of a man who would then be in the summer of his life, with all his passions in full vigour, was more than absurd – it was horrible.'[26] He remonstrated, 'firmly, but kindly', and Shelley apparently dropped the plan. Yet it shows a theoretical half-way house between the desire to proselytize his sisters – which his mother so feared – and his adult scheme for an ideological community of radicals, which were in practice to be composed largely of female disciples.

This adult scheme was of course open to the same misinterpretations that Merle made of the youthful one.

All these ideas were in the air when Shelley finally left London and the Westbrooks on Friday, 10 May, and re-entered Field Place where 'the enemy' lay, after a preparatory weekend with Captain Pilfold at Nelson Hall, Lindfield, near Cuckfield. Captain Pilfold was persuasive, and by negotiating separately with both parties he got Timothy to offer Shelley an income of £200 per annum and freedom to choose where he would live. Shelley in turn allowed his threats over the inheritance to drop, and tacitly refrained from hot-gospelling atheism at least within the confines of Field Place.[27] We learn from letters to Hogg that Shelley was allowed to settle himself independently in two rooms of the house: a bedroom and a little study. But none of the rest of the family were permitted to enter. Shelley read and wrote, walked out at night, and according to Merle used to frequent the taproom of one of the Horsham taverns where he talked atheism into any available ear. It was lonely in a different way from Poland Street. 'I am a perfect hermite, not a being to speak with, I sometimes exchange a word with my mother on the subject of the weather, upon which she is irresistibly eloquent— otherwise all is deep silence. I wander about this place, walking over the grounds with no particular object in view. I cannot write except now & then to you – sometimes to Miss Westbrook – my hand begins to hurry, & I am tired & ennued.'[28] Shelley sent Hogg poetical effusions selected from his notebook of the previous *St Irvyne* summer, and meditated on the divine character of Luxima, a beautiful Indian girl in Lady Morgan's *The Missionary*. 'What pity,' he lamented, 'that we cannot incorporate these creations of Fancy; the very thought of them thrills the soul.' The passages he chose from his own poems were appropriately melancholic:

> Hopes that bud in youthful breasts
> Live not thro the lapse of time –
> Love's rose a host of thorns invests
> And ungenial is the clime . . . .[29]

His restless sense of having no immediate purpose unsettled him as he took his midnight walks, and for Hogg's benefit he dramatized his longings, half mocking himself, half serious: 'I have been thinking of Death and Heaven for four days. What is the latter? shall we set off – Is there a future life; whom should we injure by departing? should we not benefit some – I was thinking last night when from the summer house I saw the moon, just behind one of the chimneys if she were alone to witness our departure.'[30] Years later, in a small boat on the bay of Lerici, he was to terrify his lady passenger with exactly the same brand of mournful humour, meditating on suicide.

By way of sympathy, Hogg resurrected his passion for Elizabeth Shelley, whom he had still not set eyes on, and implored Shelley to let him visit Field Place. Shelley enthused heatedly over Hogg's desire for illicit union with his sister, while simultaneously doing everything in his power to prevent Hogg coming down to Sussex to fulfil his tryst in reality. Elizabeth, he told Hogg sadly, would hear nothing of the scheme, she was 'a Christian', her mind was 'diseased'. But all the same the prospect had been glorious: 'I own it – I desired, eagerly desired to see you & my sister irrecoverably united where you have no priest but love: I pictured to myself Elysium in beholding my only perfect friend daring the vain world, smiling at its silly forms, setting an example of perfection to an universe.'[31] Elizabeth, one notes, plays a minor role in this picture of perfection. But for the two friends it would have been an achieved community of passion.

There is evidence from a letter of Hogg's to Mrs Shelley, that Hogg did eventually convince Shelley that it was safe to spend a few secret days at Field Place, and he came at the end of June. 'Do not trouble about baggage; I have plenty of clean things for you,' wrote Shelley with a sudden access of practicality. Hogg was rewarded with a single peep at Elizabeth through the window of Warnham Church.[32] But afterwards, when Shelley was about to leave for Wales, Timothy found out, and there was a further row. 'God send he does not write to yr father,' observed Shelley sententiously, '– I threw cool water on the rage of the old buck.'[33]

One further friend began to play an important part in Shelley's life in these days of interregnum at Field Place. It was another lady, a certain Miss Elizabeth Hitchener. She ran the local school at Hurstpierpoint which Captain Pilfold's daughter attended.

Miss Hitchener was an unusual figure in the neighbourhood, a girl of working-class background who had educated herself in liberal ideas, and now at 29, had established an independent intellectual standing and gained considerable respect as the local schoolmistress. She was a striking figure, tall, black-haired and dark-eyed, self-possessed and remarkably articulate. Her father was rumoured to be a retired smuggler from the Sussex coast. Miss Hitchener had risen so far beyond her background that she had already made contact with the radical Godwinian set in London. Hogg, in one of his most rumbustious passages, says she had a bony, masculine figure, with a shadow of facial hair above her lip.

Some time during June, Shelley met Miss Hitchener, and struck up an extraordinary intellectual friendship, with hours of long and candid arguments on the subjects of religion and philosophy.[34] Shelley eagerly embarked on the process of organizing Miss Hitchener's secondary education. He procured her copies of Locke, Southey's *The Curse of Kehama* and Ensor's book *On National Education* which argued that literature, and poetry in particular, had an instructive and social function, and should be considered primarily as a didactic medium: 'Poetry seems to me the most powerful means of instructing youth.'[35]

The friendship and progressive discussion soon grew into a correspondence. For Shelley this seems at first to have served a purely proselytizing function, with Miss Hitchener in the role of eager pupil. But later it became an extraordinary arena for his philosophical and political speculations, and for his attempts at emotional self-analysis and self-justification. Miss Hitchener found herself inexorably up-graded, to confidante, and finally to soul-mate. She had the great merit of being a regular and enormously prolix correspondent, as she admitted herself with pleasure, and responded with enthusiasm to her promotions, little understanding what was going on, though a good deal flattered, and half convinced that Shelley might be in love with her. Miss Hitchener seems to have been an earnest, awkward, lonely creature, without any obvious guile or malice, and the estimates of her intelligence have suffered unfairly from the fact that the copies of her letters which exist were merely first drafts, very rough and unfinished.[36] The fact that she made drafts at all is indicative of her earnestness. She was aware, more realistically than Shelley, of the social divide that existed between them, and was only talked into ignoring it by Shelley's sweeping disregard for all social forms. In the end this ruined Miss Hitchener's career, so carefully built up at Hurstpierpoint, shattered her relationship with Shelley, and turned her into the lasting butt of Shelley biographers.

Atheism was their great topic in these early days. It is interesting to compare Miss Hitchener's cool reaction to Harriet's horror. '*Self-love*, you see,' she wrote to Shelley, consciously adopting his own terminology, 'prompts me eagerly to accept the opportunity you offer me of improving my mind by a correspondence with you, though you cannot surely suppose me so *conceited* as to attempt making you a proselyte to my faith, have I not reason rather to tremble for my own; but tho' I presume not to argue I love to *discuss*. . . .'[37] This was her answer to Shelley's studiously polite and dignified offer: '. . . I know that you, like myself are a devotee at the Shrine of truth. Truth is *my* God, & *say* he is Air, Water, Earth or Electricity but I think *yours* is reducible to the same simple Divinityship. Seriously however, if you *very* widely differ, or differ indeed in the least from me on the subject of our late argument, the only reason which would induce me to object to a polemical correspondence, is that it might deprive *your* time of that application which it's value deserves: *mine* is totally vacant.'[38]

The correspondence then moved out into discussions of Christianity, the nature of God, of belief, of reason; the possibility and type of an after-life – the 'future state'. Politics only entered marginally at first, with references to Shelley's disapproval of aristocratic notions, and his belief that religious establishments were the 'formidable tho' destructible barriers' to a society politically organized in 'accordance with Nature and Reason'.[39]

On a topical issue Shelley attacked the Prince Regent's lavishly extravagant fete at Carlton House on 19 June, which included a 200-foot banqueting table along the length of which ran an artificial stream encased in banks of silver and pumped from intricately ornamented silver fountains at one end. 'What think you of the bubbling brooks, & mossy banks at Carlton House?' he exclaimed to Miss Hitchener, grimly enumerating the ludicrous magnificence and 'disgusting splendours'. 'Here are a people advanced in intellectual improvement, willfully rushing to a Revolution, the natural death of all great commercial Empires, which must plunge them in the barbarism from which they are slowly rising.'[40] Misuse of wealth in this way always outraged Shelley, for not only did it inflame his natural puritanism, but it shocked his sense of the justice of fair distribution and the self-evident claims for a reasonable economic equity.

But he did not risk telling Miss Hitchener later that he had carried out a rapid propaganda expedition against the Regent's festivities. He had dashed off a satire of some fifty lines, had it printed locally as a pamphlet, and on his way through London to Wales, stopped off at the Groves, to spend several hours tossing copies into the windows of carriages driving up to Carlton House. This was to be his first exercise in active political campaigning, half prank and half serious propaganda. His pupil Miss Hitchener was not apprised of it, nor did Shelley's promise to visit her in London on the first stage of his journey actually materialize. He afterwards explained that he had been prevented by several nights of sleeplessness and days of pressing business, which ended by giving him 'a short but violent nervous illness' on his arrival in Wales.[41] All this, though perhaps conveniently exaggerated, suggests that he had been living at Field Place under considerable nervous stress.

The plan to go to Wales had been worked out with his cousins the Groves at the end of June. It came as both an escape and a relief, for he wished to take stock of his position on neutral ground. Shelley left Field Place for London, and then travelled to Thomas Grove's remote house at the top of the valley of Cwm Elan, near Rhayader, in the county of Radnorshire. He arrived about 9 July, immediately sending off a note to Hogg.

Thomas Grove, Harriet Grove's eldest brother, was aged 27, and a gentleman farmer with an estate of 10,000 acres. His house lay some four miles south-west of Rhayader, and not far from the tiny country village of Elan. The Elan valley which surrounds it is a formation of bleak and rocky hills, covered in mauve heather and flowering gorse with the pink sandy Radnorshire stone peering through. In fine weather it is very beautiful and dramatic, especially the curving view from the road leading back into Rhayader; but the geography of the area is essentially closed and gloomy. The population in 1811 was extremely sparse, consisting largely of the semi-wild breed of mountain sheep, with their long thin muzzles, narrow close-set eyes and vivid splashes of marker dye maintained by the seasonal visits of the reddleman. The kind of *enclosure* offered by this landscape, with its steeply sheltered sides, the wall of rock or hillside at its back, and the single dramatically channelled vista through the open end of the valley seems to have exercised a quite extraordinary and hitherto unremarked attraction for Shelley. As his travels took him further afield and eventually on to the Continent, this curiously symbolic geographical setting became the recurrent and dominant motif of the many different houses in which he chose to stay. The airy remoteness, the cradling protection, and the single dramatic view recur like some kind of subliminal theme. His houses were, for choice, like the encastellated strongholds of chivalric romance, each one an ultimate retreat in which he seemed to be waiting, back to the wall, for the inevitable pursuer who will appear at first a great way off, but inexorably advancing through the only route that is not barred. Once again, this is a central image in the mature poetry.

To Hogg, Shelley wrote with unusually bluff brevity that the scenery was 'divine, but all very stale flat and unprofitable – indeed this place is a very great bore'.[42] But to Miss Hitchener, who had already channelled off a good deal of the enthusiastic froth previously reserved for his college friend, Shelley was rather more thoughtfully forthcoming: 'Rocks piled on to each other to tremendous heights, rivers formed into cataracts by their projections, & valleys clothed with woods, present an appearance of enchantment – but *why* do they enchant, *why* is it more affecting than a plain, it cannot be innate, is it acquired?' Already he seems to have felt some response in himself to this kind of landscape, some particular reflection of his own mind. He went on, meditatively: 'Thus does knowledge lose all pleasure which involuntarily arises, by attempting to arrest the fleeting Phantom as it passes – vain almost like the chemist's aether it evaporates under our observation; it flies from all but the slaves of passion and sickly sensibility who will not analyse a feeling.'[43]

This contempt for 'sickly sensibility' was new and growing in Shelley. He attempted to replace it by a more objective concern with facts around him, especially the social facts of oppression and hardship. He had told Miss Hitchener that he was going to travel around 'on foot' to view the manner and conditions of the peasantry. He produced an immediate report on an incident concerning a Welsh beggar whom he had heard asking for bread at Grove's kitchen door while he was dressing by his window in the morning. He hurried downstairs, caught the old man, and 'gave him something' which was received with due grace. Then, thinking no doubt of Wordsworth's philosophic vagrants, he tried to get the beggar to talk. 'I followed him a mile asking a thousand questions; at length I quitted him finding by this remarkable observation that perseverance was useless. "I see by your dress that you are a rich man – they have injured me and mine a million times. You appear to be well intentioned but I have no security of it while you live in such a house as that, or wear such clothes as those. It would be charity to quit me." [44] Shelley learnt one of his first genuine political lessons from the unexpectedly abrupt and prosaic denouement of this romantic encounter.

Cwm Elan was not all social study. It was mostly boredom and indecision and self-doubt. 'I am what the sailors call banyaning. I do not see a soul. All is gloomy and desolate. I amuse myself however with reading Darwin,* climbing rocks and exploring this scenery.' [45] Various plans were fermenting in Shelley's mind. The Westbrooks were on holiday at Aberystwyth, only thirty miles away to the west, and part of Shelley's undeclared reason for coming to Wales was to arrange a visit to Harriet and Eliza. [46] To Edward Graham he wrote that he was still planning surgical studies, in emulation of John Grove, but was hindered by being 'as poor as a rat'. [47] To Hogg, he wrote drily that if he knew anything about love then he knew he was not in love with Harriet; he planned, on the other hand, to come to see Hogg at York as soon as his strengthened finances might allow, and added that it would be necessary to come under a false name to avoid irritating his father 'needlessly'. He found the deception easily justified in his newly adopted tone of brisk objectivity: 'we must *live* if we intend to live, that is we must eat drink & sleep, & money is the necessary procurer of these things'. [48] He was scathing about Timothy's unfortunate discovery of Hogg's visit to Field Place in June. 'I regard the whole as a finesse to which I *had* supposed the Honourable Member's headpiece unequal.' [49]

As he steeled himself to fling back into the centre of action and events, Shelley's thoughts turned increasingly to politics, and it was of these that he wrote to Miss Hitchener rather than disclosing his ambitions for Harriet. His discussions were now rapidly moving from the notion of atheism to the idea of equality in society:

> You are willing to dismiss for the present the subject of Religion. As to its influence in individuals we will – but it is so intimately connected with politics, & augments in so vivid a degree the evils resulting from the system before us, that I will make a few remarks on it. [50]

*Erasmus Darwin, 1731–1802, one of the archetypes of Shelley's much admired scholars. Darwin was a free-thinker, physician, botanist and poet; a man of strong Quakerish principles, and much admired where he practised in Lichfield and Derby. He married twice (and thereby became the grandfather of both Charles Darwin and Francis Galton, the geneticist). Shelley read his long poem *The Botanic Garden* (1792), and probably glanced at his prose work *Zoonomia* (1796) in which an early theory of evolution was propounded. Darwin's fusion of Science, philosophy and poetry was to prove an inspiration to Shelley. See Chapter 9.

Shelley was now determined to view religion in the wider context of the English society of 1811, and indeed within the context of the whole history of social oppression. His mind ran over the St Bartholomew's Day Massacre and the Gordon Riots. His conclusion was a crude building-block version of Rousseau, that a naturally egalitarian society had been continually corrupted by the hereditary power-pyramids of Religion, Monarchy and Aristocracy.

> It is this empire of terror which is established by Religion, Monarchy is its prototype, Aristocracy may be regarded as symbolising its very essence. They are mixed – one can now be scarce distinguished from the other, & equality in politics like perfection in morality appears now far removed from even the visionary anticipations of what is called the wildest theorist. *I* then am wilder than the wildest.[51]

In other letters he looked at the idea of equality more closely, and tried to answer the objection that his views on a just society were 'visionary': 'Why is it visionary, have you tried?' If Locke's argument that there are no 'innate ideas' is correct, it proved to him that all mankind started out equal before nature, 'intellect varies but in the impressions with which casualty or intention has marked it'.[52] At any rate, he felt, whatever the objections to complete equality as an attainable political situation, any advance in this direction would be an improvement. 'What can be worse than the present aristocratical system? there are in England ten millions only 500,000 of whom live in a state of ease; the rest earn their livelihood with toil and care.'

As yet Shelley's grasp of the problem was primitive, not to say naïve. He had no real experience of how the majority lived; he had suffered no real economic deprivation; he had no realization of the problems of educating ignorance and bigotry at the lowest level; and, like most of his contemporaries, he had no idea that industrialization and urbanization were far more at the roots of an unjust society than a lazy, pleasure-loving aristocracy, or a fat quiescent clergy. The Welsh beggar had been right to take his alms and distrust his intentions.

It was not politics, but the romantic interest of Harriet's situation which finally brought Shelley out of Radnorshire. A rapid correspondence moved between Cwm Elan and Aberystwyth, though the post was maddeningly irregular, 'like the waves in Hell were to Tantalus'.[53] Scenting the wind, Eliza, through Harriet, had sent him a novel extolling the virtues of matrimony, by Amelia Opie.[54] It was entitled suggestively *Adeline Mowbray, or The Mother and Daughter*.

Walking alone through the rocks and waterfalls of Wales, Shelley felt ready to embark on some new form of life, to grapple with it: '. . . a thousand shadowy trees form the principal features of the scenery, I am not wholly uninfluenced by its magic in my lonely walks, but I long for a thunder storm.'[55] Thus he wrote at the end of July.

By the end of August the thunderstorm had occurred; he was in Edinburgh and married. Events had moved quickly. In late July Shelley had received letters from Harriet in London saying that her father had 'persecuted her in the most horrible way', and was forcing her to go back to school. He wrote back and urged resistance. Harriet became so upset that she now wrote to him, talking of suicide, and threw herself on Shelley's 'protection'. On Monday, 5 August, Shelley dashed to London by coach, but on arrival he could not persuade Harriet to take any decisive action. He put up at Charles Grove's in Lincoln's Inn for the weekend, anxious and perplexed. News that John Grove was proposing to his sister Elizabeth further disturbed him and he made a whirlwind visit to Field Place the following Thursday, 15 August. His note apprising Hogg of the disaster, and reassuring him that Elizabeth would not accept Grove went off the same day to York.

Meanwhile Harriet hung fire for a further ten days of intimate negotiations, undecided 'not with respect to me but herself' – as Shelley put it.[56] But finally on the morning of Sunday, 25 August, Shelley and Harriet, abetted by Charles Grove, slipped away from Chapel Street in a Hackney carriage, and spent the day hiding in coffee houses near Cannon Street. The two elopers caught the night mail from the Green Dragon Inn, Gracechurch Street, bound for Edinburgh via York. Shelley had in his pocket ten pounds borrowed from Hogg, and twenty-five pounds from Tom Medwin's father, the estate lawyer at Horsham. Behind him he left a diversionary note for his father, saying without explanation that he was making a sudden trip to Ireland via Holyhead, and asking for his 'clothes papers gun &c' to be forwarded to Charles Grove's in London. The coup was complete. As with most of the crucial events of Shelley's biography, his own version of the facts gradually became distorted. Two months later Shelley was writing to Elizabeth Hitchener, to explain that the whole thing had really occurred because of Harriet. Harriet had fallen in love with him, rather than vice versa; she had been made so ill and miserable by persecution that she had become suicidal and he had been forced, first to 'promise to unite' his fate with hers, and finally to contradict his whole anti-matrimonial position so far as to propose marriage. The protection of the woman was finally, he felt, an overwhelming argument in the case.[57] His role thus became that of the rational Godwinian, who had unwittingly been caught up in Harriet's circumstances, but had responded coolly and disinterestedly in a point-by-point fight for her freedom. Certainly Shelley came to believe this about himself.

The actual facts, as far as we can recover them, do not suggest this is the truth. The evidence seems to show that Shelley far more than Harriet was the instigator of events, and it was he who pressed them to their final conclusion, even though this was not exactly what he had intended. In his last letter to Hogg from Cwm Elan, it is clear that he was already passionately involved with Harriet and determined to carry her off, though on the basis of free love if he could manage it. 'We shall have £200 a year, when we find it run short we must live I suppose on love. Gratitude and admiration all demand that I should love her *forever*. We shall see you at York. I will hear your arguments for matrimonialism by which I am now almost convinced. I can get lodgings at York I suppose. . . . Your enclosure of £10 has arrived. I am *now* indebted to you £30.'[58] This letter clearly shows that Shelley intended to carry off Harriet even before he left Wales. He went to London with the immediate intention of liberating her from Chapel Street and taking her to York to meet Hogg and get lodgings. Afterwards they might then argue about 'matrimonialism'. When Shelley arrived in London and put his case, however, it did not work. Harriet refused. Far from abandoning herself to him and his 'protection', for more than two weeks she refused to leave Chapel Street at all.

Shelley's note of about 14 August, some seven days after he had arrived in London, shows him perplexed and depressed in the middle of this unexpected predicament. 'My arguments have been *yours*,' he wrote to Hogg, 'they have been urged by the force of the gratitude which their occasion excited – but I yet remain in London, I remain embarrassed & melancholy.' Characteristically in this moment of reverse, he turned back to his old fondness for Hogg, continuing in the same note: '*Your* noble and exalted friendship, the prosecution of your happiness, can alone engross my impassioned interest.' Reverting to the struggle to capture Harriet, he concluded: 'I never was so fit for calm argument as now. This I fear more resembles exerted action than inspired passion.'[59]

The 'arguments' which Shelley keeps referring to here are the arguments for marriage as against free love. What seems to have happened, therefore, is that Harriet refused to leave on a free-love basis, and that Shelley had to talk himself into a proposal of marriage and her into an acceptance. To do this Shelley had to alter his plans radically. Discussions with Charles Grove, the only friend who was fully Shelley's confidant at this point, revealed that such an elopement would have to be solemnized in Scotland in order to avoid lengthy qualifications and parental approvals. This necessitated abandoning the York plan, and obtaining further travelling money – which Shelley did under some pretext from Mr Medwin when he visited Sussex. In all this it is again clear that Shelley was the instigator. Although one may also feel that it was the elder and more 'refined' Eliza Westbrook who was shrewdly bargaining marriage into the Sussex aristocracy for the consummation of Shelley's youthful passion. This was Hogg's opinion, and also the explanation given by Shelley's counsel during the trial for custody of the children, six years later.[60] If such was the case, by her own lights, Eliza did very well.

As the negotiations drew to a conclusion in the last week of August, Shelley seems to have had a slight sense of getting rather more than he had bargained for. There is a story that may be taken as a slight indication of Shelley's mood at the actual moment of his elopement. The anecdote goes that as he and Charles waited for Harriet at a prearranged coffee house in Mount Street, the two young men breakfasted on oysters and then Shelley stood in the doorway distractedly skimming the empty shells across the street, repeating over and over to Charles with an ironic sigh: 'Grove, this is a *Shelley* business!'[61] Besides the mournful pun, he probably intended a reference to his grandfather's marital exploits. It also seems from this account that Harriet was late.

Shelley and Harriet travelled non-stop, leaving a note for Hogg, requesting further money, as they went through York at midnight on Monday. They reached Edinburgh on the morning of Wednesday, 28 August 1811, and immediately took out a marriage licence, having been advised on the exact procedure by a Scottish lawyer they met on the coach. Shelley described himself in the marriage book as 'Farmer, of Sussex'.[62] They moved from the coaching inn to lodgings, and Hogg came up from York to join them, probably during the following weekend. It must have been some time before Hogg arrived that the wedding night incident occurred which Peacock later described, when Shelley drew his pistols on a party of well-wishers and threatened to shoot them if they crossed the threshold.

Altogether it is unlikely that Shelley was alone with Harriet for much more than seven days, three of which were spent in non-stop coach travel. It was a strange honeymoon *à trois* and showed from the outset Shelley's disinclination to live entirely in the company of one woman for more than a few hours at a time. It was only gradually that Shelley came to accept this about himself, and ask what it was that caused it. Harriet, at this time, it must be remembered, was only just 16 years old, and still really a schoolgirl.

The Shelleys and Hogg spent the whole of September in Edinburgh. Hogg has many droll anecdotes, a few of which can be gingerly interpreted. Shelley had taken handsome lodgings on the ground floor of a house in George Street, and the moment Hogg arrived Shelley insisted that his friend must immediately have a bed in the same house. ' "We have met at last once more!" Shelley exclaimed, "and we will never part again! You must have a bed in the house!" It was deemed necessary, indispensable . . . the landlord was summoned, he came instantly; a bed in the house; the necessity was so urgent that they did not give him time to speak.'[63]

All three walked joyfully about Edinburgh, Shelley collecting regular letters from the post office in 'prodigious number', and doting on large supplies of comb honey that they found in the shops. A special treat was to visit the dour Edinburgh kirks to hear the sermons, which caused Shelley an exquisite mixture of amusement and outrage. On one memorable and embarrassing occasion Shelley and Hogg attended a Presbyterian catechism class, in which the catechist got more and more angry as his pupils failed to answer the questions correctly. After interrogating them on the identity of Adam, and receiving no satisfactory reply, he went on to sterner stuff. 'The indignation of the Catechist waxing hot, in a still louder and very angry tone he broke forth with: "Wha's the Deel?" This was too much; Shelley burst into a shrieking laugh, and rushed wildly out of doors. I slowly followed him, thinking seriously of Elders, Presbyters, and Kirk Synods. However, nothing came of it; we were not cast into prison.'[64] From this tale one may gather that both Shelley and Hogg were indulging in a priest-baiting game partly for their own amusement, partly out of genuine ideological outrage and partly no doubt for the benefit of the beautiful, simple and easily impressionable Harriet. On another occasion Shelley was reprimanded in the streets for giving vent to his piercing, fiendish laughter on the Sabbath.[65]

Shelley was now studying furiously once more, as he had done at Oxford. Hogg recalls how he managed to discover a source of free books in Edinburgh – either at the excellent circulating library, or possibly through the young lawyer whom he had met on the coach. Shelley was continually going out to get new ones. He read French philosophers of the Enlightenment, and discovered Buffon, one of whose treatises he began to translate in the evenings. Harriet fitted very well into this routine, and for her part took up a French romance which she translated and copied out with characteristic style, 'without blot or blemish, upon the smoothest, whitest, finest paper, in a small, neat, flowing and legible feminine hand'.[66] When not employed in this, Harriet used to read aloud to Hogg and Shelley, 'remarkably well, very correctly, and with a clear, distinct, agreeable voice, and often emphatically'. She would keep this up for hours, well into the night, and Hogg implies that he appreciated this exercise rather more than Shelley who was inclined to grow drowsy and drop off to sleep on the hearth-rug.

Shelley, immersed in the scientific speculations of Buffon, was particularly fascinated by the stars seen so clearly in the northern summer latitude, and the three of them would walk the night streets gazing upwards, talking of constellations, modern astronomy and Greek mythologies of the zodiac. For several nights the sky was marked by a startling comet.

Edinburgh itself gradually palled on Shelley and he was soon to refer to their being 'chained to the filth and *commerce*' of the Scottish capital.[67] The chain that bound them was money, or rather, it was lack of money. Financial difficulties began to occupy an important part in Shelley's plans, and he was never really to be free of them for the rest of his life. At the time of his elopement with Harriet, Shelley was living on the £200 annuity from his father. His journey to Edinburgh, and much of his stay there, seems to have been subsidized by money from Captain Pilfold, who generously stuck by his wayward nephew at this time. Hogg also had lent his friend several small sums.

The day after his marriage at Edinburgh, Shelley attempted to secure the quarterly fifty pounds due to him from Timothy on 1 September. Realizing that once the news of his marriage reached Field Place his allowance would probably be cut, he hurried off an innocent filial appeal, explaining that he had (somehow, on his way to Ireland) been detained at Edinburgh 'in consequence of having incurred a slight debt', and anxiously awaited his allowance which could be sent through Graham in London. With the brisk calculation he had already decided upon in Wales, Shelley masked all reference to Harriet and wrote in a style of anxious and trusting respect: 'My dear Father – I know of no one to whom I can apply with greater certainty of success when in distress than you. I must own that I am not so frugal as could be wished, but I know you are kind enough to enclose me a Dft for £50.'[68] It is extraordinary, considering what had already taken place between him and his father, that Shelley did not realize – if nothing else – the transparent untruth of this address would alert his father. In the event, Timothy quickly had news of the elopement, stopped the allowance, and wrote an angry and distraught letter to Hogg's father at Durham: 'God knows what can be the end of all this disobedience.'[69]

As the days and then weeks passed and no money reached him, Shelley's letters to Field Place escalated from a tone of frigid politeness, through heavy sarcasm, into paeans of insult and accusation. More than anything, it was Timothy's refusal to make a response of any kind, the operative effect of his original threat to 'withdraw himself', which enraged and goaded Shelley. It is easy to sympathize with Shelley in this, for he was in an awkward and entirely unknown situation, for the first time responsible for someone besides himself; quite bereft of reliable resources, and yet apparently writing to a brick wall.

Two weeks after his unsuccessful attempt to secure the £50, Shelley again wrote to Timothy in a vein of ceremonious and ostentatious reasonableness: 'Proceeding on the idea suggested, the vague information above alluded to that you were displeased with me, permit me with the utmost humility to deprecate any anger on your part, perhaps also I may succeed in pointing out its inutility, & inadequacy to the happiness of any one whom it may concern.'[70] Ten days later, on 27 August, he was writing with greater urgency and more open sarcasm: 'Father, are you a Christian? ... do not rather these hypocritical assumptions of the Christian character lower you in real virtue beneath the *libertine* atheist, for a real one would practise what you preach, & quietly put in practice that forgiveness. . . .'71

By 12 October, having moved with Harriet and Hogg back to York, his letters show that he had now given up any immediate hope of financial support from Timothy, but was more than ever determined to press home his case, and make his reproaches sting. '*Obedience* is in my opinion a word which should have no existence – you regard it as necessary. – Yes, you can command it. The institutions of society have made you, tho' liable to be misled by passion and prejudice like others, the *Head of the family*; and I confess it is most natural for minds not of the highest order to value even the errors whence they derive their importance.'72 In this letter one can hear for perhaps the first time the ring of what can be called a truly Shelleyan note: that mixture of intense anger, glowing libertarian principle, and the bitter reproachfulness of the abandoned and the outcast.

A day later, Shelley was writing to his grandfather Sir Bysshe in a similar vein, though with more hope and therefore with more dignity. 'Language is given us to express ideas – he who fetters it is a BIGOT and a TYRANT, from these have my misfortune arisen. – I expect from your liberality and justice no unfavourable construction of what fools in power would denominate *insolence*. This is not the spirit in which I write. I write in the spirit of truth and candor. If you will send me some money to help me and my wife (and I know you are not ungenerous) I will add to my respect for a grandfather my love for a preserver.'73 Sir Bysshe did not respond any more than Timothy, for it seems that he too regarded a *mésalliance* as something unspeakable, and Shelley's high tone to be a mockery.

The battery of letters to his father had not quite been discharged. The final letter, like the whole series, has something deeply characteristic of Shelley's primary range of emotional reactions, which were to reappear in other more complicated, more diverse and more sophisticated situations. It is an outcry, against which there can be no turning away, but equally no real answer. It is not finally an accusation, a blow, or even a threat: it is a kind of self-consecration – it is a curse. Shelley wrote to Timothy on 15 October from York:

You have treated me ill, vilely. When I was expelled for atheism you wished I had been killed in Spain. The desire of its consummation is very like the crime, perhaps it is well for me that the laws of England punish murder, & that *cowardice* shrinks from their animadversion. I shall take the first opportunity of seeing you – if *you* will not hear my name, *I* will pronounce it. Think not I am an insect whom injuries destroy – had I money enough I would meet you in London, & hollow in your ears Bysshe, Bysshe, Bysshe, – aye Bysshe till you're deaf.[74]

The curse was significantly his own name: significantly, for it betrays the fact that he regarded himself at some level as his father's own blunder, his own damnation. At this extremity, fears, suspicions and guilts took on the solidity of facts for Shelley. Thus the story that Timothy had wanted his son to be conscripted to fight in the Peninsular War and be killed in action, which has no evidence or even likelihood behind it, now becomes one of Shelley's permanent grievances against him. The idea that Timothy was pursuing him – tragic, for the reverse was so obviously true – also became a recurrent obsession. Peacock, who did not get to know Shelley until a year later, refers particularly to this as an ingrained apprehension, himself knowing that it was totally unfounded.

After this cathartic letter Shelley let silence fall between them, wrote through the solicitor Whitton, and adopted an altogether more oblique, calculating and offhand style. The gulf was now irrevocable between father and son at an emotional level; and a particular pattern of response between Shelley and the outside world of established society had been forged, if not for ever, then at least for many years to come. Shelley had his nineteenth birthday on 4 August 1811.

The move to York, which lies in the background of this correspondence, took place in the first days of October. Their resources were now very low, and arriving one evening in the autumn rain, they hunted miserably about for cheap lodgings which they found in the house of two 'weird sisters' as Hogg called them, retired dressmakers. On the journey Shelley had been dispirited and distracted, and once, at Berwick, Hogg had found him missing from his seat when the coach was about to start. 'He was standing on the Walls in a drizzling rain, gazing mournfully at the wild and dreary sea, with looks not less wild and dreary.'[75]

4
Harriet Westbrook

The early days at York were bad for Shelley and he needed considerable personal courage to face them. He had taken the decisive step away from his family, especially from his sisters and his father; away from the financial and social stability of the class he had been brought up in; and away from the structure of beliefs, and especially the unquestioned assumptions of privilege, which that class had deeply in its bones. He was already paying a heavy emotional price for all this, and he was probably aware that there was more to follow. Years later, Leigh Hunt used to enumerate with admiration all the worldly goods that Shelley had renounced: the family fortune, the respectability, the seat in Parliament. But Hunt tended perhaps to over-emphasize the material deprivation which at this moment in York in October 1811 was so clearly secondary to the emotional and psychological one. For a young man, material difficulties are the easiest. Yet Shelley's final reaction to all this was one that had already become characteristic. He fought back.

The first sign of this was his reopening of the correspondence with Elizabeth Hitchener. Writing on 8 October from 'Miss Dancer's, Coney Street, York', he apprised her of the fact that he, the convinced atheist and anti-matrimonialist, was now married. He defended his action vigorously, on the grounds that in the present state of society both the reputation of the woman and the 'political rights' of both would otherwise suffer; yet he confirmed his opposition to the *principle* of marriage. 'How useless,' he wrote, with one of his earliest sparks of pragmatism, 'to attempt by singular examples to renovate the face of society'; arguing that the proper weapons were 'reasoning' and the struggle for a 'comprehensive change'. Nevertheless, he continued, it was still necessary to ignore the prejudices of society wherever practical and his married status gave him a new power to do this. He therefore issued for the first time a remarkable invitation to Miss Hitchener. 'Will you write to me?...Nay more – will you be my friend, may I be your's – the shadow of worldly impropriety is effaced by *my* situation; our strictest intercourse would excite none of those disgusting remarks with which *females* of the present day think right to load the friendships of the opposite sexes. Nothing would be transgressed by your even living with us – could you not pay me a visit. My dear friend Hogg that noble being is with me, & will be always, but my wife will abstract from our intercourse the shadow of impropriety.'[1] Here for the first time Shelley was groping towards his idea of the community of like-spirits, the radical commune of reformers who could live together on an equal basis and attempt that 'comprehensive change' of society which the ideal of 'perfectibility' constantly held out. Also, on a more personal level, one sees his increasing discomfort in the narrow confines of the closed married relationship: Hogg will 'always' be with them, and others like Miss Hitchener will soon follow.

Shelley need not have worried about the Sussex schoolmistress. She reacted with kindness, and positively overwhelming enthusiasm. She thought there was 'no equivocation' in Shelley's action and as to the marriage, that was certainly 'due to Mrs Shelley' in the circumstances. 'May your life ever protect her, to say how sincerely I wish you both every happiness does not convey half my feeling for it.' She had however certain instinctive social misgivings concerning Shelley's invitation, and gently diverted it into a more ethereal kind of sympathy. 'With the greatest and sincerest pleasure should I accept your invitation if in my power, but situated as I am it is not possible, tho' at some future period I anticipate accepting it. . . . I long to be introduced to *your Harriet* will she ever permit me to call her so, she shall have a Sister's affection, for are you not the Brother of my soul; *see!* I have profited by *your instructions*, & levelled you with as much, (nay perhaps more) facility than you can wish.'[2]

This warming reply reached Shelley the day after he had delivered his final epistolary blast of 'Bysshe, Bysshe, Bysshe' into his father's ear. It is perhaps by the reaction away from his family that one can account for the extreme outburst of tender and passionate feelings with which he at once replied to Miss Hitchener. One may also perhaps detect a hint of dissatisfaction, if not actual disillusionment, with the intimate relationship that he should normally have been developing with his young and beautiful girl-bride, Harriet. There is a certain physical distaste, a Hamlet-like sneer at the fleshly fact that indicates this. 'You who can contemn the world's prejudices, whose views are mine,' he carolled to Miss Hitchener, 'I will dare to say I *love*, nor do I risk the possibility of that degrading and contemptible interpretation of this sacred word, nor do I risk the supposition that the lump or organized matter which enshrines *thy* soul excites the love which that soul alone *dare* claim. Henceforth I will be yours, yours with truth sincerity & unreserve.'[3]

The first fruit of this 'unreserve' was a wild declaration of a plan to use his inheritance for the foundation of some kind of egalitarian community, which should feature Hogg and Miss Hitchener – and presumably Harriet, though it is remarkable that in his enthusiasm he forgets to mention her. 'I still desire money, and I desire it because I think I know the use of it. It commands labour, it gives leisure, & to give leisure to those who will employ it in the forwarding of truth is the noblest present an individual can make to the whole. . . . Justice demands that it shd be shared between my [real – *deleted*] sisters? Does it or does it not? Mankind are as much my brethren & sisters as they, *all* ought to share – this cannot be, it must be confined. But thou art the sister of *my soul* – *he* is its brother – surely these have a right.' The reference to justice here is implicitly Godwinian 'political' justice, which always insists that property is not rightfully owned by he who possesses it in law, but only by he whose need or personal worth can make best use of it in the ordinary course of events. The little detail of Shelley's deletion of 'real' sisters shows how clearly he was substituting his own chosen 'philosophical family' for the family of flesh and blood at Field Place, who had betrayed him. Hogg and himself, Shelley explained, already considered 'our property as common', and they were eagerly anticipating the moment when Miss Hitchener would do the same. He signed off rapturously, 'Sister of my soul adieu. With I hope *eternal* love your – Percy Shelley.' The usual 'Bysshe' was dropped presumably as a gesture of democratic good faith; for Bysshe, after all, had become a weapon to beat the aristocracy with their own misdeeds.

An explosion of egalitarian ideas now began to take place in the little cramped lodgings at York. In the idea of his little community, Shelley had discovered a philosophic plan of action, and he was rapidly organizing new egalitarian principles to back it up with. These theories began to make him see even his own day-to-day existence in a transformed light, and he raged against the waste of time and effort expended on trivial domestic labour which had no meaning. He looked at the rooms around him like a revolutionary designer who is appalled by the lack of purity of function. 'Every useless ornament, the pillars, the iron railings, the juttings of the wainscot, & as Southey says the cleaning of grates are all exertions of bodily labour, which tho' trivial separately considered when united destroy a vast proportion of this valuable leisure – how many things could we do without, how unnecessary are *mahogany* tables, silver vases, myriads of viands & liquors, expensive printing that worst of all. Look even around some little habitation, the dirtiest cottage which has myriads of instances where ornament is sacrificed to cleanliness, or leisure.'[4] Here once more, his natural puritanism was reasserting itself, and came to dominate the organization of his own menage. He loved a certain kind of scrubbed simplicity, as a Nonconformist loves a bare, blanched altar.

Yet Shelley could be extravagant in his own way: he always spent heavily on books, on the most rapid available forms of transport, and occasionally on individual articles of clothing; he gave away money with reckless generosity, but he often promised far more than he could perform, and retained until the end of his life the old contemptuous aristocratic habit of running up local bills from small shopkeepers, merchants, agents and printers without scrupling to pay them if he could get away with it. 'Vile as aristocracy is,' he was inclined to say, 'commerce, purse-proud ignorance & illiterateness is more contemptible.'[5] This was all very well, but it pointed to a severe weakness in his temperament, not to mention his egalitarianism, and partly explains why in later years many of the middle-class radicals and writers, men as diverse as Hazlitt, Francis Place and John Keats, instinctively disliked and distrusted him. Someone, after all, has to clean the grates, and if Shelley was really after a new form of natural and functional existence, it would have to be himself. This was a fact of life he had yet to face.

But for the moment he was preparing to do battle, rather than to settle into poverty-stricken domesticity. He decided to go to Field Place in person, as he had threatened, and attempt to get his allowance reinstated by 'that mistaken man'. He went no longer as an eldest son claiming his right, but as an enemy of the vile aristocracy who was fighting for political justice on behalf of his little community of elect spirits, to pursue the 'hateful task of combating prejudice and mistake'.[6] Shelley left York on Thursday, 17 October, and, by travelling non-stop, reached his uncle's house at Cuckfield on the night of Friday, 18 October. In his absence, Hogg was to care for Harriet. News of this arrangement reached Hogg's family, and Mrs Hogg wrote instantly to Harriet warning her of the imprudence of remaining alone with her son. Besides, explained Mrs Hogg, Tom could not possibly support her; would she not prefer to go and stay with friends of Mrs Hogg's acquaintance? Harriet replied with one of her short, admirably simple letters, and, to Mrs Hogg's evident surprise, 'much in the style of a gentlewoman'. She politely declined Mrs Hogg's services; but she thanked her for her kindness in a situation which Mrs Hogg clearly did not understand. Mrs Hogg thought she understood the situation only too well. Her husband wrote gloomily to Timothy Shelley: the worst of it was that their two sons had resolved 'never to part'.[7] None the less this warning may have encouraged Harriet to make the fateful move of summoning Eliza, who arrived in York post-haste, and before Shelley's own return.

Shelley's whirlwind campaign lasted four days, and by Tuesday, 23 October, he was again boarding the evening coach for York. In this short space of time he renewed relations with his champion, Captain Pilfold, and the Sister of his Soul, Miss Hitchener. He wrote to Thomas Medwin and asked him to organize a marriage settlement of £700 a year for Harriet. He sent a seething letter to his mother accusing her of an adulterous relationship with Edward Graham, the music-master,* and bombarded Timothy with demands for the £200, putting the whole Field Place household in a state of uproar and panic. Failing to achieve anything concrete in Sussex, he took the captain with him to London and tried to frighten the solicitor Whitton, but without success. Whitton and Shelley then mutually insulted each other by post, the latter writing on the outside page which formed the envelope: 'Mr S. commends Mr W. when he deals with gentlemen (which opportunity perhaps may not often occur) to refrain from opening private letters, or impudence may draw down chastisement upon contemptibility.'[8] Whitton who had been ordered specifically by Timothy Shelley to open all private letters addressed to him by his son, was considerably shaken by this threat which seemed to be a complicated way of saying he would be beaten up. He wrote to his employer that he thought Shelley was a 'mad viper'.[9]

Timothy in his turn was also shaken, and actually intimidated – a significant fact. In his more intimate relationships, Shelley frequently if unconsciously exerted an element of fear as a way of establishing his own importance and authority. But during this visit to Sussex, inflamed by his new principles and outraged by the alienation of his family, Shelley seems to have been constantly on the brink of overt physical violence. Potentially Shelley had a murderous temper, and this was one of several incidents in his life when he came dangerously near to unleashing it. Two days after he had left London, Timothy wrote to Whitton about his son's visit, and the picture he draws, though brief, is sufficiently clear. 'From the present disturbed state of PB's mind, which will not suffer it to rest until it has completely and entirely disordered his whole spiritual past, I will not open a letter from him, and be cautious how I open any in other handwriting for fear he should endeavour to deceive. I shall most decidedly keep my resolution with him, and had he stay'd in Sussex I would have sworn in especial Constables around me. He frightened his mother and sister exceedingly, and now if they hear a Dog Bark they run up stairs. He has nothing to say but

* After acting faithfully as Shelley's literary agent in London during 1810 and spring 1811, Graham had fallen from favour. Like John Grove, he had apparently made an offer for Elizabeth Shelley's hand, and Shelley was overwhelmed by feelings of betrayal. Stories of adultery between Graham and Mrs Timothy Shelley – which Shelley had dismissed as a joke in May (*Letters*, 1, No. 71, p. 85) – were now resurrected as hard facts, and Shelley wrote bitterly to his mother: 'I suspect your motives for *so violently so persecutingly* desiring to unite my sister Elizabeth to the music master Graham, I suspect that it was intended to shield *yourself*. . . .' Mrs Shelley, like Timothy, was now also seen as a sexual hypocrite and family tyrant; and Graham's role was that of a mere pawn in the emotional drama. There is no independent evidence of adultery, nor did Elizabeth marry the unfortunate music-master. The episode throws light on the intensity of Shelley's feelings both for his mother and his sister, and the frailty of his early friendships.

the £200 a year.'[10] To his family Shelley appeared to have become a criminal lunatic without any interest in them except obtaining money. It should never be forgotten that his own father feared that Shelley might break into the house and assault them.

Some echo of this state of mind was caught in one of Shelley's notes to Miss Hitchener, dashed off when he had arrived at Field Place. He said that he had been planning how to use the money for the little group at York all the way down on the overnight coach. He was filled with millennial visions, and there was an unmistakable note of hysteria in his expectations. 'I shall come to live in this county. My friend Hogg, Harriet, my new sister – could but be added to these the sister of my soul, *that* I cannot hope, but still she may visit us. – I have long been convinced of the eventual omnipotence of mind over matter; adequacy of motive is sufficient to anything, & *my* golden age is when the present potence will become omnipotence: this will be the millennium of Xtians "when the lion shall lay down with the lamb".'[11]

The millennium had not yet arrived, and Shelley went back empty-handed to York. The whole visit had been an unrelieved disaster. In London, Charles Grove advised Shelley that the Duke of Norfolk, who had tried to mediate during the expulsion crisis, might again be worth applying to for aid. When Shelley arrived back in York he wrote to the duke, explaining the new crisis over the marriage, and asking for the duke's 'intervention' on his behalf.[12] The duke had in fact already heard of the renewed trouble, probably through Timothy, and had sent a message through Whitton suggesting that Shelley might like to call on him in London. But the message had unfortunately reached Shelley's address at the Turk's Head too late, and he was already whirling northwards.

Shelley's rapid travels were not yet over, for about eight days after returning to York he was again on the road, this time to Cumberland, with Hogg left behind in disgrace. The events leading up to this sudden departure from York have been exhaustively discussed by Shelley biographers, but beyond establishing that Hogg had made a pass at Harriet, there has not been very much agreement as to what really occurred.

Two facts stand out. The first is that Eliza Westbrook had arrived in York. She immediately re-established her maternal hold over her sister Harriet, and completely altered the balance of the little group. Eliza took a quick dislike to Hogg who returned the emotion with vivacity; he left a memorably malicious account of her delphic silences, her long hair-combing sessions in front of the mirror, and her governessy commands to Harriet to take care of her health, and to 'think what Miss Warne would say'. Most important of all, Eliza arrived in York with a considerable sum of money, which, in Shelley's precarious state of finances, gave her the lead, not to say the whip-hand. This has usually been overlooked, but it is clear from what Hogg says,[13] and from the fact that after Eliza's arrival they immediately moved to more salubrious lodgings in Blake Street. It is obvious that Eliza came to York with the determination to regulate Harriet's marriage, and this she quickly succeeded in doing.

The second outstanding fact is that Hogg had been carrying on a flirtation with the 16-year-old Harriet ever since they met in Edinburgh. He had actually 'declared himself' – probably jokingly, in Scotland, and Harriet had laughed him off without awkwardness. Since they had all been living closely together for some six weeks, it is impossible that Shelley had not noticed Hogg's growing infatuation. In view of the opinions that Shelley subsequently expressed about free love and the un-exclusiveness of marriage in a sexual sense, an arrangement which he sometimes referred to as the 'Godwinian system', it would seem likely that not only did he accept this, but that he may have encouraged it. When he wrote to Miss Hitchener about the community of property, and Hogg and he sharing everything in common, there was an implied suggestion of sexual communality. Indeed it seems possible that his journey to London, leaving Hogg and Harriet alone, was made partly with the intention of fostering the relationship between them, his sister and his brother.*

If this was indeed part of the plan, it too misfired, for Hogg pressed his suit too warmly until finally Harriet was alarmed, and told him that the whole thing was immoral and must stop. The situation had now become awkward. 'At last Harriet talked to him much of its immorality and (tho I fear her arguments were such as *could not* be logically superior to his) Hogg confessed to her his conviction of having acted wrongly, & as some expiation proposed instantly to inform *me* by letter of the whole. – This Harriet refused to permit, fearing its effect upon my mind at such a distance.'[14] Hogg wanted to clear up the whole matter with Shelley instantly, but Harriet prevaricated and it is interesting that she doubted Shelley's mental stability in Sussex. In fact Shelley was *not* told of the disagreement immediately after he had returned from York, and possibly as much as a week elapsed. Finally, 'dark hints' were made, Harriet was 'greatly altered' towards Hogg, and Shelley questioned her and finally had the whole thing out with Hogg in a long walk together in the fields outside York.

In an explanatory letter to Miss Hitchener, Shelley makes no mention of Eliza's role in all this, but he might well be expected to play it down. It is impossible to believe that Eliza's presence did not materially alter the outcome of the affair. It can only have been her presence that prevented a free and frank discussion of what had occurred, when Shelley returned, as both Harriet and

---

* This interpretation is strongly supported by comparable events and liaisons in spring 1813, and again in spring 1815. See Chapters 9 and 11.

Hogg had wanted this. By covering up the matter, misunderstandings were allowed to fester; and this suited Eliza very well.

Once Shelley did finally have the matter out with Hogg, the interview was traumatic, though, as he emphasized to Miss Hitchener, nothing had actually *happened* between Hogg and Harriet. 'I sought him and we walked to the fields beyond York. I desired to know fully the account of this affair, I heard it *from him* and I believe he was sincere. All I can recollect of that terrible day was that I said I pardoned him, freely, fully pardoned him, that I would still be a friend to him and hoped soon to convince him how lovely virtue was . . . that I hoped the time would come when he would regard this horrible error with as much disgust as I did – He said little, he was pale terrorstruck, remorseful.'[15] One concludes that the decision to abandon Hogg in York was made over Shelley's head at the insistence of Harriet; and this really meant at the insistence of Eliza Westbrook. Propriety had got her foot back in the door.

The Shelleys departed from Blake Street suddenly in mid-afternoon some eight days after Shelley had returned from London. They left without Hogg's knowledge, and a 'blind' note was propped on the mantelpiece saying that they were going to Richmond, where Hogg might like to follow. In fact they were already on the road to Cumberland. Shelley apparently did not know about this note,[16] so it must have been left by Harriet – or by Eliza. Hogg also found that he had been delegated to deal with the landlord's bill.

Once Shelley had arrived in Keswick a passionate exchange of letters took place between him and the deserted Hogg. It was a series of recriminations, explanations and avowals which continued for most of November. In one of the last and longest, Shelley insisted: 'I am not jealous. – Heaven knows that if the possession of Harriet's person, or the attainment of her love was all that intervened between our meeting again tomorrow, willingly would I return to York, aye willingly, to be happy thus to prove my friendship. Jealousy has no place in my bosom; I am indeed at times very much inclined to think the Godwinian plan is best, particularly since the late events. But Harriet does not think so. She is prejudiced; tho' I hope she will not always be so, – and on her opinions of right and wrong alone does the morality of the present case depend.'[17] This was how Shelley interpreted events when he rationalized them at a distance.

Yet the real emotional shock for him was not the seduction of Harriet, but the loss of Hogg as a friend, and almost – one must insist – as a lover. Shelley's letters from Keswick give a vivid impression of the battle fought out in his mind between Hogg and Harriet for his ultimate allegiance. It was more than the usual rivalry between the young wife and the best friend of the young husband, and it was a close thing. Eliza certainly realized that it could only be won by separating the two friends first. In writing to Miss Hitchener, the painful affection with which Shelley looks back at Hogg was heartfelt, if partially veiled: 'never could you conceive never having experienced it that resistless & pathetic eloquence of his, never the illumination of that countenance on which I have sometimes gazed till I fancied the world could be reformed by gazing too'.[18]

In addressing Hogg himself, Shelley completely broke down, and he became passionate and agonized:

> I am dismayed. I tremble – is it so? Are we parted, you – I – Forgive this wildness. I am half mad. I am wretchedly miserable. I look on Harriet. I start – she is before me – Has *she* convinced you? . . . Will you come – dearest, best beloved of friends, will *you* come? Will you share my fortune, enter into my schemes – love me as I love you; be inseparable as once I fondly hoped you were. . . . Ah! how I have loved you. I was even ashamed to tell you how! & now to leave you *forever*, – no, not forever. Night comes, – Death comes – Cold, calm death, almost I would it were tomorrow. There is another life. – Are you not to be the first there – Assuredly. Dearest, dearest friend, reason with me – I am like a child in weakness. . . .[19]

This was, in many respects, the letter of one lover to another, written at the most bewildering moment of a major upheaval and breach.

Hogg, in his turn, was writing distractedly, threatening to pursue them to Keswick, sending letters directly to Harriet herself, which Shelley had to intercept – the parallel with Elizabeth Shelley is obvious – swearing that he would blow his brains out at Harriet's feet. This side of the correspondence has not survived, but its nature is clear from Shelley's return comments in his own letters. He wrote back: 'Can I not feel? are not those throbbing temples that bursting heart chained to mine . . . do they not sympathize. Cannot I read your soul as I have done your letter which I believe especially considered to be a copy of the former – little must you know me if now I appear to you otherwise than the most wretched of men. . . .'

Referring to his friend's passion for Harriet, which Hogg was still urging and declaring, Shelley wrote to Hogg in the same letter: 'But how tyrannic is that feeling do I not know; how restless its influence, how sophisticated its inductions. And shall I eager to avoid prejudice, by the vanity of disinterestedness expose you to the possibility of a renewal of this. . . . Shall I to gratify your present feelings expose you to the lasting scorpion sting. . . .'[20] For the duration of the letter, at least, Shelley considered Hogg's physical passion for a woman as a poison, a scorpion's sting.

In one matter Shelley remained firm. Here again the parallel with the earlier love-triangle with Elizabeth Shelley is obvious. He always refused to have Hogg join them in Cumberland. However distracted his letters became in those first two weeks, he always ended them with an absolute injunction not to come, on one occasion waiting until the flap of the outer cover to write: 'Do not come *now*.'[21] Continually he upbraided Hogg for his weakness in letting a woman, the implication is a *mere* woman, come between them. 'Oh! how the sophistry of the passions has changed you, the sport of a woman's whim; the plaything of her inconsistencies, the bauble with which she is angry, the footstool of her exaltation. Assert yourself be what you were Love! Adore! It will exalt your nature, bid you a Man be a God.'[22]

Shelley became extraordinarily dependent on Elizabeth Hitchener's support during these early days at Keswick, writing, 'I am immersed in a labyrinth of doubt. My friend, I need your advice your reason, my own seems almost withered. Will you come here in your Christmas holydays.'[23] He was almost surprised to find himself immersed in the green, tranquil depths of the Lake District, in sole command of a grateful and adoring Harriet, and a strangely good-humoured Eliza. He walked out alone over the cold and beautiful upland pastures, gazing down on the ruffled waters and brooding on mutability. He felt his friendship with Hogg was one more example of an intimate emotional relationship that had failed him. Paradoxically he came to believe that it was Hogg who had deserted him, and not he who had allowed himself to be spirited away from Hogg at York. He wrote plaintively: 'I know how much I owe to you . . . but it is not my fault, indeed it is not.'[24]

Transformed into mythical pattern, the desertion of his first friend was to appear in the opening cantos of the long poem *The Revolt of Islam* of 1817. At the time it left him little that was illuminating about his own nature. There was the clear statement on free love: 'I attach little value to the monopoly of exclusive cohabitation. You know that I have frequently spoken slightingly of it.'[25] But even this was overshadowed by the ambiguity of his feelings towards his new wife. As he wrote to Hogg about his sexual relations with Harriet: 'suppose not that I would have envied you what I too might share, what I should not much care utterly to resign (you see I am explicit as you were)'.[26] There was still too little that seemed settled or explicit in his own mind. Without Hogg his marriage began to take on a different complexion; while with Eliza the old problem of Harriet's dependence threatened to return. Yet it was no good looking back: the letters to his old friend tailed off in mid-November, and the correspondence gradually ceased as the passion burnt itself out with nothing left to feed on. The silence that came between them was to last for almost a year.

At Keswick they had taken a small house, Chesnut Cottage, about two miles outside Keswick on the Penrith road. They were now in the region of the Lake poets, and Shelley expected as his immediate neighbours Wordsworth, Coleridge, Southey and de Quincey. It was, perhaps, one of the greatest strokes of ill-luck that in all his time at Chesnut Cottage he was only to meet Southey. Coleridge was away lecturing in London that winter, and Wordsworth remained deep in hibernation at Grasmere.* Wordsworth does not seem to have been aware that Shelley was ever in his vicinity, and in all probability would not have relished the idea very much. But Coleridge was to recall the missed opportunity long afterwards with a mixture of wistful regret and gentle patronizing complacency. 'Poor Shelley,' he confided to John Frere in 1830, 'it is a pity I think that I never met him. I could have done him good. He went to Keswick on purpose to see me. . . . Southey had no understanding for a toleration of such principles as Shelley's. I should have laughed at his Atheism. I could have sympathized with him, and shown him that I did so, and he would have felt that I did so. I could have shown him that I had been in the same state myself, and I could have guided him through it. I have often bitterly regretted in my heart that I never did meet with Shelley.'[27] In this interview, not published until 1917, Coleridge added an acute general comment on Shelley's predicament as he had seen it unfolding. 'Shelley was a man of great power as a poet,' he told Frere, 'and could he only have had some notion of order, could you only have given him some plane whereon to stand, and look down upon his mind, he would have succeeded.' The strange thing was that Shelley himself soon wrote about his difficulties in a very similar way. De Quincey, who was burrowed into Grasmere at Dove Cottage, missed Shelley and commented impishly on his own library, which, 'being rich in the wickedest of German speculations, would naturally have been more to Shelley's taste than the Spanish library of Southey'.[28] It was, then, Southey alone that Shelley chanced to meet during his four months' stay in the Lake District.

In the meantime, the Shelleyan routine reestablished itself at Chesnut Cottage. The house was divided with another family, but the Shelleys were allowed to use the little garden, or as Harriet naïvely explained to some visitors, 'the people let us run about in it, whenever Percy and I are tired of sitting in the house'.[29] The post came in daily at Keswick at 7 o'clock in the morning, and went out again at 9, and on urgent occasions Shelley would be waiting for letters – especially from Hogg – and dash off his replies in time to go by return. This in itself may account sometimes for their breathless wildness. Shelley walked about the lakes and peaks, often alone, and his reflections on the deserted and magnificent scenery were soon flooding out to Miss Hitchener. A small sum of money came from old Westbrook, perhaps in response to a request from Eliza, but Shelley

---

* Both poets were in the middle of a bitter quarrel, which seems to have been started by a misunderstanding of certain remarks that Wordsworth made to Coleridge's host in London Basil Montagu, about Coleridge being 'a rotten drunkard' and 'an absolute nuisance in his family'. See Mary Moorman, *Wordsworth: A Biography*, 1965, II, pp. 199–201.

was soon on the verge of penury again despite the fact that his rent only came to thirty shillings a week. By 30 November he was writing to Medwin, who had been severely taxed by Timothy for helping with Harriet's marriage settlement, to inquire about the possibilities of raising some money by loan with his inheritance as security. It is interesting that Shelley did not yet stoop to entertaining the idea of getting work himself.

Despite being 'so poor as to be actually in danger of every day being deprived of the necessaries of life',[30] Shelley was able to gird himself and his ladies up to visit the Duke of Norfolk at Greystoke at his lordship's invitation in the first week of December. The weekend was extended to one of more than seven days. The meeting did not help solve family difficulties as the duke had hoped, but it gave Shelley an introduction to the Lake District notables. Unexpectedly Shelley enjoyed himself, showing off the pretty and very presentable Harriet, and arguing everyone into corners. The duke, who remembered his own radical days when he had proposed the notorious toast to 'our Sovereign, the People' was by all accounts friendly and tolerant of his fiery young guest, and Shelley recovered much of the resilience and self-confidence which the break with Hogg had weakened. 'I held the arguments which I do everywhere.'[31]

On his return to Chesnut Cottage, about 9 December, he wrote to Miss Hitchener that he was 'fatigued by aristocratical insipidity', but that was only to reassure her that he was still of the egalitarian faith. More indicative was the short, low-toned and refreshingly simple note he sent to Hogg, the epilogue to the agonized series, and its dismissal. Here at last he put all the vaporous emotions, tortuous moral distinctions and defensive Godwinian theories firmly aside, and admitted it had been a straight fight. A fight which by the nature of things Hogg had lost. 'If I were free,' he told Hogg gently but firmly, 'I were yours – tho' I don't think you sinless, I think you capable of great things, and in truth as well as in the stores of such a mind as yours can I conceive no pleasure equal to the participation. But I *am* Harriet's. I am devoted to her happiness; *this* is entrusted to me, nor will I resign it. Would you desire me to desert her and live with you?'[32] There could be only one answer to this. For the time being, T. J. Hogg, his first great friend, dropped out of his life.

As Shelley recovered, the radical mission which he had first clearly perceived at York reasserted itself, and now more comprehensively than before. In the letters to Miss Hitchener, the image of 'sister of his soul' was subtly replaced by a more politicized one in which he saw the mirror of his own aspirations: 'I consider you one of those beings who carry happiness, reform, liberty wherever they go – to me you are as my better genius, the judge of my reasonings, the guide of my actions, the influencer of my usefulness. Great responsibility is the consequence of high powers.'[33]

His genius for disturbance began to make itself felt at Keswick. There was talk of strange lights and noises in the cottage, and rumours of the devilish consequences of Shelley's atheism soon went abroad. 'Strange prejudices have these country people!' remarked Shelley innocently, as he set out to project the sinister reputation for alchemy that he had marketed at Oxford. The occult influences of childhood were growing up with him. Shelley's landlord finally came knocking at the door to protest. 'Mr Dare entered our cottage and said he had something to say to me. "Why Sir," said he, "I am not satisfied with you. I wish you to leave my house." – "Why Sir?" "Because the country talks very strangely of your proceedings. – Odd things have been seen at night near your dwelling. I am very ill satisfied with this – Sir I don't like to talk of it. I wish you to provide for yourself elsewhere."' Shelley succeeded in quieting Mr Dare's fears with 'much difficulty', but realized that he was not welcome as a permanent tenant, and would eventually have to move. His explanation for the strange night-time proceedings was disarmingly simple. He had been discussing physics with Harriet and Eliza and demonstrating the nature of the atmosphere: 'to illustrate my theory I made some experiments on hydrogen gas, one of its constituent parts. – This was in the garden, and the vivid flame was seen at some distance.'[34] He concluded his account to Miss Hitchener with a rather more mocking gleam, 'I wish to stay at Keswick . . . to see Southey. You may imagine then that I was very humble to Mr Dare, I should think he was tolerable afraid of the Devil.'[35]

Shelley now began to think of taking a house in Sussex again, but not near any 'populous manufacturing dissipated town' or near any barracks. In travelling between Edinburgh, York and Keswick he had already gained new experience of the poverty and exploitation which existed in the great cities of the North and Midlands, and had observed the ubiquity of soldiers wherever social conditions were worst.

At this time the occupation army stationed at trouble spots in England exceeded in number the whole of Wellington's force fighting on the Spanish peninsula.[36] The war itself was increasingly unpopular, and the country was in the throes of a severe economic crisis, brought on partly by the Continental blockade, and partly by the internal disruption of trade and the soaring of wartime prices. Harvests were bad, and the cost of basic foods rose sharply. Petitions for minimum wages were drawn up by thousands of weavers in Scotland, Manchester and Bolton.[37] Discontent boiled over in local disturbances, food riots and outbreaks of frame-breaking, especially in Lancashire. All this came together in the phenomenon of Luddism, which shook the country in the spring and summer of 1812. The symptoms were not merely temporary economic ones: they arose from deep-seated social grievances, the appalling lack of proper housing, savage working hours and factory conditions, and the complete absence of educational or medical facilities among the manufacturing populations. Class antagonisms were sharpened by the indiscriminate use of troops to 'keep the peace' for the local employers and property-owners.

These extreme economic conditions were helping to give birth to a quite new kind of radicalism, not the old radicalism of the Foxite Whigs and men like the Duke of Norfolk, but a working-class radicalism, concerned fundamentally with economic and social grievances rather than party political ones, and without as yet any kind of parliamentary representation. In the country as a whole, and especially in the parts of it through which Shelley had been travelling as an outcast from his family and from his class of southern Whig aristocrats, a new political awareness was growing. Class identities were solidified as they came into opposition and finally into open and violent conflict with the forces of local justice and property ownership, and ultimately with the forces of government.*

In the December of 1811, a steady politicizing of Shelley's views was going on at Keswick, reflecting the developments in the nation at large. To begin with he was concerned primarily with the settling of his own little community in such a remote and beautiful region. 'Oh! how you will delight in this scenery. The mountains are now capped with snow. The lake as I see it hence is glassy and calm. Snow vapours tinted by the loveliest refractions pass far below the summit of these gigantic rocks. The scene even in winer is inexpressibly lovely. The clouds assume shapes which seem peculiar to these regions; what will it be in summer, what when *you* are here. Oh! give me a little cottage in *that* scene, let all live in peaceful little houses, let temples and palaces rot with their perishing masters.'[38] Yet even in this pastoral Rousseauesque dream, the note of political discontent crept in. Shelley was planning a poem, a long one, which would be 'by anticipation a picture of the manners simplicity and delights of a perfect state of society: tho still earthly'.[39] He realized, half laughingly, that at such a time, even so poetical a plan might be regarded as subversive. 'What think you of my undertaking. Shall I not get into Prison. Harriet is sadly afraid that his Majesty will provide me a lodging in consideration of the zeal which I evince for the bettering of his subjects.'[40]

The works of Godwin now began to fill more and more of Shelley's vision of the struggle for reform and the ideal society. He listed to Miss Hitchener what he considered were Godwin's most valuable contributions in the following order of

---

* E.P. Thompson has written: 'It is true that Napoleon's Continental System and the retaliatory Orders in Council [of Lord Liverpool's administration] had so disrupted the market for British textiles that the industries of Lancashire, Yorkshire and the Midlands were stagnant. Both war and successive bad harvests had contributed to the raising of the price of provisions to "famine" heights. But this will not do as an explanation of Luddism; it may help to explain its occasion, but not its character.' *The Making of the English Working Class*, 1968, p. 593.

importance: *The Enquirer, St Leon, Political Justice* and *Caleb Williams*. It was characteristic of Shelley's temperament that as his thinking became politically active he should immediately be attracted to the work of an extreme anarchist idealist, who had once been trained for the Presbyterian ministry at Hoxton Academy, and always retained the passionate puritan logic of the dedicated religious missionary. Shelley's championship of atheism was now almost lackadaisical: 'I annihilate God; you destroy the Devil and then we make a Heaven entirely to our own mind – It must be owned that we are tolerably independent. . . .' But it began to take its place in a wider pattern of intellectual rejection and social criticism, that grew in self-confidence and anger.

On Christmas Day 1811, Shelley wrote to Miss Hitchener, now the perfect sounding-board for his ideas, what was really a classic statement of the new emergent radicalism. Coming from Shelley, at this early stage, it inevitably lacked any definite objectives in reform terms; yet the depth, the fury and the social disillusionment of the criticism is unmistakably cast in the language of the Luddite period.

> I have been led into reasonings which make me *hate* more and more the existing establishment of every kind. I gasp when I think of plate & balls & tables & kings. – I have beheld scenes of misery. – The manufacturers are reduced to starvation. My friend, the military are gone to Nottingham – Curses light on them for their motives if they destroy *one* of its famine wasted inhabitants. – But if I were a friend to the destroyed myself about to perish, I fancy that I could bless them for saving my friend the bitter mockery of a trial. – Southey thinks that a revolution is inevitable; this is one of his reasons for supporting things as they are. – But let *us* not belie our principles. – They may feed & may riot & may sin to the last moment. – The groans of the wretched may pass unheeded till the latest moment of this infamous revelry, till the storm burst upon them and the oppressed take furious vengeance on the oppressors.[41]

Shelley now saw a lifetime's task opening up before him. The awareness that he showed in this Christmas Day letter of 1811, though as yet naïve and to some extent melodramatic, was to lie behind his work and thinking for the rest of his career. One must also remember its formulation: 'I have been led into reasonings which make me *hate*. . . .' This hate remained steadily behind the main thrust and energy of much of his most powerful and characteristic work.

At this point in Keswick, he thought of the methods for circulating ideas which he had learnt from Lind at Eton, and practised at Oxford. He began to consider propaganda and more active forms of political intervention. At once he planned to put out a small collection of poems which would celebrate the cause of liberty. 'The minor Poems I mentioned you will see soon. They are about to be sent to the Printers. – I think it wrong to publish anything anonymously. I shall annexe my name, and a preface in which I shall lay open my intentions as the poems are not wholly useless. "I sing, and liberty may love the song." Can you assist my grave labours. Harriet complains that I hurt my health, and fancies that I shall get into prison.'[42] The accent on prison was partly to impress on Miss Hitchener the seriousness of his intentions, but also to show that he anticipated taking issue with the established authorities of society. The determination to publish under his own name also showed he had changed and learnt from the Oxford days. Shelley was not able to find a publisher in England, and eventually took the collection to Ireland instead, where the manuscript was left with R. and J. Stockdale of Abbey Street, Dublin.*

The idea of visiting Ireland was first vaguely mentioned on 10 December, but it was not until January that it began to form in Shelley's mind. It seemed the obvious place to get his propaganda poems printed, and to make his first venture into political activism.

Yet it was the meeting and talks with the poet Robert Southey at Greta Hall which supplied the decisive political catalyst. It has usually been thought that the relationship between Southey and Shelley was wholly antagonistic: the young idealist revolutionary set against the middle-aged, soured and hypocritical Tory. Southey remarked in a letter to his friend Grosvenor Bedford that 'It had surprised him [Shelley] a good deal to meet for the first time in his life with a man who perfectly understands him, and does him full justice. I tell him that all the difference between us is, that he is nineteen, and I am thirty-seven.'[43] This was written on 4 January 1812, at an early stage of their acquaintance. It has sometimes been taken that Southey began by patronizing Shelley; or that, alternatively, as in Hogg's ridiculous story, Shelley began by offending Southey and falling asleep in the middle of Southey's talk.[44] Yet Shelley, on the contrary, makes it quite clear that at this time he was deeply fascinated and influenced by Southey; they disagreed on many points, but this was precisely the attraction.

The Christmas Day letter, where one first becomes aware of Shelley grappling with contemporary political issues on any extended scale, in fact commences as a discussion of Southey, whom he had just met after 'contemplating the outisde of his house' for several days.

I have also been much engaged in talking to Southey. You may conjecture that a man must possess high and estimable qualities, if with the prejudice of such total difference from my sentiments I can regard him great and worthy. –

* It went through varied vicissitudes but it was never finally printed in Shelley's lifetime though some of the poems appeared in the Esdaile MS Notebook. See Chapter 3, Ref. 7.

In fact Southey is an advocate of liberty and equality; he looks forward to a state when all shall be perfected, and matter become subjected to the omnipotence of mind; but he is now an advocate for existing establishments. . . . Southey hates the Irish, he speaks against Catholic Emancipation, & Parliamentary reform. In all these things we differ, & our differences were the subject of a long conversation. . . . But Southey tho' far from being a man of great reasoning powers is a great Man. He has all that characterizes the poet – great eloquence though obstinacy in opinion which arguments are the last things that can shake. He is a man of virtue, he never will belie what he thinks. His professions are in strict compatibility with his practice.[45]

Shelley was later to reverse the end part of this appraisal, but not at once, and not before Southey had had a considerable effect upon him.*

Southey was at this time, as he says, a man of 37, living at Greta Hall, originally Coleridge's house, with his wife, Mrs Coleridge and her three children, and the wife of the poet Robert Lovell. All three ladies were sisters: Edith, Sara and Mary Fricker. Southey supported all these by journalism in the Tory periodicals,[46] and by writing voluminous biographies and histories, the most lasting of which has been his *Life of Nelson*. Southey was acutely aware of the serious condition of the social question in England, and wrote at length on issues such as Poor Law relief, unemployment, national education and Luddism. Though his opinions were, as Shelley already knew, quite different from his own, Southey was better informed on these issues than anyone Shelley had met before. The long conversations Shelley had with him gave his own vague ideological loyalties to 'liberty' and egalitarianism a new clarity and immediacy. They also led, inevitably, to a break with Southey himself. Poetically though, Southey was to remain an influence on Shelley, and *The Curse of Kehama* (1810), especially, was to be one of the primary sources for the long poem Shelley was beginning to contemplate.

Seven days after the Christmas letter, Shelley was still reporting long, though somewhat one-sided conversations with Southey; one-sided on Shelley's side. Southey 'says I ought not to call myself an Atheist, since in reality I believe that the Universe is God. – I tell him I believe that God is another signification for the Universe. – I then explain –' Southey was then treated to a description of Shelley's view of the universe. 'Southey agrees in my idea of the Deity, the mass

---

* Shelley had been introduced to Southey by William Calvert, whom he had met at Greystoke. Calvert, whose brother had befriended Wordsworth, had instantly struck both Shelley and Harriet with his earnest, sympathetic gaze, so that they remarked upon it in their letters. Calvert seemed to know all about the Field Place and Oxford background; he helped the Shelleys with practical details like getting the rent on Chesnut Cottage reduced to a guinea a week, and supplying linen. Shelley, incidentally, wrote to Medwin that the rent was 30 shillings.

of infinite intelligence. I, you, & he are constituent parts of this immeasurable whole.'[47] Shelley was to make this idea – a development of the eighteenth-century 'Great Chain of Being' – central to his long poem. It was at this point that Southey tried to put Shelley on to 'a course of Berkeley', the great Idealist philosopher.[48] This may have caught Shelley's attention; at any rate he was given the run of Southey's library.

Southey helped to strengthen the link between Shelley's religious and social criticism. 'Southey is no believer in original sin: he thinks that which appears to be a taint of our nature is in effect the result of unnatural political institutions – there we agree – he thinks the prejudices of education and sinister influence of political institutions adequate to account for all Specimens of vice which have fallen within his observation.'[49] Thus Shelley was firmly across the bridge travelled by most of the confirmed radicals of the period: they saw atheism or at least 'Deism' as the precondition for social reform. Only if human nature was freed from the religious definition of its potential, freed from all concepts of its 'fallen' or 'subjected' state, did it become genuinely open to political and social improvement. God's Will could no longer be used to justify the ways of Man to men. Finally, it was Southey who recommended that he write to James Mont-gomery, the radical poet and editor of the *Sheffield Iris,* about political pamph-leteering; and Southey who reminded him – he may not have known before – that William Godwin was still alive, and working in London.

This last piece of news filled Shelley with 'inconceivable emotions', and he decided at once to write to the philosopher. Very soon the false prophet would be abandoned for the true, and Shelley would refer with disgust to Southey, as previously he had written with delight. By 16 January he had read a piece of Southey's heavy Tory time-serving in the *Edinburgh Annual Register* and was already describing him to Miss Hitchener as a 'hateful prostitution of talents'.[50] To Godwin he was to write dismissively: 'Southey the Poet whose principles were pure & elevated once, is now the servile champion of every abuse and absurdity. – I have had much conversation with him. He says "You will think as I do when you are as old." I do not feel the least disposition to be Mr S's proselyte.'[51] The swiftness and violence of this reaction might have warned Godwin of what was eventually in store for him too.

Southey never met Shelley again, but he does not drop out of Shelley's life. What Southey had written about meeting himself was true: the young idealist who wrote *Wat Tyler* and planned a utopian community on the banks of the Susquehannah with Coleridge, had indeed been a kind of previous Shelley.*

---

* It is remarkable to compare the impressions of William Hazlitt, who saw both men in their youth, and described them in similar language and tone. Of Southey he wrote 'Mr Southey, as we formerly remember to have seen him, had a hectic flush upon his cheek, a roving fire in his eye, a

Equally, Shelley was haunted by Southey as an image of what he might himself come to in *his* middle age, surrounded by domestic commitments and forced to make some kind of compromise with society. Southey in turn felt some degree of reproach from this vision of his younger self, and turned away in comfortable clichés, unable to face it. Shelley for his part could not accept that Southey's 'apostacy', his revulsion from the revolutionary principles in 1797, was part of the revulsion and shattering disappointment of a whole generation, a bitter historical fact, which had very little to do with 'corruption' or middle-aged hypocrisy. That he was at least aware of the historical problem is shown by his planning at this time a novel designed to 'exhibit the cause of the failure of the French Revolution'.[52] But it was typical of him that he would not let this moderate in any way his sudden sweeping condemnation of Southey. The novel, entitled 'Hubert Cauvin', never materialized; but the problem recurs in Shelley's writing. Thus the two faced each other, and bitter unretractable words passed between them. When Shelley left Keswick he passed by Greta Hall 'without a sting' of regret, but years later, in Italy, Southey rose up again in Shelley's life, and stood in his turn like an accusing ghost. In its own way, though by no means the most influential, it was one of the most significant confrontations in Shelley's whole life.

Shelley's lights were now beamed on Godwin. On 3 January he wrote his famous letter of philosophic introduction.

> You will be surprised at hearing from a stranger. . . . The name of Godwin has been used to excite in me feelings of reverence and admiration, I have been accustomed to consider him a luminary too dazzling for the darkness which surrounds him; and from the earliest period of my knowledge of his principles I have ardently desired to share on the footing of intimacy that intellect which I have delighted to contemplate in its emanations. . . . I am young – I am ardent in the cause of philanthropy and truth, do not suppose that this is vanity. I am not conscious that it influences this portraiture. I imagine myself dispassionately describing the state of my mind. I am young – you have gone before me, I doubt not are a veteran to me in the years of persecution – is it strange that defying prejudice as I have done, I should outstep the limits of custom's prescription, and endeavour to make my desire useful by a friendship with William Godwin. . . . I am convinced I could represent myself to you in such terms as not to be thought wholly unworthy of your friendship. At least

falcon glance, a look at once aspiring and dejected. . . . It was the dawn of Liberty that still tinged his cheek, a smile between hope and sadness that still played upon his quivering lip. . . . He was an enthusiast, a fanatic, a leveller; he stuck at nothing that he thought would banish all pain and misery from the world.' (From *The Spirit of the Age*, 1824.) Compare this with p. 362.

if desire for universal happiness has any claim upon your preference that desire I can exhibit. – Adieu. I shall earnestly await your answer.[53]

In writing thus out of the blue to William Godwin, Shelley decided to adopt the 'Godwinian style' of discourse, in which all sentiments are considered and expressed as impersonal and objective facts according to the universal principles of Reason. The final effect of this style is a curious kind of vertigo, as if Shelley was looking down at himself from a very great height, and yet was all the time fearful of falling. Godwin, who doubtless recognized this tribute to his own manner in *Political Justice*, wrote back at once, but complained with some justification, that Shelley's letter was too 'generalizing' in character. Shelley then sent a second, more autobiographical letter on 10 January.

The 'Godwinian style' nevertheless remained to infect much of Shelley's correspondence for the next three or four years, making him at times almost unreadably periphrastic. Most dangerously, the style gave Shelley a temporary substitute for precisely that quality which Coleridge noted that he lacked: that 'plane whereon to stand, and look down upon his own mind'.

Shelley's second letter to Godwin has often been understood as the classic inside description of his own childhood, and in particular of Shelley's development from Gothic adolescence to Godwinian maturity.

I was haunted with a passion for the wildest and most extravagant romances: ancient books of Chemistry and Magic were perused with an enthusiasm of wonder almost amounting to belief. . . . From a reader I became a writer of Romances; before the age of seventeen I had published two 'St Irvyne' and 'Zastrozzi' each of which tho quite uncharacteristic of me as I now am, yet serve to mark the state of my mind at the period of their composition. . . . It is now a period of more than two years since first I saw your inestimable book on 'Political Justice'; it opened to my mind fresh & more extensive views, it materially influenced my character, and I rose from its perusal a wiser and a better man. – I was no longer a votary of Romance; till then I had existed in an ideal world; now I found that in this universe of ours was enough to excite the interest of the heart, enough to employ the discussions of Reason. I beheld in short that I had duties to perform.[54]

But this is really a description of what had happened to Shelley's mind only very recently, since his elopement, and especially since coming to Keswick. That is, it was a description of what Shelley wanted Godwin to think had happened to his mind. Yet in truth, the shedding of Gothic shadows and the putting on of luminous Reason was not to be accomplished so easily in one of Shelley's temperament.

The autobiographical letter has quite another interest. For what is perhaps most remarkable about it, as a piece of serious self-description by a 19-year-old, is the number of facts that are distorted or embellished. Shelley says he published his romances 'before the age of seventeen'; actually he published *Zastrozzi* three months after his seventeenth birthday (November 1810), and *St Irvyne* at Oxford when he was 18. He says he first saw *Political Justice* 'more than two years since' and implies that it 'materially' influenced him from that date. Actually the first time there is any solid evidence that he read the book is when he ordered it from Stockdale at Oxford on 19 November 1810, and references to Godwin remain very slight,[55] before the development of the Hitchener correspondence in the summer of 1811. Even then, the main point of remark is the 'Godwinian' anti-matrimonial system.

Later in the letter Shelley says he was 'twice expelled' from Eton. There is no evidence for this dramatic occurrence, though it is possible his 'feverish illness' related to a *threat* of expulsion on one occasion. Over his Oxford expulsion, he says, 'It was never my intention to deny' the 'Atheism' pamphlet; yet as we have seen, he took great care that it should remain anonymous, and probably ruined his own case by refusing to come out with an open avowal of his authorship. To Godwin he implies strongly that he was expelled for the reverse, for 'refusing' to deny authorship.

At the end of the letter Shelley again resurrects the story that his father had wanted to kill him off in the Peninsular War, but with a different twist: 'He wished to induce me by poverty to accept of some commission in a distant regiment, and in the interim of my absence to prosecute the pamphlet that a process of outlawry might make the estate on his death devolve on my younger brother.' Again there is no evidence at all for this, and the most that can be said is that immediately on hearing news of Shelley's elopement, Timothy consulted with his solicitor Whitton and may, among other things, have looked into the possibility of disinheriting his son, though he could not do this by law, since the estate was entailed.[56]

Finally Shelley gives a strong general impression of an utterly subjugated childhood: 'Passive obedience was inculcated and enforced in my childhood: I was required to love because it was my duty to love.' Again, this does not fit the facts of his Field Place upbringing, as we now know them, though it is consistent with Shelley's mythical interpretation of them. These are all small points, but together they show that at the very time when Shelley was attempting to be most rational and Godwinian in his self-description, he was shifting and remoulding the image of himself to fit a preconceived picture of how he felt he ought to be. A good deal of this remoulding can be accounted for by Shelley's enthusiastic wish to prove himself as a true pupil of Godwin's: the shifting of the dates, the background of persecution. But one concludes on this and other occasions that Shelley could be very unscrupulous in adjusting the truth when the need arose. What is most disturbing is that it is difficult to tell how far Shelley really realized – or admitted to himself – what he was doing.

This second letter was a success with Godwin, and Shelley was soon engaged in a rapid philosophic correspondence, occasionally interjected by *frissons* of pure delight: 'that William Godwin should have a "deep and earnest interest in *my* welfare" cannot but produce the most intoxicating sensations',[57] as he wrote back. Godwin's first move, it seems, was to try to discourage Shelley from any pre-mature publication, or worse, from any political activity. He urged him to proceed with due philosophical calm and modesty. It was one of the fundamen-tal principles of *Political Justice* that change was not to be brought about by active political association or campaigning, but by the process of reading, reasoning and discussion carried on by a broad front of the intelligentsia, and carried on peacefully and privately. Godwin also reasoned with Shelley over his hardened attitude towards his father, quickly realizing that Shelley would in every way be less useful to himself and to others if he forfeited his inheritance.

Shelley's reply, in which he conceded a good deal, is interesting. 'You mistake me if you think that I am angry with my father, I have ever been desirous of a reconciliation with him, but the price which he demands for it is a renunciation of my opinions. . . . It is probable that my father has *acted* for my welfare, but the manner in which he has done so will not allow me to suppose that he has *felt* for it, unconnectedly with certain considerations of birth; and feeling for these things was not feeling for me.'[58] This emphasis on Timothy's failure of feeling for him, on his *failure of love*, is extremely revealing. Beside this omission, Shelley seems to be admitting, all Timothy's 'tyrannical' actions pale into insignificance. It was the crucial, unforgivable failure of fatherly love that really counted. Shelley's next remark to Godwin immediately reflects this: 'I never loved my father; it is not from hardness of heart for I have loved, and I do love warmly.'[59]

In this opening phase of the correspondence, in which Shelley wrote four letters from Keswick, he respectfully took issue with Godwin over his own desire to proselytize, though he assured him that he hoped 'in the course of our communication to acquire that sobriety of spirit which is the characteristic of true heroism'; adding with a sententiousness that might have warned Godwin, 'I have not heard without benefit that Newton was a modest man.'[60]

Sobriety of spirit was not exactly what Shelley had immediately in mind. He and Harriet had been busy planning the trip to Dublin. It was not to be a pleasure trip, but was intended to be a serious and indeed possibly dangerous propaganda campaign. 'We go principally to forward as much as we can the Catholic Emancipation.'[61] The idea had grown since December, when Ireland had seemed to be a good place to publish Shelley's collection of poems in the cause of liberty. On 16 January Shelley was busy writing a pamphlet on Catholic Emancipation which he planned to distribute in the capital. This now absorbed his interest rather than the novel 'Hubert Cauvin', which was thrown aside, and the collection of metaphysical essays he had been tinkering with in December. The as yet unnamed long poem was again postponed. The pamphlet eventually became *An Address to the Irish People*, a rather disorganized popular tract of some 12,000 words, with sceptical ideas drawn from Hume, and spruced with punchy political formulations taken from Tom Paine's propaganda masterpiece *The Rights of Man*. Shelley's recent reading also showed up in echoes of *Political Justice* and Holbach's *Système de la Nature*. General information on the Irish background Shelley culled from the published speeches of John Philpot Curran, a fiery Irish lawyer who had defended Wolfe Tone, Hamilton Rowan and Peter Finnerty in the courts.[62] Some of his more striking passages Shelley cleverly incorporated, though without acknowledgement.

Beside this pamphlet and the poems, Shelley was also preparing a broadside ballad for sticking on walls and pinning up in meeting-halls, after the propaganda methods of Paine. This was called 'The Devil's Walk', admiringly plagiarized from Coleridge's 'The Devil's Thoughts'.* It described a natty *beau-monde* Devil who takes a stroll to review the activities of his faithful servants in the earthly metropolis: the politicians, lawyers and courtiers in London. This was the first notable time that Shelley used the Devil as his satirical protagonist, a poetic role that eventually bordered on a strange kind of self-identification. For the time being the verse was very rough and ready stuff, unevenly handled and lacking sufficient striking power, but some of the images have a lively presence:

> Once, early in the morning,
>   Beelzebub arose,
> With care his sweet person adorning,
>   He put on his Sunday clothes.
>
> He drew on his boot to hide his hoof,
>   He drew on a glove to hide his claw,
> His horns were concealed by a *Bras Chapeau*,
> And the Devil went forth as natty a *Beau*
>   As Bond-street ever saw.

* It had first been published in *The Morning Post*, 6 September 1799.

Then at the Inns of Court . . .

> He peeped in each hole, to each chamber stole,
>   His promising live-stock to view;
> Grinning applause, he just showed them his claws,
> And they shrunk with affright from his ugly sight,
>   Whose work they delighted to do.

Then observing the Prince Regent . . .

> For he is fat,—his waistcoat gay,
> When strained upon a levee day,
>   Scarce meets across his princely paunch;
> And pantaloons are like half-moons
>   Upon each brawny haunch.[63]

It has been suggested that this sort of work was merely characteristic of Shelley's juvenilia. But Shelley was to return to the raw material and style of 'The Devil's Walk' nine years later, and to use it with vastly more sophisticated effect, though with an essentially similar target, in *Peter Bell the Third* and in *The Mask of Anarchy*. In 1812 it served to make the simple propaganda point that the established officials of the English rule were corrupt, cowardly and obscene, as they busied themselves with the satanic task of cheating and oppressing the under-privileged masses of society.

The 'Esdaile Notebook' shows evidence of other, more private poems also written on political themes during these weeks. In all of them one can sense Shelley trying to work towards an expression of his new-found awareness of the radical cause. In 'The Crisis' he attempted to produce a kind of litany of his new beliefs, a sapphic chant with an oddly psalmic, stumbling rhythm. But as yet it is hollow and rhetorical:

> When we see Despots prosper in their weakness,
> When we see Falsehood triumph in its folly,
> When we see Evil, Tyranny, Corruption,
>   Grin, grow and fatten;
> When Virtue toileth through a world of sorrow,
> When Freedom dwelleth in the deepest dungeon,
> When Truth, in chains and infamy, bewaileth
>   O'er a world's ruin;
> When Monarchs laugh upon their throne securely
> Mocking the woes which are to them a treasure,
> Hear the deep curse, and quench the Mother's hunger
>   In her child's murder;

> Then we may hope the consummating hour
> Dreadfully, sweetly, swiftly is arriving,
> When light from Darkness, peace from desolation,
>   Bursts unresisted. . . .[64]

What Shelley meant by all these capitalized abstracts, and in particular the line about the child's murder, is partly clarified by his observations on Keswick and its surroundings. Though the Lake District was beautiful in itself, he found that man's presence made it morally and socially *ugly*. 'The manufacturers with their contamination have crept into the peaceful vale and deformed the loveliness of Nature with human taint,' he observed, as many a tourist has done since. But then he continued with that characteristic puritanism, 'The debauched servants of the great families who resort contribute to the total extinction of morality. Keswick seems more like a suburb of London than a village of Cumberland. Children are frequently found in the River which the unfortunate women employed at the manufactory destroy.'[65] From this situation, Shelley in his poem was trying to extrapolate a broad picture of England in that bad winter of 1811–12, and vaguely invoking that 'dreadfully, sweetly, swiftly' arriving moment of revolution. Of his Irish campaign he had written to Miss Hitchener: 'You see my friend what I am about. I consider the State of Ireland as constituting a part of a great crisis in opinions.'[66]

In another poem, Shelley tried to relate the Irish social conditions more closely to his own political ambitions. Imitating Southey's oriental frames of mythology, he created an Indian tale involving two lovers, Zeinab and Kathema, who are separated by tyrannic authority. The girl, Zeinab, is eventually hanged at a crossroad gibbet, and Kathema later hangs himself by the same chain in a moment of despairing desire to rejoin her. At the end of the poem, Shelley turns Zeinab's career into an apocalyptic symbol of revolt, burning like a fiery comet through the darkness of society. It is clear that he was partially identifying himself with this early heroine of rebellion against the great 'Them' of established society:

> Therefore against them she waged ruthless war
> With their own arms of bold and bloody crime, –
> Even like a mild and sweetly beaming star
> Whose rays were wont to grace the matin-prime
> Changed to a comet, horrible and bright,
> Which wild careers awhile then sinks in dark-red night.
>
> Thus, like its God, unjust and pityless,
> Crimes first are made and then avenged by man,

For where's the tender heart, whose hopes can bless
Or man or God's unprofitable plan, –
A universe of horror and decay,
Gibbets, disease, and wars, and hearts as hard as they.[67]

In Edinburgh, during the autumn, Shelley, Hogg and Harriet had watched a comet that appeared for some days in the evening sky.

Of all Shelley's Keswick poems, easily the most striking is the long Wordsworthian 'A Tale of Society as It Is', which he posted to Miss Hitchener on 7 January. It deserves to be counted as the first of Shelley's important poems, though it is undramatic, indeed markedly flat and factual in its narrative style. It keeps as close as possible to the story of a poor woman whose only son is pressed into the Army, while she is left in solitude and poverty; Shelley had learnt of the incident at Keswick. This style, with its plain-faced, austere quality of statement and reflection was to mature gradually, like the other satiric style, until Shelley used it in his Italian poems to carry and present some of his finest human material. It is quite different from the gaseous, hyperbolic manner traditionally associated with Shelley's lyricism.

For seven years did this poor woman live
In unparticipated solitude.
Thou might have seen her in the desert rude
Picking the scattered remnants of its wood.
If human, thou might'st there have learned to grieve.[68]*

While Shelley was arming himself for the Irish expedition with propaganda pamphlets and poems, he had received more practical aid in the form of an unexpected stabilization of his finances. Both Timothy Shelley and old Westbrook, after hearing of Shelley's successful visit to the Duke of Norfolk's at Greystoke, had agreed to contribute an allowance of £200 a year each. As Timothy put it, it was to prevent his son 'cheating strangers'.[69] The money was important, for it at last gave Shelley a degree of freedom of choice and movement, however ironically Timothy chose to concede it.

Timothy's irony had some point, for the final gaining of this allowance has its own special twist. Immediately after returning from Greystoke, Shelley wrote to his father to broach the question of the £200. He stated his own point of view with an air of calm resolution which perhaps owed something to the duke's influence. 'Now let me say', he wrote, 'that a reconciliation with you is a thing which I very much desire, accept my apologies for the uneasiness which I have

---

* The original of this poem was probably the one Shelley tried to sell at Oxford for Peter Finnerty's benefit; its subject of the social injustice of warfare would have been particularly suitable. The poem is worth reading in full.

occasioned, believe that my wishes to repair any uneasiness is firm, & sincere – I regard family differences as a very great evil. . . . I hope you will not consider what I am about to say an insulting want of respect or contempt, but I think it my duty to say that however great advantages might result from such concessions, I can make no promise of concealing my opinions in political and religious matters.'[70] On the face of it this looked admirably fair and sincere.

Yet on the very same day Shelley posted a secret letter to his little sister Hellen, who was then 12 years old. He sent it clandestinely via Sir Bysshe Shelley's huntsman, Mr Allen Etheridge, with instructions to leave it in the summer-house at Field Place where Hellen might find it. Etheridge was to pick up the return correspondence. As a reward, there was a promise of favours to come: 'Remember Allen, that I shall *not* forget you.'[71] The contents of this remarkable cloak and dagger missive were not exactly consistent with a 'sincere & firm' wish to repair the 'uneasiness' among the senior members of the family. It was imaginatively written from 'Summer House. Evening.', in order to convince little Hellen of her brother's magical powers, liable to appear at a window or in the shadow of the redwoods at any moment. 'Show this letter to no one,' Shelley began dramatically. 'Because everybody else hates me, that is no reason that you should. Think for yourself my dear girl, and write to me to tell me what you think. Where you are now you cannot do as you please. – You are obliged to submit to other people. – They will not let you walk and read and think (if they knew your thoughts) just as you like tho' you have as good a right to do it as they. – But if you were with me you would be with some one who loved you, you might run & skip read write think just as you liked.'[72] The simplicity of this appeal, its offer of unimpeded love and freedom, is in one way exquisitely Shelleyan. But it is also, in the context of what he had been promising to his father at the same day and at the same desk, exquisitely treacherous – a machiavellian attempt to take the stronghold from within.

Later in the letter Shelley touched, very lightly and subtly, on the note of fear, as in the old days: '. . . nobody can suspect you, you may easily write and put your letter into the Summer House where I shall be sure to get it. I watch over you, tho' you do not think I am near, I need not tell you how I love you. – I know all that is said of me – but do not believe it. You will perhaps think *I'm* the Devil, but no, I am only your brother who is obliged to be put to these shifts to get a letter from you.'[73] He aroused the fear by denying it.

Needless to say, Etheridge the huntsman saw how the land lay, and turned over both this letter and the covering one to Sir Bysshe, who passed it on to Timothy. Timothy was, naturally, infuriated. Once again, he turned all correspondence over to his solicitor Whitton, and refused to have any more direct contact with his son. Later in the spring, when Shelley was trying to raise capital to set himself up in a farmhouse for his little community, he found all his overtures peremptorily rejected. His father was disillusioned with him. Ever after he seems to have felt that Shelley might have designs on his other children. One recalls the plan that Shelley outlined to Merle. Certainly in 1814 Shelley was to consider a plan to kidnap Hellen and Mary.

The violent disagreement with Southey, combined with the nervous tension of planning a semi-subversive campaign, began to put considerable stress on Shelley. This made itself apparent in the middle of January. The references to the possibility of prison and government persecution lose their lightheartedness in his letters to Miss Hitchener. On 16 January he refers in passing to a 'terrible headache'. 'I have been obliged by an accession of nervous attack to take a quantity of laudanum which I did very unwillingly and reluctantly, and which I should not have done had I been alone. – I am now quite recovered.'[74] But he was not really; the symptom passed, but the cause remained. He compared what he was planning to the radical work of Godwin, Tom Paine and Sir Francis Burdett, and, as he said, 'Tom Paine died a natural death – his writings were far more violently in opposition to government than mine perhaps will ever be.' Thus he tried to reassure both Miss Hitchener and himself.

Yet his anxiety showed through in other ways. The gothic imagination, which he had been assuring Godwin he no longer possessed, crept back into his conversation. He began to frighten Harriet again with ghostly talk. He was planning his radical community once more, but he gave it a nightmare twist. 'I shall try to domesticate in some antique feudal castle,' he told Miss Hitchener, 'whose mouldering turrets are fit emblems of decaying inequality and oppression. . . . As to the ghosts I shall welcome them, altho Harriet protests against my invoking them, but they would tell tales of old, and it would add to the picturesqueness of the scenery to see their thin forms flitting thro the vaulted charnels.'[75] Of course, he was joking; and yet, not entirely.

Fears and suspicions began to grow in the little household at Chesnut Cottage. Shelley could not keep quiet about his plans; he certainly told all the Calvert family and the Southeys. Opinion in the locality had been gradually polarizing against him, ever since it had been first aroused by the strange night-time activities of which Mr Dare had complained.

On 19 January this was brought to a head by a violent incident. It was reported in the local *Cumberland Pacquet* for 28 January 1812, as follows:

Several attempts at robbery have been made within the last fortnight, at Keswick and in its neighbourhood. One of the most remarkable was about seven o'clock, on the night of Sunday 19th inst. at Chesnut Cottage near Keswick, the seat of Gideon Dare, Esq. – A part of the house, it seems, is occupied by Mr Shelley and his family. – Mr Shelley being alarmed by an unusual noise, (but not knowing, or suspecting the cause) went to the door; was knocked down by some ruffians, and had remained senseless for a time, when Mr Dare, hearing the disturbance, rushed out of the house. The villains, no doubt perceiving that he was armed, fled immediately. It could not be ascertained how many the gang consisted of; but the attack was of a very formidable nature, and must stimulate the magistrates and inhabitants of the vicinity to make the most speedy exertions, and adopt the most effectual measures for the security of the town and of the neighbourhood.[76]

The report is written from the point of view of Mr Dare, who appears to be the main source of information, and there seems to be no doubt at all in the reporter's mind that such a 'very formidable' attack did actually take place. The motives of the ruffians is of course a moot point, since the reporter has no evidence that Shelley was robbed.*

Harriet, frightened that Miss Hitchener might hear the story by rumour 'much more dreadful than it really was', wrote at once to her 'sister' in Sussex. A week later she wrote again, in a more reassured tone, 'quite angry' that she might have frightened Miss Hitchener with her own fears: 'but do not my dear Madam suffer yourself to be alarmed at it; for now all is quiet and tranquil; nor do we expect any more alarms, and if we have which is not at all likely, we are well guarded'.[77] The guard must refer to Shelley's pistols, which he always carried in his personal baggage from the time of his elopement onwards. This letter is the first we have in Harriet's hand, and it shows at once her direct and pleasant frankness, combined with the sort of *naïveté* which might be put upon. Harriet's note, included in one of Shelley's, indicated that Shelley had a strong nervous reaction to this attack, and it was probably for this reason that he did not himself write to Elizabeth Hitchener with the news. 'He is much better than he has been for some time,' confided Harriet, 'and I hope as he gets stronger he will outgrow his nervous complaints – next week we think of going to Ireland.'[78]

Shelley, when he finally felt up to writing himself, on 26 January, seven days after the attack, tried to dismiss the incident, but he did so in an ambiguous way. 'Harriet has told you of the circumstance which has alarmed her. I consider it as a complete casual occurrence which having met with once we are more likely not to meet with again. The man evidently wanted to rifle my pockets; my falling within the house defeated his intention. There is nothing in this to alarm you. I was afraid you might see it in the newspaper or fancy that the blow had

---

* Dowden's 'summary' of this report, which has been consistently given in previous biographies, altered the whole emphasis of the news article, and by suppressing circumstantial details, contrived to make the whole incident inherently unlikely. (Dowden, I, p. 227.) Like many other writers, Dowden found Shelley's 'hallucinations' very convenient. See also Ref. 76.

injured me. Dismiss all fears of assassins, and spies and prisons, let me have your confident hopes of safety and success. . . .'[79] But by the very fact of mentioning what they all feared, the spies and assassins, Shelley managed to sound an ominous note. Once again, he may have done this deliberately, for at the very end of this letter, in his postscript, he touches the delicate spot once more: 'I am now as Harriet can tell you quite recovered from the little nervous attack I mentioned. Do not alarm yourself either about murderers, spies, governments, prisons, or nerves. – I must as I said have hopes and those very confident ones from *you* to fill the sails of our Packet to Dublin.'[80] Noticing the alarm in the little household, the Calverts kindly offered to put them up during these final weeks in Keswick. The offer was gratefully accepted.[81] The weather was stormy.

The pressures of Shelley's last days at Keswick, leading to the climactic attack, were to be repeated more than once at later residences. Since they are bio-graphically controversial, it is important to note the overall pattern. The first thing is the growing evidence of the friction between the Shelley household and the neighbourhood. Shelley, with his strange, deliberately 'devilish' ways, his outspoken political views and his unusual menage of ladies, clearly came into confrontation with much of the traditionally respectable and conservative element at Keswick. The row with Southey is just one of the symptoms of this which happens to be well documented; but it is highly probable, remembering for example his conduct in Edinburgh with Hogg, that he also publicly affronted or mocked the owners of the manufactory for which he had expressed so much distaste in private correspondence. The difficulty with Mr Dare, his landlord, is another case in point. Shelley was frequently outspoken in every kind of com-pany, and if aroused, he could show a furious temper and contempt for his opponents. It is not surprising that his behaviour eventually met with retaliation.

As this social friction built up, it also began to have its psychological effect on Shelley. He reacted, despite himself, to the hostility around him. His sensitive, fundamentally unstable disposition produced a painful state of nerves, and 'nervous attacks'. Shelley tried to combat these with laudanum, which would normally only be taken to kill a specific physiological pain. The combined effect was to produce morbid trains of fantasy, suspicions and fears. Quite often he was able to joke about these, and this admirable presence of humour and distancing appears sporadically in his letters. But at the same time his fears, reflecting the suspicion and dislike of his neighbours, tended to grow upon him.

Next appeared an intensification of the 'ghostly' talk, the grim gothic fan-tasies, with which he partly amused and partly frightened Harriet. At their most extreme, the fantasies came near to hallucinations, but this was rare, and Shelley knew when they had occurred, and distinguished them from reality. The outlet for his own tension, found in the tendency to terrorize his feminine companions, has been noted from his earliest childhood. The themes of ghosts and hauntings were endemic to his poetry, providing a powerful source of private imagery, which reflected his alienation from the society around him. Moreover, the imaginative investigation of these abnormal states in himself and in others, conducted almost in the spirit of the psychologist, had a permanent fascination for him, and later informed many of his prose speculations. The 'antique castle' and its 'ghosts' with which he taunted and discomforted Harriet at Keswick was a fairly mild example of what Shelley was capable of doing in this respect.

The actual attack on Shelley that Sunday evening brought all this to a climax. The anger and dislike of the community finally manifested itself in a real assault. Shelley, always brave in the moment of physical crisis, was subsequently overcome by extreme 'nerves'. By this one can understand that he probably had attacks of hysteria; at its most extreme this could involve a screaming fit and complete prostration, and he would have to be put to bed and nursed.* It was doubtless to help Harriet to cope with all this that the Calverts extended their timely invitation. After this Shelley would be weak, listless, unable to work, and have a tendency to sleepwalk at night and be plagued by bad dreams.

As he recovered, Shelley began to dramatize what had actually occurred; Harriet's anger seems to have been partly caused by the realization that she had been unduly frightened by Shelley's accounts. Gradually, as he completely regained his normal state, the dramatized accounts would attain a more overtly gothic twist, making them both more grim and more humorously exaggerated. Thus the experience was brought more easily under control. Another, and more obvious defence mechanism was the way in which Shelley moved out of the district as soon as possible after the climactic incident. The definite decision that they were leaving for Dublin was given in Shelley's first letter to Miss Hitchener after the attack, on 26 January.

Just before they had left Keswick, there was a slight excitement about Harriet being pregnant. But it turned out to be a false alarm. Both were disappointed, Shelley saying that it was 'a piece of good fortune I could not expect'.[82] Children definitely fitted into Shelley's idea of the commune. 'I hope to have a large family of children,' he confided to Miss Hitchener. 'It will bind *you* and me close & Harriet.' It was perhaps a slightly curious way of explaining his enthusiasm. Harriet was more immediately practical, but slightly wistful about it. 'Now I can bear the Journey better than if I were you know what, which I do not expect will be the case for some time, years perhaps – but now adieu to that subject.'[83] There is no further hint why Harriet did not expect to be pregnant for 'years

* Later, when Shelley was on the Continent, we have several detailed records of such hysterical attacks; they are also connected with the early somnambulism which Medwin noted.

perhaps', though writing from Dublin in February, Shelley again mentions the possibility of a 'little stranger'.[84] From the very beginning there is evidence in the Hitchener correspondence, that Shelley's sexual life with Harriet was not satisfying. Subsequent remarks made by Shelley confirm this. Harriet always remained silent. Nevertheless Shelley found her deeply attractive, and made a motif of her radiant glance and gorgeous hair. At Keswick he wrote her a little clumsy two stanza poem which is full of gratitude and reassurance. The second stanza is:

O Ever while this frail brain has life
Will it thrill to thy love-beaming gaze,
And whilst thine eyes with affection gleam
    It will worship the spirit within.
    And when death comes
    To quench their fire
A sorrowful rapture their dimness will shed
    As I bind me tight
    With thine auburn hair
And die, as I lived, with thee.[85]

Harriet came out well from the crisis at Keswick. It was the first time in her life that she had been called upon to act with some independence. Instead of being organized by Shelley, she had had to organize him; to arrange the move to the Calverts, to judge the seriousness of Shelley's symptoms and the general situation, to correspond with Shelley's intellectual partner Miss Hitchener. She did all this effectively, and Shelley found a new appreciation for her. From this time on her letters and postscripts became a central part of Shelley's story.

Harriet was not as politically radical as Shelley, but she had her own strong sympathies which she could express with boldness and simplicity. 'I cannot wait till Summer,' she wrote to Miss Hitchener, 'you must come to us in Ireland. I am Irish, I claim kindred with them; I have done with the English, I have witnessed too much of John Bull and I am ashamed of him.'[86] Often in her talk and her actions she unconsciously mimicked her husband, using his phrases and gestures and references. But she was distinguished from him by her thoroughly feminine sense of proportion, and a very quick sense of the ridiculous. She even managed to tease Shelley in her own quiet way, which must have been very good for him; but she was too young and too inexperienced to stand up to him completely. She was easily overruled or overawed by him, and often refers, rather pathetically, to her own youth and ignorance in comparison with someone like Miss Hitchener.

On 29 January, Shelley's mood was fluctuating between expectancy and gloom. 'I hope to be compelled to have recourse to laudanum no more; my health is reestablished and I am strong in hope and nerve; your hopes must go with me. I must have no horrible forebodings. Everybody is not killed that goes to Dublin – perhaps many are now on the road for the very same purpose as that which we propose.'[87] Harriet also noted that the reports from Ireland were bad, but still she hoped 'Percy will escape all prosecutions'.[88] Leaving the neighbourhood, in which they had made both known and unknown enemies, was clearly a relief to them all. They loaded several stout trunks with books and belongings; Shelley carried pistols and laudanum; and the manuscripts of the pamphlet, the broadsheet, and the collection of poems – the sacred words of liberty – were stowed safely away in their baggage.

On 3 February, as the little party waited for their boat in the unsettled weather and rain at Whitehaven, they drew together all their physical and emotional resources, and concentrated, as Shelley said, on the greater object, 'the welfare of general man'.[89] The new contact opened with Godwin was a great inspiration at this time. As they embarked, Shelley fired off one last letter to Miss Hitchener. The packet was to leave at 12 midnight, stopping at the Isle of Man on the way. They were glad to leave Whitehaven, 'a miserable manufacturing seaport Town', where the Inn was horrible. The sea looked rough and there was talk of a storm. Shelley's thoughts dwelt briefly on the lost comforts of the Calverts' house and especially Mrs Calvert's kindness. But their spirits were excellent, their purpose determined, and Shelley struck a note of valiant confidence. 'To give you an idea of the perfect fearlessness with which Harriet and Eliza accompany my attempt, they think of no inconveniences but those of a wet night and sea-sickness, which in fact we find to be the only real ones. – Assassination either by private or public enemies appears to me to be the phantoms of a mind whose affectionate friendship has outrun the real state of the case.'[90] He closed the note with an unexpected little sally. 'Pray what are you to be *called* when you come to us for Eliza's name is Eliza and Miss Hitchener is too long too broad and too deep. Adieu. Your P. B. Shelley.'[91]

The crossing was very rough. It took nearly thirty hours, and they were swept far up into the North of Ireland. They were all exhausted on arrival. But no one was sick; and there were no assassinations. Their mission had begun.

5
Irish Revolutionaries: 1812

The Shelleys finally reached Dublin, after a laborious coach-journey southwards, late on the night of 12 February 1812, and put up at the first available hotel. The next day Shelley took first-floor rooms at No. 7 Sackville Street, with a wrought-iron balcony suspended elegantly over the busy thoroughfare. The house was owned by a prosperous woollen draper, and Sackville Street was in the thriving commercial quarter, with the city centre just a few minutes' walk away. Shelley posted a five-line note to Miss Hitchener to say that they had all arrived safely, but forgot to include their new address; Harriet slipped it in as a postscript with the injunction, 'write soon'. In the evening the three of them stood on their balcony and gazed round at the bustling city which, over the next six weeks, was to provide Shelley with the most intensive period of practical political education that he experienced in his life.

The following morning, St Valentine's Day, Shelley made his opening moves. He took the introductory letter that Godwin had sent him at Keswick, and left it at the house of the Irish barrister and Master of the Rolls, John Philpot Curran, on St Stephen's Green.* On his way back, at Winetavern Street he found a printer, Isaac Eton, who was prepared to set up the manuscript of his first Irish pamphlet, *An Address to the Irish People*. Eton promised delivery of 1,500 copies within the week. During the afternoon Shelley picked up a newspaper, probably an American one, as these were available in Dublin, and read with ecstatic delight an article on the republican revolution that had broken out in Mexico at the end of 1810, led first by the liberal priest Miguel Hidalgo, and, after his execution, by José Morelos. He rushed back to Sackville Street to tell Harriet and Eliza, and in the enthusiasm of the moment they felt as if the forces of

---

* John Philpot Curran (1750–1817), lawyer and one-time radical whose appointment as Master of the Rolls (1806) signified the end of active social dissent. His itinerant daughter Aemelia later painted the famous flat-faced sentimental portrait of Shelley in Rome in 1819. See Chapter 20.

freedom were breaking out simultaneously all over the globe. Shelley sat down
and wrote:

> Earth's remotest bounds shall start
> Every despot's bloated cheek,
> Pallid as his bloodless heart
> Frenzy, woe, and dread shall speak . . .

The poem, 'To the Republicans of North America', as he wrote it that day in
five stanzas, celebrated his American 'brothers' and called on the great Ecuadorian
volcano Cotopaxi to blast out the news of freedom across the mountain-tops of
the whole American continent:

> Cotopaxi! bid the sound
>   Through thy sister mountains ring,
> Till each valley smile around
>   At the blissful welcoming!

This was the first time that he used one of his favourite images, the erupting
volcano which symbolizes the egalitarian revolution in society and the revolution of love in the human heart.* The idea of worldwide revolution constantly
recurred to Shelley in moments of optimism throughout his life, and he eventually incorporated it in his theory of the evolution of Liberty through human
history. Worldwide revolution was also one of the secret articles of the Illuminists.

In this poem Shelley also touched on the problem that was to haunt him with
increasing perplexity during his time in Dublin, the question of violent revolution. Could bloodshed ever be justified in the cause of freedom? Using the
renowned image of the Liberty Tree, which had been on the lips of both Thomas
Jefferson and Barère in the National Convention,[1] Shelley wrote confidently:

> Blood may fertilize the tree
> Of new bursting Liberty
> Let the guiltiness then be
> On the slaves that ruin wreak
> On the unnatural tyrant-brood
> Slow to peace and swift to blood.[2]

---

* Like many untested revolutionaries, Shelley believed for a time that the two things were necessarily consequent upon one another. Though his beliefs changed, the eruptive symbol of the volcano
remained, and he eventually drew an ink sketch of it in an Italian Notebook of 1821: Bod. MS
Shelley Adds. e. 9, p. 336.

Writing to Miss Hitchener that evening, and uncertain 'whether our letters be inspected or not', he adopted a less fiery tone and promised her that his conduct in Dublin would be marked by 'openness and sincerity', and that his writings should 'breathe the spirit of peace, toleration, and patience'. When he copied out the poem for her, he omitted the blood-fertilizing stanza, which in his notebook is the penultimate one. But he could not suppress his enthusiasm which was so great that he had actually persuaded Eliza to agree to edit a selection of Tom Paine's works that they might print in Dublin to help educate the working classes, though just at that moment Eliza was 'making a red cloak which will be finished before dinner'. He was full of printing schemes, and was trying to get hold of the works of Benjamin Flower, the radical propagandist and agitator who had edited the *Cambridge Intelligencer* during the French Revolution, and later founded the *Political Register* which was eventually taken over by William Cobbett. His own pamphlets, wrote Shelley, would contain 'downright proposals for instituting associations for bettering the condition of human kind. *I* even I, weak young poor as I am will attempt to organize them. The society of peace and love! . . . This is a crisis for the attempt.'[3]

Four days later the first sheets came off Eton's press; they were almost illegibly printed on bad paper, and the whole pamphlet ran to the absurd length of thirty pages. Shelley was delighted nevertheless, and sent off proofs to Miss Hitchener. The style, he assured her, 'is adapted to the lowest comprehension that can read'.[4] By the 24th, the *Address* was published, and he sent a copy to her, with a rapturous letter: 'let us mingle our identities inseparably, and burst upon tyrants with the accumulated impetuosity of our acquirements and resolutions. I am eager, firm, convinced.' Godwin too was immediately sent a copy, with the promise of a second pamphlet already in the press: 'a crisis like this', Shelley repeated enthusiastically to Godwin, 'ought not to be permitted to pass unoccupied or unimproved'.[5]

The *Address* now had to be distributed, and the vigour with which Shelley undertook this is one of the most impressive features of his whole stay. Scores of copies were mailed to prominent liberals like Curran and Hamilton Rowan.* No less than sixty copies were sent out to public houses in the centre and surrounds of the city – an apt method in Dublin, which he had learnt from Paine's experiences. He hired a servant especially to distribute copies, with instructions when to give them away and when to sell them, depending on the look of the potential customer. Shelley himself took copies into the streets, throwing them into passing carriages and open windows, pushing them into the hands of beggars, drunkards and street ladies. Harriet sometimes went with him, delighting

---

* Archibald Hamilton Rowan (1751–1834), an erstwhile member of the Society of United Irishmen, pamphleteer and propagandist.

in Shelley's passionate eagerness, and yet laughing at him too: 'We throw them out of [the] window and give them to men that we pass in the streets; for myself I am ready to die of laughter when it is done and Percy looks so grave. Yesterday he put one into a woman's hood of a cloak. She knew nothing of it and we passed her. I could hardly get on my muscles were so irritated.'[6] In the evenings Shelley stood on the balcony at Sackville Street watching for a passer-by who looked 'likely', and then tossing down a pamphlet.

He took advertising space in the *Dublin Evening Post*, and a summary of the *Address* appeared on 25 and 29 February, and again on 3 March. It mentioned Catholic Emancipation, Repeal of the Union with England, and the setting up of 'associations' to press for these and other measures. Most important, and most controversially, it stressed the attempt to reach the lowest levels of society: 'The lowest possible price is set on this publication, because it is the intention of the Author to awaken in the minds of the Irish poor a knowledge of their real state, and suggesting rational means of remedy.'[7]

In the first three days after publication, Shelley succeeded in distributing 400 copies. No reaction seemed forthcoming from Curran or Rowan, but he was promptly invited by the Catholic Committee, a powerful liberal pressure group, to address one of their open Aggregate Meetings the following evening, 28 February, at Fishamble Street. This was to prove the most striking success of the expedition, and Shelley wrote to Miss Hitchener, 'The persons with whom I have got acquainted, approve of my principles, & think the truths of the equality of man, the necessity of a reform and the probability of a revolution undeniable.'[8]

Yet his pamphlet *An Address to the Irish People* was far too long to have any impact on its intended popular readership. Ideologically it shifted uneasily between the sobriety of the Catholic Committee's gradualism, and the hectic rhetoric of bloody popular revolution. This ambiguity reflected a deep split in Shelley's own political thinking.

Ostensibly, the *Address* proclaimed a mild policy of peaceful self-education, and sober political thinking which would remove from the men's minds the prejudice of religious division and sectarian hatred. The targets to be striven for, by peaceful means, were repeal of the Union, Catholic Emancipation and political self-education. Change by violent means was repeatedly repudiated. 'I do not wish to see things changed now, because it cannot be done without violence, and we may assure ourselves that none of us are fit for any change, however good, if we condescend to employ force in a cause we think right.'[9] The real method of change must be slower and more severe. 'Temperance, sobriety, charity, and independence will give you virtue; and reading, talking, thinking and searching will give you wisdom; when you have those things you may defy the tyrant.'[10] All this, though Godwinian in flavour, was thoroughly amenable to the Catholic Committee's strategy.

But the pamphlet was not quite as innocent as it looked, for it had two messages, an overt one and a secret one. The secret one was in effect revolutionary. While preparing it in Keswick, Shelley had explained that the pamphlet 'is intended to familiarize to uneducated apprehensions ideas of liberty, benevolence, *peace* and toleration. It is *secretly* intended also as a preliminary to other pamphlets to shake Catholicism at its basis, and to induce Quakerish and Socinian principles of politics without objecting to the Christian Religion, which would do no good to the vulgar just now, and cast an odium over the other principles which are advanced.'[11] Socinus's politics, like those of the Quakers, were stoutly democratic, independent and egalitarian, with a strong puritan drive.* To think in these terms, and to plan to 'shake Catholicism at its basis' in an Irish context, could only be regarded as courting violence and revolution. The 'secret' intentions were concealed in the body of the pamphlet.

Shelley explicitly opposed the government's legislation on meetings, and followed with an outright call to resistance.

> Although I deprecate violence, and the cause which depends for its influence on force, yet I can by no means think that assembling together merely to talk of how things go on, I can by no means think that societies formed for talking on any subject, however Government may dislike them, come in any way under the head of force or violence. . . . Are you slaves, or are you men? If slaves, then crouch to the rod and lick the feet of your oppressors; glory in your shame; it will become you, if brutes, to act according to your nature. But you are men; a real man is free, so far as circumstances will permit him. . . . The discussion of any subject is a right that you have brought into the world with your heart and tongue. Resign your heart's blood before you part with this inestimable privilege of man.[12]

Shelley attacked aristocrats and legislators, irrespective of their religion or nationality, and condemned the political system wholesale as oppressive, corrupt and unrepresentative.

> It is horrible that the lower classes must waste their lives and liberty to furnish means for their oppressors to oppress them yet more terribly. It is horrible that the poor must give in taxes what would save them and their

---

* The sixteenth-century Italian philosopher Faustus Socinus (nephew of Laelius Socinus), a figure calculated to appeal to Shelley. Socinus travelled from Siena to Cracow attacking fundamental Christian dogma such as the Divinity of Christ, the Trinity and Original Sin. He was a personality of hectic charm and welcome enlightenment in European university circles.

families from hunger and cold; it is still more horrible that they should do this to furnish further means of their own abjectness and misery.[13]

This was no longer the language of the Catholic Committee; nor the language of Godwinism. This was the language of the nineties once more – Godwin recognized it instantly – the language of the French Revolutionary Convention, of Painites, of Wolfe Tone, of radical republicans. When Godwin received his copy of the pamphlet in early March, he read passages like this with open horror. 'You talk of awakening them,' he wrote, 'they will rise up like Cadmus' seed of dragon's teeth, and their first act will be to destroy each other.'[14]

Godwin's own position, which was reflected by many of the old guard radicals like Curran and Rowan, was that in the present conditions of society, reform could only be propagated *safely* through individual discussion and 'congenial intercourse' at 'each other's fireside'. It was in effect armchair radicalism, and the thing it most feared was mob violence among the lower orders. There was some good reason for this, since the experience of the French Revolution had taught them that revolutionary mobs do not in the end bring liberty, but civil war followed by some form of tyranny. Having digested his pamphlet, Godwin made this point to Shelley with some acidity: ' . . . Your views and mine as to the improvement of mankind are decisively at issue. You profess the immediate object of your efforts to be "the organisation of a society, whose institution shall serve as a bond to its members". If I may be allowed to understand my book on *Political Justice*, its pervading principle is, that association is a most ill-chosen and ill-qualified mode of endeavouring to promote the political happiness of mankind.'

Godwin was also quick to see the ambiguity of Shelley's position between inoffensive gradualism and dangerous violence. 'I think of your pamphlet, however commendable and lovely are many of the sentiments it contains, that it will be either ineffective to its immediate object, or that it has no very remote tendency to light again the flames of rebellion and civil war. It is painful for me to differ so much from your views on the subject, but it is my duty to tell you that such is the case.'[15] Godwin noted finally that his supposed disciple must have been 'infected' by the Irish air, since his last letter had £1 1s 8d extra to pay on the postage.

Shelley responded briskly to Godwin's criticisms. 'I am not forgetful or un-heeding of what you said of Associations. – But Political Justice was first pub-lished in 1793; nearly twenty years have elapsed since the general diffusion of its doctrines. What has followed? Have men ceased to fight, have vice and misery vanished from the earth? – Have the fireside communications which it recom-mends taken place? . . . I think of the last twenty years with impatient scepticism as to the progress which the human mind has made during this period. I will own that I am eager that something should be done.'[16] Nevertheless, the letter afforded him 'much food for thought'.

Shelley had arrived in Dublin with little more knowledge of the true state of Irish politics than that which could be gleaned from the Duke of Norfolk's drawing-room and the library of Robert Southey. With the immediate prospect of addressing the Fishamble Street meeting, and committed to his own scheme for 'associations', he made a rapid survey and study of the Irish liberation movement as it had been developing since before the French Revolution. The sectarian rivalry between Protestant and Catholic was abhorrent to him, and attempting to ignore this traditional backbone of reform politics, he anxiously examined the various historical phases of the Irish movement in an effort to establish principles and personalities with which he could align himself. It was a painful education in political reality.

Phase one had been led by Henry Grattan, a member of the Dublin Parliament, and was essentially an aristocratic struggle to bring political power to the Catholic peers and landowners. It commenced in 1778 and ended in 1793 when Grattan's army of 'volunteers' was forcibly dissolved. The episode had little interest for Shelley.

The second phase, championed by Wolfe Tone, one of the greatest of all Irish revolutionaries, had started in the year of Shelley's own birth. Tone's United Irishmen were a product of the French Revolutionary decade, republican in aspiration, schooled on the French philosophers and Tom Paine, middle-class in origin but egalitarian in outlook. The leaders of the United Irishmen were the figures whom Shelley, twenty years after, still worshipped and revered: Tone himself, who committed suicide in a Dublin prison; Hamilton Rowan, a wealthy Whig by background, but an extremist of the cause, who wore his green uniform in public, and was tried for sedition in 1794; John Philpot Curran, the liberal lawyer, who defended Rowan and many others in the courts; Arthur O'Connor, a radical intellectual and freethinker, who was arrested and tried in England, and later married Condorcet's daughter.

The United Irishmen were finally provoked into armed rebellion in 1798; support from France failed to materialize, and like many subsequent Irish liberation movements they were savagely crushed by English forces. Pitt pushed through the Act of Union and the Irish MPs and Peers moved to the comforts of Westminster.

The United Irishmen are important because they link together many of the older figures who feature in Shelley's life. Curran and Godwin were fast friends from the heady days of the nineties when the radicals of Dublin, Paris and London formed an intimate circle which stretched to include their American brothers from the East Coast. The two main defence witnesses at O'Connor's trial – he was acquitted – were Charles James Fox and the Duke of Norfolk, precisely those English Whigs to whom Shelley's family were allied.

Shelley's Irish expedition lay within the context of what was, by 1812, almost a venerable tradition of co-operation between Irish freedom fighters, English Whig aristocrats of the liberal wing and radical and revolutionary intellectuals of the nineties with backgrounds as diverse as Godwin, Condorcet, Paine and Mary Wollstonecraft.* Shelley was to keep coming across this influential network in later life, in locations as far apart as London, Paris, Pisa and Rome.

In Dublin Shelley inquired after the scattered members of the illegal organization, and wrote to Arthur O'Connor's brother. He reported to Miss Hitchener: 'The remnant of the United Irishmen whose wrongs make them hate England I have more hopes of. – I have met with no determined Republicans, but I have found some who are DEMOCRATIFIABLE.'[17]

The Catholic Committee, which Shelley was preparing to address, formed the third and modern phase of the liberation movement and was organized by Daniel O'Connell. It was composed of a powerful and ambitious group of young Dublin barristers, doctors, merchants and other professions of the middle class. They made their two unifying targets repeal of the Union and Catholic Emancipation.† This was a new and powerful political force, educated, well-informed, conscious of their own increasing importance and prosperity, businesslike and undoctrinaire. It was neither republican nor revolutionary nor 'continental'. It wanted parliamentary democracy with both Lords and Commons, and O'Connell even spoke of an Irish king. It was the most politically active opposition in Dublin.

It had become the strategy of the Catholic Committee to hold what were termed 'aggregate meetings' to circumvent the laws against political societies. They were staged in public theatres, and open to all including the government reporters and police. A list of speakers was informally announced without actually stating that they were guests or officials of the committee. Shelley's invitation was to one of these semi-legal political gatherings.

The Fishamble Street meeting of 28 February gave Shelley his first clear indication of the gap between his own aspirations and the practicalities and expediences of reform politics. He went down that evening, with Harriet and

---

* Mary Wollstonecraft Godwin (1759–97), Author, radical feminist, educationalist. traveller. One of the most remarkable intellectual figures in the background of Shelley's career. Here it is sufficient to note that she was a tutor in Ireland with the Mountcashell family (see Chapter 24); lived with the American Imlay in Paris during the Terror; published *The Rights of Women* in 1792; travelled alone through Scandinavia; and married William Godwin a few months before her death in 1797. Their love-child, also Mary, was aged 14 at the time of Shelley's Irish trip.

† The latter was achieved in 1829; the former has proved a rather more difficult objective.

Eliza on each arm, to a narrow ill-smelling lane near the Liffey, crowded by beggars and drunkards at the entrance, which was up a rickety wooden verandah. The Fishamble Theatre had once been a church, but later was converted into a music hall with stalls and boxes, where Handel was reputed to have played. Inside, he was surprised to find everything brilliantly illuminated by candlelit chandeliers, the boxes crowded with fashionable ladies, and the stalls packed out with several hundred rumbustious but highly respectable and well-dressed Irishmen from the smarter part of town. The doormen made every effort to keep out the lower orders. Daniel O'Connell himself spoke first, and Shelley – his voice cracking with nervousness and sincerity – third or fourth. He had prepared himself carefully with material from the *Address*, an outline of his proposed association, and several sharp and well-turned attacks on the English government and the Prince Regent. Startled by his pale, youthful face, his vehement manner, and his sudden felicitous bursts of Oxford rhetoric, the audience listened for more than an hour, though not always with good humour. They cheered loudly when he voiced anti-English sentiment and vague idealisms of brotherhood, but booed and hissed when he discussed political reform, associations or religion. His speech was later reported in three Irish newspapers, and drew a polemical correspondence in the *Dublin Journal*.

Among the audience were two English special agents, Michael Farrell and Thomas Manning, who later dispatched an abbreviated report of the meeting to Lord Sidmouth's Home Office in Whitehall. This was to be the first time that Shelley's name was officially filed for subversive activity. Manning's note, now in the State Papers of the Public Records Office, read: 'On this resolution . . . a young boy, delivered a speech of considerable length and replete with much elegant language; the principle matter it contained of notice was, that he lamented that the Regent should abandon Mr Fox's principles and join in a shameful coalition, or that he had been so far *womanized* – here he was interrupted by a question of order.' Farrell added that Mr Shelley 'stated himself to be a native of England', and forwarded with the report a copy of the *Dublin Evening Post* for the following day. 'Mr Shelley requested a hearing. He was an Englishman, and when he reflected on *the crimes committed by his nation on Ireland*, he could not but blush for his countrymen, did he not know that arbitrary power never failed to corrupt the heart of man. (Loud applause for several minutes) . . . He walked through the streets, and he saw the *fane of liberty converted into a temple of Mammon*. He beheld beggary and famine in the country, and he could lay his hand on his heart and say that the cause of such sights was the union with Great Britain.' The report was stamped by the Lord Lieutenant and sent on to London.[18]

After the initial euphoria of the night, and the dispatch of duplicate newspaper cuttings to Godwin and Miss Hitchener the next day, Shelley's intelligence began to warn him that the whole affair had been a hollow one. His considered verdict was severe: 'My speech was misinterpreted . . . the hisses with which they greeted me when I spoke of *religion*, tho in terms of respect, were mixed with applause when I avowed my mission. The newspapers have only noted that which did not excite disapprobation.'[19]

Shelley now began to realize the wild disorganization of the liberal wing, the severity of sectarian divisions and the nervousness of the opposition newspapers which strove to give a false impression of 'fictitious unanimity'. He also guessed that many of the old radicals had traded in their green coats for government sinecures. Yet he found it difficult to discuss the implications of this with Harriet, and he did not at first like to admit it in correspondence with Miss Hitchener – and certainly not in his philosophic letters to Godwin. For the time being he found it difficult to admit to himself.

On 2 March, two days after Fishamble Street and nearly three weeks after his arrival in Dublin, Shelley's second pamphlet *Proposals for an Association of Philanthropists* was duly published. Casting all doubts aside, Shelley once again began vigorous distribution. But he had now shifted the field of his attention away from the ordinary man in the street. His plan was now for 'proselyting (*sic*) the young men at Dublin College', and for reaching a generally more educated Dublin readership. He imagined the possibility of founding not merely one, but a whole chain of associations relying wholly on the support of young intellectuals and enlightened members of the middle class. 'This Philanthropic Association of ours is intended to unite both of these,' he informed Miss Hitchener. He allowed his thoughts to play for a moment over a wide horizon. 'Whilst you are with us in Wales, I shall attempt to organize one *there*, which shall correspond with the Dublin one. Might I not extend them all over England, and *quietly* revolutionise the country?'[20]

Behind Shelley's idea of the 'quiet revolution', the revolution from within, rising silently through society like a yeast from an ever-extending chain of linked associations, lay the unmistakable form of Illuminism. At a time when the Corresponding Societies and early Union clubs had been suppressed, and even William Godwin could not conceive of anything in the middle ground between fireside discussion and mob violence, Shelley secretly turned to the Masonic conception of revolutionary brotherhood as a viable form of reform organization. He was attracted especially by its occultism, its tight communal solidarity, and 'seeding' of subversive political ideas. He never wrote of Illuminism to Godwin, who would have been appalled, but to Miss Hitchener in this same letter he recommended the authoritative book on the subject, by the Abbé Barruel, *Memoirs Illustrating the History of Jacobinism*, a translation in four volumes,

1797-8. 'To you who know how to distinguish truth, I recommend it.'[21]* This letter marked the high point of Shelley's political hopes in Ireland.

But from March onwards, Shelley knew the tide was turning inexorably against his whole mission. He gradually became disillusioned by the lessons of the Fishamble Street meeting, although it had brought him into contact with the liberal editor and publicist John Lawless.† Moreover, he was shaken by Godwin's first reactions to his campaign which were just beginning to reach him. For the first time too, he seemed suddenly to become aware of just how bad the conditions were in Dublin itself. On 8 March he wrote bitterly to Godwin, as if his eyes had been opened for the first time:

> I had no conception of the depth of human misery until now. – The poor of Dublin are assuredly the meanest and most miserable of all. In their narrow streets thousands seem huddled together – one mass of animated filth! ... These were the persons to whom in my fancy I had addressed myself; how quickly were my views on this subject changed! ... I do not think that my book can in the slightest degree tend to violence. ... A remedy must somewhere have a beginning.[22]

By 10 March, the impressions of physical suffering and degradation had become almost overwhelming. Shelley's letters to Miss Hitchener were now steadily emptied of political theory which was replaced by detailed descriptions of human squalor, poverty and individual injustice. He explained that he was writing to Sir Francis Burdett to help prosecute the case of a man called Redfern, an expatriate Irishman who had been 'torn from his wife and family in Lisbon' and pressed into the army. On one occasion Shelley had found a little boy, 'starving with his mother, in a hiding place of unutterable filth and misery' and had rescued him and was 'about to teach him to read' when they were seized by constables. The boy 'has been snatched on a charge of false and villainous effrontery to a magistrate of *Hell*, who gave him the choice of the *tender* or military service. He preferred neither yet was compelled to be a soldier.' It was the poor Cumberland woman's story all over again.

Everywhere Shelley met the horrors of poverty and cruelty on the streets, and whenever he intervened, the result only increased his anger and despair. 'A widow woman with three infants were taken up by two constables. – I remonstrated, I pleaded. – I was everything that my powers could make me. The landlady was overcome. The constable relented, and when I asked him if he had

---

* Shelley's autographed and annotated copy of Vol. 2 of Barruel is in the Berg Collection, New York Public Library. Its condition suggests that it was a constant source of reference.

† John Lawless (1773–1837), a stagey radical, who cultivated the use of his quizzing glass and his nickname 'Honest Jack'. He published *A Compendium of the History of Ireland* in 1814, a republican view of the English colonization.

a heart, he said "to be sure he had as well as another man, but – that he was called out to business of this nature sometimes twenty times in a night". The woman's crime was stealing a penny loaf. – She is however drunken, & nothing that I or anyone can do can save her from ultimate ruin and starvation.'[23] He was also disenchanted with the Irish reformers whom he had originally been so eager to contact: 'I have daily numbers of people calling on me; *none* will do. The Spirit of Bigotry is high.'

At the very moment when he realized just how radical a reform was required to reach these poor miseries on the street, he found his own idealistic schemes were faltering. 'The Association proceeds slowly, and I fear will not be estab-- lished. Prejudices are so violent in contradiction to my principles that more hate me as a freethinker, than love me as a votary of Freedom. . . . I have at least made a stir here, and set some men's minds afloat. I may succeed, but I fear I shall not in the main object of Associations.' Walking round the streets he had entered so eagerly, he felt disgusted and angry. 'I am sick of this city & long to be with you and peace,' he told Miss Hitchener. 'The rich *grind* the poor into abjectness and then complain that they are abject. – They goad them to famine and hang them if they steal a loaf. . . . My own dearest friend in the midst of these horrors thou art our star of peace.'[24] He vented some of his frustration by writing a violent letter to the 'Editor of the panegyrizing paper', the *Dublin Weekly Messenger*, which had carried an article describing his mission in glowing terms, on 7 March.*

Few of Shelley's contacts in Dublin had turned out well. His introduction to Curran did not mature, and though he dined with him twice, Curran refused to talk politics and only angered Shelley with his ribald humour. Godwin told Shelley that his pamphlet had probably 'frightened him'. John Lawless, the editor, sensing that Shelley had money to spend, promised him 'a share in the management of a paper', and as March drew on, interested him in the publication of his *Compendium of the History of Ireland* which he was planning. Shelley undertook to raise some money for this venture, and it was some time before he learnt to distrust 'Honest Jack'. Lawless turned out to be the author of the 'panegerizing' article.

The best friend that the Shelleys made in Dublin was Catherine Nugent, a spinster of solid artisan background and strong republican sympathies. During the United Irishmen's rebellion she had regularly visited the political prisoners awaiting trial or execution in Dublin jail. She now supported herself by doing needlework at a furrier's, and had met Shelley through reading one of his

---

* For once Shelley's political instinct was sound: the editor of the *Weekly Messenger* was William Conway, a supposed liberal, who secretly corresponded with Lord Sidmouth at the Home Office on radical activities in Ireland. See MacCarthy, *Shelley's Early Life: From Original Sources*, pp. 305-7.

pamphlets. Catherine Nugent was a great practical help and support to them all during the difficult month of March, and by the 10th they had moved from Sackville Street to take new rooms at 17 Grafton Street, since Mrs Nugent lived at No. 101.

When Shelley, with his usual attentiveness to new female company, inquired if Mrs Nugent was married, he received the conclusive reply that 'her country was her only love'.[25] Harriet found her 'an agreeable, sensible woman', and formed a close friendship with her that lasted over several years.* She corresponded freely with Mrs Nugent until her death, and did not hesitate to write frankly or even jokingly of Shelley. Harriet never quite liked to do this when writing to Miss Hitchener, the Sister of his Soul. Shelley had recently taken up vegetarianism, almost an act of defiance, at this time, and Harriet joined the 'Pythagorean' system. On 15 March she wrote, 'Mrs Shelley's comps. to Mrs Nugent, and expects the pleasure of her company to dinner, 5 o'clock, as a murdered chicken has been prepared for her repast.'[26] Three days later Mrs Nugent was again visiting, and sat in their room 'talking to Percy about Virtue', as Harriet put it for Miss Hitchener's benefit.

During these mid-March days Shelley's political optimism continued to wane. 'As to an Association my hopes grow daily fainter on the subject, as my perceptions of its necessity increase.'[27] He still looked forward to the 'command of a paper, with Mr Lawless', though even Lawless had made it clear that he regarded Shelley's ultimate hopes as 'visionary'. A new note of despondency crept in with the rumour that Habeas Corpus was about to be suspended, and there were possibilities of surprise arrests. Harriet had been 'very much alarmed at the intelligence' of this, though she hoped it was ill-founded: 'if it is not where we shall be is not known, as from Percy's having made himself so busy in the cause of this poor Country, he has raised himself many enemies who would take advantage of such a time & instantly execute their vengeance upon him'. To anger and disgust, fear had now been added; Shelley's period of education in practical politics was continuing rapidly towards its end.

On 18 March, almost exactly five weeks after Shelley's arrival, a letter of grand remonstrance arrived from Godwin. He had read with mounting horror an extract from Shelley's second pamphlet, *Proposals for an Association* in the *Weekly Messenger*. The Advertisement had read: 'I propose an Association for the following purposes: first, of debating the propriety of whatever measures may be agitated; and, secondly, for carrying, by united and individual exertion, such measures into effect when determined on. That it should be an Association

---

* Harriet's letters to Mrs Nugent thus become one of our main sources of information concerning Shelley's domestic affairs during the years 1811–14. Sadly, Harriet never saw Mrs Nugent again after this first acquaintance.

diffusing knowledge and virtue throughout the poorer classes of society in Ireland. . . .' To these activist proposals, Godwin demanded:

> Can anything be plainer than this? Do you not here exhort persons, who you say 'are of scarcely greater elevation in the scale of intellectual being than the oyster: thousands huddled together, one mass of animated filth' to take the redress of grievances into their own hands. . . . Shelley, you are preparing a scene of blood! If your associations take effect to any extensive degree, tremendous consequences will follow, and hundreds, by their calamities and premature fate, will expiate your error. And then what will it avail you to say, 'I warned them against this; when I put the seed into the ground, I laid my solemn injunctions upon it, that it should not germinate?'[28]

From this time forth Shelley was never absolutely frank in his letters to Godwin about his most extreme political views. In the *Proposals* Shelley had specifically derided the Godwinian approach to reform. Speaking of liberty, Shelley had written: 'It will not be kept alive by each citizen sitting quietly by his own fireside and saying that things are going on well, because the rain does not beat on him, because *he* has books and leisure to read them, because *he* has money and is at liberty to accumulate luxuries to *himself.*'[29] And again: 'I think that individuals acting singly with whatever energy can never effect so much as a society.'

Yet Shelley had seen enough of Dublin, and he was contemplating departure. Godwin's letter, though he did not agree with it, was the final stroke. 'I have withdrawn from circulation the publications wherein I erred & am preparing to quit Dublin,' he wrote repentantly to Godwin from Grafton Street. 'The part of the City called the Liberty exhibits a spectacle of squalidness and misery such as might reasonably excite impatience in a cooler temperament than mine. But I submit. I shall address myself no more to the illiterate, I will look to events in which it will be impossible that I can share, and make myself the cause of an effect which will take place ages after *I* shall have mouldered into dust.'[30] Reading this passage, Godwin later remarked that his disciple was going 'from one extreme to the other'. This was true, for Shelley wanted to convince Godwin that he had acquiesced in his reasoning, while in fact he found Godwin's remonstrance merely gave him a convenient way out of a position he had already decided to abandon.

He did not give up the argument over associations though: they were ill-timed, but not dangerous. 'My mind is by no means settled on the subject.' He also omitted to tell Godwin about the newspaper and publishing scheme with Lawless, or the fact that he was already printing a new radical document, a *Declaration of Rights* which was soon to see very active service in Devon. 'Fear no more for any violence or hurtful measures in which I may be instrumental in Dublin,' he told Godwin soothingly, 'I acquiesce in your decisions. I am neither haughty reserved or unpersuadable.'[31]

Shelley now began a strategic retreat from Dublin. He sent instructions and explanations through Harriet to Miss Hitchener at Hurstpierpoint the same day. 'Dispense the Declarations. Percy says the farmers are very fond of having something posted on their walls. Percy has sent you all his Pamphlets with the Declaration of Rights, which you will disperse to advantage. . . . All thoughts of an Association are given up as impracticable. We shall leave this noisy town on the 7th of April, unless the Habeas Corpus Act should be suspended, and then we shall be obliged to leave here *as soon as possible*.' On the 20th Shelley hurried off a note to Medwin, his faithful financial standby, asking him to arrange a loan of £250 over eighteen months for Lawless's book. 'As you will see by the Lewes paper, I am in the midst of overwhelming engagements.'[32] Miss Hitchener had been keeping the local Sussex press well primed with cuttings from the Dublin papers with a view to softening up the ground for Shelley's next campaign, and his activities sounded more impressive in England than they really were in Dublin.

For the Irish mission was a defeat. When Shelley did return to England it was not to carry the fight into any of the disturbed urban centres of the North or West – Bristol, Liverpool, Manchester or Carlisle. He sought rural seclusion to recoup his energies and meditate on what he had experienced. But if it was a defeat, it was also an invaluable lesson. The confrontation with the physical facts of poverty, disease and brute ignorance was an experience which never left Shelley, and they were to fill his best writing with images of macabre force. The issue of violent change was brought forward as a central question in his political thinking. The idea of the 'association', and of political change fertilized by tight-knit communities of advanced thought, was one that never left him, and he continued to experiment with it in his own pattern of living for the next ten years. Looking back at the whole thing two weeks later, he summed it up without prevarication or bravado. 'The Habeas Corpus has not been suspended, nor probably will they do it. We left Dublin because I had done all that I could do, if its effects were beneficial they were not greatly so, I am dissatisfied with my success, but not with the attempt.'[33]

The Shelleys finally departed from Dublin on Saturday, 4 April. They had sent ahead a large deal box containing the pamphlets, the broadsheets, the *Declaration* and a printed version of poor Redfern's letter from the Portuguese army, the whole thing directed to Miss Hitchener as material for the development of the Lewes Association. They tried to persuade Mrs Nugent to join their little errant commune, but she looked up from her needlework and said simply 'she had never been out of her country, and [had] no wish to leave it'.[34] They did take with them the Irish servant who had first been employed in giving out pamphlets: his name was Dan Healy and Shelley had forgiven him for announcing that his master had peculiar political views since he was only '15 years of age'.[35] Dan was now a dedicated member of the cause, and their only Irish convert. They left Dublin harbour tacking out to sea in a heavy headwind.

6
A Radical Commune

The crossing took them thirty-six hours of extremely rough sailing, during which time they had nothing to eat. They arrived off Holyhead at 2 a.m. on Monday, 6 April, and were put ashore on the beach nearly a mile from the inn. The sailors led the way with storm lanterns across the rocks and shingle in the pouring rain. Harriet survived the best, for she had curled up in a dry corner of the boat and slept placidly for almost the entire voyage. Both Shelley and Eliza were almost too weak and exhausted to cover the ground, but when at last they reached the inn Shelley surprised Harriet by ordering a large meal including *meat*. 'You will think this very extraordinary,' she wrote to Catherine Nugent.[1]

Once recovered, they set off to find a new home and base for their activities. Shelley had long been planning to get Miss Hitchener to join them in Wales, and if possible to get Godwin and his family to come as well. But it was not easy to find the kind of place that would suit them; Shelley wanted considerably more than a cottage, but at the same time he could afford almost nothing in ready cash. Some kind of arrangement would have to be made to get a lease on security, or on borrowed capital. This meant finding a sympathetic landlord. They travelled rapidly southwards through Caernarvonshire and Merionethshire – 'every Inn we stopped at was the subject of new hopes, and new disappointments'.[2]

At Barmouth they discovered that travelling into Cardiganshire would be cheaper by boat than by following the tortuous coastal road which turns to follow the inlets and river mouths for several miles inland and snakes among the foothills of the Cader Idris range. Nothing daunted, they took to the sea again. The boat was open, but they had fine sparkling spring weather, and they slipped easily down the coast for thirty miles into the harbour at Aberystwyth. Later Shelley used the experience as the background for a rambling poem, 'The Voyage', which contains praise for the 'peculiarly engaging and frank generosity of seafaring men'. Although Harriet and Eliza had spent their previous summer holiday there, Aberystwyth did not attract them. Shelley had finished with large towns for the time being. As he wrote feelingly in 'The Voyage':

Lo! here a populous Town
Two dark rocks either side defend,
The quiet water sleeps within
Reflecting every roof and every mast.
A populous town! it is a den
Where wolves keep lambs to fatten on their blood.
Tis a distempered spot. Should there be one,
Just, dauntless, rational, he would appear
A madman to the rest.[3]

So they pressed on, taking the eastern road that climbs away from the coast into the hills in a series of coiling hairpins, and catching a last glimpse of the sea, descended gradually into the rolling plains and valleys of Radnorshire. They reached Rhayader, where Shelley, knowing the district from the previous year, at last discovered that there was a house unoccupied no more than a mile from his cousin's estate in Cwm Elan. He had come a full circle.

They arrived at Nantgwillt, near Rhayader, on 14 April, and within forty-eight hours had begun negotiations to secure the lease, stock and grounds consisting of 200 acres of arable land and some woodlands. In the meantime the land-lord allowed them to occupy the farm, as the Shelleys' family name carried a respectable weight in the locality. Harriet and Shelley were suddenly overflow-ing with delight, gazing upon a place that might become their own, and they bubbled with plans for the coming summer. The farm land could be sub-let, thereby paying three-quarters of the annual rent on the whole property, which anyway was cheap, as Shelley said, at £98 a year. The £500 to purchase the stock could be borrowed in Sussex. There were enough rooms to put up not only Miss Hitchener, but the Godwins, and even Mrs Nugent if she could be persuaded to come. The largest room could be fitted out as a library of classical and radical texts – 'this luxury is one that we are entitled to'.[4] The whole place, with its beautiful views, its blue woodland full of spring flowers, and its 'moun-tains & rocks seeming to form a barrier around this quiet valley which the tumult of the world may never overleap'[5] might at last become the physical basis of the commune which they had so long desired to establish, both the 'asylum of distressed virtue' and more militantly, the 'rendez-vous of the friends of liberty and truth'.[6]

From this place of retirement and concealment, Shelley's eye continued to play watchfully over the scenes of political development. He urged Miss

Hitchener to distribute the *Declaration of Rights* to the houses of the Sussex farmers: 'it was by a similar expedient that Franklin propagated his commercial opinions among the Americans'. He himself planned to circulate the Redfern letter in Wales.[7] He observed that 'Manchester, Carlisle, Bristol & other great towns are in a state of disturbance', and cursed the Prince Regent for his demands of money from the people. 'If the murderer of Marr's family containing 6 persons deserves a gibbet, how much more does a Prince whose conduct destroys millions deserve it.'[8] Later, however, seeing how the disturbance progressed, he was inclined to fear that 'hunger is the only excitement of our English riotings'. This was a sharp disappointment, for, as he noted shrewdly, 'the Local Militia that body of soldiery nearest approaching & immediately mingling with the character of citizen have been called out near Carlisle & other great towns to quell the populace. That the government has dared to call the Local into action appears to be an evidence that at least they do not think that disaffection to Government (except so far as directly connected with starvation) has any share in these tumults.'[9] When the Prime Minister, Spencer Percival, was shot down in the lobby of the House of Commons, Shelley and Harriet could only wish that it had been Castlereagh who had been killed instead – 'it had been better'.[10]

Shelley was soon fully concerned with the immediate plans for the future of his own 'little circle', although Cwm Elan haunted him with memories of Harriet Grove and the time before his complete break with Field Place. 'The ghosts of these old friends', he wrote to Godwin, 'have a dim and strange appearance when resuscitated in a situation so altered as mine is.'[11] To Miss Hitchener he recounted his feelings in whimsical terms. 'We are now embosomed in the solitude of mountains woods and rivers, silent, solitary, and old, far from any town, 6 miles from Rhayader, which is nearest. – A ghost haunts this house, which has frequently been seen by the servants. We have several witches in our neighbourhood, & are quite stocked with fairies, & hobgoblins of every description.'[12] Yet in his present frame of mind, this merely added to the attractions of the house, and he was soon writing busily to Timothy Shelley and to T. C. Medwin in an attempt to raise loans or security on the £500 capital necessary to purchase the stock and furniture at Nantgwillt. To his father, he put the proposition with considerable diplomacy. 'If you would advance [the £500] to me, I should at once by your means be settled where my yearly income would amply suffice, which would otherwise be dissipated in searching for a situation where it might maintain myself and my wife. You have now an opportunity of settling the heir to your property where he may quietly and gentlemanly pursue those avocations which are calculated hereafter to render him no disgrace to your family on a more extended theatre of action.'[13]

Yet none of their optimistic plans were to mature. Unexpected setbacks met them from every quarter, and by the first week in June they were preparing to leave the lovely Cwm Elan valley.

In the first place there was illness. Harriet had hardly been in Nantgwillt more than a few days when she showed signs of strain from their journeyings. She went down with a severe bilious attack, and this developed into an unpleasant fever, 'intermittent' but severe enough to make her too weak to walk about, or help properly with the domestic arrangements, or even to write letters. She was not properly recovered until the end of May, and during most of their residence at Nantgwillt she had relapses, perhaps brought on by the chill valley air, which sent her back to her bedroom or the library couch.[14]

Moreover, the security for the farm was not immediately forthcoming as they had hoped. Timothy Shelley, on receiving his son's request, sent a curt refusal through Whitton. Medwin showed more interest, but he discovered that the previous landlord, a Mr Hooper who had gone bankrupt, did not have it in his power to transfer the lease of Nantgwillt, and that an entirely new lease with many restrictive clauses would have to be drawn up with agents in Kingston. There were two immediate objections to this. In the first place, the new lease would not give Medwin the right to assign it to Shelley, legally a minor; Medwin would have to farm Nantgwillt himself, and maintain personal responsibility for it. In the second place, under closer appraisal it became clear from the Nantgwillt accounts that the value of the stock was not a mere £500, but a sum approaching very nearly £1,000. At this point, Medwin decided to consult with Shelley's old friend and supporter, Captain Pilfold, and during May Shelley waited anxiously for the outcome of these negotiations in Sussex.

Another misfortune, which was ultimately to endanger the whole communal scheme, concerned the large box of subversive propaganda material which had been sent from Dublin to Miss Hitchener, and which Shelley supposed had long ago reached Hurstpierpoint in safety. The box contained the Irish pamphlets and a long open letter from Harriet to Miss Hitchener in which the latter was addressed by the assumed name 'Portia'. Harriet's letter contained reference to two previous letters smuggled illegally inside newspapers (at a much cheaper rate); sympathetic description of the popular discontent in Dublin and the possibilities of a rising when the Horse Guards were in the streets; and directions for Miss Hitchener to disperse the *Declaration of Rights* around Lewes. Altogether, it added up to what Harriet herself called 'a large box so full of inflammable matter'.

Shelley had only paid the carriage on this box as far as Holyhead, trusting that it would then be forwarded to Hurstpierpoint, where Miss Hitchener might pay the remainder. But the box lay for some days at the Holyhead customs house, and finally was opened to check what charges should be made. The surveyor of customs, Mr Pierce Thomas, was appalled by what he found. His opposite number, Mr William Fellowes, the post office agent at Holyhead, was immediately alerted, and together they examined the 'inflammatories'. Both decided that the matter was serious enough to be reported direct to their superiors in London: Thomas wrote to the Secretary of State for the Home Department, and Fellowes wrote to the Secretary of the General Post Office in London. Copies of the pamphlet and Harriet's letter were taken and enclosed. Fellowes' letter reads in part: '[the box] contained, besides a great quantity of Pamphlets and printed papers, an *open letter*, of a tendency so dangerous to Government, that I urged [Mr Thomas] to write without further loss of time, a confidential letter, either to the Secretary of State, or to Mr Percival (the Prime Minister). . . .'[15] On the government side, copies of the papers eventually reached the office of the Home Secretary in London, Lord Sidmouth, and the Department of the Secretary for Ireland in Dublin, Mr Wellesley Pole.[16]

No prosecution was immediately forthcoming, and the papers were noted and returned. But the informal intelligence system of the Home Office was alerted. The papers reached the Earl of Chichester, joint Postmaster-General, in Sussex, and he set certain inquiries on foot which were reported to the General Post Office Secretary as follows. 'I hear that [Mr Shelley] has married a Servant, or some person of very low birth; he has been in Ireland some time, and I heard of his speaking at the Catholic Convention. Miss Hitchener, of Hurstpierpoint, keeps a school there, and is well spoken of; her Father keeps a Publick House in the neighbourhood, he was originally a smuggler, and changed his name from Yorke to Tichener [*sic*], before he took the Publick House. I shall have a watch upon the daughter, and discover if there is any connexion between her and Shelley.'[17] This is the first definite evidence that Shelley's activities had aroused the active attention of the Home Office and an agent had been especially assigned to watch his 'connection' with Miss Hitchener. The Postmaster-General's letter is dated 5 April 1812. Hogg has suggested that Shelley had in fact left Ireland on a 'hint' from the police, but this earlier incident is not certain.

The technique of identifying and then watching subversive groups, rather than immediately prosecuting them, was characteristic of government policy until the end of the Napoleonic War. From 1816 to 1820 it was to be more active, introducing *agents provocateurs* with the intention of catching treasonous schemes at a premature stage. The government thus hoped to draw the maximum publicity from them as part of its more severe campaign of repression in the deteriorating post-war social climate. The Pentridge Revolution and the Cato Street Conspiracy were results of this latter policy. But at this period the Home Office had very little administrative machinery, and Sidmouth himself only employed seven officials. It functioned effectively enough through personal communication between Westminster and local landlords, officials and JPs, relying on them for its often startling efficiency in gathering information and dealing with *personae non gratae*.

As far as the Home Office was concerned, it was not so much the pamphlets as Harriet's letter with its reflections on Irish discontent, and its instructions to distribute the *Declaration* in Sussex which aroused the greatest alarm. What did the *Declaration* consist of? It was printed as a broadsheet poster, in double column, with thirty-one Rights numbered and stated. These were mostly drawn from radical principles referred to in Shelley's Irish pamphlets, recognizably influenced by Godwin and Paine. There was also a rather more vague and disturbing atmosphere of fundamentalism reflecting similar declarations by the revolutionary governments in France and America. Some of the more forceful and characteristically Shelleyan of the thirty-one Rights were as follows:

1. Government has no rights; it is a delegation from several individuals for the purpose of securing their own. It is therefore just only so far as it exists by their consent, useful only so far as it operates to their well-being.

6. All have a right to an equal share in the benefits and burdens of Government. Any disabilities for opinion imply, by their existence, barefaced tyranny on the side of Government, ignorant slavishness on the side of the governed.

9. No man has a right to disturb the public peace by personally resisting the execution of a law, however bad. He ought to acquiesce, using at the same time the utmost powers of his reason to promote its repeal.

12. A man has a right to unrestricted liberty of discussion. Falsehood is a scorpion that will sting itself to death.

19. Man has no right to kill his brother. It is no excuse that he does so in uniform; he only adds the infamy of servitude to the crime of murder.

26. Those who believe that Heaven is, what earth has been, a monopoly in the hands of favoured few, would do well to reconsider their opinion; if they find that it came from their priest or their grandmother, they could not do better than reject it.

27. No man has a right to be respected for any other possessions but those of virtue and talents. Titles are tinsel, power a corrupter, glory a bubble, and excessive wealth a libel on its possessor.

28. No man has a right to monopolize more than he can enjoy; what the rich give to the poor, whilst millions are starving, is not a perfect favor, but an imperfect right.

30. Sobriety of body and mind is necessary to those who would be free; because without sobriety, a high sense of philanthropy cannot actuate the heart, nor cool and determined courage execute its dictates.

What is perhaps most remarkable about this *Declaration* is the extreme variety or source, of tone and of implication. It seems to face in several different directions at once, and suggests the confused state in which the Dublin experience had left Shelley. The opening points, No. 1 and No. 6, are almost pure Paine, seditious but philosophical. Later points like No. 27 and No. 28 are aggressively egalitarian and clearly suggest a militant line of action reminiscent of the French intellectuals of the early Revolution.

Point No. 9 seems in contrast a thoroughly law-abiding and expedient approach to the *status quo*. Points No. 19 and No. 26 are different again, with a sharp polemic edge deliberately aimed at arousing and provoking. Point No. 30 is a fine example of Shelley's more quakerish, practical side, the tone of a man who has seen political action and faces realities. Altogether it is difficult to see what the farmers would make of it; but certainly there was enough to convince a government department during the Napoleonic War that Shelley was a trouble-maker to be watched.

The *Declaration* ends with a curious piece of rhetoric, in which Shelley both exhorts and insults his reader to 'think of thy rights'. 'They are declared to thee', he concludes, 'by one who knows thy dignity, for every hour does his heart swell with honourable pride in the contemplation of what thou mayest attain – by one who is not forgetful of thy degeneracy, for every moment brings home to him the bitter conviction of what thou art. *Awake! – arise! – or be forever fallen.*'[18] One can see here the double edge of his Dublin experience at work, aware simultaneously of the ideal possibility and the bitter reality. It is also the first time that Shelley consciously identified himself with the Satanic outcast, the angel who has rebelled against the government of the Almighty; for the final call to action comes from the first book of *Paradise Lost*, Satan calling the infernal host to gather themselves up from the burning lake where they lie prostrated after the Great Battle.

This call to 'awake' – to stand up for your rights, to think for yourself, and to band together with your fellowmen – was to become for Shelley a central part of his mature political credo. It occurs here, like the Satanic identification, almost one feels by chance, a premonition of the attitudes which lived experience would make real and solid. The *Declaration* did manage to circulate among working-class radicals eventually, for it was printed complete in R. Carlile's paper *The Republican*, the fifth number, published from 55 Fleet Street on 24 September 1819.

The effect of the interference of central government in Shelley's plans was to become apparent by the end of May.

Apart from securing Nantgwillt as his base, Shelley's other main objective was to get Elizabeth Hitchener to join them in Radnorshire. For months he had been planning to bring his most faithful and intimate correspondent, the Sister of his Soul, into the little circle. Two days after settling in Nantgwillt Shelley had already begun to plan the practical details of the arrangement. Miss Hitchener – 'Portia' in the commune dialect* – should come at the end of June. With the seven bedrooms of Nantgwillt, Portia's father could come as well and manage the farm, which would be an amusement to him.[19] This seemed to settle all personal difficulties, provided Portia would give up the little school she had worked so hard in establishing at Hurstpierpoint. Perhaps even she could bring some of her pupils with her, preferably 'the little Americans'. Money of course was to be shared: 'our income is by right, natural right, the property of all the members of our society, of which you are henceforth considered as one'.[20]

Working on the basis of equality, armed with their own library, farming their own farm, encircled even with their own pupils, they thus hoped to make Nantgwillt a truly radical centre dedicated to 'plans, ideas communicated ameliorated & passed through the fire of *unbiased* discussions', and to no less than the 'immediate energizing of these reforms which the thoughtless and the everyday beings cannot conceive of as practicable or useful'.[21] For the first time since his elopement, Shelley saw immediately within his grasp the possibility of setting up a living community of like spirits.

But it was not to be. The first hint of trouble to come appeared in a letter from Miss Hitchener at the end of April. People in Sussex were *talking*; there were rumours going about concerning her and Shelley. Captain Pilfold, their own mentor, was looking doubtful and she herself was worried. At first Shelley reacted scornfully, dismissing her worries with an indignant flourish. 'Oh my dearest friend do not think of *not* living with us. What! because a few paltry village gossips repeat some silliness of their own invention till they believe it shall those resolves be shaken which ought to survive the shock of elements and crush of worlds? What is there in the Capt.'s disapproval? he has been an uncle to me, I owe him gratitude for his kindness – but am I prescribed to take his word. I have examined this affair on every side, & withdraw not an iota of my former convictions.'[22]

Further letters reached Nantgwillt, and it emerged that Portia's father was throwing his weight against the plan too. On 30 April Shelley wrote to him. Shelley must have realized how delicate was the situation. There was the relationship between father and unmarried daughter; the class division between the son of a baronet and a smuggler turned publican; and the ever-present problem of sexual scandal. Yet he wrote to Thomas Hitchener of Friar's Oak without a

---

* Miss Hitchener, after considerable thought had chosen it herself. As Harriet said: 'I do not like the name you have taken but mind only the *name*.' Subsequently Portia became 'Bessy', an apt indicator that she had passed her perihelion.

vestige of tact: 'Sir – I am your daughters friend, of whom you may have heard her speak. . . . Sir, *my* moral character is unimpeached & unimpeachable. I hate not calumny so much as I despise it. What the world thinks of my actions ever has, & I trust ever will be a matter of the completest indifference. Your daughter shares this sentiment with me, & we both are resolved to refer our actions to one tribunal only, that which Nature has implanted in us.' This was a disastrous lapse and can only have confirmed Mr Hitchener's worst fears. It was a lapse typical of Shelley, typical of his blind self-assertion and sudden explosions of high mind-edness. The letter went on to assure Mr Hitchener that Mrs Shelley was equally determined that Elizabeth should 'share the prosperity or adversity of her lot with us'. He concluded with a remark that was probably well-intentioned, but somehow came out in the context as a patronizing sneer. 'I understand that there is woven in the composition of your character a jealous watchfulness over the encroachments of those who happen to be borne to more wealth and name than yourself. – You are perhaps right. It need not be exerted now. I have no taste for displaying genealogies, nor do I wish to seem more important than I am.'[23]

The following evening Shelley sat up late, with Harriet once more tossing feverishly in her bed, 'so languid that she can scarcely speak', and wrote passion-ately to Miss Hitchener. He told her about his letter-writing to her father and also to Captain Pilfold. 'I can think with no patience,' he wrote, his anger grow-ing once more, 'my toleration to the hateful race of vipers that *crawl* upon this earth is almost exhausted when I find they have stung thee.' Then, growing calmer again with the act of writing, he advised her more sensibly: 'Your father and the Capt. are near you, we are far; & yet my friend when you hear *their* arguments, persuasions, & threats, I think you sometimes turn your mind to-wards us, & ask, "What would Percy's little circle think of this; what would they say?" Adieu. You will hear from me soon at greater length as I have much to say, & much to answer. Yours indissolubly P B S.'[24]

By the end of May, Harriet was convalescing, and the fever had gone. Shelley was immensely relieved at this, and more confident at the outcome of events. Quoting *Macbeth* he told Miss Hitchener – 'but screw your courage to the sticking place and we'll not fail'. Yet the rumours going around Hurstpierpoint continued to grow. As Shelley put it, acidly: 'That you are to be my *Mistress*! that you refused it whilst I was single, but that my marriage takes away all objections that before stood in the way of this singular passion. – They certainly seem to have acquired a taste for fabricating the most whimsical and impossible crimes.'[25]

Shelley explained the opposition to his plans not in terms of moral bigotry or Mrs Pilfold's 'extemporaneous effusions', but in specifically *political* terms. He

believed that what he had excited was, ultimately, the force of political reaction-
ism, and he put it as such to Miss Hitchener. 'Now my friend are we or are we
not to sacrifice an attachment in which far more than you & I are immediately
implicated, in which far more than these dear beings are remotely concerned;
and to sacrifice to what? – To the *world*. – To the swinish multitude, to the un-
discriminate million such as burnt the House of Priestly, such as murdered
Fitzgerald,* such as erect Barracks in Marylebone, such as began, & such as
continue this libertycide war, such wretches as dragged Redfern to slavery – or
(equal in unprincipled cowardice) the slaves who permit such things. . . .'[26]

From what is now known of the Home Office and Post Office investigation
at the end of April, it seems that Shelley was more right than he realized. It
seems highly likely that the inquiry instigated in Sussex by the Postmaster-
General, and the decision to set a watch on Elizabeth Hitchener, was the real
source of the 'rumours' which began to circulate at this time. The order to
discover if there was any connection between her and Shelley can only have
meant that their correspondence was being intercepted and opened, and that
inquiries were being made locally about Miss Hitchener's day-to-day activities.
In small rural communities such as those at Hurstpierpoint and Cuckfield, it is
unlikely that news of this had not crept around the social grapevine.

Shelley now tried to convince Captain Pilfold that what he was planning need
not upset established morality. But Pilfold, who was still considering Shelley's
financial affairs, remained uneasy. 'The Capt. told me that the reports were
as you stated them to be,' Shelley informed Miss Hitchener in rather a more
grave tone. 'He professed to disbelieve the Mistress-business, but asserted that I
certainly was very much attached to you. I certainly should feel quite as inclined
to deny my own existence as to deny this latter charge. . . .' Immediately
following this news of Captain Pilfold's objections, Shelley sent a caution to
Miss Hitchener which suggests that the Captain had made some reference to
rumours of government investigation. 'Tell me in your next how your political
affairs get on. Who are your agents? What have you done? Take care of letting
any of the Declarations get into the hands of priests or aristocrats. Adieu.'[27] But
of course it was too late.

Shelley had now effectively alienated what little support he had in Sussex.
Mr Hitchener wrote a stiff refusal to allow his daughter to go to Wales, which
Shelley answered with furious and fruitless rhetoric, expending his question
marks on the unresponsive air. 'How are you entitled to do this? who made you
her governor? Did you receive this refusal from her to communicate to me?
. . . Your ideas of Propriety (or to express myself clearer, of *morals*) are all
founded on considerations of *profit*.' Perhaps Shelley thought the best policy now

* Lord Edward Fitzgerald (1763–1804) who headed the military committee of the United Irishmen.

was to force an angry separation between father and daughter, since it would at least help to make up Miss Hitchener's mind for her.

But much more important than Mr Hitchener's disapproval was Captain Pilfold's. It struck at the root of Shelley's plans. Medwin and Captain Pilfold met on 23 May to discuss the lease of Nantgwillt. Despite the £1,000 of to stock be purchased, Captain Pilfold might still have been disposed to help his nephew if he had been convinced that the Nantgwillt scheme was a sound one. But instead he saw all manner of social and political disgrace threatening. The following day Medwin wrote to inform Shelley that 'Captain Pilfold and myself are under the Necessity of Declining any further Concern in the Transaction'.[28] The draft lease was returned to James Davies, the owner's solicitors in Kingston, by the next post. In effect this meant the end of Shelley's Welsh plan. The chance for setting up the Nantgwillt community had been lost.

On Saturday, 6 June, Mr Hooper forced them to quit the lovely farmhouse, and a disconsolate baggage train crossed over the valley and put up rather shame-facedly at Thomas Grove's house of Cwm Elan. They found Mrs Grove to be pleasant, 'tho too formal to be agreeable' on this occasion; and Mr Grove seemed to act rather distantly. Altogether, as Harriet put it, 'you may guess how we pass our time'.[29] For a moment their plans were chaotic. Shelley's first reaction was to throw everything up and talk of going to Italy until he came of age in 1814, for until then 'the same difficulty will attend us wherever we go'. Italy might also be beneficial to Shelley's health which had come to worry them both as other plans went astray. He had recently been writing to Godwin that 'until my marriage my life had been a series of illness, as it was of a nervous, or spasmodic nature, it in a degree incapacitated me for study . . .' [30]* The Italian plan depended on securing passports during a time of war, and Shelley realized that these might be difficult to obtain. In the meantime they might go to the seaside, in Cardiganshire perhaps, or further south, in Devon.

Miss Hitchener wrote to suggest that they might all go and settle in Sussex, perhaps even at her own house in Hurstpierpoint? This might be cheap, but there were obvious strategic objections. 'Might not our central situation with relation to all our *well-meaning* enemies expose us, & our views continually to

---

* The question of Shelley's ill-health is a problematic one, and becomes increasingly important after 1815. It seems to have three elements: hysterical and nervous attacks after periods of great strain and emotional upheaval; the spasmodic symptoms of a chronic disease associated with his kidneys and bladder; and a shadowy, psychosomatic area in which the two inter-reacted and fed upon each other's symptoms. In general, Shelley was healthy when he was happy; none the less in Italy he became subject to periods of nephritic spasms which caused the most acute physical pain, and probably required surgical treatment. The first medical description we have of Shelley dates from 1816, where he is described as 'consumptive'. As a young man, he showed traces of hypochondria and undoubtedly cultivated the pose of ill-health for the benefit of such as Godwin; his childhood was certainly *not* 'a series of illness'.

their aggressions, which contemptible as they might be with respect to our own peace of mind, would assume an entirely different aspect with regard to our usefullness?' – by which he meant political usefullness.[31] There was also the possibility that Timothy might be so angry at their residence in Sussex that he would withdraw the vital quarterly allowance of fifty pounds.

The last few letters from Cwm Elan were full of calculations about the expense of travelling in various directions. A journey to Sussex would cost them thirty pounds, but to Ilfracombe in Devon only eight pounds, and this was finally decisive. 'With the difference of these two sums, a house is procurable at Ilfracombe or near it which shall be the sanctuary of happiness.' It was decided that Miss Hitchener must take a coach to London as soon as she could arrange her affairs. She could stop the night at Mr Westbrook's in Chapel Street, who was still regarded as a neutral party, and the next morning he could see her safely on to the Barnstaple coach. No doubt the well-meaning enemies would attempt to prevent her departure, but 'there is no necessity either to conceal or make public your departure. I recommend not secrecy, but calm firmness.'[32] It was sad to be leaving their Welsh valley, and despite her fevers Harriet said she was 'tied Leg and Wing' to 'this enchanting place'. For years afterwards she dreamed of returning.

Shelley still managed to look ahead for possible directions in which he could be *useful* – a word he used a lot during this period. He noticed an article in Hunt's *Examiner*[33] about radical publisher Daniel Eaton who had recently been tried and sentenced for publishing the third part of Tom Paine's attack on revealed religion in *The Age of Reason*, in a cheap mass-circulation edition. The Lord Chief Justice Ellenborough had sentenced Eaton to the relatively hard punishment of eighteen months imprisonment, with the unpleasant and rather medieval addition of two hours' in the public pillory each month. Shelley saw the opportunity for a third public pamphlet and began to draft a defence of the free press.

Meanwhile he took care to reaffirm his loyalty to Godwin, partly eclipsed since Dublin. He was responding to the need for a fatherly and authoritative figure which he still felt in moments of crisis, though he did not admit it to himself. The declaration of loyalty stemmed from quite genuine feelings of respect on his part, although it did not have quite so much doctrinal agreement behind it as Godwin might have wished. On 11 June he wrote from Cwm Elan: 'I will no longer delay returning my grateful & cordial acknowledgements for your inestimable letter of March 31st. That it is most affectionate & kind I deeply feel & thankfully confess. I can return no other answer than that I will become all that you believe & wish me to be.' He was anxious now to make amends. 'I will endeavour to subdue the impatience of my nature so incompatible with true benevolence. I know that genuine Philanthropy does not permit its votaries to relax even when hope appears to languish, or to indulge bitterness of feeling against the worst the most mistaken of men. – To these faults in a considerable degree I plead guilty, at all events I have now a stimulus adequate to excite me to the conquest of them.'[34] It was a warm and touching letter. In the intellectual presence of one he felt he could trust, Shelley's sense of personal inadequacies was revealing. He was rarely able to admit his own impatience and his own bitterness of feeling; more usually he was 'unimpeached and unimpeachable'.

They left Cwm Elan about 20 June, planning to break their journey at the market town of Chepstow, in Monmouthshire, on the river Wye. At the last moment there was a panic concerning Miss Hitchener. It is not quite clear what this was, but it seems as if Shelley finally got to hear definite news of the Post Office investigation. On 18 June he dashed a quick note to her, more urgent than anything before. 'Something on which we cannot calculate has happened. Means utterly unknown to us, have been practised upon you. – Friendship & justice command that we should do all that can be done.'[35] He promised that once at Chepstow, Eliza would stay with the baggage, and he and Harriet would hurry by coach 'across the country to *you*'. Meanwhile Miss Hitchener was to try and borrow money for the return journey with them from a Mr Howel at Hurstpierpoint. Shelley treated it as a break for liberty. 'Affairs have now arrived at a crisis, I perceive by your letter the necessity of our journey, it is playing a momentous game, it demands coolness & resolution – such coolness as contempt for our adversaries has given Harriet and me. Calm yourself collect yourself my dearest friend. . . .' As for 'Mr & Mrs Pilfold & Co', 'even now I can sometimes not help smiling tho the smile is a bitter one, when the train of their conspiracies comes across me.' The liberation date was fixed as Thursday, 25 June; perhaps not that very day, but positively that week, Shelley promised. 'Prepare yourself to leave a scene rendered hateful by impotent malice,' he crowed.[36]

But in the event, and despite all his protestations, he never went to Hurstpierpoint at all. Arriving at Chepstow about 24 June, the little party – Shelley, Harriet, Eliza and Dan their Irish servant – went to look over a house that Godwin had heard of from a friend. But they found the house 'not half built', as Harriet said, 'and by no means large enough for our family', by which she meant all those whom Shelley intended to invite to join them. Moreover the country around Chepstow was dismal after Cwm Elan. They wrote the owner, a certain Mr Eton, a refusal, and posted it via Skinner Street. After anxiously checking their remaining money, they turned westwards and headed along the north Somerset and Devon coast with the vague target of Ilfracombe. It is not known what excuse was sent to Miss Hitchener for this failure of the promised liberation party.

About 28 June they left the main coastal road and began to descend a precipitous track through the cliffs, engulfed in rich flowering foliage, with a little river curling and rushing in the gorges below them. After nearly an hour's dusty descent, for the track wound down for about two miles, a beautiful vista of glittering blue sea, rocky foreshore and beached fishing boats, enclosed in a tiny shingle bay, suddenly opened in front of the eyes of the tired travellers. They had arrived at Lynmouth. It was natural Shelley country.

Among the cluster of little stone and whitewash houses, with their low thatch roofs and deeply recessed windows and doorways, peering out to sea under shaded brows, they found a single cottage unoccupied. It stood a little way back from the beach on rising ground where the trackway met the two branches of the Lyn river, crossed and ran down parallel to the sea. The cottage was roughly built, but sprawled into a pleasant series of adjoining rooms which provided Shelley once more with the chance to bring his friends together. 'The poverty and humbleness of the apartments is compensated for by their *number*, & we can invite our friends with a consciousness that there is *enclosed* space wherein they may sleep.'[37] Around them the cliffs were covered in a wild profusion of plants and bushes, with trees shimmering through various shades of green and mauve, and dotted by vivid clumps of pink and purple rhododendrons. The sun slid round the rim of the steeply wooded cove, which faced north, never far from the over-arching treetops. As its angle flattened towards mid-afternoon the village was filled with a curious blue-green haze. The stone shoulders of the cliffs hunched tightly and defensively around the village and the cottage windows gazed out on the sharply restricted band of open sea to the north.

Harriet was radiant with surprise and delight; it was as beautiful as Nantgwillt and it had 'a fine bold sea' as well. She wrote joyfully to Mrs Nugent: 'We have taken the only cottage there was, which is most beautifully situated, commanding a fine view of the sea, with mountains at the side and behind us. Vegetation is more luxuriant here than in any part of England. We have roses and myrtles creeping up the sides of the house, which is thatched at the top. It is such a little place that it seems more like a fairy scene than anything in reality. All the houses are built in the cottage style, and I suppose there are not more than 30 in all.'[38] The post came in twice a week from Barnstaple, some eighteen miles away to the south-west. The trackway was so steep no carriage would venture down it, but a horse could be ridden up with care. Getting Shelley's heavy trunks of books and pamphlets down the hill was a memorable business which required local labour. It was an event that aroused a certain amount of speculation in the village, and caused sufficient remark for it to appear in a government report that reached Lord Sidmouth's desk two and a half months later. 'Mr Shelley had with him large chests, which were so heavy scarcely three men could lift them, which were supposed to contain papers.'[39] Shelley also made his mark on the bi-weekly postal system, supplying it with more letters than the rest of the village put together, usually more than a dozen at a time and on one occasion, as Sidmouth was informed, 'so many as sixteen letters by the same post'. It was generally felt that Shelley must be, for all his youthful looks, a 'somebody', and as like as not a somebody up to no good. He was watched at Lynmouth from the start.

Both Shelley and Harriet were too busy to notice. Harriet arranged their books and papers, wrote letters to Mrs Nugent, and fussed around trying to find something for Dan to do. Shelley was now in the middle of writing his pamphlet on the Eaton case. He was organizing his philosophic reading more carefully again, and had embarked on a translation of d'Holbach's *Système de la Nature*, the implications of which he was eager to discuss with Godwin. He arranged for liberal and radical papers to be sent over weekly from Barnstaple, including Cobbett's *Political Register* and Hunt's *Examiner*, and he was searching about for a London bookseller.* It was probably Godwin who put Shelley on to Thomas Hookham and Sons, of 15 Old Bond Street.[40]

Shelley was again anxious to get his commune together. Miss Hitchener at last set out from Sussex about 14 July, and Shelley wrote a long eulogy on her self-made republican and Deist virtues in a letter to Godwin. This was by way of an introduction, for Miss Hitchener spent the stop-over night in London, not at the Westbrooks' but at Skinner Street. 'She is a woman with whom her excellent qualities made me acquainted – tho deriving her birth from a very humble source she contracted during youth a very deep & refined habit of thinking; her mind naturally inquisitive and penetrating overleaped the bounds of prejudice – she formed for herself an unbeaten path of life.'[41] One cannot help being struck by the difference between this apparently cool Godwinian assessment of Miss Hitchener's 'worthy' virtues, and the passionate outpourings which Shelley had lavished upon her so often in correspondence, calling her nothing less than 'the rock' in all his storm.

Shelley attempted to get one of Godwin's own household to come down to Devon with Miss Hitchener. 'Why may not Fanny† come to Lynmouth with Miss Hitchener ... and return with us all to London in the autumn?' Godwin was not happy with this suggestion, explaining that he did not really *know* Shelley, he had not 'seen his face', and that such a move might be premature. Yet Shelley already had a feminine following at Skinner Street, as was clear from

---

* Booksellers at this time performed a wide range of functions: publishing their own and private editions; mail order; organizing extensive circulating libraries which often reached as far as the Continent; and functioning as author's post office and coffee shop.

† Fanny (Imlay), Mary Wollstonecraft's child by the American in Paris, and Godwin's eldest stepdaughter.

Godwin's observation about Shelley's letter from Chepstow: 'the moment when what I may now call the well-known hand was seen, all the females were on the tiptoe to know'.[42] In the event, Miss Hitchener left at long last on the Barnstaple coach alone on 15 July to join her fate to the Shelleys.

One can imagine the interest aroused in Lynmouth as a third female, travelling unescorted, arrived to join young Mr Shelley's party at Hooper's Lodging, as his cottage was known locally. She was joyfully received, a tall, thin figure with her rather pocked and ravaged complexion, very talkative and anxious to please. She obviously worshipped Shelley. The villagers never discovered quite what the set-up was, but it was concluded that she was some kind of 'female servant' and 'supposed a foreigner'.[43] This was reported to Lord Sidmouth too, though his Sussex sources had probably already informed him that Miss Hitchener had left to stay with 'her connection' in the West Country.

Once Miss Hitchener had arrived, Shelley began active local propaganda work for the first time since he had left Dublin. There was another change which was also indicative of businesslike activity: Portia's name was changed to 'Bessie'. After Miss Hitchener had been with them for a fortnight, Harriet wrote one of her exact and amusing descriptions to Mrs Nugent in Dublin. She was kindly about her, though slightly mocking her earnestness. It was not altogether easy to have another woman in Shelley's life. 'Our friend Miss Hitchener is come to us,' Harriet wrote on 4 August. 'She is very busy writing for the good of mankind. She is dark in complexion, with a great quantity of long black hair. She talks a great deal. If you like great talkers she will suit you. She is taller than me or my sister, and as thin as it is possible to be. I hope you will see her one day. . . . Miss Hitchener had read your letter and loves you in good earnest. Her own expression. I know you would love her did you know her. Her age is 30. She looks like as if she was only 24 and her spirits are excellent. She laughs and talks and writes all day.' Miss Hitchener also brought doubtful news of Godwin. 'She has seen the Godwins, and thinks Godwin different to what he seems, he lives so much from his family, only seeing them at stated hours. We do not like that, and he thinks himself such a very great *man*. He would not let one of his own children come to *us* just because he had not seen our faces. Just as if writing to a person in which we express all our thoughts, was not a sufficient knowledge of them. I knew our friend, whom we call Bessy, just as well when we corresponded as I do now.'[44] However, that opinion was to change shortly too.

Lynmouth, so cut off from all communications, might not be thought the ideal centre for distributing propaganda. But there was one ever-ready mode of transport and dispersion waiting their command, as Shelley suddenly realized: the sea, and the wind that blew over it. The result was that in the early mornings and late evenings, Shelley and the supposed foreigner could be seen picking their way along the rocks and shingle with arms and pockets full of bottles. Carefully waiting for the right turn of the tide, and the right shift of the wind so it blew from the west into Avonmouth, or south-west across to Wales, they lobbed far out to sea a fleet of bobbing vessels, 'vessels of heavenly medicine' as Shelley called them in a sonnet, 'On Launching some bottles filled with Knowledge into the Bristol Channel'. The medicine consisted of the *Declaration of Rights* and the broadsheet ballad 'The Devil's Walk'.

Another of Shelley's methods, which had in its elaborateness a curious element of game-playing, was to build a miniature boat. Again, Lord Sidmouth was to receive a detailed description of one of these, picked up off-shore by a local fisherman. The little box was 'carefully covered over with bladder, and well-rosined and waxed to keep out the water, and, in order to attract attention at sea, there was a little upright stick fastened to it at each end, and a little sail fastened to them, as well as some lead at the bottom to keep it upright'.[45] The contents of seditious paper was duly reported. A third method was more prosaic. Their Irish servant, simple blundering Dan Healy, was loaded up with broadsheets and sent off into the surrounding byways to post them up on the wall and barn doors when no one was about. Shelley gave him a cover story, about meeting two travelling gentlemen on the road, if he happened to be stopped and questioned.

The last method can only be called perfectly Shelleyan. Harriet and Bessie and he would spend hours by the windows of their cottage cutting out sections of silk, and sewing and gluing them with cowgum. The result was a fire balloon, a globe of silk which was inflated by the operation of a spirit-soaked wick suspended under the open neck. These are tricky machines to fly, as they tend to ignite, but Shelley managed to get many radiant balloons to lift copies of the *Declaration of Rights* and sail through the evening sky north-eastwards across the Bristol Channel, until their tiny spark was lost in the dusk. He recorded this in one of the best of his early poems, 'To a Balloon, laden with Knowledge':

Bright ball of flame that thro the gloom of even
Silently takest thine ethereal way
And with surpassing glory dimmst each ray
Twinkling amid the dark blue depths of Heaven;
Unlike the Fire thou bearest, soon shalt thou
Fade like a meteor in surrounding gloom,
Whilst that, unquenchable, is doomed to glow
A watch light by the patriots lonely tomb,
A ray of courage to the opprest and poor,
A spark, tho' gleaming on the hovel's hearth,

Which thro' the tyrant's guilded domes shall roar,
A beacon in the darkness of the earth,
A sun which o'er the renovated scene
Shall dart like Truth where Falsehood yet has been.[46]

One remembers how he berated one of his friends at Eton as *apyros*, a man who has no love for fire. In this poem, every image is shot through by the presence of flame, and the fire-balloon itself becomes a metaphor of the life of the revolutionary or philanthropist, whose body is burnt away and destroyed, but whose message survives and kindles those around. The poem weakens and falls off towards the end, until the distinctive image of fire in darkness succumbs to the almost meaninglessly general 'renovation of the scene' by Truth replacing Falsehood. This was a very apt reflection of Shelley's own limitations in understanding the philosophy of political change, at this point in his life.

The 1st of August was Harriet's seventeenth birthday, and the 4th was Shelley's twentieth. They let off balloons to celebrate. Afterwards this became one of Shelley's customs, and he was continuing it four years later in Switzerland.

Living all together at Lynmouth, Shelley again began to think about the communal life, and how it was best organized for his own little circle. All the time while he campaigned for egalitarian principles, he kept a regular servant in Dan. It is not known if Dan ate at table with the rest of the household, but it is certain that Shelley liked to employ local servants to cook and housekeep wherever he went. The wages for such services were tiny. The plan to run the farm at Nantgwillt had been part of a general idea that manual labour and a certain degree of self-sufficiency should be a necessary feature of communal living. Carried through into action, this would have been a truly revolutionary scheme, reminiscent of the Southey–Coleridge Pantisocratic plan formed at Cambridge and Bristol during the 1790s, and a premonition of the breakaway groups from the Owenite factory townships in the 1820s.*

But at Lynmouth, writing to Godwin, Shelley stated his views differently, and showed a surprising willingness to reflect the current morality and class stratification of his own day. It is, however, important to remember that he was trying to get Godwin's daughter down to stay with them, and that Shelley consistently put on a more conservative and respectful front for the master's benefit than he did in real life. 'I do not mean', Shelley wrote to Godwin, 'that a splendid mansion, or an equipage is in any degree essential to life, – but that, if I was

---

* Notably the egalitarian communities of New Harmony in Indiana, and Orbiston in Scotland, 1825–8. For a detailed account of these utopian experiments, which throw considerable light on Shelley's communal ideas at this time, see J.F.C. Harrison, *Robert Owen and the Owenites in Britain and America* (1969); and W.H.G. Armytage, *Heavens Below: Utopian Experiments in England 1560–1960* (1961).

employed at the loom or the plough, & my wife in culinary business and house-wifery we should in the present state of society quickly become very different beings, & I may add, less useful to our species. Nor consistently with invincible ideas of delicacy, can two persons of opposite sexes unconnected by certain ties sleep in the same apartment. Probably, in a regenerated state of society agri-culture & manufacture would be compatible with the most powerful intellect and polished manners; – probably delicacy as it relates to sexual distinction would disappear. Yet now, a ploughboy can with difficulty acquire refinement of intellect, & promiscuous sexual intercourse under the present system of thinking would inevitably lead to consequences the most injurious to the hap-piness of mankind.'47

These arguments reflect the assumptions of Shelley's social background. It was certainly true that a ploughboy in 1812 would be extraordinarily lucky to achieve any degree of education, even literacy. Although even here, there were distinguished exceptions in the working-men's movement, which threw up writers of the calibre of Samuel Bamford, William Lovett and Richard Carlile.★ But Shelley's argument that if *he*, the educated man, the man of intellectual refinement, were put to the plough, he 'would quickly become a very different being', suggests a very deep sense of class differentiation, so deep as to be almost a *biological* differentiation. He seemed to believe that the mere act of manual labour destroyed a man's mental capacity for thought and the intellectual life. Again, on the sexual issue, the slightly embarrassed consideration of the physical details of undressing and sleeping in the same room, which lies behind Shelley's idea of invincible delicacy, is another deeply ingrained idea of his own class stratum, dependent on the simple fact of spacious living.

William Cobbett, the editor and journalist who proudly proclaimed his ploughboy origins, featured in the discussions which were going on at the cottage about his paper the *Weekly Register* and his attitudes as a political popularist. Both Shelley and Harriet were furious that Cobbett had attacked Sir Francis Burdett in his recent stand over the building of barracks in disturbed areas. Harriet thought that 'Cobbett merely changes his sentiments as occasion requires', and that his political manners were abusive and contradictory.48 Both were anti-Cobbett because of his popularist appeal and style, precisely that bridgehead to the 'poor and opprest' that Shelley had failed to establish in his Dublin pamphlet. Shelley enlisted Cobbett's name rather sneeringly in a general

★ Samuel Bamford (1788–1872), Manchester weaver and poet, author of the classic *Passages in the Life of a Radical* (1841). William Lovett (1800–77), Cornish carpenter, radical leader and author of *Life and Struggles in Pursuit of Bread, Knowledge and Freedom* (1871). Richard Carlile (1790–1843), publisher, polemicist, editor of the *Republican*, and one of the great figures in the history of the struggle for a free press in England. From 1821 he was to play an important role in the publishing and popularizing of Shelley's writing.

attack on the irrelevancy of classical education, suggesting that men like Cobbett were really beyond all hope of refinement. 'I have as great a contempt for Cobbett as you have', he wrote to Godwin, 'but it is because he is a dastard & a time server; he has no humanity, no refinement, but were he a classical scholar would he have more?'⁴⁹ As Shelley began to understand the political process more broadly and with more insight, so his admiration for Cobbett steadily increased. He eventually came to regard him as a 'mischievous' and delightful bull-baiter of authority, and almost exactly seven years after Lynmouth, he was writing 'Cobbett still more & more delights me, with all my horror of the sanguinary commonplaces of his creed. His design to overthrow Bank notes by forgery is very comic.'⁵⁰

At Lynmouth in July, Shelley embarked on a concentrated period of reading and study. He began a debate with Godwin over the materialist philosophy and the principles behind *Political Justice*. They discussed Helvetius and Berkeley, and Shelley once more found himself at issue with Godwin. They had agreed on the 'omnipotence of education' and were united in antagonism towards the 'system of self-love', which they understood to be the operating principle behind contemporary society. But in more purely philosophical regions, Shelley disagreed with Godwin that 'the loftiest disinterestedness is incompatible with the strictest materialism'. Shelley at this stage regarded himself as a strict 'necessitarian', with a rigidly mechanical view of the moral universe, whereas Godwin tended towards a more flexible philosophy. Shelley held his ground without compunction. 'If I err in what I say, or if I differ from you (though in this point I think I do not) Reason stands arbiter between us. Reason (if I may be permitted to personify it) is as much your superior, as you are mine.'⁵¹

Shelley took issue with Godwin over the content of education, and argued that Godwin's ideas were too literary and fettered by undue respect for a classical education and sophisticated linguistic training. 'You say that words will neither debauch our understandings, nor distort our moral feelings. – You say that the time of youth could not be better employed than in the acquisition of classical learning. But *words* are the very things that so eminently contribute to the growth and establishment of prejudice: the learning of *words* before the mind is capable of attaching correspondent ideas to them, is like possessing machinery with the use of which we are so unacquainted as to be in danger of misusing it.' Shelley here hit upon a powerful critique not only of literary education in general, but of eighteenth-century literature in particular; his argument is not unrelated to the advocacy by both Wordsworth and Coleridge of the 'plain style' in their essays and prefaces.

Shelley was at this moment most concerned with education, and he therefore concluded his argument with a suggestion for an adolescent syllabus: 'I should think that natural philosophy,* medicine, astronomy, & above all History would be sufficient employments for immaturity, employments which would completely fill up the era of tutelage, & render unnecessary all expedients for losing time well, by gaining it safely.'[52] The subjects which Shelley chose as the basis for a true education show he was once again turning over in his mind the background for his long poem which he had projected at Keswick. The 'Notes to Queen Mab', which he finally put down in definite form in London the following year, are based on exactly these categories. Shelley was 're-educating' himself with all these disciplines at Lynmouth. A book order to Hookham dated 29 July included a collection of *Medical Extracts*, Sir Humphry Davy's *Elements of Chemical Philosophy*, Mary Wollstonecraft's *Rights of Women* and David Hartley's study of 'mental association', an early psychological thesis, *Observations on Man*.[53]

At Lynmouth Shelley also read for the first time J.H.Lawrence's four-volume romance, *The Empire of the Nairs; or The Rights of Women*. It was based on a study of the matriarchal caste of the Nairs in Malabar, and was one of the most influential of feminist tracts.† Shelley at once wrote enthusiastically to Lawrence that his book had 'succeeded in making me a perfect convert to its doctrines. I then retained no doubts as to the evils of marriage, – Mrs Wollstonecraft reasons too well for that; but I had been dull enough not to perceive the greatest argument against it, until developed in the "Nairs", viz. prostitution both legal and illegal.'[54] The fundamental exemplum of Lawrence's book was that a healthy and happy community could only be formed by the abolition of a sexually monogamous morality. This chimed with the kind of theories Shelley had been developing ever since Oxford; yet he was acutely aware of the dangers of practising such a theory in the present society. For this reason he defended his own marriage as he had done previously to Miss Hitchener, remarking cheerfully that 'Love seems inclined to stay in the prison'.

Yet his further comments on seduction, with their curiously over-sensitive shudder of recoil, reflect much less on Harriet than on his relationship with Miss Hitchener, and the accusations which had been levelled from Sussex: ' . . . Seduction, which term could have no meaning in a rational society, has now a most tremendous one; the fictitious merit attached to chastity has made that a forerunner of the most terrible of ruins, which, in Malabar, would be a pledge of honour and homage. If there is any enormous and desolating crime, of which I should shudder to be accused, it is seduction.'[55] For all his shuddering however, one notes that, quite firmly, chastity was a 'fictitious merit'.

---

* The forerunner of classical nineteenth-century physics, chemistry and botany.

† First published in Germany in 1800; later translated into French; finally published in England by Thomas Hookham in 1811.

This period of summer study gradually bore fruit. In a package to Hookham, dated 29 July, Shelley delivered twenty-five copies of his completed pamphlet, the *Letter to Lord Ellenborough*; and on 18 August, he sent fifty more. The work, printed locally in Barnstaple, was an essay of some 4,000 words, in which Shelley argued the case for complete freedom of the press and toleration of all published opinion on the classic ground that 'That which is false will ultimately be controverted by its own falsehood. That which is true needs but publicity to be acknowledged.'[56]

Eaton had been tried and found guilty of 'blasphemous libel' by a jury directed by Lord Ellenborough. His defence had been that he was a deist, and not an atheist; that the Scriptures were open to the kind of criticism that Tom Paine was making, since the God of the Old Testament was a revengeful and primitive deity, and Christ was 'an exceedingly virtuous, good man, but nothing super-natural or divine'.[57] With great relish Shelley chose to defend a highly polemic version of this position. 'Mr Eaton asserted that the Scriptures were, from beginning to end, a fable and imposture, that the Apostles were liars and deceivers. He denied the miracles, the resurrection, and ascension of Christ. He did so, and the Attorney General denied the propositions which he asserted, and asserted those which he denied. What singular conclusion is deducible from this fact? None, but that the Attorney General and Mr Eaton sustained two opposite opinions.'[58]

There are several other passages in which Shelley writes with this kind of clarity and verve. But as in the Irish pamphlets, he still had no clear idea what kind of audience he was speaking to, and his argument shows little coherent development, but swirls away to itself without ever reaching any definite set of conclusions, except the need to raise his 'solitary voice' in 'disapprobation'.* Shelley missed one crucial point about the larger significance of Eaton's trial. His letter was based on the idea that Eaton's persecution was, strictly speaking, theological. 'Wherefore, I repeat, is Mr Eaton punished? Because he is a Deist? And what are you, my Lord? A Christian. Ha then! the mask is fallen off; you persecute him because his faith differs from yours.' But in fact the legal instru-ment of 'blasphemous libel' had become far more a political weapon used by the government to suppress socially subversive ideas. The very name of Tom Paine signified social subversion. Eaton's trial for publishing Paine was really the opening of the second phase of political repression – the first had been con-ducted by Pitt in the nineties – which took place between 1812 and 1824, and involved all the most distinguished members of the early free press movement:

---

* Shelley's voice was actually far from 'solitary'; both Cobbett and Hunt roundly attacked the trial in their papers and the *Examiner* reported that when Eaton appeared for his statutory two hours in the public pillory, he was greeted by a barrage of cheers and applause.

Wooler, Hone, Carlile, Cobbett, Burdett and Hunt. In every case prosecutions were mounted on one of two counts: blasphemous libel or seditious libel. Shelley did not see, at the time of writing his *Letter to Lord Ellenborough*, the full political implications of what was taking place. Later he came to see only too well: the open letter he wrote for Hunt's *Examiner* on the occasion of Carlile's trial in 1819 is a far more penetrating and forceful plea for liberty of the press and published opinion than this early pamphlet.

But Shelley did see that the central issue was not one of a true or false opinion, as it would be in, say, a purely scientific debate over Newton's laws, but a question of relative standards, of values developing historically with a society. He saw that ways must be kept open for one system of belief to lose its sectarian and institutionalized character and broadened out to embrace a much wider and more diverse kind of society. He wrote:

> The thinking part of the community has not received as indisputable the truth of Christianity as they have that of the Newtonian system. A very large portion of society, and that powerfully and extensively connected, derives its sole emolument from the belief of Christianity as a popular faith. To torture and imprison the asserter of a dogma, however ridiculous and false, is highly barbarous and impolitic. How, then, does not the cruelty of persecution become aggravated when it is directed against the opposer of an opinion *yet under dispute*, and which men of unrivalled acquirements, penetrating genius, and stainless virtue, have spent, and at last sacrificed, their lives in combating.[59]

He closed the pamphlet on a high note: 'The time is rapidly approaching, I hope, that you, my Lord, may live to behold its arrival, when the Mahometan, the Jew, the Christian, the Deist, and the Atheist will live together in one community, equally sharing the benefits which arise from its association, and united in the bonds of brotherly love.'[60]

Altogether, Shelley's *Letter to Lord Ellenborough*, though a much more lively and economic piece of work than the Irish pamphlets, was still too politically naïve to carry much weight. It begged too many questions. Where it was most lively, his style had become almost colloquial, and this was promising, and undoubtedly reflected the 'fire of discussion' that was taking place in the little circle at Lynmouth. The pamphlet was a brave piece of work to circulate, for in its boisterous lack of deference either to the machinery of justice, in the person of Lord Ellenborough, or to the tenets of the Christian religion, it was itself open to possible prosecution.*

---

* The *Letter to Lord Ellenborough* reappeared twice on its own merits as part of later campaigns against blasphemous libel. In New York, 1897, when the editor of the *Truth Seeker* was imprisoned for thirteen months; and in London, 1883, when the editor and staff of the *Free Thinker* suffered similar persecution.

Of the seventy-five copies which Shelley sent to Hookham for 'gratuitous distribution',[61] only one is still known to exist, in the Bodleian Library. Hookham would not publish the pamphlet under his own imprint, because it was too dangerous. Shelley himself, who did not sign the work, was only too aware of the possibilities of government interference, and wrote prudently: 'I beg you to accept of them that you may shew your friends who *are not informers.*' Copies were mailed to Godwin, Mrs Nugent, Chevalier Lawrence, Lord Stanhope, Sir Francis Burdett and many others, and this partly accounted for the stream of Shelley's mail which left Lynmouth by the twice-weekly post, and which subsequently so intrigued the Home Office.

August at Lynmouth also saw other literary projects in the making, for the attentions of Godwin as a reader, and Hookham as a possible publisher, encouraged Shelley to collect what material he already had, and to get down to composing new works. Stockdale, his publisher in Dublin, still held the manuscripts of Shelley's collection of 'songs of liberty', but he refused to complete the printing or to render up the manuscript until Shelley paid his outstanding bills. Shelley, with no intention of paying bills that he could no longer afford, tried to get John Lawless to intercede for him, but without apparent success. Stockdale also held manuscripts of a collection of 'essays moral and religious'[62] which Shelley had been preparing. Lawless's reputation dropped steadily in the Shelley household as he failed to procure these manuscripts. Later Mrs Nugent was to be importuned, but with no greater success.

Shelley hoped to persuade Hookham to publish his two Irish pamphlets, with 'annexed suggestions', altogether in one cheap volume 'with an explanatory preface, in *London*'. The work could then be secretly conveyed into Ireland and circulated.[63] A second venture was to involve polishing and expanding the 'essays moral and religious' from the Stockdale manuscript for Hookham to publish. But in the event Shelley never retrieved it. The idea for such a collection of essays remained with Shelley, and in the next ten years he wrote on such varied subjects as vegetarianism, religious belief, free love, marriage, Christianity, poetry, the Devil and methods of political reform.* The subjects were ones that Shelley returned to again and again throughout his life, continually re-examining and reappraising them. For precisely this reason they form some of the most intimate autobiographical material that we have from him. 'My publications will present to the moralist and the metaphysician a picture of a

---

* These essays mostly remained in his MS Notebooks during his lifetime, and they are still the least known or appreciated part of his work. They are often difficult to date, since the surrounding poems and notes were written at different times, sometimes quite haphazardly, in margins, upside down, and even occasionally right across the original entry. Shelley seems to have seized whatever notebook was nearest. Several early notebooks were re-used years later in Italy, e.g. Bod. MS Shelley Adds. e. 8; and Bod. MS Shelley Adds. e. 11.

mind however uncultured and unpruned which had at the dawn of its knowledge taken a singular turn, and to leave out the early lineaments of its appearance could be to efface those which the attrition of the world had not deprived of right angled originality.'[64] Egotistical or not, he was quite correct.

A third scheme which Shelley had lined up for Hookham was the publication by subscription of an American history of Irish republicanism, extremely antagonistic towards the English colonists, called 'Pieces of Irish History'.[65] Shelley thought it was an excellent piece of radical propaganda, and Miss Hitchener was 'so much enraged with the characters there mentioned' – these would be English landlords and politicians – 'that nothing will satisfy her desire of revenge but the printing & publishing of them, to exhibit to the world those characters which are (shameful to say) held up as beings possessing every amiable quality, whilst their hearts are as bad as possible to be'.[66] In fact the book put Miss Hitchener in such low spirits about the fate of Ireland and the Irish that Harriet was quite worried about her. 'I shall print proposals for publishing it by subscription', Shelley wrote to Mrs Nugent, 'if you cd send us any names you would benefit the Cause.'[67] But the work did not materialize.

During these summer weeks at Lynmouth, the long poem which Shelley had contemplated at Keswick in the winter was finally taking shape. He worked at it on the beach in the daytime, and in the cottage in the evening. On 18 August Shelley was able to send Hookham a 'specimen' consisting of about 700 lines. He had been writing this, his first major work, very much aware of the political climate, the need for propaganda and the dangers of persecution. The Irish expedition was fresh in his mind, and the potentially violent condition throughout the depressed regions of England. His letters to Godwin from Dublin had shown how Shelley fluctuated between the extremes of revolutionary political association and despairing political quietism. *Queen Mab* as the poem was called, offered a third alternative, a third way. It was politics conducted by propaganda; polemics, visions, prophecies and philosophical disquisitions. Because it was also politics parading as poetry, Shelley hoped it might find a weak spot in the government's armour.

He wrote to Hookham: 'I enclose also by way of specimen all that I have written of a little poem begun since my arrival in England. I conceive I have matter enough for 6 more cantos. You will perceive that I have not attempted to temper my constitutional enthusiasm in that Poem. Indeed a Poem is safe, the iron-souled Attorney General would scarcely dare to attack "Genus irritabile vatum". The Past, the Present, & the Future are the grand and comprehensive topics of this Poem. I have not yet half exhausted the second of them.'[68]

But, even as he wrote, the attack was closing on him. Of all the propaganda methods he had been employing, the simplest and most prosaic let him down. The following evening, 19 August, Dan Healy was caught putting up posters in Barnstaple, and taken into custody by the magistrates. When the posters which Dan was carrying, the *Declaration* and 'The Devil's Walk', were read, the case was treated as a matter of urgency. Dan was called before the mayor of Barnstaple later that night and interrogated.

The correspondence between the Home Office and the town clerk has survived in the Public Records Office, so we know fairly accurately what happened. Dan did not inform on Shelley, but he faithfully gave the cover story. 'On being asked how he became possessed of these papers, he said, on his road from Linton to Barnstaple yesterday, he met a gentleman dressed in black, whom he had never seen before, who asked him to take the papers to Barnstaple, and post and distribute them; and on Hill [sic] consenting, the gentleman gave him five shillings for his trouble.'[69] Barnstaple is seventeen miles from Lynmouth, so one must suppose that if Dan was found there in the evening, as the clerk reported, he must have been spending at least two days in the area on a distributing expedition; Shelley might well have been with him, but of this we have no information. The mayor, 'interrogating him more particularly concerning his master', elicited various details about Shelley's residence in Lynmouth, his travels in Dublin, his marriage to Harriet and his family connections in Sussex. But he obtained nothing further on Shelley's political activities.

The mayor then instituted immediate inquiries about Shelley's activities in Lynmouth. It is interesting, and slightly disquieting, how quickly this information was obtained. By the following morning, 20 August, the mayor knew all about Shelley's massive correspondence, about the bottle-launching expeditions, and what the bottles contained. He was, in general, informed that 'Mr Shelley had been regarded with a suspicious eye since he has been at Lynmouth'. Armed with this background, the mayor again summoned Dan before him and, acting in his capacity as magistrate, he tried and convicted him 'in ten penalties of £20 each for publishing and dispersing papers printed without the printer's name being on them, under the Act of 39 George III c. 79'. Dan was then 'committed to the common gaol of this borough for not paying the penalties, and having no goods on which they could be levied'.[70] The town clerk wrote his report to Lord Sidmouth, dating and dispatching it 'Barnstaple, August 20th, 1812'. This was an extremely rapid and astute piece of legal work. Dan had been convicted on a technical, not a political offence. The penalty for not paying the £200 fine was six months' imprisonment. The fine was too heavy for him to be able to pay it himself, but not too heavy for his well-connected master. The mayor therefore confidently sat back and awaited the appearance of Mr Shelley, and the chance to conduct a further discreet interrogation.

Shelley came at once; either on that day, or the following. But, to the authorities' surprise, he did not offer to pay the fine, nor did he volunteer any further information. The interview between Dan and Shelley was apparently brief, and calm, as if the whole thing was already understood between them. 'Mr Shelley came here to apply for his discharge; and, on visiting the jail, did not, I apprehend, express any astonishment at his situation, or reprove him for his conduct, which appears rather extraordinary.'[71] Shelley then returned alone to Lynmouth. It was impossible for him to pay that size of fine – exactly half his annual income.

While the authorities at Barnstaple awaited Home Office instructions, they also alerted the Post Office. Sir Francis Freeling was once again informed, as Secretary to the Post Office in London, of Shelley's activities. Once again the papers were passed on to Lord Chichester. This time Lord Chichester felt it was really a matter for official action. He endorsed Freeling's covering letter: 'I think it right to communicate the circumstances to the Secretary of State. It will have no effect to speak to Mr Shelley's family, they suffer enough already from his conduct.'[72] But Chichester may nevertheless have passed on a word of warning to the Shelley family in Sussex, and it is possible that this news reached Shelley at Lynmouth and so alerted him in time to what was afoot.

The first official reaction was a note from Lord Sidmouth, in his capacity as Secretary of State for the Home Office. It was dated 22 August, and probably reached Barnstaple about the 24th. It was short and to the point. 'Recommend that Mr Shelley's proceedings be watched if he is still at Linton. It would also be desirable to procure the address of his different correspondents, to whom he writes from the post-office. Lord S. will be obliged for any further information respecting Mr S., and, in the meantime, inquiries will be made about him here. Lord S. quite approves of the steps that have been taken respecting Daniel Hill [*sic*].'[73]

The Post Office at Barnstaple were informed of the Home Office's instructions, and the town clerk, Henry Drake, set about collecting a dossier on Shelley. But this time he was not quick enough. About ten days after receiving his instructions, he found his sources of information were beginning to dry up, and that no more news of Shelley was arriving in Barnstaple. After another three or four days had elapsed, the suspicions of the mayor were aroused, and Henry Drake was rapidly dispatched to Lynmouth to make first-hand inquiries. Drake arrived in Lynmouth on 7 September. His report to the Home Office, dated 9th, speaks for itself: 'I beg to inform your lordship, that not being enabled to obtain here sufficient information respecting Mr Shelley, I went to Lynmouth, where he resided, and returned yesterday. On my arrival there, I found he, with his family, after attempting in vain to cross the Channel to Swansea from that place, had lately left Lynmouth for Ilfracombe; and, on my following him there, found he had gone to Swansea, where I imagine he at present is.'[74] Further details followed about Shelley's menage, and his political propaganda methods. There was also a description: 'Mr Shelley is rather thin, and very young; indeed, his appearance is, I understand, almost that of a boy.' But the fact remained, despite the assiduity of the authorities at Barnstaple, Shelley had managed to escape from under their noses.

At this juncture, Sidmouth had all the relevant papers passed along to his legal department, the standing council who advised on matters of public prosecution. The last note in the Records Office collection is addressed from a Mr Litchfield, at Lincoln's Inn on 18 September, and states the result of a legal conference on the Shelley affair. One of the factors which must have played an important role in the decision was Shelley's legal minority. Counsel advised not to prosecute, but to have Shelley closely followed and observed. Mr Litchfield wrote: 'It did not appear either to Mr Becket or himself that any steps could with propriety be taken with respect to Mr Shelley, in consequence of his very extraordinary and unaccountable conduct; but that it would be proper to instruct some person to observe his future behaviour, and to transmit any information which might be obtained respecting him.' A note on this memorandum adds: 'Write to the Mayor of Barnstaple accordingly.'[75]

In view of events the following winter in Wales, it is important to see these exchanges, and the final instructions, in their full perspective. The Home Office had now received information on Shelley's subversive and possibly seditious activities on three separate occasions: from Dublin, from Holyhead and from Barnstaple. They also knew a good deal about his Sussex background, his 'unsuitable' marriage, and his 'connection' with Miss Hitchener. He was politically suspect, and there was no hope of curbing him through his family. Prosecution had been considered, but he was a minor. The temporary solution to this dilemma was typical of Sidmouth's policy of establishing a network of spies and informers during this period. Addresses of his correspondents must be noted and filed, and Shelley's activities must be closely observed. The difficulty now was that Shelley had successfully disappeared. The security system, though surprisingly quick and efficient locally, had one outstanding weakness; it was not co-ordinated nationally. The chances of trailing Shelley after Swansea were negligible. The Home Office had therefore, for the time being at least, lost their contact. Two possibilities now remained. Either Shelley would be informed on yet again, from whatever new locality he settled in. Or else, failing this, in five months' time, when Dan Healy was released, the servant would unwittingly lead the authorities' spies to his new residence. But one way or the other, Shelley's pursuing shadows would eventually catch up with him.

Meanwhile, what had happened to Shelley and his three ladies? Almost immediately after returning from seeing Dan in Barnstaple, they had started discreet preparations for leaving. For transport, a boat to Wales was the obvious answer. But as Henry Drake discovered, the fishermen at Lynmouth would not co-operate, and in the end they had to bargain for a boat further up the coast at Ilfracombe. Money was also difficult, but here they were more lucky. The lady at Hooper's Lodgings, who did their domestic work, had befriended them. Shelley managed to borrow twenty-nine shillings directly from her, and through her good offices, a further three pounds from a helpful neighbour. Shelley also borrowed a further small sum from one of the Lynmouth people, but how much is not known.[76] In exchange, he left a surely rather optimistic draft on 'the Honourable Mr Lawless'. The tiny amounts here involved suggest Shelley was very nearly penniless, and one wonders how he was even able to leave fifteen shillings a week to keep Dan in necessary comforts during his six months' imprisonment. However, it was not quite as bad as it seemed, for Shelley had received through the post one half of a large banknote (in the usual manner of splitting large denominations for safe keeping), and it was merely a question of waiting for the other half. This banknote was probably one of the quarterly payments of fifty pounds due from either Timothy or Mr Westbrook on 1 September. When they got to Ilfracombe, the split banknote was apparently cashed, and Shelley faithfully returned all the borrowed money.* It is clear that whatever the general hostility of the Lynmouth population, Shelley had, as ever, charmed at least a few of its poorer residents. When questions were asked in Lynmouth, Shelley's domestic lady gave little information beyond the fact that they had left for Ilfracombe and would be 'in London within a fortnight'.[77] This was clearly a diversion, for the Shelleys went north, not east. The actual date of Shelley's departure remains a mystery: somewhere, at any rate, between 28 and 31 August. From Swansea, they hurried north deep into the mountains of Wales, and steering clear of Rhayader, they headed for the long rolling valley of Llangollen, a strategic spot on the main connecting route between North Wales and London. They could then decide what to do next.

Much of the detail of Shelley's rapid and secretive departure has reached us by a strange irony. For William Godwin had at last decided to visit the Shelleys himself, and after writing to them on 31 August, he set out on 9 September on an autumn tour of the South-West, via Bristol and Tintern Abbey, which eventually brought him to Lynmouth at 3 o'clock in the afternoon of the 18th. To his great surprise and disappointment he found: 'The Shelleys are gone! They have

* A letter of 19 December 1812 which Shelley wrote from London appears to show that he borrowed a further thirty pounds from Mrs Hooper, of which twenty pounds was only then being returned. But the dating and provenance of this note are uncertain. See *Letters*, I, No. 207, p. 331.

been gone these three weeks. . . . I have been to the house where Shelley lodged, and I bring good news. I saw the woman of the house, and I was delighted with her. She is a good creature, and quite loved the Shelleys . . . the best news is that the woman says they will be in London in a fortnight.'[78]* Godwin thereafter continued his tour in a leisurely fashion via Salisbury and Stonehenge, and arrived back at Skinner Street in time for tea on Friday, 25 September, confidently expecting his peripatetic friends to appear at any moment on his doorstep.

* Neither Godwin at this moment, nor Hogg much later, were fully informed of Shelley's political activities at Lynmouth, or the real reasons for his sudden flight. Their understanding of Shelley's political fears and commitments, and how serious they were, suffered in consequence.

7
The Tan-yr-allt Affair

But from Llangollen the Shelleys had travelled east, deeper and deeper into Wales. Passing by the famous traveller's inn and bridge of Dolgelley, on the edge of Merionethshire, and still hearing of no suitable accommodation, they moved northwards into the wilds of Caernarvonshire and forded the great tidal estuary of Treath Bach. They were now in desolate country, of rocks and heather and sea, with a few tiny farmsteads and villages. Welsh, not English, was universally spoken. Ahead of them lay the Caernarvon peninsula, barely inhabited, which stretched out dividing Caernarvon Bay from Cardigan Bay, thus forming the upper claw of the Welsh seacoast. At the end of the peninsula lay Hell's Mouth and Bardsey Island. It was a bleak moment, and the Shelleys felt that they were beyond civilization. At this very time, rumours were flying from village to village of the savage murder of a young farmhouse maid, Mary Jones, which had recently been committed in the area. She was found hacked to death with a pair of sheep-shears. The assailant was said to be a giant man, well over six foot, who was known locally as 'the King of the Mountains'. In late August and early September, armed bands were enlisted to protect the scattered populace and search out the killer.*

Crossing a second, sand-bound estuary, Treath Mawr, they discovered them-selves to be on the site of an enormous building operation, involving nearly a hundred workmen, who were reinforcing a massive embankment across the mouth of the estuary to the little port of Portmadoc, and draining and clearing the land behind it. Continuing some two miles inland, they found themselves in the main street of a trim, newly built grey-stone village, with a central market

---

* Thomas Edwards, a six-foot-two quarry-worker from the Parry Mines, was captured while trying to cross Treath Bach at low tide below Portmeirion. While being escorted at night by six constables to Dolgelley, he again escaped, and terrorized the district for several days. He was prose-cuted by David Ellis-Nanney in the 1813 sessions, and was convicted and executed. For further macabre details, see the *Chester Chronicle*, 18 September 1812. The indictment remained in Shelley's mind during the winter.

square, two chapels, several shops, a tavern and a surprisingly imposing town hall with a classically pillared portico. All these buildings were geometrically arranged on a spacious T-shaped ground plan, and were clearly part of a harmonious and integrated design. The head of the T, formed by the town hall and the tavern, faced southwards down the length of the village, and was set flushly up against the base of a dramatic cliff of rocks and undergrowth which rose several hundred feet above the village, ending in jagged tips and pinnacles, beyond which, far out of sight, lay a stony upland moor and a natural reservoir.[1] They had fallen by chance on the site of one of the most advanced community and commercial experiments of the period. They put up at the tavern, which was called the Madoc Arms. The village was the contemporary 'wonder of Wales', the brain-child of William Alexander Madocks, Foxite Whig, reformer and speculator, and its name was, naturally, Tremadoc. Moreover, there was a house for sale.

In 1794, Madocks had rebuilt a little cottage high up on the mountainside above Tremadoc known as Tan-yr-allt (Under-the-hill). The new design was simple and delicate: a set of large, gently vaulted south-facing parlours, with bedrooms above, commanding a magnificent view across the Treath and into Merionethshire. Madocks had added a new slate roof, not conventionally steep and square, but hipped outwards in a gentle flare which formed a ground floor verandah on three sides, supported by an elegant colonnade of carved wood and lattice work. The refurbished windows were not conventional sash, but unexpectedly large casements, opening in a series of glass doors or French windows on to the verandah, and filling the rooms with air and light. To offset the bleak and mountainous aspect of its position, the house was surrounded by freshly planted lawns, vines and a rich vegetable garden, sheltering behind sun-trap walls. The verandah was encircled with thousands of old-fashioned roses (according to Madocks's specification), and the lattice-work clothed in honeysuckle, clematis and other clambering blossoms. Tan-yr-allt had originally been intended as the throne from which Madocks could watch his Great Scheme unfold in the valley below. But in 1812, threatened by accumulated debts, he was forced to sell the lease to a creditor, Girdlestone, and the house was now unoccupied.* Shelley instantly applied for the property.

After their long and uncertain travels, the Shelleys were delighted with the prospect of staying at Tan-yr-allt. The New Town and the Embankment project appealed to Shelley as a direct attempt to reform both man and his surroundings, and promised a wider and more practical view of how an ideal community might be developed. Moreover Madocks, who was at that time in London, brought

---

* Tan-yr-allt boasted the first operating water closet in the principality, although this did not prove a great sales attraction locally.

Shelley back into the orbit of the Whig ginger-group. When Shelley met Madocks's manager on the spot, John Williams, they struck up an immediate rapport. Williams promised he would do all in his power to obtain the lease of Tan-yr-allt from Girdlestone, while Shelley in his turn promised his enthusiastic support for the Embankment and appointed himself as a sort of unofficial chief of fund-raising. He also made it clear to Williams that his own prospects, once he had come of age, would be a great asset to the fund. Shelley rapidly assimilated the history of Tremadoc. William Madocks's scheme had been to reclaim and cultivate the whole estuary, by building a Grand Cob across the mile-long sea mouth. He intended to turn the new township into a centre of culture and entertainment in North Wales, with the Grand Cob as its living masterpiece, along which he hoped would run the main north–south road between Caernarvon and London. Tremadoc had been steadily built up during the Napoleonic Wars; the Grand Cob was started in 1808 and finished in September 1811, when a 'Tremadoc Embankment Jubilee', complete with roast ox, Eisteddfod and Horse Races was held. Much of the success was due to the steadiness of the local manager John Williams, who became Madocks's aide-de-camp and bosom friend. Meanwhile Madocks, entering Parliament in 1802, allied himself with the reforming wing of the Whigs, forming a close alliance with the circle of Norfolk and Sir Francis Burdett, attacking the corrupt management of the Peninsular War, and finally, seconding Burdett in the dramatic impeachment of Spencer Percival and Castlereagh in 1809. Continuing his alliance with Burdett and Cartwright, and outside Parliament with Cobbett, Madocks became a founder member of that very Shelleyan kind of association, the Hampden Clubs, in 1810.*

In February 1812 (when Shelley had been in Keswick) disaster struck when the Grand Cob's central section collapsed in the high spring tides. Madocks and Williams summoned the whole county to their aid, and put pressure on the *North Wales Gazette* to play down the possibilities of bankruptcy and failure. (This ability to muzzle the local press is important in the light of later events.) No less than 892 men with 727 horses came in response. For the time being the dam was saved, but Madocks was now in severe financial straits, and much of his property, including Tan-yr-allt, had been sold or leased over to his main London debtor, Mr Girdlestone.

So rapidly and enthusiastically did Shelley identify himself with the Embank-

---

* The Hampden Clubs were founded by Major John Cartwright (1740–1824), one of the great radical figures of the nineties. They acted both as political meeting centres and corresponding societies and were the first notable reform organizations to emerge in England since the Treason Trials of 1794. The most notable Clubs were in the industrial Midlands and North, especially Manchester and Birmingham. Shelley's idea for 'associations' reflected the Hampden pattern, and he mailed copies of his later pamphlets directly to them. See Chapters 14–15.

ment cause, that John Williams took him to an important public meeting with the Corporation of Beaumaris on Monday, 29 September, to drum up more money. Having listened to accounts of the Fishamble Street meeting, Williams presented Shelley as his main guest speaker to plead for the Embankment fund. Shelley's speech, which glowingly reflected his new-found feelings for the Tremadoc community, caused considerable local excitement and was reported at great length in the *North Wales Gazette* of the following Wednesday. The reporter himself was so enchanted that he slipped into direct speech and the present tense without noticing it. In the next issue the editor of the *Gazette* had to apologize for giving disproportionate coverage to the meeting. As reported Shelley's speech read in part:

Mr J. Williams, who had just sat down, would testify to them the sincerity and disinterestedness of his (Mr Shelley's) intentions. That man he was proud to call his friend – he was proud that Mr Williams permitted him to place himself on an equality with him; inasmuch as one yet a novice in the great drama of life, whose integrity was untried, whose strength was unascertained, must consider himself honoured when admitted on an equal footing with one who had struggled for twelve years with incessant and unparallelled difficulties, in honesty, faithfulness, and fortitude. As to Mr Madocks, he had never seen him – but if unshaken public spirit and patriotism – if zeal to accomplish a work of national benefit, be a claim, then has *he* the strongest. The Embankment at Tremadoc, is one of the noblest works of human power – it is an exhibition of human nature as it appears in its noblest and most natural state – benevolence – it saves, it does not destroy. Yes! the unfruitful sea once rolled where human beings now live and earn their honest livelihood. Cast a look round these islands, through the perspective of these times, – behold famine driving millions even to madness; and own how excellent, how glorious, is the work which will give no less than three thousand souls the means of competence. How can anyone look upon that work and hesitate to join me, when I here publicly pledge myself to spend the last shilling of my fortune, and devote the last breath of my life to this great, this glorious cause.[2]

This was certainly a valiant performance, and Shelley's health was drunk by the assembled company. To give weight to his words, Shelley's name appeared heading the list with that of William Madocks, and the local Solicitor-General David Ellis-Nanney, pledging £100 each to boost a new public subscription advertised in the same number of the *Gazette.* John Williams and Ellis-Nanney must have been delighted at the prospect of a substantial Sussex fortune being transfused into the Embankment so unexpectedly. But Shelley's financial promises were not altogether substantial. Even on the way back from this meeting, Shelley was arrested for sixty or seventy pounds of debts by the authorities in Caernarvon, and would have been immediately committed to prison if John Williams and a certain Dr William Roberts had not volunteered bail to exculpate their new found champion.*

When Shelley returned from Beaumaris a second difficulty awaited him. Mr Girdlestone had been making inquiries about his prospective tenants, and concluded that they were most unsuitable: 'you must take especial care not to let Mr Shelley into possession of the House or Furniture', he wrote to John Williams from London, 'for if he gets in, we may have great difficulties in getting him out again'.³ Girdlestone had had an unsatisfactory interview with old Westbrook – who would underwrite nothing – and he had discovered all about Shelley being 'at variance with his own family', and having offended them by marrying, as he suspected, 'much beneath him'. Girdlestone summarized: 'with a confined & dependent income, [Mr Shelley] wd. most probably be ill able to pay his rent, & wd. besides incur debts with all the tradesmen in the town which he wd. be unable to pay'. In all this, he was proved perfectly correct.

John Williams, now equally determined that Shelley live at Tan-yr-allt and organize the fund, asked Madocks to intercede with Girdlestone. Shelley explained, with doubtful veracity, that there was a 'deed in doctors' commons' stating that he should come into a large property automatically on attaining his majority. This changed Girdlestone's tune, and by 28 September he was temporizing and trying to trace the deed.† Madocks, having heard of Shelley through Williams and perhaps Burdett, was now keen for him to join the project. Williams and Shelley decided that he must at once go to London, to press his case with Madocks, to clinch the lease and to settle the Caernarvon debt. The whole party took the coach road south again.

The Shelleys put up at Lewis's Hotel, St James' Street, and remained in London for some five-and-a-half weeks, between 4 October and 13 November. On that first evening, a longed-for meeting took place, and the Shelleys dined at Godwin's in Skinner Street. It was a great success. The Godwins were pleased and intrigued by Shelley, and enchanted with Harriet. Godwin himself was immediately confirmed in the role of mentor. He approved of Tremadoc as a much safer and more solid project than Irish campaigning; but he advised Shelley to set his finances in order, especially if he wanted to contribute to the fund himself. There is some evidence that Godwin was instrumental in having

---

* The source of this debt is still a mystery. It was paid off in October with the aid of a solicitor Mr John Bedwell in London, and bail was recovered. But Dr Roberts was still applying to Shelley's executors for repayment of a further loan of thirty pounds as late as 1844.

† The 'deed' was never traced; nevertheless Shelley was definitely expecting to inherit money on his majority in August 1813.

Shelley consult the lawyer John Bedwell to advise him on his affairs and negotiate a loan of cash. Shelley applied to the Vicar of Warnham for his birth
certificate, so that a loan until his majority could be formally drawn up. At the
same time Shelley wrote to Field Place for his galvanic generator and solar
microscope, so he could set up a proper study at Tan-yr-allt.[4]

Godwin explained at some length to Shelley his own hopes for the bookshop
which Mrs Godwin was running. It was intended to supply liberal and rational
textbooks and encyclopaedias for children's education. The great problem, as
Godwin said, was an acute lack of capital financing to put the business on a solid
footing. Even Harriet understood that 'they are sometimes very much pressed
for enough ready money. They require such an immense capital. . . .'[5] It had already occurred to Godwin that his young disciple might eventually be of great
use to him in this department. Godwin borrowed on principle, for he believed
his work had a *right* to financing and was valuable to the community, justifying
his belief with the egalitarian arguments of *Political Justice*. Shelley, in his turn,
forced his acts of generosity upon others, strangely like Godwin in his disregard
for practical consequences, and insisted on the virtue of the generous act in
itself. This was, perhaps, another kind of blindness. Ironically, both men subscribed to the doctrine stated in Book III of *Political Justice* that 'morality as
has been frequently observed, consists entirely in an estimate of consequences'.[6]
The one thing that neither Shelley nor Godwin ever managed to do with any
consistency was to estimate consequences.

The Shelleys, for their part, were jubilant with their conquest. Godwin at
this time was aged 56, small, balding, well rounded, and comfortable looking,
but with narrow piercing eyes, sometimes encircled with fine round gold
spectacles, looking steadily out from a deep brow. The peak of his career had
been reached nearly twenty years previously, with the publication of *Political
Justice* and his novel of pursuit, *Caleb Williams*, in 1793-4. His daring defence of
Horne Tooke at the Pittite treason trials long afterwards endeared him to the
radical cause. Another minor peak of creative and intellectual output still
awaited him, for between 1817 and 1820, in the midst of personal and financial
crises, he published *Mandeville* and his excellent polemic, *Answer to Malthus*. At
the moment the prophet had become, as Harriet noted, 'quite a family man'.
Though somewhat brooding and imperious with his own children, and frequently strained in the company of his second wife, Mrs Clairmont, Godwin
was yet a charming and hospitable host. He enjoyed the way his own slow and
oracular manner was complemented by the rapid volleys and ascending monologues of Shelley's conversation. Again, Harriet's immediate reaction was indicative: 'We have seen the Godwins. Need I tell you that we love them all? . . .
His manners are so soft and pleasing that I defy even an enemy to be displeased

with him. We have the pleasure of seeing him daily, and upon his account we determine to settle near London. . . . G. is very much taken up with Percy. He seems to delight so much in his society. He has given up everything for the sake of our society. It gives me so much pleasure to sit and look at him. Have you ever seen a bust of Socrates, for his head is very much like that?'[7] It must have given Godwin great pleasure to have Harriet sitting looking at him, and thinking how like Socrates he was.

Hazlitt, whose little biographical essay is by far the most vivid and just contemporary portrait of Godwin in old age, observed the same gentleness as Harriet, though with more acidity. 'In private, the author of Political Justice, at one time reminded those who knew him of the Metaphysician engrafted on the Dissenting Minister. There was a dictatorial, captious, quibbling pettiness of manner. He lost this with the first blush and awkwardness of popularity, which surprised him in the retirement of his study; and he has since, with the wear and tear of society, from being too pragmatical, become somewhat too careless. He is, at present, as easy as an old glove. Perhaps there is a little attention to effect in this, and he wishes to appear a foil to himself.'[8] The remark on Godwin's clerical dissenting background is shrewd; Godwin had been educated at the seminary at Hoxton, and as a young man was a fervent disciple of the Sandemanian, John Glas.* The missionary touch of the dissenting minister never entirely left Godwin's cast of mind and personality. Equally his philosophical work always has the piercing single-mindedness of the inspired campaigning journalist, writing for a small circulation newspaper. Hazlitt wrote his essay in 1824; but at the time the Shelleys first met Godwin he was just entering his old glove period.

The menage at Skinner Street was somewhat complicated by Godwin's two marriages. The first had been in 1797 to Mary Wollstonecraft, after her desertion by the American Imlay and her return from Scandinavia. The relationship had been intensely happy and tragically brief; Mary was dead a few months later after giving birth to Godwin's first child, named after her mother. Godwin also found himself responsible for Mary Wollstonecraft's earlier child by Imlay, another girl, named Fanny. His daughter Mary and his stepdaughter Fanny were in 1812 aged 15 and 19 respectively. Mary was in Scotland, staying with relatives for most of Shelley's visit, but Fanny was at home, 'very plain, but very sensible', observed Harriet. She quickly made friends with Shelley, though strangely she seems to have been rather in awe of Harriet, almost jealous, thinking her rather a

---

* John Glas (1695–1773), a Scottish minister, founder of an extreme sect of millennial and egalitarian dissenters known as Glassites or Sandemanians. They were distinguished from their brother Moravians, Inghamites, Muggletonians, etc., by their intellectual rigour and approval of theatre and literature for didactic purposes.

'fine lady'. She was shy, slightly bullied by her father's second wife, and full of her own inferiority; Shelley's interest dazzled her, he talked to her, teased her, explained things to her, and gave her glimpses of the poet and iconoclast. Shelley spoke freely of himself, and his 'dreadful sardonic grins'.[9] It was the sort of relationship in which he was at his most gentle, most frank and most winning. The results were to be tragic.

Godwin remarried in 1803. His second wife was a widow with a powerful and determined personality, and it was a practical rather than a romantic match. Mrs Clairmont, now Mrs Godwin, ran the bookshop and wore green-tinted spectacles like Robespierre. She brought with her two children, Charles and Jane, now aged 18 and 15. A son was born to her and Godwin in 1805: William was the baby and darling of the family, and much time was spent on his education, including the construction of a miniature pulpit from which he could deliver lectures especially written by the older children.[10]

Skinner Street thus contained five children: Fanny and Mary, from Godwin's first marriage, and Charles, Jane and William, from the second. All of them were encouraged to eschew fashionable things and society; instead from an early age the Godwins took them out to dinner and theatre with their own adult friends, and taught them to be hosts to the stream of distinguished visitors: Holcroft, the playwright, and his daughter Fanny; Curran and his daughter Aemelia; Coleridge; Hazlitt; the Lambs and later Wordsworth. Characteristically all three girls went regularly to Coleridge's lectures in the winter of 1811.[11]

Godwin's most intense emotional relationship was not with Mrs Clairmont, but with his own daughter by the first marriage. The young Mary was darkly handsome, cool and precocious for her age, well read and painstakingly educated in the radical tradition by her father. Much of the affection which had been aroused in Godwin originally by the headstrong, mercurial Mary Wollstonecraft had been insensibly transferred to the daughter after her death. Mary returned this love with great warmth, luxuriating in the pride her father took in her. In many ways the relationship became too close during Mary's adolescence, and in later life it was to give her a strangely chilly detachment, as if something had been drawn out of her by her father. Later still, after Godwin's death, she reacted, and became flirtatious and capricious in a genteel slightly old-maidish way, which often embarrassed both her admirers and herself. But Mary was also fiercely intelligent, with a curiously masculine, penetrating and abstract quality to her thought, inherited from her mother, and this enabled her to be aware of her own emotional difficulties.

Mary was not spoilt as a child, however; Godwin was far too conscientious a father, treating her stringently, and deliberately sending her away for lengthy periods to stay with his friends, the Baxters, in Scotland. The other children looked up to Mary, depended on her and confided in her. This was especially true of the younger girl Jane, and the older girl Fanny: both Mary's stepsisters. Mrs Clairmont, on the other hand, distrusted her and her influence.

At the time of Shelley's first visit of 1812, Mary was away with the Baxters. Harriet merely learnt that Mary was 'another daughter in Scotland', and that she looked very much like her mother. Shelley and Harriet gazed at the picture of Mary Wollstonecraft which dominated Godwin's study. 'She is very much like her mother, whose picture hangs up in his study. She must have been a most lovely woman. Her countenance speaks her a woman who would dare to think and act for herself.'[12]

Mrs Godwin the second has largely been preserved in the venom of Charles Lamb's pen. In 1803, he had written: 'The Professor [Godwin] is COURTING. The lady is a Widow with green spectacles and one child, and the Professor is grown quite juvenile.'[13] Later, summing up her disagreeableness, her inquisitiveness, her gossiping and her managing manners, he coined the ultimate formula: 'That damn'd infernal bitch Mrs Godwin.' None the less it required considerable character to stand up to the boundless egoism of the philosopher and the relentless conditions of his financial affairs – a fact which Shelley only gradually came to appreciate for himself. Harriet's first impression was strong: 'The many trials that Mrs Godwin has had to encounter makes me very much inclined to believe her a woman of great fortitude and unyielding temper of mind. There is a very great sweetness marked in her countenance. In many instances she has shown herself a woman of very great magnanimity and independence of character.'[14] By the following summer, however, Harriet found her so disagreeable that she preferred not to visit Skinner Street. Shelley succeeded in evading her odium for slightly longer.

By the end of October the two families had become close friends, and they walked, talked and dined together. Skinner Street became Shelley's centre of gravity in London for two years. Apart from advising him how to organize his finances, Godwin was urging Shelley to adopt a thorough and systematic programme of reading and study: Shelley's correspondence and book-lists from Tan-yr-allt show the immediate fruits of this. The subjects discussed, which Godwin noted in his diary, were: 'matter and spirit, atheism, utility and truth, the clergy, Church Government, and the characteristics of German thought and literature'.[15]

One casualty of the new friendship was almost certainly Miss Hitchener, whose role as soul-mate and spiritual advisor was rapidly superseded by the influence of the greater prophet. There had already been considerable domestic friction between her and Harriet in the stress of the flight from Lynmouth, and one may suspect again, as in the case of Hogg, the steady subterranean influence of Eliza Westbrook, mining away at her sister's rivals. The inevitable consequences did not immediately come to a head, for Shelley was preoccupied with many different affairs. He was working on the Embankment fund, and appears to have tried his local influence in Sussex, though without much success. Possibly this was the last plan he and the doomed Miss Hitchener co-operated on, and he may have tried to re-install her conveniently as his agent in Hurstpierpoint.

Shelley reported back to John Williams at Tremadoc: 'I see no hope of effecting on my part any grand or decisive scheme until the expiration of my minority. In Sussex I meet with no encouragement, they are a parcel of cold selfish & calculating animals who seem to have no other aim or business on earth but to eat drink and sleep.' However he assured Williams that there was no slackening on his own behalf. 'My fervid hopes, my ardent desires, my unremitting personal exertions (so far as my health will allow) are all engaged in that cause which I will *desert but with my life*.'[16] The parenthesis about his health suggests that during the days at Beaumaris and Caernarvon he had been under considerable strain, and he was falling back on ill health as an escape clause in the way he had done at Keswick. In London, however, he was 'much better',[17] and the discussions with William Madocks were clearly accounted satisfactory on both sides, though no personal record of an interview has survived.

Another notable meeting, or rather reunion, which Shelley fitted into these busy weeks, was with his old friend Hogg. That Shelley should seek Hogg out in unknown chambers, as he did, shows the degree to which his relationship with Harriet had matured. Shelley was now confident enough to wish tentatively to draw Hogg back into his circle; but Hogg too had changed, for the discipline and the drudgery of the legal circuit had burnt off much of his undergraduate radicalism, and left him in rather bitter humour. His description of their reunion, though brief and clearly coloured up, is one of the finest and most suggestive passages in his biography. He had not seen or heard of Shelley for almost exactly a year. 'I had returned from the country at the end of October 1812, and had resumed the duties of a pleader: I was sitting in my quiet lodgings with my tea and a book before me; it was one evening at the beginning of November, probably about ten o'clock. I was roused by a violent knocking at the street door, as if the watchman was giving the alarm of fire; some one ran furiously upstairs, the door flew open, and Bysshe rushed into the middle of the room. . . . Bysshe looked, as he always looked, wild, intellectual, unearthly; like a spirit that had just descended from the sky; like a demon risen at that moment out of the ground. How had he found me out?'

The answer was that Shelley had gone to Hogg's offices at the Middle Temple. Hogg's superior was unwilling at first to give Shelley his friend's address, because he did not like the look of him, and Shelley was in one of his flashing, peremptory moods. Finally, as was later explained to Hogg, 'My clerk thought, that in a frequented part of London there could not be much danger, so I permitted him, though rather unwillingly, to write down your lodgings, and at last I gave it him. . . . I hope he did not do you any harm.' Shelley's reaction to this caution was scornful: 'Like all lawyers, he is a narrow-minded fool! How can you bear the society of such a wretch? The old fellow looked at me, as if he thought I was going to cut his throat; the clerk was rather better, but he is an ass!'[18]

With that he launched into his own affairs, 'a thousand at least of them at a time', says Hogg, 'without order, and with his natural vehemence and volubility'. Shelley stayed late, making a great noise, and finally Hogg, for fear of disturbing the people of the house, led him by the arm down into the street, where he continued talking. They arranged to meet again the next day, and Hogg, Shelley, Harriet and Eliza dined at 6 together near St James's Palace. Harriet shook hands and talked of Irish revolutions; Eliza smiled 'faintly upon me in silence'; and Shelley was late. When he came thundering upstairs he would talk of nothing but Welsh waterfalls and a new plan for them all to live together again in London. Hogg implies this was in his manner of 'habitual mystery', but in fact Shelley had reasons for keeping quiet on all subjects with political implications. He told Hogg about the Tremadoc scheme in the very vaguest terms,[19] but he said nothing of the Lynmouth affair, and – what was even more remarkable – he told Hogg nothing about his friendship with Godwin. Thirty years later when Hogg came to complete this part of Shelley's life, he was still unaware that Shelley and Godwin had ever met during that autumn. Nothing of course was mentioned about *Queen Mab*. A spring meeting was enthusiastically agreed on, and in the meantime, correspondence was re-opened.

The preparation of material for his pamphlet on Eaton, and for 'Queen Mab', had brought Shelley a new circle of friends grouped around the bookseller Thomas Hookham of New Bond Street. Unlike Hogg, they were fully apprised of Shelley's active radicalism. The most important of these was Thomas Love Peacock, then aged 27, who had already published two long poems with Hookham, *Palmyra* (1806) and *The Genius of the Thames* (1810). Peacock had been born at Weymouth, of a merchant family, and moved to London with his mother at the age of 16, where he was privately educated. He was made independent by a small annuity. His stringent scholarly humour, his prickly attitude to contemporary politics, and his immense range of reading in Italian and Greek, made him one of the most promising of the younger authors on Hookham's list. Shelley was amused to hear the stories of Peacock's own experiences in Merionethshire, where he had stayed as a kind of literary hermit the previous year, walking the mountains with a pack, reading classical authors, writing verses and staying first at a cottage near Maentwrog, and then at local inns. The seven years between them gave Peacock the authority of experience, as well as the proven ability to remain intellectually and socially self-sufficient. Shelley very much admired this and was impressed by his poetry. The friendship remained slightly formal at this time, with Shelley sending 'best Compts to Mr Peacock' via Hookham. Later he wrote directly from Wales to tell Peacock with sly amusement how he had spoken to one Welsh lady, 'in many respects a woman of considerable merits', who recalled Peacock with a frisson of disapproval. ' "Ah!" said she, "there Mr Peacock lived in a cottage near Tanybwlch, associating with no one, & hiding his head like a murderer, but" she added altering her voice to a tone of appropriate gravity, "he was *worse than that*, he was an *Atheist*." I exclaimed much against the intolerance of her remark, without producing the slightest effect. She knows very well that I am an infidel and a democrat but perhaps she *does not do me justice*.'[20] The mischievous solemnity with which Shelley narrated this little incident, with its wry conclusion about his own atheism, suggests some of the strength Peacock's friendship would eventually give him: the ability to mock his own enthusiasms, and to laugh gently at his own eccentricities. This gift was to be more important as a personal influence than a literary one. Shelley, in his turn, gave Peacock the inspiration to transform his taste for mocking personal and intellectual foibles, into a complete new literary sub-genre – the crotchet novel – with its brilliant manipulation of dialogue and polemic debate.*

Besides Godwin, Hookham and Peacock, a fourth figure was added to Shelley's London repertoire. John Frank Newton, vegetarian, naturist and Zoroastrian, was such a perfectly embodied crotchet that it is sometimes difficult to believe that he was not one of Peacock's own inventions. Shelley's meeting with him, as described by Hogg (who mistakenly set it at a later date) suitably took place on 5 November. Abandoning Godwin's drawing-room, as the sound of fireworks filled the evening air, Shelley shot out of Skinner Street with William Godwin junior, aged 9, and was led hot on the trail of the fiercest flashes and detonations, to Dr Newton's house. Newton was an old friend of the Godwin family, and he was agreeably surprised to find that young William's friend was really rather well read. Later he found out from Godwin who Shelley was, and in the following year in London they formed a regular acquaintance.

* The first of these, *Headlong Hall*, appeared in 1816, and contained recognizable caricatures of William Madocks (Squire Headlong), Southey (Mr Night Shade), Coleridge (Mr Panoscope), Hogg (Mr Jenkinson). The wildly fluctuating debates between Mr Foster the perfectibilian and Mr Enscott who believes in material degeneracy, reflect one aspect of the intellectual clash between Godwin and Shelley.

He had a large family brought up on strict naturist principles, and a neurotic wife whom Hogg idolized.

The Shelleys were now preparing to return to Wales. Harriet and Eliza had determined that Elizabeth Hitchener could no longer be a member of the group, and they saw that a showdown had to be brought off before returning to Tan-yr-allt, and Hogg's aid was enlisted. On Sunday, the 8th, Miss Hitchener was given a farewell dinner, which Hogg also attended, and it was agreed that Shelley should pay her a stipend of £100 a year, for her troubles. The private arrangement between her and Shelley was probably that she should continue to work for the cause in Sussex. But the stipend was not paid more than once, and there is evidence that a separate sum of £100 which she had loaned them in June was applied for but never refunded.[21]

When she returned to Hurstpierpoint, Miss Hitchener found that she was the subject of much laughter and scandal, and generally regarded as Shelley's cast-off mistress. Merle heard that she insisted that 'their union was purely platonic', but felt she was not generally believed. In her disappointment and shame, Miss Hitchener rather understandably turned on Shelley, writing letters threatening vengeance, the worst of which was denunciation to the government of his political schemes. Merle found her the next year in such a state that he would not have been surprised 'had her wanderings led to insanity'. In fact, Miss Hitchener's whole life showed her toughness and spirit, and it did not fail her here. She went abroad, married an Austrian officer, and finally returned to run a successful school at Edmonton, dying in 1822.[22] She looked back at her time with Shelley with fondness and regret, and referred to him as her one inspiration in life in her Poems.

Nevertheless Shelley did not come well out of this incident. It indicated a certain callous indifference to those he had grown disenchanted with, an ill omen for the future. After the way he had hymned her and begged her to join them a mere five months previously, there was a coldness about his concern, and hypocrisy in his fair-mindedness. He wrote to Hogg in jocular vein: 'The Brown Demon, as we call our late tormentor and schoolmistress, must receive her stipend. I pay it with a heavy heart and an unwilling hand; but it must be so. She was deprived by our misjudging haste of a situation, where she was going on smoothly: and now she says, that her reputation is gone, her health ruined, her peace of mind destroyed by my barbarity; a complete victim to all the woes mental and bodily that heroine ever suffered! This is not all fact: but certainly she is embarrassed and poor, and we being in some degree the cause, we ought to obviate it.' Thus far he seemed fair, but he could not forbear to add with a sudden grimace and stab: 'She is an artful, superficial, ugly, hermaphroditical beast of a woman, and my astonishment at my fatuity, inconsistency, and bad taste was never so great, as after living four months with her as an inmate. What would Hell be, were such a woman in Heaven?'[23] It has been suggested that this passage was produced for the benefit of Harriet and Eliza, who certainly read Shelley's letters to Hogg. But the phrase 'hermaphroditical beast' is a spontaneous one, and suggests a degree of sharp sexual revulsion. It is likely that Miss Hitchener met Shelley's own passionate outpourings with what amounted to a frank physical offer, since she was already the Sister of his Soul, and both were agreed on the 'Godwinian system'. Shelley may or may not have taken it up with any seriousness – the limited circumstances of their lives at this period suggest that if so, it was clandestinely done, the consequence of their walks along the rocky shores of Lynmouth, when they were observed together by the locals. In all events, poor Miss Hitchener quite clearly bore the markings of a woman scorned.

Harriet, writing to Miss Nugent in November of the once-beloved Portia, expressed a note of sharpness quite new to her, the note of a woman who is jealous. 'We were entirely deceived in her character as to her republicanism, and in short everything else which she pretended to be. We were not long in finding out our great disappointment in her. As to any noble disinterested views, it is utterly impossible for a selfish character to feel them. She built all her hopes on being able to separate me from my dearly beloved Percy, and had the artfulness to say that Percy was really in love with her, and [it] was only his being married that could keep her within bounds now.' It was clear from this, at any rate, that the sexual issue had been brought out into the open, though it was convenient for Harriet (or Eliza) to see Shelley as the victim of assault, rather than vice versa. 'It was a long time ere we could possibly get her away,' concluded Harriet, 'till at last Percy said he would give her £100 per annum. And now, thank God, she has left us, never more to return.'[24]

On 13 November 1812 the newly purified party of utopians set out for Wales stopping over night at Stratford. Shelley's mind had already moved beyond Miss Hitchener and he was turning over the radical cause once again, shaking off the dust of the city, the hateful sights of its poverty and the softness and compromises of the social round. He wrote a poem, 'On Leaving London for Wales':

Hail to thee, Cambria, for the unfettered wind
Which from the wilds even now methinks I feel
Chasing the clouds that roll in wrath behind
And tightening the soul's laxest nerves to steel!

Again he confirmed the revolutionary goal he had set himself, although now mediated through the Tremadoc project:

> . . . the weapon that I burn to wield
> I seek amid thy rocks to ruin hurled
> That Reason's flag may over Freedom's field,
> Symbol of bloodless victory, wave unfurled –
> A meteor-sign of love effulgent o'er the world.

The verse was not notably better than the Lynmouth sonnets, but the sense of a real problem being worked into expression had become more vivid. Shelley confronted his wild and undisciplined hatred of poverty and exploitation, and the dangers of involving himself in a movement that led towards violence, with greater clarity:

> Do thou, wild Cambria, calm each struggling thought;
>   Cast thy sweet veil of rocks and woods between
> That by the soul to indignation wrought
>   Mountains and dells be mingled with the scene;
> Let me forever be what I have been,
>   But not forever at my needy door
> Let Misery linger, speechless, pale and lean.
>   I am the friend of the unfriended poor;
> Let me not madly stain their righteous cause in gore.[25]

His head full of these 'visions' and 'sad realities', Shelley and his party plunged back into Wales, leaving the coachline at Capel Curig, and 'jumbled in a chaise' down the wild valley to Tremadoc, and Tan-yr-allt on the hill. 'The road passes at the foot of Snowdon; all around you see lofty peaks lifting their summits far above the clouds, wildly wooded vallies below, and dark tarns reflecting every tint & shape of the scenery above them.'[26] Three newly hired maidservants awaited them. Books and papers were unpacked; Harriet and Shelley established themselves in one of the large bedrooms with a view south over Tremadoc and the Treath, the curt square façade of Morpha Lodge, owned by the local quarry owner, the Hon. Robert Leeson, facing them across the valley on the further hill. The Ellis-Nanneys, who had helped them with domestic arrangements, paid a formal neighbourly call, and Harriet and Mrs Nanney soon struck up amicable relations, with Harriet sending over the latest London scores, music and songs. As December drew in, the weather grew wilder and colder, and the mail coaches reached them with less and less frequency.[27]

8

One Dark Night

During the winter months Shelley established a regular pattern of life that was quite new to him. He put himself under Williams's command, and walked or rode each morning to the site-office at the edge of the Embankment to help with the work. His main job seems to have been following up the promised payments made by local farmers and gentry into the Embankment fund. Some of his letter reminders still exist, and they show that Shelley took the work seriously, indeed with a degree of zeal that quickly made him several enemies. The Caernarvon solicitor, John Evans, was a person of some weight in the district who handled Madocks's financial affairs, while also acting as local agent for Madocks's creditors, such as Girdlestone. But Shelley adopted an imperious and really rather offensive manner with Evans, who had promised £50 to the fund. Shelley wrote him one reminder soon after returning to Tremadoc on 3 December 1812. About a week later, he sent a second reminder. It was hardly a masterpiece of public relations. 'Sir, In reply to a message which I sent you by Mr John Williams you asserted that you had never received my letter. – To obviate the repetition of so *singular* an occurrence I send this by personal messenger. – The substance of my former letter, was to remind you, by right of being a fellow subscriber, of your debt to the Tremadoc Embankment, which being a debt of honour ought to be of all others the most imperious, & to press the necessity of its immediate payment, to lament also the apathy & backwardness of defaulters in such a case. Sir Your Humble Sert.'[1] Turning the tables on Evans, and using the jargon of the debt-collecting agency to *him*, gave Shelley undisguised satisfaction. For it was Evans who had dealt with Shelley's own £70 debt at Caernarvon. Evans was a dangerous man to alienate, for he was influential with the local forces of law and order, and it so happened that he also was clerk to the sheriff of Caernarvon.[2]

Another of the important figures in the Tremadoc community whom Shelley managed to antagonize was the Honourable Robert Leeson. Leeson owned and directed the local quarry at Innys Towyn which supplied the Embankment with most of its stone.[3] He was the largest employer of manual labour in the area, and his attitude was tough and 'realistic', typical of the new class of capitalist owners who had lost the old eighteenth-century paternalism without gaining the new social evangelicalism – one hesitates to call it socialism – of Robert Owen of New Lanark. He was sensitive to Madocks's own financial precariousness, and while viewing the Embankment itself as a shrewd capital investment, continually put pressure on Madocks's agent, Williams, to adopt a more stringent policy towards local labour. One note he sent to Williams at this time reads typically: 'Money *must be got* as some people who never complained before are now clamorous. . . . I think John it is madness feeding so many mouths if it could be dispensed with, as most of the men eat more than their work is worth.'[4] Politically, Leeson was a hard-line Tory and a fanatical admirer of Wellington,[5] and his attitude to his labour force was characteristic of the son of a great Irish landowner,* who had been brought up to regard men on the land as nothing more than feudal peasantry. In private, he seems to have been a man of culture and intelligence, and it is perhaps significant in the light of subsequent events that Leeson had a passion for amateur dramatics, and later, when he returned to Dublin, he bought a house which contained a small theatre on its upper floor.[6]

The men themselves were not wholly inarticulate, and there is evidence of the formation of embryo unions at Tremadoc, and attempts to bargain *en masse*, with the use of strikes and walkouts. Little of this story has been preserved in documents, for like so much other early labour history of the period it was overlooked or suppressed by the educated as a peripheral movement of malcontents. One document at least, preserved on the Caernarvonshire county records, and tentatively dated May 1812 or 1813, indicates quite clearly what was going on. The note is from an unnamed local overseer, to John Williams, who was on business in London at the time.

Today about 3 clock in the afternoon all of the Towyn men Rise and Leave off the Work. My men Come Back intent to do the same. I have grate trouble to Persuade them to stop at Work and this is the very speech that I have from them. 'We are all Willing to work but we cannot work without meat and we Cannot get meat without money' – you know the terms very well. But however them did promise to stop at Work untill I have an answer to this Letter. For God sake trie to come home. It is a great pitty that all [?] are same as we is with this Great Concern at this time of the year. Indeed I am longing more for see you than I never did for my father.[7]

* Robert Leeson was the second son of the third marriage of the First Earl of Milltown, the great landowner of County Wicklow.

In such a dispute between owner and labourers, there can be no doubt with which side Shelley aligned himself. Harriet was to summarize their feelings about Leeson, that from his character and 'from many acts of his' they found him 'malignant and cruel to the greatest degree'. Shelley, with his natural bias against this kind of aristocrat, refused to have any social relations with Leeson, and the occupant of Morpha Lodge was never allowed to cross the threshold of Tan-yr-allt.[8] In such a small circle of local gentry, such a refusal was a most signal insult. Leeson, for his part, quickly came to suspect Shelley's financial probity, and distrusted his influence among the labourers in Tremadoc. Later, he was to discover, through Williams, the story of Shelley's propagandizing and pamphleteering in Dublin. His reaction to this was, not unnaturally, extremely hostile. Ultimately he came to regard Shelley as little better than a financial adventurer, a professional agitator and an unprincipled subversive. He acted accordingly.

The situation at Tremadoc quickly came to resemble the previous situations at Keswick and Lynmouth. The difference was that Shelley was no longer a visitor, but an important and active member of the community, whose very occupation in connection with the fund took him legitimately to all areas of the district. It is difficult to know how far Shelley really involved himself with the working people of Tremadoc. One commentator[9] imagines him riding from door to door; while another wonders, 'Did he dispense anti-militarism, anti-capitalism, egalitarianism, republicanism, perhaps atheism, with his five pound notes?'[10] His interest in Luddism generally, and the particular fate of persecuted Luddites during that hard winter of 1812, shows at least that he could not have been indifferent to the 'violent rioting' in the Leyn Peninsula, a mere two hours ride away, during these weeks. (Two men were subsequently executed for their part in these disturbances, in 1813.) His own letters show that he was sufficiently intimate with the local people to know about individual cases of hardships and illness, and already on 11 December he was writing to Dr William Roberts in Caernarvon asking him to make Tan-yr-allt 'your headquarters' since Shelley had 'a patient or two' in the neighbourhood.[11] This reminds one of his activities with the poor in Dublin, which always had a very decided political slant to them. Shelley made a habit of walking out at night – and talking to the labourers who used the time to cultivate their little garden patches by moonlight – an occupation at that time and that season which vividly suggests their hardship, and the inevitable subject of Shelley's conversations with them. In a note appended to one of the passages of *Queen Mab*, which Shelley was writing all this time, he observed pointedly: 'It has come under the author's experience that some of the workmen on an embankment in North Wales, who, in consequence of the inability of the proprietor to pay them, seldom received their wages, have supported large families by cultivating small spots of sterile ground by moonlight.'[12]

He argued further in the note that manual labour was constantly exploited: 'The labour requisite to support a family is far lighter than is generally supposed. The peasantry work, not only for themselves, but for the aristocracy, the army, and the manufacturers.'[13]

It was soon apparent that Shelley was resented strongly in those sections of the community influenced by men like Leeson and Evans, and that he in turn was angry and critical about much that met his eyes locally. From the start he felt that he was likely to be hounded and persecuted. 'The society in Wales is very stupid,' he wrote to Hogg, shortly before Christmas, 'they are all aristocrats and saints: but that, I tell you, I do not mind in the least; the unpleasant part of the business is, that they hunt people to death, who are not likewise.'[14] Although Williams remained friendly to Shelley, and was helping him with such things as his winter coal stock, Madocks himself does not seem to have been at Tremadoc to exert a moderating influence among the various parties. The business was to get very unpleasant indeed by the next spring.

While Shelley worked for the Embankment he was also turning his spare hours into an intensive period of study, under Godwin's general direction. The broad field was to be history, what Shelley sardonically called that 'record of crimes and miseries'.[15] Godwin argued that it depended on the selection of events one chose to make – 'it is our own fault, therefore, if we do not select and dwell upon the best'. Godwin inspired Shelley with an ambitious and active approach to his self-education which ever after informed Shelley's raging and voracious appetite for books. He especially encouraged him to ignore secondary and minor work as a substitute for the grand originals. 'A true student', Godwin told him, 'is a man seated in a chair, and surrounded with a sort of intrenchment and breast-work of books. It is for boarding-school misses to read one book at one time.' Did Shelley smile at that, thinking of Miss Hitchener? 'Particularly when I am sifting out facts, either of science or history, I must place myself in the situation of a man making a book, rather than reading books. When I have studied the Grecian history in Homer, in Herodotus, Thucydides, Xenophon, and Plutarch, together with those of the moderns that are most capable, or most elaborate, in unfolding or appreciating the materials the ancients have left us, I shall then begin to know what Greece was. I need not, of course, mention how superior is the information and representation of contemporaries to those who come after-wards. . . .'[16] Godwin firmly put Shakespeare and Milton 'at the head of our poetry', and Bacon and Milton 'at the head of our prose'. These preferences were also passed on to Shelley, though as yet he read Greek only in translation. Of Shelley's own taste, Godwin noted: '*You* have what appears to me a false taste in poetry. You love a perpetual sparkle and glittering, such as are to be found in Darwin, and Southey, and Scott and Campbell.'[17]

The immediate result of Godwin's advice and strictures was a series of enormous book-lists which went out to Hookham, and, spreading the load and also the debt, to Thomas 'Clio' Rickman, the bookseller and contributor to the *Yellow Dwarf*. Besides the works of the Greek and English classics which Godwin had recommended, Shelley was organizing his own intellectual odyssey. He ordered Aeschylus and Euripides, Sappho, Confucius, Plato, Kant and Spinoza, and various English historians including Gibbon, whose sour elegance, surprisingly, attracted him throughout his life. Next came Moore's *Hindu Pantheon* and Southey on Brazil, which interested Shelley as a revolutionary centre. There were also selected semi-scientific works, Erasmus Darwin's *Zoonomia* and *The Temple of Nature*; Lord Monboddo on *The Origin and Process of Language*; the French encyclopaedists; Trotter on *The Nervous Temperament* and on *Drunkenness*.[18] Shelley made various astronomical inquiries: 'You would very much oblige me if you would collect all possible documents on the Precession of the Equinoxes; as also anything that may throw light upon the question whether or no the position of the Earth on its poles is not yearly becoming less oblique?'[19] Shelley digested this vast load rather unevenly, as might be expected. Nevertheless, the intensive period of research bore fruit in the quite extraordinarily ranging 'Notes' which he attached to *Queen Mab*, which were to run from classical authors on atheism to essays on vegetarianism and speculations on the astronomical layout of the universe.

Despite the difficulties which Embankment affairs involved Shelley in, the composition of *Queen Mab* went on steadily. By the end of January 1813, Shelley was writing to Hookham that *Queen Mab* would be finished by March in ten cantos, and that the collection of short poems would also be ready. 'The notes to QM will be long & philosophical. I shall take the opportunity which I judge to be a safe one of propagating my principles, which I decline to do syllogistically in a poem. A poem very didactic is I think very stupid.'[20]

Of the short poems he remarked: 'Some of the later ones have the merit of conveying a meaning in every word, and these all are faithful pictures of my feelings at the time of writing them, but they are in great measure abrupt & obscure. All breathing hatred to government & religion, but I think not too openly for publication. – One fault they are indisputably exempt from, that of being a volume of *fashionable literature*.'[21]

Shelley was in an extremely didactic mood, inflamed no doubt by the visible contrast between the living conditions of the 'aristocrats and saints', and the labourers of Tremadoc who were now in the hardest part of winter, and always on the edge of starvation. It was a 'Russian' cold.[22] The persistent story, unsupported by any documentary evidence, that Shelley went out and shot a farmer's sheep caught in a bramble, may have its origin in one of Shelley's more desperate attempts to help the labourers with food. Most of his own supplies, including food and coal, were only obtained on credit from the local shopkeepers – a fact that was to make him vulnerable to better-heeled opponents. In these spartan conditions, Shelley's fanaticism was daily inflamed.

To Hogg, he was beginning to posture again in his old manner of melodramatic self-projection. Writing of his adherence to 'republicanism' he delivered a superior flourish: 'It certainly is far removed from pothouse democracy, & knows with what smile to hear the servile applause of an inconstant mob. – but though its cheek could feel without a blush the hand of insult strike, its soul would shrink neither from the scaffold nor the stake, nor from those deeds and habits which are obnoxious to slaves in Power.'[23] Through this, suitably generalized for Hogg's consumption, one can make out the lineaments of the struggle at Tremadoc.

Harriet, speaking for them all, voiced a more general disenchantment in one of her missives to Mrs Nugent, which reflected in a feminine way much of the righteous fury with which Shelley himself judged the deleterious human effect of the Embankment on the very people it was designed to benefit. 'All the good I wrote of Mr Madocks I now recant. I find I have been dreadfully deceived respecting that man.' Gazing down from the south windows of Tan-yr-allt, she wrote: 'The sea, which used to dash against the most beautiful grand rocks . . . was, to please his stupid vanity and to celebrate his name, turned from its course, and now we have for a fine bold sea, which there used to be, nothing but a sandy marsh uncultivated and ugly to the view.' She added scornfully that the Embankment 'viewed from the height looks as if a puff of wind from the mountains would send it to oblivion like its founder's name.' She deliberately took a remote and careless attitude to the very event which Williams, Leeson, Ellis-Nanney and the others most feared. Though the household at Tan-yr-allt was proud to consider itself 'the means of saving the bank from utter destruction', it was increasingly restless about the motives of the owners.[24] Shelley's passage in the affairs of Tremadoc grew less and less harmonious, and by early February he was saying that he had been 'teazed to death for the last fortnight'.[25]

Yet despite it all, Shelley still seems to have been remarkably happy at Tan-yr-allt. Harriet was now visibly pregnant, the baby was due in June, and the house seemed to him 'extensive and tasty enough for the villa of an Italian prince.'[26] In the evenings, 'when I come home to Harriet I am the happiest of the happy'.[27] He does not seem to have even considered leaving. Hogg was already invited to come to stay as early as possible in March, and to remain as long as he could. Hookham and his family had also been invited, for Shelley felt the young publisher was an important man to draw into his radical circle, and on 15 February Shelley was writing to convince him that August was much too late to arrive, why not June?[28] The only unexpected absentee from these spring plans was Godwin, who had once again fallen temporarily out of favour. Harriet summarized: 'He wanted Mr Shelley to join the Wig [*sic*] party, and do just as they pleased, which made me very angry, as we know what men the Wigs are now.' Both the Sussex Whigs, and the Duke of Norfolk himself had turned down support for Madocks's Embankment,[29] and of course Madocks himself was in disgrace. '[Godwin] is grown old and unimpassioned, therefore is not in the least calculated for such enthusiasts as we are. He has suffered a great deal for his principles, but that ought to make him more staunch in them, at least it would me.' In keeping with the spirit of the times, Harriet closed her letter to Mrs Nugent – 'Adieu, dearest friend to liberty and truth.'[30]

But around his own fireside, all was well. Shelley had even grown quite complacent about his family at Field Place, and his inheritance. 'I do not see that it is in the interest of my Father to come to terms during my nonage, perhaps even not after. – Do you know I cannot prevail upon myself to care much about it. – Harriet is very happy as we are, & I am very happy.' The regularity of retired country life seemed to suit him, and he mocked Hogg gently for his unhealthy existence. 'I continue vegetable. Harriet means to be slightly animal until the arrival of spring. – My health is much improved by it, tho partly perhaps by my removal from your nerve racking & spirit quelling metropolis.'[31] He was teaching Harriet Horace, and made Hogg promise to bring with him a copy of Ovid's *Metamorphoses* for her; in the meantime she had a 'bold scheme' of writing Hogg a Latin letter.[32] But before their schemes for self-improvement, and for uniting the little circle, could come to fruition, circumstances once again overwhelmed them.

February was a time of increasing tension at Tremadoc, for it was the month of the high spring tides. The previous year, the first winter of the completed Embankment, the disastrous breach had occurred on 14 February. Another breach this year would probably have been fatal for Madocks, who was already deeply in debt, and he would have been forced to declare himself bankrupt and abandon his whole North Wales scheme. It was absolutely essential that the workmen manned the Embankment, and kept up running repairs, with complete dedication and loyalty. Any form of labour unrest was anathema. John Williams, Leeson and the Ellis-Nanneys were all in a state of intense nervous expectation, as was the whole community. Matters were so tense that Mr Ellis-Nanney, on hearing vague rumours that part of the Embankment was improperly finished, had his wife write to Williams. Williams's reply still exists,[33] repeatedly reassuring them that nothing possible had been left undone: 'God Forbid that he should have any such an idea,' as Williams put it.

But it was just at this time that Shelley, excited by other events elsewhere in

England made a most inopportune display of his violent radical sympathies, which were greeted, in the circumstances, with more than usual outrage and horror. At the end of January, the newspapers carried reports of the execution of fourteen frame-workers, who were convicted at York for Luddite activities. Among the local gentry, such news was naturally greeted with deep satisfaction; and at Tremadoc especially there was appreciation of stern punishment meted out to mutinous labourers. But Shelley, on the contrary, was furious. No doubt he aired his views publicly at Tremadoc, and he soon decided to go further than this. On 31 January Harriet wrote to Hookham, with Shelley's direction: 'I see by the Papers that those poor men who were executed at York have left a great many children. Do you think a subscription would be attended to for their relief? If you think it would, pray put down our names and advertise it in the Papers. Put down my Sister's name, Mr Shelley's and mine for two guineas each; if this meets with your approbation we will enclose the sum.'[34] Although this was not a direct expression of solidarity with the Luddite cause, it made Shelley's sympathies only too clear.

On top of this, Shelley now began to distribute his Irish pamphlets to those he regarded as 'likely'. We do not know how far this dangerous process went, except in one vital instance. Copies were given to John Williams, whom Shelley persisted in regarding as friendly to all his ideas. From Williams, at least one pamphlet got into the hands of Leeson. We know this from the one letter surviving of an exchange between Shelley and Leeson. Leeson wrote: 'I beg to tell you that [the pamphlet] was not given to me by Mr Ashstone, nor taken by him from John Williams's house, – *but* was handed to me by John *Williams* with a remark that it contained matter dangerous to the State, and that you had been in the practise of haranguing 500 people at a time when in Ireland. So much for your friend.'[35] The fact that such inflammatory material reached Leeson, particularly with his own personal interest in Ireland and the Tremadoc labour-force, may have produced the decisive polarization of feeling within the neighbourhood. It seems clear that Leeson, presumably after serious consultation with other important figures in the district like Evans and the aforesaid Mr Ashstone, must have come to the conclusion that Shelley should be forced out of the district as rapidly as possible. There is no definite evidence for such a consultation, but subsequent events strongly substantiate it. Whether Williams himself knew anything of this, it is difficult to say; but in his position as Madocks's manager, it is easy to see how he might have had to play a double part. His essential loyalty was always to the Embankment, and not to any clique or individual. Equally, it is easy to see the motives of the Leeson faction, who disliked Shelley both in his person and in his principles, distrusted his financial promises, and feared his influence on the embryo labour movement in the village. Leeson's first move was strictly correct. He sent Shelley's pamphlet 'up to Government', together with the circumstances of the case.[36] It was the Barnstaple situation all over again.

Shelley had not learnt caution, however. As always, sensing opposition, he plunged forward. On 15 February he discovered another radical cause to champion. He had been following throughout the winter the case of the Hunt brothers, John and Leigh, who had been prosecuted for libel as the result of an attack on the character of the Prince Regent in the *Examiner* for 22 March. The case had been defended by Brougham, and Shelley had already voiced a trenchant opinion on the liberal side to Hogg: '[Brougham] was compelled to hesitate when truth was rising to his lips; he could utter that which he did utter only by circumlocution and irony. – The Solicitor General's speech appeared to me the consummation of all shameless insolence. & the address of Ld. Ellenborough, so barefaced a piece of timeservingness, that I'm sure his heart must have laughed at his lips as he pronounced it.'[37] Now he learnt that the Hunts had each been imprisoned for two years, fined £500 and ordered to supply £750 securities for good conduct over the next five years. Once again he felt required to commit himself in the most public way possible. The letter he wrote to Hookham, with its high, lashing, unshakeably righteous tone, gives us as clear an indication as anything of his mood in the last ten days at Tan-yr-allt. The violent uncompromising manner was the same, both in his letters to London and his dealings at Tremadoc; he was at bay, and he knew it.

> My dear Sir, I am boiling with indignation at the horrible injustice and tyranny of the sentence pronounced on Hunt and his brother, & it is on this subject that I write to you. Surely the seal of abjectness and slavery is indelibly stamped upon the character of England. – Altho I do not retract in the slightest degree my wish for a subscription for the widows and children of those poor men hung at York yet this £1000 which the Hunts are sentenced to pay is an affair of more consequence. – Hunt is a brave, a good, & an enlightened man. – Surely the public for whom Hunt has done so much will repay in part the great debt of obligation which they owe the champion of their liberties & virtues or are they dead, cold, stonehearted & insensible, brutalized by centuries of unremitting bondage? . . . Well. – I am rather poor at present but I have £20 which is not immediately wanted. – Pray begin a subscription for the Hunts, put my name for that sum, & when I hear that you have complied with my request I will send it to you. – Now if there are any difficulties in the way of this scheme of ours, for the love of liberty and virtue overcome them.[38]

Liberty and, characteristically, Virtue were now the watchwords. On second thoughts Shelley, ignoring his grocery bills, suggested a public advertisement in the papers, and enclosed a twenty-pound note for good measure, a daring piece of generosity.[39] With Shelley in this mood, the tides at their peak, Leeson and his friends acutely sensitive to the least shift of opinion in Tremadoc and conscious that the defence of the social order lay completely in their hands, the least incident would have been enough to bring matters to a crisis.

The week of Sunday, 19 February, blew dark and stormy; gale-force winds came in from Caernarvon Bay, and rains lashed the roads into rivers of mud. Water poured through the gullies and clefts from the surrounding mountains; communications virtually closed down; and the *North Wales Gazette* reported that a coach-driver had been blown off the top of the Capel-Curig to Shrewsbury mail.[40] The papers in February also carried another notice which either Shelley or Leeson might have observed: 'Associations for the Prosecution of Felons' were being formed in several Caernarvonshire districts, as a defence against the increasingly unsettled state of the county. Rewards for arrest were advertised, the highest of which was five guineas for information concerning 'Feloniously Breaking and Entering any Dwelling House, in the night time.'

On Friday, 26 February a triggering incident occurred. It was of an unexpected kind. Dan Healy arrived in Tremadoc, fresh from his six months' sentence in Barnstaple gaol for posting unlicensed and seditious papers. He must have been very dedicated to travel in such weather. The Shelleys welcomed him with open arms, and in Tremadoc, the story spread that Shelley's personal servant, an ex-convict, had arrived to abet his master's activities. Whether Dan himself had suspicions that the authorities had trailed him from Devon to Wales, or whether Shelley simply feared the reaction of the Leeson faction, is not known. But it is certain that Shelley expected immediate repercussions, and prepared for trouble. When he went upstairs to bed that stormy night with Harriet, he took his pair of pistols, and he loaded them.[41]

What happened next has been one of the most fiercely disputed points in Shelley biography. Afterwards, Shelley's closest friends, Peacock and Hogg, both concluded that he was suffering from hallucinations, one of the 'thick-coming fancies' which they found so convenient to cover up those parts of his career which they did not know, did not approve of, or which they simply did not understand. Their evidence is obviously partial, but they successfully distorted all subsequent interpretations.*

---

* Those adhering to the total hallucination theory include Hogg (1858), Peacock (1858) and White (1940). Jeaffreson (1885) and Cameron (1950) believe the events were fictional in a different sense: deliberately staged to extricate himself from the Embankment scheme and his Tremadoc debts. Dowden (1886), Blunden (1945) and J. Overton Fuller (1968), with a characteristically English kind of compromise, prefer to believe in an indefinite mixture of fantasy, fact and stage managing. The decisive reinterpretation was by H. M. Dowling (1961), who first recognized and explored the tense political and social circumstances at Tremadoc. For full details of all these works, see References.

The external events seem clear. During the night the house was twice disturbed; several shots were fired; at least two, and possibly more, of the large glass windows on the ground floor were smashed; the lawn outside the east front of the house was trampled and Shelley rolled in the mud; Shelley's nightgown was shot through; and one pistol ball was found embedded in the wainscot under one of the windows in the main drawing-room. By the next morning the whole household was in a state of terror and exhaustion. Shelley especially was in a state of severe nervous shock, amounting to something like nervous breakdown, and his stomach seems to have been strained or kicked during a violent struggle.[42] John Williams was called, and the Shelleys moved at once some seven miles out of Tremadoc to stay with the Solicitor General, Ellis-Nanney; they moved the same day (Saturday) without waiting for the weather to abate, or their things to be packed. Shelley wrote the following partially coherent note as they left, to Hookham. 'I have just escaped an atrocious assassination. – Oh send the £20 if you have it. – you will perhaps hear of me no more. friend Percy Shelley.'[43] To this Harriet appended a hurried explanation. 'Mr Shelley is so dreadfully nervous today from having been up all night that I am afraid what he has written will alarm you very much. We intend to leave this place as soon as possible as our lives are not safe so long as we remain. – it is no common Robber we dread but a person who is actuated by revenge & who threatens my life & my Sisters as well. – if you can send us the money it will greatly add to our comfort.'[44]

The Shelleys stayed with the Solicitor General and his wife between 27 February and 6 March.* During this time Shelley slowly recovered; he was increasingly anxious to obtain money to get himself out of Wales, and in vain he attempted to have proper inquiries into the affair instigated. But under no circumstances would he himself go back to Tan-yr-allt. One surviving letter from these ten days, to Williams, reads: 'I am surprised that the wretch who attacked me has not been heard of. – Surely the inquiries have not been sufficiently general or particular? Mr Nanney requests that you will order that some boards should be nailed against the broken windows of Tanyrallt.' He also asked Williams for a loan of twenty-five pounds. All report of the attack was suppressed from the local papers, despite the fact that their columns were showing great interest in such night incidents. By 6 March Shelley was ready to leave for Ireland. He had recovered his health, but he was now convinced that some kind of conspiracy of silence was being organized, and he had little hope of justice. News that Leeson, who was putting about a story that Shelley was only

---

* It was at this time, when he was still suffering from shock, that Shelley was supposed to have drawn the picture of the 'devil' which attacked him. He then apparently tried to burn it. For a 'copy' of this drawing, see plate 13.

trying to avoid paying his bills, had originally obtained the Irish pamphlet through John Williams only confirmed his worst suspicions.[45]

From Bangor, on the first stage of the Dublin mail, Shelley wrote to Williams that unless he did not know 'the unalterable goodness' of his heart, he would have felt 'staggered at this deceit' over the pamphlet. 'As I told you when we parted unless you are explicit and unreserved to me I am fighting in the dark.' But Shelley was no longer fighting, he was running. The moment he left the district, it was clearly to everyone's advantage to smooth things over and ask no awkward questions: the reputation of the Embankment could best be served in this way. If Shelley had stubbornly remained, the matter could not have been hushed up. At Bangor, Shelley picked up Hookham's loan, and was cheered that he was not entirely surrounded by 'the suspicion coldness and villainy of the world'. As the miles unrolled between him and Tremadoc, his confidence returned. 'I am now recovered from an illness brought on by watching fatigues and alarm,' he told Hookham, '& we are proceeding to Dublin to dissipate the unpleasing impressions associated with the scene of our alarm. We expect to be there on the 8th. You shall then hear the details of our distresses. The ball of the assassin's pistol (he fired at me twice) penetrated my night gown & pierced the wainscot. He is yet undiscovered tho' not unsuspected as you will learn from my next.' In a P.S., Shelley was once again talking of 'liberty and virtue', saying he still wanted to contribute the twenty-pound subscription to Hunt. The sight of the sea had cheered him up.[46]

After a rough and unpleasant crossing, they were safely in Dublin by 9 March, and took rooms with John Lawless at 35 Cuffe Street. The following days were spent sending a series of letters to friends, such as Hogg and Hookham, explaining in detail what had occurred at Tan-yr-allt and asking for money. It does not appear that Shelley got the twenty-five pounds from Williams. The full explanatory letter to Hookham, written by Harriet, since Shelley still felt unable to recount the events coolly and accurately without her aid, is our chief source for Shelley's version of the occurrence. As they waited for their books to arrive from Wales, Shelley was able to complete a fair copy of the manuscript of *Queen Mab* and send it to Hookham for a first reading. His comment was dry. 'I expect no success. – Let only 250 copies be printed. A small neat Quarto, on fine paper & so as to catch the aristocrats: They will not read it, but their sons and daughters may.'[47] With that, the whole party – he and Harriet, Eliza and Dan – swept out of the capital and headed for a western fastness. As far as is known Shelley took a cottage on one of the islands of the Killarney lakes, and stocked it with his library; he covered his traces well, and for the time being left behind fears of Welsh assassins, debtors and Home Office spies. There were even the 'wiles of a scorned disappointed woman' to escape, for letters had been arriving, containing news of 'desperate views and dreadful passions' from poor, abandoned Miss Hitchener.

From the mere outline of these events, it is quite clear that Shelley's actions were motivated by something far more substantial than 'a hallucination', that night at Tan-yr-allt. The overall pattern of physical shock and fear, helpless suspicion and headlong flight is only consistent with a genuine assault. Though points of detail may remain at issue, it is evident that the whole incident was a product not of psychological, but of social and political pressures, building up within Tremadoc itself, as a result of the tension connected with the Embankment, and the deep feelings of resentment and hostility which Shelley's views and actions had attracted.

Despite the contrary evidence of Peacock and Hogg, the reports extracted years after from John Williams's widow,* and the story of 'Shelley's ghost',† all the evidence which is contemporaneous with the incident unites to confirm the reality of the assault. The evidence comes under six heads. First, there are Shelley's brief notes of that fortnight to Williams and Hookham, which we have already seen. Second, there is Harriet's long and circumstantial account to Hookham written from Dublin. Third, there is a letter from Eliza Westbrook to John Williams, also written from Dublin. Fourth, there is a significant note from William Madocks to John Williams at Tremadoc commenting on the attack. Fifth, there is the suggestion of a local conspiracy of silence, supported by the actions of Williams, Leeson and Ellis-Nanney, and the extraordinary silence of the local press over the incident. Sixth, there are the serious flaws and omissions in Peacock's own version of the so-called 'hallucinations', which tend to invalidate his whole position. From the combination of all this evidence, it is possible to reconstruct in some detail, and with a good degree of certainty, the sequence of singular and unpleasant events which finally drove Shelley from Wales.

Harriet's letter of 12 March is the most detailed exposition of the events of that night. It is addressed to Hookham, but according to Hogg is one of a series of identical 'descriptive circulars'[48] which Shelley had sent to his friends, to explain what had happened. The account is therefore not tailored to one particular correspondent, but represents Shelley's absolute version of the attack. This is important, and the whole letter has the air of a careful, detailed, coldly factual deposition; at no point does it refer to the feelings of those concerned, except in the first paragraph where Harriet explains why she, and not Shelley, is writing. It is

---

* Taken perhaps twenty or thirty years after: Dowden, I, pp. 354-5.

† The ghost theory was elaborated and then 'explained' by reference to a local farmer, 'Old Robert Pant Evan', in Margaret L. Croft's article, 'The Century Magazine', October 1905. A letter from Captain S. Livingstone-Learmonth, the present owner of Tan-yr-allt, to the author, (1971), further elaborates on the family tradition of a haunting.

1 Field Place, south façade: Shelley's windows are on the first floor, to the right (*photograph by Adrian Holmes*)

2 Sir Bysshe Shelley by Sir William Beechey

3 Sir Timothy Shelley by George Romney

4 Lady Elizabeth Shelley by
George Romney

5 Margaret and Hellen Shelley
by an unknown artist

6 'The Nightmare' by Henry Fuseli

7 Robert Southey in 1804
by H. Edridge

8 T. L. Peacock by R. Jean

9 *above* Lynmouth, Devon: harbour and village. The site of Shelley's house is on the extreme left
10 Tan-y-rallt, Tremadoc: general view from the south

11 *above* Tan-y-rallt, the east windows and lawn

12 Assailant's target-view diagonally across drawing-room, from the east window to the south

13 *left* Copy of a drawing Shelley supposedly made of his Tan-y-rallt assailant. First published in *Century Magazine* 1905 — a myth in the making

14 William Godwin by James Northcote

necessary to distinguish where Harriet is recounting what she herself observed, and where she is merely giving Shelley's version. Harriet's own evidence can be regarded, *prima facie*, as sound; while Shelley's requires corroboration. The first half of the letter is as follows:

> Mr S. promised you a recital of the horrible events that caused us to leave Wales. I have undertaken the task, as I wish to spare him, in the present nervous state of his health, every thing that can recal to his mind the horrors of that night, which I will relate.* On Friday night, the 26th February, we retired to bed between ten and eleven o'clock. We had been in bed about half an hour, when Mr S. heard a noise proceeding from one of the parlours.† He immediately went down stairs with two pistols, which he had loaded that night, expecting to have occasion for them.‡ He went into the billiard room, where he heard footsteps retreating. He followed into another little room, which was called an office. He there saw a man in the act of quitting the room through a glass window which opens into the shrubbery.§ The man fired at Mr S., which he avoided. Bysshe then fired, but it flashed in the pan. The man then knocked Bysshe down, and they struggled on the ground. ‖ Bysshe then fired his second pistol, which he thought wounded him in the shoulder, as he uttered a shriek and got up, when he said these words: By God I will be revenged! I will murder your wife. I will ravish your sister. By God. I will be revenged.‖ He then fled – as we hoped for the night. Our servants were not gone to bed, but were just going, when this horrible affair happened. This was about eleven o'clock. We all assembled in the parlour, where we remained for two hours. Mr S. then advised us to retire, thinking it impossible he would make a second attack.

* His disturbed state is confirmed by Shelley's own letter of 13 March 1813. *Letters*, I, No. 230, p. 360.

† The main bedrooms are still directly above the main parlours at Tan-yr-allt.

‡ This is a clear indication of the nature of the expected crisis precipitated by the arrival of Dan at Tremadoc.

§ At this stage it is vital to notice that Shelley is dealing not with an assassin, but an intruder who is trying to escape. An intruder could only have two motives: to steal valuables, or to gather incriminating papers and pamphlets. Shelley specifically discounted the first motive; after all the household was in debt. The second motive would explain why the intruder moved from the parlour to the 'office', where Shelley's paperwork was presumably kept. We know who was interested in Shelley's paperwork at Tremadoc.

¶ This was evidently outside the glass door, on the lawn.

‖ We notice that the intruder's instinctive language is English, not Welsh; and that he is aware of the relationships within the household, though he muddled Eliza's sisterhood, and transferred it to Shelley. The stilted melodrama of the words is faintly ludicrous because of the contrasting sobriety of Harriet's account. Some commentators have suggested that this was Shelley's *alter ego* expressing his subliminal desire to murder Harriet and rape Eliza.

Up to this point, it is clear that we are really dealing with an intrusion rather than an attack. By his prudent act of assembling all his servants, and by his confident decision not to send to the village for help, Shelley showed that he was still entirely capable and in command of the situation at this point. There are two slight anomalies: the misfiring of Shelley's carefully prepared pistol, and the intruder's cry of 'revenge'.

These may be accounted for together. Other evidence indicates that the glass window of the office was smashed in the shooting; and yet strangely there is no mention by either Shelley or Harriet, or later Peacock, of any bullet mark *within* the office or billiard room. This surely suggests that the glass was smashed by a bullet travelling *outwards*, i.e. fired by Shelley as he chased his retreating enemy 'in the act of quitting the room by the glass window'. It is therefore possible that either deliberately, or in the rush of action, Shelley was muddled over the shooting roles, and reversed them in his account. In that case, what may have happened was that Shelley rushed into the office with pistols ready, and fired first. Moreover an intruder, who had come in from a storm, was more likely to have misfiring pistols than Shelley who had carefully prepared his indoors. The actual sequence would therefore read: 'Mr S. then saw a man in the act of quitting the room through a glass window which opens into the shrubbery. Bysshe fired, which he avoided. (*The glass door smashed.*) The man fired at Mr S. but it flashed in the pan. (*No bullet entered the house.*) The man then knocked Bysshe down, and they struggled on the ground.' The crucial switch involved here has the effect of making Shelley to some extent the aggressor, having used fire-arms first. This is perfectly in character. It fits the evidence better, and is the best way of explaining why the intruder threatened *revenge* as he did. Most significant of all, it explains how what began as a simple night intrusion, a search for incriminating papers, was transformed into an outright attempt at murder, preceded by a terrifying ordeal of vigilance. Harriet's letter continues:

> We left Bysshe and our manservant, who had only arrived that day, and who knew nothing of the house, to sit up.* I had been in bed three hours when I heard a pistol go off. I immediately ran downstairs, when I perceived that Bysshe's flannel gown had been shot through, and the window curtain.† Bysshe had sent Daniel to see what hour it was, when he heard a noise at the window. He went there, and a man thrust his arm through the glass and fired

---

* This caveat concerning Dan implies that in Shelley's or Harriet's opinion he could not have had anything to do with the attack. The fact that he continued in the household for several months after confirms this.

† The evidence of the nightgown is elaborated in Shelley's letter of 6 March 1813. *Letters*, I, No. 228, pp. 358–9. The hole in the curtain is not mentioned elsewhere, but if Harriet was correct in hearing only one shot, both holes must have been caused by the same bullet.

at him. Thank heaven! the ball went through his gown and he remained unhurt, Mr S. happened to stand sideways; had he stood fronting, the ball must have killed him. Bysshe fired his pistol, but it would not go off.* He then aimed a blow at him with an old sword which we found in the house.† The assassin attempted to get the sword from him, and just as he was pulling it away Dan rushed into the room, when he made his escape.‡

This was at four in the morning. It had been a most dreadful night; the wind was as loud as thunder, and the rain descended in torrents. Nothing has been heard of him; and we have every reason to believe it was no stranger, as there is a man of the name of Leeson, who the next morning that it happened went and told the shopkeepers of Tremadoc that it was a tale of Mr Shelley's to impose upon them, that he might leave the country without paying his bills. This they believed, and none of them attempted to do anything towards his discovery. We left Tanyrallt on Saturday, and staid till every thing was ready for our leaving the place, at the Sol. General of the county's house, who lived seven miles from us.[49]

This concludes the account of the second part of the attack. It seems clear that the intruder had retired after the midnight incident, and either returned himself some hours later, or, more likely, sent a friend or servant to take his 'revenge' by attempting to kill Shelley. He had waited outside the window for an opportune moment, and when Dan left the room, he broke the glass with his pistol for a clear shot and fired. A bullet that passes through the target's nightgown is not intended in jest. The evidence of the bullet hole is conclusive. One shot was fired; it passed through Shelley's nightgown, through the curtain, and into the wainscot. The physical evidence is confirmed by Harriet, and later, incidentally, by Peacock. The 'hallucination' theory finally collapses here, unless one concludes either that Harriet was deliberately lying, or that Shelley had deliberately staged this second attack and fired the shot himself. This first objection makes no sense either with regard to Harriet's known character, or her situation. The second objection assumes that in the few seconds that Dan was out of the room, Shelley had the time, the motivation and the forethought to smash in the window and

* There is no reason to dispute this misfire, if Harriet heard only one report. Shelley had probably reloaded his pistols in a hurry after the first incident; the second pistol was presumably with Dan.

† There is a tradition that Shelley used to practise his sabre cuts on a beech tree outside on the east lawn; for many years after it was said to have carried deep scars. The present beech tree is too young to remember.

‡ This seems to imply that Dan caught a glimpse of Shelley and the assailant struggling on either side of the smashed window, with the latter just getting the upper hand. Some commentators have felt that Dan discovered Shelley wrestling with his *doppelgänger*. Dan himself left no known written record.

fire a single shot that penetrated at convincing heights and angles his own night-gown, the curtain and the wainscot; then to rush back, seize the sword, smash out a window and put on a convincing display of fighting with a non-existent assailant. This makes even less sense.

In the third and last part of the letter, which follows, Harriet put her own interpretation on the events. It is here that textual evidence becomes suggestive. In his published version of the letter, Hogg had already altered the day of leaving Tan-yr-allt from 'Saturday' to 'Sunday' in order to make their flight look less urgent.[50] Peacock, in his reprinting of the letter, sustained the alteration of the date, and carefully omitted the reference to Leeson.[51] He then closed his excerpt having omitted all the subsequent part of Harriet's explanation, without a single word of comment. This effectively served to distort the whole incident for a generation of subsequent readers and biographers, by giving it the appearance of a totally unexplained, unmotivated, nightmare experience. Harriet's final paragraphs, omitted by Peacock, read:

> This Mr Leeson had been heard to say that he was determined to drive us out of the country. He once happened to get hold of a little pamphlet which Mr S. had printed in Dublin; this he sent up to Government. In fact, he was forever saying something against us, and that because we were determined not to admit him to our house, because we had heard his character and from many acts of his we found he was malignant and cruel to the greatest degree.
>
> The pleasure we experience at reading your letter you may conceive, at the time when everyone seemed to be plotting against us. When those whom we had [. . . *manuscript torn* . . .] the horrible suspicion [. . .] from the task when called upon in a moment like that. Pardon me if I wound your feelings by dwelling on this subject. Your conduct has made a deep impression on our minds, which no length of time can erase. Would that all mankind were like thee.

This, even as it stands, shows in a candid light the Shelleys' distrust of people like the Nanneys and Williams as a result of their failure to prosecute investigations. The manuscript, as it now exists in the Bodleian, has had a quarter of the last leaf torn out, effectively destroying several sentences. But that one phrase alone, 'horrible suspicion', suggests the degree of feeling and sense of betrayal. Hogg silently suppressed this phrase in his printing of the letter.[52] Hogg himself claims to have had a 'precisely similar' letter from Harriet, but lost it. This is doubtful. He admits that although he saw them both in London within a matter of weeks, 'neither Bysshe nor Harriet ever spoke to me of the assassination; and the lovely Eliza observed on this subject, as on all others, her wonted silence'.[53] Altogether, this shows Hogg's complete unreliability as a witness in the case, as he was neither Shelley's confidant, nor was he honest with what evidence he did hold.

Peacock, with his suppression of the Leeson references, is little better. He is more damaging though, for while Hogg is frequently untrustworthy, Peacock is usually not only reliable, but psychologically perceptive. His own statement of denial on the matter, which has been very influential, concludes the physical evidence.

> I was in North Wales in the summer of 1813, and heard the matter much talked of. Persons who had examined the premises on the following morning had found that the grass of the lawn appeared to have been much trampled and rolled on, but there were no footmarks on the wet ground, except between the beaten spot and the window; and the impression of the ball on the wainscot showed that the pistol had been fired towards the window, and not from it. This appeared conclusive as to the whole series of operations having taken place from within. The mental phenomena in which this sort of semi-delusion originated will be better illustrated by one which occurred at a later period. . . .[54]

Thus Peacock originated the 'hallucination' theory.

Peacock's objections, by themselves so apparently complete, disappear at once when they are placed in context. Since 'torrents of rain' had been pouring down all night, a single set of footprints across a lawn made at about 11 p.m. would certainly have disappeared by daylight eight or nine hours later. Besides, Tan-yr-allt was – and still is – flagged on three sides by large paving stones nearly six feet broad which make up the floor of the verandah. There was nothing to prevent the intruder from dodging around the corner of the house on these flagstones and plunging into the shrubbery without trace.

The impression of the ball on the wainscot is explained by the layout of the house. It appears that Peacock was shown a bullet mark on the wainscot *below one of the windows*, and he concluded that the pistol had been fired by Shelley *at that window*. On the contrary, the layout of the windows in this corner room is such that if a shot were fired directly through one of the eastern windows it would – unobstructed – cross the room diagonally and go out of the southern window. The shot in this case was fired through the eastern window, on a downward trajectory, holed Shelley's nightgown, and passing through the curtains of the southern window finally embedded itself just below in the wooden wainscot. This is the mark that Peacock saw. In effect then, Peacock's evidence, far from discrediting Shelley's story, actually goes to prove in detail how the shooting occurred: precisely as Shelley himself stated, 'the ball of the assassin's pistol . . . penetrated my nightgown and pierced the wainscot'.[55]

Both Peacock and Hogg claimed that 'persons acquainted with the localities and the circumstances' did not believe any shooting had taken place. In particular Peacock seems to imply by 'persons who had examined the premises on the following morning', the Embankment manager John Williams. (He was however, like Hogg, studiously careful to avoid all names.) This claim was allowed to stand, and was assumed to be true by all biographers until in 1961 conclusive evidence to the contrary was obtained.[56] There is an undated letter from William Madocks to Williams, which internal evidence shows was probably written from London in the late spring or early summer of 1813. After referring to various business matters, Madocks wrote: 'How could Shelly [sic] mind such a contemptible trick as had been played off on him to get him out of the Country on account of his liberal principles. Whoever the hoxters are, it is a transportable Offence, if discovered. I will write fully in a day or two after Monday, when the Committee of Creditors meet again.' This letter not only shows conclusively that Madocks believed an attack had occurred (which Medwin later denied[57]), but much more important, it shows that his manager John Williams, the chief man on the spot, had sent a full account of the affair, *also believing in it at the time.* The one discrepancy seems to be in the reported seriousness of the matter, for Madocks calls 'a contemptible trick' what was clearly a murderous attack in the second instance. Probably Williams had implied that the shooting had been meant as an attempt to frighten, thus starting in embryo what gradually became the fully fledged joke of the 'ghost' at Tan-yr-allt.* Nevertheless, Madocks realized that what had occurred was 'a transportable Offence, if discovered'. In his last caveat, the conspiracy hunter might perhaps find a hint from Madocks to his manager that things would be best smoothed over.

The 'hoxters', needless to say, have never been discovered. Circumstantial evidence, and the undoubted suspicion of the Shelleys, point towards some kind of sortie organized either by Leeson himself or those within his sphere of influence. There is also the possibility that Home Office agents were involved, though these speculations are very far from proof. What does emerge is the certainty that an intrusion, and then a murderous attack did take place at Tan-yr-allt on the night of 26 February 1813, and that these were motivated by personal and political hostility to Shelley's radicalism. It is my own belief that Harriet's letter is substantially accurate on all points, except for the details of the exchange of shots during the first intrusion.

It also seems possible that Shelley was not only shot at during the second

---

* H. M. Dowling has followed up some interesting letters where the reward for the 'Tan-yr-allt ghost', dead or alive, was humorously discussed: but these all date from several years after, like the best legends. Talking of ghosts, however, one recalls Leeson's propensity for amateur theatricals.

encounter, but was taunted and terrified by some deliberately contrived theatrical 'apparition'. Because it succeeded to a great degree, he and Harriet may have chosen to suppress reference to this side of the affair, although imaginatively the experience remained with him. Certainly something horrific entered a number of his poems and was later to colour his account of the affair as he gave it in Italy when 'the scene at the inn in "Count Fathom" was hardly surpassed in horror by the recital Shelley used to make of the circumstances'.[58]

In April, from Dublin, Eliza Westbrook, who always insisted that the shooting had been 'a frightful fact',[59] wrote to Williams herself. 'My good friend though disappointed you cannot be surprised at our not returning, the unpleasant scenes which occurred there, would ever make that situation disagreeable, lovely as is the spot by nature, the neighbourhood is too corrupt for us ever to take delight in Tan-y-rallt [sic] again, particularly as a fixed residence.'[60] Even as Eliza signed and directed this letter from Cuffe Street, Harriet was sealing up the last of their baggage, Shelley was scrawling a note, and the coach was drawn up at the door ready to whisk them to Killarney.

Later, resting in their hidden lakeside cottage, in the windy March days, Shelley had time to look over the last twelve unstable months of their lives, with all its sudden arrivals and hasty departures, its schemes and its failures and its alarms. Above all, he brooded over the Tremadoc project, the moral and political corruption of this ideal progressive community, and the terrifying sequel of revenge that the tyrants of the community had unleashed upon him, almost costing him his own life – not to mention the threat to Harriet's. Moreover, it was more than his and Harriet's lives at stake now; there was the unborn child to be considered. Gradually, the centre of his mental gravity was shifting. It was one of the decisive changes of his life. He wanted to settle down again; the draw of London, the draw of the centre, the draw of Godwin and Hookham's bookshop, the draw of a reconciliation with his family even, became stronger and stronger. He felt he wanted to have done with travel, exile, missionary schemes. He wanted to work, to project reform and to write. He wanted security for his wife and child. He wanted no more terrors in the night. Political activism, the direct action of Dublin and Lynmouth and Tremadoc, had lost its attraction and its force. His radicalism was becoming more tempered, more sophisticated, more patient, more oblique. In conformity with the great principle he recognized in material nature around him, he himself was changing according to Necessity. The real importance of the Tan-yr-allt affair, its final reality, lay in the painful force with which all these considerations were brought home to him.

Their effect was lasting. For the next twelve months, in complete contrast to the previous twelve, Shelley's life was to centre fundamentally on London and the Home Counties. Not until another spring came round did the old restlessness finally reassert itself. As for political activism, he never again returned to it. His interest in politics, his commitment to the radical cause and his relentless drive to publicize subversive viewpoints, were established and consecrated for the rest of his life. But from now on Shelley regarded himself as a mouthpiece rather than as an instrument for political change. In a famous later phrase, he became the 'trumpet of a prophecy', but not the sword. Though his old Illuminist belief in the political force of the small, radical community, the commune of like spirits, did not slacken – in fact it increased steadily – his trust and confidence in the larger democratic community was shaken. It came to depend very much on his personal mood; when he was well and optimistic he trusted it implicitly; but when he was, as so often, ill or depressed, he regarded it and its leaders with distrust, and a cynicism close to despair.

9
A Poem and a Wife:
Queen Mab 1813

Shelley's reveries were suddenly interrupted towards the end of March by the arrival of a note from Hogg, who had come to Dublin, and was impatiently awaiting them at Lawless's. His old friend Hogg, and the lights of the metropolis, suddenly looked infinitely attractive. Leaving Eliza with Dan to follow at a more normal pace, Shelley and Harriet seized a chaise and horses and set out on the evening of the 28th. Without Eliza's matronly presence it was quite like a second elopement. Driving through the night, they reached Cork at 1 a.m. on the 29th,[1] and without pausing for sleep took their seats on the Dublin mail that Tuesday morning. By 3 o'clock on Wednesday afternoon they had reached the city, only to find that Hogg had himself departed for London the previous day. Shelley roundly blamed 'the inconceivable blindness and matter of fact stupidity of Lawless' – 'had you stayed one day longer, you would have heard the words of sincerity and friendship from my own lips'.[2] It appears that in his anxiety to cover his tracks, Shelley asked Lawless to keep his Killarney address secret from all inquiries – and had forgotten or omitted to except Hogg. Shelley was not in the mood to be obstructed by minor considerations of time and distance. He borrowed 'a small sum of money', arranged a sea-passage for Harriet and himself, and sailed out of Dublin on Friday morning, 2 April. Eliza, Dan, books and luggage were all forgotten, left to make there own journey to England by the Freight Route from Cork to Bristol.[3] Ahead of him raced a message: '. . . Tomorrow evening we embark for Holyhead. . . . Of course you will not write to us here. Above all do not send, or dream of procuring for us any money; we will do these matters very well. The property of friends at least is in common. On Monday evening we shall be in London. . . . My dear friend, all happiness attend you.'[4]

Harriet and Shelley reached London late on the evening of Monday, 5 April, and drove straight to Westbrook's at Chapel Street. Shelley fired off a quick greeting to Hogg, and the two friends were united early the next morning.

With Harriet's baby due in June, Shelley's majority in August and *Queen Mab* to be put through the press, Shelley decided to take up strategic but neutral ground in central London where Harriet could be comfortable and he could quietly write letters, correct proofs and compose his 'Notes'. They took a suite of rooms at Cook's Hotel in Albemarle Street, and settled in. They were eventually joined by Dan and a disgruntled Eliza. Little record remains of these months, except 'the bustle of the city' and Harriet's slightly irritable complaints about the noise made by the two waiters who came to set and serve dinner in their rooms.[5] Hogg, Hookham and probably Peacock were regular visitors. But they did not bother to write to Lawless (who had since been committed to prison) or their other friends in Dublin; and strangest of all it appears from Godwin's Diary that he and Shelley did not meet until 8 June when Godwin found him at John Newton's taking tea and discussing vegetarianism. During this period they had all, according to Harriet, 'taken to the vegetable regimen again'.

The next few weeks Shelley spent editing and correcting *Queen Mab*, and drafting the 'Notes'. Two hundred and fifty copies were run off, probably towards the end of May, 'Printed by P.B.Shelley, 23 Chapel Street, Grosvenor Square, 1813.' Hookham had, in the end, concluded that it was too dangerous to carry such a work under his own imprint. The full title page was given: 'Queen Mab; a Philosophical Poem; with Notes. By Percy Bysshe Shelley. Ecrasez l'Infame!, *Correspondance de Voltaire.*' The 'infame' of Voltaire was the Church in general; but the same phrase had also been adopted by the Illuminists as its motto referring specifically to Christ. The title was complete with a Latin tag from Lucretius, and Archimedes's famous aphorism in Greek: 'Only give me a place on which to stand, and I shall move the whole world.' The idea of the search for a *place*, from which he could launch his ideas of changing society, was to become increasingly important for Shelley. It meant both the search for a philosophical standpoint, and the search for a literal geographical location where he could live and write unmolested. *Queen Mab* was being distributed by July.

The whole work was dedicated to Harriet with a typically Shelleyan flourish of generosity:

> . . . thou wert my purer mind;
> Thou wert the inspiration of my song;
> Thine are these early wilding flowers,
> Though garlanded by me.

On 21 May she broke her silence to Dublin, writing to Catherine Nugent from Cook's Hotel: 'Mr Shelley continues perfectly well, and his Poem of "Queen Mab" is begun [to be printed], tho it must not be published under pain of death, because it is too much against every existing establishment. It is to be privately distributed to his friends, and some copies sent over to America. Do you [know] any one that would wish for so dangerous a gift?'[6]

This was very much the light in which Shelley himself regarded his first major production. *Queen Mab* is essentially subversive in intent, vigorously polemic in attack, and revolutionary in content and implication. Its main targets, constantly expressed in abstract categories, are, in order of importance: established religion; political tyranny; the destructive forces of war and commerce; and the perversion of human love caused by such chains and barriers as the marriage institution and prostitution. Secondary themes carry a strong puritan undercurrent, involving temperance and vegetarianism, republican austerity, and righteous moral independence of judgement. For all its irreligion, which is in many places extremely violent, the poem and the 'Notes' are fundamentally missionary in their manner of address with many overtones of sectarian tract writing. This is the real substance of *Queen Mab*, and it is only partly softened and obscured by the introductory machinery of the Fairy Queen, the sparkling cosmological settings, and the eruptions of exotic phrases, imagery and rhythms which are imitated from Southey's oriental epics. Shelley had commented to Hogg: '. . . I have not been able to bring myself to rhyme. The didactic is in blank heroic verse, & the descriptive in blank lyrical measure. If authority is of any weight in support of this singularity, Milton's Samson Agonistes, the Greek Choruses, & (you will laugh) Southey's Thalaba may be adduced. . . . I have not abated an iota of the infidelity or cosmopolicy of it.'[7]

What Shelley was preaching came to be understood by his friends, and by his enemies, as a vision of the good life built on atheism, free love, republicanism and vegetarianism: a combination of the enlightened, the millennial and the cranky.

The poem consists of nine cantos. After the two introductory cantos, Canto III attacks Monarchy; Canto IV attacks warfare and political Tyranny; Canto V attacks economic and commercial exploitation; Cantos VI and VII attack priestcraft and religion in general, and Christianity in particular. The remaining cantos enclose the whole poem in visionary machinery of past and future civilizations.

There are seventeen notes, eleven of which are quite brief, and six of which are fully developed essays. The six essays are on the labour theory of value (Note 7); on the theory and practice of free love (Note 9); on Necessity in the moral and material universe (Note 12); on atheism (Note 13, a reprint of the Oxford pamphlet); on Christ and Christian doctrine (Note 15); and on vegetarianism (Note 17). As parts of these essays, the 'Notes' also contain long quotations in the original from Pliny, Lucretius, d'Holbach, Spinoza,

Bacon and Plutarch. Altogether the 'Notes' are almost equally as long as the poem.

The poetry and the prose are closely interwoven in argument, and the reader is constantly aware of a strong pressure of cross-reference which forces him to move back and forth between the two forms, and between the various cantos. The aim of the whole work is argumentative and philosophical rather than poetical. Everywhere the poetry is subordinated to the ideas. The poetry lies not so much in the surface effects of the language, but in the sustained and occasionally brilliant attempt to bring together, relating, comparing and combining, information from enormously varied sources: historical, ethical, astronomical, theological, political and biological. The poetry lies in the energy and fire with which Shelley attempts to weld unity out of diversity. *Queen Mab* is no less than an attempt to state the basis for an entire philosophy of life, an active and militant view of man confronting his society and his universe.

The attitudes expressed in the work are drawn from many previous writers, and clearly reflect the pattern of Shelley's reading since spring 1811. But these writers are not in fact those normally accredited with influencing Shelley. In particular the influence of Godwin is local, rather than, as usually stated, dominant. Shelley's attitude to nature, the material universe and the functioning of natural processes is drawn from Lucretius's *On the Nature of Things* and Baron d'Holbach's *Système de la Nature*, backed up with detailed information and statistics from the new range of 'Encyclopedias'. With regard to man's role in society, its political, ethical and economic aspects, the influences are more diverse, but the most powerful shapers of Shelley's thinking are the scepticism of Hume and the militant republicanism of Tom Paine. These are supported on specific issues such as free love and labour theory by writers as different as Adam Smith, Mary Wollstonecraft, Lord Monboddo, Godwin, Lawrence and Trotter (*On Nervous Diseases*).

The conception of such a total approach to human knowledge was encouraged in Shelley by the reading of Count Volney's notorious vision of corrupt society, *The Ruins of Empire*, and Erasmus Darwin's poems of science and society. Many of these influences are not wholly absorbed or digested, and the 'Notes' especially have something of the texture of a private anthology. Nevertheless, there is no poem of the period in England to compare in originality of reach and conception with *Queen Mab* as a whole, and it entered the small radical repertoire of key books recognized by the next generation along with Volney's *Ruins*, Paine's works and Byron's *Cain*.[8] It was an eccentric, uneven and very immature work; and yet it was unique.

Despite its incidentally poetical 'beauties' and exotica, the overwhelming impression is one of anger and accusation. In this the poem reflects much of the personality of the author. At its best this can reach oracular heights of eloquent indignation:

'Then grave and hoary-headed hypocrites,
  Without a hope, a passion, or a love,
  Who, through a life of luxury and lies,
  Have crept by flattery to the seats of power,
  Support the system whence their honours flow. . . .'[9]

Harnessed to Shelley's fundamentally egalitarian outlook, this indignation takes on the quality of driving political polemic:

'Nature rejects the monarch, not the man;
  The subject, not the citizen: for kings
  And subjects, mutual foes, forever play
  A losing game into each other's hands,
  Whose stakes are vice and misery.
  The man
  Of virtuous soul commands not, nor obeys.
  Power, like a desolating pestilence,
  Pollutes whate'er it touches; and obedience
  Bane of all genius, virtue, freedom, truth,
  Makes slaves of men, and, of the human frame,
  A mechanized automaton. . . .'[10]

The sharp sting of Shelley's puritanism is never very far from the argument, and frequently breaks out with all the rhythms and menaces of religious revivalism. Here, for instance, he addresses the priests and princes of political and commercial power:

'. . . Are not thy days
  Days of unsatisfying listlessness?
  Dost thou not cry, ere night's long rack is o'er,
  "When will the morning come?" Is not thy youth
  A vain and feverish dream of sensualism?
  Thy manhood blighted with unripe disease?
  Are not thy views of unregretted death
  Drear, comfortless and horrible? Thy mind,
  Is it not morbid as thy nerveless frame,
  Incapable of judgement, hope, or love?'[11]

The posture of attack is carried over into the 'Notes', where it is often expressed with sardonic scorn. Shelley observed that the sun is 95 million miles from the earth, and that light, which 'consists either of vibrations propagated through a subtle medium, or of numerous minute particles' takes a mere eight minutes seven seconds to pass between them. In contrast it takes 'many years' for the light to travel from the nearest star, and hence the material universe must surely contain a 'plurality of worlds' within 'indefinite immensity' (Note 2). Taking into account these modern astronomical considerations, he concludes:

It is impossible to believe that the Spirit that pervades this infinite machine begat a son upon the body of a Jewish woman; or is angered at the consequences of that necessity, which is a synonym of itself. All that miserable tale of the Devil, and Eve, and an Intercessor, with the childish mummeries of the God of the Jews, is irreconcilable with the knowledge of the stars. The works of His fingers have borne witness against Him.[12]

The theme of free love provides the most successful example of the way in which Shelley managed to interrelate his poetry and his prose. *Queen Mab* opens in Canto I with the presentation of the sleeping girl, Ianthe, a picture of Harriet, whose dream is to form the substance of the poem. The lover regards her with deep physical tenderness and desire:

Her dewy eyes are closed,
And on their lids, whose texture fine
Scarce hides the dark blue orbs beneath,
The baby Sleep is pillowed:
Her golden tresses shade
The bosom's stainless pride,
Curling like tendrils of the parasite
Around a marble column.[13]

This description is echoed at the close of the last canto, when Ianthe awakes from her dream, and the blue eyes open to confront and welcome Henry's (Shelley's) 'looks of speechless love'. The theme of free love is thus argued against the background of a warm and personal realization of a love relationship between two individuals. In the opening four cantos there are many references to the perversion, frustration and incapacitating effect of love caused by tyrannical systems of power and belief, both theological and political. In canto v, the cheapening of sexual love is presented directly as one of the consequences of a corrupt commercial system:

Even love is sold; the solace of all woe
Is turned to deadliest agony, old age
Shivers in selfish beauty's loathing arms,
And youth's corrupted impulses prepare
A life of horror from the blighting bane
Of commerce; whilst the pestilence that springs
From unenjoying sensualism, has filled
All human life with hydra-headed woes.[14]

Shelley's position here would at first appear to be fairly orthodox; he is attacking prostitution, venereal disease and promiscuity – all three of which were commonplaces of Regency society. But he then appends a note, which opens up the subject in a far more radical way. This is perhaps the greatest short statement on the subject of free love. It begins with a paean:

> Love is inevitably consequent upon the perception of loveliness. Love withers under constraint; its very essence is liberty; it is compatible neither with obedience, jealousy, nor fear: it is there most pure, perfect, and unlimited, where its votaries live in confidence, equality and unreserve.[15]

From here, Shelley goes on to argue that the 'sexual connection' should only last as long as partners love each other. 'Any law which should bind them to cohabitation for one moment after the decay of their affection would be a most intolerable tyranny.' The marriage institution – let alone the Christian idea of 'mortifying the flesh for the love of God' – is just such an intolerable tyranny. Constancy itself has no virtue, and 'there is nothing immoral in separation'. Shelley summarizes this argument:

> Love is free: to promise for ever to love the same woman is not less absurd than to promise to believe the same creed: such a vow in both cases excludes us from all enquiry. The language of the votarist [of marriage] is this: the woman I now love may be infinitely inferior to many others; the creed I now profess may be a mass of errors and absurdities; but I exclude myself from all future information as to the amiability of the one and the truth of the other, resolving blindly and in spite of conviction to adhere to them. Is this the language of delicacy and reason? Is the love of such a frigid heart of more worth than its belief?

Considering this belief in its domestic light, Shelley makes shrewd points about the children of unhappy marriages, and the erosive effects of domestic quarrelling. 'The early education of their children takes its colour from the squabbles of the parents; they are nursed in a systematic school of ill-humour, violence and falsehood.' Of the relations between husband and wife, he writes with equal perception: 'The conviction that wedlock is indissoluble holds out the strongest of all temptations to the perverse: they indulge without restraint in acrimony and all the little tyrannies of domestic life, when they know that their victim is without appeal.'

Next Shelley attacks the 'fanatical idea of chastity', which he always argued led necessarily to prostitution, 'destroying thereby all those exquisite and delicate sensibilities whose existence cold hearted worldings have denied; annihilating all genuine passion, and debasing that to a selfish feeling which is the excess of generosity and devotedness'. Of the convention of chastity outside marriage, he writes:

> Chastity is a monkish and evangelical superstition, a greater foe to natural temperance even than unintellectual sensuality; it strikes at the root of all domestic happiness, and consigns more than half the human race to misery, that some few may monopolize according to law. A system could not well have been devised more studiously hostile to human happiness than marriage.

What then did Shelley propose to put in its place? Shelley was aware that he would be accused of preaching promiscuity and the destruction of the social network, but he would not be drawn to speculate far on the wider implications of his views.

> I conceive that from the abolition of marriage, the fit and natural arrangement of sexual connection would result. I by no means assert that the intercourse would be promiscuous: on the contrary, it appears, from the relation of parent to child, that this union is generally of long duration, and marked above all others with generosity and self-devotion. But this is a subject which it is perhaps premature to discuss. That which will result from the abolition of marriage will be natural and right; because choice and change will be exempted from restraint.

This essay on free love typifies Shelley's method of drawing on and combining several writers. The emphasis on the psychological and spiritual importance of 'freedom' and 'choice' comes from Godwin; the critique of the destructive effects of the conventional marriage relationship comes from Wollstonecraft and Chevalier Lawrence; the appeal to the 'natural' processes of change and constancy reflect Lucretius and Rousseau; the violent cut at the 'monkish' and 'christian' attitudes to physical love have Gibbon for their historical authority. But the passion and edge in the tone of the argument, the mixture of logic, sarcasm and urgency, is wholly Shelley's. The essay ends with a memorable, and faintly mischievous image:

How would morality, dressed up in stiff stays and finery, start from her own disgusting image should she look in the mirror of nature!

The theme is now returned to the poem, where it is picked up again in the final Canto IX, in which Shelley is celebrating the vision of a politically and morally revolutionized world, in which 'the habitable earth is full of bliss',[16] and 'all things are recreated, and the flame / Of consentaneous love inspires all life'.[17] Describing sexual love under this new dispensation, Shelley imagines how the conventionally profane has become naturally sacred:

'Then, that sweet bondage which is Freedom's self,
And rivets with sensation's softest tie
The kindred sympathies of human souls,
Needed no fetters of tyrannic law:
Those delicate and timid impulses
In Nature's primal modesty arose,
And with undoubted confidence disclosed
The growing longings of its dawning love,
Unchecked by dull and selfish chastity,
That virtue of the cheaply virtuous,
Who pride themselves in senselessness and frost. . . .

Woman and man, in confidence and love,
Equal and free and pure together trod
The mountain-paths of virtue, which no more
Were stained with blood from many a pilgrim's feet. . . .'[18]

The handling of the free love theme is characteristic of much of the strength and weakness of the whole work. The prose notes are constantly more powerful and effective than the long-drawn Miltonic or Southeyan rhetoric of the verse. Ideas are diffused by abstraction and repetition. The reader, however much he sympathizes with Shelley's position, cannot be unaware of immaturity and inconsistency of thought, and a tendency to approach real human problems in a spirit of scornful, bookish brilliance. Shelley's attitude to love is marred by two obvious blank spots. The first is his blindness to the intrinsic value of constancy in human relations, so that loving has the chance to develop from a static 'sweet sensation' into a cumulative process of discovery and exploration. We notice that Henry's love is 'speechless'. An earlier moralist and lover, Richard Steele, had observed, 'to love her is a liberal education'. Shelley, less experienced, believed that 'affection' could simply 'decay' – presumably he imagined a painless, balanced and simultaneous process on both sides. His second blindness was to the way in which children made a fundamental alteration to the direction and responsibilities of a love relationship. Shelley was to remain faithful to his free love principles throughout his life, but he was to pay dearly – and make others pay dearly – for his personal blindness in both these respects.

Queen Mab was, however, to have a life quite independent of its author's. In the twenty-five years from its first printing, this was undoubtedly the most widely read, the most notorious, and the most influential of all Shelley's works. It was not read by 'the sons and daughters of aristocrats', nor was it read for its poetic qualities; it was read by middle-class and working-class radicals in cheap pirate editions. The poem was advertised, extracted and discussed in the radical papers such as Richard Carlile's *Champion* and *Republican*; and established itself as a basic text in the self-taught working-class culture from which the early trade union movement of the 1820s, and the Chartism of the thirties and forties was to spring. The Owenite interest in Shelley is well known, and Thomas Cooper, the 'Chartist Rhymer' placed Shelley in the pantheon of republican and visionary poets alongside Milton and Byron.* Bernard Shaw was told by an old Chartist that 'Queen Mab was known as the Chartists' Bible' – an evangelical role for which it was well-suited.[19]

Apart from these hints, it is difficult to show exactly how important Shelley's poem became in circles that have left little written historical record, despite the brilliant pioneering work of E.P.Thompson. But the complicated and largely underground printing history of *Queen Mab* gives some indication. Of the original 250 copies Shelley distributed about seventy in England, Ireland and America. When the radical booksellers bought up the remainder in spring 1821, Richard Carlile says there were 180 left.[20] The publisher Clark brought these out of the genteel selling market, and under his own imprint (which he simply pasted over the title page) he found he was able to sell them off among the radical working-class readership of the *Republican* within a few months. When he was prosecuted by the Vice Society, he desisted and Carlile then set up and printed a new edition towards the end of 1821; Trelawny found one copy in a Geneva bookshop and took it over the Alps to Shelley. (Shelley's reaction belongs to another part of the story.) This sold so well, and was so satisfactorily threatened by the same Vice Society that Carlile was bringing out his second edition in boards at the 'reduced price' of 7s. 6d. in February 1822. By December 1822 there were no less than four entirely separate editions of *Queen Mab* on sale, and Carlile was cautioning readers against other 'imperfect editions', and advertising his own which now had the 'Notes' 'all translated'. This was a great advance. Carlile's advocacy was straightforward:

---

* It is also interesting to note Cooper's admiring reference to another of Shelley's political poems, *The Revolt of Islam* (1817). See his *Purgatory of Suicides*, written in Stafford jail, 1845, Canto II, stanza 7. Chapter 15.

Queen Mab is a philosophical poem in nine cantos, and is remarkably strong in its exposure and denunciation of Kingcraft and Priestcraft. Lord Byron calls it a poem of great strength and wonderful powers of imagination; and, with his Lordship, we differ from some of the Author's metaphysical opinions. However it is upon the principle of free discussion and giving currency to every thing that is valuable, that the present publisher has taken up the publication. . . . In addition to the Poem itself, there are Notes by the Author, of equal bulk, equal beauties, and equal merit. Every thing that is mischievous to society is painted in this work in the highest colours.[21]

Carlile, though suggesting reservations regarding Shelley's outright attitudes to atheism, marriage and vegetarianism, cheerfully went ahead with the dangerous business of combating the Vice Society in the courts; he had been to jail before, and it held no terrors. Altogether Carlile published four separate editions in the twenties. Other important editions in this decade were Brook's reprint of 1829 from an original 1813 copy, and the mysterious 'New York' edition of 1821 under the imprint of William Baldwin.[22] * In the thirties, the first definitive American edition appeared, published by Wright and Owen, New York 1831, with translated 'Notes'. The following year, 1832 – the year of Reform – saw the appearance of perhaps the most important underground edition of all, under the imprints of Mrs Carlile and Sons (Mr Carlile being in jail). This was a cheap, pocket-size version, intended for serious study, with the 'Notes' appended directly to the verse as footnotes or prose commentary, and the long quotations from French, Greek and Latin fully translated. This was the classic Chartist's copy, taken over in 1833 by the Owenites, and reprinted constantly by the great radical publishers of the 1840s, Heatherington and Watson.[23] The number is not certain, but between 1821 and 1845 it has been reckoned 'fourteen or more' separate editions were published. At the same time, it has been calculated that between 1823 and 1841, the working-class and radical periodicals such as those edited and published by Carlile and Heatherington carried '140 items' on Shelley, most of which were excerpts from or discussions of *Queen Mab*.[24] Besides reaching American radicals, it is known that the poem was influential in liberal and revolutionary circles on the Continent, and the young Frederick Engels began a translation before the 1848 upheavals.[25] All this is bitterly ironic in the light of Shelley's own laments in Italy about his failure to reach an audience; and the subsequent attempts by the Shelley dynasty and the established publisher

---

* These should not be confused with Benbow's pirate edition of 1826, which was a book that Robert Browning later picked up on a London bookstall, thus changing his whole life, and precipitating *Pauline* (1833). This was entitled *Miscellaneous Poems*, and did *not* contain *Queen Mab*, which in the circumstances was a pity for Browning. See Frederick A. Pottle, *Shelley and Browning*, 1965; and Ref. 22.

Moxon, to keep the official collections of Shelley's poetry clean and respectable. In the end Heatherington took a test case for blasphemous libel against Moxon in 1841 to establish the principle that *Queen Mab* could be printed in full and remain beyond the reach of the law. The case was lost, but as no sentence was forthcoming from the Bench, the principle was won.

Queen Mab's reputation was of course quite otherwise in the established press. A middle-of-the-road periodical, the *Investigator* of 1822, summed up the feelings of 'unmingled horror and disgust' at that 'most execrable publication' to which Byron's *Cain* was 'a homily'.[26] A long pamphlet of the previous year, entitled an *Answer to Queen Mab* significantly addressed the first of its two parts to 'The Anti-Matrimonial Thesis' and the second to 'The Supposed Atheism'. The political and commercial critique had less power to shock, for it was only really taken seriously by the radicals.[27] The exception to these reactions were Hunt's *Examiner* and a rather mysterious periodical entitled the *Theological Enquirer* which carried excerpts amounting to one-third of the whole poem in eight numbers between March and July 1815, together with favourable discussion and correspondence. The paper then disappeared without trace. The enigma of this astute, mushroom publication, edited by an Irish radical under the unlikely name of Erasmus Perkins was not solved until 1955.[28] This forms a later part of the story, together with Shelley's curious love–hate relationship with his own creation.[29] In June 1822, eight days before they died together, Shelley's intimate friend Edward Williams was given a pirate copy of the poem and sat under the boat sails in the 'excessive heat' reading it. His note in his journal reads: 'Read some of S's Queen Mab – an astonishing work. The enthusiasm of his spirit breaks out in some admirable passages in the poetry and the notes are subtle and elegant as he could now write.'[30] *Queen Mab* followed Shelley to the end, almost it seemed, with a will and spirit of its own. What had happened was that in his first major work, he had captured something of the spirit of the coming age, and it had sailed on beyond him.

Yet from a literary point of view, there is perhaps only one passage in all the nine cantos that presages the best of the poetry to come. It is not one of the diffuse visions of future Utopian light, but one of the visions of darkness. In it, Shelley manages to find a poetic image powerful enough to reflect his own arguments and indignation concerning the state of the majority of men he had seen in the society around him. The image is of primitive man in his pre-social state, abandoned on the face of a hostile and freezing globe, in a region where neither sunlight or intelligence has penetrated. It is terminated with a scowling, ironic twist which only Shelley could have conceived. As so often with Shelley, it was an image that once seized he never let go, but returned to it, altering and enriching, as a painter might work on a canvas, or a teacher on a child. The final transformation was to appear six years later, in Act II Scene IV of *Prometheus Unbound*. In *Queen Mab* it stands in its crudest, angular form, full of the awkward transitions and bald insistencies which everywhere flaw the poem. Yet the power to fuse passionate abstract argument with large visionary scenes and mythic projections of deep social or psychological significance is already present in this passage. This is the power that made Shelley a great poet. Here we see it struggling to dominate the material of its conception:

'Man, where the gloom of the long polar night
Lowers o'er the snow-clad rocks and frozen soil,
Where scarce the hardiest herb that braves the frost
Basks in the moonlight's ineffectual glow,
Shrank with the plants, and darkened with the night;
His chilled and narrow energies, his heart,
Insensible to courage, truth, or love,
His stunted stature and imbecile frame,
Marked him for some abortion of the earth,
Fit compeer of the bears that roamed around,
Whose habits and enjoyments were his own:
His life a feverish dream of stagnant woe,
Whose meagre wants, but scantily fulfilled,
Apprised him ever of the joyless length
Which his short being's wretchedness had reached;
His death a pang which famine, cold and toil
Long on the mind, whilst yet the vital spark
Clung to the body stubbornly, had brought:
All was inflicted here that Earth's revenge
Could wreak on the infringers of her law;
One curse alone was spared – the name of God. . . [31]

That summer in London, largely spent in hotels, was for Shelley a season of births and prospects. Besides *Queen Mab* there was Harriet's baby. This was due towards the end of June, and with Shelley's twenty-first only a month later, there were hopes of turning it into a time of reconciliation with Field Place. But Shelley's feelings in this respect were not quite the same as Harriet's, and for the first time one is aware of a definite difference of opinion between them. At the end of May, Harriet was writing with half-disguised excitement: 'Mr Shelley's family are very eager to be reconciled with him, and I should not in the least wonder if my next letter was not sent from his Paternal roof, as we expect to be there in a week or two.'[32] Timothy had come up to town, and Tom Medwin, perhaps with promptings from his father, urged Shelley to get in touch with him once more. Possibly it was Medwin too who alerted the Duke of Norfolk to the timely possibility of a reconciliation between father and son. The duke paid a visit to Cook's Hotel, and left an invitation to a meeting the following morning. Shelley did not go, later explaining that 'illness prevented him'. This was not a good omen. Yet Harriet still dreamt of giving birth to her first-born under her father-in-law's roof, and Eliza and her own father encouraged her sensible aspirations. When Shelley had actually been persuaded to write to Timothy on the 18th, Harriet felt she could afford to view Field Place with a certain condescension. '[Timothy Shelley] has not yet answered the letter; but we expect it daily. Their conduct is most surprising, after treating us like dogs they wish for our Society.'[33]

Shelley's letter might well have misled her into this false confidence, opening as gracefully as it did. 'My Dear Father, I once more presume to address you, to state to you my Sincere desire of being consider'd worthy of a Restoration to the intercourse with yourself and my Family which I have forfeited by my Follies.'[34] But for both father and son these were the opening moves of a chess game which had been played out to stalemate long since. Timothy replied with equal grace, inquiring if Shelley was prepared to state publicly the renunciation of his said 'Follies'. Shelley, whose follies were at that very moment attaining permanent form on Hookham's printing press, answered that indeed he was not. We do not have his letter, but Timothy's reply to it makes it quite clear that neither side was the least interested in compromise. 'As you now avow there is no change in [your opinions], I must decline all further Communication, or any Personal Interview, until that shall be Effected, and I desire you will consider this my final answer to anything you may have to offer.'[35] Despite all Harriet's hopes, the exchange had lasted a mere eight days. It was, after all, a formality. On 28 May Shelley sent off a courtesy note to the Duke of Norfolk, in which he revealed his willingness to man the old barricades of two years previously. 'My Lord Duke . . . I was prepared to make my father every reasonable concession, but I am not so degraded and miserable a slave as publicly to disavow an opinion which I believe to be true. Every man of common sense must plainly see that a sudden renunciation of sentiments seriously taken up is as unfortunate a test of intellectual uprightness as can possibly be devised.'[36] It was difficult to contradict.

What could the duke, or Medwin or even Harriet urge against this? When Shelley chose to defend his 'intellectual uprightness' no pressure could force him out. Wisely, Harriet chose to adopt an attitude of brisk defiance towards Field Place, yet her disappointment is eloquent. 'Mr Shelley has broken off the negotiation, and will have no more to say to his son because that son will not write to the people of Oxford, and declare his return to Christianity. Did you ever hear of such an old dotard? It seems that so long as he lives, Bysshe must never hope to see or hear anything of his family. This is certainly an unpleasant circumstance, particularly as his mother wishes to see him, and has great affection for him.'[37] But it was to be more unpleasant than either Shelley or Harriet supposed, for at this date, and certainly well on into July, Shelley had no notion that such a breach could endanger the financial side of the inheritance. The complete trans-formation of their expectations in this respect was to put severe pressure on a point that was now revealed as a weak one in their relationship. To this, Harriet was to bring all the claims of a young mother without house or security, and the emotional support of Eliza and her father Mr Westbrook. Surely some reason-able formula could be patched up with Timothy, and at least a small degree of financial independence secured? Yet what Harriet attempted to alter was a cardinal stubbornness in Shelley's character, and an emotional decision about his family the roots of which stretched back well beyond his marriage.

But for the time being, Shelley looked confidently on his economic prospects. The expensive rooms at Cook's were continued, while lodgings in Half Moon Street, a hundred yards down Piccadilly were taken, probably as an extra for Harriet's confinement. Shelley decided that some regular form of transport was now in order, and he went to the fashionable coach-maker Thomas Charters of New Bond Street and ordered the construction of a carriage. This was a solid vehicle which was to take him to the continent in 1816. The bill for construction and servicing was expected to amount to several hundred pounds, which Shelley confidently hoped to pay in the autumn. In the event, nothing was paid at all, and in the following year Charters became one of Shelley's most pressing creditors. Still nothing was paid, but in November 1815 Shelley was threatened with imminent arrest and finally signed a bill of exchange 'which committed him to the payment of £532 11s. 6d. four years from that date'.[38] * In 1844, twenty-two years after his death, Shelley's executor Peacock received an applica-tion from Thomas Charters for the payment of a bill of exchange to the value of '£532 11s. 6d.'. This saga can be taken as exemplary of the history of many lesser bills and obligations which Shelley contracted throughout his life. Shelley's conduct in this respect, which has only gradually been revealed by extensive investigations of secondary documents† must be set against his much better publicized acts of flagrant generosity. Overall one has the impression that he owed rather more than he gave away.

Shelley's confidence at this time also extended to the Tan-yr-allt bills, and he

* By November 1816 this sum had somehow risen to £1,000 in respect to further borrowings which Shelley apparently secured from Charters. There is no evidence that at any time did Shelley repay this extra sum. See Ingpen, *Shelley in England,* p. 638.

† The honours for this patient and not altogether edifying research must go to Roger Ingpen, op. cit. For Shelley's own estimate of his debts by 1822, see pp. 710-11.

had several meetings with 'Williams the Welchman' who was down in London taking instructions from Madocks at the end of June.[39] But Shelley's Welsh creditors were to fare no better. By May a list of Shelley's unpaid bills had been drawn up, of which the amount owed to Williams and Nanney alone amounted to £350.[40] Apparently Shelley then signed a bond which made him liable for £700 in default of payment after an agreed date. By June 1815, part of these debts had been paid, but Nanney was writing to Williams in exasperation about the rest:

> I have been informed that you have received £150 of the debt due from Shelley: all the money provided for the payment of Shelley's debts is now exhausted; and that act of justice must be suspended till more money comes in which will be in November next: – the money has failed in consequence of Shelley's stating his debts less than they are; & in order to justify this statement, he is actually guilty of abundant falsities: – in order to get rid of the £100, due to me for hire of furniture, he said, that he had resided at Tanyrallt only *two months*, & that *the instant he had quitted it*, I *sold the furniture*; did you ever hear of a more ungrateful fellow! – his attorney however promises that *all* his debts will be paid by the Father: – in November next.[41]

Unfortunately, but not unexpectedly, there is no evidence that the remainder of this debt was ever cleared either.*

At Half Moon Street, one is aware of the presence of Hogg again in the little circle. While Shelley pursued business at the press, and his new intimacies with Peacock and the vegetarian and naturist John Frank Newton, Hogg was left to entertain Harriet. From certain of Hogg's insinuations, one is tempted to wonder how far the situation at York in 1811 repeated itself, and how far Shelley, once again, was encouraging an intimacy between his best friend and his wife. The advanced state of Harriet's pregnancy might appear to make this unlikely except for the curious fact that an exactly similar episode, of which we have slightly fuller record, was to occur during the pregnancy of Shelley's second wife in 1815. Hogg paints a picture of himself dining and taking tea alone with Harriet, or of Harriet reading to him for long periods, until Shelley would come 'tumbling up the stairs, with a mighty sound, treading upon his nose, as I accused him of doing, and throwing off his neckcloth, according to custom'. Then he would stand 'staring around for some moments, as wondering why he had been in such a hurry'.[42] On one occasion he recounts how he was sitting alone with Harriet after dinner when a Quaker physician 'Dr S.' arrived to examine Harriet and

---

* One cannot altogether dismiss the possibility that the exasperation of Ellis-Nanney and others in the district had some effect on the way in which the history of the Tan-yr-allt affair in February 1813 was eventually transmitted to posterity.

the condition of her pregnancy. Hogg rose to go, but, according to his narration, Harriet made a great show of forcing him to stay: ' "You need not go away! Dr S. does not desire it, I am sure. He rather wishes you to stay!" ' Hogg implies that he found the position 'delicate and distressing'. Although in the event the Quaker physician, in a *volte face* typical of Hogg's humorous narrative, did nothing except sit down next to Harriet and gaze intently at her for ten minutes murmuring 'softly and inarticulately'.[43]

The development of a somewhat awkward relationship, awkward for Harriet, rather than for Shelley, is indicated by one of Shelley's notes, simply dated 'Cook's Hotel, Wednesday Morn'. 'My Dearest Friend, I have felt myself extremely hurt by Harriet's conduct towards you. She writes in this. I only desire that she were as anxious to confer on you all possible happiness as I am. She tells you that she invites you this evening. It will be better than our lonesome and melancholy interviews.'[44] The first sentence was suppressed by Hogg when he published it in his own biography; the last sentence seems to suggest that Hogg had been moping to Shelley about Harriet. Shelley added a P.S. 'I am sure that Harriet will be as kind as ever. I could see when I spoke to her (if my eye were not blinded by love) that it was an error not of the feelings but of reason. I entreat you to come this evening.' That 'error of reason' recalls of course the long passionate exchange on sexual sharing which had passed between Keswick and York in 1811. But for the moment, these considerations were dissolved by the birth of Harriet and Shelley's first child, Eliza Ianthe, on 23 June 1813. She was christened at St George's, Hanover Square: her names were drawn from both sides: Eliza after Miss Westbrook, and Ianthe after the dream heroine of *Queen Mab*. The services of Dr S. were apparently satisfactory, despite, or perhaps because of, his murmuring, and within a few hours Shelley noted she was 'rapidly recovering'. He was now a father; but at once it was a father with worries. He had begun to understand through Medwin how his financial prospects were endangered, and he was assailed, as he told Medwin on the 28th, by 'a most unpleasant feeling of embarrassment and uncertainty'.[45]

For the first time Shelley felt the thick cloak of domestic responsibility begin to settle about his shoulders. He stayed up so late talking to Medwin that his meetings with Hogg were frequently missed or forgotten. But the Newtons distracted him, and Shelley soon found himself being whisked off to late-night parties at the Vauxhall.[46]

Shelley's feelings towards his first child are not easy to establish. Hogg says that the little blue-eyed, fair-haired baby did not 'appear to afford him any gratification, or to create an interest'.[47] Peacock on the other hand says Shelley was extremely fond of it, and 'would walk up and down a room with it in his arms for a long time together, singing to it a monotonous melody of his own making'.[48] Yet even Peacock admits that the child was always a source of worry and disagreement between Shelley and Harriet. The child had brought them family responsibility without bringing them back into the security of the family inheritance. At a more personal level, Shelley wished the child to be brought up along 'naturist' lines, as he had observed in the Newton household where, among other things, the children were encouraged to run around the house naked.* Particularly, Shelley wished Harriet to breast-feed the child and look after it herself, but instead, as Peacock observed, 'the child had a wet-nurse whom he did not like, and was much looked after by his wife's sister, whom he intensely disliked'. It was the arrival of Ianthe which first brought the latent antagonism between Shelley and Eliza clearly into the open. Eliza had all the faults of an over-managing mother-in-law.

By the end of July, it was clear that Shelley's inheritance was to be obstructed, and the settlement was put into Chancery – by Timothy's solicitors – a move that promised virtually indefinite delay. It was now imperative for Shelley to reduce his expenditure; the debts he owed to the Tremadoc creditors and Charters were already beyond hope of immediate repayment. As a temporary measure, the Newtons suggested that he could take his family to stay with another member of their set who owned a large country house in Bracknell, Berkshire. By the 27th they were installed at High Elms, the property of Mrs Boinville, a handsome and prosperous widow, the elder sister of Mrs Newton. Peacock, who had just returned from a summer holiday in North Wales (when he made his investigations at Tan-yr-allt), joined Shelley at Bracknell, and together they planned an autumn trip to the North as a method of escaping Shelley's immediate creditors and reducing his expenditure. Healy had to be discharged from service, but as his conduct had become 'so unprincipled' in London Harriet was glad to dismiss him. On Dan's side, it seems that he was owed ten pounds' wages, but these too fell victim to the new economizing. Servants were never to have a smooth run in Shelley's unorthodox households; their attitudes fluctuated between sublime dedication and vilest recriminations.

Harriet wrote miserably to Mrs Nugent of the loss of 'the immense property of his sires', and the Chancery manoeuvre, which she felt was a concerted plan by Timothy, the Duke of Norfolk and the family solicitors to keep it out of Shelley's hands. This was probably near the mark. 'We are now in a house 30 miles from London, merely for convenience. How long we remain is uncertain, as I fear our necessities will oblige us to remove to a greater distance. Our friends the Newtons are trying to do everything in their power to serve us; but our

---

* In a footnote to *Queen Mab* he praised Newton's children as 'the most beautiful and healthy creatures it is possible to conceive; the girls are perfect models for a sculptor; their dispositions are also the most gentle and conciliating'. *Poetical Works*, p. 834.

doom is decided. . . . To have all our plans set aside in this manner is a miserable thing. Not that I regret the loss, but for the sake of those I intended to benefit.'[49] Shelley was soothed by the new household, where he found himself among sympathetic spirits. Mrs Boinville was the wife of a French revolutionary *emigré*, a friend of Lafayette's, who had recently been killed during retreat from Moscow in February 1813. She was a young-looking woman for her age, but her hair was absolutely white. Shelley called her teasingly, 'Maimuna', partly to imply the maternal relationship, and partly romantically, to recall the lady of Southey's 'Thalaba', with grey hair and 'a damsel's face'. They discussed vegetarianism, atheism, naturism and French politics in the slightly rarefied intellectual air of Madame Boinville's *salon*. Shelley was also charmed by Mademoiselle Boinville, who at 18 was bilingual, intelligent and very pretty. Her name was Cornelia.

Harriet was less relaxed. She found ideas that she had been taught by Shelley to treat with reverence now chattered over by armchair radicals in an effete society she did not respect. She found an unexpected ally in Peacock, whose dry, rather donnish humour and respect for solid scholarship had little patience with the Bracknell set. Peacock, who was 28 in October, unmarried and introverted, hid under bland good manners an acidly observant eye for everything that went on around him. He had unhappily broken off a love-affair in North Wales, and now turned with pleasure and relief to the task of cheering and amusing Shelley's young wife. They made a private joke of the Bracknell people, which later became for Peacock one of the inspirations for his first comic novel. 'At Bracknell,' he recalled, 'Shelley was surrounded by a numerous society, all in a great measure of his own opinions in relation to religion, and politics, and the larger portion of them in relation to vegetable diet . . . each [had] nevertheless some predominant crotchet of his or her own, which left a number of open questions for earnest and not always temperate discussion. I was sometime irreverent enough to laugh at the fervour with which opinions utterly unconducive to any practical result were battled for as matters of the highest importance to the well-being of mankind; Harriet Shelley was always ready to laugh with me, and we thereby both lost caste with some of the more hotheaded of the party.'[50] Peacock, whose evidence becomes increasingly important in the next four years of Shelley's life, never took Shelley absolutely seriously, though he admired him in many ways and found him a fruitful source of ideas for his own work. He regarded Shelley as an extraordinary human being, rather than as an extraordinary writer; unlike Hogg he had little awe – either genuine or false – for the 'Divine Poet'. He was fascinated by the 'crotchety' side of Shelley's personality, yet he was frequently inclined to overlook its deeper driving forces and motives. Like Shelley, he loved a mysterious occurrence more than a prosaic one, and their sense of the macabre was mutual – a great source of amusement and private understanding in later years.

During this Bracknell period of late summer 1813, Shelley found himself entering on one of the most uncertain and upsetting periods of his life. All his immediate goals were dissipated; the inheritance with which he had planned so much philanthropy had slipped from his grasp; his wife and child were slowly changing from a source of peace and hope into one of anxiety and dissatisfaction; his political interests were being swamped and diverted by the endless talk of the Boinville set. It is from this unsettled period that one of Hogg's most extraordinary tales of Shelley emanates. According to Hogg, Shelley believed he had caught elephantiasis during a coach journey, and was perpetually worrying over it and examining himself. As Hogg tells the story, Shelley is made to seem merely an amusing and childlike eccentric, going through the strange routine of examining others' skin to compare with his own. But if the story has any basis in fact, and Peacock's evidence supports it, it seems that Shelley was deliberately acting up to the artificialities of the society in which he had marooned himself and Harriet. The madness is that of a pet eccentric, a drawing-room poet indulging himself, a charade.

> His imagination was so much disturbed, that he was perpetually examining his own skin, and feeling and looking at that of others. One evening, during the access of his fancied disorder, when many young ladies were standing up for a country dance, he caused wonderful consternation amongst these charming creatures by walking slowly along the row of girls and curiously surveying them, placing his eyes close to their necks and bosoms, and feeling their breasts and bare arms, in order to ascertain whether any of the fair ones had taken the horrible disease. He proceeded with so much gravity and seriousness, and his looks were so woebegone, that they did not resist, or resent, the extraordinary liberties, but looked terrified and as if they were about to undergo some severe surgical operation at his hands.[51]

Hogg seems to want to imply also, that Shelley was inexorably breaking loose from sexual loyalty to Harriet. Once more the undercurrent of fear, used as a catalyst in his relations with the opposite sex, makes itself felt in Shelley's behaviour.

As September wore on, Harriet found that she and Shelley were having 'many arguments concerning the respect that all men pay to property'.[52] They seemed to agree, but it was a sore subject. Debtors had now begun to inquire after Shelley in London, and there was talk of his arrest. Shelley was bitterly resigned to his father's withholding of the inheritance, and was already thinking of alternative ways of raising funds. Harriet still clung to every sign of goodwill from Field Place, writing pathetically to Mrs Nugent: 'The post has just brought me a letter from Mr Shelley's sister, who says her father is doing all in his power to prevent his being arrested. I think even his family pride must long to give way on the present occasion. ... Mrs Shelley tells her son everything she hears.'[53] Yet in reality, there was neither help nor even sympathy forthcoming from Field Place. It was becoming imperative to leave the Home Counties for the time being. Harriet, anxious for the security of her child, suggested that they might try once more to lease the lovely farm at Nantgwillt, but the plan was ephemeral without ready capital to secure the stock. Harriet continued to dream of a home at Nantgwillt for many months, and it became her ideal setting for a family life with Shelley. Shelley on the other hand was increasingly unsettled and unsatisfied, and sometimes he was finding it easier to talk to Cornelia Boinville than his wife. Their new friend Peacock found himself steadily drawn into a mediating role.

At the end of September, Shelley decided that they must attempt to establish their own residence for the winter. Apparently through Hogg, he contacted a money-lender in London, called Starling, and began negotiations for a large loan. The coach built by Charters was packed up with belongings, while Shelley convinced Harriet that the child – still only three months old – would be safe to travel, and persuaded Peacock to accompany them. On Saturday, 2 October, he clinched a ruinous *post obit* loan for £500 payable on Sir Bysshe Shelley's death at the rate of 300 per cent, which amounted to £2,000.* On Monday 4 October, the coach which was laden down with Shelley, Harriet and the baby, Eliza and Peacock and all their books and luggage, trundled slowly out of Bracknell and headed for Cumberland and the Lake District. At Warwick, Shelley posted back a note to Hogg informing him of their destination, the *post obit* loan and stressing the need for secrecy. 'I *wish you to* consider all communications made to you on this subject as secret. I may confide to you surmises probably rash, & possibly ill-founded. To your secrecy and friendship I shall commit them.'[54] There was also the more humdrum business of Peacock's 'small trunk' of books, which required forwarding, as Shelley had off-loaded it at the last moment in deference to his coach springs. The same fate, presumably, had also overtaken little Ianthe's wet nurse.

Shelley drove the coach quite hard, and they reached Low Wood Inn, Ambleside, within the week. Ianthe remained healthy, and Harriet seeing the mountains, was once more dreaming of 'our dear Nantgwillt'.[55] Shelley contacted the Calverts at Keswick, and began to ask around for a house for the winter. To his

---

* The bond was eventually settled by Timothy Shelley in May 1815 for £833 7s. 6d., a mere 33 per cent. This reflects on the comparative sagacity with which father and son chose their respective lawyers.

surprise, none was forthcoming. Memories of the winter of 1811 probably lingered on about Shelley locally, and Shelley and Harriet in turn soon decided that 'such a set of human beings' occupied the Lakes that they would move on. North Wales held no attractions, so they set out on the road to Scotland and within sixteen days of leaving London found themselves in Edinburgh. Shelley took lodgings for them all at 36 Frederick Street, planning to remain for the winter. Peacock's books arrived, and Shelley was encouraged to embark on a solid course of study, now mixing ancient with modern: notably Homer's *Odyssey* and Laplace's *Système du Monde*.[56] The coach went in to John Dumbreck, Coach-maker, for service which it badly needed since Shelley had managed to break eight main plates, four steel springs, and smash two of the lamps so they had to be completely replaced. The bill came to £8 11s. which Mr Dumbreck was still trying to collect ten years later.[57] Meanwhile Shelley translated two of Plutarch's essays on vegetarianism, and busied himself, to Peacock's bemused fascination, with preparing one of his most peculiar and crotchety productions, a pamphlet *On the Vegetable System of Diet*. In its thin, high-flown rhetoric, and its subordination of political and philosophical questions to those of speculative 'dietetics' one catches something of the tone and quality of the talk among the Newton–Boinville set:

> With [what] arguments shall philosophy assail superstition, so long as terrifying phantoms crowd round the couch of its pale and prostrate victim, refuting with the indisputable evidence of sense the metaphysical scepticism of reason, while politician's dreams and reveries of indiscribable horror testify? How shall we inspire the miserable man with kindness and humanity whose social feelings are jaundiced by a torture that lurks within his vitals. . . .[58]

For the time being, Shelley seemed to be content to argue that political injustice and oppression was the consequence of indigestion. Like the elephantiasis episode, it showed how he had been thrown off course since Tan-yr-allt, and turned in a restless, absurd circle of self-doubt and uncertainty which he had not experienced since the post-Oxford days in Poland Street. Parts of the essay also suggest the beginning of a constant worry about his own health (as again in the elephantiasis episode), which showed its symptoms in a combination of mental anxiety and physical discomfort in the region of the stomach and abdomen, perhaps accompanied by his first minor spasms.* 'Groundless terrors, vertigo, and delirium are frequently consequent upon a disease of the digestive organs; tremors and spasmodic affections, remote both in their nature and position from

---

* There is still no definite record of this chronic disorder until some eighteen months later. But it does seem likely that Shelley's increasing interest in vegetarianism was as much prompted by misplaced medical considerations as by ideological ones.

disorders of the stomach, are yet in many cases to be traced to its derangement. . . .'[59] Nevertheless he was not too caught up in his own concerns to let a novel by Hogg, *The Memoirs of Prince Alexy Haimatoff*, just published, go by unremarked; he wrote warmly to Hogg, praising the 'extraordinary and animated tale' and a hero 'so natural and energetic as Alexy'.[60] 'Believe me,' he concluded, 'to be ever sincerely attached to you.'

As the November days drew in at Frederick Street, Shelley and Peacock found themselves thrown together, studying, talking and reading Peacock's beloved Greeks, while the women busied themselves with the baby. Peacock was at his most discreet and diplomatic, and Shelley had not yet penetrated into the wittiest and most original side of his character; his immediate impression was of the bland, well-mannered pedant. 'He is a very mild, agreeable man, and a good scholar. His enthusiasm is not very ardent, nor his views very comprehensive: but he is neither superstitious, ill-tempered, dogmatical, nor proud.'[61] Which, coming from Shelley, was apt praise.

Peacock, if we are to believe his own evidence, quickly seized on the more extraordinary and eccentric elements of Shelley's personality. He noted that Shelley was 'especially fond' of the horror-romances of Charles Brockden Brown, the American novelist* whose tales were 'remarkable for the way in which natural causes were made to produce supernatural effects'. Shelley was 'captivated by the picture of Clitheroe in his sleep digging a grave under a tree' in *Edgar Huntley*; and he was always searching for a summerhouse like the one in *Wieland* where the hero's father 'died of spontaneous combustion'. Peacock argued that this gothic element, the mysterious and 'superstitious terror of romance' were permanent and central features of Shelley's personality. Many years after Shelley's death, Peacock still held the same view, and summarized it by literary analogy:

> [Charles Brockden] Brown's four novels, Schiller's *Robbers*, and Goethe's *Faust*, were, of all the works with which he was familiar, those which took the deepest root in his mind, and had the strongest influence in the formation of his character. . . . He devotedly admired Wordsworth and Coleridge, and in a minor degree Southey . . . but admiration is one thing and assimilation is another; and nothing so blended itself with the structure of his interior mind as the creations of Brown.[62]

* Charles Brockden Brown (1771–1810). *Wieland* (1789); *Ormond* (1799), *Edgar Huntley* (1799). From a Philadelphian Quaker background, he worked in New York and supported himself by magazine articles and fiction. His psychosomatic interests, and his gothic penetrations into the world of horror, obsession, seduction, cruelty and mania, make him the direct precursor of Edgar Allen Poe. He had a genius for complex plot-lines. Characteristically it was Peacock, not Hogg, who first realized his fascination for Shelley, and who noticed how Shelley playfully named many of his friends after Brown's heroes and heroines. It was however not altogether play.

But for the time being, Peacock was really closer to Harriet than to Shelley, and perhaps not altogether consciously he was helping her to get a slightly more mature and objective opinion of her husband. Certainly by 23 November she showed in a letter to Mrs Nugent that she had no more illusions about how far father and son were divided over the inheritance, and an acid note has crept in: 'There has been no conciliation between Mr S. and his father. Their opinions are so contrary, that I do not think there is the least chance of their being reconciled. His father is now ill with the gout; but there is no danger I suppose. If there was he would send for his son and be reconciled to him.' [63]

Shelley was cheered by one chance meeting in Edinburgh, with a young Brazilian medical student called Joachim Baptista Pereira, who qualified as a doctor in 1815. Pereir talked to Shelley about the revolutionary movements in South America, the news of which had so excited him in Dublin in 1812, and they compared notes on cordially abominated fathers. Pereira was swept off his feet by Shelley, and began a translation of *Queen Mab* into Portuguese as his contribution to the cause in South America. He showed Peacock a sonnet he had written as a preface to the translation, of which Peacock remembered two lines, the first and the last:

Sublime Shelley, cantor di verdade! . . .
Surja *Queen Mab* a restaurar o mundo

The two remained in touch for several months, and there is a letter from Shelley as late as September 1815 which seems to suggest that Pereira was going to Europe, and from there home to Brazil. Peacock says he 'died early' from a disease of the lungs.

The enthusiasm of Pereira, and the agreeableness of Peacock were not enough to see Shelley through the winter in Edinburgh. He seems to have discussed with Harriet the possibility of their spending Christmas apart. Within three days of each other, Harriet wrote to Mrs Nugent, who was poorly, suggesting that she might come to Dublin to 'attend' her; while Shelley wrote briskly to Hogg, on the 26th: 'I am happy to hear that you have returned to London, as I shall shortly have pleasure of seeing you again. I shall return to London alone. My evenings will often be spent at the Newtons', where, I presume, you are no unfrequent visitor.' [64] Shelley was also drawn by Godwin, who although he had not featured much in their social life in London during the summer, had been writing to Shelley assiduously, as his diary shows. Since Shelley had left Bracknell in October, Godwin had dispatched six missives, most of which, as later evidence shows, were concerned not so much with political justice, as with the problems of Shelley's inheritance, and the ways in which he might still raise money on his prospects.

Shelley finally decided, perhaps on the advice of Peacock, that it would be better if they all went south together, and at the very end of November the coach was once again loaded up and they rattled south through the foul weather on their brand-new springs. Peacock, Harriet and the baby, and Eliza were deposited at Bracknell, and on 10 December Godwin's diary records that Shelley took breakfast with him alone at Skinner Street. This meeting marked a new stage in the relationship between Shelley and his philosophical mentor; William Godwin was now elevated to the position of paternal adviser in matters both spiritual and financial – an odd combination which produced some otherwise inexplicable results. Shelley's filial dependence on Godwin lasted only in complete form for six months, until June 1814, when it was dramatically broken. But in fragmentary forms of guilt, admiration and the sense of accountability, this dependency hung on for many years after, with the direst consequences for Shelley's financial affairs. For the time being, Godwin was the fount of wisdom and sympathy.

For the next four months, that is to say until mid-March of 1814, Shelley's life is very largely a mystery. We do not know in any detail or with any certainty where he was living, who his companions were, or what he was thinking and writing. What evidence we do have suggests that this was one of the most desperately unhappy periods of his whole adult life, when he was constantly racked by worries about money and his inheritance, when his relationship with Harriet was inexorably breaking down in mutual dissatisfaction and bitterness, and when he could find no steady place of residence, but moved restlessly between addresses in Berkshire and London, alternatively leaning on his friends' shoulders and quarrelling violently with them. Godwin alone remained beyond reproach.

On 13 December, Shelley had the first of many financial conferences with his new solicitor, Amory, of 59 Old Bond Street. Godwin's diary records that this was held at Took's Court with himself, Dr Newton, the publisher Hookham, and a gentleman called Sorrel in attendance.[65] Both Godwin and Hookham certainly had their own interests as well as Shelley's at heart: Hookham was owed money on the printing of *Queen Mab*, and Godwin was already taking up Shelley's repeated offers of support, since, despite the success of Mrs Godwin's library his position was very precarious. Shelley had first promised to help him in the summer, when he had still thought that his majority would automatically bring extensive funds. At this meeting, only tentative plans and immediate needs were met. Before returning to the country, Shelley had a long talk with Hookham and arranged to keep a private room for himself in Hookham's house at 15 Old Bond Street. He was already thinking in terms of a retreat.

On 19 December, just in time to make arrangements for a family Christmas,

Shelley took a house at Windsor, some eight miles and an easy ride from the Boinvilles' at Bracknell. We have no record of this Christmas, the last one he spent with Harriet and his child. Likewise, January and February 1814 are largely a blank. Godwin's diary shows that he was writing to Shelley about once a week, except at the end of February when letters stopped for a while.[66] On short trips to London, when Shelley was beginning to think in terms of procuring a really large *post obit* loan in the region of £3,000 (about seven times his annual income), he saw Godwin several times, and dined with him thrice. At the Newtons' there was a quarrel, and relations were broken off.[67] In Berkshire, domestic relations became more and more difficult, and increasingly Shelley took to riding over to Bracknell, and sometimes he stayed the night. As the spring approached, Cornelia Boinville suggested that she give him regular lessons in Italian to help pass the time.

At the beginning of March, things seemed to be approaching a crisis, and Mrs Boinville and Shelley decided that for a temporary period at least Shelley should leave Harriet and Eliza at Windsor. Shelley packed a few things and moved over to Bracknell, while Mrs Boinville wrote to apprise his friend Hogg of the situation in a lightly handled letter: 'I will not have you despite homespun pleasures. Shelley is making a trial of them with us, and likes them so well, that he is resolved to leave off rambling, and to begin a course of them himself. Seriously, I think his mind and body want rest. His journeys after what he has never found have racked his purse and his tranquillity. He is resolved to take a little care of the former in pity to the latter, which I applaud, and shall second with all my might. He has deeply interested us. In the course of your intimacy he must have made you feel what we feel for him now.'[68] To give Shelley's visit a certain propriety, Mrs Boinville explained that he was seeking a house in the district. 'Excuse a thousand blunders and much confusion of expression,' she wrote in an expressive P.S., '... for I write, talking occasionally to Shelley of twenty different subjects.'

Hogg seems to have visited Bracknell during this month, but happened to miss Shelley, who was visiting London. In one of his most elusive passages Hogg describes Shelley's bedroom scattered over with clothes and books – mostly French – turned face downwards at the point where he had broken off reading; and he relates some strange history of Shelley using the wooden wash-tubs to go boating on the stream at the bottom of the garden. Apparently, he managed to knock out the bottoms of all the washtubs in the house. There is also a description of Shelley being given endless cups of tea in the drawing-room by 'a lovely young creature', presumably Cornelia. The intention is, as ever with Hogg, comic; but the physical facts described suggest Shelley was on the verge of breakdown: 'He was greedily swallowing the nectar, discussing and disputing the while, and trembling with emotion; and pouring the precious liquor into his bosom, upon his knees, and into his shoes, and spilling it on the carpet.' Meanwhile, Cornelia stood by him listening, refilling his cup, and mopping him gently with a white cambric handkerchief.[69]

From Bracknell, Shelley wrote to his father, after Amory had gone to negotiate with him at Field Place. Timothy had politely turned Amory off with the explanation that the settlement now lay in Chancery and only Shelley's grandfather, old Sir Bysshe, had it in his power to remove the impediments. Shelley coldly deployed his most pointed argument: 'I lament to inform you that the posture of my affairs is so critical that I can no longer delay to raise money by the sale of Post Obit bonds to a considerable amount . . . surely my Grandfather must perceive that his hopes of preserving and perpetuating the integrity of the estate will be frustrated by neglecting to relieve my necessities; he knows that I have the power, which however reluctantly I shall be driven to exert of dismembering the property should I survive himself & you.'[70] The letter was received in silence, and despite Amory's own remonstrations,[71] Shelley now decided he would clinch the biggest loan he could conveniently get his hands on in London. A large part of this was destined for Godwin.

Shelley's state of mind in March and April was enough to cause those who were still in touch with him increasing uneasiness. A rare letter to Hogg of 16 March reveals febrile and conflicting emotions, and fluctuates between apathy and something like hysteria. Referring to Bracknell Shelley wrote, 'I have escaped, in the society of all that philosophy and friendship combine, from the dismaying solitude of myself. They have revived in my heart the expiring flame of life. I have felt myself translated to a paradise, which has nothing of mortality but its transitoriness. . . .' But only a few lines later he is writing: 'I have sunk into a premature old age of exhaustion, which renders me dead to everything, but the unenviable capacity of indulging the vanity of hope, and a terrible susceptibility to objects of disgust and hatred.' Looking back over his life to the Oxford days, he glanced 'with wonder at the hopes which in the excess of my madness I there encouraged'. Harriet is simply not mentioned, but Shelley is bitterly explicit about his feelings for Eliza Westbrook, which had been building up for months: 'I certainly hate her with all my heart and soul. It is a sight which wakens an inexpressible sensation of disgust and horror, to see her caress my poor little Ianthe, in whom I may hereafter find the consolation of sympathy. I sometimes feel faint with the fatigue of checking the overflowings of my unbounded abhorrence for this miserable wretch. But she is no more than a blind & loathsome worm, that cannot see to sting.' All barriers of pretence and politeness were now down.

Yet not all, for astonishingly, a mere week after this letter was written,

Shelley agreed to go through the form of a second marriage with Harriet to remove possible legal irregularities resulting from the Scottish marriage of 1811. This may have been the result of a request from John Westbrook, who attended the ceremony and was determined to have his daughter's legal position in relation to Shelley's inheritance made absolutely certain, especially since the emotional position was steadily deteriorating for all to see. But Shelley himself may also have needed the clarification of the legal position for tying up his *post obit* arrangements. Shelley called with Godwin at Doctors Commons for the licence on 22 March, and two days later he was remarried to Harriet at St George's Church, Hanover Square – where little Ianthe had been christened – with Westbrook and others as witnesses. Whether this hollow rite, which Shelley still abominated on principle, served to increase or reduce the tension between them is not known.* The only writing we have from him at this period is a note to his father imperiously requesting that a certain Mr Shourbridge should be granted shooting rights on the Field Place estate. Possibly this was in exchange for an introduction to useful financiers. Timothy's note scrawled angrily on the back of the letter when he received it reads: 'Hatter in Bond Street, Dashing Man, the latter goes to Brighthelmstone in his Barouche & fine Blood Horses in Summer. No sort of acquaintance with them [the Shourbridge brothers] whatever.' The letter was written from 16 Charing Cross, which was Francis Place's address, and suggests that Godwin was busy introducing Shelley into the radical London set. At around this time Shelley found two money-lenders, the brothers Andrew and George Nash, and negotiations for a sum in the region of £3,000 were commenced. Godwin hoped to collect about half of this figure.

By the end of the month Shelley was again back in Bracknell, sheltering with the Boinvilles. It is not certain at what date he returned, but he was not long enough in London to witness the arrival of Godwin's daughter Mary at Skinner Street. She had returned from one of her stays with the Baxter family in Scotland on 30 March, and dined that evening with her beloved father.[72]

At Bracknell during April, Shelley continued his conversations with Mrs Boinville, and his Italian lessons with Cornelia. Relations with Harriet showed little signs of improvement, and Harriet herself decided to leave Windsor and take a spring holiday. Accompanied by Ianthe and Eliza, she travelled down to the West Country, staying first at Southampton, and later at Bath, according to Mrs Boinville's letter of 18 April to Hogg. Thus the separation which had tacitly existed between Shelley and Harriet since the beginning of March was now openly recognized. There is no evidence that Harriet was in London again before

---

* However, in late March, it may be observed that Shelley and Harriet were still on terms of sexual intimacy. For in July Harriet announced that she was again pregnant, and her second child by Shelley was eventually born on 30 November 1814, one month premature.

July. Mrs Boinville's attitude to these developments may be gathered from what Shelley later wrote to Harriet: 'Mrs Boinville deeply knows the human heart; she predicted that these struggles would one day arrive; she saw that friendship & not passion was the bond of our attachment.'[73]

Taking tea with Godwin and Shelley and several others at about this time, Hogg heard a voice inquire of the author of *Political Justice* what he considered the nature of love to be? Godwin remained silent, but Shelley with a half mocking, half defiant glance interrupted the master's cogitations: 'My opinion of love is that it acts upon the human heart precisely as a nutmeg grater acts upon a nutmeg.' The company waited solemnly for this piece of levity to be rebuked, but Godwin merely looked across the room and nodded silently.[74]

At Bracknell Shelley moved in a dream world, totally disillusioned with Harriet's love, but desperately seeking some alternative relationship. He half thought he had fallen in love with Cornelia Boinville, and to Hogg he sent a poem addressed in secret to her, 'I have written nothing but one stanza':

> Thy dewy looks sink in my breast;
>   Thy gentle words stir poison there;
> Thou hast disturbed the only rest
>   That was the portion of despair!

But then, with a moan, he dismissed it: 'This is the vision of a delirious and distempered dream, which passes away at the cold clear light of morning. Its surpassing excellence and exquisite perfections have no more reality than the colour of an autumnal sunset.'[75]

But there was more reality in this transient passion for Cornelia than he admitted to Hogg. In the first few pages of a notebook dating from this period, and subsequently given to Jane Clairmont for her journal in August,[76] there are several fragmentary entries, in Latin, in Italian and in English which were the product of this half-suppressed passion. He copied out the section of Dante's *Inferno*, Canto v, in which Paulo and Francesca fall violently in love while innocently studying a book together; and from Augustine's *Confessions* he drew one of his favourite tags which he afterwards used as the epigraph to *Alastor*: 'I was not yet in love, but I was in love with love itself; and I sought for something to love, since I loved loving.'* Then in a piece of rather stumbling Latin dog prose, he constructed a vague erotic fantasy of desire and fulfilment. Part of this may be rendered: 'She (he) pressed kisses upon my lips! Suddenly the whole world was clothed with the everlasting colours of heaven. . . . Out of a terrible solitude I contemplated love, as if I were a prisoner, both wretched and

---

* 'Nondum amabam, sed amare amabam, quiesebar quid amarem amans amare.' St Augustine, *Confessions*, Book III, Chap. I.

contented. . . . I rose up from sleep, denied all delicious desires. . . . She (he) held me in her (his) arms in bed, and I nearly died from delirium and delight. Sweet lips called back the mutual kisses of life! She (he) calmed my fears.' The gender of the narrator is not clear from the Latin. The manuscript has been burnt in several places. There are also several lines of blank verse in this section of the notebook, most of which are loose and undistinguished; but the opening three lines present with simple force a familiar image:

> – The thoughts of my past life
> Rise like the ghosts of an unquiet dream
> Blackening the cheerful morn.

Much of the 'feverish dream' of these weeks was used the following year for Shelley's study of unrealized sexual desire in *Alastor*.

One other quotation from Dante in the notebook, referred not to Cornelia, but to Harriet: the inscription over the Gate into Hell, 'Lasciate ogni Speranza, voi che intrate [*sic*]'. We know this, because five months later, looking back at this period of 'two months at Mrs Boinville's without my wife', Shelley described his feelings to Hogg as follows:

> I saw the full extent of the calamity which my rash & heartless union with Harriet: an union over whose entrance might justly be inscribed
>
> Lasciate ogni speranza voi ch'entrate!
>
> had produced. I felt as if a dead & living body had been linked together in loathsome and horrible communion. It was no longer possible to practise self-deception: I believed that one revolting duty yet remained, to continue to deceive my wife.[77]

This appalling feeling of physical revulsion, so strong that he felt that the act of love had become like an act of necrophilia, had its roots as far back as the earliest letters to Miss Hitchener from York in 1811. Shelley had at last managed to do the thing that all his life he found most difficult: to face up to one of the deep and often unpalatable truths of his own feelings and temperament. But this he achieved only in retrospect: in October 1814, and not in April or May.

What was revulsion on one side, became painfully vivid longing and projection on the other. One has the impression that the air round Shelley was heavy with what can only be described as sexual static. Cornelia was merely a temporary conductor for this super-charged atmosphere. Shelley's description of the sensations which surrounded and overwhelmed him are finely, and even touchingly caught in an incident he related to Hogg. It is important to understand that

Shelley makes it quite clear that this happened *before* he went to Skinner Street in June, and therefore *before* he had met Mary Godwin:

> I wandered in the fields alone. The season was most beautiful. The evenings were so serene & mild – I never had before felt so intensely the subduing voluptuousness of the impulses of spring. Manifestations of my approaching change tinged my waking thoughts, & afforded inexhaustible subject for the visions of my sleep. I recollect that one day I undertook to walk from Bracknell to my father's (40 miles). A train of visionary events arranged themselves in my imagination until ideas almost acquired the intensity of sensations. Already I had met the female who was destined to be mine, already had she replied to my exulting recognition, already were the difficulties surmounted that opposed an entire union. I had even proceeded so far as to compose a letter to Harriet on the subject of my passion for another. Thus was my walk beguiled, at the conclusion of which I was hardly sensible of fatigue.[78]

Hogg records that a friend saw him at Field Place on this occasion, when he was welcomed clandestinely by his mother; he leant on a grand piano in the drawing-room and with one hand playing over and over again a little melody which was said to have been a favourite of Harriet Grove's.[79]

Shelley was drawn from Bracknell and the dream by the humdrum reality of money. His Welsh creditors had been pressing him in May, as two brief notes to John Williams show.[80] With creditors on one hand, and Godwin on the other, and both getting restless, it was time to realize the *post obit* bond with the Nash brothers. On 5 May he dined with Godwin, where fleetingly he may have glimpsed Mary. On the 6th he wrote to Nash's solicitor to guarantee that 'there has been no portion of the Shelley Estate sold under the Settlement of 1791'.* He also had to declare the previous *post obit* acquired from Starling in October 1813. On the 14th he was again in London, and writing to Williams, asking him to appoint an official representative for the Tremadoc creditors in London. He stayed at his room in Old Bond Street with Hookham.[81]

By the beginning of June, Shelley's negotiations kept him more frequently in London than in Bracknell. A desultory correspondence with Harriet at Bath was still continuing, for the plan to lease Nantgwillt had once again been resurrected; and apparently for her peace of mind Shelley went through the motions of acquiring the lease stock. On 12 June he wrote to the solicitor Davies in Kingston, Herefordshire, to request his acceptance as the prospective tenant.[82] There is no other evidence that Shelley seriously intended to take Nantgwillt, but it may have remained a vague possibility in his mind. What it does show is that Harriet still dreamt of going there, and considered the separation from

---

* The somewhat involved terms and implications of this settlement are discussed on pp. 283-5.

Shelley as only temporary. It is impossible to say how far Shelley was deliberately deceiving Harriet at this stage; it is most likely that he regarded the Nantgwillt plan as a convenient way of preventing her from worrying too much, or from worrying him too much. For his mind, indeed his whole being, was elsewhere.

It was June 1814 when Mary Godwin entered his life, and Shelley's world shifted on its axis. With the experiences of the previous five months, and with the state of mind which he had described to Hogg, it is not surprising that the sudden recognition of friendship between himself and the intensely intellectual daughter of Mary Wollstonecraft took him by storm. Mary was three months short of 17, and strikingly pretty. Like Harriet, Mary had an extremely attractive and characteristic aureole of hair, which seemed to draw Shelley as if it were the emanation of her own spirit burning above the broad pale forehead. Jane Clairmont later described it, as though it were a kind of spiritual presence: 'Mary's hair is light brown, of sunny and burnished brightness like the autumnal foliage when played upon by the rays of the setting sun; / it sets in round her face and falls upon her shoulders in gauzy wavings and is so fine it looks as if the wind had tangled it together into a golden network . . . it was so fine one feared / to disturb the beauty. . . .'[83] Jane, her half-sister and adoring shadow, was a few months younger. From the start, the friendship grew on a triangular basis.

When Shelley came to talk and dine with Godwin at Skinner Street, with the topic rarely shifting from the *post obit* negotiations, it seemed natural that Godwin's two girls should help to entertain him and cheer his spirits in the interludes. Shelley had also offered to teach Jane Italian, and Mary was a kind of chaperone. Neither Mr nor Mrs Godwin suspected the power of the alchemy that was brewing. Shelley and the two girls enjoyed long afternoon walks around London in the radiant June weather, and their favourite rendezvous was Mary Wollstonecraft's grave in Old St Pancras Church Yard. Mary, Jane and Shelley sat on the grave and talked for hours. We do not know what they talked of: could it have been other than the rights of women, free love, atheism, political and social tyranny, the community of radical spirits? How far Shelley, sensing the abnormally close relationship between Mary and her father, felt that he had discovered another paternal tyranny that required liberation, we cannot tell either, though it is hinted at in one of his letters. He presented a copy of *Queen Mab* to her with a facetious joke on the fly leaf, but she wrote secretly in it: 'I am thine, exclusively thine. I have pledged myself to thee and sacred is the gift.'

By mid-June, Shelley had taken rooms 'at an Inn in Fleet Street', and from 19 to 29 June he dined at Skinner Street every day. During these very few days, the friendship had exploded into mutual passion.

There can be no doubt that Shelley was entirely swept off his feet by the sudden vision of the daughter of William Godwin and Mary Wollstonecraft: physical passion, brotherly affinity, spiritual identity burst upon him like a thunderclap. After the grinding months of Edinburgh and Bracknell, after the naggings of unsatisfactory fatherhood and the tramels of the disappointed inheritance, it was as if he could start his youth all over again, a dazzling second chance. Mary offered fresh, 16-year-old sexuality combined in the most extra-ordinary way with the precocious intellectual flair of her Godwinian upbringing. She was both naïve and knowing, both flesh and spirit, burning with a youth and intelligence which blazed out all the more hypnotically against the gloomy, hopeless, complicated collapse of Shelley's married relationship with Harriet. With only momentary hesitations and misgivings, he fled from the shadow into the sun. Love was free, and to promise for ever to love the same woman was absurd.

An agonized, self-dramatizing little poem written 'To Mary Wollstonecraft Godwin' in mid-June, and clandestinely slipped across the book counter at Skinner Street, openly displayed the alternative chances of life that Harriet and Mary seemed to offer him –

> To sit and curb the soul's mute rage
>   Which preys upon itself alone;
> To curse the life which is the cage
>   Of fettered grief that dares not groan,
> Hiding from many a careless eye
> The scornèd load of agony. . . .
>
> To spend years thus, and be rewarded,
>   As thou, sweet love, requited me
> When none were near – Oh! I did wake
>   From torture for that moment's sake.
>
> Upon my heart thy accents sweet
>   Of peace and pity fell like dew
> On flowers half dead; – thy lips did meet
>   Mine tremblingly; thy dark eyes threw
> Their soft persuasion on my brain,
> Charming away its dream of pain.[84]

For Mary the passion seems to have been equally sudden and overwhelming, though of a different order. She had already heard much of Shelley's daring exploits from her sisters Fanny and Jane, especially Jane, and he was the kind of figure her whole education had brought her up to admire: a poet, an intellectual, a radical and an activist. But to find his attention turned so fiercely upon her within the very first days of their meeting, to find him so passionate and yet so bitter, so tender and yet so frightening, was an experience that pierced her to the very heart. The childhood security of the Godwin household, dominated by the heavy emotional demands of her father and yet made comfortless by the jealousy of her stepmother, was broken open for her by his restless, pursuing presence and the quick, unmistakable sound of his footsteps darting up the stairs at the back of the shop and the sudden low call – Mary! He spoke to her with a directness and intensity which was so new to her, and yet she instantly recognized it as love. With a singlemindedness that later proved wholly characteristic, Mary soon found the irresistible moment at her mother's graveside in Old St Pancras Churchyard, and then simply and explicitly declared her own love for Shelley, offered him both body and soul, and then, almost calmly, awaited the consequences.* It was Sunday, 26 June, and they walked back arm in arm. Beside them, a little puzzled and a little envious, walked Jane who had been waiting patiently on a distant tombstone.

Mary entered in her copy of *Queen Mab*: 'This book is sacred to me and as no other creature shall ever look into it, I may write what I please. Yet what shall I write? That I love the author beyond all power of expression and that I am parted from him. Dearest and only love, by that love we have promised to each other although I may not be yours I can never be another's.'[86] It sounded almost like a challenge.

The following day, 27 June, Shelley revealed their love to Godwin. To his surprise, the philosopher was appalled. Godwin was now in an unenviable position. The loan from Nash, which he had been assiduously helping Shelley to negotiate, was very nearly completed; and yet all prudence bid him shut his house to a married man who had openly declared his designs on his daughter. After agonized thought, he decided to try and temporize. He described in a letter to an old friend how Shelley had 'had the madness to disclose his plans to me, and to ask my consent. I expostulated with him with all the energy of which I was master, and with so much effect that for the moment he promised to give up his licentious love, and return to virtue.'[87] He asked Shelley to visit Skinner Street less often, and the regular dining stopped after 29 June; however Shelley continued to call and take occasional meals until 7 July. On the previous day, the transactions for a loan of £2,593 10s. 0d. were completed with Nash, of which half was to be made over direct to Godwin. Godwin later said that it was only on

---

* Godwin later implied that Shelley there and then 'seduced' his daughter on top of Mary Wollstonecraft's gravestone. In one of her subsequent novels, *Falkner* (1837), Mary staged a passionate declaration of love in a cemetery. The girl declares her love first, and the man responds by weeping on the girl's breasts. In a letter of October 1814, Shelley wrote emphatically that 'no expressions' could convey 'the *manner*' in which Mary declared herself.[85]

this evening, 6 July, that Shelley declared himself, when the loan had already been finalized, but this was not so. The actual money did not reach Godwin until thirteen days later, on 19 July.[88] From 8 July, it seems that Shelley was no longer welcome at Skinner Street except for formal meetings with Godwin. Meanwhile, he had stopped writing to Harriet altogether for a week, and Hookham received an anxious inquiry from Bath. Godwin began to compose a ten-page letter to Shelley, which took him two days to write.[89]

There is no reliable account of the next fraught ten days of Shelley's life. Mrs Godwin recalled awful scenes at Skinner Street, with Shelley bursting in furious and hysterical, and on one occasion threatening to commit suicide by poisoning himself with an overdose of laudanum in their front room.* The bottle had to be wrested from him by Mary. Godwin's diary records serious 'Talks' held first with Mary, and then with Jane. Peacock remembered Shelley in the grip of 'a sudden, violent, irresistible, uncontrollable passion', torn between loyalty to Harriet and love for Mary. 'His eyes were bloodshot, his hair and dress disordered. He caught up a bottle of laudanum, and said: "I never part from this." '[90] He also implies that Shelley considered suicide.

As a result of Hookham's news, Shelley summoned Harriet from Bath, and she arrived in London about 13 July. Harriet, in her own person, was now Godwin's last hope of avoiding either tragedy or scandal, and there is evidence that he tried to bring all available forces to control the situation. He had private consultations with Harriet, took Shelley out on a coach drive, and even summoned Mrs Boinville from Bracknell for her advice and support. But Shelley, at his first meeting, had effectively stunned Harriet, by withholding nothing and insisting that he loved Mary with passion while he had only ever felt a brotherly attachment to *her*. Yet he insisted that he was remaining loyal to Harriet. His explanation was devastatingly simple:

> I repeat (& believe me, for I am sincere) that my attachment to you is unimpaired: I conceive that it has acquired even a deeper & more lasting

---

* Mrs Godwin's account, though not altogether reliable, gives some impression of Shelley's alarming force when roused. 'Then, one day when Godwin was out, Shelley suddenly entered the shop and went upstairs. I perceived him from the counting-house and hastened after him, and overtook him at the schoolroom door. I entreated him not to enter. He looked extremely wild. He pushed me aside with extreme violence, and entering, walked straight to Mary. "They wish to separate us, my beloved; but Death shall unite us," and offered her a bottle of laudanum. "By this you can escape from tyranny; and this," taking a small pistol from his pocket, "shall reunite me to you." Poor Mary turned as pale as a ghost, and my poor silly [Jane], who is so timid even at trifles, at the sight of the pistol filled the room with her shrieks. . . . With tears streaming down her cheeks, [Mary] entreated him to calm himself and go home. . . . "I won't take this laudanum; but if you will only be reasonable and calm, I will promise to be ever faithful to you." This seemed to calm him, and he left the house leaving the phial of laudanum on the table.' Mrs Godwin to Lady Mountcashell, 20 August 1814. Dowden II, Appendix A, p. 544.

character, that it is now less exposed than ever to the fluctuations of phantasy or caprice. Our connection was not one of passion & impulse. Friendship was its basis, & on this basis it has enlarged & strengthened. It is no reproach to me that you have never filled my heart with an all sufficing passion ... may you find a lover as passionate and faithful, as I shall ever be a friend affectionate & sincere![91]

If this struck coldly into Harriet's heart, the more so because it was basically true, with what an icy chill she recognized the ghost of her former self in Shelley's description of Mary: 'I wish you could see Mary; to the most indifferent eyes she would be interesting only from her sufferings, & the tyranny which is exercised upon her. I murmur not if you feel incapable of compassion & love for the object & sharer of my passion.' Shelley later discovered that, probably on Godwin's advice, Harriet wrote to Mary about him in a letter which recommended that Mary should write to Shelley asking her lover to 'calm' himself and 'subdue' his passion for her.[92] It does not seem likely that Mary wrote such a letter. Harriet, who saw the Chapel Street history repeating itself at Skinner Street, at once suspected the denouement. As far as one can gather, she took shelter in the idea that this was a passing infatuation, and that Shelley would eventually be drawn back by the ties of loyalty to his legal wife, and above all by the ties of affection for his children: for Harriet had told Shelley that she was pregnant again. She was consoled by Peacock.

Having received his share of the *post obit* on the 19th, Godwin was more than ever determined to crush Shelley's fatal and inconvenient passion. Both Mary and Jane were confined to the house, and Godwin wrote long letters to Harriet on the 22nd, and Shelley on the 25th. But it was all in vain. When he rose early on the morning of 28 July, he found a letter leaning on his mantelpiece. Shelley had gone one better than his great-grandfather: on his second elopement he had taken two girls.

10
Three for the Road: Europe 1814

Shelley ordered a chaise for 4 a.m. and stood waiting at the corner of Skinner Street 'until the lightening and the stars became pale'.[1] The air was still and oppressive, and the city seemed to slumber uneasily. At long last Mary and Jane appeared at a side-door clutching small bundles, their faces drawn and pale from lack of sleep. They mounted up and clattered away over the cobbles. At Dartford, they hired four horses to outstrip pursuit, but Mary became ill with the stormy summer heat and the speed, so that they had to halt at each stage for her to recover, while Shelley like a character out of one of his own romances, was 'divided between anxiety for her health and terror lest our pursuers should arrive'. Jane gazed listlessly from the carriage window, silent and close to tears. At 4 p.m. they had reached Dover, and by six they hired a small open channel boat, and were drawing out from the white cliffs while the sun set and the sails flapped in the flagging breeze. Jane looked at the English cliffs and thought 'I shall never see these more'.[2] As the moon came up, a heavy swell set in, and the sailors debated whether to make for Calais or Boulogne. The wind moved to the opposing quarter, and blew stiffly all night, while the summer sheet lightning shook out constantly from an ominous horizon. Mary sat exhausted between Shelley's knees, and slept fitfully. At dawn, the wind veered and waves broke violently into the undecked boat, and the three of them huddled together under travelling cloaks, too tired to feel more than discomfort and disappointment at the prospect of being drowned. Mary did not speak or look, but Shelley was content merely to feel her presence. Then suddenly the wind was blowing them fast into Calais, and the boat drove upon the sands, and they were safe. Shelley looked down and found Mary was asleep. He woke her gently and said: 'Look, Mary, the sun rises over France.' Together they disembarked and the three of them walked wearily and happily over the sands to the inn.

By the evening their pursuers in the shape of Mrs Godwin had arrived. Shelley refused to allow her to see Mary, but Jane spent the night with her mother, and was almost persuaded to return by the 'pathos of Mrs Godwin's appeal'. But the next morning, Saturday the 30th, after Shelley had talked to Jane and advised her to reconsider for half an hour, she told her mother she would continue with Shelley and Mary. Mrs Godwin, speechless with fury, returned to England on the next boat: it was complete victory for Shelley. Refreshed and heartened by sleep, the three set out for Paris, with a vague scheme to travel to Switzerland, and take a house on Lake Lucerne where their friends might join them to form the community of like spirits as Shelley had attempted at Lynmouth, Tan-yr-allt and Nantgwillt. Now after the fears and uncertainties they were over-whelmed by a sense of relief and everything seemed strange and delightful. Mary recalled: 'We saw with extasy the strange costume of the French women, read with delight our own descriptions in the passport, looked with curiosity on every *plât*, fancying that the fried-leaves of artichokes were frogs; we saw shepherds in opera-hats, post-boys in jack-boots, and (*pour comble de merveille*) heard little boys and girls talk French: it was acting a novel, being an incarnate romance.'[3] That, at any rate, was how she remembered it twelve years after-wards.

At the time, however, their continental expedition was very far from being all marvels and delights. Once in Paris, they took cheap lodgings in the Hotel Vienne, and Shelley and Mary were too happy to sleep. Then they embarked on a frustrating week trying to arrange passports with the police, and to borrow money. Shelley was forced to sell his watch, chain and various personal valuables, for amazingly he had not waited long enough in London to secure any actual coin from the Nash *post obit*. He had hoped that Hookham might be persuaded to forward a bridging loan from London, but all they received was 'a dull and insolent letter'; Hookham had apparently joined the general condemna-tion of Shelley's behaviour, with Peacock, Godwin and the Boinvilles (to whom Shelley was in debt for forty pounds). Negotiations with a French banker came to nothing, but finally a lawyer called Tavernier, 'an insupportable fool' according to Shelley, promised to secure them sixty pounds of credit, while arranging their passports, and providing a forwarding address for their English letters. Jane, who could speak the most French of the three, helped Shelley with his negotiations, and was sent out to walk with Tavernier on the boulevard.

During this time, while they were prisoners in Paris, they walked in the Tuileries, 'formal and uninteresting', gazed at Notre Dame and had a glimpse of the pictures in the Louvre. Mary remained rather weak and ill and could not be made to eat much. But her world now revolved round Shelley, and she was perfectly content to curl up in his embrace, resting upon his bosom, indifferent to food and, according to their shared journal, 'insensible to all future evil'. Sometimes she read him passages from Byron's poems. 'Our own perceptions are the world to us,' noted Shelley dreamily. On their first evening at the Hotel Vienne, Mary had opened to Shelley her precious box of papers, hitherto kept secret, which contained among other things her own earliest writings, and the love letters between Mary Wollstonecraft and Godwin. Though Mary was not well, Shelley and she slept together on the sofa. On 4 August she reminded him that it was his birthday; he had forgotten. He was 22.

By Sunday, 7 August, the sixty pounds was secured in French money, and they determined on the plan to walk to Uri on Lake Lucerne, despite the fact that their host at the hotel thought they were mad to go alone in a countryside that was still disordered by the ravages of war. 'Madame Sa Hote could not be persuaded', wrote Mary in her first personal contribution to the journal, 'that it was secure and delightful to walk in solitude in the mountains.' But they were in high spirits and Mary was feeling better.

On Monday the 8th, Shelley and Jane went to the stables and purchased an ass, upon which they hopefully mounted their baggage, and departed from Paris. Over the next four days they walked steadily south-east through Guignes, where Napoleon had slept at the inn, Provins with its ruined citadel, Nogent and St Aubin, with vines in the fields, the first evidence of cultivation for many leagues, though the grapes were not ripe enough to pick. By Saturday they had reached Troyes, in the Haute Marne. They covered about thirty miles a day. Shelley sprained his ankle, and the ass refused to pull its weight and had to be exchanged for a mule, which was if anything less co-operative. They took turns riding it, until Shelley's sprain made the girls refuse to let him dismount. The *auberges* were mostly filthy and not altogether friendly, the beds were 'infinitely detestable', and one evening they had nothing for supper but milk and sour bread. At the inn near Troyes, the innkeeper thought he had sized up the little party, and strongly insinuated that the unattached young lady, Jane, was destined to share his bed. Shelley dealt brusquely with the man, language on such occasion being no barrier; but the innkeeper's rats were less easily deterred. Finally Jane shared Shelley's bed as the solution to all problems. In the morning Mary wrote up the journal: 'Jane was not able to sleep all night for the rats who as she said put their cold paws on her face – she however rested on our bed which her four-footed enemies dared not invade perhaps having heard the threat that Shelley terrified the man with who said he would sleep with Jane.'[4] The countryside throughout their walk showed evidence of war, famine and crippling poverty. On the last long leg into Troyes, on Friday afternoon, they fell in with a man whose children had all been murdered by the Cossacks. They walked on through the gathering dusk and Shelley, riding on the mule, told them the story of the Seven Sleepers to beguile the time.

On Saturday morning Shelley and Jane went out and sold their mule, buying in exchange a *voiture* which cost them five napoleons. They planned that this should take them as far as Neufchatel, where it could be resold. They had already lost fifteen napoleons on the ass, the mule and the saddles, and their finances were again looking very thin. Mary stayed behind at the inn and wrote letters. Shelley joined her and wrote to Harriet. He took up the theme of his last conversations with her, quite calmly and composedly, insisting that he was still completely true to her as a friend, and that he wanted her to rejoin him in his search for a community of like spirits which he hoped to set up on the Swiss lakes.

> My dearest Harriet, I write to you from this detestable Town. I write to show you that I do not forget you. I write to urge you to come to Switzerland, where you will at least find one firm & constant friend, to whom your interests will be always dear, by whom your feelings will never be willfully injured. From none can you expect this but me. All else are either unfeeling & selfish. ... I will write at length from Neufchatel or Uri. ... Direct your letters 'd'etre laisses à la Bureau de Poste Neufchatel' [*sic*] until you hear again. ... You shall know our adventures more detailed, if I do not hear at Neufchatel that I am soon to have the pleasure of communicating to you in person, & of welcoming you to some sweet retreat I will procure for you in the mountains.[5]

To this he added that she should bring two deeds, connected with their legal separation, and the settlement of an annuity on Harriet and the children. Supported by the love and affection of Mary and Jane, and busy with the excitement of their expedition, Harriet's pain and misery was obviously quite unreal to him. His letter was perfectly genuine in intention, and yet perfectly unfeeling. Only in reference to Peacock, who had sided sharply with Harriet during the separation crisis, did Shelley display any emotion. He knew that Peacock was helping Harriet: 'I have written to Peacock to superintend money affairs – He is expensive inconsiderate & cold; but surely not utterly perfidious & unfriendly and unmindful of our kindness to him. Besides interest will secure his attention to these things.'* Peacock was unmoved by Shelley's bitterness at this time, and always took his swings of mood for granted, though between Harriet and Mary Godwin, there was never any doubt as to his preference.

Harriet had moved back to her father's at Chapel Street, and continued to correspond with Mrs Nugent in Dublin, and to look after her child. She kept in

---

* It seems that Shelley may have pressed money on Peacock during their stay in Edinburgh, the previous winter. Leigh Hunt says that Shelley gave Peacock 'a pension of a hundred a year', but Shelley would not have been able to do this – a quarter of his income – until summer 1815 at earliest when there was a family settlement. Possibly Peacock, like Godwin, benefited from the money realized by the ruinous *post orbit* with Nash; or again Harriet, who had access to Shelley's account for paying off some of his numerous bills, rewarded Peacock for his good offices on her behalf.

touch with John Williams at Tremadoc, and tried to sort out Shelley's unpaid bills there, and also in London. She drew heavily on the remainder of the loan in Shelley's bank account. A week after receiving Shelley's letter from Troyes, she wrote to Mrs Nugent: 'Mr Shelley is in France. You will be surprised to find I am not with him: but times are altered, dear friend, and tho' I will not tell you what has passed, still do not think that you cloud your mind with your sorrows. Every age has its cares. God knows, I have mine. Dear Ianthe is quite well. She is fourteen months old, and has six teeth.'[6] Nothing on earth would have dragged her to visit the Godwin daughters on the Swiss lakes.

Meanwhile, collecting his impressions of France at the inn at Troyes, Shelley was appalled by the frightful desolation they had witnessed. 'Village after village entirely ruined & burned; the white ruins towering in innumerable forms of destruction among the beautiful trees. The inhabitants were famished; families once perfectly independent now beg their bread in this wretched country. No provisions, no accommodation; filth, misery & famine everywhere.'[7] They determined to make as rapidly as they could for Switzerland, and left in their little carriage at 4 on Sunday morning.

Trundling down the valley of the river Aube, where the country changed abruptly, they found themselves surrounded by sunlit, vine-hung hillsides, with sudden little expanses of green meadows, 'intermixed with groves of poplars and white willow, and spires of village churches which the Cossacks had still spared'. It filled them with delight, and suddenly relaxed, they got out of the carriage and slept for two hours in the shade of a wood belonging to a neighbouring château. Shelley rummaged in his baggage at Jane's request, and gave her one of his notebooks to use as a diary. It was the one he had started at Bracknell in the spring, when studying Italian with Cornelia Turner. She turned it round and started at the other end, heading it on the inside cover: 'Will you try what Fortune will for you', and sketching a face.[8]

During the next three days they pushed on through Langres, where there was a numerous and vulgar set come for the fair; through Champlitte, where Shelley found a little girl so lovely that he tried to persuade her father to let them take her in the carriage; through Besançon with its 'stupendous brown rocks' – the first hint of the Alpine foothills – and a ruined castle perched above the gorge; and up as far as Mort, where they passed the night fitfully, on Wednesday, 17 August, in the inn kitchen, the beds too crawling with lice to sleep in. During the evening, Shelley and Mary went out and sat on the rocks, and read Mary Wollstonecraft's *Mary, a Fiction*. 'We sleep all night by the Kitchen fire,' recorded Jane, 'Shelley much disturbed by the creaking door, the screams of a poor smothered child & the fille who washed the glasses.'[9]

On Thursday they hoped to get to Pontarlier, within striking distance of the

Swiss border, but when they stopped in a pinewood at midday to rest in the shade, their *voiturier*, who had become increasingly irritated with Shelley during the last few days, drove on ahead without them. Mary's journal merely says that the driver pretended that it was all a mistake, and told many lies. What actually happened was recorded by Jane when she wrote up her diary, probably several years later. It made a telling *vignette*.

> On our way to Pontarlier, we came to a clear running shallow stream, and Shelley entreated the Driver to stop while he from under a bank could bathe himself – and he wanted Mary to do the same as the Bank sheltered one from every eye – but Mary would not – first, she said it would be most indecent, and then also she had no towel and could not dry herself – He said he would gather leaves from the trees and she could dry herself with those but she refused and said how could he think of such a thing.[10]

Shelley behaved, said Jane delightedly, 'just as if he were Adam in Paradise before his fall'. Clearly Mary was not so delighted. As for the *voiturier*, he thought Shelley was touched. They walked on during the afternoon, and took a lift in a hay-cart. The moon slid down below the woody horizon before they reached Pontarlier, where the *voiturier* had a thousand excuses – all falsehood.[11] But the beds were clean for the first time in France.

The next day, Friday the 19th, they caught their first glimpse of the Alps. 'Hill after hill is seen extending its craggy outline before the other, and, far behind all, towering above every feature of the scene, the snowy Alps; they are 100 miles distant; they look like those accumulated clouds of dazzling white that arrange themselves on the horizon in summer.' Jane thought they were white flaky clouds too at first sight, but then after a long and steady examination – 'yes, they were really the Alps'. They gazed and gazed as their carriage rattled down towards Neufchatel, through upland meadows and pines and outcrops of bare rock. Their new Swiss *voiturier* insisted on talking though: 'it was like discord in music,' thought Jane, 'his associations with the mountains were those of butter and cheese – how good the pasturage was for the cows – & the cows yielded good milk & then the good milk made good cheese . . .'.[12] But still, after the French, there was freedom in his countenance.

Shelley had the idea for a romance forming in his mind, about a small community of idealists living cut off from the world in a secret valley somewhere in the Near East. The Alps were transformed into an even more exotic vision, as he wrote a few days later:

> After many days of wandering the Assassins pitched their tents in the valley of Bethzatanai. . . . The mountains of Lebanon had been divided to their base

to form this happy valley; on every side their icy summits darted their white pinnacles into the clear blue sky, imaging, in their grotesque outline, minarets, and ruined domes, and columns worn with time. . . . Meteoric shapes, more effulgent than the moonlight, hung on the wandering clouds and mixed in discordant dance around the spiral fountains. Blue vapours assumed strange lineaments under the rocks and among the ruins, lingering like ghosts with slow and solemn step.[13]

At Neufchatel on Saturday morning, they found nothing at the Poste Restante; nothing from Harriet, and much more serious, no remittances from Hookham or Peacock or Shelley's solicitor. Once again, they were virtually without money. Shelley hastily sold off their carriage to the *voiturier*, and went into town to negotiate a loan at a bank. He was not very hopeful, but to the astonishment and consolation of Jane and Mary at the inn, he returned within two hours 'staggering under the weight of a large canvas bag full of silver'. Shelley later wrote in the journal, referring to himself in the third person, as was the communal idiom: 'Shelley alone looks grave on the occasion, for he alone clearly apprehends that francs and louis d'or are like the white and flying clouds of noon, that is gone before one can say "Jack Robinson".' The Swiss banker's advance was worth about thirty-eight pounds, though Jane had the vague idea that it was a round fifty pounds. Shelley booked cheap seats on the local diligence, and they left at dawn on Sunday, travelling towards Lucerne, with misty views of the St Gothard. Their inn room, after Zoffingen, was graced with a glass case of stuffed birds, which they glared at disapprovingly, and Shelley was in a 'jocosely horrible' humour. On this day, there was the first sign of Jane's moody temperament; there was a brief quarrel, and Mary and Shelley went to look at the cathedral at Soleure alone, and, in an irritable state themselves, they found it very modern and stupid. The disagreement was patched up by Shelley: Mary recorded, 'Shelley and Jane talk concerning Jane's character', without further comment. Jane's diary has the page torn between Sunday the 21st and Tuesday the 23rd.[14]

This was to be the beginning of a recurrent pattern, which had an enormous influence on Shelley's domestic life for the next six years. Jane and Mary, though very close to each other in childhood and adolescence, and with only six months' age between them, were nevertheless almost absolute temperamental opposites. Jane had undergone neither the intellectual awakening, nor the emotional strain of having Godwin as her childhood father. With thick, black unruly ringlets of hair parted round an oval face, a compact and generously moulded figure verging on chubbiness, and large dark bright eyes, she was volatile, childish and outgoing. On her father's side, she was half Swiss, and she always felt at home in

Europe, eventually remaining for many years as a governess in Moscow. Although without Mary's intelligence, she wrote letters and diaries always more lively and more immediately observant than her half-sister's, bursting with life and feeling, and as she grew older, sharpened with wit. By nature she was passionate and generous, but she could also hate – as subsequent events proved – with a sustained and fiery anger where Mary could only freeze and turn away. She was always very much at the mercy of her feelings, while Mary frequently felt divorced from sentiment. She was sexually attractive to men (the disappointed innkeeper at Troyes was the first of many), more obviously so than Mary, and it was characteristic that one of her accomplishments, besides languages, was singing, which she did with verve and confidence.* Throughout their tour through France and Switzerland, Jane's mood fluctuated wildly between the sullen and the ecstatic. At 16 she was full of unharnessed energies and interests, and unfocused passion. She was fond of Shelley from the start, and competed mildly – and occasionally more than mildly – for his attentions, against Mary. For his part, the relationship with Jane, which was built up gradually and through many vicissitudes and crises over the next eight years of his life, was if not the most intimate, yet perhaps the kindest and most successful of all his relationships with the opposite sex – a field in which his successes were sometimes startling, but rarely lasting. Jane and Mary grew steadily apart from this time onwards, and not the least reason for this was Shelley; though, as now at Soleure, it was always he who, perhaps surprisingly, supplied the necessary patience and understanding and contrived the many reconciliations.

On Tuesday morning, the 23rd, they arrived at last at Lucerne and, now in reach of their projected residence, they bought needful supplies with their dwindling sum of money, and embarked on a boat for Bessen on the further side. The weather was hot and clear, and they gazed with rapture at the rocks and pine forests covering the feet of the immense mountains. As their thoughts turned to the community they hoped vaguely to form, Shelley bought out his precious copy of Barruel's *History of Jacobinism* and they read together of the Illuminists' secret societies on the boat. The book and its ideas were probably new both to Jane and to Mary; Jane records that they studied it over the next three days. The boat put in at Bessen, and after a comical scene in the wrong inn, they moved up the road to Brunnen, situated on the far end of the lake opposite Uri. From their room they gazed down at lake waters, breaking in a stiff evening wind below the house. Around them towered the pine-covered mountains and rocky peaks. Now they had to find a home.

It was not easy. The next morning, as they took stock of their money and

* In 1817 Shelley was to write a poem in praise of her singing, where the musical and sexual gift are successfully united in evocation. See 'To Constantia, Singing' in Chapter 15.

their expensive but none too salubrious surroundings, they were depressed: 'We cannot procure a house; we are in despair; the filth of the apartment is terrible to Mary; she cannot bear it all winter.' They thought of moving on round the lake, but the wind was contrary. Finally they found an apartment of two rooms to rent in 'an ugly house they call the Chateau', set back from Brunnen on a small hill; it cost one louis a month, and they took it for six months, starting from the next day. Shelley and Mary walked by the lake and read Tacitus's account of the Siege of Jerusalem, yet another beleaguered community. Shelley turned the idea over in his mind. Jane went to bed early and had 'very curious dreams or perhaps they were realities'.[15]

On the 25th they moved to their new apartment, and were visited by their landlord, the local abbé, whom Shelley treated with ostentatious ill grace. Jane heard without enjoyment of a local legend at Brunnen, that a renegade priest had taken his mistress across to the mountains opposite the village, only to meet divine retribution in the form of an avalanche that overwhelmed both of them. On some nights, it was said, their moans could be heard drifting across the waters on the wind.[16] Shelley noticed Jane's fright; but he encouraged her to work at Barruel in the evening as the rain fell, and the clouds came down far below the mountain tops. Meanwhile, with Mary's help, he was beginning his own peculiar fable, a romance which they had immediately entitled *The Assassins*. He worked on it that evening, and most of the rest of the next day.

The Assassins as we now have it is a story of four chapters, of which the last is unfinished. The main part of the narrative, which alternates between exotic description and discussions of abstract ethical principles, tells how a small breakaway sect of primitive Christians, 'an obscure community of speculators',* escaped the sack of Jerusalem by the Romans and fled to safety. 'Attached from principle to peace, despising and hating the pleasures and customs of degenerate mankind, this unostentatious community of good and happy men fled to the

---

* Historically, the Assassins were a sect of Ismaeli extremists of the eleventh century commanded by the Persian Hassan-ben-Sabbah (Sheikh el Djebel – the Lord of the Mountains) and based on the mountain stronghold of Alamut. According to Mary in her notes of 1840, Shelley first read about them in Sales de Lisle's *The Old Man of the Mountain* – *Le Vieux de la Montaigne*, printed in 1799. It was a book that Shelley probably picked up during their week in Paris. Shelley was attracted by three elements in the Assassins' history: the tradition that Hassan had been educated by a mystic sub-cult of primitive, communist Christians known as the Druses who lived in a secret valley of the Lebanon; the idea that Hassan was dedicated to political terrorism intended to destroy religious and state authorities; and finally the curious legend of the Garden of Earthly Paradise, administered by beautiful girls and youths, in which each Assassin was allowed to spend one perfect day of complete licence on the eve of his mission, as a foretaste of eternal ecstasy. The garden was said originally to have been created by Hassan at Alamut. Such heretical and antinomian splinter groups as the Assassins, the Druses, the Gnostics and the Manicheans became important in the development of Shelley's mature political thought and poetic imagery. They illustrated for him the endless historical struggle between Revolution and Tyranny, Satan and God, Light and Darkness.

solitudes of Lebanon.' In Lebanon they find the happy valley, with its tropical alpine setting, 'the flowering orange tree, the balsam, and innumerable odiferous shrubs', where the fantastic broken sculptural remains of a previous civilization are hidden by the vegetation. Here they settle, unaffected by previous history, and quietly survive the Fall of Rome:

> Four centuries had passed thus terribly characterized by the most calamitous revolutions. The Assassins, meanwhile, undisturbed by surrounding tumult, possessed and cultivated their fertile valley. The gradual operation of their peculiar condition had matured and perfected the singularity of their charac-ter. . . . Their republic was the scene of perpetual contentions of benevolence; not the heartless and assumed kindness of commercial man, but the genuine virtue. . . . Little embarrassed by the complexities of civilized society, they knew not to conceive any happiness that can be satiated without participation, or that thirsts not to reproduce and perpetually generate itself. . . . They clearly acknowledged in every case that conduct to be entitled to preference which would obviously produce the greatest pleasure. They could not conceive an instance in which it would be their duty to hesitate in causing, at whatever expense, the greatest and most unmixed delight.[17]

The final one-and-a-half chapters embark on an unfinished and semi-allegoric account of how a member of the Assassins' community one day finds the body of a mangled man hanging in the trees, having apparently just dropped into their valley from the sky. The stranger, who is still alive, is being assaulted by a monstrous snake, which he regards with 'a bitter smile of mingled abhorrence and scorn', and complete self-possession. The snake is driven off, and he is succoured by the young Assassin who found him.* Though mild and kind, the stranger occasionally breaks out into demoniac monologues: 'Delight and exultation sit before the closed gates of death! I fear not to dwell beneath their black and mighty shadow. Here thy power may not avail! Thou createst – tis mine to ruin and destroy. I was thy slave – I am thy equal and thy foe. Thou-sands tremble before thy throne, who, at my voice, shall dare to pluck the golden crown from thy unholy head!' He is clearly some semi-divine personage, half Satan, half Illuminist revolutionary. Later, as he convalesces, he watches with delight the Assassin's children at play, while they make a toy boat for another snake – this time a friendly one – to sail in. The snake curls itself in the

---

* The incident of the stranger dropping from the sky is taken directly from Sales de Lisle's romance, and initiates the beginning of the hero's picaresque adventures with his Arab guide. The full sig-nificance of Shelley's use of the Assassins material and de Lisle was first discovered and examined by Jean Overton Fuller, op. cit., pp. 156–61, a fine discursive chapter concluding with the suggestive revelation that the 15-year-old hero of de Lisle's book was named Ariel.

little girl's bosom. Here, without the least hint of a conclusion, the narrative breaks off.*

It is clear that, apart from its literary sources, the themes of *The Assassins* reflect many of the issues on Shelley's own mind during his time in Switzerland, in connection with his flight from London and his plan for a community. The most interesting part of the story concerns his speculation on how the behaviour of the Assassins, once withdrawn from the religious and moral conventions of a large society, would develop under the influence of natural surroundings. The Assassins became rationalists, but also hedonists, whose conduct is only measured by what causes the 'most unmixed delight'. Their natural behaviour is marked by physical gentleness and imaginative energy, they achieve a state of almost complete intellectual and sexual freedom, and at times reach a condition of ecstatic and virtually hallucinogenic perception of the beauties of the physical universe.

> Thus securely excluded from an abhorred world, all thought of its judgement was cancelled by the rapidity of their fervid imaginations. ... A new and sacred fire was kindled in their hearts and sparkled in their eyes. Every gesture, every feature, the minutest action was modelled to beneficence and beauty by the holy inspiration that had descended on their searching spirits. The epidemic transport communicated itself through every heart with the rapidity of a blast from heaven. They were already disembodied spirits; they were already the inhabitants of paradise. To live, to breathe, to move was itself a sensation of immeasurable transport. ... To love, to be loved, suddenly became an insatiable famine of his nature, which the wide circle of the universe, comprehending beings of such inexhaustible variety and stupendous magnitude of excellence, appeared too narrow and confined to satiate.[18]

This is the language of mystical transport, private and ecstatic, and one notes how Shelley has slipped from describing how 'they' felt, to how 'he' felt. It has risen beyond political or social description, to a purely poetical one. From the journal, it is clear that Mary and Shelley worked on it together, with Shelley probably dictating and Mary transcribing.

In Chapter 11, at the heart of the story, Shelley begins to speculate on what would happen if this community of Assassins, once secured in their principles, were to return to the corrupt society outside. Would they remain the same

* This is the first time that snakes appear in Shelley's writings; thereafter they play a large symbolic role in many of the political poems. The snake symbol does not seem to be primarily sexual in Shelley, and although frequently ambiguous, it is usually associated with positive forces of Reason, Freedom or Revolt, as in the Gnostics. In Egyptian mythology, as Shelley later discovered, the serpent swallowing its own tail is the symbol of eternity. Shelley always ridiculed the Hebrew serpent of the Book of Genesis; most memorably in his 'Essay on the Devil' written in Italy, 1821.

peace-loving, free, ecstatic human beings? 'It would be difficult for men of such a sincere and simple faith to estimate the final results of their intentions among the corrupt and slavish multitude.' Here the narrative takes on a specifically political slant again. Shelley argued that there would in fact be a state of war between the two communities: 'against their predilections and distastes an Assassin, accidentally the inhabitant of a civilized community, would wage unremitting hostility from principle'. The Assassin would not accept the right of established government and authority to control and mislead the lower orders. 'Can the power derived from the weakness of the oppressed, or the ignorance of the deceived, confer the right in security to tyrannize and defraud?' No, on the contrary, 'the religion of the Assassin imposes other virtues than endurance when his fellow-men groan under tyranny, or have become so bestial and abject that they cannot feel their chains'. Shelley concludes this argument, and the chapter, with an extraordinary passage in which he invokes a condition of wholesale political terrorism and violence as the justifiable and indeed glorious means towards liberating and freeing a 'civilized' society. This is, undoubtedly, the unspoken coda to his Irish experience which William Godwin, for one, was never allowed to glimpse. With its grim and fantastic gothic imagery, and its fiery, energetic, hate-filled language, it brings Shelley one step further towards his best political poetry.

No Assassin would submissively temporize with vice, and in cold charity become a pandar to falsehood and desolation. His path through the wilderness of civilized society would be marked with the blood of the oppressor and the ruiner. The wretch whom nations tremblingly adore would expiate in his throttling grasp a thousand licensed and venerable crimes.

How many holy liars and parasites, in solemn guise, would his saviour arm drag from their luxurious couches, and plunge in the cold charnel, that the green and many-legged monsters of the slimy grave might eat off at their leisure the lineaments of rooted malignity and detested cunning. The respectable man – smooth, smiling, polished villain whom all the city honours; whose very trade is lies and murder; who buys his daily bread with the blood and tears of men – would feed the ravens with his limbs. The Assassin would cater nobly for the eyeless worms of earth and carrion fowls of heaven.[19]

It is important to remember that *The Assassins* is a work of fiction, and that it is unfinished for the simple reason that Shelley had reached an impasse. It has been one of the most neglected of Shelley's works, although it is clear that it occupies a significant place in the mainstream of his political thought, and centres on questions of freedom, love and violence. The appearance of the outcast, heroic leader in the final chapters, although not pursued, points to the direction in which Shelley was to attempt to resolve his dilemma in the visionary work of the years 1815-19. His ultimate projection is Prometheus himself. The desperate longing for a transcending and paradisal form of love, for ever unsatisfied, which appears in the description of the Assassins' life, also points towards the more inward and psychologically orientated work which Shelley began in the spring of the following year and displayed at length in his notebook essays 'On Love' and 'On Life', and his *rite de passage* of adolescent sexuality, *Alastor*. That Shelley managed to take up and pursue these themes again, after a lapse of almost two years, can be largely attributed to the confidence and affection which his relationships with Mary, and also Jane Clairmont, had brought back into his world.

Shelley was to add to and rework his romance desultorily over the coming days and weeks, but Mary's dislike of their house and surroundings and Brunnen, and their increasingly frail finances, quickly interrupted his first burst after only two days. On Friday, 26 August, a mere three days after their arrival on the lake, they suddenly decided that they had had enough. Arguing through the afternoon, as the rain fell miserably on the waters below them, they decided first to go over the St Gothard, and finally, quite abruptly, to return to England and London. They could manage it, Shelley calculated, if they took the risk of travelling by the 'water-diligence' used mostly by local peasants, merchants and students, down the length of the Rhine to a Channel port. The next morning, the 27th, they flitted from Brunnen at dawn on the first boat available, having packed their bags and omitted to inform or pay their landlord, and gazed back on the receding shore ironically imagining 'the astonishment of the good people of Brunnen'. 'Most laughable to think', as Jane put it, 'of our going to England the second day after we entered a new house for six months – All because the stove don't suit.'[20] From Lucerne they launched on a headlong river journey in a series of local boats and water-buses of varying degrees of discomfort and precariousness, which took them breathlessly, travelling day and night without respite, on often swollen and dangerous waterways, down the river Reuss through Dettingen to Mumpf, and switching to the Rhine at Rheinfelden, on down through Basle, Strasbourg, Mannheim and Mayence as far as Bonn, which they reached nine days later on Monday, 5 September. From there they crawled at a maddening snail's pace over the border into Holland by carriage, arriving at Rotterdam on the evening of the 8th, exhausted, and with barely enough money to buy a meal.

During this whirling river-trip they fluctuated wildly, as lonely travellers often do, between moods of elation and desperation. Jane, over-excited by Shelley's talk of terrorism and political revenge as he continued to work on *The Assassins*,[21] had a fit of 'horrors' while reading the passage in *King Lear* where

Gloucester's eyes are torn out. 'Such refinement in wickedness and cruelty', she wrote in her diary, '[it] produces almost stupendous despair on the reader.' Mary noted briefly in the journal, 'interrupted by Jane's horrors; pack up'. It was Shelley who had to calm Jane down and put her to sleep, though it seems as if he was partly responsible for her unsettled state. In her diary she wrote, '"What shall poor Cordelia do – love & be silent" – Oh this is true – Real Love will never shew itself to the eye of broad day – it courts the secret glades – Go to bed after. . . .'[22] The rest of the entry, where she describes Shelley's talk with her, is thoroughly crossed out. He could not help being intrigued by Jane's susceptibilities to the macabre, which made her particularly vulnerable to his old cultivation of feminine fears. This episode was not to be the last.

On board the local boats, their democratic spirit was often strained by the coarseness and proximity of their fellow-travellers, and a peculiarly English kind of fastidiousness emerged. The horrid and slimy faces of the people on one boat made them 'only wish to absolutely annihilate such uncleanly animals', while on another Shelley flew at a German who took their seats and when the man continued to remonstrate in a loud voice, Shelley turned on him and knocked him down.[23] All Shelley's puritan instincts were outraged by what Jane described, with suitable sternness, as 'the licentiousness of the Manners that prevailed in the Cabin below – Drinking, smoking, singing and cracking jokes of a risqué nature'.[24] They stuck firmly on the top deck, except when the wind was too cold to bear. Beyond Mayence, with the banks lined with rocks and mountains, crowned with lonely castles, they were happier, and when someone suggested fearfully that they should pray as the boat entered a particularly dangerous, foaming defile of the river, they laughed him down, until a good-natured schoolmaster broke in, 'Eh! bien donc il faut chanter,' and did so much to Jane's delight.[25] Mary and Shelley were cornered by a disagreeable man who spoke a little English, but their response was pointed: 'We frightened [him] from us . . . by talking of cutting off kings' heads.' At their lowest moments, when they were unable to buy enough to eat, or the delay and discomforts seemed overwhelming, Shelley read Shakespeare and Mary Wollstonecraft to the two girls. Mary's seventeenth birthday passed, almost unnoticed, on 30 August.

But behind everything there was the river, with its ceaseless, dream-like unfolding of the landscape, its broad calm sweeps dotted with little islands, green and beautiful, and its sudden, swollen rapids dashing among the rocks. It was the images from this unbroken, ever-changing scenario of the Rhine, moving like a superior reality around the discomfort and bustle of their boats, which entered most deeply into Shelley's mind. In his long poem of the following year, *Alastor*, these returned to dominate the vision of the poet's journey, and the changing river which controlled the poem's symbolism. It was the vision of the river which also filled Mary's reworking of their journal which she published in England in 1817 under the title of *History of a Six Weeks Tour*, her first book.

At Rotterdam they bargained with an English captain to take them to Gravesend for three guineas apiece; most of this fare had to be taken on trust. The boat left Rotterdam on Friday, 9 September, but they were held back in the harbour at Marsluys until Sunday, by a violent storm. They had almost nothing to eat, but Shelley returned to writing *The Assassins*, and Mary and Jane were both encouraged to start stories. Mary's was called 'Hate', and Jane's 'Idiot'; they were not to be outdone by Shelley's gothic fiction. The packet finally crossed the Channel in forty-eight hours of heavy swell, while Mary huddled below and Shelley and Jane sat doggedly on deck, with alarming waves battering the boat and occasionally breaking over them. There was an easterly gale during the night, which they recorded in the journal, 'nearly kills us, whilst it carries us nearer our journey's end'. But in the morning Shelley argued loudly with a fellow-passenger against the slave trade. They docked at Gravesend at 10 o'clock, on Tuesday the 13th, and with great trouble convinced the captain and the watermen that payment would be immediately forthcoming in the city. 'Every one of the passengers was sick except myself,' recorded Jane brightly. It suddenly seemed nice to be back. But what of Harriet, what of the Godwins?

11
Bad Dreams: Kentish Town 1814

When Shelley, Mary and Jane got back into London on the afternoon of Tuesday, 13 September 1814, one consideration dominated all others: the pressing need to obtain money. At the bank Shelley found he had no credit left. This was scarcely surprising since the payment of the gift to Godwin, and the personal withdrawals that Harriet had made with Peacock's aid in an attempt to meet twelve months' accumulated bills in London. There were also his own withdrawals made at Paris and Neufchatel. In Old Bond Street they found Hookham was out, while his brother was sarcastic and unhelpful, keeping them 'a long time at the door'.[1] A friend of Mary's, Henry Voisey, was unable to lend anything substantial. Shelley felt quite unable to apply to the Boinvilles, to Godwin or the Newtons; and Hogg was away on the northern legal circuit. The situation was now desperate, and decisive action was required. Shelley hired a closed hackney carriage, drove to Chapel Street, and spent two hours in the house with Harriet, while Mary and Jane waited outside in awful suspense sitting well back from the carriage windows. It was an extremely delicate situation, since Harriet's first startled reaction was that Shelley had returned to her. Somehow he convinced her that everything could be arranged if only she would trust him, but it is not known exactly what he promised. Finally, Shelley emerged alone after dark triumphant, and they collected their baggage, paid off the channel fare and the carriage, and put up for the night at the Stratford Hotel in Oxford Street. The next day Shelley took cheap lodgings at 56 Margaret Street, off Cavendish Square and about five minutes' walk from the Westbrooks. It was to prove the first of many such temporary addresses in the coming eight months.

The address at Margaret Street was a deliberately strategic choice on Shelley's part. Until a fortnight later, at the beginning of October, when he moved away north-eastwards across the city to St Pancras, he was determined to come to a working arrangement with Harriet. The acute shortage of day-to-day money remained, and even by the 16th he was having to cancel a meeting at Chapel Street because of dangers of arrest by bailiffs.[2] Gone too was Skinner Street as his old centre of gravity in London, and complete social ostracism now threatened. Both Mary and Jane stood by him under increasingly trying circumstances, and through the medium of Jane's brother, Charles Clairmont, and through Fanny, they managed to keep themselves informed of the feelings and events in the Godwin household. But Godwin himself refused absolutely to have anything to do with Shelley, rejected his letters and let it be known that he bitterly reproached his daughter Mary. Three days after their arrival, Mrs Godwin, accompanied by an anxious Fanny, called at the window of 56 Margaret Street to talk with Mary, but when Shelley appeared they walked away down the street, refusing to speak.[3] Later, in the evening, Charles threw stones at the window, and stayed talking until 3 a.m.[4] But he could be of no practical aid and everything depended on what could be arranged with Harriet.

Between 13 September and 12 October Shelley wrote at least nine letters to his wife. He saw her in private at least three times, on 13, 14 and 15 September, and thereafter he had news of her through personal intermediaries, notably his publisher Hookham and Peacock. This four-week period did not mark the end of his communications with Harriet, but it did mark what was in retrospect the decisive quarrel. Till the end of October Harriet was still hoping to recover Shelley from the arms of Mary. She could not believe that Shelley was really in love with the Godwin girl; sometimes she felt that Shelley had been dazzled intellectually by the Wollstonecraft connection; sometimes that Mary had mischievously set out to seduce him; and sometimes in her wildest moments, that Godwin had simply sold Mary to Shelley in return for the financial gift of July. It is significant that Harriet did not choose to tell her old friend and correspondent, Mrs Nugent, what had occurred in any detail, until a letter of 20 November. Shelley took great pains to dispel these ideas, one by one, from Harriet's head, though each contained an element of truth. But what Harriet could never believe, and what Shelley never attempted to explain to her in forthright terms, was that for him the marriage had been falling apart ever since the birth of the first child, and that Harriet's longing for security and her dependence on Eliza had become hateful to him. Instead he told his wife that she had always failed to satisfy him intellectually or emotionally, and that her commitment to his principles had been hollow. He embarked on long disquisitions about the difference between love and friendship, and claimed that from the beginning he had never felt passionately about her. He offered Harriet the benefit of his perpetual care, protection and solicitude, but failed to specify any practical means to bring this about. The only definite conclusion that Harriet could draw from his first few letters was that Shelley was anxious for her to keep all their negotiations secret from her family and her friends, and that whatever she did she must on no account apply to solicitors. It was véry cold comfort.

In his first letter, written on the afternoon they took lodgings at Margaret Street, he wrote: 'Indeed my dear friend I cannot write to you in confidence unless my letters are sacredly confined to yourself. . . . I know not what is the nature and extent of the intercourse which is hereafter to take place between us. Whatever it be let it not be contaminated by the comments and interference of others. Suffice to your own self, and despise the miserable compassion of those who cannot esteem or love – Forgive this frankness Harriet. Let us understand each other and ourselves. I deem myself far worthier and better than any of your nominal friends. . . . We must agree on certain points, or our intimacy will be the mere gibe and mockery of affection. – Are you above the world & to what extent? – My attachment to Mary neither could nor ought to have been over-come: our spirits and our bodies★ are united. We met with passion, she has resigned all for me. But I shall probably see you tomorrow. I wish you to answer this letter.'[5]

What answer could Harriet make to this? Shelley did meet her the next day, and it gradually became clear to both parties what was at issue, and how far 'above the world' Harriet was required to be. Shelley, on his side, still wanted Harriet to join him and live under his protection with Mary and Jane as 'a sister'. He also wished for a private and informal settlement over the terms of Harriet's support. How Mary would have taken to this we can only guess; her sole comment in her journal had so far been that Harriet was 'certainly a very odd creature'. Yet without her positive enthusiasm the plan was a hopeless one, necessarily fated to founder on every sort of jealousy and insecurity, between her and Harriet. Harriet, on her side, was at first prepared to appear interested in anything Shelley might suggest. But what she hoped was to draw Shelley's interest away from the younger girl, supposing that he would still còme to his senses. She hoped above all to press Shelley into making some formal arrange-ment over money, which would provide the necessary independence for herself and her children, and have the effect of still acknowledging her as the true Mrs Shelley. But in this she completely misunderstood the precariousness of Shelley's financial state, and her actions to secure a legal settlement had the opposite effect from that which she had intended. She inadvertently disorganized all Shelley's arrangements for securing an immediate loan, which only infuriated him and drove him even more firmly into the arms of Mary, where solidarity was

---

★ Omitted in Public Records Office transcript, where Shelley's letters to Harriet were discovered by Leslie Hotson in 1930.

confirmed by adversity. Harriet also lost the moral advantage of her pregnancy, for in October Mary announced that she was expecting a child as well.

Until about 20 September the situation was still evenly balanced. Shelley was attempting to secure money through his lawyer Amory, who seems to have agreed to try and sell the reversion of part of the inheritance which was ultimately due, without being fully informed of Shelley's and Harriet's situation. Shelley was still writing in a conciliatory tone to Harriet, begging her secrecy, promising his aid and urging her to reconsider her position: 'I am anxious for an answer to my letter – Collect your maturest judgement & acquit yourself with justice towards me and Mary. United as we are we cannot be considered separately. Consider how far you would desire your future life to be placed within the influence of my superintending mind, whether you still confide sufficiently in my tried and unalterable integrity to submit to the laws which any friendship would create between us: whether we are to meet in entire and unreserved faith or allow our intimacy to subside.'[6] But Harriet, who had been finding the high-minded and condescending tone increasingly insufferable, finally doubted the genuineness of Shelley's intentions, and despite his requests, she went direct to the lawyer, overwhelmed by misery and bitterness and uncertainty. She proceeded to explain the full nature of Shelley's position, and demanded that he be forced to come to a formal legal settlement. She then closed all communication with Margaret Street, and appears to have left London for several days. When Shelley called at Chapel Street on the 22nd, he found Harriet was 'out of town'. No doubt her father and Eliza were strongly influential in this determined action on her part, and there was talk that Eliza had told Hookham that a legal action against Shelley was about to be put in motion by Mr Westbrook. The results were fatal for any reconciliation. In Shelley's mind she had reverted to her original status, a puppet of the Westbrooks.

Four days later, Shelley wrote her a stinging, furious letter, which showed that at last she too, the beautiful Harriet, had joined the ranks of those who had finally and irrevocably fallen from grace. He began with pointed coolness. 'In the first place I find that you have detailed the circumstances of our separation to Amory in opposition to your own agreement with me, in contradiction to your own sense of right, & with the most perfect contempt for my safety or comfort. He, as you foresaw, has determined to resign the affairs of mine that were on the point of completion.'

This, as Shelley implied, cut Harriet's throat as effectively as it cut his own. Certainly it was true that from this time onwards Shelley had to abandon ordinary legal channels, and engage in a desperate game of dodging bailiffs and warrants of arrest for debt. His negotiations were forced to descend into the seedy world of money-lenders and property speculators. Realizing this, he now turned on Harriet the full force of his anger. 'I was an idiot to expect greatness or generosity from you, that when an occasion of the sublimest virtue occurred, you would fail to play a part of mean and despicable selfishness. The pure & liberal principles of which you used to boast that you were a disciple, served only for display. In your heart it seems you were always enslaved to the vilest superstitions, or ready to accept their support for your own narrow & worldly views. You are plainly lost to me forever. I foresee no probability of change.'7 This was, among many unwise and unfortunate outbursts, perhaps the unkindest and most arrogant in his life. Perhaps some of his bitterness was called forth by what he called the 'wanton cruelty & injustice' of Harriet circulating to various persons false reports about Godwin favouring Shelley's passion for Mary. But one can understand how it must have looked to Harriet. Shelley concluded his letter with the observation that 'the subject of money alone remains', and signed himself with pointed brevity 'PBShelley'.

Harriet apparently* replied to this letter, attempting to 'vindicate' herself as Shelley put it, the same day; yet he wrote again on the 27th, in much the same tone. 'You have applied to an attorney the consequence is obvious – you are plainly lost to me, lost to the principles which are the guide and hope of my life.' As to her remarks about Mary, and her 'appeal to the vilest superstitions', he considered it 'an insult that you address such Cant to me'. His own sense of moral superiority remained unshaken, and, if anything, further enhanced. 'If you feel yet any ambition to be ranked among the wise and good, write to me. I am hardly anxious however to hear from you, as I despair of any generosity or virtue on your part. ... PB Shelley.'8 Shelley was preparing to move to St Pancras that afternoon at 5 o'clock, but deliberately omitted to give Harriet the new address, advising her instead to communicate through Hookham. In retrospect this really marked the decisive collapse of the relationship. There was a break of some six days in the correspondence, and thereafter Shelley's letters, though never again so bitter, remained frigidly aloof. Yet Harriet still had hopes.

The new lodgings were on two floors at No. 5 Church Terrace, St Pancras, beyond what is now the Euston Road, a shabby-genteel district bordered by open fields, to which Godwin himself was to retire much later in old age. Peacock began to call regularly, and he helped Shelley with the early stages of his negotiations with a money-lender called Ballechy, while discussing his own amatory complications in the shape of an enthusiastic heiress, and his old friend Marianne St Croix. Shelley accepted Peacock's new position as an intermediary,

---

* All Harriet's side of this correspondence is lost, and one must allow for bitter or short-sighted remarks which Harriet herself must have made.

and was now glad of his friendship in a London that had suddenly become hostile. He reacted curiously to the break with Harriet, and plunged into a volatile mood of mischievous scheming. Shelley and the two girls and Peacock walked over Hampstead Heath and Primrose Hill, launched fleet after fleet of paper fireboats, read aloud from *Political Justice*, set off fireworks in the fields, discussed a renewed Irish expedition and concocted an extraordinary plan to kidnap his two younger sisters, Hellen and Elizabeth, from their boarding school at Mrs Hugford's in Hackney. Jane and Mary were even sent to the school anonymously to reconnoitre.[9]

On 3 October, Shelley wrote a long retrospective letter to Harriet. Although he told her that he would have liked to have 'superintended' the progress of her mind, and have assisted her in 'cultivating an elevated philosophy', he was now broadly dismissive. 'I am united to another; you are no longer my wife. Perhaps I have done you injury, but surely most innocently & unintentionally in having commenced any connection with you. – That injury whatever be its amount was not to be avoided. If ever in any degree there was sympathy in our feelings & opinions wherefore deprive ourselves in future of the satisfaction which may result, by this contemptible cavil – these unworthy bickerings. Unless a sincere confidence be accorded by you to my undesigning truth, our intercourse for the present must be discontinued.' He cancelled an arrangement for them to meet the following afternoon, apparently to settle mutual debts, since he had heard rumours of bailiffs.

Harriet had perhaps counted on one last appeal: the forthcoming birth of their second child. But underneath the signature, 'Affectionately yours, P B Shelley', she read a coldly courteous P.S. 'I do not apprehend the slightest danger from your approaching labour: I think you may safely repose confidence in [Dr] Sim's skill. Your last labour was painful, but auspicious. I understand that cases of difficulty after that are very rare.' He closed by asking her to send on to Hookham 'stockings, hanks & Mrs Wollstonecraft's posthumous works'.[10]

Two days later it was the same thing: he hoped she would find another lover, 'capable of being to you as the brother of your soul', meanwhile he remained her true friend, and 'enough your friend to make the employment of a lawyer quite unnecessary'. He still refused to see her, refused to meet a lawyer or to give his address. He felt he could be rational about Ianthe too. 'I know that by the law of nature she is yours, & not mine – that your feelings towards her depend on physical sympathy, whilst mine are the result of habit & self-persuasion.' Now at last Harriet began to see how hopeless it was.[11]

Shelley's letters to Harriet over this period had totally lacked understanding or sympathy towards his wife's feelings. Her own point of view was merely 'superstition', and her own need for support and advice merely weakness and treachery. Compared with his letters to Hogg of 1811, or his letters to Miss Hitchener of 1812, they were chill, high-minded and emotionally empty. It is difficult to believe that anyone could really have taken seriously those beneficent plans for Harriet's future life and welfare. The Westbrooks and Amory certainly did not. Did Mary? Did Peacock?

In striking contrast, when writing to Hogg in Norton on 3 and 4 October, Shelley revealed his feelings freely, and surveyed the whole pattern of his life as it had shifted in the last year from Harriet to Mary Godwin. He wrote that Harriet had diverted the true and natural course of his career and task in life. There is no talk of beneficence. 'You will rejoice that after struggles and privations which almost withered me to idiotism . . . I am restored to energy and enterprise, that I have become again what I once promised to become. . . . I suddenly perceived that the entire devotion with which I had resigned all prospects of utility or happiness to the single purpose of cultivating Harriet was a gross & despicable superstition.' By contrast, his union with Mary had given him an overwhelming sense of both intellectual and sexual liberation and fulfilment, amounting to a revelation. 'How wonderfully I am changed! Not a dis-embodied spirit can have undergone a stranger revolution! I never knew until now that contentment was anything but a word denoting an unmeaning abstraction. I never before felt the integrity of my nature, its various dependencies, & learned to consider myself as a whole accurately united rather than an assemblage of inconsistent and dis-cordant portions.' Most important of all, the liberation that his love for Mary had brought freed him to continue with his life's work. 'I am deeply persuaded that thus ennobled, I shall become a more true and constant friend, a more useful lover of mankind, a more ardent asserter of truth and virtue – above all, more consistent, more intelligible more true.'

The nature and intensity of his passion for Mary were well expressed in the way he recalled his first impressions of her at Skinner Street, though remember-ing that Hogg had never seen the girl whom Shelley was now presenting as his lover, it had a curious physical disembodiment. 'The originality & loveliness of Mary's character was apparent to me from her very motions and tones of voice. The irresistible wildness and sublimity of her feelings shewed itself in her gestures and her looks. – Her smile, how persuasive it was, and how pathetic! She is gentle, to be convinced and tender; yet not incapable of ardent indigna-tion and hatred. . . . I speedily conceived an ardent passion to possess this inestimable treasure.* In my own mind this feeling assumed a variety of shapes. I disguised from myself the true nature of affection. I endeavoured also to

---

* It is important for the interpretation of later events to note Shelley's use of the phrase 'possess the treasure' in a sexual context.

conceal it from Mary: but without success. . . . No expressions can convey the remotest conception of the *manner* in which she dispelled my delusions.'

Shelley was himself beginning to be aware of the self-reflecting nature of his feelings, adding to Hogg with a sudden flash of recognition: 'I speak thus of Mary now – & so intimately are our natures now united, that I feel whilst I describe her excellencies as if I were an egoist expatiating on his own perfections.' The extraordinary delusive, subjective, nature of sexual feelings, and the complications of self-projection which can so easily dominate passionate relationships between a man and a woman, became the subject of several of Shelley's prose speculations, and the long poem *Alastor* the following year.

Writing to Hogg he omitted much that was still painful and difficult, and mentioned nothing about his expected children by both Harriet and Mary, or his ostracism by Godwin and the Boinville set. Yet he was anxious for Hogg's tacit approval, and asked if 'any degree of our ancient affection is yet cherished by you for a being apparently so inconsistent and indisciplinable as me'. He ended his letter with a partially veiled appeal. 'My dear friend I entreat you to write to me soon. Even in this pure & celestial felicity I am not contented until I hear from you.'[12] Hogg replied to this letter on 17 October, and first met Shelley again in London some three weeks later on 7 November.

Shelley's felicity was now indeed very far from that pure and celestial state he wished to suggest. Apart from the pressures and anxieties caused by his wife and his creditors, there was increasing tension within the *ménage à trois* at Church Terrace. The state of affairs between himself and Jane was reaching a critical stage. On the night of October 7, there took place an extremely bizarre incident, with ingredients of mystery, sexuality and terror which made it almost a paradigm of Shelley's relationships with young women. It is particularly interesting, because it is relatively well documented, with a full account both by Shelley himself in the journal, and by Jane in her diary.

On the 5th the threesome had gone to Hampstead Ponds to sail fireboats, and in the evening Shelley had excited the two girls with a melodramatic reading of Coleridge's 'Ancient Mariner', and Wordsworth's macabre tale 'The Mad Mother'. Mary went to bed early, as she tended to do at this time, and Shelley and Jane sat up 'till one over the fire' talking, while Shelley wrote to Harriet. This entry Jane later tried to delete from her diary.[13]

The next day, the 6th, Peacock came to breakfast and Shelley went off to negotiate with Ballechy, and came back feeling 'very unwell'.[14] Peacock had stayed at Church Terrace 'wearying us all morning', according to Jane. They dined at 6, Shelley read a canto of *Queen Mab* and some of Mary Wollstonecraft's love letters out loud to them, and they all retired to bed early.

On the morning of the 7th, Shelley, Mary and Peacock walked over the fields towards Hampstead, while Jane, for some reason, 'refuses to walk', as Shelley wrote in the journal. Actually, we know from Jane's diary that she slipped out after they had gone and walked by herself 'in the Squares'. The friction between Mary and Jane was now tacitly recognized. Shelley's entry continues, with faintly disquieting touches. 'We traverse the fields towards Hampstead. Under an expansive oak lies a dead calf. (Contemplate subject for a poem.) The sunset is beautiful. Return at 9. Peacock departs. Mary goes to bed at half-past 8; Shelley sits up with Jane. Talk of oppression and reform, of cutting squares of skin from the soldiers' backs. Jane states her conception of a subterranean community of women.* Talk of Hogg, Harriet, Miss Hitchener &c.' The last part of this indicates the degree of confidentiality now reached between Shelley and Jane.

Jane's own entry makes this even clearer, and also sounds the first note of sinister implications. 'Mary goes to bed – Shelley & myself sit over the fire – we talk of making an Association of Philosophical people – of Eliza and Helen – of Hogg and Harriet – at one the conversation turned upon those unaccountable & mysterious feelings about supernatural things that we are sometimes subject to – Shelley looks beyond all passing strange –'

To understand what happened next it is necessary to recall Shelley's skilled manipulation of feminine sensitivities ever since the legends of the Great Snake among his sisters at Field Place. It is also necessary to observe very carefully the small, probably unconscious clues in his gestures and questions, which show that Shelley subtly diverted the potentially sexual elements of the fireside intimacy into the path of horror. Jane, as he had previously discovered in France, was peculiarly susceptible to this diversion. Shelley's journal continues, referring to himself in the third person. 'At 1 o'clock Shelley observes that it is the witching time of night; he inquires soon after if it is not horrible to feel the silence of night tingling in our ears; in half an hour the question is repeated in a different form; at 2 they retire awe-struck and hardly daring to breathe. Shelley says to Jane "Good night"; his hand is leaning on the table; he is conscious of an expression in his countenance which he cannot repress. Jane hesitates. "Good night" again. She still hesitates. "Did you ever read the tragedy of Orra?" said Shelley. "Yes – How horrible you look – take your eyes off." "Good night" again, and Jane ran to her room.'[15]

What Shelley's entry explicitly fails to mention at this point is the extreme

* To divert the radicalism of this reference to a feminist community, probably drawn from the female province of 'Cocklecu' in Ludwig Holbert's *A Journey to the World Underground* (1742), Lady Shelley altered it to the charming 'Sublime community of women' in *Shelley and Mary*, 1882.

pitch of nervousness to which he had now succeeded in bringing Jane. Her own entry makes this painfully clear, and also makes the deeply disturbing effect of the facial expression which Shelley 'could not repress' quite definite. Jane wrote: 'Shelley looks beyond all passing strange – a look of impressive deep & melancholy awe – I cannot describe it I well know how I felt it – I ran upstairs to bed – I placed the candle on the drawers & stood looking at a pillow that lay in the very middle of the Bed – I turned my head round to the window & then back again to the Bed – the pillow was no longer there – it had been removed to the chair* – I stood thinking for two moments – how did this come? Was it possible that I had deluded myself so far as to place it there myself & then forget the action? This was not likely – Every passed at it were in a moment† – I ran downstairs – Shelley heard me & came out of his room – He gives the most horrible description of my countenance – I did not feel the way he thinks I did – We sat up all night – I was ill.'[16]

Towards the end of this entry, it is Jane who is omitting details, and we have to turn back to Shelley's journal to gain a fuller picture. It is helpful to see the passage at length, to understand quite clearly how Shelley managed to aggravate rather than calm Jane. It is notable that almost every action which he performed, ostensibly in order to soothe her, has the actual result of further increasing her terror. Just how far Shelley consciously realized what he was doing is difficult to decide; there is an element of game-playing in his account. One presumes that the ghastly description of Jane's face, a portrait far more macabre than anything to be found in *Zastrozzi*, is the same description which he gave to Jane *at the time*. This surely was a calculated piece of witch-raising, and Jane herself says that she 'did not feel in the way he thinks I did'. This is what Shelley wrote in the journal which he shared with Mary.

Shelley, unable to sleep, kissed Mary and prepared to sit beside her & read until morning, when rapid footsteps descended the stairs. Jane was there; her countenance was distorted most unnaturally by horrible dismay – it beamed with a whiteness that seemed almost like light; her lips and cheeks were of one deadly hue; the skin of her face and forehead was drawn into unnumerable

* The possible significance of this sprightly pillow is variable. It has been ingeniously suggested that lying there in the middle of the bed it was for Jane a symbol or substitute for Shelley. In another direction one can observe that Jane was of the ideal age and temperament for those mischief-making phenomena usually referred to as 'poltergeists'. Students of the works of M. R. James will know that bed-linen *in propria persona*, so to speak, provides the classic form of supernatural apparition. See *Oh Whistle and I'll Come to You My Lad* (1908), a tale with sexual undertones not inappropriate to the present case, and especially his comments on the *expressions* of linen.

† I gloss this broken but eloquent sentence as meaning something like, 'Every [minute] passed [looking] at it were [gone] in a moment', even though ungrammatical. The sensation of uncontrollably accelerating or decelerating time flow is a primary ingredient of nightmare terror.

wrinkles – the lineaments of terror that could not be contained;* her hair came prominent and erect; her eyes were wide and staring, drawn almost from the sockets by the convulsion of the muscles; the eyelids were forced in, and the eyeballs, without any relief, seemed as if they had been newly inserted, in ghastly sport, in the sockets of a lifeless head. This frightful spectacle endured but for a few moments – it was displaced by terror and confusion, violent, indeed, and full of dismay, but human. She asked me (Shelley) if I had touched her pillow (her tone was that of dreadful alarm). I said, 'No, no! if you come into the room I will tell you'† I informed her of Mary's pregnancy; this seemed to check her violence.‡ She told me that a pillow placed upon her bed had been removed, in the moment that she turned her eyes away to a chair at some distance, and evidently by no human power. She was positive as to the fact of her self-possession and calmness. Her manner convinced me that she was not deceived. We continued to sit by the fire, at intervals engaging in awful conversation relative to the nature of these mysteries. . . . I repeated one of my own poems. Our conversation, though intentionally directed to other topics, irresistibly recurred to these. Our candles burned low, we feared they would not last until daylight. Just as dawn was struggling with moonlight, Jane remarked in me that unutterable expression which had affected her with so much horror before; she described it as expressing a mixture of deep sadness and conscious power over her. I covered my face with my hands, and spoke to her in the most studied gentleness. It was ineffectual; her horror and agony increased even to the most dreadful convulsions. She shrieked and writhed on the floor. I ran to Mary; I communicated in a few words the state of Jane. I brought her to Mary. The convulsions gradually ceased, and she slept. At daybreak we examined her apartment and found her pillow on the chair.[17]

One can tell from various cryptic entries later in the journal and Jane's diary that these ritual horror sessions were regular features of the menage at Church Terrace throughout October. Mary never took part in them, but neither did she

---

* Five years later in Italy, Shelley was to write of another female face in a not dissimilar state:

Its horror and its beauty are divine.
Upon its lips and eyelids seems to lie
Loveliness like a shadow, from which shine,
Fiery and lurid, struggling underneath,
The agonies of anguish and of death.

See 'On the Medusa of Leonardo da Vinci', *Poetical Works*, p. 582.

† That is, back into the little parlour. If Shelley had chosen of course, he could have gone up to Jane's room to reassure her that nothing was really amiss. But he did not.

‡ Again, there is a slight suggestion of sexual diversion here, suggesting that Mary's pregnancy must somehow isolate Shelley from further attachment to Jane.

interfere; she seems to have taken the attitude that this was something to be worked out strictly between Shelley and Jane, and retained a certain ironic detachment. Ten days later, on the 18th, for example, she noted 'I go to bed soon, but Shelley and Jane sit up, and, for a wonder do not frighten themselves.'[18] Jane's diary for this day has a deleted entry, 'Mary goes to bed – Talk with Shelley over the fire until two – Hogg – his letter – friendship – Dante – Tasso & various other subjects.'[19] Peacock was told on a walk to the 'Withered Tree' at Hampstead, and apparently laughed at them. Nevertheless they had another session that same night, when Jane's diary reads: 'Mary [*deleted for* We] goes to bed at eight – sit up with Shelley over the fire – get rather in a horrid mood – go to bed at eleven thinking of ghosts cannot sleep all night.'[20] Shelley directed her reading to *Zastrozzi*, the Abbé Barruel and *Queen Mab*.

Apart from the light which these occurrences throw on the darker side of Shelley's personality, they are also of great interest in connection with the development of his poetry. Up to 1814 his writing had mainly a political source of inspiration, but now gradually it was turning inwards as well, and drawing upon psychological or even psychic materials and imagery. Shelley began to extend his lifelong fascination with ghosts, monsters and gothic machinery into a more exact appreciation of abnormal mental states, when the faculties of perception appeared to be in some sense heightened and acutely sensitized. The 'aesthetic of terror', the idea that terror and beauty are closely linked, had become almost a commonplace of Romantic painters, epitomized by the work of Blake and Fuseli. Several passages in the childhood sections of Wordsworth's *Prelude* and many of the *Lyrical Ballads* link the state of terror and the state of visionary enlightenment.*

Shelley pursued the theme much further and much more grotesquely than any poet had done previously. For him, the state of terror was one of literally 'aweful' hypersensitivity to the phenomenon of the natural universe. The mind's receptive powers were enormously increased, like the tautened strings of a musical instrument, and certain clues and hints about invisible and possibly supernatural forces might just enter the abnormally increased range of mental perception. The analogy of the musical instrument is one he himself used, and the sensation of night silence 'tingling' in the ears, as if even the very hearing faculty had become enhanced, appears both in his journal entries of this month

---

* The aesthetics and psychology of nineteenth-century Terror literature have not received much serious study. Interesting texts to begin with are Edmund Burke's *A Philosophical Enquiry into the Origins of Our Ideas of the Sublime and the Beautiful*, 2 vols, 1756; Freud's short essay 'The Uncanny', in *Collected Papers*, Vol. IV, 1919; and Eino Railo's little-known work, *The Haunted Castle: Studies in Romanticism*, London, 1927. The only modern critic who seems genuinely aware of the problem specifically in Shelley's poetry is James Reiger, in *The Mutiny Within*, 1967, a wayward and masterly book full of curious resonance.

and the poetry of the following year. To a lesser degree, one can also infer that an 'abnormal' state of sexual excitement or tension seemed to Shelley to have similar sensitizing and visionary properties. The word 'properties' is particularly appropriate here, for Shelley continued for some time to use the old student concept of the alchemical experiment to describe this kind of exploration. He was also interested in the dream, and the sudden 'flash' of imagination during ordinary daylight affairs, as similar abnormal conditions of vision.

Such incidents as these horror sessions with Jane, fortuitously well documented at Church Terrace, suggest the direction in which Shelley's writing began to develop. In particular the journal and diary entries for the night of 7 October provide an excellent critical gloss for such passages as the opening invocation of *Alastor*, which would otherwise remain a largely inert and over-stylized piece of gothic machinery. Although this poem was not first drafted for at least another nine months, the verbal echoes are explicit, and it is most appropriately given in this place as an example of the way Shelley was learning to transform his daily experiences into a new kind of poetry.

> Mother of this unfathomable world!
> Favour my solemn song, for I have loved
> Thee ever, and thee only; I have watched
> Thy shadow, and the darkness of thy steps,
> And my heart ever gazes on the depth
> Of thy deep mysteries. I have made my bed
> In charnels and on coffins, where black death
> Keeps records of the trophies won from thee,
> Hoping to still these obstinate questionings
> Of thee and thine, by forcing some lone ghost
> Thy messenger, to render up the tale
> Of what we are. In lone and silent hours,
> When night makes a weird sound of its own stillness,
> Like an inspired and desperate alchymist
> Staking his very life on some dark hope,
> Have I mixed awful talk and asking looks
> With my most innocent love, until strange tears
> Uniting with those breathless kisses, made
> Such magic as compels the charmèd night
> To render up thy charge: ... and, though ne'er yet
> Thou hast unveiled thy inmost sanctuary,
> Enough from incommunicable dream,
> And twilight phantasms, and deep noon-day thought,

Has shone within me, that serenely now
And moveless, as a long-forgotten lyre
Suspended in the solitary dome
Of some mysterious and deserted fane,
I wait thy breath, Great Parent. . . .[21]

At a personal level, however, the stress between Shelley and Jane could not really be sustained at this pitch for long, and on 14 October there was a violent quarrel. The previous evening they had been to see Kean playing Hamlet at Covent Garden (an interesting sidelight on Shelley's budgeting), and had walked out at the end of the second act because, as Shelley put it, of 'the extreme depravity and disgusting nature of the scene'. But when they returned to Church Terrace, something about the feeling in the house so upset them that they finally left it late in the evening and spent the night at the Stratford Hotel.

This extraordinary move was even more remarkable because of their thin financial resources. But Shelley simply wrote in the journal 'alarm'; and Jane wrote cryptically 'we don't like the house – get a Coach & sleep at the Stratford Hotel'. Probably Jane had got herself into another horror fit, and refused to go to bed in the house. She got up very late the next morning, and came down 'in a very ill humour' and immediately quarrelled with Shelley. They set out to walk home across Regent's Park, and Jane stalked off by herself. When Shelley and Mary got to the house Peacock arrived, and Jane soon after. Peacock tried to cheer them up in his usual laughing manner, but Jane retired to her room. Finally Shelley went up to her room and made up with her, at the same time trying to explain what was wrong between them.

Jane wrote, 'Shelley comes into my room & thinks he was to blame – but I don't – how I like good explaining people.' Later Shelley told her that he had thought she despised him, and that he had been angry with her. He also told her some home truths, but they were gratefully received. 'To know ones faults is to mend them,' Jane confided to her diary, 'perhaps this morning though productive of very painful feelings has in reality been of more essential benefit to me than any I ever yet passed – how hateful it is to quarrell – to say a thousand unkind things – meaning none – things produced by the bitterness of disappointment.'[22]

But later that night she was again disturbed and frightened, walking in her sleep and 'groaning horribly'. Shelley finally went up and took her down to sleep with Mary on the floor below. 'Can't think what the deuce is the matter with me,' she wrote pathetically, '"I weep yet never know why – I sigh yet feel no pain." Go to sleep at ½ past two.' Shelley wrote with a certain irony that 'the next morning the chimney-board in Jane's room is found to have walked leisurely into the middle of the room, accompanied by the pillow, who, being very sleepy, tried to get into bed again, but fell down on his back.'[23]

News of some of these disturbances had apparently filtered back to Skinner Street, for the following day a letter arrived from Godwin while Shelley was out, suggesting that Jane leave Shelley and Mary and return to her mother and step-father. Mary seems to have thought this was an excellent idea, but when Shelley returned with Peacock from financial negotiations, he advised Jane strongly not to go, and she wrote a letter of refusal the same evening. Mary wrote slightly irritably in the journal, 'Talk about going away, and, as usual, settle nothing.'[24] This fluctuating situation was to remain virtually unchanged, with the occasional crisis and reconciliation, until the following spring.

The pressures of the triangular relationship produced a long self-analytic note which Shelley wrote in the shared journal for 14 October. Though ostensibly about Jane's shortcomings, it also showed the philosophic gravity with which Shelley approached his relationship with the two teenage girls. Its sternness and moral earnestness was revealing, though doubtless Shelley was writing partly for Mary's benefit. He did not hint at warm feelings for Jane, though the lack of philosophic 'severity' was perhaps meant to confess them. Shelley began his note briskly: 'Jane's insensibility and incapacity for the slightest degree of friendship. The feelings occasioned by this discovery prevent me (Shelley) from maintaining any measure in severity. This highly incorrect, subversion of the first principles of true philosophy; characters, particularly those which are unformed, may change. Beware of weakly giving way to trivial sympathies.'

After this admonitory introduction, Shelley turned to his love for Mary, though he did not actually use the word 'love'. 'Content yourself with one great affection – with a single mighty hope; let the rest of mankind be the subjects of your benevolence, your justice, and, as human beings, of your sensibility; but, as you value many hours of peace, never suffer more than one even to approach the hallowed circle. Nothing should shake the truly great spirit which is not sufficiently mighty to destroy it.'

From these considerations, which betray a heroic and almost military view of his own life and task in society, he turned back to Jane, and also with surprising coldness, to Peacock. Here again the puritan fibre in Shelley's pattern of moral judgements asserted itself. 'Peacock calls. I take some interest in this man, but no possible conduct of his would disturb my tranquillity. Hear that Eliza and Helen go to Norfolk in three weeks. Converse with Jane; her mind unsettled; her character unformed; occasion of hope from some instances of softness and feel-ing; she is not entirely insensible to concessions; new proofs that the most exalted philosophy, the truest virtue, consists in an habitual contempt of self; a subduing of all angry feelings; a sacrifice of pride and selfishness. When you attempt benefit to either an individual or a community, abstain from imputing it an error that they despise or overlook your virtue.'

This had perhaps been the text of his bedroom talks with Jane.

The final part of Shelley's note returned to the texture of everyday life at Church Terrace, with its peculiar mixture of elevated ethical discussion and extreme emotional upheaval. (Marianne St Croix had become Peacock's mistress.) 'These are incidental reflections which arise only indirectly from the circumstances recorded. Walk with Peacock to the pond; talk of Marian and Greek metre. Peacock dines. In the evening read Cicero and the "Paradoxa". Night comes; Jane walks in her sleep, and groans horribly, listen for two hours; at length bring her to Mary.'[25]

Their self-engrossed life at Church Terrace did not continue for more than a few days longer. Shelley's creditors, notably Charters the Coach-maker, the money-lender Starling, and Mrs Stewart, one of their previous landladies, had decided to employ bailiffs to track down Shelley's address and arrest him. To his fury and dismay, Hookham, in an ill-judged moment of irritation and impatience, revealed the address in St Pancras, which had hitherto been kept secret. It is not clear if either of the households at Chapel Street or Skinner Street had any responsibility for the betrayal; but a veiled warning first arrived through the faithful Fanny Godwin, on Saturday 22 October, when she sent an anonymous note into Church Terrace.

Fanny got little thanks except for a bad fright. Shelley and Jane rushed wildly out to the field opposite where she was waiting to give more information: 'I catch hold of her,' Jane related afterwards. 'She foolishly screams & runs away – She escapes – Shelley and I hasten to Skinner St. We watch through the window.' The following day, Sunday, they got up at dawn and waited like spies until the shutters were open at the Godwins' shop, then rang the bell and seized Fanny, who had come unsuspecting to the door. Cornered, and yet anxious not to give them away, Fanny admitted the 'surprising treachery of the Hookhams', and they realized for certain that the bailiffs were now alerted.[26] The only respite was the fact that through a technicality of Lord's day observance, bailiffs were not empowered to arrest between midnight on Saturdays and midnight on Sundays. This gave them some twelve hours to work out a plan.

They hurried over to Old Bond Street to confront Hookham, but he was out: 'the little sly rascal got out of the way', as Jane expressed it, echoing Shelley's anger. Back at Church Terrace, they tried to consult together to make a plan, but ended up only by quarrelling until 'Shelley makes all right again in his usual Way'. Peacock came in, and it was at last agreed that Shelley would have to separate from the two girls and go to ground while he and Peacock tried to speed the negotiation of a loan. Mary and Jane, with much foreboding, were left alone at Church Terrace, and Shelley departed with Peacock as soon as it got dark, to stay the night at Southampton Street, where Peacock lived with his mother. For the next fortnight or so, until 9 November, a game of cat and mouse was played out with the bailiffs. Shelley stayed secretly with Peacock in Holborn, or at City coffee-houses, met with Mary or Jane at prearranged rendezvous, and slipped home on Sundays to sleep with Mary. The pain of separation frequently tempted him to throw caution to the winds and return to Church Terrace during the week; Mary, on the other hand, mixed prudence with passion.

After about four days of their separation Shelley wrote, 'Oh my dearest love why are our pleasures so short and so uninterrupted [*sic*]? How long is this to last? – Know you my best Mary that I feel myself almost degraded to the level of the vulgar & impure. I feel their vacant stiff eyeballs fixed upon me – until I seem to have been infected with the loathsome meaning – to inhale a sickness that subdues me to languor. Oh! those redeeming eyes of Mary that they might beam upon me before I sleep! Praise my forbearance oh beloved one that I do not rashly fly to you – & at least secure a *moments* bliss. . . . Meet tomorrow at 3 o'clock in St Paul's if you do not hear before. Adieu remember love at vespers – before sleep. I do not omit *my* prayers.'[27] In their intense mutual frustration, they had fixed on a private ceremony of making love to each other in imagination before they went to sleep. 'I did not forget to kiss your *eidwlov kevov*★ before I slept,' he wrote forlornly on another occasion.[28]

Shelley and Peacock were now involved in a hectic, ceaseless round of negotiations. Their main hope was still Ballechy, but other names who featured were a 'somewhat benevolent baldheaded man' called Mr Watts; a farmer from Sussex, possibly William Bryant of Worth Rectory, East Grinstead; Starling, the veteran from the negotiations of 1813; Lambert, a rich merchant who was also one of Godwin's creditors; and a property speculator called Pike, who was interested in obtaining the reversion on old Sir Bysshe Shelley's seat at Goring Castle. Most of these schemes were to prove quite fruitless, and the people involved were little better than sharks. But Shelley's anger was still reserved for the Hookhams, whose hearts he intended to tear out 'by the roots with irony and sarcasm'.

Nevertheless, it was Thomas Hookham who had helped Shelley most with ready money up till October,[29] and it was finally to be Hookham who helped him clinch and distribute the deal with Ballechy between 5 and 8 November. Shelley's outrage was in consequence tempered by a certain self-interested and

---

★ Shelleyan Greek, roughly translated as 'The immaterial image of your body'. For the importance of these 'immaterial images' in love-making, see the exposition of 'idols' in Lucretius's chapter on Love, Book IV, *De Rerum Nature*, a lifelong favourite of Shelley's.

rather cynical caution: 'If you see Hookham, do not insult him openly,' he wrote to Mary on 25 October. 'I still have hopes. We must not resign an inch of hope. I will make this remorseless villain loathe his own flesh – in good time. He shall be cut down in his season. His pride shall be trampled into atoms. I will wither up his selfish soul by piecemeal. Your own only love –' This note closed with an epigraph from Aeschylus' *Prometheus Bound*: 'he hisses murder with ghastly jaws'.[30]

Their circumstances during these days were indeed frequently very strained. At the Cross Keys Inn on 1 November, where Mary and Shelley were meeting in secret, Mary noted, 'People want their money; won't send up dinner; and we are all very hungry.'[31] On one occasion Shelley fed them with cakes taken from Mrs Peacock. The bailiffs, 'Shelley's old friends', pounced frequently at Church Terrace, but always missed their prey, and went away 'much disappointed and very angry'. Shelley wrote to Harriet towards the very end of the month, demanding thirty pounds urgently, and with some excusable exaggeration: 'These vexations have induced my ancient illness. I am perfectly free from danger but so exhausted as scarcely to be able to walk. This however does not matter. I have not a friend in the world who can assist me. My endeavours have been in vain. If once in a prison, confined in a damp cell, without a sixpence, without a friend. . . . I must inevitably be starved to death. We have even now sold all that we have to buy bread. I am with a friend who supplies me with food and lodging, but I think you will shudder to hear that before I could sell the last valuable Mary and her sister very nearly perished with hunger – My dear Harriet send quick supplies –'[32] But it seems unlikely that this, Shelley's last recorded appeal to Harriet, had much result. Mary at any rate was writing to Shelley that 'it is impossible to knock into some people's heads that Harriet is selfish and unfeeling'.[33]

With much regret, Shelley decided to sell his solar microscope, and took Jane for support. 'We go to Harris the optician – he won't have our microscope – I go to Peacock to fetch him and the microscope – He talks to Shelley a little while in Holborn – Shelley & I go to Davison's in Skinner Street. We are sent away for half an hour – Walk up and down Chatham Place though we are both so tired we can hardly stand – I am so hungry for I had nothing since breakfast & it is now six o'clock – Return to Davison's get 5 Pounds – for our microscope – In my absence Peacock has gone all the way to Pancras we were not at home – he sees the waiter at St James' Hotel there – much frightened and returns home.'[34] A few days later, Shelley, after much hesitation, sold his pistols to Davison as well. There really was no one to turn to.

The two girls stuck together, despite several misunderstandings and reproachful scenes. Shelley failed to arrive at meeting places on time or at all; Jane got left behind when Shelley and Mary were trying to find a hotel room for the day. It was perhaps hardest on Jane, who had the least support, and inevitably tended to feel on the outside of the intimacy between Shelley and Mary. 'He says he is unhappy,' she exploded once in her diary, 'God in heaven what has he to be unhappy about! Go to Bed at ten.' One of his brief Sunday visits she summed up: 'Shelley writes many letters. Dine at four. Mary & Shelley & I sleep all evening – Shelley goes at ten – Very philosophical way of spending the day – To sleep & talk – why this is merely vegetating.'[35] On 9 November Mary noted with a certain satisfaction in the journal, 'Jane gloomy; she is very sullen with Shelley. Well, never mind, my love – we are happy.' Perhaps Jane's mood was partly explained by a meeting Shelley had just had with Hogg who was returned to London. 'Hogg had been with him the evening before & asked him after his *two Wives*. He joked all the time and talked of the pleasures of Hunting.'[36] In the circumstances it must have seemed a cruel jest.

But even between Shelley and Mary the strain sometimes showed. His passionate letters were all very well, but Mary found he was often maddeningly vague about what actual progress had been made in negotiations. 'You don't say a word in your letter – you naughty love to ease one of my anxieties, not a word of Lambert of Harriet of Mrs Stewart of money or anything – but all the reasonings which you used to persuade Mr Peacock love was a good thing. Now you know I did not want converting. . . .'[37] Yet sometimes, when Shelley had to contemplate the long week ahead without her, his notes broke into a kind of spontaneous lyricism. Under their poignancy, they contained a characteristic psychological penetration into the way his desire fluctuated in its objects.

'Mary love – we must be united. I will not part from you again after Saturday night. We must devise some scheme. I must return. Your thoughts alone can waken mine to energy. My mind without yours is dead & cold as the dark midnight river when the moon is down. It seems as if you alone could shield me from impurity and vice. If I were absent from you long I should shudder with horror at myself. My understanding becomes undisciplined without you.'[38]

Ever after, he considered the moon to be Mary's emblem. Six years later in Italy, looking back at the way the whole relationship had developed, he wrote with infinitely sad understanding in the classical austerity of his matured style:

She led me to a cave in that wild place
And sate beside me, with her downward face
Illumining my slumbers, like the Moon
Waxing and waning o'er Endymion.
And I was laid asleep, spirit and limb,
And all my being became bright or dim

As the Moon's image in a summer sea,
According as she smiled or frowned on me;
And there I lay, within a chaste cold bed:
Alas, I then was nor alive nor dead. . . .[39]

The period of limbo was finally broken on 8 November by the securing of a loan, with the co-operation of Ballechy and Hookham and Peacock, for a sum somewhere in the region of £500. It is not known to what extortionate rate of interest Shelley was forced to agree. The following morning, Jane and Mary packed up their few books and belongings in a hired coach, picked Shelley up from Peacock's, and drove southwards across the city shaking off the dust of St Pancras. Their new lodgings were more select, in the residential area off the Blackfriars Road, at No. 2 Nelson Square. Mary had arranged these, having first tried Pimlico and Sloane Street.

Soon after their arrival, Shelley was out in the city planning a further loan with Hookham. For almost unbelievably, Godwin had sent word through a third party that further financial aid was acceptable, since Shelley had achieved such striking success with Ballechy. That Godwin had the cold audacity to claim money at this juncture, and even more that Shelley was prepared to recognize the claim, gives some indication of the perverse influence that the philosopher still exercised over his erstwhile pupil. The Godwins also made one more attempt to extract Jane, when they heard that since moving she was in a sullen mood with Shelley. In Shelley's absence a note arrived, brought by Fanny Godwin. Apparently, 'the reason she comes is to ask Jane to Skinner Street to see Mrs Godwin, who they say is dying'.[40] Mary did not oppose this obvious overture, and Fanny was sent back to pick up some suitable clothes for Jane to wear. She returned to Nelson Square and with Mary's blessing, the two went off together. When Shelley, too late, came back, 'he disapproves'. But Mary was rather pleased. 'In the evening talk with my love about a great many things. We receive a letter from Jane saying she is very happy, and she does not know when she will return.' This happened on the 13th; two days of silent suspense followed, during which Shelley noted 'disgusting dreams' in the journal. On the 15th, Shelley recorded: 'Jane calls; converse with her. She goes back to Skinner Street; tells Papa that she will not return; comes back to Nelson Square with Shelley.' Mary had been ill in bed and was unable to contribute much to the decision.

It turned out that Godwin had proposed to Jane a scheme that she should go and stay with his friends, the Taylors of Norwich, as a kind of governess. Jane had shown no enthusiasm for such a post, so Godwin suggested merely that she go to stay as a paying guest with some family outside London, where she could find her own feet. But Shelley had liberated his young protegée too well. Jane had agreed to go, but only on two conditions: 'That she should in all situations openly proclaim and earnestly support, a total contempt for the laws and institutions of society, and that no restraint should be imposed upon her correspondence and intercourse with those from whom she was separated.' That at any rate was how the Godwins remembered her outrageous response when the scheme had been abandoned, and Shelley had reclaimed Jane. Mrs Godwin was genuinely distraught for her daughter, and regarded Shelley as a madman and an immoralist. Among other things, Jane told her that she could not leave Shelley since he was fearful of walking alone in the streets in case a revengeful enemy called Leeson should ambush him with a knife.[41] It was the sort of macabre joke only she and Shelley could fully appreciate.

Jane had resoundingly established her independence of Skinner Street and her parents, and she began to experiment with a new name, in a manner that resembled Miss Hitchener's less fortunate changes of nomenclature. Various forms were tried: Clare, Clara, Claire, and these gradually entered their journal. Finally she settled on the firm and musically satisfying Claire Clairmont, and as such she is known to history. It is precisely at this point that Jane's, or rather Claire's diary would become of maximum interest. But the remaining pages of the notebook which Shelley had originally given her in France are torn away from 9 November 1814 onwards, and there is nothing left for the rest of the year. It is not known what hand destroyed this vital and fascinating record of her relationship with Shelley, but such wholesale annihilation is unlikely to have been her own. No further manuscript of Claire's diary is known to exist, until that beginning on 1 January 1818.[42]

With the move to Nelson Square, the worst of Shelley's financial tribulations were over. Yet there was still no definite source of a permanent income in sight. He was unable to set up proper house with Mary and Claire; he could not leave the network of lawyers and money-lenders so painfully built up in London; he could afford no journey, nor could he find in the countryside the tranquillity and concentration to embark on any solid piece of composition. There was no gleam of a reconciliation with Godwin, although his old philosophical master continued to make pressing inquiries about a loan through Thomas Turner, Cornelia Boinville's husband. This was an intolerable situation which was eventually to goad Shelley to open fury, though not before he had surrendered further payments. Reconciliation with Field Place was more than ever unthinkable. Political action in any sphere was impossible, even a brotherly kidnapping, with his hands so tied. In the immediate future lay the birth of his second child by Harriet, and only slightly more distantly, in the spring, Mary's child. He was hemmed in on all sides by personal responsibilities. It was ironic that the result of all his efforts to liberate himself and those around him from the trammels of morality and society seemed so far to be an almost total entrapment in the complications of his own daily existence.

It seemed certain now that Shelley, Mary and Claire would have to winter in London, and little remained to do, with Shelley visiting the money-lenders daily, except to cultivate books and friends. Mary seems to have been almost constantly unwell in November and December, and since Shelley liked to take Claire with him on his city visits, the reappearance of Hogg on the horizon promised to fill a social gap in their little community. Hogg first visited Nelson Square on 14 November. He had changed a good deal, Shelley found. Many of his liberal political sympathies had dropped away, and his shyness had been replaced by a jovial ironic mask behind which Hogg posed as a worldly-wise raconteur. 'Perhaps he may still be my friend', Shelley wrote in the journal, 'in spite of the radical differences of sympathy between us; he was pleased with Mary; this was the test by which I had previously determined to judge his character. We converse on many interesting subjects, and Mary's illness disappears for a time.'[43]

Hogg called again on the 16th, the 20th, 24th and 29th, and gradually assimilated himself to the household. At first Mary was inclined to be glacial, and only took pleasure in engaging and beating him in chess-like games of intellectual argument. 'Get into an argument about virtue, in which Hogg makes a sad bungle – quite muddled on the point, I perceive.' Several days later, when Shelley was out, Hogg called in the evening and 'we have an argument upon the Love of Wisdom, and Free Will, and Necessity; he quite wrong, but quite puzzled; his arguments are very weak'. Slowly Hogg realized that he would do better by omitting to run the Wollstonecraft intellectual gauntlet. On 1 December when he called, they talked about 'heaps of things, but do not argue tonight'; and three days later, Shelley was gratified to read Mary's entry in the journal, which observed: 'Walk about dusk a few times round the Square. Hogg comes in the evening. I like him better tonight than before, but still fear he is an *enfant perdu*.' Provided Mary thought of Hogg as an *enfant*, whether *perdu* or not, all would be well. Soon he was calling regularly every few evenings, being 'sincere', and amusing them all with droll recollections of their early life together, like the 'funny account of Shelley's Father, particularly of his vision and the matrimonial morning'. This was very apt stuff.[44]

Hogg had brought with him a copy of his novel, *Prince Alexy Haimatoff*, and Shelley thought it would be suitable to sit down and write a critique. This was one of the very few pieces of composition he produced between their return from the Continent in September and the following spring. It was subsequently published in the *Critical Review* of December 1814. Shelley singled out for attention Hogg's daring description of the advice given by young Prince Alexy's tutor on matters of sexual morality. He attacked vigorously what he regarded as a debased version of 'free love', and the argument was partly *ad hominem*:

> But we cannot regard his commendation to his pupil to indulge in promiscuous concubinage without horror and detestation. The author appears to deem the loveless intercourse of brutal appetite a venial offense against delicacy and virtue! He asserts that a transient connection with a cultivated female may contribute to form the heart without essentially vitiating the sensibilities. It is our duty to protest against so pernicious and disgusting an opinion. No man can rise pure from the poisonous embraces of a prostitute, or sinless from the desolated hopes of a confiding heart. Whatever may be the claims of chastity, whatever the advantages of simple and pure affection, these ties, these benefits are of equal obligation to either sex. Domestic relations depend for their integrity upon a complete reciprocity of duties.[45]

A 'transient connection with a cultivated female' would be, surely, a reasonably adequate description of 'free love' as normally understood. But Shelley attacked it with peculiar force on this occasion. The new emphasis on reciprocity and equal obligation within sexual relations was not entirely caused by Hogg's reappearance. Shelley was thinking of his experience with Harriet, and the reproof of Hogg's moral levity contained more than an element of self-reproach. Yet he was divided by the implications of Prince Alexy's sentimental education, and concluded that the narrative was 'an unweeded garden where nightshade is interwoven with sweet jessamine'. Shelley praised Hogg for his perceptive handling of female characters, and again stressed the need for moral sensitivity. Above all, the crudeness of conventional morality and the brutal slavishness of desire must be banished from intimate human relations.

> In the delineation of the more evanescent feelings and uncommon instances of strong and delicate passion we conceive the author to have exhibited new and unparallelled powers. He has noticed some peculiarities of female character, with a delicacy and truth singularly exquisite. We think that the interesting subject of sexual relations requires for its successful development the application of a mind thus organized and endowed. Yet even here how great the deficiencies; this mind must be pure from the fashionable superstition of gallantry, must be exempt from the sordid feelings which with blind idolatry worship the image and blaspheme the deity, reverence the type and degrade the reality of which it is an emblem.[46]

This was, in its way, a formal if guarded invitation to Hogg.

By a curious irony, in the same week that Shelley was writing this review and gradually introducing Hogg back into his household, Harriet was writing to her old friend Mrs Nugent from Chapel Street. In a detailed letter dated 20 November, she finally revealed the full extent of the disaster that had wrecked her life. She took her own view of domestic reciprocity. 'My dear Mrs Nugent, Your fears are verified. Mr Shelley has become profligate and sensual, owing entirely to Godwin's *Political Justice*. The very great evil that book has done is not to be told. The false doctrines there contained have poisoned many a young and virtuous mind. Mr Shelley is living with Godwin's two daughters – one by Mary Wollstonecraft, the other the daughter of his present wife, called Clairmont. I told you some time back Mr S. was to give Godwin three thousand pounds. It was in effecting the accomplishment of this scheme that he was obliged to be at Godwin's house, and Mary was determined to seduce him. She is to blame . . . and here I am, my dear friend, waiting to bring another infant into this woeful world. Next month I shall be confined. He will not be near me. No, he cares not for me now. He never asks after me or sends me word how he is going on. In short, the man I once loved is dead. This is a vampire.'[47]

Shelley's last letter, a request for thirty pounds to save him from prison, had been written to Harriet about a month previously, on 25 October. He had not informed her of his change of address, to Nelson Square, and he knew nothing about the state of her health or finances as the birth of the second child approached. Harriet in fact gave birth to a boy, rather sooner than she expected, on 30 November. She called him Charles. News only filtered through to Shelley a week later via Hookham. Shelley was walking out with Claire 'as usual, to heaps of places', as Mary put it, when a note arrived in the evening. Mary treated the event with considerable bitchiness in their shared journal. 'A letter from Hookham, to say that Harriet has been brought to bed of a son and heir. Shelley writes a number of circular letters of this event, which ought to be ushered in with ringing of bells, &c, for it is the son of his *wife*. Hogg comes in the evening; I like him better, though he vexed me by his attachment to sporting. A letter from Harriet confirming the news, in a letter from a *deserted wife!!* and telling us he has been born a week.'[48] Mary's tone is understandable, considering her own pregnancy, her growing jealousy of Claire and the ill-health that kept her frequently marooned in the parlour at Nelson Square. The next day, Shelley went out with Claire to visit the lawyers, and then on to Harriet in Chapel Street. They came home irritable and dispirited, having been caught in the rain. He told Mary that Harriet had treated him 'with insulting selfishness', and as far as one can tell, he did not try to see Harriet again until the following April.

Harriet's side of this last brief interview, as given to Mrs Nugent four days later, was profoundly miserable. 'Ianthe has a brother. He is an eight month child, and very like his unfortunate father, who is more depraved than ever. Oh, my dear friend, what a dreadful trial it is to bring children into the world so utterly helpless as he is, with no kind father's care to heal the wounded frame. After so much suffering my labour was a very good one, from nine in the morning till nine at night. He is a very fine healthy child for the time. I have seen his father; he came to see me as soon as he knew of the event; but as to his tenderness to me, none remains. He said he was glad it was a boy, because he would make money cheaper. You see how the noble soul is debased. Money now, not philosophy, is the grand spring of his actions.'[49] There was a certain truth in what she said about money. It did fill most of Shelley's day, as the journal showed, and as far as he was concerned, she and her children were now just one more of his financial problems.

As Christmas approached, they went out less, except to Pike's the money-lender, and much of the day was spent reading. Their reading lists have survived, a macabre mixture: political philosophy and horror novels. The works of Tom Paine, Godwin, Voltaire and Mary Wollstonecraft stand beside Weber's *The Sorcerer*, Lewis's *The Monk*, *Edgar Huntley* and other Brockden Brown novels, Joanna Baillie's *Plays*, and Ann Radcliffe's *The Italian*. They also read travel books, and *The Lives of the Revolutionists* by John Adolphus. Shelley cleansed his palate in private with Cicero, Petronius and Suetonius's *Lives of the Caesars*.

Wordsworth's *Excursion*, which Hookham had published that autumn, was passed from hand to hand with frowns of disapproval. Shelley still admired the spiritual penetration of Wordsworth's poetry, and the quality of high moral austerity in his style was something that corresponded with a growing need in his own creative development. Yet Wordsworth was for Shelley a political traitor, a deserter of the French Revolution, branded with the same mark as Southey. It was about now that he first sketched out the lines which finally became his sonnet 'To Wordsworth', in which he expressed both his admiration and his disgust. The image of what Wordsworth once had been, reflected a continuing literary-political ambition for what Shelley himself might become.

> Poet of Nature, thou hast wept to know
> That things depart which never may return:
> Childhood and youth, friendship and love's first glow,
> Have fled like sweet dreams, leaving thee to mourn.
> These common woes I feel. One loss is mine
> Which thou too feel'st, yet I alone deplore.
> Thou wert as a lone star, whose light did shine
> On some frail bark in winter's midnight roar:

Thou hast like to a rock-built refuge stood
Above the blind and battling multitude:
In honoured poverty thy voice did weave
Songs consecrate to truth and liberty, –
Deserting these, thou leavest me to grieve,
Thus having been, that thou shouldst cease to be.[50]

The complete poem was first published in 1816. His conception of what Wordsworth's 'desertion' involved, in personal and historical terms, was still immature. Six years later in Italy, he was to return to the theme with real understanding, in one of his most colourful and brilliant satirical pieces, *Peter Bell the Third*.*

Hogg was now rapidly finding his feet at Nelson Square. Adaptable to his old friend's interests, he soon helped to resuscitate the horror sessions in a slightly lighter and more sociable vein that was more to Mary's taste. Three days before Christmas he spent the evening with great success. 'Hogg comes. He describes an apparition of a lady, whom he had loved, appearing to him after her death; she came in the twilight summer night, and was hardly visible; she touched his cheek with her hands, and visited him many successive nights; he was always unaware of her approach, and passed many waking hours in expectation of it. Interesting conversation interrupted by Clara's childish superstition. Hogg departs at 12.' Mary remembered the story, and years later she wrote it up and published it with three others, collected from a later period of 'horrors', in the *London Magazine* for March 1824.

On Boxing Day, a significant note appeared in the journal: Shelley referred to Mary as 'sweet Maie', one of several cosy nicknames, including 'Pecksie' and 'the Dormouse' (because she always seemed to be in bed), which Hogg had introduced into the household. An intimacy was now developing between her and Hogg, and this appropriately complemented the time which Shelley and Claire spent away together in town. In the last days of December, they went several times in the evenings to lectures given at one of the city institutes by a Mr Garnerin, 'on electricity, the gasses, and the phantasmagoria'. On 30 December, Shelley and Claire did not return 'till past 7, having been locked into Kensington Gardens; both very tired'. But Hogg came to cheer Mary up in the evening.[51]

One week into the new year saw a sudden and wholly unexpected change in Shelley's prospects. On 7 January 1815, while Shelley and Claire were out walking in search of new lodgings, Mary and Hogg found the death of Sir Bysshe

---

* To gain a deeply felt, though deeply republican view of Wordsworth's difficulties, one has to turn once again to William Hazlitt, in his essay in *The Spirit of the Age*, 1824.

Shelley announced in the papers. Almost immediately Hookham appeared on a social call, and to Mary's wry amusement, 'is very gracious'.

When Shelley heard the news, he was wholly delighted. The death of old Bysshe meant nothing to him emotionally, but it promised to mean very much financially. He moved rapidly. A large apartment was taken at Hans Place, in the fashionable area of Chelsea and Kensington, and they moved there, with Hogg's help, on the 10th. Shelley then left Mary in Hogg's care, and took Claire with him to the formal reading of Sir Bysshe's will at Field Place. He did not go to the funeral, but the trip took two days and they stopped the night at Kingston, returning for a late breakfast with Mary on Friday the 13th. Shelley related with glee how he had been forbidden to enter the house, so sat instead ostentatiously on the doorstep, where all the relatives and servants could see, reading a copy of Milton's *Comus* with Mary's name prominently written in the fly-sheet. Mary recorded the scene: 'The will has been opened, and Shelley is referred to Whitton. His Father would not allow him to enter Field Place; he sits before the door and reads [my] "Comus". Dr Blocksome comes out; tells him his father is very angry with him. Sees my name in Milton. Shelley Sidney comes out; says that it is a most extraordinary will. Shelley returns to Slinfold. Shelley and Clara set out, and reach Kingston that night. Shelley goes to Whitton, who tells him that he is to have the income of £100,000 after his father's death if he will entail his estate.'[52] The question of the entail was one which would eventually cause enormous difficulty and complication. Shelley had always said he wished to break up the estate from the time he left Oxford and quarrelled with Timothy; but for the moment his prospects looked glowing. A preliminary settlement was not to come into Shelley's hands until three months later.

The story of these early weeks of 1815 is obscured by one of the most strange and suggestive destructions of the manuscript record as it has come down to us. For the period of 7 January to 6 May 1815, no less than nine separate sections have been torn from the manuscript of Mary and Shelley's shared journal. The deletions fall fairly evenly through January, February and April; but between 14 and 28 January, two weeks are missing; between 29 March and 6 April eight days are missing; and between 23 April and 4 May, another eleven days are missing. Apart from these three extended sections, it is notable that the suppressions tend to fall over weekends. Altogether, in the four-monthly period between January and May, no less than thirty days have been deleted.[53]

It is also intriguing that other primary sources suddenly become very thin. In the same period, between January and May, there are only seven extant Shelley letters, all of which are brief notes, most of them to solicitors. Claire's diary has not survived. Hogg's second and last volume of his unfinished *Life* breaks off, perhaps significantly, in the middle of spring 1815. The only other informative source is a series of eleven love-notes written from Mary to Hogg between 1 January and 26 April, which show that Hogg had been fully accepted into the household as Shelley's closest friend and Mary's proposed lover.

In January Hogg was a regular, usually daily, visitor, and from 10 March onwards, when the law vacation began, he lived continually with Mary, Shelley and Claire, and slept at the house.[54] From this same date, Mary's exasperation with Claire was openly expressed in the journal: 'Friday 10th March. – Hogg's holidays begin. Shelley, Hogg and Clara go to town. Hogg comes back soon. Talk and net. Hogg now remains with us. Put room to rights. *11th March.* – Very unwell. Hogg goes to town. Talk about Clara's going away; nothing settled; I fear it is hopeless. She will not go to Skinner Street; then our house is the only remaining place, I see plainly. What is to be done? Hogg returns. Talk, and Hogg reads the "Life of Goldoni" aloud. *12th March.* – Talk a great deal. Not well, but better. Very quiet all the morning, and happy, for Clara does not get up till 4.'[55]

Yet despite Mary's irritation, Shelley continued to take Claire out with him during these months, to shop in the town, to negotiate with the solicitors and to disappear on long walks in Kensington Gardens and round the Serpentine. Had both Shelley and Mary mutually agreed to send her away, she would not have stayed. But Claire did stay, at least until the break-up of the London *ménage* in May.

One can conclude from these circumstances that the destruction of the journal was intended to obliterate the best documented of Shelley's attempts at setting up a radical community of friends, in which everything was shared in common. Around the central relationship between himself and Mary, he tried to encourage secondary intimacies between Mary and Hogg, and himself and Claire. While Hogg adopted a slightly chivalric role of confidant and lover towards Mary, Shelley in turn adopted the tutorial one of philosophic friend and lover towards Claire.

Around their experimental household, there were satellite figures from Skinner Street: Fanny, and Claire's brother Charles Clairmont – rather wild in the 'Clairmont style' as Mary noted. There was also Peacock, torn between his mistress Marianne St Croix and the unknown heiress who appeared briefly on his horizon, and equally troubled by summonses for debt. In January he went one worse than Shelley and landed himself briefly in prison.[56] Further off there were rumblings from Chapel Street, for Harriet had also heard of the death of Sir Bysshe, and was now pressing hard for a definite legal settlement from Shelley. Shelley was all the time anxiously awaiting the outcome of two decisive events: the birth of Mary's child, due in April, and the distribution of the settlement of Sir Bysshe's will.

The emotional development of the *ménage* at Hans Place was effectively commanded by Mary. At the beginning of January, when only five months pregnant, yet almost permanently confined to bed, or at least the parlour, she was writing to Hogg: 'You love me you say, – I think I could return it with the passion you deserve – but you are very good to me and tell me that you are quite happy with the affection which from the bottom of my heart I feel for you . . . you are so generous, so disinterested, that no one can help loving you. But, you know, Hogg, that we have known each other for so short a time, and I did not think about love, so that I think that *that* also will come in time & then we shall be happier, I do think, than the angels who sing for ever and ever, the lovers of Jane's [Claire's] world of perfection. There is a bright prospect before us, my dear friend – lovely – and – which renders it certain – wholly dependent on our own selves – for Shelley & myself I need promise nothing. . . .'[57]

Mary wrote in the language of Shelley, and echoed his emphasis on the due delicacy and sensitivity required in sexual matters – '*that* also will come in time'. Shelley's steady attempt to set up a pattern of secondary pairing appeared in two notes sent simultaneously to Hogg a few days later, the first from Mary. 'Shelley and Jane [Claire] are both gone out & from the number & distance of the places that they are going to I do not expect them till very late. Perhaps you can come and console a solitary lady in the mean time – but I do not wish to make you a truant against your conscience. . . . With one kiss Good bye Affectionately yours Mary.' Meanwhile Shelley had sent round a brief note: 'My dear friend, Mary wished to speak with you alone, for which purpose I have gone out & removed [her *deleted*] Clare. If you should return before this evening & are at leisure I need not direct your steps. Affectionately yours, PBS.'[58]

With her pregnancy, and the uncertainty of her position in relation to Shelley's 'deserted wife', Mary was inclined to be cautious about full sexual intimacy with Hogg. On 7 January, the day when Sir Bysshe's death was announced, Mary wrote to him. 'My affection for you, although it is not now exactly as you would wish will I think daily become more so – then, what can you have to add to your happiness. I ask but for time, time which for other causes beside this – phisical [*sic*] causes – that must be given – Shelley will be subject to these also, & this, dear Hogg, will give time for that love to spring up which you deserve and will one day have.'[59]

But Claire was given no part in the picture of happiness which Mary began to anticipate. Where Shelley seems to have been genuinely unjealous of Hogg's part in his life, the possessive instinct was already working powerfully in Mary. She was content with a *ménage à trois*, but not *à quatre*. Shelley was to find this a permanent difficulty in his social arrangements and experiments. By the end of

January Hogg had rechristened himself in the commune fashion, with the name of his sentimental hero.

> When you return to your lodgings this evening, dearest Alexy, I hope it will cheer your solitude to find this letter from me, that you may read & kiss before you go to sleep. My own Alexy, I know how much and how tenderly you love me, and I rejoice to think that I am capable of constituting your happiness. We look forward to joy & delight in the summer when the trees are green, when the suns brightly & joyfully [*sic*] when, dearest Hogg, I have my little baby, with what exquisite pleasure shall we pass the time. You are to teach me Italian, you know, & how many books we will read together, but our still greater happiness will be in Shelley – I who love him so tenderly & entirely, whose life hangs on the beam of his eye, and whose whole soul is entirely wrapped up in him – you who have so sincere a friendship for him to make him happy – no, we need not try to do that, for every thing we do will make him that without exertion, but to see him so – to see his love, his tenderness, – dear, dearest Alexy, these are joys that fill your heart almost to bursting and draw tears more delicious than the smiles of love from your eyes. When I think of all that we three in. . . .

Here Mary broke off, and later finished the letter, adding briefly, 'now Shelley and Clara are talking beside me, which is not a very good accompaniment when one is writing a letter to one one loves'.[60]

By another sad irony, on the very same day that Mary was conjuring this vision of mutual bliss, Harriet wrote to Mrs Nugent a miserable and hopeless letter.

> I am sorry to tell you my poor little boy (Charles) has been very ill. . . . I am truly miserable my dear friend. I really see no termination to my sorrows. As to Mr Shelley I know nothing of him. He neither sends nor comes to see me. I am still at my father's, which is very wretched. When I shall quit this house I know not. Everything goes against me. . . . At nineteen I could descend a willing victim to the tomb. How I wish those dear children had never been born. . . . Mr Shelley has much to answer for. He has been the cause of great misery to me and mine. I shall never live with him again. 'Tis impossible. I have been so deceived, so cruelly treated, that I can never forget it. . . . Is it wrong, do you think, to put an end to one's sorrow? I often think of it, all is so gloomy and desolate.[61]

Harriet remained alone, with her children, and this gloomy question.

At Hans Place, the end of January and the beginning of February saw the start of the sole literary scheme of this period. Shelley had a series of what seemed to be highly unpromising talks with an Irish radical and editor called George Cannon, who planned to start up a monthly paper called *The Theological Inquirer, or, Polemical Magazine*. Cannon seems to have wanted both contributions and financial backing from Shelley. On the 29th they looked over Cannon's papers, but concluded he was 'a very foolish man'; and again, on 7 February, Cannon came and stayed the evening, a 'vulgar brute' as Shelley put it. Apparently his radicalism was too Irish for Shelley's taste: 'it is disgusting to hear such a beast speak of philosophy, &c. Let refinement and benevolence convey these ideas.' In the end, however, Cannon performed an unexpected service for Shelley. Between March and July, his magazine published, with editorial comments under the name of 'Erasmus Perkins', nearly a third of the verse section of *Queen Mab*, and the whole of one of Shelley's attacks on revealed religion, *A Refutation of Deism* .[62] Shelley was still anxious to keep in circulation the political ideas set out in his early poem. The magazine announced, doubtless fictionally, that the poem had been discovered 'during an excursion on the Continent', and had been put into a correspondent's hands by 'the celebrated Kotzebue', who 'considered it too bold a production to issue from the British press'.

On 8 February, perhaps to absorb their enlarged household more comfortably, Shelley took new apartments in Hans Place, at No. 41. Mary was irritable and unwell, the child in the womb beginning to give her some anxiety and discomfort. The journal for the 9th records: 'Prate with Shelley all day. After dinner talk; put things away. Finish Gibbons Letters. . . . Shelley and Clara sleep, as usual. Hogg does not come till 10. Work and talk. Shelley writes letters. Go to bed. A mess. . . .'[63] Here the manuscript is torn out, and recommences only four days later.

On the 22nd Mary was suddenly and unexpectedly delivered of a child, the doctor arriving five minutes too late. It was a little girl, very tiny, and nearly two months premature. 'Maie perfectly well', noted Shelley; but the baby was not expected to live. Surprisingly though, it suckled properly, and began after five days to look strong. Shelley rather than Mary was exhausted by the strain. He was continually 'unwell', and his side gave him one of the first recorded spasms on the 26th after Fanny Godwin had kept him up talking until half past three in the morning. The next day he and Claire went out to get a cradle. It seemed as if the baby would live, and Mary had triumphed in the permanent bond between her and Shelley.

Shelley decided to leave Hans Place, and move to yet another apartment, this time nearer the river, in Pimlico. The place had become 'horrid', and the landlady was apparently determined to fleece them. No doubt she disapproved of illegitimate children. On 2 March, a mere ten days after the child's birth, there was the bustle of moving to 13 Arabella Road. Mary and the baby went alone at 3 in the afternoon, but Shelley and Claire did not arrive until 6. Four days later Mary woke to find the child dead; it looked as if it had had convulsions and Mary was appalled. Her reaction tells a good deal about the disposition of Shelley's household at this time. She wrote immediately to Hogg: 'My dearest Hogg my baby is dead – will you come to me as soon as you can – I wish to see you. . . . Will you come – you are so calm a creature & Shelley is afraid of a fever from the milk – for I am no longer a mother now Mary.'[64] Her journal entry makes no mention of Shelley. 'Find my baby dead. Send for Hogg. Talk. A miserable day. In the evening read *Fall of the Jesuits*. Hogg sleeps here.'[65] Four days later Hogg also moved into Arabella Road, and Mary began to press Shelley to make Claire leave. But 'the prospect appears to me more dismal than ever; not the least hope. This is, indeed, hard to bear.' Shelley did at least get Claire to advertise under the initials 'AZ' in the papers for a position, but there were no results. They read together, drank tea, played endless games of chess, and when the weather looked up they walked to the park or to the museums, or to the animals on show at the Exeter Change. Shelley noted a panther, a lynx, monkeys, a cassowary and tortoises, and a 'very pretty antelope'. The antelope appeared six years later, in a superb glowing image:

> An antelope,
> In the suspended impulse of its lightness,
> Were less aethereally light. . . . [66]

Godwin glimpsed them by chance near the cages, and later remarked to Charles Clairmont that 'Shelley was so beautiful, it was a pity he was so wicked'.[67] Meanwhile Mary had nightmares about her dead baby, and dreamt that it was still alive. For the first time she felt what was never quite to leave her, the shadow of Harriet. Harriet, after all, had borne Shelley a son. Shelley sailed paper boats with Claire on the Serpentine.

On 10 April Shelley passed the morning with Harriet, who was in 'a surprisingly good humour', discussing legal arrangements. Throughout the month, Shelley's new solicitors P. W. Longdill were busy organizing his claims and debts to be presented to Sir Timothy for discharge. On the 21st and 22nd, Shelley again saw Harriet about presenting his little son Charles in court as part of the legal formalities; but this time, as Mary noted, 'he was much teased with Harriet'. Eventually it was agreed that Shelley's and Sir Timothy's solicitors, Longdill and Whitton, should complete the arrangements between them. Shelley made no attempt to get custody of the children.

Instead he decided to take Mary away for a brief spring holiday in Berkshire, as the completion of legal matters was now nearly in sight. Claire was left to look after the apartment. They departed on 24 April, to stay at the Windmill Inn at Salt Hill near Windsor, a part of the country which, despite its proximity to Eton, held considerable attractions for Shelley. They took a room overlooking a neat little garden planted with cypresses and enclosed by white palings. Hogg, whose law term had started again, could not come with them, though Mary made several coquettish attempts to get him out of London, saying that when his 'letters arrived Shelley's distitch was truly applicable –'

> 'On her hind paws the Dormouse stood
> In a wild & mingled mood
> Of Maieishness & Pecksietude.'[68]

On the 25th Shelley returned to London to consult with Longdill, and probably spent the night at Arabella Road with Claire. He came back with the news that Harriet's attorney said she 'meant (if he did not make a handsome settlement on her) to prosecute him for Atheism'.[69] This was a threat which was later renewed, but its source was the Westbrooks rather than Harriet herself. Hogg did not come down despite further solicitations from 'A Runaway Dormouse', but Mary and Shelley returned to London on 27 April, and took new lodgings at 26 Marchmont Street, in Bloomsbury. Shelley sent on ahead the last note which refers to the intimacy between Mary and Hogg, strongly suggesting that it had reached a sexual stage and that Mary, at least briefly, had been shared. 'I shall be very happy to see you again, & to give you your share of our common treasure of which you have been cheated for several days. The Maie knows how highly you prize this exquisite possession, & takes occasion to quiz you in saying that it is necessary for me to absent from London, from your sensibility to its value.'[70]

One result of this short holiday was that Shelley and Mary came back agreed to send Claire away to stay with friends. As the last few days passed by before the settlement, they walked about London in the May sunshine, Mary still with Hogg, who was now more severely known as 'Jefferson', and Shelley, to Mary's chagrin, still with Claire. After the failure of a plan to send Claire to an acquaintance of Godwin's, a certain Mrs Knapp, it was decided that she should go right away from London to stay by the sea, and Lynmouth was eventually decided upon. Possibly Shelley wrote to the lodgings he had stayed at in 1812; at any rate Claire was determined to go by herself, to prove her independence. On 12 May, the day before her departure, Mary noted with undisguised irritability, 'Shelley and the lady walk out. After tea, talk; write Greek characters. Shelley and his friend have a last conversation.' On the Saturday morning, Shelley went alone to see Claire on to the coach. He did not come back for a long time, and in the middle of the afternoon the awful suspicion that he might have gone off with Claire crossed Mary's mind. Suddenly 'very anxious', she hurried out to meet him, but was unable to find him and returned in the rain. Finally Shelley reappeared at half past six, very tired, and went to sleep immediately after dinner. 'The business is finished,' wrote Mary. She closed her journal on that day, adding as an epigraph, 'I begin a new Journal with our regeneration.' Just above, Shelley scrawled in with a whimsical touch of the macabre, a witch's recipe: '9 drops of human blood, 7 grains of gunpowder, ½ oz. of putrified brain, 13 mashed grave worms.' But below this Mary added, 'The Maie and her Elfin Knight' – which was Shelley.

The day of their regeneration also saw the conclusion of the lengthy financial negotiations between Shelley's solicitors and Sir Timothy's. Things had been much complicated by two factors. First the collection and assessment of Shelley's bills and *post obit* bonds, which ran to several thousand pounds. Second, the disagreement between Sir Timothy and Shelley over the eventual fate of the two parts of the Shelley estate, which were by now of very considerable value. A final decision over these estates could not be taken, by the terms of Sir Bysshe's will, for twelve months, but in the meantime Longdill pushed successfully – applying pressure on both father and son – for a temporary agreement.

Exactly a year and a day after the announcement of his grandfather's death, Shelley wrote the following letter to Godwin which set out the crux of the business. 'My grandfather had left me the option of receiving a life estate in some very large sum (I think £140,000) on condition that I would prolong the entail so as to possess only a life estate in my original patrimony.* These conditions I never intended to accept, although Longdill considered them very favourable to me, & urged me by all means to grasp at the offer. It was my father's interest and wish that I should refuse the conditions, because my younger brother [John], *would* then inherit in default of my compliance with them, this life estate. Longdill & Whitton therefore, made an agreement that I should resign my rights to this property, & that my father in exchange for this concession should give me the full price for my reversion. In compliance with the terms of this agreement I signed a deed importing that I disclaimed my grandfather's property.'[71] The consequence of this agreement, if it went smoothly into effect in spring 1816, would have been to guarantee Shelley an

---

* Both old Sir Bysshe, and Sir Timothy, were ambitious to pass on intact a large landed estate, and the method of entail was the traditional legal means of preventing it from being broken up by a fractious elder son. It is necessary to distinguish between (a) the life estate in the large capital sum from Sir Bysshe's residual personal estate, which was used essentially as a bribe; and (b) the actual landed 'patrimony' which Shelley would inalienably inherit provided he did not entail it and outlived his father.

annuity from Sir Timothy, the power to encumber the estate freely, and the eventual inheritance of the Shelley estates proper on the death of Sir Timothy.* The estates proper were valued at an income of £8,000 per annum. Shelley, with the connivance of Longdill, achieved these terms, largely by hiding from his father the fact that he had never intended to accept the bribe of his grandfather's legacy, and therefore forcing Sir Timothy – who was most anxious to obtain the legacy for his other son – to agree to more immediately generous terms than he might otherwise have done. Timothy also agreed to give Shelley an immediate annuity, and pay off his debts.

A typical piece of Shelley's sharp practice appeared in the listing of these debts. Sir Timothy's solicitor, Whitton, eventually agreed to honour £2,900-worth of unpaid bills and loans; but, of this, £1,200 was actually intended by Shelley to be used as another massive payment to Godwin, though listed as a debt. Moreover Shelley had promised Godwin only £1,000 and intended to pick up the remaining £200 for his own pocket. This, again, only became clear a year later, when Godwin complained about the loan, and Shelley wrote on 23 January 1816, with unblushing frankness: 'My meaning was, that you should receive no more than that £1000 until the second settlement with my father which was then expected in November (1815); & I considered your giving in your debt at 1200 as an accommodation to me, enabling me to procure as it did 200 which I should not otherwise have received.'[72] Another curiosity about the listing of Shelley's debts was the number of items which were not finally dealt with.†

The immediate result of the settlement put a small but significant sum of money in Shelley's control but postponed the final arrangement of the estates until spring 1816. Shelley collected a lump sum of £4,500‡ and was granted an

* But in thus purchasing freedom in the future use of his unentailed inheritance of approximately £80,000, Shelley was paying a high price for himself and his heirs. He threw away approximately another £70,000 of Sir Bysshe's residual personal estate. Thus, if he had agreed to his grandfather's plan, in all the life interest on an estate of some £150,000 (yielding £14,000 per annum) would have been his and his heirs' after Sir Timothy's death. But this did not fit in with his idea of responsible estate management; nor, incidentally, did it leave him free to borrow cash on the estate in the meantime.

† Later, in the 1817 Chancery case, Shelley claimed that his true debts should have been valued in May 1815 at £5,000. At any rate, major creditors not fully settled included Williams and Ellis-Nanney at Tremadoc; Charters the coach-maker; and Nash, with whom Shelley had made the *post obit* bond for £3,000 before eloping in July 1814. Sir Timothy in fact offered to pay off Nash, but at a lower rate than the exorbitant one blithely agreed by his son, which was £8,000. Nash refused an offer of £4,500, there was a court case in 1816 and Shelley lost.

‡ It is notable that the £4,500 cash 'gift' is the same figure as that offered to Nash: Sir Timothy no doubt intended Shelley to deal with the debt from this fund. That Nash ruthlessly stuck to his original bond was perhaps more exasperating for father than for son, since Shelley rapidly converted the money for other uses. A final judgement in favour of Nash was made in May 1818, but since this was

annual income in the shape of an annuity of £1,000 to be paid until his death, or Sir Timothy's. For the first time in his life, he was made reasonably independent, though the ability to wield money with any power, by encumbering the estate or raising normal *post obit* loans was also postponed until the following year. On 15 May he wrote to Whitton directing that, from his annuity, £200 should be paid in quarterly sums to Harriet, for her upkeep. This does not seem very large, as no separate provision was made for the feeding, clothing or education of his two children Ianthe and Charles, or for finding Harriet her own house or lodgings. Nevertheless it was one-fifth of his income. Harriet also received a cash present of £200, largely to pay off bills incurred over the winter. Mary was given a draft on his new bankers, Messrs Brookes & Co. of Chancery Lane, for £300 cashable on request. The one mystery is Claire, who was staying on her own in Lynmouth. Charles Clairmont, who had been asking Shelley for a £100 travelling allowance, was probably given money with which he was also to look after his younger sister. Of this there is no record, but later in the summer Charles and Claire went together to Ireland.

Meanwhile Shelley did what he had been longing to do for many months, and escaped into the country. He took Mary on a leisurely tour of the West Country, and by the end of June had settled at comfortable lodgings in Torquay. At last they had escaped London. But Shelley had not escaped himself.

---

the time that Shelley left England there is no definite evidence that the debt was honoured by him. Eventually though, the Shelley estate would have been legally constrained to pay: the family disagreements of the aristocracy were the best class of business.

12

Up the River: Bishopsgate
1815

During the summer months of June and July 1815, Shelley's whereabouts in England is largely unknown. But what has survived suggests that he was in a state of great uncertainty about his immediate future. This was complicated by the first serious bout of his chronic abdominal illness, together with consumptive symptoms, which led him in July or August to put himself under the care of Sir William Lawrence, the eminent London consultant surgeon and medical author who wrote one of the early essays on modern evolutionary theory. It is not until the very end of August that he sent a calm, but strangely soulful letter to Hogg, announcing that he had finally taken a house near Peacock in Bishopsgate, and was living there quietly reading and writing with Mary. During the intervening months he had undergone a decisive change, one of the effects of which was the recommencement of his creative output. Another expression of this change was his decision to set up house properly with Mary, and to start a second family.

This decision was not easily made. From Torquay, on 22 June, he had written to John Williams in North Wales inquiring if there was 'any remote or solitary situation of a house *to let* for a time, with the prospect of purchase when my affairs will permit'. On the 24th he received the first quarterly payment of his £1,000 annuity. With funds actually in hand, he changed his mind about going to Wales and sealing himself off alone with Mary. On the 30th he sent a brief note to Williams saying he had altered his plans and was leaving Torquay early the following day 'for Windsor in whose neighbourhood a friend has seen & highly recommended a furnished house'.[1] This was a result of correspondence with Peacock, who was already living in a house at Marlow on the Thames. But Mary was only told that he was going house hunting, and he left her behind in rooms at Clifton. More than three weeks later she was still writing miserably and now rather desperately to him, asking when he would find a house, and when she would see him again. She was particularly upset by the fact that they were to be apart on 28 July, the anniversary of their elopement. She could see only small hope of seeing him on his birthday on 4 August – and then only if she forced matters, and jumped into a London coach herself, which he obviously did not want. Her letter is eloquent of her distress, and shows in places that she had real fears of losing him:

> We ought not to be absent any longer – indeed we ought not – I am not happy at it – when I retire to my room no sweet Love – after dinner no Shelley – though I have heaps of things *very particular* to say – in fine either you must come back or I must come to you directly – You will say shall we neglect taking a house – a dear home? No my love I would not for worlds give up that. . . . Dearest, I know how it will be – we shall both of us be put off day after day with the hopes of the success of the next days search for I am frightened to think how long – do you not see it in this light my own love.

She added a few lines later with rather more force, 'indeed, my love, I cannot bear to remain so long without you – so if you will not give me leave – expect me without it some day'.[2]

The real basis of her fears was revealed in a brief paragraph that came unexpectedly in the middle of her letter. 'Pray is Clary with you? for I have enquired several times & no letters – but seriously it would not in the least surprise me if you have written to her from London & let her know that you are there without me that she should have taken some such freak –'. Whether Mary's fears were unfounded or not, there is no way of knowing, as Claire's exact whereabouts are a mystery all this summer. Not until October, when Shelley sent her a draft for ten pounds at Enniscorthy, County Wexford, is it known that she was definitely in Ireland with her brother Charles. Peacock has no remarks upon the point.

For the most part, it would seem that Shelley spent July alone with Peacock, visiting his doctor, Lawrence, and arranging for a house. He was assailed by a curious sense of detachment and vacancy, as if suddenly he had seen through life and all it had to offer. One anecdote of Peacock's seems to belong to the month which he spent coming to the decision to take the house at Bishopsgate, and join his life irreparably with Mary.

> He had many schemes of life [recalled Peacock] amongst them all, the most singular that ever crossed his mind was that of entering the church. . . . We were walking in the early summer through a village where there was a good vicarage house, with a nice garden, and the front wall of the vicarage was covered with corchorus in full flower, a plant less common then than it has

since become. He stood some time admiring the vicarage wall. The extreme quietness of the scene, the pleasant pathway through the village churchyard, and the brightness of the summer morning, apparently concurred to produce the impression under which he suddenly said to me, – 'I feel strongly inclined to enter the church.' 'What,' I said, 'to become a clergyman with your ideas of the faith?' 'Assent to the supernatural part of it', he said, 'is merely technical. Of the moral doctrines of Christianity I am a more decided disciple than many of its more ostentatious professors. And consider for a moment how much good a clergyman may do. In his teaching as a scholar and a moralist; in his example as a gentleman and a man of regular life; in the consolation of his personal intercourse and of his charity among the poor, to whom he may often prove a most beneficial friend when they have no other to comfort them.'

Peacock answered in his usual mode of gentle irony that he thought Shelley would find 'more restraint in the office than would suit his aspirations', and he walked on in thoughtful silence, and then turned to another subject.[3]

The decision to be taken about his mode of life was really a decision to be taken about his own character and temperament. In the effort to face certain aspects of himself, his attempts and failures to set up constant and happy relations with those around him, he made a breakthrough into a new kind of reflective poetry. Probably the first short lyric which dates from the transition period of this summer is a six-stanza poem beginning 'Oh, there are spirits of the air'. When it was published the following year, it was simply entitled 'To –', and in her notes of 1839, Mary was to claim that it was 'addressed in idea to Mr Coleridge, whom he never knew'. But she always found it difficult to accept that Shelley suffered from deep personal doubts which inevitably reflected on her own relationship with him. Shelley's subsequent editors, including William Rossetti and Hutchinson, have generally accepted that the poem must have been addressed to himself. The stanzas have a Greek epigraph, from Euripides's *Hippolytus*.* Like all the poems from the period of summer and autumn 1815, it has the hallmark of psychological introspection, and attempts to reach a position of philosophic balance. This is matched by the balance and simplicity of its rhythms and phrasing. It also has the elegiac note, a nostalgia for a way of life lost, which was the result of looking back and trying to understand certain elements in his own

---

* It comes from a Choric Epode, in which Hippolytus's fate is bemoaned, lines 1144 ff:

Sad mother, you bore him in vain!
I am angry at the gods.
Sister Graces, why did you let him go
Guiltless, out of his native land,
Out of his father's house?

developing personality. Throughout, the imagery draws on the world of ghosts and spirits, which it begins by affirming.

> Oh! there are spirits of the air,
>   And genii of the evening breeze,
> And gentle ghosts, with eyes as fair
>   As star-beams among twilight trees: –
> Such lovely ministers to meet
> Oft hast thou turned from men thy lonely feet.
>
> With mountain winds, and babbling springs,
>   And moonlight seas, that are the voice
> Of these inexplicable things,
>   Thou didst hold commune, and rejoice
> When they did answer thee; but they
> Cast, like a worthless boon, thy love away.
>
> And thou hast sought in starry eyes
>   Beams that were never meant for thine,
> Another's wealth! – tame sacrifice
>   To a fond faith! still dost thou pine?
> Still dost thou hope that greeting hands,
> Voice, looks, or lips, may answer thy demands?

At this point, the poem turns sharply upon itself, and considers the damaging consequence of trying to live in isolation and spiritual solitude, purely in 'thine own mind'. This was to be the theme he explored fully in *Alastor* during the autumn. But here, it merely leads to a terrible image of deadlock, drawn from a reservoir far back in his earliest poetry and experience. It is the image of the relentlessly pursuing fiend.

> Yes, all the faithless smiles are fled
>   Whose falsehood left thee broken-hearted;
> The glory of the moon is dead;
>   Night's ghosts and dreams have now departed;
> Thine own soul still is true to thee,
> But changed to a foul fiend through misery.
>
> This fiend, whose ghastly presence ever
>   Beside thee like thy shadow hangs,

Dream not to chase; – the mad endeavour
  Would scourge thee to severer pangs.
Be as thou art. Thy settled fate,
Dark as it is, all change would aggravate.[4]

Ghosts, dreams, pursuit, the difficulty of stable human relationships, and the terror and destruction implicit in the solitary 'settled fate' were to be the broad. terms within which Shelley worked for the rest of the year.

After some four weeks with Peacock at Marlow, he decided to take a house in the neighbourhood, at Bishopsgate, and settle down. The lease was signed on 3 August for a neat, two-storey cottage, with a little verandah and trellised porch, which stood at the eastern entrance to Windsor Park. Mary joined him from Clifton, within a week, and they established themselves in a quiet, regular routine, surrounded by books, and varied with long walks by the river and day-long expeditions into the leafy caverns of the Great Park. Here Shelley established one of his outdoor studies and read for hours surrounded by a litter of books with their pages blowing open in the wind. To begin with he read little but classics, mostly Lucan and Cicero, and began to teach Mary Latin by going through a section of the *Aeneid* each day. By the end of the month he was writing to Hogg, 'My life has been very regular and undisturbed by new occurrences since your departure. My health has been considerably improved under Lawrence's care, and I am so much more free from the continual irritation which I lived, as to devote myself with more effect and consistency to study.'[5]

But the sense of detachment, almost of disillusion, remained. Commenting on a fanatical missionary whom Hogg had met on the law circuit, Shelley remarked generally on the illusions of ambition in a way that seemed to reflect upon himself. 'Yet who is there that will not pursue phantoms, spend his choicest hours in hunting after dreams, and wake only to perceive his error and regret that death is so near. . . . Even the men who hold dominion over nations fatigue themselves by the interminable pursuit of emptiest visions; the honour and power which they seek is enjoyed neither in acquirement, possession, or retrospect; for what is the fame which attends the most skilful deceiver or destroyer?' His observations on politics, and particularly on the final denouement of the Napoleonic struggle in Europe, are distanced to the point of indifference. 'In considering the political events of the day I endeavour to divest my mind of temporary sensations, to consider them as already historical. This is difficult. Spite of ourselves the human beings which surround us infect us with their opinions; so much as to forbid us to be dispassionate observers of the questions arising out of the events of the age.' Although he later wrote a sonnet celebrating Bonaparte's defeat, it is difficult to believe these were the words of a political radical aged 23, who had elected to live with the daughter of Mary Wollstonecraft. It is also extraordinary that in writing to Hogg, who had in the spring been living as an intimate part of his household, he should make absolutely no mention of Mary.

His farewell to Hogg is itself an elegy. 'It is already the end of August. Those leaves have lost their summer glossiness which, when I see you again, will be fluttering in the wind of autumn. Such is mortal life. Your affectionate friend –'.[6]

Shelley was finally aroused from his state of almost permanent brown study by an unexpectedly successful boating expedition, in the first fortnight of September. It was organized by Peacock, and included Mary and Charles Clairmont in the party. They decided they would try to reach the source of the Thames, and Shelley was forced to abandon his strict vegetarian régime by Peacock, who said it was inconvenient and fed him 'mutton chops, well-peppered'. The four of them started in a wherry from Old Windsor, and the whole expedition lasted ten days. Charles wrote a long letter to Claire, describing their progress. The weather was hot, and the river wound smoothly through chalk hills, woodland and Oxfordshire Downs. Arriving at Oxford one evening, they put up for the night and Shelley spent the next day showing them round the scene of his former campaigns. In company he was cheerful and good-humoured during this *recherche du temps perdu*. 'We saw the Bodleian Library, the Clarendon Press, and walked through the quadrangles of the different colleges,' Charles told Claire, adding, with the echo of Shelley's own voice, 'We visited the very rooms where the two noted infidels, Shelley and Hogg, (now, happily, excluded from the society of the present residents), pored, with the incessant and un-wearied application of the alchymist, over the certified and natural boundaries of human knowledge.'[7] Perhaps something Shelley said on this day first laid the germ of an idea in Mary's mind for a story involving an 'infidel' student, working secretly in the heart of a respectable university, to bring forth a diabolic creation.

They returned to their wherry that evening, and pushed on towards Lechlade, in Gloucestershire; the last town before the river curls away to its hidden sources and headstreams in the Cotswolds. A characteristic fancy took hold of Shelley's mind as they rowed in turn, and he began to talk, half humorously, half seriously, of prolonging the expedition throughout England. 'We had in the course of our voyage conceived the scheme of not stopping there, but, by going along a canal which here joins the Thames, to get into the Severn, and so also follow up that river to its source. Shelley even proposed, in his wildness, that there should be no halting place even there; he even proposed, by the help of divers canals and rivers, to leave North Wales, and traversing the inland counties, to reach Durham and the Lakes, so on to the Tweed, and hence to come out on the Forth, nor rest till we reached the Falls of the Clyde, when by the time we returned we should have voyaged two thousand miles.'[8]

As it turned out, they could not manage the Severn Canal sailing fee of twenty pounds, and above Lechlade, 'the weeds became so enormously thick and high, that all three of us tugging could not move the boat an inch'. Mary stayed demurely aboard the boat during these struggles. 'We did not get much beyond Inglesham Weir,' Peacock recalled, 'a solitary sluice was hanging by a chain, swinging in the wind and creaking dismally. Our voyage terminated at a spot where the cattle stood entirely across the stream, with the water scarcely covering their hooves.'[9] They turned back, and drifted quietly downstream again under the hot September sun, towards Lechlade. Shelley continued to talk about his endless river expedition, and years later, in 1831, Peacock gently conjured up a nostalgic, afternoon portrait of him in the middle of the mad river voyage of *Crotchet Castle*, 'Mr Philpot would lie alone for hours, listening to the gurgling of the water around the prow, and would occasionally edify the company with speculations on the great changes that would be effected in the world by the steam navigation of rivers: sketching the course of a steam-boat up and down some mighty stream which civilisation had either never visited, or long since deserted; the Missouri and the Columbia, the Oronoko and the Amazon, the Nile and the Niger, the Euphrates and the Tigris . . . under the overcanopying forests of the new, or by the long-silent ruins of the ancient world; through the shapeless mounds of Babylon, or the gigantic temples of Thebes.'[10]

While Shelley was publicly amusing the party and playing the eccentric dreamer, he was privately brooding on the river imagery as an analogue, a poetic metaphor, for an entirely different kind of journey. It was a journey into the past, and into his own personality. This combination of public joking and private poetic meditation can be seen to recur as a pre-creative condition both in England and later in Italy. In a notebook of September, he made a number of haphazard jottings, attempting to define something which he tentatively called 'the science of mind'. In one of these fragments, taking up an idea he had first mentioned several years ago in a letter to Godwin, of 1812, he wrote:

If it were possible that a person should give a faithful history of his being from the earliest epochs of his recollection, a picture would be presented such as the world has never contemplated before. A mirror would be held up to all men in which they might behold their own recollections and, in dim perspective, their shadowy hopes and fears – all that they dare not, or that daring and desiring, they could not expose to the open eyes of day. But thought can with difficulty visit the intricate and winding chambers which it inhabits. It is like a river whose rapid and perpetual stream flows outwards – like one in dread who speeds through the recesses of some haunted pile and dares not look behind. ... If it were possible to be where we have been, vitally and indeed – if, at the moment of our presence there, we could define the results of our experience – if the passage from sensation to reflection – from a state of passive perception to voluntary contemplation were not so dizzying and so tumultuous, this attempt would be less difficult.[11]*

In this thoughtful mood he returned with the rest of the party to the village of Lechlade, where they put up for two nights at the secluded little inn. Mary began to write up a diary of the trip, and Shelley, wandering alone through the little churchyard during the evening began to draft his second poem of the year. The calm, reflective tone and pace of the opening stanzas are full of echoes of Gray, and other eighteenth-century churchyard verses. Only the supple freedom with which the iambic pentameter line is shaped and run over, and the faintly disturbing literalness with which the personifications of Evening, Silence and Twilight are used – as if they really were gigantic, floating figures like something out of a medieval pageant – suggest that 'A Summer Evening Churchyard, Lechlade, Gloucestershire', was not written fifty years before.

> The wind has swept from the wide atmosphere
> Each vapour that obscured the sunset's ray;
> And pallid Evening twines its beaming hair
> In duskier braids about the languid eyes of Day:
> Silence and Twilight, unbeloved of men,
> Creep hand in hand from yon obscurest glen.

> They breathe their spells towards the departing day,
> Encompassing the earth, air, stars, and sea;
> Light, sound, and motion own the potent sway,
> Responding to the charm with its own mystery.
> The winds are still, or the dry church-tower grass
> Knows not their gentle motions as they pass.

In the last two stanzas the pulse of the verse quickens, and Shelley's familiar concern with the abnormal state of acute perception, the potential force of terror hovering at the margins of thought, makes itself felt. The overt 'softening'

---

* This, and other prose fragments of the period, come from a loose collection of Shelley's foolscap notes in the Bodleian MS. Shelley Adds. c. 4. Folder 21–23. They were never formally edited or titled by Shelley. Mrs Shelley later grouped them, including a fragment on Shelley's recurrent dreams, under two headings: 'Speculations on Metaphysics' and 'Speculations of Morals'. Since they are clearly held together by the central theme of the study of mental change and development – both generally in society, and specifically in Shelley's own life – it is more appropriate to title them with his own phrase: 'On the Science of Mind'.

of these forces, and the faintly ironic dismissal of the experience as an 'inquiring child's' game, though beautiful and tantalizing, reflects the unusual warmth and security which the company of Mary, Peacock and Charles brought to him during this expedition. It is perhaps the most relaxed and harmonious poem he ever wrote.

> The dead are sleeping in their sepulchres:
> And, mouldering as they sleep, a thrilling sound,
> Half sense, half thought, among the darkness stirs,
> Breathed from their wormy beds all living things around,
> And mingling with the still night and mute sky
> Its awful hush is felt inaudibly.
>
> Thus solemnized and softened, death is mild
> And terrorless as this serenest night:
> Here could I hope, like some inquiring child
> Sporting on graves, that death did hide from human sight
> Sweet secrets, or beside its breathless sleep
> That loveliest dreams perpetual watch did keep.[12]

They set off down-river next morning at 6, and had reached Old Windsor again in four days, on 10 September. 'We all felt the good effects of this jaunt,' Charles wrote to Claire, 'but in Shelley the change is quite remarkable; he now has the ruddy, healthy complexion of the autumn upon his countenance, and is twice as fat as he used to be.'[13] 'He . . . rowed vigorously, was cheerful, merry, overflowing with animal spirits, and had certainly one week of thorough enjoyment of life,' said Peacock, who was inclined to attribute it to his diagnostic prescription of mutton chops.

Returned to the house at Bishopsgate, Shelley sent off lists of classical and philosophical authors to booksellers in London and Edinburgh, and got down to developing his speculations 'On the Science of Mind' with fresh determination. 'Let us contemplate facts,' he wrote. 'Let us in the great study of ourselves resolutely compel the mind to a rigid consideration of itself. We are not content with conjecture, and inductions, and syllogisms in sciences regarding external objects. As in these, let us also, in considering the phenomena of the mind, severely collect those facts which cannot be disputed. Metaphysics will thus possess this conspicuous advantage over every other science that each student by attentively referring to his own mind may ascertain the authorities upon which any assertions regarding it are supported. . . . Metaphysics may be defined as an inquiry concerning those things belonging to, or connected with, the internal nature of man.'[14] With the emphasis on severely factual inquiry into mental phenomena, Shelley was clearly advancing towards the notion of an objective psychology, which despite the work of the philosopher David Hartley, was still not generally current.* He was himself aware that some new descriptive term was needed, though he hesitated to supply it. 'Metaphysics is a word which has been so long applied to denote an enquiry into the phenomena of mind that it would justly be considered presumptious to employ another. But etymologically considered it is very ill adapted to express the science of mind.'[15]

Shelley's first attempt to exploit the realization that 'we are ourselves the depositories of the evidence of the subject which we consider', was to embark on an analysis of his own dreams. He called this a 'Catalogue of the Phenomena of Dreams, As Connecting Sleeping and Waking'. For the moment he was content to work away at these 'obscure and shadowy' caverns of the mind in prose rather than in verse. 'Let us reflect on our infancy, and give as faithfully as possible a relation of the events of sleep. And I am first bound to present a faithful picture of my own peculiar nature relative to sleep. . . . I shall employ caution, indeed, as to the facts which I state, that they contain nothing false or exaggerated.' The main interest of this 'Catalogue' lies in the dramatic way in which it proved how difficult Shelley found it to analyse himself, to follow the stream to its source.

His first recurrent dream is presented with little comment, 'the single image, unconnected with all other images, of a youth who was educated at the same school as myself'. He merely remarks that he had dreamed of this youth 'between intervals of two or more years', and that he could never hear his name without instantly remembering the dreams and the places where he dreamt them. This dream obviously refers to the early romantic attachment at Syon House, which the sight of a statue in the Uffizi Gallery, Florence, was also to recall.†

The next dream that he discussed produced on the contrary an extraordinary commentary, one of the most peculiar records of composition that he ever made.

> I have beheld scenes, with the intimate and unaccountable connection of which to the obscure parts of my own nature, I have been irresistibly impressed. I have beheld a scene which has produced no unusual effect on my thoughts. After the lapse of many years I have dreamed of this scene. It has

---

* David Hartley (1705–57), educated at Cambridge, doctor and medical writer, philosopher. His major work, *Observations on Man, his Frame, his Duty, and his Expectations* (1749) is perhaps the first work of English psychology. He advanced a curious theory of physical vibrations (probably due for revival), as well as his famous theory of individual morality depending upon the 'association of ideas'. He was influential among many later writers, including Wordsworth, Coleridge and J.S.Mill. Shelley first read Hartley's *Observations* at Lynmouth in the summer of 1812.

† Shelley finally accepted the sexual significance of this dream three years later, in his preface to a translation of the *Symposium* (1818).

hung on my memory; it has haunted my thoughts at intervals with the pertinacity of an object connected with human affections. I have visited this scene again. Neither the dream could be dissociated from the landscape, nor the landscape from the dream, nor feelings, such as neither singly could have awakened, from both. But the most remarkable event of this nature which ever occurred to me happened five years ago at Oxford. I was walking with a friend in the neighbourhood of that city engaged in earnest and interesting conversation. We suddenly turned the corner of a lane, and the view which its banks and hedges had concealed presented itself. The view consisted of a windmill, standing in one among many plashy meadows, inclosed with stone walls; the irregular and broken ground between the wall and the road on which we stood; a long low hill behind the windmill, and a grey covering of uniform cloud spread over the evening sky. It was that season when the last leaf had just fallen from the scant and stunted ash. The scene surely was a common scene; the season and the hour little calculated to kindle lawless thought; it was a tame uninteresting assemblage of objects, such as would drive the imagination for refuge in serious and sober talk, to the evening fireside and the dessert of winter fruits and wine. The effect which it produced on me was not such as could have been expected. I suddenly remembered to have seen that exact scene in some dream of long . . .

At this point the manuscript breaks off, and the whole 'Catalogue' ends, with the single startling note by Shelley: 'Here I was obliged to leave off, overcome by thrilling horror.' Mrs Shelley, in her later editorial footnote, remarks: 'I remember well his coming to me from writing it, pale and agitated, to seek refuge in conversation from the fearful emotions it excited. No man, as these fragments prove, had such keen sensations as Shelley.'[16]

This curious incident, recalled as it obviously is, from a walk with Hogg in the autumn of 1810, is difficult to interpret. Hogg's *Life* offers no clues, and the image of the windmill, with its outstretched vanes, against the long low hill and grey sky, does not recur anywhere in the rest of Shelley's writing. The only clue to the nature of the 'lawless thought' is Shelley's earlier remark about the pertinacity of objects 'connected with human affection'. It is perhaps possible that something revisited at Oxford during the river trip recalled his passionate feelings for Hogg, and set off this powerful reaction.

Despite this surprising setback, Shelley was able to write to Hogg at the end of the month that the boat trip had done him good, and he was now busily at work. 'The exercise & dissipation of mind attached to such an expedition have produced so favourable an effect on my health, that my habitual dejection & irritability have almost deserted me, & I can devote 6 hours in the day to study without difficulty. I have been engaged lately in the commencement of several literary plans, which if my present temper of mind endures I shall probably complete in the winter. . . . The East Wind, the wind of Autumn is abroad, & even now the leaves of the forest are shattered at every gust. When may we expect you?'[17] From October onwards, Hogg made several visits, walking down from London, while Peacock walked across from Marlow frequently. Otherwise Shelley was alone with Mary.

This was the first time since his marriage to Harriet that he had lived alone in one other woman's company for more than a few days at a stretch. This was a decisive change in itself, and indicates the increased emotional maturity of the relationship. Mary was pregnant again, which she probably knew for certain at the end of July, and the baby was due early in the following year. She fitted in easily with Shelley's studious routine, not troubling him when he spent hours alone in Windsor Park, and coped well with both Hogg and Peacock. Both remained slightly in awe of her, the demure intellectual who remained in Shelley's boat. She went on with her study of Latin authors under Shelley's direction. In the evenings they read out loud to each other. For his part Shelley was embarking on his first concentrated study of Greek writers, especially the dramatists Aeschylus and Euripides, with the encouragement of Peacock who already read and translated fluently and was able to lend and recommend him texts. Hogg called this winter 'a mere Atticism'.

Peacock recalled that 'one or two persons called upon him', but they were not to his mind, and were not encouraged to reappear. The only exception was a physician whom he had called in; the Quaker, Dr Pope of Staines. This worthy old gentleman came more than once, not as a doctor, but as a friend. He liked to discuss theology with Shelley. Shelley at first avoided the discussion, saying his opinions would not be to the doctor's taste, but the doctor answered, 'I like to hear thee talk, friend Shelley; I see thee art very deep.'[18] The friendship is not so surprising, considering Shelley's natural reverence for eccentric doctors and sages, and the zealous, puritan cast to his own temperament.

With these few interruptions, Shelley continued the course of his exploration into the caverns of the mind. It was now apparent to him that the way was blocked through a straightforward autobiographical account of his own sensations and dreams, and he turned to more formal types of philosophical essay to describe the problems. These, equally, had little success. In a 2,000-word essay 'On Life', he moved awkwardly between academic notes on the distinction between Berkeleian idealism and Humean scepticism as philosophical systems, and much broader semi-poetic formulations. 'What is life? Thoughts and feelings arise, with or without our will, and we employ words to express them. We are born, and our birth is unremembered, and our infancy remembered but in

fragments; we live on, and in living we lose the apprehension of life. How vain
it is to think that words can penetrate the mystery of our being!'[19] But this was
merely to surrender the problem as an insoluble one, and apart from rejecting
a simple materialist philosophy – which he had never really held anyway – and
remarking on the book of philosophical commentaries which he always subsequently stood by, *Academical Questions* by Sir William Drummond, the essay
took him little further.* Towards the end of the essay, Shelley once again found
himself turning back upon his own past, and suddenly, almost unexpectedly,
for it links with little that had gone before, Shelley managed to define the
condition of one of those 'abnormal states' which seemed to him to offer the
key, both to self-knowledge and to artistic creation.

> Let us recollect our sensations as children. What a distinct and intense
> apprehension had we of the world and of ourselves. Many of the circum-
> stances of social life were then important to us which are now no longer so.
> But that is not the point of comparison on which I mean to insist. We less
> habitually distinguished all that we saw and felt, from ourselves! They seemed,
> as it were, to constitute one mass. There are some persons who in this respect
> are always children. Those who are subject to the state called reverie feel as if
> their nature were dissolved into the surrounding universe, or as if the sur-
> rounding universe were absorbed into their being. They are conscious of no
> distinction. And these are states which precede, or accompany, or follow an
> unusually intense and vivid apprehension of life. As men grow up this power
> commonly decays, and they become mechanical and habitual agents.[20]

The identification of this creative condition of 'reverie', linked with the con-
tinuation of childhood states and the cultivation of the 'intense' experience in
adult life was a striking personal discovery, though one already made for themselves by poets of the previous generation, such as Wordsworth and Coleridge.
But it gave Shelley no satisfaction for it led immediately to two further problems. How far was the state of self-absorbing reverie a genuinely creative or
valuable one? And how far was it a state peculiar to himself, one that cut off his
experiences from those of people and society around him? How far indeed, was
it precisely that state in which 'Thine own soul still is true to thee, But changed
to a foul fiend through misery'?

---

* William Drummond (1770?–1828), essayist and amateur geologist. *Academical Questions*, Vol. I,
was published in 1805; the projected Vol. II never appeared. Drummond studied the work of
Descartes, Newton, Locke and Hume, and glanced critically at the contributions of Spinoza and Kant.
His exposition of ideas was fluent and gentlemanly, with a strong, English flavour of scepticism. But
he was eccentric enough for his times to write approvingly of Plato and Lucretius, and this particularly attracted Shelley. Drummond was in Italy during this decade, and finally met Shelley in Rome.
He was making a study, appropriately enough, of volcanoes.

Shelley was now on the frontier which led immediately into that country and river of the mind to be described in the poem *Alastor*. He made one last effort to push his prose investigations further, in a second essay, 'On Love'. This differs from the previous work in that he was now addressing in imagination at least a specific reader who was beyond doubt Mary.* It also differs in that the terms he uses are in places virtually identical with those used in the prose preface to *Alastor*, and one can assume that he was already drafting sections of the poem. This final prose trial is very brief, less than a thousand words, and opens with the directness which is characteristic of Shelley when he has tracked down what he wished to say. 'I know not the internal constitution of other men, nor even yours whom I now address. I see that in some external attributes they resemble me, but when misled by that appearance I have thought to appeal to something in common and unburden my inmost soul to them, I have found my language misunderstood like one in a distant and savage land. . . . Thou demandest, What is Love? It is that powerful attraction towards all that we conceive, or fear, or hope beyond ourselves, when we find within our own thoughts the chasm of an insufficient void *and seek to awaken in all things that are a community with what we experience within ourselves.*' Within this broad idea of a 'community' of attraction and sympathy, Shelley specified the particular human direction in which his own idea of love had developed. Its peculiar egoism is immediately apparent.

We dimly see within our intellectual nature a miniature as it were of our entire self, yet deprived of all we condemn or despise, the ideal prototype of everything excellent or lovely that we are capable of conceiving. . . . To this we eagerly refer all sensations, thirsting that they should resemble or correspond with it. The discovery of its anti-type; the meeting with an understanding capable of clearly estimating our own; an imagination which should enter into and seize upon the subtle and delicate peculiarities which we have delighted to cherish and unfold in secret. . . . this is the invisible and unattainable point to which Love tends.[21]

In this short essay, directed at Mary, which already admitted from a personal point of view the existence of the gap between them, Shelley had pressed the search into the caverns of his own mind as far as he could go in prose. He now sought the even greater formality and distancing of poetry, and composed the

---

* The dating of both the essays 'On Love' and 'On Life' is not absolutely certain. Shelley used and re-used the notebooks in which they appear both in England and in Italy. For example the Notebook Bodleian MS Shelley Adds. e. II contains both 'On Love' (pp. 1–9) and a draft preface to *Prometheus Unbound* (pp. 56–61) though they are certainly not contemporary. In the end, style, tone and sophistication of argument are important factors in assigning them to the summer of 1815, while the similarity of the material to that discussed in the 'Preface to Alastor' can be regarded as decisive.

700-line blank verse poem *Alastor*, the second long poem of his career. This was the final point which these months of introspection and self-assessment reached, and his own comment, as a poet, on the inner significance of the events of 1814. The subject of the poem is, specifically, the picture of a developing psychological state. 'The poem entitled *Alastor* may be considered as allegorical of one of the most interesting situations of the human mind,' Shelley wrote. To which Mary shrewdly added in a later editorial note, 'the poem ought rather to be considered didactic than narrative'. It is not known how long Shelley took to draft or revise it, but a good deal of it was written in his open-air study, sitting under the autumnal oaks of Windsor Great Park, during September and October.

The myth that shapes the broad outline of the story is that of Narcissus and Echo. The youth, 'the Poet', goes in search of an ideal vision of beauty, which leads him eventually to his death. It is a *rite de passage*. On the way he is helped by an Arab girl who falls in love with him, but is ignored; at night he dreams intensely erotic visions of a girl who can satisfy him; but unable to bring the dream and the fleshly reality together, he embarks on a wild and hopeless boat trip up the river, through fantastic landscapes and caverns, seeking the visionary beauty. Both pursuer and pursued, he is tortured by unattainable desires, grows ill and old, passes into more and more grotesque and macabre landscapes, and finally finds himself gazing at his own image in a pool.

> His eyes beheld
> Their own wan light through the reflected lines
> Of his thin hair, distinct in the dark depth
> Of that still fountain; as the human heart,
> Gazing in dreams over the gloomy grave,
> Sees its own treacherous likeness there.[22]

All these settings, Shelley stresses from the outset, are mental landscapes, which reflect directly the spiritual state of the protagonist. There is now nothing left for him but to pursue the course of the river, which is itself a journey further inwards. 'O stream!' says the Poet,

> Whose source is inaccessibly profound,
> Whither do thy mysterious waters tend?
> Thou imagest my life.[23]

The river takes him into an utterly barren land of rocks and precipices, and, on the edge of one of these, overlooking a night landscape of jagged hills and stars, he lies down in exhaustion and dies, incapable of further emotion or feeling.

> Hope and despair,
> The torturers, slept; no mortal pain or fear
> Marred his repose, the influxes of sense,
> And his own being unalloyed by pain,
> Yet feebler and more feeble, calmly fed
> The stream of thought, till he lay breathing there
> At peace, and faintly smiling: – his last sight
> Was the great moon, which o'er the western line
> Of the wide world her mighty horn suspended. . . .[24]

The final verse paragraph of the poem stands as a coda, an elegy regretting the death of the Poet and the passing of his special vision of the world, with further Shelleyan references to dreams, alchemy and God – 'profuse of poisons'.

Shelley is careful, both in the preface and the verse prologue, to distinguish himself from the Poet. Yet it is clear that the value of the poem to him was the degree to which it allowed him to extend the investigations into his own psychology further than he had managed in prose. In his preface, he draws a clear judgement *against* the experience of the Poet, condemning it as limited and destructive. In this, he was attempting to come to terms with and reject tendencies which he had found in his past life. 'The picture is not barren of instruction to actual men. The Poet's self-centred seclusion was avenged by the furies of an irresistible passion pursuing him to speedy ruin.' But the text of the poem does not underwrite this judgement, especially in its coda, and there is evidence of some sense of contradiction in Shelley's own mind. The references to the furies of solitude, the pursuing fiends of his earlier poems, remain consistent. In one passage he writes,

> At night the passion came,
> Like the fierce fiend of a distempered dream,
> And shook him from his rest, and led him forth
> Into the darkness.[25]

And in another, just as the Poet prepares to embark on the river from which he can never return,

> Startled by his own thoughts he looked around.
> There was no fair fiend near him, not a sight
> Or sound of awe but in his own deep mind.[26]

The preface also draws the wider conclusion, already set out in the essay 'On Love', that satisfactory love can only be found within the context of a human community of responsible relationships. 'Among those who attempt to exist without human sympathy, the pure and tender-hearted perish through the intensity and passion of their search after its communities, when the vacancy of their spirit suddenly makes itself felt.' Yet again, this conclusion is not explicitly drawn within the text of the poem.

Something of this contradiction made itself felt in Shelley's inability to find a name for the work. Finally, he allowed Peacock to read it, and asked his opinion. Peacock's choice, with its careful derivation, shows how well he understood Shelley's difficulties, and also passes an implicit comment on Shelley's character. 'He was at a loss for a title, and I proposed that which he adopted: "Alastor; or, the Spirit of Solitude". The Greek word αλαστωρ is an evil genius, κακοδάιμων though the sense of the two words is somewhat different, as in . . . Aeschylus. The poem treated the spirit of solitude as a spirit of evil. I mention the true meaning of the word because many have supposed "Alastor" to be the name of the hero of the poem.'27 The distinction between 'daimon', the classical concept of the supernatural spirit either benevolent or neutral towards man, and the 'kaka-daimon', the specifically *evil* and pursuing spirit, was to become important to Shelley in his own increasingly sophisticated catalogue of wraiths and fiends.

Poetically, the main advance of the poem was the flexibility of the verse, and Shelley's new-found ability to suggest scenes and landscapes which corresponded to mental atmospheres he wanted to define. Besides these gains, the advance in constructive skill is not very great, and the language suffers from lack of density and directive power. Although much of the description is distinctly overwrought, with that curious suggestion of the Baroque, which in his finest work is tightened to a much wirier, plainer line, there are places where his scenarios presage the direct simplicity of his mature style. Yet Milton's epic drone is still overpoweringly loud.

> At length upon the lone Chorasmian shore
> He paused, a wide and melancholy waste
> Of putrid marshes. A strong impulse urged
> His steps to the sea-shore. A swan was there,
> Beside a sluggish stream among the reeds.
> It rose as he approached, and with strong wings
> Scaling the upward sky, bent its bright course
> High over the immeasurable main.
> His eyes pursued its flight.

But Shelley got closest to what he was after, and achieved his most sustained passage in the contrasting descriptions of the Arab maiden of reality and the visionary dancing girl of the erotic dream. Here he stated clearly the main dilemma of the poem, the choice between sexual reality and sexual fantasy.

Alastor in this sense is a presentation of adolescent sexuality. The poem itself is purely an exploration of such a state but, when taken within the context of the preface, the prose fragments 'On the Science of Mind', and the essays 'On Life' and 'On Love', it is clear that Shelley was intending to present it as a critique of such a 'situation of the human mind'. However the terms of this critique, and the form in which such a wider community of human sympathies might be reached, do not appear in the poem. His ambiguous attitude to sexual narcissism also appears in the terminology of the essay 'On Love', where the object of love yet remains merely the 'anti-type' of that ideal self or 'prototype' to be discovered within the lover's own heart. The beloved remains, in other words, an ideal projection of the self, which by definition must be unchanging, self-sufficient and therefore ultimately sterile. The terms of this contradiction are set out with surprising frankness in the picture of the two girls. The first, the Arab maiden, represents what one may call domestic sexuality, a genuine human relationship which the Poet's dreaming 'self-centred seclusion' cruelly frustrates:

> Meanwhile an Arab maiden brought his food,
> Her daily portion, from her father's tent,
> And spread her matting for his couch, and stole
> From duties and repose to tend his steps: –
> Enamoured, yet not daring for deep awe
> To speak her love: – and watched his nightly sleep,
> Sleepless herself, to gaze upon his lips
> Parted in slumber, whence the regular breath
> Of innocent dreams arose: then, when red morn
> Made paler the pale moon, to her cold home
> Wildered, and wan, and panting, she returned.[28]

The main peculiarity of this portrait is the completely slavish function Shelley assigns to the girl, an inarticulate servant to the Poet's vagaries. Later he was to write consistently and powerfully that the sexual relationship could only be satisfactory when the woman was herself completely liberated from social and intellectual servitude.

The second portrait, of the dancing girl, is clearly related to that of the Arab maiden, whom the Poet had left to continue his journeying through 'Arabie, And Persia, and the wild Carmanian waste'. She is in fact the same girl, but conjured up in dream and gradually and subtly distorted into an object of exclusively sexual desire. The dream ends in what are clearly the sensations and motions of orgasm, and the Poet's detumescent feelings of waste and emptiness on waking immediately afterwards are brilliantly evoked. The description may well suggest why in his prose writings Shelley had consistently shied away from pursuing some of the more intimate dream-tracks into the caverns of his mind. The passage is the most sustained and successful piece of work in the poem, depending notably on radiating images of light and music, and powerfully active, driving verbs.

> Beside a sparkling rivulet he stretched
> His languid limbs. A vision on his sleep
> There came, a dream of hopes that never yet
> Had flushed his cheek. He dreamed a veilèd maid
> Sate near him, talking in low solemn tones.
> Her voice was like the voice of his own soul
> Heard in the calm of thought. . . .
> Knowledge and truth and virtue were her theme,
> And lofty hopes of divine liberty,
> Thoughts the most dear to him, and poesy,
> Herself a poet. Soon the solemn mood
> Of her pure mind kindled through all her frame
> A permeating fire: wild numbers then
> She raised, with voice stifled in tremulous sobs
> Subdued by its own pathos: her fair hands
> Were bare alone, sweeping from some strange harp
> Strange symphony, and in their branching veins
> The eloquent blood told an ineffable tale.
> The beating of her heart was heard to fill
> The pauses of her music, and her breath
> Tumultuously accorded with those fits
> Of intermitted song. Sudden she rose,
> As if her heart impatiently endured
> Its bursting burthen: at the sound he turned,
> And saw by the warm light of their own life
> Her glowing limbs beneath the sinuous veil
> Of woven wind, her outspread arms now bare,
> Her dark locks floating in the breath of night,
> Her beamy bending eyes, her parted lips
> Outstretched, and pale, and quivering eagerly.
> His strong heart sunk and sickened with excess
> Of love. He reared his shuddering limbs and quelled

His gasping breath, and spread his arms to meet
Her panting bosom: . . . she drew back a while,
Then, yielding to the irresistible joy,
With frantic gesture and short breathless cry
Folded his frame in her dissolving arms.
Now blackness veiled his dizzy eyes, and night
Involved and swallowed up the vision; sleep,
Like a dark flood suspended in its course,
Rolled back its impulse on his vacant brain.

  Roused by the shock he started from his trance —
The cold white light of morning, the blue moon
Low in the west, the clear and garish hills,
The distinct valley and the vacant woods,
Spread round him where he stood.[29]

Considered together, these two passages represent a considerable intellectual and artistic advance. Shelley had indeed managed to penetrate far upstream in his own mind, and one begins to understand the force of the image he gave to the difficult process, 'like one in dread who speeds through the recesses of some haunted pile and dares not look behind'. A directly autobiographical interpretation is possible, for one can see in turn the shadowy reference first to Harriet, then to Mary and finally, perhaps to Claire. These have indeed been attempted exhaustively by scholars, but they are not in the end satisfactory: Shelley wrote the poem precisely in order to *distance* himself from his own lived experience. More general observations do however throw light on his own psychological development. The Poet rejects sexual experience in the waking, domestic world, and the girl is turned away, speechless, panting and frustrated. But in the fantasy world, in the world of 'dream' or 'waking reverie' or 'trance' or 'vision', the sexual experience, and specifically the sexual act – what Shelley called in *Queen Mab* the 'sexual connection' – is celebrated and indulged.

Shelley was in two minds about condemning this. In the overall context of *Alastor* composition, he condemns it as not only socially inadequate but also destructive, opening the poet to the 'furies'. Yet within the poem the ambiguity remains. One remembers his recommendation to Mary about 'kissing the insubstantial image' when they were separated. It was a subject to which he was to return frequently, but there is one passage, part of a prose essay written three years later in Italy, which is immediately relevant. It came in the preface to his translation of Plato's *Symposium* and was suppressed by Mary in her edition of 1840. Shelley is somewhat circumspectly discussing modes of the 'sexual act' which might take place without physical penetration. The context is homosexuality, but this is not significant here.

> If we consider the facility with which certain phenomena connected with sleep, at the age of puberty, associate themselves with those images which are the objects of our waking desires; and even that in some persons of an exalted state of sensibility that a similar process may take place in reverie, it will not be difficult to conceive the almost involuntary consequences of a state of abandonment in the society of a person of surpassing attractions, when the sexual connection cannot exist. . . .[30]

Clearly, the second *Alastor* passage is his first attempt to describe such an 'involuntary consequence of a state of abandonment'. There were to be many subsequent ones in his work, and it became one of his most powerful images. It is one of the triumphs of *Alastor* that Shelley succeeded in isolating this split in sexual nature as he had experienced it, and further, implied that it was a type or metaphor for a universal 'split' between the actual and the ideal, between the act and the desire. It was not merely the metaphor, either; it was part of the condition itself.

Another suggestive thing about the dream is the passive role which it assigns to the Poet in the sexual encounter. It is the girl who 'Folded *his* frame in her dissolving arms'. Throughout it is the female figures who are active, and more or less aggressive, and the Poet who is passive and receptive. This also was to become a feature of later descriptions, and may have something to do with the context of the dream or reverie itself.

When Mary edited *Alastor*, it is suggestive that she tried to draw a veil across the subject matter and implications of the poem, and referred instead to the general difficulties of Shelley's life in 1814 and 1815. Following her lead, most critics have been prepared subsequently to look at the poem in vague terms of a 'search for ideal beauty and ideal truth'.[31] Mary wrote in 1839, 'This is neither the time nor the place to speak of the misfortunes that chequered his life. It will be sufficient to say that, in all he did, he at the time of doing it believed himself justified to his own conscience; while the various ills of poverty and loss of friends brought home to him the sad realities of life. Physical suffering had also considerable influence in causing him to turn his eyes inward; inclining him rather to brood over the thoughts and emotions of his own soul than to glance abroad, and to make, as in *Queen Mab*, the whole universe the object and subject of his song.'[32]

Alastor was finished by the end of autumn, and Shelley did not attempt to pursue his introspection any further. He turned instead to concentrate on his Greek reading, which now widened to include his introduction to Homer, the historians Thucydides and Herodotus, and several Greek lyric poets. He was also teaching Mary, and his book-lists to Lackington, Allen and Co., include Locke's *An Essay Concerning Human Understanding*, Bacon's *Essays* and Lemprière's *Classical Dictionary*.

Outside events were pressing once again, mainly in the shape of Godwin, who began to write to him directly once more on 11 November about a £250 debt to a certain Hogan who threatened to sue him.[33] Claire almost certainly came back from Ireland before Christmas, and she seems to have shuttled rapidly between the Godwins at Skinner Street, Shelley's old flat in Arabella Road and Bishopsgate. We know from Godwin's diary that she spent the New Year, 1816, with Shelley and Mary, and it is clear from the cheques which he paid out to her that Shelley regarded her as his own responsibility. In March alone he drew her three cheques totalling £41.[34] In the six months between October 1815 and March 1816, Claire had received cash equivalent to one-third of the money Shelley was paying his wife Harriet annually. Harriet herself had applied for an increase in Shelley's annuity, but he had turned her down, and demanded custody of his daughter Ianthe by way of reply. In return the Westbrooks threatened to bring him to court on settlement proceedings and expose his atheism. On both sides these seem to have been strategic moves in the hope of obtaining more funds from Sir Timothy, rather than genuinely intended threats. At any rate, there was no reaction from Field Place, stalemate was reached, and no further advances were made on either side. There is no evidence that Shelley attempted to visit his children, or make any special provision for them. Nor is there anything on record at this time to show he had any particular feeling or attachment for either Ianthe or Charles. This is significant in the light of Shelley's subsequent actions in the winter of 1816–17.

Encouraged by Mary and Peacock, Shelley decided to publish his first volume of poetry, consisting largely of the title poem, *Alastor*, with its preface, and the other introspective poems of the previous summer. His sonnets to Wordsworth, and on the fall of Bonaparte were also included. The opening lyric section to *Queen Mab* – 'How wonderful is Death, Death and his brother Sleep!' – in prudently edited form, filled out the end of the collection, together with a shorter but rather more daring statement of atheism, also taken from *Queen Mab*, and re-entitled 'Superstition'. Finally there were two charming pieces of translation which hinted at the increasingly serious and agile scholarship upon which Shelley was embarked. The first was from the Greek of Moschus; and the second a sonnet from Dante. The Dante, which is a beautiful piece of craftsmanship, shows how quickly Shelley recognized and assimilated what was congenial to his temper in a foreign author. The longing for a community of intimate friends, combined with the surprising and perfectly Shelleyan image of a magic airship, is brilliantly caught in one of the few and one of the best sonnets he ever wrote: 'Dante Alighieri to Guido Cavalcanti' –

> Guido, I would that Lapo, thou, and I,
> Led by some strong enchantment, might ascend
> A magic ship, whose charmèd sails should fly
> With winds at will where'er our thoughts might wend,
> And that no change, nor any evil chance
> Should mar our joyous voyage; but it might be,
> That even satiety should still enhance
> Between our hearts their strict community:
> And that the bounteous wizard then would place
> Vanna and Bice and my gentle love,
> Companions of our wandering, and would grace
> With passionate talk, wherever we might rove,
> Our time, and each were as content and free
> As I believe that thou and I should be.[35]

Shelley also translated a sonnet from Cavalcanti to Dante, which was not published until 1876, in which another bitterer facet of Dante's relationship is revealed:

> Once thou didst loathe the multitude
> Of blind and madding men – I then loved thee –
> I loved thy lofty songs and that sweet mood
> When thou wert faithful to thyself and me. . . .
> > Again and yet again
> Ponder my words: so the false Spirit shall fly
> And leave to thee thy true integrity.[36]

Shelley chose to translate it because of its obvious connection with his attitude to Wordsworth; and also, perhaps, in a more oblique way, to his old and unreliable friend Hogg.*

In December 1815 Shelley sent the manuscript of this slim volume to Samuel Hamilton, printers, in Weybridge, Surrey, for 250 copies to be run off. On 6 January, with high hopes, he sent a complete set of unbound sheets – all but the title page and last sheet – to John Murray at Albemarle Street, in the hope that no less than Byron's publisher might consent to bring the work out under their imprint. Sadly, Murray did not make any offer; but by the first week in February,

---

* Claire Clairmont's literary judgement is surprisingly good. 'Alastor is a most evident proof of improvement; but I think his merit lies in translation – the sonnets from the Greek of Moschus and from Dante are the best. . . .' Claire to Lord Byron, spring 1816, Murray MSS.

Shelley had managed to get two lesser publishers to take on the book jointly; Baldwin, Cradock, & Joy of Paternoster Row, and Carpenter & Son, of Old Bond Street. It is significant that Thomas Hookham, also of Old Bond Street, did not take on *Alastor*, for the personal breach caused by the events of 1814 was not really healed, nor would it ever be. Shelley suffered unnecessarily from this, for he never achieved another close or long-standing friendship with his publishers, and, especially after he had left London, this was to mean that his manuscripts were never treated with any particular care or enthusiasm. As for the Weybridge printer, his bill was still unpaid in July 1820.

Counting *Queen Mab*, but not counting the juvenile novels and poems, Shelley was to publish ten separate volumes of work during his lifetime. The last seven of these appeared only in the final three years of his life, when Shelley was isolated from his reading public, in Italy. The first three alone appeared in England while he was still living there, and *Alastor* is the second of these. As *Queen Mab* remained for several more years an underground poem, the critical and public reception of *Alastor* thus takes on very considerable importance. In the event, the book sold badly, and the reviews were scanty, uncomprehending and hostile. In April 1816, the *Monthly Review* carried a brief paragraph, without quotation from any of the poems, in which the anonymous reviewer remarked: 'We perceive, through the "darkness visible" in the which Mr Shelley veils his subject, some beautiful imagery and poetical expressions; but ... we entreat him, for the sake of his reviewers as well of his other readers (if he has any), to subjoin to his next publication an *ordo*, a glossary, and copious notes, illustrative of his allusions and explanatory of his meaning.'[37] Relatively, this was good-natured, although the stupid sarcasm of the closing jab – after the extensive Notes of *Queen Mab* – must have wounded Shelley. In May, the *British Critic*, a stolid Tory cudgel, decided to give its reviewer a little space for a facetious interlude, and it genially quoted from *Alastor*: 'we are therefore not a little delighted with the nonesense which mounts, which rises, which spurns the earth, and all its dull realities'. Extracting the Narcissus passage, where the Poet gazes through his hair at his own image in the stream, the reviewer commented: 'Vastly intelligible. Perhaps, if his poet had worn a wig, the case might have been clearer ...'[38]

Only much later, in October 1816, did the *Eclectic Review* show the beginnings of some serious understanding. 'The poem is adapted to show the dangerous, the fatal tendency of that morbid ascendancy of the imagination over the other faculties, which incapacitates the mind for bestowing an adequate attention on the real objects of this "work-day" life, and for discharging the relative and social duties. ... It cannot be denied that very considerable talent for descriptive poetry is displayed in several parts.' Yet even here the reviewer concluded that

Alastor was a 'heartless fiction', 'wild and specious, untangible and incoherent as a dream'.[39] But it seems unlikely that either Shelley or any of his immediate circle ever saw this review, and anyway it was really too late to affect the public sale of the book. Shelley was to write to Godwin in December 1816, 'You will say that ... I am morbidly sensitive to what I esteem the injustice of neglect – but I do not say that I am unjustly neglected, the oblivion which overtook my little attempt of Alastor I am ready to acknowledge was sufficiently merited in *itself*; but then it was not accorded in the correct proportion considering the success of the most contemptible drivellings.'[40] Yet whatever explanation he protested, it was a bad blow, and one to be repeated over and over again in Italy, until he was almost dumb. The terrible bitterness against reviewers was finally put to work in *Adonais*, on the death of John Keats. The failure to reach a regular readership, even a small one, was to have the most important consequences for the direction in which Shelley's work developed. Nor can it ever be forgotten as an underlying element in the friendship with Byron, the best-selling author of the age, which was to commence in the coming summer.

One curious anomaly was the copy which Shelley suddenly sent to Southey at Keswick. He decided apparently on the spur of the moment, and posted it on 7 March 1816 from his lawyers, Messrs Longdill & Co, in Gray's Inn. Remembering the opinions which Shelley had expressed to Miss Hitchener in 1812, and was again to give vent to in 1817, it seems strange that he should have treated Southey with such deference. But perhaps it is not so strange when one recalls his tactics with his father. The letter demonstrates how important Southey's opinion still was to him, and the significance that Shelley had always attached to their early conversations. Shelley enclosed a copy of *Alastor* with his note: 'I shall never forget the pleasure which I derived from your conversation, or the kindness with which I was received in your hospitable circle during the short period of my stay in Cumberland some years ago. The disappointment of some youthful hopes, and subsequent misfortunes of a heavier nature, are all that I can plead as my excuse for neglecting to write to you, as I had promised from Ireland. ... Let it be sufficient that, regarding you with admiration as a poet, and with respect as a man, I send you, as an intimation of those sentiments, my first serious attempt to interest the best feelings of the human heart, believing that you have so much general charity as to forget, like me, how widely in moral and political opinions we disagree. ... Very sincerely yours, Percy B Shelley.'[41] He received no response; but Southey was alerted, and watched the press for any subsequent publications. His vigilance was to be rewarded in the following spring of 1817.

The publication of *Alastor* coincided roughly with the birth of Shelley's first surviving child by Mary, a little boy, on 24 January 1816. He was christened

William, after his grandfather. Of all his children, this first grandson of Mary Wollstonecraft and William Godwin was the one to whom Shelley was most obviously and most intensely attached. Beside William, his other children, whom he often treated with such careless unconcern, sometimes seem like mere domestic appendages. William is the only child who features in his poetry. The happy birth of this son, and the depressing failure of *Alastor*, also mark one of the main watersheds in Shelley's creative output.

For the next twelve months Shelley was to write virtually nothing except one poem of rather less than 150 lines, and a few scattered slight or fragmentary effusions. Of prose essays, pamphlets or speculations, he produced nothing at all. Mary noted that his normal practice of study-reading declined except for a few select classical authors like Aeschylus and Lucretius. Even his private correspondence thinned out, and except for four long descriptive letters to Peacock in the middle of the summer, his letters are concerned almost exclusively with matters of his own inheritance and complicated negotiations to settle Godwin's apparently bottomless debts. The greatest part of his effort and energy was transferred into his family life, and turned to the minds and faculties of those around him. It is not coincidental that 1816 was a highly creative year for his immediate companions – Peacock completed *Headlong Hall* and commenced *Melincourt*; Mary embarked on the sensational novel that was to make her own literary career at a single stroke; and Lord Byron, after two years of relative inactivity, dabbling in Oriental Tales and marriage, at last took up and completed his Third Canto of *Childe Harold* and his celebrated bad poem 'The Prisoner of Chillon'. There is a sense indeed in which the year 1816 almost lost Shelley altogether as a writer, and relegated him to the ranks of the comfortable, domesticated *littérateurs*, who encourage the glow of creativity in others and are then content to bask in it themselves. This did not happen, because the old core of disturbance was still active, as certain strange occurrences were to show; and events at the end of 1816 threw Shelley mercilessly back into the maelstrom. But it nearly happened.

The idea of settling down to domesticity, which he had struggled against in the previous summer, and had now, with the birth of his son, tacitly accepted, was also in his own mind connected with an increasingly bitter feeling of social rejection. When he did want to settle down, he found he was unable to. This gradually became clear in the exhausting and acerbic correspondence with Godwin concerning debts which occupied a great deal of Shelley's time in January, February and March of this year. The question of Shelley's responsibility for Godwin's finances was emotionally complicated in the extreme Godwin still persisted in an attitude of unrelenting condemnation of the elopement which had taken place nearly two years before; at the same time he was desperate enough to keep applying for Shelley's financial aid. His position was further complicated by Mrs Godwin, who felt that her own daughter Claire had been seduced by Shelley with Mary's tacit connivance. Mary, in turn, felt that Mrs Godwin was forcing her father to be harder towards them than he wished. Both the Godwins thought that not only Mary but also Claire and Fanny had fallen ruinously in love with Shelley. Four years later these attitudes were still basically unchanged, and a mutual friend of both parties, talking at Skinner Street in July 1820, noted in her diary: '[Godwin] then expatiated much on the tender maternal affection of Mrs G. for her daughter, and the bitter disappointment of all her hopes in the person to whom she looked for comfort and happiness in the decline of her life; he described her as being of the most irritable disposition possible, and therefore suffering the keenest anguish on account of this misfortune, of which M[ary] is the sole cause, as she pretends; she regards M[ary] as the greatest enemy she has in the world. Mr G[odwin] told me that the three girls were all equally in love with [*blank*].'[42] There is no doubt from the context of these remarks that the blank stands for Shelley.

On Shelley's side, the straightforward desire to help a philosopher and political figure whom he still admired immensely had become layered over with secondary motives. He could no longer avoid the realization that Godwin was venal and opportunist where money was concerned. Yet paradoxically, the need to prove himself in Godwin's eyes had increased, and he was prepared to try and buy his father-in-law's approbation at almost any price. He felt the need to prove himself worthy of Godwin's principles, to be more Godwinian than Godwin in his social conduct. Yet why this need drove him to such lengths is still not altogether clear. To an extent, Shelley must have felt that Godwin was his own father by adoption and the idea of a second failure, a second withdrawal of love filled him with terrible dismay. But perhaps stronger than this was the influence of both Mary and Claire. Mary especially felt that Godwin ought to be helped, whatever his apparent attitude, for only thereby could he be saved from the clutches of Mrs Godwin. It was, significantly, Mary and not Shelley who became Godwin's final court of appeal when he was writing for yet more money to them in Italy. The intensity of the bond between Mary and her father was something that Shelley only slowly realized. But it is this which finally explains the inordinate lengths that Shelley went to to satisfy Godwin's financial requests, and the mixture of patience and fury with which he persisted.

Shelley first began to negotiate seriously with Godwin on 7 January 1816. He explained the half-completed terms of the settlement of May 1815, and continued: 'You say that you will receive no more than £1250 for the payment of those incumbrances from which you think I may be considered as *specially* bound to relieve you. I would not desire to persuade you to sell the approbation of your friends for the difference between this sum, & that which your necessities actually require. . . .'[43]

This sum of £1,250 was of course in addition to the £1,000 which Shelley had procured for Godwin as a 'debt' the previous year. Shelley was in fact unable to provide such a large sum until either the settlement with his father to buy the reversion of old Sir Bysshe's legacy was complete, or else the legal state of his own inheritance without entail was sufficiently clarified for him to raise *post obit* bonds upon it. This latter course required the strictest secrecy from Whitton and Sir Timothy, and there were even doubts in Shelley's mind as to whether his own solicitor Longdill could be trusted. But Shelley's grasp of these worldly difficulties was quite confident and steady.

By the end of the month, the two other main figures in the negotiation, Hayward, Godwin's solicitor, and William Bryant, a money-lender, were deeply involved, and Shelley was steadily applying pressure on Godwin to meet him. He carefully let the personal note creep back into the business letters, as the prelude to a *rapprochement*. 'But I shall leave this subject henceforth, entirely to your own feelings. Probably my feelings on such an occasion would be no less distressing than your own. . . . Fanny & Mrs Godwin will probably be glad to hear that Mary has safely recovered from a very favourable confinement, & that her child is well.'[44]

By mid-February, the solicitors had discovered that the sale of the reversion to Sir Timothy might actually break the terms of Sir Bysshe's will as a whole, and disqualify both Sir Timothy and his son, so that a test case was now required in Chancery. Shelley was in difficulties once again over his own 'domestic expenditure' at Bishopsgate, and he came briefly to London to see if anything could be hastened. It seems that Claire, who was staying at Bishopsgate, accompanied him, and went to stay for several days at Skinner Street, perhaps as part of the plan to melt Godwin and assuage Mrs Godwin. Shelley wrote to Godwin in much more openly warm terms from Hogg's rooms on 16 February. 'I intended to have left Town at 2 o'clock tomorrow. I will not do so if you wish to see me. In that latter case send a letter *by a porter* to Mr Hoggs, 1 Garden Temple Court, making your own appointment. Yet I do not know that it is best for you to see me. On me it would inflict deep dejection. But I would not refuse anything which I can do, so that I may benefit a man whom in spite of his wrongs to me I respect & love. Besides, I shall certainly not delay to depart from the haunts of men.'[45] But these hopes were ill-founded, Godwin refused bluntly to see Shelley, and moreover, Longdill gave him a most depressing analysis of his prospects in the Chancery case.

One thing which did strike an anxious cord in Godwin's heart was Shelley's vague threat to depart from the haunts of men. Shelley had hinted before to

Godwin that he might shortly die from a recurrence of supposed consumption, but Godwin had been used to these prognostications of doom ever since he first corresponded with Shelley in 1812, and they had little effect. But the threat simply to *leave* English society, and go into voluntary exile did terrify Godwin, for he realized that Shelley had already adopted this course twice previously. At worst Shelley might choose to leave England altogether, and Godwin would be left to fend for himself among the money-lenders and buyers. At the end of February, he detailed Thomas Turner, the husband of Shelley's old friend of the Bracknell days, Cornelia Boinville, to act as a personal intermediary on his behalf. After the first of Turner's visits on 20 February, Shelley had detected Godwin's concern which indicated softening, and played upon it with considerable skill in a long letter of the following day. First, he sweepingly denied that he had any such intention. 'I shall certainly not leave this country, or even remove to a greater distance from the neighbourhood of London, until the unfavourable aspect assumed by my affairs shall appear to be unalterable, or until all has been done by me which it is possible for me to do for the relief of yours.'

But then, carefully moving in the opposite direction, he allowed Godwin to see further into his mind. For the first time Shelley explicitly stated the full implications of a lifelong exile. This was an important moment of realization in his own mind, and he approached it first of all as a personal and family matter, rather than a literary one. The moral which Godwin was intended to draw about his own ostracism of Shelley was unavoidable.

'You are perhaps aware that one of the chief motives which strongly urges me either to desert my native country, dear to me from many considerations, or resort to its most distant and solitary regions, is the perpetual experience of neglect or enmity from almost everyone but those who are supported by my resources.' This last was indeed a formidable realization, and contained a great deal of truth.

'I shall cling, perhaps, during the infancy of my children to all the prepossessions attached to the country of my birth, hiding myself and Mary from that contempt which we so unjustly endure. I think, therefore, at present only of settling in Cumberland or Scotland. In the event the evils which will flow to my children from our desolate and solitary situation here point out an exile as the only resource to them against that injustice which we can easily despise.'[46] Godwin had much food for thought.

In the beginning of March, negotiations demanded Shelley's presence in London so frequently that he took lodgings first at 13 and then at 32 Norfolk Street. Preliminaries for the Chancery case were already on hand, and Shelley had among other things to present in court his son by Harriet, little Charles, in order to have a legal guardian assigned. Harriet prevented him from doing this until an order of attachment was delivered by the Messenger of the Court and the child was apprehended.[47] No immediate decision was forthcoming, and, even more frustrating, Godwin still refused to grant a personal interview. Without Mary's calming influence, for she was still at Bishopsgate with William, Shelley's patience finally gave way and he wrote to Godwin from Norfolk Street in a fury of reproach and scorn. The letter reminds one instantly of his notes to Sir Timothy of 1811. Whatever social arrangements were subsequently patched up, neither Shelley nor Godwin ever recrossed the emotional gulf opened up by this explosive letter. The explosion had, in effect, been delayed since the winter of 1814.

In my judgement neither I, nor your daughter, nor her offspring ought to receive the treatment which we encounter on every side. It has perpetually appeared to me to have been your especial duty to see that, so far as mankind value your good opinion, we were dealt justly by, and that a young family, innocent and benevolent and united, should not be confounded with prostitutes and seducers. My astonishment, and I will confess when I have been treated with most harshness and cruelty by you, my indignation has been extreme, that, knowing as you do my nature, any considerations should have prevailed on you to be thus harsh and cruel. I lamented also over my ruined hopes, of all that your genius once taught me to expect from your virtue, when I found that for yourself, your family, and your creditors, you would submit to that communication with me which you once rejected and abhorred, and which no pity for my poverty or sufferings, assumed willingly for you, could avail to extort. Do not talk of *forgiveness* again to me, for my blood boils in my veins, and my gall rises against all that bears the human form, when I think of what I, their benefactor and ardent lover, have endured of enmity and contempt from you and from all mankind.[48]

But Shelley was still trapped in his own emotional contradictions. The following day, he sent Godwin a note, confirming that the financial negotiations were still continuing, and pitifully asking for understanding. 'I must appear the reverse of what I really am, haughty & hard, if I am not to see myself & all that I love trampled upon and outraged.'[49] Yet still Godwin did not relent, and several days later, when Shelley actually called at Skinner Street, he was refused admittance: not once, but three times.[50] Gradually and painfully the resolution to see the Chancery case through, and leave Godwin to his fate was forming in Shelley's mind.

March too saw another event which was decisive in Shelley's departure from England. Claire, after shuttling between London and Bishopsgate, took advantage of Shelley's residence in London to make the first moves in a little project of her own. This was the invasion, storm and capture of Byron. It says much for Claire, still only just 18, that where many others, more powerful and more beautiful, had failed, she – at least temporarily – succeeded.

Lord Byron was at this time aged 28. His life had been disordered and made directionless by a desperately unhappy marriage to Anne Isabella Milbanke in 1815. The legal separation proceedings were now drawing to a close in a storm of bills and claims after months of separations and *rapprochements*. The basis of the settlement was agreed on 17 March.[51] His emotional tangle was further complicated by an intimate relationship with his half-sister Augusta, in an advanced state of pregnancy, who had just removed from his house at 13 Piccadilly Terrace to lie in at her rooms at St James's Palace. The friendship had caused Byron endless public acrimony. He wished above all to leave England before he should be caught in further scandals, legal complications or even in the clutches of the bailiffs. He planned his escape for April. His old friends Scrope Daves and John Cam Hobhouse were making preparations for a secret departure, and Byron's faithful valet Fletcher was discreetly preparing trunks at No. 13. The city firm of Baxter's were engaged to construct a new Napoleonic carriage for his travels, for which he paid £500. Byron hoped that escape to the Continent in the spring might also restart the creative mechanism which had faltered in 1813, after the completion of two cantos of *Childe Harold*. The delights of marriage and the glitter of social and literary celebrity both seemed to him intolerably faded. He desperately needed the break.

At that moment, in March, his life seemed to be suspended between two distinct theatres of action, and, without indicating his intention to depart, he was in the mood to write to James Hogg in Scotland: 'And so you want to come to London? It's a damned place to be sure, but the only one in the world (at least the English world) for fun; though I have seen parts of the globe that I like better, still upon the whole it is the completest either to help one in feeling oneself – alive – or forgetting that one is so.'[52] By luck, by ill-luck or by instinct, it was in this fatalistic mood that Claire and Byron's paths crossed; and their lives irretrievably tangled.

Claire first came to Byron's attention, very mildly, with a series of pseudonymous notes addressed to him in his capacity as a member of the Drury Lane Theatre Committee. After achieving a first interview, which was rather more prosaic than she would have desired, she followed up her advantageous opening with a spirited correspondence. Claire filled her *billets doux* with discussions of new poetry, her own fiction, and advanced ideas on social institutions, including, scornfully, marriage: 'I can never resist the temptation of throwing a pebble at it as I pass by.'[53] Of the story she sent him, probably 'The Idiot' of 1814, she noted progressively that 'the story might appear to be a highly moral warning to young people about irregular opinions', but nevertheless 'atheists might see and understand my meaning'. Shelley's teaching and influence were being put to good use.

How far Shelley was actively engaged in Claire's campaign can only be judged from minor details. But it is important in the light of Shelley's subsequent behaviour towards Claire. During the six weeks she was conducting her siege of Byron, Claire was staying at least part of the time with Shelley in Norfolk Street. In March alone she received notes of hand from him providing her with no less than forty-one pounds. Moreover, Shelley, though he had not yet met Byron, featured actively in Claire's correspondence. She explained to Byron about the events of 1814; about Mary and Godwin; and about the underground publication of *Queen Mab*. Byron was prepared to be impressed, and Claire wrote in reply: 'Shelley is now turned three and twenty, and interested as I am in all he does, it is with the greatest pleasure I receive your approbation.'[54] The news was passed on to Shelley, and later Claire sent Byron a copy of *Alastor* as well.

Claire next asked Shelley for a summation of her own character, and Shelley provided an apt one. She passed this on to Byron verbatim; she implies that Shelley did not know to what use she was putting the description, but if so, it is curiously appropriate to the situation. 'My Sweet Child,' Shelley said, adopting his best tones of guide and mentor, 'there are two Clares – one of them I should call irritable if it were not for the nervous disorder, the effects of which you still retain: the nervous Clare is reserved and melancholy and more sarcastic than violent; the good Clare is gentle yet cheerful; and to me the most engaging of human creatures; one thing I will say for you that you are easily managed by the person you love as the reed is by the wind; it is your weak side.'[55]

Charmed by Claire's quickness, her warmth, her lightness of touch, and her apparently totally free attitude to sexual relations, Byron saw her with increasing frequency, usually in the evenings in his private rooms at the theatre. On one evening, when he could not be there, Byron offered her his box, but she refused as much as she wanted to go, because Shelley disliked the theatre and 'declares he could not endure it'. At other *soirées* Claire probably sang to Byron, as she knew her voice was her greatest asset, and he wrote one of his most famous lyrics at this time, dating the manuscript 28 March 1816. It has traditionally been taken as addressed to Claire.

> There be none of Beauty's daughters
> With a magic like thee;
> And like music on the waters
> Is thy sweet voice to me;

When, as if its sound were causing
The charmed Ocean's pausing,
The waves lie still and gleaming,
And the lulled winds seem dreaming. . . .

It was a long time since Shelley had written such a love poem.

13
The Byron Summer:
Switzerland 1816

April 1816 promised to be a decisive month in more ways than one. The test case over the Shelley inheritance was finally to go into Chancery; Byron's separation papers were due; Mary came up to London with the child and Shelley moved to new and more spacious lodgings at 26 Marchmont Street; Godwin's financial fate hung in the balance. Shelley, like Byron, was waiting only for a legal decision before breaking away from London completely. Claire, for her part, realized that her own freedom of action depended very largely on Shelley's financial independence; especially when she discovered that Byron would never agree to take her with him as his travelling mistress to Geneva. She therefore planned hopefully to seduce Byron before he left, but the timing was tricky. 'I steal a moment to write to you to know whether you go tomorrow,' she wrote in mid-April. 'It is not through selfishness that I pray something may prevent your departure. But tomorrow Shelley's chancery suit will be decided & so much of my fate depends on the decision; beside tomorrow will inform me whether I should be able to offer you *that* which it has long been the passionate wish of my heart to offer you.'[1]

In the event, Byron's separation papers did not come through until the 21st, and Shelley's chancery decision was not given until the 23rd. This was the day on which Byron fled from 13 Piccadilly Terrace with his valet Fletcher and his new amanuensis Dr William Polidori, and made headlong for Dover with the bailiffs expected hourly on his trail. But by this time Claire was already Byron's mistress. According to one of her notes, she had arranged a first romantic night with Byron at a discreet inn ten miles outside London, probably on Thursday, 18 April. She had waited for a reply in Hamilton Place, and it had been in the affirmative.[2] Later Mary had been taken to meet Byron formally in the green room at Drury Lane, though Claire had emphasized to Byron that the nature of their connection should not be hinted at. Mary indeed does not seem to have realized fully what was afoot until quite late in the summer, as remarks in her Geneva journal indicate.

Shelley on the other hand must have been *au fait* from the start. When Byron, after the first flush of physical delight, began to remark more critically on Claire's 'fiendish temper', she countered with her recommendation from Shelley, which seemed to implicate his judgement in the affair. 'I know Shelley is too fond of me not to be indulgent, yet I think it an honourable testament to that part of my character you have accused that the man whom I have loved & for whom I have suffered much should report this of me. Some time hence you will say the same about my temper. . . . Now pray answer me kindly & do not put any little sarcastic speeches in it. . . .'[3]

The ease with which Shelley fell in with Claire's plans to follow Byron to Geneva even suggests that he may have been using Claire as an introduction to Byron. The engineering of Mary's visit to Drury Lane was designed to make the whole scheme seem more natural and innocent. The different degrees to which Claire took Mary and Shelley into her confidence in this respect is a good indication of her instinctive assessment of their real attitudes and sympathies.

On the 23rd, Shelley was in court to hear a surprise decision given *against* any rearrangement of the estates by Sir Timothy, and consequently against the intended sale of Shelley's reversion. Sir Timothy's solicitor, Whitton, also in court, noticed the great disappointment on Shelley's face with ill-disguised satisfaction.[4] But Sir Timothy behaved with perhaps unexpected generosity on hearing of the decision, which went equally against his own plans for his other children, and against Shelley's plans. Doubtless the dependency of Harriet and her two children had some bearing on his action. He informed Shelley that the £1,000 annuity would continue as agreed, despite the fact that the business basis for it had collapsed, now the reversion could not be sold. Furthermore he would pay off more of Shelley's bills.

Shelley presented the situation in its gloomiest light in a letter to Godwin: 'Chancery has decided that I and my father may not touch the estates. . . . All this reduces me very nearly to the situation I described to you in March, so far as relates to your share in the question. I shall receive nothing from my father except in the way of charity. Post Obit considerations are very doubtful, & annuity transactions are confined within an obvious & very narrow limit. My father is to advance me, a sum to meet as I have alleged engagements contracted during the dependence of the late negotiation. This sum is extremely small, & is swallowed up, almost, in such of my debts & the liquidation of such securities as I have been compelled to state in order to obtain the money at all. A few hundred pounds will remain; you shall have £300 from this source in the course of the summer.'[5] Shelley had hoped to obtain at least another £600 by this disengenuous method,[6] though in the event, largely through Longdill's sense of legal propriety, this was reduced to less than half such a sum. Godwin never saw any of it, let alone the hoped-for £1,250. Most depressing of all, he saw his worst fears confirmed, despite Shelley's promises, when he noted that the letter, dated 3 May, was addressed from Dover. Shelley was abroad again.

His choice of Geneva, indeed his choice to go across the Channel at all, rather than northwards into Cumberland or Scotland as he had previously intended, was very largely decided by Claire's wishes. Shelley departed – like Byron ten days previously – with speed and silence, taking the two girls and little William. Godwin was not forewarned. The financial negotiators Bryant and Hayward were given a cover story that Shelley was to be in the country for a week. Even Hogg, with whom Shelley dined on the eve of their departure, was not enlightened until a note arrived asking him to forward an explanatory letter to Longdill. Hogg had been led to expect that he was going to live with them again in communal fashion as in the previous spring, and Shelley felt considerably embarrassed on the point. He explained obliquely: 'Seal, & dispatch for me the enclosed letter to Longdill. It will give you that information which *mauvaise honte* or awkwardness, or anything which you please except a want of regard made me conceal last night. In fact I had determined on the plan; & felt pained that the commencement of it, fell at a time when it was impossible that you should be partaker in it.'[7] There is no evidence that Harriet was in any way informed of Shelley's plans or whereabouts, and this final act of disregard was to have grim consequences.

Characteristically, Peacock in his 'Memoir' preferred to make no reference at all to either the Godwin debt, or Claire's affair. Instead he gave a long circumstantial and totally irrelevant account of Shelley having left England because of a hallucination that Williams of Tremadoc had come to Bishopsgate to warn him of a plot by Sir Timothy and Captain Pilfold to imprison him. There is in fact a rather more mundane basis for this story in the circumstances of Shelley's debts *two years later* in 1818 at Great Marlow. Peacock's delightfully eccentric anecdote seems to be a mixture of polite subterfuge and the genuine confusion of aging memory.

When he wrote from Dover to Godwin, Shelley did not explain that Claire was with them, and he implied that he and Mary had been driven into exile 'perhaps forever'. Perhaps he might return alone, for a few days, on strictly business affairs, but 'to see no friend, to do no office of friendship, to engage in nothing which can soothe the sentiments of regret almost like remorse . . .'. He appealed once more to Godwin's better feelings: 'But I have been too indignant, I have been unjust to you. – forgive me. – Burn those letters which contain the records of my violence, & believe that however what you erroneously call fame

& honour separate us, I shall always feel towards you as the most affectionate of friends.'[8] Godwin did not write to Shelley for a month, and then it was only to receive no reply for a further four weeks. Shelley had dismissed him.

They caught the packet out of Dover on the afternoon of 3 May, Shelley just managing to seal and dispatch his letter to Godwin before the ropes were cast off. Travelling at a leisurely rate, they arrived in Paris on the 8th. Here they were held up by passport difficulties, since regulations had been tightened because of an escaped political prisoner. From their rooms in the rue Richelieu, Claire wrote amusingly to Byron that she had persuaded the 'whole tribe of Otaheite philosophers' to come with her – a laughing reference to the sunny pleasure-loving islanders of Tahiti. She also assured him that she had ten times rather be his male friend than his mistress. The letter was sealed in red wax with the impression of the Judgement of Paris – Shelley's signet.

They were all glad, for their individual reasons, to be on the Continent again. Shelley was immensely relieved to escape the pressures of London, which had been making him physically ill with consumptive symptoms once more. He was also looking forward to the meeting with Byron which Claire promised. Much of Mary's attention was taken up by the child, but she recalled the happy times of 1814, though noting shrewdly that the French population seemed more hang-dog and oppressed since the restitution of the Bourbon dynasty of tyrants: 'the discontent and sullenness of their minds perpetually betrays itself'.[9] Her phrase was taken from Shelley, the first significant political observation he had made for more than a year.

Claire's thoughts were of course exclusively on Byron. She knew that making love with him had not changed his essentially casual attitude towards her, and already she had picked up, with that sensitivity which so delighted Shelley, a perfect echo of the Byronic *dégagement*. 'I know not how to address you,' she wrote, 'I cannot call you friend for though I love you you do not feel even interest for me; fate has ordained that the slightest accident that should befall you should be agony to me; but were I to float by your window drowned all you would say would be "Ah voila". . . .' She knew that perhaps her greatest hold over him was simply her youth, and she played that card with delicacy and sincerity '. . . a few days ago I was eighteen; people of eighteen always love truly & tenderly; & I who was educated by Godwin however erroneous my creed have the highest adoration for truth.'[10] Between her and Shelley it seemed like a kind of conspiracy.

The journey to Geneva took another six days. They followed the main tourist route south-eastwards through Troyes, which now bored them, then Dijon and Poligny. In the Jura they found that spring was late in arriving. Tourists were not yet expected, and reluctant hospitality and snow greeted them.

But they pressed on, divided between awe at the scenery and irritation at the local population. At Les Rousses they hired a four-horse closed carriage, ten men to dig them out of drifts, and scandalized everyone by setting off at 6 in the evening. They huddled in stale rugs, snow pelting against the windows of the carriage, and darkness falling rapidly.[11] Through the freezing windows, Mary recorded the first note in a theme that was to come to dominate her imagination during the next five months, 'Never was a scene more awefully desolate. The trees in these regions are incredibly large, and stand in scattered clumps over the white wilderness; the vast expanse of snow was chequered only by these gigantic pines, and the poles that marked our road: no river or rock-encircled lawn relieved the eye, by adding the picturesque to the sublime. The natural silence of that uninhabited desert contrasted strangely with the voices of the men who conducted us, who, with animated tones and gestures called to one another in a patois composed of French and Italian, creating disturbance, where but for them, there was none.'[12]

Then suddenly, they came down out of the snow and foreboding pines, and were jogging through the sweet lake air in the outskirts of Geneva. They forgot the icy desert wilderness, a dream of premonition, and gazed eagerly upon the bustling illuminated prettiness of the lake. But writing to Peacock the next morning, 15 May, Shelley recalled the same grim passage: 'The trees in this region are incredibly large, but stand in scattered clumps in the white wilderness. Never was scene more awefully desolate as that which we passed in one evening of our last days journey.'[13]

They drove straight to Monsieur Dejean's Hotel d'Angleterre in the fashionable suburb of Secheron, the regular stopping point for all well-to-do English travellers passing by the Lake, and also Byron's expected port of call. Shelley took an inexpensive set of rooms on the upper floor, and hired a small sailing boat for the duration of their stay. Their windows looked pleasantly southwards over the blueness of the lake, with the terraced vine fields opposite as yet showing no crop. Above them the haze of Alps stretched backwards and upwards in darker and darker tones until finally, above and beyond them all – when the morning light was clear – the single glittering white fang of Mont Blanc appeared. 'We do not enter society here,' wrote Mary, 'yet our time passes swiftly and delightfully. We read Italian and Latin during the heats of noon, and when the sun declines we walk in the garden of the hotel, looking at the rabbits relieving fallen cockchaffers, and watching the motions of a myriad of lizards, who inhabit a southern wall of the garden.' On most evenings, at about 6 p.m., all three of them embarked on the little boat and drifted over the lake for an hour or two. As they came in towards land, about 10 o'clock, Mary noted how the sweet scents of spring flowers and new-mown grass would blow across the water to meet them. They hung limply over the sides of the boat and gazed down into the clear water as the pebbled bottom and innumerable fish rose up silently towards them. These details were later to be transferred into the mind of Victor Frankenstein as he ferried his young wife across the lake on the evening of his doomed marriage day.[14]

Briefly, Shelley was overwhelmed by a strong feeling of homesickness which he himself found strange, and he expanded it in his letter to Peacock. The very beauty of the country around him reminded him of his feeling for English scenes, and he thought of the Lake poets, especially Wordsworth. 'Our Poets & our Philosophers our mountains & our lakes, the rural lanes & fields which are ours so especially, are ties which unless I become utterly senseless can never be broken asunder. These and the memory of them if I never should return, these & the affections of the mind with which having once been united they are inseparably united, will make the name of England, my country dear to me forever, even if I should permanently return to it no more.'

Then, feeling better, he dismissed thoughts of exile and 'sentimental gossip', and ended briskly, 'We are now at Geneva, where or in the neighbourhood we shall remain probably until the autumn. I shall return almost immediately, within a fortnight or three weeks, to attend to the least exertions which Longdill is to make for the settlement of my affairs – of course I shall see you then.' Mary he noted was busy writing up a journal, otherwise she would have sent him a letter in Latin.[15]

The long-awaited arrival of Byron, ten days later, soon put all thoughts of returning to grapple with business affairs far from Shelley's mind. The Napoleonic carriage appeared at about midnight on 25 May, spattered with mud from a vigorous sightseeing trip. Byron and Dr Polidori had been over the battlefield of Waterloo, and up the Rhine among the wild and beautiful scenery that Shelley had observed in rather less comfort two summers before.

Polidori, who had been commissioned for £500 by Murray to keep a private diary of the trip, tended to give the impression that while he had been visiting the galleries, Byron had visited the chambermaids. In fact, Byron's thoughts had been turning constantly and sadly to Augusta, who alone would have appreciated the sights that he did, the Rhine crags and castles, and in the loneliness of the early hours he had at last turned to poetry again. The opening section of Canto III of *Childe Harold* was already under way in his notebook. It was on the Rhine that a famous altercation between Byron and Polidori had already taken place. The young Polidori, still only aged 21, had turned abruptly on the poet after sourly reading a eulogium of Byron's works, and asked what, pray, could Byron do better than *he* except write poetry. 'First . . . I can hit with a pistol the keyhole of that door – Secondly, I can swim across that river to yonder point – and thirdly, I can give you a d—d good thrashing.'[16] That, at any rate, was how Byron cared to recall the incident six years later. Byron was ready for a change of society.

Claire knew of their arrival within half an hour, for she had heard the carriage noise and bustle of servants, and checked the register where Byron, overcome with weariness, had put his age as 100. In the anxious note she sent up, Shelley's complicity was again useful: 'Direct under cover to Shelley for I do not wish to appear either in love or curious.' But Byron went off to Geneva the following morning on business, and there was no contact between the two parties for the rest of the day, the Shelleys pursuing their usual routine on the lake in the evening. Claire decided that this diffidence on both sides was too ridiculous, and after staying up late that night, she wrote a piqued but thoroughly practical and straightforward note to him at 2 in the morning. 'I have been in this weary hotel this fortnight and it seems so unkind, so cruel of you to treat me with such marked indifference. Will you go straight up to the top of the house this evening at ½ past seven & I will infallibly be on the landing place and show you the room.'[17] With that she went to bed.

The next morning, spotting Byron and Polidori rowing in from an excursion on the lake, she seized the opportunity and brought Shelley and Mary to walk along the *plage*. Byron disembarked, leaving Polidori to float offshore, and splashed up the beach with his slight limp. Here the famous introduction was at last made, Mr Shelley very formal and Lord Byron a little cool. The two poets were shy with each other, Claire's presence adding awkwardness, but Byron hastily invited Shelley to dine alone with him that evening and with a quick bow to Mary and Claire, stumped back to see to the boat.

Polidori made up the third member of the party in the evening, and noted in his diary: 'P[ercy] S[helley], the author of *Queen Mab*, came; bashful, shy consumptive; twenty-six; separated from his wife; keeps the two daughters of Godwin, who practise his theories; one L[ord] B[yron]'s.'[18] Shelley, with his pallor and his silence and his advanced theories, appeared to Polidori older than he was, but Byron felt he could relax in his company and the dinner was a success. From the final part of Polidori's entry, it seems as if Claire's invitation was finally taken up. Later Byron was to write with a rather assumed shrug to Augusta: 'I was not in love, nor have any love left for any, but I could not exactly play the stoic with a woman who had scrambled eight hundred miles to unphilosophize me.' He added, with a touch of self-pity which was more to the point, 'beside I had been regaled of late with so many "two courses and a *desert*" (Alas!) of aversion, that I was fain to take a little love (if pressed particularly) by way of novelty.'[19] Claire did press particularly.

The next day, Polidori was properly introduced all round, and Byron and the

Shelleys began a regular arrangement of breakfasting together – a meal that was not altogether familiar to Byron. Polidori noted: 'Was introduced by Shelley to Mary Wollstonecraft Godwin, called here Mrs Shelley. . . . No names announced, no ceremony, – each speaks when he pleases.' There was something to be said for Shelley's 'theories' after all. They boated and dined together with increasing frequency, and Shelley and Byron began to plan a whole summer spent together. At the Plainpalais, outside Geneva, they visited the bust and memorial of Jean Jacques Rousseau, and discovered a common enthusiasm.

The first thing was to get clear of the Hotel d'Angleterre, which was expensive and inconvenient; already stories were beginning to circulate about their curious *entente*. Shelley talked Byron into splitting the purchase of a properly rigged sailing boat, with a sufficiently deep keel and draught to withstand the occasionally violent squalls. Byron discovered a possible set of residences with a harbour, on the opposite southern side of the lake, near Compegny, about three miles beyond Geneva. There was a large porticoed house, with an extensive shaded balcony along its length, commanding a broad view of the Lake and the Jura. It was known as the Villa Diodati, and Milton had once occupied it. Below, about eight minutes' walk down a narrow, tortuous track through the vine fields, was a smaller, two-storied chalet which gave directly on to the lake and commanded the small private harbour. This was known by the cheerful name of Montalègre. These seemed almost ideal properties for Byron and Shelley respectively, though the leases were rather high in the best Swiss fashion. Negotiations were opened with the landlords.

Meanwhile the talk continued between the two poets, and became more intimate. Shelley fascinated Byron with the lurid details of his career, which he narrated as commonplace, and Byron listened with amused sympathy. Polidori, who seems to have been present at many of these dicussions, noted down the topics, some of them characteristically distorted by Shelley, and sometimes added his own caustic commentary. Of Harriet and Mary and Claire, he noted on the 30th: '[Shelley] gone through much misery, thinking he was dying; married a girl for the mere sake of letting her have the jointure that would accrue to her; recovered; found he could not agree; separated; paid Godwin's debts, and seduced his daughter; then wondered that he would not see him. The sister [i.e. Claire] left the father to go with the other. Got a child. All clever, and no meretricious appearance. He is very clever and the more I read his "Queen Mab" the more beauties I find.'[20]

The next day, Shelley's reminiscences went even further back into the mythologies of Dr Lind and Harriet Grove. 'Shelley is another instance of wealth inducing relations to confine for madness, and was only saved by his physician being honest. He was betrothed from a boy to his cousin, for age;

another came who had as much [money] as he *would* have, and she left him "because he was an atheist".'[21] Of Godwin Shelley talked bitterly. 'When starving, a friend to whom he had given £2000 though he knew it, would not come near him.' Mary impressed Polidori by reciting Coleridge's grim satire against Pitt, 'A War Eclogue', in which the three voices of Fire, Famine and Slaughter chant of the statesman's damnation – 'which persuades me [Coleridge] is a poet'. Polidori was surprised by the taste among the Shelleys for the macabre, but glad when Shelley requested him to vaccinate little William, which he did on 2 June. The doctor received in thanks a gold chain and seal.

Shelley took Montalègre without more ado at the beginning of June, and Byron, whose negotiations had been more protracted, moved into the Villa Diodati, above them on the hill, ten days later. Their new boat arrived on 8 June, and Shelley established its moorings in the little harbour. Polidori noted: 'Into the new boat – Shelley's – and talked till the ladies' brains whizzed with giddiness about idealism. Back; rain; puffs of wind.' Other subjects Polidori noted were madness, and names involved in the Irish revolutionary movement. Shelley was also, according to Byron, busy 'dosing' him with Wordsworth. In the evenings sometimes Claire managed to slip away up to the Diodati. But it was not altogether easy, for she found Polidori's presence awkward, and she was anxious, she wrote in a note to Byron, that his suspicions should not be aroused. This was clearly a defensive device of Byron's, for we know that he had told Polidori of the relationship on the first night they dined with Shelley. But by June there was also another piece of information that Polidori may or may not have known. Claire was pregnant. For Shelley it was a cloud, but a distant one.*

Things became easier for Claire when the two households drew together as a result of a spell of bad weather in the last fortnight of June. There was less sailing to be done, and they joined together in literary discussions and projects at the Diodati. The talk went on late into the evenings, and when the rain was falling, Shelley's party often stopped over the night. Polidori was laid up on a couch, having slipped and sprained his ankle attempting to perform a gallantry for Mary on the path through the vine fields on 15 June. He had begun a play, which 'all agreed was worth nothing', but the conversation with Shelley on that same night led in intriguing directions. 'Shelley and I had a conversation about principles – whether man was to be thought merely an instrument.'

Sitting in the long, candlelit drawing-room at the Diodati, with rain beating

---

* Byron did raise the question of paternity with Shelley, but only briefly, and he soon dismissed it as certainly his child. But writing to his friend Douglas Kinnaird, he implied that Shelley did not deny *previous* sexual relations with Claire: '. . . Is the brat mine? I have reason to think so, for I know as much as one can know such a thing – that she had not lived with S[helley] during the time of our acquaintance – and that she had a good deal of that same with me.'

at the large balcony windows, and thunder and lightning frequently descending across the lake from the Jura, the subjects turned upon the life force, galvanism and the principles of animation. Polidori had qualified in Edinburgh at the exceptional age of 19, and the discussion was balanced between his considerable knowledge of contemporary medicine and Shelley's more speculative interest in Erasmus Darwin's work, and the possible applications of the kind of electrical instruments Shelley had experimented with at Oxford. Mary, who sat silently with Claire, half drawn back in the flickering shadows, listened with fascination as the men talked and theorized. She recalled: 'Many and long were the conversations between Lord Byron and Shelley to which I was a devout but nearly silent listener. During one of these, various philosophical doctrines were discussed, and among others the nature of the principle of life, and whether there was any probability of it ever being discovered and communicated. They talked of the experiments of Dr Darwin . . . who preserved a piece of vermicelli in a glass case till by some extraordinary means it began to move with voluntary motion. Not thus, after all, would life be given. Perhaps a corpse would be reanimated; galvanism had given token of such things: perhaps the component parts of a creature might be manufactured, brought together, and endued with vital warmth.'[22]

These speculative discussions, which continued on the nights of 16 and 17 June, became merged with the idea that, after the disappointment of Polidori's play, they should all try their hands at writing a ghost story. The previous week Polidori had been discussing problems of somnambulism with Dr Odier in Geneva, and someone, perhaps Byron, had brought in a copy of a very rare collection of German horror stories, translated under the title of *Fantasmagoriana*. On the 17th they all went to a ball at Madame Odier's for part of the evening, except Polidori with his bad ankle, and these subjects were continued. Polidori was annoyed to be left out, since he had taken a fancy to Mary and her free thinking, though she responded drily enough to his gallantries by saying that she thought of him as a younger brother. Surrounded by the irritability and frustrations of the young doctor and also Claire's tensions, and deep in the world of horror stories and speculations, Shelley found himself slipping into a mood of morbidity and oppression. Mary too was assailed by disturbing ideas and fantasies, and for once she felt threatened by Shelley's power to frighten and unsettle.

Shelley's ghost story was never written down, but received a single explosive performance, on the night of the 18th. They were all sitting in the long room at the Diodati, and Polidori records what happened. 'Twelve o'clock really began to talk ghostly. L[ord] B[yron] repeated some verses of Coleridge's "Christabel", of the witch's breast; when silence ensued, and Shelley suddenly shrieking and putting his hands to his head, ran out of the room with a candle.' In Coleridge's poem, the witch, Geraldine, first appears as a beautiful and benighted princess, lost in the forest. But in reality she is a Lamia – a disguised serpent – and she is intent on both the spiritual and physical possession of the young girl, Christabel. Christabel's father mistakenly gives Geraldine shelter in the castle. The witch is actually lodged in Christabel's chamber, and when they retire to bed, she casts a kind of dreaming spell on her, and then proceeds to undress in front of her sleepy, half-closed eyes. The verse runs:

> Beneath the lamp the lady bowed,
> And slowly rolled her eyes around;
> Then drawing in her breath aloud
> Like one that shuddered, she unbound
> The cincture from beneath her breast;
> Her silken robe, and inner vest
> Dropt to her feet, and in full view,
> Behold! her bosom and half her side –
> Hideous, deformed, and pale of hue –
> O shield her! shield sweet Christabel!*

The others were much shaken by the suddenness and violence of Shelley's outburst, and it was Polidori who went to Shelley and treated him in his capacity as a doctor. He managed to calm him, and with considerable tact succeeded in extracting the story of Shelley's hallucination. 'Threw water in his face, and after gave him ether. He was looking at Mrs S[helley], and suddenly thought of a woman he had heard of who had eyes instead of nipples, which taking hold of his mind, horrified him.' Polidori continued to talk to Shelley, as he lay on a couch recovering, and several of Shelley's persistent fears were candidly revealed in these unguarded minutes. Polidori recorded: '– He married; and a friend of his liking his wife, he tried all he could to induce her to love him in turn. He is surrounded by friends who feed upon him, and draw upon him as their banker. Once, having hired a house, a man wanted to make him pay more, and came trying to bully him, and at last challenged him. Shelley refused, and was knocked down; coolly said that would not gain him his object, and was knocked down again.'[23]

The emotional pressures resulting from Shelley's communal attempts are clear from Dr Polidori's notes, and it seems that he had at least partly succeeded in 'interpreting' Shelley's hallucination in terms of the social and sexual contradictions in Shelley's life. But there is no episode in Shelley's career that exactly

---

* Coleridge himself was somewhat concerned at the witch's revelation of the ghastly deformity of her breasts, and in later editions changed the penultimate line to, 'A sight to dream of, not to tell!'

matches the last incident. Shelley seems to have been trying to explain how he felt continually persecuted at places like Keswick, Lynmouth, Tremadoc and Kentish Town. Above all, he was trying to indicate to Polidori his absolute refusal to indulge in physical violence; a refusal that Polidori vaguely realized denied some important element in his temperament. Later, because of an incident during a sailing race, Polidori, who was himself extremely hot-tempered, threatened to challenge Shelley to a duel, until Byron intervened to say that he would accept any challenge on Shelley's behalf. Polidori withdrew, as Byron had intended; but perhaps Byron would have done better to leave Shelley to deal with the matter himself.

Polidori later made use of this 'fit of fantasy', as Byron called it, in the ghost story he wrote, adapted from one thrown aside by Byron. It was published in 1819 as a pamphlet with a lurid woodcut, *The Vampyre*. Byron commented on this gothic tale in a letter to Murray in the same year, to the effect that Shelley 'certainly had the fit of phantasy which Polidori describes, though *not exactly* as he describes it'.[24] But at the time, writing from the Diodati to his publisher he was more puzzled; he could not understand what had got into Shelley, 'for he don't want courage'. The friendship between him and Shelley had not yet broken the barriers of gentlemanly good form.

Nonetheless Shelley's 'fit' did not stop Byron going off alone with Shelley four days later on a sailing trip round the lake. The weather had improved on the 19th, and the Shelleys had gone back to more regular residence at Montalègre. The late night talks still continued at the Diodati, and it was probably on one of those days before Shelley's departure that Mary experienced the awful nightmare that gave her the central idea for her own, most famous story: *Frankenstein, or, The Modern Prometheus*. Her description of how this occurred, though clearly formalized for the occasion of her preface, is a classic example of the way in which the heightened consciousness of terror, which Shelley had so often played upon, was transmuted into creative inspiration. Mary had managed this, where neither Harriet nor Claire had survived the stress.

> Night waned upon this talk, and even the witching hour had gone by before we retired to rest. When I placed me head on my pillow I did not sleep, nor could I be said to think. My imagination, unbidden, possessed and guided me, gifting the successive images that arose in my mind with a vividness far beyond the usual bounds of reverie.* I saw – with shut eyes, but acute mental vision – I saw the pale student of unhallowed arts kneeling beside the thing he had put together. I saw the hideous phantasm of a man stretched out, and

---

* A close connection with Shelley's earlier description of such states, in the writings of 1815, is manifest here.

then, on the working of some powerful engine show signs of life and stir with an uneasy, half-vital motion. . . . His success would terrify the artist; he would rush away from his odious handiwork, horror-stricken. He would hope that, left to itself, the slight spark of life which he had communicated would fade, that this thing which had received such imperfect animation, would subside into dead matter. . . . He sleeps; but he is awakened; he opens his eyes; behold, the horrid thing stands at his bedside, opening his curtains and looking on him with yellow, watery, but speculative eyes.

I opened mine in terror. The idea so possessed my mind that a thrill of fear ran through me, and I wished to exchange the ghastly image of my fancy for the realities around. I see them still: the very room, the dark parquet, the closed shutters with the moonlight struggling through, and the sense I had that the glassy lake and white high Alps were beyond.* I could not so easily get rid of my hideous phantom; still it haunted me. I must try to think of something else. I recurred to my ghost story – my tiresome, unlucky ghost story! Oh! If I could only contrive one which would frighten my reader as I myself had been frightened that night!

Swift as light and as cheering was the idea that broke in upon me. 'I have found it! What terrified me will terrify others; and I need only describe the spectre that haunted my midnight pillow.' On the morrow I announced that I had *thought of a story*. I began that day with the words 'It was on a dreary night of November', making only a transcript of the grim terrors of my waking dream.[25]

The first words that Mary wrote now correspond to the opening of the fifth chapter of *Frankenstein* as it was finally completed, and describes Dr Frankenstein's awakening of the monster. The setting is the German university town of Ingolstadt, known mainly to the Shelleys as the birthplace of the Illuminist conspiracy, a suggestive hint.

Mary later described how Shelley had urged her to develop the full implications of the story into a novel: 'but for his incitement it would have never taken the form in which it was presented to the world'. She worked on the book steadily through the rest of the summer, and began to redraft it after they had returned to England during the winter. In its theme and settings, if not its actual plot-line, the book is closely related to the circumstances of Mary's private life with Shelley and sometimes the resemblances are uncanny.

The description of Dr Frankenstein's education developing from alchemical

* Mary's solitariness during this night, if accurately recalled, suggests that it occurred when Shelley was already away on the lake with Byron; however this may have been a literary device, as was the imagined landscape – it was the Jura that were 'beyond' the lake; the Alps lay behind Montalègre, to the south.

and magical interests in authors such as Albertus Magnus and Paracelsus, to a more strictly scientific concentration on 'natural philosophy', galvanism and anatomy is deliberately intended to parallel Shelley's own story of his intellectual development from romance to philosophy, as told for example in his introductory letters to Godwin of 1812.[26] The monster's first murder, of Frankenstein's baby brother, who is called William, takes place on the Plainpalais which Shelley and Mary had visited twice in May.[27] The central confrontation between Frankenstein and his ghastly creation, when the monster demands a wife to compensate him for his rejection by human society, is staged on the Mer de Glace, at Chamonix, which Mary, Shelley and Claire visited in July.[28] Dr Frankenstein's second laboratory, where he builds and then destroys the second, female monster – thus breaking his pact and putting both himself and the monster under a similar curse – is located in Scotland where Mary had spent much of her late childhood.[29] The books on which the monster educates himself are Goethe's *Young Werther*, Plutarch's *Lives* and Milton's *Paradise Lost*.[30] The descent of the Rhine by boat of Frankenstein and his bosom friend Clerval (who is also murdered) recalls their journeyings of 1814.[31] The many other boating scenes reflect impressions of Shelley and Mary on the water, not least perhaps the tranquil journey across the lake through the twilight to Evian, on the eve before the monster murders Frankenstein's bride, Elizabeth.[32] The monster's leering face through the window of the Inn after the murder, and Frankenstein's distraught attempt to shoot it, is an obvious reference to what Shelley had told Mary of the assassination attempt at Tan-yr-allt in 1813.[33]

Mary's most brilliant structural innovation in the book is the way in which, after the murder of Elizabeth, she reverses the roles of pursuer and pursued. It is now Frankenstein who pursues the monster. This creates a *doppelgänger* theme, in which Frankenstein and his creation are made to form antagonistic parts of a single spiritual entity. The theme of demonic pursuit had become by then a central image in Shelley's poetry. Frankenstein's obsessional pursuit of the monster into the Arctic wastes, with which the book both begins and ends, reflects in mood and imagery much of the reversal and pursuit of narcissistic ideals which Shelley had studied in *Alastor*. It also draws heavily, with an explicit reference in Chapter 5, on Shelley's favourite poem by Coleridge, 'The Ancient Mariner'. Like these two poems, *Frankenstein* is a study in spiritual isolation, and the monster sometimes seems to be an almost programmatic attempt to present the *kaka-daimon* of Shelley's poem, the evil spirit of solitude itself.

The plotting of *Frankenstein*, like that of *Alastor*, turns on the destructive effects of the perversion of the sexual forces which bring people together and hold them within a human community. The creation of the monster himself is undertaken by Frankenstein at Ingolstadt in an inhuman and obsessional mood. He perversely rejects the appeals of his cousin Elizabeth, the beloved friend of his childhood, who he nevertheless passionately desires to marry. His father explicitly warns him against the destructive effect of such intense and specialized studies. The moment after he has rushed from the laboratory, having seen the appalling sight of the monster coming to life, he tries to shield himself in sleep, only to dream a ghastly and symbolic incident. 'I slept indeed, but I was disturbed by the wildest dreams. I thought I saw Elizabeth, in the bloom of health, walking in the streets of Ingolstadt. Delighted and surprised, I embraced her, but as I imprinted the first kiss on her lips, they became livid with the hue of death; her features appeared to change, and I thought I held the corpse of my dead mother in my arms; a shroud enveloped her form, and I saw the grave worms crawling in the folds of the flannel. I started from my sleep with horror.'[34]

When Frankenstein meets the monster again, in the great confrontation at Chamonix, the monster makes the demand which controls the rest of the story: 'You must create a female for me with whom I can live in the interchange of those sympathies necessary for my being. This alone you can do, and I demand it as a right which you must not refuse to concede.' Frankenstein at first recognizes this right, and does make the female monster in his Scottish laboratory. But then, in the presence of the monster, he tears the body apart just before completion. The monster's response, when he has recovered from his howls of anguish and despair, is simple: 'Remember – I will be with you on your wedding night.' This threat is duly carried out during the grim scene at Evian, where Elizabeth is throttled on her bridal bed. Thus both creator and created destroy each other's hopes of sexual happiness, and with that their links with human society are shattered. Both become outcasts and pariahs, tortured equally by the knowledge of what they have done, and the desire to be revenged for what they have lost. It is a gloomy denouement, and one wonders at it all the more remembering that Mary was only just 19 at the time of writing.

The core of the book dramatizes that mythic projection of the condition of exile which was already becoming a major preoccupation of Shelley's. When at the Mer de Glace the monster appeals to its master for help and understanding, Mary states with an extraordinary premonition the theme which was to dominate so much of Shelley's later poetry in Italy. 'Oh Frankenstein . . . Remember that I am thy creature; I ought to be thy Adam, but I am rather the fallen angel, whom thou drivest from joy for no misdeed. Everywhere I see bliss, from which I alone am irrevocably excluded. I was benevolent and good; misery made me a fiend. Make me happy, and I shall again be virtuous.' To which Frankenstein replies, answering for authority and society, 'Begone! I will not hear you. There can be no community between you and me; we are enemies.'[35]

Shelley was well aware of the many autobiographical influences which shaped Mary's book, besides the night of terror at Montalègre which saw its inception. Their experiences in England; his own poetry; Mary's relationship with her father; their continued readings of Godwin's own novels of pursuit, especially *Caleb Williams*; all played an important part. But in writing, anonymously, the preface to the novel a year later, and in reviewing it for the magazines under his own name, he made only passing references to these, and concentrated once again on the central issues of spiritual solitariness and social ostracism. Of the monster's crimes, he wrote in his review that they were, 'the children, as it were, of Necessity and Human Nature. In this the direct moral of the book consists. . . . Treat a person ill and he will become wicked. Requite affection with scorn; let one being be selected for whatever cause as the refuse of his kind – divide him, a social being, from society, and you impose upon him the irresistible obligations – malevolence and selfishness.' It is impossible to believe that he was not thinking at least partly of himself when he added, 'It is thus that too often in society those who are best qualified to be its benefactors and its ornaments are branded by some accident with scorn, and changed by neglect and solitude of heart into a scourge and a curse.'[36] Implicitly, Shelley accepted his own identification as Frankenstein's monster.

On the afternoon of Sunday, 23 June, Shelley, Byron and their boatman set out on a leisurely sailing tour of Leman, heading eastwards towards Evian. The tour took eight days, and despite uneven weather, including one unpleasantly dangerous storm, and another day of unbroken rain, it was a great success. Shelley was reading Rousseau's *Nouvelle Héloïse* for most of the journey, which, being set around the various lakeside villages, turned the trip for him into something of a literary pilgrimage. The 'ghostly visions', as he called them in the preface to *Frankenstein*, gave way to sentimental ones. 'Meillerie, the castle of Chillon, Clarens, the mountains of La Valaise and Savoy, present themselves to the imagination as monuments of things that were once familiar, and of beings that were once dear to it. They were created indeed by one mind, but a mind so powerfully bright as to cast a shade of falsehood on the records that are called reality.'

Shelley was unusually subdued in the elder poet's presence. While Byron absorbed his impressions apparently without effort into *Childe Harold* and the 'Prisoner of Chillon', Shelley was content to keep a mild, sightseer's diary-letter, which he subsequently posted to Peacock.[37] In the evenings they talked for hours about each other's childhood, but neither kept a written record of what was said. Yet it changed the formal friendship into the beginning of a real intimacy. Byron was delighted to be free from the company of both Claire and Polidori, and once in the middle of a beautiful wood he broke out, 'Thank God Polidori is not here.' Shelley also felt freed, and at Evian, surprisingly, he turned his attention to a number of business letters to Godwin and London lawyers that he had been putting off for weeks. He rapidly wrote and dispatched them, and Godwin received a cheque for five pounds, under the name of 'Martin'. Byron, according to his normal practice, rarely got up much before midday, while Shelley liked to rise soon after dawn, and explore the various sites of the romance between Julie and St Preux. He walked reverently along the 'terraced roads' and through the groves where they had wandered. He gathered a nosegay of wild flowers at St Gingoux, and at Clarens he was delighted when their land-lady pointed out the 'bosquet de Julie' from the window of their lodgings.

Another memorial of Rousseau was more dramatic. Their boat was caught in a squall off the rocks of St Gingoux and nearly swamped, as Shelley wrote afterwards with ill-disguised satisfaction, 'precisely in the spot where Julie and her lover were nearly overset, and where St Preux was tempted to plunge with her into the lake.' Twenty-five years later, Moore, in his *Life of Byron* described how Shelley imperiously refused his companion's offer to save him, as Shelley could not swim: 'Shelley positively refused; and seating himself quietly upon a locker, and grasping the rings at each end firmly in his hands, declared his de-termination to go down in that position, without a struggle.'[38]

But the incident had been coloured up. At the time, Shelley himself noted that when the rudder broke, and the waves began to fall into the boat, 'My com-panion, an excellent swimmer, took off his coat, I did the same, and we sat with our arms crossed, every instant expecting to be swamped.' Nothing seems to have been spoken between them until afterwards, though Shelley was painfully conscious that Byron knew he could not swim. 'I felt in this near prospect of death a mixture of sensations, among which terror entered though but subordin-ately. My feelings would have been less painful had I been alone; but I knew that my companion would have attempted to save me, and I was overcome with humiliation. . . .' Byron himself observed Shelley's coolness, and merely com-mented to Murray that since the boat was so near the rocks he himself ran 'no risk'. The most extraordinary thing is that after this incident, Shelley did not ask Byron to teach him to swim.

At Chillon, Shelley counted the columns in the dungeon, noted the depth of the lake, the dates of the graffiti on the walls, and gazed up in horror at the black and rotten hanging beam which has since been replaced by a stouter, but less suggestive timber. 'I never saw a monument more terrible of that cold and in-human tyranny, which it has been the delight of man to exercise over man,' he noted sententiously. Byron carved his name abstractedly on a column, while listening to the guide's tale of François Bonivard. Bonivard was imprisoned in the dungeons for rebelling against Duke Charles III of Savoy in the sixteenth century. Byron brooded on the story. Two days later, on 28 June, they were detained at Ouchy by rainy weather, and Byron scribbled off the fourteen stanzas of his 'Prisoner of Chillon', emphatically casting himself into Bonivard's predicament, and reaching the curiously bitter and ironic denouement:

> My very chains and I grew friends,
> So much a long communion tends
> To make us what we are: – even I
> Regained my freedom with a sigh.

In contrast Shelley found he could draw no direct inspiration from their surroundings, but continued to read *La Nouvelle Héloïse*, and began to sketch out the autobiographical opening of his 'Hymn to Intellectual Beauty', with its romantic memories of ghosts and terrors and self-dedications in early childhood.

Byron's presence continued to inhibit Shelley. He noted with curious regret how he had been unable to let himself cry openly when they walked in the beautiful vineyards above the bosquet de Julie at Clarens. It also affected his writing, and it is characteristic that while Byron scribbled verse, Shelley walked and read and wrote letters.* There was however one passage in the long diary-letter to Peacock, which achieved a strong autobiographical resonance, and rose nearly to the intensity of a prose poem. Besides this, the dates and statistics concerning the Chateau Chillon look stiff and unfeeling. Shelley had noticed the cruel deformation of the children on the Savoy side of the lake. This was a thyroid condition caused by an iodine deficiency in the water, not discovered until nearly a hundred years later. To Shelley, the sight of one child who was a striking exception to this grim malformation seemed to have a strong symbolic overtone. He described the scene with a new combination of perception and delicacy, in a dreamy, pre-occupied mood that suggests his own boyhood was much in his mind.

> On returning to the village, we sat on a wall beside the lake, looking at some children who were playing at a game like ninepins. The children here appeared in an extraordinary way deformed and diseased. Most of them were crooked, and with enlarged throats; but one little boy had such

---

* Shelley kept a small sketch book with him in which he pencilled rough drawings of the lake and drafts of his diary-letter to Peacock, (Bodleian MS Shelley Adds. e. 16.) On p. 37, perhaps after his return to Montalègre, he wrote cross-wise in ink:

> My thoughts arise and fade in solitude,
> The verse that would invest them melts away
> Like moonlight in the heaven of spreading day:
> How beautiful they were, how firm they stood,
> Flecking the starry sky like woven pearl!

exquisite grace in his mien and motions, as I never before saw equalled in a child. His countenance was beautiful for the expression with which it over-flowed. There was a mixture of pride and gentleness in his eyes and lips, the indications of sensibility, which his education will probably subvert to misery or seduce to crime; but there was more of gentleness than of pride, and it seemed that the pride was tamed from its original wildness by the habitual exericse of milder feelings. My companion gave him a piece of money, which he took without speaking, with a sweet smile of easy thankfulness, and then with an unembarrassed air turned to his play. All this might scarcely be; but the imagination surely could not forbear to breath into the most inanimate forms, some likeness of its own visions, on such a serene and glowing evening, in this remote and romantic village, beside the calm lake that bore us hither.

At Lausanne they walked on the terrace of Gibbon's house where he had finished the *Decline and Fall of the Roman Empire*. Byron was deeply moved, but Shelley again drew himself back from the experience. 'My companion gathered some acacia leaves to preserve in remembrance of him. I refrained from doing so, fearing to outrage the greater and more sacred name of Rousseau; the con-templation of whose imperishable creations had left no vacancy in my heart for mortal things. Gibbon had a cold and unimpassioned spirit.' Byron entered his tribute to Gibbon in his *Childe Harold* notebook, calling him the 'Lord of irony', 'sapping a solemn creed with solemn sneer', and dispatched the acacia leaves to Murray. Shelley walked back down to the pier, where the waves still lashed the anchored boat and stood gazing out across the lake. Suddenly the sun came out, for the only time that day. 'A rainbow spanned the lake, or rather rested one extremity of its arch upon the water, and the other at the foot of the mountains of Savoy. Some white houses, I know not if they were those of Meillerie, shone through the yellow fire.' Two days later, on the evening of Sunday, 30 June, Mary and Claire spotted the little sail curving across the lake towards the har-bour at Montalègre.

This boat trip created an understanding between Shelley and Byron, which from now on continued to work at a level above the ordinary domestic re-lationships established through Mary and Claire. Yet there was still no complete intimacy between them, and both continued to observe the other as a somewhat curious specimen. They said one thing to each other's faces and another behind each other's backs. Byron wrote that Shelley had dosed him with Wordsworth, 'even to nausea', while Shelley wrote to Peacock after their return that 'Lord Byron is an exceedingly interesting person, and as such it is to be regretted that he is a slave to the vilest and most vulgar prejudices, and as mad as the winds'. Whether, when referring to Byron's prejudices, he had Gibbon or Claire in mind, is not completely clear. But the way for intimacy was opened, and this was to occur immediately on the next occasion that they were alone together: at Venice in 1818.

After Shelley and Byron's return, the routine of boating and visiting settled down again between Montalègre and the Villa Diodati. Shelley completed his 'Hymn to Intellectual Beauty', Byron his Third Canto, and Claire was gratified to be given the task of fair copying the 'Prisoner of Chillon'. To Peacock, Shelley wrote to say that they planned to remain probably until next spring. In the meantime would Peacock sell the furniture and goods at Bishopsgate, relinquish the possession and inquire after 'an unfurnished house, with as good a garden as may be, near Windsor Forest', to be taken on a long lease of fourteen or preferably twenty-one years. 'My present intention is to return to England and make that most excellent of nations my perpetual resting place.' Peacock was probably receiving a small stipend from Shelley by this time, which is indicated by his unhesitating use of Peacock as an amanuensis. Shelley had now clearly rejected any ideas of permanent exile, and indeed his letter is full of nostalgic references which fall strangely from his pen: 'good wood fires, or window frames intertwined with creeping plants; . . . purring of kittens, the hissing of kettles; the long talks over the past and dead, laugh of children, . . . and the pelting storm of winter struggling in vain for entrance'.[39] Shelley also asked for news of the political state in England.

Meanwhile he was vaguely planning another of his epic river voyages which never materialized, this time descending the Danube as far as Constantinople, and then back through Athens and Rome, '. . . Always following great rivers. The Danube, the Po, the Rhone, and the Garonne; rivers are not like roads, the work of the hands of man; they imitate mind, which wanders at will over pathless deserts, and flows through nature's loveliest recesses, which are inaccessible to anything besides.' When he had read through this letter, Peacock shrewdly decided to postpone purchase of 'a fixed, settled, eternal home' until Shelley had definitely set foot in England again.

On 17 and 18 July, Shelley also wrote to Godwin and Hogg. To the former, he hinted that he would not remain at Geneva for much longer, so that complicated postal negotiations were impossible. Hogg was now told definitely that the plan for him to join their community again would have to be postponed. Shelley suggested rather wildly that he should address his letters in future to *poste restante* at Avignon. Shelley was perhaps thinking of the river Rhône; but in fact he never visited Avignon in his life. He wrote briefly, somewhat airily, of Byron, and of Madame de Staël and the literary people whom he had 'no great curiosity to see'.

On Sunday, 21 July, three weeks after he had returned from his lake tour,

Shelley suddenly set off again with Mary and Claire to visit the valley at Chamonix, a popular and picturesque resort among the Alps, dramatically situated at the head of the river Arve. Little William was left behind at Montalègre to be cared for by a Swiss maidservant Shelley had hired, Elise. Mary took with her instead the manuscript of *Frankenstein*.

Mary's journal, after an interval of over a year, now recommences, and is full of descriptive passages. Many of these served as drafts for settings of the confrontation scene between Dr Frankenstein and the monster in the Mer de Glace. She wrote now with a new power and irony. On the long road up the valley of the Arve between Bonneville and Chamonix, she observed: 'This cataract fell in to the Arve, which dashed against its banks like a wild animal who is furious in constraint. As we continued our route to Cerveaux, the mountains increased in height and beauty; the summits of the highest were hid in clouds, but they sometimes peeped out into the blue sky, higher one would think than the safety of God would permit, since it is well known that the Tower of Babel did not nearly equal them in immensity.' Another rock, over which a waterfall divided, seemed to her like the visionary image of 'a colossal Egyptian statue of a female deity'.[40] Shelley bought a squirrel for the girls, which bit him while trying to escape.

They arrived at Chamonix, exhausted, at 7 on Monday evening, and were startled by the unearthly thunder of an avalanche from the further mountain. Shelley was not too tired to note a proclamation of the King of Sardinia's 'prohibiting his subjects from holding private assemblies, on pain of a fine of 12 Francs, and, in default of payment, imprisonment'.[41] Shelley wrote briefly to Byron from their Hotel de Ville de Londres, suggesting he hire mules and join them. Then he began the second of his long descriptive diary-letters to Peacock, filled with the immensity and grandeur of the icy peaks. During the following days they visited the glaciers at Boisson and at Montavert. The impact which the sheer mass and cruel simplicity of the Alps at close quarters had on Shelley was profound. It entered immediately into the store of his fundamental imagery, like the rivers, and the sea, and the sky. On the first day in Chamonix he wrote to Peacock. 'Pinnacles of snow, intolerably bright, part of the chain connected with Mont Blanc shone through the clouds at intervals on high. I never knew I never imagined what mountains were before. The immensity of these ariel summits excited, when they suddenly burst upon the sight, a sentiment of extatic wonder, not unallied to madness.'[42] Already, crossing the bridge over the river Arve, he had begun to work over the outline of a philosophic meditation on the Alpine experience. His overall impression was one of overwhelming power, gigantic but infinitely remote force. It frightened and fascinated him. He was filled with awe and the sense of his own limited, human intelligence brought face to face with enormous natural energies and processes beyond anything he had previously imagined. The meditation became a poem called simply, 'Mont Blanc'.

The experience which Shelley underwent at Chamonix, something close to a religious experience, was in fact a recognized feature of such visits to the Alps. Unearthly revelations were soon to become a regular part of the Englishman's tour. Writing in 1825 William Hazlitt noted wrily: 'The Crossing of the Alps has, I believe, given some of our fashionables a shivering-fit of morality; as the sight of Mont Blanc convinced our author [in this case Tom Moore] of the Being of God – they are seized with an amiable horror and remorse for the vices of others (of course so much worse than their own) so that several of our *bluestockings* have got the *blue-devils*. . . .' The only difference was that Shelley was in contrast convinced by this experience of the *non-existence* of God.*

Indeed, the emotions he experienced depended entirely on his intellectual position as an atheist. What he saw seemed to him both a symbol, and an actual example, of the sublime but utterly impersonal Power which functioned through nature. Describing the slow but irresistible advance of the glacier towards Chamonix, and the 'inexpressibly dreadful' aspect presented by the shattered pines which were overwhelmed one by one by its relentless progress, a few feet each year, he wrote to Peacock that he tended to believe Buffon's theory of Nature's inevitable self-destruction, of its inherent entropy. He saw this as yet another example of a tyranny, of power functioning inhumanely to crush and destroy, and likened it to the esoteric Indian dualism which Peacock had used in his earlier poetry. This was the eternal struggle between Oromazes, the spirit of life and warmth, and Ahrimanes, the spirit of darkness, cold and death.

After a superb description of the terror of the glacier's advance, he concluded: 'I will not pursue Buffon's sublime but gloomy theory, that this earth which we inhabit will at some future period be changed into a mass of frost. Do you who assert the supremacy of Ahriman imagine him throned among these desolating snows, among these palaces of death and frost, sculptured in this their terrible magnificence by the unsparing hand of necessity, & that he casts around him as the first essays of his final usurpation avalanches, torrents, rocks & thunders – and above all, these deadly glaciers at once the proofs and symbols of his reign. – Add to this the degradation of the human species, who in these regions are half deformed or idiotic & all of whom are deprived of anything that can excite interest & admiration. This is a part of the subject more mournful & less sublime; – but such as neither the poet not the philosopher should disdain.'[43]

These reflections formed the basis of Shelley's descriptive and meditative poem

---

* Here, too, Coleridge had been before him, and had come back with his 'Hymn before Sunrise in the Vale of Chamouni'. But for Coleridge the almighty God was safely in residence 'On thy bald aweful head, O sovran Blanc!'

'Mont Blanc'. The river Arve, the glaciers and the mountain are loosely organized into a system of images to represent three levels of the human consciousness as it speculates on, respectively, human imagination, material phenomena and on a hypothetical divinity. The poem is Wordsworthian in its verse phrasing, and its apparent subject matter; yet the tone has a grimness, and a sense of disruptive uncontrollable forces, which is peculiar to Shelley alone. Characteristically, the philosophic conclusions which he tries to draw from his imagery are continuously left suspended in dread or doubt. Both at the beginning and the end of the poem, it is this sense of baffled, fearful and yet heroic confrontation between sensitive mind and brutal matter which is dominant.

> For the very spirit fails,
> Driven like a homeless cloud from steep to steep
> That vanishes among the viewless gales!
> Far, far above, piercing the infinite sky,
> Mont Blanc appears, – still, snowy, and serene –
> Its subject mountains their unearthly forms
> Pile around it, ice and rock. . . .[44]

Despite its essentially philosophic and sceptic pitch, the poem is not without its monsters and ghosts. Shelley refers to the 'old Earthquake-daemon'; the glaciers are at one point described as serpents creeping on their prey; and the snowy peaks as 'A city of death, distinct with many a tower'. In his letter to Peacock, which he subsequently adapted for Mary's book *A History of a Six Weeks Tour*, Shelley expressed this feeling of the monstrous – closely connected with Mary's *Frankenstein* – in a memorable image. 'One would think that Mont Blanc, like the god of the Stoics, was a vast animal, and the frozen blood forever circulated through his stony veins.' Yet the poem ends finally, with its focus neither on the mountain, nor the monster, nor God, but on the poised, unflinching attention of the human mind itself which embraces all, and is in this sense the ultimate power:

> And what were thou, and earth, and stars, and sea,
> If to the human mind's imaginings
> Silence and solitude were vacancy?[45]

As far as he could press the question in this poem, Mont Blanc proved for Shelley that the natural world held no other intelligent divinity except the mind of man. The effect of this prolonged and intense meditation was to induce in Shelley a feeling of irritable and mocking superiority towards his fellow tourists, and the locals of Chamonix. The Swiss guide, Ducrée, who took him over the glacier of Boisson, he called 'the only tolerable person I have seen in this country'.

To Peacock he wrote acidly: 'There is a Cabinet d'Histoire Naturelle at Chamouni, just as at Matlock & Keswick & Clifton; the proprietor of which is the very vilest specimen, of that vile species of quack that together with the whole army of aubergistes & guides & indeed the entire mass of the population subsist on the weakness & credulity of travellers as leeches subsist on the blood of the sick.' When in September, Byron came to Chamonix, he was more infuriated by the general philistinism of his compatriots, and raged about an English woman who exclaimed how *rural* the mountains looked – 'as if it was Highgate, or Hampstead, or Brompton, or Hayes'.[46]

But Shelley was not content with registering merely private indignation. In the hotel register at Chamonix, and in another at Montavert, and possibly in a third on the return journey down the Arve valley, he made a celebrated entry in Greek. Under the 'Occupation' column, he inscribed the deliberately provocative tag: 'Δημοκρατικος, Φιλάνθρωποτατος, κάι 'αθεος' – Democrat, Philanthropist and Atheist. Under the destination column, for him and the two girls, he wrote succinctly 'L'Enfer'.[47] Only by considering the reputation Chamonix had among the travelling English at this time, as a natural temple of the Lord and a proof of the Deity by design, is it possible to realize the spirit in which Shelley wrote these entries, and the astounding fury with which they were greeted. Fifty years later, Swinburne noted that the entry in the register previous to Shelley's was 'fervid with ghostly grease and rancid religion'.[48] Yet when Byron himself came across one of Shelley's three entries with Hobhouse in September, he immediately felt obliged to cross it out as indelibly as possible for Shelley's own protection. Byron missed the other registers, and the scandalous annotation was soon a regular notoriety. Thomas Raffles noted it in his *Letters During a Tour* of 1818, together with a retort: 'If an atheist, a fool – if not, a liar.' Southey, among others, seized upon it and spread the story, and it played a prominent part in the major newspaper attacks on Shelley in the *Quarterly* of January 1818, and the *London Chronicle* of June 1819. It was the word 'αθεος which caused the original offence; but in such a context, the word Δημοκρατικος was mentally read as 'revolutionary', and the word Φιλάνθρωπος as 'pervert'.

On Thursday the 25th, they returned from Montavert, picnicking in an Alpine meadow, among wild rhododendron and mountain roses. Friday was wet, and Shelley spent much time cross-questioning the guide about his work, his pay, Swiss politics and conscription laws. He noted with interest that Ducrée married a girl of 16 when he himself was only 18. Mary and Shelley collected Alpine seeds to plant in the garden of their proposed home at Windsor. The following day they returned down the valley for Lake Leman. 'Did I tell you that there are troops of wolves among these mountains?' Shelley closed his letter to Peacock. 'In the winter they descend into the valleys which the snow occupies during six months of the year, & devour everything they find outside of the doors. A wolf is more powerful than the fiercest & strongest dog.'[49]

On Shelley's return to Montalègre, at the beginning of August, it was soon clear that the summer with Byron was coming to an end. From London the tentacles of his financial affairs were at last closing around him again, and a letter from his solicitor Longdill received on the 2nd convinced him that he would have to return. A cheque for twenty-five pounds was sent off to Peacock to help tidy up bills at Bishopsgate, for the sale of the furniture had realized little. Charles Clairmont had also written from Bordeaux begging Shelley to support his studies, and Shelley contributed ten pounds. But the deciding factor was Claire.

Claire was now three or four months pregnant, and it was obvious that the moment had come to settle the arrangements about the child with Byron. Perhaps he would agree to set up a regular *ménage* with her? She hoped so, desperately; but Shelley was doubtful, already knowing Byron far better than she did. He had never loved her; and now even physical love had become irritating, and Claire's very presence at the Diodati seemed intolerable. With a good deal of sense, and much kindness, Shelley undertook to negotiate with Byron on Claire's behalf. Mary was kept out of the discussions and she noted in her journal for 2 August: 'In the evening Lord Byron and [Shelley] go out in the boat, and after their return, Shelley and Claire go up to Diodati; I do not, for Lord Byron did not seem to wish it.'[50] Shelley finally managed to arrange an unhappy, but not altogether unsatisfactory compromise. Byron would recognize the child when it was born, and would bring it up himself in Europe; but meanwhile Claire would treat the pregnancy discreetly, and go to England for the birth. Byron refused to have Claire in his household, but he agreed to allow her to visit the child regularly under the designation of an aunt, once it had been settled under the paternal roof. Exact dates and places remained vague, but there was talk of summer 1817 in Italy.

What gave force to this agreement was Shelley's determined and courageous offer to look after Claire during the period of her pregnancy and childbirth, and support her as one of his own household. This was an offer which he put forward, fully realizing from his past experience the difficulties with Mary, the Godwins and other outsiders he would encounter. He must also have considered the inevitable rumours of 'incest' which would attach to himself. He did not blanch at these in the least, and for once acted both from principle and from experience. It was an act of great personal generosity, and imagination, far more distinctive than many of his philanthropic declarations and wild disbursements of his father's money. It was also a frank recognition of personal responsibility for Claire. Claire never forgot this. One of the first fruits was that Shelley had now no choice but to leave Switzerland.

Mary says nothing in her journal of her reaction to these events. On 4 August she gave Shelley a telescope which she had bought in Geneva for his 24th birthday, and they celebrated by going out in the boat to launch a fire balloon from the lake. But there was too much wind, and they had to try from the shore. From the lawn in front of Montalègre, the silken balloon inflated, rose unsteadily, caught the wind and burst instantly into flame and was consumed.

The little community was inexorably breaking up. But the arrival of M.G. Lewis on the 18th, with a colourful train of Jamaican servants, whom he treated with genial kindness, temporarily lifted the Byronic gloom at the Diodati, and they all went up in the evening to discuss ghosts again. Shelley, who was now constantly discussing with Mary the plotting of *Frankenstein*, carefully questioned Lewis about 'the mysteries of his trade'. In the journal he entered a long note on four stories, 'all grim', which Lewis told, and Mary years later wrote one of these for her article 'On Ghosts' for the *London Magazine* of March 1824. Shelley was curious to find that personally speaking, Lewis was a sceptic with regard to ghosts, and that Byron sided with him in the argument. 'We talk of Ghosts; neither Lord Byron nor Monk G. Lewis seem to believe in them; and they both agree, in the very face of reason, that none could believe in ghosts without also believing in God. I do not think that all the persons who profess to discredit these visitations really discredit them, or if they do, in daylight, are not admonished by the approach of loneliness and midnight to think more respectably of the world of shadows.' Shelley took Byron and Lewis out in the boat, during the next few days, and among the subjects discussed was Goethe's *Faust*. Shelley continued to escort Claire to the Diodati where she was being allowed to fair copy *Childe Harold*. But Byron still refused absolutely to see her alone. Yet he frequently came down from the Diodati, to talk with Shelley at Montalègre, partly to escape Polidori who was constantly getting drunk or involving himself in affrays in Geneva; and partly because he regretted Shelley's departure. One Saturday evening, they sat on the wall overlooking the little harbour, talking quietly till the light faded and they parted for dinner. More and more rumours were now circulating back to them from Geneva, and five years later, writing to an Italian friend of Byron's, Shelley recalled:

> The natives of Geneva and the English people who were living there did not hesitate to affirm that we were leading the life of the most unbridled libertinism. They said that we had found a pact to outrage all that is regarded as most sacred in human society. Allow me, Madam, to spare you the details. I will only tell you that atheism, incest, and many other things – sometimes ridiculous and sometimes terrible – were imputed to us. The English papers

did not delay to spread the scandal, and the people believed it. . . . The inhabitants on the banks of the lake opposite Lord Byron's house used telescopes to spy on his movements. One English lady fainted with horror (or pretended to!) on seeing him enter a drawing room. . . . You cannot, Madam, conceive the excessive violence with which a certain class of the English detest those whose conduct and opinions are not precisely modelled on their own. The systems of those ideas forms a superstition, which constantly demands and constantly finds fresh victims. Strong as theological hatred may be, it always yields to social hatred.[51]

Shelley did not, however, choose to recall the hotel registers.

The arrival of Byron's old friends from London on 26 August, John Cam Hobhouse and Scrope Daves, effectively marked the changing of the guard. Shelley now felt he was *de trop*, and packing and coaching arrangements began. Byron and Polidori came down for farewells, and the two poets took a last sail on the lake in their boat which was thenceforward handed over to the Diodati. A copy of Coleridge's 'Christabel' had arrived from London, and Shelley gave it a quiet memorial reading to Mary before going to bed. By the 28th they were packed up, and left on the 9 o'clock coach from Geneva the following morning. The fair copy of *Childe Harold* was locked in Shelley's portmanteau for personal delivery to Murray's at Albemarle Street. The Swiss nursemaid, Elise, came with them to look after little William. They glanced back regretfully at the shining lake, as they rose into the Jura, and gazed thoughtfully at the rocks, and the pines and meadows that had been under snow at the time of their arrival long ago in the spring.

The departure was hardest for Claire. There is a brief undated note of hers to Byron, probably written in the last few days of August. It tells everything about that brief liaison. 'I would have come to you tonight if I thought I could be *any use* to you. If you *want* me or anything of, or belonging to me I am sure Shelley would come and fetch me if you ask him. I am afraid to come dearest for fear of meeting anyone. Can you pretext the copying? Tell me anytime I shall come & I will because you will have then made your arrangements. Every thing is so awkward. We go soon. Dearest pray come and see us pray do.'[52] But Byron had not come.

Yet as the coach rolled slowly through Dijon and Fontainebleau towards Le Havre, Shelley was already looking and planning ahead. The friendship with Byron, though it had brought him responsibilities and had banked up much of his creative impulse, had also given him a matured and confident sense of new purpose. He felt alive again to the wider pattern of events in England, and at the back of his mind a long-buried theme for his writing was beginning to stir. One of the last books he had read at Montalègre was the *Histoire de la Révolution*, by Rabault.[53] Dispatching a brief letter to Byron, he expressed the idea obliquely, as something for Byron rather than for himself. 'We passed, not through Paris, but by a shorter route through Versailles, and Fontainebleau, and stayed to visit those famous Palaces, which, as I will hereafter tell you, are well worth visiting as monuments of human power; grand, yet somewhat faded; the latter is the scene of some of the most interesting events of what may be called the master theme of the epoch in which we live – the French Revolution.'[54]

At Le Havre, they embarked for Portsmouth, as Shelley knew that arrival in London with Claire would only complicate matters unnecessarily. They docked on 8 September, and Shelley watched anxiously while the customs officer leafed through the MS of *Childe Harold*, apparently looking for lace concealed between the pages. He drove into Somerset, and quickly established Mary and Claire in a house at No. 5 Abbey Churchyard, a discreet corner of Bath, and within three days was himself in his old London lodgings at 26 Marchmont Street. He had much business. There was Murray to deal with; and Peacock's negotiations for a house at Windsor; and the old, endless wrangle with Godwin over money he could not supply, and loans he could not convincingly underwrite. While he stayed in London between the 10th and 14th, Fanny Godwin came to visit him in the evenings, partly as Godwin's messenger, and partly on her own account. Then he went to Peacock's at Marlow, and Mary joined him, but no house was immediately available, so they determined to winter in Bath.*

From there, at the end of the month, Shelley wrote to Byron, apprising him of their plans, the 2,000 guineas Murray had agreed on for 'the Childe', and their hopes for all meeting again in the spring. The picture was cosy and domestic: 'We are all now at Bath, well and content. Claire is writing to you at this instant. Mary is reading over the fire; our cat and kitten are sleeping under the sofa; and little Willy is just gone to sleep. We are looking out for a house in some lone place; and one chief pleasure which we shall expect then, will be a visit from you.'[55] But as autumn darkened into winter, the little household was shaken and transformed by a series of disastrous blows, and they were drawn back, one more time, into the whirlpool of London. The summer was long over.

* On 24 September 1816, Shelley delivered his will to the solicitor Longdill. It gives an interesting indication of his sense of attachments and responsibilities at this time. The residue of his estate was left directly to Mary Godwin. Harriet Shelley was to receive a sum of £6,000, and her children Ianthe and Charles £5,000 each. Claire Clairmont was to receive a sum of £6,000, together with an invested annuity of a further £6,000 which Shelley perhaps intended to make the care and upbringing of the forthcoming child independent of Byron if Claire so chose. Peacock was to receive £500, and an invested annuity of £2,000. Hogg and Lord Byron were each left gifts of £2,000. Byron and Peacock were appointed the trustees. The comparative provisions made for Claire and for Harriet are especially suggestive of Shelley's feelings; as is also the complete absence of William Godwin's name from the document.

14
The Suicides: London 1816

On the 9 October 1816, an extremely depressed note from Fanny Godwin arrived at Abbey Churchyard. To their surprise the Shelleys saw it carried a Bristol postmark. Both Claire and Mary were familiar with Fanny's profound depressions, and Shelley was immediately dispatched to Bristol to seek out the girl. He returned at 2 a.m. without news. That night, in a small upper room in the Mackworth Arms, Swansea, Fanny committed suicide by overdosing herself with opium. Her pathetic suicide note explained nothing, and the Godwins were left to conclude that she had killed herself because of unrequited love for Shelley. There were in fact several other possible motives, including the recent discovery of her own illegitimacy, but her agonizing and loveless suspension between the Godwin and Shelley households was clearly the root circumstance. Godwin himself reacted by imposing a complete silence on the matter both at Skinner Street and on the Shelleys at Bath. Someone tore off the name from the suicide note, and Fanny's identity never reached the local papers. Godwin forbade the Shelleys to go to Swansea or claim the body, and he himself was so discreet as to turn back his own journey at Bristol. No one went to see Fanny buried, and relatives were at first told that she had gone to Ireland; and later that she had died from a severe cold. Charles, her half-brother, was still not informed of her death by the following summer.

Neither Shelley's nor Mary's correspondence contain the least overt reference to Fanny's death at this time, which demonstrates among other things how secretive they could be about personal matters if they so chose. Claire wrote to Byron that Shelley's health was upset by Fanny's death (she did not herself mention suicide), and it has normally been assumed that Shelley was distraught. But there is no other evidence for this in Mary's journal, or elsewhere. Shelley continued to read *Don Quixote* out loud, and began to keep records of the amount he ate, in grams. Mary took drawing lessons, and began to study chemistry with Shelley, reading Sir Humphry Davy's *Elements of Chemical Philosophy*. Claire was moved to a nearby address at 12 New Bond Street, for her approaching confinement, probably with Elise in attendance. It seems that only months later, when Shelley looked back at the grim pattern of that autumn and winter, did he accept the full implications of Fanny's death. Several poems he wrote in the following year seem to grope towards realization and acceptance. There is the famous, 'Her voice did quiver as we parted', but also the following lyric in which he himself is pictured and placed:

> They die – the dead return not – Misery
>   Sits near an open grave and calls them over,
> A Youth with hoary hair and haggard eye –
>   They are the names of kindred, friend and lover,
> Which he so feebly calls – they all are gone –
> Fond wretch, all dead! those vacant names alone,
>   This most familiar scene, my pain –
>   These tombs – alone remain.[1]

But of course, in reality, Shelley did not sit over Fanny's poor anonymous grave.

The rest of October and November passed in an ominous calm. The retired domesticity of Shelley's life at Bath was almost unbroken. He moved between Mary at Abbey Churchyard and Claire at New Bond Street, writing letters from both addresses. Claire was now expecting her child within six or eight weeks and his presence was her main comfort. They all walked up to the Royal Crescent to view the solar eclipse, but it was cloudy, and Mary amused herself watching the many disconsolate people with burnt glass.[2] Shelley put forward a few tentative literary feelers, writing to a Monsieur Pascoud in Geneva concerning a French translation of *Political Justice* he had undertaken, and sending a fair copy of his 'Hymn to Intellectual Beauty' to Hunt at the *Examiner*'s offices in London. For the time being there was no response from either quarter. He noted that Murray was rapidly preparing to bring out *Childe Harold*, though he himself had been ousted from the job of proof-reading by the critic Gifford. This minor professional snub, which Shelley passed off as best he could, was caused by Byron pretending to take him further into his confidence about the poem at the Diodati than he actually had. Shelley diverted his spleen by attacking the *Edinburgh Review*'s criticism of Coleridge's 'Christabel'. There was some genuine comfort for the author of *Alastor* in the fact that this volume, which also contained 'Kubla Khan', was so superciliously dismissed by a liberal review: ' . . . there is literally not one couplet in the volume before us which would be reckoned poetry, or even sense, were it found in the corner of a newspaper, or upon the window of an inn.'[3] Lord Byron and he could sympathize equally in the callous treatment of Coleridge.

At Bath, Shelley had time to take in and read much of the liberal press, including the *Examiner* and Cobbett's *Register*. More and more, he was drawn back into the reform movement. The revival of the political impulse, which had begun at the end of the summer in Switzerland, showed in the increasing space it took up in his letters. Throughout England generally there was a powerful renaissance of the reform movement in the autumn of 1816. Men like Cobbett, Henry Hunt the orator, Francis Burdett the MP for Westminster and Francis Place the radical, re-emerged as public leaders who were prepared to encourage at the grass roots a new pattern of mass meetings and local associations. New figures also arose, who had not been soured by the experiences of the nineties, and believed passionately in the processes of self-education and democratic reform. These were men like Samuel Bamford the radical weaver from Manchester, and Richard Carlile the London publisher. They were not revolutionaries in the conspiratorial or Jacobin sense, though they held the monarchy and Liverpool's administration in contempt. They did not believe in the Tory nightmares of mass violence of Parisian-style revolution, but they were doggedly prepared to go to jail in the name of democratic rights that had not yet become English laws. They also believed in the power of class solidarity in a new way. Shelley clearly saw a major confrontation on the horizon, and described his attitude, in terms of deliberate moderation, in his letters to Byron.

Of course you have received intimations of the tumultuous state of England. The whole fabric of society presents a most threatening aspect. What is most ominous of an approaching change is the strength which the popular party have suddenly acquired, and the importance which the violence of demagogues has assumed. But the people appear calm, and steady even under situations of great excitement; and reform may come without revolution. Parliament will meet on 28th January; until which – for the populace have committed no violence – they only meet, resolve and petition – all classes will probably remain in a sullen and moody expectation of what the session will produce. The taxes, it is said, cannot be collected – if so, the national debt cannot be payed – and are not the landed proprietors virtually pledged to the payment? I earnestly hope that, without such an utter overthrow as should leave us the prey of anarchy, and give us illiterate demagogues for masters, a most radical reform of the institutions of England may result from the approaching context.[4]

Shelley's *caveats* are almost as interesting as his hopes. His distrust of democratic leadership – automatically 'demagogic' – was still typical of the Whig-liberal pattern which he himself had rejected; and his attitude to the arm-lever which the tax-payers could assert over the landowners was still markedly ambiguous. Such political attitudes remained in a state of flux, and only matured slowly and painfully. But his feeling that reform must be 'most radical' never changed; nor his fear that a revolution, though he himself might support it in principle, could easily overreach itself and run through the grim dialectical pattern exemplified by the Paris Revolution: anarchy followed by military dictatorship. But even this fear itself matured, for finally Shelley was to recognize that under certain degrees of social extremity the risk of anarchy, and even civil war, not only could be but must be embraced, in order to prevent the moral and political suppression of an entire stratum of the population.

Some light is thrown on Shelley's more private feelings in this matter, in the remarkable friendship with Leigh Hunt which sprang up at the end of November and the beginning of December. The opening was not altogether auspicious. A letter from Hunt arrived at Bath on 1 December, which apparently stated that Hunt had mislaid the manuscript of the 'Hymn to Intellectual Beauty', though he wished to publish it in the *Examiner*. At the same time Hunt asked Shelley for help in a financial matter. From Shelley's cheques,[5] it would appear that Hunt had asked for a loan, rather than an outright gift, probably in aid of a reform cause or prison fund that he was organizing, and Shelley immediately sent fifty pounds, explaining that it came from 'a friend' who required no interest. Hunt then wrote back, feeling slightly awkward at Shelley's 'precipitancy' and insisting that at least he would pay interest in a proper businesslike fashion.[6] His letter contained five pounds. As Hunt had just given Shelley a favourable notice in the famous Young Poets issue of the *Examiner* on 1 December, which also mentioned Keats and John Reynolds, he found the situation was potentially embarrassing. But Shelley was in no way abashed. He wrote back on the 8th that he had actually missed the current number of the *Examiner* by 'some fatality', and that though his friend 'accepts the *interest* & is contented to be a Hebrew',[7] he was himself returning a gift of five pounds. This happened conveniently to match Hunt's ten per cent 'interest' on the loan. Shelley's two cheques were cashed on the 9th and the 19th, the fifty pounds last, suggesting that it had indeed been transferred to some other account or fund. But how far Shelley was making a personal payment to Hunt remains a mystery, for Hunt had also mentioned personal 'distress'.

The exciting breakthrough of a favourable review in the *Examiner*, and the kindly interest of an important editor, led Shelley to unburden himself in the long personal letter of the 8th. Compared with the elegant formality of his letters to Byron, and the icy business tone of his exchanges with Godwin, the correspondence with Hunt was from the start passionately confidential. The letter was written from Peacock's house at Marlow, where Shelley had gone to choose a new house, leaving Mary and Claire at Bath.

Shelley wrote:

I am undeceived in the belief that I have powers deeply to interest, or substantially to improve, mankind. How far my conduct and my opinions have rendered the zeal & ardour with which I have engaged in the attempt ineffectual, I know not. ... But thus much I do not seek to conceal from myself, that I am an outcast from human society; my name is execrated by all who understand its entire import, – by those very beings whose happiness I ardently desire. – I am an object of compassion to a few more benevolent than the rest, all else abhor and avoid me. With you, & perhaps some others (tho in a less degree, I fear) my gentleness & sincerity finds favour, because they are themselves gentle & sincere; they believe in self-devotion and generosity because they are themselves generous & self-devoted. Perhaps I should have shrunk from persisting in the task which I had undertaken in early life, of opposing myself, in these evil times and among these evil tongues, to what I esteem misery & vice; if [so] I must have lived in the solitude of the heart.[8]

This personal confession is no less remarkable for the fact that it was sent to a man that Shelley had only once seen, more than five years before. It is to be classed with Shelley's introductory letter to Godwin, written from Keswick in 1812. Shelley still identified himself primarily as a reformer. although the persecution of the world in general had replaced the persecution of his father in particular. Like his letter to Godwin, it was a leap in the dark towards a man he admired intellectually. Like Godwin, though to a lesser extent, Hunt was to accept the role of mentor and father figure. In return, though with infinitely more grace than Godwin, he received financial aid.

While Shelley stayed house-hunting in Marlow, Mary wrote with a mixture of sourness and sentimentality she frequently employed when unsure of herself: 'Ah – were you indeed a winged Elf and could soar over mountains & seas and could pounce on the little spot – A house with a lawn a river or lake – noble trees and divine mountains that should be our little mousehole to retire to. But never mind this – give me a garden & *absentia Clariae* and I will thank my love for many favours.'[9]

For two days, between the 11th and 14th, Shelley left Marlow and travelled to the Vale of Health in Hampstead, where he was eagerly welcomed by Hunt, his wife Marianne, the children and also at least two members of the Hunt circle, Horace Smith and John Keats. Hunt, though he was an editor, essayist and poet of some distinction, had one overwhelming art: the art of hospitality. Shelley travelled back to Bath on the 15th in the highest spirits, his entrance into

London literary and liberal circles suddenly and delightfully assured. Hunt more-over promised to review *Alastor* and publish the 'Hymn'. The latter appeared in the *Examiner* for 19 January 1817.

But even as Shelley returned with his good news to Mary and Claire at Bath, the second blow fell. His old publisher Thomas Hookham wrote from London in reply to a casual inquiry which Shelley had made about Harriet and the children in a letter of mid-November. Shelley had not bothered to follow up this letter, busy as he was with Mary and Claire and Hunt. Now Hookham's answer finally arrived. In September Harriet had left the children with their grandparents at Chapel Street and taken lodgings in Chelsea near the barracks, under the name of Harriet Smith. A month later, on 9 November, she had disappeared; her body had been discovered in the lower reach of the Serpentine on 10 December. On receiving this news, Shelley went instantly to London: the jury had returned a kindly verdict of 'found drowned', but the Times had stated bluntly that the 'respectable lady with an expensive ring on her finger' was 'far advanced in pregnancy' and had committed suicide. Her landlady at Elizabeth Street also testified to Harriet's solitary state, her depression and her appearance of being in the family way.

The death of Harriet presented Shelley with one of the most severe emotional crises of his life. The circumstances were so appalling, and Harriet was still officially his wife, with all that that implied in terms of social and moral responsi-bility. A confrontation with the Westbrooks was immediately necessary in order to obtain custody of the children, but it was soon clear that this would be fiercely contested. Further, there was the sudden alteration of his position with regards to Mary, who knew that if she was to marry Shelley the critical moment had now arrived. Enormous pressures were put on him from every side. In the event Shelley reacted, as he always did in emergency, with energy and determina-tion. His first move, on the 15th, was to call upon the aid and friendship of Hunt, who knew nothing of Harriet or the Westbrooks. Hunt responded magnificently and stood by Shelley during the last fortnight of the year with unfailing sympathy and kindness. Shelley stayed with the Hunts at the Vale of Health for much of the time, and later when Mary came to London she also stayed with them. Shelley's second cheque to Hunt, for fifty pounds, is dated 18 December.

Shelley consulted with his solicitors immediately, and was told that legalizing his union with Mary would make the custody of the children automatic. Otherwise Longdill saw severe complications and the need to proceed with 'utmost caution and resolution'. Shelley did not realize at the time that his marriage to Mary would make little difference if the Westbrooks decided to contest. After talking the implications over with Hunt, Shelley wrote decisively to Mary on the 16th. 'I told [Longdill] that I was under contract of marriage to you; & he said that in such an event all pretences to detain the children would cease. Hunt said very delicately that this would be soothing intelligence for you.'[10] Mrs Godwin, in a letter years later, endorsed by Claire, wrote to her friend Lady Mountcashell that Mary forced Shelley into the marriage by threatening suicide: a kind of reversal of the situation in July 1814. It seems exceedingly unlikely that Mary would resort to such a melodramatic gesture, and Mrs Godwin's evidence was notoriously unreliable about Mary whom she hated. Yet there is a certain psychological truth in the accusation, and to Claire, Shelley was to write at the time in very different and mocking tones about the marriage. Claire herself regarded the marriage as unnecessary. It is characteristic of Shelley that he showed quite different aspects of himself and his feelings during this crisis to his various friends.

No difference is more marked than over the vexed question of blame and responsibility for Harriet's death. In a letter to Mary, he repudiated all feelings of guilt, and turned them on to the Westbrooks with a blind fury reminiscent of some of his letters of 1811. Considerable dispute has arisen of the authenticity of the manuscript, and Lady Shelley, who could never accept this facet of Shelley's personality, became involved with printing a forgery.* Shelley wrote to Mary: 'It seems that this poor woman [Harriet] – the most innocent of her abhorred & unnatural family – was driven from her father's house, & descended the steps of prostitution until she lived with a groom of the name of Smith, who deserting her, she killed herself. – There can be no question that the beastly viper her sister [Eliza], unable to gain profit from her connection with me – has secured to herself the fortune of the old man – who is now dying – by the murder of this poor creature. Everything tends to prove, however, that beyond the mere shock of so hideous a catastrophe having fallen on a human being once so nearly connected with me, there would, in any case, have been little to regret. Hookham, Longdill, – every one does *me* full justice; – bears testimony to the uprightness & liberality of my conduct to her: – There is but one voice in condemnation of the detestable Westbrooks.'[11] That Shelley should write like this was perfectly in character. The only doubtful thing is whether he really had any idea of the care and affection the detestable Westbrooks had lavished on the children when Harriet could not longer cope; or of the loyal efforts that Eliza

---

* At the present time two manuscripts of this letter are extant, one in the British Museum (Ashley 5021), and the other in the Bodleian (Bod. MS Shelley c. 1, F135–138): both have doubtful postmarks or signatures. For a lively discussion, see Robert M. Smith, *The Shelley Legend*, New York, 1945, with a gentlemanly reply by the distinguished trio of Shelley scholars N.I. White, K.N. Cameron and F.L. Jones. The overall point is exemplary of Shelley sources: where events reveal Shelley in an unpleasant light, the original texts and commentaries have attracted suppressions, distortions and questions of doubtful authenticity, originating from Victorian apologists.

had made to keep Harriet's illegitimate pregnancy a secret and to help her with finding decent lodgings.

It was Claire alone of the intimate Shelley circle who came to view these circumstances in a reasonably balanced light.

After calling on Eliza unsuccessfully twice on the following day, 17 December, Shelley wrote to her expressing his feelings in a totally different manner. It seems from the way in which he discussed only the eldest child Ianthe, that the West-brooks had offered him the uncontested custody of little Charles, provided he would respect a last wish which Harriet had expressed that he should allow Ianthe to continue to live with Eliza. It seems certain that they must have shown Shelley Harriet's last letter, addressed to Eliza and with clear indications that she was about to commit suicide; for it contributed to their case over the children. But if Shelley saw it, he was unmoved. It was, nevertheless, a painfully moving and absolutely direct appeal. The central paragraph read: 'My dear Bysshe, let me conjure you by the rememberance of our days of happiness to grant my last wish, Do not take your innocent child from Eliza who has been more than I have, who has watched over her with such unceasing care. Do not refuse my last request. I never could refuse you & if you had never left me I might have lived, but as it is I freely forgive you & may you enjoy that happiness which you have deprived me of. There is your beautiful boy. Oh! be careful of him, & his love may prove one day a rich reward. As you form his infant mind so will you reap the fruits hereafter. Now comes the sad task of saying farewell – oh! I must be quick. God bless and watch over you all. You dear Bysshe & you dear Eliza. May all happiness attend ye both is the last wish of her who loved ye more than all others.'[12] Perhaps Shelley could not accept the request so clearly and poignantly made, without also accepting the accusation of guilt, a grim piece of blackmail from beyond the grave, inextricably bound up in it. At any rate, Shelley was adamant towards this proposal, though quite prepared to absolve the West-brooks from blameworthy conduct. He was even prepared to accept that he and Mary had some responsibility. The *volte face* is indeed remarkable. Shelley wrote to Eliza Westbrook:

> You will spare me & yourself useless struggles on this occasion when you
> learn, that there is no earthly consideration which would induce me to forgo
> the exclusive & entire charge of my child. She has only one parent, & that
> parent, if he could ever be supposed to have forgotten them,* – is awakened
> to a sense of his duties & his claims which at whatever price must be asserted
> & performed. . . . As it is, allow me to assure you that I give no faith to any

---

* Shelley had some cause for this caveat: there is no proof that he had even seen Ianthe since spring 1814, two and a half years before.

of the imputations generally cast on your conduct or that of Mr Westbrook towards the unhappy victim. I cannot help thinking that you might have acted more judiciously but I do not doubt that you intended well – My friend Mr Leigh Hunt, will take charge of my children & prepare them for their residence with me. I cannot expect that your feelings towards the lady whose union with me you may excusably regard as the cause of your sister's ruin should permit you to mention her with the honour with which Ianthe must be accustomed to regard the wife of her father's heart.[13]

Mary Godwin herself might have been more than surprised to find Shelley now describing the Westbrooks' view of *her* guilt 'excusable'.

Shelley's diplomacy however came to nothing as far as the Westbrooks were concerned. If they did ever offer him the uncontested custody of Charles, the offer was now withdrawn. Hunt, and others, may have rightly urged that the sanest course was, in the end, to draw a line and to start again with Mary and not look back. Perhaps they were right. He decided to marry Mary at once, and then fight for his children in the courts.

On 30 December, Shelley and Mary were married at St Mildred's Church, Bread Street in the City. They had dined, for the first time, at Skinner Street on the previous evening, and Godwin was present and beaming at the church. 'Call on Mildred' he entered in his diary, and wrote self-satisfied letters to his friends, stressing Shelley's family and wealth. Armed now with legitimacy to fight the law, Shelley returned immediately with Mary to Bath. Ahead of him, a letter reached Claire which suggests at least a touch of cynicism about what he had done. He seemed to be admitting her into confidences he had not revealed to Mary. 'Dearest Claire . . . Thank you too, my kind girl, for not expressing much of what you must feel – the loneliness and the low spirits which arise from being entirely left. Nothing could be more provoking than to find all this unnecessary. However, they will now be satisfied and quiet.' Shelley's 'they' is clearly the Godwins, but it is not evident if he included Mary among their number. He appeared to be referring to the 'necessity' of marriage in order to secure Ianthe and Charles legally. He implied to Claire that this, beyond anything else, was why he succumbed a second time to an institution which he still in theory rejected. He continued: '. . . The ceremony, so magical in its effects, was undergone this morning at St Mildred's Church in the City. Mrs G. and G. were both present, and appeared to feel no little satisfaction. Indeed Godwin throughout has shown the most polished and cautious attentions to me and Mary. He seems to think no kindness too great in compensation for what has past. I confess I am not entirely deceived by this, though I cannot make my vanity wholly insensible to certain attentions paid in a manner studiously flattering. Mrs G.

presents herself to me in her real attributes of affectation, prejudice, and heartless pride.'[14]

Sixty years later, Claire was to write acidly of those who had tried to defend Shelley's actions as if he could do no wrong. '[Harriet] did not form after S.'s leaving her, a connexion with some low man, as Mr Rossetti in his desire of making S. a model of moral perfection hints and more than hints. Her lover was a Captain in the Indian or Wellington Army I forget which, and he was ordered abroad. His letters did not reach her – with her sister's concurrence, she retired for her accouchement to live with a decent couple in a Mews near Chapel Street. . . . The parents were told that H. – was gone on a visit of some weeks to a friend in the country – it was of consequence in Miss W.'s opinion to conceal the affair from Shelley.' Claire went on to describe Harriet's increasing loneliness and depressions, the suicide itself and the burial in a small cemetery off the Bayswater Road. Perhaps she recalled how Shelley's own role *vis-à-vis* the concealment of her pregnancy from the Godwins mirrored that of Eliza's concealment of Harriet's pregnancy from the Westbrooks. If Shelley himself was aware of this, he did not say so. Claire concluded: 'To me it appears that Mr Rossetti has written his memoir to suit Lady [Jane] Shelley's predilections – and she is a warm partisan of Shelley and Mary, and like all warm partisans does not care much about Truth. Miss [Eliza] Westbrook related all the above particulars to my Mother. Harriet's suicide had a beneficial effect on Shelley – he became much less confident in himself and not so wild as he had been before.'[15] For Claire, it was Shelley's recognition of his own degree of responsibility – a slow and painful recognition – which matured him. But with the advantage of hindsight Claire did not include his marriage to Mary as one of the 'benefits'.

Back at Bath, Shelley tried to concentrate on practical matters: Claire's baby, a little girl, was born safely on 12 January 1817. At first they called her Alba, and later at Byron's request, Allegra. His 'Hymn to Intellectual Beauty' was published by Hunt in the *Examiner* of the 19th, and consolidated his *entrée* into London literary life. On the 24th the Chancery case for custody of the two children, Ianthe and Charles, began under Lord Eldon, and Shelley spent many afternoons consulting in London with his counsel Basil Montagu, and Lord Brougham. Both Hunt and Godwin were at their most solicitous, but Shelley and his friends badly underestimated the determination and the sense of justice of the Westbrooks. Old John Westbrook, ill as he was, but ably advised by his solicitor Deesse and supported by Eliza, assembled a powerful case for custody of the children. First, he settled £2,000-worth of four-per-cent annuities on both children, irrespective of the outcome of the case. Secondly, he drew up a dossier of letters which Shelley had sent to Harriet during the time of their separation in autumn 1814. These reflected badly on the irregularity of his conduct and compounded Shelley's complete failure to visit the children. Thirdly, he began to assemble, with Eliza's critical advice, several of Shelley's ideological writings – notably *Queen Mab* – which showed his political and religious views at their most heretical. It was characteristic of Shelley that he failed to see the social and legal force of the first two aspects of the case, and concentrated entirely on the third. It was of course over the matter of heresy that he felt most justified, and most righteous. Writing to Byron on 17 January to inform him of the birth of Claire's child, most of the letter was spent defending this position. Again, he reverted to the accusation that Eliza, 'a libidinous and vindictive woman'* had 'not in law, yet in fact' murdered Harriet. Shelley continued:

> The sister has now instituted a Chancery process against me, the intended effect of which is to deprive me of my unfortunate children, now more than ever dear to me; of my inheritance, and to throw me into prison, and expose me in the pillory, on the ground of my being a REVOLUTIONIST, and an *Atheist*. It seems while she lived in my house she possessed herself of such papers as go to establish these allegations. The opinion of Council is, that she will certainly exceed to a considerable extent, but that I may probably escape entire ruin, in the worldly sense of it. So I am here, dragged before the tribunals of tyranny and superstition, to answer with my children, my property, my liberty, and my fame, for having exposed their frauds, and scorned the influence of their power. Yet I will not fail; though I have been given to understand that I could purchase victory by recantation. Indeed, I have too much pride in the selection of their victim.[16]

The last part of this letter, in its melodramatic posturing, might have been written while Shelley was still at Oxford. There was no real sense in which he could have 'purchased victory by recantation': the essence of the Westbrook case lay not in what he had done as a writer but in what he had omitted to do as a father. In the event the case dragged on for many weeks: judgement against Shelley was given on 17 March, but the actual custody of the children was not finally awarded until the autumn. The Westbrooks did not get them either, but they were farmed out to respectable foster parents, a certain Dr and Mrs Thomas Hume, who lived in the Home Counties. Strictly limited visiting rights were granted to Shelley, and slightly more flexible ones to the Westbrooks. There is no evidence that Shelley ever made use of this right. It was, in the end, probably the least satisfactory solution for the children themselves, and a far cry from Harriet's last request.

Peacock, whom Shelley visited frequently at Marlow during this time, observed that he was 'calm and self-possessed', except for one curious incident

* Like Elizabeth Hitchener presumably.

when he flew at a gardener who had topped off a holly bush to sell as Christmas decorations. This was in the grounds of the new house which Shelley intended to take. 'As soon as Shelley saw it, he asked the gardener, "What had possessed him to ruin that beautiful tree?" The gardener said, he thought he had improved its appearance. Shelley said: "It is impossible that you can be such a fool." The culprit stood twiddling his thumbs along the seams of his trousers, receiving a fulminating denunciation, which ended in his peremptory dismissal. . . . Nothing disturbed his serenity but the unfortunate holly. Subsequently, the feeling for Harriet's death grew into a deep and abiding sorrow: but it was not in the beginning that it was felt most strongly.'[17]

Writing four years later in *Epipsychidion*, Shelley faced much of that which he had hidden from Peacock, from Byron and from Mary. Most of all he faced the appalling effect that 'abiding sorrow' had on his own feelings, and on his relationship with Mary. Guilt for Harriet's suicide itself he never accepted, and perhaps he was right not to do so and true to himself. He wrote of Mary as the Moon; Ianthe and Charles the 'twin babes', and Harriet 'the planet of that hour'. He described the deadening of his emotions, as if part of his mind had iced over.

And there I lay, within a chaste cold bed:
Alas, I then was nor alive nor dead: –
For at her silver voice came Death and Life,
Unmindful each of their accustomed strife,
Masked like twin babes, a sister and a brother,
The wandering hopes of one abandoned mother,
And through the cavern without wings they flew,
And cried 'Away, he is not of our crew.'
I wept, and though it be a dream, I weep.

What storms then shook the ocean of my sleep,
Blotting that Moon, whose pale and waning lips
Then shrank as in the sickness of eclipse; –
And how my soul was as a lampless sea,
And who was then its Tempest; and when She,
The Planet of that hour, was quenched, what frost
Crept o'er those waters, till from coast to coast,
The moving billows of my being fell
Into a death of ice, immovable; –
And then – what earthquakes made it gape and split,
The white Moon smiling all the while on it,
These words conceal: – If not, each word would be
The key of staunchless tears. Weep not for me![18]

In later letters to Byron, Shelley wrote that Harriet's death communicated a shock 'which I know not how I have survived'.

But Shelley's powers of survival were, as he had shown many times before, very great. He threw himself with enthusiasm into the new circle of writers, journalists and poets which Hunt's friendship had brought him. From the end of January 1817, while seeing the case through Chancery, Shelley and Mary came to stay for four weeks at the Vale of Health. On the 26th, Hunt invited the critic William Hazlitt and the editor Walter Coulson up to dine with the Shelleys, reinforced by Hogg. On 5 February Hunt organized a special dinner for the three members of his 'Young Poets' article, and Shelley again met Reynolds and John Keats. Four days later Shelley, Hazlitt and Hunt were up to 3 in the morning arguing about Monarchy and Republicanism. Hunt was determined to keep his new friend well occupied.

There were many other acquaintances who came to Hunt's fireside, to drink tea, or eat supper, or pass musical evenings surrounded by the literary busts by Shout, the pots of trailing flowers, the elegant engravings, the piles of books and galley proofs, the comfortably battered chairs and settees, and the charming suite of female cousins. Among them were Charles and Mary Lamb, the painter Benjamin Haydon and the two literary lawyers who were recognized as sympathetic satellites of the Hampstead set, Basil Montagu and Horace Smith. Shelley also met the man who was to take Hookham's place as his future publisher, Charles Ollier. The circumstances of Shelley's Chancery case were generally known and he was treated with kindness and understanding. Besides, Shelley at once felt perfectly at ease in the liberal–radical atmosphere of the group, and the genteel quality of Hunt's tea-drinking, 'neat disorder' and eternal literary puns did not jar him as it tended to jar Hazlitt and Keats. Shelley found it kindly and comfortable and slightly quaint, and he responded to the faint shade of sychophancy in Hunt's warm personality. In contrast, Hazlitt felt at bottom that Hunt was only playing at radicalism; and Keats was slowly coming to distrust the poetaster element in Hunt's make up. Shelley, after his initial shyness had worn off, entered loudly and vigorously into both political and literary discussions which filled the evenings throughout February. He seemed to be unaware that both Keats and Hazlitt found him, in their different ways, rather overbearing. Keats was sensitive to his tendency to insist on a point with a hint of aristocratic superiority; and Hazlitt distrusted his political fervour.

It is remarkable that on the whole the reminiscences of Shelley left by the Hampstead set – by Keats, Hazlitt and Haydon especially – were sharply unfavourable. This contrasts with the idealizing that Hunt always indulged in towards Shelley, but most notably after his death.

Perhaps the most kindly was that of Horace Smith, the literary lawyer, who afterwards looked after Shelley's financial affairs in England with great efficiency. Meeting him for the first time at Hunt's in January, his immediate impression was of the curious combination of fashionable clothes worn carelessly with 'no thought for modish adjustment', yet 'it was impossible to doubt, even for a moment, that you were gazing upon a gentleman'. Smith noticed that Shelley smiled but took no part in the 'playful and bantering' antics of Hunt. The weather was fine, and they all walked out on Hampstead Heath; Smith attached himself to Shelley, and gradually drew him into conversation. He was surprised at once by the extent of his reading, and the force and fearless disregard with which he asserted his opinions. 'My companion, who, as he became interested in his subjects, talked much and eagerly, seemed to me a psychological curiosity, infinitely more curious than Coleridge's Kubla Khan, to which strange vision he made reference. His principle discourse was, however, of Plato. . . .'[19]

The painter, Benjamin Robert Haydon, erratic friend of both Hunt and Keats, met Shelley at a memorable dinner at Hampstead on 20 January 1817, when he found himself set upon and severely baited for his Christian belief. His memories of Shelley, who took an active part in this baiting, recorded in his diary were not pleasant. First of all, he found Shelley to be hypocritical: 'Shelley said he could not bear the inhumanity of Wordsworth in talking about the beauty of the shining trout as they lay after being caught, that he had such a horror of torturing animals it was impossible to express it.'[20] Haydon felt this compared badly with the pain Shelley had caused in his own domestic life. Shelley later returned to this criticism of Wordsworth in 1819.[21] Haydon felt that all Shelley's attitudes and actions were perverse in this way, and he was one among many who were appalled by the story of 'his writing $\alpha\theta\epsilon os$ on Mont Blanc'.[22] 'He would lie with his sister & sophisticate himself into a conviction of its innocence, and then sell his coat for his Friend, if the produce would relieve his Friend's necessities! He would kill his wife by infidelity, or himself by continence, whichever would make him most singular by appearing to suffer on principles not vulgarly acknowledged; pride was the foundation of his heart, I suspect, though I certainly [saw] little of him.'

Compiling his autobiography in 1846, Haydon considerably dilated on his first impressions of Shelley at that dinner in January, when he was gored for his Christianity. Allowing for retrospective colouring, the picture of Shelley at his most domineering and insensitive is very vivid.

I went a little after the time, and seated myself in the place kept for me at [Hunt's] table right opposite Shelley himself, as I was told after, for I did not know what hectic, spare, weakly, yet intellectual-looking creature it was carving a bit of brocoli or cabbage on his plate, as if it had been the substantial wing of a chicken. Hunt and his wife [Marianne] and her sister [Elizabeth Kent], Keats, Horace Smith and myself made up the party. In a few minutes Shelley opened the conversation by saying in a most feminine and gentle voice, 'As to that detestable religion, the Christian . . .' I looked astounded, but casting a glance round the table, easily saw by Hunt's expression of ecstasy and the women's simper, I was to be set at that evening *vi et armis*. No reply, however, was made to this sally during dinner, but when the desert came and the servants were gone, to it we went like fiends. —— and —— were deists. I felt exactly like a stag at bay and resolved to gore without mercy. Shelley said the Mosaic and Christian dispensations were inconsistent. I swore they were . . . neither of us using an atom of logic. Neither —— Keats nor all codes of law in the earth. Shelley denied it. [Hunt] backed him. I affirmed they were . . . neither of us using an atom of logic [*sic*]. Neither —— Keats nor —— said a word to this; but still Shelley, and [Hunt] and —— kept at it till, finding I was a match for them in argument, they became personal, and so did I. We said unpleasant things to each other, and when I retired to the other room for a moment I overheard them say, 'Haydon is fierce.' 'Yes' said Hunt, 'the question always irritates him.'[23]

It was this sort of scene, far more than the sense of class distinction which Hunt hinted at, that made Keats wary of Shelley. At first his attitude was merely playful, taking after Hunt, but with a touch of Keatsian sarcasm: 'Does Shelley go on telling strange Stories of the Death of Kings?' he asked in May 1817; 'Tell him there are strange Stories of the death of Poets – some have died before they were conceived. . . . Does Mrs S[helley] cut Bread and Butter as neatly as ever? Tell her to procure some fatal Scissars and cut the thread of Life of all to be disappointed Poets.'[24] Later, in the summer, he definitely refused to be drawn into the Shelley *ménage* at Marlow: 'I refused to visit Shelley, that I might have my own unfettered scope.'[25]* Discussing 'Endymion' which he had been working on at the same time as Shelley wrote *Laon and Cythna*, he made his antagonism clearer, though without any of Haydon's defensive malice: 'the fact is [Hunt] & Shelley are hurt & perhaps justly, at my not having showed them the affair officiously & from several hints I have had they appear much disposed to dissect & anatomize, any trip or slip I may have made. – but whose afraid Ay! Tom! demme if I am.'[26]

William Hazlitt felt no such reticence as Keats, and his description of Shelley

---

* '[Shelley] went to Charles Richards, the printer in St Martin's Lane . . . about the printing of a little volume of Keats' first poems . . . the printer told me that he had never had so strange a visitor. He was gaunt, and had peculiar starts and gestures and a way of fixing his eyes and his whole attitude for a good while, like the abstracted apathy of a musing madman.' The opinion of Mr John Dix in his *Pen and Ink Sketches of Poets, Preachers and Politicians* (1846).

in an essay of 1821 aroused the anger of Hunt, and shadowed the friendship for some time to come. In a celebrated rodomontade Hazlitt displayed with ironic gusto much that had been merely implied by Keats and Smith.

> Mr Shelley ... has a fire in his eye, a fever in his blood, a maggot in his brain, a hectic flutter in his speech, which mark out the philosophic fanatic. He is sanguine-complexioned, and shrill-voiced. As is often observable in the case of religious enthusiasts, there is a slenderness of constitutional *stamina*, which renders the flesh no match for the spirit. . . . The shock of accident, the weight of authority make no impression on his opinions, which retire like a feather, or rise from the encounter unhurt, through their own buoyancy. . . . There is no *caput mortuum* of worn-out, thread-bare experience to serve as ballast to his mind; it is all volatile intellectual salt of tartar, that refuses to combine its evanescent, inflammable essence with any thing solid or any thing lasting. . . . Curiosity is the only proper category of his mind, and though a man in knowledge, he is a child in feeling. . . . He strives to overturn all established creeds and systems: but this is in him an effect of constitution. He runs before the most extravagant opinions, but this is because he is held back by none of the merely mechanical checks of sympathy and habit. He tampers with all sorts of obnoxious subjects, but it is less because he is gratified with the rankness of the taint, than captivated with the intellectual phosphoric light they emit.[27]

With Hunt's family however, Shelley was indulged as a great favourite. Hunt's wife, Marianne, looked on Mary and Shelley simply as a misunderstood and persecuted couple, and she was delighted with the way Shelley played with the children. Hunt's eldest son, Thornton, then 11, afterwards remembered how he frequently went boating and walking on the Heath with Shelley. His father's new strange friend filled him with a mixture of fascination and fear. He remembered one of his alarming physical spasms 'when he suddenly threw up his book and hands, and fell back, the chair sliding steeply from under him, and he poured forth shrieks, loud and continuous, stamping his feet madly on the ground'.

Contrasting him with his own father, Thornton recalled: 'Shelley entered more unreservedly into the sports and even the thoughts of the children. I had probably awakened interest in him, not only because I was my father's eldest child, but still more, because I had already begun to read with great avidity, and with an especial sense of imaginative wonders and horrors. . . . I can remember well one day when we were both for some long time engaged in gambols, broken off by my terror at his screwing up his long and curling hair into a horn, and approaching me with rampant paws and frightful gestures as some imaginative monster. . . . Shelley often called me for a long ramble on the heath, or into regions which I then thought far distant; and I went with him rather than with my father, because he walked faster, and talked with me while he walked . . . and when I was "done up", he carried me home in his arms, on his shoulder, or pickback. Our communion was not always concord; as I have intimated, he took a pleasure in frightening me, though I never really lost my confidence in his protection, if he would only drop the fantastic aspects that he delighted to assume. Sometimes, but much more rarely, he teased me with exasperating banter. . . . I am well aware that he *had* suffered severely, and that he continued to be haunted by certain recollections, partly real and partly imaginative, which pursued him like an Orestes. He frequently talked on such subjects. . . .'[28] Young Hunt's memories are remarkable, and have the candid, unflinching penetration of a child's glance. Thornton was, incidentally, one of those who was always convinced of the reality of the attack at Tan-yr-allt. Perhaps more than any of the adult Hampstead friends, Shelley allowed him into the dark side of his mind.

But for Shelley, the games, the sociable dinners, the late-night arguments, the comfortable breakfasts with Hunt joking and punning genially in his flowered dressing-gown, all served as stimulating distractions. A sense of purpose was hardening secretly inside him. Both the Chancery case, and the reform meetings which had been sweeping the country had crystallized within him a new determination to express himself politically. The creative and the political impulse worked, as before, together.

In February, Lord Liverpool's administration had again announced a national state of alarm, as it had done in 1812. Government secret committees, commissioned to examine agitational and insurrectional movements and the levelling propaganda of the Spenceans, reported to both Houses of Parliament in the middle of the month. On 3 March Habeas Corpus was suspended, and on the 29th the Seditious Meetings Act was passed.[29] On 30 January the deputies of the Hampden Clubs had held a special conference in London, and a contest for command of the reform movement was fought out between Francis Place, William Hone the editor of *Reformist's Register*, and Cobbett. The fundamental principle at issue was whether it was best to press at once for full manhood suffrage, by working-class agitation throughout the nation, or whether to try and increase merely the middle-class representation. Francis Place advocated the second course, arguing that they might then carry the final stage of reform through from the floor of the Commons itself. Shelley was deeply involved with these issues. When Shelley and Mary moved from Hampstead to stay with Peacock at Marlow, she wrote to Hunt that the house was 'very political as well as poetical', and somewhat nervously asked his advice on a scheme which Shelley and Peacock were planning to start a local protest movement based on a refusal, as householders, to pay their rates and taxes.[30]

Nothing can better capture the popular political feeling of this early spring of 1817 than the reports which Cobbett's *Weekly Political Pamphlet* and the *Black Dwarf* carried of the execution of a sailor called Cashman who had been convicted as a result of the Spa Fields Riot of December 1816. The execution itself acted as the trigger for a large and spontaneous demonstration, in which Cashman gallantly played the jocular democratic hero to the very last. 'As the Sherriffs advanced, the mob expressed the strongest feelings of indignation; groans and hisses burst from all quarters, and attempts were made to rush forward. . . . Cashman . . . seemed to enter into the spirit of the spectators, and joined in their exclamations with a terrific shout . . . "Hurra, my hearties in the cause! success! cheer up!"' He brushed away two Anglican clergymen, and the execution hood, with derision, stepped on to the trap with the noose around his neck and bellowed amiably at the crowd. ' "Now you buggers, give me three cheers when I trip"; and, after telling the executioner to "let go the jib-boom", Cashman "was cheering at the instant the fatal board fell from beneath his feet".' The crowd fell silent, and the constables shifted uneasily at the barricades. Then with growing force they cried 'Murder' and 'Shame', and would not disperse for several hours.[31]

It was in this month also that Samuel Bamford was arrested near Manchester and brought south for a trial and imprisonment that led to his personal examination by Sidmouth and other members of the Cabinet, of which he has left a brilliant and celebrated description.[32]

In mid-February, Shelley suddenly began to work on a political pamphlet, his first since 1812. He showed the draft to Hunt's friend Ollier, who agreed to print and publish it at Shelley's expense. Shelley took the manuscript with him to Marlow, where he revised it, in discussion with Peacock. Its final title was *A Proposal for Putting Reform to the Vote throughout the Kingdom*, and it was signed with the vatic pseudonym, 'The Hermit of Marlow'. The pamphlet itself is short and to the point, and deliberately reasonable and moderate. Shelley suggested that a Crown and Anchor Meeting should be assembled of all the Friends of Liberty, whatever their particular bias, in order to set up what was in effect a national plebiscite. Funds and representatives should be organized to ask every 'adult individual of Great Britain' one simple question: whether or not they were in favour of the proposal that the House of Commons 'should originate such measure of reform as would render its members the actual representatives of the nation'. This single question should be canvassed, without any further details or particulars. 'It is trivial to discuss what species of reform shall have place when it remains a question whether there will be any reform or no.' But if the answer was a majority 'yes', then all pressures could be brought to bear on Parliament to put through some immediate measure of reform, as this would then indisputably be the 'will of the nation'.

Beyond this simple target, towards which Shelley himself made a characteristic offer of £100 to set up an action fund, the meeting should disclaim 'revolutionary and disorganizing schemes', and declare its object to be 'purely constitutional'. Indeed he stated that for his part, he did not believe that it was the right time to press matters further than instituting annual Parliaments, and a limited middle-class extension of the electoral base. He had, it seemed, no wish to be counted, in this contest at least, a democrat or demagogue. 'With respect to universal suffrage, I confess I consider its adoption in the present unprepared state of public knowledge and feeling a measure fraught with peril. I think that none but those who register their names as paying a certain small sum in *direct taxes* ought, at present, to send members to Parliament. The consequences of the immediate extension of the elective franchise to every male adult would be to place power in the hands of men who have been rendered brutal and torpid and ferocious by ages of slavery. It is to suppose that the qualities belonging to a demagogue are such as are sufficient to endow a legislator.'[33]

It would appear from this that Shelley was quite deliberately setting out to align himself with the liberals of Hunt's *Examiner*, rather than with the real radicals of the *Political Register* and the *Black Dwarf*. But in private, Shelley's views were much further left than he admitted in this pamphlet. His scheme with Peacock to withhold payment of taxes – a highly unusual piece of direct action at that time – demonstrates this well; as also his tendency to side in political argument with the republican Hazlitt; and much of his private writings. This split between public and private attitudes gives some indication of the intense difficulty with which men like Shelley entertained the idea of a real English democracy.

But there was hidden in the Hermit's pamphlet a single logical trick which made the radical democratic point well enough. For, ideologically speaking, Shelley's proposal in fact *assumed already* what it pretended to question. Once the reader found himself agreeing that the whole of the 'individual adult' population of Great Britain had a right to be consulted on the reform issue – that is, on a fundamental political issue – then the principle of universal adult franchise was already in practice established.

Five hundred copies of the pamphlet were advertised by Ollier (together with Keats's first volume of poems), and began to appear in the first fortnight of March. Shelley pressed Ollier to advertise unsparingly, and drew up for him a mailing list which shows clearly that he was addressing himself to the very centre of the controversy. Among those who received his pamphlet were Cob-

bett, Major Cartwright, Francis Burdett, Place, Brougham and Robert Owen.
Bundles of copies were also sent to Hunt at the *Examiner*, and the Hampden
Clubs of London and Birmingham. In April Shelley had some direct negotia-
tions with Hone, probably about reprinting this or another of Shelley's political
works, but as far as is known nothing came of it directly. But this is perhaps how
Shelley's name came into the circle of working-class radical publishers, and how
Richard Carlile himself approached Shelley in the summer about publishing
Queen Mab.[34] A copy eventually reached the *Quarterly*, and was later scathingly
reviewed in a collection of anonymous and semi-seditious pamphlets by Robert
Southey.

The publication of the pamphlet brought Shelley no personal reactions outside
the circle at Marlow and Hampstead, but from now on he felt himself back
inside the reform movement and he followed the process of public meetings,
political trials of editors, publishers and working leaders, with close attention.
As he settled into the spring at Marlow, he turned the whole question of radical
political and social change over in his mind and began to read further studies of
the French Revolution. More and more he came to believe that the way in
which he and his contemporaries interpreted the French Revolution would
decide the way in which they would fight for or oppose the present struggle for
democratic reform.

15
The Garden Days: Marlow 1817

By the end of February 1817, Shelley had at last secured a twenty-one-year lease on Albion House, and after several delays, on 18 March Shelley and Mary took possession of their new home. Claire had come up from Bath, bringing with her Elise, little William and her own beloved Alba. Albion House was the most determined effort at a permanent residence that Shelley ever made in England. It was a rather long, low, two-storey building roughly finished in a kind of white pebble-dash, with tiny attic windows peering over the top of a mock gothic balustrade. The slightly quaint impression was enhanced by the curious shape of the window frames, which were also mock gothic, each one rising to a pair of gnomish points. The front door, which gave directly on to the street, was fenced round and embowered by a lattice-work porch and balustrade over which wisteria and wild ivies climbed in profusion. The rooms were large inside, though they tended to be slightly dark and damp. The pride of the house was an enormous library which gave on to the back garden, and Shelley immediately began stocking it with books from Ollier and furnishing it in the approved Hunt fashion with full-size statues of Venus and Apollo. The garden itself at the back was very fine, about an acre in size, partly enclosed by a high, mellow red-brick wall, and already set out with neat lawns and dominated by a floating, dark green cedar tree. Its peripheries were somewhat darkened by firs and cypresses, closely planted. At the bottom of the lawn was a mound, where they sometimes sat in the evenings to see the view over the meadows, and behind this a vegetable garden where ornamental plants were inclined to appear idiosyncratically among the cabbages. At the end of the garden, the ground fell away down a steep chalk bank into a hidden lane. There are several records of Shelley hiding from uninvited visitors in this lane; of his leading his ladies up the chalk bank after walks; and using it as a slide to shoot past the enraptured Hunt children 'in a cloud of chalk dust'.[1] One of the first books Shelley ordered was Mawe's *Gardening Calendar*, and his newly engaged gardener, Harry, was put to work sowing the Alpine seeds they had brought back from Switzerland. Mary also hired a cook and a housemaid.

Albion House stood on the main London coaching route to Henley, about 200 yards to the west of the centre of Marlow and the solid three-storey brick establishment where Peacock lived with his mother. Across the road, and about three minutes over a hayfield, was the Thames, Marlow steps and the weir. Shelley kept a small skiff permanently moored here throughout the spring and summer for his water expeditions. Southwards from the Thames, across about a mile of shining water-meadows rose the steep green escarpment of Bisham Woods, loosely timbered with beech, birch and fir trees. Here Shelley loved to walk, turning secluded spots into open-air studies, or indulging in horse-play with Peacock and Hogg and the Hunt children, slithering down more dust slides and carving Greek hieroglyphics and revolutionary slogans on the trees. They even set up an altar to Pan, which Hogg and Peacock were solemnly to visit long after Shelley had gone abroad.

Mary was anxious to play the hostess from the start, and in March she invited the Hunts: 'I am now writing in the Library of our house in which we are to sleep tonight for the first time – It is very comfortable and expectant of its promised guests. The statues are arrived and everything is getting on. Come then, dear, good creatures, and let us enjoy with you the beauty of the Marlow sun and the pleasant walks that will give you all health spirits & *industry*.' Hogg and Peacock, however, were a reminder of former things, and Mary was not unduly enthusiastic about Shelley's old friends from the unsettled days. 'Hogg is at present a visitor of Peacock. I do not like him and I think he is more disagreeable than ever. I would not have him come every week to disturb our peace by his illhumour and noise for all the world. Both of the menagerie were very much scandalised by the praise & sonnet of Keats and mean I believe to petition against the publication of any more.'[2] Mary omitted to mention that Shelley's opinion of Keats was correspondingly low; or that at Hampstead, with his own *Queen Mab* and *Alastor* behind him, he had solemnly advised Keats to avoid publishing young.

The first proper guest was Godwin, who came in the early days of April. The weather had turned cold, and the whole visit was something of a strain, but Shelley manfully organized boating trips to Medmenham Abbey, Henley and Maidenhead, and talked with his father-in-law about the progress of his new novel *Mandeville* and the old issues of 'perfectibility'. Claire had deposited Alba with Marianne Hunt and her sister Bessy Kent at Hampstead, and came down to Marlow immaculate again under her maiden name. A few hours after Godwin's departure, the whole Hunt family arrived, bringing besides their own children, a little 'cousin' of theirs whom Aunt Claire had kindly agreed to take care of for the summer. Thus with Shelley's careful management Alba was slipped easily into the Marlow household. With the arrival of the Hunts, the weather seemed to improve, regular expeditions took to the water or disappeared for the day into Bisham Woods. Shelley set himself on a concentrated course of Spenser's poetry and Lacretelle's *Short History of the French Revolution*, with the idea for a big political poem steadily forming in his mind. Mary meanwhile began to revise and fair copy her *Frankenstein* which had been thrown aside during the crises of the winter.

Shelley took much trouble to fit Claire smoothly into the household. He wrote twice to Ollier to secure her 'a print done from a drawing by Harlowe of Lord Byron', specifying carefully how it should be framed. At the end of April he negotiated a loan of seventy-five pounds to buy a first-class concert piano from Vincent Novello upon which Hunt and others might accompany her singing. This piano, needless to say, was still not paid for in 1821.

He wrote to Byron a cheerful but somewhat wry description of Claire and her little baby at Marlow. '[Alba] is very beautiful, and though her frame is of a somewhat delicate texture, enjoys excellent health. Her eyes are the most intelligent I ever saw in so young an infant. Her hair is black, her eyes deeply blue, and her mouth exquisitely shaped. She passes here for the child of a friend in London, sent into the country for her health, while Claire has reassumed her maiden character. Indeed all these precautions have now become more necessary than before on account of our renewed intimacy with Godwin, which has taken place in consequence of my marriage with Mary, a change (if it be a change) which had principally her feelings in respect to Godwin for its object. I need not inform you that this is simply with us a measure of convenience, and that our opinions as to the importance of this pretended sanction, and all the prejudices connected with it, remain the same.' Shelley went on to discuss in general terms Alba's future. He assumed without question that Byron would honour his obligations to the child herself, but tacitly admitted that Byron might well feel less obliged towards the mother. He and Mary would, of course, he said, give 'all our care' to the child in Byron's absence. Shelley did not add that Mary regarded Claire as one of the main burdens of her life: '*absentia Clariae*' still being one of the preconditions of her happiness. All in all, he felt it best that Byron should try to come back to England to settle the matter himself. In the event Byron was to be fully occupied in Venice.[3]

For the rest, Shelley drew a picture of tranquillity. Though he feared that 'a criminal information' might arise from the Chancery case concerning the political and religious contents of *Queen Mab*, for the time being he was determined to extinguish rather than be extinguished by the anxiety.* He was content,

* He had good reason for this fear. 1817 saw twenty-six prosecutions for seditious and blasphemous

he told Byron, with his garden, his books and the boat. At Marlow, the apple trees were in blossom.

Marianne Hunt, Bessy and the children seem to have stayed on at Albion House for most of May and June, with Hunt himself paying flying visits whenever he could get away from the *Examiner*. The children were happy in each other's company, and with the combined nursery forces of Bessy, Elise and Claire to look after them, they played for long sunny hours in the enclosed garden. William soon became attached to little Alba, and together they endured the rigours of Shelley's cold-bath routine. Shelley would escape alone, or with Hunt and Peacock, for whole days on end in the boat.

It was during May that he began the first autobiographical cantos of the long political poem which he intended to call *Laon and Cythna, or, The Revolution in the Golden City*. Much of it was actually written in the boat, or sitting on the leafy heights in Bisham Woods. Shelley used a series of thick, small sketching books, and wrote at tremendous scrawling speed in soft pencil, each page rarely containing more than two of the nine-lined Spenserian stanzas he had adopted for the work.[4] His protagonists were to be a brother and a sister, who were also lovers, and who became leaders of a city insurrection and revolution apparently in the Far East, but actually modelled on the Paris Revolution. Some of the later passages were written more carefully, in pen, and suggest that Shelley also worked occasionally in the library at Albion House. It is notable that these sections contain the most dense and finely worked poetry, in a work that suffers overall from the diffusion of its loose philosophical narrative. There is no indication that Shelley, as he began the poem in May, had any clear outline of the shape and pattern of the plot. After a formal Spenserian allegory of an eagle fighting a serpent, in Canto 1, the poem moves through several layers of autobiographical narrative about Shelley's childhood, much of it extended into a semi-heroic disguise of epic and myth. After some 1,500 lines, it gradually begins to concentrate on recognizably contemporary public and political events in Canto IV. Altogether the poem was to last 4,818 lines, over eleven cantos, and to occupy Shelley until September. It was the longest work he ever wrote, and served the purpose of completely clearing the creative block which had hindered him since the spring of 1816. He was in fact trying to write that poem on the French Revolution, the 'master theme of the epoch', which he had originally recommended to Byron.

libel, among which were the trials of William Hone, Tom Wooler and Richard Carlile. *Queen Mab* was peculiarly open to the kind of disguised political prosecution which the government mounted during this period. Shelley realized that further involvement with the courts on *civil* charges might well bring with it a *criminal* 'information' with the threat of crippling fines and perhaps even imprisonment. In 1821 *Queen Mab* was indeed successfully prosecuted and its publisher heavily fined. See Chapter 27.

When Shelley came home in the evenings, he spent much of his time reading and talking with Mary, and the household tended to retire early, before 10. When Hunt was down, or Hogg and Peacock came over, they had lively musical evenings and the conversation ranged freely. Mary recalled, 'He was eloquent when philosophy or politics or taste were the subjects of conversation. He was playful; and indulged in the wild spirit that mocked itself and others – not in bitterness, but in sport.'[5] When little William learned to walk, Shelley wrote characteristically to Hogg amid discussion of Homer and Apuleius: 'My τετραπους [quadruped] has been metamorphosed since you were here, into a featherless biped; he lives, & inhabits his father's house but he has ceased to creep. He walks with great alacrity.'[6]

At the end of May, Shelley and Mary spent a few days in London with Hunt, and delivered the manuscript of *Frankenstein* to Murray at 50 Albemarle Street. They went to see *Don Giovanni* at the Opera, and an exhibition of Turner landscapes, and dined once again with Hazlitt. They discussed the forthcoming trial of Wooler, editor of the *Black Dwarf*, which was to open on 5 June, and eagerly speculated on the popular disturbances which were coming to a head in the Midlands.*

The Shelleys returned to Marlow, and through the length of June they and the Hunts mounted a series of idyllic picnicking expeditions with the children on the river and in Clifton Woods.

Claire was absorbed by the new demands and fascinations of her baby, although she was sometimes moody and sullen in the old manner, and was depressed by the rarity of Byron's letters, which were always addressed to Shelley and always excluded her. There is some evidence that both Hogg and Peacock made advances to Claire, but found her inaccessible. On good evenings though, she could be persuaded to sing, and it is thus that Shelley described her, with surprisingly overt passion, in a poem of this summer 'To Constantia, Singing'.†

Constantia, turn!
In thy dark eyes a power like light doth lie,

---

* The night of 9 June 1817 saw disturbances in Derbyshire which became known as the Pentridge Revolution. Shelley later wrote his most brilliant political pamphlet in defence of the men involved in this most successful of Lord Sidmouth's political exercises with *agents provocateurs*.

† In the Silsbee–Harvard MS Notebook, Claire's copy of the poem contains an indicative notation in pencil which she later added: 'written at Marlow 1817 – wd. not let Mary see it – sent it to Oxford Gazette or some Oxford or county paper without his name'. The version printed by the *Oxford University and City Herald* in its issue of 31 January 1818 was first recovered and republished by Judith Chernaik, *The Lyrics of Shelley*, Case Western Reserve University Press 1972, pp. 195–7. It contains a number of minor textual variants and is signed 'Pleyel'. Pleyel is the rationalist and lover of Clara Wieland in Charles Brockden Brown's romance, *Wieland*.

> Even though the sounds which were thy voice, which burn
> Between thy lips, are laid to sleep;
> Within thy breath, and on thy hair, like odour, it is yet,
> And from thy touch like fire doth leap.
> Even while I write, my burning cheeks are wet,
> Alas, that the torn heart can bleed, but not forget![7]

Written across the manuscript of the last stanza, in the notebook which Shelley started keeping for occasional pieces at Albion House, is a fragment which he later incorporated into one of the speeches of his play of 1819, *The Cenci*. One cannot place any definite autobiographical significance on it, but it suggests that Claire's music reminded him only too harshly that the cravings expressed in *Alastor* were still powerfully at work.

> To thirst and find no fill – to wail and wander
> With short unsteady steps – to pause and ponder –
> To feel the blood run through the veins and tingle
> Where busy thought and blind sensation mingle;
> To nurse the image of unfelt caresses
> Till dim imagination just possesses
> The half-created shadow, then all night
> Sick . . .[8]★

Another occasional poem, 'Marianne's Dream' was produced by Mrs Hunt's labours in scraping down and restoring the plaster statues in the library. In Shelley's vision, which is full of eruptive political symbols of earthquakes and floods and volcanic explosions, the statues come alive in a blazing city.

At the end of June, after a brief visit to London again with Hunt, Shelley returned to Marlow feeling suddenly ill. For several days he had to break off from his writing of *Laon and Cythna*. He grew irritable. It was the chronic pain in his side, and spasmodic attacks, and in a letter to Byron, he seemed to feel that they were connected with the strains of the Chancery case and the general

---

★ In *The Cenci*, Shelley adapted the fragment to the speech of Orsino in which he explicitly describes the overwhelming force of his physical lust for Beatrice, in the last soliloquy of Act II, Scene II, l. 132:

> Her bright form kneels beside me at the altar
> And follows me to the resort of men,
> And fills my slumber with tumultuous dreams,
> So when I wake my blood seems liquid fire;
> . . . and thus unprofitably
> I clasp the phantom of unfelt delights
> Till weak imagination half possesses
> The self-created shadow.

political situation in England. 'I have lately had a relapse of my constitutional disease, and if the Chancellor should threaten to invade my domestic circle, I shall seek Italy; as a refuge at once from the stupid tyranny of these laws and my disorder.' To Hunt, he wrote with more of the acid 'spirit that mocked itself', which Mary remembered: 'Do not mention that I am unwell to your nephew; for the advocate of a new system of diet is held bound to be invulnerable by disease, in the same manner as the sectaries of a new system of religion are held to be more moral than other people, or as a reformed parliament must at least be assumed as the remedy of all political evils. No one will change the diet, adopt the religion, or reform parliament else.'9 Mary added a note at the bottom of the letter, 'he always writes in this manner when ill'.

But the long, lazy July days in the garden at Albion House and in the boat soon brought him back to health, and he returned eagerly to composition. Betty Kent remembered the way he would be seen drifting on the river, lying flat down in the bottom of the boat to read, 'his face upwards to the sunshine'. Sometimes when he came back from Bisham Woods he brought the girls bunches of wild flowers, or appeared with trailers of green and white convolvulus draped round his straw sun hat.10 Thornton Hunt remembered walking alongside him on the river bank, as panting with exertion, he pulled a boat-load of visitors home against the current. Both Hunts, father and son, noticed how quickly he became known in the village, talking among the poor families, handing out money and giving simple medical advice. Mary wrote: 'Marlow was inhabited . . . by a very poor population. The women are lacemakers, and lose their health by sedentary labour, for which they are very ill paid. The Poorlaws ground to the dust not only the paupers, but those who had risen just above that state, and were obliged to pay poor-rates. The changes produced by peace following a long war, and a bad harvest, brought with them the most heartrending evils to the poor. Shelley afforded what alleviation he could. In the winter, while bringing out his poem, he had a severe attack of ophthalmia, caught while visiting the poor cottages.'11

Bursting out of Bisham Woods one day, Shelley ran across one of the little village girls called Polly Rose. She was brown-eyed, pretty and dressed virtually in rags. After a brief conference with Mary, and with Polly Rose's mother, Polly was invited to visit Albion House as regularly as she wished, where Shelley promised to educate her. She played with the babies in the garden, and had long talks with Mary, and frequently slept at the house, being allowed to stay up until 10 o'clock. What Shelley actually taught her is not on record, but as an old lady she remembered best his mad horse-play. One game was sitting her on a polished wooden dining-table, and then tilting it up so she slid down shrieking with delight into his arms. Claire was also encouraged to join in these games, and sometimes she and Polly would perch on the long-suffering table, shouting and screeching in delight, while Shelley with prodigious energy and enthusiasm 'ran it from one end of the room to the other'.[12]

Polly Rose was also subjected to the terror treatment. She remembered the way Shelley used to come suddenly surging out of the woods, his hair stuck full of old man's beard and other wild plants, 'his long brown coat with curling lambs' wool collar and cuffs' flying behind him, his shirt pulled open and his gaze distracted. At that time, for a gentleman to be seen outdoors in public without a hat was unusual, and to be without stock or cravat of any kind was to be virtually *déshabillé*. Moreover Shelley was inclined to return from his rambles in a state of total self-absorption, which was equally weird and ungentlemanlike, 'and he dashed along regardless of all he met or passed'.[13]

At Albion House some of the games were liable to turn nasty, and Shelley concocted various tales of terror, including his oldest one of all, that what he was really trying to do in Bisham Woods was to raise the devil by necromantic efforts, 'veryfying his aweful statement by a recital of the opprobrious names used in the evocation'.[14] He also introduced Polly to gothic horrors, which reached a suitable climax in the Christmas of 1817. 'On Christmas Eve Shelley related the ghostly tale of Bürger's ballad of Leonore, a copy of which in Spencer's translation with Lady Diana Beauclerc's designs, he possessed, working up the horror to such a height of fearful interest that Polly "quite expected to see Wilhelm walk into the drawing room".'[15]

By the end of the year, Bisham Woods had been established by local repute as Mr Shelley's peculiar woodland empire. When walking there once with Horace Smith, they came across two village 'urchins' who were stoning a squirrel from bough to bough in the elms overhead. Without even raising his voice he made them throw down their missiles and they 'slunk away'.[16]

Shelley's status as eccentric squire of the district, enhanced perhaps by rumours of incest and illegitimate children, gave him a new though somewhat curious kind of dignity in the eyes of his friends. Hogg was inclined to write to Peacock, indirectly asking for news about 'the Conchoid, Demogorgon & my other Marlow friends', by which he meant Shelley and Mary and the Albion household. To Hunt, Shelley wrote: 'It is the most comical thing in the world: You write accounts of your good behaviour to me as if I were some ancient and wrinkled, but rather good-natured grand-uncle. Now this is a new feeling for me. I have been accustomed to consider myself as the most imprudent and unaccountable of mankind.'[17]

Peacock's picture of the bustling madcap household of his novel *Nightmare Abbey* (1818) is drawn from his impressions of Albion House during this high summer, and for the sake of fiction he turned its gothic battlements into a mystic tower, 'ruined and full of owls', and imported not only Byron but also Coleridge into the household. Mary clearly recognized Shelley in the character of Scythrop with his mysterious mannerism, half comic and half grotesque, his secret and divided love-life, and his obsession with conspiratorial plans for revolutionary reform movements. This portrait-parody was a free, affectionate and nostalgic play of satire around Shelley during the period he was writing *Laon and Cythna*, and the political pamphlets.

> [Scythrop] now became troubled with the *passion for reforming the world*. He built many castles in the air, and peopled them with secret tribunals, and bands of illuminati, who were always the imaginary instruments of his projected regeneration of the human species. As he intended to institute a perfect republic, he invested himself with absolute sovreignty over these mystical dispensers of liberty. He slept with Horrid Mysteries under his pillow, and dreamed of venerable eleutherarchs and ghastly confederates holding midnight conventions in subterranean caves. . . . Scythrop proceded to meditate on the practicability of reviving a confederation of regenerators. To get a clear view of his own ideas, and to feel the pulse of the wisdom and genius of the age, he wrote and published a treatise, in which his meanings were carefully wrapped up in the monk's hood of transcendental technology, but filled with hints of matter deep and dangerous, which he thought would set the whole nation in a ferment; and he awaited the result in awful expectation, as a miner who has fired a train awaits the explosion of a rock.[18]

The result, says Peacock, was not a detonation but merely a letter from his bookseller, informing him that only seven copies had been sold, and concluding with a polite request 'for the balance'. Scythrop did not despair, but 'foresaw that a great leader of human regeneration would be involved in fearful dilemmas, and determined, for the benefit of mankind in general, to adopt all possible precautions for the preservation of himself'. He smuggled a dumb carpenter into Nightmare Abbey to fit secret passages and sliding doors, and tutored the servants, 'even the women', to be absolutely silent. The Scythrop chapter closes with a memorable cameo. 'In his evening meditations on the terrace, under the ivy of the ruined tower, the only sounds that came to his ear were the rustling of the wind in the ivy, the plaintive voices of the feathered choristers, the owls, the occasional striking of the Abbey clock, and the monotonous dash of the sea on its low and level shore. In the mean time, he drank Madeira, and laid deep schemes for a thorough repair of the crazy fabric of human nature.'[19]

Shelley himself did not see the completed novel until June 1819, but then he wrote to Peacock and described his reactions with an unexpected gravity, for he took the essential subject of the satire seriously. 'I am delighted with Nightmare

Abbey. I think Scythrop a character admirably conceived and executed, & I know not how to praise sufficiently the lightness chastity & strength of the language of the whole. . . . I suppose the moral is contained in what Falstaff says "For Gods sake talk like a man of this world" and yet looking deeper into it, is not the misdirected enthusiasm of Scythrop what J[esus] C[hrist] calls the salt of the earth?'[20] But he made no reference to Scythrop's shuttlecock love between the raven-haired intellectual Stella, and the fair-haired musical Marionetta, a cunning amalgam of Shelley's torn affections between Harriet, Mary and Claire.[21] Mary, in her 'Note on the Poems of 1817', agreed that Peacock had 'seized on some points of his character and some habits of his life when he painted Scythrop'; but she made it clear that Shelley was 'not addicted to port or madeira'.

While Shelley's boating expeditions continued to take Claire, the Hunts and the children to Hampden, Virginia Water and Egham, Mary tended to remain behind. She was expecting another child, and liked to stay quietly at Albion House, making jellies for the children, and reading Brockden Brown's horror novels. On 4 August they celebrated Shelley's twenty-fifth birthday, and on the 30th, Mary's twentieth.

First Murray, and then Charles Ollier turned down *Frankenstein*, but at the end of the month Shelley's persistence as Mary's agent was rewarded by a contract with Lackington, Allen and Co., and the novel was hurried off to the printers. Lackington's was a good catch, for their circulating library and bookshop, with its splendid circular display tables and book galleries, was one of the most popular in London. Shelley insisted on a tight and highly commercial contract, writing to Lackington: 'You should take the risk of printing and advertising etc. entirely on yourselves and, after full deduction being made from the profits of the work to cover these expenses, that the clear produce, both of the first edition and of every succeeding edition should be divided between you and the author.'[22] Shelley was never able to insist on a similar contract for any of his own works.

With the coming of September, the golden chain of summer days began to dissolve, and the atmosphere seemed to grow chilly in Albion House. Mary noted that the lowered declination of the sun prevented it from reaching over the roof into the garden, and the rooms seemed to become perpetually dark and damp. Later she discovered that all Shelley's books in the library had gathered a sinister blue mould.[23] Her child was born on the 2nd, and though both mother and baby remained well, Mary was constantly troubled by inability to provide sufficient milk. She knew that Shelley would not consider a wet-nurse, and the child had constant upsets from attempts to feed it cow's milk. Shelley struggled on to finish his poem, but he could no longer spend the day comfortably outside, and he began to feel ill again, and now his chest especially troubled him.

His new daughter did not move him as the birth of little William had done. He wrote archly to Byron: 'Since I wrote to you last, Mary has presented me with a little girl. We call it Clara. Little Alba and William, who are fast friends, and amuse themselves with talking a most unintelligible language together, are dreadfully puzzled by the stranger, whom they consider very stupid for not coming to play with them on the floor.'[24] With a great effort, Shelley pushed *Laon and Cythna* to a conclusion on 20 September. He wrote a dedication 'To Mary' –

> So now my summer task is ended, Mary,
>   And I return to thee, mine own heart's home;
> As to his Queen some victor Knight of Faëry,
>   Earning bright spoils for her enchanted dome . . . .[25]

But far from returning to his 'heart's home', Shelley immediately left for London, arriving with Claire at Hunt's on the evening of the 23rd. Suddenly he was immersed in business: correcting the proofs of *Frankenstein*, negotiating the publication of his poem with Ollier, and dealing with debts which had been growing ominously at Longdill's office. Once again he put himself under the treatment of Sir William Lawrence. His health was in a 'miserable state' and he gloomily told Mary that he was consumptive and sometimes feared that he would die during the coming winter. His separation from Mary was to last, apart from fleeting weekend visits, for almost the whole of the rest of September and October, and was to worry her into a state of irritation and nervous anxiety reminiscent of the separation of 1815.

Shelley's sudden plunge into the gloom and despondency of September was caused by the sense of circumstances closing around him once more. There were his debts; the responsibility of Alba and Mary's complaints about Claire which had increased since the birth of her own little Clara; and the collapse of his health in the autumnal damps of Albion House. A mood of martyrdom and self-sacrifice assailed him, and writing to Byron from Hunt's new address in Paddington, he described the future of *Laon and Cythna* with lurid relish. 'I have been engaged this summer, heart and soul, in one pursuit. I have completed a poem . . . in the style and for the same object as "Queen Mab", but interwoven with a story of human passion. . . . It *is* to be *published* – for I am not of your opinion as to religion, etc, and for this simple reason, that I am careless of the consequences as they regard myself. I only feel persecution bitterly, because I bitterly lament the depravity and mistake of those who persecute. As to me, I can but die; I can but be torn to pieces, or devoted to infamy most undeserved. . . .'[26]

Shelley now decided that the house at Marlow could never be their permanent home. This was to be a momentous decision. By the end of September, he was already advertising the lease for sale, and asking Mary to decide between wintering in Italy or somewhere on the Kent coast. Mary was aware that details of their financial difficulties were being kept from her, and when Claire returned from London without Shelley, Mary cross-questioned her. Afterwards she wrote anxiously to Shelley, 'whether it might be that [Claire] was in a croaking humour (in ill spirits she certainly was) or whether she represented things as they really were I know not but certainly affairs did not seem to wear a very good face – She talks of Harriet's debts to a large amount & something about Longdill's having undertaken for them so that they must be payed – She mentioned also that you were entering into a post-obit transaction. . . .'[27]

In other letters to Shelley she urged him in turn to come to a decision about Italy, and in the meantime badgered him with domestic requests, telling him to get his hair cut, and demanding his immediate return to Marlow. Mary in her domestic mood is well illustrated by her instructions concerning a hat for William. 'I wish Willy to be my companion in my future walks – to further which plan will you send down if possible by Monday's coach (and if you go to Longdill's it will be very possible – for you can buy it at the corner of Southampton buildings and send it to the coach at the Old Bailey) a seal skin fur hat for him it must be a fashionable round shape *for a boy* mention particularly and have a narrow gold riband round it, that it may be taken in if too large; it must measure [blank] round & let it rather be too large than too small – but exactly the thing would be best – He cannot walk with me until it comes. . . .' Several paragraphs later, she cancels the whole request, 'as it may not fit him or please me'.[28] This nagging, carping side of Mary's personality gradually emerged through her craving for complete emotional security, which Shelley's temperament could never satisfy.

From trivial complaints about Peacock 'drinking his bottle', and Claire's moods, and her own depressions with the children she turned increasingly to his own lack of efficiency and decision. On 2 October her letter began, 'My dear Love, Your letter received per parcel tonight was very unsatisfactory. You decide nothing and tell me *nothing*. – You say – "the Chancery expenses must be paid" but you do not say whether our going to Italy would obviate this necessity.'[29]

Shelley wrote back four days later, with a variety of explanations. 'We must go to Italy, on every ground. This weather does me great mischief. I nurse myself, & these kind people [the Hunts] nurse me with great care. I think of you my own beloved & study the minutest things relative to my health. I suffer today under a violent bowel complaint attended with pain in the side which I daresay will relieve me but which prevents me today from going out at all. I have thus put off engagements with Longdill & Godwin which must be done tomorrow. I have borrowed £250 from Horace Smith which is now at my bankers.'[30] Mary answered this briskly by return of post, remarking that she could not understand his complaints about the weather since she had 'seldom known any more pleasant'. She was not impressed by Horace Smith's timely loan. 'Your account of our expenses is by very much too favourable. You say that you have only borrowed £250 – our debts at Marlow are greater than you are aware of besides living in the mean time and articles of dress that I must buy – Now we cannot hope to sell the house for £1200 – And to think of going abroad with only about £200 would be madness. . . .' She ended her note affectionately, but to the point. 'Adieu my own love – Get rid of that nasty side ache – You will tell me the Italian sun will be the best physician – be it so – but money money. . . .'[31]

To these frictions, as the month dragged on, were added Godwin's request for cash in London, and a swelling number of local creditors who started calling at Albion House demanding bills rendered. The news of the house sale had quickly got about. Some time about 15 October Shelley was actually arrested for debt and detained for two days on the instance of his father and his old ally of the Irish days, Captain Pilfold. Sir Timothy's solicitor Whitton estimated Shelley's debts in this affair alone at some £1,500.[32]

But despite everything, Shelley pushed firmly ahead with his own literary projects. His main effort was still concentrated on finding *Laon and Cythna* a publisher. But he also found time to draft the beginning of an eclogue, to be called *Rosalind and Helen*, based on Mary's relationship with her old Scottish schoolfriend Isabel Baxter. The poem is weak, and Shelley only forced himself to finish it at Mary's request the following year, at the Bagni di Lucca. It is based on two stories told respectively by two sisters, Rosalind and Helen, which combine many of the private and public issues facing Shelley during 1817, and cover sketchily much of the material handled with infinitely greater skill and perception in *Laon and Cythna*. Rosalind's story concerns an incestuous love-match, and a tyrannical father; Helen's story narrates the tribulations of a family life destroyed by her husband Lionel's political persecution. The emphasis on exile is also notable, and the two sisters meet each other at the beginning of the poem on the banks of Lake Como, where Shelley was to search for a house in spring 1818.

Lionel, like Laon, reflects Shelley's own ambitions for radical political leadership, and his own state of spiritual exile. Crude as the workmanship is, frequently descending to a kind of fumbling sub-Skeltonic doggerel, it shows something of the way in which Shelley now saw his role as a writer. Lionel attacked the conventions and superstitions of 'the priests' in verses 'wild and queer':

> So this grew a proverb: 'Don't get old
> Till Lionel's "Banquet in Hell" you hear,
> And then you will laugh yourself young again.'
> So the priests hated him, and he
> Repaid their hate with cheerful glee.

Frustrated by the collapse of political hopes, Lionel became

> A spirit of unresting flame,
> Which goaded him in his distress
> Over the world's vast wilderness.[33]

The single important thing about this minor work, was the creative pattern it established in Shelley's mind of repeating a theme from one of the public 'visionary' poems, in a second, more intimate, 'domestic' poem. Thus *Laon and Cythna* and *Rosalind and Helen* are not unlike parallel texts. Many of his Italian poems were later to be paired in this way.

Of *Laon and Cythna* itself Shelley wrote a clear descriptive letter to Longmans, enclosing the first four sheets – 64 pages – which he had had set up in print, in the hope of catching the attention of Longmans' chief reader, Thomaş Moore. 'The scene is supposed to be laid in Constantinople & modern Greece, but . . . it is in fact a tale illustrative of such a Revolution as might be supposed to take place in an European nation. . . . It is a Revolution of this kind, that is, the *beau ideal* as it were of the French Revolution, but produced by the influence of individual genius, and out of general knowledge. The authors of it are supposed to be my hero & heroine whose names appear in the title.'[34]

Shelley was careful to make no reference to the incestuous relationship between Laon and Cythna; but in a prose preface he wrote that the introduction of the theme of incest 'was intended to startle the reader from the trance of ordinary life. It was my object to break through the crust of those outworn opinions on which established institutions depend.'[35] It was a straight case of *épater les bourgeois*, and illustrated well what was implied by Lionel who 'repaid their hate with cheerful glee'.

In the last week of October, Shelley came down to spend several days at Albion House, bringing with him Walter Coulson, as a weekend guest. Coulson was a protégé of Jeremy Bentham's, and a journalist of the liberal-intellectual wing. His presence, with his enthusiastic and encyclopaedic talk, eased the atmosphere, and after his return to London Shelley spent a quiet final week with Mary and Claire and the children, 'writing, reading and walking' and dictating to Mary a rough translation of a piece of Spinoza.[36]

The preface to *Laon and Cythna*, was now completed; although it is only 3,000 words long, it touches many essential matters, and it shows that behind the sustained and perhaps overdrawn creative effort of the summer, an intense critical process had been at work. It represents the first emergence of his mature thought as a writer, and contains the seed of nearly all the literary arguments he was later to develop in his separate essays.

His description of his own education as a poet, while being a remarkable statement of the Romantic position, is also interesting for its emphasis on physical experience and travel.

There is an education peculiarly fitted for a Poet, without which genius and sensibility can hardly fill the circle of their capacities. . . . The circumstances of my accidental education have been favourable to this ambition. I have been familiar from boyhood with mountains and lakes and the sea, and the solitude of forests: Danger, which sports upon the brink of precipices, has been my playmate. I have trodden the glaciers of the Alps, and lived under the eye of Mont Blanc. I have been a wanderer among distant fields. I have sailed down mighty rivers, and seen the sun rise and set, and the stars come forth, whilst I have sailed night and day down a rapid stream among mountains. I have seen populous cities, and have watched the passions which rise and spread, and sink and change, amongst assembled multitudes of men. I have seen the theatre of the more visible ravages of tyranny and war; cities and villages reduced to scattered groups of black and roofless houses, and the naked inhabitants sitting famished upon their desolate thresholds. I have conversed with living men of genius. The poetry of ancient Greece and Rome, and modern Italy, and our own country, has been to me, like external nature, a passion and an enjoyment. Such are the sources from which the materials for the imagery of my Poem have been drawn. I have considered Poetry in its most comprehensive sense; and have read the Poets and the Historians and the Metaphysicians whose writings have been accessible to me, and have looked upon the beautiful and majestic scenery of the earth, as common sources of those elements which it is the province of the Poet to embody and combine. . . . How far I shall be found to possess that more essential attribute of Poetry, the power of awakening in others sensations like those which animate my own bosom, is that which, to speak sincerely, I know not. . . .[37]

Most striking about this affirmation is its sweeping, measured, prose reminiscent of the authorised version of the Bible; and its quality of dauntless dignity containing neither self-aggrandisement or self-pity. It has an almost heroic note. The quality of confidence, and the old missionary note of *Queen*

Mab,* is repeated and amplified, in Shelley's declaration of intent, about writing 'in the cause of liberal and comprehensive morality'.

> I have made no attempt to recommend the motives which I would substitute for those at present governing mankind, by methodical and systematic argument. I would only awaken the feelings, so that the reader should see the beauty of true virtue, and be incited to those inquiries which have led to my moral and political creed, and that of some of the sublimest intellects in the world. The Poem therefore (with the exception of the first canto, which is purely introductory) is narrative, not didactic. It is a succession of pictures illustrating the growth and progress of individual mind aspiring after excellence, and devoted to the love of mankind. . . .[38]

From 1817 onwards Shelley relied more frequently than before on prose to advance the 'methodical and systematic argument' for altering the present government of mankind.

Finally, in his preface, Shelley tried to make some overall assessment of the social, political and spiritual climate in which he now wrote. His assessment is essentially post-Godwinian. His analysis shows strongly the influence of discussions with Byron in 1816, and Hunt and Peacock and to some extent Hazlitt in 1817. It is not only historically mature, but we can now see that it was also extremely perceptive.

> . . . those who now live have survived an age of despair.
>
> The French Revolution may be considered as one of those manifestations of a general state of feeling among civilised mankind produced by a defect of correspondence between the knowledge existing in society and the improvement or gradual abolition of political institutions. The year 1788 may be assumed as the epoch of one of the most important crises produced by this feeling. . . . The revulsion occasioned by the atrocities of the demagogues, and the re-establishment of successive tyrannies in France, was terrible, and felt in the remotest corner of the civilised world. Could they listen to the plea of reason who had groaned under the calamities of a social state according to the provisions of which one man riots in luxury whilst another famishes for want of bread? Can he who the day before was a trampled slave suddenly become liberal-minded, forbearing, and independent? This is the consequence

---

* On 22 November 1817, Shelley sent a copy of *Queen Mab* to a certain Mr Wailer, writing in the flyleaf: 'It is the Author's boast . . . that after 6 years of added experience and reflection, the doctrines of equality and liberty and disinterestedness, and entire unbelief in religion of any sort to which this Poem is devoted have gained rather than lost that beauty and that grandeur which first determined him to devote his life to the investigation and inculcation of them. – P B S.' Bod. MS Shelley Adds. c. 4, F303.

of the habits of a state of society to be produced by resolute perseverance and indefatigable hope, and long-suffering and long-believing courage, and the systematic efforts of generations of men of intellect and virtue.

Such is the lesson which experience teaches us now. But, on the first reverses of hope in the progress of French liberty, the sanguine eagerness for good overleaped the solution of these questions, and for a time extinguished itself in the unexpectedness of their result. Thus, many of the most ardent and tender-hearted of the worshippers of public good have been morally ruined by what a partial glimpse of the events they deplored appeared to show as the melan-choly desolation of all their cherished hopes. Hence gloom and misanthropy have become the characteristics of an age in which we live, the solace of a disappointment that unconsciously finds relief only in the wilful exaggeration of its own despair. This influence has tainted the literature of the age with the hopelessness of the minds from which it flows. Metaphysics, and enquiries into moral and political science, have become little else than vain attempts to revive exploded superstitions, or sophisms like those of Mr Malthus, calculated to lull the oppressors of mankind into a security of everlasting triumph. Our works of fiction and poetry have been overshadowed by the same infectious gloom. But mankind appear to me to be emerging from their trance. I am aware, methinks, of a slow, gradual, silent change. In that belief I have composed the following Poem.[39]

On 2 November Shelley returned alone to London, and on the 8th he took temporary lodgings for a month at 19 Mabledon Place, off the Euston Road, where Mary joined him, leaving the children with Claire at Marlow. Mary and Shelley were now both busy in the task of supervising their respective works for publication. For the fortnight that Mary remained much time was spent dining and taking tea with the publishers Ollier and Hookham; and also with the Godwins, the Hunts and the Baxters. There was one visit to Mabledon Place on the 18th from Keats and Walter Coulson. After the 19th, the guard changed, and Mary returned to Marlow while Claire came up to London; she and Shelley dined together at the Godwins on the 24th.

Whatever Shelley wrote to Mary or Byron of his sickness and depression, he was deeply excited about the forthcoming publication of his poem, which Ollier now agreed should appear around Christmas time. The domineering self-confident attitudes in company that he had manifested at Hunt's in the spring, were again in evidence. When Henry Crabb Robinson dined at Godwin's on 6 November, he found Shelley very much at home. 'I went to Godwin's,' he recorded in his diary that evening, 'Mr Shelley was there. I had never seen him before. His youth, and a resemblance to Southey, particularly in his voice, raised a pleasing impression, which was not altogether destroyed by his conversation, though it was vehement, and arrogant, and intolerant. He was very abusive towards Southey, who he spoke of as having sold himself to the Court. And this he maintained with the usual party slang. . . . Shelley spoke of Wordsworth with less bitterness, but with an insinuation of his insincerity, etc.'[40]

As the author of *Laon and Cythna*, Shelley had committed himself to a public political statement, and 'party slang' and radical politics occupied much of his talk and thought throughout November, and was the occasion of his second Hermit of Marlow pamphlet. This was the best political pamphlet he ever wrote.

The idea was triggered off in an unexpected way. At the Crabb Robinson dinner Shelley heard that Princess Charlotte, the much-loved only daughter of the much-hated Prince Regent, had died suddenly in childbirth that morning. Public mourning was officially declared. This event ironically coincided with the trial of the Pentridge Revolution leaders, and their conviction and execution at Derby on 8 November.

Shelley had been following the trial closely in the *Examiner* and other more radical journals. The case was notorious both in liberal and working-class circles. The jury had been picked, the prosecution were assigned ten lawyers and the defence only two, and all the prisoners were held for weeks previously on a bread and water diet with no visitors permitted. Most disturbing of all, though the man's name appears nowhere in the transcripts of the trial, it was widely known that one of the ring-leaders and anchor-men of the insurrection was the government spy Oliver.[41] Jeremiah Brandreth was convicted of high treason, and with two other insurrectionists, Isaac Ludlam and William Turner, they were publicly hanged and quartered on 8 November. Contrary to popular belief, these men were not 'half-starved, illiterate, and unemployed' labourers.[42] Brandreth was a stern, self-educated Baptist, who had probably served as a Luddite captain in 1812. Turner was a 47-year-old stonemason, a man of steady and independent character who had served during the war in Egypt. Ludlam was a Methodist preacher, and part-owner of a local stone quarry. They were all examples of the new wave of self-educated and politically conscious working class from whom Cobbett, Carlile and Samuel Bamford had also sprung.*

. * E.P.Thompson's summary is definitive. 'We may see the Pentridge rising as one of the first attempts in history to mount a wholly proletarian insurrection, without any middle-class support. The objectives of this revolutionary movement cannot perhaps be better characterized than in the words of the Belper Street song – "The Levelution is begun".... And yet the longer-term influence of the Oliver affair was to strengthen the constitutionalist, as opposed to the revolutionary, wing of the reform movement.. . . For three years the crucial political contests centered upon the defence of civil liberties, and the rights of the Press, where the middle class was itself most sensitive. . . . the failure of Pentridge emphasized the extreme danger of conspiracy. Only the shock of Peterloo (August 1819)

Shelley was immediately struck by the grim discordance between the official reception given to the two pieces of news; the death of the three Pentridge conspirators, and the death of Princess Charlotte. Turning the matter over in his mind, he had already begun to think in terms of a pamphlet, when on the evening of the 11th he and Mary walked along the Marylebone fields from Mabledon Place to take tea with Hunt in Lisson Grove. Godwin and Charles Ollier also dropped in on Hunt, and in the political discussion that followed Shelley's plan was well received. He began his pamphlet, *An Address to the People on the Death of Princess Charlotte* the same evening and writing with intense concentration continued it the following day. By midday on the 12th he had most of it finished, and hurried off the manuscript to Ollier. 'I enclose you what I have written of a pamphlet on the subject of our conversation the other evening. I wish it to be sent to press without an hours delay . . . the printer can go on with this & send me a proof & the rest of the manuscript shall be sent before evening.' Shelley thought the subject 'tho treated boldly is treated delicately', and hoped Ollier would have no objections.[43] He wrote on during the afternoon, and walked over with Mary and the completed manuscript as he had promised in the evening. He had given it a subtitle, a famous revolutionary jibe from Tom Paine: *We Pity the Plumage, but Forget the Dying Bird*. Paine had been attacking Burke's sentimental eulogy on the execution of Marie Antoinette in 1793, when the Revolution was in danger. Shelley was attacking the attention given to the Princess's death, when political liberty itself was dying.

On the Death of Princess Charlotte is the last political pamphlet Shelley ever wrote in England. It bears the distinctive mark of a single, rapid, informed and passionate reaction to a public issue of moment. It goes straight to its mark, without philosophical extenuations, and is brilliantly readable. Shelley's real target was, as before, the urgent need for sweeping political reform; but now he added to this the need for economic reform as well. Like the preface to *Laon and Cythna*, it shows for the first time Shelley's attitudes reaching their mature formulation. It is outstanding in his political writing for its flexibility and directness of style. Shelley used the lurid data of the popular press with immense effect. Thus he makes his main, and of course seditious, political point:

> On the 7th November, Brandreth, Turner and Ludlam ascended the scaffold. We feel for Brandreth the less, because it seems he killed a man. But recollect who instigated him to the proceedings which led to murder. On the

threw a part of the movement back into revolutionary courses; and the Cato Street Conspiracy (February 1820) served to reinforce the lesson of Oliver and Pentridge. From 1817 until Chartist times, the central working-class tradition was that which exploited every means of agitation and protest short of active insurrectionary preparation.' *The Making of the English Working Class*, 1968 pp. 733–5.

word of a dying man, Brandreth tells us, that 'OLIVER brought him to this' – that 'but for OLIVER, he would not have been there.' See, too, Ludlam and Turner, with their sons and brothers and sisters, how they kneel together in a dreadful agony of prayer. Hell is before their eyes, and they shudder and feel sick with fear lest some unrepented or some wilful sin should seal their doom in everlasting fire. With that dreadful penalty before their eyes – with that tremendous sanction for the truth of all he spoke, Turner exclaimed loudly and distinctly *while the executioner was putting the rope round his neck*, 'THIS IS ALL OLIVER AND THE GOVERNMENT'.[44]

Shelley's indictment of the Liverpool ministry's role in the whole affair is no less forthright and trenchant. It is in many ways surprising that Ollier was prepared to let the pamphlet go out under his imprint unaltered at such a time. The risk of a prosecution for seditious libel must have been very considerable.

The Government had a desperate game to play. In the manufacturing districts of England discontent and disaffection had prevailed for many years; this was the consequence of that system of double aristocracy produced by the causes before mentioned. The manufacturers, the helots of luxury, are left by this system famished, without affections, without health, without leisure or opportunity. . . . Here was a ready field for any adventurer who should wish for whatever purpose to incite a few ignorant men to acts of illegal outrage. So soon as it was plainly seen that the demands of the people for a free representation must be conceded, if some intimidation and prejudice were not conjured up, a conspiracy of the most horrible atrocity was laid in train. It is impossible to know how far the higher members of the government are involved in the guilt of their infernal agents. . . . But thus much is known that so soon as the whole nation lifted up its voice for parliamentary reform, spies were sent forth. . . . It was their business to find victims, no matter whether right or wrong. It was their business to produce upon the public an impression that, if any attempt to attain national freedom, or to diminish the burdens of debt and taxation under which we groan, were successful the starving multitude would rush in and confound all orders and distinctions, and institutions and laws in common ruin.[45]

This was clear, forceful argument and it showed once again the benefit of Shelley's long summer of sustained composition.

The pamphlet also contains effective though simplified passages of economic analysis, in which Shelley locates the root cause of political oppression in the economic exploitation of labourers and factory hands ('manufacturers'). The prime factors in this exploitation he suggests were the national debt which had grown phenomenally in the previous twenty-five years; and the 'second aristocracy' of capitalists, businessmen and bureaucrats. These were men who had taken advantage of the growing system of stocks and loans, 'petty piddling slaves who have gained a right to the title of public creditors, either by gambling in the funds, or by subservience to government, or some other villainous trade'. This is one of the earliest pieces of recognizably 'pre-Marxist' analysis to be found in English. Shelley drew the political lesson that democratic revolution was required in bold and vivid terms:

> The effect of this system is that the day-laborer gains no more now by working sixteen hours a day than he gained before by working eight. I put the thing in its simplest and most intelligible shape. The laborer, he that tills the ground and manufactures cloth, is the man who has to provide out of what he would bring home to his wife and children, for the luxuries and comforts of those whose claims are represented by an annuity of forty-four millions a year levied upon the English nation . . . the public voice loudly demanded a free representation of the people. It began to be felt that no other constituted body of men could meet the difficulties which impend.[46]

His steady move away from the conspiratorial Illuminist beliefs, towards a more open and aggressive confidence in democratic and extra-Parliamentary mass movements perfectly reflects the movement of the times.

Shelley brought together his two central themes of the death of Princess Charlotte, and the death of the Derbyshire men tricked in their struggle for political liberty, in a masterly closing elegy. The passage is especially important in that for the first time Shelley specifically addresses himself to a mass and working-class audience, 'People of England'. Its processional imagery, and the phoenix trope of the 'glorious Phantom' Liberty, were to re-occur in the great political ballads and poems of 1819.

> Mourn then, People of England. Clothe yourselves in solemn black. Let the bells be tolled. Think of mortality and change. Shroud yourselves in solitude and the gloom of sacred sorrow. Spare no symbol of universal grief. Weep – mourn – lament. Fill the great City – fill the boundless fields with lamentation and the echo of groans. A beautiful Princess is dead: she who should have been the Queen of her beloved nation and whose posterity should have ruled it forever. . . . She was amiable and would have become wise, but she was young, and in the flower of youth the despoiler came. LIBERTY is dead.

> If One has died who was like her that should have ruled over this land, like Liberty, young, innocent, and lovely, know that the power through which that one perished was God, and that it was a private grief. But *man* has murdered Liberty. . . . Let us follow the corpse of British Liberty slowly and

reverentially to its tomb; and if some glorious Phantom should appear and make its throne of broken swords and sceptres and royal crowns trampled in the dust, let us say that the Spirit of Liberty has arisen from its grave and left all that was gross and mortal there, and kneel down and worship it as our Queen.[47]

Shelley's pamphlet, printed in sixteen quarto pages, appeared on Saturday morning, 15 November, and was eagerly read by Mary, as she records in her journal, and by members of the Hunt circle. But there is a mystery about its wider distribution. Unlike the *Proposals*, there is no record of a mailing list, or of how many copies were run off, and no copy of the original edition remains extant. The modern text is from a 'facsimile reprint' published in the 1840s. It seems likely that Ollier did finally baulk at having a large edition printed for extensive circulation. Unlike *Queen Mab*, the pamphlet did not have the good but dangerous fortune of falling into the hands of Richard Carlile or other members of the working-class radical press.*

Back at Marlow, Mary wrote to her old friend Isabel Baxter encouraging her to visit Shelley and Claire, and they subsequently met at Godwin's on 23 November. Isabel's father, William Baxter, who admired Shelley, was there; and also Isabel's husband, David Booth, an elderly Scottish brewer with strong Presbyterian views, who did not. The evening provided the opportunity for another piece of direct action. Shelley agreed with Baxter that he should purchase on his behalf twenty thick ex-army blankets, together with material for sheets, and send them down to Marlow in time for Shelley to present them as Christmas presents to the poor of the district. They were embroidered with his name, presumably so that they could not be sold off: 'PBS Esq., Marlow, Bucks'. The bill, which he did honour, came to £17 2s. 9d.[48] Baxter highly approved of this apparently Christian act, but later he was advised by David Booth that he should not allow his family to take up socially with the Shelleys at Marlow. Baxter wrote tactfully to Shelley: '[Your] independence of fortune, too, has given you a freedom of thought and action entirely inconsistent with the customs, manners, and prejudices of European society with which I have been at pains to imbue their minds and which I wish not to see eradicated.'[49]

Shelley instantly sensed a social rebuff and wrote back a touchy letter: 'Though I have not a spark of pride or resentment in this matter, I disdain to say a word that should tend to *persuade* you to change your decision.'[50]

* The 'fac-simile reprint' was published by Thomas Rodd, who stated that 'The author printed only twenty copies of this Address'. There is no way of checking this, but certainly the strong political views Shelley expressed in this pamphlet, as with the *Philosophical View of Reform*, were generally unavailable to his contemporaries, and for many years after his death. See T.J. Wise, *A Shelley Library*, 1924.

The connection between the Baxters and the Shelleys was broken, and Shelley thought gloomily of how relentlessly he was prevented from forming social connections outside the small Godwinian circle of writers and Hunt's set of liberals.

Shelley returned to Marlow with Claire at the end of November to prepare for Christmas. He wrote to Ollier demanding a publication date as soon as possible in December, and the immediate advertisement of *Laon and Cythna* in the public papers. The edition he knew was already completed by the printers, and merely needed binding and distribution. 'I wish a parcel of *twelve* to be sent to me as soon as you can get them into boards. If you will send me an account of the expense of the advertisements I will transmit you the money the moment they and it appear –'[51]

Without mentioning *Laon and Cythna*, he pressed an invitation for Hogg to come down and stay at Marlow: 'the weather is delightful and so unseasonably fine that yellow and blue flowers are blooming in the hedges, and the primroses are blowing in the garden as if it were spring: a few more days may cover them all with snow' [52] Hogg stayed over the whole Christmas break, but based himself at Peacock's in deference to Mary's coolness. Mary's own book was moving smoothly towards publication at Lackington's who proposed to produce it in January of the New Year. On 3 December Shelley sent them her dedication: it was not to himself. 'To William Godwin, author of *Political Justice*, *Caleb Williams* etc, These volumes are respectfully inscribed by the author.' They distributed the Christmas blankets in the village, and prepared for festivities. Shelley began to feel ill again.

Only a fortnight before Christmas, Charles Ollier suddenly became nervous about *Laon and Cythna*. Yet he was a bit late: Shelley was already urging more advertisements in *The Times* and the *Morning Chronicle*; Godwin, the Hunts and the Marlow circle were all reading it, and some bound copies had reached the booksellers. One copy eventually reached the *Quarterly Review*. But the printer McMillan had begun to make doubtful noises to Ollier. At first Shelley tried to bluster it out. 'That McMillan is an obstinate old dog as troublesome as he is impudent. 'Tis a mercy as the old women say that I got him through the poem at all – Let him print the errata, & say at top if he likes, that it was all the Author's fault, & that he is as immaculate as the Lamb of God.'[53]

Then he busied himself with an impassioned defence of his own motives for Godwin's benefit. 'The Poem was produced by a series of thoughts which filled my mind with an unbounded and sustained enthusiasm. I felt the precariousness of my life, & I engaged in this task resolved to leave some record of myself. Much of what the volume contains was written with the same feeling, as real, though not so prophetic, as the communications of a dying man. . . .' Godwin had criticized the poem in London, and Shelley wished to outflank such criticism. What he wanted most of all was to impress Godwin with his unassailable sincerity. 'I felt that it was in many respects a genuine picture of my own mind. I felt that the sentiments were true, not assumed. And in this I have long believed that my power consists: in sympathy & that part of imagination which relates to sentiment & contemplation. . . .'

Shelley felt that he had grasped and understood something fundamental about his own writing gift. He continued, 'I am formed, – if for anything not in common with the herd of mankind – to apprehend remote and minute distinctions of feeling whether relative to external nature, or the living beings which surround us, & to communicate the conceptions which result from considering either the moral or the material universe as a whole.' But Godwin was not over-impressed: he told Shelley that his review of *Mandeville*, Godwin's new novel, was a better specimen of his powers than the poem. Shelley was appalled that he could discount the 'agony & bloody sweat of intellectual travail' which had produced the poem for a mere scrap of journalism.[54]

On the 11th, Ollier wrote to inform Shelley that he was withdrawing the poem from sale, on the pretext that an old customer had walked out of his shop in disgust. He could not consider publishing it in its present form. He had reasons to fear a government prosecution. Shelley responded in a long, coolly-argued, letter in which one can feel the result of thoughtful discussions with Mary, and perhaps Peacock.

As far as the disgusted customer was concerned, Shelley argued with calm logic: 'The people who visit your shop, and the wretched bigot who gave his worthless custom to some other bookseller, are not the public. The public respect talent, and a large proportion of them are already undeceived with regard to the prejudices which my book attacks. You would lose some customers, but you would gain others. Your trade would be diverted into channels more consistent with your principles.'

Shelley's further argument was that only an author, and not a publisher, could be held responsible for a book: but legally this was unsound. He added, with more relevance, that Thomas Moore had already read and commented favourably on a copy of the poem which Shelley had sent him, and that it now lay in Ollier's hands to 'blast' his reputation and literary character.[55] 'I do hope you will have too much regard to the well chosen motto of your seal to permit the murmurs of a few bigots to outweigh the serious and permanent considerations presented in this letter.' The Ollier seal was, 'In omnibus libertas'.

Ollier's reply arrived two days later. Shelley was surprised to discover that the publisher's only objections apparently lay in the specific statements of the blood relation between the two lovers, Laon and Cythna, and the implicit defence of incest in the preface. It was merely a question of a few individual lines and phrases, and Ollier did not mention politics. Shelley replied that his explanation 'certainly alters the question' and hastened to invite Ollier down to Marlow to help with the alterations on the spot. Ollier came at once, on 14 December, to find 'a friendly welcome and a warm fire' at the end of his journey, and the corrected manuscript was completed in two days, when Ollier returned with it to London.[56]

The ease with which this was accomplished is perhaps surprising. On the day of Ollier's departure, Shelley wrote defensively to Moore that *Laon and Cythna* was to be suppressed and republished shortly after Christmas as *The Revolt of Islam*. There were 'some alterations which consist in little else than the substitution of the words *friend* or *lover* for that of *brother & sister*'.[57]

Yet Shelley was being less than frank. Though sixty-three lines of the poem were corrected, only thirteen were cancelled because of the incest reference. The rest were cancelled because of their controversial references to God, Hell, Christ, republicanism and atheism. In every case Shelley had to retreat to a vague and unsatisfactory circumlocution.* Much that had been politically explicit was now weakened and obscured.

These kind of alterations must have caused Shelley considerable heart-searching. But it is clear that once Ollier had forced him to accept alterations in principle, the rest followed. 'His friends', wrote Peacock, 'finally prevailed on him to submit. Still he could not, or would not, sit down by himself to alter it, and the whole of the alterations were actually made in successive sittings of what I may call a literary committee. He contested the proposed alterations step by step. . . .'[58] When he wrote to Byron on the next day, Shelley merely told him that 'My long poem under the title of "The Revolt of Islam" is almost printed'.[59]

Horace Smith came down on Boxing Day to cheer up the now permanently damp and twilit rooms of Albion House, but he only remained for two days. Mary persuaded Shelley to go on a meat diet, but he soon gave it up. Shelley's health was bad again, and certain of his letters to Godwin suggest that he may

---

* A typical alteration came at the climax of the death-speech of one of Laon's supporters in Canto XII, stanza 30. Shelley had originally written:

'For me the world is grown too void and cold,
Since hope pursues immortal destiny
With steps thus slow – therefore shall ye behold
How Atheists and Republicans can die;
Tell to your children this!' Then suddenly
He sheathed a dagger in his heart and fell. . . .

But, bending to Ollier's wishes, the fourth line was finally reduced to the inoffensive and unremarkable

How those who love, yet fear not, dare to die.

have been relying heavily on laudanum, for the symptoms they describe are characteristic of the extreme fluctuations of mood and sensation usually associated with narcosis. If so, this suggests a state of mental exhaustion comparable to the winter of 1811 when Shelley stated explicitly that he had been taking too much opium at Keswick. 'My health has been materially worse,' he wrote to Godwin. 'My feelings at intervals are of a deadly & torpid kind, or awakened to a state of such unnatural & keen excitement that only to instance the organ of sight, I find the very blades of grass & the boughs of distant trees present themselves to me with microscopical distinctness. Towards evening I sink into a state of lethargy & inanimation, & often remain for hours on the sofa between sleep & waking a prey to the most painful irritability of thought. Such with little intermission is my condition. The hours devoted to study are selected with vigilant caution from among these periods of endurance.'[60] The thoughts which were preying upon Shelley's mind centred especially on the decision to go to Italy, which he had now put off irretrievably, until the spring. The hopes attached to his poem kept him in England; but fears that he had consumption, fears that he might again be prosecuted and lose his children by Mary, fears that Godwin was yet again preparing a massive financial demand, and fears that he would be subject more and more to social sneers both public and private; – all these weighed upon his mind.

The winter of 1817–18 had become a time of deep depression and self-doubt, which sunk many of the days of December and January in the deepest gloom. Shelley could not help lumping together the possible failure of both his poetical and political hopes. On 4 January he roused himself sufficiently to donate five guineas to a 'subscription for the permanent Welfare of Mr Hone and his family'. Hone had been prosecuted and acquitted for seditious libel three times in 1817 as part of the government's policy of active repression. He was almost penniless by the end. The Friends of the Liberty of the Press, a radical and popular group, had advertised the subscription in the radical '*Champion*'. The Hunts subscribed too.

The Revolt of Islam, with its new title leaf, and twenty-seven substituted pages, was finally released in the first days of the new year, 1818. The poem is in twelve cantos, and besides its preface, contains no notes. Canto I contains a formal allegory of the struggle between Revolution and Oppression, in the conflict of a serpent and an eagle above a stormy sea. The serpent, which symbolizes Revolution, drops wounded into the water, and swims into the arms of a beautiful lady, who on being questioned by the Poet, explains the historical development of Liberty from Athens down to the French Revolution, in terms of the eternal struggle. In the manuscript, over the stanza in which the lady first speaks, Shelley wrote: 'Demon Lover'.[61]

Cantos II to IV comprise the mythological projection of Shelley's own persecuted youth in the person of Laon. The passage which describes his friendship with the 12-year-old Cythna, became a favourite of the early reviewers, notably *Blackwoods* and the *Quarterly*. It is a good indication of what his contemporaries valued him for; though this is ironic, for it was originally intended to describe an incestuous passion.

> She moved upon this earth a shape of brightness,
>   A power, that from its objects scarcely drew
> One impulse of her being – in her lightness
>   Most like some radiant cloud of morning dew,
>   Which wanders through the waste air's pathless blue,
> To nourish some far desert: she did seem
>   Beside me, gathering beauty as she grew,
> Like the bright shade of some immortal dream
> Which walks, when tempest sleeps, the wave of life's dark stream.[62]

Less to their taste, though more to Shelley's purpose, was the conclusion about women's freedom which Shelley drew from this friendship. He put it into Cythna's mouth:

> 'Can man be free if woman be a slave?
>   Chain one who lives, and breathes this boundless air,
> To the corruption of a closèd grave!
>   Can they whose mates are beasts, condemned to bear
>   Scorn, heavier far than toil or anguish, dare
> To trample their oppressors? in their home
>   Among their babes, thou knowest a curse would wear
> The shape of woman . . .'[63]

It is for this reason that Cythna goes to start the struggle for freedom in the city on her own, independently of Laon. She is immediately captured by a troop of the tyrant's armed men. Laon is also captured. His incarceration, madness and escape, and his nursing by the wise old hermit, is based on the familiar mythological pattern with which Shelley explained his own youthful struggles.

In Canto V, Shelley presents the taking of the city by the revolutionary army. It is led by Laon, who is wounded. He manages to plead for the life of the Tyrant. In the evening Cythna, who has also escaped and reappeared under her new revolutionary name of Laone, harangues the troops about victory, political freedom, free love and atheism. Her language contains much of the crude rhetoric of Shelley's Irish poems. But his description, part realistic and part symbolic, of the emotional effect of her words upon the audience, points forward to the mature lyric style.

> Her voice was as a mountain-stream which sweeps
>   The withered leaves of Autumn to the lake,
> And in some deep and narrow bay then sleeps
>   In the shadow of the shores; as dead leaves wake
>   Under the wave, in flowers and herbs which make
> Those green depths beautiful when skies are blue,
>   The multitude so moveless did partake
> Such living change, and kindling murmurs flew
> As o'er that speechless calm delight and wonder grew.[64]

One recognizes at once here the gathering imagery of the 'Ode to the West Wind'.

In Canto VI, the Tyrant's troops make a surprise counter-attack at dawn, burn the city and massacre the revolutionaries. This marks what Shelley saw as the almost inevitable counter-reaction of violent revolution. All Laon's supporters, including even the white-haired old hermit, are killed round him. The scenes of battle are described with violent disgust. Laon notices how in combat the faces of friend and foe are equally distorted with exhaustion and fear and hatred –

>   ... their eyes started with cracking stare,
> And impotent their tongues they lolled into the air,
>   Flaccid and foamy, like a mad dog's hanging. . . .[65]

At the last moment Laon himself is saved by Laone who appears on a giant black Tartarian horse, and sweeps him out of the butchery. As they ride into the mountains, in a characteristic image, the wind spreads and lashes her dark hair over Laon's eyes.

She then reveals, what he had already guessed, that she is in fact Cythna. In the original draft, this meant his sister. Lying together on the mossy floor of an old ruin under 'the eastern stars' they console each other for the terrible political catastrophe by making love for the first time, 'the solace of all sorrow'.

The five stanzas which follow are one of Shelley's most direct attempts to describe the physical and mental sensations of love-making. Although his poetry generally is full of images and metaphors of kissing, caressing, penetration and orgasm it is rare for him to present the actions of lovers very explicitly; but here he does so. He writes with great deliberateness and tenderness. The synonymous physical meanings of words like 'frame', 'heart', 'limb' and 'life' are obvious from the context, so that the poetry is biologically explicit. But a sense of wonder, even of amazement, is pervasive. The ruins are first illuminated by the symbolic light of a 'wandering Meteor', hung 'high in the green dome' which presages a storm.

The Meteor showed the leaves on which we sate,
    And Cythna's glowing arms, and the thick ties
Of her soft hair, which bent with gathered weight
    My neck near hers, her dark and deepening eyes,
    Which, as twin phantoms of one star that lies
O'er a dim well, move, though the star reposes,
    Swam in our mute and liquid ecstasies,
Her marble brow, and eager lips, like roses,
With their own fragrance pale, which Spring but half uncloses.

The Meteor to its far morass returned:
    The beating of our veins one interval
Made still; and then I felt the blood that burned
    Within her frame, mingle with mine, and fall
    Around my heart like fire; and over all
A mist was spread, the sickness of a deep
    And speechless swoon of joy, as might befall
Two disunited spirits when they leap
In union from this earth's obscure and fading sleep.

Was it one moment that confounded thus
    All thought, all sense, all feeling, into one
Unutterable power, which shielded us
    Even from our own cold looks, when we had gone
    Into a wide and wild oblivion
Of tumult and of tenderness? or now
    Had ages, such as make the moon and sun,
The seasons, and mankind their changes know,
Left fear and time unfelt by us alone below?

I know not. What are kisses whose fire clasps
    The failing heart in languishment, or limb
Twined within limb? or the quick dying gasps
    Of the life meeting, when the faint eyes swim
    Through tears of a wide mist boundless and dim,
In one caress? What is the strong control
    Which leads the heart that dizzy steep to climb,
Where far over the world those vapours roll,
Which blend two restless frames in one reposing soul? . . .

395

Cythna's sweet lips seemed lurid in the moon,
　　Her fairest limbs with the night wind were chill,
And her dark tresses were all loosely strewn
　　O'er her pale bosom: – all within was still,
　　And the sweet peace of joy did almost fill
The depth of her unfathomable look; –
　　And we sate calmly, though that rocky hill,
The waves contending in its caverns strook,
For they foreknew the storm, and the gray ruin shook.[66]

The psychological acuity retained in 'even from our own cold looks' in the
third stanza, and of '*almost* fill' in the last stanza, is remarkable in such a molten
passage of lyric and erotic intensity. Again, it is characteristic of the mature
Shelley.

In the next two cantos, VII and VIII, Cythna relates to Laon the story of her
own capture, incarceration, madness and final escape to the city with the help
of friendly mariners. Her hallucinations include the grim fact that she is raped,
and gives birth to a child; and she also is convinced that she has been forced to
eat bits of Laon's murdered body. On board ship, she rapidly recovers and con-
verts the mariners to Atheism. She then persuades them to release their cargo of
chained slaves and slavegirls, and encourages the crew and the slaves to put the
principles of free love into practice. They do so, and on arrival at the city
harbour, they are the first to join the revolution. Sexual liberation precedes
political liberation. In the city, Cythna triggers off the start of the insurrection by
her speeches, appealing chiefly to the women 'who my voice did waken From
their cold, careless, willing slavery'. It is at this point that Laon arrives to take
charge of the revolutionary forces. Cythna's reminiscences finish. Together,
they contemplate the possible future for the revolution and for their own lives.
Neither appears very promising. But Laon breaks into an impassioned paean of
hope and love. This ends the Canto IX, and forms one of the great climaxes of
the poem.

'The seeds are sleeping in the soil: meanwhile
　　The Tyrant peoples dungeons with his prey,
Pale victims on the guarded scaffold smile
　　Because they cannot speak; and, day by day,
　　The moon of wasting Science wanes away
Among her stars, and in that darkness vast
　　The sons of earth to their foul idols pray,
And gray Priests triumph, and like blight or blast
A shade of selfish care o'er human looks is cast.

'This is the winter of the world; – and here
    We die, even as the winds of Autumn fade,
Expiring in the frore and foggy air. –
    Behold! Spring comes, though we must pass, who made
    The promise of its birth, – even as the shade
Which from our death, as from a mountain, flings
    The future, a broad sunrise; thus arrayed
As with the plumes of overshadowing wings,
From its dark gulf of chains, Earth like an eagle springs.'[67]

The extraordinarily free and forceful command of the metric pattern and
cross-rhythms of the difficult Spenserian stanza is a great technical achievement,
while much of the gaseous abstraction has been taken out of the rhetoric. The
condemned man, like Cashman, smiling grimly on the scaffold, is a new kind of
detailing, and the seasonal imagery has gained new intellectual precision,
especially in lines like 'The moon of wasting Science wanes away'. Moreover
not only the style but the actual argument has grown austere. Shelley allows
Laon to contemplate a long and severe political 'winter', and even the destruction of his own personal hopes, without despairing of the eventual spring of
political and social liberty.

The image of 'Earth like an eagle springs' illustrates the range at which
Shelley's imagination was now working. The comparison of Earth and eagle
appears at first sight to have no *visual* component, but seems merely to be a
vague invocation of power, action, natural grandeur. Yet in fact the visual
comparison is the primary one. In earlier stanzas Shelley wrote of the 'winged
seeds', and the 'wind-winged emblem'.* These 'wings' produce the dispersion
of the seeds on the wind, and in the 'eagle' image, Shelley is imagining the whole
earth as a 'winged seed'. The round globe is the central pod, and the *earth shadow*,
cast into space by the alternative paths of solar and lunar light, becomes the wings.

> thus arrayed
> As with the plumes of overshadowing wings

The whole earth, tipped by its seasonal wings of solar and lunar shadow-casts,
becomes one enormous 'wind-winged emblem'. It thus becomes like a bird. The
earth *looks* like an eagle, and in Shelley's full image is transformed into a gigantic
space-bird of the solar system. So the pun on 'spring' gains its full force: the
global bird leaps into the sunlight; the global seed fructifies – 'springs' – as one

---

* These became a favourite symbol of Shelley's and in his later Italian notebooks he made frequent
sketches of them, often resembling sycamore seeds with a round central pod and a single or double
fibrous wing extension. See, for example, Bod. MS Shelley Adds. e. 6, p. 97 rev.

might say something winters, or indeed, summers. The two will happen simultaneously at the season of the revolution.*

Canto x describes the fate of the people in the city under the new tyranny, which Laon discovers during his clandestine ride from the mountain. They are being destroyed by plagues and famines and droughts, while their new rulers are reverting to the old superstitions of divine appeasement. The priests have ruled that the capture and execution of Laon and Cythna alone will save the remnant of the populace from divine vengeance. This canto contains some of Shelley's most powerful and most violent writing. It shows clearly the continuing strength of the gothic and grotesque inheritance which had run through his poetry and prose from the beginning. The sense of horror, physical revulsion and disgust are strongly at work. Ugliness and anger bring out a deadly accuracy in Shelley's language.

> First Want, then Plague came on the beasts; their food
>> Failed, and they drew the breath of its decay.
> Millions on millions, whom the scent of blood
>> Had lured, or who, from regions far away,
>> Had tracked the hosts in festival array,
> From their dark deserts; gaunt and wasting now,
>> Stalked like fell shades among their perilous prey;
> In their green eyes a strange disease did glow,
> They sank in hideous spasm, or pains severe and slow.
>
> The fish were poisoned in the streams; the birds
>> In the green woods perished; the insect race
> Was withered up; the scattered flocks and herds
>> Who had survived the wild beasts' hungry chase
>> Died moaning, each upon the other's face
> In helpless agony gazing; round the City
>> All night, the lean hyaenas their sad case
> Like starving infants wailed; a woeful ditty!
> And many a mother wept, pierced with unnatural pity.[68]

The macabre implication of this last image, the mothers weeping for the starving hyenas, presages the fate which is about to overrun all society. The whole system of nature breaks down. Oppression is unnatural, so it actually destroys Nature.

* In Shelley's manuscript notebook (Bod. MS Shelley Adds. e. 10), this whole passage of Canto IX from stanzas 19 to 26 is written very carefully in ink and much corrected; while the surrounding body of the canto is written in his usual racing pencil scrawl, as Trelawny later said, for all the world like a marsh overgrown with bulrushes and blotted with wild ducks.

There was no food, the corn was trampled down,
　　The flocks and herds had perished; on the shore
The dead and putrid fish were ever thrown;
　　The deeps were foodless, and the winds no more
　　Creaked with the weight of birds, but, as before
Those wingèd things sprang forth, were void of shade;
　　The vines and orchards, Autumn's golden store,
Were burned; – so that the meanest food was weighed
With gold, and Avarice died before the god it made.

There was no corn – in the wide market-place
　　All loathliest things, even human flesh, was sold;
They weighed it in small scales – and many a face
　　Was fixed in eager horror then: his gold
　　The miser brought; the tender maid, grown bold
Through hunger, bared her scorned charms in vain;
　　The mother brought her eldest-born, controlled
By instinct blind as love, but turned again
And bade her infant suck, and died in silent pain.[69]

The small, exact verbal touches are specially noticeable, such as the winds that 'creaked' with the birds. Such stories of famine, forced prostitution, even cannibalism, had been rife in the parts of France which Shelley had travelled through in 1814, utterly ravaged by the post-Revolutionary wars. Shelley now shows plague, sickness and mental derangement sweeping through the streets of the city. This is the final breakdown of both outer and inner order. There is a brief glimpse of a familiar, fiendish *doppelgänger*.

It was not hunger now, but thirst. Each well
　　Was choked with rotting corpses, and became
A cauldron of green mist made visible
　　At sunrise. Thither still the myriads came,
　　Seeking to quench the agony of the flame,
Which raged like poison through their bursting veins;
　　Naked they were from torture, without shame,
Spotted with nameless scars and lurid blains,
Childhood, and youth, and age, writhing in savage pains.

It was not thirst but madness! Many saw
　　Their own lean image everywhere, it went
A ghastlier self beside them, till the awe

> Of that dread sight to self-destruction sent
> Those shrieking victims; some, ere life was spent,
> Sought, with a horrid sympathy, to shed
> Contagion on the sound; and others rent
> Their matted hair, and cried aloud, 'We tread
> On fire! the avenging Power his hell on earth has spread!'[70]

The texture of the verse and imagery here has finally become coarse. It borders on the sensational, as Shelley pushes towards the ultimate extremities, and one feels the deliberate straining. Nevertheless, there is a power and accuracy, which presses on the surreal: the 'lean image' of the self, the contagion shed 'on the sound'. In the original manuscript Shelley's last line had read, 'We tread On fire! Almighty God his hell on earth has spread!'[71]

It is at this point in Canto X, that the historical and social part of Shelley's poem ends. The city is plunged in disease, famine, despotism and bigotry; superstitious terrors dominate the Tyrant's court, and the 'Priests' are everywhere regaining control of the minds of a cowed population. Against this are set the radical and atheist values and aspirations portrayed in the personal lives of Laon and Cythna, and affirmed especially in Cantos VI and IX.

Shelley's poem has been completely purged of any crude social optimism or 'perfectibility' in the popular sense. It is fundamentally a grim poem, and it presents hope and love as growing and flourishing only in the very teeth of despair and hatred. It is moreover a post-Godwinian poem, in that it is as much about counter-revolution as revolution. Though it accepts joyfully the principles and the historical achievements of the French Revolution, it rejects that revolution as a model for further political and social change.

In the brief penultimate Canto XI, Laon and Cythna part at their mountainous stronghold, and Laon goes down to the city, and bargains his own life in sworn exchange for Cythna's. She is allowed to go unharmed to America. In Canto XII, Laon is led chained through the streets in a manner that recalls some of the executions of 1817, while a silent crowd looks on. He is taken up to be burnt alive.

> I, Laon, led by mutes, ascend my bier
> Of fire, and look around: each distant isle
> Is dark in the bright dawn; towers far and near,
> Pierce like reposing flames the tremulous atmosphere.[72]

At the last moment, Cythna arrives on her huge Tartarian charger, scattering the crowd in terror. She reaches the execution pyre, dismounts and without a word – but smiling – climbs to Laon's side at the stake.

> Cythna sprung
> From her gigantic steed, who, like a shade
>   Chased by the winds, those vacant streets among
>   Fled tameless, as the brazen rein she flung
> Upon his neck, and kissed his moonèd brow.[73]

Laon and Cythna are burnt together on the pyre.

There remains an epilogue of twenty-five stanzas, which returns to the schematic allegorical world of Canto I. The two lovers and revolutionaries awake to find themselves sailing rapidly down an exotic river in a glittering, translucent boat 'one curved shell of hollow pearl'. It is skippered by a seraphic child, who is loosely connected with the child Cythna believed she gave birth to in prison. The child reports the death by suicide of Laon's follower, the 'Atheist and Republican' which Shelley had to suppress, who symbolizes the vast following which has been left behind among the youth, ready to forward the cause, when the time is ripe again on earth. The boat sails into a sunlit ocean towards a visionary Hesperides.

The Revolt of Islam is the longest poem Shelley ever wrote. He intended it to be a political epic of modern revolution, but its literary model, in so far as it has one, is Spenser's *Faerie Queene*. It has little in common with the historical dramas inspired directly by the French Revolution: Southey's *Wat Tyler*, or Coleridge's *Fall of Robespierre*. Politically, it shows little grasp of the revolutionary process, beyond the important dialectical principle that revolutionary anarchy breeds revolutionary dictatorship, a principle that every other reader of the *Examiner* would have subscribed to. But it shows no understanding yet of a genuinely democratic process or popular movement. Laon and Cythna are heroic leaders out of an ancient, aristocratic mould that owes more to Spenser's mythical knights than to the world of Brandreth, or Henry Hunt, or Sir Francis Burdett. The prose of Shelley's preface, and the political pamphlet, showed far more progressive thought and intellectual penetration than his poem. Only in the grotesque scenarios of Canto X, with its extraordinary expressionist picture of Nature and society collapsing under terrorism and oppression, did he find any adequate political image of his age: and it was an image of reaction, not of revolution.

The real revolution celebrated in *The Revolt of Islam* is a moral and social one. The heart of that revolution lies in the new kind of freedom and independent partnership expressed in the relationship between Laon and Cythna. They grow up together as equals; they talk, struggle for the cause, and make love, as equals. They attack religious belief and moral prudery, as equals. They are both sexually passionate, but both ethically and actively independent. Moreover it is the woman, Cythna, who actually triggers the revolution, not the man Laon. Shelley's original intention to make the relationship explicitly incestuous was deliberately meant to draw maximum attention to its revolutionary and socially iconoclastic nature. The suppression of the incest theme was therefore a major blow to the ideology of the poem. The very change of title shows Charles Ollier's wish to draw attention away from the moral to the political events. But it is this relationship which contains and celebrates all the genuinely revolutionary values in the poem: its atheism, its free love, its social equality between men and women, and its selfless dedication to the people. It is only in describing these values that Shelley's poetry achieves its briefly sustained passages of brilliance, and successfully contains the uneasy balance between mythic and realistic presentation. Otherwise the poem is a failure. But for Shelley, paradoxically, it achieved the major breakthrough into his mature work. Written at 25, *The Revolt of Islam* was the last poem of his youth. It also contains the first work of his maturity.

The poem was not to prove influential, except in the sub-genre of workers' propaganda poems written by later nineteenth-century poets such as Thomas Cooper the Chartist Rhymer, William Morris and Thomas Hood. Cooper lectured extensively on Shelley at working men's clubs and institutes during the 1840s. He included *The Revolt of Islam*, as well as Byron's *Childe Harold*, in the sacred roll call in his own political epic *The Purgatory of Suicides*. It gives some indication of Shelley's importance as a prophetic figure in the eyes of the Chartists:

Or thou, immortal Childe, with him that saw
Islam's Revolt, in rapt prophetic trance, –
Did fear of harsh reception overawe
Your fervid souls from fervid utterance
Of Freedom's fearless shout? – your scathing glance
On priestly rottennes, did ye tame down
Till priests could brook that lightning's mitigance?
Knowing your cold reward would be the frown
Of Power and Priestcraft, – ye your sternest thoughts made known.[74]*

---

* One curious and unexpected influence was on the German Expressionist writers of a century later, who wrote in the climate of social upheaval and desperation of the years 1917–22. *The Revolt of Islam* is particularly reflected in the Expressionist revolutionary *Ich-dramas* written by Ernst Toller and Georg Kaiser, where epic scenarios are combined with political and utopian imagery and intense mythological projections of the individual self. Like Shelley they relied on violent and luridly distorted images, combined with highly abstract rhetoric; but like Shelley too they found it impossible to integrate fully heroic myth and political reality. The Expressionist novelist B. Traven, author of *The Death Ship* (1926), proclaimed his main influences as Max Steiner and Shelley.[75]

Shelley counted a great deal on the public reception of his poem. One of the reasons which held him back from going to Italy was the hope that his literary reputation might at last be put on a sound footing. With the tantalizing example of Byron's sweeping sales of *Childe Harold* before him, he longed desperately to find recognition among the liberal English readership. His submission to the editorial changes by Ollier could only be truly justified by reaching a broad audience.

It is transparently clear from his letters to Ollier how concerned he was about both the advertising and reviewing of his work. On 11 January he wrote, 'keep it well *advertized*, and write for money directly the other is gone'. Four days later he sent ten pounds to Ollier 'that no delay may take place in vigorously advertising. I think I said that I wish under the new circumstances that a copy should be sent to each of the Reviews.'[76] On the 22nd he wrote yet again. 'Don't relax in the advertizing – I suppose at present that it scarcely sells at all. – If you see any reviews or notices of it in any periodical paper pray send it me, – it is part of my reward – the amusement of hearing the abuse of bigots.'[77] At the end of the month he was still urging, 'you ought to continue to advertise the poem vigourously', and he added as a casual P.S. that Ollier might send the current number of the *Quarterly*.[78] But it was all in vain. The sales were bad, and the reviews were worse, despite Hunt's most vigorous efforts for him in the pages of the *Examiner*.

First, as a trailer, Hunt ran two large extracts from the poem, each over fifty lines, in the issues of 30 November 1817 and 25 January 1818. Then in February and March he ran two parts of a massive and favourable review, including a summary of the entire plot, and extensive quotation. 'If the author's genius reminds us of any other poets, it is of two very opposite ones, Lucretius and Dante. The former he resembles in the Daedalian part of it, in the boldness of his speculations, and in his love of virtue, of external nature, and of love itself. It is his gloomier or more imaginative passages that sometimes remind us of Dante.'[79]

But Hunt's praise, though very welcome, was from the inside. His advocacy may even have hindered Shelley's cause in wider circles, for outside the liberal camp Hunt was regarded as a genteel charlatan, and writers associated with the 'Cockney School' got rough handling. Keats was also to suffer from this reaction. The *Monthly Magazine* quoted a modest couple of stanzas of *The Revolt of Islam* in its March issue, merely observing that there was 'an almost total neglect of harmonious modulation and quantity', and leaving the rest in silence. In May the *Quarterly*, turning aside from a scathing review of Hunt's 'Foliage' – which was dedicated to Shelley – lambasted Shelley without naming him. After referring to a disreputable career at Eton and Oxford, the anonymous reviewer (probably John Taylor Coleridge) continued: 'according to our understandings it is not a proof of a very affectionate heart to break that of a wife by cruelty and infidelity; and if we were told of a man who, placed on a wild rock among the clouds, yet even in that height surrounded by a loftier amphitheatre of spire-like mountains, hanging over a valley of eternal ice and snow . . . if we were told of a man who, thus witnessing the sublimest assemblage of natural objects, should retire to a cabin near and write *atheos* after his name in the album, we hope our own feelings would be pity rather than disgust; but we should think it imbecility indeed to court that man's friendship, or to celebrate his intellect or his heart as the wisest or warmest of the age'.[80] This story was retold in 1819 by both the *London Chronicle* and the *Commercial Chronicle*. In London society Shelley's name gained currency for atheism and immorality rather than for poetry. But the *Quarterly* saved its main attack on *The Revolt of Islam* for April 1819, having prepared itself with a copy of the suppressed 'incestuous' edition, *Laon and Cythna*.

The third journal which commented in 1818 was the right-wing *British Critic*, which produced a masterpiece of innuendo in preference to literary comment. 'Mr Percy Bysshe Shelley – but we will not trust ourselves with this person; Tacitus has taught us that there are some offences so flagitious in their nature, that it is necessary, for the benefit of public morals, to conceal their punishment; we leave them, therefore, to the silent vengeance which vice sooner or later *must* wreak upon itself.'[81] It is this kind of smear journalism which must be borne in mind when considering the development of Shelley's almost pathological hatred for reviewers.

The most penetrating review of *The Revolt of Islam* appeared exactly twelve months later in *Blackwood's Magazine*. Sadly this was far too late to change Shelley's feeling that the poem had done nothing but bring him hatred and notoriety. Nevertheless it shows that intelligent contemporaries could indeed appreciate his work. The review began by distinguishing sharply between Shelley's work and the 'Cockney School' poetry of Hunt and the immature Keats. It commented shrewdly on 'the silence observed by our professional critics' which it attributed to fear, in the present political climate, of praising the literary merits of poetry which professed a radical ideology: 'by giving to his genius its due praise, they might only be lending the means of currency to the opinions in whose service [Mr Shelley] has unwisely enlisted his energies'. Equally, *Blackwood's* felt the Hunt connection had frightened off other critics, fearful of 'public disgust'.

For his own part, the *Blackwood's* reviewer J. G. Lockhart,* carefully separated

---

* John Gibson Lockhart (1794–1854), critic, editor and biographer. An almost exact contemporary of Shelley's, he revived *Blackwood's Magazine* with John Wilson, with whom much of his review work has been confused, and later edited the *Quarterly Review* from 1825 to 1853. Though he was to

the poetry from the politics. 'As a philosopher, our author is weak and worth-less; – our business is with him as a poet, and, as such, he is strong, nervous, original; well entitled to take his place near to the great creative masters, whose works have shed its truest glory around the age wherein we live. As a political and infidel treatise, the Revolt of Islam is contemptible; – happily a great part of it has no necessary connexion either with politics or with infidelity.' This was disingenuous, to say the least, but it served its purpose. Lockhart continued, like Hunt, by summarizing the plot and quoting extensively, but in a way that really showed a finer and more ranging appreciation. Passages were drawn from the description of the childhood love between Laon and Cythna in Canto II; the battle and arrival of the black Tartarian horse in Canto VI, 'a power and energy altogether admirable'; and from the whole of the love-making sequence in the mountains. This last, especially, was an apt and courageous piece of reviewing. Lockhart's commentary has not really been bettered in modern criticism. 'It is in the portraying of this intense, overmastering, unfearing, unfading love, that Mr Shelley has proved himself to be a great poet. Around his lovers, moreover, in the midst of all their fervours, he has shed an air of calm gracefullness, a certain majestic monumental stillness, which realizes in them our ideas of Greeks . . . . struggling for freedom in the best spirit of their fathers.'[82]

If Shelley had read this paragraph while he was still in England, it is conceivable that he might never have chosen exile. But it was all too late. *The Revolt of Islam* seemed to be nothing but a devastating failure. His whole life appeared to have been misdirected.

During January 1818, Shelley was again attacked by ophthalmia, probably the result of his Christmas visits to the Marlow cottagers distributing the blankets. The disease was so bad that he was virtually unable to read and had to forgo the long immersions in Gibbon and *Paradise Lost* with which he had been sooth-ing himself. Mary brought in Hogg and Peacock to distract him, but in the evenings she banished everyone from the room and had long, serious talks with him which she noted briefly in her journal. After a few days, the ophthalmia eased, and they went for walks together by the grey Thames and Shelley began translating Homer's 'Hymns'.[83]

He was haunted by the problem of little Alba. How should she be sent to Italy? Who could take her if they could not? He had no peace from Mary until this could be settled. Only when the child had been presented to Byron, could it be guaranteed the kind of upbringing that it deserved; only then could Claire's ambiguous position in Shelley's household be clarified; and only then would

prove Shelley's most intelligent reviewer, his sympathies were unreliable and he was partly responsible for the notorious attack on Keats's *Endymion* in 1818. His great *Life of Scott* (1837–8) is remembered for its brilliant inaccuracies.

Mary be satisfied. 'Can you suggest a plan?' he wrote to Byron, explaining his 'constant and gradual delay'. 'Have you any friend, or person of trust, who is leaving England for Italy?'[84] Besides, he wrote, with that curiously open and paternal affection he always displayed towards Claire's child, as if he and not Byron were the real father, how 'exquisitely beautiful' she had become. 'Her temper has lost much of its *vivacité*, and has become affectionate, and mild.' Some of the only happy hours of these dreary winter weeks were spent watching Alba and his beloved William play together on the nursery floor. When William, now nearly two years old and highly mobile, was given raisins or sweetmeats he always hastened to put at least half, or even more, into little Alba's mouth, a practice that delighted his father.[85]

Yet these charming distractions served in the end only to remind Shelley of the fragility and difficulties of his situation. These little children, and both their mothers, depended so completely on him for their ultimate happiness. 'It is not health but life that I should seek in Italy,' he told Godwin earnestly '& that not for my own sake, – I feel I am capable of trampling on all such weakness – but for the sake of those to whom my life may be a source of happiness utility security & honour – & to some of whom my death might be all that is the reverse.'[86]

In this winter mood of gloom and indecision Shelley began to compose the autobiographical fragments which make up the poem 'Prince Athanase', and most of which bear on the very early part of his life. None the less Part I of the poem reflects much of his feelings at Marlow, and the attempts of his friends to get at the root of his depression. One phrase, about the 'mysterious grief' inflicted on those who 'owned no higher law Than love', conjures up the whole disastrous complication of his enmeshed relationships with Harriet, Mary and Claire. When Prince Athanase's friends speculate on his grief, and try to draw him out in conversation, he does not attempt to evade the subject. But in the end this makes his life appear only more painful, more hopeless and more enchained:

> . . . nor did he,
> Like one who labours with a human woe,
> Decline this talk: as if its theme might be
>
> Another, not himself, he to and fro
> Questioned and canvassed it with subtlest wit;
> And none but those who loved him best could know
>
> That which he knew not, how it galled and bit
> His weary mind, this converse vain and cold;
> For like an eyeless nightmare grief did sit

Upon his being; a snake which fold by fold
Pressed out the life of life, a clinging fiend
Which clenched him if he stirred with deadlier hold; -
And so his grief remained – let it remain – untold.[87]

Yet the final image is strikingly close to the poems of 1815, and this itself suggests a direct interpolation of the immediate worries of the winter 1817–18 is inappropriate. In his manuscript, Shelley added a dry and not altogether unironic comment. 'The Author was pursuing a fuller development of the ideal character of Athanase, when it struck him that in an attempt at extreme refinement and analysis, his conceptions might be betrayed into assuming a morbid character. The reader will judge whether he is a loser or gainer by the difference.'[88] It is clear that he was struggling to get a grip on himself.

On 20 January, Godwin, after lengthy and cautious inquiries about the possibilities of ophthalmia being infectious, arrived with his son William to spend two days with the Shelleys. William Godwin junior was then 15, and ignoring the rather solemn conversations of his half-sister and brother-in-law, he immediately attached himself to Claire. He spent the whole time laughing, and teasing her. Shelley was pleased to see her cheer up. In the afternoons they all went for a walk in the woods, and in the evening they played chess round the fire.[89] Godwin was once again determinedly angling for money. He had worked out a plan for Shelley to secure a large *post obit* loan, and a life insurance from William Willats, a London financier. The Godwins hastily departed from Marlow on the 22nd when Shelley's ophthalmia broke out again. But the visit was decisive in another way. It at last brought home to him that it was time to put the Italian plan into operation. He wrote letters to Hogg, and to solicitors in London, using Mary as an amanuensis. On the 25th, much to everyone's surprise and delight, it was discovered that Albion House, which had been advertised on the market for sale since the previous November, had found a definite buyer. The decision to go to Italy was now made. Four days later, Shelley, all ophthalmia forgotten, was bundling into the London coach with Claire and Peacock. For the next five weeks their life was transformed into a sudden, ceaseless, whirl of social activity; legal conferences, tea parties, operas, visits to the museum, dinners at Hunt's and Godwin's, packing, casing up of books and fitting the children out with all those clothes and conveniences of which the Italians had surely never heard.

Shelley arranged to install himself at 119 Great Russell Street, a pleasant set of rooms near the British Museum, just off the bustle and thunder of carriages down the Tottenham Court Road. It was his last address in England. He was down in Marlow again on the 6th, helping Mary with the packing, and having

407

arranged to leave the final winding up of Albion House affairs with the local agent, Mr Madocks. There were several bills outstanding, both on the house itself, and at local suppliers. Shelley undertook to settle them through Madocks before he left England. To Madocks, and to the financier Willats, he gave assurances that he was unlikely to leave England until April, 'if so soon'.[90] None of these assurances and arrangements were fully honoured. On the 7th Shelley returned to London, having taken leave of his library, his garden and his statues of Venus and Apollo for the last time. Keats's schoolmaster patron, the genial Cowden Clarke, revisiting the neighbourhood several years later was told by one of the richer residents that 'they all considered Shelley a madman'. He had not made the usual formal calls, either on arrival or departure.[91]

Mary, the children and the rest of the *ménage* arrived in the city three days later. Accompanied by Peacock they celebrated their first night in town by a grand visit to *Don Giovanni*. Peacock was paying special attentions to Claire, and on one of their shopping expeditions he seems to have told her about the Brazilian student Shelley had met many years ago in Edinburgh. At any rate, she wrote into her diary with evident relish, the proud lines of Pereira's sonnet in his praise: 'Sublimi Shelley – Cantor di verdade, Sorge Queen Mab a ristorar il mondo.'[92] The next evening when they were all over at Paddington with the Hunts, Hogg dropped in, and also Keats, and Shelley once more failed to convert the younger poet into a disciple. There was music, Hunt played the piano, and Claire sang, like Constantia. On the 14th, St Valentine's Day, Shelley took Claire once again to *Don Giovanni* at Covent Garden, and Hogg and Peacock made up the foursome. From then on almost every night of February was spent in festive mood. They went continually to hear Mozart at the opera, to see the prima ballerina Mademoiselle Milanie dance at the ballet, and to the theatre. During the day Peacock conducted them round the museums. They paid an admiring visit to the recently acquired Marbles that Lord Elgin had shipped from Greece. They saw an exhibition of painted glass, which Hunt then reviewed for the *Examiner*, while Shelley contributed a charitable critique of Peacock's newly published *Rhododaphne*. They saw casts of Canova's Castor and Melpomene in Bond Street, as a kind of aperitif before the piazzas and galleries of Italy. They went to see a lioness and her cubs in one of the travelling zoos, and they paid several visits to the Apollonicon, a monstrous barrel organ housed in St Martin's Lane. It was reputed to have cost £10,000 to build, and no less than six organists could play upon it simultaneously, with results that sent Claire Clairmont, and several thousand others, into a marvelling ecstasy.

This was perhaps the most lively, sociable and urbane month Shelley ever spent in his life. After the weeks of depression and indecision, he threw himself into it with energy and delight. The world of Bisham Woods, and Laon and Cythna, and the solitary skiff on the Thames seemed far away. Equally, he seemed to have forgotten, the decision once made, that he was about to uproot his whole life, and to go into what was in effect a forced exile. February was a charmed limbo. His old friend Hogg, bustling out regularly to join the celebrations from his legal apartments in Garden Temple, especially appreciated the change. He wrote in his oracular fashion to a friend that Shelley 'had lately parted with his house at Marlow for an advantageous price & with his opinion gratis that a wise man can only benefit his species by dwelling upon a wold in the midst of a morass or on the highest summit of a mountain'.

Shelley was no longer the aloof, critical observer of city pleasures, that he had been of old. 'He is now in town arrayed in purple and fine linen, in a blue coat & white waistcoat; for three weeks he has been a punctual attendant at the Opera; he condescends to admire Madame Fodor & Mademoiselle Millanie & to haunt Exhibitions, Concerts & Theatres.' His wine bill at Messrs Gilbey & Co. rose to the unprecedented heights of nine guineas. Meanwhile the carriage was being prepared at a coaching house in Long Acre.[93] Hogg could not avoid a few twinges of doubt, but he brushed them off as briskly as he could. 'In a short time he intends to go abroad to visit Paris & perhaps Italy; it seems unjust to leave our native country where only he can be of great utility, & such being his sentiments, his absense will not I believe be very long, but he will return to reside in the vicinity of London.'[94]

For Mary, this was a taste of the city life with Shelley she never forgot. She had, after all, been brought up by Godwin to officiate at evening dinners and entertainments, and to enjoy the public glare of theatres and concerts. Her *Frankenstein* had finally been published, and sensational reviews were coming in from the journals, and distinguished writers like Scott and Tom Moore were signifying their approval of the unknown author. Mary adored the theatre and the opera. Despite Peacock's opinion that Shelley hated stage comedies, he too enjoyed these nights out immensely, and he took a regular box at Covent Garden. Hunt nostalgically recalled such evenings long after Shelley had departed. 'We look up to your box almost hoping to see a thin, patrician-looking cosmopolite leaning out upon us, and a sedate-faced young lady bending in a similar direction, with her great tablet of a forehead, and her white shoulders unconscious of a crimson gown.'[95] Shelley also visited the pantomime with Claire, and its garish magic completely entranced him. Shelley loved stage contrivances and melodrama. Many years later, after Mary had visited the German Opera, she wrote to Hogg: 'We liked the music, & the incantation scene would have made Shelley scream with delight, flapping owls, ravens, hopping toads, queer reptiles, fiery serpents, skeleton huntsmen. . . .'⁹⁶

Apart from review contributions for the *Examiner*, Shelley wrote little or nothing. But in Hunt circles poetry was a social art, and on 14 February three competitive sonnets on the subject of the Nile were written during an evening party at Lisson Grove. The competitors were Hunt, Keats and Shelley.⁹⁷ Not surprisingly perhaps, Hunt's is far the most competent while both Keats's and Shelley's betray embarrassment. Egyptian subjects were very much in vogue, for in the autumn of 1817 the British Museum had taken receipt of fragments and sculptures from the Empire of the Ramases, some dating from *circa* 2000 BC. Among these were the celebrated Rosetta Stone, and the massive figure of Ramases II taken from the King's Funerary Temple at Thebes and presented by Henry Salt and J.L.Burckhardt. This figure, perhaps the most famous of all Egyptian fragments, is carved in blue and white granite. Much was also being written in the press about the startling Egyptian finds, and when Walter Coulson, the editor, visited Marlow over Christmas it had been often discussed. Visits to the British Museum with Horace Smith prompted Shelley to suggest that they might both produce a sonnet on the subject. Smith, the stockbroker poet who had agreed to be Shelley's financial agent in London, faithfully produced a workmanlike poem. Shelley produced 'Ozymandias'. It is the finest sonnet he ever wrote: harsh, dramatic and deeply expressive of his eternal hatred of tyranny and his brooding philosophic scepticism. The poem was published in Hunt's *Examiner* shortly before he left England, *ave atque vale*:

> I met a traveller from an antique land
> Who said: Two vast and trunkless legs of stone
> Stand in the desert . . . Near them, on the sand,
> Half sunk, a shattered visage lies, whose frown,
> And wrinkled lip, and sneer of cold command,
> Tell that its sculptor well those passions read
> Which yet survive, stamped on these lifeless things,
> The hand that mocked them, and the heart that fed:
> And on the pedestal these words appear:
> 'My name is Ozymandias, king of kings:
> Look on my works, ye Mighty, and despair!'
> Nothing beside remains. Round the decay
> Of that colossal wreck, boundless and bare
> The lone and level sands stretch far away.⁹⁸

Apart from business connected with the house at Marlow, and the immediate arrangements for the coach and the journey, Shelley had only one other important affair to arrange: Godwin's finances. By the technical device of having his own life insured against the possibility of dying before Sir Timothy, Shelley was able to secure a very substantial *post obit*, and Godwin expected to benefit handsomely. It is not quite clear how much the sum amounted to, but it may have been a sum as large as £4,500; at any rate the liability to Willats was £9,000.[99] Godwin's delight at hearing of this agreement was quickly dashed when he discovered that Shelley, as in 1815, had decided to make use of a good part of this money for his own expenses. He wrote acknowledging the receipt of 'the sum mentioned in your letter. I acknowledge with equal explicitness my complete disappointment. I observe the expression you use, that you are "resolved to keep in your hands the power conferred by the difference of the two sums".'[100]

Godwin pressed Shelley to leave all the *post obit* money in England, under a joint account, requiring joint signatures; but Shelley would not accept this, for he had learnt his lesson and was not leaving financial hostages behind. Godwin's bitter reaction brought out much of that mixture of shame and hostility towards Shelley that he had tried to suppress since the marriage of 1816. His letter, the last one we have from him to Shelley in England, sadly recalls the declining course which the relationship between master and protégé had run, ever since 1812. Godwin wrote that he had 'reflected much on the subject. I am ashamed of the tone I have taken with you in all our late conversations. I have played the part of a supplicant, and deserted that of a philosopher. It was not thus I talked with you when I first knew you. I will talk so no more. I will talk principles; I will talk *Political Justice*; whether it makes for me or against me, no matter. I am fully capable of this. . . . I have nothing to say to you of a passionate nature; least of all do I wish to move your feelings; less than the least to wound you. All that I have to say in the calmness of philosophy, and moves far above the atmosphere of vulgar sensations. If you have the courage to hear me, come; if you have not, be it so.'[101]

This final appeal, intended by Godwin to be dignified and even majestic, had to Shelley's ear a mixture of hypocrisy and pathos, and his answer was eloquent. Having assured himself that Godwin had received the allotted money, he broke off contact. Throughout the month of February, his last in England, while he was lodging at Great Russell Street and visiting friends virtually every evening, he did not once call on Godwin. Meanwhile, abandoning every restraint, Godwin wrote to him again and again, on the 2, 3, 5 and 10 February; and renewed the onslaught on the 17th, 22nd, 24th and 25th. There is no record of Shelley replying, and Godwin's own letters have not survived, probably because Shelley tore them up.[102] As a last resort, five days before they left London, Godwin slipped in to see his daughter while Shelley was out. By chance, or perhaps by Godwin's calculation, Shelley returned while he was still there, and a stiff but polite reconciliation followed.

Over their last weekend, the 7 and 8 March, Shelley called briefly on Godwin, and stayed to tea. But he visited in company with Hogg, Peacock and Horace Smith, so it was impossible to talk business. Claire also visited her mother, Mrs Godwin, to say farewell. On Monday the 9th, Godwin was permitted to come to the christening of William and little Clara at St Giles-in-the-Fields. Claire also had Alba baptized according to Byron's instructions, 'Clara Allegra', adding: 'reputed daughter of Rt Hon. George Gordon, Lord Byron, Peer of no fixed residence, travelling on the continent'. They all returned to Russell Street, but once again Shelley had Peacock and Horace Smith on hand, and the visitors left early. Later in the evening Hunt and Bessy Kent walked down from Paddington, and arranged a farewell dinner for the following day. On Tuesday the 11th they were busy packing, and various friends looked in to say goodbye. The children were put to bed early in precaution for the next day's journey, and Hunt and Marianne came down to celebrate Shelley's last night. After supper, exhausted, Shelley fell asleep on the couch, and the Hunts crept away without finally saying goodbye at all.

The next morning they were up before first light, and left the capital still in darkness. They breakfasted at Dartford, and by nightfall came down the long Dover hill from Canterbury, with Claire pointing out to the children all the lights below then, the castle and the sea, 'almost like a fair city'. It was the largest household Shelley had ever taken abroad, consisting of eight people: Mary and Claire, little William, the babies Clara and Allegra, their faithful Swiss nurse Elise and Milly Shields, a servant girl from Marlow. This time they were not pursued, and put up comfortably at York House, intending to sail the next day. In the morning, Claire and the maids walked with the children on the beach, and Allegra had her first experience of sea bathing.[103]

While waiting for the captain of their packet to decide if they could manage the stiff north-easterly, Shelley suddenly remembered that he had not left his bankers, Brookes, full instructions concerning unpaid bills. He hurried off a note, specifying four applicants only, and 'no other bills to be honoured'. Peacock was put down first, for thirty pounds. Towards the printing of *The Revolt of Islam*, Shelley also stipulated thirty pounds for Charles Ollier. Godwin got a handshake of £150. Finally, 'Mr Madocks (for accounts at Marlow). £117'.[104] The last thing Shelley wrote in England concerned bills, not poetry.

They embarked. The sea was very rough and they left Dover on the wings of a March storm. Claire watched waves 'mountains high', but the sail over to Calais took just two hours and forty minutes, and was the quickest crossing Shelley had ever had. The babies were ill, but behaved beautifully, and slept below deck with the servants. Shelley, Mary and Claire leaned on the deck rail. Next to them, a military gentleman's wife became so frightened she began to repeat the Lord's Prayer out loud. Each time she was sick, she ordered her servant to continue repeating it for her.[105] Shelley looked away towards France: it seemed to him that spring was hastening to meet them from the south.[106]

16
The Platonist: Bagni di Lucca 1818

As Mary noted in her new journal, they were now at Calais for the third time in their lives. Shelley did not wish to linger in France, where he had learnt to expect dirty inns, unreliable coaches and 'the nasal and abbreviated cacophony of the French'.[1] Instead he decided to make with all possible speed for the Alps. Having decided after all to purchase a carriage at Calais on Friday, 13 March 1818, they mounted their baggage and set out to travel towards the Swiss border through Artois and Burgundy, deliberately circumventing Paris. The first leg of the journey was made largely by moonlight, and they had to tip the guards heavily at St Omer in order to enter the city walls so late at night. A woman shrieked from across the moat, demanding who the invaders were.[2] From St Omer, they passed through Rheims, Châlons-sur-Marne and Dijon, finally reaching Lyons at nearly midnight on the following Saturday, 21 March, where they had their first rest. Shelley wrote of their rapid progress to Hunt and Byron, and negotiated with a *voiturier* to drive them over the Alps to Milan.

Throughout the journey Shelley ignored French books, and concentrated on reading Schlegel's essays on Shakespeare and the theatre, turning over in his mind the idea for a poetic drama. The weather was hot, and the sky over the Midi a radiant blue, and Shelley's spirits rose steadily. On the evening before their departure from Lyons they sat discussing the Revolutionary times in the city with the *voiturier* who had witnessed action; and then went out to see the moon rise over the distant Alps and glitter in the water where the Saône flows into the Rhône.[3] The next day they drove into the foothills, and crossed the frontier at Les Echelles. Shelley's books had to be submitted to the Sardinian censor, 'a Priest who admits nothing of Rousseau, Voltaire etc. in the province'. 'All such books', he noted acidly, 'are burned.'[4] As an Englishman on his travels, however, the eccentricities of Shelley's library were eventually allowed to pass by.

The delay was eclipsed by the fantastic rockscapes and cliffs of the mountain pass outside Les Echelles, which reminded Shelley of a famous *mise en scène* in

Aeschylus: 'The rocks which cannot be less than 1000 feet in perpendicular height, sometimes overhang the road on each side, and almost shut out the sky. The scene is like that described in the "Prometheus" of Aeschylus; vast rifts and caverns in granite precipices; wintry mountains, with ice and snow above; the loud sounds of unseen waters within the caverns; and walls of toppling rocks, only to be scaled, as he describes, by the winged chariot of the Ocean Nymphs.'[5] This image, and other ones from the previous Alpine expedition in summer 1816, now began to coalesce in Shelley's mind around the subject of the Titan Prometheus, chained and welded to his rocky precipice. It was a mythic image which went back to the earliest of Shelley's childhood romances, and now suddenly it found its appropriate physical setting. Mary's outcast monster and her modern Prometheus had also been conceived in the mountains. But for the moment, surrounded by the bustle and irritation and delights of travel, the Aeschylean image lay dormant in Shelley's imagination.

At Chambéry their carriage was again halted, half-way across the bridge, the French soldiers at one end, and Piedmontese at the other. Passports and books were pored over by customs men who maddened Shelley with their officiousness. For over an hour they refused to allow the carriage to move either backwards or forwards, and all the time it rained steadily. Finally a Swiss canon who had met Sir Timothy Shelley at the Duke of Norfolk's, passed through the customs post, and with more charity than honesty assured the officials of Percy Shelley's respectability and good connections. The carriage was allowed through, with its crates of heresy undisturbed. The rest of the day was spent at Chambéry, where the parents of their Swiss maid Elise had arranged to meet their daughter.

Elise was to play an important part in Shelley's life in Italy during the next years, and something of her background is now known. Elise's mother had married twice. The family life had been a disturbed one, and in her early twenties Elise had had an illegitimate child. Her mother and her stepfather had agreed to look after it, when Elise went off to make a new life with the Shelleys in 1816. This fact perhaps accounts for her willingness to leave Switzerland in the first place, and also why Shelley himself regarded her as a highly suitable nurse for both Mary's and Claire's children. She understood such extra-matrimonial matters. Her own little girl, whose age is uncertain, was called Aimée, and the stepfather's name was Romieux. But Elise's maiden name is unknown.[6] Claire liked Elise, and described her as 'a very superior Swiss woman of about thirty, a mother herself'.[7] Elise was not, as has often been conjectured, an innocent working-class maidservant in her teens. She was a woman of some education, with sexual experience, and was in fact the oldest member of Shelley's party by four or five years. The parallel with Elizabeth Hitchener is obvious, and her possible importance in the triangular relationship between Mary, Claire and Shelley thus becomes partially evident. There is no record of Elise's personal appearance, or of her attractions, and nothing that Shelley wrote at this time seems to imply more than his complete trust in her. She was almost one of the family.

After Chambéry, which they left on Saturday, 28 March, the carriage ploughed through the snow over Mount Cenis and along the Napoleonic route across the Pont du Diable. Shelley was in high spirits, and sang all the way according to Claire, his voice echoing off the cascades of frozen ice, the snow cliffs and the precipices. His songs were improvised snatches of atheistical verse, about gods being 'hung on every tree', and he joked gleefully about the Promethean possibilities of the landscape, and the world of mythic monsters, asserting 'that the Mountains are God's *Corps de Ballet* of which the Jungfrau is Mademoiselle Milanie'.[8] They came down into the sunlit meadows and primroses of Susa the next day, and reached Turin and went to the opera on 1 April. Finally, on the 4th, they reached their first objective in Italy, Milan, with its splendid theatre, its opera house and its cathedral bristling with white pinnacles and statuary. Their first monument in Italy was a symbolic one: 'a ruined arch of magnificent proportions in the Greek taste standing in a kind of road of green lawn overgrown with violets and primroses'. Shelley was delighted to be shown round it by a *blonde* Italian girl, as he stressed to Peacock, who seemed to him like Fuseli's Eve.[9] Perhaps he had re-entered the Paradise.

Settling themselves at a small apartment in the Locande Reale, they embarked on a whirl of operatic and balletic evenings in Milan. Shelley wrote to England to inform his friends of their safe arrival, and general health and high spirits. He was planning, he told Peacock, a tragedy on the subject of Tasso's madness, which he intended to take the whole summer writing, once they got settled in a house: 'I thirst to be settled that I may begin.' During the day Claire wrote long notes on the power of the Italian ballet, which swept both her and Shelley off their feet. 'It is full of mad and intoxicating joy, which nevertheless is accompanied by voluptuousness.' They saw an adaptation of *Othello*, and Maria Pallerini, dancing Desdemona, was described by Claire in terms that reflect upon Shelley's poetry: 'Her walk is more like the sweepings of the wind than the steps of a mortal, and her attitudes are pictures.'[10] It was something of this combination of liquid line and sculptural frieze that Shelley was trying to achieve in his writing. Italy at first acquaintance seemed to awake so many correspondences and resonances in Shelley's mind that it came like a revelation; he barely had time to ask after 'Cobbett and politics', or the proofs for his own forthcoming volume, to be entitled *Rosalind and Helen*. Even the papist cathedral offered itself to him in the most vivid and sympathetic way. 'It is built of white marble

& cut into pinnacles of immense height & the utmost delicacy of workmanship, & loaded with sculpture. The effect of it, piercing the solid blue with those groups of dazzling spires relieved by the serene depth of this Italian Heaven, or by moonlight when the stars seem gathered among those sculptured shapes is beyond anything I had imagined architecture capable of producing.' Inside, the sombre luxury of the stained glass, the 'massy granite columns overloaded with antique figures & the silver lamps that burn forever' seemed to him like a 'gorgeous sepulchre'. Curiously none of this repelled him, and there was one particular spot in the aisles behind the high altar where the light was 'dim and yellow under the storied window', which he visited regularly in the afternoons to read Dante whom he had selected for his guide into Italian literature. He was reading the *Purgatorio*.[11]

More mundane things pleased him and Mary too: the pensione was very reasonable, and the cost of basic foods seemed very low, 'the finest bread, made of sifted flour the whitest & the best I ever tasted is only *one English penny* a pound'.[12] Only a few luxuries – including, unfortunately, tea – were ludicrously expensive.

Now Shelley had finally arrived in Italy with his not inconsiderable entourage, two problems immediately presented themselves. First, to find and lease a house where they might all settle in congenial surroundings. Second, to present little Allegra to Lord Byron and help reach a satisfactory agreement for Claire. Until these things were settled, the possibility of getting on with his drama on the madness of Tasso remained at a distance, although he was busily reading up 'Lives' by Giovanni Manso (1619) and Pietro Serassi (1785), which he had found in the Milan bookshops.[13] Shelley and Mary decided that if they could find a suitable house on Lake Como, which lay some six hours' ride to the north, both problems would be solved. Byron could be invited to visit them there from Venice and collect his child. Accordingly over the weekend of 10–13 April, leaving Claire with the nurses and the children, they visited the steep surrounds of the lake together. They admired the masses of laurel and wild fig trees, the plantantions of olives and lemons, and the smart villas of the Milanese nobility, and they decided to lease the Villa Pliniana, 'so called from a fountain which ebbs & flows every three hours described by the younger Pliny which is in the courtyard'. The rooms of the villa were huge, empty and echoing and in an advanced state of disrepair; it stood in a solitary position giving precipitously on to the lake, surrounded by gloomy black rocks, waterfalls and huge cypress trees. The garden was full of snakes.

Shelley at least was enthusiastic and applied for the lease; but Mary seems to have felt uncomfortable in the place, and there was a curious incident involving Shelley's pistols which did not reassure her. She carefully omitted all reference to it in her journal, but on their return to Milan on Sunday evening Shelley told Claire one version of it which was noted in her diary.

> When they were at Como S thought he would take a walk to some solitary place that he might fire off his pistol which had been loaded during our whole Journey. In walking he observed two men to follow him & when he had got pretty far he stopped till they came up to him. They said they were Police & must take him into Custody as it was forbidden to any one to be carrying Arms about as he was. He expostulated but they persisted in carrying him before the Prefect. This gentleman when he heard that Shelley was an Englishman and his intention with regard to the pistol behaved with the greatest politeness but said he should keep the pistol safe in his custody till he had heard from Madame Shelley that her husband had no intention of shooting himself through the head. Mary having certified this – the Pistol was rendered.[14]

No explanation of why Shelley was followed in the first place by the police, or why the prefect thought Shelley was contemplating blowing out his own brains was forthcoming. Claire merely noted that it was 'a curious adventure'.

Writing the following day to Peacock, Shelley seems to have undergone a temporary disillusionment with the Italians: 'The men are hardly men, they look like a tribe of stupid and shrivelled slaves, & I do not think I have seen a gleam of intelligence in the countenance of man since I passed the Alps. The women in enslaved countries are always better than the men; but they have tight laced figures, & features & mien which express (O how unlike the French!) a mixture of the coquette and the prude that reminds one of the worst characteristics of English women.'[15] They now spent their time reading, or playing chess or taking evening carriage rides round the Corso while waiting for the result of the lease application. Shelley wrote to Byron and invited him, somewhat prematurely, to the Villa Pliniani: 'If you would come and visit us – and I don't know where you could find a heartier welcome – little Allegra might return with you.'[16] From Claire he passed on a message asking if Byron had received the lock of Allegra's hair which she had sent. He moved on from the *Purgatorio* to the *Paradiso*.

After some ten days of delay, during which time no news was heard from Como, Shelley received a letter from Byron announcing somewhat abruptly that the invitation to Milan was unsuitable and ill-advised, that he had no wish to see Claire, but that he would send a messenger to collect the child. Some indication of Byron's attitude is revealed in another letter, to his friend Cam Hobhouse, in which he referred to the subject of Allegra with studied flippancy: 'A clark can bring the papers', he wrote, talking of necessities to be brought from England in the spring, '(and, bye-the-bye, my *shild*, by Clare, at the same time.

Pray desire Shelley to pack it carefully), with *tooth-powder, red only*; magnesia, soda-powders, tooth-brushes, diachylon plaster, and any new novels good for anything.'[17] Byron seems to have been particularly sensitive to the scandalous talk that was circulating about his life in the *demi-monde* of Venice; and the Shelleys themselves had heard much colourful gossip even in Milan.

Caught between Byron and Claire, and with the immediate prospect of Byron's messenger arriving to collect the child, Shelley was once again placed in a position where he could only mediate. His response, given at length in a letter written back to Byron on the same day, 22 April, was prompt and well judged, expressed in terms both graceful and firm that showed Shelley at his most diplomatic and mature. On the immediate issue he was definite: 'If your messenger arrives before Clare [*sic*] and you have come to an understanding on this subject, I shall detain him until further orders, unless your instructions are explicit that he shall not stay.' To this he added: 'You write as if from the instant of its departure all future intercourse were to cease between Clare and her child. This I cannot think you ought to have expected, or even to have desired.' He then argued with disarming candour against Byron's attempt to shirk the real nature of his emotional responsibilities towards both child and mother. 'I know the arguments present in your mind on this subject; but surely, rank and reputation, and prudence are as nothing in comparison to a mother's claims. . . . I assure you, my dear Lord Byron, I speak earnestly, and sincerely. It is not that I wish to make out a case for Clare; my *interest*, as you must be aware, is entirely on the opposite side. Nor have I in any manner influenced her. I have esteemed it a duty to leave her to the impulse of her own feelings in a case where, if she has no feeling, she has no claim. But in truth, if she is to be brought to part with her child, she requires reassurance and tenderness. A tie so near the heart should not be rudely snapt. It was in this persuasion that I hoped (I had a thousand other reasons for wishing to see you) that you would have accepted our invitation to the Pliniana. Clare's pain would then have been mitigated by the prospect of seeing her child with you, and she would have been reassured of the fears which your letter had just confirmed, by the idea of a repetition of the visit. Your conduct must at present wear the aspect of great cruelty, however you justify it to yourself. Surely, it is better if we err, to err on the side of kindness, than of rigour. You can stop when you please; and you are not so infirm of purpose that soothing words, and gentle conduct need betray you in essential matters further than you mean to go.'*

---

* This letter is also important evidence of Shelley's general attitude to the responsibilities of a father, and the rights of a mother, in the case of an illegitimate child. It was to have an application in other circumstances during the winter of the year. The phrase, 'if she has no feeling, she has no claim' is particularly relevant.

Byron may have felt that Shelley was more *interested* in Claire's cause than he pretended to be; and for himself, he was not at all sure how firm his purpose was in 'essential matters'. In any case, to stay under the same roof with Claire was now an impossibility. Whatever other concessions he made, he always steadfastly refused to see Claire again. Nevertheless Shelley's calm reasonings and reproaches had considerable effect. When Byron wrote again, on the 27th, it was in a kinder and more compromising tone, promising to take the greatest personal interest in the child if she came to Venice, and assuring Shelley that Claire would be permitted to visit Allegra during the summer. Subsequently Shelley held him to his word, and the arrangement was honoured.[18]

Shelley's letter had also succeeded in amusing and flattering Byron on the question of scandalous gossip, with which Byron was initially concerned. 'This is the common lot of all who have distinguished themselves among men,' he informed Byron. 'When Dante walked through the streets, the old women pointed at him, and said, "That is the man who went to Hell with Virgil; see how his beard is singed." Stories unlike this, but to the full as improbable and monstrous, are propagated of you at Venice; but I know not wherefore you should regard them.'[19]

Shelley might have been less nonchalant if he had known some of the details of Byron's *modus vivendi* at Venice. The massive grey-stone Palazzo Mocenigo on the Grand Canal, a few hundred yards from San Marco, had seen a stream of buxom and disreputable ladies, and was the centre of much brawling, drinking and political subversion. At this time Byron had just broken off with one courtesan, Marianna La Segati, and attached himself to another, Margarita Cogni. The latter was a voluptuous black-eyed baker's wife, 'fit to breed gladiators from', as he had boasted to a friend. He added drily, in a letter to Hobhouse: '. . . my old "relazione" is over, but I have got several new ones (and a Clap, which is nearly well at present).'[20] Byron, now 30 years old, was indulging in what was to be in fact his last thoroughly libidinous household, with a wildness that began to approach desperation. By the end of the year 1818, in which he had begun his greatest poem, *Don Juan*, he was to be discovered morosely climbing the balcony of an 18-year-old Italian heiress at midnight. He afterwards told Medwin that he was indifferent to the outcome of the affair, and did not care whether the police officer had come to have him shot or married.[21] Flippancy had become a last refuge. If Byron had not visited Hell with Virgil, it was nevertheless a curiously Venetian kind of Paradise, some of the squalid sublimity of which was caught in the first poem of his maturity, *Beppo*.*

---

* Murray published *Beppo* in February 1818; Shelley was asked to bring a copy to Lord Byron in his book box, but he forgot it.

Shelley added in his letter of the 22nd two strictly practical offers. One was to waive all questions of Allegra's expenses, which in the circumstances was a generosity he could ill afford. The other was that Allegra's nurse Milly Shields should go with the child to Venice; 'Allegra has an English nurse, a very clean and good-tempered woman, whom, in case of a termination of these melancholy differences, I can safely recommend to you.'

On 27 April Claire celebrated her twentieth birthday in a rather dismal way, and news reached Shelley that the application for the lease on Villa Pliniana had not succeeded. This was possibly something to do with the unfortunate impression he had made on the local prefect, but the exact reason is not known. The failure of the Lake Como plan had a decisive influence on the shape of Shelley's life for the next nine months. He became virtually a tourist, constantly on the move, and until his arrival at Naples in the winter of 1818–19, rarely stayed for more than a few weeks in any one part of the country. Shelley revelled in the constant change of scenery and impressions, and wrote a series of long letters to Peacock which together compose a brilliant Italian travelogue, and are comparable with the great travel letters of Dickens, Trollope and Lawrence. Yet the restless life of the tourist, with its discomforts and expense, was certainly not what Mary and Shelley had planned in the previous autumn. The loss of the Pliniana was eventually to have another more terrible effect, on the children of the family. The immediate consequence of this came on the 28th, when Shelley, unable to press Byron any further with the Lake Como plan, persuaded Claire to release Allegra, and the child departed for Venice in company with Byron's messenger Merryweather and a nurse. Claire, wrote Shelley, 'is wretchedly disconsolate, and I know not how I shall calm her, until the return of post'. He planned with Mary to leave Milan at once, to travel southwards to Pisa where 'I shall attempt to divert Claire's melancholy by availing myself of some introductions'.

There was one interesting, and perhaps significant minor change of plan. It was not Milly Shields, but Elise who was sent with Allegra. This was despite the fact that it was Milly who had always been Allegra's nurse. Shelley's explanation is given in passing to Byron, but it suggests that the decision was perhaps Mary's rather than Claire's or his own. 'Her attendant is not the servant I alluded to in my last letter; but a Swiss, who has attended my own children, in whom Mrs S. entirely confides, and who even quits us somewhat unwillingly, and whom Mary parts with solely that Clare and yourself may be assured that Allegra will be attended almost with a mother's care.'[22] Why Mary should have thought it more suitable and convenient that Elise should leave their entourage is not immediately evident. Perhaps it was simply felt that as a 'superior woman' Elise might be better able to cope with the exigencies of Byron's household than the young Milly. But one may also detect in the sudden reversal of Shelley's stated plan a degree of force in Mary's decision. From subsequent events it seems clear that by the end of April 1818, Mary was glad to have the chance of removing Elise to a safer distance from their circle.

After a last night at the opera, and the dispatch of brief letters of direction to Hogg and Peacock, they left Milan on the morning of 1 May. To Hogg, Shelley wrote in his old *Alastor* style, that the lake had 'those green banks for the sake of which you represented me as wandering over the world. You are more interested in the human part of the experience of travelling; a thing which I see little and understand less, and which if I saw and understood more I fear I should be little able to describe.'[23] Later on, however, he was to write amusingly both to Peacock and to Hogg of his impressions of the Italians, especially the Italian women.

The depleted party, with Claire huddled miserably in the carriage corner, giving vent to fits of moodiness and pique, travelled south-westwards through the plain of Palma. They gazed at the panorama of high meadow grass and wild festoons of vines, which were trained to climb the trees like ivy; and after stopping off at Modena and Bologna, they climbed into the Apennines, before finally descending into the chestnut valleys of the Arno towards Pisa. Amid the Apennines, where they spent one night in a desolate inn, Shelley was struck by the wildness of the landscape, and felt that 'the imagination cannot find a home in it'.[24] Claire listened to the wind which howled dismally, and was taken by a sudden terror that the whole carriage would be blown away.[25] Shelley once more drew them together with a grimly humorous speculation about mountain monsters. He jotted down a fragment beginning, 'Listen, listen, Mary mine, To the whisper of the Apennine', in which when night falls the mountain itself comes alive and 'walks abroad with the storm'. The thought seemed to cheer them up.[26]

Skirting the Florentine plain, they followed the road along the Arno and came directly into Pisa on 7 May, putting up at the main inn, the Tre Donazelle. The Tre Donzelle stood just across the Ponte Mezzo, at the centre of the long curve of riverside buildings which has made up the city of Pisa since medieval times.* They visited the Leaning Tower and the Baptistry, but despondently observed the chain gangs of Italian convicts working in the streets under armed guard, and the curious ghost-like emptiness and dilapidation of the streets – 'a large disagreeable city almost without inhabitants'. They moved on after a few days towards the sea. This was their first unpromising introduction to the city,

---

* The Tre Donzelle still stands there, virtually unchanged in appearance, the left corner building of what is now the Piazza Garibaldi. Its ground floor has been metamorphosed into an English tea-room. See plate 27.

apparently so inhospitable, which was eventually to become their home in Italy.

The port of Livorno, three hours' ride to the east on the 'blue and tranquil Mediterranean', was at least more sociable with a small but semi-permanent colony of expatriate English, among whom were Shelley's connections, the Gisbornes. This was his first contact in Italy with the international set of radicals and liberals who had moved in the Godwinian circles during the heady days of the nineties, and some of whom he had met, more locally, in Ireland six years before. At the age of 20 Maria Gisborne had been drawn into friendship with Godwin and Holcroft in London through her first husband, Mr Reveley, a merchant with liberal tendencies. After Mary Wollstonecraft's death, Maria had helped Godwin nurse his young daughter Mary. She was a beautiful and educated woman, and after Reveley's own death in 1799, Godwin had actually proposed marriage to her. Although she had refused, the friendship had been maintained. In 1800, she married John Gisborne, also a businessman, and went abroad with him and her young son, the following year, to Rome. Letters had continued to pass between the Gisborne and Godwin households. The Gisbornes had been living in Livorno since 1815, and Maria, now aged 48, was widely read in both Spanish and Italian literature, and held something of a minor *salon* among the more cultivated English at the port. For his part, John Gisborne had been somewhat overshadowed by his clever and maturely attractive wife, and had been forced into the role of retired *homme d'affaires* and tolerated bore. His letters however show him to have been quite otherwise, an intelligent and reasonable man, and a reliable ally. The Gisbornes were to become some of Shelley's closest friends in Italy, and to help him both with his writing and with his ceaseless domestic complications. None the less it was characteristic that he accepted from the start the boorish estimate of John, while making use of his services, and addressed most of his conversation and letters to Maria. Only four years later did John Gisborne's true value become plain to Shelley. Henry Reveley, Maria's son by her first marriage, training as a marine engineer in Livorno, was also to be involved in Shelley's affairs.

On that first evening, Shelley, Mary and Claire at once made their introductions, and during the following fortnight the Gisbornes walked and took tea with them constantly. The Gisbornes' house, the Casa Ricci in Via Genesi, quickly became their postal address, and they were advised about the surrounding countryside and spas, and recommended to take advantage of the fresh vegetables and unseasonable strawberries with which Mary regaled Marianne and Leigh Hunt.[27] Mary's first impression of them was, 'reserved, yet with easy manners', which she liked.[28] Shelley's was more resplendent: 'we have made some acquaintance with a very amiable and accomplished lady Mrs Gisborne, who is the sole attraction in this most unattractive of cities'.[29] On the Gisbornes' advice, Shelley left Livorno on his own on 26 May to make inquiries for a house at the popular and at that time fashionable spa at the Bagni di Lucca, one day's ride away, high in the valley of the Lima which flows through the centre of the Apennines. Besides its remedial springs, the Bagni di Lucca boasted several comfortable inns, a casino where dances and dinners were given regularly, and a score of solid summer villas discreetly withdrawn into their separate gardens among the steep, wooded slopes which clustered above the town and its bridge. Among many other English people, Byron was to spend a season here, ensconced in one of the largest villas set back into the hillside.

The house that Shelley found, the Casa Bertini, was on a modest scale. It had three floors, an elegantly tiled roof, new furnishings and freshly painted shutters, yet it was in its appointments little more than a large country cottage. It was owned by a local businessman, Signor G.B.del Chiappi, and was available for lease for the whole summer. Its greatest attraction was its neatness and its position, tucked away almost at the top of the unpaved, dusty yellow, hairpin road, which snaked up through the village and lost itself in the surrounding hills. While the front of the Casa Bertini commanded a curve of this road from its own small terrace garden, the back was shrouded in a densely overgrown little garden about twenty yards long, at the end of which was a rough arbour constructed out of laurel bushes. Only by parting this wall of half-tamed foliage with the hand could glimpses of the Lima be caught, glittering far below, through its sinuous margins of white shingle thrown up by the winter floods. Shelley realized at once that he had found a perfect setting to resume his work, and rode back two days later to tell the girls the good news. But nothing could be hurried in Tuscany at that, or any other time of the year. It was nearly another three weeks before the Casa Bertini was ready to receive them and the formalities complete. In the meantime, they adapted themselves to the pleasant, gossipy expatriate life of Livorno – 'Leghorn' to the literal-minded English – reading and studying in the mornings, walking out round the piazza and the old drum-like medieval fortifications of the harbour in the afternoon and taking tea and *conversazione* in the evening. Shelley had laid Dante aside for the time being, and was concentrating on the Greek dramatists. He read *Hippolytus* of Euripides, and then turned to Sophocles, whose measured philosophy and sensitive psychological characterization he found a revelation. He read *Electra*, *Ajax* and then *Philoctetes*, finding that he could translate with increasing swiftness and fluency. This last, with its symbolic themes of isolation, sickness and madness connected in Shelley's mind with the research he had already undertaken into Tasso's life.*

---

* Philoctetes, the great Athenian bowman, was marooned on an island by the Greek expedition who sailed to destroy Troy, because of the demoralization caused by the appalling wound in his foot.

He sketched out one or two scenes for this drama which he hoped to write at Bagni di Lucca, including a 'Song' about Tasso's love for the Princess Leonora.

> Sometimes I see before me flee
> A silver spirit's form, like thee,
> O Leonora, and I sit
> . . . still watching it,
> Till by the grated casement's ledge
> It fades, with such a sigh, as sedge
> Breathes o'er the breezy streamlet's edge.[30]

The dramatic fragment of 'Tasso' is interesting, for it foreshadows how all Shelley's attempts to create a poetic drama for the stage were to be overwhelmed, as both Coleridge and Keats were overwhelmed, by the massive presence of Shakespeare. Even the little song here carries the melancholy echo of Hamlet's Ophelia. It was only when Shelley further developed the new modes already created in *Queen Mab* and *The Revolt of Islam* that he was to be able to break free into entirely original and individual forms of dramatic confrontation, set within epic or balladic frames. His most fruitful models were not to be the Elizabethan or Jacobean drama, but the Greek plays, Milton's *Paradise Regained*, and Coleridge's *The Ancient Mariner*.

'Tasso' did however indicate the directions in which Shelley was to turn his efforts later in 1818. It contained a poet called Count Maddalo, who became a major figure in one of Shelley's greatest poems, written in the autumn. But it served especially to focus his attention on the mythological complex of ideas persistently recurring in the stories of Laon, of Philoctetes, of Tasso himself and of Prometheus – both Aeschylus's and Mary Shelley's.

A sensational Renaissance story, already circulating among the English at Livorno, was added to this repertoire of source materials before Shelley departed for the Bagni. Mrs Gisborne had spent one evening talking to Mary about 'a strange story that happened to her concerning a mad girl'.[31] Finding the Shelleys' interests were peculiarly adapted to such things, the next day she passed a copy of the 'Cenci Manuscript', the grim story of the evil Count Cenci of Rome, who had committed incest with his daughter the beautiful Beatrice, and was subsequently murdered by her. Mary was copying the manuscript into a small,

---

He lived in solitude for nearly ten years, a prey to hallucinations and recurring spasms of terrible pain when the abscess burst. Finally he was rescued by Odysseus and the young Neoptolemus, because an oracle had warned the Greeks that Troy would not fall without Philoctetes and his Bow. Sophocles's drama turns on the terrible effect that solitude has had on Philoctetes's mind, and the difficulty with which he is persuaded to accept the inevitability of past injustice and the necessity of returning to a society which had once persecuted him but now desperately needs him. The divine intervention of Herakles is eventually required to persuade him to return.

dark calf notebook in a rounded copper-plate hand for Shelley to brood on, at the end of May. The villain is introduced in bold gothic fashion with the memorable sentence, 'Sodomy was the least and Atheism the greatest of the vices of Francisco [Cenci] . . .'[32]

Claire had been somewhat taken out of herself by Maria Gisborne's pleasant though slightly strait-laced 28-year-old son Henry Reveley, a clever if submissive man who seemed, like his stepfather, to be over-shadowed by his mother. Mary was later to write of him, 'he is under as complete a subordination as few boys of twelve are', and again: 'the pattern of good boys'.[33] For Claire he already seemed the perfect subject for teasing, if not actually enticing; and how could one tease without being cheerful? Henry told Shelley of his education under John Rennie, the architect and engineer of Waterloo Bridge,[34] and eagerly showed him round his waterside workshops where he was planning to construct a revolutionary marine engine powered by steam. Shelley's interest was caught, and Henry joined their walks in the clear June evenings regularly, until they departed for the Bagni di Lucca and Casa Bertini. Shelley and Mary felt at last that their lives were beginning to take on the shape they had envisaged. Late at night they taught themselves Italian by reading together the comic and amorous cantos of Ariosto.

Shelley, Mary, Claire, Milly Shields and the two children arrived at the Casa Bertini on 11 June, when the spa season was already well under way. They were all delighted. Signor Chiappi had hired them a full-time cook, and a cleaning maid who came every day, and Mary approved of the spick paintwork. Shelley chose as his study a small room looking out over the wooded hills of the Apennines, and unpacked his books fully for the first time since he had arrived in Italy. They quickly settled into a relaxed routine of studying, bathing at the spa and walking in the chestnut woods, and this remained virtually unbroken for the next seven weeks. Sometimes they hired horses and rode out into the surrounding hills, and occasionally they dressed and went down to the Casino where there were lively dances two evenings a week: 'English and French country dances; quadrilles; waltzes; & Italian dances', as Mary observed carefully.

As he felt the heat of the Italian sun bringing back his health, Shelley frequently disappeared for whole days into the woods with his books, enjoying the open-air studies which he had originated at Bishopsgate and Marlow, usually beside some stream or waterfall. He continued to read steadily through his Greek authors, turning also now to Aristophanes and Plato, and began to build up a homogeneous impression of Athenian society in its golden age. Still perhaps thinking of 'Tasso', he read more sporadically among the Jacobeans, especially Jonson and Beaumont and Fletcher. He sent a memorable and not altogether unmischievous portrait of himself at work in his open air study to Peacock, transforming himself gradually from a scholar into a dryad.

[My pool] is surrounded on all sides by precipitous rocks, and the waterfall of the stream which forms it falls into it on one side with perpetual dashing. Close to it, on the top of the rocks, are alders, and above the great chestnut trees, whose long and pointed leaves pierce the deep blue sky in strong relief. The water of this pool . . . is as transparent as the air, so that the stones and sand at the bottom seem, as it were, trembling in the light of noonday. It is exceedingly cold also. My custom is to undress and sit on the rocks, reading Herodotus, until the perspiration has subsided, and then to leap from the edge of the rock into this fountain – a practice in the hot weather exceedingly refreshing. This torrent is composed, as it were, of a succession of pools and waterfalls, up which I sometimes amuse myself by climbing when I bathe, and receiving the spray over all my body, whilst I clamber up the moist crags with difficulty.[35]

Thus began Shelley's long love-affair with the waters of Italy; wherever he stayed, the waters received as much attention and enthusiasm as the architecture. But whether he was joined in these aquatic sports he does not mention, and neither Mary's journal nor Claire's diary remark on them.[36]

Mary now longed for the Gisbornes to join them, and make a somewhat remote existence slightly more sociable. She wrote to them in early July, happy with everything but the *gran turismo*. 'I am sure you would be enchanted with everything but the English that are crowded here to the almost entire exclusion of the Italians. . . . We see none but the English, we hear nothing but English spoken. The walks are filled with English nurserymaids, a kind of animal I by no means like, & dashing staring Englishwomen, who surprise the Italians who are always carried about in Sedan Chairs, by riding on horseback. – For us we generally walk except last Tuesday, when Shelley and I took a long ride to *il prato fiorito*; a flowery meadow on the top of one of the neighbouring Apennines – We rode among chestnut woods hearing the noisy cicala, and there was nothing disagreeable in it except the steepness of the ascent. . . . Not long ago we heard a Cuckoo.'[37]

For Shelley, the bustling life was invisible. 'We have spent a month here already in our accustomed solitude (with the exception of one night at the Casino) and the choice society of all ages which I took care to pack up in a large trunk before we left England. . . .' The trip to the Prato Fiorito filled him with delight at its sudden vistas of torrents and green ravines, and he planned at once to make a more extensive trip of two or three days to Monte San Peligrano, an ancient centre of summer pilgrimage. But Mary was not keen on complete immersion in rural pleasures, and he was unable to make the trip until two years later, when he went by himself. However he gradually persuaded her to come out riding in the evening more often.[38]

Above all it was the climate and the countryside of the Italian Apennines that fascinated and attracted Shelley. He spent hours and hours simply gazing upwards at the changing skyscapes, and the shifting light values in the trees, and the blue-green transformations of the air in the Lima valley. 'I take great delight in watching the changes of the atmosphere here,' he told Mrs Gisborne, '& the growth of the thunder showers with which the noon is often over shadowed, & which break & fade away towards evening into flocks of delicate clouds. Our fire flies are fading away fast, but there is the planet Jupiter who rises majestically over the rift in the forest-covered mountains to the south, & the pale summer lightning which is spread out every night at intervals over the sky. No doubt Providence has contrived these things, that when the fire flies go out the low flying owl may see her way home.'[39] Nearly every one of these details, the cloud growths, the storms, the sheet lightning, the planets, the fireflies, even the owl, were later to find their places in his poems. A letter he wrote to Godwin at this time, though it is short, and mostly taken up with politics, books and reviews, begins with the Italian sky. To Peacock he noted that the storms produced hail sometimes 'about the size of a pigeon's egg', and observed how the clouds varied between 'those finely woven webs of vapour which we see in English skies, and flocks of fleecy and slowly moving clouds, which all vanish before sunset'. The planets too came in for further notice in the clear evening skies, though when writing to Peacock there was again a certain mischievousness in his commentary. 'We see a star in the east at sunset – I think it is Jupiter – almost as fine as Venus was last summer; but it wants a certain silver and aerial radiance, and soft yet piercing splendour which belongs, I suppose, to the latter planet by virtue of its at once divine and female nature. I have forgotten to ask the ladies if Jupiter produces on them the same effect.'[40]

Shelley's visits to the casino, rare as they were, apparently gave him more pleasure than they did Mary or even Claire. Shelley was much amused that although they looked forward to their outings so much, neither of the girls, when it came to the point, would actually dance: 'I do not know whether they refrain from philosophy or protestantism.'[41] He himself had no such scruples, though he told Peacock mockingly that there was pitifully little chance of being swept off one's feet: 'the women being far removed from anything which the most liberal annotator could interpret into beauty or grace, and apparently possessing no intellectual excellencies to compensate the deficiency. I assure you it is well that it is so, for the dances, especially the waltz, are so exquisitely beautiful that it would be a little dangerous to the newly unfrozen senses and imagination of us migrators from the neighbourhood of the pole. As it is – except in the dark – there could be no peril.'[42]

But these frivolities barely rippled the surface of his days at the Casa Bertini. He luxuriated in the remoteness of everyday affairs, especially affairs in England, and hardly paused to note the news of the Westminster elections, or the political apostasy of the 'beastly and pitiful wretch that Wordsworth!' The generally favourable run of reviews which Mary's *Frankenstein* was receiving, and his own pillorying in the *Quarterly* as a civil and religious pervert, evoked slightly more interest; but the anticipation of Peacock's *Nightmare Abbey* alone aroused something like enthusiasm, and he suggested a motto from Ben Jonson, 'Have you a stool there to be melancholy upon?' Understanding from Peacock that the book was to be an attack on the pessimism and conservatism of modern English authors, he urged: 'I hope you have given the enemy no quarter. Remember, it is a sacred war.'[43] Later, in August, having received vague forewarning from Peacock, or having himself guessed that his own circle was involved, he wrote with sudden sharpness: 'Well, what is in it? What is it? You are as secret as if the priest of Ceres had dictated its sacred pages.'[44]

The mixture of moods which his letters from Casa Bertini reflect – the sense of well-being and amused detachment, suddenly cut across by moments of irritations or self-mockery – betray the difficulty he was having through June and July with his own writing. He had come to the Bagni primarily, as he had planned in Milan, to get a major piece of work done. But beyond the few fragments already begun at Livorno, his projected drama of 'Tasso' yielded nothing, and Mary's suggestion that he take up and complete *Rosalind and Helen* – which he did – neither freed his creative faculties nor satisfied them. His reading, especially in the Greeks, went ahead rapidly; but his notebooks remained empty. Finally, almost as a kind of distraction, he started to put down translations of what he was reading. Though he did not fully realize it at the time, this almost casual act was his first significant literary step since his arrival in Italy. Translation was to prove an immensely important catalyst. Not only was he to produce several translated texts, excellent and highly significant in their own right; but a number of his own works were to be triggered by, or actually based upon, translations.

Shelley's reading of the Greek dramatists had given way by the end of June to reading Plato. Restlessness at being unable to write had set in, and on the first Saturday in July he hired a horse and rode alone down the long winding valley of the Lima as far as Lucca, where rivers combine and become the Serchio. It was a distance of about eighteen miles, but Shelley covered it in the course of the long evening, stopped the night, and returned on Sunday, when they all went to the casino. During this interlude, a plan had suddenly formed in his mind to translate the *Symposium*, and by Thursday the 9th he was at work. Occasionally reading sections to Mary as he went, he continued for a week, and by Friday the 17th he had completed a rough draft. He started off again to ride to Lucca, this time taking Claire with him, but she fell off her horse and they had to go back to the Casa Bertini to recover. The next day the trip was made successfully. Mary's journal is not explicit on the point, but judging by the distance of the ride, and Claire's evident inexpertise, it seems likely that she and Shelley spent the night together at Lucca, and returned the next day, as Shelley had done alone the week previously. Claire's riding technique at least was not improved, for she fell off her horse again in August.[45]

Shelley now handed the whole of his text over to Mary, who began a careful transcription on Monday the 20th. Discussion of various points of social and literary background, many of which were obscure to Mary, led him on to consider writing an introductory essay. This he found more difficult, and he was still adding to it and clarifying it on 16 August, when outside events called his attention away.

Shelley's *The Banquet Translated from Plato*, together with his introduction, 'A Discourse on the Manners of the Ancient Greeks Relative to the Subject of Love', are the two works which of his whole output show most clearly his qualities as a pure scholar. When Hogg referred to the summer at Marlow as 'a mere Atticism', it is by these two works that one can assess the real value of that essentially gentlemanly classicism. The value is high. Shelley's translation shows him perfectly in control of the overall sweep of the philosophic dialogue, masterly with the more impassioned sections of Socrates's and Agathon's speeches, and with a considerable gift for drawing out the individual character and style of each speaker. The general directness and limpidity of his style, while retaining a certain elegant formality, especially in its rhythms, is particularly pleasing. A comparison with Jowett's great Victorian translation, and a popular modern one by W.D.Rouse, shows how Shelley holds the Attic balance between pedanticism and breezy familiarity, even at the most mundane level.* It has also been noted how the translations reflected the milieu in which they were made, and how, in this too, Shelley's version is especially rich with the resonances of lived experience: 'Jowett, for instance, somehow imparts to his Alcibiades the atmosphere together with the locutions of an English under-

---

* Here for example are their respective opening sentences, as Apollodorus begins his account of how the banquet came to be held. Jowett: 'Concerning the things about which you ask to be informed, I believe that I am not ill-prepared to answer,' which sounds irretrievably donnish. W.D. Rouse has more the air of a schoolboy in a police court: 'I think I am pretty well word-perfect in what you are inquiring about.' While Shelley simply gives the impression of one gentleman stopped by another while strolling across a sunlit piazza: 'I think that the subject of your enquiries is still fresh in my memory,' which is perfect.

15 Mary Shelley, sketch by an unknown artist, about 1814

16 Claire Clairmont in 1819 by Amelia Curran

17 Byron in 1818 by James Holmes

18 Château Chillon and Lac Leman from an early nineteenth-century engraving

19 *left* Leigh Hunt by Samuel Lawrence

20 John Keats by C. A. Brown

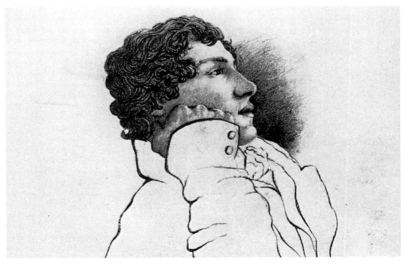

21 William Hazlitt by William Bewick

22 Ramasses II
(*photograph by Adrian Holmes*)

23 *above* Garden at Casa Bertini, Bagni di Lucca where Shelley translated Plato's Symposium

24 Beatrice Cenci, by Guido Reni

25 *above* 'Massacre at St Peter's',
cartoon by F. Fogg, 1819

26 Venus Anodyomene,
Florence

graduate, while Shelley's Alcibiades carries about him, with something of a Byronic air and with an incommunicable verve and charm and freshness, the atmosphere of an accomplished man of the world, a spoilt darling of the gods.'[46] Where Shelley is occasionally inaccurate, in more philosophic passages, it is because he has preferred to abandon the use of Scapula's Greek lexicon, and rely on the interpretation given by Plato's great Renaissance student, Marsilio Ficino, whose Latin text Shelley had alongside him at Casa Bertini as he worked.[47]

Shelley's interest in Plato had existed since he was introduced to him as an hermetic and subversive text by Dr Lind at Eton. One of the most interesting facts about Shelley's translation is that both he and Mary still regarded the text as controversial. The *Symposium* had the reputation of being improper to the point of indelicacy, and despite Thomas Taylor's translation (1792) it was still academically suspect in the English universities. Plato was not included in the papers set for the Humanities at Oxford until 1847.[48] Mary wrote privately to Mrs Gisborne that 'Shelley translated the Symposium in ten days (an anecdote for Mr Bielby). It is a most beautiful piece of writing – I think you will be delighted with it – It is true that in many particulars it shocks our present manners, but no one can be a reader of the works of antiquity unless they can transport themselves from these to other times and judge not by our but by their morality.'[49] It was not Plato's idealism, but the homosexual undertone to the whole work which called forth this *caveat*. Shelley quite appreciated the force of this, and his 'Discourse' was mainly concerned with putting the matter into its historical perspective. He explained to Peacock that it was a 'subject to be handled with that delicate caution which either I cannot or I will not practise in other matters, but which here I acknowledge to be necessary. Not that I have any serious thoughts of publishing either this discourse or the *Symposium*, at least till I return to England, when we may discuss the propriety of it.'[50]

The thought of Shelley discussing the *propriety* of a publication is surprising, and has led to some speculation that the subject of homosexuality was a particularly delicate one for Shelley himself. But Shelley's estimate of publication difficulties was perfectly correct. Editorial caution on the part of Moxon and Leigh Hunt allowed only a mutilated version of each to be published in the official edition of Shelley's prose in 1840, despite Mary's struggle to retain a reasonably open text.* The mutilated version of both, with glaring omissions,

---

* Mary wrote to Hunt in October 1839, 'You said: "Do as Mills, who has just phrased it so that the common reader will think common love is meant – the learned alone will know what is meant." Accordingly I read [Mill's] *Phaedrus* & found less of a veil even than I expected – thus I was emboldened to leave it so that our sort of civilized love should be understood – Now you change all back into friendship – which makes the difficulty as great as ever . . . I have left some & not others – where you seemed very vehement . . . but I could not bring myself to leave the word *love* out entirely from a treatise on Love . . . It is puzzling – *that's a fact* as the Americans say.'

continued in all editions into the present century,[51] and was mistakenly used by psychologist–critics as *prima facie* evidence of Shelley's 'suppressed homosexuality', the argument being that he could not face translating certain sections.[52] As it is, the full text of Shelley's 'Discourse' from his own manuscript, and the full text of *The Banquet*, from Mary's own transcription of August 1818 first appeared in a limited scholars' edition of 100 copies, printed 'for private circulation' in 1931.[53]

Shelley's fascination with Plato influenced his work throughout his years in Italy, especially between 1818 and 1820. He also translated Plato's *Ion*, part of his *Phaedo*, and several epigrams. It is a main element in the development of his thought, especially in politics, religious scepticism and that special mixture of moral and psychological speculation which Shelley called metaphysics. Yet Shelley was at no point completely converted to 'Platonism', any more than he had been previously to Godwinism. His attitude from the start was critical and comparative. He selected, disregarded and explored as he went: it is precisely that sense of the *historical relativity* of ideas and social values which Plato brought to Shelley, for which he is most important. The combination of logic and poetry in Plato especially delighted him, and led him to the comparison with Bacon's essays. Yet even in the introductory 'Discourse', Shelley was always careful to define Plato's virtues against a background of critical reservations. '[Plato's] views into the nature of mind and existence are often obscure, only because they are profound; and though his theories respecting the government of the world, and the elementary laws of moral action, are not always correct, yet there is scarcely any of his treatise which do not, however stained by puerile sophisms, contain the most remarkable intuitions into all that can be the subject of the human mind. . . . The dialogue entitled The Banquet was selected by the translator as the most beautiful and the most perfect among all the works of Plato.'[54] Moreover it is clear from Shelley's subsequent remarks on Plato, that he approached the *Symposium* as much as a great piece of Greek poetry as as a piece of philosophic dogma. 'Plato was essentially a poet,' he wrote some three years later, 'the truth and splendour of his imagery and the melody of his language is the most intense that it is possible to conceive. He rejected the harmony of the epic, dramatic and lyrical forms, because he sought to kindle a harmony in thoughts divested of shape and action, and he forbore to invent any regular plan of rhythm which would include under determinate forms the varied pauses of his style.'[55] The observation on prose rhythm is interesting, for the corresponding rhythm of Shelley's translation is part of his most striking achievement, and distinguishes it from later versions.

Apart from its literary value, the main interest of Shelley's translation and commentary on Plato derives from the broad and steady light which it throws on Shelley's own theories and personal feelings about sexual love. There is no other text anywhere in his writing which shows these so clearly.

In the first place, Shelley examined the problem of homosexuality.

> The passion which [the Greek] poets and philosophers described and felt seems inconsistent with this latter maxim [*i.e. according to nature*], in a degree inconceivable to the imagination of a modern European. But let us not exaggerate the matter. We are not exactly aware – and the laws of modern composition scarcely permit a modest writer to investigate the subject with philosophical accuracy, – what the action was by which the Greeks expressed this passion. I am persuaded that it was totally different from the ridiculous and disgusting conceptions which the vulgar have formed on the subject, at least except among the more debased and abandoned of mankind. It is impossible that a lover could usually have subjected the object of his attachment to so detestable a violation or have consented to associate his own remembrance in the beloved mind with images of pain and horror.[56]

Dismissing the direct physical expression of homosexual love – an 'operose and diabolical machination', as he graphically described the act of buggery – Shelley explains his own theory of 'certain phenomena connected with sleep', which has already been examined in relation to *Alastor*. He then developed his critique of Greek homosexuality as an index of an unjust and distorted society.

> Probably there were innumerable instances among that exalted and refined people, in which never any circumstance happens [to] the lover and his beloved by which natural modesty was wronged. The lover appeased his physical instinct with his wife or his slave; or was engrossed in such lofty thoughts and feelings as admitted of no compromise between them and less intense emotions. Thus much is to be admitted, that represent this passion as you will, there is something totally irreconcileable in its cultivation to the beautiful order of social life, to an equal participation in which all human beings have an indefeasible claim, and from which half of the human race [*i.e.* the female half], by the Greek arrangement, were excluded. This invidious distinction of human kind, as a class of beings of intellectual nature, into two sexes, is a remnant of savage barbarism which we have less excuse than they for not having totally abolished.[57]

Through the issue of homosexuality, Shelley wished to direct his readers' attention on to the specific limitations of Plato's thought in particular, and Greek society in general, with respect to slaves and women. He regarded this Greek exploitation of slaves and women as mere property as the fundamental anachronism of their social and intellectual life. Referring to heterosexual love, he summarized:

The fact is, that the modern Europeans have in this circumstance, and in the abolition of slavery, made an improvement the most decisive in the regulation of human society; and all the virtue and the wisdom of the Periclean age arose under other institutions, *in spite of* the diminution which personal slavery and the inferiority of women, recognized by law and by opinion, must have produced in moral, political and metaphysical science. . . .[58]

Next, Shelley wished to compare this failure of the Greeks with what he regarded as an equal failure and distortion in modern European society.

The action by which this [homosexual] passion was expressed, taken in its grossest sense, is indeed sufficiently detestable. But a person must be blinded by superstition to conceive of it as more horrible than the usual intercourse endured by almost every youth of England with a diseased and insensible, prostitute. It cannot be more unnatural, for nothing defeats and violates nature, or the purposes for which the sexual instincts are supposed to have existed, than prostitution. Nor is it possible that the society into which the one plunges its victim should be more pernicious than the other.[59]

He defended the Greek erotic writing as compared with modern obscenity.

The ideas suggested by Catullus, Martial, Juvenal and Suetonius never occur among the Greeks; or even among those Romans, who, like Lucretius, Virgil, Horace, imitated them. The Romans were brutally obscene; the Greeks seem hardly capable of obscenity in a strict sense. How innocent is even the Lysistrata of Aristophanes compared with the infamous perversions of Catullus! The earlier dramatic English writers are often frightfully obscene, exceeding even the Romans. I should consider obscenity to consist in the capability of associating disgusting images with the act of the sexual instinct. Luxury produced for the Romans what the venereal disease did for the writers of James [I], and after the redeeming interval over which Milton presided the effects of both were united, under Charles II, to infect literature.[60]*

After this critical and historically comparative approach which Shelley urged towards Plato and Greek society, the 'Discourse' is finally focused on the moral,

* The curiously overemphasized stress on venereal disease, which recurs in later works, suggests possibly that Shelley had some contact with a prostitute earlier in life. There is a further fragmentary note in the MS Notebook which contains the 'Discourse': 'Loathsome diseases the cause of modern obscenity exceeding the worst of antiquity in hideousness and horrors. . . .' Bod. MS Shelley Adds. e. 2, p. 73 rev.

psychological and ideal nature of Love as the universal and dominant human passion. Here Shelley picked out certain favourite passages in the *Symposium* itself. Of the speeches, those of Pausanias (2nd), Aristophanes (4th), Agathon (5th) and Socrates (6th) touched him most closely.

From Pausanias he drew the distinction between Pandemic and Uranian love which frequently underlies much of his love poetry. The first is fleshly, promiscuous, temporal and concerned equally with young women and young boys. The second, Uranian love, is essentially masculine, deeply felt with the whole personality, both fleshly and spiritual, faithful over long periods and perhaps for life, and fundamentally improving and educative. According to the limited Greek system, Uranian love could only be held between two men, or a man and a youth of equal social status. It could not concern women or young boys, or slaves. The distinction between Pandemic and Uranian love was very important to Shelley, though he considered its homosexual and class interpretation as a characteristic piece of Greek barbarism. It was the matured, heterosexual and egalitarian form of Uranian love which Mary Shelley later referred to as 'our sort of civilized love' in the letter to Hunt. The two kinds of love are also referred to in Mary's interpretative note on 'Prince Athanase'. 'The idea Shelley had formed of Prince Athanase was a good deal modelled on *Alastor*. In the first sketch of the poem, he named it *Pandemos and Urania*. Athanase seeks through the world the One whom he may love. He meets, in the ship in which he is embarked, a lady who appears to him to embody his ideal of love and beauty. But she proves to be Pandemos, or the earthly and unworthy Venus; who, after disappointing his cherished dreams and hopes, deserts him. . . . "On his deathbed, the lady who can really reply to his soul comes and kisses his lips.' "61 Urania, if she exists, is also a woman. This Platonic, or strictly speaking, Pausanian, interpretation also reflects a good deal on the structure of Shelley's *Epipsychidion*, to be written two and a half years later, though it by no means explains the theme.

In translating Pausanias's description of Uranian Aphrodite, Shelley made a notable adjustment and addition to the text, pointing it towards his own constant concern with the small, intimate and progressive community of friends:

And it is easy to distinguish those who especially exist under the influence of this power [*Urania*], by their choosing in early youth as the objects of their love those in whom the intellectual faculties have begun to develop: in preference to mere youths. For those who begin to love in this manner, seem to me to be preparing to pass their whole life together in a community of good and evil, and not ever lightly deceiving those who love them, to be faithless to their vows.62

The enigmatic and thoughtful phrase about the 'community of good and evil' is entirely Shelley's own. He has also widened the application of the Greek, which clearly talks about 'young boys in their green thoughtlessness', in order to make the Uranian qualities of dedication and loyalty apply to both young men and young women.*

Aristophanes's daring and comic parable of man's dual nature – divided by the gods 'as I have seen [hard-boiled] eggs cut with hairs' – was Shelley's second key text. He was fascinated by the psychological acuity of the Greek. Several concepts rapidly reinforced the lines along which Shelley's thought had naturally been developing. There were the ideas of the divided self; the self in search of its tally (*lispae*) or double; and the fear of yet a further division within the psyche, 'like those figures painted on the columns, divided through the middle of our nostrils', which was the threat of insanity from the gods. But perhaps the greatest curiosity to him in Aristophanes's speech was that of the third unnamed sex, the Hermaphrodite.

> The androgynous sex, both in appearance and in name, was common both to male and female; its name alone remains, which labours under a reproach . . . the male was produced from the Sun, the female from the Earth; and that sex which participated in both sexes, from the Moon, by reason of the androgynous nature of the Moon.[63]

Shelley later saw a fine Greek copy of the Hermaphrodite in Rome, and explored both its psychological and poetic possibilities in later writing, especially 'The Witch of Atlas' and *Epipsychidion*.

Shelley left a special notation in a manuscript notebook, on the speech of Agathon, the young tragic poet of 31 in whose house the banquet was held. He wrote that it was a 'wonderful description of love', and marked the passages on the tenderness and delicacy of Love's transit through 'the souls and inmost natures of Gods and men'. He considered 'Agathon a poem', and later incorporated a section of his speech in *Prometheus Unbound*.[64]

But it was finally the sage Diotima's philosophy, given in Socrates's speech, which drew Shelley's overwhelming interest. He marked six separate passages in his notebook, under the general heading of approval, 'Diotima's Atheism'.[65] He was fascinated above all else by the argument between Diotima and Socrates

---

* Shelley normally keeps the sexual distinction quite candid in his text, as for example: 'But the attendant on the other, the Uranian, whose nature is entirely masculine, is the Love who inspires us with affection towards men. . . .' In fact Shelley very rarely altered or even softened the text out of considerations of sexual propriety; but in more than a score of places he added a single word or phrase to extend its meaning philosophically. Occasionally he relied on Ficino to help him over a technically difficult passage.

which proves that Love cannot, after all, be a divine god. Love is, rather, a special *intermediary* force, in that strange daemonic level which exists between the known human world, and the perfect and for ever unknowable divine one. In this passage, Shelley found Plato penetrating directly into his own most private, inner obsession with the world of demons, which had always hovered uneasily in his mind between gothic metaphor and psychological reality. Given at length, it makes perhaps the finest example of Shelley's translation skills, and the most suggestive indication of how one level of his creative writing was going to develop after leaving the Bagni di Lucca.

'But', [said Socrates], 'Love is confessed by all to be a great God'. .... 'Do you not call those alone happy who possess all things that are beautiful and good?' – 'Certainly' – 'You have confessed that Love, through his desire for things beautiful and good, possesses not those materials of happiness'. – 'Indeed such was my concession.' – 'But how can we conceive a God to be without the possession of what is beautiful and good?' – 'In no manner, I confess.' – 'Observe, then, that you do not consider Love to be a God.' – 'What then', I said, 'is Love a mortal?' – 'By no means.' – 'But what, then?' – 'Like those things which I have before instanced, he is neither mortal or immortal, but something intermediate.' – 'What is that, O Diotima?' – 'A great Daemon, Socrates; and every thing daemoniacal holds an intermediate place between what is divine and what is mortal.'

'What is his power and nature?' I enquired. – 'He interprets and makes a communication between divine and human things, conveying the prayers and sacrifices of men to the Gods, and communicating the commands and directions concerning the mode of worship most pleasing to them, from Gods to men. ... Through him subsist all divination, and the science of sacred things as it relates to sacrifices, and expiations, and disenchantments, and prophecy, and magic. The divine nature cannot immediately communicate with what is human, but all that intercourse and converse which is conceded by the Gods to men, both whilst they sleep and when they wake, subsists through the intervention of Love; and he who is wise in the science of this intercourse is supremely happy, and participates in the daemoniacal nature; whilst he is who wise in any other science or art, remains a mere ordinary slave. These daemons are, indeed, many and various, and one of them is Love.[66]

It was to this study, 'this science', of the intermediary sphere, and to the recognition of Love and the other daemons 'many and various', some good and some evil, that Shelley was to direct much of the more obscure and private parts of his thought and writing in Italy. This Platonic passage provided the occult key. The *Symposium* as a whole, made especially his own through this brilliant summer translation of 1818, formed for Shelley a symbolic guide to the perplexities and paradoxes of his own mental processes. Given the sceptical cast of Shelley's mind, Plato remained for him, over the next four years, the nearest thing to his Bible. In times of distress – and there were to be many – Plato was never far from his thoughts.

17

An Evening with Count Maddalo: Venice

Theoretical discussion and meditation on the subject of love under the chestnut trees of the Lima, and in the laurel bower of Casa Bertini, suddenly gave way, in the middle of August 1818, to pressing practical demands. With the departure of Allegra to Venice in April, the old closeness between Shelley and Claire had been partly reconstituted. Shelley's almost paternal sympathy with Claire's depression and anxieties about the child had encouraged him to identify with her circumstances as much as with Mary's. News from Venice was scarce, and Claire's health and spirits had been steadily recovering. But now two urgent letters from Elise arrived in rapid succession, on Friday the 14th, and Sunday the 16th, which threw Claire once again into a desperate panic about the welfare of her child.[1] She began to insist that they must go at once to Venice. Parts of Elise's letters were impossible to decipher, according to Claire, and this only made things worse.[2] It was of doubtful value to let Claire lay siege to Byron again, and besides, Venice was over 200 miles away and would require a long and expensive journey. Yet surprisingly, Shelley agreed at once that Claire should go. Moreover, he decided to accompany her. Allowing barely time to pack their bags, Shelley and Claire hired a one-horse cabriolet without springs and set out at dawn on Monday the 17th, to drive the first stage of the journey eastwards, to Florence. A capable Italian servant called Paolo Foggi, whom Mary had employed at Casa Bertini since June, went with them on the first leg of their journey. Mary was left rather forlornly to write to the Gisbornes, asking them to come and 'cheer her solitude' in a house empty except for the servants and the two babies.

But for Shelley and Claire, it was quite like the old days. The journey took in all the best part of the week, though they drove hard sometimes sixty miles a day. Shelley was, judging by his letters, in admirably good form throughout. The sudden relief of leaving the pastoral hermitage of Casa Bertini, the prospect of seeing Byron, and no doubt the anxious but excited company of Claire on the open road all filled him with a sense of freedom and exhilaration. His first sight of Florence, the elegant Lung' Arno, the bridges, the sails on the river, the haze of 'bright villas . . . Domes & steeples on all sides' delighted them both. They swept into the Austrian Minister's office to demand passports, which they got in the space of four hours, and gorged themselves on figs and peaches like 'Paradise flowers' while waiting. Paolo's theatrical bargaining secured a *vetturino* for Padua, to leave at about midday on Tuesday, 'a comfortable carriage & two mules'. Shelley then sent Paolo back to Bagni di Lucca and posted a letter to Mary. He sent his love to Willmouse and little Ca, as the babies were now known, and told Mary breezily, 'I assure you I am not of a disposition to be flattered by your sorrow though I should be by your cheerfullness, & above all by seeing such fruits of my absence as were produced when we were at Geneva.' Perhaps she could manage another *Frankenstein*?

Meanwhile he and Claire eagerly discussed various plans to cope with Byron, which underwent 'a good deal of modification', as Shelley gradually persuaded her to abandon the idea of a personal confrontation. By letter he informed Mary that Claire would be dropped off to await events at Padua or Fucina, but whether this was ever really intended seems doubtful. At any rate, when they reached Padua on Friday, 21 August, the badness of the beds, full of 'those insects inexpressible by Italian delicacy', as Shelley gaily explained, and Claire's unwillingness to part from him 'in the strangeness & solitude of the place', led to yet another change of plan.

So it was they sailed into Venice together in a black gondola, late on Saturday night. They huddled in the cabin on the soft, inviting couches and grey carpets, while rain lashed the windows and lightning flashed across the *laguna*. The sea foam broke around, sparkling like stars, and 'Venice now hidden & now disclosed by the driving rain shone dimly with its lights'. Inside they were warm and comfortable, 'except that Claire was now & then a little frightened in our cabin', as Shelley always liked her to be. For some reason Shelley was fascinated by the construction of the gondola's windows, and pulling the strings to show Claire, he demonstrated how they could have 'at will either Venetian plate glass flowered, or Venetian blinds or blinds of black cloth to shut out the light'.[3] They reached their inn at Venice at midnight.

The next day, Sunday, was a critical one which Shelley, by a combination of stealth and candour, managed to bring off successfully. From the moment of their entry into Venice, talk of Byron's scandalous exploits was to be heard continuously on the lips of both gondoliers and innkeepers. Shelley realized the need to proceed with extreme tact. Elise's letters had informed Claire that Allegra was, for the time being, in the care of the English consul-general's wife, Mrs Richard Belgrave Hoppner, at the consular building. Starting immediately after breakfast, when he knew Byron would still be asleep at the Palazzo

Mocenigo, he hired a gondola and went at once with Claire to the Hoppners. Claire was then sent into the consular building on her own, to make inquiries about the child, and to sound out the Hoppners' sympathies. Shrewdly realizing that his presence at this point could only complicate matters, Shelley remained discreetly in the cabin of the gondola, examining the window glass. After a few minutes, much to his surprise, a servant came down to the mooring steps to ask for Mr Shelley. All was well. Claire had found Mrs Hoppner to be immediately 'agreeable and admirable', and full of sympathetic interest in their journey and their worries. Introductions were made, Elise was summoned to bring little Allegra, who appeared looking pale and slightly subdued, Shelley thought, but 'as beautiful as ever', and mother and child were happily reunited. An invitation to dine was extended, and Mr Hoppner took Shelley aside in a friendly way. 'We discussed a long time the mode in which I had better proceed with [Byron], & at length determined that Claire's being here should be concealed, as Mr H. says that he often expresses his extreme horror at her arrival, & the necessity which it would impose on him of instantly quitting Venice.'[4] The Hoppners entered into the arrangements for this concealment 'as if it were their own dearest concern', and explained with a certain relish some of the more outland-ish features of Byron's household. Shelley was inclined to feel that there was 'doubtless some exaggeration'.

After dinner Shelley embarked on the second stage of the plan: his unan-nounced visit to Palazzo Mocenigo. This too went unexpectedly well, though not quite as he had intended. Shelley had himself announced at three in the afternoon, when he calculated that Byron would have disembarrassed himself of any lady guests, and would have had time to complete his traditionally extended toilet and his sparse breakfast. Fletcher showed him in. Byron was delighted and surprised, sat Shelley down, and good-humouredly quizzed him on the subject of his visit. Shelley explained in his frankest and most measured manner that he had recently toured with Mary and Claire and the children as far as Padua. Since Claire was rather worried about her child's health and anxious to see her again if it should now be convenient, Shelley had thought to come on alone to Venice, and to have the pleasure of renewing his acquaintance with Lord Byron while discussing this matter privately between themselves.

Byron remained good-humoured. He was genuinely pleased and relieved to see Shelley again. He relished the prospect of renewing the Diodati style of speculative talk. He even began to excuse himself for not having Allegra sent to Florence: he feared, apparently, that 'the Venetians will think he has grown tired of her & dismissed her, & he has already the reputation of caprice'. Shelley later told Mary how the conversation went on: 'But if you like she shall go to Clare at Padua for a week (when he said this he supposed that you & the family were there). And in fact said he after all I have no right over the child. If Clare likes to take it – let her take it – I do not say what most people would in that situation that I will refuse to provide for it, or abandon it, if she does this; but she must surely be aware herself how very imprudent such a measure would be.'[5] Shelley found the anxiety which Byron showed to satisfy him and Claire most unexpected, and he was relieved at the spirit in which Byron dealt with the whole matter, and the conversation began to run more easily. With one of his abrupt and generous decisions, Byron suddenly suggested that Shelley should bring Mary and Claire and the children across from Padua to a country villa which he had taken at Este. Este was a decaying medieval fortress town in the Euganean hills, known locally for its pottery, some forty miles southwest of Venice. Byron had leased the largest house there, a summer villa known as 'I Capuccini' because it was built on the ruins of a Capuchin monastery; he had intended it as a possible retreat if life at the Palazzo Mocenigo with the Fornarina should become too hectic. Now, with a rapid gesture he dismissed the problem of Claire and Allegra by putting I Capuccini entirely at Shelley's service for the remainder of the summer, making it clear that while Allegra might visit Este, he should stay in Venice untroubled by Claire's solicitations.

By this time the conversation had moved from Byron's parlour in the Palazzo, to a gondola on the grand canal; and from the gondola across the *laguna* to the sandy reaches of the Venetian Lido, where Byron had horses waiting for his regular afternoon ride. They mounted up and 'rode along the sands of the sea talking'. The subject of Claire gave way to more personal matters: Harriet Shelley, Byron's sister Augusta, the composition of the new fourth canto of *Childe Harold*, Hunt and the attacks of the *Quarterly*. Byron was in a mood for confessions and confidences. 'Our conversation consisted in histories of his wounded feelings, & questions as to my affairs, & great professions of friendship & regard for me. He said that if he had been in England at the time of the Chancery affair, he would have moved Heaven & Earth to have prevented such a decision.'[6] Once Byron was in such a mood, and Shelley was in correspondingly good spirits, there was little that could stop them. The interview which had begun rather tentatively at 3 in the afternoon concluded at 5 a.m. the next morning, after a session of fourteen hours of non-stop talk. This included Byron reciting *Childe Harold* with abandoned energy. The fact that Claire had been waiting anxiously since dinner the previous day at the Hoppners' for news had become irrelevant. After all, she was meant to be at Padua. So, even more disconcertingly, were Mary and the children.

However, Shelley was not in the mood to be deterred by time or space. Arriving back at his inn as the first grey light broke over the canal, he seized pen and paper and dashed off an enormous letter to Mary, explaining everything that had happened in the last twenty-four hours, and demanding her immediate presence in Este to bring his plan for Claire into fruition. The final success of this, he wrote, 'is still doubtful', and everything depended on Mary making his story about Padua appear true, and Byron not learning about Claire's presence in Venice. It was a matter of speed. 'Pray come instantly to Este, where I shall be waiting with Claire & Elise in the utmost anxiety for your arrival. You can pack up directly you get this letter & employ the next day in that. The day after get up at four o'clock, & go post to Lucca where you will arrive at 6. Then take Vetturino for Florence to arrive the same evening. From Florence to Este is three days. . . . Este is a little place & the house found without difficulty. I shall count 4 days for this letter 1 day for packing 4 for coming here – On the ninth or tenth day we shall meet.'[7]

That these arrangements, the packing, the pre-dawn departure, and the five days of hard travelling in the blazing August weather, with the children, would be very hard for Mary did not really occur to Shelley. He thought, perhaps rightly, that Claire's happiness was at stake, and on such an occasion Mary must defer to it. His gentle excuses were not altogether serious: 'I have done for the best & my own beloved Mary you must soon come & scold me if I have done wrong & kiss me if I have done right – for I am sure I do not know which – & it is only the event can shew.' This did not soften the timetable.

The letter broke off as a gondola arrived to take Shelley to the bank to obtain an order of fifty pounds for Mary's travelling expenses. Later at the bank he scrawled a P.S.: 'Kiss the blue darlings for me & don't let William forget me – *Ca* cant recollect me.' He missed the post, but the letter went express. Later perhaps, he woke Claire with the good news.

On the 25th or 26th they quietly departed from Venice for Este with Elise and Allegra and the good wishes of the Hoppners. They did not know, because in the situation there was no way of knowing, that at the Bagni di Lucca little Clara was ill, slightly feverish and unable to take food, and Mary was intensely anxious about her. For ten days Shelley and Claire basked in the sun at the Villa Capuccini, awaiting Mary's arrival. They found the house cheerful and full of the radiant Italian light, set on the brow of one of the rolling foothills of the Euganean range, and commanding a view southwards over the plain of Lombardy. In the mornings, to westwards, before the heat of the day had filled the air with a blue haze, they could make out the distant line of the Apennines. Once again Shelley spent many hours observing the rising and setting of the sun and moon and evening star, and studying the slow architectural developments of 'the golden magnificence of autumnal clouds'. 'Behind us here', he wrote to Peacock, 'are the Euganean hills, not so beautiful as those of Bagni di Lucca, with Arqua where Petrarch's house and tomb are religiously preserved & visited. At the end of our garden is an extensive Gothic castle, now the habitation of owls and bats, where the Medici family resided before they came to Florence.'[8] Shelley found that, at night, when the moon 'sunk behind the black and heavy battlements', he could call up the owls, and obtain a satisfactory echo from the massive looming wall of the crumbling fortress.[9]

But the great feature of the Villa Capuccini was its summerhouse, situated at the end of a stone-flagged path stretching across the little back garden and reached by a glass doorway in the hall at the back of the house. The path was shaded by a trellis of vines trained across wooden frames to make one of the charming pergolas typical of the region. Shelley set up his study in this little summerhouse, scattering it with his few books and papers, and each morning he would make his way through the tunnel of sunlight and shade to write.

After the translation of the *Symposium*, his mind was again turning to the Promethean theme which he had unsuccessfully attempted to develop at Livorno and at Lucca in the stage play about Tasso. Realizing that the act of translation had both released and sustained his creative powers, he now turned to another Greek text, the *Prometheus Bound* of Aeschylus, and began to work some of it over into English. He no longer attempted to work methodically at a strict translation, but played around with certain images and speeches, adapting, extending and improvising as he went. He gradually came to the conclusion that by using the Aeschylean play as a base, he could attempt to re-create in English a version of the missing third part of the Aeschylean trilogy, the *Prometheus Unbound*. He could adapt the Aeschylean mythology and symbolism to the themes of political revolution and moral regeneration which had consistently concerned him in his previous epic poems, *Queen Mab* and *The Revolt of Islam*.

The process of adaption was to prove a slow and immensely arduous one. Upon no other of his poems did Shelley lavish such concentrated work over such a long period. By 22 September he had written twenty-six manuscript pages, and by 8 October he was writing to Peacock that he had 'just finished the first act of a lyric & classical drama to be called "Prometheus Unbound"'. Yet two months later in Naples, he was still redrafting this first act, and he wrote that it had been 'completed' at the end of January 1819. The second and third acts of *Prometheus* were finished in Rome by June 1819, but the fourth and final act was not conceived or added until the winter of 1819 in Florence. In all, *Prometheus Unbound* was sixteen months in composition. Yet the original idea, grounded upon Aeschylus' *Prometheus* remains as he first conceived it in September, living quietly with Claire at Este, and writing in the shaded summerhouse of the Villa Capuccini.

Meanwhile, as Mary pressed to conform to Shelley's gruelling travel scheme, aided as far as Lucca by Mrs Gisborne, little Clara became increasingly ill. By a kind of sympathy at the Villa Capuccini, Shelley made himself sick by eating some Italian cakes which he thought – for no apparent reason – must have been poisoned. Mary arrived on Saturday, 5 September, six days after her twenty-first birthday which she had celebrated alone by packing their books at the Casa Bertini. She was greeted by Shelley and Claire, who had been alone together, with Allegra and Elise, for three weeks. The 5th September is also important for it is the first time that Paolo Foggi met Elise. Little Clara was rather worryingly ill, and Shelley's stomach upset was turning into dysentery. Claire too seems to have been ill, and on the 16th the two of them went into Padua, to consult a doctor, since a proper *medico* could not be found in the country. Mary noted anxiously '[Shelley] is very ill from the effects of his poison'; and of the baby, 'Poor Clara is dangerously ill'.[10] Little Clara's condition was aggravated by her weakness from travelling and her teething. Shelley was the first to recover fully, and Mary noted that he was again writing hard in the summerhouse, and reading Sophocles's *Oedipus* to her in the evenings. He wrote to Byron that he had been 'four or five times on the point of setting out to Venice', but that Clara's illness had kept him 'an anxious prisoner' at Este. 'We have domesticated ourselves un-ceremoniously here, and find it, as I think you would find it, a most delightful residence.'[11] But Byron did not take the hint.

On Tuesday, 22 September, Shelley again took Claire into Padua to visit the doctor, but arriving too late in the morning, they missed her appointment. They had also intended to ask the *medico*'s advice about little Clara. Shelley was not unduly concerned, and he decided to go on alone to keep his long-promised visit to Byron at the Palazzo Mocenigo, and stay until Thursday. He sent Claire back to Este with a note to Mary, once again issuing a rather severe travelling time-table. 'Clare says she is obliged to come to see the Medico whom we missed this morning, & who has appointed as the only hour at which he can be at leisure, ½ past 8 in the morning. – You must therefore arrange matters so that you should come to the *Stella d'Oro* a little before that hour – a thing only to be accomplished by setting out at ½ past 3 in the morning.' Shelley intended to meet them at Padua, and then take Mary back to see Byron at Venice, while Claire returned to Este. Despite an explanation about avoiding the heat, this did not really alter the fact that Mary and the baby were again being fitted to Claire's convenience. Shelley was not entirely happy about his treatment of Mary and the child. 'My poor little Clara how is she today? Indeed I am somewhat uneasy about her, and though I feel secure there is no danger, it would be very com-fortable to have some reasonable person's opinion about her. The Medico at Padua is certainly a man in great practise, but I confess he does not satisfy me. – Am I not like a wild swan to be gone so suddenly?' He added a mysterious re-mark about not addressing her yet as 'Lady Shelley' – which was perhaps intended to remind her of the favours of fortune to come. Shelley finished his instructions by urging Mary to continue a translation of Ariosto which she had been attempting to work on since his departure from the Bagni di Lucca; and also for her to bring the manuscript of his own poem '. . . the sheets of "Prometheus Unbound" which you will find numbered 1 to 26 on the table of the pavilion'.[12] With that, he set off for Venice, and the intoxication of Byron's late night conversation, and the long rides across the deserted Lido.

How far Shelley was underestimating or simply ignoring Mary's worries about the child can be seen by the entirely different tone of one of her own letters to Maria Gisborne, which had arrived in Livorno four days previously. '. . . the fatigue has given my poor little *Ca* an attack of dysentery and although she is now somewhat recovered from that disorder she is still in a frightful state of weakness and fever and is reduced to be so thin in this short time that you would hardly know her again – the physician of Este is a stupid fellow but there is one come from Padua & who appears clever so I hope under his care she will soon get well, although we are still in great anxiety concerning her.'[13] A forced journey from Este to Venice, which was to begin at 3.30 in the morning and end at 5 in the afternoon was not perhaps the most suitable treatment in the circumstances.[14]

The upshot was rapid, and surely foreseeable. By the time little Clara had reached the Stella d'Oro at Padua on Thursday morning, she was again seriously ill. Shelley however insisted on continuing the prearranged journey into Venice, rather than put her under the care of the Paduan *medico* who had treated her previously. As the journey continued, Clara showed 'symptoms of increased weakness and even convulsive motions of the mouth and eyes', which as Shelley said made him 'anxious to see the physician'. At Fusina, where travellers boarded the gondolas to cross the lagoon into Venice, Shelley found he had forgotten their travel permit and was held up by the customs guards on duty. Mary was now frantic with the difficulties and delays, and Shelley forced their way on to the boat with a characteristic outburst. 'They could not resist [his] impetuosity at such a moment,' Mary wrote afterwards.[15] In the gondola, the child grew worse. They reached the inn, and Shelley immediately took another boat to find Byron's physician, Dr Aglietti. But he had made no previous arrangement, and the doctor was not to be found at home. Meanwhile Mary remained alone in the hall of the Venetian inn, in the 'most dreadful distress', as the child's convulsions grew worse. Before Shelley had returned, in a state of desperation, Mary had managed to summon a local doctor through the servants. But all he could tell was that there was no hope. Little Clara's convulsions ceased, and she grew quiet, and died silently about one hour after they had arrived in Venice. Shelley returned to see her die in Mary's arms. A few minutes later, the Hoppners arrived by gondola, having been alerted by a messenger, and took off the stunned and weeping party to the consulate. Clara was buried the next morning. Shelley wrote to Claire that Mary was by this 'unexpected stroke reduced to a kind of despair. She is better today.'[16]

But Mary was not really 'better' for another twelve months. The death of little Clara, to which Shelley's carelessness and unconcern had distinctly contributed, brought to a state of crisis the already strained relations between husband and wife. Other events were to compound further the situation during the winter, and Mary went into a long period of decline and isolated misery. When the birth of a new child, in November 1819, finally brought her back into full engagement with her life in Italy, she was a matured and rather hardened woman, who had come to accept both more realistically and more coldly the nature and limitations of her relationship with Shelley. Between young Mary and the matured one there is a distinct emotional caesura. Something of it can be seen in the comparison of the two portraits of her, the first drawn before her departure for Italy, and the second painted after her return to England. She worked herself through this crisis, a sort of mental breakdown, partly with the help of a long autobiographical novel which she wrote but retained in manuscript, called 'Mathilda'.[17] Many side-effects flowed from this 'kind of despair' which overwhelmed her, but one of the most important was the end of the state of confidentiality which had hitherto existed between her and Shelley. Certain parts of Shelley's emotional life were now forever closed from her. He found it easier to turn to Claire, and to others, for understanding. From the death of little Clara until the spring of 1819, there is only one complete letter of Mary's extant, although her journal continues in its usual laconic fashion. For 25 September she entered, 'This is the Journal of misfortune.'[18]

After Clara's burial, and a weekend during which Lord Byron and the Hoppners kindly attempted to distract Shelley and Mary with tours round the palaces, bridges and museums of Venice, the couple returned subdued to Este. Byron gave Mary the manuscript of his new poem 'Mazeppa' and told her gravely how helpful it would be if she could find time to fair-copy it. Shelley returned to the summerhouse and continued work sporadically on *Prometheus Unbound*, and made a draft of the 'Lines Written Among the Euganean Hills', a poem of great personal unhappiness.

After the first fortnight of October Mary seems to have found the atmosphere at the Villa Capuccini too melancholy, and she and Shelley returned to Venice for the rest of the month, dutifully distracting themselves with gondola trips, visits to the opera and a regular dinner engagement at the Hoppners'. Claire remained at Este with Allegra and Elise. One of the Hoppners' Italian acquaintances, the Chevalier Mengaldo, learning of Mary's authorship of *Frankenstein*, enthusiastically retold in detail several ghost stories, three of which Mary transcribed woodenly into her journal for 20 October. She later used them in her *London Magazine* article of 1824. The Chevalier, who had fought and been honourably wounded in Napoleon's Russian campaign, gallantly escorted Mary out to opera and comedies, although privately she was dismissing them as 'wretched' and 'stupid beyond measure'.[19] Shelley took the opportunity to slip away in a gondola, spending many afternoons riding with Byron along their favourite windswept Lido, and most evenings talking far into the night in the inner sanctum of Palazzo Mocenigo. Besides more personal matters, Shelley discussed Plato's *Symposium* and *The Republic* with Byron, and lent him a text. He was always anxious to improve Byron's mind, if not his morals, when he got the chance. In return, Byron drew his attention to a violent attack on Mr Hunt and Mr Shelley in the *Quarterly*, perhaps from his own version of the improving motive.[20]

Shelley's first delight with the gondolas and waterways and palaces of Venice slowly gave way to a deep disgust and aversion. To begin with it was largely political; he was appalled by the dungeons of the Doge's Palace, 'where the sufferers were roasted to death or madness by the ardours of an Italian sun, and others called the Pozzi, or wells, deep underneath, and communicating with those on the roof by secret passages where the prisoners were confined sometimes half up to their middles in stinking water'. As at Chillon, one suspects that the image of claustrophobic confinement was particularly appalling to him. Yet these signs of ancient tyranny were as nothing to the abject spirit of the place under its present occupation by Austrian troops. The Austrians, he noted, levied sixty per cent taxes and were quartered freely on the inhabitants; their soldiers swaggered brutally through the city, and dominated the public entertainments.[21]*

But politics formed only the objectionable dress of Venetian society, for there was also the repulsive flesh beneath. Shelley's hypersensitive nerves prickled with the Venetian combination of the beautiful and the disgusting, the graceful and the vile. He was both impressed and horrified by the gradual revelation of Byron's private life, and the extraordinary mixture of energy and cynicism with which it affected Byron's mental outlook. He wrote a long analysis to Peacock, which shows, besides his own acuteness of observation, that continuing puritan combination of revulsion and fascination in Shelley's own make-up.

> I entirely agree with what you say about Childe Harold [Canto IV]. The
> spirit in which it is written is, if insane, the most wicked & mischievous insanity
> that ever was given forth. It is a kind of obstinate & self-willed folly in which

---

* Dr Polidori was arrested in 1817 for asking a trooper to remove his busby at the opera.

he hardens himself. I remonstrated with him in vain on the tone of mind from which such a view of things alone arises. For its real root is very different from its apparent one, & nothing can be less sublime than the true source of these expressions of contempt & desperation. The fact is, that first, the Italian women are perhaps the most contemptible of all who exist under the moon; the most ignorant the most disgusting, the most bigoted, the most filthy. Countesses smell so of garlick that an ordinary Englishman cannot approach them. Well, LB is familiar with the lowest sort of these women, the people his gondolieri pick up in the streets. He allows fathers & mothers to bargain with him for their daughters, & though this is common enough in Italy, yet for an Englishman to encourage such sickening vice is a melancholy thing. He associates with wretches who seem almost to have lost the gait and physiognomy of man, & who do not scruple to avow practices which are not only not named but I believe seldom even conceived in England. He says he disapproves, but he endures. He is not yet an Italian & is heartily & deeply discontented with himself, & contemplating in the distorted mirror of his own thoughts, the nature & the destiny of man, what can he behold but objects of contempt & despair?[22]

Yet despite this degradation, and even perhaps partly because of it, Shelley's estimate of Byron's greatness as a poet and potential greatness as a public figure, were enormously enhanced by his Venetian visit. He already recognized that *Don Juan* was going to be 'infinitely better' than *Beppo*, and had the makings of one of the great satirical poems of the age. The paradoxes and contradictions of the situation troubled him deeply. He knew also that while their own friendship had been sealed by the past weeks in Venice, the fundamental opposition of their temperaments and tastes had been sharply revealed. How could he account for these things, and what, if any, was their wider philosophic significance? Shelley turned these questions over in his mind.

Claire was still at Este with Allegra, and on the last Saturday in October Shelley went back alone to the Villa Capuccini to sort out his books and papers and collect the child, who was due to be returned to the Hoppners. He took the opportunity to spend four quiet days at the villa, writing in the summerhouse and talking with Claire, and playing with the child in the evenings. He may also have had reasons to talk seriously with Elise. By the time he returned to Venice, on Thursday, 29 October, he had completed the first draft of his great Venetian poem 'Julian and Maddalo'. This is the first of his masterworks, one of the four best long poems he ever wrote.

'Julian and Maddalo' arose directly from Shelley's meditation on his visit to Byron. The simple outlines of the poem are deliberately and intensely realistic:

Julian is Shelley, and Count Maddalo – his name extracted from the Tasso manuscript – is Lord Byron. The setting of the poem is Venice, their own Venice of leisurely gondola trips, of rides on the Lido, of discussions at the Palazzo Mocenigo. The graceful philosophic argument and the strong clash of temperaments from which the dialogue of the poem is constructed form Shelley's attempt to evaluate as exactly as possible the full human significance of his own disagreement with Byron's approach to life. Maddalo is a philosophic pessimist and cynic, who pretends to believe that most men are mere sheep and that all men are at the mercy of chance and circumstance and their own passions. Julian chooses to argue as a progressive and an optimist, believing that men's circumstances can be changed, that society is capable of continuous improvement, and that individuals can in the end command their own faculties and fates. Maddalo argues as a behaviourist, Julian as an evolutionist. Maddalo is essentially apolitical, Julian is a reformer if not a revolutionary. The confrontation is brought into poetry with extraordinary ease and skill.

> This day had been cheerful but cold, and now
> The sun was sinking, and the wind also.
> Our talk grew somewhat serious, as may be
> Talk interrupted with such raillery
> As mocks itself, because it cannot scorn
> The thoughts it would extinguish: – 'twas forlorn,
> Yet pleasing, such as once, so poets tell,
> The devils held within the dales of Hell
> Concerning God, freewill and destiny:
> Of all that earth has been or yet may be,
> All that vain men imagine or believe,
> Or hope can paint or suffering may achieve,
> We descanted, and I (for ever still
> Is it not wise to make the best of ill?)
> Argued against despondency, but pride
> Made my companion take the darker side.[23]

The contrast in the personalities of his protagonists is carefully pointed out in a prose preface. The description of Maddalo is little more than a softened and generalized version of the analysis of Byron sent to Peacock.

> Count Maddalo is a Venetian nobleman of ancient family . . . [who] resides chiefly at his magnificent palace in that city. He is a person of the most consummate genius, and capable, if he would direct his energies to such an end, of becoming the redeemer of his degraded country. But it is his weak-

ness to be proud: he derives from a comparison of his own extraordinary mind with the dwarfish intellects that surround him, an intense apprehension of the nothingness of human life. . . . but . . . in social life no human being can be more gentle, patient, and unassuming than Maddalo. He is cheerful, frank, and witty. His more serious conversation is a sort of intoxication; men are held by it as by a spell.[24]

The description of Julian is instantly recognizable as a self-portrait, though edged by what Mary Shelley called the 'spirit that mocked itself'.

> Julian is an Englishman of good family, passionately attached to those philosophical notions which assert the power of man over his own mind, and the immense improvements of which, by the extinction of certain moral superstitions, human society may be yet susceptible. Without concealing the evil in the world, he is forever speculating how good may be made superior. He is a complete infidel, and a scoffer at all things reputed holy; and Maddalo takes a wicked pleasure in drawing out his taunts against religion. What Maddalo thinks on these matters is not exactly known. Julian, in spite of his heterodox opinions, is conjectured by his friends to possess some good qualities. How far this is possible the pious reader will determine. Julian is rather serious.[25]

The sense of lucid control and objective irony, almost of wit, is carried over into the narration and dialogue of the poem, and the fluency and natural simplicity of the verse movement is from the opening lines a masterly and artful achievement which Shelley had been working towards for years. Nothing could be more memorable in image and phrase than the fine austerity of the opening scenario, in which the atmosphere and the feelings of the Venetian landscape is brought slowly to bear on the human characterization.

> I rode one evening with Count Maddalo
> Upon the bank of land which breaks the flow
> Of Adria towards Venice: a bare strand
> Of hillocks, heaped from ever-shifting sand,
> Matted with thistles and amphibious weeds,
> Such as from earth's embrace the salt ooze breeds,
> Is this; an uninhabited sea-side,
> Which the lone fisher, when his nets are dried,
> Abandons; and no other object breaks
> The waste, but one dwarf tree and some few stakes
> Broken and unrepaired, and the tide makes
> A narrow space of level sand thereon,
> Where 'twas our wont to ride while day went down.

> This ride was my delight. I love all waste
> And solitary places; where we taste
> The pleasure of believing what we see
> Is boundless, as we wish our souls to be. . . .[26]

Julian and Maddalo are crossing back over the laguna from the Lido when Maddalo points out the dark windowless shape of the lunatic asylum which is to play a central role in the second section of the poem. Maddalo's comment on Julian's scoffing reaction to communal prayers at the asylum is, in the light of subsequent events, slightly uncanny:

>   'What we behold
> Shall be the madhouse and its belfry tower,'
> Said Maddalo, 'and ever at this hour
> Those who may cross the water, hear that bell
> Which calls the maniacs, each one from his cell,
> To vespers.' – 'As much skill as need to pray
> In thanks or hope for their dark lot have they
> To their stern maker,' I replied. 'O ho!
> You talk as in years past,' said Maddalo.
> ''Tis strange men change not. You were ever still
> Among Christ's flock a perilous infidel,
> A wolf for the meek lambs – if you can't swim
> Beware of Providence.' I looked on him,
> But the gay smile had faded in his eye.[27]

The next day, Julian calls on Maddalo at his palace to continue their discussions. Maddalo is naturally still in bed, and there is an apparently unimportant interlude while Julian plays with Maddalo's little girl, an obvious and charming portrait of Allegra. Here the scene is described with remarkable simplicity and directness of feeling. It is the product of intense artistic control, and the figure of the little girl is placed with deceptive ease, for she is to play a major part in the resolution of the poem.

> The following morn was rainy, cold and dim:
> Ere Maddalo arose, I called on him,
> And whilst I waited with his child I played;
> A lovelier toy sweet Nature never made,
> A serious, subtle, wild, yet gentle being,
> Graceful without design and unforeseeing,
> With eyes – Oh speak not of her eyes! – which seem

Twin mirrors of Italian Heaven, yet gleam
With such deep meaning, as we never see
But in the human countenance: with me
She was a special favourite: I had nursed
Her fine and feeble limbs when she came first
To this bleak world; and she yet seemed to know
On second sight her ancient playfellow,
Less changed than she was by six months or so;
For after her first shyness was worn out
We sate there, rolling billiard balls about,
When the Count entered.[28]

The child does not appear again until the final fifty lines of the poem; but Shelley places her here carefully in the thematic development of the work, as a kind of hostage both against fortune and against the purely intellectual side of Julian and Maddalo's argument.

This debate now continues at the palace, when Julian takes up the thread of their previous night's talk. He again attacks religion and forms of faith which 'break a teachless nature to the yoke', and continues to argue that progress is within the control of the individual, whose mind remains free and open.

                                         'See
This lovely child, blithe, innocent and free;
She spends a happy time with little care,
While we to such sick thoughts subjected are
As came on you last night – it is our will
That thus enchains us to permitted ill –
We might be otherwise – we might be all
We dream of happy, high, majestical.
Where is the love, beauty, and truth we seek
But in our mind? . . .'[29]

As it stands, Julian's argument is obviously weak, and his recourse to the example of the child is a very superficial kind of Wordsworthian platitude. Maddalo replies briskly and to the point: 'You talk Utopia.' Julian rejoins that these things remain to be tried: 'So taught those kings of old philosophy Who reigned, before Religion made men blind.' Adroitly refusing to embroil himself in an argument about Greek and Christian ethics, Maddalo again replies realistically that Julian can make 'such a system refutation-tight As far as words go', but that individual lives do not in fact work out like that. To illustrate his argument, Maddalo introduces the fourth major figure in the poem, the Maniac:

> '. . . I knew one like you
> Who to this city came some months ago,
> With whom I argued in this sort, and he
> Is now gone mad. . . .'

With this dry introduction, Maddalo once again whirls Julian into his gondola and they sail off through the 'fast-falling rain and high-wrought sea' to visit the asylum which Maddalo had pointed out the evening before.

The poem now reaches its central section, and the whole texture of the verse and the argument is imperceptibly and cunningly transformed. The violence of the weather and the sea begins to carry over into the human landscape, and the language abandons its fine-drawn austerity of style:

> We disembarked. The clap of tortured hands,
> Fierce yells and howlings and lamentings keen,
> And laughter where complaint had merrier been,
> Moans, shrieks, and curses, and blaspheming prayers
> Accosted us. We climbed the oozy stairs
> Into an old courtyard.[30]

They are taken to the Maniac who is in an upper chamber, sitting at a piano by the open window, while the wind blows in spatters of rain and spray from the *laguna*, and disorders his long hair. He is leaning his head against a book of music. His hands are twined together and he mutters quietly to himself. For the next 200 lines, the poem consists of his monologue, which is broken off several times, and recommences without apparent logic or connection. He talks and shouts and weeps. In his prose preface, Shelley defined with deliberate brevity the role of the Maniac, in which the lack of personal history or personal characterization is emphasized.

> Of the Maniac I can give no information. He seems, by his own account, to have been disappointed in love. He was evidently a very cultivated and amiable person when in his right senses. His story, told at length, might be like many other stories of the same kind: the unconnected exclamations of his agony will perhaps be found a sufficient comment for the text of every heart.[31]

Maddalo's commentary on the Maniac reinforces this mysterious lack of information. 'Alas, what drove him mad?' asks Julian:

> 'I cannot say:
> A lady came with him from France, and when
> She left him and returned, he wandered then
> About yon lonely isles of desert sand

> Till he grew wild – he had no cash or land
> Remaining, – the police had brought him here –
> Some fancy took him and he would not bear
> Removal; so I fitted up for him
> Those rooms beside the sea, to please his whim,
> And sent him busts and books and urns for flowers. . .'[32]

The Maniac's monologue makes an extraordinarily powerful and effective contract with the coolness, the disinterestedness, of the rest of the poem. This effect is carefully planned by Shelley. The reader is at once aware that in the asylum he is moving into a region which is, strictly speaking, paranormal. The scenario has already warned him of this. The monologue is saturated with ideas of pathological sexual disturbance: sadistic torture, necrophilia, self-castration, suicide, revulsion from familiarity without love. Yet none of these ideas are pursued or explained by the Maniac: they bubble up, burst and subside.

> 'That you had never seen me – never heard
> My voice, and more than all had ne'er endured
> The deep pollution of my loathed embrace –
> That your eyes ne'er had lied love in my face –
> That, like some maniac monk, I had torn out
> The nerves of manhood by their bleeding root
> With mine own quivering fingers, so that ne'er
> Our hearts had for a moment mingled there
> To disunite in horror – these were not
> With thee, like some suppressed and hideous thought
> Which flits athwart our musings, but can find
> No rest within a pure and gentle mind . . .'[33]

The Maniac never entirely gives way to these feelings at any point; he always insists in brief lucid moments that he intends no harm, that he casts away 'All human passions, all revenge, all pride'. Yet his resolution and his lucidity never lasts for very long, and in the end he exhausts himself, breaks off, smiles sadly, and goes to lie down on a sofa where he falls into a heavy sleep, disturbed only by weeping. The effect of the whole passage is brilliant and traumatic. The Maniac is like a dream that visits Julian and Maddalo simultaneously, and some of what he says refers indirectly to their own conscious or waking experience. Rather than a real character or person, he is *part* of a person, the part which lies below the threshold of consciousness. It is symbolic that he is both found and left asleep by his visitors. Shelley stresses in the preface that the Maniac's experience is *exemplary*, 'a comment for the text of every heart'.

Julian's reaction to the Maniac is that he never was 'impressed so much', and that for both of them 'our argument was quite forgot'. They return to the palace, and talk till dawn about the meaning of what they have witnessed. They are inconclusive. Julian observes that the root of the Maniac's suffering seemed to come from 'some deadly change in love Of one vowed so deeply that he dreamed not of'. Maddalo recalls the power of his language, 'the colours of his mind seemed yet unworn':

> And I remember one remark which then
> Maddalo made. He said: 'Most wretched men
> Are cradled into poetry by wrong,
> They learn in suffering what they teach in song.'[34]

The final section of the poem draws rapidly to its conclusion. There is another radiant description of the Venice which so attracted Julian, the gondolas, the buildings and statues, Maddalo's conversation. Julian wishes to stay, but he is called back to London. He is unable to put into action a plan to help the Maniac, but he describes it. He is now thinking in terms of human psychology far more than philosophic argument:

> ... I imagined that if day by day
> I watched him, and but seldom went away,
> And studied all the beatings of his heart
> With zeal, as men study some stubborn art
> For their own good, and could by patience find
> An entrance to the caverns of his mind,
> I might reclaim him from his dark estate . . .[35]

The underground cavern or labyrinth was to recur again and again in Shelley's Italian writing, as an image of the spiritual quest for the truth about oneself.

The poem ends with Julian's return, years later, to Venice. Maddalo had travelled far away in the mountains of Armenia, and 'his dog was dead'. But the little girl has grown up into a fine young woman, 'Like one of Shakespeare's', and she retells how the Maniac was visited again by his lover and then died. 'And was this not enough? They met – they parted.' The calm, beautiful, courtly presence of the girl comes through strongly and positively as a human value opposed to the pathological ravings of the Maniac. Yet there is no final confirmation at the end, for the Maniac's sufferings are not explained or justified. The note is elegiac, austere and confidential, and Shelley breaks off the poem with effective suddenness, giving no moral or conclusion overtly.

> I urged and questioned still, she told me how
> All happened – but the cold world shall not know.[36]

Of Shelley's major poems, 'Julian and Maddalo' remains perhaps the most subtle, the most oblique and the most suggestive in terms of psychological analysis. It is also the poem in which human characterization and the expressiveness of the Italian landscape are most delicately and harmoniously fused. The skill, light-ness, elegance and emotional control of the verse indicate that he had reached a new level of maturity.

The subsequent history of the manuscript is strange, as with nearly all Shelley's best works. Although he sent a fair copy to Hunt for printing in the *Examiner* at the end of the year, and several times wrote to Ollier in 1820, suggesting how it might be published both separately and with other poems, it was not in fact printed until after his death.[37] In August 1819 he wrote to Hunt introducing the poem as 'in some degrees consistent with your own ideas of the manner in which Poetry ought to be written. I have employed a certain familiar style of language to express the actual way in which people talk with each other. . . .' Of Julian, Maddalo and the Maniac he wrote: 'two of the characters you will recognise; the third is also in some degree a painting from nature, but, with respect to time and place, ideal'. Hunt did nothing.

In Florence, a year later, in 1819, he was planning to use the Venetian poem as a model for further work: 'I mean to write three other poems, the scenes of which will be laid at Rome, Florence, and Naples, but the subjects of which will all be drawn from dreadful or beautiful realities, as that of this was.'[38] So, al-though it remained unpublished, the poem came to represent for Shelley an important standard of 'realistic' writing which was opposed to the general rhetoric and idealistic drift of much of his own until the completion of *Prometheus*.* The poem indeed in its critique of Julian's idealism – for Shelley a form of self-criticism – and its insistence on the values of psychological under-standing, self-knowledge and personal experience, had already reached what was in many ways a far more advanced intellectual position than the Manichean ideology of *Prometheus*. It is in its *human* penetration and subtlety of self-discovery that 'Julian and Maddalo's' greatness lies: an achievement for which Shelley had suffered much, and on account of which much suffering was still in store for all of them.

---

* Beyond Shelley's lifetime, 'Julian and Maddalo' was to have a strong influence on the develop-ment of Robert Browning's best work, especially in the Italian Monologues such as 'Fra Lippo Lippi'.

18
The Tombs of Naples: 1818

Shelley and Elise returned Allegra to the care of the Hoppners, and on Saturday, 31 October 1818, he and Mary took leave of Byron. They were not to meet him again for nearly three years. Elise pressed to return to the Shelley household, and although this was awkward, it was allowed. The party, now consisting of little Willmouse, Milly Shields, Elise and Paolo Foggi, rejoined Claire at Este, and after five days of packing and preparation they set out to travel steadily southwards and take up winter lodgings in Naples. Not caring to keep a personal journal, Shelley began his series of long travel letters to Peacock. They show an eager and unselfconscious delight in the tourism which took his mind off other things, and a steadily increasing eye for the small, telling detail. At a farm north of Ferrara, 'the country of Pasiphaes', he counted sixty-three white and dove-grey oxen in their stalls. He noted the strange look of the closed and unpainted window shutters of the farmhouse; the flattened threshing floor still like that described in the *Georgics*, so that 'neither the mole nor the toad nor the ant' could hide in crevices; the heaps of coloured *zucki* or pumpkins stored for feeding the hogs; and the turkeys and fowls walking free in the yard, '& two or three dogs who bark with a sharp hylactism'. The farm-hands had a blunt incivility of manners which had 'an English air with it, very encouraging to those accustomed to the impudent & polished lying of the inhabitants of the cities'.[1]

At Ferrara Shelley went eagerly to view the souvenirs of Ariosto and Tasso. He prised off a splinter of wood from the door of Tasso's grated prison, remarking grimly that 'when I say it is really a very decent dungeon, I speak as one who has seen the prisons in the Doges palace at Venice'. He observed Ariosto's plain wooden chair, which 'has survived its cushion as it has its master', and peered at the three voluptuous bronze nymphs perched sportively on the circumference of his decorative ink-stand. Considering the two poets' manuscripts, he launched into a mild essay in graphology.

458

The handwriting of Ariosto is a small firm & pointed character expressing as I should say a strong & keen but circumscribed energy of mind, that of Tasso is large free & flowing except that there is a checked expression in the midst of its flow which brings the letters into a smaller compass than one expected from the beginning of the word.

On Tasso's script, which is not unlike his own, he commented: 'It is the symbol of an intense and earnest mind exceeding at times its own depth, and admonished to return by the chilliness of the waters of oblivion striking upon its adventurous feet.' Seeing in his mind's eye Peacock's eyebrows raised amusedly, he dipped his pen and added: '– You know I always seek in what I see the manifestation of something beyond the present & tangible object: and as we do not agree in physiognomy so we may not agree now.'[2]

Coming out of the museum library, Shelley stopped short at the door when a hand appeared rattling a wooden box for charity. He gazed for a moment with horror at a figure like some apparition from one of his own dreams, a shape enveloped from head to ankle in 'a ghost like drapery of white flannel', with even its face masked by a kind of network visor of cloth, the eyes alone glittering through the slits. 'I imagine this man had been adjudged to suffer this penance for some crime known only to himself & his confessor,' Shelley wrote afterwards, adding more briskly, 'this kind of exhibition is a striking instance of the power of the Catholic superstition over the human mind.'[3] The draped figure reappeared in the fragment of a story, 'The Colosseum', which Shelley began several weeks later at Rome.

From Ferrara they travelled to Bologna, 'a city of Colonnades', with its large picture gallery, and its Corinthian Madonna di Luca on the hill. Shelley enjoyed walking round it in the moonlight, and observing the sinister effect of its huge leaning brick towers built by the military-minded nobility. 'There are two towers here one 400 foot high ugly things built of brick, which lean both different ways, & with the delusion of moonlight shadows you almost fancy the city is rocked by an earthquake.' At the gallery Shelley gazed at pictures by Correggio, Guido, Domenichino and Guercino which he enthusiastically described to Peacock, though ridiculing their religious implications. His eye was caught by Guido's delicately suggestive picture of Love chasing Fortune. Love was 'trying to catch her by the hair and her face was half turned towards him, her long chestnut hair was floating in the stream of the wind and threw its shadow over her fair forehead'.[4] It was an image of desire that he himself had used frequently in his poetry, and it struck him almost with a kind of nostalgia.

After two days at Bologna, they travelled on by the coastal road through Fossombrone, Spoleto with its magnificent aqueduct, Terni and its famous waterfall, and finally reached Rome on Friday, 20 November. They had decided to hire their own horses and let Paolo do the driving, which, as Mary said, was very economical and very disagreeable.

Shelley thought the Terni waterfall the grandest natural spectacle he had ever seen except for the glaciers of Montanvert, and described with minute care the strange hallucinatory effect of the light and movement of the great mass of water as it fell 300 feet into the valley of the Velino. 'It comes in thick & tawny folds flaking off like solid snow gliding down a mountain. . . . Your eye follows it & is lost below. . . . The very imagination is bewildered in it. . . . We past half an hour in one spot looking at it, & thought but a few minutes had gone by.'⁵ Mary was put in mind of Sappho leaping from a rock, 'and her form vanishing as in the shape of a swan in the distance'. It was almost her only personal observation throughout the whole journey.⁶ Their arrival in Rome was greeted by an immense hawk sailing in the sky high above the Campagna di Roma searching for prey.

They remained in Rome for a week. Shelley was obviously overwhelmed by his first impressions and was content to be swept round the standard sights with the other visitors: St Peter's, the Colosseum, the Forum, the Capitol, the fountains and the piazzas. More than anything he was struck by the way that Nature had reasserted herself among the ruins: within the sixteen-mile circuit of the ancient wall were to be found whole fields of wild flowers, grassy lanes, green knolls overlooking the Tiber and copses of fig trees among the ruins.* The Colosseum especially amazed Shelley in this respect, for it had become an immense garden ruin, a *hortus conclusus*, in which nature and civilization had reached a kind of harmony. 'It has been changed by time into the image of an ampitheatre of rocky hills overgrown by the wild olive the myrtle & the fig tree, & threaded by little paths which wind among its ruined stairs & immeasurable galleries; the copse-wood overshadows you as you wander through its labyrinths & the wild weeds of this climate of flowers bloom under your feet. . . . I can scarcely believe that when encrusted with Dorian marble & ornamented by columns of Egyptian granite its effect could have been so sublime and so impressive. . . .'⁷ Mary found that the ruins disappointed 'in quantity', and the opera Shelley took her to on their second evening was 'the worst I ever saw'.⁸ The next two mornings she spent sketching in the Colosseum with Willmouse while Shelley took Claire to view the grosser aspects of the Vatican.

Shelley found time during this week to sketch out 2,000 words of his fragmentary story, 'The Colosseum'. A blind old man, accompanied by his daughter in a

---

* In some ways the situation had reverted to the time when Filippo Brunelleschi first entered the Holy City to study the architecture of the Pantheon, and found foxes running through the streets. See Vincent Cronin, *The Flowering of the Renaissance*, 1969, Ch. 1.

manner vaguely reminiscent of Sophocles's *Oedipus at Colonus*, is taken into the ruins of the Colosseum. The old man imagines the Colosseum as a magic cavern filled with exotic beasts. 'Are they not caverns such as the untamed elephant might choose, amid the Indian wilderness, wherein to hide her cubs; such as, were the sea to overflow the earth, the mightiest monsters of the deep would change into their spacious chambers?'[9] They meet there a stranger whose figure Shelley drew from the penitent at Ferrara. The strange youth, who inhabits the Colosseum like a ghost, attempts to introduce himself to the pair, having heard the old man speak mystically of the circle round 'the internal nature of each being' which prevents human contact. But here, just as a theme is beginning to appear, the manuscript ends, leaving one interesting detail. On the youth's shoes there is carved an image which was to appear in later letters from Rome and finally in Shelley's poem *Prometheus Unbound*. 'His snow white feet were fitted with ivory sandals, delicately sculptured in the likeness of two female figures, whose wings met upon the heel, and whose eager and half-divided lips seem quivering to meet.'[10] The long, slow crystallization of apparently disparate images like this was to give Shelley's mature poetry much of its richness in the coming months. For the time being it remained dormant.

On 27 November, Shelley decided to go ahead of his party, and travel alone to Naples, ostensibly to arrange rooms, without the expense of all of them having to 'alight at an Inn' in Naples while accommodation was found. Whether Shelley had any other private business to attend to in Naples was not immediately apparent. He travelled day and night by *vetturino*, crossing the notorious Pontine Marshes after dark in the company of a Lombard merchant and a gross Calabrian priest. The priest expressed frantic terror of robbers on the road, while the merchant talked genially of the recent murder of two bishops.[11] The priest was further terrified by the sight of Shelley withdrawing his customary brace of pistols from his travelling bag. Shelley did this with deliberate display, and the coach-driver had to be called down to quiet the priest's 'hysterics'. The Calabrian had his revenge when, on arrival at Naples, they witnessed at close quarters a youth stabbed to death in the neck as he ran out of a shop. Shelley reacted with horror and the priest, showing the true courage and dignity of his cloth, laughed heartily in Shelley's face. Shelley was furious: 'the priest attempted to quiz me as what the English call a *flat*. I never felt such an inclination to beat anyone, Heaven knows I have little power, but he saw that I looked extremely displeased & was silent'.[12] The incident confirmed Shelley's opinion of the Italian church, although this was neither the first nor last time that the way he brandished his pistols got him into difficulties.

Shelley took lodgings in the respectable tourist quarter of Naples, at No. 250 Riviera di Chiaia. The rooms appear to have been on the first or second floor, with a splendid view from the tall windows, overlooking the Royal Gardens, and beyond 'the blue waters of the bay, forever changing yet forever the same, & encompassed by the mountainous island of Capreae [*sic*], the lofty peaks which overhang Salerno, & the woody hill of Posilypo whose promontories hide from us Misenum & the lofty isle Inarime which with its divided summit forms the opposite horn of the bay'. Mary and Claire and the entourage arrived two days later, on 1 December. They could not but be pleased with the rooms, and consider themselves 'well off'; but Mary was tired and in low spirits. Shelley walked her in the Royal Gardens, pointed out the smoke from Vesuvius, and enthused about the delicious March wildness of the climate, which allowed them to sit in the evenings without a fire and with the windows open. They had 'almost all the productions of an English summer'. But Mary could not be cheered, and ten days later she was writing to Maria Gisborne that she still felt wearied and overcome by the fatigue of the long journey – 'so you must expect a very stupid letter'.[13] Claire was ill, with a return of the complaint which had apparently been troubling her when she attended the Paduan *medico* in early October.

On top of everything, Mary now discovered that there was some sort of romantic intrigue afoot between the Italian, Paolo Foggi and Elise. This attachment had first become obvious during the journey from Venice and the week spent in Rome, and Mary tried strongly to discourage it. So did Shelley. 'We all tried to dissuade her,' Mary wrote afterwards, 'we knew Paolo to be a rascal, and we thought so well of her that we believed him to be unworthy of her.'[14] As far as she could tell, they had at least temporarily succeeded. But it did not make the atmosphere at Riviera di Chiaia any less strained. Moreover, in between bouts of enthusiastic sightseeing, Shelley himself appeared to lapse into a mysterious gloom. He noted that at night, from their windows, the plume of smoke above Vesuvius was transformed into a dull red glow.[15] The old nephritic trouble in his side began relentlessly to return.

The only day-to-day record of the Shelley household during the months of December and January is Mary's journal. This shows that Shelley made a great effort to busy them all with sightseeing during the first three weeks, and visits were arranged to the ancient theatre at Herculaneum on Saturday the 5th, and by boat through the Bay of Baiae on Tuesday the 8th, calling at the Mare Morto, the Elysian Fields, and the Cavern of the Sibyl. Shelley was still gathering images to reappear in his poems: 'the sea . . . was so translucent that you could see the hollow caverns clothed with the glaucous sea-moss, & the leaves & branches of those delicate weeds that pave the unequal bottom of the water';[16] while Mary merely noted, 'The Bay of Baiae is beautiful; but we are disappointed by the various places we visit.'[17] On Sunday the 13th they went to the opera, and the next Tuesday they visited Virgil's tomb. On Wednesday the 17th they made an afternoon and evening expedition to the volcanic head of Vesuvius, which turned out to be almost traumatic. Mary exhausted herself, Claire was practically abandoned by her guides in the dark, and Shelley became extremely ill during the descent by torchlight, with an agonizing pain in his side, and virtually collapsed at the guides' hermitage in 'a state of intense bodily suffering'. He nevertheless managed to write it up in one of his most brilliant descriptive letters to Peacock the following morning.

Three days before Christmas, Shelley organized yet one more expedition, this time to Pompeii. In the ruined city, Shelley walked brooding through the streets, mentally noting the mosaics, the 'little winged figures & small ornaments of exquisite elegance', and the Greek bas-reliefs of Egyptian angels in the temples. He approved of the number and grandeur of the public buildings. Under the portico of the Temple of Jupiter, the party camped for luncheon, 'we sate & pulled out our oranges & figs & bread & apples (sorry fare you will say) & rested to eat'.[18] They munched in silence, gazing out over the blueness of the bay and the mountains of Sorrento. It was beautiful and yet disquieting. 'Every now & then we heard the subterranean thunder of Vesuvius; its distant deep peals seemed to shake the very air & light of day which interpenetrated our frames with the sullen & tremendous sound.'

They returned by the eastern gate, as the sun set and the shadows lengthened, and walked among the exquisitely carved marble tombs which stand along either side of the consular road. He noted on the stucco wall of one of the tombs 'little emblematic figures of a relief exceedingly low, of dead or dying animals & little winged genii, & female forms bending in groups in some funeral office'. It seemed to him suddenly as if these were not like English tombs, hiding decay, but like 'voluptuous chambers for immortal spirits'.

Mary's journal for the rest of December and all January is confined to the barest entries, usually recording books read by her or Shelley – Dante, Livy and Winckelmann's *History of Ancient Art* – and frequently entering nothing more than the date. This silence in fact covers an extreme personal crisis for Shelley, and December 1818 is the date attached to one of his most despairing and self-pitying lyrics, 'Stanzas Written in Dejection, Near Naples'.

> Alas! I have nor hope nor health,
>   Nor peace within nor calm around,
> Nor that content surpassing wealth
>   The sage in meditation found,
>   And walked with inward glory crowned. . . .
>
> I could lie down like a tired child,
>   And weep away the life of care. . . .[19]

Other manuscript fragments dating from this period included the 'Invocation to Misery', and the unfinished stanza beginning 'My head is wild with weeping'.[20] Shelley was also probably working on the Maniac section of 'Julian and Maddalo' at this time, and the story of the Pisan 'Marenghi' who was forced into life-long exile in the Maremma in reparation for an unknown crime.[21]

Writing twenty years afterwards, Mary chose to indicate this period of crisis without fully explaining the cause. But of her own emotional separation from Shelley she is remarkably frank.

> At this time, Shelley suffered greatly in health. He put himself under the care of a medical man, who promised great things, and made him endure severe bodily pain, without any good results.* Constant and poignant physical suffering exhausted him; and though he preserved the appearance of cheerfulness, and often greatly enjoyed our wanderings in the environs of Naples, and our excursions on its sunny sea, yet many hours were passed when his thoughts, shadowed by illness, became gloomy, – and then he escaped to solitude, and in verses, which he hid from fear of wounding me, poured forth morbid but too natural bursts of discontent and sadness. One looks back with unspeakable regret and gnawing remorse to such periods; fancying that, had one been more alive to the nature of his feelings, and more attentive to soothe them, such would not have existed. And yet, enjoying as he appeared to do every sight or influence of earth or sky, it was difficult to imagine that any melancholy he showed was aught but the effect of the constant pain to which he was a martyr.
>
> We lived in utter solitude.[22]

After the disastrous expedition to Vesuvius on the 17th, Shelley wrote three letters to friends in England just before Christmas. They were to Peacock, to Hunt and to Hogg, and they show, without giving any direct reason, that Shelley was extremely depressed and, for the first time in Italy, lonely and homesick. His letter to Peacock, after completing the magnificent Vesuvius description, ended mournfully: 'I have depression enough of spirits & not good health, though I believe the warm air of Naples does me good. We see absolutely no one here – Adieu.'[23] Most of his letter to Hunt, the first one for many weeks, consisted of a rather morbid defence of his own character against the supposed attacks of Southey in the *Quarterly Review*. It ended somewhat abruptly urging

---

* The medical man was a Scottish surgeon, Dr J. Bell, but Shelley did not actually put himself under his direction until about the middle of January 1819. Dr Bell diagnosed 'a disease of the liver' for which he prescribed 'mercury and Cheltenham salts' to be be used with much caution, together with daily riding exercise. Shelley was not under a medical man during the first five or six weeks of their stay in Naples, as Mary seeks to imply, and his physical disease was clearly in part the result of mental stress during these weeks, as Mary largely seeks to disguise.

that Hunt should bring himself and Peacock as soon as possible to Italy in the spring: 'Now pray write directly, addressed as usual to Livorno, because I shall be in a fever till I know whether you are coming or no. I ought to say, I have neither good health or spirits just now, & that your visit wd be a relief to both.'[24] The letter to Hogg, briefest of all, contained a sketch of their journeyings and a violent attack on Italian women, who 'are disgusting with ignorance and prostitution', and the strong implication that somehow 'We shall meet again soon'.[25] Neither the letter to Hunt or Hogg mentioned Claire, or any of the servants, or gave any indication of Mary's bad spirits. In fact nothing that Shelley wrote at the time goes any way to explain the real causes of his misery. Yet physical illness and depression were symptoms, rather than causes, of Shelley's unhappiness. His mysterious troubles at Naples arose from practical problems and difficulties of the most tangible human kind. Not until eighteen months after he had left Naples, did Shelley write a confidential letter to the Gisbornes which gives the basis for an explanation. 'My Neapolitan charge is dead. It seems as if the destruction that is consuming me were as an atmosphere which wrapt & infected everything connected with me. The rascal Paolo has been taking advantage of my situation at Naples in December 1818 to attempt to extort money by threatening to charge me with the most horrible crimes. He is connected with some English here [i.e. Livorno] who hate me with a fervour that almost does credit to their phlegmatic brains, & listen & vent the most prodigious falsehoods. An ounce of civet good apothecary to sweeten this dunghill of a world.'[26]

This brief paragraph, despite references which may at first appear obscure, gives the essence of Shelley's problem. It indicates that he was in some kind of personal entanglement during the winter at Naples – 'my situation'; that the result of this was a child whom he regarded as his responsibility – 'my Neapolitan charge' and that there had been an element of impropriety which was grave enough for his servant Paolo Foggi to threaten to use his knowledge as the basis for blackmail. The blackmail element is important, for it affected a good deal of Shelley's subsequent life in Italy. Paolo was sufficiently sure of his knowledge and advantage to require Shelley to employ against him an Italian lawyer, Signor del Rosso of Livorno, from June 1820 until at least February 1821.[27]

Of the child, we now know certain definite facts. It was a little girl, and Shelley twice registered himself as her father in official documents at Naples. The first document was a state registration paper, signed on 27 February 1819. It states that Elena Adelaide Shelley, daughter of Percy B. Shelley, was born at 250 Riviera di Chiaia on 27 December 1818 at 7 p.m. The second document was a certificate of baptism, which states that the child of Percy B. Shelley was baptized Elena Adelaide Shelley on 27 February 1819. There is also a third document in the Neapolitan State archive. This is a death certificate that states that Elena Schelly [*sic*] died at No. 45 Via Vico Canale, Naples on 9 June 1820, giving her age as 15 months 12 days.[28]*

To the bare dates in these documents, it is also possible to add a number of circumstantial facts of equal certainty. On 27 December, the day given as Elena's birth, Shelley, Mary, Claire, Milly Shields, Elise and Paolo were all resident at 250 Riviera di Chiaia.[29] On 28 February 1819, the day after Elena was registered by Shelley and baptized, the Shelley household left Naples, never to return.[30] That is to say, Shelley, Mary, Claire and Milly left; for Paolo and Elise had married and were no longer with them. On 9 June 1820, the day of Elena's death in Naples, the Shelleys were at the Bagni di Pisa; and three days later, on the 12th, Paolo Foggi first began his blackmail attempts by letter.[31] Elise's whereabouts is not known at this time; she may have been in Naples, Rome or Florence; but later in the summer of 1820 she was back in Venice working at her old job as a servant and companion to an English lady, probably a Miss Fairhill. Paolo no longer seems to have been with her.[32] So much then, is clear about the general outline of Shelley's 'situation at Naples in December 1818'.

But from this point, the evidence is highly confusing. Shelley had registered as Elena's father. But then who was her mother? Why did the circumstances of her birth make him so desperately unhappy, and leave him open to blackmail? Why did he not register her birth until two months after the event? And why did he leave her behind in Naples with, presumably, the Italian foster parents who lived at 45 Vico Canale?

The documents in the state archive do not help to answer the question of Elena's maternity. For they state that Elena's mother was Mary Godwin Shelley. This was patently a falsification on Shelley's part, for otherwise the child would never have been left in Naples, and there would be no mystery and no blackmail. Moreover there is no mention of Elena in any of Mary's letters or journal at this or any other time, and one cannot be certain that she knew about the baby's existence until the beginning of the Foggi blackmail in June 1820. Even then there is no absolute evidence that Shelley gave her all the details of Foggi's threatened revelations; though it seems likely that she knew of Elena, who was

---

* The birth registration in the State Archives of Naples was first discovered and printed in photostat by N.I.White in 1947. There are a number of interesting minor points about this document. It is made out in official hand, and signed personally by Shelley and two witnesses, but not by Mary Shelley. Mary's name is given on the document as 'Maria Padurin', an Italian mispronunciation of Mary Godwin which Shelley did not bother to correct. Shelley correctly gave his own age and address, but he allowed Mary's age to be entered as 27 – when she was in fact 21. The only woman in Shelley's household who was in her late 20s was Elise. In the certificate of baptism, which was made out by the parish priest of St Joseph at Chiaia, and not signed by Shelley, Mary's name is more correctly given as Maria Godwin. When the death certificate was made out on 10 June 1820, little Elena's age was given as from the day of baptism.

by then dead. On the whole, though, it would appear that Mary probably knew about this baby and Shelley's 'situation' from the time that they were in Naples in December.

If Elena Adelaide Shelley's mother was not Mary, who was she? One answer to this question appears in a notorious exchange of letters written in September 1820 on the other side of Italy, between Shelley's old friend the British Consul at Venice, and Lord Byron. During the intervening period, the Hoppners had for a time looked after Allegra, while Claire had struggled with Byron (by post) to reassert her right to visit her child. On 10 September 1820, Byron wrote from Ravenna to Richard Belgrave Hoppner at Venice: '. . . I regret that you have such a bad opinion of Shiloh [Shelley]; you used to have a good one. Surely he has talent and honour, but is crazy against religion and morality. . . . His *Islam* had much poetry. You seem lately to have got some notion against him. Clare writes me the most insolent letters about Allegra; see what a man gets by taking care of natural children! Were it not for the poor little child's sake, I am almost tempted to send her back to her atheistical mother. . . .'[33]

Hoppner, who had originally been so helpful and sympathetic to the Shelleys had indeed contracted 'a notion' against them, as he proceeded to elaborate in a return letter to Byron, of 16 September 1820. It will be observed that the date on which he says he first heard his revelation falls somewhere in the period of June or July of 1820, and thus corresponds to the commencement of Paolo's blackmail threats to Shelley at this period. The letter is given at length, for despite its obvious antagonism towards Shelley, it vividly substantiates what is already known about the stresses and strains within his household, and confirms and clarifies what have up to now remained at best hints and clues in the narrative. Belgrave Hoppner wrote to Byron:

My dear Lord. . . . You are surprised, and with reason, at the change of my opinion respecting Shiloe; it is certainly not that which I once entertained of him; but if I disclose to you my fearful secret, I trust, for his unfortunate wife's sake, if not out of regard to Mrs Hoppner and me, that you will not let the Shelleys know that we are acquainted with it. . . .

You must know then that at the time the Shelleys were here Clare was with child by Shelley: you may remember to have heard that she was constantly unwell, and under the care of a Physician, and I am uncharitable enough to believe that the quantity of medicine she then took was not for the mere purpose of restoring her health. I perceive too why she preferred remaining alone at Este, notwithstanding her fear of ghosts and robbers, to being here with the Shelleys. Be this as it may, they proceeded from here to Naples, where one night Shelley was called up to see Clara who was very ill. His wife, naturally, thought it very strange that he should be sent for; but although she was not aware of the nature of the connection between them, she had had sufficient proof of Shelley's indifference, and of Clara's hatred for her: besides as Shelley desired her to remain quiet she did not dare to interfere.

A Mid-wife was sent for, and the worthy pair, who had made no preparation for the reception of the unfortunate being she was bringing into the world, bribed the woman to carry it to the Pietà, where the child was taken half an hour after its birth, being obliged likewise to purchase the physician's silence with a considerable sum. During all the time of her confinement Mrs Shelley, who expressed great anxiety on her account, was not allowed to approach her, and these beasts, instead of requiting her uneasiness on Clara's account by at least a few expressions of kindness, have since increased in their hatred to her, behaving in the most brutal manner, and Clara doing everything she can to engage her husband to abandon her. Poor Mrs Shelley, whatever suspicions she may entertain of the nature of their connection, knows nothing of their adventure at Naples. . . . This account we had from Elise, who passed here this summer with an English lady who spoke very highly of her. She likewise told us that Clara does not scruple to tell Mrs Shelley she wishes her dead, and to say to Shelley in her presence that she wonders how he can live with such a creature.

Thus you see that your expression with regard to her is *even too delicate*; and I think with you, not only that she is a —— ——,* but anything worse even that you can say of her. I hope this account will encourage you to persevere in your kind intentions to poor little Allegra, who has no one else to look up to. . . .[34]

The last paragraph of this letter explains much of its high-minded and malicious relish, by showing how Hoppner considered himself to be carrying out a Christian duty towards Allegra. It also indicates that he was anxious to interpret matters in the light that he imagined would most please Byron. One can be certain that nothing that Elise said about Claire was softened in the retelling, and one may reasonably suspect, as in the admitted case of his own 'uncharitable' supposition about the abortion attempt, that some details were added or coloured up.

Byron allowed three weeks to elapse and then replied shortly and evenly, that the 'Shiloh story is true no doubt, though Elise is but a sort of *Queen's evidence*. You remember how eager she was to return to them, and then she goes away and abuses them. Of the facts, however, there can be little doubt; it is just like them. You may be sure that I keep your counsel. . . .'[35]

* Byron had called her, simply, 'a damned bitch' which was for him almost an endearment.

At first sight, despite the obvious attempt to make as unpleasant and damaging as possible a story that could, after all, have been narrated with sympathy and understanding, Hoppner's version of Paolo and Elise's 'fearful secret' appears to fit convincingly the known facts about the Shelley household. That there was an increase in intimacy between Claire and Shelley from the time Allegra was dispatched from Milan to the time they spent three weeks by themselves together at I Capuccini in August and September, is certain. Moreover Elise alone was with them on this occasion.

Equally certain is the evidence for the increasing rift between Shelley and Mary, marked especially by the death of little Clara. That these things ever amounted to 'indifference' on Shelley's part, and 'hatred' on Claire's seems unlikely: they had all three, after all, been coping with this situation for four years, though Elise had been with them for more than two of those years. But no doubt there were scenes, and Claire certainly had a sharp tongue when she wanted.

That Claire attended a *medico* at Padua frequently, and was seriously 'ill' at Naples, is also certain. On 17 December, during their expedition to Vesuvius, Shelley noted that while he and Mary rode on donkeys, Claire 'was carried in a chair on the shoulders of four men, much like a member of parliament after he has gained his election, & looking with less reason quite as frightened'.[36] To Peacock, Shelley tried to make a joke of it, but it could only have been because Claire was unwell, and incapable of violent exertion on a mule like the others. A few days later, she was indeed ill in bed, as Mary herself later admitted to Mrs Hoppner: 'I now remember that Clare did keep her bed for two days – but I attended on her – I saw the physician – her illness was one that she had been accustomed to for years.'[37] Hoppner said that Elise said specifically that Shelley and not Mary attended Claire on this occasion. Mary realized that Claire's illness was an awkward point, for when she wrote privately to Shelley about the scandal, she remarked: 'Do not think me imprudent in mentioning Clare's illness at Naples – It is well to meet facts – they are as cunning as wicked. . . .'[38]

But even more suggestive than this is the date which Mary's own journal at the time gives for Claire's illness. Her entry for the day of Sunday 27 December 1818, at Naples: 'Finish 2nd book of the Georgics. Clare is not well. Shelley reads Winckelmann. Walk in Gardens.'[39] 27 December is of course the date given on the birth registration of Elena Shelley. From this evidence it seems very difficult not to conclude that little Elena was indeed the illegitimate child of Shelley and Claire Clairmont.

Yet despite these highly circumstantial facts, there are overwhelming reasons against it. In the first place, everything we know of Claire's character, and her feelings and actions with regard to her first child Allegra, totally contradict the idea that she would ever abandon a child of hers, least of all by Shelley, to be brought up by Neapolitan step-parents. Unless all the rest of the evidence of her life, her friendship with Shelley, and her known letters and diaries is to be regarded as completely misleading, there are no conceivable circumstances under which she would be party to such an abandonment. The evidence of her diaries, which are extant for 1820, fully underwrites this view. There is no sign that she was unduly upset when Shelley received news of Elena's death in June or early July – Shelley was deeply upset – and there is no evidence that she tried to go back to Naples at any time between February 1819 and June 1820. On the other hand the diary clearly suggests that Claire was taken into Shelley's confidence more fully than Mary on this matter, that she was concerned for his own sake, and that Claire later had exchanges with Elise about her revelations to the Hoppners. It also shows by contrast that Claire *was* occasionally bitter towards Shelley about Allegra's fate. This of course is not to say that Claire could never have fallen in love with Shelley, or slept with him; simply that Elena could not have been her child.

In the second place, Elise's story – as told by Hoppner – does not bear close examination as far as the actual details of Claire's alleged secret baby are concerned. We are asked to believe that Claire was seven months pregnant when she and Mary were together at Este; eight months pregnant when they were together at Rome sightseeing without Shelley; and nine months pregnant when they were touring Vesuvius, Pompeii and the sights of Naples – all without Mary realizing Claire was carrying a child. It is not very convincing. In her strenuous denials to Mrs Hoppner that Claire ever had a baby, Mary herself made exactly this point: 'at the time specified in Elise's letter, the winter after we quitted Este, I suppose while she was with us, and that was at Naples, we lived in lodgings where I had momentary entrance to every room, and such a thing could not have passed unknown to me'.[40]

Moreover there are the inherently unlikely parts of the story: that Shelley had made no preparations to receive the child; that Claire allowed it to be taken from her breast on the very day it was born; that it was sent to a common Foundling Hospital rather than – as Elena – to decent foster parents. None of this adds up.

Apart from the authentic, but unkind and exaggerated account of the relations between Claire and Mary and Shelley, only two parts of the whole story remain sound. First, the fact that Mary could not know what, if anything, happened between Shelley and Claire at I Capuccini, while Elise might have known, for she was there. But this of course was in August and September 1818, and could have no relevance to Elena who was born only four months later, in December. Second, there is the curious coincidence of Claire's day of 'illness' – as recorded by Mary herself – with Elena's date of birth as entered by Shelley in the documents of registration and baptism. But perhaps this was exactly that – a curious coincidence.

The question now arises why Elise, the Shelleys' faithful servant and companion through all their vicissitudes since the Byron summer of 1816, should have attempted to damage Claire and Shelley through this wild story. The answer is that in all probability it was Elise herself who was the mother of Shelley's 'Neapolitan charge', Elena.

The evidence for this is by no means absolutely certain or complete. Neither Shelley, nor Mary, nor Elise herself ever explicitly said so. But it looks very probable; its fits all the known facts, and contradicts none. Above all it is, humanly speaking, convincing at every point.

Elise was definitely pregnant at Naples in December 1818. It is Mary herself who gives the evidence for this. When she discovered it she immediately changed her previous attitude to Paolo; she firmly encouraged him, if she did not command him, to marry Elise; then afterwards dismissed them both. She wrote later, in the same letter to Mrs Hoppner: 'An accident led me to the knowledge that without marrying they had formed a connection; she was ill, we sent for a doctor who said there was danger of a miscarriage. I would not turn the girl on the world without in some degree binding her to this man. We had them married at Sir W. A'Court's – she left us; turned Catholic at Rome, married him, and then went to Florence.'[41]

Elise was therefore pregnant and had to be married off urgently. But it is impossible that the child was Foggi's. Paolo, although very capable, had only first set eyes on Elise on 5 September at Este. Mary herself says elsewhere in the letter that 'Elise formed an attachment to Paolo when we proceeded to Rome'. They had left Venice on 31 October, and arrived in Rome on 20 November. If Elise had conceived by Paolo during this time, she could barely even have known she was pregnant by Christmas, for she would only have missed one, or at the most two periods. In these circumstances, for Mary to imply a threatened miscarriage of *Foggi's* child was absurd.* Moreover, no single mention of a Foggi child has been found in subsequent registration records, diaries or letters. The only child known to have been born at 250 Riviera di Chiaia at this time was the child which Shelley registered as his own, Elena Adelaide.

Yet one may continue to suppose that Elise was Elena's mother. It is surprising how many details then explain themselves and fit into place. If Elena was

---

* It is probable that a good doctor at this time, without having the aid of chemical tests, could have diagnosed a definite pregnancy by the end of ten weeks. But even this goes outside the timescale for Foggi's paternity, and it still does not cover illness caused by a threatened *miscarriage*. Mary, incidentally, announced *her* pregnancies to Shelley as definite after three months. They conceived a child in February 1819, she announced at the end of May; and it was born in November.

born at the end of December, she was presumably conceived sometime in April 1818, when the Shelleys first came to Italy. This would perhaps throw light on Mary's sudden decision to send Elise rather than Milly with Allegra to Venice; and perhaps also on the curious 'suicide' incident with the pistol at Lake Como. She probably had some suspicion of an intimacy and she wished to curtail it. Four months later, in August 1818, it was Elise's letters to the Bagni di Lucca that brought Claire and Shelley so precipitously to Venice. Besides information about Allegra they could also have contained the first definite news of Elise's pregnancy. Shelley, now alarmed, seized the opportunity to attempt to arrange things on the spot. But Elise's attachment to Paolo Foggi, which developed in October and November, added enormous complications, and the death of little Clara would have made the news terribly difficult to break to Mary.

At Naples, Mary might well have come to see in Paolo the possible practical solution to their difficulties, and so, no doubt, might Elise. Mary urged them to marry. Shelley on the contrary, would have preferred a more personal and less obviously 'respectable' solution, and was extremely unhappy about the match.[42] He wanted to keep the child; Mary, who had just lost Clara, could not apparently bear it. But Paolo's presence tended to force the decision. The gap between Elena's birth on 27 December 1818 and her registration on 27 February 1819 represents a time while this was still under discussion. Paolo and Elise's marriage in the third week of January falls at a half-way point.[43] One suspects that only at the very moment when the Shelleys finally decided to leave Naples did Mary's opinion prevail. But Shelley, while leaving the child with its mother and stepfather, decided to have the child registered in his own name, and it is clear from what he wrote later that he occasionally still hoped to bring it back into his household at Pisa.[44] The child would have to be registered as Shelley or Foggi to be legitimate; Shelley deliberately chose the first course, leaving himself wide open to Paolo's later blackmail. Mary says that Elise became an Italian Catholic, and this would explain why the child was baptized.

Shelley might have agreed to pay Foggi an allowance, and we know that he did indeed have 'expenses at Naples'.[45] In 1820, however, it would seem that Elise herself left the child with the Neapolitan foster parents at Vico Canale. It sickened with 'a fever of dentition', and died. Immediately, Foggi could no longer claim an allowance, and then the claim turned to blackmail in June 1820.

After Elena's death, Elise must have felt some pangs of guilt and remorse, as Shelley himself so obviously did in his letter to the Gisbornes. So while Paolo's blackmailing attempts to extort more money logically commenced in June 1820, Elise's story to the Hoppners was given that summer not for financial gain, like Paolo, but under the influence of her own sense of guilt, and her apparently deep bitterness towards Shelley. Both of these were strong emotional reactions.

But more than this, Elise, as the mother of Shelley's 'Neapolitan charge' – or, as he elsewhere called the child, 'my Neapolitan' – showed in her story that she was intensely jealous of Claire. She was always closer to Claire than to Mary, and in some senses she seemed to consider herself Claire's rival for Shelley's affections, while Mary stood beyond either of them.

Perhaps Elise genuinely did believe her own story about Claire being Shelley's mistress. The details of the clandestine birth are perhaps a transference of her own remorseful memory of the birth of Elena. No doubt Shelley did surreptitiously employ and reward a discreet physician and midwife when Elena was born. A midwife's name appears on the baptism certificate, Gaetana Musto. Moreover Elise told her story to her old employers, the Hoppners, out of guilt and grief and jealousy, not out of any desire to reap a reward. She was not, after all, like Paolo, who knew that the financial value of such scandals lay purely in the fact that it has not yet been disclosed. Elise, in her own way like Shelley, was miserable at being the victim of circumstances. Would she have grieved, any less than Shelley, that her poor child was dead?

Neither Shelley nor Mary ever saw Elise again, though Elise sometimes applied to Mary and Shelley for money, since Paolo was not supporting her properly. This was done, according to Mary, in a quite innocent and beseeching way, and without a hint of blackmail. But Mary, apparently, disapproved of Shelley answering these requests with help.[46]

Three years later, in February and March of 1822, Claire and Elise met in Florence and became intimate once more. For several weeks they were meeting almost every other day.[47] At the beginning of this intimacy, on 10 February 1822, Elise talked to Claire about her story to the Hoppners. Claire was deeply upset by certain things Elise told her, and wrote of her 'miserable spirits'; but it was news of Byron's attitude to Allegra which apparently caused this. At any rate, Claire's anger against Elise must have been short-lived, judging from their continued friendship, and suggests that Claire sympathized strongly with her over Elena. Yet Claire made Elise agree to write letters denying an illicit connection between Shelley and Claire, both to Mary and to Mrs Hoppner as a legal weapon against further scandal.* But these letters do not mention Elena, who had been dead for two years.

This then, as far as one can reasonably judge, was the true background to Shelley's deep misery, ill-health and sometimes suicidal depressions during the winter at Naples of 1818–19. One inference becomes more and more overwhelming as the facts and probabilities of the case slip into place. This inference is that little Elena was more than Elise's illegitimate child and Shelley's 'charge'.

* On 19 April 1822, Claire wrote to Mary: 'I wish you would write me back what you wish Elise to say to you and what she is to say to Mad. H. I have tried in vain to compose it.' *Claire*, p. 279, h. 3.

It is that when Shelley registered with the Neapolitan authorities as Elena's father, what he stated and signed was not – as in the case of 'Maria Padurin's' maternity – a convenient falsehood; but, on the contrary, it was a painful and highly inconvenient statement of fact. Elena Adelaide Shelley, that poor little creature of fate, was Shelley's own illegitimate daughter by the 'superior' and sexually experienced woman, Elise Foggi.

In the very nature of the case, absolute certainty will always remain elusive. In the unlikely event that the papers of the Livornese lawyer del Rosso, who later dealt with Shelley's allowance for Elena and Paolo Foggi's persistent blackmail attempts, should eventually be unearthed, it is still doubtful if further light could be thrown on the matter. That Shelley, with the history of his previous relations with Elizabeth Hitchener, and the Boinvilles, not to mention Claire Clairmont herself, should have become deliberately or accidentally embroiled with Elise seems, on reflection, not altogether surprising; nor was it to be the last of such interludes in Italy. It is perhaps disconcerting that such a tract of his emotional life should be so largely – yet so understandably – obscured from view, although there is the continuous strand of ambiguous elusions in his poetry from 'Julian and Maddalo' onwards which seems to refer to his sense of guilt and misery. Yet it is the very persistence of otherwise inexplicable elements in his story which are finally convincing: the persistence of Shelley's deep personal interest and involvement with the child; the persistence of Foggi's blackmail which otherwise could have been so rapidly disarmed and, on a signal occasion in 1821, publicly disclaimed; the persistence of Elise's bitterness towards Shelley; and finally the persistent sense of some continuing and radical rupture in the relationship between Shelley and Mary. The very fact of the illegitimate child would have immeasurably deepened the wound already opened by little Clara's death at Venice. But that their old friend and companion Elise was the child's mother, and even worse, that the untrustworthy Paolo Foggi had been drawn inextricably into such an intimate emotional entanglement, sufficiently explains the stresses and tensions within the household in December, and in January 1819. Even if this is not the whole story, it is enough.*

By the end of January 1819, Shelley at least was struggling hard with his

* For the background to the problem posed by Elena Adelaide Shelley, see Medwin's extraordinary account of the 'lady' who followed Shelley to Naples and died there, *The Life of Percy Bysshe Shelley*, pp. 204–10 which seems to suggest some confused knowledge of the affair; also N.I. White's discussion, *Shelley*, II, pp. 71–83; Ivan Roe, *Shelley, the Last Phase*, 1953, pp. 161–81; and Ursula Orange, 'Elise, Nursemaid to the Shelleys', *Keats–Shelley Memorial Bulletin VI*, 1955. White's hypothesis that Elena was simply a casual 'adoption' is inadequate to meet the mysteriousness of the affair, the persistence of blackmail and many other contradictory factors, or the emotional intensity and complication of the case. It was Miss Orange who first suggested the liaison between Shelley and Elise, and sketched the salient considerations of the solution. For further remarks concerning Shelley and Claire at this time, see Appendix I.

illness and depression, and beginning to take regular rides through Naples and into the surrounding countryside. He again visited the galleries, though the standing and walking still exhausted him. He heaved his mind away from his own troubles to write to Peacock with a good attempt at his old political satire. 'I am writing as from among sepulchres, you from the habitations of men yet unburied; tho the Sexton Castlereagh after having dug their grave stands with his spade in his hand evidently doubting whether he will not be forced to occupy it himself.' Peacock's news from England concerning the increasing political tension served at first as a relief and diversion; but slowly it began to rouse Shelley to a political consciousness that had been slumbering for virtually twelve months. This arousal was to be the keynote of his great work in 1819.

Shelley inquired if it was Cobbett's excellent influence he detected in the refusal of juries to convict in four government prosecutions over forged paper money, and added majestically: 'Cobbet is a fine ὑμτοποιος [popular hymn-writer] – does his influence increase or diminish? What a pity that so powerful a genius should be combined with the most odious moral qualities.'[48] He fed Peacock European political news, especially the first rumours of a Catalan rising against the Spanish monarchy. Then he began to consider his own writing with respect to the political movements for liberation that seemed to be in the wind. Apropos of his first act of *Prometheus*, which Mary had clean-copied just before Christmas, he wrote one of his most deliberate literary declarations of the year.

> I consider Poetry very subordinate to moral & political science, & if I were well, certainly I should aspire to the latter; for I can conceive a great work, embodying the discoveries of all ages, & harmonizing the contending creeds by which mankind have been ruled. Far from me is such an attempt & I shall be content by exercising my fancy to amuse myself & perhaps some others, & cast what weight I can into the right scale of that balance which the Giant (of Arthegall) holds.[49]

Shelley was here recalling a conversation he had once had with Peacock in which he interpreted Sir Arthegall's iron-man Talus, in Spenser's *Faerie Queene*, as the brute force of repressive government. The Giant on the other hand he regarded as the radical and popular protagonist, and it was with the Giant that Shelley sided.*

---

* Spenser's meaning, as also his bias, is plain. The Giant observes that 'realmes and nations run awry',

> All which he undertooke for to repaire
> In sort as they were formed aunciently,
> And all things would reduce unto equality.
> Therefore the vulgar did about him flocke . . .
> Like foolish flies about a honey-crocke,

Thoughts of Castlereagh, and rumours of a change in Liverpool's administration – for the Duke of Wellington had been brought into the Cabinet in 1818, and among liberals there was growing fear of a military dictatorship – brought Shelley's attention back for a moment to his own problems: 'To what does it amount?' he asked Peacock, 'for besides my natural interest in it, I am on the watch to vindicate my most sacred rights invaded by the Chancery.' The birth of Elena Shelley had set him thinking once more about Ianthe and Charles.

The image that he had conjured up of Sexton Castlereagh standing over graves lingered in Shelley's mind, and combined grotesquely with other images peculiar to his residence at Naples, to produce the first and one of the most violent of his own popular hymns on the state of political oppression in England. This appears to be the first time Shelley had returned to the genre since his pastiche of Coleridge in 1812, 'The Devil's Walk'. It is interesting that it was probably thoughts of Cobbett which brought him back to a style of writing which through this year he made peculiarly and brilliantly his own. The poem that Shelley now sketched is venomous in tone, livid with hatred and yet perfectly controlled in its rhythms. The short balladic stanzas roll out flatly in the first three lines and then plunge home through the last two with a single long murderous thrust. This control, together with the exploitation of dissonance and half-rhyme to set up a continual humming and whining among the vowels is characteristic of the mature Shelley and produces a grim undercurrent of sound like a kind of tribal keening. The poem is nothing if not savage. 'Lines Written During the Castlereagh Administration':

> Corpses are cold in the tomb;
> Stones on the pavement are dumb;
> Abortions are dead in the womb,
> And their mothers look pale – like the death-white shore
>   Of Albion, free no more.

> Her sons are as stones in the way –
> They are masses of senseless clay –
> They are trodden, and move not away –
> The abortion with which *she* travaileth
>   Is Liberty, smitten to death.

> In hope by him great benefite to gaine,
> And uncontrolled freedome to obtaine.

Faerie Queene, Book V, Canto II, *xxxii–iii*.

Talus eventually bludgeons the Giant over a cliff into the sea, which as Shelley observed, 'is the usual way in which power deals with opinion'. Spenser did not have Shelley's egalitarian sympathies.

Then trample and dance, thou Oppressor!
For thy victim is no redresser;
Thou art sole lord and possessor
Of her corpses, and clods, and abortions – they pave
    Thy path to the grave. . . .

Ay, marry thy ghastly wife!
Let Fear and Disquiet and Strife
Spread thy couch in the chamber of Life!
Marry Ruin, thou Tyrant! and God be thy guide
    To the bed of the bride![50]

Thoughts of tombs and sepulchres took Shelley back to the pre-Christmas expedition to Pompeii, and using John Eustace's *A Classical Tour* for his guidebook, he carefully reconstructed their visit for Peacock's benefit. Recalling the return along the road of Neapolitan tombs, with the long shadows of sunset and a chill evening wind stirring, he forgot the guidebook and threw off almost casually to Peacock perhaps the best piece of prose he ever wrote in Italy. It is steeped in the elegiac imagery that was to fill his poems at a later date, and yet radiant with that sense of Greek energy and harmony which was his greatest source of intellectual hope. His anger against the Christian and imperial cultures of guilt and violence which had threatened to destroy the Greek ideal, is also powerfully present.

These tombs were the most impressive things of all. The wild woods surround them on either side and along the broad stones of the paved road which divides them, you hear the late leaves of autumn shiver & rustle in the stream of the inconstant wind as it were like the step of ghosts. The radiance and magnificence of these dwellings of the dead, the white freshness of the scarcely finished marble, the impassioned or imaginative life of the figures which adorn them contrast strangely with the simplicity of the houses of those who were living when Vesuvius overwhelmed their city. . . . I now understand why the Greeks were such great Poets, & above all I can account, it seems to me, for the harmony the unity the perfection the uniform excellence of all their works of art. They lived in a perpetual commerce with external nature and nourished themselves upon the spirit of its forms. Their theatres were all open to the mountains & the sky. Their columns, that ideal type of a sacred forest, with its roof of interwoven tracery admitted the light & wind, the odour & the freshness of the country penetrated the cities. Their temples were mostly upaithric; & the flying clouds the stars or the deep sky were seen above. O, but for that series of wretched wars which terminated in the Roman conquest of the world, but for the Christian religion which put a finishing stroke to the ancient system; but for those changes which conducted Athens to its ruin, to what an eminence might not humanity have arrived![51]

This was a statement both of a poetical and a political credo, and it was for this direct and personal understanding of the classical world that Shelley had come to Italy.* His stay at Naples, disastrous and terrible in many other respects, nevertheless added this new dimension to his philosophy and provided him with the fundamental sense of the reality of Hellenic ideals and impulses from which the final stage of his writing was to be generated.

By February, a sense of movement started slowly and painfully to penetrate the Shelley household once more, and Shelley began organizing expeditions again. They all went to admire the wild water-birds on the Lago d'Agnano, and made two day-trips to the royal chase of the Caccia d'Astroni, with its pine-fringed lakes and forest of massive oaks engulfed in 'purple darkness like an Italian midnight'. These were a success, and on the 23rd of the month he hired a *calèse*, with two lively black horses, one running on free-harness in the Italian style, and drove sixty miles south to the Etruscan remains of Paestum. Shelley included in the party a young Englishman, Charles MacFarlane, who remembered years later how fast Shelley drove and how the wind and speed brought a flush to his pale cheeks.[52]

On this expedition they slept at Salerno, and rising well before dawn the next day drove rapidly along the shore road. 'It was utterly dark, except when the long line of wave burst with a sound like thunder beneath the starless sky and cast up a kind of mist of cold white lustre.' A broken bridge stopped the carriage seven miles outside the city, but Shelley ordered everyone out and they walked along the muddy road through the *maremma*, collecting bunches of huge, sweet-smelling violets until they reached the three temples. He pointed out to MacFarlane the way in which the yellow fluted columns were carefully slimmed towards the top, so as to produce an independent scale of perspective, 'not that this symmetry diminishes your apprehension of their magnitude, but that it overpowers the idea of relative greatness'.[53] On the return journey they stopped off at Tore Annunziata where MacFarlane was amazed to see Shelley leaping into a macaroni factory and watching with wild delight and equal attention the mechanical plunging of one of the pasta-pressing levers. Outside they were

---

* In his celebration of the 'perpetual commerce with external nature', Shelley forgot or at least suppressed the great limitations to Greek society with respect to women and slaves, which he had so carefully defined in his introduction to the *Symposium*. The neologism 'unpaithric', from the Greek 'upaithrios' meaning 'open-air, roofless' is correctly assigned to Shelley in the *Oxford English Dictionary*.

besieged by beggars, and Shelley emptied his pockets of loose *scudi*. MacFarlane, hardly knowing what to expect next and deeply impressed by this flamboyant gesture of generosity, remarked feelingly to Shelley on the wretched condition of the Neapolitan poor. Shelley fixed him with his sudden earnest stare and observed that they at least had physical freedom. 'I had ten times rather be a Neapolitan beggar than an English artisan or maid-of-all-work.'[54] The *calèsse* was driven furiously back into Naples, calling in at Pompeii on the way to hear Vesuvius rumble.

The refreshment of this journey now decided Shelley that it was time to leave Naples, and move northwards with the spring, to Rome again. A last day was spent in the *studii* re-examining statues and paintings. He was both fascinated and repelled by Michelangelo's study for the *Last Judgement*, which was in the royal collection, and commented on it with loaded atheistical humour. Moses was only less monstrous than his historical prototype; Christ was in an attitude of haranguing the assembly and showing signs of 'common place resentment'; the heavenly host looked very like 'ordinary people', and those in Purgatory were 'half-suspended in that Mahomet-coffin kind of attitude which most moderate Christians I believe expect to assume'. Only Hell was truly impressive as every step towards it 'approximates to the region of the artist's exclusive power. . . . Hell & Death are his real sphere.' Shelley observed the devils and the damned, writhing in their knotted serpents, with a connoisseur's eye, and concluded: 'a kind of Titus Andronicus in painting – but the author surely no Shakespeare'. Thinking of the Inferno, he added the thoughtful observation: 'What is terror without a contrast with & a connection with loveliness? How well Dante understood this secret.'[55] He himself was to try it in a later poem on one of Leonardo's pictures, the *Medusa*.

Peacock's letter sealed, and other notes sent off to his bankers, Brookes & Co., and to his publisher Ollier, Shelley helped with packing their trunks. He had a row with the landlord who wanted them to pay for panes of glass broken by the sirocco, but Shelley had preferred to sit in the draught.[56] On the 27th he made the final arrangements for little Elena and signed the forms of birth registration and baptism. The next day they set off late, at 2 in the afternoon, with a new Italian servant, Vincenzo, driving the carriage, which was harnessed with their own horses.

The time for hurrying had long since passed, and the Shelleys spent five nights on the road to Rome. At Gaeta they passed a whole day walking by the seashore in the sunshine, picnicking in the woods. They stayed at an old inn built on the site of one of Cicero's summer villas, precipitously overhanging the sea, and skirted in groves of olives and oranges. They played chess on the inn terrace, and Shelley leant back in his chair gazing at 'an emerald sky of leaves starred with innumerable globes of ripening fruit'. In the bay was an island which was called the 'promontory of Circe'.

In the afternoon of 5 March they at last drew towards the Celestial City whose presence was announced by the wild, melancholy landscape of shattered aqueducts which commences at Albano, 'arches after arches in unending lines stretching across the uninhabited wilderness, the blue defined outline of the mountains seen between them; masses of nameless ruins standing like rocks out of the plain; and the plain itself with its billowy & unequal surface announced the neighbourhood of Rome'.[57] This time there was no hawk.

Appendix to Chapter 18

It is my belief that this story of Shelley's 'situation at Naples' in the winter of 1818, constructed from logical inferences based on a survey of the known facts, is the truth *as far as it goes*. There are however two further broad lines of consideration.

In the first place, it has to be accepted that because of the thinness of our knowledge about Elise Foggi, there are certain unresolved problems. These may be summarized as follows:

1. It is difficult to know out of what mixture of bitterness and loyalty towards the Shelleys Elise should tell the Hoppners the 'Claire scandal' without mentioning her own illegitimate child. The desire for revenge, 'transference' from her own case, and very probably jealousy of Claire – but *not*, significantly enough, blackmail (like Paolo) – obviously motivated her. But one would like to know more, especially of Elise's movements through Italy in 1819–20, and of her 'superior' character as Claire called it years afterwards. It is still possible that some information remains to be gleaned from hitherto unknown records of Elise's family at Chambéry.

2. One would also like to know more of the day-to-day life of Shelley's travelling entourage in April 1818. The relevant evidence here is very scanty. The only noticeable points are Mary's sudden decision to send away Elise rather than Milly Shields to Venice; Shelley's alarming and apparently suicidal behaviour in the woods near Lake Como; and Shelley's remarks in his letters *passim* about the sexual attractiveness of Italian women, who seemed at one moment to delight him and the next to disgust him. There is also his statement to Byron about the rights of the mother of an illegitimate child – 'if she has no feeling, she has no claim' – but at the time this was clearly directed at Claire, and could have no bearing until the decision to send Elena Adelaide out to foster parents in December. Mary's letters and journal are not helpful; nor is the only other

source, Claire's diary, which merely describes opera-going, sightseeing and endless games of chess. It is true that the diary is not yet available in manuscript for the last eight days of April (Elise departed from Milan on 28 April), but this is less promising than it might be supposed (*vide* Chapter 16, reference no. 36). Altogether the evidence for April, though in some ways suggestive, is really very bare; nor is it likely that there is anything further to be found by way of sources.

It is unlikely that either of these problem areas will ever be fully resolved; but as they are essentially questions not of *contrary* evidence, but simply of paucity of evidence, they cannot in the final consideration be taken as substantial objections. The great weight of the other factual and circumstantial evidence very largely overwhelms them.

In the second place, there is the further broad consideration that this is still *not the whole story*. I have deliberately left out from the body of the narrative any further speculation on Claire's and Shelley's relations at this time. I have done this because, whereas I regard the inference that Shelley and Elise were the parents of Elena Adelaide as not only warrantable but virtually certain from the facts, I do not feel there is anything like sufficient evidence to make similar kinds of inference about Claire's possible pregnancy. For the record, however my belief, after considering all relevant facts at present available,[1] and also the general pattern of Shelley's and Claire's life in Italy, stands as follows.

Brought closely together by the mutual worries over Allegra and Elise, Shelley and Claire became lovers during the nineteen days spent alone on the road to Venice, and at Este in August and September 1818. Claire conceived a child by Shelley. She may then have made some early attempts to bring on her period, probably without Shelley's knowledge, at Padua. Elise, who was with Claire, may have known or suspected this. Later in September, they were dismayed at the turn of events caused by little Clara's death, and agreed not to tell Mary until some later date. The child, after all, would not be due until June 1819. But the pregnancy made Claire frequently ill and weak, and such exertion as the expedition to Vesuvius endangered it. On 26–27 December at Naples, as recorded in Mary's journal, Claire was 'unwell'. I believe that her 'illness' was in fact a miscarriage at four months, but that Mary remained ignorant of it exactly as Elise had said. The reason for Mary being told and further upset had now disappeared. She was never told; at least not until after 1820. Elise's child might conceivably have been born on that very same day; or, far more likely, shortly afterwards, in January 1819. But at any rate Shelley decided to commemorate that grim day, 27 December, with the more joyful fact of little Elena's safe arrival, by registering the child's birth at that date. This also served to cover up the reasons for medical attendance at 250 Riviera di Chiaia after Christmas. Hence the otherwise inexplicable coincidence of Elena's birth and registration and Claire's illness coming on the same day.

Yet Claire and Elise *may well* have been brought to bed simultaneously, unlikely as this might appear. It is given a curious kind of support in one of the poems that Shelley wrote a few months later at Rome. Biographical evidence drawn directly from a literary work is always highly suspect, but the reader must consider for himself how far the reference could possibly be coincidental. In the notorious Act I Scene 3 of Shelley's Italian horror play, *The Cenci*, the perverse Count delivers the news of his two sons' death at a festive banquet at which his wife, daughter and fellow-nobles are in attendance. He announces these deaths as if it were a piece of good news, and proposes a toast. His wife faints, and the whole assembly rise up in confusion and horror. What somehow makes the Count's announcement doubly macabre is the fact that both Rocco and Cristofano are reported to have died on the *same* night, one stabbed and one crushed. This coincidence Cenci gloatingly refers to as the work of 'most favouring Providence'. But the shock awaits in the last lines of his speech. Both his children died, says Cenci –

All in the self-same hour of the same night;
Which shows that Heaven has special care of me.
I beg those friends who love me, that they mark
The day a feast upon their calendars.
It was the twenty-seventh of December:
Ay, read the letters if you doubt my oath.[2]

In my opinion the only reason for Shelley to single out that crucial date with such transparent bitterness was to commemorate, once more, *the loss of two of his own children*, both delivered on the same night. One by Claire through miscarriage, and the other by Elise, through the marriage and machinations of Paolo Foggi. Two children lost to him on 27 December, through Heaven's special care.

Finally, if it is objected that Shelley would never have made two women pregnant simultaneously, and certainly not in the same household, it is as well to consider his situation in the winter of 1814–15. Harriet's and Mary's babies were born at approximately two and a half months interval; moreover Mary's being only seven months was so premature that it was virtually a miscarriage, and of course it died. The similarity could hardly have escaped Shelley, and his sense of being hounded by fate – if not by anything more diabolic – could hardly have been lessened. I believe this double-horror was the direct source of some of Shelley's imagery in the poetry of early 1819, and in a more diffused way, throughout his later Italian writing.

Be all this as it may, the biographical proof remains completely inadequate, and I have not incorporated it or referred to it again in the body of my text. I leave this sad subject to the keeping of later, and I hope, kindly, scholars. For the time being the reader must judge for himself how far the narrative tends to confirm or contradict this further hypothesis, and in particular how far the emotional stress between Shelley, Mary and Claire is commensurate with the bitter and unhappy memories of such an event.

19
A Roman Spring: 1819

In Rome Shelley took rooms at the Palazzo Verospi, No. 300 Corso. The Corso was perhaps the most fashionable address in the city, an immensely long narrow street of hotels, churches, palazzos, banks and villas diversified by small colonnaded piazzas swarming with market stalls and barrows. It was really an extension of the Via Flamini, stretching from the northern gate to the foot of the Capitoline Hill, and it had become the social centre of the city, so that in the evenings the close stucco walls and yellow stone façades echoed with the continuous clatter of smart carriages taking the air. To the west, across the Tiber, lay the Vatican, and to the south stretched the ruins of ancient Rome, the Forum and Colosseum, the Palatine Hill and about a mile beyond the massive arched remains of the Baths of Caracalla. The Palazzo Verospi stood on the west side of the Corso, just below the Piazza Colonna, some ten minutes' walk from the Forum and only about three minutes from what was to become Shelley's favourite building in Rome, the Pantheon.

For all of them the return to Rome seemed like a return to life. They embarked on a massive and strenuous routine of high tourism, in the mornings concentrating on the Roman ruins, the galleries and the private collections of paintings and statues like those in the Villa Borghese. Sculpture and carving of every kind especially attracted them. In the afternoons and evenings they joined the fashionable routes as well, driving through the Monte Cavallo and the Gardens of the Quirinal and the Borghese, and visiting the great marble fountains of Piazza Navona and the Trevi. Perhaps surprisingly, both Shelley and Mary were fascinated by the ritual aspects of the Vatican, and they attended Papal services at St Peter's on several festive occasions. Mary wrote in her journal for the second Saturday in Rome, 'Walk to the Baths of Caracalla. Meet the Pope.'[1]

Claire now began a new diary, Mary started writing letters again, and Shelley abandoned Winckelmann's *History of Art* to read Euripides and Lucretius. His thoughts had turned back to *Prometheus Unbound*. Mary took drawing lessons,

Claire took singing lessons and little Willmouse became vociferously Italian crying out 'O Dio che bella' whenever he saw anything he liked or was supposed to like.[2] Social calls were paid by Lord Guildford, Dr and Mrs Bell and later by Sir William Drummond. The Shelleys' most regular port of visitation became the *salon* of the ageing Signora Marianna Dioniga, 'a distinguished painter, antiquary, authoress, and member of academies innumerable' who held mild soirées at No. 310 Corso.[3] Judging by the regularity of their evenings spent there, this Roman blue-stocking must have been a favourite of Shelley's; though Mary, who was slightly jealous of her, later described her to Maria Gisborne as 'very old, very miserly, & very mean'. Claire described one perhaps typical evening, 'go to the conversazione of the Signora Marianna Dioniga where there is a Cardinal and many unfortunate Englishmen who after having crossed their legs & said nothing the whole Evening, rose all up at once, made their bows, & filed off. . . .'[4] Though no doubt she was cheerfully making the worst of it.

But Mary was echoing the general sentiment when she wrote to Marianne Hunt, 'Rome repays for everything. – How you would like to be here! We pass our days in viewing the divinest statues in the world . . . my letter would never be at an end if I were to try to tell a millionth part of the delights of Rome – but it has such an effect on me that my past life before I saw it appears a blank & now I begin to live – In the churches you hear the music of heaven & the singing of Angels.' In mentioning William's Italian, Mary revealed a glimpse of past troubles: '[Willmouse] has quite forgotten French for Elise has left us – She married a rogue of an Italian servant that we had and turned Catholic – Venice quite spoiled her and she appears in the high road to be as Italian as any of them. She has settled at Florence.' But her high spirits and relief after Naples was well caught in her P.S.: 'Shelley & Clare desire with me a thousand kind loves to Hunt & Bessy – Do you ever see Hogg – how he would scream & beat his sides at all the fine things in Rome – it is well that he is not or he would have broken many a rib in his delights or at least bruised them sorely.'[5]

For Shelley Rome too worked steadily on his health with restorative powers. By the end of March it was 'materially better' though his spirits were 'not the most brilliant in the world'. He seems to have attributed this to the continuing solitariness of their situation from English society, though at other times he expressed his relief at avoiding the English. Italian society offered some compensations, however, as he explained to Peacock in a gently provocative description of Italian women. He had, once again, changed his opinion on that score, and garlic was less in evidence.

The Romans please me much, especially the women: . . . Their extreme innocence & naïveté, the freedom and gentleness of their manners, the total absence of affectation makes an intercourse with them very like an intercourse with uncorrupted children, whom they resemble often in loveliness as well as simplicity. I have seen two women in society here of the highest beauty, their brows & lips and the moulding of the face modelled with sculptural exactness, & the dark luxuriance of their hair floating over their fine complexions – and the lips – you must hear the commonplaces which escape from them before they cease to be dangerous.[6]

After the initial burst of touristic enthusiasm, the Shelley household began to fall into a regular routine. A drive or a ride in the Borghese Gardens became an almost daily custom, and Claire frequently spent whole mornings there delighting in the mixture of formality and wilderness, 'extensive with a variety of green shady nooks, with fountains and statues'. She found a special place on the steps of the Temple of Aesculapius where she would sit and read Wordsworth.[7] Mary also liked the carriage part of these visits, but one has the impression that she tired easily, and preferred visits to galleries and museums nearer the Corso, and sketching expeditions with little Willmouse in the Forum or the Colosseum. She was also reading a lot, Shakespeare and Livy.

For Shelley, the spirit of Rome gradually came to condense itself into three magical gardens of archaeology: – the Forum, the Colosseum and the Baths of Caracalla. He walked over the first two daily and prompted Claire to write in her diary: 'In ancient times the Forum was to a city what the soul is to the Body.' Shelley's favourite was moonlight walks, and on these he would sometimes go alone, and sometimes take one or other of the girls. From a comparison of Mary's journal and Claire's diary it would seem that he preferred on the whole not to take them together. Best of all he preferred to go alone. 'I walk forth in the purple & golden light of an Italian evening & return by star or moonlight thro this scene. The elms are just budding, & the warm spring winds bring unknown odours, all sweet from the country. I see the radiant Orion through the mighty columns of the temple of Concord,* & the mellow fading light softens down the modern buildings of the Capitol the only ones that interfere with the sublime desolation of the scene. On the steps of the Capitol itself stand two colossal statues of Castor & Pollux, each with his horse; finely executed though far inferior to those of Monte Cavallo, the cast of one of which you know we saw together in London – This walk is close to our lodging, & this is my evening walk.'[8]

---

* Shelley's 'Temple of Concord' is now called the Temple of Saturn by modern classical archaeologists, and stands at the base of the Capitoline Hill, dominating the northern end of the Via Sacra. The god's statue was filled with olive oil, and in his hand he held a pruning knife, symbols of Agriculture and Husbandry. His temple was suitably used as the state treasury, but was also the centre of the annual winter Saturnalia, a time of carnival and goodwill. Eight massive granite columns alone remain.

Of all the monuments and marble fragments in the Forum, it was the Arch of Titus, standing at the eastern end of the Via Sacra, and the Arch of Constantine standing below it in the south-western corner of the Piazza di Colosseo, which exerted the most deep and continuous interest. Titus, a single triumphal arch erected in AD 81 to commemorate the capture of Jerusalem, was called in medieval times the Arch of the Seven Lamps, because of the magnificent reliefs on the interior of the portico depicting the triumphal Roman chariot carrying off slave and spoils and the huge seven-branched Jewish candlestick. Constantine, a massively vulgar triple arch erected in AD 315, shows the decline of the Roman classic ideal, but is luxuriously decorated by a brilliant series of earlier reliefs, ripped from the monuments of Trajan, Hadrian and Marcus Aurelius, and packed between the eight Corinthian columns of the supporting façade. It was this marvellously clear, vigorous, set of epic reliefs and sculptures which filled Shelley's imagination with a vision of effortlessly achieved symbolic power. He was deeply impressed by the clarity of their carved line, and the grace of their hovering presences. They were not merely sculpture, they were ballet suspended in stone, and they offered him an example and an inspiration. From these he saw how images could be made both to retain their humanity, and express divinity, superhuman force and eternal power or potential. In two of the carvings he found specific images – the triumph, the chariot and the winged angels – which he was able to incorporate directly into his work. Shelley first described these carvings in detail in his letters and his Roman notebook, and later transferred them into his poetry.

Walking back from the Forum one evening he entered in his notebook on the imperial destruction of Jerusalem:

> Titus is represented standing in a chariot drawn by four horses, crowned with laurel, and surrounded by the tumultuous members of his triumphant army, and the magistrates, and priests, and generals, and philosophers, dragged in chains beside his wheels. Behind him stands a Victory eagle-winged.
>
> The arch is now mouldering into ruins, and the imagery almost ceased with the lapse of fifty generations. Beyond this obscure monument of Hebrew desolation, is seen the tomb of the Destroyer's family, now a mountain of ruins.
>
> The Flavian amphitheatre has become a habitation for owls and dragons. The power, of whose possession it was once the type, and of whose departure it is now the emblem, is become a dream and a memory. Rome is no more than Jerusalem.[9]

The Forum was itself too populated with tourists, and too close to No. 300 Corso to serve as one of Shelley's open-air studies; but by walking on for some thirty minutes, over the Palatine hill, leaving the Circo Maximo and the Tiber on his right hand, he could reach the fantastic, jungled ruins of the Termi di Caracalla. As he had done at Marlow, he made this expedition into the wilderness the beginning of his writing routine every morning, with his pockets stuffed with books, portable pen and ink, and one of his small sketching notebooks bound in black leather.* The huge Baths of Caracalla, which could accommodate over 1,500 people, had been begun by Septimus Severus in AD 206 and continued to serve the Romans as bathing place, gymnasium, sports club and community centre until the Goths cut the aqueducts in the sixth century. Completely ruined by the nineteenth century, they still retained massive surrounding walls, and huge fragments of brick archways and vaulting, many of them towering over 200 feet into the air. These were entirely overgrown with plants and shrubs, but were still secure enough to be climbed by one or two remaining staircases. The effect was like an enormous hanging garden. The floor of the ruins was covered with the red clay of Rome, through which pieces of brilliantly coloured mosaic glowed after rain. Shelley made this deserted but luxuriant site his headquarters, and soon found he could disappear within its labyrinth for as long as he chose, climbing high into some aerial grove, perched among the blossom. He took up the *Prometheus* drama once more and later he wrote his preface, 'This Poem was chiefly written upon the mountainous ruins of the Baths of Caracalla, among the flowery glades, and the thickets of odoriferous blossoming trees, which are extended in ever winding labyrinths upon its immense platforms and dizzy arches suspended in the air. The bright blue sky of Rome, and the effect of the vigorous awakening spring in that divinest climate, and the new life with which it drenches the spirits even to intoxication, were the inspiration of this drama.'[10]

To Peacock at the end of March, he attempted in a long descriptive passage to capture the extraordinary atmosphere of the baths, which was producing on him an almost mystical effect.

Never was any desolation more sublime and lovely. The perpendicular wall of ruin is cloven into steep ravines filled with flowering shrubs whose thick twisted roots are knotted in the rifts of the stones. At every step the aerial pinnacles of shattered stone group into new combinations of effect, & tower above the lofty yet level walls, as the distant mountains change their aspect to one rapidly travelling along the plain. The perpendicular walls resemble nothing more than that cliff in Bisham wood which is overgrown with wood, & yet is stony & precipitous – you know the one I mean, – not

---

* Probably what is now Bod. MS Shelley Adds. e. 12, a small black leather notebook which contains a draft of *Prometheus* Acts I–IV, though this may have been Shelley's clean copy book.

the chalk pit, but the spot which has that pretty copse of fir trees & privet bushes at its base, & where Hogg & I scrambled up & you – to my infinite discontent – would go home.

He went on to explain how one could ascend by 'an antique winding staircase', dangerously open to the precipice at many turns, and come out some hundred feet up on the summit of the walls.

Here grow on every side thick entangled wildernesses of myrtle & the myrtelus & bay & the flowering laurustinus whose white blossoms are just developed, the wild fig & a thousand nameless plants sown by the wandering winds. These woods are intersected on every side by paths, like sheep tracks thro the copse wood of steep mountains, which wind to every part of these immense labyrinths. . . . Around rise other crags & other peaks all arrayed & the deformity of their vast desolation softened down by the undecaying investiture of nature. Come to Rome. It is a scene by which expression is overpowered: which words cannot convey.[11]

For Shelley, Rome presented overwhelming evidence, both literal and symbolic, that the schema which he had dimly revealed in the colossal wreck of Ozymandias was a permanent and historic truth. Power and imperialism *were* destroyed. The forces of human love and freedom, and of Nature, which he regarded as allies, did in the end reassert themselves, just as the beautiful and innocent white blossoms of the laurustinus covered over the desolation of Caracalla. Fresh from his terrible experiences at Naples, which had brought him to the verge of breakdown, the recovery of this vision swept over him with the force and conviction of a religious revelation. It was this force, this empassioned wish-fulfilment, that he tried to structure and express in the poetic drama of *Prometheus Unbound*. He found himself writing now, not as an English tourist but as a Greek visionary. He wrote on a Greek text, with a Greek theme and within a Greek *upaithric* temple of Nature.

Once he began writing, Shelley wrote as ever, with immense speed. Only four weeks after their arrival in Rome, he notified Peacock: 'My Prometheus Unbound is just finished, & in a month or two I shall send it. It is a drama, with characters & mechanism of a kind yet unattempted; & I think the execution is better than any of my former attempts.'[12]

The myth of Prometheus the fire-bringer and liberator of mankind was already a familiar force in the liberal culture of the nineteenth century, quite apart from the poems of Goethe and Byron. The success of Mary Shelley's own modernization of the myth clearly demonstrated its popular currency to Shelley. Politically too, the myth of Prometheus had always been present in the 'progressive philosophy' of rationality and revolution which had swept over Europe since the date of Shelley's own birth. The French Revolutionaries had been Promethean by adoption. Shelley was acutely conscious of his predecessors, but he intended to reconstruct the Aeschylean drama in a new form.

> . . . I was averse from a catastrophe so feeble as that of reconciling the Champion with the Oppressor of mankind. The moral interest of the fable, which is so powerfully sustained by the sufferings and endurance of Prometheus, would be annihilated if we could conceive of him as unsaying his high language and quailing before his successful and perfidious adversary. The only imaginary being resembling in any degree Prometheus, is Satan; and Prometheus is, in my judgement, a more poetical character than Satan, because, in addition to courage, and majesty, and firm and patient opposition to omnipotent force, he is susceptible of being described as exempt from the taints of ambition, envy, revenge, and a desire for personal aggrandisement. . . . [he] is, as it were, the type of the highest perfection of moral and intellectual nature. . . .[13]

Jupiter (God) was to be conceived as wholly evil, Prometheus (Satan) as a type of human perfection. There were to be none of the slow, monumental moral dawnings of Aeschylus, or the central and strictly speaking tragic recognition of necessity by Prometheus. Shelley's schema would be more melodramatic, but also more rigid: two totally alienated moral principles would oppose each other within a Manichean framework. The universe was to be polarized into the extreme gnostic oppositions, dark and light, tyranny and freedom, Ahrimanes and Oromazes.

Moreover, Shelley wanted to attempt something new in his use of poetic language. He wrote:

> The imagery which I have employed will be found, in many instances, to have been drawn from the operations of the human mind, or from those external actions by which they are expressed.

To this he added a literary observation which confirms that his Italian reading had been creatively important.

> This is unusual in modern poetry, although Dante and Shakespeare are full of instances of the same kind: Dante indeed more than any other poet, and with greater success. But the Greek poets . . . were in the habitual use of this power.[14]

Physically external images which express mental states and processes, dominate the language of the poem. There is a sense in which the whole action is metaphysical rather than physical, and in which the setting of the drama is not so much the universe at large but the dome of a single human skull, so that the ruins of Caracalla sometimes seemed to him like an immense cranial chamber. The technique of using a physical scene as 'evocation' of a mental state was one Shelley had first discovered and used in *Alastor* four years previously and perfected in 'Julian and Maddalo'. But now Shelley wanted to go one stage further, as he believed the Greeks had done. He wanted his poetry to be so highly wrought that a physical image, while attaining completeness in itself, *simultaneously* offered meanings at several other levels. He wanted a mythic image, for example, to present also a psychological, or political, or modern scientific meaning: or perhaps all three at once. When the Furies come to torment Prometheus in Act I, they first announce themselves purely in terms of mythic action:

> *First Fury.* We are the ministers of pain, and fear,
>   And disappointment, and mistrust, and hate,
>   And clinging crime; and as lean dogs pursue
>   Through wood and lake some struck and throbbing fawn,
>   We track all things that weep, and bleed, and live. . . .[15]

But very soon, they threaten Prometheus with psychological torment and their language begins to carry a strictly *medical* meaning as well as the mythic one:

>   . . . we will be dread thought beneath thy brain,
>   And foul desire round thine astonished heart,
>   And blood within thy labyrinthine veins
>   Crawling like agony.[16]

The physiological suggestiveness of these lines, the implications of the adrenalin 'shock' to the heart and the literally 'monstrous' invasion of venereal infection through the delicate network of the blood system (an image conceived as long ago as 'Mont Blanc') give the Furies of guilt and remorse a wholly new and contemporary presence. The medical base of this image was to be characteristic of the whole poem, whose other major image sources are also from the natural sciences: geology, climatology and electrophysics especially.

Some of these new 'multiple' images are so brilliantly sustained that they threaten to detach themselves from the text. In the second act, two fauns sit on a rock at the entrance to Asia's cave, and question each other about the nature of the animating forces within the universe. (One thinks of Shelley and Byron at the Diodati.) 'Canst thou imagine where those spirits live Which make such delicate music in the woods?' one asks. The second faun's reply is not only a speculation about the creative forces within Nature – 'the music in the woods' – but also about the creative forces within the mind. At a mythic level, Shelley draws upon the sprite world of Shakespeare's *Tempest*; but he simultaneously achieves a wonderful psychological image of the 'act of creation' in man. It is interesting to note that it is presented as an act of pure elated 'play'. The image is also given a scientific base. This is drawn from the action of marsh gas rising from within submerged and decomposing vegetation as a result of solar radiation and igniting on contact with the air. Shelley had doubtless observed this phenomenon many times in the *maremma* surrounding Naples and Livorno. Strictly speaking this is methane, a gas formed from decaying organic matter, which spontaneously combusts on contact with oxygen. The phenomenon is sometimes known as will 'o the wisp or *ignis fatuus*, but Shelley's image can also be transcribed: $CH_4 + O_2$:

> I have heard those more skilled in spirits say,
> The bubbles, which the enchantment of the sun
> Sucks from the pale faint water-flowers that pave
> The oozy bottom of clear lakes and pools,
> Are the pavillions where such dwell and float
> Under the green and golden atmosphere
> Which noontide kindles through the woven leaves;
> And when these burst, and the thin fiery air,
> The which they breathed within those lucent domes,
> Ascends to flow like meteors through the night,
> They ride on them, and rein their headlong speed,
> And bow their burning crests, and glide in fire
> Under the waters of the earth again.[17]

The 'multiple' image is here moving on three perfectly interpenetrated levels of myth, natural science and psychology. The idea of 'natural fire' as a creative force forms a central theme in the Prometheus drama. The use of the 'multiple' image, directly inspired by Shelley's reading of the Greeks, was one of the most ambitious elements in the poem he had set out to write.

Finally, Shelley intended to give his *Prometheus* a political dimension. His position was as ever progressive, anti-authoritarian and radical, though he wrote that 'it is a mistake to suppose that I dedicate my poetical compositions solely to the direct enforcement of reform . . .'.[18]

Shelley nonetheless wanted his reader to see the drama in a definitely public context, for exactly this, he argued, was what made possible the transformation of private writing into great literature.

> We owe the great writers of the golden age of our literature to that fervid awakening of the public mind which shook to dust the oldest and most

oppressive form of the Christian religion. We owe Milton to the progress and development of the same spirit: the sacred Milton was, let it ever be remembered, a republican, and a bold inquirer into morals and religion. The great writers of our own age are, we have reason to suppose, the companions and forerunners of some unimagined change in our social condition or the opinions which cement it. The cloud of mind is discharging its collected lightning, and the equilibrium between institutions and opinions is now restoring, or is about to be restored.[19]

The use of the electrical image, even here in the preface, was not coincidental in a drama about Prometheus the fire-bringer. Besides using myth, natural science and psychology, Shelley set out to write a great drama that depicted in its action and its images the vision of political freedom.

The plot of *Prometheus Unbound*, as completed in three acts at Rome, is a symbolic story of man's liberation from tyranny. The drama opens 'in a ravine of Icy rocks in the Indian Caucasus'; Prometheus is bound to the rockface over the precipice, while two of the Daughters of Ocean, Panthea and Ione sit silently at his feet. It is a bitter winter season which we understand has lasted over the whole earth for a thousand years. Prometheus's long opening monologue, a series of superb variations on the Aeschylean text, describes this state in a magnificent example of the multiple images with several frames of geophysical and psychological reference:

> The crawling glaciers pierce me with the spears
> Of their moon-freezing crystals, the bright chains
> Eat with their burning cold into my bones.
> Heaven's wingèd hound, polluting from thy lips
> His beak in poison not his own, tears up
> My heart; and shapeless sights come wandering by,
> The ghastly people of the realm of dream,
> Mocking me. . . .[20]

The grim addition to the myth, that the eagle dips its beak in Jupiter's poisonous saliva before flying to tear out Prometheus's *innards*, is a characteristic Shelleyan innovation. It implies whole dimensions of verbal slander, sneers and rumours by which established authority can sting and corrode the non-conforming individual.

A chorus of Earth Spirits, and the Earth herself, answer Prometheus and from them we understand that both his and their suffering is the result of the ancient deadlock between Prometheus and Jupiter. Earth's monologue is rich with echoes of Aeschylus, Lucretius and Shelley's own 'Mont Blanc':

I am the Earth,
Thy mother; she within whose stony veins,
To the last fibre of the loftiest tree
Whose thin leaves trembled in the frozen air,
Joy ran, as blood within a living frame. . . .[21]

From Earth we learn that, paradoxically, her own suffering is the result of a curse laid by her child Prometheus upon Jupiter in revenge for his persecution. Prometheus wishes to recall this curse, but to do this it has literally to be 'recalled': to be uttered a second time, in an act of exorcism. Neither Prometheus himself, nor any of the Spirits of the Earth, is able to face this appalling prospect. In an extraordinary passage, Earth reveals how these words can be recovered by calling on a 'second world' of spiritual existence. Here Shelley achieves a fantastic combination of classical ideas of Hades, Platonic ideas of the 'intermediary' world of daemons and *kaka-daimons*, Dantean visions of the Christian Inferno, and modern ideas of the individual and collective unconscious recoverable through psychoanalysis. On top of all this, he introduces the magician Zoroaster, a gnostic figure, attractive to Shelley for his perverse antinomian and mystic associations. This is one of the great cruxes of the drama, and deserves consideration at length. It is part of Shelley's achievement that virtually nothing about the ideological background of this 'second world' concept needs to be known by the reader, except for the broad outline of the Aeschylean plot:

Ere Babylon was dust,
The Magus Zoroaster, my dead child,
Met his own image walking in the garden.
That apparition, sole of men, he saw.
For know there are two worlds of life and death:
One that which thou beholdest; but the other
Is underneath the grave, where do inhabit
The shadows of all forms that think and live
Till death unite them and they part no more;
Dreams and the light imaginings of men,
And all that faith creates or love desires . . .

. . . all the gods
Are there, and all the powers of nameless worlds,
Vast, sceptred phantoms; heroes, men, and beasts;
And Demogorgon, a tremendous gloom;
And he, the supreme Tyrant, on his throne
Of burning gold. Son, one of these shall utter

> The curse which all remember. Call at will
> Thine own ghost, or the ghost of Jupiter. . . .
> Ask, and they must reply: so the revenge
> Of the Supreme may sweep through vacant shades,
> As rainy wind through the abandoned gate
> Of a fallen palace.[22]

The phantasm of Jupiter is called, and repeats Prometheus's curse, 'Fiend I defy thee.' Prometheus is suddenly overcome by hearing his own words thus repeated, and at this moment of weakness Mercury the messenger of Jupiter arrives, accompanied by the Furies, again following the Aeschylean plot. When the mediations and diplomacy of Mercury are rejected, then the Fiends close around Prometheus. The visions of horror and remorse they bring are public as well as private. Visions of war and famine pass before Prometheus, and the bloody failure of the French Revolution. The massive cruel conglomerations of trapped humanity brought together by industrial urbanization are already recognized:

> Look! where round the wide horizon
>   Many a million-peopled city
> Vomits smoke in the bright air.
> Hark that outcry of despair![22]

The poisonous distortions of the message of 'truth, peace and pity' brought by the historical Christ, whom Shelley understands as a simple human and political figure 'a youth with patient looks nailed to a crucifix' are presented as a further pathological perversion by the forces of Jupiter. Prometheus, the all-knowing and all-seeing, seems bowed in final despair. The whole world seems in chains.

Only when Earth summons a troop of spirits, 'whose homes are the dim caves of human thought', and who are associated with the eternally recurring force of Spring, is Prometheus partially rescued from his hopelessness. The Sixth Spirit is questioned about 'The form of Love' which is the most powerful of human psychic forces. Her answer is deeply ambiguous, but heralds the next step towards breaking the deadlock between Prometheus and Jupiter, after the recall of the curse. The imagery is drawn by Shelley directly from Agathon's speech in the *Symposium*. The Spirit begins not with love, but with its absence – Desolation.

> Ah, sister! Desolation is a delicate thing:
>   It walks not on the earth, it floats not in the air,
> But treads with lulling footstep, and fans with silent wing
>   The tender hopes which in their hearts the best and gentlest bear;

Who, soothed to false repose by the fanning plumes above
  And the music-stirring motion of its soft and busy feet,
Dream visions of aëreal joy, and call the monster, Love,
  And wake, and find the shadow Pain, as he whom now we greet.[24]

This introduction of the 'monster Love', at first nothing more than a dream, the counterpart or counterfeit of Pain, is seized upon by Panthea. She reminds Prometheus – it is perhaps significant that he had forgotten – of his own eternal love Asia, the third daughter of Oceanus, and Panthea's sister. Panthea also proclaims her own love for Asia, and we glimpse for a moment a familiar emotional triangle. Panthea goes off to the 'far Indian vale' to waken Asia. This brings Shelley to the end of Act I.

Act I has no scene divisions, and moves forward with a steady, unhurried, operatic development. The main characters are introduced, the scene is set, the confrontation is clarified. The drama is still recognizably Aeschylean. There is, however, an entirely original Shelleyan theme working like a kind of yeast in the unleavened classical text. This is the familiar idea of the double nature, the pursuer and pursued, the *doppelgänger*.

Everywhere the reader is aware of nature's split, Nature herself divided. The permanent winter of fruitlessness, disease and icy colds has divided Earth from the warm, productive side of her seasonable self. There is even an indication that the geophysical tilt of the planet earth from a ninety-degree polar axis is taken by Shelley as an image of internal contradiction and disharmony. Zoroaster's underworld of Unconscious, his universe of disunited doubles, indicates that Prometheus is himself a divided personality. What is he divided from? When Earth explains that he can call up either his own or Jupiter's ghost to repeat the curse, there is an indication that paradoxically the very condition of the polar opposition between Prometheus and Jupiter proves that they were once equal parts of a single, harmonious nature. Like Frankenstein and his monster, it is the failure of 'a community' between the two that has turned them alternatively into persecutor and victim, pursuer and pursued.

The Sixth Spirit in her strange Desolation speech, one of the most mysterious in the whole drama, seems to emphasize the duality of existence, the transformation of opposites between dream and waking, between desire and reality. The 'monster Love' can be transformed in a single shift of action or attention into the 'shadow Pain'. Panthea's journey to Asia proclaims clearly that, at a mythic level at least, Prometheus is separated from Love.

This mystic separation or alienation, according to the Shelleyan interpretation of the whole drama, must have psychological and political dimensions as well. The first act therefore presents a whole world of disassociated, dispossessed, schizophrenic and alienated beings. Their 'desolation' is also the winter of political hope, the frozen misery of the sick and hungry and the ignorant. For Prometheus to unbind mankind and unite the opposed terms of the spiritual equation, he has to confront those parts of himself represented by Jupiter and by Asia, by tyrannic authority and by Love, and to re-embody in some new medium the gift of his 'creative fire' to man.

Act II shifts the focus of attention to Prometheus's lover Asia. Prometheus himself does not appear. The setting of Scene I is 'a lovely vale in the Indian Caucasus' and the season is Shelley's Roman spring. It is Asia herself who first speaks, in rhythms that recall the Song of Songs:

> From all the blasts of Heaven thou hast descended:
> Yes, like a spirit, like a thought, which makes
> Unwonted tears throng to the horny eyes,
> And beatings haunt the desolated heart,
> Which should have learnt repose; thou hast descended
> Cradled in tempests; thou dost wake, O Spring!
> O child of many winds![25]

The cold, hard, almost strident epic language of the first act is transformed into a rich, pliant, highly wrought medium heavily loaded with sensuous and erotic imagery. Panthea, describing to Asia her peaceful state as one of Ocean's daughters before Prometheus's 'fall' is given a characteristic passage:

> . . . I slept . . .
> Within dim bowers of green and purple moss,
> Our young Ione's soft and milky arms
> Locked then, as now, behind my dark, moist hair. . . .[26]

Panthea needs to rouse Asia, as she had roused Prometheus, with remembrance of their separated love. She does this in another extraordinary passage where Asia is reminded of Prometheus's emotional and sexual potency by seeing one of *Panthea's dreams* of Prometheus mirrored in the 'dark, far, measureless Orb within orb', of Panthea's eyes. Here Panthea is made both a kind of messenger and a spiritual medium. Her memory of Prometheus's love-making is one of Shelley's finest presentations of the dream-orgasm since the dancing maid of *Alastor*.

> I saw not, heard not, moved not, only felt
> His presence flow and mingle through my blood
> Till it became his life, and his grew mine,
> And I was thus absorbed, until it passed.

And like the vapours when the sun sinks down,
Gathering again in drops upon the pines,
And tremulous as they, in the deep night
My being was condensed. . . .[27]

Panthea and Asia are now drawn from the Indian vale by the dream, which
first becomes personified, ('*Dream:* Follow! Follow!') and finally transforms
itself into a chorus of ever-changing Echoes, Spirits and Fauns. Through three
rapid scenes, Panthea and Asia are led irresistibly towards the hidden, deep,
volcanic layer of Demogorgon. The descriptions are drawn from Shelley's
visit to Vesuvius. As in Act I, the importance of this movement downwards,
inwards, backwards, into the abysms of memory and the earth, is stressed. They
are looking, as it were, into the seeds of time, the cauldron of the unformed
world. At the beginning of Scene IV they arrive in the underground realm of
Demogorgon, an adaption of Aeschylus's Typhon, who represents the forces of
Necessity, Change and Revolution, and where

>   rays of gloom
> Dart round, as light from the meridian sun.[28]

This is a reference to the infra-red and ultra-violet ends of the spectrum of
radiation beyond the reach of human vision, which Shelley loosely understood
as a form of 'creative fire', and it provides a clue to the nature of the 'new fire'
which Prometheus will give to man in Shelley's adaption of the myth.

Act II Scene IV is unquestionably the finest and most effortlessly sustained in
the whole drama. It is 172 lines long, and consists mainly of an exchange between
Asia and Demogorgon. It contains Asia's marvellous monologue on the gifts
which Prometheus gave to man according to the Aeschylean version of the
story. All of the scene except the very end stays extremely close to the Aeschylean text, lines 435 to 525. Asia, the incarnation of Love, questions Demogorgon
about the nature of power in the natural universe. Her questions finally narrow
down to one: who is the author of evil within the universe? and is this author –
she implies Jupiter, a Manichean, evil God – finally master or slave of his own
creation? Demogorgon's dismissal of the question, and Asia's reply, is a celebrated philosophic crux of Shelley's poem.

Asia. Who is the master of the slave?

Demogorgon.   If the abysm
    Could vomit forth its secrets. . . . But a voice
    Is wanting, the deep truth is imageless;
    For what would it avail to bid thee gaze

> On the revolving world? What to bid speak
> Fate, Time, Occasion, Chance, and Change? To these
> All things are subject but eternal Love.

> *Asia.* So much I asked before, and my heart gave
> The response thou hast given; and of such truths
> Each to itself must be the oracle.[29]

Through Demogorgon, Shelley confirms his scepticism and denies absolute knowledge either in the religious or scientific sense; he believed that both science and religion were only images of the 'imageless' truth. Demogorgon's reply nevertheless confirms the freedom of Asia herself, in as far as she represents or embodies the 'eternal Love' which is subject to nothing. The identification between Love and Freedom, though it stands in Act II as little more than a poetic formula, points towards the kind of liberated world which Shelley hoped to depict and celebrate in the third act. The whole dialogue between Asia and Demogorgon is recreated from the Aeschylean text with immense force and authority, and an urgency which moves far beyond the classical, mythic base. The terms of the debate are modern. Asia has all her sister Panthea's warmth and ardour, but none of her softness or languor. She is Love militant, as she rapidly shows in the development of the argument.

> *Asia.* Who made that sense which, when the winds of Spring
> In rarest visitation, or the voice
> Of one belovèd heard in youth alone,
> Fills the faint eyes with falling tears which dim
> The radiant looks of unbewailing flowers,
> And leaves this peopled earth a solitude
> When it returns no more?

> *Demogorgon.* Merciful God.

> *Asia.* And who made terror, madness, crime, remorse,
> Which from the links of the great chain of things,
> To every thought within the mind of man
> Sway and drag heavily, and each one reels
> Under the load towards the pit of death;
> Abandoned hope, and love that turns to hate;
> And self-contempt, bitterer to drink than blood;
> Pain, whose unheeded and familiar speech
> Is howling, and keen shrieks, day after day;
> And Hell, or the sharp fear of Hell?

Demogorgon.   He reigns.

Asia. Utter his name: a world pining in pain
         Asks but his name: curses shall drag him down.[30]

This is how Love can talk when Shelley required it. If Act II Scene IV is the centre and strong point of the drama, Asia's Promethean speech is the masterpiece of the scene. One of the strangest comments on Shelley's own creative process is the degree to which he had anticipated this speech, even before he had read Aeschylus, six years previously in the final canto of *Queen Mab*. The high, sinuous clarity of the verse, its almost perfect balance between intellectual abstraction and vividly localized images, and its immense energy concentrated in a silvery plainness of statement shows Shelley writing at the very height of his poetic powers.

And Jove now reigned; for on the race of man
First famine, and then toil, and then disease,
Strife, wounds, and ghastly death unseen before,
Fell; and the unseasonable seasons drove
With alternating shafts of frost and fire,
Their shelterless, pale tribes to mountain caves:
And in their desert hearts fierce wants he sent,
And mad disquietudes, and shadows idle
Of unreal good, which levied mutual war,
So ruining the lair wherein they raged.
Prometheus saw, and waked the legioned hopes
Which sleep within folded Elysian flowers,
Nepenthe, Moly, Amaranth, fadeless blooms,★
That they might hide with thin and rainbow wings
The shape of Death; and Love he sent to bind
The disunited tendrils of that vine
Which bears the wine of life, the human heart;
And he tamed fire which, like some beast of prey,
Most terrible, but lovely, played beneath

★ Moly is the legendary herb, sometimes identified with the wild garlic, which Homer tells us that the god Hermes gave to Odysseus to inoculate him against the bestial sorceries of Circe. The flower was white, the root jet black. For Shelley, Moly seems to represent that power of control over one's own mind which prevents a man from reverting into a beast. Amaranth, the purple flower sometimes identified with love-lies-bleeding, is traditionally associated with immortality; it is 'fadeless' in Spenser and Milton, and brings man the fruitful illusion of personal immortality. Nepenthe is also mentioned by Homer as a drug used by Odysseus to banish pain, grief and trouble from the mind; it has an Egyptian origin and Shelley probably associated it with a narcotic such as opium or hashish.

The frown of man; and tortured to his will
Iron and gold, the slaves and signs of power,
And gems and poisons, and all subtlest forms
Hidden beneath the mountains and the waves.
He gave man speech, and speech created thought,
Which is the measure of the universe;
And Science struck the thrones of earth and heaven,
Which shook, but fell not; and the harmonious mind
Poured itself forth in all-prophetic song;
And music lifted up the listening spirit
Until it walked, exempt from mortal care,
Godlike, o'er the clear billows of sweet sound;
And human hands first mimicked and then mocked,
With moulded limbs more lovely than its own,
The human form, till marble grew divine;
And mothers, gazing, drank the love men see
Reflected in their race, behold, and perish.
He told the hidden power of herbs and springs,
And Disease drank and slept. Death grew like sleep.
He taught the implicated orbits woven
Of the wide-wandering stars; and how the sun
Changes his lair, and by what secret spell
The pale moon is transformed, when her broad eye
Gazes not on the interlunar sea:
He taught to rule, as life directs the limbs,
The tempest-wingèd chariots of the Ocean,
And the Celt knew the Indian. Cities then
Were built, and through their snow-like columns flowed
The warm winds, and the azure aether shone,
And the blue sea and shadowy hills were seen.
Such, the alleviations of his state,
Prometheus gave to man, for which he hangs
Withering in destined pain. . . .[31]

This great scene ends without the least diminution in poetic power. Asia's questioning of Demogorgon and her celebration of Prometheus's historic role, precipitate the moment of destiny for which the whole earth has been waiting. The volcanic fire of history begins to erupt. In a memorable image, Demogorgon shows the constant stream of the chariots of the Hours pouring up through the purple night, like sparks hurtling up a flue. One of these carries the grim destiny of Jupiter; another the happy reunion of Asia and Prometheus. Both in their political aspect are revolutionary.

Shelley drew the picture of these chariots directly from the classical carving on the Arch of Constantine. By comparing it with his prose notes made in the Forum it is possible to see exactly the process of imaginative transformation. Shelley had first observed:

> The keystone of these arches is supported each by two winged figures of Victory, whose hair floats on the wind of their own speed, & whose arms are outstretched bearing trophies, as if impatient to meet. They look as it were born from the subject extremities of the earth on the breath which is the exhalation of that battle & desolation which it is their mission to commemorate.[32]

Returning later to the same carved relief, he further elaborated the visual details and the symbolism.

> The figures of Victory with unfolded wings & each spurning back a globe with outstretched feet are perhaps more beautiful than those on either of the others. Their lips are parted; a delicate mode of indicating the fervour of their desire to arrive at their destined resting place, & to express the eager respiration of their speed.[33]

This was now recast in the poem as a completed image, of peculiar force and beauty. Taking courage from the massive but simple dignity of the classical carving, Shelley boldly embodied the extremely abstract idea of the 'great historical moment', the great turning-point in the development of civilization, in a simple iconographic picture:

Demogorgon.   Behold!

Asia. The rocks are cloven, and through the purple night
      I see cars drawn by rainbow-wingèd steeds
      Which trample the dim winds: in each there stands
      A wild-eyed charioteer urging their flight.
      Some look behind, as fiends pursued them there,
      And yet I see no shapes but the keen stars:
      Others, with burning eyes, lean forth, and drink
      With eager lips the wind of their own speed,
      As if the thing they loved fled on before,
      And now, even now, they clasped it. Their bright locks
      Stream like a comet's flashing hair: they all
      Sweep onward.[34]

This is one of the great Shelleyan images. The writing here is richer, more ornate than in the Promethean speech; yet it still retains the immense energy of movement, and its clarity of visual line really does remind one of stone-carving. It is also extraordinary how many of his most familiar themes Shelley has managed to pack into it: – the chariot–boat–airship; the fiends; the pursuer and the pursued; the sexual fire of the comet and the streaming hair. There is a unique combination of simplicity and suggestiveness achieved in such a line as 'And yet I see no shapes but the keen stars'.

This close of Scene iv brings the climax of the whole drama. In mythic terms, Demogorgon is about to end the reign of Jupiter and restore Prometheus to his liberty. He ascends in the Chariot of the Hour driven by a spirit with 'dreadful countenance'.

> *Panthea.*   That terrible shadow floats
>   Up from its throne, as may the lurid smoke
>   Of earthquake-ruined cities o'er the sea.
>   Lo! it ascends the car; the coursers fly
>   Terrified: watch its path among the stars
>   Blackening the night![35]

In physical terms, Shelley is describing a gigantic volcanic and geophysical upheaval, a Vesuvian explosion, and the restoration of Nature to her golden equilibrium of fruitful and seasonal fluctuations.

In psychological terms, Asia, the principle of Love, has discovered her own freedom and is about to be re-united – by a second chariot, 'an ivory shell inlaid with crimson fire' – driven by a young and beautiful spirit, with the Promethean aspect of man's mind. Love, the private creative and sexual part of human relationships, is freed from its inhibitions and repressions, and recombined with the social elements. It forms the unity of mind which Shelley believed could alone produce the great scientist, the artist, the doctor, the architect and the law-giver. The divided nature is healed.

Finally, in political terms, this is the moment of uprising and revolution against tyranny and imposed authority. Shelley is here not being nationally or even historically explicit. It is perhaps the old Illuminist ideal of world revolution, originally symbolized by a string of volcanic eruptions. But with the reference to the French Revolution in Act I, it is possible to believe that he was thinking of Europe; and within Europe, of England.

Was he celebrating a violent, 'democratic', revolution? The text, like the preface, is ambiguous. There are two chariots mentioned: the one that brings Demogorgon to Jupiter is undoubtedly terrible and violent: Jupiter, authoritarian government, is to be overwhelmed by massive force, and the process in

society is to be like a volcanic eruption and an earthquake which 'ruins' cities.*
The etymological reading is surely relevant here. It is the eruption of 'demos-
gorgon', the 'people-monster'.[36]

Yet there is also the second chariot, with its 'delicate strange tracery', and its
gentle charioteer with 'dove-like eyes of hope'. This is the chariot which carries
Asia and Panthea back to Prometheus, and it seems to indicate that political
freedom transforms man's own nature and substitutes an ethic of love for the
ideology of revenge and destruction represented by Prometheus's curse. The
end of Act II leaves both these possibilities open historically. Revolution will
come, but how it will come depends on man himself. There are always two
chariots. In either case it is inevitable, and it is to be celebrated.

The act ends with a short, final choric Scene v. Panthea describes the transformation of Asia as they fly upwards and forwards in the chariot, and compares
her to the pagan Venus Anodyomene, the creative force of Love rising from the
sea like 'the atmosphere of the sun's fire'. The famous hymns, 'Child of Light!
thy limbs are burning' and 'My soul is an enchanted boat' form parts of this
chorus. The final lines of the act envisage a fantastic journey through reversed-
time into a metempsychotic Paradise, part womb, part regenerated planet.

> We have passed Age's icy caves,
>   And Manhood's dark and tossing waves,
> And Youth's smooth ocean, smiling to betray:
>   Beyond the glassy gulfs we flee
>   Of shadow-peopled Infancy,
> Through Death and Birth, to a diviner day;
>   A paradise of vaulted bowers,
>   Lit by downward-gazing flowers,
>   And watery paths that wind between
>   Wildernesses calm and green,
> Peopled by shapes too bright to see. . . .[37]

We are in fact back where we began, the vision has dissolved, and Shelley is
sitting within the blossoming labyrinths of the Baths of Caracalla.

From the Third Act onwards, the poem no longer has the strong architectonic
plotting of Aeschylus's drama behind it. The moment Shelley attempts to
develop the myth in a conscious way, by artificially adding to the structure of
the action, the poem comes apart in his hands. The Prometheus who actually

* Alexander von Humboldt, Sir Humphry Davy and Sir William Hamilton all carried out major
research into volcanic activity during Shelley's lifetime. Mount Etna erupted in 1792, and again at
the end of 1819; Vesuvius erupted in 1794, and was partly active again during the period of Shelley's
visit to Naples in 1818.

and finally liberates man from the powers of Jupiter is no longer Prometheus. Prometheus represents suffering, hope, creative skill and the eternal struggle for a potential freedom. He is the symbol of those who struggle for the future; he is the symbol of those who wait the revolution, the new golden age; but he cannot be the symbol of Victory itself.

The one genuinely creative departure of Acts III and IV lies in the development of the imagery of Promethean fire. This is both poetically and intellectually a brilliant transformation. The new fire that Prometheus brings is electricity.

> *Ione.* Sister, it is not earthly: how it glides
>   Under the leaves! how on its head there burns
>   A light, like a green star, whose emerald beams
>   Are twined with its fair hair! how, as it moves,
>   The splendour drops in flakes upon the grass!
>   Knowest thou it?

> *Panthea.*   It is the delicate spirit
>   That guides the earth through heaven. From afar
>   The populous constellations call that light
>   The loveliest of the planets; and sometimes
>   It floats along the spray of the salt sea,
>   Or makes its chariot of a foggy cloud,
>   Or walks through fields or cities while men sleep,
>   Or o'er the mountain tops, or down the rivers,
>   Or through the green waste wilderness, as now,
>   Wondering at all it sees. . . .[38]

Shelley was not of course scientifically exact, and wrote without the benefit of Faraday's work. He included indiscriminately in the electric phenomena of this 'delicate spirit' glow worms, phosphorescences, *ignis fatuus*, lightning, the 'long blue meteors cleansing the dull night', the aurora borealis, and even the 'polar Paradise' which 'Magnet-like of lovers eyes' keeps the moon in its field of attraction round the Earth. But his apparently inspired prevision of electron shells in the atomic structure of matter is celebrated:

> A sphere, which is as many thousand spheres,
> Solid as crystal, yet through all its mass
> Flow, as through empty space, music and light:
> Ten thousand orbs involving and involved,
> Purple and azure, white, and green, and golden . . .
> Upon a thousand sightless axles spinning. . . .[39]

Electricity as the new fire beautifully satisfied the extension of the plot both mythically and scientifically. Electricity would be the great new power source to liberate man from physical servitude. But as a metaphor of the liberation of spiritual and political energies it suffers, like the whole of Acts III and IV, from irresolution. This could signify any kind of vague radiation of goodwill. It cannot hold together the remainder of the poem, though it served later in 1820 to give Shelley the core image of physical and psychological freedom for 'The Witch of Atlas'.

From the opening of Act III onwards the poem completely disintegrates. The dethronement of Jupiter is a piece of creaking epic stage machinery; there is no confrontation between him and Prometheus, and thence no reconciliation. The evil principle is merely dismissed. The reunification of Prometheus and Asia when it comes is empty and anticlimactic. The vision of the world and Nature revolutionized is almost entirely a failure, anyway poetically an impossible task. The language as a whole becomes increasingly rhetorical, and the imagery depends on successive reworking and weakening of tropes and metaphors discovered in the first two acts. Prometheus's reaction to his liberation and the revolution of human society is to retire into a kind of rural hermitage, 'a cave, All overgrown with trailing odorous plants, Which curtain out the day with leaves and flowers'. This is yet another recycling of the image of the Baths of Caracalla, a *hortus conclusus*, and it symbolizes a rejection of the world rather than universal social revolution. In this sense Shelley's poetry remains more honest than his ideology, for the actions of Prometheus in Act III are those of a leader who has escaped defeat and gone into a jaded exile, rather than those of a genuine victor.

Shelley himself had increasingly nagging doubts about Act III. In the autumn of the year, at Florence, he returned to it, and added a Fourth Act. This was really a confession of artistic failure. He abandoned the mythic structure altogether, banished Prometheus and Asia to a forest cave from which they do not emerge at all or speak, and attempted to create a cosmic operetta of lyric duets and trios between Earth, Moon and Demogorgon. It is like the libretto for a great piece of music that he never managed to compose.

The great achievement of *Prometheus Unbound* therefore rests securely in the first two acts which together form a complete and unified poem of some 1,500 lines. The rest remains superfluous and second-rate. But the essential two-act work is undoubtedly the second of Shelley's four Italian masterpieces. At every level it is a poem of hope achieved agonizingly through suffering: but it is not broadly an optimistic poem. It is in many ways obsessed with the evil and pain and tyranny in the world, like all Shelley's previous writing. More than in *The Revolt of Islam*, and more perhaps than in *Queen Mab*, it sees the definite imminence of a moral and political revolution: in this sense it is more aggressive and confident. But it also presents clearly the possibilities of both a peaceful and a violent revolution: the choice remains ahead, and in a sense, always remains ahead. Finally, says the poem and the myth, there will be Victory. But the Victory is not there in Shelley's poem. The Revolution remains to be made.

20

The Palace of the Dark

Prometheus Unbound was near completion early in April 1819. Shelley relaxed by going to see the Easter illumination of St Peter's in the Vatican with Mary and Claire. On the 16th he began to read *Paradise Lost* out loud in the evenings, and on the 25th he gave Mary the manuscript of *Prometheus* to read. She makes no comment in her journal.

Mary was still feeling depressed and withdrawn. 'God knows why but I have suffered more from [ill spirits] ten times over than I ever did before I came to Italy evil thoughts will hang about me – but this is only now and then –'[1]. She was cheered a little by the *entrée* of a bluff English eccentric, the Revd Colonel Finch, 'a mixture of Abelard & old Blucher', into their small circle of acquaintances. The Shelleys christened him Calicot, after one of Tom Moore's story characters. At least he was someone for Mary to laugh at. There was also the Emperor of Austria, who came to give a feast at the Capitol at the end of April. The galleries of the palazzos were hung with coloured silks, and there were fireworks in the evening. 'I have not room to tell you,' Mary gossiped to Maria Gisborne in her letter, 'how gracefully the old venerable Pope fulfilled the Church ceremonies.' Shelley asked Mary to inquire about herbs for flea powder.[2]

Shelley had few thoughts of publication. The effort of composition had exhausted him, and he walked out much less. He stayed at the Corso reading, or took leisurely turns in a carriage content to observe the constant flux of the Italians going about their daily business. He consigned his manuscript to the bottom of his trunk after Mary had read it, and it is not mentioned again in his letters for several months. Not until September did he write to Charles Ollier, who knew of the poem from Peacock: 'My "Prometheus" which has been long finished, is now being transcribed, & will soon be forwarded to you for publication. It is in my judgement, of a higher character than any thing I have yet attempted. . . .'[3] He had confidence and satisfaction in it; but he was not confident of his audience.* In the meantime he needed a subject with a more obvious appeal: something more extroverted, more popular. Perhaps Italian life might provide it?

Shelley looked around him carefully. For the first time he was beginning to see Rome as a living city rather than an enormous museum. He had ceased to be a tourist. 'In the square of St Peter's there are about 300 fettered criminals at work, hoeing out the weeds that grow between the stones of the pavement. Their legs are heavily ironed, & some are chained two by two. They sit in long rows hoeing out the weeds, dressed in party-coloured clothes. Near them sit or saunter, groups of soldiers armed with loaded muskets. . . . It is the emblem of Italy: moral degradation contrasted with the glory of nature & the arts.'[4]

Simultaneously with this growing identification with the real Italy, came the bitter realization that since he was not a tourist, he really was an exile. After receiving the depressed and anxious letters from Naples, Peacock had written strongly suggesting that Shelley would be wise to return to England. 'How is it possible!' Shelley replied. 'Health competence, tranquility all these Italy permits & England takes away.' Perhaps there were five people alone, he wrote, who did not regard him 'as a rare prodigy of crime & pollution whose look even might infect'. Events at Naples no doubt contributed to this gloomy self-accusation. They still planned to return south in the summer to Naples where presumably they would visit Elena, but no mention of this was made to Peacock. Instead Shelley sent greetings via him to Mrs Boinville, 'I desire such remembrances to her as an exile & a *Pariah* may be permitted to address to an acknowledged member of the community of mankind.' Was this a conscious echo of Frankenstein's monster talking on the glacier? Perhaps; at any rate it was not entirely unsarcastic. 'It was hardly possible for a person of the extreme subtlety & delicacy of Mrs Boinville's understanding & affections,' wrote Shelley cordially, 'to be quite sincere & constant.' There are other indications in his letters that the 'spirit of the English abroad' was becoming increasingly uncongenial to him, and the fashionable Corso, and the sociable soirées of Signora Dioniga had become distasteful.

However, some sort of relief was at hand. On 23 April Claire's sharp and roving eye spotted the disappearing shape of Aemilia Curran in the Borghese

---

* *Prometheus Unbound* did not reach England until the end of 1819, and was not published until the summer of 1820. It was then printed as the title poem to a collection of Shelley's Italian poetry. It was reviewed steadily from June 1820 until the end of 1821. Despite the fact that the reviews were mixed – the *Quarterly* crucified it, *Blackwood's* praised and generously defended it – the book did not sell. Public opinion was against Shelley's work in London, and the book was regarded as disreputable rather than daring. It is not certain how much money Ollier lost on the edition, but the jibe went that Prometheus was unbound because the publisher could not afford to bind it up. This was undoubtedly the greatest of Shelley collections printed during his lifetime.

Gardens. Miss Curran was the eloquent, independent and high-spirited elder daughter of John Philpot Curran, the Irish politician. Claire and Mary knew her through Curran's friendship with the Godwins; and Shelley had also met her during his expedition to Dublin in 1812. Inquiries were made, and a card left.[5] It was indeed Miss Curran, and she was delighted to meet them. Visits were exchanged and she soon became a frequent companion of their carriage rides and gallery visits.

Miss Curran was a good example of the Godwinian breed: an Irish radical in politics, and sturdily independent in person, she had decided to go abroad and educate herself. She lived completely alone at No. 64 Via Sestina, a narrow but elegant street of closely packed stone houses on the northern heights of Rome and giving immediately on to the commanding and beautiful piazza of the Trinità dei Monti. Her main occupation was painting. She seems to have supported herself partly by turning out competent society portraits in oils. She spoke Italian fluently and adapted herself well to European life. She was still living like a hermit in Rome in 1821, and in the summer of 1822 she was to be found living with equal satisfaction in the *faubourg* of St Germain in Paris. She had a revivifying effect on the Shelleys. A few days after this new acquaintanceship, Mary gave up her drawing for painting; and on 5 May Claire began to sit for her portrait by Miss Curran. Claire and Shelley went up to see her at Via Sestina on several afternoons, and Shelley learnt that there were rooms to be had next door at No. 65.

On 5 May also occurred an unpleasant incident which made the society of the Corso definitely unwelcome. Mary and Claire recorded cryptically: 'S.'s adventure at the Post Office.'[6] Tom Medwin, who met Shelley at Pisa in 1821, was told the story, and recorded it, muddling the date and place (he thought it was Pisa) in his usual fashion. The essential facts seem to have been that Shelley 'was at the Post Office asking for his letters, addressed, as is usual in Italy, Poste-Restante, when a stranger in a military cloak, on hearing him pronounce his name, said "What, are you that damned atheist, Shelley?" and without more preamble, being a tall, powerful man, struck him such a blow that it felled him to the ground, and stunned him. On coming to himself, Shelley found the ruffian had disappeared.'[7] Medwin adds various fanciful details about a mysterious pursuit to Genoa, which seem to be pure invention. Claire's word 'adventure' suggests, however, that Shelley may not have allowed himself to be knocked unconscious quite so docilely as Medwin pretends, and recalling the incident on the Rhine boat in 1814 it sounds unlikely. The damned atheist probably gave as much as he got. They moved to No. 65 Via Sestina the next day.

The house was the last one before the Trinità, and immediately below it were the three graceful landings of the Spanish Steps – already the haunt of flower-sellers – and the Piazza di Spagna containing the elegant ochre scallop of the Bernini fountain. Beyond was laid out one of the finest Baroque vistas in Rome, stretching south-eastwards over the Palazzo Borghese and across the Tiber to the huge machicolated drum of Castel San Angelo, where Cellini had once manned the guns, and beyond that again to the hovering silver green dome of St Peter's and the dark walls of the Città del Vaticano. The area of the Trinità and the Spanish Steps was to become known eventually as the 'Romantic' or 'English quarter', and to fill in consequence with Victorian travel agencies and tea-rooms. But in 1819 it was relatively undiscovered. Two winters later, when Keats and Joseph Severn arrived in Rome, they took a cheap apartment in the first house at the bottom of the Steps. Keats's room directly overlooked the Bernini fountain, and at night it was full of the sound of splashing water. Claire entered in her diary for 6 May: 'L'Ultima Casa sulla Trinità dei Monti. In the evening walk on the Trinità with S. . . .' They admired the view as the light faded. They were joined by Dr Bell, the distinguished Scottish physician who Shelley had decided to consult about his health.

The next morning Shelley was sitting for his portrait at No. 64. In the follow-ing month Aemilia Curran produced or at least started portraits of Mary and little Willmouse, besides those of Claire and Shelley. It is a great pity that this completed set has not survived. The first two have been lost; Claire's was finished and is certainly the best, though she herself disliked it.[8] Perhaps she thought she looked too irritable; or that there was too much flesh under her chin.

The portrait of Shelley is the most famous painting Miss Curran ever exe-cuted. It is not generally known, however, that the work was unfinished, and the artist herself felt that it was a very bad likeness indeed. It remained stacked in her studio until 1822, awaiting an opportunity for alteration and completion. When Mary sent for it in July 1822, Miss Curran replied: 'The [portrait] you now write for I thought was not to be enquired for; it was so ill done, and I was on the point of burning it with others before I left Italy. I luckily saved it just as the fire was scorching it, and it is packed it up with my other pictures at Rome. . . .'[9]*

The month of May in Rome not only marked Shelley's escape from the society of the Corso but also an artistic shift of address. It was now Renaissance and not ancient Classical Rome which held Shelley's attention. There are almost no records of walks in the Capitol and Forum, but several visits to the great

---

* Perhaps it was not so lucky. The present painting in the National Portrait Gallery shows no sign of scorching, which suggests that Miss Curran touched it up after hearing of Shelley's death. The 'official' portrait is both wooden and querulous, and the mouth and neck are sentimentally finished. It is interesting to compare the style with the buxom life and energy in Miss Curran's painting of Claire.

palazzos. At the end of April Shelley had first seen the portrait of Beatrice Cenci, and in May he returned to the seed idea which he had found in the Cenci manuscript at Livorno. On the 11th he spent the afternoon visiting the grim buildings of the Palazzo Cenci down by the Tiber Island, with its iron-fenced windows and its small dim courtyard. The building is sinister in a retiring rather than an imposing way: it is hidden at the centre of a labyrinth of old blackened houses and dark alleys, which crowd tightly round it so that it is impossible to get a clear view of the shape and size of the whole. One always ends up under the shadow of one of its walls. It worked quickly on Shelley's imagination, and on the 14th Mary noted that he was already drafting 'his Tragedy'. He had found his popular subject. He would write a melodrama, specifically for the London stage, intending the actress Mademoiselle O'Neil to take the leading role of Beatrice Cenci at Covent Garden.

It was an ambitious project for all its popular intention. It required gifts of stage plotting and dialogue that Shelley had not previously exercised, and of course he intended to write verse drama. The whole subject was under discussion in the Shelley household, and kindled considerable emotion. At first there was even some doubt who should write it. Mary recalled: 'Shelley's imagination became strongly excited, and he urged the subject to me as one fitted for a tragedy. More than ever I felt my incompetence; but I entreated him to write it instead. . . . This tragedy is the only one of his works that he communicated to me during its progress. We talked over the arrangement of the scenes together.'[10] Claire was also reading the Cenci manuscript and on the evening of the 12th she, Shelley, Mary and Miss Curran had a discussion 'concerning Jealousy' at the studio at No. 64.

On the following day Claire wrote the first letter to Byron after a long silence: 'Did you ever read the history of the Cenci's a most frightful & horrible story? I am sorely afraid to say that in the elder Cenci you may behold yourself in twenty years . . . but if I live Allegra shall never be a Beatrice.' Since Count Cenci, besides being an atheist, a sodomite and a rapacious materialist, had also murdered his two eldest sons, and raped his eldest daughter Beatrice, this was fairly strong stuff from Claire. On reflection she crossed out the second sentence; but it was still legible.[11]

The picture Claire gives of the Shelley household at Via Sestina in mid-May is fairly morbid. 'Mr Bell, one of the first English surgeons has seen Shelley (who has been very ill) and he has ordered him to pass the summer at Naples & says if S has any consumptive symptoms left by the approach of next winter he must pass the cold season at Tunis. . . . And if Shelley were to die there is nothing left for us but dying.'[12] That Claire was orchestrating things somewhat for Byron's benefit, is indicated by the fact that two days earlier she had been with Shelley and Aemilia Curran on a day's expedition to Tivoli, and described it in her diary that evening as 'one of the pleasantest [days] of my life and one as only Italy can give'.[13] None the less, the plan to go further south, to North Africa or even the Near East, remained at the back of Shelley's mind throughout his time in Italy, as one further place of retreat. In 1821 he was to talk seriously to Claire about it; though not to Mary.

The decision to return to Naples depended on Shelley's health and the news of Elena. Mary clearly wished to go north to rejoin the Gisbornes in Tuscany, and except for Shelley's consumptive symptoms, one has the strong impression that she wanted no more to do with Naples. Shelley made her write to the Gisbornes, begging them to come south too for the summer, as a kind of compromise; he had also written himself, promising 'a piano & some books, & little else, – besides ourselves: but . . . it is intolerable to think of you being buried in Livorno'.[14] The Gisbornes in the end declined, and nothing remained but to see what June would bring. Meanwhile Shelley continued working sporadically at *The Cenci*, while Mary read Boccaccio's *Decameron*, and Claire flicked rapidly through Dante's *Purgatorio*, keeping an eye out for suitable locations for herself and Byron.[15]

What was it that attracted Shelley so persistently to the theme of *The Cenci*? Partly it was a reaction to the prolonged work on the Promethean theme: it was a complete change of scale and style. From cosmic drama, with its intricate meshing of symbolic levels, he turned to domestic melodrama, with a bold simple plot of outrage and revenge, and a language almost entirely bare of all imagery. He later wrote: 'I have avoided with great care in writing this play the introduction of what is commonly called mere poetry, and I imagine there will scarcely be found a detached simile or a single isolated description. . . .'[16] In many respects he had written 'carelessly', that is 'without an over-fastidious and learned use of words'. Artistically, this was a relief. But above all the Cencis' history offered him a subject which he knew already had a lurid popularity among the expatriate English: indeed there is some evidence that he wrote partly under the fear that someone else would take the idea back to London before he did. But few other writers would have felt confident enough of their powers, or careless enough of their reputation, to try and put a story of incest and parricide on the London stage under their own name. The experience with *Laon and Cynthia* had already taught Shelley that incest was a profoundly controversial and sensitive subject with the London public, and one can certainly trace in its choice an impulse that goes back to the Oxford days of *The Necessity of Atheism*. It is interesting that Shelley did not make Count Cenci an atheist too, though there is authority for it in the manuscript. Instead he makes him a fervent Catholic, as Shelley put it, 'deeply tinged with religion'. This was, in the end, a more subtle and provocative choice than atheism, and much more to Shelley's avowedly shocking purpose. His comments on religion in the preface to the play are suggestive; and show his shrewd penetration into the daily life of Rome:

> To a Protestant apprehension there will appear something unnatural in the earnest and perpetual sentiment of the relations between God and men which pervade the tragedy of the Cenci. It will especially be startled at the combination of an undoubting persuasion of the truth of the popular religion with a cool and determined perseverance in enormous guilt. But religion in Italy is not, as in Protestant countries, a cloak to be worn on particular days; or a passport which those who do not wish to be railed at carry with them to exhibit; or a gloomy passion for penetrating the impenetrable mysteries of our being, which terrifies its possessor at the darkness of the abyss to the brink of which it has conducted him. ... It has no necessary connection with any one virtue. The most atrocious villain may be rigidly devout, and without any shock to established faith, confess himself to be so. Religion pervades intensely the whole frame of society, and is according to the temper of the mind which it inhabits, a passion, a persuasion, an excuse, a refuge; never a check. Cenci himself built a chapel in the court of his Palace, and dedicated it to St Thomas the Apostle, and established masses for the peace of his soul.[17]

The personal horror with which Shelley clearly reacted to this 'culture of hypocrisy' shows his own deeply puritan root. Moreover, his description of the 'passion for penetrating into the mysteries of our being', as a *religious* impulse (a Protestant one), is perhaps one of the few times he formally admitted the religious element in his own nature. Such powerful and lurid ingredients strongly attracted Shelley to the evil tale of Renaissance family brutality.

The two living Roman monuments to the Cenci story – the palazzo and the picture of Beatrice – were also attracting him at a different and probably less conscious level. The Cenci Palace itself filled his mind with a disturbing symbolic force. He wrote later of it as if it had been one of the specimens in his dream catalogue. 'The Palace is situated in an obscure corner of Rome, near the quarter of the Jews, and from the upper windows you see the immense ruins of Mount Palatine half hidden under their profuse overgrowth of trees. There is a court in one part of the Palace (perhaps that in which Cenci built the Chapel to St Thomas), supported by granite columns and adorned with antique friezes of fine workmanship, and built up, according to the ancient Italian fashion, with balcony over balcony of open-work. One of the gates of the Palace formed of immense stones and leading through a passage, dark and lofty and opening into gloomy subterranean chambers, struck me particularly.'[18] The palace was for him like the gateway into an underground Inferno, a metaphysical rather than physical one, a hell of the mind.

Throughout *The Cenci* as he finally completed it, there are passages of monologue – not only from Beatrice but also from Giacomo her brother, and Orsino a fellow-plotter – which describe in an intensely personal way the effects of evil actions on the mind. At several points one is aware that Shelley is writing dramatized autobiography. The motivations and the consequences of evil, in psychological and analytic terms, form the main theme of the drama. In this the play runs a direct parallel with the central scene of *Prometheus*, the confrontation between Asia and Demogorgon in Act II. In one, evil is examined at a domestic level, in the other, at a cosmic one. In contrast the Count himself, the only completely evil figure in the play, is psychologically insignificant, and has many of the grosser attributes of a pantomime demon. Shelley wrote that the events of the play in 'all conspiring to one tremendous end', would be 'as a light to make apparent some of the most dark and secret caverns of the human heart'. It was an idea that seemed to haunt him.

The other Roman memorial, the portrait of Beatrice Cenci, also had a peculiar attraction. Shelley not only visited it at the Colonna Palace but had his own copy which he kept on the wall of his room at Via Sestina, and was delighted when the Italian servants instantly recognized it as *La Cenci*.[19] It is by Guido Reni, said to be painted while she was actually in prison awaiting trial; it was subsequently moved to the Barberini Palace, and finally to the Galleria Nazionale d'Arte Antica. From the way Shelley described this portrait, it is obvious that not only was he deeply moved by it but also that he strongly empathized with her personality:

> There is a fixed and pale composure upon the features. . . . Her head is bound with folds of white drapery from which the yellow strings of her golden hair escape, and fall about her neck. The moulding of her face is exquisitely delicate; the eyebrows are distinct and arched; the lips have that permanent meaning of imagination and sensibility which suffering has not repressed. . . . Her forehead is large and clear; her eyes, which we are told were remarkable for their vivacity, are swollen with weeping and lustreless, but beautifully tender and serene. . . . Beatrice Cenci appears to have been one of those rare persons in whom energy and gentleness dwell together without destroying one another. . . .[20]

But the most remarkable thing about the Reni portrait is something Shelley did not mention, and we have no hint if he ever consciously realized it; or if anyone else in the household did. But it is immediately apparent to an outside observer that there is a most striking resemblance between the Reni portrait of La Cenci and the Curran portrait of Shelley.

Both are oddly androgynous creations, whose glance is a mixture of defiance and pathos; the broad, pale forehead; the delicately arched brows; the large almond-shaped eyes; and finally the long faintly aquiline nose – these upper features are so markedly similar that it seems almost certain that Aemilia Curran was influenced by the Reni, even if she was not aware of the common elements between the two subjects.* As Shelley developed his drama so too did he develop his identification with Beatrice, and Miss Curran seems to have discovered this in a strangely unconscious way in her painting.

The identity between male and female, or at least the transposable or interchangeable elements between the two sexes had long been an under-theme of Shelley's writing. The masculine role frequently assigned to his heroines like Cythna or Asia, and the passivity of his male lovers like the poet of *Alastor*, is one of the constant and original features of his poetry. With his work on *The Cenci*, Shelley showed signs of developing this feature further into the realization and acceptance of certain elements in his own personality and temperament. Again, the importance of the play lies in its character as a psychological documentary. In later poems, especially 'The Witch of Atlas' and *Epipsychidion*, he was to pursue questions of bisexuality and androgynous creative powers with more deliberation.

Shelley worked on *The Cenci* quietly for a week at Via Sestina, and on 23 May, went by himself on a visit to Albano. Mary continued with her Boccaccio, and Claire eagerly consumed a copy of *The Infernal Quixote*, a novel about a young woman corrupted by Mary Wollstonecraft's principles.[21] Three days after Shelley's return, little William fell ill with a stomach complaint which quickly threatened to make him dangerously feverish. He had perhaps caught some germ from Aemilia Curran who had been painting his portrait the previous week, and had then fallen ill for several days.[22] Dr Bell called on the 27th, and his diagnosis was encouraging, for Shelley took Claire out for a social evening at the Academy of Music in the Piazza di Spagna. By the 29th Willmouse appeared to be better and Shelley dated his completion of the first draft of *The Cenci* on this day.[23] Mary used their temporary fright to persuade Shelley not to go southwards again to Naples, where it would be too hot during the summer for the little boy. Instead she successfully urged the mountain cool of the Bagni di Lucca, which was within riding distance of the Gisbornes as she had originally wanted. Another argument was the fact that Bell, for whom they had now developed a great trust and personal liking, was himself going north during the

---

* In September 1819 Shelley commissioned Miss Curran to execute a copy of the Reni portrait, to be used in England as the frontispiece to the first edition of *The Cenci* (1820).

summer to attend a valued patient, the Princess Paulina Borghese. Mary told Shelley that she wanted Dr Bell to be present at the birth of her next child, for she had recently disclosed that she had become pregnant in February. All this news Mary wrote with some semblance of her former enthusiasm to Mrs Gisborne, adding detailed requests about cooks and houseservants. She even looked forward to doing a little entertaining.[24]

But on 2 June, only five days before their planned departure from Rome, William had a serious relapse. On the 4th he started serious convulsions, as little Clara had done the previous year at Venice. Dr Bell was in constant attendance, and Shelley exhausted himself by sitting up in the room for three consecutive days and nights.[25] He was determined not to let this child die, his 4-year-old son, the most precious child of his life. Claire wrote a brief note to the Gisbornes on the 5th. Two days later, at midday, Willmouse died, silently, without fuss. He was buried at once in the Protestant Cemetery.

On 10 June the Shelleys left Rome. They drove slowly northwards, and arrived in Livorno seven days later. Mary gave up writing her journal. Shelley wrote numbly to Peacock: 'You will be kind enough to tell all my friends. . . . It is a great exertion to me to write this, & it seems to me as if, hunted by calamity as I have been, that I should never recover any cheerfulness again.'[26] Claire noted without comment their arrival at the Aquila Nera Inn at Livorno, and a visit to the Gisbornes. She refers to a small country house Shelley took on the outskirts of Livorno in the third week of June, the Villa Valsovano near the village of Monte Nero some 3 kilometres to the south of the port. Then her diary too breaks off. Mary did not begin her journal again till August 1819; and Claire's diary does not recommence until January of 1820. The Roman spring had deceived them; they were almost crushed by life.

21
The Hothouse: Livorno 1819

The summer of 1819 at Monte Nero was a time of great unhappiness in Shelley's household. The bustling *ménage* that had left Dover in 1818 was now grimly depleted. The sense of childlessness affected all three of them: Claire had lost her darling Allegra at Milan; Clara had died at Venice; Shelley's little Elena had been left behind at Naples; and now finally their favourite, their only son, Willmouse was buried at Rome. The household seemed to be infected, it was a ruin, a graveyard.

Shelley, as ever, fought strongly against the crisis of feeling. Though he wrote miserably to Peacock at the end of the month about the heavy weight of 'misfortune added to exile, & solitude', and spoke secretly of his desperate longing to return to England he soon drew a line with a curt 'Enough of melancholy', and would talk only of books and politics.[1] Claire busied herself with looking after Mary, for she too, like Shelley, always showed herself unexpectedly strong and stubborn in times of emergency. But it was Mary, who had just begun to recover during the spring from the depression of Naples, who was hardest hit. She had a total relapse of feeling, and plunged into an even greater mood of despair and isolation which was in effect a severe nervous breakdown. She wrote few letters during these months, and these as she wrote to Miss Curran were 'stupid'. 'I no sooner take up my pen than my thoughts run away with me & I cannot guide it except about *one* subject & that I must avoid.'[2] And more succinctly: 'I never shall recover that blow. . . . Everything on earth has lost its interest to me.' To Marianne Hunt she showed perhaps unconsciously how she again blamed Shelley: 'We came to Italy thinking to do Shelley's health good – but the Climate is not any means warm enough to be of benefit to him & yet it is that that has destroyed my two children.' This letter too was short: 'if I would write anything else about myself it would only be a list of hours spent tears & grief [*sic*].'[3]

The following March, Claire explained to Byron how bad things had been.

'Last May I had promised to go to Venice but Shelley could not do it. Our little boy died and we came to Livorno – here I was nearer [to you] but Mary was so melancholy and so sickly that I cannot imagine how she could have been left alone.'[4] For Claire to have thrown away a chance of seeing Allegra, Mary must have been desperate indeed.

Shelley realized clearly enough what was happening to Mary, but he took a deliberate decision to remain beyond the radius of her misery, and to help her from the outside only. He decided that it was best to leave her to live out her own feelings and despair by herself. He continued his reading and writing through the summer, and took certain practical measures to establish his routine independently of hers. It was a harsh but characteristic commitment to his own craft. A fragment of a poem he wrote puts the matter simply:

> My dearest Mary, wherefore hast thou gone,
> And left me in this dreary world alone?
> Thy form is here indeed – a lovely one –
> But thou art fled, gone down the dreary road,
> That leads to Sorrow's most obscure abode;
> Thou sittest on the hearth of pale despair,
> $\qquad\qquad\qquad\qquad$ Where
> For thine own sake I cannot follow thee
> Do thou return for mine.[5]

This poem Shelley wrote to her directly, like a letter; but Mary did not allow it to be published until the second edition of the *Poetical Works* of 1839. He also twice tried to write of William's death itself, but the two poems came out stiffened and formalized by grief, and remain unfinished. One breaks off on the brink of the discovery of one of Shelley's most celebrated elegiac phrases:

> Let me think that through low seeds
> Of sweet flowers and sunny grass
> Into their hues and scents may pass
> A portion——[6]

It was only two years later, in *Adonais* that Shelley finally found the completion of that line of thought and verse.

The Villa Valsovano, where with the help of the Gisbornes the stunned household found themselves residing by the end of June, provided Shelley with the ideal place to embark on a period of recuperation. It was a spacious, simple stone building, dating back at least two centuries, part country villa and part farmhouse. It was within sight of the sea, but set in its own garden and

olive plantation on rising ground which gave a magnificent view of the surrounding countryside. It was outside the bustle of Livorno, but close enough
to the municipal walls to make the walk to the Gisbornes' house an easy and
pleasurable daily excursion.

Mary described it listlessly as 'an airy house', but judging by her letters she
barely seems to have taken it in until the end of August. It was only then that
she began to notice the charm of the deep green lane that led up to the villa
gate, and the sleepy singing of the local peasants who worked in the surrounding
fields. The furrowed rows contained a fascinating mixture of vines, cabbages,
olives, fig and peach trees, corn and even apparently celery. It was a typical
podère, a mixture of farm and kitchen garden, perfectly calculated, Mary
thought, to appeal to Leigh Hunt. Mary spent much time sitting on one or
other of the many stone arbour seats which were concealed round the garden,
watching the peasants at work. It seemed to soothe her: 'they work this hot
weather in their shorts or smock frocks (but their breasts are bare) their brown
legs nearly the colour only with a rich tinge of red in it with the earth they turn
up. – They sing not very melodiously but very loud – Rossini's music *Mi
revedrai, ti revedro*, and they are accompanied by the cicada . . .'[7]

But for Shelley the great thing about the Villa Valsovano was its tower. It
was really a kind of balcony placed on the roof. It was glassed in on all sides,
and suspended Shelley in the blazing sunlight above the landscape of the farm
and the blue curving line of the bay, as if he were encased in one of his solitary
floating airships. The design is characteristic of the Livorno region, and can still
be seen more or less elaborately incorporated into the modern buildings along
the front. For Shelley it became his fortress of physical and intellectual light.
He ascended into it, closing behind him the darkness and human misery below.
Mary much later recalled: 'Shelley made [this] his study; it looked out on a
wide prospect of fertile country, and commanded a view of the near sea. The
storms that sometimes varied our day showed themselves most picturesquely
as they were driven across the ocean; sometimes the dark lurid clouds dipped
towards the waves, and became water-spouts that churned up the waters beneath, as they were chased onward and scattered by the tempest. At other times
the dazzling sunlight and heat made it almost intolerable to every other; but
Shelley basked in both, and his health and spirits revived under their influence.
In this airy cell he wrote the principal part of "The Cenci".'[8] It was now the
second draft of his poem that Shelley was slowly labouring over. But sealed off in
his cell, too hot for anyone else to stand the direct sunlight, he worked on alone.

Shelley forced himself to adopt a regular routine. He awoke usually at 7 in
the morning, and lay reading in bed for half an hour; he then dressed and breakfasted alone. 'After breakfast, *ascend my tower*, and read or write until two. Then

we dine – after dinner I read Dante with Mary, gossip a little, eat grapes & figs, sometimes walk, though seldom; and at ½ past 5 pay a visit to Mrs Gisborne who reads Spanish with me until near seven. We then come for Mary & stroll about until suppertime.'9 Shelley, who could already read and translate Lucretius, Plato and Dante from the original, had decided that it was a good moment to turn to a fourth language in order to read the work of the great Spanish playwright Calderón. Maria Gisborne was also a great help to Shelley with Mary, and the suppers which rounded off the day were frequently eaten *en partie*. When Shelley did decide to walk out, it was either to visit the Gisbornes alone, or else to take Claire to the sea. He found Mary a difficult companion. Claire was the best, but she was sometimes moody and unreliable in the old manner, and as Shelley said, 'sometimes does not dress in exactly the right time'. Claire had always had a weakness for sleeping through not only breakfast but also *dinner*; however, when she did manage to come, she was Shelley's closest company. Milly Shields, their English servant, also seems to have supplied Shelley with a mild diversion, when she took to star-gazing in the garden after dark. Shelley wrote: 'Milly surprised us the other day by first discovering a comet, on which we have been speculating. "She may make a stir, like a great astronomer."'10

Another instrument of Shelley's recuperation was Peacock's first box of books, which having been sent off by sea in November the previous year, had finally arrived at Livorno harbour. Shelley was especially interested by eight back numbers of Cobbett's *Political Register*, and a copy of his lively democratic and agrarian sermon *A Year's Residence in the United States of America*, about his period of exile in 1817. Cobbett had been chased out of England by the threat of a government prosecution for seditious or blasphemous libel, but was now back at work in the Home Counties. Shelley's opinion of Cobbett was markedly changing, along with his whole approach to the mass democratic movement in England. 'Cobbett still more and more delights me, with all my horror of the sanguinary commonplaces of his creed. His design to overthrow Bank notes by forgery is very comic.'11 Shelley could not have written these two sentences eighteen months previously.

The box also contained, besides the works of Scott, which were handed over to Mary, the first copy of Peacock's *Nightmare Abbey*. The book was passed eagerly round from hand to hand, even to the Gisbornes, and they all thought back to the summer at Marlow in 1817. It seemed long ago. Shelley wrote his serious and complimentary appreciation to Peacock: 'I suppose the moral is contained in what Falstaff says: "For God's sake talk like a man of the world."' He had no resentment, so much else had happened since the garden days at Marlow.12

Later he told Peacock: 'I have a study here in a tower something like Scythrop's – where I am just beginning to recover the faculties of reading and writing. My health, whenever no Libecchio blows, improves. – From my tower I see the sea with its islands, Gorgona, Capria, Elba & Corsica on one side, & the Apennines on the other.'[13]

Things were made more difficult at this time by the unreliability of the post from England. Shelley had received no news from Peacock since March, and he knew that at least three letters had gone astray at Naples. He wondered if Peacock had married, and inquired after Marianne St Croix. From Hogg he learned later in the month that Peacock had not married, but had found himself an excellent position in India House. Hogg noted with the old Oxford inflection: 'He is well pleased with his change of fortune, and has taken a house in Stamford Street, which, as you might expect from a Republican, he has furnished very handsomely.'[14] In subsequent letters Shelley inquired assiduously after the development of both Peacock's and Hogg's professional careers. 'The race indeed,' he remarked wistfully, 'is not to the swift.'[15]

Throughout July Shelley continued to work regularly at *The Cenci* in the glazing solitude of his tower each morning. In the scenes where Orsino attempts to persuade Giacomo – Beatrice's brother – to the murder of his father Count Cenci, the psychoanalytic theme, the obsessive examination of conscience, becomes more and more explicitly stated: Orsino mutters in a stage monologue:

> . . . 'tis a trick of this same family
> To analyse their own and other minds.
> Such self-anatomy shall teach the will
> Dangerous secrets: for it tempts our powers,
> Knowing what must be thought, and may be done,
> Into the depth of darkest purposes:
> So Cenci fell into the pit. . . .[16]

By Act v, Giacomo has realized, though too late, Orsino's role of infernal analyst and tempter, and rounds furiously though vainly on him:

> O, had I never
> Found in thy smooth and ready countenance
> The mirror of my darkest thoughts; hadst thou
> Never with hints and questions made me look
> Upon the monster of my thought, until
> It grew familiar to desire . . .[17]

Shelley also incorporated into Orsino's monologues autobiographic material he had originally written without dramatic intention at Marlow in 1817. The finest extensions of Beatrice's character, and the most immediate pieces of dramatic verse, again lie in the moments of intense self-analysis, accompanied as always by very deep fear. When questioned obliquely by her mother about the insanity which her father's act of rape had produced in her, and which in turn eventually produces the Count's murder, Beatrice answers:

> What are the words which you would have me speak?
> I, who can feign no image in my mind
> Of that which has transformed me: I, whose thought
> Is like a ghost shrouded and folded up
> In its own formless horror: of all words,
> That minister to mortal intercourse,
> Which wouldst thou hear?[18]

Beatrice's character changes and hardens throughout the play, so that by the trial scene, although she has reached heroic stature, she also has a cold cruelty of purpose which is in its own way as vicious as her father's. This gives the play both its dramatic balance and irony, and equally, its failure to contain the least human warmth or moral richness. There is no figure with whom one can easily empathize. Beatrice is as much villain as heroine, and as Shelley noted, 'It is in the restless and anatomizing casuistry with which men seek the justification of Beatrice . . . that the dramatic character of what she did and suffered, consists.'[19] The whole drama is comfortless and pitiless and cold.

In Act v, after Beatrice has finally been condemned to death for Cenci's murder, her habitual coolness and singlemindedness breaks down for a few moments, and she delivers perhaps the most celebrated speech of the play, 'Can it be possible I have To die so suddenly? So young to go Under the obscure, cold rotting, wormy ground!' The opening of this speech is almost entirely vitiated by its unconscious but massive plagiarism of Claudio's speech in Shakespeare's *Measure for Measure*: 'Aye, but to die, and go we know not where, To lie in cold obstruction and to rot.'[20]

But after some eight lines it moves out of the Shakespearian orbit, and presents a perceptive glimpse into Beatrice's identification between the God of her religion and the father of her family. The acuteness of this perception, and the relevance of it to Shelley's examination of his own beliefs as a continuing atheist do not need emphasizing:

> If there should be
> No God, no Heaven, no Earth in the void world;
> The wide, gray, lampless, deep, unpeopled world!

If all things then should be . . . my father's spirit,
His eye, his voice, his touch surrounding me;
The atmosphere and breath of my dead life!
If sometimes, as a shape more like himself,
Even the form which tortured me on earth,
Masked in gray hairs and wrinkles, he should come
And wind me in his hellish arms, and fix
His eyes on mine, and drag me down, down, down![21]

Yet here, and at other emotional heights, the coarse melodrama of Shelley's stage writing is painfully evident, and from a literary point of view *The Cenci* remains almost entirely a pastiche of Shakespearian and Jacobean drama. After the tremendous advances of 'Julian and Maddalo' and *Prometheus*, it marks a sharp decline of imaginative power. For the time being, his emotions were exhausted and the drama served him largely as a vehicle for private documentation and mental relief. It is curious that Mary Shelley's later opinion was that Act v of *The Cenci* is 'the finest thing he ever wrote'.[22]

The final draft of *The Cenci* was finished on 8 August. A popular success had been very much in the front of Shelley's mind all the time he wrote, and perhaps for this reason he seemed extraordinarily unaware of the real nature and quality of the work he had produced. At the end of July he had even taken the precaution of alerting Peacock, sending a copy of the Italian manuscript, and secretly revealing his ambitions for Covent Garden, Miss O'Neil and Edmund Kean. He described his copy of the Reni portrait, but ostentatiously drew back from connecting himself with an actual performance of the play. He wanted it to be anonymous, or else his name would drag it down into disrepute, and anyway, 'God forbid that I shd. see [Miss O'Neil] play it – it would tear my nerves to pieces.'[23] At the beginning of August Shelley began to write to his publisher Charles Ollier after a silence of many months, and no less than four letters were dispatched from Livorno in rapid succession. His tone was now changed, and he spoke of interesting manuscripts without sending them: 'I have *more poetry* if you like, but you shall have it not without asking.'[24] With the three acts of *Prometheus Unbound*, the five acts of *The Cenci* and 'Julian and Maddalo', on his desk, he felt justifiably confident. As far as Ollier remaining his publisher was concerned, he wrote, '*I* have no inclination to change unless you wish it, as your neglect might give me reason to suppose.'[25]

As a second line of attack, he sent the manuscript of 'Julian and Maddalo' to Hunt on 15 August, asking him to give it to Ollier for publication 'but *without my Name*'.[26]

While Shelley busied himself with his campaign for a popular readership in

England, Mary struggled towards the surface of her depression. It was a slow process. On 4 August, Shelley's twenty-seventh birthday, she began her journal again largely to please him. It commenced: 'LEGHORN – I begin my Journal on Shelley's birthday. We have now lived five years together; and if all the events of the five years were blotted out, I might be happy; but to have won, and then cruelly to have lost, the associations of four years, is not an accident to which the human mind can bend without much suffering.'[27] The wish that all the years of her life with Shelley were blotted out marked the extreme point of Mary's crisis. From the moment when she accepted the reality of this feeling, she began very gradually to rebuild her life in Italy once again.

Throughout August she noted 'write' in her journal, and this almost certainly refers to her intensely private and self-exploratory novel *Mathilda* which served as a therapeutic instrument for her. In this, it was not unlike *The Cenci*.[28] By August, she was some six months pregnant, and the palpable presence of this new life steadily became the focus of new hopes and new confidence. For Shelley the new child helped to restore a more understanding and sympathetic relationship with Mary, and the symbolic hope of the new birth entered into his poetry of the autumn.

But the improvement seemed agonizingly slow. It was not helped by Godwin, who wrote to Mary with little sympathy for her loss, and even less appreciation of her state, urging his own need for further money, and abusing Shelley for not supplying it. He had detected something of Mary's own bitterness towards Shelley, and tried, quite literally, to capitalize on it. Shelley intercepted his letters, and wrote angrily to Hunt: '. . . I cannot expose her to Godwin in this state . . . [the letter] received yesterday, and addressed to her, called her husband (me) "a disgraceful and flagrant person" tried to persuade her that I was under great engagements to give him *more* money (after having given him £4,700), and urged her if she ever wished a connection to continue between him and her to force me to get money for him. . . . I have not yet shewn her the letter – but I must. I doubt whether I ought not to expose this solemn lie; for such, and not a man, is Godwin. . . . I have bought bitter knowledge with £4,700. I wish it were all yours now!' Later, when Godwin was threatened with the loss of his house because of unpaid bills, Shelley decided to suppress all his letters to Mary.[29] When he wrote to Aemilia Curran to inquire about a small pyramidical stone monument for the little grave in Rome, Shelley explained: 'Mary's spirits still continue wretchedly depressed – more so than a stranger (tho' perhaps I should not call you so) could imagine.' He could not forbear, however, to brighten the picture with news of *The Cenci* – 'which Mary likes' – and detailed inquiries about having an engraving made of the Reni portrait to go on the frontispiece of the popular edition with which he intended to take London by storm.

At Livorno, the main sources of activity remained Claire and the Gisbornes. Claire had embarked on a vigorous series of music and singing lessons, taken three times a week with the best music-master in the city. One of the earliest signs of Mary's recovery were her complaints about the expense – 4 crowns a month – as against three shillings a lesson in Rome. Shelley thought it well spent. Claire had also continued her teasing friendship with the Gisbornes' 30-year-old son, the well-behaved engineer Henry Reveley. They were joined on 4 September by Charles Clairmont, who suddenly arrived after fifteen months of study in Spain to see his sister and the Shelleys. He rapidly adapted himself to the Shelley household, and contrived to aid Claire in her campaign to make poor Henry rather less well behaved. By the end of September Claire had a proposal of marriage from Henry; but the Gisbornes apparently thought it unsuitable, and anyway Claire turned him down.[30] Shelley took a paternal interest in Reveley, despite the fact that he was three years his senior. He listened to Henry's dream of designing and manufacturing a prototype ocean-going steamboat, to run a service between Livorno, Genoa and Marseilles and became convinced of Henry's talents as an engineer. He announced that he would back the project financially, and by the end of October Henry's dream had turned into the reality of a signed contract with local boat-builders, a work-shop full of models for casting and forging, and a negotiated loan for ship's timber.[31] The Gisbornes, who agreed to share in the financing, regarded this project as more satisfactory than the marital one.

Although Shelley was sometimes inclined to compare Maria in her earnest culture and sensibility to Mrs Boinville, he was kindly disposed towards the Gisbornes as a family, and they were kind to him in return. Yet Shelley felt he could indulge himself a little at their expense. To Peacock, he wrote as if they might have passed untransformed into the pages of *Nightmare Abbey*. 'Mrs Gisborne is a sufficiently amiable & very accomplished woman she is δημοκρατικη & αθεη – how far she may be φιλανθρωπη I don't know for she is the antipodes of enthusiasm. Her husband a man with little thin lips receding forehead & a prodigious nose is an excessive bore. His nose is something quite Slawkenbur-gian – it weighs on the imagination to look at it, – it is that sort of nose which transforms all the *gs* its wearer utters into *ks*. It is a nose once seen never to be forgotten and which requires the utmost stretch of Christian charity to forgive. I, you know, have a little turn up nose; Hogg has a large hook one but add them both together, square them, cube them, you would have but a faint idea of the nose to which I refer.'[32] The Gisbornes also had a large, amiable dog called Oscar which doted on Mary.[33]

A real portrait which gave Shelley much pleasure at this time, was a long-requested one of Leigh Hunt. This finally arrived from London in the third week of August.[34] The thought of Hunt and his family, and the great support they had been to him in the crisis of the winter of 1816, helped Shelley considerably during the solitary hours in the tower at Villa Valsovano. Shortly after receiving the picture, Shelley propped it in front of his desk and wrote the letter which dedicated *The Cenci* to Hunt. He concluded it on a heroic note:

> In that patient ánd irreconcilable enmity with domestic and political tyranny and imposture, which the tenor of your life has illustrated, and which, had I the health and talents, should illustrate mine, let us, comforting each other in our task, live and die.[35]

He dated it from Rome, where the play had first been conceived and drafted. Hunt did not read this generous dedication until an edition of 250 copies had been printed in Leghorn during October and shipped in unbound sheets to Peacock at Stamford Street in London.[36]

Together with Hunt's picture, more books, reviews and the first of a steady stream of *Examiners* had arrived in August. Shelley took these up to his Scythrop's tower, and many days at the end of August were spent catching up on English political and literary news, and musing on the loneliness of his self-imposed Italian banishment. In a letter to Peacock of the 24th, he launched into a long fantasy about living again in England. 'I most devoutly wish that I were living near London. – I don't think I shall settle so far off as Richmond, & to inhabit any intermediate spot on the Thames would be to expose myself to the river damps, not to mention that it is not much to my taste – My inclinations point to Hampstead, but I dont know. . . .'

Here Shelley appeared to break off the letter, and walk round his glass tower, looking westwards over the bay, and northwards across the *maremma* between Livorno and Pisa to the distant Apennines. For a moment it all seemed unreal to him, as if he was only half-awake and dreaming. He picked up his pen again and wrote rapidly: 'All that I see in Italy – and from my tower window I now see the magnificent peaks of the Apennine half enclosing the plain – is nothing – it dwindles to smoke in the mind, when I think of some familiar forms of scenery little perhaps in themselves over which old remembrances have thrown a delightful colour. How we prize what we despised when present! So the ghosts of our dead associations rise & haunt us in revenge for our having let them starve, & abandoned them to perish.'[37] Peacock would know how literally this was to be interpreted. The mood hung on in Shelley's mind, and deepened in September as the summer sun blazed on and on, and life seemed to move more and more slowly, and only the nights were cool.

22

The West Wind: Florence 1819

Up in the glass tower, Shelley leafed through the reviews and journals that the Gisbornes took from Paris. The impression he had already gained from Hunt's *Examiner* pieces about the state of English politics was strengthened. A crisis comparable to, or even greater than, those of 1812 and 1817 seemed to be in the making, though it was difficult to be sure. 'England seems to be in a very disturbed state, if we may judge by some Paris Papers,' he mused to Peacock. 'I suspect it is rather overrated, but when I hear them talk of paying in gold – nay I dare say take steps towards it, confess that the sinking fund is a fraud &c. I no longer wonder.' He reverted briefly to the old Whig–liberal *sententiae*: 'But the change should commence among the higher orders, or anarchy will only be the last flash before despotism. I wonder & tremble.' Yet no political change Shelley could foresee at that moment could ever touch Peacock in the East India Company: '*You* are well sheltered.'[1]

The mood of permanent summer siesta, and the long solitary mornings spent reading and musing, were suddenly broken by dramatic news from England. Peacock had especially posted a set of English papers by the coach mail from London which only took two weeks. These arrived on 5 September, and almost entirely swamped the appearance of a long-awaited box from Ollier, containing a first edition of *Rosalind and Helen*, and Keats's *Endymion*, the same day.

The news from England concerned politics: on 16 August at St Peter's Field, on the outskirts of Manchester, a public meeting of some 60,000 working men and women had been brutally attacked and dispersed by mounted militiamen. The result had been a massacre of unarmed civilians which went down in history as Peterloo. It looked like the beginning of the English Revolution.

There was not much Whig–liberalism in Shelley's immediate reaction to Ollier on the 6th: 'The same day that your letter came, came news of the Manchester work, & the torrent of my indignation has not yet done boiling in my veins. I await anxiously to hear how the Country will express its sense of this bloody murderous oppression of its destroyers. "Something must be done ...What yet I know not."[2] In his fury, he had quoted from his own *Cenci*, where Beatrice first conceives the assassination of her father. The passage continues: '... something which shall make The thing that I have suffered but a shadow In the dread lightning which avenges it; Brief, rapid, irreversible, destroying The consequence of what it cannot cure.'[3]

The news was certainly bad enough, and with the number of eye-witnesses and trained journalists on the spot, all the significant details had been available to the readers in the reports of the immediately following week of 17–22 August. *The Times*, the *Manchester Observer* and the *Examiner* were especially full in their coverage; the editor of the *Observer* was one of those in prison awaiting trial by the end of the autumn.* The St Peter's Field meeting had been called by Henry Hunt and advertised in local papers several weeks in advance. The avowed and published intention was to consider and support 'the propriety of adopting the most *legal and effectual* means of obtaining Reform of the Commons House of Parliament'.[4] Upwards of 60,000 working people and union representatives arrived during the morning of 16 August from a region of some fifty miles' radius. Many came in organized bands, marching in orderly groups, behind banners and flags, and led by 'radical drill-sergeants' whose experience had been gained during the Napoleonic wars. But all reports agree that the people were totally unarmed. Banner and flag mottoes recorded by the press give a clear indication of the issues and the strength of political feeling: – 'Liberty and Fraternity'; 'Parliaments Annual, Suffrage Universal'; 'Unity and Strength'. Samuel Bamford noted several Women's Suffrage banners, and the way the 'handsomest girls' placed themselves at key positions in the front of marching bands, and around the central hustings where Henry Hunt was to speak.[5] He also remarked on the Lees and Saddleworth Union banner, notable for its stark-white lettering on a pitch-black cloth, 'Equal Representation or Death', with below, in red, two hands clasped and adorned with the word LOVE. This must be one of the very earliest recordings of the English anarchist colours, red and black, which for the next 150 years were traditionally associated with Manchester in protest demonstrations. For Shelley, it must have seemed as if certain scenes out of *The Revolt of Islam* had come alive, and that Demogorgon's chariot was launched towards Jupiter.

Jupiter however was armed and prepared. The magistracy had six troops of the 15th Hussars, several companies of the 88th, the whole of the 31st (Infantry)

---

* The hour-by-hour account may be reconstructed from reports by Tyas in *The Times*; Baines in the *Leeds Mercury*, and Richard Carlile in the *Political Register*. There is also the evidence given in court in *The Trial* of Henry Hunt; and three excellent eye-witness accounts, one from a lieutenant in the 15th Hussars, eventually published in *Three Accounts of Peterloo*, edited by F.A. Bruton (1921). Samuel Bamford was one of the organizers of the meeting.

and one troop of Horse Artillery, stationed within ten minutes' call. The whole detachment was under the military command of Colonel Guy L'Estrange.[6] There was a prearranged plan with the Home Secretary Sidmouth to use local Yeomanry first to disperse the crowds and arrest Hunt, and only to put in the military if necessary.[7]

Henry Hunt arrived at the hustings, wearing his white top-hat, in the early afternoon. Almost as soon as he began to speak, the local magistrates ordered a force of the local Manchester and Salford Yeomanry to ride into the dense crowd and arrest him. With much difficulty, they did so, Hunt being pulled off the hustings without resistance. Regrettably, however, they knocked down a woman as they charged, and trampled her child to death.[8] The crowd surged, and while Hunt was escorted out to the magistrates' house (he was clubbed on the way by a line of special constables, and the white hat 'packed over his face'),[9] the rest of the Yeomanry were isolated in the Field, hemmed in by a jeering crowd. They drew their swords. At this point the magistrates sent in the mounted Hussars to retrieve the Yeomanry and disperse the crowds. They went in with drawn sabres, at first sweeping only with the flat of the blade, according to training. The Yeomanry were incapable of such subtleties, but anyway in a few moments it was unnecessary. Bamford says the massacre only lasted ten minutes. At the end of this time the field was virtually deserted except for bodies, abandoned hats and flags, and dismounted Yeomanry wiping their swords and easing their horse girths.[10] The afternoon light of August was orange with the dust.

Lord Sidmouth, the whole of the Liverpool administration and the Prince Regent publicly endorsed the action, and praised the decision of the magistracy and the calm of the military. The total death-roll, including the child trampled by the Yeomanry, was eleven. Official committees authenticated 421 cases of serious injury sustained on the Field, including more than 100 women and children; in 162 individual cases these injuries were identified as sabre wounds. The unofficial number of injuries, and deaths caused by injury, was of course far higher.[11]

Shelley plunged into his Scythrop's tower. Words could not describe his feelings; or perhaps they could. On the 9th he wrote very briefly to Peacock, referring to the 'terrible and important news' from Manchester. 'These are, as it were, the distant thunders of the terrible storm which is approaching. The tyrants here, as in the French Revolution, have first shed blood. May their execrable lessons not be learnt with equal docility! I still think there will be no coming to close quarters until financial affairs decidedly bring the oppressors and the oppressed together. Pray let me have the *earliest* political news which you consider of importance at this crisis.'[12] At such a moment, the acuteness of

Shelley's observation on the decisive importance of the general economic situation is remarkable. For the next twelve days he wrote no letters. His attention was not concerned with letters. He had embarked, almost without realizing it, on the most intensely creative eight weeks of his whole life.

In the first twelve days he wrote and clean-copied the ninety-one stanzas of *The Mask of Anarchy*. This is the greatest poem of political protest ever written in English. It also has claims to be considered as the most powerfully conceived the most economically executed and the most perfectly sustained piece of poetry of his life. With 'Julian and Maddalo', and *Prometheus Unbound* (Acts I and II), it ranks as the third of his four Italian masterpieces. It begins with unhesitating simplicity, in the very phrase and cadence of Shelley's letter to Peacock, as if he had put pen to paper the moment he drew up his chair in the tower:

> As I lay asleep in Italy
> There came a voice from over the Sea. . . .[13]

He found himself writing immediately in the colloquial ballad stanzas he had not used since 1812, except for the brief premonitory poem at Naples. The lines were terse, flexible, rapid, based on the simple four-stress verse of the broadsheets, sometimes end-stopping, sometimes running on unchecked for a whole stanza, using a bewildering variety of full rhymes, half rhymes, assonance, the curious minor-key of half-assonance, and sudden bursts of brutal, merciless alliteration. His images are drawn recognizably from almost all his previous political poems, right back to 'The Devil's Walk', and the reader has the sense of a mass of unconsciously prepared material leaping forward into unity at a single demand. The dominant material comes from the pamphlet of 1817, *On the Death of Princess Charlotte*, and from the immediate news reports of the day. The most important single image Shelley took from the newspapers was that of the unarmed mother, whose child was trampled to death as the Yeomanry first charged.

The ninety-one stanzas develop naturally in three sections. In the first thirty-four stanzas there is a viciously satirical picture of Lord Liverpool's ministers riding the horses which trample down the English crowd. Each stanza is drawn in a single stroke. It is done with a unique combination of Coleridge and Cruikshank, that transcends both:

> I met Murder on the way
> He had a mask like Castlereagh –
> Very smooth he looked, yet grim;
> Seven blood-hounds followed him:

All were fat; and well they might
Be in admirable plight,
For one by one, and two by two,
He tossed them human hearts to chew
Which from his wide cloak he drew.

Next came Fraud, and he had on,
Like Eldon, an ermined gown;
His big tears, for he wept well,
Turned to mill-stones as they fell.

And the little children, who
Round his feet played to and fro,
Thinking every tear a gem,
Had their brains knocked out by them.

Clothed with the Bible, as with light,
And the shadows of the night,
Like Sidmouth, next, Hypocrisy
On a crocodile rode by.

And many more Destructions played
In this ghastly masquerade,
All disguised, even to the eyes,
Like Bishops, lawyers, peers, or spies.[14]

These distinguished members of the government and the Establishment are
commanded by another, even more sinister figure on a horse, a figure out of
a gothic engraving, or perhaps even out of Dante's Hell:

Last came Anarchy: he rode
On a white horse, splashed with blood;
He was pale even to the lips,
Like Death in the Apocalypse.

And he wore a kingly crown;
And in his grasp a sceptre shone;
On his brow this mark I saw –
'I AM GOD AND KING AND LAW!'

> With a pace stately and fast,
> Over the English land he passed,
> Trampling to a mire of blood
> The adoring multitude.[15]

The multitude, though trampled and killed, Shelley says, is *adoring*. Here is the first intellectual twist in a poem which underneath its hard, brilliantly active surface, contains a structure of complicated ideological reasoning. 'Anarchy, the Skeleton', who is the prize exhibit in the governmental masquerade of murderers, is also the insane deity who 'bowed and grinned to everyone' and leads the adoring multitude to an attack on the Palace, the Bank and the Tower

> And was proceeding with intent
> To meet his pensioned Parliament

when he is halted. Shelley meant that Anarchy, a savage god outside any human law, is already the idol of the government's train; he could easily become the leader of the people's too. But Shelley halts him. He is halted by a woman who lies under the horses' hooves,

> a maniac maid,
> And her name was Hope, she said:
> But she looked more like Despair,
> And she cried out in the air:
>
> 'My father Time is weak and gray
> With waiting for a better day;
> See how idiot-like he stands,
> Fumbling with his palsied hands!
>
> 'He has had child after child,
> And the dust of death is piled
> Over every one but me –
> Misery, oh, Misery!'
>
> Then she lay down in the street,
> Right before the horses' feet,
> Expecting, with a patient eye,
> Murder, Fraud, and Anarchy.[16]

The starkness and emotional clarity of this figure is very great. There is complete realism in that 'patient eye'. As she lies there, something begins to materialize between her and Anarchy: at first a mist, then a vapour, then a cloud, then a storm anvil with lightning head until finally

> It grew – a Shape arrayed in mail
> Brighter than the viper's scale

and sweeps over the heads of the crowd and in an instant leaves Anarchy unhorsed and lifeless

> And the prostrate multitude
> Looked – and ankle-deep in blood,
> Hope, that maiden most serene,
> Was walking with a quiet mien[17]

With this blinding deliverance, the first section of the poem ends.

In the second section, between stanzas 34 and 63, the maid talks to the crowd and gives her description first of false freedom, and then of true political freedom. She talks of food, clothes, fire, a proper home:

> 'For the labourer thou art bread,
> And a comely table spread
> From his daily labour come
> In a neat and happy home.

> 'Thou art clothes, and fire, and food
> For the trampled multitude –
> No – in countries that are free
> Such starvation cannot be
> As in England now we see.

> 'To the rich thou art a check,
> When his foot is on the neck
> Of his victim, thou dost make
> That he treads upon a snake. . . .'[18]

To this she adds broader considerations: protection against exploitation by wealth; justice available without money; intellectual freedom from religious bigotry; national peace; voluntary expenditure of wealth to improve bad conditions, and 'Science, Poetry, and Thought'.

In the last section of the poem, the maid issues a celebrated call for a series of massive demonstrations of English working people to claim their political rights:

'Let a great Assembly be
Of the fearless and the free
On some spot of English ground
Where the plains stretch wide around. . . .

'From the corners uttermost
Of the bounds of English coast;
From every hut, village, and town
Where those who live and suffer moan
For others' misery or their own,

'From the workhouse and the prison
Where pale as corpses newly risen,
Women, children, young and old
Groan for pain, and weep for cold. . . .'[19]

When faced with the 'tyrants' troops', the artillery, the fixed bayonet, or the horsemen's sabres

'Stand ye calm and resolute,
Like a forest close and mute,
With folded arms and looks which are
Weapons of unvanquished war. . . .

'Let the laws of your own land,
Good or ill, between ye stand
Hand to hand, and foot to foot,
Arbiters of the dispute,

'The old laws of England – they
Whose reverend heads with age are gray,
Children of a wiser day;
And whose solemn voice must be
Thine own echo – Liberty!

'On those who first should violate
Such sacred heralds in their state
Rest the blood that must ensue,
And it will not rest on you. . . .'[20]

This heroic but yet stoic belief in the power of the mass demonstration, using passive resistance as an instrument of political change, is remarkable enough in itself, as far as the evolution of Shelley's radical thought is concerned. There would be very few outside the circles of the working-class radical leadership who would have come anywhere near avowing such a policy publicly. Yet this is not quite the end of the poem. There is one more twist, which leaves it not on a note of stoicism, but one of triumphant solidarity with the underprivileged, oppressed and unrepresented, against the *élite* class in power. These are the last three stanzas, which refer back again to Peterloo itself:

> 'And that slaughter to the Nation
> Shall steam up like inspiration,
> Eloquent, oracular;
> A volcano heard afar.

> 'And these words shall then become
> Like Oppression's thundered doom
> Ringing through each heart and brain,
> Heard again – again – again –

> 'Rise like Lions after slumber
> In unvanquishable number –
> Shake your chains to earth like dew
> Which in sleep had fallen on you –
> Ye are many – they are few.'[21]

Shelley worked hard on the poem, anxious to get it published in England as soon as possible. It was one of those crises which a writer must seize. On 21 September, in another short note to Peacock, he remarked merely: 'What an infernal business this of Manchester! What is to be done? Something assuredly. Henry Hunt has behaved I think with great spirit & coolness in the whole affair.'[22]* He did not mention *The Mask*, though by now it was virtually complete.

In fact Shelley seems to have been working largely in secret. Nothing shows Mary's remoteness from him, busy with her own *Mathilda*, more than the emptiness of her journal at this time. There are references to Shelley reading Calderón, taking tea with Madame Merveilleux du Plantis and her daughter Zoïde, and discussing the move to Florence for Mary's approaching lying in. The domestic life crept on.[23] Afterwards, Mary wrote that she remembered hearing him sometimes in the house repeating the stanzas beginning 'My Father Time is

---

* When Henry Hunt entered London for his trial on 15 September 1819, an observer noted: 'The whole distance from the Angel at Islington to the Crown and Anchor [Strand] was lined with multitudes.' The anxious onlooker was John Keats.

old and gray', and admired them, although she did not know to what poem they belonged.[24]

Finally Shelley announced that he had a poem called 'The Mask of Anarchy' for posting to Hunt at the *Examiner*. Mary was given the manuscript to fair copy, and with Shelley's corrections added at the last moment, it was taken to Florence on the 23rd and put on the mail. He took Charles Clairmont with him, and also arranged for them all to take lodgings for the winter in Madame du Plantis's house, starting in October.

Shelley returned to Villa Valsovano on Saturday, 25 September, tired, and feeling very unwell. Mary wrote that the weather was beginning to fluctuate: sometimes too hot to go out at midday, sometimes as cold as Christmas in England. The wind shifted, and came in from every side, and there were 'no fireplaces & stone floors'. The Italians seem to take no precaution against the cold, 'except holding a little earthenware pot with charcoal in it in their hands'.[25]

During the last days at Villa Valsovano, Shelley again retired into his tower. Mary spent her time packing, and visiting Maria Gisborne. Mr Gisborne, much to her relief, had set out on a trip to England before the weather broke, intending to inquire after prospects in London for Henry. She warned the Hunts in a letter of his impending arrival, adding miserably that her own 'life & freshness' was lost to her, 'on my last birthday when I was 21 – I repined that time should fly so quickly . . . now I am 22 . . . I ought to have died on 7th June last'.[26] She did not show this letter to Shelley.[27]

Three days later Shelley also wrote to the Hunts from his tower. He was in high spirits again. 'Ollier tells me that the Quarterly are going to review me; I suppose it will be a pretty morsel, and as I am acquiring a taste for humour and drollery I confess I am curious to see it.' He discussed the merits of Boccaccio at length, laughing and half approving of his system of love, and ending in a positive dumb-show of exclamation marks. 'Boccaccio seems to me to have possessed a deep sense of the fair ideal of human life considered in its social relations. His more serious theories of love agree especially with mine . . . He is a moral casuist, the opposite of the Christian, Stoical, ready made and worldly system of morals. Do you remember one little remark or rather maxim of his, the application of which might do some good to the common narrow-minded conceptions of love? "Bocca baciata non perde ventura; anzi rinnuova, come fa la luna." If you show this to Marianne give my love to her and tell her that I don't mean xxxxx . . .—!!?? [*sic*]' Of Mary, he wrote simply, 'We expect Mary to be confined towards the end of October, and one of our motives in going to Florence is to have the attendance of Mr Bell, a famous Scotch surgeon, who will be there . . . The birth of a child will probably relieve her from some part of her present melancholy depression.' The impersonal use of 'we' may have puzzled the Hunts.[28]

Shelley's good spirits, despite uncertain health, were produced by the knowledge of the quality of his work which was now reaching London for publication. Indeed the posting of *The Mask* at the end of September 1819 marks the most critical single moment of his entire professional career. Hunt had already received 'Julian and Maddalo', posted in August; manuscript copies of *Prometheus* had gone both to Peacock and Ollier earlier in September, and a clean copy of *The Cenci* had been posted ahead of the printed edition to Peacock on 21 September. Thus, four major works, the fruit of Shelley's first eighteen months in Italy, were all arriving in London virtually within a few days of each other. In retrospect one can see that everything turned on Hunt's acceptance of *The Mask* for immediate publication in the *Examiner* as Shelley intended.

The question was whether Shelley's work would now finally reach a broad readership. The publication of *The Mask* would undoubtedly have had explosive effect, all the more because it was to be first detonated among a liberal rather than a strictly radical readership. Even among the radicals, who saw published in September Hone's pamphlet *The Political House that Jack Built* with vicious illustrations by Cruikshank, as part of the massive wave of post-Peterloo protest, the absolutely explicit attack and power of Shelley's poem would have struck home with unique impact. Moreover it spoke to the people in the street, not merely to the reviewer or the politician or the Hampstead drawing-room. The very roughness of the verse, the deliberate ruggedness of grammar and style, pushed aside the dillettante and the littérateur.

This was a significant legal point. When Sir Francis Burdett, as part of his Peterloo protest, sent to the press an open letter, 'To the Electors of Westminster', he was subsequently prosecuted for seditious libel and convicted. In directing the jury at Leicester to convict, Mr Justice Best made what is one of the most significant literary and political distinctions of the age: 'If you find in [his writing] an appeal to the passions of the lower orders of the people, and not having a tendency to inform those who can correct abuses, it is a libel.'[29] In other words, if such a composition as Burdett's was addressed to the ruling classes, it was allowable; if it was addressed to the working classes, it was libellous. There can be no doubt into which category Shelley's *The Mask of Anarchy* fell. Burdett was eventually sentenced to three months' imprisonment and fined £2,000. This was only for sending a letter to the papers.

If therefore Shelley's poem had been printed in the *Examiner*, as he intended, there would undoubtedly have been a violent public controversy, and almost certainly a prosecution. But besides being a highly tendentious work, *The*

Mask is also a great poem, and Shelley's name would at last have begun to be generally known in liberal and radical circles and among the discerning of every political colour in England. With the beginnings of a real public reputation, it was quite possible that Harris, the director of Covent Garden, would have accepted *The Cenci* at least for a short run, and the two other major poems already on their way to Ollier, 'Julian and Maddalo' and *Prometheus Unbound* would surely have found a ready audience and promising sales.

In the event, exactly the reverse happened. Hunt, after consultation with his brother John Hunt, put *The Mask of Anarchy* aside. It was never published in Shelley's lifetime. Following this, and despite Peacock's good offices, both Covent Garden and apparently Drury Lane turned down *The Cenci* – a dangerous subject by an unknown author. 'Julian and Maddalo' was never published in Shelley's lifetime either. *Prometheus Unbound* appeared much later in 1820, almost unnoticed except among a handful of reviewers. It sold hardly a score of copies. The chance of popular recognition, so near in the autumn of 1819, and certainly never nearer, slipped from Shelley's fingers, through the prudence of friends and publishers.

Why did Hunt not publish *The Mask*? The short answer is clearly that he feared political prosecution. He feared with good reason. 1819 marked the height of the government's attack on the free press, and there were no less than seventy-five prosecutions for seditious or blasphemous libel during that year.[30] They resulted in heavy or crippling fines, and prison sentences ranging between a few months and five years. Hunt himself had done time as a guest of His Majesty's Hospitality ten years previously; his brother John Hunt, the managing editor of the *Examiner*, was to serve a sentence of twelve months for attacking the monarchy in 1820. But on this occasion, Hunt was no longer prepared to risk his neck, and at the moment of crisis and decision he revealed his true colours as a liberal rather than a committed radical.

When he brought out *The Mask of Anarchy* in 1832, to coincide with the passing of the first Parliamentary Reform Bill, he explained his decision of 1819 in these words. 'I did not insert it because I thought that the public at large had not become sufficiently discerning to do justice to the sincerity and kindheartedness of the spirit that walked in this flaming robe of verse.'[31] In other words, that the man in the street might recognize that Shelley had written a radical poem; and the Home Office also. But Hunt genuinely thought that the time was not ripe to inflame the 'people at large'*, and that Shelley's belief in passive resistance was incompatible at that time with massive democratic demonstrations.

---

* It was exactly this kind of liberalism that Hazlitt ridiculed in a retrospective essay of autumn 1825: 'But the great thing was to be genteel, and keep out of the rabble. They that touch pitch are

Nevertheless one notes the roll-call of those who did protest and were prosecuted as a result of Peterloo; among many, Samuel Bamford, Sir Francis Burdett, Major Cartwright, Sir Charles Wolseley, James Wroe of the *Manchester Observer*, a fearless pamphleteer Joseph Swann of Macclesfield (who was sentenced to four and a half years, which he served in chains), and above all Richard Carlile, now editor of the most notable radical paper of the period, the *Republican.** Yet in every case these men were prosecuted for material that they themselves had both written and caused to be published. One cannot blame Hunt if his author was not in England. Shelley was not there to stand by his editor, and to take legal responsibility on his own shoulders; or indeed to choose alternative means of publication. It was Shelley's own self-exile in Italy, his failure to be on the spot, that provided the ultimate cause of the critical sequence of failed publications in late 1819 and early 1820. This in turn was to dictate the obscure fortunes of the remaining works printed in his lifetime. But these things were not clear to Shelley for many months. On the contrary, he now felt on the offensive, for the moment of crisis had found him prepared. There was a brief interlude of house-moving and resettling for the winter.

On 30 September, Shelley's household, with the addition of Charles, left the Villa Valsovano. They took leave of Mrs Gisborne and Henry, with many promises concerning the steamboat, and set out on the road for Pisa and Florence. As the carriage began to bounce eastwards over the rough track, the dog Oscar leapt after it and ran alongside, his slender tail wagging, and his bright teeth smiling up to where Mary sat, eight months pregnant and trembling slightly, with the strain of travel.[32]

'Poor Oscar!' wrote Shelley later to Mrs Gisborne. 'I feel a kind of remorse to think of the unequal love with which two animated beings regard each other, when I experience no such sensations for him as those which he manifested for us. His importunate regret is however a type of ours as regards you. Our memory – if you will accept so humble a metaphor – is forever scratching at the door of your absence.'[33]

At Pisa, they broke their journey briefly to call upon another expatriate lady, a Mrs Mason who lived in the Via Managonella. Like Aemilia Curran, she had Godwinian and Irish republican connections. She was married, and her house, the Casa Silva at Pisa, was to become in the spring one of Shelley's most

defiled. "No connection with the mob", was labelled on the back of every friend of the People. Every faithful retainer of the Opposition took care to disclaim all affinity with such fellows as [Henry] Hunt, Carlile, or Cobbett . . . the chief dread of the Minority was to be confounded with the populace, the *Canaille* etc.'

* The only piece of Shelley's writing published at this critical time in England in fact appeared in the fifth issue of the *Republican*, on 24 December 1819. Ironically, it was his old *Declaration of Rights* dating from 1812, and Carlile did not know the name of the author.

important addresses in Italy. The roads to Florence were very bad, and Mary found the going exhausting, so they stopped one night at Pisa, and another at Empoli, finally arriving on 2 October. They moved in at once to their apartment in Madame du Plantis's house, the Palazzo Marini at No. 4395 Via Valfonda, near Santa Maria Novella. Mary found the rooms comfortable and secure, and she was glad to hear that there were other English people in the building. She sent a note to Livorno, telling Mrs Gisborne of their safe arrival, and asking for several of their books – Cobbett, Byron's *Childe Harold* and *The Revolt of Islam* – to be sent to Mrs Mason at Pisa, together with half a pound of 'the very best green tea'. On second thoughts, she crossed *The Revolt* off the list. 'Clare & Shelley send their best love to you & I would say to Henry but that would not do from the young lady so take out her name & only *remember her kindly* to him as well as my self.'[34]

During their first week in Florence, they went out on visits to the ballet and the opera, and Claire arranged for more music lessons. Mary could not long manage these excursions, and she stayed more and more on the sofa and in bed. Charles flirted with Zoïde du Plantis, and Shelley with an amused and practised eye observed that Zoïde was 'not so fair but I fear as cold as the snowy Florimel in Spenser [and] is in & out of love with Charles as the winds happen to blow'.[35] For the time being Charles was in a 'high state of transitory contentment', but he was intending to leave in November for further study in Vienna.

Shelley was much by himself. After a preliminary tour round Florence he decided to concentrate on the Uffizi Gallery, and he concocted 'a design of studying [it] piecemeal' through the winter. His solitary visits became almost as regular as those to the Forum and the Baths of Caracalla in Rome had been. His aim, he said, was to observe especially in the sculpture the rules by which 'that ideal beauty of which we have so intense yet so obscure an apprehension' was realized in external form.[36] Later he assembled an interesting series of manuscript notes on the subject.

But politics and the English Revolution remained steadily in the forefront of his mind. In these weeks of October and November, he produced a whole series of brilliant political ballads, songs and elegies in which the enormous energy and angry directness of *The Mask* continued to flow and coruscate. These are some of the best short poems Shelley ever wrote. He also wrote a full-length verse satire on contemporary English poetry and politics; and in early November a long open letter for the *Examiner* attacking the prosecution of Richard Carlile for sedition. He was reading Clarendon's three-volume *The History of the Rebellion and Civil Wars in England*, and also Plato's *Republic*.[37]

The impulse which the horror of the Peterloo massacre had given Shelley was now immeasurably deepened and intensified by the discovery of a savage personal attack in the *Quarterly*. The two pieces of violence – although to an outsider totally disconnected in kind – fused in his mind with the most extraordinary and creative force. Public and private sufferings were made identical in the heat of his imagination.

Shelley had already heard from both Hunt and Ollier of the review of *The Revolt of Islam* in the *Quarterly* for April 1819 and he had written for a copy from Livorno. But before this arrived, he came across the article unexpectedly one afternoon in the second week of October at Delesert's English Library.

The article is long[38] and the author, John Taylor Coleridge, a distant relative of the poet and a man who had been at school with Shelley at Eton, had clearly assembled a personal dossier on his subject. There are explicit references in the piece to Shelley's misery at school, his expulsion from Oxford, his friendship with Godwin, and his withdrawal of *Laon and Cythna*–the 'incestuous' version – from circulation. On this last, the reviewer wrote with both texts before him, and made considerable and not unjustified play with Shelley's 'wholly prudential' but still blasphemous alterations, and his penchant for incest. He also accused him of plagiarizing Wordsworth. It seems too that the reviewer knew of the existence of *Queen Mab*, and the 'Hermit of Marlow' pamphlets, and had made inquiries about Shelley's relationships with Harriet, Mary and Claire between 1814 and 1816.

Some of this background detail was so close that Shelley was convinced for the rest of his life that the writer responsible was his former acquaintance and early confidant Robert Southey.[39] Who else, he wondered, could have written: '[Mr Shelley's] speculations and his disappointments [began] in early childhood, and even from that period he has carried about with him a soured and discontented spirit – unteachable in boyhood, unamiable in youth, querulous and unmanly in manhood – singularly unhappy in all three.' Who else could have paternally decided that '[Mr Shelley] is really too young, too ignorant, too inexperienced, and too vicious to undertake the task of reforming any world, but the little world within his own breast'?[40] The *Quarterly*'s actual criticism of Shelley's poetry was marginal, even flattering; its main case was against his 'theories', political, social, religious and sexual. There is an unmistakable air of gusto in the way it reduced Shelley's radicalism *ad absurdum*. Taylor Coleridge was arguing from the very heart of the *Quarterly* belief in sound government, law and order, the social hierarchies, institutionalized religion and benevolent but firm paternalism. He intended to attack Shelley both as an individual and as a political and philosophic *type*, a new and dangerous species of post-Jacobin democrat and leveller. Far from making his article a mere piece of philistine viciousness, this gives it genuine social interest, the more so when one considers that the *Quarterly* was the most widely read and most authoritative review of the day. The article was not, as Hunt liked to make out, a mere lampoon.

> Mr Shelley would abrogate our laws – this would put an end to felonies and misdemenours at a blow; he would abolish the rights of property, of course there could thenceforward be no violation of them, no heart-burnings between the poor and the rich, no disputed wills, no litigated inheritances . . . he would overthrow the constitution, and then we should have no expensive court, no pensions or sinecures . . . no army or navy; he would pull down our churches, level our Establishment, and burn our bibles . . . marriage he cannot endure, and there would at once be a stop put to the lamented increase of adulterous connections amongst us, whilst repealing the canon of heaven against incest, he would add to the purity and heighten the ardour of those feelings with which brother and sister now regard each other; finally, as the basis of the whole scheme, he would have us renounce our belief in our religion. . . .
>
> This is at least intelligible; but it is not so easy to describe the structure, which Mr Shelley would build upon this vast heap of ruins. 'Love', he says, 'is the sole law which shall govern the moral world'; but Love is a wide word with many significations, and we are at a loss as to which of them he would have it now bear. We are loath to understand it in its lowest sense, though we believe that as to the issue this would be the correctest mode of interpreting it. But this at least is clear, that Mr Shelley does not mean it in its highest sense: he does not mean that love, which is the fulfilling of the law, and which walks after the commandments, for he would erase the Decalogue, and every other code of laws.[41]

This attack puts the *Quarterly* position very well, especially in its definition of the 'highest love', and also shows what it most feared. Like few other reviews it was prepared to argue *ideas*, or at least admit of their existence. It is also interesting that such an attack was written long before the reviewer could have even heard of *Prometheus Unbound* or *The Cenci*; or have expected the dramatic political development of Peterloo.

The article's final paragraph contains a memorable attempt at a personal *coup de grâce* in the highest style. Having referred to Shelley's 'proud and rebel mind', his 'thousand sophisms' and his 'impurity of practice', it delivered itself with Ozymandian finality. We shall never know by what curious premonition John Taylor Coleridge found his biblical image:

> Like the Egyptian of old, the wheels of his chariot are broken, the path of mighty waters closes in upon him behind, and a still deepening ocean is before

him: – for a short time are seen his impotent struggles against a resistless power, his blasphemous execrations are heard, his despair but poorly assumes the tone of triumph and defiance, and he calls ineffectually on others to follow him to the same ruin – finally, he sinks 'like lead' to the bottom, and is forgotten. So it is now in part, so shortly will it be entirely with Mr Shelley.[42]

This fortissimo passage was given a final cadenza of domestic innuendo, in which reference is made to the 'disgusting picture' of Shelley's private life over which the reviewer chose to draw a veil. 'It is not easy', concluded the *Quarterly*, 'for those who *read only*, to conceive how much low pride, how much cold selfishness, how much unmanly cruelty are consistent with the laws of this "universal" and "lawless love".' This was intended to be the last twist of the knife. For Shelley at Delesert's it was certainly the most unpleasant one.*

It so happened on this particular afternoon that a certain Lord Dillon 'observed at Delesert's reading room, a young man very earnestly bent over the last "Quarterly". When he came to the end, he straightened up suddenly and burst into a convulsive laughter, closed the book with an hysteric laugh, and hastily left the room, his Ha! Ha's! ringing down the stairs.'[43] The fiendish laugh that had troubled the Presbyterians of Glasgow on the sabbath ten years previously had not become any more discreet.

Shelley was shaken more than he cared to admit, but he was not outwardly cast down. Hearing on 14 October that Peacock had doubts about *The Cenci* which he had just read, he wrote bluffly to Maria Gisborne: 'he don't much like it – But I ought to say, to blunt the edge of his criticism, that he is a nursling of the exact & superficial school in poetry'. This was true enough.[44] On the following day, he wrote directly to Ollier about the attack in the *Quarterly*, 'well aware' that it was by Southey: it was 'all nothing' – 'trash' – particularly that 'lame attack on my personal character, which was meant so ill'. He was determined to show Ollier that he could ride out such stuff, and he composed an excellent comic improvisation on the *coup de grâce*. 'I was amused too with the finale; it is like the end of the first act of an opera, when that tremendous concordant discord sets up from the orchestra, and everybody talks and sings at once. It describes the result of my battle with their Omnipotent God; his pulling me under the sea by the hair of my head, like Pharaoh; my calling out like the devil who was game to the last; swearing and cursing in all comic and horrid oaths, like a French postillion on Mount Cenis; entreating everybody to drown themselves; pretending not to be drowned myself when I *am* drowned; and, lastly, *being* drowned.'[45] Ollier no doubt was convinced.

---

* John Taylor Coleridge, after this suitable debut, became a King's Bench judge and the biographer of Keble.

Yet the criticism was also working more slowly, at a deeper level of Shelley's mind. He brooded on it, though he appears to have spoken to nobody for the time being. Mary records that he visited the galleries constantly on his own, during these mid-October days. The weather was beginning to break up in earnest now, and though the temperature in Florence remained fairly mild, the wind began to get up in the afternoons, and high cloud raced across the sky from the west, sweeping in from the sea beyond Pisa. Shelley went for walks along the banks of the Arno thinking of everything that the *Quarterly* attack represented, thinking of his own exile, his 'passion for reforming the world', his apparent impotence to help the downtrodden people of England, the disasters of his private life and inevitably, at 27, the beginning of the end of his youth. He had noticed, with a slight shock, that he already had premature threads of grey hair. Yet everything was still to be done. His walks sometimes took him beyond the city walls into the wooded regions by the river, where the autumnal leaves streamed among the silver grey trunks of birch and plane trees. He carried a new notebook with him.[46] On the seventh page, he jotted a fragmentary entry:

Twas the 20th of October
And the woods had all grown sober
As a man does when his hair
Looks as theirs did grey & spare
When the dead leaves
As to mock the stupid
Like ghosts in . . .[47]

The 20th was a Tuesday. On one of the following days, towards the end of the week, he again took the notebook out, and began a second fragment, jotted down at the other end. It was a longer piece altogether, elegiac, but less pessimistic in tone, with the line length extended, and the rough couplet altered to the English terza rima. After twenty-three lines it too faltered and came to a halt, ending:

And this is my distinction, if I fall
I shall not creep out of the vital day
To common dust nor wear a common pall
But as my hopes were fire, so my decay
Shall be as ashes covering them. Oh, Earth
Oh friends, if when my   has ebbed away

One spark be unextinguished of that hearth
Kindled in . . .[48]

It was now the weekend of 23–24 October. On Sunday Shelley again went to Delesert's reading-room, and saw there a copy of Reynolds's satirical pastiche of Wordsworth's poem of the same title, 'Peter Bell II'.[49] Shelley's scorn and confidence were returning; moreover he had a poem in the making.

On Monday morning, 25 October, he began a cold but angry letter to the editor of the *Quarterly*, drafting it in what usually served as his fair-copy notebook.[50] 'Sir. . . . I hereby call upon the Author of that Article or you as his responsible agent publickly to produce your proofs of that assertion [to the disadvantage of my personal character], or as you have thrust yourselves forward to deserve the character of a slandered, to acquiesce also in. . . .' But the letter would not do, and he threw down his pen.

On Monday afternoon he went for another solitary walk along the Arno, and watched in the sky above Casciano the gathering of a violent storm against the clear cold blue. The wind was hard from the west. When he returned to the Palazzo Marini he had his poem. 'This poem was conceived and chiefly written in a wood that skirts the Arno . . . on a day when that tempestuous wind, whose temperature is at once mild and animating, was collecting the vapours which pour down the autumnal rains. They began, as I foresaw, at sunset with a violent tempest of hail and rain, attended by that magnificent thunder and lightning peculiar to the Cisalpine regions.'[51]

Shelley picked up the same pen[52] with which he had been writing to the *Quarterly*, turned the notebook upside down, and entered a clean draft of his poem. He dated it at the head 'Oct 25', and gave its title.[53] But he was still having a little trouble with the last stanza, and pulling a second notebook at random on to his table, he ran through another draft across two pages. The lines seemed almost right:

> . . . Those ashes from an unextinguished hearth . . .
> . . . For through my lips to the frozen earth . . .
> . . . O Wind
> When winter comes Spring lags not far behind . . .[54]

Then, in triumph and defiance, he scrawled below in Greek a tag from Euripides, as if he had just won a tremendous victory. "$\alpha\rho\epsilon\tau\hat{\eta}$ $\sigma\epsilon$ $\nu\iota\kappa\hat{\omega}$ $\theta\nu\eta\tau\grave{o}s$ $\overset{\circ}{\omega}\nu$ $\theta\epsilon\grave{o}\nu$ $\mu\acute{\epsilon}\gamma\alpha\nu$.'[55] 'By virtuous power, I a mortal, vanquish thee a mighty god.' The poem was complete.

I

> O wild West Wind, thou breath of Autumn's being,
> Thou, from whose unseen presence the leaves dead
> Are driven, like ghosts from an enchanter fleeing,

Yellow, and black, and pale, and hectic red,
Pestilence-stricken multitudes: O thou,
Who chariotest to their dark wintry bed

The wingèd seeds, where they lie cold and low,
Each like a corpse within its grave, until
Thine azure sister of the Spring shall blow

Her clarion o'er the dreaming earth, and fill
(Driving sweet buds like flocks to feed in air)
With living hues and odours plain and hill:

Wild Spirit, which art moving everywhere;
Destroyer and preserver; hear, oh, hear!

II

Thou on whose stream, mid the steep sky's commotion,
Loose clouds like earth's decaying leaves are shed,
Shook from the tangled boughs of Heaven and Ocean,

Angels of rain and lightning: there are spread
On the blue surface of thine aëry surge,
Like the bright hair uplifted from the head

Of some fierce Maenad, even from the dim verge
Of the horizon to the zenith's height,
The locks of the approaching storm. Thou dirge

Of the dying year, to which this closing night
Will be the dome of a vast sepulchre,
Vaulted with all thy congregated might

Of vapours, from whose solid atmosphere
Black rain, and fire, and hail will burst: oh, hear!

III

Thou who didst waken from his summer dreams
The blue Mediterranean, where he lay,
Lulled by the coil of his crystàlline streams,

Beside a pumice isle in Baiae's bay,
And saw in sleep old palaces and towers
Quivering within the wave's intenser day,

All overgrown with azure moss and flowers
So sweet, the sense faints picturing them! Thou
For whose path the Atlantic's level powers

Clear themselves into chasms, while far below
The sea-blooms and the oozy woods which wear
The sapless foliage of the ocean, know

Thy voice, and suddenly grow gray with fear,
And tremble and despoil themselves: oh, hear!

IV

If I were a dead leaf thou mightest bear;
If I were a swift cloud to fly with thee;
A wave to pant beneath thy power, and share

The impulse of thy strength, only less free
Than thou, O uncontrollable! If even
I were as in my boyhood, and could be

The comrade of thy wanderings over Heaven,
As then, when to outstrip thy skiey speed
Scarce seemed a vision; I would ne'er have striven

As thus with thee in prayer in my sore need.
Oh, lift me as a wave, a leaf, a cloud!
I fall upon the thorns of life! I bleed!

A heavy weight of hours has chained and bowed
One too like thee: tameless, and swift, and proud.

V

Make me thy lyre, even as the forest is:
What if my leaves are falling like its own!
The tumult of thy mighty harmonies

Will take from both a deep, autumnal tone,
Sweet though in sadness. Be thou, Spirit fierce
My spirit! Be thou me, impetuous one!

Drive my dead thoughts over the universe
Like withered leaves to quicken a new birth!
And, by the incantation of this verse,

Scatter, as from an unextinguished hearth
Ashes and sparks, my words among mankind!
Be through my lips to unawakened earth

The trumpet of a prophecy! O, Wind,
If Winter comes, can Spring be far behind?

· · · · ·

The last week of October and the first of November continued for Shelley
in a whirl of creative and business activity. He seemed to find time for everything. The arrangements to organize the financing of Henry Reveley's steam-
boat had run into unexpected complications connected with Shelley's account
at Brookes in London, which was suddenly found to be overdrawn. A cheque
for fifty pounds in Italian sequins had already been forwarded to Livorno as a
first payment towards the steamboat expenses on 21 October, with a promise
of £200 to follow immediately. On 28 October, much to his surprise, he received the bill of £200 back from his English agent explaining that it had been
bounced by Brookes. Explanatory letters flew off to Maria Gisborne and Henry,
while inquiries and demands were sent post-haste to his solicitor Longdill, to
Peacock and to his faithful financial adviser and aid in London, Horace Smith.
Due to carelessness between Sir Timothy, Whitton and Longdill, Shelley's
annuity had simply not been paid into his London account. Smith rapidly put
all this to rights by the end of November.[56] Reveley's £200 eventually reached
him before Christmas. Meanwhile Shelley sent him improving letters, 'let you &
I try if we cannot be as punctual and business like as the best of them', and
urged the importance of Reveley learning to write a good business letter. He
also advised Mr Gisborne, through Henry, of the inadvisability of keeping his
family's investments in British state bonds 'at this crisis of approaching
Revolution'.[57]

Meanwhile he did his best to support Mary through her fourth pregnancy,
and relenting on her account, to make movements towards helping Godwin
who had been convicted in the autumn of owing £1,500 in arrears on his rent

at Skinner Street. Claire was not forgotten either, and inquiries went out to the new vice-consul at Venice during the Hoppners' absence in Switzerland, asking about Allegra's health and education, 'and where Lord Byron is, or where he is next expected to be'.[58] A plan even began to form in his mind about making a rapid visit to England after Christmas, travelling on his own. Both from the point of view of politics and poetry, London seemed to be the most interesting place in the world to be; and with so many people anxious to see him – Hunt, Peacock, Hogg, certainly Godwin and probably Ollier, not to mention Mr Harris of Covent Garden – it no longer seemed such a hostile spot. Of course there was the problem that Mary was set against the idea, from the first moment that he vaguely mentioned it to her.[59]

This same week, the week after the writing of the 'Ode to the West Wind', and the week before the expected arrival of Mary's baby, saw the composition of the 152 stanzas of *Peter Bell the Third*. It was in Shelley's words, 'a *very heroic* poem', and intended like *The Mask*, but for different reasons, for immediate publication; though to Ollier he wrote that 'perhaps no one will believe in anything in the shape of a joke from me'.[60] Shelley had read Hunt's witty review of both Wordsworth's original 'Peter Bell', and Hamilton Reynolds's smart parody, 'Peter Bell II' at Livorno in the *Examiner*.[61] But it was not until he read the originals at Delesert's that the idea for a third Peter Bell came into his mind. He wrote the whole work, poem and preface, and pseudo-pedantic footnotes, in a wild spirit of mockery and seriousness combined. It had much of the tone and *élan* of his comic transformation of the *Quarterly*'s attack in his letter to Ollier.

The core of *Peter Bell the Third* is a political attack on Wordsworth, and to a lesser extent Coleridge: 'He was at first sublime, pathetic, impressive, profound . . . and now dull – oh so very dull! it is an ultra-legitimate dullness.' It was written at breakneck speed, more than twenty stanzas a day, as Shelley explained in his preface. 'Let me observe that I have spent six or seven days in composing this sublime piece; the orb of my moonlike genius has made the fourth part of its revolution round the dull earth which you inhabit, driving you mad . . .'[62]

It is dedicated, under a pseudonym, to Tom Moore, and turns satirically upon the issues of public reputation and fame which Shelley was in fact deeply concerned about. Shelley's manner is both comic, and strangely sad:

> Hoping that the immortality which you have given to the Fudges,* you will receive from them; and in the firm expectation, that when London shall

* The Fudge family were characters in a popular children's series of stories that Tom Moore had written.

be an habitation of bitterns; when St Paul's and Westminster Abbey shall stand, shapeless and nameless ruins, in the midst of an unpeopled marsh; when the piers of Waterloo Bridge shall become the nuclei of islets of reeds and osiers, and cast the jagged shadows of their broken arches on the solitary stream, some transatlantic commentator will be weighing in the scales of some new and now unimagined system of criticism, the respective merits of the Bells and the Fudges, and their historians. I remain, dear Tom, yours sincerely, Miching Mallecho.[63]

The poem has the rough, rapid-moving, colloquial surface of *The Mask*, though its satire, being less forceful and single-minded, is also lighter and nimbler, moving to the attack simultaneously on several points. It has genuine wit, and it is the one poem of Shelley's life where one can clearly discern the acrid elegance of Pope. It is in seven parts, entitled severely: 'Death', 'The Devil', 'Hell', 'Sin', 'Grace', 'Damnation' and 'Double Damnation'. The poem is set throughout – in as much as it has a location – in a kind of nightmare London, a Zoroastrian double of the real city. Half-familiar figures and distortions flit past including Coleridge lost in Germanic reveries, Cobbett inciting the mob to a festival of murder, several of Lord Liverpool's ministry, the Prince Regent, Sir William Drummond, reviewers, lawyers, bishops and society ladies all swept along in a wild phantasmagoria of lost souls, 'a pestilence-stricken multitude'. The most strange and Protean of all is the protagonist Peter, who is sometimes clearly Wordsworth pinned with an acute critical phrase – 'turned to a formal puritan, a solemn and unsexual man'; sometimes he is a kind of composite poet, a Wordosoutheridge betraying both his political and poetical creed; and sometimes he is even Shelley himself crucified in the reviews:

> Then *seriatim*, month and quarter,
>   Appeared such mad tirades. – One said –
> 'Peter seduced Mrs. Foy's daughter,
> Then drowned the mother in Ullswater,
>   The last thing as he went to bed.' . . .

> One more, 'Is incest not enough?
>   And must there be adultery too? . . .
> By that last book of yours WE think
>   You've double damned yourself to scorn;
> We warned you whilst yet on the brink
> You stood. From your black name will shrink
>   The babe that is unborn.'[64]

But this was mockery that ran almost masochistically close to the bone. Yet the best of the work, and the best is very good indeed, lies in the two short sections: No. 3, 'Hell'; and No. 5 – 'Grace'. Both have an extraordinary kind of intellectual gaiety, which flourishes amid the grimness of the setting. The writing of 'Hell' has an unflinching eye, which seems both childlike and lethal. Hell is of course London.

> Hell is a city much like London –
> A populous and a smoky city;
> There are all sorts of people undone,
> And there is little or no fun done;
> Small justice shown, and still less pity. . . .
>
> There is a ***, who has lost
> His wits, or sold them, none knows which;
> He walks about a double ghost,
> And though as thin as Fraud almost –
> Ever grows more grim and rich.
>
> There is a Chancery Court; a King;
> A manufacturing mob; a set
> Of thieves who by themselves are sent
> Similar thieves to represent;*
> An army; and a public debt. . . .
>
> There is a great talk of revolution –
> And a great chance of despotism –
> German soldiers – camps – confusion –
> Tumults – lotteries – rage – delusion –
> Gin – suicide – and methodism; . . .
>
> There are mincing women, mewing,
> (Like cats, who *amant miserè*,)
> Of their own virtue, and pursuing
> Their gentler sisters to that ruin,
> Without which – what were chastity? . . .†

* The unreformed House of Commons.

† The 'gentler sisters' are of course the London prostitutes, and Shelley wrote in his own footnote: 'What would the husk and excuse for virtue be without its kernel prostitution?' *Chastity* in order to rhyme with *miserè* has to be pronounced genteelly.

> And all these meet at levees; –
>   Dinners convivial and political; –
> Suppers of epic poets; – teas,
> Where small talk dies in agonies; –
>   Breakfasts professional and critical. . . .
>
> At conversazioni – balls –
>   Conventicles – and drawing-rooms –
> Courts of law – committees – calls
> Of a morning – clubs – book-stalls –
>   Churches – masquerades – and tombs.
>
> And this is Hell – and in this smother
>   All are damnable and damned;
> Each one damning, damns the other;
> They are damned by one another,
>   By none other are they damned.[65]

Shelley's hatred for the hypocrisies, cruelties, injustices and genteel class-layerings of metropolitan life, which first made itself shown in his early broadsheet 'The Devil's Walk', had found its purest political expression in *The Mask*. Here it found a satiric one, something closer to Pope, and Byron and Peacock. But Shelley had not done with the theme in *Peter Bell the Third*. A celebrated sonnet written right at the end of 1819 as a kind of retrospective, returns to this passage, condensing it and embittering it; and the transformation of the impulse continued in later poems. The very last long poem of Shelley's life, 'The Triumph of Life', still shows a continuity of theme with this section of *Peter Bell*, developing especially the idea of a grotesque ceaseless procession of vain human activity. The ultimate classical model for such writing is Juvenal.

Section 5 of the poem, 'Grace', is by contrast a thoroughly individualized portrait of Wordsworth himself, as he appeared as a great poet before his Zoroastrian 'damnation' overtook him. Shelley gradually fades out the sharpness and acidity of the writing, the lines flow more smoothly and the rhymes take on lyric rather than epigrammatic force. Finally we are given a poetic assessment and celebration of Wordsworth's gift which is as fine as anything rendered by Coleridge or Hazlitt, or later in the essays of J.S. Mill or Arnold.

> For in his thought he visited
>   The spots in which, ere dead and damned,
> He his wayward life had led;
> Yet knew not whence the thoughts were fed
>   Which thus his fancy crammed.

And these obscure remembrances
   Stirred such harmony in Peter,
That, whensoever he should please,
He could speak of rocks and trees
   In poetic metre.

For though it was without a sense
   Of memory, yet he remembered well
Many a ditch and quick-set fence;
Of lakes he had intelligence,
   He knew something of heath and fell.

He had also dim recollections
   Of pedlars tramping on their rounds;
Milk-pans and pails; and odd collections
Of saws, and proverbs; and reflections
   Old parsons make in burying-grounds.

But Peter's verse was clear, and came
   Announcing from the frozen hearth
Of a cold age, that none might tame
The soul of that diviner flame
   It augured to the Earth:

Like gentle rains, on the dry plains,
   Making that green which late was gray,
Or like the sudden moon, that stains
Some gloomy chamber's window-panes
   With a broad light this day.

For language was in Peter's hand
   Like clay while he was yet a potter;
And he made songs for all the land,
Sweet both to feel and understand,
   As pipkins late to mountain Cotter.[66]

In the variety of Shelley's explosive creativity during these weeks it is sometimes difficult to reconcile the idea of him writing 'Ode to the West Wind' and *Peter Bell the Third*, within not merely days, but possibly within hours of each other. Yet here, in the wonderful bright expansion of feeling, and the flowing verse lines of stanzas 5 and 6, the harmonious and almost unbroken continuity of the inspiration between the two poems is unmistakable.

Shelley gave the poem to Mary on 1 November to fair-copy in preparation for immediate publication in London. She finished it the following day, despite the momentary expectation of labour pains. Later she wrote that although it must be looked upon as a plaything, it had 'much merit and poetry – so much of *himself* in it'.[67] The manuscript was posted directly to Hunt, 'you being kind enough to take upon yourself the correction of the press'. But *Peter Bell the Third* was not published until Mary's collected edition of 1839. Though Shelley asked after it throughout the winter, no real explanation was ever forthcoming from either Ollier or Hunt.

For the first time really since June, in this covering letter of Shelley's the positive presence of Mary was felt again, as if she had now returned to his life. 'Next post day you may hear from me again, as I have many things to say, & expect to have to announce Mary's *new work*, now in the press. – She has written out as you will observe, *my* Peter & this is, I suspect the last thing she will do before the *new birth*.'[68] The connection between Mary's baby and his own sources of creativity and hope, runs deeply through all the poetry of this autumn, gradually emerging in the imagery, and finally becoming explicit in these letters of November.

Yet the baby was not yet born, and Shelley's fantastic writing output continued through the first week of November. From the 1st, Shelley began drafting a long open letter of protest for the *Examiner* on the subject of Richard Carlile's trial in London which had begun on 10 October and had become a *cause célèbre* of both the liberal and radical press. Shelley was especially interested in Carlile since of the ten indictments to be faced for blasphemous and seditious libel, one concerned the publication of a popular edition of Tom Paine's *Age of Reason*, and another Carlile's brilliant reporting of the Peterloo affair in Sherwin's *Political Register*.

Shelley took five days to write the densely argued composition, which ran in the end to over 6,000 words in length, and became virtually a pamphlet on the legal basis of the freedom of the press. He appears to have begun it on the same day that he completed *Peter Bell the Third*.[69] The astonishing speed and range of his creative output, which had now run in an unbroken curve from 6 September when he first received news of Peterloo, until 5 November, embracing such widely different genres of poetry and prose, and simultaneously throwing off a comet's tail of ballad fragments and songs, suggest a state of exultant energy and vision, a consciousness of formidable active powers that it is difficult to conceive in ordinary terms.

The outcome of Carlile's trial was especially significant for Shelley for it marked the first decisive check of political hopes. Carlile was convicted on two counts of 'wicked malicious and blasphemous libel': his sentence totalled three years, and his fine £1,500. This in itself was sufficiently crippling in personal terms: but on top of it, the local authorities managed to seize his entire stock of 70,000 books, thus ruining at a stroke his whole capital investment. At the time, it looked to Shelley and many other observers that in the silencing of Carlile the government had won a tactical victory.* Shelley did not for a moment believe this would divert the inevitable course of radical reform; but he believed that it made the chances of a bloody and insurrectionary confrontation more likely between the popular party and the government. Such a confrontation he felt – as he had always felt – made the danger of a military despotism very great, in which the mass of the people would be no better off and no more democratically represented than before.

His Carlile letter makes three major points. First, that Carlile, as a Deist, was being tried essentially for his religious opinions; but since he was being judged by a jury of staunch Christians they could not by legal definition be regarded as 'his peers'. Therefore the jury was not valid. Secondly, that it was nonsense to prosecute Carlile for publishing Tom Paine, if the government did not equally prosecute middle-class booksellers, who published deistical writings by Hume, Gibbon, Sir William Drummond, Godwin or Jeremy Bentham. Thirdly, that though it might be assumed, correctly or incorrectly, that Carlile published with the intention of making money, 'with the innocent design of maintaining his wife and children', there was not a shred of legal evidence to prove that Carlile published with an intention that was either 'wicked' or 'malicious'. All three of these points are solid legal arguments against the conviction; indeed the last has a distinct ring of the Inner Temple about it.

Shelley's summary – though in the hurry of composition he did not manage to assign it to the end – is masterly. It seems to have been written to be declaimed. Its great and characteristic strength is its unhesitating penetration through the particular legal case to the general political one.

In prosecuting Carlile they have used the superstition of the Jury as their instrument for crushing a political enemy, or rather they strike in his person at all their political enemies. They know that the Established Church is based upon the belief in certain events of a supernatural character having occurred in Judea eighteen centuries ago; that but for his belief the farmer would refuse to pay the tenth of the produce of his labours to maintain its numbers in

---

* In the event Richard Carlile was to prove indomitable, and he published and was damned for many more years; during this imprisonment, at Dorchester jail, he wrote one of the earliest popular features on family planning and birth control, called *What is Love*, based on an illegal pamphlet by the young John Stuart Mill.

idleness; that this class of persons if not maintained in idleness would have something else to do than to divert the attention of the people from obtaining a Reform in the oppressive government, & that consequently the government would be reformed, & that the people would receive a just price for their labours. . . .[70]

The Carlile letter, like everything that Shelley had composed especially for publication during this autumn, was never published in his lifetime. Indeed it was only first printed, complete in 1926.[71]

For the first time Shelley seemed to realize in considering Carlile's fate what would happen to his own political writing in the hands of Hunt and Ollier. In proposing a public subscription for Carlile's benefit, he remarked wistfully to Hunt, 'I know the value of your occupation & the delicacy of your health, & I am sorry [that] this winter time I cannot be with you to [assist] in the performance of this duty.' This was, as he gradually realized, the crucial point.[72]

At the end of the Carlile letter, Shelley took the opportunity of looking across the broad panorama of political development during the autumn of 1819, and he openly referred to the difference in degree between his own radicalism and Hunt's liberalism, while still acknowledging the fundamental unity of their objectives. It was one of his great avowals of permanent political commitment. 'These my dear Hunt are awful times. The tremendous question is now agitating, whether a military & judicial despotism is to be established by our present rulers, or some form of government less unfavourable to the real & permanent interests of all men is to arise from the conflict of passions now gathering to overturn them: *We* cannot hesitate which party to embrace; and whatever revolutions are to occur, though oppression should change names & names cease to be oppressions, our party will be that of liberty & of the oppressed. Whatever you may imagine to be our differences in political theory, I trust that I shall be able to prove that they are less than you imagine, by agreeing, as from my soul I do, with your principles of political practice.' Shelley began to analyse further their differences of 'theory & practice', but on second thoughts he crossed the sentence out. It was not the moment for disquisitions; it was time for men to stand together. Shelley stood by Hunt in spirit amid the 'despicable tyrants & imposters'; but would Hunt stand by Shelley in practice? Would he publish?

Shelley put down his pen. For the time being, there was no more to write. He read aloud to Mary as she rested on the sofa, waiting for the labour pains to begin.[73] He took Hunt's portrait from his desk, and hung it on the wall opposite Mary's bed.[74] On 6 November a brief letter went off to the Gisbornes, again advising them against leaving their investments in government bonds. 'I have deserted the odorous gardens of literature to journey across the great sandy desert of Politics; not, you may imagine, without the hope of finding some enchanted paradise.' Then, extravagantly developing the metaphor, as he had learnt to do from Calderón – 'Calderonizing' as he called it to Maria Gisborne – he continued cheerfully: 'In all probability, I shall be overwhelmed by one of the tempestuous columns which are forever traversing with the speed of a storm & the confusion of a chaos that pathless wilderness. You meanwhile will be lamenting in some happy Oasis that I do not return.' The weather had now broken completely. There was frequent rain and lightning in the afternoons and evenings. But Shelley still liked to slip out when he could to the gardens of the Cascini, 'where I often walk alone watching the leaves & the rising & falling of the Arno'. He was, he said, full of all kinds of literary plans.[75]

23
From the Gallery: Florence 1820

Mary's fourth child was born on the morning of 12 November 1819. After all their arrangements, Dr Bell did not manage to be present, but the labour was an easy one, over in two hours. To Shelley's great delight the child was a boy: small, but healthy and pretty. Much of Shelley's relief and pleasure came from the evident effect on Mary. 'Poor Mary begins (for the first time) to look a little consoled. For we have spent as you may imagine a miserable five months.'[1] They christened him after his father and his birthplace, Percy Florence Shelley.

Both Shelley and Mary found the child very absorbing, and the days being shorter, and darker, they slipped by unnoticed. Shelley went out less by himself, and Mary again omitted to keep her journal. After a week or so, he began slowly to send off letters, but he did not hurry to complete them. To Maria Gisborne, he calderonized on Calderón. 'I have been lately voyaging in a sea without my pilot, & although my sail has often been torn, my boat become leaky, & the log lost, I have yet sailed in a kind of way from island to island. . . . *I have been reading Calderon without you.*' By way of a P.S. he copied out four stanzas from the *Cisma de Inglaterra*, a play about incestuous love, without bothering to translate them from the Spanish.[2] To John Gisborne he wrote sagely of Theocritus and the British Funds and the follies of youth. 'All of us who are worth any thing spend our manhood in unlearning the follies, or expiating the mistakes of our youth.'[3] To Aemilia Curran in Rome, he spoke of the new baby, and Godwin's debts, and his vague plan to go secretly to England in the spring.[4]

After receiving news from Henry Reveley of another birth, that of an eighty-three-pound bronze air cylinder for the steam-boat in the workshop at Livorno, he calderonized on the Creation. Anxious to please Shelley, Reveley had described in great detail the casting of the mould and the 'massy stream of a bluish dazzling whiteness' of molten metal rushing in like 'the twinkling of a shooting star'. Shelley replied in kind: 'Your volcanic description of the birth of the Cylinder is very characteristic both of you & of it. One might imagine God when he made the earth, & saw the granite mountains & flinty promontories flow into their craggy forms, & the splendour of their fusion filling millions of miles of void space, like the tail of a comet, so looking & so delighting in his work. God sees his machine spinning round the sun & delights in its success, & has taken out patents to supply all the suns in space with the same manufacture. – Your boat will be to the Ocean of Water what the earth is to the Ocean of Aether – a prosperous & swift voyager.' The metal steamer had been transformed into one of Shelley's luminous airships. Charles Clairmont, who had left the Palazzo Marini on 10 November 'not without many lamentations as all true lovers pay', had been commissioned to write an account of the Trieste Steam Boat especially for Reveley.[5]

A letter to Hunt of the 18th discussed baby clothes and the difficulties of translation. In between were slipped tentative literary inquiries: 'You do not tell me whether you have received my lines on the Manchester affair. . . . The "Julian and Maddalo" I do not know how it ought to be published. What do you think best to do with it? Do as you like.' There were a few sentences on politics, the need to hold the balance between 'popular impatience and tyrannical obstinacy'. The great thing to do, Shelley wrote, pressing the cause of moderation in a way designed to appeal to the editor of the *Examiner*, 'is to inculcate with fervour both the right of resistance and the duty of forbearance'. But even on this occasion he could not quite restrain his radicalism. 'You know my principles incite me to take all the good I can get in politics, for ever aspiring to something more. I am one of those whom nothing will fully satisfy, but who am ready to be partially satisfied by all that is practicable. We shall see.'[6]

By the end of November Mary was slowly beginning to return to something like her old self. When she looked back at the five months at Livorno it was to 'shudder with horror': yet it was also to be capable of looking back. Practical details began to absorb her attention. She worried about getting flannel for Percy Florence to wrap him against the Italian winter; and she began to complain loudly over the remissness of Hunt's le ter-writing. She joined Shelley in inquiries about the poems: what of *The Mask* sent a few days before they left Leghorn, 'which is now 2 months ago'? and what of *Peter Bell the Third*, which she herself had copied? Mary took pleasure in the calderonizing game which Shelley played with Maria Gisborne. She reported how one day he stood at the window and announced that the weather of late had been 'an epic of rain with an episode of frost & a few similes concerning fine weather'.[7] She felt calmer in herself now, and enjoyed the improvement in Claire's singing under her new Florentine music-master. She asked after the 'rustics' at Marlow and on learning that Peacock had not married Marianne St Croix observed with something of her old archness, 'this shepherd King has I am afraid forgotten his crook & his mistress'. One cloud on the horizon was the distant prospect of Shelley's trip to England in the spring. This was ostensibly to help Godwin. But Mary had reached a new assessment of her father, and she was less easily made guilty by his ceaseless financial troubles. She felt determined to set her face against Shelley's leaving Italy without her, for this reason or any other. She enlisted Marianne Hunt's sympathy. 'Shelley in his last letter mentioned something about his return to England – but this is very vague – I hope – how ardently you may guess, that it will not be . . . his return would be in so many ways so dreadful a thing that I cannot dwell long enough upon the idea to conceive it possible. – We do not think of all returning.'[8] Part of the difficulty here was money. Mary's control of the housekeeping showed that they had lived for the first time 'in an economical manner' in Italy, only since they had taken up residence in Tuscany. To break up the household, and incur travelling expenses would be 'madness'. Whether Mary feared that Shelley might embroil himself politically in London is not clear: but she wrote to Marianne of the danger of his visit if it were known, and 'arrests & a thousand other things'. It was probably arrests for debt, rather than for seditious libel, that she feared.[9]

For the time being Shelley did not press the point. He was delighted with the new-found harmony produced by the presence of the child. On 2 December Mary was writing that she felt well and strong, and that Percy Florence was nearly three times as big as when he was born, though there were still no flannel petticoats for him from Genoa.[10]

Perhaps the sight of such a blooming mother and child prompted Shelley to think back to the death of that unknown mother's baby which had so appalled him at Peterloo. The image had run right through his poems of September and October, and he had reverted to it in the opening of his letter concerning the trial of Richard Carlile in November. At any rate, immediately over the page in the white-backed notebook in which he had worked on the last stanzas of the 'Ode to the West Wind', he began to sketch out stanzas for a ballad concerning a starving mother with an infant at her breast. The first verse arrived without explanation, but urgently:

Give me a piece of that fine white bread
   I would give you some blood for it
Before I faint & my infant is dead
   Oh, give me a little bit [11]

Gradually the poem established itself as the appeal of a starving woman to a parish priest, young Parson Richards. The woman explains how she was ruined – seduced – by a 'trinket of gold', and gradually sickened in hunger and penury, until her need became shameless and desperate. Holding her baby in her arms, she appeals to the parson across the rectory gate.

> . . . the single blanket of threadbare woof
>   Under which we both cried to sleep
> Is gone – the rain drenches us through the roof
>   And I moan – but no longer weep
>
> What would it avail me to prostitute
>   This lean body squalid and wild
> And yet by the God who made me I'd do't
>   If I could but save my child
>
> Perhaps you would like – but alas you are
>   A staid and a holy man
> And, if you were not, . . . would any one care
>   For these limbs so meagre and wan

The frankness, the unintentional irony, and the stumbling simplicity of her speaking voice, show the urgent impulse which had inspired the forms and style of *The Mask* and *Peter Bell the Third* driven to a final extremity of directness. It is as if the message of man's inhumanity to man had become so overwhelming in Shelley's mind that every intervening form – politics, satire, even the decorum of poetry, had eventually to fall back before the simple, agonizing, human speech of suffering and need. The man who was later to become famed as the greatest rhetorician and the most sublime lyricist of all the English Romantic poets, was actually driven to writing like this in order to say what he really had to say:

> The poor thing sucks and no milk will come,
>   He would cry but his strength is gone, –
> His wasting weakness has left him dumb,
>   Ye can hardly hear him moan.
>
> The skin round his eyes is pale and blue,
>   His eyes are glazed, not with tears –
> I wish for a little moment that you
>   Could know what a mother fears.

Shelley continued this poem in other manuscripts. In his final draft the young parson never speaks; he walks down frowning to the wicket gate, and by the time he gets there both mother and child have collapsed. The poem ends abruptly, with a lethal twist so quietly understated it almost escapes observation:

> The man of God with a surly frown
> To the garden wicket paced
> And he saw the woman had fallen down
> With her face below her waist.

> The child lay stiff as a frozen straw
> In the woman's white cold breast –
> And the parson in its dead features saw
> His own to the truth expressed.

> He turned from the bosom whose heart was broke
> Once it pillowed him as he slept. –
> He turned from the lips that no longer spoke
> From the eyes that no longer wept. –

> And how that parson . . .
> Becomes thy . . .
> More than my words to say . . .[12]

Shelley made little attempt to integrate his versions, though he did later fair copy one into a notebook for Claire. Perhaps she liked it better than Mary. He did not bother to send it to Hunt or Ollier. The poem was still being rejected as unsuitable for printing by editors in 1889.

In December life became more social and frivolous at the Palazzo Marini under the influence of a charming young English girl, Miss Sophia Stacey, and her dragon-like elderly chaperone, Miss Corbet Parry-Jones, who had arrived on a cultural grand tour. Their appearance was not entirely by chance, since Miss Stacey was a ward of one of Shelley's Sussex uncles, and she had heard that the intriguing not to say disreputable black sheep of the clan, the atheist, eloper and poet Percy Bysshe, was in winter residence at Florence. Miss Parry-Jones was finally persuaded by Miss Stacey to pay a formal visit to the Shelleys, and interpreting the situation instantly, he set out to charm them both off their feet. There was not much difficulty, as Mary observed with amusement. 'The younger one was entousiasmée to see him – the elder said he was a very shocking man – but finding that we became the mode she melted.'

Miss Parry-Jones was a little elderly Welshwoman 'without the slightest education' who valiantly learnt French and Italian which she spoke with a strong Welsh lilt and mixed indiscriminately with her own native tongue. Sophia

Stacey was attractive, lively and relatively unaffected, as Mary was prepared to admit, and 'sings well for an english dilettante'. Though in Mary's opinion, she paid too much attention to her 'sweet voice', and not enough to her scales. Claire immediately joined Shelley's campaign, and rapidly made herself indispensable as a companion and interpreter during lessons with the Italian music-master. One or two other young English ladies appear to have joined the group. One of them, a certain Miss Jones, had had a very severe music-master in England, and when asked by her suave Italian Gaspero Pelleschi to sing the scales, promptly burst into floods of tears. The poor Pelleschi was aghast at this strange English reaction and exclaimed hopelessly to Claire, 'non capisco questo effeto'. The Shelleys, as confirmed expatriates, were highly amused.[13] Claire was 'as busy as a bee', and Madame du Plantis's common sitting-room at the palazzo, with its tiny marble fireplace, now became a place of great popular resort.[14]

The weather in Florence during December and much of January 1820 turned bitterly cold, and there were severe frosts. Mary stayed at home much of the time, busy with her child, and Sophia Stacey recalled in her diary how Mrs Shelley seemed to be permanently in bed with a little night table on her knees, elegantly equipped with pen and ink and blotter.[15] Shelley on the other hand was continually plunging out on energetic expeditions to the galleries, and frequently called for Miss Stacey and the other English girls. He had adopted a huge serge winter cloak, topped off with an extravagant grey fur collar which encased his pale, smiling face up to the ears, and kept him warm in the narrow blustery alleys of Florence. Despite the freezing winds, he continued to keep his neck open without scarf or cravat in the old *déshabillé* manner. These details were noticed by an amateur English artist, a Mr Tompkyns, who became friendly with the family and painted Shelley's portrait in early January.[16] Sophia was obviously most flattered by Shelley's attentions. He made a point of helping her with her Italian, and taught her the words of a Carbonari ballad and a local love-song. They seem to have gone visiting the galleries together, probably with Claire and Miss Jones as well, making a voluble and attractive female party, and perfectly adapted to Shelley's social tastes. Sophia records carefully in her diary the two occasions when Shelley lifted her bodily down from a carriage; and also the evening when she had a 'dreadfull tooth ache' at the Palazzo Marini, and Shelley came downstairs especially from his apartment and with great gentleness applied a cotton lint to the offending molar at the back of her mouth.[17]

Shelley's 'Notes on Sculptures in Florence' written during this time afford some idea of the liveliness and attraction of his conversation during the visits to the Uffizi with Sophia and Claire. One of his earliest notes, on an unidentified athlete, begins: 'Curse these fig leaves; why is a round tin thing more decent than a cylindrical marble one? An exceedingly fine statue. . . .'[18] Another, on a

Venus Genetrix observes: 'Remarkable for the voluptuous effect of her finely proportioned form seen through the folds of a drapery, the original of which must have been the "woven wind" of Chios.'[19] A third, on another *Venus*, comments: 'A very insipid person in the usual insipid attitude of this lady. The body and hips and where the lines of the —— fade into the thighs is exquisitely imagined and executed.'[20] On a *Leda*, the judgement is made in two sentences: 'Leda with a very ugly face. I should be a long time before I should make love with her.'[21]

Shelley's descriptions, where they are developed beyond these apt and provoking conversational gambits, tend to concentrate on two aspects of the sculpture. One is the technical details of drapery, limb-joint, and posed gesture by which a voluptuous or explicitly sexual effect is achieved by the sculptor. The other is the emotional, or more especially, the *moral* characterization expressed by a figure or group. His remarks show very little strictly aesthetic appreciation, and almost no interest in the purely formal relations of line, plane or volume. He writes, in effect, as if the stone statues were living theatrical *tableaux*. The sense that the statues were actually alive is one of the most interesting parts of his appreciation, and frequently gives such a personal twist to his remarks that they tell far more about his own feelings than about the way the piece of stone has been carved. Sometimes they approach the condition of prose poems. Of 'A Youth said to be Apollo', he wrote:

> The countenance though exquisite, lovely and gentle is not divine. There is a womanish vivacity of winning yet passive happiness and yet a boyish inexperience exceedingly delightful. . . . It is like a spirit even in dreams. The neck is long yet full and sustains the head with its profuse and knotted hair as if it needed no sustaining.[22]

Here Shelley seemed to have moved himself into a world of half-conscious revery, and one is aware of the presence of bisexual themes which had first been consciously liberated and recognized by the sight of the *Sleeping Hermaphrodite* in the Borghese Palace at Rome. Shelley's longest notes are confined to three subjects: 'The Bacchus and Ampelus', with its comment on adolescent friendships; 'A Statue of Minerva', representing the uniquely Greek form of maenadic insanity; and the statue of 'The Niobe'. The latter is one of the great pieces of the gallery and shows Niobe drawing to the safety of her body her last child before it is murdered by Zeus. The sculptor 'seems in the marble to have scarcely suspended her terror', and it had the most profound effect on Shelley. His description is not in fact very good, since it is too emotionally involved, but both his own and Mary's letters frequently spoke of it as the most impressive single work of sculpture that he ever saw in Italy, and he remembered it ever after with a kind of awe. The reason lay partly in its connection with the figure of the mother and child at Peterloo which had developed into a dominating poetic motif during the autumn. Further study of the artistic effect of combining beauty with great pain or revulsion produced the unfinished poem 'On the Medusa', which meditates on the qualities of a repulsive picture attributed to Leonardo.

Perhaps the most delightful and characteristic of his gallery notes is on the little statue of the *Venus Anodyomene*, a beautiful Greek copy dating from the third century AD and standing a little over three feet high. It is carved in marble which is richly stained and flecked with areas of dark amber and gold, and has a polished surface which shines in sunlight almost like water. The girl is naked except for two simple armbands.* Shelley responded with a fine essay on erotic suggestion.

She seems to have just issued from the bath, and yet to be animated with the [joy] of it. She seems all soft and mild enjoyment, and the curved lines of her fine limbs flow into each other with never-ending continuity of sweetness. Her face expresses a breathless yet passive and innocent voluptuousness without affection, without doubt; it is at once desire and enjoyment and the pleasure arising from both. Her lips . . . have the tenderness of arch yet pure and affectionate desire, and the mode in which the ends are drawn in yet opened by the smile which forever circles round them, and the tremulous curve into which they are wrought by inextinguishable desire, and the tongue lying against the lower lip as in the listlessness of passive joy, express love, still love.

Her eyes seem heavy and swimming with pleasure, and her small forehead fades on both sides into that sweet swelling and then declension of the bone over the eye and prolongs itself to the cheek in that mode which expresses simple and tender feelings.

The neck is full and swollen as with the respiration of delight and flows with gentle curves into her perfect form.

Her form is indeed perfect. She is half sitting on and half rising from a shell, and the fullness of her limbs, and their complete roundness and perfection, do not diminish the vital energy with which they seem to be embued. The mode in which the lines of the curved back flow into and around the thighs, and the wrinkled muscles of the belly, wrinkled by the attitude, is truly astonishing. . . . This perhaps is the finest personification of Venus, the Deity of superficial desire, in all antique statuary. Her pointed and pear-like bosom ever virgin – the virgin Mary might have this beauty, but alas! . . .[23]

* The sculpture is now catalogued as No. 188, *Venere di Bagni*, and stands in the south gallery of the Uffizi overlooking the Arno. See plate 26.

How much of all these 'Notes on Sculpture' were personally explained to Sophia Stacey is not known, but Shelley did write especially for her several short love-lyrics intended to be sung to music. These included the famous 'Song Written for an Indian Air', adapted from an Oriental love-lyric and beginning

> When I arise from dreams of thee
> In the first sweet sleep of night . . .

Others were 'Love's Philosophy', 'To Sophia' and probably the little song 'I fear thy kisses gentle maiden'.[24]

Miss Stacey and Miss Parry-Jones were required to continue on their cultural tour to Rome after Christmas, and Shelley took much trouble in arranging introductions to Signora Dioniga before they eventually departed at the end of December.[25] Shelley later sent Sophia a copy of Hunt's anthology *The Literary Pocket-Book*. In it he inscribed a three-stanza song, 'Buona Notte', which he had first composed in Italian. It ended:

> The hearts that on each other beat
> From evening close to morning light
> Have nights as good as they are sweet
> But never *say* good night.[26]

He hoped to see her once more in Tuscany, and Mary later wrote in the spring from Pisa, but they never met again.

With these diversions, much of the urgency went out of Shelley's writing during December, and in the absence of any more dramatic or decisive news from England, the immediate pressure of politics seemed to relax, and his letters took on a more distant tone. Much of his bitterness had for the moment been exorcized from the *Quarterly*'s attack, mostly by the poem 'Ode to the West Wind', but also by reading a copy of Lockhart's fine defence of *The Revolt of Islam* in *Blackwood's* which Ollier thoughtfully sent. The two magazines were later circulated to the Gisbornes as 'bane and antidote'.

Shelley continued to ask Ollier about the fate of *The Cenci* and *Peter Bell the Third* and 'Julian and Maddalo', but he seemed almost resigned to hearing nothing definite until the spring, perhaps guessing that much must have been rejected.[27] Yet he continued to dwell on the political theme, and December saw the completion of the fourth and last act of *Prometheus Unbound*, written at noticeably low poetic pressure. It was perhaps difficult to compose a great operatic finale to Revolution and Victory when actual political conditions in England were in such a critical state of suspension. Mary transcribed the final act, and it was dispatched to Ollier around Christmas time.[28]

The need to face up to a realistic appraisal of the English situation, decided

Shelley to embark on a prose essay on the history of the growth of individual liberty and free institutions in society; and more especially on the methods of democratic reform immediately available in England. This work, one of the most intellectually demanding he ever embarked upon, was begun in mid-December and eventually finished in May 1820. It was entitled *A Philosophical View of Reform.*

On the 15th Shelley alerted Ollier. 'I am preparing an octavo on reform – a commonplace kind of book – which, now that I see the passion of party will postpone the great struggle till another year, I shall not trouble myself to finish for this season. I intend it to be an instructive and readable book, appealing from the passions to the reasons of men.'[29] The pace of Shelley's political hopes, and of his poetic production was slowing down simultaneously. The moderation into prose and 'reason' marks the clear end of the great creative burst of autumn 1819. Yet this tapped undercurrent of power and vision was to remain a permanent if hidden resource of Shelley's imagination for the rest of his life. Like the great creative efforts of 1812 and 1817 – which were, equally, responses to political and social crises in society – the effort of 1819 pushed forward the range of Shelley's literary powers. It established in his mind more mature conceptions both of the actions and sufferings of other men, and of his own. In artistic terms the greatest gains were in economy and intensity of style.

At the end of the year he wrote a short letter to Hunt, which consciously marks the end of this period. He asked, without much hope of getting a real answer, why Hunt still wouldn't write regular letters to them? Furthermore, when he did write, why wouldn't he write about politics? And why, at least, wouldn't he write about politics and the actual 'State of the country' in his own paper the *Examiner*? – for after the trial of Carlile in November, the Liberal press had fallen very quiet. 'Every word a man has to say is valuable to the public now, and thus you will at once gratify your friend, nay instruct, and either exhilarate him or force him to be resigned, and awaken the minds of the people.' His own writings he made as if to dismiss; 'I have been a drone instead of a bee in this business, thinking that perhaps, as you did not acknowledge any of my late enclosures another would not be welcome to you.' He felt resignation rather than resentment. At the end of the letter he concluded, without much conviction, 'I suppose we shall soon have to fight in England. Affectionate love to and from all.' In a postscript he included a sonnet, 'England in 1819', though he now had no illusions about its reception. 'I do not expect you to publish it, but you may show it to whom you please.'[30] The poem looks back over the crowded events of that autumn, and is one of the strongest, sparest pieces he ever wrote. The handling of the rhythms is particularly powerful. It is bitter and disenchanted, yet the ghost of hope still walks, as she did under the hooves of Anarchy.

An old, mad, blind, despised and dying king;
Princes, the dregs of their dull race, who flow
Through public scorn, – mud from a muddy spring;
Rulers who neither see, nor feel, nor know,
But leech-like to their fainting country cling,
Till they drop, blind in blood, without a blow;
A people starved and stabbed in the untilled field;
An army, which liberticide and prey
Makes as a two-edged sword to all who wield;
Golden and sanguine laws which tempt and slay;
Religion, Christless, Godless – a book sealed;
A Senate, – Time's worst statute unrepealed;
Are graves, from which a glorious Phantom may
Burst to illumine our tempestuous day.[31]

The stress in the penultimate line falls with deliberate intention on *may*; the Promethean future possibility which always remains open. Leigh Hunt of course did not publish this poem, though oddly enough a piece did appear over Shelley's name in Hunt's literary paper the *Indicator* in the last issue of the year. It was one of the little two-stanza love-songs written for Miss Sophia Stacey.

What is all this sweet work worth
    If thou kiss not me?[32]

So the year 1819 ended.

24
The Reformer: Pisa 1820

The cold of January 1820, and the departure of their young English friends from Florence drew the Shelley household in upon itself at Palazzo Marini. Shelley developed a rheumatic pain in his side, which was solicitously reported by Mary to Mrs Gisborne: his plans for a new year excursion to Livorno had to be cancelled. Instead Shelley stayed in and read aloud to Mary: Sophocles, and the New Testament – each Evangelist in turn. It was probably these days which saw the drafts of his unfinished 'Essay on Christianity', a sketch of Jesus Christ as an enemy of institutionalized religion and the Old Law, and as one of the first of the great social reformers. Reflecting on what he saw as Christ's compromises with the old society, and his calculated adaptation of his message to the understanding of simple people, Shelley recalled his own experiences during the previous months and concluded: 'All reformers have been compelled to practise this misrepresentation of their own true feelings and opinions.'[1]

Claire began her diary again, and she recorded a busy social life with the other English residents in the house, notably the families of the Hardings and the Meadows. Her lessons with the gentle Pelleschi continued, but when she went out to the galleries it was usually with the Meadows or the du Plantis daughters, Zoïde and Louisa. Shelley did not go any more. On the 12th, she noted without comment Allegra's third birthday. She had already heard that Byron had moved from Venice to Ravenna with his new mistress, Countess Teresa Guiccioli.

There were heavy falls of snow on the 13th and 14th and Florence lay under whiteness. Claire led Zoïde, Louisa and the Harding children out into the garden to throw snowballs during a spell of sunshine, but again Shelley did not join them. Instead he remained in doors, reading *The Tempest* with Mary. Pelleschi said it was the hardest winter in Florence for seventy years.[2]

Claire's own reading, when she found time for it, still showed Shelley's guiding presence. While studying social life in classical Greece, she noted the superior freedom of Graecian women compared with Roman ones. She entered thoughtfully: 'Pythagoras says when you sacrifice to the celestial gods let it be with an odd number, & when to the terrestial – with an even – "for the odd number is most perfect because it cannot be divided into two equal parts as the even number may which is therefore the symbol of division" – let this rule be applied to marriage and we shall find the cause of its unhappy querulous state.'³ On such a view, a *ménage à trois* formed the smallest stable social unit. Claire may have hoped this issue was reasonably settled for the time being in her life with Shelley and Mary. But in fact the old trouble of *absentia Clariae* was to raise itself again in an unexpected and threatening fashion during the coming spring. There was little to indicate this, except that Claire noted for 23 January: 'Elise calls. Take a short walk.'⁴ There was no equivalent entry in Mary's journal; only, the following day: 'Walk with Shelley' – which implied private discussion.

Throughout January, Mary and Shelley had been debating in which direction they should turn their steps during the new year. The cold had made impossible any immediate move after Christmas, and the idea of Shelley's secret visit to London had been made impracticable by the pains in his side. Rome seemed too distant, and anyway its unhealthy climate and unhappy associations made it unthinkable for Mary. There remained therefore Tuscany, where they had already established close friends: the Gisbornes at Livorno and perhaps too the Masons at Pisa. The Gisbornes obviously wished them to return to the Villa Valsovano, and Reveley would have liked his patron on the spot during the boat-building. Yet various factors pointed to Pisa: it was an ancient Italian university city, rather than a commercial centre like Livorno; it was much less of an expatriate English colony than 'Leghorn'; and it was strategically placed on the main coaching route between Florence and Livorno, allowing relatively rapid journeys in either direction or northwards through the Apennines to Bagni di Lucca. Pisa also had the great attraction for Shelley of being built along a curve of the river Arno, which was eminently navigable for small boats from this point. A further consideration was the fact that the most distinguished Italian doctor and surgeon in the region, Andrea Vaccà, was resident at Pisa, where he held a professorship at the university. Vaccà had studied at Paris and London, and was renowned as a distinguished writer on medical topics and a man of broad European culture.

Over Christmas, several letters from Shelley's old boyhood friend and cousin Tom Medwin had reached Florence from Geneva, and in mid-January, Shelley wrote, inviting him to join them: 'we are fixed for the ensuing year in Tuscany'. Shelley wrote as one who no longer thought of returning to England, and had given himself up to the delights of Italy. 'You used, I remember, to paint very well; & you were remarkable, if I do not mistake, for a peculiar taste in, & knowledge of the *belle arti* – Italy is the place for you – the very place – The

Paradise of exiles – the retreat of Pariahs – but I am thinking of myself rather than of you.' Of his own writing, he said little, though he still set it clearly in a political context: 'I have enough of unrebuked hope remaining to be struck with horror at the proceedings in England. . . . These are not times in which one has much spirit for writing Poetry; although there is a keen air in them that sharpens the wits of men and makes them imagine vividly even in the midst of despondence.'[5] This was precisely what he had achieved at Florence.

Now in the last fortnight of January, a sudden thaw set in, and from the 23rd Florence was bathed in long hours of mild spring sunshine. After two days, Shelley promptly decided to move to Pisa without further delay. He did not even bother to inquire about lodgings ahead, but ordered the girls to pack, and walking down to the Arno booked a passage by river to Empoli on the 26th. They started at 8 in the morning, and the Meadows and Zoïde du Plantis came to wave them off at the quay in the thin morning sunlight. A stiff, piercing east wind blew down the river, and though it froze them through, it had the effect of whisking them the thirty-odd miles to Empoli in five hours.[6] At just after 5 o'clock the same evening, they crossed by coach over the main bridge into Pisa, and put up at the first inn on the left of the Lung' Arno Regio, the Albergo delle Tre Donzelle.

The Tre Donzelle stands on the north side of the Arno, at the edge of the little piazza where the Ponte Mezzo deposits the main coach road from Florence and Empoli. Like many other of the riverside buildings, it presents a bleached façade of mellow orange stone standing three stories high, its windows shuttered and its roof covered in large curved tiles. From its windows the Shelleys could see the Arno bending away in a long bow shape to left and right, the banks clustered by an unbroken line of elegant buildings and palaces, many of them with marble frontages and balconies, intricately mullioned windows, and finely ornamented coping stones of terracotta. Several of the palaces dated from the fifteenth and sixteenth centuries, among them the Palazzo Medici, the Palazzo Toscanelli and the Palazzo Reale. This curving vista of stone, duplicated in muted yellows and oranges in the curve of the river, presented an aspect that was serene and aristocratic, with a simplicity of line recalling classical rather than Renaissance Rome.

It pleased Shelley very much. Yet for all its aristocratic graces, the city was faded. Originally a flourishing marine centre, Pisa had slowly been enclosed by the *maremma*, in much the same way as Rye in England had been enclosed by marshes. Its eminence and its population had steadily declined since the seventeenth century. The stonework of the façades was cracked and crumbling, many of the large palazzos – including the Medici – were not in full use, and in the areas near the city walls, whole streets were crumbling into the ground and overrun by wild vegetation. The ancient *cittadèlla vècchia*, with its huge club-like tower, stood guarding the western approaches by the Ponte al Mare amid the ruins of medieval prosperity and faded glories of Galileo Galilei, Count Ugolino and the Pisanos. It was a city in its dotage, a city as Shelley soon appreciated, of memories and ghosts.

Yet the core of the city still flourished. Behind the Lung'Arno Mediceo and the Tre Donzelle stood the towers of numerous churches, and the buildings of the university, founded in the twelfth century, with its famous medical faculty and botanical gardens, and its lively eccentric circle of students and professors. There was a semi-active opera and theatre, and the great architectural monuments of the cathedral, the *battistèro* and the Leaning Tower in the Piazza dei Miracoli continued to draw a steadily increasing stream of English, French and German tourists from the end of the eighteenth century onwards. This served to keep the pulse of the city's commerce alive when all else stagnated.

The strangely dream-like, other-worldly quality of the city during the time of Shelley's residence was emphasized by the distinctive quality of the architecture, which had earned itself separate recognition as the Pisan style. It was a hybrid, an evocative mixture of influences. The bold and simple arches and columns of the Romanesque were laid against flat surfaces of undecorated stone, and austerely repeated across whole façades and upon several levels. Against this were sudden bursts of Gothic extravagance, ornate clusters of pinnacles, intricate mullioning, characterized by the dense and busy carving of the octagonal pulpit or the great cathedral gates. Then there was a third element, an undertone of something altogether more exotic and pagan. This could be seen especially in the gourd-like doming on the *battistero*, and in the mosque-like simplicity of the interior of the Camposanto Monumentale. It was a recognizably Moorish influence, which recalled Pisa's ancient connection with the trade routes to Africa and the Eastern Mediterranean, and which must have found a profound echo in Shelley's mind. It is interesting that, alone among Italian cities, Shelley never looked on Pisa with a tourist's eye. He wrote no architectural or artistic notes on its great showpieces, and nowhere did he record comment on its paintings or carvings. Yet he wrote several poems and prose fragments about the city, which caught the atmosphere of the place, at certain times and in certain lights. In this unexpected way Pisa was to serve as a mirror of his own deepest feelings.

After three days at the Tre Donzelle, the Shelleys, with the help and advice of their new friends the Masons at the Casa Silva, took spacious apartments on the mezzanine floor at the Casa Frassi on the north-west and sunny side of the Lung'Arno. Mary particularly was delighted with these rooms and the economy. 'We have two bed rooms, 2 sitting rooms kitchen servants rooms nicely furnished – & very clean & *new* (a great thing on this country) for 4 guineas and a ½ a month – the rooms are light and airy – so you see we begin to profit by

Italian prices – one learns this very slowly but I assure you a crown here goes as far in the conveniences & necessaries of life as £1 in England.' Milly was not, incidentally, any longer with them, having changed her employer in Florence, so that their servants were now all Italian and Mary tended to give much more personal attention to her child. The Italians were not entirely satisfactory, they 'teaze us out of our lives', and Mary thought of engaging another Swiss. But in the end they managed to adapt to Italian ways.

Shelley's arrival at Pisa in January 1820 marked an important change in the manner of his life. Since leaving Marlow almost exactly two years earlier in 1818, it had really been that of a nomad. He had been constantly on the move: London, Milan, Bagni di Lucca, Venice, Naples, Rome, Livorno, Florence – eight residences in rather less than twenty-four months. The restlessness of his journeyings, and the inherent sense of rootlessness, was obscured by the day-to-day details of his life, for there seemed such a multiplicity of reasons and motives – domestic, financial and political ones – to explain why he should always move on. But the deep cause of this need to move is certainly one of the profoundest questions which can be asked about his life. Like the poet in *Alastor*, one is left always with a dilemma: was Shelley running away from something, or was he running after something?

The residence at Pisa, which was to last, off and on, for well over two years, cut decisively across this pattern of movement. Pisa became the nearest thing Shelley ever had to a home anywhere since leaving Field Place. Yet there is evidence that the need for movement had been stabilized at Pisa, rather than permanently outgrown. Shelley was to make a series of excursions from Pisa between 1820 and 1822, and to live temporarily at various houses within the vicinity. The desire for an ever-expanding field of journeyings returned: after England, it had been Europe; but after Europe, it was to become – in his mind at least – Africa and the Near East. Significantly, the confidante for these new urges was no longer Mary, but Claire; and in a more literary and dreamy way, certain of his new lady acquaintances at Pisa.

Once they had settled at the Casa Frassi, Shelley made a quick visit to the Gisbornes at Livorno on his own, partly to see the latest developments of the steam-boat, and partly to explain why he had settled on Pisa rather than at Villa Valsovano again. He returned on 2 February, and from this time dates the growing intimacy with the Masons, which gradually surplanted the influence of the Gisbornes and calderonizing.

Mrs Mason, of the Casa Silva, was not in fact Mrs Mason at all, but the Countess, Lady Margaret Mountcashell. She had grown up on extensive family estates in Ireland, and during adolescence, her governess had been Mary Wollstonecraft. The effect of this was lasting. She became a correspondent of

Godwin's, an ardent republican and one of the few feminist members of the United Irishmen movement. She had been marginally involved in the uprisings of the nineties, and had attended in London the famous trial for treason of the working-men's leaders Hardy, Horne Tooke and Thelwall. Later she had published political pamphlets and books in Godwin's Juvenile Library. During the Napoleonic wars she had abandoned Earl Mountcashell, and gone to live in Pisa under the name of Mason with a talented expatriate agronomist of similar political sympathies, George William Tighe.

Tighe was universally liked by the Shelleys and affectionately known as 'Tatty' because of his scientific interest in agriculture. Tatty's advanced knowledge of the chemistry of soil compounds and organic growth both amused and delighted Shelley, who kept extensive notes in the back of the same notebook in which he had drafted the last stanzas of the 'Ode to the West Wind', and the unfinished 'Ballad' of the starving mother.

Shelley's agricultural notes included a list of the forty-seven known chemical elements, descriptions of the action of electrolysis, capillary attraction and the use of acid as a fertilizer. There are references to magnesium, silica and 'hexagonal cells'; remarks on the 'dairy system', human food consumption and elementary statistics on the productivity of land per acre in comparative terms of potatoes, milk and butter. It is also clear from these notes that Tatty Tighe had encouraged Shelley to read Davy's lectures on agriculture, and to consider the problems set by Malthusian social theory in terms of population figures and food production. It is very characteristic of Shelley that he did not feel the need to separate this scientific information from his poetry by starting another notebook.[7]

When the friendship with the Masons commenced in 1820, they had two daughters, Laurette aged 10½, and Nerina aged 4½. Claire was very kind and friendly towards these two little girls, and Mrs Mason in turn, came to look on Claire as something of a grown-up daughter. She developed both social and intellectual ambitions for Claire, and Claire came to call Mrs Mason her 'Minerva'. Lady Mountcashell was at this time a tall, gaunt, rather brusque and distinctly Celtic woman in her mid-forties, a great *raconteuse*, of considerable charm and with much force of character.[8]

During the early part of February, she deluged the Shelley household with pamphlets about Ireland. At the Casa Silva there were long, lively discussions about the Irish Rebellion and the horror of Castlereagh's influence both in Ireland and in England. After one of these powerful discussions, Claire recorded that she had a 'horrid dream about Skinner Street & apoplectic fits'.[9] A letter from Mary to Marianne Hunt also showed the Mountcashell influence since it was almost entirely filled by a long Jeremiad against 'King Cant', and those

'Castlereaghish men', who were detested by all radicals.[10] Visits between the Casa Frassi and the Casa Silva became a daily feature of the life at Pisa, and the Shelleys and the Masons soon began to dine frequently in one another's company.

Mary took up riding, and Shelley was visited by Vaccà. The astute doctor, who spoke fluent English, observed Shelley closely and examined and questioned him on his symptoms. His diagnosis was simple: that Shelley should refrain from special medicines, take plenty of exercise and take care of himself – all would then be well. In the season he recommended the pleasant advantages of the *bagni*, either at Lucca or locally. He seemed at once very *simpàtico* both to Mary and to Shelley: 'a great republican & no Christian'.[11] In passing, he also diagnosed an indisposition of Claire's, much to her disgust: 'Vaccà says I am scrofulous and I say he is ridiculous.'[12] But actually he was perfectly right, and she had to have treatment in Florence a year later. A friendship with Vaccà gradually grew up, and the Shelleys sometimes met him socially with other doctors at the Casa Silva. They had thus gained an *entrée* into the circle of the university by the autumn of 1820.

The Pisan Carnival, which ended on the day after St Valentine's day, gave them an early chance to see the city take to the streets in festive mood. The place filled with 'scamps, raffs etc.' with tousled hair and torn shirts, many of them apparently university students. There were bargees, and beggars, and galley slaves cheerfully dressed in yellow and red cloth over their chains. The Italian notables showed a weakness for pink silk hats, large whiskers, twirling canes and white satin shoes, with party-coloured ribands in their buttonholes, which Mary perceived were symbols of nobility.[13] She found it all singularly garish, but Claire took a carriage and rode down the Lung'Arno with the Mason children, all of them shrieking with delight behind paper masks.[14]

After the excitement of the Carnival, Shelley and Mary settled down at the Casa Frassi. The new servant arrived on the 28th, and Claire kept full diary entries which record the discussions which became a regular feature of the Shelley–Mason households. The subjects were highly varied. On one day the interest centred around Locke's remark about the social persecution of intellectual dissenters: 'And where is the man to be found that can patiently prepare himself to bear the name of Whimsical, Sceptical, or Atheist which he is sure to meet with who does in the least scruple any of the Common opinions?' On another occasion Mrs Mason and Professor Vaccà discussed the powers of the human nose. On a third, they talked of Lord Edward Fitzgerald, the legendary republican Irish aristocrat who had been executed for plotting a mass assassination attempt against the English ministers in Dublin in 1798. In the light of subsequent news from England, this was an odd coincidence.[15]

The spell of fine weather broke, and during the last week of February Shelley was unwell again, despite the attentions of Vaccà. For Mary it was 'days of idleness and nursing'.[16] That this illness was entirely the effect of the Pisan climate seems unlikely. On 3 March, when he had recovered, Shelley immediately rode over to Livorno, where he stayed until the 6th, and having returned, wrote the following short letter to John and Maria Gisborne: 'My dear friends, I have written at a venture the letters which it seems to me are requisite. — I have ordered my Florence Banker to send you all that remains in his hands; you will receive it in a day or two & tell me the amount, & I will make up the deficiency from Pisa. – I enclose an outside calculation of the expenses at Naples calculated in ducats – I think it as well to put into the hands of Del Rosso or whoever engages to do the business 150 ducats. – or more, as you see occasion. – but on this you will favour me so far as to allow your judgement to regulate mine.'[17] Shelley's trip to Livorno had concerned the baby Elena, who was now 14 months old. For some reason it had now become necessary to administer further money in her connection, and Shelley had decided to take the Gisbornes into his confidence. That Mary was not told of these latest developments is shown by Shelley's next letter of 19 March, in which he refers to the use of a pseudonym to maintain secrecy: 'If it is necessary to *write* again on the subject of Del Rosso, address not *Medwin*, nor Shelley, but simply "Mr Jones".'[18]

Shelley's application for the services of a lawyer suggests that some complication had arisen in Naples, and it seems likely that this was connected with Elise Foggi's presence in Florence during January. Obviously more money was required for the support of the child: Shelley's letter makes it quite clear that the money was to be paid *by* the lawyer, (not to him, for any legal service) on account of – possibly disputed – 'expenses at Naples'. Despite the precautions for secrecy, there is no indication that either Elise or her husband were at this point engaged in anything approaching blackmail; yet from this time on Shelley's sense of responsibility towards the child seems to have become an increasing burden. Possibly one part of del Rosso's commission was to find new foster parents for Elena in Naples, or else confirm that those at No. 45 Vico Canale were satisfactory. This might also explain the subject of Shelley's other letters 'written at a venture'; but there is no definite evidence.

Why should Shelley have involved the Gisbornes in this business, while taking great precautions to keep it secret from Mary? Since the child was inextricably linked with Mary's miseries in Naples and Rome, it is not difficult to understand why he should want to keep further thought of it from her. He also wanted peace in his own household. His later decision to keep her own father's correspondence from her shows a similar kind of motive. The Gisbornes on the other hand, with their knowledge of Italy and their independence of mind, were in an extremely practical position to help him. Shelley would not have had much misgiving about their 'social prejudices' concerning an illegitimate offspring, considering as he did that Maria was both 'atheistic' and 'democratic'. In completely discounting social prejudice, Shelley may have been in the long run over-optimistic. But immediate practical aid and advice the Gisbornes did provide, and arrangements seemed to be running smoothly in March and April; Shelley after all was supporting the steam-boat.

Mary seemed blissfully unaware of these developments. She wrote to Maria Gisborne only of darning needles, arrowroot tea and little Percy's mild attack of measles. While she organized domestic affairs – the new servant, the cooking and the clothes at the Casa Frassi – Shelley and Claire were more frequently out roving through Pisa together. They had a brush with the ubiquitous Colonel Calicot Finch, who had now appeared in Tuscany. Shelley and Claire had spotted a long-legged gentleman with an umbrella pursuing a little dirty blacksmith's boy through the streets calling 'thief!' When he caught up with him, the gentleman shook the child by the collar, and roared at him 'with the greatest vehemence'. Shelley decided to intervene; but the umbrella man swung round and roared in turn at Shelley in Italian that it was none of his business. Mary continued the little scenario with evident amusement: 'A crowd collected – Claire twitched Shelley & remonstrated – Don Quixote did not like to leave the boy in thrawl but deafened by the tall strider's vociferations & overcome by Claire's importunities he departed – & then Claire out of breath with terror as you may well suppose said "for mercy's sake have nothing to do with those people it's the reverend Colonel Calicot Finch" so they escaped the attack.'[19] Subsequently Calicot Finch was 'impudent' to one of the university doctor's wives and was given his *congé*.[20] But on the whole life at Pisa suited them all, and by the end of the month they had moved to new and even more 'lightsome & spacious' rooms at the very top of the Casa Frassi overlooking the vista of the Arno. Mary wrote to Sophia Stacey in Rome, 'we shall remain here stationary until the end of May, when Mr.S is ordered to the Baths of Lucca, where we shall accordingly pass the summer – I am afraid that it does not accord with your plans, *bella Sofia*, to pass it there likewise: will not you also be one of the swallows to return to see his new most excellent and most gracious majesty [George IV] crowned?' Shelley added a poem: 'On a Dead Violet' and a post-script which countermanded Mary's tacit refusal of an invitation: 'When you come to Pisa continue to see us – Casa Frassi, Lung'Arno.'[21]

Apart from news of George IV's forthcoming coronation, letters and papers from England brought one highly dramatic story: the Cato Street conspiracy. Thistlewood and his four fellow-conspirators had been arrested on 23 February, on the very eve of their plot to assassinate Lord Liverpool's ministry in London. At the Casa Silva this provoked animated discussion for several days, the talk turning to the fate of conspirators in general. Madame Mason told a story of the Irish conspirator Jackson who 'swallowed a strong poison and expired in torture before his judges' rather than endanger his fellow-prisoners by an escape attempt. Then she mentioned a particular kind of poison – her knowledge originating from Tatty – which was both deadly and painless. Claire recorded: 'Talk with Madame M. of the Prussic Acid distilled from Laurel leaves which kills without pain in a few minutes.'[22] Shelley listened to this with great interest, and put it at the back of his mind.

Shelley's considered reaction to the Cato Street affair was anything but enthusiastic. He saw it as a victory for useless extremism which would only put the political intiative even further into the hands of the government. It was the final act of that tragedy which had begun with Peterloo – Thistlewood had publicly stated that revenge for the deaths at Peterloo was one of his objectives – and Shelley now saw the hopes for any immediate degree of democratic reform receding into an uncertain future. To Peacock he wrote: 'I see with deep regret in today's Papers the attempt to assassinate the Ministry. Every thing seems to conspire against Reform. – How Cobbett must laugh at the "resumption of gold payments". I long to see him. I have a motto on a ring in Italian – "Il buon tempo verra" – There is a tide both in public & in private affairs, which awaits both men & nations.'[23] For the rest of his life Shelley wore that ring, which promised the good times to come.

When Shelley wrote to Ollier to ask once more about *The Cenci* he made half-mocking inquiries. 'I hope you are not implicated in the late plot. – Not having heard from Hunt, I am afraid that he at least has something to do with it. – It is well known since the time of Jaffier that a conspirator has no time – to think about his friends.' It was a slightly bitter jest – that Hunt, who would not even publish political poems, might have involved himself in a political conspiracy was not exactly likely.[24]

It was only at the beginning of April that Shelley finally received letters from Hunt and Bessy Kent explaining that the silence of three months' duration was due to financial 'torments'. But this still did not explain or excuse Hunt's total failure to react to Shelley's stream of contributions during the autumn and winter, and Shelley asked pointedly after *The Cenci*, adding: 'I don't remember if I acknowledged the receipt of [your] "Robin Hood" – no more did you of "Peter Bell". There's tit for tat! . . . Then on my side is the letter to Carlile, in which I must tell you I was considerably interested.'[25]

Shelley was no longer talking of coming to England; instead he returned to the old invitation for Hunt to come to Italy. Two weeks later, on 20 April, he also issued an invitation to Hogg with whom he had not corresponded for over a year. He wanted Hogg to come for the summer and to stay until the beginning of the law term in November. He was obviously serious, discussing the best mode of travel which was by coach to Marseilles, and then by boat to Livorno. He nostalgically recalled old friends. 'Do you ever see the Boinvilles now? Or Newton? If so, tell them, especially Mrs Boinville, that I have not forgotten them. I wonder none of them stray to this Elysian climate, and, like the sailors of Ulysses, eat the lotus and remain as I have done.'[26] When Hogg eventually replied from Garden Court, it was to say that the coronation prevented such a visit for that year, 'though I should like to see Percy Shelley the younger, and to steal behind some laurel bush where you are singing shrilly like a king; but that cannot be'.[27]

A third invitation sent in April, and the only one that bore fruit, was a repetition of Shelley's demand that Tom Medwin should move south from Geneva. He had now heard that Medwin was living with a brother-officer, Edward Williams, who like him was retired from the army in India on half pay. Shelley extended the invitation to Williams, and to his beautiful wife Jane with faintly ribald good humour. 'I hope, if they come to Italy, I may see the lovely lady & your friend. – Though I have never had the ague, I have found these sort of beings, especially the former, of infinite service in the maladies to which I am subject. . . . Forgive me joking on what all poets ought to consider a sacred subject.' But even Medwin and the Williamses did not come for several months.

In the new spacious apartments at the Casa Frassi, Shelley had at last established a completely private study for himself, which he had been missing ever since he left the airy sunlit cell at Villa Valsovano. He already had on hand the outline of his 'octavo on reform', and a scattered collection of political lyrics left over from the autumn. The news of Cato Street had been balanced at the beginning of April by unexpected good tidings of a successful insurrection of republicans in Madrid, and the proclamation of the liberal constitution of 1812 throughout the Spanish peninsula. The motto on his ring seemed true, and Shelley half thought of going to Madrid for the winter.[28] Mary eagerly expressed both their feelings: 'The inquisition is abolished – The dungeons opened & the Patriots pouring out – This is good. I should like to be in Madrid now.'[29] The talk was animated at Casa Silva.

The political news helped to steady his attention. What little writing Shelley had already produced at Pisa during March and April was spoilt by diffuseness and marked by an extreme but aimless violence of language and metaphor. Partly this was a reaction from the intense creative period of the previous three months. His powers now seemed to be turning over too fast, without properly engaging with solid or deeply felt subject-matter. The language seemed to expend energies of disgust and hatred on itself until it was performing an almost purgative, therapeutic function. In 'The Sensitive Plant', a poem traditionally associated with Shelley's first impressions of Lady Mountcashell, the autumnal and winter imagery reaches a peculiar pitch of ugliness and horror.

And plants, at whose names the verse feels loath,
Filled the place with a monstrous undergrowth,
Prickly, and pulpous, and blistering, and blue,
Livid, and starred with a lurid dew.

And agarics, and fungi, with mildew and mould
Started like mist from the wet ground cold;
Pale, fleshy, as if the decaying dead
With a spirit of growth had been animated!

Spawn, weeds, and filth, a leprous scum,
Made the running rivulet thick and dumb,
And at its outlet flags huge as stakes
Dammed it up with roots knotted like water-snakes. . . .

For Winter came: the wind was his whip:
One choppy finger was on his lip:
He had torn the cataracts from the hills
And they clanked at his girdle like manacles [30]

In these verses, Shelley felt that Spring was indeed far behind, and they contain much of the personal anger, revulsion and despair that he refused to acknowledge or give way to in his letters.

Another lengthy but unfinished poem, dated in April, was an even more grotesque and shapeless piece of writing, 'A Vision of the Sea'. It describes a tempest in which a boat – for a perhaps autobiographical reason carrying wild tigers, together with the familiar figure of a mother with child at breast – is wrecked and overwhelmed. The stormy sea is inhabited by sea-snakes and sharks. The whole fragment reads like a piece of 'automatic' or dream writing. Vaguely one can distinguish familiar shapes, like Henry Reveley's steam-boat used as image to describe a tiger and a sea monster fighting in the foam:

the whirl and the splash
As of some hideous engine whose brazen teeth smash
The thin winds and soft waves into thunder; the screams
And hissings crawl fast o'er the smooth ocean-streams,
Each sound like a centipede.[31]

The painful and empty brilliance of this excruciated writing was perhaps partly symptomatic of the kind of 'bad nervous attacks' which Mary noted briefly in her journal and letters during these weeks.[32] These probably took the form of hysterical outbreaks, usually preceded by particularly bad and vivid nightmares, of the kind that Mary much later described in detail in 1822; or the sort of sudden overwhelming nervous seizures which Shelley himself alluded to during his work on the 'Catalogue of Dreams' in 1815. There is no indication that they were epileptic; or even the kind of nephritic convulsions Thornton Hunt had once witnessed at Hampstead, but they give some indication of the hidden strains under which he was living.

Shelley slowly returned to the political theme, and picked up the thread of *A Philosophical Review of Reform*, continuing it into three chapters, which together form a substantial essay of 20,000 words. At the same time, he began to draft as a kind of parallel text, a formal 'Ode to Liberty'. It began by celebrating the Spanish Rebellion, and then described the growth of Liberty throughout human history from the pre-Promethean period, to Athens, and finally to the revolutions in France, South America and Europe during Shelley's own lifetime. The prose work and the poem cross at several points, and Shelley worked steadily at both for the rest of April and May. The essay was ready for a prospective publisher by 26 May, when Shelley again wrote to Hunt about it.[33] The ode was sent to Ollier for inclusion in the *Prometheus* volume.

By a *philosophical* view, Shelley meant that he intended to study the world history of political change and revolution, and the corresponding evolution in men's ideas concerning their own intellectual, social and religious freedom. He believed that the gradual emergence of Liberty in human thought and institutions was a recognizable 'law' of social development. This had nothing to do with a belief in material progress, nor did it discount the fact that terrible political 'winters' and cycles of tyrannical and bloody reaction frequently intervened. Shelley normally identified such periods of reaction with the triumph of imperialisms which included the Roman Empire, the Catholic Church, the Spanish Slave Empire in South America and the Indies, the Turkish Empire and the European despotisms of the eighteenth century.

Nevertheless the gradual change to more and more liberated forms of life and government he believed to be a historical *necessity*, and as such capable of study and acceleration. This broad argument forms the substance of his first chapter, and it includes in its scope reference to China, India, Persia, North and South America, the Jews in Palestine, the Turks, Greece, Syria and Egypt; and France, Germany, Italy and Spain. The argument settled most sharply on Europe as the current focus of historical change, and within Europe, on England – 'the particular object for the sake of which these general considerations have been stated'. England, Shelley believed, was to be considered in this sense 'at a crisis in its destiny'.[34] In this first chapter Shelley also stated his belief in the connection – again, philosophically speaking, the *necessary* connection – between periods of national upheaval and social revolution, and periods of outstanding literary greatness. 'For the most unfailing herald, or companion, or follower, of an universal employment of the sentiments of a nation to the production of beneficial change is poetry, meaning by poetry an intense and impassioned power of communicating intense and impassioned impressions respecting man and nature.'[35]

Shelley was not, in sociological terms, very specific about the nature of this connection. He did not say that great literature actually produced great revolutions; or vice versa. He seemed rather to feel that the two ran a mysteriously parallel course – 'herald, or companion, or follower' – and that the common factor was not so much direct social causation or didactic intent, but a certain quality of imaginative power, as it were, 'let loose'.

This was a controversial assertion, for there is clearly a case for arguing the opposite, that great periods of literature are only produced by periods of national stability which frequently occur in the very midst of an authoritarian or imperialist régime. Shelley cited as part of his historical case, the great dramatists and philosophers of fourth-century Athens; 'Shakespeare and Lord Bacon and the great writers of the age of Elizabeth and James 1st'; the painters and poets of the Italian republics of the Lombard league *before* the domination of the Medicis in Florence; and finally the English poets and philosophers of his own age, which he defined as dating from the French Revolutionary period of the 1790s. There is too some evidence that Shelley felt the four books of the New Testament and some of the earliest Apostolic and Apocalyptic writings, all produced in Asia Minor during the first century AD, also served in this argument and 'heralded' the collapse of the Roman Empire.[36] Altogether he makes this a powerful position, and it may subsequently be found developed in the work of later nineteenth-century theorists of literature and society, notably Arnold, Taine and Marx.

Turning to his English contemporaries, whom Shelley believed passionately, and surely rightly, occupied one of the great 'moments' of literature, he tried to define more carefully the operations of the forces of imagination which he understood to be at work. Two points are specially remarkable about what he wrote. First, that not only poets but many other classes of imaginative writer are included in his description. Second, that the *conscious intention* of a writer, or even his formal philosophic and political loyalties, did not in the end affect their inevitable tendency to serve 'the interests of liberty'. This was later to be the position of Marx.

The persons in whom this power takes its abode may often, as far as regards many portions of their nature, have little tendency to the spirit of good of which it is the minister. But although they may deny and abjure, they are yet compelled to serve that which is seated on the throne of their own soul. And whatever systems they may have professed by support, they actually advance the interests of liberty.

It is impossible to read the productions of our most celebrated writers, whatever may be their system relating to thought or expression, without being startled by the electric life which there is in their words. They measure the circumference or sound the depths of human nature with a comprehensive and all-penetrating spirit at which they are themselves perhaps most sincerely astonished, for it is less their own spirit than the spirit of their age.

They are the priests of an unapprehended inspiration, the mirrors of gigantic shadows which futurity casts upon the present; the words which express what they conceive not; the trumpet which sings to battle and feels not what it inspires; the influence which is moved not, but moves. Poets and philosophers are the unacknowledged legislators of the world.[37]

The idea that poets should be the legislators was not a new one. It may be found explicitly stated as early as George Puttenham's *Arte of Englishe Poesie* (c. 1585), or as late as Samuel Johnson's *Rasselas* (1759). Shelley's innovation was to see that they were 'unacknowledged': not merely unacknowledged by politicians and businessmen, which was obvious; but unknowing, unaware of their historical role, *themselves*. It was the writers who 'are themselves perhaps most sincerely astonished'; they *themselves* did not apprehend the true source of their inspiration and its ultimate social effect.

The most difficult, and in effect the most metaphysical idea in Shelley's analysis, was the idea of the writer as a mirror of the future. His image is complicated: writers are 'the mirrors of gigantic *shadows* which futurity casts upon the *present*'. There is nothing here about the conscious intention of a writer in predicting new inventions or social institutions; nor about the writer as some kind of clairvoyant. It is rather that in what the great writer produces naturally, the future pressures and contradictions and achievements of his society are *unconsciously expressed*. The writer is a kind of tuning-fork for a melody yet to be composed.

This difficult and sophisticated idea of Shelley's can be seen at work at a more personal level in something he wrote to Peacock during May. Commenting on Peacock's unexpected marriage, he remarked thoughtfully: 'I was very much amused by your laconic account of the affair. It is altogether extremely like the *denouement* of one of your own novels, and as such serves to a theory I once imagined, that in everything any man ever wrote, spoke, acted, or imagined, is contained, as it were the allegorical idea of his own future life, as the acorn contains the oak.'[38] The argument can be seen – itself an acorn – already emerging in the prose prefaces of *The Revolt of Islam* and *Prometheus Unbound*. Several months later Shelley used a simplified version of it as his peroration to a magazine article written for Peacock's benefit. This was the famous passage in his *A Defence of Poetry*.

Chapter II of *A Philosophical View of Reform* was entitled 'On the Sentiment of the Necessity of Change'. In it Shelley examined at length the outstanding features of the political and social conditions in England in 1819–20 which had created 'the dilemma of submitting to a despotism which is notoriously gathering like an avalanche year by year, or taking the risk of something which it must be confessed bears the aspect of revolution'.[39] He discussed the subject under several heads: the shift of the 'real constitutional presence' of the majority away from parliamentary representation; the corruption in the new financial system of 'Public Credit', the national debt and capital investment; the increase in the average daily hours of agricultural and manufacturing labour which corresponded to a severe decrease in real worth of the average daily wage; the class interest enshrined in the fashionable theories of Malthusian population control; the distinction between property acquired through 'labour, industry, skill' and that acquired through inheritance and capital investment; and finally the issue of universal male and female suffrage.

Shelley set out these issues with a skill and simplicity which can only be bettered in the professional writings of the Smithians and Benthamites of the period, and the pages of the *Westminster Review*. He drew conclusions from it which in their political penetration and courageous originality are rare in England until the writings of the Chartist period and the early work of Engels.★

Concerning the kind of exploitation of labour through capital investment, Shelley wrote:

★ The growth of a full economic analysis of the forces which were transforming the conditions of the English lower classes was painfully slow at this time. The main landmarks were David Ricardo's *Principles of Political Economy and Taxation* (1817); James Mill's *Elements of Political Economy* (1821) and the radical journal the *Westminster Review* founded by Bentham, Mill, Brougham and others in 1824. The 1830s brought the on-the-spot *Blue Book* reports of Sir Edwin Chadwick and Anthony Ashley Cooper, 7th Earl of Shaftesbury. These separate analytic traditions combined in the two classics of the late-Chartist period, Frederick Engels's *The Condition of the Working Class in England* (1844) and John Stuart Mill's *Principles of Political Economy* (1848). Both J.S. Mill and Engels acknowledged the profound influence of Shelley in their twenties. For a general survey, see J.L. and B. Hammond, *The Skilled Labourer* (1919); E. Halevy, *The Growth of Philosophic Radicalism* (1928) and J.P. Guinn, *Shelley's Political Thought* (1969).

One of the vaunted effects of this system is to increase the national industry: that is, to increase the labours of the poor and those luxuries of the rich which they supply; to make a manufacturer [*factory hand*] work 16 hours where he only worked 8; to turn children into lifeless and bloodless machines at an age when otherwise they would be at play before the cottage doors of their parents; to augment indefinitely the proportion of those who enjoy the profit of labour. ... The consequences of this transaction have been the establishment of a new aristocracy, which has its basis in fraud ... an aristocracy of attorneys and excisemen and directors and government pensioners, usurers, stock jobbers, country bankers, with their dependents and descendants.[40]

Of the decline in the real 'constitutional presence' of the people, Shelley began from the calculation that the Cromwellian Revolution, as enshrined in the new electorate of the Long Parliament in 1641, had signified that one man in every eight carried the democratic power of the vote. This had been a good start towards 'actual representation'. But the figure had got worse, not better, in the following 170 years. By the 'Glorious Revolution' of 1688, it had fallen to something in the region of one man in twenty carrying the vote. This was because 'population increased, a greater number of hands were employed in the labour of agriculture and commerce, [unrepresented] towns rose where villages had been ... a fourth class therefore appeared in the nation, the unrepresented multitude'.[41] By 1819 Shelley reckoned the ratio of enfranchisement had plunged to something like 'one in several hundreds', and that the House of Commons was so far from being even a 'virtual representation' of the English people that politically England could be accurately described as a despotic oligarchy. '... A sufficiently just measure is afforded of the degree in which a country is enslaved or free, by the consideration of the relative numbers of individuals who are admitted to the exercise of political rights.' By this measure, England was neither democratic nor free, and without reform became less so every year.

One of Shelley's most radical positions was revealed in his analysis of the 'national debt' which had been contracted over the period of the American and Napoleonic wars, the interest of which was being paid back in the form of national taxes at the rate of £45 million a year. Shelley argued that this money was in effect only a war investment by the rich and propertied class, and that it was neither just nor constitutional to attempt to pay off the *interest* on it by a national tax affecting all classes. There was no justice in the poor paying for the war profits of the rich. Shelley's solution was to dissolve the debt at a stroke: no profits or interest at all should be paid, and the remaining capital sum should be dispersed among the original stock-holders and investors who would have to share their own losses: 'It would be a mere transfer among persons of property.

Such a gentleman must lose a third of his estate, such a citizen a fourth of his money in the funds; the persons who borrowed would have paid, and the juggling and complicated system of paper finance be suddenly at an end.'[42] This severely egalitarian argument reflected Shelley's view on the fundamental injustice of vast inherited properties, and of rich personal estates created out of capital investment profits.

Private property as such, and inheritance, he accepted within certain vigorously defined limits of social justice. Only the active, productive member of society had a real right to property:

> Every man whose scope in society has a plebian and intelligible utility, whose personal exertions are more valuable to him than his capital; every trades man who is not a monopolist, all surgeons and physicians and those mechanics and editors and literary men and artists, and farmers, all those persons whose profits spring from honourably and honestly exerting their own skill and wisdom or strength. ... Labour, industry, economy, skill, genius, or any similar powers honourably and innocently exerted are the foundations of one description of property, and all true political institutions ought to defend every man in the exercise of his discretion with respect to property so acquired.[43]

Against this he set the established view of property which he regarded as abhorrent:

> But there is another species of property which has its foundation in usurpation, or imposture, or violence, without which, by the nature of things, immense possessions of gold or land could never have been accumulated. Of this nature is the principal part of the property enjoyed by the aristocracy and by the great fundholders, the great majority of whose ancestors never either deserved it by their skill and talents, or acquired and created it by their personal labour. . . .[44]

There was only one genuine and just source of property:

> Labour and skill and the immediate wages of labour and skill is a property of the most sacred and indisputable right and the foundation of all other property.[45]

With this broad analysis of the conditions of labour, wages, property and electoral franchise in England in 1819 set out, Shelley summarized the conclusions of his second chapter. There were five:

> (1) That the majority of the people of England are destitute and miserable, ill-clothed, ill-fed, ill-educated.

(2) That they know this, and that they are impatient to procure a reform of the cause of their abject and wretched state.

(3) That the cause of this peculiar misery is the unequal distribution which, under the form of the national debt, has been surreptitiously made of the products of their labour and the products of the labour of their ancestors; for all property is the produce of labour.

(4) That the cause of that cause is a defect in the government.

(5) That . . . every enlightened and honourable person, whatever may be the imagined interest of his peculiar class, ought to excite them to the discovery of the true state of the case and to the temperate but irresistible vindication of their rights.[46]

It is clear from this chapter how Shelley's powers of political thought and analysis had developed steadily from the heady days of *Proposals for an Association* and *A Declaration of Rights* (1812) and through the first dawning of an economic analysis in the Hermit of Marlow pamphlets of 1817. Far from declining into the Whig–liberal background from which he had come, Shelley had moved steadily – though sometimes painfully – into a more and more truly radical position. He had now come to realize the implications of capital exploitation, the real need for a mass democratic movement, and the necessary commitment of writers and educated men to address themselves to the people, as well as to their own class.

Shelley's final chapter applied these considerations to the immediate political situation in the spring of 1820. It is entitled 'Probable Means'. He was thinking in terms of a working political strategy for radicals in England over the period of perhaps the next four or five years: 'our present business is with the difficulties and unbending realities of actual life'. The fundamental principle of the strategy is what may be called the principle of graduated response.

His first point was simply that parliamentary reform was necessary at once: 'That representative assembly called the House of Commons ought questionless to be *immediately* nominated by the great mass of the people.' But he was by no means certain that this immediate reform should attempt to make the franchise universal at a single stroke. He felt that the Benthamites 'might seem somewhat immature' in their call for immediate female suffrage. Perhaps this hesitation is surprising. But Shelley was now quite literally considering the case for universal male and female suffrage in the year 1820, and considering the lack of general education in England, it is understandable.* However: 'should my opinion be the result of despondency, the writer of these pages would be the last to withhold

---

* A Bill granting equal voting rights to men and women was not put through the English House of Commons until 1928.

his vote from any system which might tend to an equal and full development of the capacities of all living beings'. If the government of the day should yield to even part of these demands, they should be accepted as strategically the quickest way to achieve the full reform: 'let us be contented with a limited *beginning* . . . it is no matter how slow, gradual, and cautious be the change; we shall demand more and more with firmness and moderation, never anticipating but never deferring the moment of successful opposition . . .'.[47] Shelley knew, as in his disagreements with Hunt, that this could be confused with a mere liberal outlook in point of day-to-day tactics. But the strategy behind it was both severely realistic and intensely radical. '. . . Nothing is more idle than to reject a limited benefit because we cannot without great sacrifice obtain an unlimited one.' Once the government could be moved, they would never be able to stop again. This was the first level of Shelley's principle of graduated response.

However, in reality Shelley believed that after the failure of the 1817 and 1819 agitations, the likelihood of the government moving forward was already past, and that the two parties were already too polarized. This had been grimly illustrated by Peterloo, and by Cato Street. Such a consideration brought the second level of graduated response. It was quite clear: 'If the House of Parliament obstinately and perpetually refuse to concede any reform, my vote is for universal suffrage and equal representation.' This should be achieved by a strategy of constant legal and parliamentary confrontation, ceaseless intellectual attack and a programme of public meetings and civil disobedience. Shelley's outline of this campaign is a most remarkable description of precisely the methods which afterwards succeeded in changing the political face of England in the nineteenth and twentieth centuries.

> For this purpose government ought to be defied, in cases of questionable result, to prosecute for political libel. All questions relating to the jurisdiction of magistrates and courts of law respecting which any doubt could be raised ought to be agitated with indefatigable pertinacity. Some two or three of the popular leaders have shown the best spirit in this respect;* they only want system and cooperation. The tax-gatherer ought to be compelled in every practicable instance to distrain, while the right to impose taxes . . . is formally contested by an overwhelming multitude of defendants before the common law. . . .[48]

While this campaign advanced, petitions 'couched in the actual language of the petitioners' should load the tables of the House of Commons. Poets, philosophers

---

* Here Shelley was clearly thinking of the recent trials of William Hone, Richard Carlile, Henry Hunt, Sir Francis Burdett and Thomas Wooler of the *Black Dwarf*; and also no doubt of the failure of his own editor and publisher to appear in the lists.

and artists should remonstrate directly with the government, and also by writing 'memorials' showing the 'inevitable connection between national prosperity and freedom, and the cultivation of imagination and the cultivation of scientific truth'. Shelley specifically named Godwin, Hazlitt, Bentham and Leigh Hunt as obvious candidates for this task; and the very book he was writing fitted into such a category.[49]

Finally the radical patriots and working-class leaders should help to organize the mass contribution to such a campaign:

> He will urge the necessity of exciting the people frequently to exercise their right of assembling in such limited numbers as that all present may be actual parties to the proceedings of the day. Lastly, if circumstances had collected a more considerable number as at Manchester on the memorable 16th of August, if the tyrants command their troops to fire upon them or cut them down unless they disperse, he will exhort them peacably to risk the danger, and to expect without resistance the onset of the cavalry, and wait with folded arms the event of the fire of the artillery. . . . The soldier is a man and an Englishman. This unexpected reception would probably throw him back upon a recollection of the true nature of the measures of which he was made the instrument, and the enemy might be converted into the ally.[50]

Here, once again, was the passive resistance doctrine of *The Mask of Anarchy*, though with the shrewd addition that given all the other agitation surrounding the circumstances of such a confrontation, the common soldier was highly likely to join such a demonstration himself. This has always proved the crucial shift of power which has triggered every successful city revolution in Western and Eastern Europe since 1792.

Shelley was writing with his eye on the actualities of English politics, and he knew that other confrontations such as Peterloo could not be indefinitely sustained by passive resistance. Such acts of physical repression brought a nation to the very brink of violent revolution.

This recognition led him irresistibly to the third stage of his strategy of graduated response, which concludes Chapter III. The prospect of bloodshed and violence appalled Shelley, and the horrors of civil war and military reaction so vividly described in *The Revolt of Islam* remained with him in painful clarity, and he enumerated them once more at length. But he had always recognized that there were two chariots, and if one could not be taken, then the other was demanded by necessity. He faced and stated the conclusion with simplicity and great intellectual integrity. 'The last resort of resistance is undoubtedly insurrection. The right of insurrection is derived from the employment of armed force to counteract the will of the nation.'[51] The essay ended on a note of muted but determined hope and triumph. 'When the people shall have obtained, by whatever means, the victory over their oppressors, and when persons appointed by them shall have taken their seats in the Representative Assembly of the nation and assumed the control of public affairs according to constitutional rules, there will remain the great task. . . .'[52]

Shelley's *A Philosophical View of Reform* is undoubtedly one of the most remarkable political documents written by any poet of the Romantic period.* It offers not only the broad ground-plan of a coherent philosophy of political change and evolution but a particularized, humane and intelligent description of conditions in England at the end of the first crucial phase of the Industrial Revolution. It combines a clear-headed and determined commitment to radical and egalitarian principles with a vivid and practical grasp of political realities. Even more than this, in its first and its third chapters it proposes two highly original and important arguments. The first is an attempt to define the relationship between imaginative literature and social and political change. The second is in effect a blueprint for a political programme designed to achieve radical change against varying degrees of opposition and repression. In this sense the work is not merely 'A Philosophical View of Reform', but an actual philosophy of revolution, and specifically a philosophy of *English* revolution. This 'Octavo on Reform' which Shelley was completing at Casa Frassi in mid-May of 1820 is one of the great examples of his powers of self-education and intellectual resilience, and of the unusually broad range of his imaginative gifts.

During the first week of May he had written to Peacock that he had little current news of immediate events except through the *Galignani's Messenger*, a Paris paper which printed extracts from the *Courier*. 'From those accounts it appears probable that there is but little unanimity in the mass of the people; and that a civil war impends from the success of ministers and the exasperation of the poor. I wait anxiously for your Cobbetts. . . . Cobbett persuaded you, you persuaded me, and I have persuaded the Gisbornes that the British funds are very insecure. They come to England accordingly to sell out their property.'[53] After their departure, Shelley adopted a large folio encyclopedia which Reveley had left for his use, and Claire observed him wandering abstractedly through Pisa deep in one of the huge volumes, with another somehow tucked away under his arm. He was probably gathering population statistics.[54]

On 26 May, after a brief visit with Tatty to the baths at Casciano, hidden in the mountains among its sprouting chestnut trees, Shelley returned to Pisa with his finished manuscript and Mary transcribed it. He announced it carefully to

---

* To obtain an enlightening and sometimes not unamusing comparative estimate of the liveliness and progressiveness of Shelley's thought, see the useful collection *Political Tracts of Wordsworth, Coleridge and Shelley*, edited by R. J. White, Cambridge University Press, 1953.

Hunt: 'One thing I want to ask you – Do you know any bookseller who would publish for me an octavo volume entitled "A Philosophical View of Reform". It is boldly but temperately written – & I think readable. – It is intended for a kind of standard book for the philosophical reformers politically considered, like Jeremy Bentham's something, but different and perhaps more systematic. – I would send it sheet by sheet. Will you ask & think for me?'[55] But Hunt did nothing, and the book was not published until one hundred years later. As far as Shelley's later reputation as a radical poet and writer was concerned, it was perhaps the most damaging suppression of all his works, and one of the very few that Mary herself later connived at.[56]

Shelley also wrote to Hunt along the same lines about a book of poems. 'I wish to ask you if you know of any bookseller who would like to publish a little volume of *popular songs* wholly political, & destined to awaken & direct the imagination of the reformers. I see you smile – but answer my question.'[57] Again Hunt did not answer and like the octavo on reform, with which it was intended to form a pair, this anthology never appeared during Shelley's life. Indeed these political poems were never published, as he intended, in a single collection. From Shelley's notebooks of the period September 1819 to May 1820 it is possible to reconstruct fairly confidently what the contents of the lost volume *Popular Songs* (1820) by P.B. Shelley, would have been if it ever reached the willing hands of Carlile, or Sherwin, or even J. Johnson of St Paul's Churchyard. The contents page would have read something like as follows (the dates of actual first publication are appended in parentheses):

'The Mask of Anarchy' (1832)
'Lines Written During the Castlereagh Administration' (1832)
'Song to the Men of England' (1839)
'Similes for 2 Political Characters' (1832)
'What Men Gain Fairly' (1839)
'A New National Anthem' (1839)
'Sonnet: England 1819' (1839)
'Ballad of the Starving Mother' (1926/1970)[58]

It also seems possible that Shelley might have considered putting two other more formal pieces in this collection, as they were written from the same source of inspiration and directed to the same ends. But these two more rapidly found their way into print elsewhere:

'Ode to Liberty' (1820)
'Ode to the West Wind' (1820)

Even without these last two poems, the collection would have been a substantial one of more than 500 lines of verse. It was a very great loss to contemporary poetry, and perhaps to contemporary politics.

> Men of England, wherefore plough
> For the lords who lay ye low?
> Wherefore weave with toil and care
> The rich robes your tyrants wear? . . .
>
> The seed ye sow, another reaps;
> The wealth ye find, another keeps;
> The robe ye weave, another wears;
> The arms ye forge, another bears. . . .
>
> With plough and spade, and hoe and loom,
> Trace your grave, and build your tomb,
> And weave your winding-sheet, till fair
> England be your sepulchre.[59]

After months of prevarication and guarded refusals to publish on the part of Ollier and Hunt, there was evidence of Shelley's growing anger, and by the summer of 1820 the thought of finishing with Ollier altogether had more than once crossed his mind. Hunt he would not break with, for Hunt was also a close personal friend, perhaps his closest in England, and he appreciated the difficulties of a literary editor who had his whole paper to consider in questions of prosecution. Instead, he used Hunt to vent his feelings about Ollier. 'As to Ollier – I am afraid his demerits are very heavy – they must have been so before *you* could have perceived them. . . . I am afraid that *I* to a certain degree am in his power; there being no other bookseller, upon whom I can depend for publishing any of my works; though if by any chance they should become popular, he would be as tame as a lamb. And in fact they are all rogues.' But even in his irritation and frustration, Shelley could not forget the political régime under which English publishers had to work. 'It is less the character of the individual than the situation in which he is placed which determines him to be honest or dishonest, perhaps we ought to regard an honest bookseller, or an honest seller of anything else in the present state of human affairs as a kind of Jesus Christ. The system of society as it exists at present must be overthrown from the foundations with all its superstructure of maxims & of forms before we shall find anything but disappointment in our intercourse with any but a few select spirits.'[60] Hunt, although no doubt counting himself as a select spirit, may well have winced a little at this short blast of Shelley's radicalism. As Shelley, no doubt, intended.

However, by the beginning of June a number of factors had combined to make Shelley more philosophical about his publications. In the first place, news had arrived that Ollier had after all brought out an edition of *The Cenci*. What is more, it was selling really quite well. It was reviewed widely through the spring and summer, and although there was a certain amount of talk about 'a dish of carrion', the reviews were lengthy and had a good deal of enthusiasm for the 'power' and 'shocking character' of the drama, while there were no personal attacks. Articles appeared at the end of April in the *Monthly Magazine*, the *Literary Gazette*, the *London Monthly Critical and Dramatic Review* and the *Theatrical Inquisitor*. This last was especially significant, because it catered for a broad theatre-going London audience and its reviewer wrote as one who had no previous knowledge of Shelley's work as a poet. Moreover the review was radiant: 'As a first dramatic effort "The Cenci" is unparalleled for the beauty of every attribute with which drama can be endowed.'[61] In May reviews followed from the *New Monthly Magazine*, the *Edinburgh Monthly Review*, the *London Magazine*, and a further panegyric from Hunt's pen in the *Indicator*.[62] Of all Shelley's publications, this was undoubtedly proving the most popular, and there was immediate talk of a second edition. Indeed, for several weeks Shelley was under the impression that Galignani had published a pirate edition in Paris for eager continental readers; but in fact he had only advertised the London edition in his paper.[63] Yet a second edition of *The Cenci* did eventually appear in 1821. Shelley had never judged his market better.

In the second place, Ollier was – as Shelley had suspected – considerably mollified by these signs of popular approval. He contracted definitely with Shelley to bring out a really handsome edition of *Prometheus Unbound* in the late summer of 1820, and he also agreed to print a small collection of short poems with it. These were to include the 'Ode to the West Wind', 'The Sensitive Plant', 'A Vision of the Sea' and 'Ode to Liberty'. Shelley continued to send other short poems for inclusion during June and July.* John Gisborne agreed to act as Shelley's proof-reader in London, and eventually became his *de facto* literary agent.[64] On top of this, Ollier had apparently intimated to Hunt that he was after all considering an anonymous publication of *Peter Bell the Third*.[65] Only by the autumn was it clear that nothing could be expected in this quarter, though Mary herself wrote asking the Gisbornes secretly to find an alternative publisher.[66]

The loss of *The Mask of Anarchy*, *A Philosophical View of Reform* and the

---

* The volume eventually appeared as *Prometheus Unbound, A Lyrical Drama, in 4 Acts, with Other Poems* in August 1820. Although accurate figures are unknown, it is reputed not to have sold more than a score of copies. But in June 1820, the name of *The Cenci* was on many readers' lips in London, and the prospect looked fair.

Popular Songs (and the actual loss of *Peter Bell*) now seemed a subject for regret, but for acquiescence. Shelley had already yielded in principle at the end of May, though with a shrug. 'It seems that I have no other alternative but to keep in with [Ollier], he having so many of my writings in his possession. . . . So I had better make the best of a bad business. . . . I must say that he has not cheated me in the commission, – but on the contrary I offered him 20 per cent, & he will accept only 10 –. So much for Ollier.'[67] Not Jesus Christ perhaps, but at least an honest Pharisee.

But there was another more personal reason for Shelley's acquiescence. For in June, after the quiet spring months at Casa Frassi, a private crisis broke over the Shelley household which required his full attention. They had intended to move for the summer to the Bagni di Lucca at about this time, but events dictated otherwise. On 9 June, according to her certificate, little Elena Adelaide Shelley died at Naples. So far as appears from Shelley's correspondence with the Gisbornes, this news did not reach him until some time between 2 and 7 July, although he knew of a 'severe fever' by 30 June. But it appears to have reached Paolo Foggi within a matter of a very few days. The affair that had previously been settled by an arrangement to administer 150 ducats now escalated into one of direct blackmail. On Monday, 12 June, the Shelleys were packing up to depart for Lucca when, by method unknown, news reached them of Paolo Foggi's threats and demands. Both Claire and Mary were now *au fait*. Claire entered in her diary: 'Bother & Confusion Packing up. – We sleep in Casa Silva. Oh Bother.' Mary entered simply 'Paolo' followed by a small drawing of a crescent moon.[68] The next day they returned to Casa Frassi while Shelley hastened over to consult Frederico del Rosso at Livorno. Claire entered: 'The king of England with all his merry men / Marched up a hill & then marched down again.'[69] Shelley returned the same evening. The next day Tatty came back from the baths at Casciano, probably to give advice at this difficult moment.*

It was decided that the move to Lucca was impossible and that they would have to stay near del Rosso in Livorno. Shelley had already inquired of the Gisbornes' servants about making over the Casa Ricci for their use. So, on the

---

* These cryptic entries by Mary and Claire are characteristic of the mysterious secrecy that always shrouded the manoeuvres of Paolo Foggi and the fate of Elena in all the extant personal documents of the Shelley household. Mary's moon symbol could refer equally to Claire herself (though elsewhere in Mary's journal she is represented by a sun symbol); to Elise Foggi; or to little Elena ('moon-child' – illegitimate child? 'moon-calf' – abortion?). But it is impossible to interpret either this – or Claire's nursery rhymes – with any certainty. Shelley's correspondence is equally delphic or circumlocutory on these matters; Paolo's motives, apart from greed, are reminiscent of Iago's; and the del Rosso papers have never been discovered. However in general there is a clear sense of the nervous tension and extreme irritability brought about by Shelley's difficulties over the illegitimate baby and what he called Paolo's 'infernal business'.

15th, they repacked and moved to Livorno, Claire being sent ahead with the child and the luggage in a *calèsse*. Percy Florence had diarrhoea, and they were all, according to Mary 'unhappy and discontented'.[70] Shelley moved into Henry's workshop study where he could be alone.

Two days later, however, del Rosso had reassured them, and things did not look quite so bad. Mary wrote to Maria Gisborne in London, explaining their presence at the Casa Ricci: 'We could not go to the baths of Lucca and finding it necessary to consult an attorney we thought of Del Rosso & came here – Are you pleased or vexed? – Our old friend Paolo was partly the cause of this – by entering into an infamous conspiracy against us – there were other circumstances which I shall not explain till we meet – That same Paolo is a most superlative rascal – I hope we have done with him but I know not – since as yet we are obliged to guess as to his accomplices.'[71] This letter clearly shows that the business with Paolo had expanded to the proportions of blackmail, and that Mary knew at least the basis of it. It would also appear that Paolo had been talking to other English in the Livorno colony.

On top of Paolo Foggi, Shelley was also being worried once more by the effect which Godwin's insistent demands for money were having on Mary. On 30 June, he wrote to the Gisbornes: 'Domestic peace I might have – I may have – if I see you, I shall have – but have not, for Mary suffers dreadfully from the state of Godwin's circumstances. I am very nervous, but better in general health. We have had a most infernal business with Paolo, whom, however, we have succeeded in crushing. I write from Henry's study, and I send you some verses I wrote the first day I came, which will show you that I struggle with despondency.'[72] Shelley was premature in supposing that Paolo, and whoever he had involved among the English, had been crushed. Nor did he yet have confirmation of Elena's death, though he grimly expected it.

The verse against despondency was his 'Letter to Maria Gisborne'. In it he drew kindly, epigrammatic portraits of his friends in London – Hunt, Hogg, Peacock, even Godwin was included, as a kind of mock-heroic Satan, 'greater none than he Though fallen – and fallen on evil times'. Shelley imagined the London streets in which they would now be walking about, and the same moon and stars over both of them, 'beautiful in every land'. But he could not forget other aspects:

But what see you beside? – a shabby stand
Of Hackney coaches – a brick house or wall
Fencing some lonely court, white with the scrawl
Of our unhappy politics; – or worse –
A wretched woman reeling by. . . .[73]

The poem is notable for its easy, talking manner, reminiscent of 'Julian and Maddalo', and its tight, purposeful grip on the physical details of the room in which Shelley wrote, Henry's study. He carefully enumerated screws, cones, grooved wooden blocks, machine designs in blue and yellow paint, a heap of rosin, a broken ink-glass, a tea-cup without handle, a paint box, a half-burnt match, a set of logarithm tables and a walnut bowl of mercury.

> And in this bowl of quicksilver – for I
> Yield to the impulse of an infancy
> Outlasting manhood – I have made to float
> A rude idealism of a paper boat: –
> A hollow screw with cogs – Henry will know
> The thing I mean and laugh at me. . . .[74]

Also enclosed as part of his letter was a cautious scheme to give Godwin £400, if the Gisbornes could first ascertain from legal papers if the sum would make any real difference to Godwin's overall situation. This offer was made as much to appease Mary as anything else, and Shelley himself was not very eager that the money should be released by the Gisbornes. He added in a postscript that she did not read: 'You know my situation; you know Godwin's implacable exactions, you know his boundless and plausible sophistry. On the other hand, if you can effect this compromise the benefits would be great.'[75] Wisely, the Gisbornes interpreted these conflicting directions correctly, and the gift was never made. It would certainly have made no lasting difference to Godwin, and would have deprived Shelley of about half a year's income. But his patience and generosity over Godwin were still extraordinary.

Consultation with del Rosso, and consideration of Godwin, led Shelley to review his whole financial position during July, a thankless task in which he was firmly encouraged by Mary. One of the first results were instructions to Hogg in his legal capacity to try to settle the large bill outstanding at Marlow. Another letter went to Messrs Baldwin the publishers of *Alastor* urging them to pay off the printer out of any profits – a piece of business more than four years outstanding.[76] Shelley embarked on a course of Lucretius which was taken in daily dosages with Mary.[77] But in the evening, he frequently took the chance to walk out from the Casa Ricci into Livorno with Claire.[78]

The early summer at the Casa Ricci saw a sharp decline in relations between Claire and Mary. On 4 July, some three weeks after their move from Pisa, things had become bad enough for Claire to note in her diary: 'Heigh-ho the Clare & the Mai/Find something to fight about every day . . .'.[79] For Claire and Shelley there had already been much strain earlier in the summer over Allegra. Doubtful reports of the child's situation had been received, and Claire had written directly to Byron threatening to intervene by going herself to Ravenna. At the end of April, a letter from Byron had been forwarded to Pisa by the Hoppners which was far from sympathetic. 'About Allegra,' Byron had written, 'I can only say to Claire – that I so totally disapprove of the mode of Children's treatment in their family, that I should look upon the Child as going into a hospital. Is it not so? Have they *reared* one? . . . I shall either send her to England, or put her in a Convent for education. . . . But the Child shall not quit me again to perish of Starvation, and green fruit, or be taught to believe that there is no Deity. Whenever there is convenience of vicinity and access, her Mother can always have her with her; otherwise no. It was so stipulated at the beginning.'[80]

Shelley had much difficulty in soothing Claire and keeping his own temper, but as ever, he found his own way of defending her to Byron. '[Claire] has consented to give up this journey to Ravenna. . . . When we meet I can explain to you some circumstances of misrepresentation respecting Allegra which, I think, will lead you to find an excuse for Claire's anxiety. What letters she writes to you I know not; perhaps they are very provoking; but at all events it is better to forgive the weak. I do not say – I do not think – that your solutions are unwise; only express them mildly – and pray don't *quote me.*'

Of the attacks upon his own household, he wrote with mild good humour, as he knew Byron would expect of him. 'I smiled at your protest about what you consider my creed. On the contrary, I think a regard to chastity is quite necessary, as things are, to a young female – that is, to her happiness – and at any time a good habit. As to Christianity – there I am vulnerable; though I should be as little inclined to teach a child disbelief, as belief, as a formal creed. You are misinformed, too, as to our system of physical education. . . .'[81]

On about 7 July – there is some uncertainty about the exact date of his letter – Shelley finally received the news that he had been dreading and he wrote to the Gisbornes about Elena Shelley's death, bitterly reproaching Paolo Foggi and the English at Livorno for their hatred and schemes and 'most prodigious falsehoods'. That evening Claire notes that she walked with Shelley. No further record of their conversation remains. 'As to us,' Shelley wrote to the Gisbornes, 'we are uncertain people who are chased by the spirit of our destiny from purpose to purpose, like clouds by the wind.'[82]

It is to these days of nagging domestic difficulties and secret gloom that Shelley's effusive and perhaps understandably sentimental lyrics 'The Cloud', and 'The Skylark' belong. They reach longingly for the idea of escape into a world of immortal and effortless creativity. Mary thought them extremely fine: 'It was on a beautiful summer evening, while wandering among the lanes whose myrtle-hedges were the bowers of the fireflies, that we heard the carolling of the skylark which inspired one of the most beautiful of his poems.' Both lyrics were dispatched to England just in time to be included in the printing of the *Prometheus* volume, probably on 12 July.[83] It is possible that Claire's acid note on the progress of the del Rosso lawsuit on 13 July contains a reference to 'The Skylark'; 'The Italians say to those who threaten to take the law, "Cantate cantate, e poi farete come la Cicala, scoppiarete" which alludes to the Cicada singing louder & louder if his stomach is rubbed until it finally hurts.'[84]

Shelley now turned to the more carefully controlled work of translating Homer's long 'Hymn to Mercury', and wrote to Peacock: 'the Libecchio here howls like a chorus of fiends all day, and the weather is just pleasant, – not at all hot, the days being very misty, and the nights divinely serene. I have been reading with much pleasure the Greek romances.'[85] There was of course nothing about del Rosso, or Elena, or Claire. But there was a book list – a Greek grammar and exercises for Mary, Godwin's *Answer to Malthus*, and optimistically, 'Six copies of the 2nd edt. of "Cenci" '.[86]

On the 15th began an odd fortnight of alternate shuttling by Shelley and Claire between Pisa and Livorno. Consultations were going on with the Masons at the Casa Silva, and there was talk of finding Claire a separate position and situation outside the Shelley household, and perhaps outside Italy. In the meantime, Shelley was looking for retired and discreet lodgings where they might pass the heat of the summer, since the Bagni di Lucca, with its large English population, was now out of the question. Shelley visited Pisa on the 15th and returned on the 17th; while Claire stayed at the Casa Silva from the 18th to the 20th, riding over at the end in a *calèsse* with Mrs Mason and the two children, which then returned the same evening with Shelley, who again stayed until the 25th.[87]

Shelley explained to the Gisbornes: 'We are about to take a villa about seven miles from Pisa – at least I think so. – Mary wishes for the mountains. Clare is yet with us, and is reading Latin and Spanish with great resolution. Poor thing! She is an excellent girl, though I don't think she will ever become a witch. Mary, who, you know, is always wise, has been lately very good. I wish she were as wise now as she will be at 45, or as misfortune has made me. She would then live on very good terms with Clare. – We hear from Paris that Clare's reception there, as an Englishwoman, is impossible: but our Irish friend [Helen Williams] is exerting herself to the utmost to discover some substitute. . . .' This was written as a postscript to a letter of Mary's, but Shelley said specifically that Mary had not read his 'transverse writing' – 'so take no notice of it in any letter intended for her inspection'. He had also enclosed another piece of secret writing, either a poem, or something in connection with del Rosso.[88] He still intended to keep Mary only partially informed of his affairs and feelings, and there were many inexplicable things in his correspondence at this time.

The scheme to get Claire away from the household was not abandoned. Various temporary measures were taken in August and September, until finally in October she was sent to Florence. This was to prove a separation as significant between Shelley and Claire, as that insisted upon by Mary in England during the spring of 1815. Shelley, as always, appeared deeply ambiguous towards these arrangements. He recognized that it was necessary for Claire to become independent, and he outwardly agreed and co-operated with Mary and the Masons when such arrangements were made. Yet he always contrived to see Claire at frequent intervals, and sometimes for several days at a time. In the private letters he wrote to her during October and November 1820, it is transparently clear that he missed her greatly, and was continually planning for her return. That a separation was finally brought about after two years together in Italy, was very largely the result of two circumstances: first, the mist of scandal that surrounded the del Rosso lawsuit; and second, the influence of Mrs Mason in her powerful personae as Lady Mountcashell and 'Minerva'.

During his absences at Pisa, Shelley somehow found time to write to John Keats in London. Sad news had reached him through the Gisbornes of Keats's first serious lung haemorrhage, which had occurred on the night after their visit to Hampstead of 22 June. He urged Keats to come to Italy to cure himself, and suggested his own household in Pisa or its environs. 'Mrs Shelley unites with myself in urging the request, that you would take up your residence with us.'[89]

He also wrote again to Medwin at Geneva. Shelley had heard that Medwin had been touring the Alps with the Williamses, and he repeated his invitation to come south, referring longingly to their freedom of movement which he himself had once enjoyed. 'How much I envy you, or rather how much I sympathise with your wandering. I have a passion for such expeditions, although partly the capriciousness of my health, and partly the want of the incitement of a companion, keep me at home. I see the mountains, the sky, and the trees from my windows and recollect, as an old man does the mistress of his youth, the raptures of a more familiar intercourse. . . .'[90]

At the end of July, Shelley succeeded in renting a good set of rooms at the little spa of the Bagni di Pisa, some four miles outside the city walls. On 2 August he returned to the Casa Ricci, bringing with him excitedly the latest news of the recent insurrection in Naples. He told Mary that he was quite happy now to forgo all thoughts of his long-delayed journey to England. '*I* have no thoughts of leaving Italy – the best thing we can do, is to save money, & if things take a decided turn (which I am convinced they will at last – but not perhaps for two or three years) it will be time for me to assert my rights and preserve my annuity. . . . Kiss sweet babe, & kiss yourself for me. I love you affectionately – P.B.S.'[91]

25
The Moons of Pisa: 1820

The road to the Bagni wound out from the northern gate of Pisa, and crossing the flat plain which is marked by occasional farm buildings and broken by the loosely cultivated lines of vines and vegetables, approached the distant curves of the Monte Pisano. On the way it picked up the line of the little canal which connects the Arno at Pisa with the Serchio at Lucca, finally crossing over by a stone bridge, shaded with plane trees, and entering the single half-crescent of stone buildings which form the tiny centre of the village, which was known locally as San Giuliano.

Huddled at the foot of the Monte Pisano, the crescent faced the solid, four-square eighteenth-century building of the *bagni* proper, which was surmounted by a large clock flanked with decorative urns. Immediately behind it rose the steep sides of the mountains, covered with wild olives, and terraced on its lower slopes with walkways and pergolas which remained from the time of its original popularity during the period of the Medici. But San Giuliano at the time of Shelley's arrival in August 1820 was like the rest of Pisa, in a period of decline, and except for local market days and fairs the village was not much frequented even by Italians from Pisa. Sporadically new researches were undertaken by the medical faculty at the university into the supposed curative properties of the waters. Traditionally it had been the resort of the Tuscan Court, but the short-ness of the season, which tended to end abruptly in September with torrential flooding from the mountainside, had long since forced it to yield in popularity and elegance to the *bagni* at Lucca.

Shelley's apartments were in the Casa Prinni, the second house on the left of the entrance to the crescent. It had large ground-floor rooms flanking an arched entrance hall, and a back garden planted with oranges and lemons which stretched right down to the banks of the canal.[1] Shelley rented the whole house at about thirteen sequins a month, which was not altogether cheap for such a retired situation: 'I could get others something cheaper & a great deal worse; but if we would write it is requisite to have space.'[2] He was to remain relatively peacefully in this retreat until the end of October.

The little household, with an Italian cook Caterina, settled in quickly enough, although Claire was ill shortly after moving, and noted cryptically that she dreamt she saw a ghost.[3] The escape to San Giuliano came as a great relief to Shelley. One of his first actions was to unburden his feelings in a long and demolishing letter to Godwin. For this, he spent one day at Pisa consulting with Tatty Tighe in his study among the shelves of sprouting potatoes in glass pots, and then carefully wrote out a five-page draft. He had at last found adequate words for what should perhaps have been said long before he left England: 'I have given you within a few years the amount of a considerable fortune, & have destituted myself, for the purpose of realising it of nearly four times the amount. Except for the *good will* which this transaction seems to have produced between you & me, this money, for any *advantage* that it ever conferred on you, might as well have been thrown into the sea. Had I kept in my own hands this £4 or £5000 & administered it in trust for your permanent advantage I should have been indeed your benefactor. The error however was greater in the man of mature age extensive experience & penetrating intellect than in the crude & impetuous boy. Such an error is seldom committed twice.'

He explained further that his present situation was delicate, and Mary had not been kept fully informed. 'My affairs are in a state of the most complicated embarrassment: added to which I am surrounded by circumstances in which any diminution of my very limited resources might involve me in personal peril. I fear that you & I are not on such terms as to justify me in exposing to you the actual state of my delicate & emergent situation which the most sacred considerations imperiously require me to conceal from Mary. . . .' This was a course of concealment that Mary herself had acquiesced in, to spare herself, and through her the baby, pain or ill-health. 'Your letters from their style & spirit (such is your erroneous notion of taste) never fail to produce an appalling effect on her frame; on one occasion, [united with other circumstances – *deleted in draft*] agitation of mind produced through her a disorder in the child, similar to that which destroyed our little girl two years ago. . . . On that occasion Mary at my request [gave me the liberty – *deleted in draft*] authorized me to intercept such letters or information as I might judge likely to disturb her mind.'[4] Besides Godwin's financial importunities, Shelley was here undoubtedly referring to the events of 14–17 June concerning Elena. There is another fragment of a draft which refers to his own severe nephritic pains on that occasion.[5]

Godwin's fury on receiving this letter was demonstrated by the long explanation and tirade to which he subjected the Gisbornes in London. There was much discussion of Claire's folly and Paolo's villainy, though as far as can be judged this concerned what Maria Gisborne called 'the old story' – that is, Byron and Allegra. Whether the Gisbornes in turn told Godwin of Elena Adelaide Shelley seems doubtful. But their good opinion of Shelley was undermined when they returned to Italy.[6]

After dispatching this letter to Godwin, Shelley decided that it was a suitable moment to fulfil an ambition of two years' standing, and make his pilgrimage to Monte San Pelegrino above Lucca. Claire and Mary accompanied him as far as the town on Friday, 11 August, where they spent the night at the Croce di Malta. He departed at dawn on Saturday, and was gone for the rest of the week-end. It was the first time he had really got away on his own since leaving Naples in the spring of 1819. The weather was blazingly hot, but he journeyed all the way on foot, and climbed to the little chapel which was sited on the peak of the Monte. He returned exhausted to San Giuliano late on Sunday evening. It was during this solitary expedition that he conceived his long and fantastic poem 'The Witch of Atlas'.

He began work on it immediately on Monday morning, and it was completed two days later, 16 August. Mary noted the progress of this work in her journal, and the rapidity of composition – more than 200 lines each day – is unmatched by any other work. Shelley himself recorded the speed of the three-day compo-sition in a set of dedicatory verses to Mary, and gave the impression of taking pride in it as a mere feat of skill. The poem has virtually no plot, but loosely recounts the wizardry and mischief of the mysterious Witch, who creates a strange and beautiful hermaphroditic companion, and a magical airship for both of them to travel in, and journeys through the world and through history. Much of the imagery of creative fire, of sailing in air and water, and of electric energy, is skimmed off from *Prometheus Unbound*. But unlike that poem, there is a deliberate absence of intellectual structure, and the verse has everywhere the air of brilliant improvisation. Especially in its stress on fire and movement and speed of line, 'The Witch of Atlas' gives the impression of a poetical aerobatics display.

> ... she would often climb
> The steepest ladder of the crudded rack
> Up to some beakèd cape of cloud sublime,
> And like Arion on the dolphin's back
> Ride singing through the shoreless air; – oft-time
> Following the serpent lightning's winding track,
> She ran upon the platforms of the wind,
> And laughed to hear the fire-balls roar behind.[7]

The manuscript of the poem is frequently decorated with sketches of boats under sail.

Mary accurately described it as 'wildly fanciful, full of brilliant imagery, and disregarding human interest and passion, to revel in the fantastic ideas that [Shelley's] imagination suggested'.[8] In fact she sharply disliked the poem, and criticized Shelley for writing in this way. She felt that it stemmed essentially from a 'morbid feeling', and represented a shrinking away from the realities of human passion and social sympathy. Shelley wrote in his dedicatory verse:

How, my dear Mary, – are you critic-bitten
  (For vipers kill, though dead) by some review,
That you condemn these verses I have written,
  Because they tell no story, false or true?[9]

Mary's distaste points towards one of the most interesting features of the poem, the further exploration of the bisexual theme. In this sense the poem does have human and passionate content, but one which Mary did not want to recognize. At the end of his dedication, Shelley warned:

If you unveil my Witch, no priest nor primate
Can shrive you of that sin, – if sin there be
In love, when it becomes idolatry.

Shelley had first consciously met the idea of the hermaphrodite in Aristophanes' speech in his translation of the *Symposium* made at the Bagni di Lucca. At Rome he had seen a statue of the hermaphrodite, which was kept at that time in the Palazzo Borghese.[10] There had been in fact two hermaphrodite statues in Rome, but one of them, the original Greek work of fifth century BC, had been sold to Napoleon and shipped to the Louvre, where it remains, though removed from the public galleries, to this day. Shelley's hermaphrodite was a much restored but nevertheless magnificent Hellenistic copy, exquisitely reworked by Andrea Bergondi.[11] The hermaphrodite is asleep, lying on its belly, with the serene face cradled on its right arm and exposed to the viewer. The large eyes are closed, and the elegant curling hair is tied in with a simple band. The sculptor has cunningly arranged the disposition of the body so that the upper torso is slightly raised to reveal one breast, while the body below the waist is twisted on the right hip and the shapely legs drawn up, to concentrate the viewer's attention on a dramatic and lavishly executed pair of curving haunches.

In his poem, the Witch herself creates a hermaphrodite. The beautiful bisexual creature is the Witch's companion and servant, a sort of sorcerer's apprentice, who symbolizes all the potential energies of Nature, sexual and electric. But for the most part the hermaphrodite remains, like its original marble image in Rome, sleeping; for its freedoms are potential only.

Then by strange art she kneaded fire and snow
  Together, tempering the repugnant mass
With liquid love – all things together grow
  Through which the harmony of love can pass;
And a fair Shape out of her hands did flow –
  A living Image, which did far surpass
In beauty that bright shape of vital stone
Which drew the heart out of Pygmalion.

A sexless thing it was, and in its growth
  It seemed to have developed no defect
Of either sex, yet all the grace of both, –
  In gentleness and strength its limbs were decked. . . .

And ever as she went, the Image lay
  With folded wings and unawakened eyes;
And o'er its gentle countenance did play
  The busy dreams, as thick as summer flies,
Chasing the rapid smiles that would not stay. . . .[12]

The idea of the sleeping potential, symbolized in the hermaphrodite, is
brought out towards the end of the poem in the Witch's interference in human
affairs. She conjures out the good or comic impulses which have lain dormant in
the characters of the evil or repressed. The Witch performs her 'magic' over
priests and kings, and soldiers (who dream they are blacksmiths); and above all
over lovers who have been restricted by the codes of their society:

And timid lovers who had been so coy,
  They hardly knew whether they loved or not,
Would rise out of their rest, and take sweet joy,
  To the fulfilment of their inmost thought;
And when next day the maiden and the boy
  Met one another, both, like sinners caught,
Blushed at the thing which each believed was done
Only in fancy – till the tenth moon shone. . . .[13]

Yet here and throughout the poem, the language is only working with intermittent force. The one exception is an extraordinary passage where the Witch
exerts her magic on those who are about to die. She creates an eternity of suspended animation for them, as if they were a species of human seed, and the
Witch was – as in an earlier phrase, – 'a horticultural adept'.

For on the night when they were buried, she
   Restored the embalmers' ruining, and shook
The light out of the funeral lamps, to be
   A mimic day within that deathy nook;
And she unwound the woven imagery
   Of second childhood's swaddling bands, and took
The coffin, its last cradle, from its niche,
And threw it with contempt into a ditch.

And there the body lay, age after age,
   Mute, breathing, beating, warm, and undecaying,
Like one asleep in a green hermitage,
   With gentle smiles about its eyelids playing,
And living in its dreams beyond the rage
   Of death or life: while they were still arraying
In liveries ever new, the rapid, blind
And fleeting generations of mankind.[14]

This finely controlled and imagined passage shows a mature transformation, not without a certain irony, of that urge to escape into a world of eternal rebirth which he had exploited sentimentally in the lyrics of July. But 'The Witch of Atlas' as a whole remains a light-weight virtuoso piece. For Shelley it served as a release of feelings, a finger-exercise in composition.

In the seclusion of the Casa Prinni, he threw the manuscript aside and turned to a second piece of serious correspondence, this time with Robert Southey. In June, he had written from Pisa to inquire if Southey was really the author of the *Quarterly* attack of the previous year, and in the course of this letter he managed to insult Southey unnecessarily by accusing him of having 'abandoned' the cause to which his early writings were devoted.[15] In his reply, the elder poet icily denied the authorship of the review, and then angrily challenged Shelley's own opinions. '. . . Have they not brought immediate misery upon others, and guilt, which is all but irremediable, upon yourself?' He urged Shelley to turn back to Christianity, and bring himself to 'a sense of your miserable condition'.[16]

This was not calculated to soothe Shelley, especially at such a juncture, and he wrote back in furious indignation. 'You select a single passage out of a life otherwise not only spotless but spent in an impassioned pursuit of virtue, which looks like a blot, merely because I regulated my domestic arrangements without deferring to the notions of the vulgar. . . .' The issue of the *Quarterly* was now far removed from Shelley's mind, but he struck back hard where he knew Southey was most vulnerable. 'I cannot hope that you will be candid enough to feel, or if you feel, to own, that you have done ill in accusing, even in your mind, an innocent and a persecuted man, whose only real offence is the holding opinions something similar to those which you once held respecting the existing state of society.'[17] Memories of the old disagreements at Keswick in 1811, and the old political resentments, had quickly flared up in Shelley's mind. On 20 August Claire made a fair copy of the letter for Shelley; one suspects that this also was information unsuitable for Mary. Yet Shelley was still not quite past the hope of softening Southey, and he sent immediate instructions to Ollier for copies of *The Cenci* and *Prometheus* to be dispatched to Keswick. He also added a postscript to Southey, that at the time of writing he was suffering from agonizing pains in his side.

When this letter eventually reached Great Hall, Southey rose to the occasion as a representative of respectable English society. He had, after all, sacrificed his own writing career to his massive domestic responsibilities. He no longer minced words, but embarked with a businesslike relish on a proper Christian demolition of Shelley's private life, starting with the expulsion from Oxford, and going on to an inquisition on the merits of Harriet Shelley's suicide: 'ask your own heart, whether you have not been the whole, sole and direct cause of her destruction. You corrupted her opinions; you robbed her of her moral and religious principles; you debauched her mind.' He summarized with dutiful force: 'you have reasoned yourself into a state of mind so pernicious that your character, with your domestic arrangements, as you term it, might furnish the subject for the drama more instructive, and scarcely less painful, than the detestable story of the Cenci, and this has proceeded directly from your principles. . . . It is the Atheist's Tragedy.'[18] With this, and further urging to the Book of Common Prayer, Southey broke off the correspondence, and it was never resumed on either side. Both men, while consistently signing themselves 'sincere well-wishers', had succeeded in deeply wounding each other, for both men had deep causes for secret bitterness and private remorse.

Yet despite these distant thunderings, the Shelley household had surmounted the crisis of June, and the beginning of a regular routine of walks and baths and carriage rides began to have its beneficial effect. Life grew lighter and more relaxed. Claire went over to stay for four days with the Masons and their children at Pisa, and in the course of this visit it was decided that she should go away to the seaside at Livorno for a few weeks. There she could get on with her studies, sea-bathe for her health and enjoy improving correspondence with Mrs Mason. On 24 August, she and the Masons rode back with another English lady, a Miss Field, to spend the festival day of St Bartholomew's at San Giuliano. The little village was rapidly filling up with people and carriages and farm animals, the windows were hung with bunting, and preparations were being made for the traditional horse-racing through the streets. After the party had arrived at the

Casa Prinni, Shelley decided to give a festival reading of one of his political odes. Mary says later that it was the 'Ode to Liberty' written the previous spring, but it seems more likely that it was an extract from his new 'Ode to Naples', which he was currently writing about the insurrection in Southern Italy.

As Shelley declaimed, the piazza under their windows gradually filled up with the loud grunting and squealing of pigs brought in for sale at the fair. Finally, the farmyard noises threatened to drown out the whole recitation, and Shelley broke off his reading with a laugh. 'He compared it to the "chorus of frogs" in the satiric drama of Aristophanes; and, it being an hour of merriment, and one ludicrous association suggesting another, he imagined a political–satirical drama on the circumstances of the day, to which the pigs would serve as chorus.'[19] At the end of August he actually began such a drama, and completed it in September. It was called *Swellfoot the Tyrant*.

In the evening of St Bartholomew's day, they all went to watch the horse-races, in a thoroughly good mood. A week later Shelley took Claire to Livorno to begin her improving month's vacation. He remained with her for two days. She probably stayed with Italian friends of the Gisbornes, and possibly even at the Casa Ricci itself. She read *Clarissa*, did Latin exercises and bathed daily, receiving regular letters from the Casa Silva and Casa Prinni, occasional news of Ravenna and once a long letter from Charles at Vienna. Weekends were frequently spent with the Masons at Pisa, and Shelley usually arrived to take her out for a talk and a walk. They read anxiously the news of the Carbonari campaigns around Naples, and discussed them animatedly.

One entry in Claire's diary describing a morning trip through the streets of Livorno gives a vivid impression of her sharp eye and violently felt reactions which remained such a permanent pleasure to Shelley. 'I see a beggar sitting at his post yawning with *ennui* – another crawling on all fours politely saluting a young washerwoman a bundle on her head & bare footed with "mi rincresce che La Mamma e ammalata" [I'm sorry to hear your Mamma is unwell]; Greeks with legs folded under them sitting upon the parapets & gazing stupidly upon the muddy current of the canal below . . . here men burning coffee before their doors, & there others beating the flock of matresses; violins squeeking and women singing. Life everywhere but like the life which is engendered of putrefaction creeping crawling worms not that wholesome strength of an agricultural product or that animation which is the child of Liberty.'[20]

September and October at the Bagni were remarkably peaceful. Shelley and Mary took the waters, rode out in the afternoons and occasionally walked among the foothills of Monte Pisano. In the evening they read Boccaccio's tales out loud to each other. At weekends, Shelley usually dined with Claire and

the Masons at Pisa. Mary began her new novel, *Valperga*, and Shelley completed
his final draft of the 'Ode to Naples', and dashed off the two comic acts of
Swellfoot the Tyrant. It ended in high style with Iona Tarina (Queen Caroline)
pulling on boots and spurs, 'and a hunting-cap, buckishly cocked on one side,
and tucking up her hair', and leaping on to the back of the Minotaur. Then, with
hunting cries and shouts, she and the Swinish Multitude pursue the evil Swellfoot
(King George) and his knavish ministers (Castlereagh, Sidmouth etc.) off the
stage; *exeunt in full cry* –

> Tallyho! tallyho!
> Through pond, ditch, and slough,
> Wind them, and find them,
> Like the Devil behind them,
> Tallyho! tallyho![21]

Altogether it was a highly successful combination of street pamphlet and revue
sketch, with material drawn equally from Aristophanes and Shelley's own *Mask
of Anarchy*. Shelley did actually manage to get it published in England, and it
is a great pity that the correspondence surrounding the publication has not
survived, for it seems to have been nothing to do with Hunt or Ollier at
all. Shelley, perhaps with the connivance and aid of Horace Smith,[22] had it
transmitted directly and anonymously to the old Godwinian publisher James
Johnson, and thus short-circuited the liberal and respectable publishing network. The burlesque appeared in London early in the autumn of 1820 with
the following title page:

> Oedipus Tyrannus
> or
> Swellfoot the Tyrant
> A Tragedy.
> In Two Acts.
> Translated from the Original Doric
>
> 'Choose Reform or Civil War
> When thro' thy streets, instead of hare with dogs,
> A consort Queen shall hunt a King with hogs,
> Riding on the IONIAN MINOTAUR.'
> London
> Published for the Author
> by J. Johnston, 98 Cheapside, and sold by
> all booksellers
> 1820.

This little edition must have made a considerable impact, for it was immediately seized by the politically motivated Society for the Suppression of Vice who threatened to prosecute Johnson. On this occasion Johnson withdrew the remaining copies, but it was just such confrontations, when persistently pursued, which Shelley himself advocated, 'defying the government to prosecute for political libel' as part of the overall radical strategy. When courageously practised by men like Carlile and Holyoake, it gradually freed the press from political control during the following fifteen years.[23]

It was one of Shelley's great tactical mistakes as a poet, a mistake for which Hunt must carry some of the blame, that he did not turn to this kind of publication sooner, or persist in it after 1820; though the choice was to be taken out of his hands on one memorable future occasion. Mary finally published the poem in her edition of 1839, by which time it was toothless.

Other poems which belong to these retired weeks of September and October are more reflective. Shelley made a five-stanza adaptation of Dante's *Purgatorio*, Canto 28, lines 1–51. He had first translated it in a fragment which Mary later entitled 'Matilda Gathering Flowers'.[24] Now he developed it into the completed poem 'The Question', with its ornate and exquisitely assembled description of a nosegay of 'visionary flowers'.

> There grew pied wind-flowers and violets,
>   Daisies, those pearled Arcturi of the earth,
> The constellated flower that never sets. . . .[25]

Other adaptions included shortened versions of the Homeric Hymns 'Apollo' and 'Pan'.

But perhaps most successful were the two lyric fragments on the Moon. They were written at harvest-time when the huge presence rose through the mists of Monte Pisano to the north-east and hung above the long flat shadows of the Pisan plain.

> And like a dying lady, lean and pale,
> Who totters forth, wrapped in a gauzy veil,
> Out of her chamber, led by the insane
> And feeble wanderings of her fading brain,
> The moon arose up in the murky East,
> A white and shapeless mass ——[26]

The second has all the Elizabethan melancholy grace of a sonnet by Philip Sidney:

     Art thou pale for weariness
Of climbing heaven and gazing on the earth,
     Wandering companionless
Among the stars that have a different birth, –
And ever changing, like a joyless eye
That finds no object worth its constancy? . . . [27]

But it was not finished. Fine as these poems are, like tiny pieces of exquisite
mantelpiece china, they represent a steady withdrawal of creative pressure and
urgency. The presence of Greek and Italian translation, as a hard core within
many of the poems of this summer and autumn of 1820, also show Shelley's need
to draw support and stimulation from more purely literary sources. In the last
eighteen months of Shelley's writing, these foreign literary presences become
more and more important in his work. Dominant are the figures of Dante,
Calderón and Goethe. They stand as powerful if shadowy figures behind his
original poems, and also are brought into clear focus in a series of masterly poetic
translations. These works, together with the prose translation of the *Symposium*
of 1818, the solid workmanlike verse rendition of Euripides's *Cyclops* of 1819,
and the 'Homeric Hymns,' combined to make Shelley by far the most outstanding
literary translator of his generation.

At the end of September, Shelley brought Claire back from Livorno, and by
agreement between Mary and Mrs Mason, she was given a room at the Casa
Silva, since Mary now preferred not to have her at the Bagni. The only sign of
disturbance was a letter from Shelley to Byron, in which he once again found
himself defending Claire's importunities. But this time a slightly firmer note had
entered into his explanations, and one now feels that his sympathies had moved
decidedly to Claire's side over the issue of Allegra. 'I wonder however at your
being provoked at what Clare writes; though that she should write what is
provoking is very probable. – You are conscious of performing your duty to
Allegra, & your refusal to allow her to visit Clare at this distance you conceive to
be part of your duty. That Clare should have wished to see her is natural. That
her disappointment should vex her, & her vexation make her write absurdly is
all in the usual order of things. But poor thing, she is very unhappy & in bad
health, & she ought to be treated with as much indulgence as possible.'

Reports had been circulating that Byron had intended to return to London.
Shelley disbelieved these, but he seized upon the possibility that Byron might at
any rate be considering leaving Italy. 'As to me, I remain in Italy for the
present. – If you really go to England, & leave Allegra in Italy, I think you had
better arrange so that Clare might see Allegra in your absence if she pleases.' This
was the first time Shelley had ever suggested how his Lordship *had better*

arrange his affairs. Equally, this was the second autumn since poor Claire had last set eyes on her child, and much future friction and unhappiness was to grow from this exacerbated situation.

Shelley's letter to Byron contains an intriguing postscript, though to Byron it probably had little significance. 'PS If I were to go to Levant & Greece, could you be of any service to me? If so, I should be very much obliged to you.'[28] This is the first time Shelley openly mentioned his scheme to set out on his travels again, and depart for the Near East. It is significant because as far as is known, it was a scheme which only Claire – and possibly also Tom Medwin – really knew about.

On 10 October the Gisbornes returned from England to Livorno and to Casa Ricci, and on the following day a package of books was left with Claire at Casa Silva. Shelley sent off a brief note welcoming them home. 'Clare tells me that you are returned, & that you even passed the Bagni without calling on us . . . we do not *quite* understand your silence.'[29] Among the books was a new volume of Keats's, *Lamia, Isabella, the Eve of St Agnes, and Other Poems*. These poems had a tremendous impact on Shelley,[30] and Claire was already quoting from 'Isabella' in her diary of the 15th.

Shelley's previous opinion of Keats's writing had not been high. He had regarded him as potentially a fine poet, but as yet a writer whose 'mannerism' and adherence to the Hunt 'system' of luxurious gentility in phrase and imagery had only shown forth his powers very indistinctly. His considered opinion of *Endymion*, given to Keats's own publisher Ollier in September 1819 was that 'much praise is due to me for having read [it], the Authors intention appearing to be that no person should possibly get to the end of it. Yet it is full of some of the highest & the finest gleams of poetry; indeed every thing seems to be viewed by the mind of a poet which is described in it. I think if he had printed about 50 pages of fragments from it I should have been led to admire Keats as a poet more than I ought, of which there is now no danger.'[31]

Shelley's main feeling about Keats's poetry was that it lacked both grandeur of design, and the classical austerity of execution that he had struggled so hard to develop in his own work. This he now saw achieved to an outstanding degree in one major poem of the new 1820 volume, and his reaction was immediate and generous, though not perhaps entirely unpatronizing. He wrote to Marianne Hunt from San Giuliano on 29 October: 'Keats' new volume has arrived to us, & the fragment called Hyperion promises for him that he is destined to become one of the first writers of the age. – His other things are imperfect enough. . . . Where is Keats now? I am anxiously expecting him in Italy where I shall take care to bestow every possible attention on him. I consider his a most valuable life, & I am deeply interested in his safety. I intend to be the physician both of his body & his soul, to keep the one warm & to teach the other Greek & Spanish. I am aware indeed in part that I am nourishing a rival who will far surpass me and this is an additional motive & will be an added pleasure.'[32] It is suggestive that the poem which Shelley liked at once is that which most closely resembles passages of his own work in *Prometheus Unbound*. Surprisingly, he made no mention of the great 'Odes'.[33]

At the time of Shelley's writing, Keats was in fact miserably spending the last two days of an enforced quarantine period on board ship in the bay of Naples with his companion Joseph Severn. But Keats never made any attempt to contact Shelley at Pisa.

On 17 October, almost exactly twelve months after the first conception of 'Ode to the West Wind', the weather began to break up over Tuscany, and the rains started.[34] Shelley and Mary knew they would have to move back into Pisa, and other social complications were impinging, but for a few days they hung on at the Casa Prinni enjoying the last few hours of their peaceful household together, and watching the rain driving over the Monte Pisano. On the 18th and 19th there are two of the longest entries in Mary's journal for many months, which give a strong impression of their serenity. The piece of verse, and the second entry, seem to have been entered in Shelley's own hand, nostalgically recalling the simple happiness of the Byron summer long ago on Lac Leman.

> Oct. 18. – Rain till 1 o'clock. At sunset the arch of cloud over the west clears away; a few black islands float in the serene; the moon rises; the clouds spot the sky; but the depth of heaven is clear. The nights are uncommonly warm. Write. Shelley reads 'Hyperion' aloud. Read Greek.

> My thoughts rise and fade in solitude;
> The verse that would invest them melts away
> Like moonlight in the heaven of spreading day.
> How beautiful they were, how firm they stood,
> Flecking the starry sky like woven pearl!

> Oct 19th. – Ride to Pisa. Read Keats' Poems. Henry Reveley calls. Walk. Read Greek. Wind N.N.W., cloudy, the sun shining at intervals. The spoils of the trees are scattered about, and the chestnuts are much browner than a week ago. In the evening the moon, with Venus just below her, sails through the clouds, but shines clearly where they are not.[35]

But times had changed. Happiness was complicated and serenity was fragile.

A visit to Livorno by Shelley and Tatty Tighe had brought back the news that the Gisbornes were acting somewhat strangely. It seems that what the Godwins had to say in London about Claire and Shelley, in some way put the affair of Elena – whom Shelley had always called circumspectly in his London letters to the Gisbornes his 'Neapolitan charge' – in a new light. Mary wrote to Maria Gisborne, but her letter does not make the matter very explicit, except to emphasize the vehemence with which she felt about it. In later correspondence between Shelley and Claire during the winter, Shelley too was to write of his erstwhile friends with savage distaste.

Mary wrote to Mrs Gisborne: 'When I saw you yesterday, you said you had written me a foolish letter, (foolish was your word, I think) but since you did not explain away any part of it, of course you meant that it should remain in full force. – A good dose on my return; – indeed I was tolerably astounded, and found Shelley in a state of considerable agitation – but this is not the purpose of this letter. – A Veil is now taken off from what was mysterious yesterday, and I now understand your refusal to visit us. . . . I see the ban of the Empire is gone out against us, and they who put it on must take it off. Of course it is quite *impossible* that we should visit you until we have first received you at our house. . . . [Henry] has chosen to join himself to your accusations. – He is young to do this. But what terms need to be made with Pariahs. And such, thank God a thousand and a million times, we are; long – very long, may we so continue. – When you said that filthy woman [*i.e.* Mrs Godwin] said she would not visit Hunt how I gloried in our infamy. Now is the time! join them, or us. . . .'[36] As on later and similar occasions, Mary here showed a great gift for expressing powerful feelings and outraged denials, without actually stating or denying anything definite at all. One also senses that she did not really seek a reconciliation with the Gisbornes. In fact the breach was serious, and there was little communication between the two households for several months, and Shelley expressed furious indignation when they dropped the steam-boat project – although he himself had earlier advised them to abandon it.[37] Henry Reveley, who had always been fond of Claire, and got on easily with Shelley, did not in the event treat the matter with such formality as his mother and stepfather and he soon started to visit Shelley regularly again at Pisa.

Spurred on by what appeared then to be the beginnings of a new scandal concerning Claire, Mary and Mrs Mason hastily completed a scheme of sending her to pass the winter with the family of Dr Bojti in Florence. The Bojti family were a contact of the Masons through the medical faculty at Pisa; Dr Bojti was the Grand Duke Ferdinand III's personal physician, and lived in a house opposite the Pitti Palace with a large family of daughters.[38] Claire went as a paying guest, ostensibly to study German and make her début in Florentine society, and the arrangement was in the first instance for one month. There is abundant later evidence that Shelley was deeply against the scheme, and that Claire herself was miserable; but circumstances had taken the decision at least temporarily out of their hands.

Shelley himself took Claire to Florence on 20 October. They arrived at six in the evening and spent a last night together at the Fontana Inn. Claire made a note in her diary that obviously reflects Shelley's bitter remarks about the Gisbornes: 'Whoever does a benefit to another buys so much envy, malice, hatred and all uncharitableness from him.'[39] The following morning introductions were made to the Bojtis, whom Claire had never met before. She entered in her diary: 'Unpack my things. Shelley takes leave of me in the evening.'[40] Eight days later she was to write: 'Think of thyself as a stranger & traveller on the earth, to whom none of the many affairs of this world belong, and who has no permanent township on the globe.'[41]

For Shelley, the drive back to Pisa was less unhappy. At long last, Tom Medwin really had come south for the winter. By chance they met in Florence, and Medwin came back with Shelley on the coach, talking non-stop about his adventures as a lieutenant in India. Medwin recalled: 'It was nearly seven years since we parted; but I should immediately have recognised him in a crowd. His figure was emaciated, and somewhat bent; owing to near-sightedness, and his being forced to lean over his books, with his eyes almost touching them; his hair, still profuse, and curling naturally, was partially interspersed with grey ... but his appearance was youthful, and his countenance, whether grave or animated, strikingly intellectual.'[42] No doubt one of the first stories Medwin told Shelley was how he had miraculously found a copy of *The Revolt of Islam* on a Parsee waste-paper stall in Bombay.[43]

They returned to Mary at San Giuliano on the 22nd, and Medwin was installed in the space vacated by Claire. Three days later, on the 25th, the constant rains flooded the little village: the baths all overflowed, and the canal broke its banks at the bottom of the garden. By nightfall their hall was four feet deep in the water, which had poured through the garden from the canal and from the piazza in front of the baths.[44] They sat in the upper windows, and watched the peasants driving the cattle off the Pisan plain to the safety of the hills. 'A fire was kept up to guide them across the ford; and the forms of the men and the animals showed in dark relief against the red glare of the flame, which was reflected again in the waters that filled the square.'[45] Shelley rode in the next day to arrange lodgings in Pisa for the winter, and with Medwin's help they moved back on the last weekend of October.

26
The Tuscan Set: 1821

The Shelleys' new winter apartments were on the Lung'Arno at the Casa Galetti, where Tom Medwin lodged with them. It stood next to one of the marble palaces, and the Shelleys occupied the whole of the mezzanine floor facing south, finding it was comfortable and warm. Shelley used Medwin's presence to secure two separate rooms higher on the fourth floor, both with open fireplaces. One of these became Medwin's bedroom, and the other Shelley's private study. Shelley was glad of his independence.[1] Medwin made himself agreeable to Shelley; they read together and played chess, and to Shelley's relief he saw that 'Mary likes him well enough'. There was a slightly invalid atmosphere in the house, for Mary had an eye inflammation and found it difficult either to read or write, while Shelley found the change in the weather – and perhaps other changes – had brought back his chronic nephritic pains. Medwin tried to amuse and distract them both with readings from his Indian journal,[2] and Shelley was sufficiently grateful and impressed to write on 10 November to Ollier recommending that the publisher take on Medwin's *Sketches in Hindoostan with Other Poems*. Unlikely as it might sound, Ollier promptly published these the following year.

With this letter, Shelley enclosed manuscripts for a new collection of his own. He intended it to be published anonymously with the title poem 'Julian and Maddalo'. They were 'all my saddest poems raked into one heap', and included some of the poems of private grief written at Naples in 1818–19; the unfinished narrative 'Marenghi', based on the history of an exile in the Pisan *maremma* during the sixteenth century;[3] and some of the fragments composed at San Giuliano. None of these were ever published in Shelley's lifetime.[4]

November was an unhappy month for Shelley, and Medwin observed his symptoms with sympathy and sometimes alarm. He later wrote, 'Shelley had . . . during that winter been subject to a prostration, physical and psychical, the most cruel to witness, though he was never querelous or out of temper, never by an irritable word hurt the feelings of those about him. . . . So sensitive was he of external impressions, so magnetic, that I have seen him, after threading the carnival crowd in the Lung-'Arno Corso, throw himself half-fainting into a chair, over-powered by the atmosphere of evil passions, as he used to say, in that sensual and unintellectual crowd . . . his physical sufferings – they, if they did not produce, tended to aggravate his mental ones. He was a martyr to the most painful complaint, Nephritis, for which he . . . was now trying Scott's vitriolic acid baths, much in vogue. This malady constantly menaced to end fatally. During its paroxysms he would roll on the floor in agony.' Medwin told Shelley that he had seen the so-called 'animal magnetism' practised in India in similar circumstances and that he himself had 'benefitted by it at Geneva'. Shelley agreed to let Medwin experiment during the next convenient attack.[5]

There is no doubt that apart from his nephritis, much of Shelley's immediate misery was caused by Claire's absence in Florence. He worried about her, and he deeply missed her friendship and company. Nine days after her departure, he wrote a l ong letter, which shows very well how he felt. They were not feelings he cared to reveal to Mary: 'My dearest Clare, I wrote you a kind of scrawl the other day merely to show that I had not forgotten you, and as it was taxed with a postscript by Mary, it contained nothing that I wished it to contain.' That word *taxed* was very expressive.

News had already reached Shelley through mutual Italian acquaintances of Claire's unhappiness at Florence. 'Keep up your spirits, my best girl, until we meet at Pisa. But for Mrs Mason, I should say, come back immediately and give up a plan so inconsistent with your feelings – as it is, I fear you had better endure – at least until you come here. You know, however, whatever you shall determine on, where to find one ever affectionate Friend, to whom your absence is too painful for your return ever to be unwelcome. I think it moreover for your own interest to observe a certain ——'. The gap is apparently in the manuscript, to indicate tiresome propriety.[6]

Shelley made no secret of his own ill-health, or his dependence on Claire's sympathy. 'I have suffered within this last week a violent access of my disease, with a return of those spasms that I used to have. . . . As to pain, I care little for it; but the nervous irritability which it leaves is a great and serious evil to me, and which, if not incessantly combated by myself and soothed by others, would leave me nothing but torment in life. – I am now much better. Medwin's cheerful conversation is of some use to me, but what would it be to your sweet consolation, my own Claire?'

He described the layout of their rooms at Casa Galetti – in which Mary 'has a very good room below, and there is plenty of space for the babe'. Shelley made a great point of his study two floors above. 'Congratulate me on my seclusion.'

Shelley next explained how the Gisbornes intended to defraud him by using the marine engine cast with his money to set up a commercial machine shop with a powered bellows. He had had a long and 'very explicit' conversation with Henry, setting out his own views, and he was even more explicit with Claire. 'The Gisbornes are people totally without faith. – I think they are altogether the most filthy and odious animals with which I ever came in contact. – They do not visit Mary as they promised, and indeed if they did, I certainly should not stay in the house to receive them.' The Gisbornes did not in the event defraud Shelley of his money, and all the evidence suggests that he was paid back a good deal of his original investment – which had, anyway, been partly in the nature of a gift. Shelley did not mention to Claire here that he had just posted an extremely polite note to Mr Gisborne requesting Arabian grammars or dictionaries, forwarding some back number of the *Galignani's Messenger*, and concluding with 'My kind regards to Mrs G., & Henry. – Yours very truly.'[7] So much, perhaps, was still due to propriety.

But the request for Arabic grammars was now repeated to Claire, 'for a purpose and a motive as you may conceive'. He dilated on his scheme: '[Medwin and I] have also been talking of a plan to be accomplished with a friend of his, a man of large fortune, who will be at Leghorn next spring, and who designs to visit Greece, Syria, and Egypt in his own ship. This man has conceived a great admiration for my verses, and wishes above all things that I could be induced to join his expedition. How far all this is practicable, considering the state of my finances I know not yet. I know that if it were it would give me the greatest pleasure, and the pleasure might be either doubled or divided by your presence or absence. All this will be explained and determined in time; meanwhile lay to your heart what I say, and do not mention it in your letter to Mary.'[8]

The idea of sailing away, of going to the East, or to distant isles, moved uneasily in Shelley's mind between poetry and reality. Did Medwin's friend 'of large fortune' really exist? Certainly he never materialized. But the journey was a plan or a vision that embraced Claire – and not much later, another girl. During this winter it was essentially the plan of a sick man, and a trapped one; it was a vision of open sea viewed from a closed harbour, but it was none the less powerful for that.

November passed painfully by. To Peacock Shelley explained that he had no taste for original composition, 'the reception the public have given me might go far enough to damp any man's enthusiasm'. He had been reading nothing but Greek and Spanish: 'Plato and Calderón have been my gods.'[9] Mary was working downstairs on her new novel *Valperga*, set in the medieval period, which, as Shelley observed evenly, 'she has raked out of fifty old books'.

At least there was Medwin's company at the Casa Galetti, and on expeditions to the Campo Santo. Once Shelley discussed Foundling Hospitals: there was one at Pisa which he took Medwin to see.[10] Shelley talked with Medwin a good deal about translation, and read Spanish and Italian with him. He discussed an idea he had had of translating the whole of the *Divina Commedia*, and showed Medwin the fragment of his version from the *Purgatorio*, 'Mathilda Gathering Flowers'. Medwin recalled: 'Shelley was well conscious of his talent for translation, and told me that disheartened as he was with the success of his Original composition, he thought of dedicating his time to throwing the grey veil of his own words over the perfect and glowing forms of other writers.'[11]

Medwin encouraged Shelley after his own fashion, and one morning brought down a rough version of *Inferno*, Canto XXXIII – the incarceration of Count Ugolino in a tower at Pisa with his two sons. All three were starved, and the grim poem implies, without explicitly stating, that Ugolino committed the act of cannibalism before he died, which he constantly and obsessively repeats, with a vulpine-like snapping of his jaws, in his infernal incarnation. Shelley gingerly corrected parts of Medwin's rough, and supplied the rewriting of several stanzas. The Ugolino Canto dwelt in Shelley's mind, especially as Ugolino's tower – La Torre della Fame – still stood in the city by the Ponte al Mare on the Arno.* The result of his brooding was 'The Tower of Famine', one of the last poems of the year, and one of the first of those admirable, short, meditative pieces which can be loosely grouped as his 'Pisan poems'. In 'The Tower of Famine' he substituted the cannibal image for one more familiar, and haunting; but the strange, displaced, faintly infernal aspect which Pisa sometimes revealed to him is clearly shown, that 'desolation of a city, which was the cradle, and is now the grave of an extinguished people'. The stanza form is the English terza rima, and it ends:

> There stands the pile, a tower amid the towers
> And sacred domes; each marble-ribbèd roof,
> The brazen-gated temples, and the bowers
>
> Of solitary wealth, – the tempest-proof
> Pavilions of the dark Italian air, –
> Are by its presence dimmed – they stand aloof,
>
> And are withdrawn – so that the world is bare;
> As if a spectre wrapped in shapeless terror
> Amid a company of ladies fair

---

* The sinister mace-like stone tower which stands isolated at the north-western gate of Pisa is not now identified as the historical Torre della Fame, which has been located as the squat municipal prison in Piazza dei Cavalieri.

Should glide and glow, till it became a mirror
Of all their beauty, and their hair and hue,
The life of their sweet eyes, with all its error,
Should be absorbed, till they to marble grew.[12]

Medwin found there was something faintly disquieting about Shelley's reading of poetry. He was confined to bed for some time by a travel illness, and Shelley frequently came up to read to him at the top of the Casa Galetti. He remembered how Shelley could produce an effect 'almost electric' with his recitation of 'The Witch of Atlas', and how he took a peculiar pleasure in Wordsworth's 'Peter Bell', and the various associations it had for him. 'Shelley used to chuckle, with his peculiar hysterical cachination, over this Nursery Tale of Wordsworth's and to repeat the stanza which forms the motto of his own "Peter Bell", with tears running down his laughing eyes, as he gave utterance to, –

This is Hell, and in this smother,
All are damnable and damned,
Each one damning, damns the other,
They are damned by one another,
By no other are they damned.'[13]

But it was probably not until January 1821 that Shelley began his essay 'On Devils and the Devil'.

Five days before Claire was due to return to Pisa from the Bojtis for the last week of November, Shelley wrote to her in Florence. He explained, several times over, that he wanted her to return to Pisa at the expiry of her first month's 'probationary' period, without definitely cancelling the arrangement with the Bojtis for the rest of the winter. 'How I long to see you again, and take what care I can of you – but do not imagine that if I did not most seriously think it best for you that I would advise you to return. I have suffered horribly from my side, but my general health decidedly improves, and there is now no doubt that it is a disease of the kidneys which, however it sometimes makes life intolerable has, Vaccà assures me, no tendency to endanger it. May it be prolonged that I may be the source of whatever consolation or happiness you are capable of receiving!'[14]

Claire did not make a practice of commenting in her diary on her letters either from Shelley or Mary, or on the news from Ravenna. But she amused herself by composing captions for imaginary cartoons of Byron, some of which were fairly savage. There is also one such caption-piece for Shelley during November.

'Caricature for poor [dear – *deleted*] S. He looking very sweet & smiling. A little [child – *deleted*] Jesus Christ playing about the room. He says:
Then grasping a small knife & looking mild
I will quietly murder that little child.

Another. Himself & God Almighty. He says If you please God Almighty, I had rather be damned with Plato & Lord Bacon than go to Heaven with Paley & Malthus. God Almighty: It shall be quite as you please, pray don't stand upon ceremony. Shelley's three aversions. God Almighty, Lord Chancellor & didactic Poetry.'15

Claire came back to Pisa on 21 November, and resumed her regular attendance on Mrs Mason at the Casa Silva. Four days later she spent the day in Livorno with Shelley, and came back late, at 9 in the evening, 'very tired'. It was during this excursion together that Shelley and Claire together convinced each other that she would have to go back to Florence in December. Medwin, who now met her for the first time, was very much struck by Claire, though he believed her to be four or five years older than she actually was. 'I remember her in 1820, living *en pension* at Florence, then twenty-six or twenty-seven years of age. She might have been mistaken for an Italian, for she was a *brunette* with very dark hair and eyes. . . . She possessed considerable accomplishments – spoke French and Italian, particularly the latter, with all its *nuances* and niceties . . . and possessed an *esprit de société* rare among our country women.'16

The acceptance of the dissolution of the old triangular *ménage* between Shelley, Mary and Claire did not have immediate or drastic repercussions. For at Pisa the *esprit de société* now suddenly and quite unexpectedly became general in the weeks before Christmas. For the first time since their arrival in Italy in 1818, the Shelley household at Casa Galetti became a genuinely open and hospitable one, and a routine of evening dinners and concert visits and *conversazione* began which had not occurred since the London spring of Madame Millanie and Mozart and the Hampstead literary tea-parties. In this sudden flurry of social activity, the departure of Claire to lead her own life in Florence somehow seemed more in the order of things. Although it was not to be without emotional consequences for Shelley.

The winter of 1820–1 at Pisa had at first promised to be a depressing one – quite apart from Shelley's nephritic attacks. Mary entered irritably in her journal on a wet afternoon in mid-November: 'It would be pleasant enough living in Pisa if one had a carriage, and could escape from one's house to the country without mingling with the inhabitants; but the Pisans and the Scolari, in short, the whole population, are such that it would sound strange to an English person if I attempted to express what I feel concerning them – crawling and crab-like through their sapping streets.'17 In other words, that Pisa would be pleasant enough except for the Pisans. But these feelings dramatically changed through the rapid blossoming of a friendship with one of the professors of the science faculty at Pisa University at the end of the month.

Francesco Pacchiani first made his appearance on 24 November, exactly one

27 *left* The Albergo *Tre Donzelle* where the Shelleys stayed when they first came to Pisa

28 The view of the Arno from Shelley's apartments at Pisa in 1821; the white façade of the Palazzo Lanfranchi is diagonally across the river with its private landing steps

29 *above* Sleeping Hermaphrodite, Rome

30 A page of Shelley's manuscript of stanzas 47–8 of 'The Witch of Atlas'

31 Detail of a sketch of Shelley made by Edward Williams in November 1821

32 Jane Williams, by George Clint

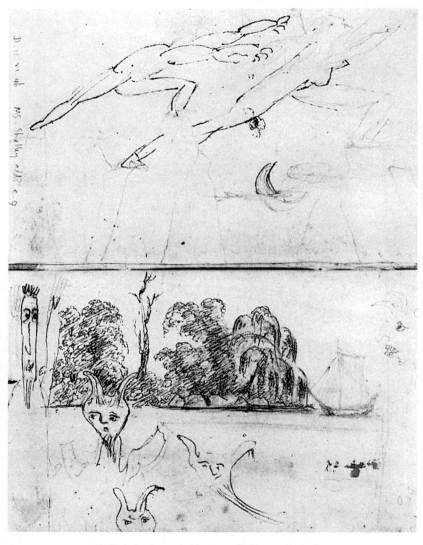

33 Shelley's sketches on inside cover of Italian notebook 1821–22

36 left Casa Magni, Lerici from a photograph taken in the 1880s

37 Manuscript sketch of the *Don Juan* and the *Bolivar*, by Edward Williams

38 Percy Bysshe Shelley in 1819 by Amelia Curran. This portrait was finished retrospectively in 1822 or 1823

39 Bust of Shelley by Marianne Leigh-Hunt.
Reproduced by permission of the Provost and Fellows of Eton College.

of those wet Fridays when they all stayed indoors and read the papers. It would seem that it was Claire who met Pacchiani at Mrs Mason's, rather than at the Casa Galetti.[18] On the following Sunday he spent the evening, and on Tuesday he supped. It was Pacchiani who introduced Shelley to a wider circle of Pisan acquaintances; he was just the man to do it. An Italian of Prato by birth, he had made a brilliant academic career, holding both the Chairs of Logic and Metaphysics at Pisa by the age of 32, while lecturing on mathematic and theoretical physics with the personal recommendations of Humboldt, Gay-Lussac and Cuvier. In 1817, Colonel Calicot Finch reported that he was still one of the two most popular lecturers among the students, with a fashionable following in Pisan society. In fact his career was on the decline, and when Shelley met him in 1820, he had, at the age of 49, just been dismissed by the university authorities, and was living among the *salons* and cafés of Pisa on his reputation as a conversationalist. He was a formidable social enemy with a lethal gift for concocting sobriquets which stuck, and was one of the best-known public eccentrics in Pisa. Medwin remembered how tall he was, with dark eyes and bony features, and a generally Moorish expression which blended well with his surroundings. Professor Pacchiani's own sobriquet was *Il Diavolo di Pisa,* an appointment which Medwin says Shelley greatly appreciated, remarking that every city should have its own. He was in fact reputed to be, as he quickly told Mary, more than a little mad.[19]

Although the friendship with Pacchiani did not remain intimate for very long, it lasted sufficiently for other introductions to follow. They were a colourful collection of human oddities, with a distinct air of the raffish. First among them was the celebrated Tommaso Sgricci, a native law student of Pisa, who had abandoned his profession to pursue his self-created career of *Improvvisatore* – a mixture of poet, stage medium and theatrical impresario. He was a highly strung personality – in fact something of a hysteric – with a natural sensibility for Greek drama and one of those rare automatic memories which could absorb dates, names, plot, quotations and whole texts with little apparent effort. In 1820, at the age of 32, he was at the height of an international career, which had triumphantly carried audiences both at Rome and Paris. At one of his evening *accademie* he could reportedly produce a three-part programme of spontaneously improvised poems: one in blank verse, one in terza rime and a complete two-and-a-half-hour tragedy on a classical theme. The inexhaustible creative faculties which this performance seemed to suggest, deeply fascinated Shelley, though he sensed the staginess of Sgricci.[20] Byron had seen him perform in Ravenna earlier in the year and wrote extenuatingly to Hobhouse: 'he is also a celebrated Sodomite, a character by no means so much respected in Italy as it should be; but they laugh instead of burning, and the women talk of it as a pity in a man of talent, but with greater tolerance than could be expected, and only express their hopes that he may yet be converted to adultery'.[21] He first spent the evening at the Casa Galetti on 1 December, and Mary said that he *improvised* with 'admirable fervour and justice', though he was too fond of female applause.[22]

Another acquaintance was Count John Taaffe, an Irish *littérateur* and traveller whose Papism had been rewarded with the honorary title of Knight Commander of the Order of St John of Jerusalem, an anachronism which suited his character. He had adopted another honorary title, 'the poet laureate of Pisa', which may have amused Shelley rather less. He was interested in the possibility of translating Dante, and had published a book of Eastern Tales, *Padilla*, in 1816. Mary regarded him as a rather ridiculous and pompous bore, but Shelley was more patient with him, since they had a common ground on the issue of translation. In the spring of 1821 he helped Taaffe with the proofs and publication of his *Comment on Dante*. Taaffe first began to call regularly with Pacchiani in the beginning of December. His role of bore seems to have had its own specialized social function in the Shelley household, for Taaffe – like Medwin, who was also to serve time in this way – seemed to ease the constant feeling of personal friction between Shelley and Mary, by the very ridiculousness of his presence. He was something to laugh about privately together – which was a great service.

A third acquaintance, of a more distinguished social background, was the young exiled Greek nobleman Prince Alexander Mavrocordato, then aged 29. His introduction, later in December, came through his cousin Prince Argyropoli, who was also within Pacchiani's circle. Mavrocordato was the leader of the Greek patriots in Europe who had been exiled because of the Turkish occupation of their native land. He had seen some service as a personal aide to the ruler of Wallachia, and he awaited anxiously the arrival of a popular Greek uprising against the Turks, when he dreamed of returning to lead his people. Many of the Philhellenic underground networks of this period centred on Mavrocordato, and in Mary's eyes especially he had the glamour of a liberator and potential hero in the field. Though small, stout, balding and bespectacled, he was both an educated and able man who had some real grasp of political action and government administration, and compared with the other potential Greek leaders, was a paradigm of personal integrity. Unexpectedly, his dream of leadership was to become reality, a very few months after he first met the Shelleys.

The last, and in some ways the most important of the new Pisan circle was, perhaps ironically, discovered by Claire. On 29 November she went with Professor Pacchiani to visit a young lady in the nearby Convent of St Anna. This was Contessa Emilia Viviani, who, at the age of 19, was undergoing the traditional Italian custom of incarceration while her parents anxiously negotiated for a husband of suitable social and financial standing. Actually Emilia was a little old for these negotiations to be still continuing, but this situation was brought about by her exceptional good looks which demanded an exceptional marital offer. A jealous mother was also involved, for Emilia's father, Count Niccolò Viviani, the present Governor of Pisa, had committed the indiscretion of marrying a wife thirty years his junior.[23] Mary described Emilia as 'romantic and pathetic . . . very beautiful, very talented, who writes Italian with an elegance and delicacy equal to the foremost authors of the best Italian epoch. . . . She sees nothing else but the servants and idiots. She never goes out, but is shut up in two small rooms which look out on the not very picturesque kitchen garden of the convent. She always laments her pitiful condition. Her only hope is to get married. . . .'[24]

The attentions of the young English Miss Clairmont were regarded as suitable by the Abbess of St Anna, and Claire was soon recording letters and visits several times a week. The letters continued even when Claire was back in Florence. Mary first saw Emilia on 1 December; and eight days later they began to read Greek and Spanish together.[25]

It is not known when Shelley was first granted visiting rights to the convent. But his first sight of Emilia in December was like a revelation. Medwin, who accompanied Shelley on his early visits, left an acute account of the impression Emilia made on his cousin. Although Medwin was always careless and unreliable in matters of names and dates and external details, he was often curiously apt in his penetration of Shelley's states of mind, and never more so than in his description of Emilia Viviani:

> Emilia was indeed lovely and interesting. Her profuse black hair, tied in the most simple knot, after the manner of a Greek Muse in the Florence Gallery, displayed to its full height her brow, fair as that of the marble of which I speak. She was also of about the same height as the antique. Her features possessed a rare faultlessness, and almost Grecian contour, the nose and forehead making a straight line, – a style of face so rare, that I remember Bartolini's telling Byron that he had scarcely an instance of such in the numerous casts of busts which his studio contained. Her eyes had the sleepy voluptuousness, if not the colour of Beatrice Cenci's. They had indeed no definite colour, changing with the changing feeling, to dark or light, as the soul animated them. Her cheek was pale, too, as marble, owing to her confinement and want of air, or perhaps 'to thought'. . . .[26]

Emilia appealed to Shelley as an incarnation of prototypes which had originally been fictions, or sculptured ideals. She was a series of artistic and imaginary conceptions made into one flesh, and she performed in Shelley's imagination the feat of Pygmalion. Further, in a way that almost alarmingly recalls Harriet Westbrook, Emilia Viviani was trapped in the proprieties of social custom and parental domination. Her situation was extremely and painfully artificial, and she was doomed to be a passive object of social and financial barter. Shelley, who was still a semi-invalid throughout December, and racked by sudden nephritic attacks, reacted as in a dream.

He was also reacting against the loss of Claire. Claire's departure before Christmas was to mark the reintroduction of ideal and partly imaginary romantic friendships in Shelley's life, of which in earlier years in England – and before Claire's presence – Elizabeth Hitchener and Cornelia Boinville had been notable victims. *Absentia Clariae* was not, after all, to bring Mary happiness.

Ten days before Christmas, during one of his nephritic spasms, Medwin tried the experiment with 'animal magnetism' that he had prearranged with Shelley. Both Mary and Claire were present, and also Taaffe and a certain Major Pittman, so it was something of a public trial. Recalling his success, Medwin wrote: 'The imposition of my hand on his forehead, instantly put a stop to his spasms, and threw him into a deep slumber, which for want of a better name has been called somnambulism. He slept with eyes open. During the continuance of it, I led him from one part of the room to the sofa in the other end; and when the trance was overpast, after the manner of all somnambulists, he would not admit that he had slept, or that he had made any replies, which I elicited from him by questioning; those replies being pitched in the same tone of voice as my own.' According to Claire, however, Shelley was rather more reticent than Medwin remembers: 'he begs them not to ask him more questions because he shall say what he ought not'. Perhaps embroidering on his achievement, Medwin also said that Shelley on his request improvised some Italian verses 'which were faultless'.[27]

The subject of mesmerism obviously fascinated the Shelleys, much as galvanism had done at the Diodati in 1816. Claire wrote as a result of their discussions, 'Magnetism is much tho secretly used in France, and they explain, the miracles which Hume speaks of as being well attested done at a french Bishop's Tomb, by a magnetic chain. To be a magnetiser it requires, a profound belief, a capacity of intense application to the act of volition and they assert, pure motives, for if he should attempt to magnetise a person upon one outward motive, with another internal & discordant, the experiment will fail.'[28]

Medwin was delighted to be a source of new information on this topic. 'Shelley had never previously heard of Mesmerism, and I showed him a treatise I composed, embodying most of the facts recorded by its adepts, and he was particularly struck by a passage in Tacitus, no incredulous historian, who seriously related two cases in Egypt. . . .' The conversation then moved on to the issue of the limitations of a strictly 'materialist' philosophy. Shelley said that mesmerism seemed to prove that 'a separation from the mind and body took place – the one being most active and the other an inert mass of matter'. Medwin adds that Shelley thought this was an argument for 'the immortality of the soul', implying perhaps theistic tendencies. But the belief in an immaterial 'soul', like the immaterial 'ghost', did not seem to Shelley to have anything to do with the existence of a Deity, as his argument with Byron and Monk Lewis had demonstrated in 1816.

Yet Shelley's illness at Pisa that winter did have the curious effect of bringing him back to old realms of speculation. The intermediary world of Plato's daemons and *kaka-daimons*, and the old haunted imagery began to reappear in his poetry with increasing power and frequency. Shelley's main notebook of this winter, which contains the draft of his essay 'On the Devil' also contains several curious diabolic sketches, the most striking of which appear on the endpapers at the back and front.[29]

Shelley's dabbling with hypnotism continued throughout 1821, and he found it especially efficacious when the 'magnetizer' was a woman. The relationship set up between therapist and patient was obviously one that appealed to him, and in its mixture of intense intimacy and clinical detachment, he found some expression of his emotional needs. The image of the beloved woman as magnetizer appears in *Epipsychidion*.

'After my departure from Pisa,' Medwin wrote, 'he was magnetised by a lady, which gave rise to the beautiful stanzas entitled "The Magnetic Lady to Her Patient", and during which operation, he made the same reply to an enquiry as to his disease, and its cure, as he had done to me, – "What would cure me would kill me," – meaning lithotomy. Mrs Shelley also magnetised him, but soon discontinued the practice, from finding that he got up in his sleep, and went one night to the window, (fortunately barred,) having taken to his old habit of sleepwalking, which I mentioned, in his boyhood, and also in London.'[30]*

Shelley was temporarily better on 21 December, and Claire played two games of chess with him before they went to visit Emilia Viviani for two hours.[31] In the evening they all went to hear one of Sgricci's performances at the Pisan theatre,

---

* Friedrich Anton Mesmer was born in Austria in 1733 and died in Switzerland in 1815. His magnetic experiments led to his ejection from Vienna by the police, and his later denunciation by an official investigating committee in Paris in 1785. Nevertheless he contributed an original theme to nineteenth-century gothic fiction, and must be regarded as the occult forefather of modern therapeutic hypnotism and psycho-analysis. 'Lithotomy' – an eighteenth-century word meaning the art of cutting out stones from the bladder. In Shelley's time it was still an agonizing and dangerous operation, depending for success entirely on the doctor's skill with a surgical knife, and for anaesthesia on the patient's own powers of endurance. Shelley dreaded having to submit to this operation, and there is some evidence that he contemplated suicide as a better alternative.

an improvisation of *Iphigenia in Tauris* over a full five acts. Shelley was impressed, but Mary was in raptures and filled most of a long letter to Hunt with Sgricci's praises. 'He is handsome – his person small but elegant – and his motions graceful beyond description. . . . I am inclined to think that in the perfection in which he possesses this art it is by no means an inferior power to that of a *printed poet*.' The theatre was half empty, except for a few university students, and talking to Sgricci afterwards Shelley remarked on the spiritual deadness of Pisa. Some of his phrases, remembered by Mary, have a curious resonance about them, and appear in later 'Pisan poems'. 'As Shelley told him . . . he appeared in Pisa as Dante among the ghosts – Pisa is a city of the dead and they are shrunk from his living presence.'[32]

Two days later Claire departed on the Florence diligence, escorted by the ubiquitous Pacchiani, and Shelley, overcome by a sudden sense of loss, was unwell all over Christmas. Sometimes Mary read to him in between his spasms. His eyes watered. Mary wrote to Maria Gisborne on the last day of the year, 'Shelley has had a cold in his eyes which has prevented him writing and reading for above a fortnight. – How does this cold weather agree with Mr Gisborne. – I hope he keeps close to the fire and lets the wind howl vainly.'[33] Meanwhile Claire wrote in her diary with her thoughts turned alternately to Shelley at Pisa and Byron at Ravenna: 'A great Poet resembles Nature – he is a Creator and a Destroyer, he presides over the birth & death of images, the prototypes of things – the torrent of his sentiments should flow like waves one after the other, each distinctly formed and visible yet linked between its predecessor and its follower as to form between them both by beauty and necessity an indissoluble connection.'[34]

Throughout January 1821 Shelley continued a prey to various infections, ophthalmia, boils and the chronic nephritis. Whenever he was well enough he paid a morning or afternoon visit to the convent of St Anna. He seems to have done little writing except his essay 'On the Devil', a finished draft of which probably belongs to this month. When it was announced that Sgricci was giving a performance at Lucca, he persuaded Mary to go alone, taking little Percy with her. His boils were bad, and his face 'swelled dreadfully',[35] so he was in no travelling condition. In a characteristic phrase of this time, Mary 'cooked up a party with Pacchiani', and was away for two days. The improvisation was a success – as Claire heard at stunning length – but Pacchiani was not, and Mary escaped from him early on. 'He would make one believe that he attracts the great as a milk pail does flies on a summer morning.'[36]

Claire had been taken ill with a scrofulous gland on reaching Florence, and Shelley wrote sadly: 'It seems that it would have been better for you to remain at Pisa. Yet being now at Florence make the best profit of your situation. . . .'

He advised her to pursue Mrs Mason's social contacts assiduously so that she might make herself more independent. Later they were to discuss a plan for Claire set to up a small school for English children at Pisa. Meanwhile he prescribed 'bustle and occupation'. His own health was still bad: 'I have suffered also considerably from my disease; and am already in imagination preparing to be cut for the stone, in spite of Vaccà's consolatory assurance.' There was one other source of comfort. 'I see Emilia sometimes, who always talks of you and laments your absence. She continues to enchant me infinitely; and I soothe myself with the idea that I make the discomfort of her captivity lighter to her by demonstration of the interest which she has awakened in me.'[37]

The relationship between the invalid Shelley and the 19-year-old prisoner of the convent was developing rather more rapidly than Shelley would quite admit to Claire. The whole thing had in his mind a strangely unreal quality, almost as if she was part of his illness, as a vivid hallucination is part of a fever. Shelley sent a little verse letter in reply to a bunch of flowers which Emilia had had delivered to the Casa Galetti, on a day when he was ill and could not visit:

> Madonna, wherefore has thou sent to me
>   Sweet-basil and mignonette?
> Embleming love and health, which never yet
> In the same wreath might be.
>   Alas, and they are wet!
> Is it with thy kisses or thy tears?[38]

It tells a good deal about his feelings for Emilia, and the way in which he tried to modulate them, when this is compared with the first draft he made in his notebook, but never sent:

> Oh my beloved why have you
>   Sent sweet basil & mignonette?
> Why when I kiss their leaves find I them wet
>   With thine adored tears dearer than heavens dew.[39]

In two other notebooks he made fragmentary drafts of five Italian letters to Emilia, though it is impossible to say on exactly which days Shelley sent them. In the second letter he promised to help her by having an influential friend write to the Prior of St Nicholas at Pisa. In the third, he wrote: 'Here we are then, bound by a few days' friendship, gathered together by some strange fortune from the ends of the earth to be perhaps a consolation to each other. . . .' In the fourth, the whole fragment consists simply of: 'tu Emilia ch'era più bella a vedere che il giglio bianco sul suo verde stelo e più fresca che la Maia quando...'

You, Emilia, who were lovelier to behold than the white lily on its green stem and fresher than May when . . .

The fifth letter fragment seems to contain the essence of the fever dream which she had become for Shelley. 'Many times you thus [appear to] me. Your dark eyes, ever most beautiful, are above me. I seem to feel your hand on mine and your lips – but then I close my eyes until you cease to love – then it will be quenched like a flame which lacks fuel. I have suffered much in health today. . . .' Most expressive of all is the fact that Shelley having written this passage struck the whole of it through with his pen, and probably never sent it.[40]

Some of Emilia's letters, both to Mary and to Shelley during these weeks, have survived.[41] They show perfectly Emilia's mixture of naïveté and charming adolescent cunning in dealing with Mary, notably in a letter of the end of December: 'You seem to me a little cold, on some occasions, and this makes me a little nervous of you [*un po' di soggezionie*]; but I realize that your Husband speaks justly, and that your apparent coldness is only the ash which covers a radiant heart [*un cuore affettuoso*].'[42] To Shelley, her notes are pitched at an altogether more impassioned level, and one can see in the almost Petrarchan use of sun and moon and stars as love-witnesses, the immediate source of the imagery which Shelley was now preparing to use in his poem about her. 'Dear Friend, and my own Brother: – I write to you by the radiance of the Moon. I cannot bear to use any other light, for that would appear as an insult to this most clear and beautiful Daughter of Heaven. What sweetness I feel when I gaze upon her. . . . I have made my usual evening prayer on my knees before the window, and I have made it with greater devotion. These stupid people here believe that I worship the Moon. . . .'[43]

Mary does not at first seem to have had any grasp of what was going on in Shelley's mind. On the 14th she wrote that she had seen little of Emilia, 'but she was in much better spirits when I did see her than I had found her for a long time before'.[44] Ten days later it was the same – surprisingly she was in 'much better spirits'. Anyway Mary was busily engaged in other directions, taking private Greek lessons from Prince Mavrocordato, and holding *tête à têtes* with Tommaso Sgricci, as she explained to Claire.[45]

Meanwhile Emilia wrote an essay for Shelley on 'Il Vero Amore', which flew effortlessly between earth and heaven on the wings of adolescence: 'But where is he, susceptible of such love? Where? Who is capable of inspiring it? Oh love! I am all love. . . . Love has no wish but for virtue. . . . Love is a fire that burns and destroys not, a mixture of pleasure and pain, a pain that brings pleasure, an essence eternal, spiritual, infinite, pure, celestial.'[46] It sounded less adolescent in Italian, and some of the phraseology was imported from Shelley's conversations.[47]

Claire, despite the distance of several score miles, seems to have been more *au fait*. The correspondence was private between her and Shelley – her letters were addressed to him at the Casa Silva, not to the Casa Galetti[48] – and she was also in touch with Emilia. In a 'kind & tender' letter towards the end of January, she appears to have quizzed Shelley mildly on the subject. His reply was warm, but slightly defensive. 'I see Emilia sometimes: & whether her presence is the source of pain or pleasure to me, I am equally ill-fated in both. I am deeply interested in her destiny, & that interest can in no manner influence it. She is not however insensible to my sympathy, & she counts it among her alleviations. As much comfort as she receives from my attachment to her, *I lose*. – There is no reason that you should fear any mixture of that which you call *love*.'[49] He slipped into this letter the fact that the secret scheme for the Eastern expedition was 'broken up'. But the letter was signed off: 'I took up the pen for an instant, only to thank you. – & if you will to kiss you for your kind attention to me, & I find I have written in ill spirits. . . . Yours most tenderly.'

On the last two days of January Mary noted that Shelley was reading Dante's essay on love and poetry, the *Vita Nuova*. Under the intense vision of his relationship with the beautiful Emilia, under the auspices of Dante, and struggling against his own ill health, he now wrote the extraordinary piece of autobiography, *Epipsychidion*. It was done within a fortnight, for a clean copy of the poem was in the post to Ollier for printing by 16 February.

Shelley's *Epipsychidion* is just over 600 lines long, written without stanza form, in couplets which often flow freely on over a dozen lines. It is a conscious piece of rhetorical improvisation partly influenced by the performances of Sgricci. The whole poem is explicitly addressed to 'the Noble and Unfortunate Lady, Emilia V——, Now imprisoned in the Convent of ——'. But it is formed from two divergent inspirations, which are in the end conflicting. The first is a courtly love-hymn to Emilia, an invitation to her to escape from the convent and take ship with him on his long-imagined expedition to the East:

> Emily,
> A ship is floating in the harbour now,
> And wind is hovering o'er the mountain's brow . . . .
> Say, my heart's sister, wilt thou sail with me?
> Our bark is as an albatross, whose nest
> Is a far Eden of the purple East;
> And we between her wings will sit. . . .[50]

This courtly invitation ends in a vision of spiritual union which is presented with great and indeed almost violent erotic intensity:

> Our breath shall intermix, our bosoms bound,
> And our veins beat together; and our lips

> With other eloquence than words, eclipse
> The soul that burns between them, and the wells
> Which boil under our being's inmost cells,
> The fountains of our deepest life, shall be
> Confused in Passion's golden purity,
> As mountain springs under the morning sun.[51]

But it is a failing vision. The difficulty which Shelley had with the word 'purity', which is a substitute word, indicates one of the characteristic weaknesses of this part of the poem. It attempts to hold simultaneously a spiritual and a physical image of human passion, like one of the 'multiple images' of *Prometheus*. Such a union was possible for Shelley, but not within the circumstances of his feverish dream relationship with a convent heiress. The contradictions were too great, and this showed vividly in the straining and flinching in the poetry of the courtly part of *Epipsychidion*. The 'invitation' was also complicated by the bisexual or hermaphroditic status which he assigned to Emilia, implicitly in the published text, and explicitly in the subsidiary fragments, one of which refers to the 'sweet marble monster' of the Borghese statue.[52] The second inspiration of *Epipsychidion* is, like *Alastor*, a retrospective review of his own emotional development since adolescence. To this extent the work is a *poème à clef*, and there are a series of references to actual women and events in Shelley's life which are only intended to be partially disguised, and were certainly meant to be interpreted by the most intimate of his circle:

> In many mortal forms I rashly sought
> The shadow of that idol of my thought.
> And some were fair – but beauty dies away:
> Others were wise – but honeyed words betray:
> And One was true – oh! why not true to me?[53]

The shadows of Elizabeth Shelley, Harriet Grove, Harriet Westbrook, Elizabeth Hitchener, Cornelia Boinville, Sophia Stacey and perhaps others all fit along the margins of the verse. The only definite identifications are Emilia herself, Mary Shelley and Claire Clairmont. Part of the general argument of the poem thus becomes the autobiographical fact, and also to Shelley the philosophical necessity, of the lifelong search among many women for a *donna ideale*: the Beautiful of Diotima's ladder in the *Symposium*; or the divine Beatrice of Dante's *Vita Nuova*; or even in one of Shelley's references to the mysterious Beloved of Shakespeare's Sonnets.[54] It is in this sense that the poem is about free love. Shelley's original tenet of physical freedom as expressed in his letters of 1811–12, and in the notes to *Queen Mab*, and *The Revolt of Islam*, is maintained and extended into a complete if heterogeneous philosophical system.

Previous to *Epipsychidion* the evidence is that Shelley's belief in free love was simply based on a liberal view of men and women's biological needs, and a violent disagreement with the social institutions which defined them in terms of monogamous property. With *Epipsychidion*, Shelley had added to these a new philosophical dimension in which free love was understood to be an integral part of a full spiritual education. Free love, as it were, led to true love or universal love – and hereby became not merely a social but a moral and philosophical necessity. Much of the language for this was taken directly from Dante.* The poem is not a very consistent literary achievement, but it is a fascinating intellectual one, and a unique picture of Shelley's emotional life at the age of 28.

> I never was attached to that great sect,
> Whose doctrine is, that each one should select
> Out of the crowd a mistress or a friend,
> And all the rest, though fair and wise, commend
> To cold oblivion, though it is in the code
> Of modern morals, and the beaten road
> Which those poor slaves with weary footsteps tread,
> Who travel to their home among the dead
> By the broad highway of the world, and so
> With one chained friend, perhaps a jealous foe,
> The dreariest and the longest journey go.[55]

The parts of the poem which formed the courtly love-hymn to Emilia were to some extent an embarrassment, and even a contradiction to the more strictly autobiographical sections. He was promising eternal courtly love in a poem which actually celebrated free love. Shelley therefore resorted to a series of four 'Advertisements', which were designed to make the whole situation of the poem – even its author – appear completely fictitious. He himself was only to appear as the 'editor' of another man's poem. The first of these prefaces which he rejected, after some consideration, ran:

> The following Poem was found amongst other papers in the Portfolio of a young Englishman with whom the Editor had contracted an intimacy at Florence, brief indeed, but sufficiently long to render the Catastrophe by which

---

* But not, as Shelley makes out in his Advertisement, from the *Vita Nuova*. The actual sources are the first *canzone* of the *Convivio*; for the free love passage, *Purgatorio*, Canto xv, where Dante questions Virgil on the nature of divine love; and for the vision of Emilia as an 'incarnation of the Sun' – the central image of the whole poem – *Purgatorio* Canto xxviii. The full moral and social implications of Shelley's mature philosophy of free love filtered gradually down through two generations of Victorian readers, and began to emerge clearly in such texts as John Stuart Mill's *The Subjection of Women* (1869), and Edward Carpenter's *Love's Coming-of-Age* (1896).

it terminated one of the most painful events of his life. . . . He had framed to himself certain opinions, founded no doubt upon the truth of things, but built up to a Babel height; they fell by their own weight, & the thoughts that were his architects, became unintelligible one to the other, as men upon whom confusion of tongues has fallen. . . . The melancholy charge of consigning the body of my poor friend to the grave, was committed to me by his desolated family.[56]

This seemed to be along the right lines, but Shelley decided to increase the realism of the 'young Englishman's' situation, and thereby make the fictitious occasion of his death appear more authentic and more closely related to the actual 'invitation' to Emilia. In this he hoped to distance himself as the 'Editor' even further from his text. In fact he inadvertently did the reverse, and this second preface is perhaps the most revealing of all about the triangular relationship between Shelley, Emilia and Mary, and reverts to his Eastern expedition:

The following Poem was found in the PF of a young Englishman, who died on his passage from Leghorn to the Levant. . . . He was accompanied by a lady supposed to be his wife, & an effeminate looking youth, to whom he shewed so [singular – *deleted*] excessive an attachment as to give rise to the suspicion, that she was a woman – At his death this suspicion was confirmed; [*blank*] object speedily found a refuge both from the taunts of the brute multitude, and from the [*blank*] of her grief in the same grave that contained her lover. – He had bought one of the Sporades, & fitted up a Saracenic castle which accident had preserved in some repair with simple elegance, & it was his intention to dedicate the remainder of his life to undisturbed intercourse with his companions.[57]

Realizing that these references to his wife and 'an effeminate looking youth' revealed far more than they disguised, he interpolated instead, in his third draft preface, a comparison with the ideal literary character of the *Vita Nuova*. The fourth & final preface of 'Advertisement', which he included in the manuscript sent to Ollier, thus read:

The Writer of the following lines died at Florence, as he was preparing for a voyage to one of the wildest of the Sporades. . . . His life was singular; less on account of the romantic vicissitudes which diversified it, than the ideal tinge which it received from his own character and feelings. The present Poem, like the *Vita Nuova* of Dante, is sufficiently intelligible to a certain class of readers without a matter-of-fact history of the circumstances to which it relates; and to a certain other class it must ever remain incomprehensible. . . .[58]

The poem itself is headed by a suitably grave and forbidding translation of the last stanza of Dante's first *canzone* in the *Convivio*;

> My Song, I fear that thou wilt find but few
> Who fitly shall conceive thy reasoning. . . .

This intricate web of precautions was further elaborated in Shelley's covering letter to Ollier on 16 February, in which he insisted that the poem be published in strictest anonymity. 'It is to be published simply for the esoteric few.' Shelley suggested an edition of 100 copies. Why should Shelley have gone to such immense trouble to obscure the sources of his poem? Especially when he afterwards insisted that it really was a piece of pure literary convention, a piece of 'philosophical idealism' of no interest except to those initiated in Platonism or the fourteenth-century conventions of *fino amore*? The answer is simply that *Epipsychidion* is the most nakedly autobiographical poem he ever wrote.

The central section of the poem, lines 277 to 320, presenting Mary as the Moon (first 'young and fair', later chaste, cold 'pale and waning'), refer to the story of the years 1814–15, together with the loss of Harriet, Ianthe and Charles, during the crisis of 1816–17. It ends with the terrible image drawn from the Mer de Glace:

> The moving billows of my being fell
> Into a death of ice, immovable; –
> And then – what earthquakes made it gape and split,
> The white Moon smiling all the while on it,
> These words conceal. . . .[59]

At length, upon this frozen prospect 'The Vision I had sought through grief and shame' appears in her cosmological and courtly form, 'Soft as an incarnation of the Sun', which finally melts Shelley. The identification is explicit –

> I knew it was the Vision veiled from me
> So many years – that it was Emily.[60]

In a remarkable passage Shelley now described the triangular relationship he wanted with Emily and Mary, which is of course very far from Dante's worshipful and singular relationship with Beatrice. The triple cosmological identifications are now, with transparent logic, Mary the Moon, Emily the Sun, Shelley the Earth. He also combined geophysical concepts of magnetic and gravitational fields affecting earth-tides and seasons, as used in Act IV of *Prometheus*, with the new ideas of Dr Mesmer's 'animal magnetism' introduced to him by Medwin. The result is a spectacular 'multiple image' projection of the emotional and psychological forces at work in the relationship. Shelley is, as ever, essentially passive:

> Twin Spheres of light who rule this passive Earth,
> This world of love, this *me*; and into birth
> Awaken all its fruits and flowers, and dart
> Magnetic might into its central heart;
> And lift its billows, and its mists, and guide
> By everlasting laws, each wind and tide
> To its fit cloud, and its appointed cave. . . .
> And all their many-mingled influence blend,
> If equal, yet unlike, to one sweet end; –
> So ye, bright regents, with alternate sway
> Govern my sphere of being, night and day!

What Mary thought of her shared role as 'bright regent' – after the long, long struggle for *absentia Clariae* – may well be imagined. She did not mention the poem in her letters for many months, and then it was with a mixture of bitterness and relief at the outcome of the affair.[61] She called it 'Shelley's Italian Platonics' and quoted a popular song about Cranbourne Lane. It is the one long poem of Shelley's she did not choose to comment on in her edition of 1839.

But what of Claire? Was she lost finally from the Shelleyan solar system? On the contrary, Shelley found her a brilliant place, in the succeeding verse passage, which is one of the high points in the uneven flow of the improvisation. While retaining its courtly grandeur, its 'ideal tinge', the poetry when turned towards the dark handsome features of Claire takes on a certain wit – almost irony – in the reference to their volatile relationship, and to the Moon. Though it is painful, it is altogether more sprightly. If Emilia was Sun, and Mary was Moon, then with a flash of inspiration,* Claire was

> Thou too, O Comet beautiful and fierce,
> Who drew the heart of this frail Universe
> Towards thine own; till, wrecked in that convulsion,
> Alternating attraction and repulsion,
> Thine went astray and that was rent in twain;
> Oh, float into our azure heaven again!

---

* The comet image, like most of Shelley's best, had been long germinating. It is the same comet – no doubt a pure anticipated cognition – that Shelley first saw in 1811 at Edinburgh; first described in the 'dark-red night' of the revolutionary poem 'Zeinab and Kathema' also of 1811. It flashes through *Prometheus* in the lovely line of Act III, scene 3, 'And long blue meteors cleansing the dull night'. The MS Notebook, Bod. MS Shelley Adds. e. 9, which contains the draft of the comet passage (p. 196 rev.) also has a dramatic ink drawing of a comet drawn diagonally across the whole of p. 317.

Be there Love's folding-star at thy return;
The living Sun will feed thee from its urn
Of golden fire; the Moon will veil her horn
In thy last smiles; adoring Even and Morn
Will worship thee with incense of calm breath
And lights and shadows; as the star of Death
And Birth is worshipped by those sisters wild
Called Hope and Fear – upon the heart are piled
Their offerings, – of this sacrifice divine
A World shall be the altar.[62]

Writing in the autobiographical way that Shelley was, one can be certain that both Even and Morn have personal identifications – one might hazard little Percy Florence and Allegra. There would also be deep personal reasons for identifying Claire with the 'star of Death and Birth', and writing of a 'sacrifice divine'. But this was something that perhaps Claire alone was ever intended to interpret. The description of their lively and intimate relationship of the heart, however, could not be more clearly summarized than in 'Alternating attraction and repulsion, thine went astray and [mine] was rent in twain'. It is the openness that Shelley has found to say this which is really striking.

There is one other passage in the autobiographical sections of *Epipsychidion* which is of special interest. Judging by its position it appears to refer to an event at the very beginning of Shelley's career, and certainly before he met Mary in 1814. It seems to refer to a first sexual experience, probably in the Oxford and Poland Street period of 1810–11. At any rate it was a horrific one, and the verse takes on that bright, grotesque sharpness one associates with the best passages of *The Revolt of Islam*:

There, – One, whose voice was venomed melody
Sate by a well, under blue nightshade bowers;
The breath of her false mouth was like faint flowers,
Her touch was as electric poison, – flame
Out of her looks into my vitals came,
And from her living cheeks and bosom flew
A killing air, which pierced like honey-dew
Into the core of my green heart, and lay
Upon its leaves; until, as hair grown gray
O'er a young brow, they hid its unblown prime
With ruins of unseasonable time.[63]

The only person who claimed to interpret this passage with any authority was, surprisingly enough, Leigh Hunt's eldest son Thornton, who had first known

Shelley at Hampstead. He stated that 'accident has made me aware of facts' –
meaning presumably conversation at the Hunt household – which suggested
that Shelley had had an unhappy sexual experience during his college life which
caused him to contract a veneral disease. As Hunt puts it, 'instead of the Flori-
men, he found her venal, hideous, and fatal *simulacrum*; and [Shelley] indicates
even the material consequences to himself in his injured aspect and hair touched
with grey'. At this time prematurely grey hair was regarded as an after-effect of
some instances of venereal infection.[64] Shelley was always markedly violent in
his denunciation of prostitution and his horror of infectious and 'hideous
diseases'; though Hunt makes no specific reference to a prostitute. If what Hunt
says had any basis in fact, one might reasonably expect other references to the
incident in Shelley's work. *Queen Mab* of course contains much general discussion of the issues, but there is a passage in Canto VI of *The Revolt of Islam*
which seems to be dealing with the same incident. Certainly the odd placing
reference to the 'well' recurs, and also similar images of 'blue nightshade' and
infectious poison. The two stanzas occur at the moment when Laon has left
Cythna in her mountain stronghold, and ridden secretly back into the City
which is in the grip of famine and plague:

> Beside the fountain in the market-place
> Dismounting, I beheld those corpses stare
> With horny eyes upon each other's face,
> And on the earth and on the vacant air,
> And upon me, close to the waters where
> I stooped to slake my thirst. . . .

> No living thing was there beside one woman,
> Whom I found wandering in the streets, and she
> Was withered from a likeness of aught human
> Into a fiend, by some strange misery:
> Soon as she heard my steps she leaped on me,
> And glued her burning lips to mine, and laughed
> With a loud, long, and frantic laugh of glee,
> And cried, 'Now, Mortal, thou hast deeply quaffed
> The Plague's blue kisses – soon millions shall pledge the draught! . . .'[65]

The two passages make an interesting comparison, at the very least, in the
development they show in the vividness and economy of Shelley's writing over
the intervening period of three and a half years. Yet *Epipsychidion* is not one of
Shelley's finished and self-sufficient works. Like *Alastor*, though to a far greater

degree, it gains its main strength from the depth and accuracy with which he questioned his own life and mind.

Even on the day he posted it to Ollier, there was a suggestion of regret and retraction. 'It is a production,' he told his publisher, 'of a portion of me already dead; and in this sense the advertisement is no fiction.'[66] Yet Ollier published promptly in the summer. To John Gisborne – once again in London – Shelley was to write in October a celebrated extenuation: 'The Epipsychidion is a mystery – As to real flesh & blood, you know that I do not deal in those articles, – you might as well go to a ginshop for a leg of mutton, as expect any thing human or earthly from me. I desired Ollier not to circulate this piece except to the Σύνετοι [initiated], and even they it seems are inclined to approximate me to the circle of a servant girl & her sweetheart. – But I intend to write a Symposium of my own to set all this right.' But this was yet another defensive screen, and perhaps the fact that Shelley was writing to the Gisbornes affects the sarcastic form it took, and the surely ironic reference to a servant girl and her sweetheart.[67]

It was only a year later, in June 1822, when Gisborne had moved much further into his confidence and was acting as his *de facto* literary agent in London, that Shelley withdrew this screen, admitted to 'flesh & blood', and spoke both more frankly and more humorously of the poem. 'If you are anxious . . . to hear what I am and have been ['Epipsychidion'] will tell you something thereof. It is an idealized history of my life and feelings. I think one is always in love with something or other; the error, and I confess it is not easy for spirits cased in flesh and blood to avoid it, consists in seeking in a mortal image the likeness of what is perhaps eternal. Hogg is very droll and very wicked about this poem, which he says, he likes – he praises it and says: *Tantum de medio sumptis accedit honoris.** Now that, I contend, even in Latin, is not to be permitted.'[68] But whether that image of the beloved – the 'epi-psychidion', the 'soul out of my soul' as Shelley called her – was indeed unattainable and eternal, remained for Shelley, even at that late date, an open question.

Throughout the rest of February 1821, both Shelley and Mary continued regular visits to Emilia, and Shelley arranged to write and have presented a petition on Emilia's behalf to the Grand Duchess in Florence, begging for her release. But this was rather different from preparing an escape boat in Livorno harbour as he had suggested in his poem. In March the number of visits, according to Mary's journal, gradually fell off. Shelley, Mary and Claire all

---

* Which may be rendered, in the Hogg manner, as

From our grey worlds of commonplace
Your skills attract bright forms of grace

Horace, *Ars Poetica*, l. 243

remained in touch with Emilia through the spring until her marriage in the summer.

As the intense focus on Emilia Viviani dissolved, and Shelley's health also improved, his social circle continued to alter and expand. Medwin's long-promised friends Edward and Jane Williams had finally arrived in Pisa at the end of January, and by the end of February they had established a friendly *rapport* with the Shelleys. The slow growth of this friendship, a gradual putting down of roots, was ultimately more promising than the whirlwind intimacies with people such as Pacchiani and Emilia, which broke quickly and exotically into blossom, and then withered in the sudden alterations of emotional *sirocco* and *tramontana*. For Mary, too, they were easier: the Williamses were, after all, English.

Shelley's first impressions, as he told Claire, were not distinctive. The woman was extremely pretty, with large dark eyes and a mass of dark hair but 'apparently not *very* clever'. Williams himself, tall, open-faced with well-cut florid features, seemed pleasant, rather shy. He was a year younger than Shelley, and had done time at Eton, which no doubt put Shelley on his guard. But he had left at 11 and been sent straight to the Navy, from thence transferring like Medwin to the Eighth Dragoons of the East India Company. Like Medwin he had retired as a lieutenant on half pay and he had decided to knock about Europe for a few years. He was intensely attached to Jane Williams partly because, perhaps, she was not actually his married wife. They had lived for a little over a year at Geneva in a house with Medwin, before moving south at his incitement, partly to meet Medwin's poetical cousin. It was also partly to find a discreet location for Jane to have her second baby, which was duly born on 16 March.[69] Another of Williams's connections at Geneva was a strange piratical Cornish adventurer called Trelawny. He too had heard of the poet at Pisa, and was later to come south. Williams had vague literary ambitions, and wrote stage plays that were never performed. Politically, he was liberal. But his real gift was for being extraordinarily easy, cheerful company out of doors. He was equally fond of walking, riding and sailing. When Medwin left Pisa on 27 February – to Mary's intense relief – Williams was already established as a walking companion, and both he and Jane had dined and supped on several occasions. As the weather opened out in early March, with soft misty mornings, followed by bright invigorating days of sun and cloud and wind, Shelley and Williams walked out daily along the Arno.[70]

Shelley did not neglect Claire, for letters continued to post off to Florence, and return via Mrs Mason's. He wrote of Emilia, but now at less length; of del Rosso affairs, which still required attention; and occasionally of news from Ravenna. Byron had moved the four-year-old Allegra into a convent at

Bagnacavallo.[71] Shelley continued to sign himself through February and March with 'eternal and tender regard', though Claire could not help noticing that the letters tended to drop off in number.

Mary's life at this time was a good deal taken up with Prince Mavrocordato, who had emerged as her clear favourite among the new circle. In early March they had moved to new lodgings on the Lung'Arno, at the Casa Aulla, partly to celebrate the spring weather but mostly to have rooms more suitable for entertaining. Mavrocordato visited every day, and Mary gave him English lessons in exchange for lessons in classical Greek. What with the Prince, and the walks and rides with the Williamses, and occasional nights at the opera with the Masons, life was fairly kind to Mary. The worst of the business seemed to be over with Emilia, and it had become, as she told Claire, 'a delicious season'. She added in her grave, smiling way: 'One is not gay – at least I am not – but peaceful and at peace with all the world.'[72]

Shelley did not look on Mavrocordato with Mary's eyes, but he found him interesting on the subject of Greek politics, and discreet and distinguished in manner. The Prince was, in his own way, Mary's answer to Emilia, and also an implicit suggestion to Shelley that 'Italian Platonics' could really be managed with better taste than he had contrived to do. Shelley acquiesced. He wrote to Peacock requesting two-pounds-worth of gems from Tassi's in Leicester Square, among which he wanted a ring or cameo cut with the head of Alexander the Great. This was a present for Mavrocordato. Shelley also asked for seals to be made up with the device of a dove with outspread wings, and the Greek motto Μάντις εἰμί ἐσθλῶν ἀγωνών, 'I am the Prophet of Victorious Struggles'.[73] His expectation of a struggle in Greece was presently to be fulfilled. The faint air of romantic comedy which breathed over the Casa Aulla in March also reached out to Claire in Florence, who received a series of anonymous love-letters from Pisa embellished with charming sketches. Her immediate reaction was to accuse Shelley, and send the letters to the Casa Aulla for examination, but their author was never discovered.[74]

The writing of *Epipsychidion* had freed Shelley from the difficult winter months of ill health and listless fantasy, and with the early Pisan spring of March, he was suddenly full of literary projects. He revived the idea of an historical drama on Charles I, and began making notes on the political figures of the period, informing Ollier that this successor to *The Cenci* would soon be ready for the press. He had also heard that Peacock had published a scathing magazine article on the decline of English Poetry in the first number of Ollier's *Literary Miscellany*. He determined to reply to it, and began to ransack his notebooks for suitable material.

The gist of Peacock's clever and provoking piece had initially reached Shelley in Peacock's latest letter in January. It was that 'there is no longer a poetical audience among the higher class of minds; that moral, political and physical science have entirely withdrawn from poetry the attention of all whose attention is worth having; and that the poetical reading public, being composed of the mere dregs of the intellectual community ... [poetry] must rest on the mixture of a little easily-intelligible portion of mawkish sentiment with an absolute negation of reason and knowledge'.[75]

Shelley reacted sharply to this line of attack, for there were clearly moments in his own writing career when he himself believed it to be true. He told Peacock that his 'anathemas against poetry' had excited in him a 'sacred rage', and he intended to break a lance with him within the lists of a magazine.[76] But he had not yet read the article itself, and he sent for it from Florence, while preparing himself in the last days of February by reading Sidney's *An Apologie for Poetrie*[77] and making draft notes on the use of the imaginative faculty in literture.[78] Mary was also brought in on the undertaking, and every day from 12 to 20 March she clean-copied a new piece for the essay. Shelley was hoping to finish it in time for it to be published in the spring number of Ollier's *Miscellany*, and had it planned out in two parts: a general defence of the function of imaginative literature in society; followed by a more detailed examination of the growth of modern English poetry. There was also a vague idea for a third part.[79] In the event, only Part 1 was ever finished.

Shelley's *A Defence of Poetry* is, as it stands, an essay of some 10,000 words, and became the best-known piece of prose that he wrote. Yet its unique distinction is partly illusory, for it is in effect an anthology of his own previous writing. Besides extensive borrowing and adaption from his prefaces to *The Revolt of Islam* (1817) and *Prometheus Unbound* (1819), his preface to the *Symposium* known as 'A Discourse on the Manners of the Ancient Greeks' (1818), and his 'Essay on Christianity', the general argument of the article as a whole is largely an amplification of that set out in the first two chapters of *A Philosophical View of Reform* (1820). The famous peroration to the *Defence* on poets as 'unacknowledged legislators' comes virtually verbatim from this last essay; and the brilliant passage on Milton's Satan is also lifted directly from the text of his 'Essay on the Devil'.[80]

Throughout the *Defence*, Shelley was writing of 'poetry' in an inclusive sense; it ranged from the literary genre *per se*, through the general ideas of imaginative writing, and out as far as poetry considered as a sympathetic and humane *faculty* – a simple responsiveness to human experience which he called the 'poetry of life'. He continued, as in the *Philosophical View* to regard the issue of the function of 'poetry' as a moral and political one, rather than as a purely literary one. In an interesting formal introduction, written to Ollier in his role as

Editor of the *Miscellany*, Shelley defined very carefully the position which Peacock had taken up:

> Every person conscious of intellectual power ought studiously to wean himself from the study and the practise of poetry, & ought to apply that power to general finance, political economy to the study in short of the laws according to which the forms of the social order might be most wisely regulated for the happiness of those whom it binds together. – These are indeed high objects, [& I pledge myself to worship Themis rather than Apollo if . . . it could be found that . . .][81]

The phrases in brackets were deleted, and eventually Shelley rejected the whole introduction; but it indicates the consistency of his thought with the previous political essays, and his determination to justify poetry (Apollo) with the same 'high objects' in view as the political sciences (Themis).

Yet Shelley did not merely reiterate or rephrase his previous arguments. He succeeded in moving them forward another stage, and occasionally crystallizing them with memorable felicity. But because of the patchwork nature of the *Defence*, and the improvised swirl of its argument, the fine passages come in no very evident logical order. The *Defence*, is best picked over like the anthology that it actually was. It serves as a brilliant series of provocations and challenges to further thought and study: but it is not a treatise. Like the 'Notes on the Florentine Sculpture', its finest remarks and *aperçus* are brief, sometimes puzzling and epigrammatic, and always full of lively imagery. It was very much a *poet's Defence*.

Of translation, Shelley wrote with all the authority and humility of a great practitioner:

> . . . the vanity of translation; it were as wise to cast a violet into a crucible that you might discover the formal principle of its colour and odor, as seek to transfuse from one language into another the creations of a poet. The plant must spring again from its seed, or it will bear no flower – and this is the burthen of the curse of Babel.[82]

Of the moral function of poetry which has no didactic – or indeed, no moral – intent:

> The great secret of morals is love, or a going out of our own nature and an identification of ourselves with the beautiful which exists in thought, action, or person, not our own. A man, to be greatly good, must imagine intensely and comprehensively; he must put himself in the place of another and of many others; the pains and pleasures of his species must become his own. The great

instrument of moral good is the imagination; and poetry administers to the effect by acting on the cause. . . . Poetry strengthens that faculty which is the organ of the moral nature of man in the same manner as exercise strengthens a limb.[83]

Of erotic writing and erotic writers, he made a firm and interesting defence. His argument is that the erotic is the last and most private stronghold of the imagination against social corruption; and that when poetry and imaginative thought generally is under great social pressure, it is to the erotic that writers retire, as to a final fortress of the individual sensibility. It is only in this sense, as evidence of a rearguard battle, that erotic writing is the product of a society in decline.

> It is not what the erotic writers have, but *what they have not*, in which their imperfection consists. . . . For the end of social corruption is to destroy all sensibility to pleasure; and, therefore, it is corruption. It begins at the imagination and the intellect as at the core and distributes itself thence as a paralyzing venom through the affections into the very appetites. . . . At the approach of such a period poetry ever adresses itself to those faculties which are the last to be destroyed, and its voice is heard, like the footsteps of Astraea, departing from the world.[84]

Astraea was the goddess of Justice. The poison imagery of this passage is familiar. Apart from Shelley's defence of Milton's Satan (as a moral being 'far superior to his God'), the finest purely literary description concerned Dante. He saw him equally as a pure poet, as a political influence, and as an eternal force in European culture. Shelley's language here was so charged with his peculiar radiant imagery, and the insistent almost Biblical rhythms which recall passages of *Prometheus Unbound*, that it really takes a considerable effort to hold onto the argument. Shelley believed that a great masterpiece had a quality of self-regeneration: it took on new forms and significance for its readers as it moved beyond its own time, and its own culture. This argument was wonderfully perceptive, and showed, once again, the authority of a poet and translator who had himself proved it true.

> Dante was the first awakener of entranced Europe; he created a language, in itself music and persuasion, out of a chaos of inharmonious barbarisms. He was the congregator of those great spirits who presided over the resurrection of learning, the Lucifer of that starry flock which in the thirteenth century shone forth from republican Italy, as from a heaven, into the darkness of the benighted world. His very words are instinct with spirit; each is as a spark, a burning atom of inextinguishable thought; and many yet lie covered in the ashes of

their birth and pregnant with a lightning that has yet found no conductor. All high poetry is infinite; it is as the first acorn, which contained all oaks potentially . . . after one person and one age has exhausted all of its divine effluence which their peculiar relations enable them to share, another and yet another succeeds, and new relations are ever developed, the source of an unforeseen and an unconceived delight.[85]

Shelley's *Defence* has many weaknesses and peculiarities, most of them attributable to the circumstances under which it was hurriedly assembled in March. It is frequently repetitive and verbose, and the major passages have to be unearthed, like so many nuggets, from the surrounding rhetorical *maremma*. It also has many eccentricities of argument, as the extraordinary passage in which he gravely put forward the opinion that poets have generally been the wisest, happiest and best of men, and that 'the greatest poets have been men of the most spotless virtue, of the most consummate prudence'. However, no doubt some mischievous Scythropian humour was here at work for Peacock's benefit, for shortly afterwards he revealed among a list of poets' minor peculiarities, 'that Raphael was a libertine, that Spenser was a poet laureate'.[86]

The heart of his *Defence* turns on the role of poetry as a force for freedom in society. Freedom from what, or for what? Taking poetry in the most comprehensive sense, he defined this in a celebrated summary which was his final answer to Peacock's position.

We have more moral, political, and historical wisdom than we know how to reduce into practise; we have more scientific and economic knowledge than can be accommodated to the just distribution of the produce which it multiplies. The poetry in these systems of thought is concealed by the accumulation of facts and calculating processes. . . . We want the creative faculty to imagine that which we know; we want the generous impulse to act that which we imagine; we want the poetry of life; our calculations have outrun our conception. . . . The cultivation of those sciences which have enlarged the limits of the empire of man over the external world has for want of the poetical faculty proportionally circumscribed those of the internal world; and man, having enslaved the elements, remains himself a slave.[87]

Peacock's argument in the *Four Ages of Poetry* has usually been underestimated; it was in fact a critique of written poetry which was to have a more and more serious application as the Victorian Age drew on. Yet it is difficult to believe that Shelley's reply is not a profound one; or that in making it, he had not indeed made himself into one of those 'mirrors of the gigantic shadows which futurity casts upon the present'. Despite Shelley's hurry to prepare it, Ollier did not use the manuscript when it arrived in London, and it was eventually printed along with Shelley's other Essays in 1840.

The moment the article was dispatched with Mary's help on 20 March 1821, Shelley turned his attention back to the state of the Italian political upheavals in which Piedmont had now joined. His letter to Peacock at the end of the month was as much about this as about the problems of poetry, and the daily attendance of Prince Mavrocordato at the Casa Aulla in a turban: 'We are surrounded here in Pisa by revolutionary volcanoes.' He added, with mild sleight of hand, that Claire was passing the carnival at Florence '& has been preter-naturally gay'.[88] On the first of April Italian political excitements were joined by news from Greece that the Greek General Ypsilanti had raised the revolutionary standard in Wallachia, and was marching with an army, rumoured to contain 10,000 Greeks, on the northern provinces. Mavrocordato came to inform Mary and Shelley of this and of his impending departure for the scene of action. Mary was unusually ecstatic for her on a political issue, and wrote with many exclamation marks to Claire, 'The Morea – Epirus – Servia are in revolt. Greece will most certainly be free.' As a postscript to Mary's letter, Shelley informed Claire that in London the Bill for Catholic Emancipation had passed its second reading by a majority of 497 to 11, and inquired after her plans for the summer. '*We* are yet undecided . . . say something to fix our determination.'[89]

Shelley had been giving a good deal of thought to the summer. After his severe illness of the winter, Vaccà had advised plenty of exercise – perhaps he should buy a horse? Certainly he felt the need to free himself from the decidedly socializing existence that Mary had established at Pisa. He needed an excuse for getting outside. On 15 April he summoned his two most open-air companions, Edward Williams and Henry Reveley, and went to Livorno to see what could be found. It was a modest idea, though it was to have significant consequences. But it was not a horse: it was a small boat.

Henry Reveley remembered the occasion well.[90] 'Shelley came to me at Leghorn in an unusually excited state, and said that he was tired of walking fourteen miles backwards and forwards, and that he must have a boat of some sort, but that he had very little money to spare.' Reveley helped them purchase a slim, ten-foot boat, with a flat bottom and a very small draught of some few inches. It was of the kind that was used by huntsmen for navigating the network of local dikes and canals through the *maremma*; a very light, strong construction made of pitched canvas stretched over a pinewood frame.[91] They had a few modifications made, including the mounting of a short mast and lugger sail, with a corresponding keel fitted to the hull. This took most of the day, and after purchasing some small stores to take home to Mary and Jane Williams, Shelley proposed that they make their maiden voyage home by moonlight to Pisa. Reveley decided to come with them for the trip, particularly as he had some local knowledge of the waterways. What happened next was very much in the order of things. About half-way through their journey, and some time towards midnight, Williams stood up in the little craft to make some adjustment, lost his balance, caught at the mast and in an instant capsized the whole boat. They were all three struggling in the dark water under the moon; Reveley swimming easily, Williams paddling in small circles, Shelley floundering and shouting.[92] The section of the canal connecting Livorno and the Arno which they were then in was broad and deep, and Reveley could feel no bottom; the water was stabbingly cold.

Reveley took charge. 'I sent Williams ashore, as he could swim a little, and then caught hold of Shelley, and told him to be calm and quiet, and I would take him on shore. His answer was: "All right, never more comfortable in my life; do what you will with me."' Williams got Shelley ashore, but it was quite a near thing, and on crawling up the bank Shelley collapsed on his face in a dead faint, from a mixture of cold and shock. Williams revived him while Reveley manfully plunged back in and recovered the boat, which seems to have been damaged. They walked across the fields to a nearby farmhouse, knocked up the Italians, and spent the night sleeping in front of roaring fires, after a large supper. Shelley was in 'ecstasies of delight after his ducking' but Williams and Reveley were less amused. For some strange reason Shelley considered it a good omen.[93] The next morning Shelley and Williams walked back to Pisa with their story, and Reveley nursed the boat back to Livorno for repairs. Shelley sent detailed instructions about altering the position of the rowlocks, mounting a shallow rudder and refitting the keel so that it ran the whole length of the hull.[94] The skiff was also to be smartly painted, so that altogether she would make, as he told Claire, 'a very nice little shell, for the Nautilus your friend'.[95] He envisaged a glorious summer spent pottering up the canals with Williams from a base at San Giuliano.

The mood was broken when he got back to Pisa by tragic news: John Keats had died at Rome. An anguished letter had arrived from Hunt during his two days' absence at Livorno. At first Shelley accepted the news with curious resignation, for he had been expecting it for some time. He wrote to Byron that evening, 'Young Keats, whose "Hyperion" showed so great a promise, died lately at Rome from the consequences of breaking a blood-vessel, in paroxysms of despair at the contemptuous attack on his book in the "Quarterly Review".'[96] The *Quarterly* attack was always inextricably bound up in Shelley's mind with Keats's suffering, though in fact there was very little connection. The review had after all been published as long ago as September 1818, and there had been many favourable notices of the *Lamia* volume of 1820 since that time.[97]

Yet Shelley had been working to create this mythic connection in his own mind between Keats's consumption and the *Quarterly*. In November 1820 he had drafted, but not sent, a letter to Gifford, Editor of the *Quarterly*, in which he stated as a fact that the first effects on Keats of this review 'are described to me to have resembled insanity, & it was by assiduous watching that he was restrained from effecting purposes of suicide. The agony of his sufferings at length produced the rupturing of a blood vessel in the lungs, & the usual process of consumption appears to have begun.'[98] It is transparent from this unsent letter that Shelley was not thinking in any realistic way about Keats's reaction to a review of 1818, but rather of his own reaction to the *Quarterly* attack on himself in 1819.

Byron, when he received Shelley's letter at Ravenna, read the sentence carefully with his head on one side. 'I am very sorry to hear what you say of Keats – is it *actually* true? I did not think criticism had been so killing. . . . I read the review of "Endymion" in the "Quarterly". It was severe, – but surely not so severe as many reviews in that and other journals upon others.' Meaning of course, that he had read between the lines into the source of Shelley's pain.[99] He went on to criticize frankly what he had so far read of Keats's work. Shelley's odd but sympathetic letter served to remind Byron of other things that he and Shelley had in common besides Claire Clairmont, and he appended a tempting postscript. 'PS. – Could not you and I contrive to meet this summer. Could not you take a run here *alone*?' This idea was to bear fruit in August, but for the time being Shelley was left to brood in solitude on the death of his fellow-poet. He returned to reading 'Hyperion', but he wrote nothing.

Apart from the boat, and plans for the summer, and Claire's correspondence, there was a financial crisis which occupied much of Shelley's mind during April. News had first arrived of this on 13 April through Horace Smith, who wrote to say that Brookes and Co had suddenly refused payment of the spring quarter of the annuity, and that the account was frozen, pending a suit of £120 brought by Dr Thomas Hume – the guardian of Shelley's children. What particularly amazed and angered Smith was that the suit had been brought without prior warning either to him or Shelley, and yet with the connivance of both Sir Timothy's solicitor Whitton, *and* Shelley's solicitor Longdill. Shelley hurried over to consult his stand-by in emergencies, Tatty Tighe, at the Casa Silva, and probably some form of immediate loan was organized to tide him over.[100] Horace Smith worked hard in London to sort the matter out, sending businesslike copies of all his correspondence with Hume, the solicitors and Sir Timothy to Shelley in Pisa. His mediation as a financial agent for Shelley was invaluable at this time, and otherwise Shelley's Italian income might well have dried up altogether. The business, involving dilatory banks and inefficient arrangements to pay Dr Hume by standing order, was eventually sorted out in June.[101]* The one letter that Shelley wrote to Dr Hume at this time showed no trace of warmth or human interest in the children, and makes nothing but a formal inquiry into their 'present state of health & intellectual improvement'. It was mainly concerned with his own sense of 'the unexampled oppression' exercised over him in 'being forbidden the exercise of . . . parental duties'.[102]

In Florence, when Claire heard of Shelley's difficulties, she was alarmed for him, and was suddenly conscious of the precariousness of the life that they were all leading in Italy. On the day after she received the first explanations, she climbed alone to the top of the Boboli gardens overlooking Florence, and sat at the foot of a statue of Ceres, listening to the wind blowing through the fir trees below like the rushing of the sea. It suddenly brought to her mind 'the many solitary hours of Lynmouth: since that time five years are past, every hour of which has brought its misfortune, each worse than the other'.[103] Hearing of her depression, Shelley wrote: 'I feel, my dear girl, that in case the failure of your expectations at Florence should induce you to think of other plans, *we*, that is you & I, ought to have a conversation together.'[104] He talked to Mrs Mason about the school plan, and pondered whether he should bring Claire back to Pisa. Meanwhile Claire's thoughts increasingly turned to Allegra in the convent at Bagnacavallo, and she started to have strange dreams about various people interceding to rescue the child.[105]

Shelley's thoughts of interceding at the other convent, St Anna, had long since receded when he heard that Emilia was to be married. But he composed a verse narrative, much in the style of Keats, about the death of a young virgin on her wedding night. Themes from sources as far apart as *Frankenstein* and *The Cenci* mingled in Shelley's mind as he wrote. The piece was entitled 'Ginevra', and is written in the same notebook as *Epipsychidion*.[106] The narrative section is not very successful, but after 200 lines it concludes with an unexpectedly fine dirge, containing imagery so macabre that Hazlitt picked it out for special mention in a preface to Shelley's poems several years later.[107] Like Chatterton's celebrated song, 'Al under the wyllowe tree', it stands out vividly from its dramatic context, and there is something similar in the stark and bitter inspiration of the two pieces.

---

* Horace Smith made permanent arrangements for Shelley's quarterly payment of £220 to be remitted regularly to the Poste Restante Pisa under personal supervision, while Sir Timothy agreed to pay the £30 quarter due to Hume straight from his own account. This in effect put Sir Timothy in the position of direct financial trustee for Charles and Ianthe, and it was later to bring out his grandfatherly tendencies, especially towards Charles.

She is still, she is cold
       On the bridal couch,
One step to the white deathbed,
       And one to the bier,
And one to the charnel – and one, oh where?
       The dark arrow fled
       In the noon.

Ere the sun through heaven once more has rolled,
    The rats in her heart
    Will have made their nest,
And the worms be alive in her golden hair,
While the Spirit that guides the sun,
Sits throned in his flaming chair,
       She shall sleep.[108]

This, in its own way, was Shelley's elegy for Emilia; or if not exactly for Emilia, for his conception of her as the beloved, as his epipsyche. There is no way of knowing how bitterly Shelley felt about it, but it does not seem to have been overwhelming. The notebook also contains pages of diagrams in which Shelley was working out the differing effects of head and following winds as they hit a sailing boat steered through various points of the compass.[109]

The little skiff was brought back, in her new rig from Livorno by Reveley on the last day of April, and in the general excitement Mary and Shelley found that at long last the Gisbornes had forgotten themselves so far as to pay a visit to Pisa to watch her arrival. The Shelleys were 'gentle, but cold'. For the whole of the next week, Shelley and Williams were afloat, exploring the canals around Pisa, and learning to handle the little craft. Reveley sometimes came over to crew, and he and Shelley successfully sailed her right down to Arno to the sea, and then the two or three miles south along the coast to Livorno. Shelley sailed her back single-handed. But there was no talk of swimming lessons, and such things as life-jackets were unheard of.[110] Mary soothed any nagging worries in the company of Prince Mavrocordato, who continued to call almost daily to give his Greek lessons. He told Mary that he was preparing his military equipage and uniform, and promised to show it off before he departed.

The return of the boat seemed to herald the real beginning of summer. The Williamses took up their summer residence in a large house, the Villa Marchese Poschi at Pugnano, some seven miles outside Pisa, while Shelley negotiated for a new residence at San Giuliano. On 8 May, they packed up their belongings at the Casa Aulla and sent them ahead to the Bagni. After a visit to Livorno,

Shelley set sail with Henry Reveley to thread through the narrow waterways to their new residence, while Mary walked over with Prince Mavrocordato to dine with the Williamses at Pugnano, and then made her own way over to the Bagni. It seems to have been a different house this time, but still in the little crescent facing the Monte Pisano, with the canal conveniently running at the bottom of the garden. It was, Shelley told Claire, 'a very nice house'. The baths were almost entirely deserted at this time in the season, but Shelley looked forward gratefully to the solitude they promised from social diversions, and eagerly stabled his sea horse by the edge of the canal, ready for explorations northwards towards Lucca and the Serchio.[111]

The month of May, with one or two interruptions, was largely spent in these boating expeditions. Occasionally Mary gingerly allowed herself to be ferried up the canal for a visit to the Casa Silva, or to do shopping in Pisa, but for the most part Shelley was alone or with Edward Williams. The most ambitious of their expeditions took them through the maze of canals and cuts into the Serchio, and winding down through the desolate *maremma* with its thick rush-clumps and wild birds as far as the sea. Shelley made a loose verse-journal of the trip, describing how their course following the Serchio 'twisting forth / Between the marble barriers which it clove / At Ripafratta', and into the 'pestilential deserts wild / Of tangled marsh and woods of stunted pine' to the bay of Viareggio. It began with them going down to the skiff before dawn –

> Our boat is asleep on Serchio's stream,
> Its sails are folded like thoughts in a dream ...

and shows in its simple, prosaic narration how the friendship between Shelley and Williams was gradually ripening into an easy intimacy, based on a common background and a shared love for slightly boyish adventuring:

> 'Ay, heave the ballast overboard,
>   And stow the eatables in the aft locker.'
> 'Would not this keg be best a little lowered?'
> 'No, now all's right.' 'Those bottles of warm tea –
> (Give me some straw) – must be stowed tenderly;
> Such as we used, in summer after six,
> To cram in greatcoat pockets, and to mix
> Hard eggs and radishes and rolls at Eton,
> And, couched on stolen hay in those green harbours
> Farmers called gaps, and we schoolboys called arbours,
> Would feast till eight.'

> With a bottle in one hand,
> As if his very soul were at a stand,
> Lionel stood – when Melchior brought him steady: –
> 'Sit at the helm – fasten this sheet – all ready.' . . .[112]

It was not very good verse, but it caught the flavour of those late spring days very well. The picture of Shelley – Lionel – suspended in sudden remembrance of his days at Eton with a bottle of tea in one hand and the boat rocking perilously underfoot while Williams shouts at him to sit down at the tiller has an authentic flavour.

Shelley wrote to Claire, 'The Baths, I think do me good, but especially solitude, & not seeing polite human faces, & hearing voices. I go about twice a week to see Emilia. . . . The William's come sometimes: they have taken Pugnano. W. I like & I have got reconciled to Jane. – Mr Taaffe rides, writes, invites, complains, bows & apologises; he would be a mortal bore if he came often. The Greek Prince comes sometimes, & I reproach my own savage disposition that so agreable accomplished and amiable person is not more agreeable to me.'[113] Most of the sociable dining took place under the Williams's roof at Pugnano, where Mavrocordato appeared in full war dress – much to Mary's admiration – on 16 May. She wrote briskly to the Gisbornes of the Patriarch and Greek bishops decapitated in Constantinople, which was more than outweighed by the success of Ypsilanti's army of liberation who 'cut to pieces the forces sent against them'.[114]

San Giuliano remained for the most part a retreat from visitors, and when entirely alone, Shelley and Mary seemed to have found a rare peace together. Sometimes Mary could be persuaded to make the trips to Pugnano in the skiff, and she afterwards remembered the slow, rustling journeys through reeds and under the blossoming boughs that hung down into the water, as a magic interlude of serenity. 'By day, multitudes of ephemera darted to and fro on the surface; at night, the fireflies came out among the shrubs on the banks; the cicale at noon-day kept up their hum; the aziola cooed in the quiet evening.'[115] Sometimes, in the early evening, they would sit at the open windows of the house and Shelley would dream out loud of 'taking a farm situated on the height of one of the near hills, surrounded by chestnut and pine woods, and overlooking a wide extent of country; or settling still farther in the maritime Apennines, at Massa'.[116] The sounds from the canal and the trees drifted across to them in the twilight, and they sat in silence listening.

> 'Do you not hear the Aziola cry?
> Methinks she must be nigh,'
> Said Mary, as we sate

In dusk, ere stars were lit, or candles brought;
     And I, who thought
  This Aziola was some tedious woman,
    Asked, 'Who is Aziola?' How elate
  I felt to know that it was nothing human,
     No mockery of myself to fear or hate:
      And Mary saw my soul,
And laughed, and said 'Disquiet yourself not;
      'Tis nothing but a little downy owl.'

Sad Aziola! many an eventide
    Thy music I had heard
By wood and stream, meadow and mountain-side,
    And fields and marshes wide, –
Such as nor voice, nor lute, nor wind, nor bird,
    The soul ever stirred;
Unlike and far sweeter than them all.
Sad Aziola! from that moment I
    Loved thee and thy sad cry.[117]

27
The Colony: 1821

The peaceful solitude of summer 1821 at San Giuliano was never long without interruption. Once, Shelley had a bad attack of his nephritic spasms, and returned to Pisa to consult Vaccà; but the illness passed. Then Claire wrote from Florence, after days of 'bad spirits' and nights of unhappy dreams. She was obsessed with the idea that Allegra would catch some fatal disease in the unhealthy atmosphere of a nunnery, and she felt the moment for decisive action could be put off no longer. Shelley was as ever deeply sympathetic, and it was Shelley's sympathy and perhaps a personal visit of reassurance to Florence that Claire most wanted.

But Claire's sudden outburst was particularly awkward. Taking up Byron's postscript about the solo run to Ravenna, Shelley had recently written back, extending his own and Mary's invitation to the Bagni, where all would be discreet and solitary, and Claire would *not* be in evidence. Apart from his personal desire to extend the friendship with Byron, he had at the back of his mind the possibility of softening Byron's attitude to Allegra, simply by the process of confirming their old friendship of the Venice days of 1818. Byron had been easy enough then. Shelley wanted Byron to understand the new independence of Claire's life in Florence. 'I hope that she will be cured of the exaggerated ideas from which such conduct arises in the society with which she has now become conversant. Our solitary mode of life, and my abstract manner of thinking, were very unfit for her; and have probably been the sources of all her errors. It is well, therefore, that I should intercede for her forgiveness.'[1] But now this promising new line of diplomacy was in danger of being put in jeopardy by Claire's eternal anxiety for a decisive confrontation.

Shelley wrote to her about the idea of setting up a school under Mrs Mason's protection, suggesting that this was an altogether more constructive and plausible project than an immediate attempt to force the issue with Byron. If she showed independence and calm, she might yet recover Allegra on her own terms. He sensed that she could be cajoled out of her sudden mood perhaps more effectively than she could be argued out. 'You say that I may not have a conversation with you because you may depart in a hurry Heaven knows where – Except it be to the other world, (& I know the coachman of that road will not let the passengers wait a minute) I know of no mortal business that requires such post haste.'[2] This letter did the trick, and for the time being Claire went back to her German studies. Now that she was living apart from Shelley, the subject of Allegra was one which Claire could and did use as a method of bringing pressure to bear on him, of demanding his attention and ultimately of demanding his personal presence. It was to that extent a weapon that she could also use against Mary. This is not to say that Claire's real concern for her child had diminished, but rather that it had gained a new motive and dimension. Byron had always feared that unless he possessed Allegra and was completely responsible for her, Claire would contrive to use the child as a lever into his affections. Now ironically it was Shelley who was vulnerable to such a measure. From this moment on, he was drawn into a position of self-contradiction with regard to Allegra's presence at the convent of Bagnacavallo: writing to Byron that his conduct was honourable and justified, while writing to Claire that Byron's conduct was ruthless and cruel. But for the moment the end of May brought a temporary peace in that quarter.

On the last day of May, Shelley took off with Williams, this time for a two days' expedition to Brentina. The quiet, broken only by the dinners at Pugnano, and the twice-weekly expeditions into Pisa, encouraged Mary to return to her novel *Valperga*. It promised to develop at considerable length, and by the end of June she found she was at the seventy-first manuscript page of her third volume.[3] Spasmodic visits from Taaffe, who brought absurd offerings of guinea pigs and bad verses, and Prince Mavrocordato, his mind increasingly on the distant shores of Morea, continued. But a ship was already waiting for the prince in Livorno harbour, and he took his departure before the end of the month. 'He is a great loss to Mary,' Shelley told Claire, 'and *therefore* to me – but not otherwise.'[4]

The quiet was also working on Shelley's mind. He was frequently taking the boat out alone, and Mary's journal shows that during the first fortnight of June, his destination was as often as not Pisa. Frequently he got back late, and on the 4th he arrived at midnight, just as a thunderstorm was about to break.[5] On the following evening a note flew off to the Gisbornes: 'I have been engaged these last days in composing a poem on the death of Keats, which will shortly be finished; and I anticipate the pleasure of reading it to you, as some of the very few persons who will be interested in it and understand it. – It is a highly wrought *piece of art*, perhaps better in point of composition than anything I have written.' Three days later, on 8 June, the poem had reached the length of some forty Spenserian stanzas, and he announced it formally to Ollier. 'It is a lament on the death of poor Keats, with some interposed stabs on the assassins of his peace and of his fame; and will be preceded by a criticism of "Hyperion". . . .'[6] On the same day he told Claire what he had been working on, and explained that in writing poetry he found the only real form of mental *relief* which lifted him above 'the stormy mist of sensations'. The poem would be 'worthy both of him and me'. It seems strange that in the external peace of San Giuliano, Shelley was in fact dwelling within storms.

Once writing, Shelley worked hard, as was his custom. The poem, fifty-five stanzas in all, was rapidly completed by the 11th, and by the 16th he had both finished his critical preface, and arranged to have a small edition especially printed in Pisa using the fine Didot typeface, so that he could correct it himself before sending it to Ollier in London. It was the first time he had tried this new method of publication. The title was taken from the Greek legend of the death of Adonis, the beloved of Aphrodite. For the purpose of the Spenserian metre, Shelley had anglicized the name and extended it by a syllable to become 'Adonais'.

From the outset, Shelley intended the poem as both an elegy and a polemic. He wrote to John Gisborne and to Claire on the day he took the manuscript into the press at Pisa, 'I have dipped my pen in consuming fire to chastise his destroyers; otherwise the tone of the poem is solemn and exalted.' As with most of his sustained writing during these years, the work was deeply literary in its conception and sources. The presence of the Greek of Bion, an erotic poet of the first century BC, whose celebrated 'Elegy on the Death of Adonis' Shelley had translated during the previous winter, was very strong. Shelley's translation opened:

> I mourn Adonis dead – loveliest Adonis –
> Dead, dead Adonis – and the Loves lament. . . .
> See, his belovèd dogs are gathering round –
> The Oread nymphs are weeping – Aphrodite
> With hair unbound is wandering through the woods
> 'Wildered, ungirt, unsandalled. . . .[7]

This provided in essence the dramatic scenario for *Adonais*: the dead poet greeted by a solemn visitation of his peers. There was also the Greek of Moschus, whose reciprocal 'Elegy on the Death of Bion' Shelley had also translated in part, so showing himself conscious of an 'Adonis' tradition of elegies already established in the Greek:

> Ye Dorian woods and waves, lament aloud, –
> Augment your tide, O streams, with fruitless tears,
> For the belovèd Bion is no more.[8]

The very phrasing of this translation at once reveals yet a third level of literary predecessors to *Adonais* – the *Lycidas* of Milton. This was a reference that Horace Smith for one immediately recognized on reading the poem in London in August.[9] It was primarily this awareness of writing out of a high, classical literary tradition that Shelley meant by his phrase, 'a highly wrought *piece of art*'.

The poem was also intended as a public gesture. Besides its bitter attack on reviewers – both in the preface, and in the text of the poem – and its praise for 'Hyperion', the original drafts show that Shelley intended a whole queue of contemporary poets to pay their respects, including Byron, Tom Moore and Walter Scott. Most of these were finally rejected,[10] but clear references remained to Byron, the 'Pilgrim of Eternity' in stanza 30; to Leigh Hunt, 'gentlest of the wise' in stanza 35; and in a notorious passage to Shelley himself between stanzas 31 and 34, 'a pardlike spirit beautiful and swift' with a mark 'like Cain's or Christ's' branded on the flesh of his forehead.

The attempt to combine overwhelming personal feelings with the high, marmoreal style of a public monument did not succeed. At best, Shelley produced the rhetoric of a funeral oration – complete with Judaic–Christian echoes of the Burial Service from the Book of Common Prayer – rather than the poetry of a funeral elegy. Alone among Shelley's poems, it has a mannerism and pomposity of style that strike one as curiously reminiscent of the Baroque.

When he sent a copy of the little Pisan edition to Byron in July, his covering note showed that despite his claims to have written his best piece of composition, he was only too aware of the central weakness of the work, a weakness of conception: 'I need not be told that I have been carried too far by the enthusiasm of the moment; by my piety, and my indignation, in panegyric. But if I have erred, I console myself by reflecting that it is in defence of the weak – not in conjunction with the powerful. And perhaps I have erred from the narrow view of considering Keats rather as he surpassed *me* in particular, than as he was inferior to others: so subtle is the principle of self?'[11]

That 'principle of self' is the problem of the poem in a nutshell; and it is also why the imported Platonism of the last five stanzas has the same straining, thinness of tone associated with a far less mature and more blatant work, the 'Hymn to Intellectual Beauty'. The poem seeks to celebrate the indestructible life of the creative spirit, in art and in nature; yet its personal drive and its most intense images tend always towards consummation and death.

Nevertheless, there are isolated passages of immense strength and genuine poignancy scattered throughout *Adonais*. There are moments where Shelley seems to have found that balance of high formality and intense emotion which he so admired in 'Hyperion' and in which he was conscious – perhaps too conscious – of competing with 'Lycidas'.

> He will awake no more, oh, never more! –
> Within the twilight chamber spreads apace
> The shadow of white Death, and at the door
> Invisible Corruption waits to trace
> His extreme way to her dwelling-place;
> The eternal Hunger sits, but pity and awe
> Soothe her pale rage, nor dares she to deface
> So fair a prey, till darkness, and the law
> Of change, shall o'er his sleep the mortal curtain draw.[12]

The wonderfully exact use of such a word as 'extreme'; and the enormous sinister force in the use of the personifications – a skill that he had been maturing from his Lechlade poem of 1815, through the *Mask of Anarchy* and into *Epipsychidion* – these show Shelley's powers at their height. It continued spasmodically in some of the Spring imagery of the second section of the poem, 'Grief has made young Spring wild'. Without apparently the least effort of phrase or sharpness of adjective, individual lines seem to tap a prototypic force close to the original signification of Adonis as fertility god:

> The amorous birds now pair in every brake,
> And build their mossy homes in field and brere;
> And the green lizard, and the golden snake,
> Like unimprisoned flames, out of their trance awake.[13]

There is also an extraordinary power of sadness in the passage where he finally discovered the great elegiac phrase he had not quite been able to develop in the poem to his little son William:

> He is a portion of the loveliness
> Which once he made more lovely: he doth bear
> His part, while the one Spirit's plastic stress
> Sweeps through the dull dense world. . . .[14]

The stanzas of homage to the young poets Chatterton, Sir Philip Sidney and Lucan are also deeply moving.

Writing of the poem after his own death, Mary observed that 'there is much in the *Adonais* which seems now more applicable to Shelley himself than to the young and gifted poet whom he mourned. The poetic view he takes of death, and the lofty scorn he displays towards his calumniators, are as a prophecy on his own destiny. . . .'[15] But this confuses, though understandably, a sentimental half-truth with the real degree to which Shelley was at the time forcing the myth of Keats's death to express his own almost unbearably bitter feelings.

More and more, the extent to which his great poetry and writing of the autumn and winter of 1819–20 had been suppressed or ignored or turned aside was borne in on him. The prospect of renewed friendship with Byron, outstandingly the most successful English poet of the age, had especially brought this home, and was half exposed in the abjectness and self-effacement of the comments on his own work in letters to Byron of May and June. His claims to be 'morbidly indifferent' to praise or blame rang most painfully false. Nor had the sense of social persecution softened with time. But in none of Shelley's private correspondence is this made quite so agonizingly clear, as in certain passages of his prose preface to *Adonais*. This had originally been conceived of as a critical defence of 'Hyperion', yet that was not how it turned out the moment Shelley put pen to paper at San Giuliano:

> As a man, I shrink from notice and regard; the ebb and flow of the world vexes me; I desire to be left in peace. Persecution, contumely, and calumny have been heaped upon me in profuse measure; and domestic conspiracy and legal oppression have violated in my person the most sacred rights of nature and humanity. The bigot will say it was the recompense of my errors; the man of the world will call it the result of my imprudence; but never upon one head. . . .[16]

This was no apologia for 'Hyperion', it was *pro vita sua*. Strangely enough it was John Taaffe, the bore, the bringer of guinea pigs and bad verses, who thoughtfully and gently saved Shelley from this further humiliation. An exchange of letters in early July shows that having been given the proofs to read, Taaffe persuaded Shelley to cancel this and several other passages of the preface, and indeed almost convinced him to omit some of the more naked pieces of self-description in the poem.[17]

The sheets of the finished edition, in its elegant Didot type, were shipped from Livorno without further delay in mid-July. But Shelley retained several bound up copies for personal distribution: to the Gisbornes, to Byron, to Claire, to Joseph Severn in Rome; and no doubt to Emilia, the Masons, and other friends in Pisa. 'The poet & the man are two different natures,' he explained to the Gisbornes, 'though they exist together they may be unconscious of each other, & incapable of deciding upon each other's powers & effects by any reflex act.'[18] Perhaps this was, as in the case of *Epipsychidion*, just another line of defence and extenuation of the personal element in his work. Or perhaps it was true:

> The breath whose might I have invoked in song
> Descends on me; my spirit's bark is driven,
> Far from the shore, far from the trembling throng

Whose sails were never to the tempest given;
The massy earth and spherèd skies are riven!
I am borne darkly, fearfully, afar;
Whilst, burning through the inmost veil of Heaven,
The soul of Adonais, like a star,
Beacons from the abode where the Eternal are.[19]

In the middle of the printing arrangements for *Adonais*, news of another form of extramural publication reached Shelley from London. One of the pirate working-class publishers had brought out a cheap popular edition – of *Queen Mab*.

This interesting news – a 'droll circumstance' was Shelley's first reaction – reached him from London in a letter from Horace Smith who treated the whole matter as an unfortunate impropriety. The pirate was a certain William Clark of Cheapside, who specialized in printing cheap editions of 'dangerous' radical authors, especially Tom Paine, Palmer and Volney. He had come across a copy of Shelley's private edition of *Queen Mab* of 1813, and secretly set it up in print again. It was at once noticed by three radical working-class papers: the *Aurora Borealis*, Benbow's *John Bull's British Journal*, and none less than Wooler's own *British Gazette*, which wrote a long approving article on 6 May. '. . . the work has ever been one for which earnest enquiry has been made; and imperfect copies in manuscript have fetched extraordinary prices. A bookseller has at last been found.'[20] A flurry of reviews followed in the larger circulation papers of the literary middle class, notably in the *Literary Gazette*, the *Monthly Magazine* and the *Literary Chronicle*.[21] As in the case of *Swellfoot the Tyrant*, a prosecution by the Society for the Suppression of Vice immediately followed, and Clark after selling some fifty copies was forced to take it off the market. But it was this courageous act of piracy that brought Shelley's work once more to the attention of Richard Carlile, and it was as a result of Clark's edition of 1821 that Carlile's various editions of 1822, 1823, 1826 and 1832 followed, together with Watson and Heatherington's 'Chartist' edition of 1839, and Shelley's name was assured currency in the working movement for the next twenty years.*

This was precisely the kind of publication that much of Shelley's best work required; a fact which Shelley vaguely recognized in his chronic dissatisfaction with Ollier, and his spasmodic attempts to publish through different channels. His reaction to the piracy was complicated, and contradictory, for he was drawn

---

* Richard Carlile, although he wrote scathingly of Clark's surrender to the Society for the Suppression of Vice, always acknowledged him as the first publisher of *Queen Mab* at 'his shop near St Clement's in the Strand', and continued to print Clark's name on the backleaf of his own later editions of the poem during the 1820s.

two ways, both alarmed and delighted. His immediate reaction to Ollier, his official publisher, was to dismiss the whole thing angrily. 'I have not seen [*Queen Mab*] for some years, but inasmuch as I recollect it is villainous trash . . . pray give all manner of publicity to my disapprobation of this publication.'[22] But in a few days he told John Gisborne about it with something close to relish: '. . . Queen Mab, a poem written by me when very young, in the most furious style, with long notes against Jesus Christ, & God the Father and the King & the Bishops & marriage & the Devil knows what, is just published by one of the low booksellers in the Strand, against my wish & consent, and all the people are at loggerheads about it. – Horace Smith gives me this account. You may imagine how much I am amused.' He added that for the sake of a dignified appearance, '& really because I wish to protest against all the bad poetry in it', he had instructed Ollier to disclaim it formally and applied for a legal injunction.[23]

Public letters of formal disclaimer duly followed to Hunt, as editor of the *Examiner*, and to Ollier for insertion in the *Morning Chronicle*. 'I fear it is better fitted to injure than to serve the cause of freedom.' But as far as an injunction was concerned, Shelley found himself in the same position as Southey, when one of his early radical pieces, *Wat Tyler*, was similarly honoured: because the edition was pirated there was no legal resource except direct prosecution of the bookseller himself. The irony was not lost on Shelley; but unlike Southey, he had no deep objections to the piracy; the one thing that might have upset him, the original dedication to Harriet Shelley, had been tactfully omitted by Clark. As for the furore, he felt beyond any but its most indirect effects in Italy. What more could they do to his reputation? To Claire he remarked stoically on 'the abuse which all the government prints are pouring forth on me', but concluded: 'I enjoy & am amused with the turmoil of these poor people; but perhaps it is well for me that the Alps & the Ocean are between us.'[24] Later, in September, he quietly asked Horace Smith, and independently Hunt, to procure copies for him: 'I should like very well to see it.'[25] In fact, he had considerable interest in his earliest offspring.

The weather was now getting hotter, and the July days slipped past easily, and Shelley was soothed with the idea of *Adonais* sailing towards England. Boating in the skiff continued on the triangle between San Giuliano, Pisa and Pugnano. Mary noted fireflies and the cicada in her journal. The after-dinner walks and discussions with the Williamses now formed almost their only regular social recreation. The Gisbornes were preparing to move permanently to London, and Shelley's main contact with them consisted in buying, or helping to sell, second-hand furniture. Shelley managed to procure several useful items for himself including classical books, a German dictionary for Claire and a microscope and a target pistol.

Claire also seemed predisposed towards peaceful behaviour. She left Florence for her summer break, and Shelley and Williams took three days off to move her from Pisa to Livorno. Mary was not having her at San Giuliano. She wrote letters, studied German, tried going to church and also swimming. She found herself more adept at the latter, though when the waves were high the water always tended to jump down her throat.[26] Towards the end of the month, she was allowed to visit Pisa for a few days, and shuttled between the Casa Silva and the Williams's villa at Pugnano. She occasionally visited San Giuliano, but she does not seem to have managed to stay overnight there, though Shelley would walk over to Pisa to have breakfast with her.[27] When she visited the convent of St Anna, she was told coyly that Emilia had adopted the habit of praying to a saint, 'but every time she changes her lover, she changes her Saint'. Both Claire and Shelley considered this a fine flower of convent education.[28]

At the end of July Claire went back to the ozone of Livorno, and Shelley departed for Florence. He was accompanying the Gisbornes to bid them a final farewell on their journey to England. Shelley and the Gisbornes parted in mutual accord, or at least Shelley and John Gisborne did; the understanding was to serve as the basis for him to act as Shelley's literary agent in London. Shelley was also carrying out a commission for Horace Smith. Smith had decided to leave England and move south with his wife, partly for reasons of health, and partly because he was bored with his legal career. Shelley was anxious to find a house in Florence in return for Smith's dedicated work in his financial affairs. Shelley was delighted that after three long years of prevarication by Hunt and Hogg, he had at last seduced one member of his old circle in London to join him in Italy. He suspected, with good reason, that once one moved, the rest might follow. This, combined with the new friendliness of Byron, began to make Shelley think that the end of the year might see Tuscany – Pisa or Florence – become a permanent home for him.

The prospect of drawing together some kind of English literary colony at Pisa began to balance in his mind against the old dreams of cutting free from his commitments and going east. Thus, on the eve of his twenty-ninth birthday, his oldest scheme of all, the ideal of a radical commune of like spirits, was after many vicissitudes and transformations beginning to re-emerge in Italian colours. Throughout the alarms and excursions of the next few months, which saw almost no time for serious or sustained writing, the strenuous effort to hold together the volatile and conflicting interests of his various friends became Shelley's paramount consideration. He wanted a nucleus for the new community and he regarded himself, rightly, as the only person who could reconcile the potential factions. He worked hard at it. For the first time since he had been overwhelmed by the confusion and misery and conflicting loyalties which beset him in the winter of 1818–19 at Naples, he felt that his life had some real social purpose. The task of reconciling his friendships with three people – with Mary, with Claire and with Byron – became the first objective; as it remained the last. Yet throughout Shelley again revealed his toughness, his resource and his not inconsiderable cunning, in the depth of these human complications.

When Shelley returned from Florence to San Giuliano on 2 August, the wheels of life which had turned slowly and remotely among the green waterways of Pisa, suddenly seemed to speed up. A summons awaited him from Byron: why didn't he *run* to Ravenna at once? Shelley kissed Mary and left the following morning.[29] Mary did not like to see him go: it was, after all, his birthday the next day, and she would have preferred them to celebrate it quietly together. Instead she wrote in her journal for the 4th: 'Shelley's birthday. Seven years are now gone; what changes! what a life! We now appear tranquil; yet who knows what wind – but I will not prognosticate evil; we have had enough of it. When Shelley came to Italy, I said all is well if it were permanent; it was more passing than an Italian twilight. . . .'[30] She consoled herself by working hard at the clean copy of *Valperga*, and spending more and more time with the Williamses. For the first time they became 'Edward 'and 'Jane' in the journal, and on the 6th Mary read Edward the fictionalized history of her breakdown, *Mathilda*. She awaited the post from Ravenna.

But Shelley, for all his haste, had not gone directly on his journey. The evening of the 3rd found him not at Florence but at Livorno, where he appeared unexpectedly at Claire's. He spent the night there, and at 5 the next morning they were up and rowing in the harbour. They visited friends, and then after breakfast took a sailing boat, and celebrated Shelley's birthday on the water. Claire noted: 'Then we sail out into the sea. A very fine warm day. The white sails of ships upon the horizon looked like doves stooping over the water. Dine at the Giardinetto. Shelley goes at two.'[31] It was the last birthday that Shelley celebrated. Claire had a pain in her stomach.

From Livorno, Shelley took the diligence and spent the night at Empoli, on the way to Florence. At dawn on Sunday the 5th he travelled into Florence, hired an open *calèsse* and drove flat out for Bologna. On the way they had a crash, an event which Shelley recounted with glee. '. . . The old horse stumbled & threw me & the fat vetturino into a slope of meadow over the hedge. – My angular figure stuck where it was pitched, but my vetturino's spherical form rolled fairly to the bottom of the hill, & that with so few symptoms of reluctance in the life that animated it, that my ridicule (for it was the drollest sight in the world) was suppressed by the fear that the poor devil had been hurt.'[32] But driver, horse and *calèsse* all survived the effects of Shelley's high spirits, and he covered the road from Florence to Bologna, a distance of some seventy-five miles, in about twenty hours of non-stop driving, having departed from Florence late on Sunday morning, and arrived soon after dawn on Monday the 6th. Part of the reason for the haste was a need to cover his tracks from both Claire and Mary.

From Florence he had dispatched a note to Claire that makes it clear that he had not told her of his trip to see Byron. He recounted that he had slept at Empoli 'as one might naturally sleep after taking a double dose of opium' – a phrase that does not quite explain itself – but that he was 'in doubt about his hours' and would probably not be able to see her 'so soon as Thursday'. He signed 'Yours ever most affectionately, S.' and advised her to keep off green fruit. In other words she knew nothing of Ravenna.[33] But another note, to Mary from Bologna, also shows that she in her turn had not been told of his birthday visit to Claire at Livorno. He breathlessly explained failure to arrive in Bologna the previous evening, by 'having made an embarrasing & inexplicable arrangement for more than twelve hours' and having travelled 'all night at the rate of 2 miles an hour'. In this way, the day spent with Claire was concealed from Mary. Shelley's only mention of Claire was to suggest tactfully that now, in his absence, Mary might invite her to spend a few days at San Giuliano: but she should not be told of the visit to Albe. 'My love to the Williams's – Kiss my pretty one, & accept an affectionate one from me in return for the cold. . . .' But he deleted the last five words. Anyway his chaise for Ravenna was waiting. 'Yours ever, S.'[34] He arrived at Ravenna, a further fifty miles, at 10 that night, and was greeted by a delighted Byron who looked sleek and healthy, with a rather receding hairline. They talked, as was their custom on such occasions, till 5 in the morning.[35]

Shelley was Byron's honoured guest for the next ten days, and the reunion, despite one dramatic eruption, was a great success. At the time of Shelley's visit, Byron was still established in a splendid and extensive set of apartments within the palace of Countess Guiccioli's erstwhile husband. The count had recently divorced La Guiccioli, who had been living with Byron as her *cavaliere servente* in the palace, and she was now banished to Florence for fear of incarceration within a convent.* She was on an allowance of 1,200 crowns a year, and Byron on an income of £4,000. For once Byron was living within his means, and even – he told Shelley – giving a quarter of it to charity.

He had at Ravenna substituted for his variegated and irregular assortment of Venetian street-walkers, bakers' wives and other youthful functionaries, an equally imaginative animal menagerie, who were allowed the freedom of the corridors and rooms, and whose number only gradually revealed themselves to Shelley. After his first three days' stay, he made it 'two monkeys, five cats, eight

---

* This was the customary form of legal redress which the Papal States allowed dissatisfied husbands in place of alimony.

dogs, and ten horses'; but by the end of the week this tally had been filled out by 'three monkies, an eagle, a crow, and a falcon'. Shelley explained gravely to Peacock that 'all these except the horses, walk about the house, which every now and then resounds with their unarbitrated quarrels, as if they were the masters of it'. However, even this was not quite the true tally. '[P.S.] After I have scaled my letter, I find that my enumeration of the animals in this Circean Palace was defective, and that in a material point. I have just met on the grand staircase five peacocks, two guinea hens, and an Egyptian crane. I wonder who all these animals were before they were changed into these shapes.'[36]

Byron established Shelley in a magnificent chamber, and gave him his personal servant Tita as his valet. 'Tita the Venetian is here, & operates as my valet: a fine fellow with a prodigious black beard, who has stabbed two or three people, & is the most goodnatured looking fellow I ever saw.'[37] Shelley was also made much of by the faithful Fletcher: 'Fletcher is here, & as if like a shadow he waxed & waned with the substance of his master, Fletcher has also recovered his good looks & from amidst the unseasonable grey hairs a fresh harvest of flaxen locks put forth.'[38] Altogether the magic palace filled Shelley with delight and good humour.

Shelley rapidly adapted himself to his Lordship's hours, which were still sublunary. He rose at midday, and walked abroad in the city before breakfasting with Byron who rose usually at 2. They then talked and read and lounged until 6, when they rode out together to an area of pine forest which stood between the city and the sea, recalling the bleak and beautiful Venetian Lido of 1818. Sometimes they rode out a little earlier to shoot off pistols before the light softened. The usual targets were pumpkins, and Shelley found his eye and hand were still good, and sometimes as good as Byron's, which was excellent.[39] Afterwards, they dined lightly but choicely at 8 o'clock, and settled down to talk until 4 or 5 in the morning. The talk was ranging but demanding: Byron's women, diseases and emotional life *in extenso* – for he had been writing his memoirs;[40] politics, especially Byron's involvement in the local *Carbonari* movement which very much surprised and pleased Shelley; and of course poetry – especially Byron's fifth canto of *Don Juan* which was still in manuscript. This last filled Shelley with conflicting waves of admiration and bitter, jealous despair, the most genuine form of tribute one great poet may spontaneously pay to another. He recognized it instantly as a masterpiece, and knew that the magic palace was not merely a stage set for a pantomime, but the theatre of something genuinely wayward and great. 'He has read to me one of the unpublished Cantos of Don Juan, which is astonishingly fine. – It sets him not above but far above all the poets of the day: every word has the stamp of immortality. – I despair of rivalling Lord Byron, as well I may: and there is no other with whom it is worth contending.' Now that Keats was dead, this was an impeccable judgement. The only exception it admitted, was that of the man who made it.

However, Byron's magic palace contained at least one demon for Shelley. It rose up during the discussions of the very first night. This was the story that Elise Foggi had related to the Hoppners the previous summer, and of which Hoppner himself had written so fully to Byron. If Byron was suspected of malice or lack of frankness in the affair, it has to be admitted that he hardly lacked forthrightness once faced with Shelley. The whole story had been related within seven hours of his arrival at Ravenna.

Nor did Shelley hesitate to write instantly to Mary the following morning. He rose at 11, and dashed off six pages of quarto in time to catch the midday post. Only about half this missive concerned the Hoppner scandal; the rest good-naturedly talked of Byron, La Guiccioli and Ravenna. For all Shelley's shock and anger, he cannot really have been very much surprised, having been struggling on and off with del Rosso against Paolo's blackmail attempts since June 1820. He had mentioned del Rosso in a letter to Claire as recently as 18 February.[41]

In Shelley's letter to Mary of 7 August, and in the passionate reply of Mary written specifically for Mrs Hoppner and dated Pisa 10 August,* one fact is outstanding in its absence. In discussing the scandal, the basis of which was the production of an illegitimate baby in Naples in the winter of 1818, neither letter makes the least reference to Elena Adelaide Shelley. This means, quite simply, that neither Mary nor Shelley intended to recount the full story. Their answer, as far as Byron or the Hoppners were concerned, was to be oblique.

Another interesting aspect was that what lawyers call the 'sting' of the libel – its sharpest and most wounding element – appeared in a different light to Mary than it had done to Shelley. To the accusation that Claire had been his mistress, Shelley reacted exactly as might have been expected in the circumstances – somewhat wearily and somewhat enigmatically, as of an issue long since talked to a standstill between him and Mary. What seemed to scald him to the point of incoherent pain, was the fact that he should have been accused of *cruelty*: either to Claire, or to Mary, or worst of all to an illegitimate child.

> Elise says that Clare was my mistress – that is all very well & so far there is nothing new: all the world has heard so much & people may believe or not believe as they think good. – She then proceeds to say that Clare was with child by me – that I gave her the most violent medicines to procure abortion . . . [etc.

---

* As usual at such a crucial point, the MS sources were subsequently tampered with, and the original has not survived. Mary's letter was first printed, 'an exact copy of the holograph', by John Murray in 1922. Murray's note explains itself: 'it may be as well to state that an imperfect version of this letter was printed in Professor Dowden's "Life of Shelley" (1886), and also in Mrs Julian Marshall's "Life and Letters of Mary Shelley". In both transcripts there are many significant omissions . . .'

concerning the foundling hospital]. . . . In addition she says that both I & Clare treated *you* in the most shameful manner – that I neglected & beat you* & that Clare never let a day pass without offering you insults of the most violent kind in which she was abetted by me. . . . When persons who have known me are capable of conceiving me – not that I have fallen into a great error & imprudence as would have been the living with Clare as my mistress – but that I have committed such unutterable crimes as destroying or abandoning a child – & that my own – imagine my despair of good – imagine how it is possible that one of so weak & sensitive a nature as mine can run further the gauntlet through this hellish society of men. [*There follow three lines heavily inked out in the manuscript.*][42]

As one considers the seven long years in which Shelley had struggled to live peaceably and fruitfully with Mary and Claire, and the grimly repeated blows of the death of his children, Clara, William, Elena, to name no others, this sense of outrage and injured innocence seems wholly understandable and largely genuine. Only in the final phrases – 'this hellish society of men' – does one detect a certain melodrama. It was the same defensive melodrama which is familiar from the time of the letters to Elizabeth Hitchener right down to the letters to Southey from San Giuliano. What had Shelley to be defensive about? Surely it was that he regretted ever having agreed to foster out his 'Neapolitan charge' to Italian parents in Naples.†

Mary's letter of refutation to Mrs Hoppner is much more extensive and impassioned than Shelley's – as Shelley had intended that it should be. Yet it seems clear that for her the 'sting' of the business lay in the fundamental accusation that Shelley and Claire had been lovers. Thus at the key points of her letter, a wholly different emphasis emerges:

She says Clare was Shelley's mistress, that – upon my word, I solemnly assure you that I cannot write the words, I send you a part of Shelley's letter that you may see what I am now about to refute – but I had rather die than copy anything so vilely, so wickedly false, so beyond all imagination fiendish.

I am perfectly convinced in my own mind that Shelley never had an improper connexion with Clare . . . [etc. concerning the rooms at Naples, and Claire's illness] . . . Clare had no child – the rest must be false – but that you

---

* A deliberate exaggeration on Shelley's part: Hoppner, for all his inventiveness, never suggested that Shelley actually beat Mary.

† This is confirmed by his remark in the letter to the Gisbornes of 30 June 1820, very shortly before the news of Elena's death, that he intended to bring her to Tuscany as soon as she recovered. But of course he never got the chance.

should believe it – that my beloved Shelley should stand thus slandered in your minds – he the gentlest and most humane of creatures, is more painful to me, oh far more painful than any words can express.

It is all a lie – Claire is timid; she always showed respect even for me poor dear girl! ... [etc. concerning Mary's perfect trust in Shelley] ... I will add that Clare has been separated from us for about a year. She lives with a respectable German family at Florence....[43]

It is not necessary to go into detail about the partially false impression Mary gives on several points, for they are all wholly in character. One would not expect her to explain fully the alternating visits which had taken place constantly between Claire and Shelley since autumn 1820; nor would one expect her to say anything other than that 'the union between my husband and myself has ever been undisturbed. Love caused our first imprudence ... has increased daily, and knows no bounds.' Mary's loyalty to Shelley was always faultless.

But it is the general weight of Mary's letter that is most significant: she did not believe that Shelley and Claire were lovers, and more than this, she found even the consideration of such a possibility unbearably painful. This radical divide in feeling and response to the Hoppner accusations between Shelley and Mary is, humanly speaking, the most informative truth to emerge from this notoriously ambiguous exchange of letters.

There was finally perhaps one sentence which indicated that Mary realized that to mention Elena would explain everything, but that it was, both for her and for Shelley, too costly a revelation. At almost the end of this long letter she wrote: 'I swear by the life of my child, by my blessed and beloved child, that I know these accusations to be false.' The use of that 'know' is oddly emphatic in the context, and the particular oath by which Mary vowed it – the life of her now only remaining child – is one that is inconceivable that she would have used except in the most grave and perfect sincerity. The one way in which Mary could 'know' such a thing, is through absolute certainty about the true parentage and fate of the supposedly 'foundling' child.

Having written in the meantime to Mary about the possibility of 'prosecuting Elise in the Tuscan tribunals', Shelley was obviously relieved and delighted on the reception of Mary's letter to Mrs Hoppner which reached him on 15 or 16 August. There was no more talk of legal prosecutions, and having referred to the Hoppners as the probable source of a critical attack in the *Literary Gazette*, he dismissed the whole business: 'So much for nothing.' His letters and notes to Mary were, towards the latter end of his stay at Ravenna, notably cheerful and affectionate. In one he thanked her warmly for a kind birthday present of her picture in miniature which 'I will wear for your sake upon my heart'; and in this and other letters he dispensed with the usual 'My dear Mary', and addressed her simply as 'My dearest love'.[44]

Mary's reply was never delivered to the Hoppners as Byron promised, but was found in his Lordship's papers, with seal broken, after his death. Yet it is clear that the real value of Mary's letter for Shelley, was not *vis-à-vis* Hoppner – but *vis-à-vis* Byron. Shelley had not the slightest interest in or respect for the Hoppners; he must have known if they believed Elise's version of the truth in the first place, no amount of eloquence from Mary – whom they always regarded as the injured and innocent party anyway – would alter them. The person whose opinion he was vitally interested in was Byron. It was Byron's reading of the letter, and Byron's conviction concerning Shelley, Claire and Mary, which was all-important. Shelley's relationship with Elise was quite irrelevant to this, and something for Shelley to discuss with Byron between midnight and 5 a.m. if he so chose. Mary's letter proved above all to Byron that Mary was still completely loyal to Shelley, and that the relationship between the two, however difficult, was still alive. The importance of this fact was shown in Shelley's one reference to the Hoppner affair in later correspondence with Byron. Discussing the arrangements to be made for Claire and Allegra, Shelley wrote from Pisa: 'I speak freely on this subject, because I am sure you have seen enough to convince you that the impressions, which the Hoppners wished to give you of myself and Mary, are void of foundation.'[45] What Byron had seen was Mary's passionately loyal letter. The real outcome of the whole Hoppner scandal was simply to convince Byron of the tested solidarity between Shelley and Mary.

All the rest of Shelley's visit to Ravenna followed from this. Byron suddenly announced that he was going to move palaces to Tuscany. Shelley's aid was enlisted to persuade La Guiccioli – who wished to go to Switzerland and taste the pleasures of foreign travel – that Tuscany was preferable. After a little discussion, and considerable homework, Shelley turned in an extremely elegant letter in flowing and gallant Italian which detailed the full hideousness of English snobbery, prejudice and inquisitiveness in Switzerland, especially at Geneva, and most especially when presented with something as outlandish as Lord Byron on the Lac Leman in the company of a lady. By way of example, Shelley called to mind at length their unfortunate experiences of 1816.[46] The letter worked splendidly; the countess, together with her charming and malleable brother Pietro Gamba, acquiesced to Tuscany; in return she put Shelley under a courtly obligation not to depart from Ravenna until Lord Byron's emigration westwards was assured.

Exactly where in Tuscany Byron should establish himself was a question of some delicacy over which Shelley spent much thought. He communed on paper with Mary: 'I am afraid he would not like Florence on account of the English. –

What think you of Lucca for him – *he* would like Pisa better, if it were not for Clare, but I really can hardly recommend him either for his own sake or for hers to come into such close contact with her. – Gunpowder & fire ought to be kept at a respectable distance from each other. – There is Lucca, Florence, Pisa, Sienna, – and I think nothing more. – What think you of Prato or Pistoia for him. . . ?'[47]

Byron and Shelley worked over the possibilities together, Byron half playing with the idea, Shelley determined to get his Lordship safely transported and housed somewhere near Pisa. But it took time, and patience and tact. In the mornings, Shelley was given the freedom of Byron's state carriage, and he rode to the sites of Ravenna his face peering through the windows above the Byron coat-of-arms. In the Chiesà St Vitale he was fascinated by a section of hap-hazardly stained marble that had formed a perfect human outline, 'a pure anticipated cognition of a Capuchin' as he put it; and the excavated basement filled with 'a sort of vaporous darkness, and troops of prodigious frogs'.[48] Later he visited Dante's tomb, with its famous sculptured relief, very life-like to Shelley, with one eye half closed like Il Diavolo Pacchiani.[49]

Shelley's only source of discomfort in Byron's presence was a slight but persistent sense of social patronage. As writers he felt they could talk frankly, and as equals; they disagreed for example on Byron's supposed principles of literary criticism. As friends, they both indulged freely in confidences, especially from Byron's side. But as social animals there was a sense of strain; Shelley was always aware of the Byron coat-of-arms on the door. 'Lord Byron and I are excellent friends, & were I reduced to poverty, or were I a writer who had no claims to a higher station than I possess – or did I possess a higher than I deserve, we would appear in all things as such, & I would freely ask him any favour. Such is not now the case – The demon of mistrust & of pride lurks between two persons in our situation poisoning the freedom of their intercourse. . . .'[50] This source of friction was to increase steadily in the coming months. In this way, it is curious that Shelley's reservations about Byron in Italy were very much analogous to Keats's hesitations about Shelley in London. Byron hardly seems to have been aware of the difficulty.

On 11 August, Byron announced abruptly that he had decided on Pisa. There can be no doubt that Shelley was the decisive factor in his choice. Delighting in his victory, he immediately offered to act as Byron's agent, and lease a suitable palazzo, and so it was agreed. Shelley half expected Byron to change his mind the next day, but on the contrary Byron became more enthusiastic with every night of talk which passed. Shelley was now anxious to return to Pisa, but one expedition remained – a visit to Allegra at the convent of Bagnacavallo some forty miles outside Ravenna. This was suddenly arranged for him, after long and inexplicable delays, some three days before his departure. Shelley spent an afternoon with the little girl, now taller and more serious, and full of talk of Paradise and Angels. Shelley was prepared to indulge these nunnish fancies, though he was appalled at 'the idea of bringing up so sweet a creature in the midst of such trash till sixteen!' Drawing on his experiences of Emilia at St Anna, Shelley conveyed to Byron 'such information as to the interior construction of convents as to shake his faith in the purity of those receptacles'.

Shelley remembered Allegra with much affection from the days at Marlow, and later at Venice. He brought her a little gold chain as a present, conversed with her in Italian, gravely asked to view her little bed, her chair at dinner and her ornamented play-cart in the convent garden. She was dressed in white muslin, with a little apron and black trousers made of silk; her hair was as dark and profuse as ever, and her eyes deep blue. Later they ran about together in the garden playing hide-and-seek until finally, somewhat over-excited, Allegra was found ringing the bell to summon the nuns from their cells, but nobody seemed to be cross. As he was taking his leave, Shelley asked if she had any message he could take to her father. 'Che venga farmi un visitino, e che porta seco *la mammina*.' Shelley winced inwardly at this, and he did not deliver the latter part of the message. But Allegra, who had not seen Claire for over three years, was almost certainly referring to Teresa Guiccioli, and not her real *mammina*. Shelley did not see Allegra again, and Allegra never left her convent.[51]

On the eve of his departure, Shelley completed a long letter to Mary, in which he reviewed the prospects and consequences of Byron coming to Pisa, and debated whether they themselves should remain there during the winter months, or move to Florence with Horace Smith. '. . . With Lord Byron & the people we know at Pisa we should have a security & protection which seems to be more questionable in Florence.' But he left the ultimate decision to Mary: '– judge (*I know you like the job*).'

He then embarked on a long soliloquy on the need to choose a more definite form of social life. He saw two alternatives ahead of him: either complete retirement and obscurity with Mary and his child; or else the development of the larger community of friends, with a wider general purpose. This was the first revelation to Mary of the problem that had occupied his own mind during the summer. To an extent, the terms of the choice were a mature echo of those in the letter to Hogg, long ago in 1814, when he described the implications of the choice between Harriet – his then legal wife – and Mary Godwin (and Claire) the interlopers.[52] The result, in both cases, was a foregone conclusion by the time he came to express it on paper. But he wanted Mary to know and understand the way his mind had been working, and he was honest enough to admit to Mary that even if he had chosen the first alternative his 'imagination' would probably still have strayed:

> My greatest content would be utterly to desert all human society. I would retire with you & our child to a solitary island in the sea, would build a boat, & shut upon my retreat the floodgates of the world. – I would read no reviews & talk with no authors. – If I dared trust my imagination it would tell me that there were two or three chosen companions besides yourself whom I should desire. – But to this I would not listen. – Where two or three are gathered together the devil is among them, and good far more than evil impulses – love far more than hatred – has been to me, except as you have been its object, the source of all sorts of mischief. So on this plan I would be *alone* & would devote either to oblivion or to future generations the overflowings of [my] mind. . . . But this it does not appear that we shall do.

It was not in the end a realistic possibility for Shelley. One suspects too, that the Wollstonecraft blood would have rebelled against this retreat from 'all human society' just as much as Shelley's imagination. As for the devil, Shelley's relations with Him had always been particularly productive.

On the other hand lay the broader and preferable choice:

> The other side of the alternative (for a medium ought not to be adopted) – is to form for ourselves a society of our own class, as much as possible, in intellect or in feeling; & to connect ourselves with the interests of that society. – Our roots were never struck so deeply as at Pisa & the transplanted tree flourishes not. – People who lead the lives which we led until last winter are like a family of Wahabee Arabs pitching their tent in the midst of London. We must do one thing or the other: for yourself, for our child, for our existence. . . .[53]

Shelley underwrote this second alternative by pointing out that within a society of their own at Pisa, they would be far less vulnerable to the kind of calumnies and blackmail attempts which had plagued them since 1820. As Shelley described the 'society of our own class in intellect and feeling', there was no mention of a wider social purpose or 'utility' as there would have been in the old God-winian days. Yet his actions on returning to Pisa soon showed that political and literary projects were very much at the front of his mind.

Having assured La Guiccioli that Milord's removal from Ravenna was now inevitable, Shelley departed from the Circean Palace on 17 August. Farewells were made with great cordiality, though it emerged that Shelley had not passed his time without undergoing a bestial transmogrification – like the other in-mates. He had become *the Snake*, and is referred to as such in Byron's letters and recorded talk from this time on. Byron later explained that it was a 'buffoonery' of his: 'Goethe's Mephistopheles calls the Serpent who tempted Eve "my aunt the renowned Snake" and I always insist that Shelley is nothing but one of her Nephews walking about on the tip of his tail.'[54] But Byron omitted to mention that he had been given this joke by Shelley. In the finale to his amusing atheistic 'Essay on the Devil', Shelley had blithely described the outcome of the successful temptation in the Garden of Eden:

> God on this occasion, it is said, assigned a punishment to the Serpent that its motion should be as it now is along the ground upon its belly. We are given to suppose that, before this misconduct, it hopped along on its tail, a mode of progression which, if I was a serpent, I should think the severer punishment of the two. The Christians have turned this Serpent into their Devil. . . .[55]

There is also one fine fragment of Shelley's poetry which seems to refer to the magical associations of the name:

> Wake the serpent not – lest he
> Should not know the way to go, –
> Let him crawl which yet lies sleeping
> Through the deep grass of the meadow!
> Not a bee shall hear him creeping,
> Not a may-fly shall awaken
> From its cradling blue-bell shaken,
> Not the starlight as he's sliding
> Through the grass with silent gliding.[56]

Shelley arrived back in Pisa, full of the news of his capture of Lord Byron, on 20 August. He found Claire staying peacefully at San Giuliano, and Edward Williams completing a large portrait of Mary. Mary's clean-copying of *Valperga* was advancing rapidly, and she was in good humour. Shelley's news was greeted with much enthusiasm. Claire entered wonderingly in her diary, 'Very unexpected news of Albe's near arrival.'[57] Within two days, he was busily negotiating for the lease of Palazzo Lanfranchi on the Lung'Arno, a splendid marble palace of the sixteenth century, with its own landing steps down to the Arno. Notes in courtly Italian flew to La Guiccioli in Florence, keeping her posted of developments. On the 26th he wrote to Byron that the lease was secured at 400 crowns a year, and that he was looking for extra stables in the proximity. He asked firmly for explicit instructions concerning furnishings.[58]

With this first stage of his plan put in motion, Shelley now wrote a momentous letter to Leigh Hunt in London, the first for several months. After the failure of

Shelley's writings of 1819 and 1820 to reach their public, Hunt had become less important to Shelley in his literary capacity, and most of their dwindling correspondence had discussed domestic matters, particularly Hunt's ill-health and now chronic state of debt. To this had been added the expenses of trying to educate no less than six very lively and intelligent children. But Hunt had never been far from Shelley's mind, and he now burst upon Hampstead the second part of the plan which had taken shape at Ravenna. It was to be a major publishing venture, based on the English colony now about to form at Pisa.

Shelley put the plan in its pristine shape: 'My dearest friend, Since I last wrote to you, I have been on a visit to Lord Byron at Ravenna. . . . He proposes that you should come and go shares with him and me, in a periodical work [*The Liberal*], to be conducted here; in which each of the contracting parties should publish all their original compositions, and share the profits. . . . There can be no doubt that the *profits* of any scheme in which you and Lord Byron engage, must, from various yet co-operating reasons, be very great. As to myself, I am, for the present, only a sort of link between you and him, until you can know each other and effectuate the arrangement; since (to entrust you with a secret which, for your sake, I withhold from Lord Byron), nothing would induce me to share in the profits, and still less in the borrowed splendour of such a partnership. . . .' As far as paying off Hunt's inescapable debts, and financing the actual journey to Italy, Shelley suggested that he would 'make up an impudent face' and ask Horace Smith when he arrived in Florence during September. He preferred not to turn to the most obvious, and presumably most willing and able source, Lord Byron, because 'there are men, however excellent, from whom we would never receive an obligation, in the worldly sense of the word'.[59]

Hunt took a little time to absorb the full implications of this proposal, and his first reply from Hampstead was non-committal. But what Shelley had said about the inevitable pulling power of such a partnership in terms of readership, and the resulting profits, was perfectly realistic. A combination of the most capable and most widely disliked liberal editor of the decade, with the most celebrated and most notorious poet of his generation in England – if not in Europe – was, in terms of literary and political publicity, a virtually foregone success. The only two real problems were the organization and administration of a sufficient capital sum to launch the project (Shelley was probably thinking of Horace Smith handling Byron's money); and the setting up in the somewhat unlikely backwater of Pisa, means of printing and distributing a sufficiently rapid and regular flow of copy to the capitals of France and England. A third, less definable difficulty was the human relations between the three principals, all of whom were as prospective business partners highly explosive and unreliable material.

But Hunt soon came to see the project in a more favourable light, after weighing these factors against the possible prize, and having had realistic talks with his brother and fellow-editor John Hunt about financial affairs. He saw, very quickly, the value of his own experience in the day-to-day business of organizing such a periodical; though he also realized, no less clearly, the human problem. Shelley's own excessive modesty, and his apparently high-minded wish to remain anonymous and receive no profits, was itself – Hunt grasped at once – a divisive rather than a unifying factor.

Hunt wrote to Pisa, accepting the plan in principle, at the end of September. He commented: 'I agree to [Byron's] proposal with less scruple because I have had a good deal of experience in periodical writing, and know what the getting up of the *machine* requires, as well as the soul of it. You see I am not so modest as you are by a great deal, and do not mean to let you be so either. What! are there not three of us? And ought we not to have as much strength and variety as possible? We will divide the world between us, like the Triumvirate, and you shall be the sleeping partner, if you will; only it shall be with a Cleopatra, and your dreams shall be worth the giving of kingdoms.' Leaving the subject as if settled by this doubtful specimen of the Hunt Pun, he turned to discuss travelling methods and Mary's novel, which he awaited anxiously. Shelley was deeply pleased by the success of his strategy.[60]

Feeling in this commanding mood, Shelley addressed himself to Ollier on 25 September. The main subject of his letter was Mary's *Valperga or, Castruccio, Prince of Lucca*, for which Mary wanted a single commission on the first edition, irrespective of sales. Shelley was very specific and firm about the matter: he wanted an advance of one-third of the agreed sum by Christmas 1821, and the remaining two-thirds paid at twelve- and eighteen-monthly intervals according to a signed contract. Moreover he wanted the proofs sent to Italy by overland post for Mary's personal correction before final printing. The sum which Mary was asking seems to have been in the region of £500, and she intended to make over all profits to the assistance of her father Godwin.[61] Shelley also briskly inquired after his own works: was there any chance of a second edition of *The Revolt of Islam*, for he 'could materially improve that poem on revision'? And what was happening to the Pisan edition of *Adonais*, which Shelley considered 'the least imperfect of my compositions'? And when did Ollier require Part 11 of his *Defence of Poetry*? – as for Part 1, Ollier could do what he liked with it. These questions never received satisfactory answers. Shelley mentioned his progress on the long-projected drama 'Charles the First': 'Unless I am sure of making something good, the play will not be written.' Still, he was 'full of great plans; and, if I should tell you them, I should only add to the list of riddles.' He added in a postscript that *Valperga* had 'not the smallest tincture of any peculiar theories in politics or religion'.[62]★

During the rest of September and early October Shelley's time was largely taken in organizing Byron's palace-moving, and linking up the affairs of his other prospective Pisans. To Hunt he fired off advice about travel routes, cutlery and linen. The best itinerary for autumn travel, with its westerly winds, was to embark at the Port of London and sail directly through the Mediterranean to Livorno. But this could not be left until too late in the season. The passage should take between twelve days and three weeks. But if Hunt came by Paris and Marseilles, he should still ship 'your beds, your piano etc but not tables chairs etc – because freightage is not payed by weight but by room'. Shelley had a last throw at another old friend: 'Hogg will be inconsolable at your departure. I wish you could bring him with you – he will say that I am like Lucifer who has seduced the third part of the starry flock.' He had recently used the simile of Dante's circle of poets.[63]

To Byron he wrote of eight wagons dispatched from Florence to carry his Lordship's hand luggage (it had nearly been made sixteen by an oversight) and kept him in good humour by a dexterous employment of interesting subjects. 'My convent friend [Emilia Viviani], after a great deal of tumult, &c., is at length married, and is watched by her brother-in-law with great assiduity. . . . They have made a great fuss at Pisa about my intimacy with this lady. Pray do not mention anything of what I told you; as the whole truth is not known and Mary might be very much annoyed at it. "Don Juan" Cantos 3, 4 and 5, I see are just published in Paris. . . . "Don Juan" is your great victory over the alleged inflexibility of your powers; and interest must be made to take an embargo off such precious merchandise. I have seen the Countess [Guiccioli] frequently, and I pronounce you secure against any of my female friends here. I will trust you with Mrs Williams. Have you formed any plan for Allegra here? . . .'[64] Byron was expected any time from the beginning of October, but his Lordship had a penchant for late entries on any important social occasion.

The only setback to Shelley's plan at this stage was the disappointing news that Horace Smith's wife had been taken ill with dysentery and fever at Paris, brought on by the unaccustomed heat, and could on no account be persuaded to move further south than the suburbs of Versailles that season. Smith was obviously bitterly disappointed himself, as his ambition to visit Florence had been lifelong, and he had also quickly realized that the presence of Byron at Pisa would

---

★ In the event Mary's novel was only published two years later by W. B. Whittaker, and when her circumstances were radically altered. Some things did not change however: all the profits went to William Godwin.

'doubtless impart a little more life to the humdrumosity of that dull & learned City'.[65] Both Shelley and Mary much regretted Smith's decision, and Shelley was inclined to tempt him over Mrs Smith's head with visions of an especially lovely house on the Arno. He did not entirely give him up. In the meantime Shelley asked him the favour of purchasing three books which were to have a significant bearing on the writing of the coming winter and spring: a complete edition of Calderón, a French translation of Kant and a German *Faust*.[66]

In this bustle of arrangements, time was still found for a peaceful seaside expedition of four days duration to the Gulf of Spezia. Shelley's only companions were Mary and Claire, and on the road out, they picnicked under the olive trees, as in the old days. At Spezia they spent one afternoon sailing, and another riding; while on their leisurely return journey they visited the marble mines of Carrara, gazing up with awe at their towering cliffs of white and ochre, and walking quietly under the large autumnal moon.[67] One consequence of this little holiday was the firm tactical decision for Shelley and Mary to make their winter home at Pisa, while Claire should return alone for Christmas to Florence. For the first time ever in Italy they decided to furnish their own house, and on their return, Claire was dispatched back to Livorno with instructions to vary her German exercises with shopping expeditions for suitable chairs and beds and tables.[68]

While the Shelleys, and the Williams and La Guiccioli and most of the rest of Pisan society impatiently awaited the appearance of the Byronic carriage on the road from Florence, Shelley suddenly and rather unexpectedly found himself engaged in another long poem. Since Prince Mavrocordato's departure in the summer, news of the Grecian struggle had been filtering back into Italy. The Tuscan cities in particular found themselves the centre of the latest reports and rumours, since Livorno like Marseilles, had become one of the Philhellenes' regular ports of embarkation. The Tuscan government fed and quartered Greek patriots returning from the Wallachian struggle via the Mediterranean to the Morea. Prince Argyropoli, Mavrocordato's cousin, had remained in Pisa, and was a hot source of Greek news, while Edward Williams shared and encouraged Shelley's passionate identification with this new focus of the revolutionary struggle.[69] These circumstances combined to inspire Shelley in the composition of a verse drama on the Greek war, based on *The Persians* of Aeschylus, and later christened by Williams, *Hellas*.

Hellas seems to have been begun at Livorno. Shelley unexpectedly appeared at Claire's lodgings on the evening of 5 October, after having sent her the upsetting news that Byron would not be bringing Allegra with him to Pisa.[70] Shelley stayed alone with Claire for the next few days, and began writing his drama.

Claire's own entry states that they read Schiller's play *Joan of Arc* together in German – Claire tutoring Shelley. On the 6th there was 'Thunder & Lightning all Night', and on the 8th she and Shelley drank tea with some Italian friends. On the 9th Shelley helped Claire pack up her belongings, and that evening they arrived at San Giuliano at 8 o'clock.

Shelley announced *Hellas* to Ollier, two days after he had returned to the Bagni on 11 October, saying that its subject was 'in a certain degree transitory', and that it should be immediately advertised since it would 'soon be ready'.[71] The drama was actually posted to Ollier a month later, on 11 November, for '*immediate* publication'.

For the rest of the month, the Williamses put up Claire at Pugnano, but Shelley and Claire continued to read German together – now moving on to Goethe's *Faust* – and visits were exchanged between San Giuliano and Pugnano almost daily. For one significant moment, it was Claire who stayed with Shelley at San Giuliano, and Mary who moved to Pugnano.[72] The Hoppner affair was no doubt having its aftermath at San Giuliano during October, and the flexibility of Shelley's arrangements suggest that as a result a greater frankness of behaviour was admitted between Mary and Claire.

Shelley was also writing with great freedom and energy. The preface to *Hellas* is one of the most active political statements on the struggle for liberty which Shelley ever framed, and parts of it had to be suppressed by Ollier. It also contains the classic English statement of Philhellenism – that movement of political, literary and military idealism which swept the whole of Europe, especially between the years of 1820 and 1824. Although it is dedicated 'To His Excellency Prince Alexander Mavrocordato', yet the action of the drama is almost entirely visionary and mystic.

Its cast-list of half a dozen names includes among the speakers Christ, Mahomet, Ahasuerus the Wandering Jew and the Phantom of Mahomet II. Despite the gestures towards epic action off-stage, and lumbering reportage of battles and smoke and carrion, the real subject of the poem – and where its poetry alone begins to grip – seems to be religious guilt. It considers the effect of past evil on the present, as so often in Shelley, both in historical and psychological terms. The poem contrasts, in this light, the difference between the great rational and humane tradition of classical Greek philosophy, with the superseding ideology of guilt and punishment represented for Shelley by the supreme authoritarianism of institutionalized Christian religion. There are several interesting prose notes to the poem on this subject, and altogether the work represents one of the most sophisticated and historically mature statements of Shelley's atheism.

But the drama is rightly celebrated for its declaration of Philhellenism:

We are all Greeks. Our laws, our literature, our religion, our arts have their root in Greece. But for Greece – Rome, the instructor, the conqueror, or the metropolis of our ancestors, would have spread no illumination with her arms, and we might still have been savages and idolaters; or, what is worse, might have arrived at such a stagnant and miserable state of social institution as China and Japan possess.

The human form and the human mind attained to a perfection in Greece which has impressed its image on those faultless productions, whose very fragments are the despair of modern art, and has propagated impulses which cannot cease, through a thousand channels of manifest or imperceptible operation, to ennoble and delight mankind until the extinction of the race.[73]

This declaration, fine as it is in itself, gains immeasurably from the knowledge that its author had also written a great translation of the *Symposium*, a wonderful set of travel letters from Naples, the first two acts of *Prometheus Unbound*, and the 'Notes on Florentine Sculpture'. Occasionally, though rarely, the verse lyrics of *Hellas* also come close to Shelley's best work:

> Temples and towers,
>   Citadels and marts, and they
> Who live and die there, have been ours,
>   And may be thine, and must decay;
> But Greece and her foundations are
> Built below the tide of war,
> Based on the crystàlline sea
> Of thought and its eternity;
> Her citizens, imperials spirits,
>   Rule the present and the past,
> On all this world of men inherits
>   Their seal is set.[74]

After experimenting with the long free lines of *Epipsychidion*, and the rigid formality of the stanza patterns in 'The Witch of Atlas' and *Adonais*, Shelley was slowly returning to the tight, rapid-running line of the poetry of 1819, with its simplicity of speech and its driving, insistent rhythms. But he had not yet established his new form, and *Hellas* contained a bewildering variety of metrical variations.

The presence of Ahasuerus in the drama also showed Shelley reaching back for new developments of old ideas. The use of the Wandering Jew, a figure last found explicitly in *Queen Mab* and *The Assassins* of 1814, pointed again to that strange reversion to old themes and feelings, the recycling of old imagery, of which Shelley's illness at Pisa in the winter of 1820–1 had first given forewarning. A curious inward spiralling of Shelley's imagination seemed to be in operation, as if it had been full circle through the experience of Italy, and was now, as he began to feel the stability of Pisa, coming back at a new angle and elevation through the field of experience and psychological stress undergone in the years 1814–15.

In a scene whose mechanism recalls the summoning of the Phantom of Jupiter in *Prometheus Unbound*, but whose subject goes further back to the poetry of the *Alastor* period, Ahasuerus summons the Phantom of Mahomet II. His explanation of this ghostly phenomenon, given to the present Turkish ruler, is in purely psychological terms.

> *Ahasuerus.*   What thou seest
> Is but the ghost of thy forgotten dream.
> A dream itself, yet less, perhaps, than that
> Thou call'st reality. Thou mayst behold
> How cities, on which Empire sleeps enthroned,
> Bow their towered crests to mutability. . . .
>   The Past
> Now stands before thee like an Incarnation
> Of the To-come; yet wouldst thou commune with
> That portion of thyself which was ere thou
> Didst start for this brief race whose crown is death,
> Dissolve with that strong faith and fervent passion
> Which called it from the uncreated deep,
> Yon cloud of war . . . and draw with mighty will
> The imperial shade hither.[75]

This passage is not nearly as fine as the equivalent scene in *Prometheus Unbound*, but Shelley's prose commentary on it in the notes throws considerable light on his own personal experiences with 'visions', and goes part of the way to explaining some of the more weird occurrences of the next spring and early summer. He wrote:

> The manner of the invocation of the spirit of Mahomet the Second will be censured as over subtle. I could easily have made the Jew a regular conjuror, and the Phantom an ordinary ghost. I have preferred to represent the Jew as disclaiming all pretension, or even belief, in supernatural agency, and as tempting Mahmud to that state of mind in which ideas may be supposed to assume the force of sensations through the confusion of thought with the

objects of thought, and the excess of passion animating the creations of imagination.

It is a sort of natural magic, susceptible of being exercised in a degree by any one who should have made himself master of the secret associations of another's thoughts.[76]

One can recognize here Shelley's mind turning not only on some of his own experiences but the experiences he had created for others, as during the disturbances at Kentish Town during the latter part of 1814. He now seemed to recognize his talents in this field. As a philosophical, rather than a purely psychological observation, this note also has clear reference to the discussion of daemons and *kaka-daimons* and the 'intermediary world' of Shelley's translation of the *Symposium*.

When *Hellas* was posted to Ollier on 11 November, Shelley considered it 'written at the suggestion of the events of the moment' and as a 'mere improvise'.[77] His main object was to get it published and circulated in aid of the Greek cause as speedily as possible. He had hopes that the work might appear in Ollier's bookshop in time for Christmas, but the publisher ran true to form and a small edition appeared quietly in February 1822. One part of the preface took slightly longer to find its way into print:

> Should the English people ever become free, they will reflect upon the part which those who presume to represent their will have played in the great drama of the revival of liberty. . . . This is the age of the war of the oppressed against the oppressors, and every one of those ringleaders of the privileged gangs of murderers and swindlers, called Sovereigns, look to each other for aid against the common enemy, and suspend their mutual jealousies in the presence of a mightier fear. Of this holy alliance all the despots of the earth are virtual members. But a new race has arisen throughout Europe, nursed in the abhorrence of the opinions which are its chains, and she will continue to produce fresh generations to accomplish that destiny which tyrants forsee and dread.[78]

This avowal of political belief was first published in 1892.[79] The little edition, with its Greek Epigraph, 'I am the Prophet of Victorious Struggles' echoing the engraving on Mavrocordato's ring, reached Shelley in April 1822. It was the last of his works he ever saw in print.

Towards the end of October, Shelley and Mary had settled on the house that they would take at Pisa. It was to be a large, unfurnished apartment occupying the whole of the top of the Tre Palazzi di Chiesa, an elegant building at the extreme eastern end of the Lung'Arno, just inside the ancient city wall, and overlooking the Ponte Fortezza. Below them on the south side was the formal Giardino Scotto with its pleasant walks and carefully tended shrubs, while beyond stretched a magnificent vista through lines of pines and cypresses, across the Pisan *maremma*, and as far as the sea. Mary wrote that 'the rooms we inhabit are south, and look over the whole country to the sea, so that we are entirely out of the bustle and disagreeable *puzzi* etc, of the town, and hardly know that we are so enveloped until we descend into the street'.[80] The Williamses were also searching for unfurnished rooms, and eventually moved into the ground floor of the Tre Palazzi. From the entrance gate, at street level, the Arno curved away to the left, with its line of tethered boats and skiffs; the Palazzo Lanfranchi was clearly visible diagonally across the river at a distance of some hundred yards, marked out from the row of buildings by its landing steps, and white marble façade, and commanding balcony on the first floor.

Lord Byron had still not arrived, but his train was expected any day, and in the meantime Shelley kept up his flow of letters, switching nimbly from *Don Juan* to furniture, to the Countess Guiccioli, to Tuscan aid for Greek patriots. He never gave up Allegra: 'The Countess tells me that you think of leaving Allegra for the present at the convent. Do as you think best – but I can pledge myself to find a situation for her here. . . .'[81] Leigh Hunt and his family were expected before the end of November; Horace Smith was still a remote possibility.

Shelley sent reports both to Hogg and John Gisborne in London. It is interesting that it was Gisborne who was given the substance of Shelley's feelings. Hogg got a formal essay on Plato's *Republic* – 'surely the foundation of true politics' – and the merits of botany over game shooting. To Gisborne, Shelley wrote with a certain sardonic realism about the Pisan scheme: 'Did I tell you that Lord Byron comes to settle at Pisa, & that he has a plan of writing a periodical work in conjunction with Hunt? . . . he has been expected every day these six weeks. – La Guiccioli his cara sposa who attends him impatiently, is a very pretty sentimental, [stupid – *deleted*] innocent, superficial Italian, who has sacrificed an immense fortune to live for Lord Byron; and who, if I know anything of my friend, of her, or of human nature will hereafter have plenty of leisure and opportunity to repent of her rashness. . . . We have furnished a house in Pisa, & I mean to make it our headquarters. – I shall get all my books out [from England], & intrench myself – like a spider in a web.'[82]

It was perhaps characteristic of Shelley that he should have given a totally different impression on this last point to Hogg. 'I have some thoughts, if I could get a respectable appointment, of going to India, or any where where I might be compelled to active exertion, & at the same time enter into an entirely new sphere of action. – But this I dare say is a mere dream, & I shall probably have no opportunity of making it a reality, but finish as I have begun.'[83] This recurrence of the old Eastern scheme at the very time that he was leasing a house and buying furniture, was perhaps not unconnected with the fact that Claire was about to disappear for her winter hibernation in the society of Florence. It was Peacock, not Hogg, who rose to the practical implications of this vague restlessness, and returned a managing sort of letter which reached Shelley in mid-November, to say that East India House did not employ any functionaries outside men of its own company. For the first time one senses that Peacock had misread his old friend: 'There is nothing that would give me so much pleasure (because I think there is nothing that would be more beneficial to you) than to see you following some scheme of flesh and blood – some interesting matter connected with the business of life, in the tangible shape of a practical man: and I shall make it a point of sedulous enquiry to discover if . . .' and so on.[84] Peacock was now aged 36; it was three and a half years since he had last talked to Shelley face to face.

Dreams of his Eastern scheme, set against the rapidly materializing reality of the Pisan plan, produced the last and finest of that group of Italian landscapes which come together as Shelley's 'Pisan poems'. 'Evening: Ponte Al Mare, Pisa' may have been written at any time towards the end of summer 1821, either in September or October. But certainly it was before the breaking of the weather, the departure of Claire and the arrival of Byron. Despite its Italian setting, and the underlying reference to Pisa as one of Dante's infernal cities – a place of blown straws, of ghosts, not men – the poem is essentially English in character. Its simplicity of presentation, its easy, adept phrasing and its carefully chosen details, make it an almost perfect English tone poem. It is also an interior landscape, an exact image of a human state of mind and spirit. Pisa reflects the watching mind, as the river reflects Pisa. The image of the third stanza was one Shelley adapted from the 'Ode to Liberty' of the previous year, as he realized its full potential. 'Evening: Ponte Al Mare, Pisa':

The sun is set; the swallows are asleep;
  The bats are flitting fast in the gray air;
The slow soft toads out of damp corners creep,
  And evening's breath, wandering here and there
Over the quivering surface of the stream,
Wakes not one ripple from its summer dream.

There is no dew on the dry grass to-night,
  Nor damp within the shadow of the trees;
The wind is intermitting, dry, and light;
  And in the inconstant motion of the breeze

The dust and straws are driven up and down,
And whirled about the pavement of the town.

Within the surface of the fleeting river
    The wrinkled image of the city lay,
Immovably unquiet, and forever
    It trembles, but it never fades away;
Go to the East. . . .
You, being changed, will find it then as now.

The chasm in which the sun has sunk is shut
    By darkest barriers of cinereous cloud,
Like mountain over mountain huddled – but
    Growing and moving upwards in a crowd,
And over it a space of watery blue,
Which the keen evening star is shining through.[85]

The Ponte Al Mare was at the far end of the town from the Tre Palazzi and the Ponte Fortezza. The river flowed under it and then turned westwards to the sea.

28
The Byron Brigade: 1822

Claire was the first person to know of Byron's arrival, just as years before, she was the first person to hear his carriage wheels on the gravel and spot his name in the register of Monsieur Dejean's Hotel at Geneva. This time, they were both in carriages. Shelley had finally packed Claire off on the coach for Florence on the morning of 1 November 1821, when they parted under a radiant blue sky. 'Just before Empoli,' Claire wrote in her diary at Florence that night, 'we passed Lord B— and his travelling train. As we approached Florence we entered also a thick white fog so that the Signora Durrazzini said, "*Par che i cieli cascin addosso*".' As if the skies were about to collapse on top of you. [1]

Byron descended upon Pisa that evening, and the lights of the Palazzo Lanfranchi blazed across the waters of the Arno until late into the night. The next day, 2 November, Shelley paid a formal call, and was profusely greeted, thanked and presented with a copy of Byron's new poem *Cain*. La Guiccioli now took up her official residence: Shelley had already pointed out to Edward Williams, some days earlier, when they were arranging his Lordship's furniture, that Byron's massive bed sported the Byron arms, 'Crede Byron'. On the 6th, Byron, La Guiccioli and her brother Pietro Gamba returned the formal call to the Tre Palazzi, and social relations were now established. On the 7th Byron applied for permission to practise pistol-shooting in the grounds of the Palazzo Lanfranchi, and had his request courteously but firmly refused: no fire-arms were permitted to be used within the city walls.

This ruling resulted in one of the most distinctive social rituals of Byron's stay in Pisa: the regular afternoon shooting expeditions. He departed each day from the southern gate to fire at targets on a remote farm on the edge of the Pisan *maremma*. As news of Byron's arrival in the city spread through Tuscany, various familiar figures drifted in to Pisa to join the *équipage* in November and December. The custom became established that they assembled on horseback at the gateway of the Lanfranchi for the start of the afternoon's sports. Before

Byron himself, and Pietro Gamba, Count John Taaffe reappeared, Tom Medwin came back from Florence where he had been pursuing a 15-year-old heiress, and Shelley and Williams frequently joined the party. Shelley had introduced Williams to Byron on 5 November, and Williams had been much impressed by his Lordship's 'most unaffected and gentlemanly ease', and charmed by Byron's sudden impetuous gift of a book as they parted with the words, 'something . . . to amuse you, besides the general matter it contains, for at the end it takes infinite pains to prove that I am the Devil'. Edward Williams took this confidence as a great compliment.[2]

Under Shelley's inspiration, besides finishing his play *The Promise*, Williams had also begun a diary. In its pages, besides a record of his and Shelley's reading, he kept a close account of the shooting expeditions. On one day he recorded: 'Lord B. hit, at the distance of 14 yards, the bulls-eye four times, and a half-crown piece three. The last shot struck the piece of money so exactly in the centre that it was afterwards found with the ball enclosed within it – the sides being drawn to the centre like a three-cornered cocked hat. – Call'd in the morning on Lrd B— His pistols were Wilkinson's.'[3] Three days later it was Shelley who hit the half-crown twice: he and Byron seem to have been by far the best shots among the party and there was a certain rivalry between the two. Tom Medwin noted their different styles of shooting: Byron drew a long aim, with a hand that visibly trembled, yet usually produced a high standard of hits. Shelley, on the contrary, took a sudden, rapid aim, with a rock-steady hand – 'all firmness' – and also produced regularly good shooting.[4] Of the two, one has the impression from Williams's journal that Byron had the edge.

The shooting gradually changed from a casual exercise into a shared obsession. Byron rode out on a Hussar saddle slung with several pistols in decorated leather holsters; Shelley spent several hours a week preparing his own targets and carried them round in his pocket. Between them they even created a special shooting *patois*: 'firing, *tiring*; hitting, *colping*; missing, *mancating*; riding, *cavalling* . . .'.[5]

Pisa was at this time a garrisoned city, and the Tuscan authorities, for all their liberality towards the Greek patriots, were on constant alert for agitators and *carbonari* sympathizers. The officers and soldiers of the Pisan guard observed the English milord's daily mounted expeditions to and from the city gates with a certain professional interest, and they noted down for future reference the bearded Venetian cut-throat Tita. Relations were not altogether happy between Byron's camp-followers and the local Pisan populace, and a situation gradually grew up during the winter that had dangerous potential.

The society of the ladies became progressively more retired and feminine, as that of the men became more flamboyant and masculine. Mary, Jane Williams and La Guiccioli became constant companions, meeting together regularly at the Tre Palazzi. They too rode out together, but it was no longer in the company of the men, but usually in a close carriage with a posse of servants. There were few visitors besides Williams, and occasionally Taaffe, and none from the Pisan university set of the previous year. Mary records that in December she went only once to the opera. She filled the house with potted plants which lined the south-facing window-sills.[6] Her main outside interest was helping choose the furniture for the Hunts's apartment which was to be on the ground floor of the Palazzo Lanfranchi; yet she very rarely saw Byron to speak to.[7] Edward Williams had become Shelley's amanuensis, and it was he who clean-copied *Hellas* for the press, and he who afterwards took down at daily dictation Shelley's translation of Spinoza's *Tractatus Theologico-Politicus*. This philosophic work had been begun at Marlow in the winter of 1817, with Shelley dictating to Mary, and taken up again at Florence in 1820. It had now been decided that Williams should help him to bring it to a close, and Byron would write a biographic preface. Mary's help was no longer required in this sphere. Her letters to Maria Gisborne in London show little signs of outward life, except to observe languidly that 'My Lord is now living very sociably, giving dinners to his male acquaintance and writing divinely; perhaps by this time you have seen "Cain" and will agree with us in thinking it his finest production . . .'.[8] She was considering making mince pies for Christmas.

Byron installed a splendid billiard table at the Lanfranchi, and Shelley and Williams spent much time patrolling its green perimeter. The riding and the shooting and the billiards steadied Shelley's spirits, and his health seems to have been materially better than during previous Italian winters, while Byron's regular dinners, usually on Wednesdays, were at first a great pleasure. By contrast Shelley's writing almost completely stopped. The only poem that he began working on during these months was the draft of a translation of Goethe's *Faust*, but it went slowly.

The curiously hypnotic effect that Byron's theatrical mode of life was having on Shelley is indicated by an extraordinary incident which occurred on 12 December. News had reached Pisa late in the evening that an unknown Italian was about to be burnt by the state authorities at Lucca for an act of sacrilege: stealing a wafer-box from a church. Although the report was totally unsubstantiated, and without any corroborating details, Shelley rushed to the Lanfranchi and proposed that he and Lord Byron should organize an armed party of English to ride through the night 'and rescue the man by force'.[9] Byron demurred, but was sufficiently drawn into the conspiratorial atmosphere of Shelley's wild suggestion to sit up with him, Williams and Medwin until 2 in the morning, having dispatched Count Taaffe to ride through the frosty night and bring back a first-hand report. Since no further definite information was obtained,

Byron promised to draw up a 'memorial to the Grand Duke of Tuscany', the next day, and the party dispersed for the night. The next morning Shelley sent over a faintly sheepish note from the Tre Palazzi. 'My dear Lord Byron, I hear this morning that the design which certainly had been in contemplation of burning my fellow serpent has been abandoned & that he has been condemned to the gallies. . . .'[10] Even this was not correct: the man had escaped to Florence.

Altogether one has the impression that while Byron's presence continued to inhibit Shelley as a writer – as it had done at Geneva in 1816 – it yet acted upon him as a goad. Shelley delighted in Byron's private company, but his public presence constituted a permanent challenge and a dare. Within the field of Byron's social life, Shelley's actions frequently had a quality of exaggeration, almost of staginess. The two poets, holding separate court on either side of the Arno, rivalled each other in everything they did, and implicitly challenged each member of the Pisan circle to confer loyalties on one party or the other. At first the confrontation was exciting and mutually stimulating, but gradually it became an exhausting performance for Shelley.

One direct consequence of these feelings was the recklessness with which Shelley and Williams put their little skiff to sail on the swollen Arno, long after the weather had broken in mid-December, and violent storms and lightning burst frequently over the city. Mary remembered how the local Italians remarked on their crazy, English foolhardiness.[11] Williams's entry for 20 December is typical: 'Cloudy – strong gales from the South. S and I sail furiously against a violent current for a considerable distance up the Arno. The storm however increasing we reached the shore only just in time.'[12] On Christmas Day they made another such expedition, in 'violent wind with rain at intervals', and then landed to dine with Byron and his party. Byron observed these expeditions from his balcony with a mixture of admiration and irony. Once, on receiving a letter attacking Shelley's writings from London, he observed acidly: '[The Snake] alone, in this age of humbug, dares stem the current, as he did today the flooded Arno in his skiff, although I could not observe he made any progress. The attempt is better than being swept along as the rest are, with the filthy garbage scoured from its banks.'[13] The weather grew steadily rougher, the Serchio burst its banks, and the water on the Arno rose above the level of the arches on one of the bridges. The danger that Shelley had played with was vividly illustrated on 26 December, when a local boatman took to the river to recover a gentleman's hat, was caught in a whirlpool caused by one of the bridges, capsized and drowned.[14]

In social gatherings – at the dinner table, on the shooting expeditions, or in the billiard room – it was Shelley's and Byron's conversation which dominated the proceedings by their continual counterpoint. Both men allowed each other a formal advantage: Shelley was absolutely rigid in his recognition of Byron's superior social status – 'my dear *Lord* Byron'; Byron in turn always appeared to submit to Shelley's critical judgement on literary matters (it being understood that he regarded *Don Juan* and *Cain* as very great poems). Medwin was immensely impressed by this fact when one morning Byron handed Shelley the manuscript of a poem 'The Deformed Transformed'. Shelley took it over to the window to read, and having read it carefully, returned to where Byron leaned against the mantelpiece and announced that 'he liked it the least of all his works; that it smelt too strongly of "Faust"; and besides, that there were two lines in it, word for word from Southey.' Medwin quailed inwardly at the cool frankness of this judgement, but '. . . Byron turned deadly pale, seized the MS., and committed it to the flames, seeming to take a savage delight in seeing it consume'.[15] Yet in part, this too was a stage device. Byron had another copy safely in his desk, and a revised version was published two years later by Murray. Equally, Shelley's respect for Byron's aristocracy was strictly a formality – he did not observe it in his private letters to his friends, and he came to believe that Byron's insistence on rank was one of his most damaging faults.

Medwin recalled the contrasting styles of their conversation, which, like their shooting, were deliberately exaggerated in company to act as foils to each other.

> [Byron's] talk was at that time a dilution of his letters, full of *persiflage* and *calembourg* [sic]. Shelley used to compare him to Voltaire, to whom he would have thought it the greatest compliment to be compared. . . . Both professed the same speculative – I might say, sceptical turn of mind; the same power of changing the subject from grave to gay; the same mastery over the sublime, the pathetic, the comic. . . . Shelley frequently lamented that it was almost impossible to keep Byron to any one given point. He flew about from subject to subject like a will-o'-the-wisp. . . . Every word of Shelley's was almost oracular; his reasoning subtle and profound, his opinions, whatever they were, sincere and undisguised; whilst with Byron, such was his love of mystification, it was impossible to know when he was in earnest. . . . He dealt, too, in the gross and indelicate, of which Shelley had an utter abhorrence, and often left him in ill-disguised disgust.[16]

Some of their jokes, which Medwin recorded, though they sound lame in isolation, give an indication of the mischievous humour of both men. During one of their many conversations concerning translation, which were the result of Shelley's work on *Faust*, Byron suddenly remarked with a suggestive leer that 'Sale, the translator of the Koran, was suspected of being an Islamite, but a very different one from you, Shiloh' – a reference to the doctrines of atheism and free love in *The Revolt of Islam*.[17] While on another occasion, apropos of the translation of colloquialisms and endearments, Shelley observed in a mild voice that a letter Byron had once received from his Lady Byron beginning 'Dearest Duck' would sound curious in Italian – 'Anitra Carissima'.[18]

At one of the dinners, the two poets so far forgot themselves as to lay a public bet of £1,000 to be paid by whichever of them first came into his family inheritance. Byron of course was always laying wagers on such things: shooting, swimming, boxing, racing. But for Shelley to lay out the equivalent of one year of his Italian income on a smoking-room bet was nothing less than extra ordinary.[19]

Shelley gave a very different impression of the friendship to Claire in Florence. 'The Exotic as you please to call me droops in this frost – a frost both moral and physical – a solitude of the heart. – These late days I have been unable to ride – the cold towards sunset is so excessive & my side reminding me that I am mortal. Medwin rides almost constantly with Lord B & the party sometimes consists of Gamba, Taaffe, Medwin & the Exotic who unfortunately belonging to the order of mimosa thrives ill in so large a society. I cannot endure the company of many persons, & the society of one is either great pleasure or great pain. . . . I am employed in nothing – I read – but I have no spirits for serious composition – I have no confidence and to write in solitude or put forth thoughts without sympathy is unprofitable vanity.' He wrote to her of the storms and the floods, and of Mary's rheumatism, which now kept her even more within doors, taking laudanum – but he did not mention the boat, or the dinners, or the bets.[20]

Yet Shelley's inner despondency was, as far as Claire was concerned, quite genuine. His letters during this winter, though they were few, are perhaps the most openly affectionate and sad that he ever wrote to her. For the first time, it seemed that it was now Shelley who was importuning Claire rather than she him. Perhaps this was the significance of the October days spent together in Livorno. 'My dearest friend,' he wrote to her just before Christmas, 'I should be very glad to receive a confidential letter from you – one totally the reverse of those I write you; detailing all your present occupation and intimacies, & giving me some insight into your future plans. Do not think my affection & anxiety for you ever cease, or that I ever love you less although that love has been & still must be a source of disquietude to me. . . . Tell me [dearest – *deleted*] what you mean to do, & if it should give you pleasure come & live with us. The Williams's always speak of you with praise and affection; & regret very much that you did not spend this winter with them but neither their regret nor their affection equal mine. . . .'[21] The pointed withdrawal of the endearment could only have been done because Shelley felt Claire herself would now frown upon it. How Shelley could have coped with Byron and Mary *and* Claire simultaneously at Pisa is impossible to envisage.

At the very end of the year, he wrote again, now almost reproachfully: 'You do not tell me, my dearest Clare, anything of your plans, although you bid me be secret with respect to them. Assure yourself, my best friend, that anything you *seriously* enjoin me, that may be necessary for your happiness will be strictly observed by me. Write to me explicitly your projects and expectations. You know in some respects my sentiments both with regard to them and you. . . .'[22]

This last letter to Claire, of 31 December, also brought worrying news concerning the linch-pin of the Pisan scheme – Leigh Hunt. The storms that had swept Tuscany and the Arno had been general throughout the Mediterranean and the Bay of Biscay – wrecks had been reported all along the coast around Genoa, and three consecutive mail ships from France had not arrived. As far as Shelley knew, the Hunts had taken ship on the *Jane*, leaving the Port of London in mid-November, and had last been heard of off the Spanish coast. As Christmas arrived and passed, and still no news of their whereabouts reached Pisa, Shelley began to suspect the worst. 'You may imagine,' he told Claire, 'and I am sure you will share our anxiety about poor Hunt. . . . I shall, of course, write to tell you the moment of his arrival.'[23]

The first weeks of the new year, 1822, were equally barren. The weather became less stormy, there was a series of fine frosty days, and yet Williams records that whole afternoons and evenings – sometimes 'almost the whole day' – passed in games of billiards. On 6 January Byron came in very excited with a project that a number of professors at the university had dreamed up of getting him to lend his name and financial assistance to a one-man steam-powered flying machine. But by the end of the evening Shelley had turned the subject to steam-powered yachts.[24] On the 11th, when Shelley wrote to Peacock, there was still no news. 'Lord Byron is established now [& gives a weekly dinner – *deleted*] & we are constant companions: no small relief this after the dreary solitude of the understanding & the imagination in which we passed the first years of our expatriation. . . . We expect Hunt here every day & remain in great anxiety on account of the heavy gales which he must have encountered at Christmas. Lord Byron has fitted up the lower apartments of his palace for him. . . . I have been long idle, – & as far as writing goes, despondent – but I am now engaged in Charles the 1st & a devil of a nut it is to crack.' This last piece of Byronism merely covered the fact that Shelley had taken up the play for about the fourth time, written a few more fragments, and thrown it aside in disgust after some five days.[25] Soon after Williams received a rejection letter from the manager of Covent Garden for his play *The Promise*. It was not easy living in Byron's shadow.

The only piece of literary work that seems to have held Shelley consistently during these suspended weeks was Goethe's *Faust*. In mid-January he received a box from Paris containing among other things his Calderón, and the new edition of *Faust* (1820) illustrated with the superb gothic etchings of Moritz Retzch. These wiry, grotesque drawings had an enormous impact on Shelley, and the whole Faust story began to haunt his imagination. 'We have just got the etchings of "Faust",' he wrote animatedly to Gisborne, 'the painter is worthy of Goethe. The meeting of him and Margaret is wonderful. It makes all the pulses of my head beat – those of my heart have been quiet long ago.' The translations which came with it did not impress him, nor those he had recently read in a copy of *Blackwood's Magazine*, and he returned to his own version.[26]

The only two scenes of *Faust* which Shelley attempted and finished, were the 'Prologue in Heaven', and the celebrated Hartz Mountain scene on May Day night – *Walpurgisnacht*. Shelley managed well with this, translating carefully, but also catching the rapid, lurid distortions of the Brocken and the sense of seething night life, when any grotesque, inanimate shape or shadow may begin to squirm and crawl:

> Are the screech, the lapwing, and the jay,
> All awake as if 'twere day?
> See, with long legs and belly wide,
>   A salamander in the brake!
>   Every root is like a snake,
> And along the loose hillside,
> With strange contortions through the night,
> Curls, to seize or to affright. . . .
>   Through the dazzling gloom
> The many-coloured mice, that thread
> The dewy turf beneath our tread,
> In troops each other's motions cross,
> Through the heath and through the moss. . . .[27]

The Retzch etchings began to fascinate him more and more until they took on a life of their own. Later he wrote again to Gisborne: 'What etchings these are! I am never satiated with looking at them, & I fear it is the only sort of translation of which Faust is susceptible – I never perfectly understood the Hartz Mountain scene, until I saw the etching. – And then, Margaret in the summer house with Faust! – The artist makes one envy his happiness that he can sketch such things with calmness, which I dared only to look upon once, & which made my brain swim round only to touch the leaf on the opposite side of which I knew that it was figured.'[28] With their macabre setting of the love between Faust and Margaret, the pictures obviously found a deep correspondence in Shelley's own experiences. They are certainly weird enough.

Shelley had first read *Faust* in company with Byron and M. G. Lewis at Geneva, and Goethe's poem was clearly associated in his mind with Byron's presence. It is perhaps for this reason that one can recognize a familiar, jaunty, aristocratic ease in some of Mephistopheles's speeches. When they pause before descending into the valley to join the witches round their 'heap of glimmering coals', the following exchange takes place:

Faust. In introducing us, do you assume
　　　　The character of Wizard or of Devil?
Mephistopheles. In truth, I generally go about
　　　　in strict incognito; and yet one likes
　　　　To wear one's orders upon gala days.
　　　　I have no ribbon at my knee; but here
　　　　At home, the cloven foot is honourable.
　　　　See you that snail there? – she comes creeping up,
　　　　And with her feeling eyes hath smelt out something.
　　　　I could not, if I would, mask myself here.
　　　　Come now, we'll go about from fire to fire:
　　　　I'll be the Pimp, and you shall be the Lover.[29]

The cloven foot was of course fortuitous. But if there were elements of Byron in Mephistopheles, one begins to speculate about Shelley and Faust. The moment at the end of the scene, where Faust recognizes the animated corpse or phantom of his first love Margaret among the dancers, is translated with a kind of chilling, stony realism, and for the only time one is given to understand that Mephistopheles is not quite in control of the infernal proceedings:

Faust. 　　　　　　Seest thou not a pale,
　　　　Fair girl, standing alone, far, far, away?
　　　　She drags herself now forward with slow steps.
　　　　And seems as if she moved with shackled feet:
　　　　I cannot overcome the thought that she
　　　　Is like poor Margaret.
Mephistopheles. Let it be – pass on –
　　　　No good can come of it – it is not well
　　　　To meet it – it is an enchanted phantom,
　　　　A lifeless idol; with its numbing look,
　　　　It freezes up the blood of man; and they
　　　　Who meet its ghastly stare are turned to stone,
　　　　Like those who saw Medusa.

Faust.   Oh, too true!
      Her eyes are like the eyes of a fresh corpse
      Which no belovèd hand has closed, alas!
      That is the breast which Margaret yielded to me –
      Those are the lovely limbs which I enjoyed!
Mephistopheles. It is all magic, poor deluded fool!
      She looks to every one like his first love.[30]

The appalling implication of Mephistopheles's final line would not have been lost on Shelley; and the images throughout this closing passage – the Medusa, the unclosed eyes – would each have reached him with a shock not of surprise, but of recognition.

Shelley turned again and again to these scenes of Goethe's during the coming spring, and one can sense them moving behind many of the fragments he wrote during this unsettled and unproductive period. In April he was to write: 'I have been reading over & over again Faust, & always with sensations that no other composition excites. It deepens the gloom & augments the rapidity of the ideas, & would therefore seem to be an unfit study for any person who is a prey to the reproaches of memory, & the delusions of an imagination not to be restrained.'[31] He says no more, but the reference is obviously to himself.

It was with Claire that Shelley had first begun to re-read *Faust*, and in February and March he encouraged her to complete, as a crown to her eighteen months of German study, a finished translation of the whole of Part I, which he promised her they would get published in England. The manuscript of Claire's version has never been recovered,[32] while Shelley's was published in the first issue of the *Liberal*.

By the end of January, the disconcerting news reached Pisa that the Hunts were still in England. They had indeed boarded the *Jane* in November, but had been held up by the terrible storms, first at Ramsgate, and later at Dartmouth. Finally, after many days of waiting and seasickness, Marianne Hunt decided that the journey with the children was too dangerous, and would have to be postponed until the spring; so they wintered near Dartmouth. This decision was to have a long train of disastrous consequences. In the first place, the several hundred pounds[33] which Shelley had organized for Hunt on an extended loan from Horace Smith, was very largely dissipated on forfeited fares, extra living expenses in England and the arrival of unpaid bills from London. In the second place the Pisan circle, lacking its linch-pin for the production of the *Liberal* by the Triumvirate, began to spin in other directions. Without the unifying idea of this literary scheme, of which Hunt's presence as managing editor of the *machinery* was an absolutely indispensable part, the friction between Shelley and Byron immediately began to increase.

There was still the shooting club, and the dining club, and the late-night private conversations, but these were no longer enough. Shelley's discontent appeared quickly in a letter to Horace Smith: 'Lord Byron unites us at a weekly dinner where my nerves are generally shaken to pieces by sitting up, contemplating the rest making themselves vats of claret &c. till 3 o'Clock in the morning. – We regret *your* absence exceedingly. . . . Hunt was expected & Lord B. had fitted up a part of his palace for his accommodation, when we heard that the late violent storms had forced him to put back, & that nothing could induce Marianne to put to sea again. – This for many reasons that I cannot now explain has produced a chaos of perplexities.'[34] He wrote to Hunt direct on the same day, enclosing a draft for £150, and begging that he still try to sail at once, before 'debts, responsibilities & expenses' enmeshed him round. Without Hunt's immediate presence the whole project was in danger.

Various new figures had joined the Pisan group since the new year, and its literary atmosphere was slowly giving way to something more swashbuckling. One, a certain Captain Hay, attached himself to Byron, and spent time shooting in the *maremma* with the Gambas. He sent consignments of wild boar to the Palazzo Lanfranchi which went well with the claret at dinner.[35]

Another, more significant figure, was Edward John Trelawny. Trelawny had arrived in Pisa on 14 January from Geneva, after months of urging from Edward Williams. Trelawny was, like Shelley, in his thirtieth year: he was a Cornishman and a professional adventurer who could turn his hand to anything; boats, horses, pistols, women and memoir-writing. He was a tall, swarthy figure, with a mass of black hair cuffed rather boyishly across his forehead and very white, smiling teeth glittering through a heavy black beard. He valued his piratical appearance, and though clearly a gentleman, he affected open shirts, coloured neckclothes, a strong enigmatic manner, and an endless supply of dramatic anecdotes. It says much for his style, that although regarded with instant suspicion by Mary, he very quickly won her favour, and later her affection and trust. Her portrait of him in the journal is very good, and tells a lot about both of them at this time.

Trelawney is extravagant, – un giovane stravagante – partly natural and partly perhaps put on, but it suits him well, and if his abrupt but not unpolished manners be assumed, they are nevertheless in unison with his Moorish face (for he looks Oriental yet not Asiatic) his dark hair, his Herculean form, and then there is an air of extreme good nature which pervades his whole countenance, especially when he smiles, which assures me that his heart is good. He tells strange stories of himself, horrific ones, so that they harrow one up. . . . I believe them now I see the man, and, tired with the everyday sleepiness of human intercourse, I am glad to meet with one, who, among other valuable qualities, has the rare merit of interesting my imagination.[36]

It is indicative of Mary's manner that when he first met her, Trelawny thought she was 27, when she was really only 24.[37] Trelawny's first meeting with Shelley at the Williamses' apartment, translating a piece of Calderón, produced an opposite extreme. His celebrated description of the 'flushed, feminine, artless face' and the boyish, stripling figure in ill-fitting black jacket and trousers may be compared with the Curran portrait, as a deliberate piece of hagiography.[38] But the whole of the memoir he later wrote was, in this respect, another of his 'strange stories', and aimed at achieving the single effect which he put into the mouth of Jane Williams at that first meeting: 'Shelley? Oh, he comes and goes like a spirit, no one knows when or where.' Trelawny committed himself to Shelley's side of the Arno, and in retrospect he wished to make his chosen poet contrast as strongly as possible with the worldliness he identified in Byron's character. Byron's comment at the time was: 'Ay, the Snake has fascinated you; I am for making a man of the world of you; they will mould you into a Frankenstein monster.'[39]

Trelawny brought with him to Pisa an idea that was in the long run to be more powerful in the affairs of the Pisan circle than the original scheme for the *Liberal*. It was presented to Shelley and Williams one evening in the shape of a small model. Williams wrote: 'January 15th. Fine and frosty. Wrote a little. Trelawney called, and brought with him the model of an American schooner on which it is settled with Shelley & myself to build a boat 30 feet long, and Trelawney writes to [Captain] Roberts at Genoa to commence on it directly.'[40]

On 7 February, Shelley and Williams rode out in a light carriage to make a five-day reconnaissance of the bay of La Spezia, north of Viareggio, with a view to spending spring and summer by the sea. Two of their days were spent sailing round the little bay of Lerici, opposite Portovenere, looking for suitable houses. Nothing was definitely decided upon, but by the time they returned to Pisa the idea had reached a new stage. Trelawny had presented Byron with drawings by Captain Roberts for a larger boat, and it had now become the 'Spezia Plan'.

Mary wrote to Maria Gisborne thoughtfully, during Shelley's absence: 'Shelley is now gone to La Spezia to get houses for our Colony for the summer. – It will be a large one, too large I am afraid for unity – yet I hope not – there will be Lord Byron who will have a large and beautiful boat built on purpose by some English navy officers at Genoa. – There will be the Countess Guiccioli and her brother – the Williams, who you know – Trelawny – a kind of half Arab Englishman. . . . There will be besides a Captain Roberts whom I do not know – a very rough subject I fancy – a famous angler &c. – We are to have a smaller boat.'[41] Talk of the boats, and of houses in the bay, now dominated all other conversation; while the arrival of Hunt seemed to become a more and more distant prospect.

The early Tuscan spring was already upon them, the hedges in the Giardino Scotto began to bud, and the days were warm and clear[42] and in mid-February it was the time of Carnival again. Mary, who had regarded the pink top-hats and carnival parades so askance on their first arrival in Pisa in 1820, now took an active and delighted part in the proceedings. She promenaded along the Lung'Arno admiring and criticizing the masks with the Williamses – they voted 'a Lawyer' as the best of the season – and one evening Jane put on a Hindustani dress, and Mary garbed herself in Turkish costume.[43] On another night a foursome, Jane and Edward, Mary and Trelawny, went to the Carnival fancy-dress ball or *Veglione* and danced till 3 in the morning. At long last, Mary's period of retreat on the top floor of the Tre Palazzi seemed over. She gave small supper parties under the open windows, and looked forward with longing to the summer colony, imagining to herself the 'sparkling waves, the olive covered hills & vines shrouded *pergolas* of Spezia'.[44] Edward Trelawny's presence had undoubtedly helped the coming of the spring.

Shelley's name was notably absent from these springtime excursions. He still spent a good deal of time in Byron's company, and he was apparently the most enthusiastic advocate – apart from Trelawny, who had thus secured himself an unofficial post – of the boat-building scheme. He was perhaps aware, more clearly than any of the others, that it was the one thing that might hold the Pisan circle together long enough for Hunt to reach Italy. But his real preoccupations were elsewhere.

In the first place, the inspiration and irritation of Byron's talk on literary matters, had led him to try to make a decisive break with his own publisher Ollier. In many ways this was long overdue, but if Byron was the inspiration, John Gisborne was the invaluable instrument. Throughout January and February, Shelley wrote a series of forceful and increasingly angry letters to Ollier, backed up by a parallel series of explanations and requests to Gisborne. The remarkable change of tone in these letters showed how far his thinking on literary matters had been affected by Byron's businesslike approach: 'First, I wish to see [Ollier's] accounts, and find out what is due to me upon them, and for what sum I *may*, if I please, draw on him. Secondly, to ask him whether he will buy the copyright of "Charles the First", what he will give me, and when he will pay me. Thirdly, to discover whether he has printed and published the poem of "Hellas", and if not to give it to some other publisher. . . . Fourthly, to make up a package of four copies of each of my poems, and send them. . . . In order to make this, or whatever other arrangements with Ollier, this letter shall be your authority. I am, all citizens of the world ought to be, especially curious regarding the article of money. What news?'[45] One can hear clearly the accents of Mephistopheles, and they were probably not unwelcome to Gisborne. The titles of his poems published by Ollier, which Shelley now wished to see round his walls, along with the other books and potted plants were: *The Revolt of Islam* (1818); *Rosalind and Helen* (1819); *The Cenci* (2nd edition, 1821); *Prometheus Unbound* (1820); *Epipsychidion* (1821); and *Adonais* (Pisan imprint, 1821).

Receiving no satisfactory news from Ollier on these points, Shelley wrote Gisborne a finalizing letter which reached London in mid-February: 'I wish now to have done with Ollier as a publisher, & I should feel exceedingly grateful to you if you would undertake to extract me from his clutches. I give you hereby, full authority, to settle my accounts with him. . . . As the books are my property I would rather that they were burnt than that they remained in his possession.'[46]

In London, Gisborne set about Shelley's affairs, and inquired discreetly after a new publisher, as best he could. But it was not to prove as simple as Shelley had supposed. To begin with, Gisborne discovered that Shelley was in debt to Ollier for a sum of at least fifty or sixty pounds. The complications over settling accounts went on into the summer, and no new publisher was found.

Familiar emotional problems were also troubling Shelley, and towards these, too, he now adopted a more forthright policy. At the end of January Williams had been surprised to receive at his apartment a short letter from Shelley, enclosing a seven-stanza poem which began 'The Serpent is shut out from Paradise'. During the previous week, Shelley had showed Williams a copy of the *Epipsychidion*, and had discussed with him his feelings about Emilia Viviani; that was to say, the feelings of his *other* self, the young Englishman who had died on his journey to the Sporades, and left behind a portfolio of poems. Williams had listened with sympathy. Now he read Shelley's letter – a curious method of communication for one who lived two flights of stairs above. 'My dear Williams, Looking over the portfolio in which my friend used to keep his verses, & in which those I sent you the other day were found, – I have lit upon these; which as they are too dismal for *me* to keep I send them you. . . . If any of the stanzas should please you, you may read them to Jane, but to no one else, – and yet on second thought I had rather you would not [*six words deleted*]. Yours ever affectionately, PBS.' The appeal for help in the poem must have been fairly explicit to Williams. Its background, which Williams knew only too well, was the almost complete failure of feeling between Shelley and Mary; and the increasing strain of the friendship with Byron, which was referred to in the fourth stanza.

I

The serpent is shut out from Paradise –
The wounded deer must seek the herb no more
In which its hearts cure lies –
The widowed dove must cease to haunt a bower
Like that which from its mate with feignèd sighs,
Fled in the April hour –
I too, must seldom seek again
Near happy friends a mitigated pain. . . .

. . .

III

. . . Therefore if now I see you seldomer
Dear friends, dear *friend*, know that I only fly
Your looks, because they stir
Griefs that should sleep, and hopes that cannot die.
The very comfort which they minister
I scarce can bear; yet I,
(So deeply is the arrow gone)
Should quickly perish if it were withdrawn.

IV

When I return to my cold home, you ask
Why I am not as I have lately been?
You spoil me for the task
Of acting a forced part in life's dull scene.
Of wearing on my brow the idle mask
Of author, great or mean,
In the world's carnival. I sought
Peace thus, & but in you I found it not.

V

Full half an hour today I tried my lot
With various flowers, & every one still said
'She loves me, loves me not.'
And if this meant a vision long since fled –
If it meant Fortune, Fame, or Peace of thought
If it meant – (but I dread
To speak what you may know too well)
Still there was truth in the sad oracle. . . .[47]

Williams had in fact seen Shelley and dined or shot with him at least four times
in the previous week, and he did not take the poem altogether seriously. But he
was warned, and he showed the whole missive to Jane. His journal for that day
read: 'Shelley sent us some beautiful but too melancholy lines – Call'd on Lord
B. and accompanied him to the [shooting] ground – Broke a bottle at 30 paces.
Dined with Mary and Shelley.'[48]

During February, Williams made a point of walking alone with Shelley along
the Arno, and they instituted a new ritual – the two of them breakfasting together with Jane. A two-day trip with Trelawny to Livorno, looking over
schooners in the harbour, cheered Shelley with the thought of the fact that he
and Williams would sail together all summer long across the Gulf of Spezia. It
took definite shape in the mind's eye. In Trelawny's words to Captain Roberts:
'. . . Will you lay us down a small beautiful one of about 17 or 18 feet? to be a
thorough *Varment* at pulling and sailing . . . three luggs and a jib – *backing ones*! –
She will be used for fishing, shooting, and as a tender for [Lord Byron's]. . . .'[49]
That amount of sail for an eighteen-foot dinghy virtually implied wings; which
was rather what Shelley had in mind.

Slowly Jane Williams began to play her new part in Shelley's life. On the first
Saturday in February, she and Shelley – accompanied by Mary – made a day-
long expedition to walk from Pisa through the Cascine pine forest to the sea. He
commemorated it in a long loose letter-poem 'The Pine Forest of the Cascine
Near Pisa', which began 'Dearest, best and brightest, Come away. . . .' It is not
a notable piece of writing, but it contains – like 'The Boat on the Serchio' – vivid
passages which catch the flavour of the expedition:

We paused amid the pines that stood,
    The giants of the waste,
Tortured by storms to shapes as rude
    With stems like serpents interlaced.

How calm it was – the silence there
  By such a chain was bound,
That even the busy woodpecker
  Made stiller by her sound

The inviolable quietness. . . .
And still, it seemed, the centre of
  The magic circle there,
Was one whose being filled with love
  The breathless atmosphere.[50]

Shelley reworked this lyric narrative during the spring, and it became two poems: 'To Jane: The Invitation', and 'To Jane: The Recollection'. Jane also agreed to try her powers of 'animal magnetism' on Shelley, and one of the mesmerism sessions was recorded in his poem 'The Magnetic Lady to Her Patient'. These, and other slight pieces, were almost the only original work that Shelley was able to conceive and execute during his continued proximity to the Palazzo Lanfranchi.

Jane, like Claire before her, was musically inclined, and could sing ballads and popular tunes in her low, slightly husky voice. Shelley now applied to Horace Smith in Paris for a pedal harp to be purchased and dispatched via Marseilles and Livorno. He calculated the expenditure at seventy or eighty guineas, and asked Smith to advance him this amount immediately with his 'accustomed kindness'. This was a sum, especially remembering the requirements of the Hunts, that Shelley could ill afford, and it is the one financial favour that Horace Smith is known to have refused him.[51] Later, in March, Shelley purchased instead for Jane a beautiful Spanish guitar at Livorno; but while still waiting for the harp from Paris, he sent her a number of his lyric fragments, written during the previous years in Italy. A characteristic covering letter with one read: 'Dear Jane, if this melancholy old song suits any of your tunes, or any that humour of the moment may dictate, you are welcome to it. Do not say it is mine to any one, even if you think so; indeed, it is from the torn leaf of a book out of date. How are you today, and how is Williams? Tell him that I dreamed of nothing but sailing, and fishing up coral. Yours ever affectionately, PBS.'[52]

Almost telepathically, Claire chose this moment to burst in again on Shelley's life from Florence. On 7 February, Claire had met Elise Foggi during a social evening at the Casa Boutourlin in Florence. Three days later Elise called on Claire at the Casa Bojti. According to a heavily deleted passage in Claire's diary, she talked about her part in the Hoppner scandal. The entry appears to be:

'E's report of Naples and me.'[53] Claire remained on terms with Elise, but she was thrown into a state of great turmoil and unhappiness, and determined to leave the Shelleys and Italy altogether, and go to Vienna where her brother Charles was studying. She was convinced from talking to Elise that Byron would never voluntarily allow her to see Allegra, and she had overwhelming fears that Allegra would die at Bagnacavallo.

After rapid exchange of letters with Shelley between 12 and 14 February, the content of which is not known, Claire dispatched a series of letters to Byron, Shelley, Mary, Mrs Mason and Charles together on the 18th, announcing her intention of going to Vienna. The letter to Byron survives in a manuscript draft,[54] in which she begs to see Allegra one last time before she leaves 'upon a disagreeable and precarious life'. 'I have often entreated Shelley to intercede for me, and he invariably answers that it is utterly useless'. The letter though passionate and in many ways pitiful, is yet organized with considerable skill. Claire implies that if Byron will let her see Allegra one last time, then she will surely leave Italy for ever, and he will be rid of her; on the other hand, if he will *not*, then she will not have the strength to start her new life, she will remain in Italy, and perhaps contemplate suicide: 'it were better that I were dead'. The tone of this letter must certainly have shaken Byron, and no doubt he spent more than one uneasy night over it. But in the end these signs of policy decided him; he refused to believe that Claire was engaged in anything more than one further manoeuvre to get inside his defences again, and he remained adamant. Whether he even reconsidered Allegra's welfare cannot be known. It was one of the greatest human errors of his life, and was the result of egoism.

When Mary and Shelley received their letters on the 20th, Mary wrote back directly to Florence by special messenger commanding Claire not to leave before discussing her plans 'in the midst of friends'.[55] Claire was in Pisa by 6 o'clock the next evening. She stayed with the Williamses for four days, and talked exhaustively with them, Shelley and Mary and Mrs Mason. Her visit was concealed from Byron. After this, she returned to Florence in a calmer mood, determined to await events, and the fulfilment of a promise that Shelley had apparently made to work Byron round as the opportunity arose. The Masons were strongly in favour of Claire leaving to start her life again in Vienna; and so probably was Mary; but Shelley wanted Claire to stay on, and stay on she did. Later, at the end of March, she was to erupt with a further plan, this time to kidnap Allegra from Bagnacavallo; and this too required emergency measures at Pisa. After 13 April, however, Claire's diary is blank for five months, for a series of tragedies occurred that did not seem to her to bear recalling.[56]

During May, Shelley spent less time with Byron and more and more sailing in his skiff up and down the Arno. Williams records that he was on the river almost every day, and though usually they sailed together, he frequently met Shelley sailing back alone from a dawn trip far outside the city limits.

Shelley still shot and dined with Byron, and with every appearance of cordiality. A plan for them all to put on an amateur production of *Othello* – Byron as Iago, Trelawny as the Moor, Mary as Desdemona and Shelley directing – was taken up and later abandoned. Once at dinner, Shelley quoted enthusiastically from *Childe Harold* much of which he knew by heart, and Byron, after listening with satisfaction until the end of the stanza, laughed modestly and called across the table 'Heavens! Shelley, what infinite nonsense are you quoting?' Williams regarded this as a fine example of Byron's insensibility 'to his real merit'.[57]

Yet despite the congeniality, the issue of Allegra was a deeply divisive one between Shelley and Byron. Shelley did try, as he had promised, to change Byron's determination, but he met with coldness and even suspicion. Shelley in turn reacted with barely suppressed fury. But his position was difficult as mediator, and he had already committed himself in the previous year to approval of Byron's treatment of the child. Shelley also felt that Byron might use the Hoppner business against Claire, and even as a last resort against himself.

Much of these fears and frustrations appear in a fragmentary letter of his to Claire, which is not dated, but seems to belong to March. One sees clearly how Shelley had been forced into two almost completely contradictory positions: one expressed by his commitments at Pisa, the other by his commitment to Claire. 'It is of vital importance both to me and to yourself, to Allegra even, that I should put a period to my intimacy with LB, and that without *éclat*. No sentiments of honour or justice restrain him (as I strongly suspect) from the basest insinuations, and the only mode in which I could effectually silence him I am reluctant (even if I had proof) to employ during my father's life. But for your immediate feelings I would suddenly and irrevocably leave this country which he inhabits, nor ever enter it but as an enemy to determine our differences *without words*. But at all events I shall soon see you, and then we will weigh both your plans and mine. . . .'[58] From this, one would not be surprised if Shelley had left Pisa within the week, or had had a pistol duel with Byron the next day. No doubt Claire half awaited such events.

Yet Byron certainly did not. In the same month that Shelley wrote this to Claire, and probably within days of so writing, Shelley had successfully secured a large loan on Hunt's behalf from Byron, with his own word and inheritance as security. He had also written to Hunt of his own and Byron's renewed enthusiasm for the Pisa scheme. The loan was worth £250 in Italian money, and Shelley immediately dispatched £220 to Hunt by the exchange through Brookes; the remaining thirty pounds he kept at Pisa as an encouragement and precaution for Hunt.[59] '[Lord Byron] expresses again the greatest eagerness to undertake [the journal] & proceed with it, as well as the greatest confidence in you as his associate. He is forever dilating upon his impatience of your delay & his disappointment at your not having already arrived. . . . I imagine it will be no very difficult task to execute that which you have assigned to me – to keep him in heart with the project until your arrival.'

Yet even to Hunt, Shelley admitted that the constant proximity with Byron just across the Arno at the Lanfranchi was becoming an enormous strain. The air was too charged emotionally between them, and quite apart from the difficulties caused through social status, and the crushing reminders of Byron's fame and immense popularity as a poet, there was the curious overbearing intensity, almost a romantic intensity, with which the presence of one affected the other. It was almost as if Byron was physically too close to Shelley. 'Particular circumstances, – or rather I should say, particular dispositions in Lord B's character render the close & exclusive intimacy with him in which I find myself, intolerable to me; thus much my best friend I will confess & *confide* to you. . . . However . . . I will take care to preserve the little influence I may have over this Proteus in whom such strange extremes are reconciled until we meet.'[60] Shelley was determined to hang on at all costs at Pisa until Hunt's arrival, and the commencement of the journal. But when would Hunt come?

Meanwhile, there was still the skiff. Shelley's river sailing was now becoming much more skilful, with increased experience of the sharp current and squall winds of the Arno, and he could now accomplish extended journeys with considerable finesse. One bright, clear Saturday morning, with strong southerly winds blowing sometimes close to gale force across the *maremma*, he and Williams sailed the length of the canal from Pisa to Livorno between 11.30 and 2 in the afternoon, a distance of about eighteen miles in two and a half hours.[61] On 21 March, Trelawny arrived back in Pisa with the news that Roberts was about to launch Shelley's new sailing boat at Livorno. She was to be sailed round to Genoa for final trials and fittings, and Roberts was then to take command of Byron's larger schooner. Shelley and Mary celebrated with Jane and Edward, all four of them going on a dignified but somewhat precarious sail up the Arno in the skiff. Trelawny, much in favour, continued to visit the Tre Palazzi on most evenings.[62]

Shelley was still struggling in vain to get some large poem launched. One fragment that seems to belong to this time is an unfinished drama concerning a Lady on an Enchanted Isle. She has been abandoned by her beloved, but she is accompanied by an Indian youth: one can perhaps gloss here the Lady as Mary, and the Youth as Trelawny. Writing an interpretative note to her edition of 1839, Mary explained that the Lady 'is accompanied by a Youth, who loves the lady, but whose passion she returns only with a sisterly affection'. The drama never developed further than a dialogue between the two, which is full of spent images from *Prometheus* and a vague atmosphere of Shakespeare's *Tempest*. But the picture of the Lady among the potted plants in the south-facing windows of their apartment – the mysterious Isle – is sadly evocative. The Lady herself speaks:

> At length I rose, and went,
> Visiting my flowers from pot to pot, and thought
> To set new cuttings in the empty urns,
> And when I came to that beside the lattice,
> I saw two little dark-green leaves
> Lifting the light mould at their birth, and then
> I half-remembered my forgotten dream.
> And day by day, green as a gourd in June,
> The plant grew fresh and thick, yet no one knew
> What plant it was; its stem and tendrils seemed
> Like emerald snakes. . . .[63]

But Shelley could build up nothing which showed any real creative promise from this piece, and it too was thrown aside. March also saw the final collapse of 'Charles I', the drama he had been sketching and announcing for nearly two years. '. . . a slight circumstance gave a new train to my ideas & shattered the fragile edifice when half built,' he told Hunt. 'What motives have I to write. – I *had* motives – and I thank the god of my own heart they were totally different from those of the other apes of humanity who make mouths in the glass of time – but what are *those* motives now? The only inspiration of an ordinary kind I could descend to acknowledge would be the earning £100 for *you* – & that it seems I cannot.'[64]

There was however one small fragment that survived the wreck of 'Charles I' beautifully intact. It was a song, rich with Shakespearian associations like the 'Song from Tasso' of 1818, but transcending that and finding its own true note. Shelley's stage direction said it was to be sung by the Court Fool, Archy. Perhaps the accompaniment was that of a Spanish guitar. 'I'll go live under the ivy that overgrows the terrace, and count the tears shed on its old roots as the wind plays the song. . . .'

> Heigho! the lark and the owl!
>   One flies the morning, and one lulls the night: –
> Only the nightingale, poor fond soul,
>   Sings like the fool through darkness and light.

'A widow bird sate mourning for her love
    Upon a wintry bough;
The frozen wind crept on above,
    The freezing stream below.

'There was no leaf upon the forest bare,
    No flower upon the ground,
And little motion in the air
    Except the mill-wheel's sound.'[65]

That was all.

March which had entered quietly, went out suddenly like a lion. On the 24th, the long-smouldering resentment and suspicion of the Pisan garrison soldiers against the English gentlemen who rode out from the Lanfranchi with Lord Byron, exploded in a violent incident. The English were really to blame. A shooting party consisting of Lord Byron, Count Gamba, Taaffe, Trelawny, Captain Hay and Shelley was returning from the farmhouse where they usually practised, along the main road into Pisa. Some dozen or so yards behind them was the Countess Guiccioli's carriage with two Italian attendants and La Guiccioli and Mary Shelley inside. The whole party was moving leisurely back towards Pisa, with the riders – all six of them – in animated conversation strung out in a line across the road. When they were still a few hundred yards outside the Porta della Piazza, an Italian dragoon called Sergeant-Major Masi came beating down the same road at full gallop, also making for the Porta della Piazza. Masi was part of the Pisan garrison, and it appears that he was late coming back from off-duty and was hurrying to make up time. Shelley also said afterwards that he was probably drunk, but this is not certain. Although the English party must surely have heard the approaching hooves from behind, they made no attempt to make way on the road, but remained strung out across its whole width. The business of passing and overtaking on horse or in carriage had its own social etiquette, and lesser men were expected to give way to greater. Taaffe was on the extreme right nearest the ditch, Lord Byron next to him, then Shelley, and the others ranged across the road to the left. The dragoon Masi did not however break his gallop.

Guiding his horse over to the right-hand side Masi jinked round the Giuccioli's carriage without incident and spotting a convenient gap between Byron and Taaffe and the ditch burst through the line of English riders, and continued at full gallop for the gate. As he passed it appears that his heel, his elbow or part of his harness brushed Taaffe and Taaffe's horse shied. Lord Byron on the other hand was unmoved. Recovering himself, Taaffe shouted out to the others 'Shall we endure this man's insolence?'[66] and after a moment Byron replied with irritation to the effect that the soldier should be brought to account. Shelley called out sharply, 'As you please.'[67] All the English horses had broken into a trot, and suddenly, without anybody exactly taking the decision, the trot had become a canter and the canter a headlong pursuit. The rider who drew out rapidly ahead was Shelley. Shelley gained steadily on Sergeant-Major Masi who was anyway slowing down as he came up to the Pisan gate. Finding himself well ahead of the others he rode across Masi's path and blocked it. They shouted at each other, and Masi turned to see five other English riders arriving at the gallop.

What exactly happened next is not quite clear. There were angry exchanges, the English horses circled the dragoon, Masi threatened to call out the guard from the gate and arrest them all, Lord Byron laughed in his face, the dragoon drew his sabre and called up to the guard to arrest the *maledetto inglesi*, Byron called back that they might if they were capable and spurred for the gate, Count Gamba did the same and in passing lashed Masi hard with his whip.[68] Masi was now furious and moved into the gateway to prevent the rest of the English passing, slashing out with his sabre. Shelley, with a characteristic impulse, dashed off his riding hat and using it as a shield rode straight at the dragoon. Masi's sabre stroke was deflected, but as Shelley came under his arm the metalled hand-guard of the sword struck him in the face and knocked him from his horse.[69] Captain Hay now plunged forward wielding a riding crop, and Masi turned quickly and made a deft full-arm stroke with his sabre which cut the crop in half with its tip and caught Hay a long slicing blow across the forehead and the bridge of the nose. Hay too went down. This only left Trelawny and Taaffe, and seeing that both hesitated, Masi wheeled his horse, sheathed his sabre and trotted smartly into Pisa. It was almost twilight.

There is no doubt that Sergeant-Major Masi was, at this point, reasonably proud of himself. As he trotted rapidly down the Lung'Arno, he saw Lord Byron riding back from the Palazzo Lanfranchi. He noticed in the fading light that Byron had a servant with him and carried a sword-stick. Masi reined in his horse and greeted Byron, holding out his hand and asking 'Siete contento?'[70] But Byron on the contrary was angry, and demanded the man's name and rank, which he duly gave. As they talked, Byron's servant came round and seized Masi's bridle, and for a moment the situation looked threatening again. Other hangers-on were beginning to congregate. Apparently Byron now waved away the servant, and Masi took his chance, and spurred off down the Lung'Arno for his barracks. But there were a number of people in the darkened street by this time, and he could not move quickly enough away from the danger area. As he passed the steps of the Lanfranchi, a few yards further on, an unidentified member of Byron's Italian household ran at him suddenly with a pitchfork from the stable. It is not clear if it was this weapon that finally caught Masi in the crowd, but as he spurred desperately to get clear a blade was thrust hard through the leather belt of his uniform and deep into his side. He lurched in the saddle, recovered himself with an effort, rode clear of the crowd, called out to some friendly Italians that he had been mortally wounded and crashed into a doorway a few paces further down the Lung'Arno.[71] Sergeant-Major Masi was taken to the *misericordia*, and he was not expected to live the night.

Edward Williams, who was not on this particular shooting expedition, left a memorable picture of the wounded English riders returning from their undistinguished affray after dark. It catches the mood of the circle round Byron and Shelley very well.

> Trelawny had finished his story when Lord B. came in – the Countess fainting on his arm – Shelley sick from the blow – Lord B. and the young Count [Gamba] foaming with rage – Mrs Shelley looking philosophically upon this interesting scene – and Jane and I wondering what the Devil was to come next. – A surgeon came in, and Lord B. took him with the Countess home – where she was bled and soon came round – Taaffe next entered, and having given his deposition at the Police, returned to us with a long face saying that the Dragoon could not live out the night. – All soon again sally'd forth to be the first to accuse and according to the Italian policy not wait to be accused. – All again return mutually recriminated and recriminating. 9 o'clock – The report already in circulation about Pisa is that a party of peasants having risen in insurrection made an attack upon the guard headed by some Englishmen. . . . Trelawny left dead at the gate, and Lord B mortally wounded. . . .[72]

The next day the troops were confined to barracks, and the English – notably Taaffe – were 'guarded by bulldogs &c' at the Lanfranchi. Vaccà, after talking to both sides, significantly took a very dim view of the English role in the affair, and said he was prepared to swear in a court of law that Masi had been horsewhipped and stabbed at close quarters with a stiletto.[73]

In the end the dragoon did not die, nor were the English attacked in reprisal, but the affair rumbled on into April, with much legal documentation and a lawsuit. It was soon in the Paris and English papers, and Galignani wrote politely to Shelley asking for personal reminiscences of the affair for publication in his paper.[74] But the most important consequence was that it resulted in the eventual banishment of Byron and the Gambas from Pisa, while the Shelleys made up their minds to move to the Bay of Spezia without further delay. The Pisa circle was no longer welcome in the city.

Events in another direction also speeded the summer sailing plan. From Florence, Claire returned to the offensive, and at the end of March, announced privately to Mary and Shelley that she had concocted a plan to kidnap Allegra from the convent at Bagnacavallo. This required Shelley's aid in forging a letter which should purport to come from the Palazzo Lanfranchi. Both Shelley and Mary replied in firm letters arguing against the madcap plan. Mary set out all the difficulties, emphasizing that Byron was alert, and powerful and on the spot, and that Shelley would quickly end up with an engagement for a duel. Having exhausted reason, Mary turned to a form of persuasion she felt was perhaps better adapted to convince Claire: that they had always been ill-fated in the spring, and it was not a good time to take on such a project for astrological reasons. Mary's analysis of their 'unlucky Springs' is interesting: 'Another thing I mention which though sufficiently ridiculous may have some weight with you. Spring is our unlucky season. . . . Remember the first spring [1815] at Mrs Harbottles. The second [1816] when you became acquainted with Lord Byron. The Third [1817] when we went to Marlow – no wise things at least. The fourth [1818] our uncomfortable residence in London. The fifth [1819] our Roman misery – the sixth [1820] Paolo at Pisa – the seventh [1821] a mixture of Emilia & a Chancery suit – Now the aspect of the Autumnal Heavens has on the contrary been with few exceptions favourable to us. – What think you of this? It is in your own style, but it has often struck me.'[75]

Shelley added a note, indicating that Mary was right, and that his own relations with Lord Byron were strained to the utmost. 'I shall certainly take our house [at Spezia] *far* from Lord Byron's, although it may be possible suddenly to put an end to his detested intimacy. . . .' He could not, he said, afford the journey to Florence to see her, but instead, why didn't Claire return to them? 'Come and stay among us – If you like, come and look for houses with me in our boat – it might distract your mind.'[76]

But for once Claire was not so easily mollified. She wrote back to Shelley under the unlikely pseudonym of 'Mr Joe James' at the Pisa post office, pressing the plan further, or threatening instead to leave Italy immediately for Vienna. On hearing his part in the dragoon affair she criticized in turn his own 'rashness' and 'want of temper', and he was forced to defend himself. 'My part in the affair, if not cautious or prudent, was justifiable. . . . The fault of the affair, if there be any, began with Taaffe. . . . The man was probably drunk. – Don't be so ready to blame. Imagine that there may be more temper and prudence in the world, besides what that little person of yours contains.'[77] He did not often write like that, but Claire had wittingly or unwittingly touched on the delicate subject of his conduct in Byron's company. He told her that as far as Vienna was concerned, 'the change might have a favourable effect on your mind. . . . I must try to manage the money for your journey, if you have so decided.'[78]

But he did not really want her to go. After his show of benevolent indifference, he suddenly addressed her an urgent and deeply personal appeal to take a firmer and calmer control on her life. 'Some of yours & of my evils are in common, & I am therefore in a certain degree a judge. If you would take my advice you would give up this idle pursuit after shadows, & temper yourself to the season; seek in the daily and affectionate intercourse of friends a respite from these perpetual and irritating projects. Live from day to day, attend to your health, cultivate literature & liberal ideas to a certain extent, & expect that from time & change which no exertions of your own can give you. . . .' It was the philosophy he had been trying to practise himself for several months.[79]

By the second week of April, the Pisan circle was breaking up. Byron was to take a summer residence near Livorno, while Shelley and the Williamses agreed that they would go further up the coast north of Viareggio. They were not quite sure where they would settle, for they had been refused leases on their original houses at Spezia. But a report from Roberts via Trelawny said their boat would be ready in ten days' time. On the 10th, Shelley wrote to Claire: 'I am not well. My side torments me; my mind agitates the frame which it inhabits, and things go ill with me – that is within – for all external circumstances are auspicious. Resolve to stay with us this summer, and remain where you are till we are ready to set off – no one need know of where you are; the Williams's are secure people, and [we] are alone.'[80] Two days later Mary, who had been writing sheets and sheets narrating the dragoon affair to the Gisbornes, wrote to Leigh Hunt to know when he might be expected. 'You will find Shelley in infinitely better health; indeed he has got over this winter delightfully. . . .'

A few last desultory billiard games were played at the Lanfranchi,[81] but there was no more shooting, or dining, and the weather was wet and windy. Shelley and Williams stayed indoors talking about play-writing: '[Shelley] gave me a long lecture on the drama – put me in bad spirits with myself.' Claire arrived secretly on the 15th, and lodged quietly with the Williams. They were all now anxious to leave, but the Pisan courts had summoned each of them to appear for cross-examination in the dragoon affair. Byron's courier was asked if he struck the dragoon: 'No! [he answered] but if I had had a pistol I should have shot him.' Mary and Theresa Guiccioli themselves were examined for five hours, during the course of which the Countess offered that 'she could not swear but she thought Mr Taaffe was the person who stabbed the dragoon'. So it muddled on.[82]

The imminent dissolution of the colony at Pisa had the effect of turning Shelley's eyes for a moment to more distant personal changes. He was anxious to know what real independence he could eventually secure in Italy from his own resources. He wrote at length to John Gisborne about the Shelley estates in England, discussing his debts – which he now reckoned at £20,000 to £25,000 'principally post obits' – and his wish to escape from the hand of his old solicitor Longdill. He talked of inheriting, but 'I have altered my determination about coming to England at my father's death – I *will not* come at any rate'. Although he did not ask Gisborne directly, he obviously hoped that having started as his literary agent he might also cope with the financial side. 'What ought I to do? Is there any possibility of engaging some active & intelligent man of business, who would zealously enter into my affairs, and make himself master of my papers &c., so that on the event of the succession falling to me, he might be prepared to act with the promptitude & the spirit which my concerns demand. . . . These are questions to which I should be obliged if you would give your serious consideration, & indeed you might consult with Hogg upon them.' The list of Shelley's enemies in England seemed full: his many creditors, his solicitor Longdill, 'this thief Ollier', and of course the Godwins – who were 'forever plotting & devising pretexts for money, none of which however they get: 1st because I *can't*, & 2nd because I *won't*'.[83]

There was little news from Pisa: *Hellas* had arrived in Ollier's edition, 'prettily printed' and Shelley was continuing to read *Faust* and also Calderón's *Magico Prodigioso* which he found 'strikingly similar' to the Goethe in many respects. He had now decided to translate both for the first issue of the *Liberal*. To Ollier he sent a curt note by the same post asking him to deliver his accounts to Gisborne and authorizing Gisborne as his sole agent in London. There were also half a dozen printing errors in *Hellas*, though only one serious one: line 466 had been printed 'Death is awake! Repulsed on the waters!' *Repulsed* was wrong.[84]

To Horace Smith in Paris Shelley wrote somewhat guardedly of Byron. There had been a report circulated by Moore that the atheistical tendencies in *Cain* were the result of Shelley's influence. Shelley remarked that he would have been happy to have any influence on that 'immortal work', but 'pray assure [Moore] that I have not the smallest influence over Lord Byron in that particular; if I had I certainly should employ it to eradicate from his great mind the delusions of Christianity, which in spite of his reason, seem perpetually to recur, & to lay in ambush for the hours of sickness & distress'.[85]

To Leigh Hunt Shelley wrote more confidentially. Though the Pisan plan for the *Liberal* was still alive, and Byron still 'anxiously' awaited Hunt's arrival, Shelley's personal feelings were bitter. 'Perhaps time has corrected me, and I am become, like those whom I formerly condemned, misanthropical and suspicious. . . . Certain it is, that Lord Byron has made me bitterly feel the inferiority which the world has presumed to place between us and which subsists nowhere in reality but in our talents, which are not our own but Nature's – or in our rank, which is not our own but Fortune's. I will tell you more when we meet. . . .' In the meantime, 'sea air is necessary'.[86] The circle was broken.

29
The Gulf of Spezia

On 23 April 1822, Edward and Jane Williams took Claire off to go house-hunting in the bay of Spezia. Williams and Shelley had already decided on the little fishing village of Lerici as their summer residence. It stood on the southern tip of the bay opposite Portovenere, and for all its diminutive size and remoteness it had a proper stone quay and was a regular calling-point for mail boats. Williams had an introduction to the harbour-master, Signor Maglian, and when they arrived on the 24th, they were greeted with great politeness and shown round at least a dozen unsuitable houses. After a full day's search round the bay, there was still 'nothing that could possibly suit', and leaving the harbour-master to make further inquiries, they set out back to Pietra Santa and Pisa. But returning homeward 'we were struck with the beauty of some unfinished grounds, and on inquiry learnt that it was probable they would sell them & the dilapidated house that stood in ruins there'.[1] This was their first sight of the Casa Magni.

Back at Pisa on the 25th, Williams found Shelley standing white-faced at the door of his apartment, and hastily took him aside.[2] He had just received news from Byron that little Allegra had died of typhus fever at the convent of Bagnacavallo.

Shelley decided that the first thing to do was to leave Pisa and get settled at Lerici without a moment's pause. The whole of the next day was spent packing and boxing furniture, for he did not intend to keep the apartment at the Tre Palazzi any longer. At midday on the 27th the baggage was loaded on to two boats at the landing-stage. Shelley kept Claire's box with his personal luggage.[3] He took a tight-lipped leave of Lord Byron who was at the Lanfranchi morosely considering his own emigration to Livorno. Mary, Claire and little Percy were dispatched by coach to La Spezia in Trelawny's care, with instructions to conclude the negotiations for a house immediately. At 4 o'clock, the two luggage boats cast off and disappeared under the Ponte Al Mare and round the curve of the Arno in the fast seaward current.[4] The Williamses and Shelley followed on a separate boat ninety minutes later. Shelley, said Mary, was like a torrent hurrying everything in its course.[5] And still Claire knew nothing of Allegra.

The last three days of April were spent with Mary at La Spezia negotiating for the Casa Magni, and Shelley at Lerici with two boat-loads of luggage trying to avoid paying £300-worth of customs duties. Notes sped across from one side of the Gulf of Spezia to the other. 'I, of course, cannot leave Lerici . . . but if the Magni House is taken there is no possible reason why you should not take a row over in the boat which will bring this – but don't keep the men long. – I am anxious to hear from you on every account. . . .'[6] Finally, on the 30th, the Casa Magni was taken, and the boats were unloaded on the tiny piece of sandy beach in front of it, with everyone helping to carry the boxes up through the lapping Mediterranean surf. It only took an hour.[7] The Williamses, unable to find a house for themselves, were also quartered on the single habitable floor of the Casa Magni, together with their two babies and the servants. The customs said they would count the house as a luggage depot since it was so near the sea, and there would be no duty to pay.

Williams and Shelley spent the next afternoon fishing off the rocks; they caught nothing and found the stone was volcanic and viciously sharp, twisted into grotesque lacework and tracery. In the evening, Claire walked into the room where they were all talking about Byron and Bagnacavallo. She asked them if Allegra was dead; Shelley stood up and said yes.[8] He told Byron afterwards that what he really feared was that she would go mad.

For the first week of May, all their time was taken up in coping with Claire. Shelley wrote to Byron asking for a miniature and a lock of the child's hair, which duly appeared by the return boat. A murderous note from Claire slipped past Shelley's observation – or so he said – and also reached Byron at Livorno; but to this second letter there would be no answer.[9] Claire's only coherent request was that she should be allowed to see Allegra's coffin before it was shipped from Livorno to England. When Byron offered to give her complete charge of Allegra's funeral and burial, Shelley wrote back: 'She now seems bewildered; & whether she designs to avail herself further of your permission to regulate the funeral, I know not. In fact, I am so exhausted with the scenes through which I have passed, that I do not dare to ask.'[10]

The only relief was the extraordinary beauty of their situation in the bay of Lerici. Even in his first letter to Byron, Shelley could not avoid mentioning it: 'Nature is here as vivid and joyous as we are dismal, and we have built, as Faust says, "our little world in the great world of all".'

The Casa Magni had been built originally as a boat-house, and it was right on the seashore. Its ground floor consisted of an open stone portico with seven arches roughly whitewashed, and a stone-flagged floor running back into the building. The edge of the flagging had a low wall which formed a little jetty, with a fringe of small rocks up against it. The sea frequently splashed to the very foot of the portico. The flag-stones were always carpeted with the blown sand, and the ground floor could only be used for storing rope and tackle and oars. Above the portico was the first-floor terrace, which ran the whole length of the building and looked out westwards clear over the bay. Inside was a single large main room, reached by a staircase from the back. Off this central chamber, which the Shelleys and the Williamses shared as their dining hall, were three smaller rooms. The ones to the left and right, facing over the terrace and the sea, were Mary's and Shelley's respectively, while the Williamses were given the third room, immediately next to Shelley's, on the north side of the building. The servants and the children slept in the back of the house.

From the terrace, the bay was spread out before them. To their right, 200 yards up the sand, was the tiny hamlet of San Terenzo, with a little cupola church, and its ruined castle on a spur of rock jutting out into the sea. Beyond it, clear in the mornings but hazy by midday, was the peninsula of Portovenere, and the blue hump of the island of Palmaria. To their left, half-obscured by one of the little rocky coves of the bay, was Lerici. It stood across about a mile of glittering water, with its harbour and moored boats and quayside strung with nets. The village houses struggled up the steep hill and were lost in the woods, while the castle of Lerici, answering more grandly that of San Terenzo, jutted sharply against the skyline. The whole bay was very wild, and communications were by boat or along the beach. Behind the Casa Magni, the rocks and trees rose up steeply cutting off all access by road, in a jungle of dark foliage. Except for the sea, the situation was strangely like Tan-yr-allt.

At night, especially when the moon shone on the water, it almost seemed as if their house was ocean-going. For the first few days all of them found it difficult to sleep with the sound of the heavy swell booming on the rocks and along the beach. 'We all feel as if we were on board ship – and the roaring of the sea brings this idea even into our beds.'[11] Williams noted: 'I think if there are no tides in the Mediterranean that there are strong currents on which the moon both at the full and change have a very powerful effect. The swell this evening is evidently caused by her influence, for it is quite calm at sea.'[12]

The death of Allegra did not affect only Claire. On the eighth day at the Casa Magni, Shelley took Williams out on to the terrace to gaze at the moonlight flooding the little bay. '... While walking with Shelley on the terrace and observing the effect of moonshine on the waters, he complained of being unusually nervous, and stopping short he grasped me violently by the arm and stared steadfastly on the white surf that broke upon the beach under our feet.

Observing him sensibly affected I demanded of him if he were in pain – but he only answered, saying "There it is again! – there!" ' Williams shook Shelley and asked him what he had seen: apparently it was a naked child which kept rising out of the sea, with its hands clasped. Williams's later comment is interesting, and suggests that Shelley wanted Williams to see the ghost as much as himself. 'Our conversation which had been at first rather melancholy led to this, and my confirming his sensations by confessing that I had felt the same, gave a greater activity to his ever wandering and lively imagination.'[13] It was 'a sort of natural magic'.

But gradually the crisis passed, and Claire then recovered with a rapidity that surprised everyone. Mary even thought that she was 'more tranquil than when prophesying her disaster'. She stayed on for several days at the Casa Magni, and Shelley told Byron on the 16th that she was much better, 'after the first shock she has sustained her loss with more fortitude than I had dared to hope'. A cheering influence was Byron's bearded Venetian servant Tita, who came to stay in the back quarters of the Casa Magni after his release from prison in Pisa where he had been held as a suspect in the dragoon affair. He announced that he had given a banquet – with hired plate and chandeliers – to his fellow-inmates on the night of his release. He stayed on amiably helping out until a new passport arrived, and then he rejoined his master at Livorno.

Shelley's boat had long been expected from Genoa, and on 12 May, a strange sail was spotted rounding the point of Portovenere. It was threatening, stormy weather, and the boat made fast for Lerici harbour, cranked hard over in the wind with a crew of three crouching in the spray over her deck. Shelley and Williams watched her with admiration from the terrace: it was the *Don Juan*. She struck them instantly with her swift temperamental elegance: she was twenty-four feet long, but very slim, with twin mainmasts and schooner rigging with topsails and a selection of jibs. They hurried along the beach to take delivery of the boat, and took her out at once into the bay. There was no other craft that could match her speed. Shelley wrote to Captain Roberts: 'She is a most beautiful boat, & so far surpasses both mine and Williams' expectations that it was with some difficulty that we could persuade ourselves that you had not sent us the Bolivar by mistake.'[14]

On the 15th they gave her a first full run, in clear fresh weather, with both Mary and Jane aboard. They sailed her to Portovenere, and found in Williams's words that 'she fetches whatever she looked at'. They turned again past the point in open sea, and beat back to Lerici, the boat sailing 'like a witch'. The late storms had covered the sea with huge, purple Portuguese men-o'-war that drifted beneath the surface like opalescent apparitions.[15]

They now had their 'perfect plaything for the summer'. They retained one of the 18-year-old English boys who came with the boat from Genoa to act as their crew, which made launching and handling the massive canvas easier. Apart from insufficient reefing, their only problem was how to remove the huge black lettering *Don Juan* which had been painted on the forward mainsail. Mary said it looked like a coal barge, and Shelley said acidly to Trelawny that he 'supposed the name to have been given her during the equivocation of sex which her godfather suffered in the Harem'.[16] It was suspected that Byron had arranged this desecration through Trelawny, and Shelley was indignant out of all proportion to the crime. Hours were spent trying to remove the paint at Lerici with 'turpentine, spirits of wine, and buccata'.[17] It would not come off, but Shelley absolutely refused to sail under the title of Byron's greatest work, and finally had the section of the sail cut out altogether, and a new patch put in by a local sailmaker, disguised by a line of reefs. Shelley had fallen in love with the craft, and he arranged with Williams that he would pay for it exclusively. 'She serves me at once for a study and a carriage,' he wrote rapturously, and for him at least life at Casa Magni was slowly transformed into a waking dream.

To Horace Smith at Versailles, he wrote: 'As to me, like Anacreon's swallow, I have left my Nile, and having taken up my summer quarters here, in a lonely house close by the sea side, surrounded by the soft & sublime scenery of the Gulph of Spezia – I do not write – I have lived too long near Lord Byron & the sun has extinguished the glow worm. . . .'[18] A day or two later he posted Smith another letter with an even more mystic contents, which Smith described in his reply: '*blank*, with the exception of your handwriting in the address, which, with the postmark identified it to be from you, though you had forgotten the Promethean part of informing it with a soul. Imagining that some most mysterious secret was to be conveyed to me by the aid of sympathetic ink, I tried it against the sun, and in the fire, and in the dark, and with lemon juice. . . .'[19]

Claire left on 21 May to collect her things from the Bojtis at Florence and stay a few days at the Casa Silva, after Shelley had made her promise to return in a fortnight. The household began to settle down, and Shelley and Williams spent the rest of the month on the water. The *Don Juan* was anchored in the bay directly in front of the Casa Magni – except when the winds were too high, when she was taken into Lerici harbour for shelter. Williams spent many hours on the beach making a small rowing boat out of canvas and beech planks to act as a tender, and Shelley sat for whole mornings with his back against the *Don Juan*'s mainmast, reading *Faust* and Calderón, writing on loose scraps of paper, and lulled by the gentle swell of the Mediterranean. He became tanned and fit, and slowly his mind began to turn towards a new visionary poem. In preparation, he turned one of the servants' rooms at the back of the Casa Magni into a study for writing in the evenings away from the communal part of the house.[20] But when the moon was out, many nights found him on the water, with Williams, or with Jane, or by himself alone.

Mary, after looking forward so long to this escape to the seaside, was now very unhappy. She was three months pregnant, and frequently ill and upset, and the remoteness of their situation, the wild beauty of the bay and the ceaseless lapping of the sea under her windows filled her with a sense of helpless remoteness. Shelley wrote to Claire at the end of May that Mary suffered 'terribly from languor and hysterical affections'.[21] Although sometimes she sailed, sitting between Shelley's legs at the helm, most of her day was spent in the shade of the terrace, feeling sick and abandoned. The squabbling servants at the rear of the house worried her, and she did not like the intimate company of the Williamses. Moreover, in the first week in June, the mild sunny weather hardened into a glazing heatwave which continued day after day with 'excessive and oppressive' heat, and lurid electrical arches – as Williams called them – forming in the haze above the entrance to the bay. It was like being in an enchanted prison. Occasionally the weather would break, with a violent electrical storm, and running waves. At these times Shelley and Williams would be busy beating the *Don Juan* into the safety of Lerici harbour. The next day the heat would return.

It was during this period, at the end of May and the beginning of June, before the arrival of Byron's boat the *Bolivar* on the 13th, that Shelley began composing his last major poem 'The Triumph of Life'. He wrote it partly on the boat, and partly in his study at night. It is not, like his other poems, in a notebook, but written on a series of loose foolscap sheets, some much folded from being thrust into his pocket.[22] One of them is the back of a bill from the sailmaker at Sarzana who came to cut out the *Don Juan* lettering; another is on the back of the beginning of one of Shelley's own letters to Captain Roberts mentioning Hunt's expected arrival at Genoa in mid-June. A third sheet is covered by sketches for the new topsail rig which Shelley and Williams wanted fitted to the boat to increase the canvas even further. The writing is in ink, unusually large for Shelley, and bleached by sun. There are many corrections in a neater, firmer hand, which appear to have been made in his study. But the motley collection of Italian foolscap suggests that Shelley did not even want to think of himself as writing another serious work: he was just trying out a few ideas.

Yet the poem, rough and unfinished as it is, is the fourth of his Italian masterpieces. In one sense the poem is like nothing he had previously written. It has a hardness of style and a lack of personal emotion which is unique among his writing: it is aloof and almost disparaging, and falls on the reader's imagination with a cold, clear light like moonlight. Yet the subject draws everywhere on previous work, reassembling it and transforming it.

The dominant image of the poem is the 'triumph' – the Roman ritual of the triumphal chariot drive in procession through the streets. It is the image that he found carved on the Arches of Titus and Constantine in the Roman Forum, and first used brilliantly in the apocalyptic second act of *Prometheus Unbound*. The Roman triumph was always an essentially cruel and violent image in Shelley's mind, and here in his last poem, the 'triumph of life' is used to mean the *conquest* which Life achieves over all human beings – especially the conquests made by physical ageing, intellectual failure, guilt and remorse, and lack of spiritual self-knowledge.

The poem is a vision, and in the directness of its presentation, and its use of the carnival processions of masked, historical and demoniac figures, Shelley has adapted the method used in *The Mask of Anarchy*, and in the nightmare sections of *Peter Bell the Third*. One can also trace his experience of the spring carnivals at Pisa, which Tom Medwin noticed appalled Shelley by their undertones of malevolent hilarity and sickness and evil.

Finally, the structure of the poem owes something to the loose improvisatory flow of *Epipsychidion*, and its images of radiant female idealisms are clearly drawn from here. Yet 'The Triumph' has none of the softness or flatulence of that poem, either in verse form or theme. The verse is the English terza rima which Shelley had used in the 'Ode to the West Wind' and his adaptions of Dante. Its movement, though brilliantly varied and flexible – sometimes for speech, sometimes for narrative – always retains an Olympian dignity, 'stately and fast'. Moreover the ideal images of the poem are never allowed to dazzle, but are continually overwhelmed by darker, demoniac ones, which return to the winter of 1821 at Pisa, and the 'intermediary world' of Plato's *kaka-daimons*, and through them to the earliest image sources of Shelley's adolescent poetry.

The dominant presence behind this austerity of form and theme is undoubtedly Dante, and especially the Dante of the *Inferno*. Shelley uses Dante's metre, Dante's bold panorama of real historical characters, and something of Dante's gloomy underworld of spiritual torment. 'The Triumph' has a personal narrator, and a guide – like Dante and Virgil. Shelley's guide is Rousseau and the passage in which Shelley meets him – or rather discovers him – has that macabre matter-of-factness which is essentially Dantean:

> . . . what I thought was an old root which grew
> To strange distortion out of the hill side
> Was indeed one of that deluded crew,
>
> And that the grass which methought hung so wide
> And white, was but his thin discoloured hair,
> And that the holes it vainly sought to hide

Were or had been his eyes. – 'If thou canst forbear
To join the dance, which I had well forborne,'
Said the grim Feature, of my thought aware,

'I will now tell that which to this deep scorn
Led me & my companions, and relate
The progress of the Pageant since the morn. . . .'[23]

Yet for all these literary presences and shadows, the poem transcends Shelley's previous work, moving above it in that climbing spiral which first became obvious in the Pisa poems, so that the same material is now rediscovered and re-created from an entirely new and matured position. And everywhere it is filled with the atmosphere of Lerici, the heat, the dust, the broad sea, the foaming wake streaming away from the boat, the cold moonlight glittering on the water.

Shelley first wrote a thirty-line introductory passage which has something of the quality of one of his trial prose prefaces, which tells the reader little except that Shelley had stayed awake all night, 'wakeful as the stars that gem The cone of night', and had now lain down in the morning sun with his back against a chestnut tree – presumably the ship's mast. The poem then begins abruptly, with much of the rapid cadence and speaking immediacy with which *The Mask of Anarchy* opens. The difference is that the line length is extended into the cool, measured modulations of the terza rima; for it is a much older poet who speaks:

As in that trance of wonderous thought I lay
This was the tenour of my waking dream.
Methought I sate beside a public way

Thick strewn with summer dust, & a great stream
Of people there was hurrying to & fro
Numerous as gnats upon the evening gleam,

All hastening onward, yet none seemed to know
Whither he went, or whence he came, or why
He made one of the multitude, yet so

Was borne amid the crowd as through the sky
One of the million leaves of summer's bier. –
Old age & youth, manhood & infancy,

> Mixed in one mighty torrent did appear,
> Some flying from the thing they feared & some
> Seeking the object of another's fear. . . .[24]

Shelley (the poet is now his own narrator and observer, as Dante casts his own persona in the *Inferno*) sits under his tree and gazes upon this stream of humanity, seeing everything in 'a cold glare, intenser than the noon, But icy cold', which obscures 'with (blinding) light The Sun, as he the stars'. Gradually the scurrying, flitting activity begins to concentrate into a massive crowd, and from this, driven by a huge hooded figure, bursts forth the Chariot.

This is the central image, and the key passage of the poem. Throughout the description, Shelley is constantly reshaping the exact picture of the Chariot itself, so that it takes on a protean, hallucinatory quality, its outlines always altering and shifting as if seen through distortions of light or water. It begins clearly as one of the chariots of the Roman Forum, but gradually it turns into a kind of vast, trundling, crushing Moloch, and from that diffuses further into something simply like a great storm wave thundering through disturbed sea, and leaving behind it a creaming wake. The effect is brutal and terrifying. The Chariot is the chariot of Life, and those who dance around it are those whom Life will unhesitatingly crush, their intellectual joy and sexual energy fruitlessly sacrificed and destroyed. It is one of the great images in English poetry.

> The crowd gave way, & I arose aghast,
> Or seemed to rise, so mighty was the trance,
> And saw like clouds upon the thunder blast
>
> The million with fierce song and maniac dance
> Raging around; such seemed the jubilee
> As when to greet some conqueror's advance
>
> Imperial Rome poured forth her living sea
> From senate house & forum & theatre. . . .
>
> . . . Now swift, fierce & obscene
> The wild dance maddens in the van, & those
> Who lead it, fleet as shadows on the green,
>
> Outspeed the chariot & without repose
> Mix with each other in tempestuous measure
> To savage music . . . Wilder as it grows,

They, tortured by the agonizing pleasure,
Convulsed & on the rapid whirlwinds spun
Of that fierce Spirit, whose unholy leisure

Was soothed by mischief since the world begun,
Throw back their heads & loose their streaming hair,
And in their dance round her who dims the Sun

Maidens & youths fling their wild arms in air
As their feet twinkle; they recede, and now
Bending within each other's atmosphere

Kindle invisibly; and as they glow
Like moths by light attracted & repelled,
Oft to their bright destruction come & go.

Till like two clouds into one vale impelled
That shake the mountains when their lightnings mingle
And die in rain, – the fiery band which held

Their natures, snaps – ere the shock cease to tingle
One falls and then another in the path
Senseless, nor is the desolation single,

Yet ere I can say *where* – the Chariot hath
Past over them; nor other trace I find
But as of foam after the Ocean's wrath

Is spent upon the desert shore. – Behind,
Old men and women foully disarrayed
Shake their grey hairs in the insulting wind,

Limp in the dance & strain with limbs decayed
To reach the car of light which leaves them still
Farther behind & deeper in the shade.[25]

It is at the moment of facing this appalling image of despair that Shelley discovers Rousseau, like the old root, resting at his side. Rousseau now offers to act as Shelley's commentator and guide, and he explains the nature of the Triumph and points out many great public figures in it, including Napoleon, Catherine the Great, the Roman Emperors, the Popes, Kant, Voltaire, Bacon, even Plato. All of them, Rousseau explains, had one underlying failure: their philosophy

> Taught them not this – to know themselves; their might
> Could not repress the mutiny within,
> And for the morn of truth they feigned, deep night
>
> Caught them ere evening.[26]

This section of the poem is in many places only roughly blocked in; there are many gaps and inconsistencies in the stanzas, and in the margins of his manuscript Shelley left names and portraits whom he had not yet fitted in.

The second section of the poem is now developed. Rousseau begins to tell Shelley his own experiences of life, and especially of love, his own *Epipsychidion*. For him, the ideal woman brought disastrous knowledge of reality. Moving 'between desire & shame', Rousseau had questioned her about the true nature of human relations. In reply she gave him a cup to drink, a cup of experience. The 'multiple image' with which Shelley presents this flash of horrific discovery is unsurpassed anywhere else in his writing:

> I rose; and, bending at her sweet command,
> Touched with faint lips the cup she raised,
> And suddenly my brain became as sand
>
> Where the first wave had more than half erased
> The track of deer on desert Labrador,
> Whilst the fierce wolf from which they fled amazed
>
> Leaves his stamp visibly upon the shore
> Until the second bursts – so on my sight
> Burst a new Vision never seen before. . . .[27]

The new vision is Rousseau's own first sight of the Chariot of Life in triumph. He describes more carefully the appearance of the young people who dance around it, and especially how the air all about them is full of shadows, and spirits, dark flitting shapes, like 'a flock of vampire-bats before the glare Of the tropic sun'. Some of these shapes and phantoms come from the *faces* of the young people. It is as if layers of their youth were continually peeling away from their flesh and taking on their own grotesque forms of life, like hideous animated masks. The visage beneath gradually shrinks and twists as these masks or 'idols' fly off jibbering into the shadows.

. . . I became aware

Of whence those forms proceeded which thus stained
The track in which we moved; after brief space
From every form the beauty slowly waned,

From every firmest limb & fairest face
The stength & freshness fell like dust, & left
The action & the shape without the grace

Of life; the marble brow of youth was cleft
With care, and in the eyes where once hope shone
Desire like a lioness bereft

Of its last cub, glared ere it died; each one
Of that great crowd sent forth incessantly
These shadows, numerous as the dead leaves blown

In Autumn evening from a poplar tree.
Each like himself & like each other were
At first, but soon distorted seemed to be

Obscure clouds moulded by the casual air;
And of this stuff the car's creative ray
Wrought all the busy phantoms that were there

As the sun shapes the clouds; thus on the way
Mask after mask fell from the countenance
And form of all; and long before the day

Was old, the joy which waked like Heaven's glance
The sleepers in the oblivious valley, died;
And some grew weary of the ghastly dance

And fell, as I have fallen, by the way side. . . .[28]

This is Shelley's final explanation of his own world of ghosts and spirits: 'projections' of his own personality, parts of himself left behind, or in the name of his old sceptical master Lucretius, 'idols', self-created delusions, and none the less real for that. The poem was now over five hundred lines long. Where

Rousseau began to talk of those who 'Fell, as I have fallen by the wayside', here, on his manuscript sheet, Shelley stopped, and wrote in tiny neat lettering: 'Alas I kiss you Jane.'[29] His train of thought was broken, and writing and scratching out half a dozen more lines, he put the manuscript away in his pocket. He did not write any more of it; in the end there was no time.*

Claire had arrived back at the Casa Magni on 7 June. She was now in good spirits, talkative and teasing as in the old days: Shelley called her 'la fille aux mille projets'.[30] Two days later, Mary was very ill in the excessive, sweltering heat and almost had a miscarriage, but she recovered. She began to hate the house.[31] Then on the 13th, looking like a pirate frigate, the *Bolivar* sailed into the bay of Lerici and fired a six-gun salute to the *Don Juan*. Captain Roberts and Trelawny were aboard, taking the ship from Genoa to Lord Byron at Livorno. Mary was glad of their company and they dined and stayed on at the Casa Magni for five days, making an excuse of the heavy swell and changes in the rigging.

The sea had got up so much on the 15th that the *Bolivar* was taken into Lerici harbour, and the *Don Juan* was moored up alongside her. Shelley and Williams looked enviously at the massive American rigging of their sister ship, with its three masts and cluster of topsails. In conversation with Captain Roberts, a scheme was conceived to re-rig the *Don Juan*, and build a false stern and prow section to increase the narrow, streamlined elegance of her profile. Roberts agreed to stay behind at Lerici when the *Bolivar* sailed.

At 8 o'clock on the morning of 16 June Mary's illness did finally result in a bad miscarriage. She bled profusely and when Shelley sent for a doctor and for ice, nobody came to the remote house for seven hours. Mary thought she was going to die. 'I lay nearly lifeless – kept from fainting by brandy, vinegar eau de Cologne &c – at length ice was brought to our solitude – it came before the doctor so Claire and Jane were afraid of using it. . . .'[32] But Shelley was quite ruthless in the emergency: he had a tin hip bath filled up with the ice, and

---

* The final unfinished words of Shelley's 'The Triumph of Life' in Bod. M S Shelley Adds. c. 4, Folder 5, are on a foolscap sheet (p. 53) which has been roughly folded in two. They read:

Then, what is Life? I said . . . the cripple cast
His eye upon the car of beams which now had rolled
Onward, as if that look must be the last

And answered . . . 'Happy those for whom the fold
Of

The back of the sheet is covered with sail sketches. The whole manuscript has been finely and exhaustively examined by G.M.Matthews, 'The Triumph of Life: A New Text', *Studia Neophilo- logica*, XXXII (1960) and Donald H. Reiman, *Shelley's 'The Triumph of Life'* (1965). Reiman in his Appendix D concludes that the poem was probably begun 'late in May 1822' and returned to, after the *Bolivar's* departure, 'late in June'.

plunged Mary into it and made her sit still till all the bleeding stopped. The rest of the household looked on in helpless horror, but his method worked. Two days later he wrote to John Gisborne: 'I succeeded in checking the haemorrhage and fainting fits, so that when the physician arrived all danger was over, and he had nothing to do but applaud me for by boldness. [Mary] is now doing well, and the sea baths will soon restore her.'³³ But she did not recover quickly, and at the beginning of July was only just able to 'crawl from [her] bedroom to the terrace'.³⁴ Claire was a great help to Mary at this time; but Jane Williams was more concerned with Shelley. It was she who went out with the men in the boat, sometimes taking the guitar Shelley had given her with its inlaid fretwork of flowers, so that the music floated across the water to the Casa Magni.

On 18 June Trelawny took the *Bolivar* out of Lerici harbour, and made south for Livorno. Captain Roberts and Williams began refitting the *Don Juan*, mounting the fore and aft sections, and preparing the new topmast rigging they had designed for both masts. It took up all their time for the next week. Shelley no longer had the release of sailing, except for the little shallop, and he stayed at the Casa Magni writing letters to Trelawny and John Gisborne, and working intermittently on his poem. His letter to Trelawny, whom he had only just waved off, was very strange. Most of it consisted of a long request for a lethal dose of 'the Prussic Acid, or essential oil of bitter almonds'. He explained that he had no intention of suicide at present, 'but I confess it would be a comfort to me to hold in my possession that golden key to the chamber of perpetual rest'. The letter does not ring quite right, it is both morbid and artificial at the same time, and one has the feeling that Shelley was trying deliberately to impress Trelawny with his own uncertain state. One reason for Shelley's guilt and depression appeared in the line of postscript: 'PS. Mary is better, though still excessively weak.'³⁵ He knew Trelawny was fond of Mary, and perhaps he felt that the Cornishman blamed his treatment of her.

To John Gisborne, he wrote more freely: 'Italy is more and more delightful to me. . . . I only feel the want of those who can feel, and understand me. Whether from proximity and the continuity of domestic intercourse, Mary does not. The necessity of concealing from her thoughts that would pain her, necessitates this, perhaps. It is the curse of Tantalus. . . .' The Williamses on the other hand he found more and more pleasing, though as he aptly put it 'words are not the instruments of our intercourse'. Claire was 'vivacious and talkative, and though she teases me sometimes, I like her'. Though he was not writing – 'Imagine Demosthenes reciting a Philippic to the waves of the Atlantic' – he was feeling well, and outwardly contented. The bay of Lerici was dazzlingly fine in the changing lights, and the sailing magical. '[My boat] is swift and beautiful, and appears quite a vessel. Williams is captain, and we drive along this delightful bay in the evening wind, under the summer moon, until earth appears another world. Jane brings her guitar, and if the past and the future could be obliterated, the present would content me so well that I could say with Faust to the passing moment, "Remain, thou, thou art so beautiful." '[36]

Shelley composed little songs and poems for Jane, one of which 'The Keen Stars are Twinkling . . .' he left in her room with a note: 'I commit [it] to your secrecy and your mercy, and will try to do better another time.'[37] Other poems belonging to these few days were the dedication of her guitar, 'Ariel to Miranda . . .', 'When the Lamp is Shattered', and the 'Lines Written in the Bay of Lerici':

And the fisher with his lamp
And spear about the low rocks damp
Crept, and struck the fish which came
To worship the delusive flame. . . .[38]

He had cast his spell over Jane, and she once reported with terror that she had seen his figure walk twice along the terrace while he was actually aboard the boat.[39]

Shelley kept a small white vellum notebook[40] in his pocket in which he jotted parts of these brief lyrics and *ariettes*, as he called them to Jane. He translated a few more lines of *Faust*, and sketched boats, sailing rigs and a chariot with a rider whipping on his horse who turns to look balefully back at him.[41] He also put odd Biblical fragments in the notebook. In the middle of one page is: 'Thou shalt be hidden from the scourge of the angel – Thou shalt be in league with the stones of the field.' And at the bottom: 'Thou makest me to possess the iniquities of my youth'; and 'The mind's invisible tyranny'.[42] On the front inside cover he wrote in large, black ink: 'The Spring rebels not against winter but it succeeds it – the dawn rebels not against night but it disperses it.'

Definite news had now reached Lerici of Hunt, who had arrived at long last in Genoa and was about to sail to Livorno. Captain Roberts and Williams hurried to finish the refitting so they could sail to meet him, and the *Don Juan* was relaunched on the 22nd. She now had two complete new sets of topmast rigging, and could fly three spinnakers and a storm jib. She looked 'like a vessel of 50 tons' Williams wrote with pride. But despite all the new woodwork and rigging, she floated three inches higher on her revised ballast load.[43] Shelley told Mary that they intended to sail on the 24th, but she begged him not to go, as she felt helpless without him and worried about the health of the child Percy Florence.

On the night before the planned departure, Williams wrote in his journal that

'Shelley *sees spirits* and alarms the whole house'.[44] Mary's account, later written to Maria Gisborne, is genuinely horrifying.

> ... The fright my illness gave him caused a return of nervous sensations & visions as bad as in his worst times. I think it was the Saturday after my illness while yet unable to walk I was confined to my bed – in the middle of the night I was awoken by hearing him scream & come rushing into my room; I was sure he was asleep & tried to waken him by calling on him, but he continued to scream which inspired me with such a panic that I jumped out of bed & ran across the hall to Mrs Williams's room where I fell through weakness, though I was so frightened that I got up again immediately – she let me in & Williams went to Shelley who had been wakened by my getting out of bed – he said that he had not been asleep & that it was a vision that he saw that had frightened him –[45]

Under questioning, Shelley explained that he had seen two visions: one was of the lacerated figures of Edward and Jane covered with blood who staggered into his room supporting each other and shouted, 'Get up Shelley the sea is flooding the house & it is all coming down.' The other vision was when he rushed into Mary's room to waken her: he saw his own figure bending over the bed strangling her. Shelley did not sail for Genoa the next day, for Mary had a relapse as a result of these visitations.[46] He talked to her calmly in the morning about the many other visions that he had been seeing lately. The only one Mary records was another meeting with himself. '. . . He had seen the figure of himself which met him as he walked on the terrace & said to him – "How long do you mean to be content?" '[47] It was of course his Zoroastrian double; he had at last succeeded in thoroughly terrifying Mary.

The trip to meet Hunt was now postponed until 1 July, when Hunt should have arrived at Livorno. The heat was again oppressive, and in San Terenzo and Lerici church prayers were offered for rain. At night the Fiesta of St John was celebrated on the shore, and the local people danced and sang wildly in the surf.[48] Two days before sailing, Shelley wrote a long letter to Horace Smith in Versailles, largely about politics. 'It seems to me that things have now arrived at such a crisis as requires every man plainly to utter his sentiments on the inefficacy of the existing religions no less than political systems for restraining & guiding mankind. Let us see the truth whatever that may be –' Having finished the letter, he turned it round and wrote crosswise on top of his previous writing: 'I still inhabit this divine bay, reading Spanish dramas & sailing & listening to the most enchanting music.'[49] Shelley seems to have had some discussion with Williams on public affairs too, and on the last day of the month, Williams sat on the deck of the *Don Juan* as the topmast rigging was being reset for the final time and read Shelley's copy of *Queen Mab* under the baking sun. 'An astonishing work.'[50]

On 1 July Shelley, Williams, Captain Roberts and the boat boy Charles Vivian sailed for Livorno, covering the distance of fifty miles in seven hours. They docked at half past nine in the evening, and spent the night sleeping on deck on cushions thrown down from the *Bolivar*. The next morning the quarantine officers cleared them to come ashore. Byron, the Gambas, Hunt and his family were all at Livorno, and there was an emotional reunion between Hunt and Shelley. Hunt recalled how Shelley rushed forward to embrace him, repeating over and over with delight 'how *inexpressibly* glad' he was to see him. Shelley was in the highest spirits, and when some joke was made, he leaned against a doorway for support, laughing wildly till the tears came into his eyes.

The next day, leaving Williams at the harbour to buy provisions, Shelley and the Hunts and Byron made their way to Pisa. The Pisa plan for the *Liberal*, which was after all the real reason for their being together, did not now look promising. The Gambas were about to be permanently exiled from Tuscany, and Byron had declared that he would abandon both the Lanfranchi, and his new summer residence at Monte Nero to follow them. Trelawny was already scheming to get the *Bolivar* by land to the Lake of Geneva. Hunt was sixty crowns in debt, and his wife Marianne was dangerously ill: at Pisa Vaccà told Hunt she would probably die. Byron was appalled and irritated by the sight of Hunt's numerous offspring, and groaned inwardly and outwardly at the responsibility he had taken on at the ground floor of his palace. On top of all this, a private letter from Mary to Hunt which Shelley delivered announced that it would be 'madness' for the Hunts to come to Lerici: 'I wish I could break my chains and leave this dungeon.'[51] 'Everybody is in despair,' Shelley wrote, '& everything in confusion.'[52]

Shelley made great efforts during the next five days to mediate between all the parties, and succeeded to some degree. He pointed out to Hunt that the offer Byron had made of assigning the copyright of his 'Vision of Judgement' for the first number of the *Liberal* would almost certainly guarantee the journal's success. This offer he firmly secured from Byron 'in spite of delicacy'. When it appeared in the autumn, the *Liberal* did in fact carry Byron's poem.

Shelley's presence at Pisa, looking sun-burnt and healthy, gradually had the effect of cheering everyone, and both Byron and Hunt were anxious that he should stay. But Williams was still waiting at Livorno with the *Don Juan*, and he was impatient to return to Jane at Lerici: the wind blew constantly northwards for Spezia. 'What can I do,' he wrote in a note to Jane. 'Poor Shelley desires that I should return to you, but I know secretly wishes me not to leave him in the lurch.'[53] Besides, there was Mary still waiting on her sofa in the terrace windows, worrying about Percy Florence. Shelley wrote to her from Pisa: 'How are you my best Mary? Write especially how is your health & how your spirits are, & whether you are not more reconciled to staying at Lerici at least during the summer. . . . Ever dearest Mary, Yours affectionately S. – PS. I have found the translation of the Symposium.'[54] He also sent a brief love-note to Jane. 'I fear you are solitary & melancholy at Villa Magni. . . . How soon those hours past, & how slowly they return to pass so soon again, & perhaps for ever, in which we have lived together so intimately so happily! . . .'[55] He looked in to greet the Masons at Casa Silva before leaving Pisa on 7 July.

At Livorno, he was greeted by Williams and Trelawny. The heat was over-powering, and the weather began to look unsettled, and they were all anxious to be off. Trelawny intended to sail the *Bolivar* to Lerici alongside them, but at the last moment he was held up by port clearance papers. Shelley and Williams decided to go on without waiting longer. Shelley jumped down on to the deck of the *Don Juan*; he was wearing a double-breasted reefer jacket, white nankeen sailors' trousers and black leather boots. The ship cast off. Together with their boat boy, Charles Vivian, they drew out of the harbour at just after two in the afternoon of 8 July 1822 and hoisted full sail to make with all speed to Lerici. Trelawny waved goodbye and watched them with a spy-glass as they headed out to sea. Then he went down to his cabin to sleep. Captain Roberts, anxious about the low clouds gathering on the horizon to the west, took a large telescope and asked permission to climb the lighthouse, where he watched the sails of the *Don Juan* until they disappeared into a thickening haze. The storm came up rapidly from the south-west and broke at about half past six. The local Italian *feluccas*, wary of such summer squalls, ran for the safety of Livorno harbour, and one of the Italian captains reported having sighted the *Don Juan* in heavy seas.

The poet laureate of Pisa, Count John Taaffe, long afterwards recounted the captain's story: '. . . seeing that they could not long contend with such tremendous waves, [he] bore down upon them and offered to take them on board. A shrill voice, which is supposed to have been Shelley's, was distinctly heard to say "No". . . . The waves were running mountains high – a tremendous surf dashed over the boat which to his astonishment was still crowded with sail. "If you will not come on board for God's sake reef your sails or you are lost," cried a sailor through the speaking trumpet. One of the gentlemen (Williams it is believed) was seen to make an effort to lower the sails – his companion seized him by the arm as if in anger.'[56] The *Don Juan* went down into the Gulf of Spezia, some ten miles west of Viareggio, under full sail.

30
Coda

The bodies of Shelley, Edward Williams, and Charles Vivian were eventually washed up along the beach between Massa and Viareggio ten days after the storm. The exposed flesh of Shelley's arms and face had been entirely eaten away, but he was identifiable by the nankeen trousers, the white silk socks beneath the boots and Hunt's copy of Keats's poems doubled back in the jacket pocket. To comply with the complicated quarantine laws, Trelawny had the body temporarily buried in the sand with quick lime, and dug up again on 15 August to be placed in a portable iron furnace that had been constructed to his specification at Livorno, and burnt on the beach in the presence of Leigh Hunt, Lord Byron, some Tuscan militia and a few local fishermen. Much later Shelley's ashes were buried in a tomb, also designed by Trelawny, in the Protestant Cemetery at Rome, after having remained for several months in a mahogany chest in the British Consul's wine-cellar.

In England, the news of Shelley's death was first published by the *Examiner* on 4 August, and on the following evening by the *Courier* whose article began: 'Shelley, the writer of some infidel poetry has been drowned; *now* he knows whether there is a God or no.' Obituaries and polemic commentaries followed in many reviews and papers during the next three months.

In Tuscany, the shock of Shelley's death served temporarily to draw the old Pisan Circle together again. Mary, Claire and Jane Williams returned together to Pisa; Trelawny and Leigh Hunt placed themselves at Mary's disposal; and Byron took on financial responsibility for the whole party and determined to go through with the plan for the *Liberal*. In that summer of 1822, Mary was aged 25; Claire 24; Trelawny 29; Byron 34; and Hunt 37. It was a young and immensely gifted group of individuals, but the influences which held them together were now far weaker than the forces that drove them apart, and nothing productive was to be achieved in each other's company. As Trelawny recalled, 'we degenerated apace'.

The first to depart, not surprisingly, was Claire, who returned almost immediately to Florence, and in September travelled alone to Vienna to stay with her brother Charles, a journey she had long contemplated. With both Allegra and Shelley dead there was nothing to keep her in Italy. In 1823 she accepted a post as a governess with a wealthy family in Moscow, and remained in Russia for several years. After a silence of twelve months, she had gradually resumed her correspondence with Mary and with Trelawny, and her letters were still as lively as ever; but she was frequently lonely, and she never married.

In the autumn of 1822, the remaining Pisan Circle moved in Byron's shadow to Genoa, and took separate houses outside the gates at Albaro. Here Jane Williams left for England, with her two children, and arrived in London in November with an introduction from Mary to Hogg. True to his form of old, Hogg was soon attracted by Shelley's latest love-object, and within a year a liaison was blossoming. Jane eventually lived with Hogg as his common law wife, and bore him a daughter who was christened Prudentia. In 1832, Hogg published his first article on Shelley at Oxford in the *New Monthly Magazine*; and many years later, with Jane's help issued the first two volumes of his biography in 1858. Hogg failed to attain either of his ambitions, a Judgeship or the Chair of Civil Law at the newly founded University of London; instead he became a regular contributor to the *Edinburgh Review*, and was finally one of the Municipal Corporation Commissioners and Revising Barrister for Northumberland. He died in 1862 at the age of 72.

In October 1822, the first number of the *Liberal* containing Shelley's translations from 'Faust' and Byron's 'Vision of Judgement' was published in London, only to be received by a storm of protest. It folded quietly the following year after only four issues, the final collapse of Shelley's original Pisan plan. In July of 1823, after growing acrimony largely over financial matters, the remainder of the old Pisan party broke up. Byron and Trelawny sailed for Greece in the *Bolivar*, Mary set out for England, the Hunts were left to struggle on for two years in Florence and Teresa Guiccioli was abandoned in Genoa.

In Greece Byron spent several harsh and disillusioning months training a private army and attempting to instil some sense of brotherhood among the mixed assortment of European freedom-fighters in their motley uniforms, only to die miserably at Missolonghi of marsh fever on 19 April 1824. His valet Fletcher was still with him. Trelawny shifted for himself as a private adventurer and freebooter, joining forces with the Greek chieftain and brigand Odysseus; later he continued his escapades in Europe and America, and swum the Niagara just above the Falls. Finally he returned as a raffish member of London society, dining out on reminiscences, and publishing the autobiographic *The Adventures of a Younger Son* in 1830, and the biographical *Recollections of the Last Days of*

Shelley and Byron in 1858, both of which are semi-fictionalized accounts. In middle age he eloped with Lady Augusta Goring, and after a divorce scandal, married for the third time, and settled in Monmouthshire.

When Mary returned to London in 1823 with her precious child Percy Florence, she renewed her friendship with Jane Williams and the Gisbornes, and settled in Kentish Town near her father William Godwin. A dramatized version of *Presumption, or the Fate of Frankenstein* was playing at the English Opera House, and her role as a minor literary celebrity began, which soothed her though it did not bring financial security. She continued an endless series of negotiations with Field Place, aided somewhat coldly by Peacock, and in 1824 obtained a £100 annuity to support herself and Percy. On the publication of five hundred copies of Shelley's *Posthumous Poems*, Sir Timothy instantly threatened to remove the vital annuity, until the remaining 191 unsold copies were destroyed. A similar threat was made on the publication of *The Last Man* in 1826; but gradually Mary's situation improved, she took rooms in Regent's Park and sent Percy to Harrow, and later to Trinity College, Cambridge – an education modelled on Byron's – where to her delight his career was smooth and undistinguished. Various drawing-room affections with a number of fashionable young poets and actors, including Washington Irving, came to nothing, and she turned down an offer of marriage from Trelawny. Gradually old friends fell away: both John and Maria Gisborne died in 1835, and in April of the following year her father died at the age of 80, the end of what Mary now clearly realized as an 'excessive and romantic attachment'. She was still obsessed by Shelley's papers, and trapped by memories both idealized and remorseful, her life attained a curious stillness, interrupted only by sea-bathing at Sandgate, increasingly acid correspondence with Claire, Trelawny and Jane, and occasional expeditions to the Continent with Percy's undergraduate friends. In 1839, on the publication of the first edition of Shelley's *Poetical Works* by Moxon, Mary was bitterly attacked by Trelawny, Hogg and Peacock for her editorial omissions and suppressions.

In 1844 old Sir Timothy finally died, and the baronetcy descended upon Percy Florence, who inherited Field Place, and married Jane St John, a narrow, kindly, capable woman with literary tastes, in 1848. Tactfully Lady Jane Shelley assumed the handling and collecting of the Shelley papers from Mary, and had built a special room of remembrance at the new Shelley home of Boscombe Manor which was treated almost like a shrine, complete with life-size monument of the poet, lockets of fading hair, glass cases of letters and blue opaque pots containing fragments of bone. The meditative stillness of Mary's life now changed imperceptibly into a physical paralysis, and she died quietly in 1851 attended by her beloved Sir Percy.

During this time Peacock had risen to eminence in India House and between 1836 and 1856 was the Chief Examiner of Correspondence, a position he held directly above the young utilitarian and feminist John Stuart Mill. Peacock published his 'Memoirs' of Shelley in *Fraser's Magazine* shortly after his retirement, and while intelligently criticizing Hogg's biography and stoutly defending the honour of Harriet Shelley against the worshippers of Boscombe Manor, he unconsciously attributed to Shelley an aura of comic mystique drawn from his own fiction. It was not coincidental that 1861 saw the crown of his own literary career in the last and most mellow of his 'crotchet' novels, entitled *Gryll Grange*. Five years later he died at the age of 81.

Leigh Hunt, who had also attacked Hogg's biography, was already dead. After returning to his beloved Highgate in 1825, he had issued his Italian apologia *Lord Byron and Some of His Contemporaries* (1828) and continued producing a mass of genial literary journalism including *Stories From the Italian Poets* (1846). He moved south to Cheyne Row, befriended Thomas Carlyle, and published perhaps his best work, a three-volume *Autobiography* in 1850. He died nine years later at Putney, aged 74.

The traces of the old Italian circle were now almost entirely dissolved. Trelawny had broken with his wife, and gone to cultivate fig trees at Worthing, where as an old man he sat to Sir John Millais as the ancient sea dog in *The North West Passage*, his final gesture of romance. He was to die in 1881. There remained only Claire Clairmont, who had returned to Europe in 1828, and shuttled between Vienna, London and Italy for many years, still labouring as a governess, and still writing her sprightly correspondence, which became faintly malicious in old age. Claire's main hope of real independence had been the generous legacy of £12,000 which Shelley had intended for her many years previously; but somehow inevitably, when it eventually reached her in 1844, much of it was squandered in a series of madcap investments. At long last she returned in genteel poverty to the beautiful Italian city of her original exile, Florence, and lived peacefully there for many years attended by her niece Pauline, finally dying in 1879.

A young Harvard University graduate, Edward Silsbee, had come to Florence shortly before Claire's death in search of Shelley's supposed love-letters. He tried ineffectually to charm them from the dark-eyed old lady by parading his youthful zeal and enthusiastic knowledge of Shelley. His performance inspired Henry James's cutting story *The Aspern Papers* (1888), which is the final damnation of all biographers. Silsbee did however retrieve Claire's faircopy book, with its transcription of the poem 'To Constantia Singing' – 'Alas, that the torn heart can bleed, but not forget'.

Author's Acknowledgements

For kind permission to consult and quote from copyright materials I am very happy to thank: the Keeper of Western Mss, the Bodleian Library; John Murray of Albemarle Street; the Caernarvonshire Record Office; Lord Abinger; and the Clarendon Press, Oxford.

For further copyright permissions, my thanks and acknowledgements to: Harvard University Press; Oxford University Press; University of Oklahoma Press; University of New Mexico Press; Duke University Press; University of Illinois Press; the Bodley Head; and Victor Gollancz.

For permission to make reference to and quotation from copyright documents I am pleased to thank The Carl and Lily Pforzheimer Foundation, Inc. of New York.

For reproductions of pictures and manuscripts my thanks are due to: the Bodleian Library; the British Museum; the National Portrait Gallery; the Galleria Nazionale d'Arte Antica, Rome; the Museo Borghese, Rome; the Uffizi Gallery, Florence; Nottingham Public Libraries; Mrs Imogen Dennis and St Pancras Public Libraries; Editions Jaeger, Geneva; the Provost and Fellows of Eton College; and the Frankfurter Goethemuseum.

My special thanks to the artist David Farris; and the photographer Adrian Holmes, now of Rylands Visual Facilities Ltd.

For technical help of one kind or another I am extremely grateful to: Bryn R. Parry, of Swyddfa Archifau Caernarfon; the archivist of the University of North Wales, Bangor; the staff of the Old Bodleian Library, Oxford; the staff of the British Museum, and Carol Andrews of the Department of Egyptian Antiquities; the staff of the London Library; the staff of the Rising Sun, Lynmouth; Richard Ormond, Assistant Keeper, the National Portrait Gallery; Signora Vera Cacciatore, the Keats-Shelley Museum, Rome; Susan Bartlett, Florence and Orinda, California; and Signor Giulio Martinelli, La Fondiaria Assicuriazioni, Bagni di Lucca.

For expert comments on Greek and Latin texts my particular thanks to: Peter Jay of the Anvil Press; Barbara Goward; Wilfred Passmore, the Abbot of Downside; and Joanna Latimer, University of London, for her interpretation of Pausanias's speech in the *Symposium*.

I should like to thank G.M.Matthews for an exacting reading of the book's first draft; John Murray for his kind interest in its progress; and Dr Donald Reiman of the Carl H. Pforzheimer Library for his courteous advice. I should also like to record, more distantly, the inspiration and anguish caused by two fine teachers and writers, the critic Dr George Steiner and the poet Peter Whigham.

My gratitude to Michael Ratcliffe of the *Times* for his earliest encouragement; Captain Livingstone Learmonth of Tan-yr-allt, Tremadoc for his hospitality; and Mrs Ismena Holland for her generous help. Best thanks also to Jo Foster, my visionary typist.

I have a primary professional debt to Tony Godwin, my first English publisher, for his editorial liberality and graceful patience; and to Hal Scharlatt in New York for the exceptional sympathy and intensely personal care which he gave to an author's cloudiest aspirations. I have a more than professional debt to Peter Janson-Smith for his wise counsel, constant friendship and inexhaustible good spirits.

I do not really know how to thank Helen Rogan, who gave me so fully a fellow writer's understanding and support; but I have tried. My very warmest thanks also to Margaret Amaral, David and Linda Griffiths, Jackie and Robin Clode, and my mother and father, under all of whose roofs or in whose gardens parts of this book were written, deleted, forgotten or dreamt.

Finally I would like to greet the unknown student of Calderón who bought me a glass of brandy one stormy October night in a crumbling bar overlooking the Arno at Pisa.

R.H.

Bibliography

It is the intention of this bibliography to be exclusive. I have selected from the vast field of works connected with Shelley's life a very small number of books which throw a really penetrating and original light on either his background, his work or his character. I have also chosen books which are each in themselves exceptional pieces of writing, and many of them are classics of their period. This list is directed equally to the general reader and the student.

For more specialized and technical information, the reader may wish to consult my References which contain running discussion of source books and manuscripts, and the bibliographies set out in two pamphlets: *Shelley* by G.M.Matthews, 'Writers and Their Work' No. 214, Longmans, 1970; and *Bibliographical Index to the Keats–Shelley Memorial Bulletin, I–XX, 1910–1969*, compiled by C.Darel Sheraw, KSMB, 1970.

1 *The Autobiography of Samuel Bamford (1788–1872)*, 2 vols, W.H.Chaloner (ed.), Frank Cass, London, 1967.

2 *The Autobiography of Francis Place (1771–1854)*, Mary Thale (ed.), Cambridge University Press, 1972.

3 *The Autobiography of William Cobbett: The Progress of a Ploughboy to a Seat in Parliament (1763–1835)*, William Reitzel (ed.), Faber & Faber, London, 1947.

4 Mary Wollstonecraft: *A Vindication of the Rights of Women*, 1792, Dent, London, 1970.

5 William Godwin, *Enquiry Concerning Political Justice*, 1792. Abridged and edited by K.C.Carter, Oxford University Press, 1971.

6 Thomas Love Peacock: *Headlong Hall*, 1816; *Melincourt*, 1817; *Nightmare Abbey*, 1818, David Garnett (ed.), Rupert Hart Davis, London 1963.

7 Mary Shelley: *Frankenstein; or, The Modern Prometheus*, 1818, Oxford University Press, 1969.

8 William Hazlitt: *The Spirit of the Age*, 1824, Collins, London, 1969.

9 E.J.Hobsbawm: *The Age of Revolution: Europe, 1789–1848*, Weidenfeld & Nicolson, London, 1969.

10 E.P.Thompson: *The Making of the English Working Class*, Gollancz, London, 1963. Penguin, Harmondsworth, 1968.

11 Leslie A.Marchand: *Byron: A Biography*, 3 vols, John Murray, London, 1957.

12 *Lord Byron: Selected Prose*, Peter Gunn (ed.), Penguin, Harmondsworth, 1972.

13 Robert Gittings: *John Keats*, Heinemann, London, 1968.

14 Howard Mills: *Peacock: His Circle and His Age*, Cambridge University Press, 1969.

15 Peter Quennell: *Romantic England: Writing and Painting 1717–1851*, Weidenfeld & Nicolson, London, 1970.

16 Newman Ivey White: *Shelley*, 2 vols., Secker and Warburg, London, 1947.

17 Kenneth Neill Cameron: *Young Shelley: Genesis of a Radical*, Gollancz, London, 1951.

18 Neville Rogers: *Shelley at Work*, Oxford University Press, 1967.

19 James Rieger: *The Mutiny Within: the Heresies of Percy Bysshe Shelley*, George Braziller, New York, 1967.

20 Roland A.Duerksen: *Shelleyan Ideas in Victorian Literature*, Mouton and Co., The Hague, 1966.

21 Judith Chernaik: *The Lyrics of Shelley*, Case Western Reserve University Press, 1972.

Abbreviated references

Letters

The Letters of Percy Bysshe Shelley, edited by F.L.Jones 2 vols, Oxford University Press, 1964. (All Shelley's known letters are now numbered in this edition, and together with an indication of the page on which a cited passage occurs, I have normally regarded this as sufficient reference. Where particular letters contain doubtful readings from the MS, or the provenance of the printed text is controversial, I give further details.) Professor Jones's edition also contains a wealth of material in its footnotes, much of it drawn from Lady Jane Shelley's *Shelley and Mary*, 4 vols, privately printed in 1882. Reference to this editorial material is similarly indicated.

Poetical Works

Shelley: Poetical Works, edited by Thomas Hutchinson, Oxford University Press, 1968. This has been the standard text since 1904, and includes all Shelley's Prefaces, and much incidental material including Mary Shelley's prose 'Notes', from the first collected *Poetical Works* of 1839. It will eventually be superseded by Neville Rogers's 4-volume edition also from Oxford University Press, which is in the process of publication (Vol. 1, 1972).

Prose

Shelley's Prose: or, The Trumpet of a Prophesy, edited by David Lee Clark, University of New Mexico Press, corrected edition 1966. (There is still no single complete edition of all Shelley's prose, but I have used this as my standard text. Where transcription is doubtful, or more convenient sources are available for a particular work, I give supplementary references.)

Journal

Mary Shelley's Journal, edited by F.L.Jones, University of Oklahoma Press, 1947. This contains many entries written by Shelley, especially during the years 1814–16, when Mary and Shelley shared it. For further discussion of the MS, see Chapter 10, ref. 1.

Mary

The Letters of Mary W.Shelley, edited by F.L.Jones, 2 vols, University of Oklahoma Press, 1944. Unless otherwise stated, all references are to Vol. 1.

Claire

The Journals of Claire Clairmont, edited by Marion Kingston Stocking, Harvard University Press, 1968. The MS 1814–22 is held in the British Museum, Ashley MS 394, and Ashley MS 2819(1–3). In my text Claire's journal is referred to as her 'diary' to avoid any possible confusion with Mary's 'journal'.

Bod. MSS

Manuscripts held in the special Shelley section of the Bodleian Library Oxford; these include most notably fifteen of Shelley's working notebooks covering the period between 1816 and 1822, in which many of his major poems and prose essays can be traced from fragmentary conception to fair copy: MS Shelley Adds e. 6 – Adds e. 20.

Abinger MSS

Microfilm of Lord Abinger's entire collection of Shelley Manuscripts, including most notably Mary Shelley's 'journal', held on eleven reels at the Bodleian Library, Oxford, R.6.112. The microfilm was made by Marion Stocking in 1952, and a second copy resides at Duke University.

Murray MSS

A collection of manuscripts relating to Lord Byron, held by John Murray Esq. at 50 Albemarle Street, London.

Pforzheimer

Shelley and His Circle, 1773–1822, edited by K.N.Cameron, Vols I–IV, and subsequently by Donald H.Reiman, the Carl H.Pforzheimer Library, New York, 1961. A miscellaneous collection of Shelley letters and Shelleyana printed from the manuscript, frequently showing small and significant variations from hitherto available printed sources, and including fifteen new Shelley letters. Some of the secondary material written by Shelley's close companions and friends has not previously been published. The edition was planned in 1961 to run to ten volumes, of which six have currently been published. The editorial commentary also contains valuable material.

New Select Bibliography

As in my original bibliography, the aim here is to give an exclusive selection from a vast field of Shelley studies. I have followed developments closely from the mid-1970s, and these are the works which I believe will be particularly helpful and interesting to the general reader and student alike. More specialised and academic bibliographies may be found in the works of Donald H. Reiman and G. Kim Blank cited below. My choice includes a play, a novel and a poem.

1 G. Kim Blank (ed.): *The New Shelley: Later Twentieth-Century Views*, St. Martin's Press, New York, 1991

2 Harold Bloom: *Shelley's Mythmaking*, Cornell University Press, 1969; 'Introduction' to *Shelley's Prose*, ed. David Lee Clark, new edition, Fourth Estate, London, 1990

3 Howard Brenton: *Bloody Poetry* (play), Methuen, London, 1985

4 Nathaniel Brown: *Sexuality and Feminism in Shelley*, Harvard University Press, 1979

5 Marilyn Butler: 'The Cult of the South' in *Romantics, Rebels and Reactionaries*, Oxford, 1981

6 Judith Chernaik: *Mab's Daughters* (novel), Macmillan, London, 1991

7 Nora Crook and Derek Guiton: *Shelley's Venomed Melody*, Cambridge University Press, 1986

8 Stuart Curran: *Shelley's Annus Mirabilis: The Maturing of an Epic Vision*, Huntington Library, California, 1975

9 P.M.S. Dawson: *The Unacknowledged Legislator: Shelley and Politics*, Oxford, 1980

10 Paul de Man: 'Shelley Disfigured' in *Deconstruction and Criticism*, ed. Harold Bloom, Seabury, New York, 1979

11 Kelvin Everest: 'Shelley's Doubles' in *Shelley Revalued: Essays from the Gregynog Conference*, Barnes and Noble, New York, 1983

12 Paul Foot: *Red Shelley*, Sidgwick and Jackson, 1980

13 Barbara Charlesworth Gelpi: *Shelley's Goddess: Maternity, Language, Subjectivity*, Oxford, 1992

14 Thom Gunn: 'Lerici' (poem) in *Collected Poems*, Faber, 1993

15 Desmond Hawkins: *Shelley's First Love*, Archon Books, 1992

16 Terence A, Hoagwood: *Skepticims and Ideology: Shelley's Political Prose and Its Philosophical Context from Bacon to Marx*, University of Iowa Press, 1988

17 Jerrold E. Hogle: *Shelley's Process: Radical Transference and the Development of his Major Works*, Oxford University Press, 1980

18 William Keach: *Shelley's Style*, Methuen, New York, 1984

19 Angela Leighton: *Shelley and the Sublime*, Cambridge University Press, 1984; 'Love, Writing and Scepticism in Epipsychidion' in *The New Shelley: Later Twentieth-Century Views*, ed. G. Kim Blank, St Martin's Press, New York, 1991

20 Jerome McGann: *The Romantic Ideology*, University of Chicago Press, 1983

21 C.E. Pulos: *The Deep Truth: A Study of Shelley's Scepticism*, University of Nebraska Press, 1954

22 Donald H. Reiman: *Percy Bysshe Shelley*, Twayne's English Authors Series, updated edition, 1990. This survey also contains details of the continuing publication of *Shelley and His Circle, 1773-1822* running to 12 volumes from the Pforzheimer Library manuscripts; and the photofacsimile editions of Shelley's manuscripts in the Bodleian Library, Oxford, by Garland Publishing Inc., New York.

23 William St. Clair: *The Godwins and the Shelleys: The Biography of a Family*, Faber, 1989

24 Michael H. Scrivener: *Radical Shelley*, Princeton University Press, 1982

25 Stuart Sperry: *Shelley's Major Verse*, Harvard University Press, 1988

26 Claire Tomalin: *Shelley and his World*, Thames and Hudson, 1980

27 Earl R. Wasserman: *Shelley: A Critical Reading*, John Hopkins University Press, 1971

28 Timothy Webb: *The Violet in the Crucible: Shelley and Translation*, Oxford, 1976; *Shelley: A Voice Not Understood*, Manchester University Press, 1977; (ed) *Shelley: Selected Poems*, Everyman's Library, 1977

29 Art Young: *Shelley and Nonviolence*, Mouton, The Hague, 1975

References

Chapter 1   A Fire-Raiser

1. Field Place and the ponds still remain, though there has been considerable alteration in the layout of the gardens, and parts of the house have been rebuilt. Field Place is described in Edward Dowden, *The Life of Percy Bysshe Shelley*, 2 vols, 1866, I, pp. 5–7; also in Roger Ingpen, *Shelley in England: New Facts and Letters from the Shelley-Whitton Papers*, 1917, pp. 22–7. Both these works are important sources of detailed information and documents for the first twenty-five years of Shelley's life (while Dowden's second volume follows Shelley into Italy).

The Sussex nurse and the Great Tortoise legend are mentioned in Hellen Shelley's letters to Jane Williams; while the 'Great Old Snake' is described in Thomas Jefferson Hogg, *The Life of Percy Bysshe Shelley*, 2 vols, 1858, the edition used here and throughout being that edited by Humbert Wolfe, 2 vols, 1933, I. Reference to the 'Great Old Snake' is on p. 22.

2. Edmund Blunden, *Shelley: A Life Story*, 1946, p. 23.
3. Dowden, op. cit., I, p. 5.
4. Shelley acidly refers to the picture of Christ in letters to Hogg, winter 1810–11; the 'bad picture of the Eruption of Vesuvius' is mentioned in Thomas Medwin, *The Life of Percy Bysshe Shelley*, 1847, edited by H.B. Forman, 1913, p. 12.
5. Hellen Shelley in Hogg, op. cit., I, p. 23.
6. ibid., p. 22.
7. Walter Edwin Peck, *Shelley: His Life and Work*, 2 vols, 1927, I, p. 30.
8. Hellen Shelley in Hogg, I, p. 28.
9. ibid., p. 25.
10. ibid., p. 22.
11. ibid., pp. 22–3.
12. Medwin, op. cit., p. 16.
13. ibid., p. 17.
14. ibid.
15. ibid., p. 20.
16. ibid., p. 24.
17. ibid., p. 20.

18. Sir John Rennie, quoted in Kenneth Neill Cameron, *The Young Shelley: Genesis of a Radical*, 1951, p. 7.

19. Medwin, op. cit., p. 27.

20. *Poetical Works*, p. 535.

21. Transcribed from Shelley's working notebook, Bixby-Huntington Notebook II, in Neville Rogers, *Shelley at Work*, 1967, Appendix III, pp. 335–6.

22. Cameron, op. cit., p. 291, n. 1. It is interesting that Timothy first applied to the Royal College of Heralds for a pedigree in 1806. The somewhat spurious genealogy is discussed by Ingpen, op. cit., pp. 1–18.

23. ibid. See also John Cordy Jeaffreson, *The Real Shelley*, 2 vols, 1885, I, p. 21.

24. Ingpen, op. cit., p. 18.

25. Medwin, op. cit., p. 13.

26. Dowden, op. cit., I, p. 5.

27. Leigh Hunt, *Lord Byron and some of His Contemporaries*, 1828, vol. I, pp. 201–305.

28. Sir John Rennie, quoted in Cameron, op. cit., p. 7.

29. Medwin, op. cit., p. 23.

30. ibid., p. 16.

31. Bod. MS Shelley Adds. c. 4 f24. (c. 1822), which shows sketches of male and female faces in profile. 'An Essay on Friendship', *Prose*, p. 338.

32. 'Notes on Sculptures in Rome and Florence' (1819–20), *Prose*, pp. 347–8.

33. 'Dedication to the Revolt of Islam', stanzas 3–4; *Poetical Works*, pp. 37–8. See also 'Hymn to Intellectual Beauty', stanzas 5–6; *Poetical Works*, p. 531.

34. Medwin, op. cit., pp. 28–9.

35. Hogg, op. cit., I, p. 53.

36. The solar microscope is first mentioned in connection with Walker by Medwin, pp. 28–9; and several times subsequently by Hogg, pp. 55, 152–3, etc. Hogg says that Shelley's 'first care' on entering new lodgings was to find a southern-facing window and cut a hole in the shutter for the microscope aperture.

37. Hellen Shelley in Hogg, op. cit., I, p. 23.

38. Hogg, op. cit., I, p. 88.

39. Dowden, op. cit., I, p. 31, n. 1, who records the experiment at Eton; but Medwin, op cit., p. 72, locates the 'electrical kite' at Field Place, 'an idea borrowed from Franklin'. Perhaps there was more than one kite, and more than one cat.

40. Hellen Shelley in Hogg, op. cit., I, p. 29. *Poetical Works*, pp. 838–9.

41. *Letters*, I, No. 1, p. 1.

42. Hellen Shelley in Hogg, op. cit., I, p. 23.

43. *Letters*, I, No. 2, p. 1.

44. W.H. Merle, article in *The Athenaeum*, 1848; reprinted in Edmund Blunden, *Shelley and Keats as they Struck their Contemporaries*, 1925.

45. Thomas Love Peacock, 'Memoirs of Percy Bysshe Shelley', first printed as three articles in *Fraser's Magazine*, June 1858, January 1860 and March 1862. Howard Mills (ed.), *Peacock: Memoirs, Essays and Reviews*, 1970, p. 24.

46. *The Revolt of Islam*, Canto V, stanzas 8–9; *Poetical Works*, p. 81.

47. Mary Shelley to Leigh Hunt, 8 April 1825: *Mary*, I, No. 225, p. 317.

48. Mary's 'Notes', *Poetical Works*, p. 835.

49. Mary Shelley, *Lodore*, 1835, pp. 72–7.

50. ibid., pp. 77–8.

51. Charles Grove to Hellen Shelley, 16 February 1857. Ingpen, op. cit., pp. 49–50. Grove recalls this as occurring when Shelley was aged 12.

52. Hellen Shelley in Hogg, op. cit., I, p. 24.

53. ibid., pp. 23–4.

54. The Reverend Robert Leslie quoted in Dowden, op. cit., I, p. 26 n. 1.

55. Hellen Shelley in Hogg, op. cit., I, p. 24.

56. ibid.

57. Medwin, op. cit., p. 34.

58. Walter Halliday to Hellen Shelley, 27 February 1857. Hogg, op. cit., I, p. 41.

59. Hogg, op. cit., I, p. 36.

60. Peacock, op. cit., p. 26.

61. Hogg, op. cit., I, p. 36.

62. 'Oh! There are spirits of the air', *Poetical Works*, p. 525.

63. *Dictionary of National Biography*, Sidney Lee (ed.), 1893, Vol. XXXIII, pp. 272–3.

64. Jean Overton Fuller, *Shelley*, 1968, p. 22.

65. Cameron, op. cit., p. 13.

66. *Letters*, I, No. 30, p. 28, n. 13.

67. 'Prince Athanase', *Poetical Works*, p. 163.

68. *The Revolt of Islam*, Canto IV, stanzas 12–14; *Poetical Works*, pp. 74–5.

69. Mary Shelley in Hogg, op. cit., I, pp. 35–6.

70. *Letters*, I, No. 4, p. 3.

71. ibid., No. 6, p. 4.

72. Hellen Shelley in Hogg, op. cit., I, p. 27.

73. Charles Grove to Hellen Shelley. Ingpen, op. cit., p. 94.

74. Harriet Grove's Diary for 1810. Printed in Newman Ivey White, *Shelley*, 2 vols, 1940; I, Chapter 4.

75. *Letters*, I, No. 11, p. 11.

76. ibid., no. 15, p. 14.

77. Dr Eustace Chesser, *Shelley & Zastrozzi; Self-Revelation of a Neurotic*, 1965, p. 32. The study also reprints the entire text.

78. ibid., *Zastrozzi*, Chapter 17, pp. 156–9.

79. ibid., Chapter 15, p. 145.

80. *Letters*, I, No. 10, p. 10.

81. ibid., No. 35, p. 35.

82. 'Ghasta; or, the Avenging Demon!!!' *Poetical Works*, p. 854.

83. 'The Irishman's Song', *Poetical Works*, p. 849.

84. Medwin, op. cit., p. 13.

85. Henry Slatter to Robert Montgomery, 18 December 1833. Cameron, p. 2.

Chapter 2   Oxford: 1810–11

1. *The Clarendon Guide to Oxford*, A.R.Woolley, OUP, 1963.
2. Hogg, op. cit., I, p. 55.
3. ibid., p. 68.
4. ibid., p. 70.
5. ibid., p. 59.
6. *Letters*, I, No. 22, p. 19.
7. Hogg, op. cit., I, p. 67.
8. Taylor's cumulative account, given in Ingpen, *Shelley in England*, p. 178.
9. Medwin, *The Life of Percy Bysshe Shelley*, p. 51.
10. Hogg, op. cit., I, p. 32.
11. ibid., p. 53.
12. ibid., pp. 51–3.
13. ibid., p. 61.
14. ibid., p. 85.
15. Notably *Letters* I, No. 30 and No. 45.
16. Cameron, *The Young Shelley, Genesis of a Radical*, p. 45ff.
17. Hogg, op. cit., I, p. 72.
18. ibid., p. 80.
19. *Letters*, I, No. 64, p. 75.
20. Hogg, op. cit., I, p. 56.
21. *Letters*, I, No. 30, p. 26, n. 3.
22. ibid., pp. 26–7.
23. ibid., No. 32, p. 32.
24. ibid., No. 30, pp. 27–8.
25. ibid., No. 35, p. 36.
26. ibid., No. 36, p. 39.
27. ibid., No. 35, p. 35.
28. ibid., No. 30, p. 29.
29. ibid., No. 34, p. 34.
30. ibid., No. 36, p. 39.
31. ibid., No. 39, p. 45.
32. ibid., No. 38, p. 42.
33. ibid.
34. ibid., No. 42, p. 47.
35. ibid., No. 45, p. 51.
36. ibid., No. 48, p. 53.
37. ibid., No. 39, p. 44.
38. *Prose*, pp. 37–9. Hogg, op. cit., I, p. 165.
39. Percy Vaughan, *Early Shelley Pamphlets*, 1905, p. 17.
40. Ingpen, op. cit., pp. 231–8.
41. *Letters*, I, No. 48, p. 53.

42. ibid., No. 47, p. 52.

43. *Oxford University and City Herald*, 9 February 1811.

44. ibid., 9 March 1811.

45. ibid., 2 March 1811.

46. *Letters*, I, No. 49, p. 54.

47. Cameron, op. cit., p. 53.

48. *Letters*, I, No. 49, p. 54.

49. Peck, *Shelley: His Life and Work*, I, pp. 105–6.

50. Hogg, op. cit., I, p. 169.

51. Medwin, op. cit., p. 86.

52. Hogg, op. cit., I, p. 168.

53. C.J.Ridley, Junior Fellow of University College, quoted in Dowden, *The Life of Percy Bysshe Shelley*, I, p. 124n.

54. Hogg, op. cit., I, p. 169.

55. Medwin, op. cit., p. 88.

56. Hogg, op. cit., I, p. 171.

57. Ridley in Dowden, op. cit., I, p. 124n.

58. ibid.

59. *Letters*, I, No. 56, p. 61.

60. Joseph Gibbons Merle, 'A Newspaper Editor's Reminiscences', in *Fraser's Magazine*, June 1841, p. 704.

61. ibid., p. 702.

62. *Letters*, I, No. 50, pp. 55–6.

63. Hogg, op. cit., I, p. 182.

64. Merle, op. cit., p. 705.

65. ibid., p. 706.

66. *Letters*, I, No. 51, p. 57.

67. ibid., No. 55, p. 57.

68. ibid., No. 55, p. 60.

69. ibid., n. 3.

70. ibid., No. 57, p. 62.

71. ibid., No. 60, p. 66, n1. Timothy's letter continues: 'The insulting, ungentlemanly letter to you appears the high-ton'd, self-willed dictate of the Diabolical Publications. . . . To cast off all thoughts of his Maker, to abandon his Parents, to wish to relinquish his Fortune and to court Persecution, all seem to arise from the same source. . . .' It is printed in full in Ingpen, op. cit., pp. 253–4.

Chapter 3   Wales and Limbo: 1811

1. *Letters*, I, No. 61, p. 67.

2. ibid.

3. ibid., No. 62, p. 70.

4. ibid., No. 63, p. 71.

5. ibid., No. 64, p. 74.

6. ibid.

7. ibid., No. 63, p. 73. See *The Esdaile Notebook*, edited by K. N. Cameron, 1964, p. 124. (Shelley collected his earliest poems 1809–13 in a marbled copybook, which is now known as the Esdaile Manuscript Notebook and is presently held by the Carl H. Pforzheimer Library, New York.)

8. *Letters*, I, No. 66, pp. 76–7.

9. ibid., No. 69, p. 82.

10. ibid., p. 83.

11. ibid., No. 66, p. 77.

12. Edmund Blunden, *Shelley: A Life Story*, 1946, p. 65.

13. *Letters*, I, No. 68, p. 82.

14. ibid., No. 68, p. 81.

15. ibid., No. 66, p. 77.

16. Medwin, op. cit., p. 89.

17. ibid., p. 90.

18. Ingpen, *Shelley in England*, p. 516.

19. Hogg, op. cit., I, p. 275 ff.

20. *Letters*, I, No. 69, p. 83.

21. ibid., No. 63, p. 71.

22. ibid., No. 175, p. 274.

23. ibid.

24. Peacock: *Memoirs, Essays and Reviews*, p. 57.

25. *Letters*, I, No. 67, p. 80.

26. Merle, *Fraser's Magazine*, June 1841, p. 707.

27. *Letters*, I, No. 70, p. 84.

28. ibid., No. 85, p. 107.

29. *Esdaile*, p. 112. (See also *Poetical Works*, p. 842, with a maudlin title conferred by William Rossetti.)

30. *Letters*, I, No. 85, p. 108.

31. ibid., No. 80, p. 96.

32. See F. L. Jones, 'Hogg's Peep at Elizabeth Shelley', *Philological Quarterly*, XXIX, 1950, for a scholarly disquisition on this romantic tryst.

33. *Letters*, I, No. 92, p. 118.

34. ibid., No. 81, pp. 97–8.

35. George Ensor, *On National Education*, 1811.

36. BM. Add. MS. 37496.

37. Miss Hitchener's correspondence is also published in Professor Jones's footnotes. *Letters*, I, No. 81, pp. 98–9 n. 5.

38. ibid., No. 81, p. 98.

39. ibid., No. 90, p. 116.

40. ibid., No. 86, p. 110.

41. ibid., No. 93, p. 119.

42. ibid., No. 92, p. 118.
43. ibid., No. 93, pp. 119–20.
44. ibid., No. 93, p. 120.
45. ibid., No. 101, p. 129.
46. *Letters*, I, No. 92, p. 118.
47. ibid., No. 95, p. 121.
48. ibid., No. 98, p. 123.
49. ibid.
50. ibid., No. 99, p. 125.
51. ibid., No. 99, p. 126.
52. ibid., No. 107, p. 136.
53. ibid., No. 101, p. 128.
54. ibid., No. 96, p. 122.
55. ibid., No. 100, p. 128.
56. ibid., No. 106, p. 134.
57. ibid., No. 114, p. 144.
58. ibid., No. 103, p. 131.
59. ibid., No. 105, p. 133.
60. See the legal brief supplied by Shelley's lawyer Wetherall, quoted in Dowden, op. cit., II, p. 83.
61. Dowden, op. cit., I, p. 172.
62. Blunden, op. cit., p. 69, taken from the Scottish marriage register.
63. Hogg, op. cit., I, p. 253.
64. ibid., p. 261.
65. ibid., p. 258.
66. ibid., p. 264.
67. *Letters*, I, No. 118, p. 151.
68. ibid., No. 110, p. 139.
69. ibid., No. 108, p. 138 n. 5.
70. ibid., No. 111, p. 140.
71. ibid., No. 112, p. 142.
72. ibid., No. 115, pp. 146–7.
73. ibid., No. 116, p. 147.
74. ibid., No. 117, p. 149.
75. Hogg, op. cit., I, p. 271.

Chapter 4   Harriet Westbrook

1. *Letters*, I, No. 114, pp. 144–5.
2. Miss Hitchener in *Letters*, I, No. 114, p. 145 n. 2.
3. *Letters*, I, No. 118, p. 149.
4. ibid., No. 118, p. 151.
5. ibid.

6. ibid., No. 119, p. 152.

7. John Hogg to Timothy Shelley, in *Letters*, I, No. 117, p. 148, n. 1.

8. *Letters*, I, No. 130, p. 165.

9. William Whitton to Sir Bysshe Shelley, in *Letters*, I, No. 130, p. 165 n. 1.

10. Timothy Shelley in *Letters*, I, No. 130, p. 165 n. 3.

11. *Letters*, I, No. 119, p. 152.

12. ibid., No. 127, p. 158.

13. Hogg, op. cit., I, p. 283.

14. *Letters*, I, No. 139, p. 182.

15. ibid.

16. ibid., No. 133, p. 171.

17. ibid., No. 140, p. 184.

18. ibid., No. 132, pp. 168–9.

19. ibid., No. 134, p. 172.

20. Pforzheimer, III, pp. 46–7. Previously Hogg's bowdlerized version has been printed in *Letters*, I, No. 137.

21. *Letters*, I, No. 138, p. 181.

22. ibid.

23. ibid., No. 141, p. 186.

24. ibid., No. 140, p. 185.

25. ibid., No. 136, p. 175.

26. ibid., No. 136, p. 176.

27. Quoted in Howard Mills, *Peacock: His Circle and His Age*, 1969, p. 71. Mr Mills has succeeded in locating the interesting original of Hogg's Floskyan distortion.

28. Thomas de Quincey, *Complete Works*, 1862, Vol. v, p. 20.

29. ibid., p. 10.

30. *Letters*, I, No. 146, p. 198.

31. ibid., No. 147, p. 199.

32. ibid., No. 149, p. 203.

33. ibid., No. 144, p. 196.

34. ibid., No. 144, pp. 193–4.

35. ibid., No. 144, p. 196.

36. E.P.Thompson, *The Making of the English Working Class*, p. 617. (I have used the revised (Penguin) edition of this magnificent social history, which provides the indispensable historical background to Shelley's career in England.)

37. ibid., p. 592.

38. *Letters*, I, No. 148, p. 200.

39. ibid., No. 148, p. 201.

40. ibid., No. 148, p. 202.

41. *Letters*, I, No. 155, p. 213.

42. ibid., No. 155, p. 214.

43. The letter of 4 January 1812 to Grosvenor Bedford: *Life and Correspondence of Robert Southey*, ed. C.C.Southey, 1850, III, p. 325.

44. Hogg, op. cit., I, p. 291.

45. *Letters*, I, No. 155, pp. 210–12.

46. Mary Moorman, *William Wordsworth; A biography*, 2 vols, II, p. 239, 1965.

47. *Letters*, I, No. 156, p. 215.

48. *Letters*, I, No. 156, p. 219 n. 10.

49. *Letters*, I, No. 156, p. 216.

50. ibid., No. 161, p. 233.

51. ibid., No. 160, p. 231.

52. ibid., No. 156, p. 218.

53. ibid., No. 157, pp. 219–21.

54. ibid., No. 159, pp. 221–8.

55. That is to say: *Letters*, I, No. 24, p. 21 (19 November 1810); No. 30, p. 27 (20 December 1810); and No. 41, p. 47 (16 January 1811).

56. See Ingpen, *Shelley in England*, pp. 307–8.

57. *Letters*, I, No. 160, p. 230.

58. ibid.

59. ibid.

60. ibid., No. 160, p. 231.

61. ibid.

62. Cameron, *Young Shelley: Genesis of a Radical*, p. 142. For a careful examination of Shelley's lively plagiarisms, see Peck, *Shelley: His Life and Work*, II, pp. 341–3.

63. *Poetical Works*, pp. 878–9.

64. *Esdaile Notebook*, ed. Cameron, p. 40.

65. *Letters*, I, No. 158, p. 223.

66. ibid., No. 161, p. 234.

67. *Esdaile*, p. 154.

68. ibid., p. 63.

69. *Letters*, I, No. 163, p. 243.

70. ibid., No. 150, p. 204.

71. ibid., No. 151, p. 205.

72. ibid., No. 152, pp. 205–6.

73. ibid., No. 152, p. 206.

74. ibid., No. 161, p. 232.

75. ibid., No. 162, p. 239.

76. *Cumberland Pacquet*, 28 January 1812, from the Carlisle Public Library Archive. Note: from Dowden down to Professor Jones's edition of *Letters*, this date had been consistently given as 28 January 1811. This error now stands corrected.

77. *Letters*, I, No. 162, p. 240.

78. ibid., No. 162, p. 240.

79. ibid., No. 162, p. 241.

80. ibid.

81. ibid., No. 164, p. 244.

82. ibid., No. 162, p. 240.

83. ibid., No. 162, p. 241.
84. ibid., No. 167, p. 252.
85. *Esdaile*, p. 43.
86. *Letters*, I, No. 164, p. 247.
87. ibid., No. 164, p. 246.
88. ibid., No. 164, p. 248.
89. ibid., No. 165, p. 249.
90. ibid., No. 165, p. 248.
91. ibid., No. 165, p. 249.

Chapter 5   *Irish Revolutionaries: 1812*

1. *Esdaile Notebook*, ed. Cameron, p. 203 n. 2.
2. ibid., p. 71.
3. *Letters*, I, No. 167, p. 255.
4. ibid., No. 168, p. 256.
5. ibid., No. 170, p. 258.
6. ibid., No. 172, p. 65. (Here, as elsewhere, Harriet has shared the letter to Miss Hitchener with Shelley.)
7. *Prose*, p. 39.
8. *Letters*, I, No. 172, p. 263.
9. *Prose*, p. 51.
10. ibid., p. 49.
11. *Letters*, I, No. 162, p. 239.
12. *Prose*, p. 55.
13. ibid.
14. William Godwin to Shelley, *Letters*, I, No. 173, p. 269 n. 6. The text of this letter comes from Hogg, op. cit.
15. William Godwin to Shelley, *Letters*, I, No. 170, p. 260, n. 8. An incomplete text, also from Hogg, op. cit.
16. *Letters*, I, No. 173, p. 267.
17. *Letters*, I, No. 172, pp. 264–5.
18. Denis Florence Mac Carthy, *Shelley's Early Life: From Original Sources*, London 1870, pp. 238–41. Mac Carthy was the first writer to examine Shelley's exploits in Dublin with any care. The two English agents were Michael Farrell, a 'chief constable', and Thomas Manning, who 'held an inferior position'.
19. *Letters*, I, No. 175, p. 275.
20. ibid., No. 172, p. 264.
21. ibid.
22. ibid., No. 173, p. 268.
23. ibid., No. 174, p. 271.
24. ibid.

25. Harriet Shelley in *Letters*, I, No. 176, p. 279 n. 5. The text comes from Mac Carthy, op. cit.

26. ibid., No. 178, p. 283 n. 8. (Harriet Shelley's letters were first collected in the Julian Edition, *The Complete Works of Shelley*, ed. Ingpen and Peck, 10 vols, 1926–30. However, Harriet's letters are also given in full by F.L. Jones in his footnotes to *Letters*, I, and since these are the most easily accessible to the general reader, I have listed my references accordingly.)

27. *Letters*, I, No. 175, p. 275.

28. Godwin to Shelley, *Letters*, I, No. 173, pp. 269–70, n. 6.

29. *Prose*, p. 62.

30. *Letters*, I, No. 176, pp. 276–7.

31. ibid., No. 176, p. 278.

32. ibid., No. 177, p. 280.

33. *Letters*, I, No. 178, p. 282.

34. ibid., No. 176, p. 279 n. 5.

35. ibid., No. 172, p. 264.

Chapter 6   A Radical Commune

1. Harriet to Mrs Nugent, *Letters*, I, No. 178, p. 284 n. 8.

2. ibid., p. 281.

3. *Esdaile Notebook*, ed. Cameron, p. 105.

4. *Letters*, I, No. 190, p. 301.

5. ibid., No. 181, p. 287.

6. ibid., No. 190, p. 301.

7. ibid., No. 187, p. 296.

8. ibid., No. 178, p. 282.

9. ibid., No. 187, p. 297.

10. Harriet to Mrs Nugent, *Letters*, I, No. 192, p. 305 n. 1.

11. *Letters*, I, No. 181, p. 287.

12. ibid., No. 178, p. 283.

13. ibid., No. 180, p. 285.

14. ibid., No. 192, p. 305 n. 1.

15. Mac Carthy, *Shelley's Early Life*, p. 310.

16. ibid., p. 321.

17. ibid., p. 313.

18. *Prose*, pp. 70–2.

19. *Letters*, I, No. 178, p. 281.

20. ibid., No. 190, p. 302.

21. ibid., No. 186, p. 295.

22. ibid., No. 182, p. 288.

23. ibid., No. 184, pp. 290–1.

24. ibid., No. 185, p. 292.

25. ibid., No. 186, p. 294.

26. ibid., No. 186, pp. 294–5.

27. ibid., No. 186, p. 296.

28. Medwin to Shelley, *Letters*, I, No. 188a n. 1.

29. Harriet to Mrs Nugent, *Letters*, I, No. 192, p. 305 n. 1.

30. *Letters*, I, No. 191, pp. 302–3.

31. ibid., No. 192, p. 304.

32. *Letters*, I, No. 193, p. 306.

33. *Examiner*, 31 May 1812.

34. *Letters*, I, No. 194, p. 307.

35. ibid., No. 195, p. 308.

36. ibid., No. 195, p. 309.

37. ibid., No. 196, p. 311.

38. Harriet Shelley to Mrs Nugent, *Letters*, I, No. 195, pp. 309–10 n. 2.

39. The Home Office papers and policing instructions were first examined and published in full by William Rossetti in the *Fortnightly Review*, January 1871, p. 79.

40. *Letters*, I, No. 199, p. 319.

41. ibid., No. 196, p. 311.

42. Godwin to Shelley, *Letters*, I, No. 197, p. 313 n. 1.

43. Rossetti, op. cit., p. 78.

44. Harriet to Mrs Nugent, *Letters*, I, No. 199, p. 321 no. 6.

45. Rossetti, op. cit., p. 79.

46. *Esdaile*, p. 89.

47. *Letters*, I, No. 197, p. 314.

48. Harriet to Mrs Nugent, *Letters*, I, No. 199, p. 320 n. 6.

49. *Letters*, I, No. 198, p. 318.

50. *Letters*, II, No. 501, p. 99. To Peacock, June 1819.

51. *Letters*, I, No. 198, p. 316.

52. ibid., No. 198, p. 318.

53. ibid., No. 199, p. 319.

54. ibid., No. 201, p. 323.

55. ibid.

56. *Prose*, p. 74.

57. T. B. Howell, *A Complete Collection of State Trials*, 1823, XXI, pp. 928–9.

58. *Prose*, p. 76.

59. ibid., p. 80.

60. ibid.

61. *Letters*, I, No. 199, p. 319.

62. ibid., No. 202, p. 324.

63. ibid.

64. ibid., No. 170, p. 259.

65. ibid., No. 200, p. 321.

66. ibid.

67. *Letters*, I, No. 200, p. 322.

68. ibid., No. 202, p. 324.

69. Rossetti, op. cit., p. 68.

70. ibid.

71. ibid., p. 78.

72. ibid.

73. ibid., p. 77.

74. ibid., p. 78.

75. ibid., p. 80.

76. See Godwin's cheerful letter to Mrs Godwin, *Letters*, I, No. 202, p. 326 n. 8. Godwin, as usual, only had half the story.

77. ibid.

78. ibid.

Chapter 7   *The Tan-yr-allt Affair*

1. See the picturesque engraving in Elizabeth Beazley, *Madocks and the Wonder of Wales*, 1967, opposite p. 177. The village square has barely changed over the intervening 160 years, except for the parking lines. It is a minor Mecca for architectural students from the north-western universities, which would have pleased Madocks.

2. *North Wales Gazette*, 1 October 1812, from the archives of the University of North Wales at Bangor.

3. J.Girdlestone to John Williams, 17 September 1812. Breese, Jones and Casson; Box 168, letter 146, from County Record Office, Caernarvon.

4. *Letters*, I, No. 205, p. 328.

5. Harriet to Mrs Nugent, *Letters*, I, No. 202, p. 327 n. 8.

6. *An Inquiry Concerning Political Justice*, ed. K.C.Carter, 1971. His text is from the third edition, 1798. Book III, Chapter 6, p. 120.

7. Harriet to Mrs Nugent, *Letters*, I, No. 202, p. 327 n. 8.

8. William Hazlitt, *The Spirit of the Age*, 1824–5; essay on 'William Godwin'.

9. *Letters*, I, No. 213, p. 338. To Fanny Godwin, 10 December 1812. This letter has some curious passages, in which one can sense that Fanny too was undergoing the Shelley treatment. For example, 'I am one of those formidable & longclawed animals called a *Man*, & it is not until I have assured you that I am one of the most inoffensive of my species, that I live on vegetable food, & never bit since I was born that I venture to intrude myself on your attention.' The letter deserves reading in full.

10. See *Claire*, p. 19 n. 20. One of William's lectures was on 'The Influence of Governments on the Character of People'.

11. ibid., pp. 16–18.

12. Harriet to Mrs Nugent, *Letters*, I, No. 202, p. 327 n. 8.

13. *Claire*, p. 15.

14. Harriet to Mrs Nugent, *Letters*, I, No. 202, p. 327 n. 8. This is one of Professor Jones's admirable and epic footnotes of 97 lines length.

15. Dowden, op. cit., I, p. 304.

16. *Letters*, I, No. 206, p. 330.

17. ibid.

18. Hogg, op. cit., I, pp. 364–5.

19. ibid., p. 172.

20. *Letters*, I, No. 210, p. 334.

21. Cameron, *Young Shelley: Genesis of a Radical*, p. 366 n. 61.

22. ibid.

23. *Letters*, I, No. 211, p. 336.

24. Harriet to Mrs Nugent, *Letters*, I, No. 207, p. 331 n. 3.

25. *Esdaile Notebook*, ed. Cameron, pp. 53–5.

26. *Letters*, I, No. 223, p. 352.

27. ibid., No. 210, p. 333.

Chapter 8   One Dark Night

1. *Letters*, I, No. 214, p. 339.

2. Beazley, *Madocks and the Wonder of Wales*, p. 197.

3. ibid., p. 181.

4. Robert Leeson in Beazley, p. 181.

5. See H.M.Dowling, 'The Attack at Tanyrallt', in *Keats–Shelley Memorial Bulletin*, 1961.

6. See the hitherto unpublished typescript 'The Miltown Leesons', 1963; BM. CUP. 504. E.15.

7. Breese, Jones and Casson papers, Box. 168, letter 148, from County Record Office, Caernarvon.

8. Harriet to Hookham, *Letters*, I, No. 225, p. 356 n. 2 (12 March, 1813).

9. Beazley, op. cit.

10. Dowling, op. cit.

11. *Letters*, I, No. 215, p. 339.

12. *Poetical Works*, p. 832.

13. ibid.

14. *Letters*, I, No. 211, p. 336.

15. ibid., No. 216, p. 340.

16. Godwin to Shelley, *Letters*, I, No. 216, p. 341 n. 3 (10 December 1812).

17. ibid.

18. See booklists in *Letters*, I, No. 216, No. 217, and No. 218 (17 to 24 December 1812).

19. *Letters*, I, No. 221, p. 349.

20. ibid., No. 222, p. 350.

21. *Letters*, I, No. 220, p. 348.

22. ibid. (In fact twelve degrees below freezing.)

23. ibid., No. 223, p. 352.

24. Harriet to Mrs Nugent, *Letters*, I, No. 221, p. 349 n. 2.

25. *Letters*, I, No. 223, p. 351.
26. ibid.
27. ibid.
28. ibid., No. 224, p. 354.
29. ibid., No. 211, p. 335.
30. Harriet to Mrs Nugent, *Letters*, I, No. 221, p. 350 n. 2.
31. *Letters*, I, No. 219, p. 347.
32. ibid., No. 223, p. 353.
33. Breese, Jones and Casson papers; Box 168, letter 151, from County Record Office, Caernarvon.
34. Harriet to Hookham, *Letters*, I, No. 223, p. 351 n. 2.
35. Leeson's letter to Shelley is in *Letters*, I, No. 227, pp. 357–8 n. 2.
36. Harriet to Hookham, *Letters*, I, No. 225, pp. 355–6 n. 2.
37. *Letters*, I, No. 219, p. 346.
38. ibid., No. 224, p. 353.
39. ibid.
40. *North Wales Gazette*, 5 March 1813.
41. Harriet to Hookham, *Letters*, I, No. 225, p. 355 n. 2. This letter is henceforth referred to as 'Harriet's account, March 1813'.
42. Thornton Hunt, 'Shelley, by One Who Knew Him', *Atlantic Monthly*, February 1863.
43. *Letters*, I, No. 225, p. 355.
44. ibid. (Harriet's postscript.)
45. Leeson to Shelley, *Letters*, I, No. 227, p. 358 n. 2.
46. *Letters*, I, No. 228, p. 359.
47. ibid., No. 230, p. 361.
48. Hogg, op. cit., I, p. 389.
49. Harriet's account, Dublin, 2 March 1813, *Letters*, I, No. 225, pp. 355–6 n. 2.
50. Hogg, op. cit., I, p. 388.
51. Peacock, p. 36.
52. Hogg, I, p. 388.
53. Hogg, I, p. 389.
54. *Peacock: Memoirs, Essays and Reviews*, pp. 36–7.
55. *Letters*, I, No. 228, p. 359.
56. Breese, Jones and Casson papers; Box 168, letter 332, from County Record Office, Caernarvon. (In the manuscript, Madocks has inserted his comments on the motives for the attack on Shelley, as an afterthought, between the lines.)
57. Medwin, *The Life of Percy Bysshe Shelley*, p. 117.
58. Medwin, op. cit., p. 116.
59. Lady Jane Shelley, p. 56.
60. Breese, Jones and Casson papers; Box 168, letter 152 (April 1813), from County Record Office, Caernarvon.

Chapter 9   *A Poem and a Wife:* Queen Mab *1813*

1. *Letters*, I, No. 233, p. 364.

2. ibid.

3. Harriet to Mrs Nugent, *Letters*, I, No. 236, p. 368 n. 3.

4. *Letters*, I, No. 234, p. 365.

5. Harriet to Mrs Nugent, *Letters*, I, No. 236, p. 367 n. 3.

6. ibid., p. 368.

7. *Letters*, I, No. 223, p. 352.

8. See the excellent appendix in White, *Shelley*, II, p. 408. Also Cameron, *Young Shelley: Genesis of a Radical*, pp. 273–4.

9. *Poetical Works*, p. 777.

10. ibid., p. 773.

11. ibid., p. 778.

12. ibid., p. 801.

13. ibid., p. 763.

14. ibid., p. 782.

15. This celebrated note on Free Love is in *Poetical Works*, p. 806–8; and *Prose*, pp. 115–17.

16. ibid., p. 793.

17. ibid., p. 794.

18. ibid., pp. 797–8.

19. *Pen Portraits and Reviews*, George Bernard Shaw, Constable, 1932. 'Shaming the Devil about Shelley', (1892), pp. 236–46.

20. *Republican*, 27 December 1822. This and other contemporary newspaper articles and magazine reviews are usefully collected in *The Unextinguished Hearth*, ed. Newman Ivey White, New York, Octagon Books Inc., 1966, p. 97.

21. *The Unextinguished Hearth*, pp. 96–7.

22. H.B.Forman, *The Vicissitudes of Queen Mab*, 1887. 'Baldwin' was probably Benbow himself: see BM 11644. e. 2. (i-2).

23. ibid. For the 1832 edition, see BM 11660. a. 14. For the Chartist copies, see (1839) BM 11642. a. 70; and (1847) BM 11644. eee. 73.

24. Cameron, op. cit., p. 274.

25. Ernest Rose, *Journal of English and Germanic Philology*, XXVI, 1927.

26. *The Unextinguished Hearth*, p. 98.

27. *A Reply ... to Queen Mab*, published by William Clark, July 1821. See *The Unextinguished Hearth*, pp. 62–95.

28. E.S.Boas, *Modern Language Notes*, LXX, 1955.

29. Forman, op. cit.

30. Edward Williams, 'Journal' for Sunday, 30 June 1822; in *Maria Gisborne and Edward E.Williams: Their Journals and Letters*, ed. F.L.Jones, 1951, p. 156.

31. *Poetical Works*, pp. 794–5.

32. Harriet to Mrs Nugent, *Letters*, I, No. 236, p. 367 n. 3.

33. ibid.

34. *Letters*, I, No. 236, pp. 366–7.

35. Timothy Shelley in *Letters*, I, No. 236, p. 368 n. 4.

36. *Letters*, I, No. 237, pp. 368–9.

37. Harriet to Mrs Nugent in *Letters*, I, No. 242, p. 372 n. 1.

38. *Letters*, I, No. 238, p. 369 n. 1.

39. ibid., No. 243, pp. 372–3.

40. Breese, Jones and Casson papers; Box 168, letter 165. David Ellis-Nanney to John Williams, 20 June 1815; from County Record Office, Caernarvon.

41. ibid.

42. Hogg, *The Life of Percy Bysshe Shelley*, II, p. 5.

43. ibid., p. 3.

44. *Letters*, I, No. 239, p. 370.

45. ibid., No. 245, p. 374.

46. ibid., No. 247, p. 375.

47. Hogg quoted in *Peacock: Memoirs, Essays and Reviews*, p. 37.

48. *Peacock*, p. 37.

49. Harriet to Mrs Nugent, *Letters*, I, No. 248, p. 377 n. 2. (From High Elms, 8 August 1813.)

50. *Peacock*, p. 38.

51. Hogg, op. cit., II, p. 39.

52. Harriet to Mrs Nugent, *Letters*, I, No. 248, p. 377 n. 2. (From High Elms, 10 September 1813.)

53. ibid.

54. *Letters*, I, No. 249, p. 377.

55. Harriet to Mrs Nugent, *Letters*, I, No. 249, p. 378 n. 3. (From Ambleside, 11 October 1813.)

56. *Letters*, I, No. 250, p. 380.

57. ibid., No. 250, p. 381 n. 5.

58. *Prose*, pp. 91–2.

59. ibid., p. 94.

60. *Letters*, I, No. 250, p. 380.

61. ibid.

62. *Peacock*, p. 43.

63. Harriet to Mrs Nugent, *Letters*, I, No. 249, p. 379 n. 3. (From Edinburgh, 23 November 1813.)

64. *Letters*, I, No. 250, pp. 379–80.

65. Godwin's 'Diary' yet remains unpublished, but extracts appear in Dowden, *The Life of Percy Bysshe Shelley*. White, op. cit., and Professor Jones's footnotes in *Letters*. *Letters*, I, No. 252, p. 382 n. 2.

66. Godwin's letters to Shelley between December 1813 and April 1814 are listed in *Letters*, I, No. 255, p. 386 n. 1.

67. *Letters*, I, No. 253, p. 385.

68. Hogg, op. cit., II, p. 134.

69. ibid., pp. 143-4.

70. *Letters*, I, No. 252, p. 382.

71. See *Letters*, I, No. 255, p. 386.

72. Godwin's 'Diary' in *Letters*, I, No. 257B, p. 388 n. 2.

73. *Letters*, I, No. 258, p. 390.

74. Hogg, op. cit., I, pp. 337-8.

75. *Letters*, I, No. 253, p. 384.

76. *Claire*, pp. 60-3.

77. *Letters*, I, No. 265, p. 402.

78. ibid.

79. Hogg, op. cit., II, p. 154.

80. *Letters*, I, No. 255 (probably 14 April 1814); No. 257 (14 May, 1814).

81. *Letters*, I, No. 257, p. 387.

82. ibid., No. 257A, pp. 387-8.

83. *Claire*, p. 431. The punctuation strokes are Jane's own: I think she was attempting to write a kind of poetic prose description, which expressed something of the intensity of her feelings for her stepsister.

84. *Poetical Works*, p. 522.

85. For a preliminary discussion of Mary's fictional portraits of Shelley, see Peck, 'The Biographical Element in the Novels of Mary Shelley', in *P.M.L.A.*, xxxvi, 1923.

86. R.Glynn Grylls, *Claire Clairmont*, John Murray, 1939, p. 15.

87. Godwin to John Taylor, *Letters*, I, No. 258, p. 391, n. 3.

88. Godwin's 'Diary' in *Letters*, I, No. 256, p. 386, n. 1. The entry reads, 'M. . . . fr Nash, fin.'

89. ibid., *Letters*, I, No. 257B, p. 388 n. 1.

90. *Peacock*, p. 54.

91. *Letters*, I, No. 258, pp. 389-90.

92. Quoted in *Claire*, p. 22, from the original entry in Mary's journal, Abinger MSS.

Chapter 10   Three for the Road: Europe 1814

1. All quotations in this chapter, unless otherwise stated, are from the journal kept by Mary and Shelley together during the tour, and published in the inappropriately named *Mary Shelley's Journal*, ed. F.L.Jones, 1947. It is important to note that this edition is not taken directly from the original MS Journal now in the Abinger MSS collection, and since 1952 on microfilm at the Bodleian Library, Oxford, and the Duke University Library, North Carolina. In particular, Professor Jones's allocations of sections either to Mary or Shelley is unreliable; and occasional interesting phrases and remarks of a personal nature are missing. I have incorporated the MS rather than the published readings into my text wherever suitable. Some of the MS readings are given in M.K.Stocking's excellent footnotes in *Claire*, to which I have not hesitated to refer.

2. *Claire*, 27 August 1814, p. 31.

3. *Claire*, p. 442. Mary Shelley's whole review, 'The English in Italy' of October 1826, printed in Appendix A.

4. Abinger MS reading of the *Journal* for 12 August 1814, quoted in Stocking, p. 22.

5. *Letters*, I, No. 259, p. 392.

6. Harriet to Mrs Nugent, 25 August 1814. *Letters*, I, No. 259, p. 393 n. 5.

7. *Letters*, I, No. 259, p. 392.

8. *Claire*, August 15, 1814, p. 22.

9. ibid., 17 August, p. 26.

10. Pforzheimer III, p. 350. The Pforzheimer library's MS of Jane's (Claire's) journal is a later and revised one, separate from B.M. Ashley MS, which Marion Stocking has used.

11. *Claire*, 18 August, p. 26.

12. ibid., 19 August, p. 27.

13. *Prose*, pp. 146–7.

14. *Claire*, p. 29.

15. ibid., 24 August, p. 30.

16. In Mary's published *History of a Six Weeks Tour*, 1817.

17. *Prose*, p. 149.

18. ibid., p. 148.

19. ibid., p. 150.

20. *Claire*, 27 August, p. 31.

21. *Journal*, 27 August, p. 12.

22. *Claire*, 27 August, p. 31.

23. *The Prose Works of Percy Bysshe Shelley*, H.B.Forman (ed.), 1880. 'History of a Six Weeks Tour', (1817); Vol. II, p. 145.

24. *Claire*, 4 September, p. 36.

25. ibid.

Chapter 11   *Bad Dreams: Kentish Town 1814*

1. *Claire*, p. 43.

2. *Letters*, I, No. 261, p. 395.

3. *Journal*, p. 15.

4. *Claire*, p. 44.

5. *Letters*, I, No. 260, p. 395.

6. ibid., No. 261, p. 396.

7. ibid., No. 262, p. 397.

8. ibid., No. 263, p. 399.

9. *Journal*, p. 17.

10. *Letters*, I, No. 264, pp. 399–400.

11. ibid., No. 266, p. 405.

12. ibid., No. 265, pp. 401–3.

13. *Claire*, p. 48.

14. *Journal*, p. 17.

15. This section of the entry is taken directly from the Abinger MS. In the printed version, by the simple effect of miscopied punctuation, Professor Jones's text alters the total implication of the whole passage, by assigning the strange facial expression to Jane, and the fearful reaction to Shelley, thus: 'Did you ever read the tragedy of Orra?' said Shelley. 'Yes.' 'How horrible you look – take your eyes off.' This effectively reverses the roles. See Chapter 10, Ref. 1.

16. *Claire*, pp. 48–9.

17. *Journal*, pp. 18–19.

18. ibid., p. 20.

19. *Claire*, p. 52.

20. ibid., p. 49.

21. *Poetical Works*, p. 16.

22. *Claire*, p. 51.

23. *Journal*, p. 21.

24. ibid.

25. ibid., p. 20.

26. *Claire*, p. 53.

27. *Letters*, I, No. 273, pp. 412–13.

28. ibid., No. 280, p. 420.

29. ibid., No. 270, p. 410.

30. ibid., No. 271, p. 411.

31. *Journal*, p. 24.

32. *Letters*, I, No. 270, p. 410.

33. *Mary*, No. 4, p. 5.

34. *Claire*, p. 54.

35. ibid., p. 58.

36. ibid., p. 59.

37. *Mary*, No. 4, p. 6.

38. ibid., No. 274, p. 414.

39. 'Epipsychidion', *Poetical Works*, p. 418.

40. *Journal*, p. 25.

41. Dowden, *The Life of Percy Bysshe Shelley*, II, Appendix A, Mrs Godwin to Lady Mountcashell, p. 547. Mrs Godwin also informs us that the prices Shelley was rumoured to have paid her husband were: Mary £800 and Claire £700.

42. Stocking in *Claire*, p. 3, gives an admirable summary of the history and vicissitudes of this MS.

43. *Journal*, pp. 25–6.

44. ibid., p. 29.

45. *Prose*, p. 304.

46. ibid., pp. 305–6.

47. *Letters*, I, No. 281, p. 421 n. 2.

48. *Journal*, p. 28.

49. *Letters*, I, No. 281, p. 422 n. 2.

50. *Poetical Works*, p. 526.

51. *Journal*, p. 32.

52. ibid., pp. 35-6.

53. These omissions are noted by F.L.Jones in his edition of the journal. The original suppressions were presumably carried out by Lady Jane Shelley before she handed the MS of the journal to Dowden for his official biography; Dowden's connivance is possible, but unlikely.

54. *Journal*, p. 40.

55. ibid., p. 40.

56. ibid., p. 35.

57. Mary to Hogg in *New Shelley Letters* ed. W.S.Scott, Golden Cockerel Press, 1948, p. 80.

58. *New Shelley Letters*, p. 81. *Letters*, I, No. 283, p. 423.

59. *New Shelley Letters*, p. 82.

60. ibid., p. 83.

61. *Letters*, I, No. 284, p. 424 n. 3.

62. *The Unextinguished Hearth*, pp. 46-52; and Louise B.Boas, 'Erasmus Perkins and Shelley', *Modern Language Notes*, LXX, June 1955.

63. *Journal*, p. 37.

64. *New Shelley Letters*, pp. 84-5.

65. *Journal*, p. 39.

66. 'Epipsychidion', *Poetical Works*, p. 413.

67. *Journal*, p. 42.

68. *New Shelley Letters*, p. 86.

69. ibid., p. 87.

70. *Letters*, I, No. 287, p. 426.

71. ibid., No. 310, pp. 439-40.

72. ibid., No. 314, p. 445.

Chapter 12   Up the River: Bishopsgate 1815

1. *Letters*, I, No. 290, p. 429.

2. *Mary*, No. 17, p. 8.

3. *Peacock, Memoirs, Essays and Reviews*, pp. 41-2.

4. *Poetical Works*, pp. 525-6.

5. *Letters*, I, No. 291, p. 429.

6. ibid., No. 291, p. 430.

7. Dowden, *The Life of Percy Bysshe Shelley*, I, p. 529.

8. ibid.

9. *Peacock*, p. 59.

10. *Crotchet Castle*, by T.L.Peacock, Ch. 10, in *Works*, 1875, Vol. II, p. 244.

11. *Prose*, p. 186.

12. *Poetical Works*, pp. 524-5.

13. Dowden, op. cit., I, p. 530.

14. *Prose*, p. 184.

15. ibid., p. 185.

16. ibid., pp. 193–4.

17. *Letters*, I, No. 294, p. 432.

18. *Peacock*, p. 60.

19. *Prose*, p. 172.

20. *Prose*, p. 174. See Arthur Koestler 'A Conference on Brain Function', paper given at UCLA, 1967, republished in *Drinkers of Infinity*, 1967.

21. *Prose*, p. 170.

22. *Poetical Works*, p. 25.

23. ibid., p. 26.

24. ibid., p. 28.

25. ibid., p. 20.

26. ibid., p. 21.

27. *Peacock*, p. 60.

28. *Poetical Works*, p. 18.

29. ibid., pp. 18–19.

30. *Prose*, p. 222.

31. But see Edward E. Bostetter, *Shelley and the Mutinous Flesh*, Texas Studies in Literature and Language, I, 1959.

32. *Poetical Works*, p. 30.

33. Godwin's Diary, in *Letters*, I, No. 299, p. 435 n. 1.

34. Peck, *Shelley: His Life and Work*, II, p. 436.

35. *Poetical Works*, pp. 725–6.

36. ibid., p. 731.

37. *The Unextinguished Hearth*, p. 105.

38. ibid., pp. 105–6.

39. ibid., pp. 107–8.

40. *Letters*, I, No. 373, p. 517.

41. ibid., No. 327, p. 462.

42. From the 'Journal of Maria Gisborne' in *Maria Gisborne and Edward E. Williams: their Journals and Letters* ed. F.L. Jones, University of Oklahoma Press, 1951, p. 39.

43. *Letters*, I, No. 310, p. 440.

44. ibid., No. 315, p. 447.

45. ibid., No. 319, p. 450.

46. ibid., No. 322, p. 453.

47. Ingpen, *Shelley in England*, p. 461.

48. *Letters*, I, No. 324, p. 459.

49. ibid., No. 326, p. 460.

50. Godwin's Diary in *Letters*, I, No. 334, p. 465 n. 2.

51. Marchand, *Byron: a Biography* Vol. II, p. 590.

52. ibid., p. 591.

53. Murray MSS.
54. ibid.
55. ibid.

Chapter 13   *The Byron Summer: Switzerland 1816*

1. Murray MSS.
2. ibid.
3. ibid.
4. Ingpen, *Shelley in England*, pp. 460–2.
5. *Letters*, I, No. 346, p. 471.
6. See *Letters*, I, No. 365.
7. *Letters*, I, No. 344, p. 470.
8. ibid., No. 346, p. 473.
9. *Mary*, No. 18, p. 9.
10. Murray MSS.
11. *Mary*, No. 18, p. 10.
12. *History of a Six Weeks Tour* (1817).
13. *Letters*, I, No. 348, p. 475.
14. Mary Shelley, *Frankenstein or the Modern Prometheus*, 1817, Signet Classic, 1965, Ch. 22, pp. 183–4.
15. *Letters*, I, No. 348, p. 475. No. private journal of Mary's survived for this year until the end of July. Claire's diary for the whole of 1816 is also lost.
16. *Maria Gisborne and Edward E. Williams: their Journals and Letters*, F.L. Jones (ed.), p. 122.
17. R. Glynn Grylls (Lady Mander), *Claire Clairmont*, 1939, p. 64.
18. *The Diary of William Polidori*, ed. W. Rossetti, 1911. Entry for 27 May, 1815.
19. Marchand, *Byron: A Biography*, Vol. II, p. 627.
20. *Polidori*, 1–5 June 1816.
21. ibid.
22. *Frankenstein*, p. x.
23. *Polidori*, 18th June, 1816.
24. *The Works of Lord Byron: Letters and Journals*, Rowland E. Prothero (ed.), John Murray, 1898–1901. Vol. IV, p. 297.
25. *Frankenstein*, p. x–xi.
26. ibid., Ch. 2.
27. ibid., Ch. 7.
28. ibid., Ch. 10.
29. ibid., Ch. 20.
30. ibid., Ch. 15.
31. ibid., Ch. 18.
32. ibid., Ch. 22.
33. ibid., Ch. 23.

34. ibid., Ch. 5, p. 57.

35. ibid., Ch. 10, pp. 95–6.

36. *Prose*, pp. 307–8.

37. *Letters*, I, No. 353, pp. 480–8.

38. Thomas Moore, *A Life of Byron*, 1844, p. 320.

39. *Letters*, I, No. 354, p. 490.

40. *Journal*, p. 51.

41. ibid., p. 52.

42. *Letters*, I, No. 358, p. 497.

43. ibid., No. 358, p. 499.

44. *Poetical Works*, p. 533.

45. ibid., p. 535.

46. Marchand, op. cit., II, p. 647.

47. *On Shelley*, Edmund Blunden *et al.*, Oxford, 1938. 'The Atheist: an Incident at Chamonix', Gavin de Beer, pp. 43–54.

48. ibid.

49. *Letters*, I, No. 358, pp. 501–2.

50. *Journal*, p. 55.

51. *Letters*, II, No. 652, pp. 328–9.

52. Marchand, op. cit., II, p. 634. See also Murray MSS for a further undated fragment: 'Everything is so awkward. We go so soon. Dearest pray come and see us, pray do. Goodbye. I cannot find a wafer S[helley] says he won't look at my note so don't be offended Goodbye dearest. Pray come and see us.'

53. *Journal*, p. 61.

54. *Letters*, I, No. 361, p. 504.

55. Ibid., No. 363, p. 508.

Chapter 14   The Suicides: London 1816

1. *Poetical Works*, p. 546.

2. *Journal*, p. 69.

3. *Edinburgh Review*, XXVIII, 1816.

4. *Letters*, I, No. 370, p. 513.

5. Peck, *Shelley: His Life and Work*, II, p. 437.

6. *Letters*, I, No. 373, p. 516.

7. ibid., p. 518.

8. ibid., p. 517.

9. *Mary*, No. 20, p. 14.

10. *Letters*, I, No. 374, p. 520.

11. ibid., p. 521.

12. ibid., p. 520 n. 1.

13. ibid., No. 376, pp. 522–3.

14. *Letters*, I, No. 378, pp. 524–5.

15. Claire to Trelawney in a long letter dated 30 August to 21 September 1878. Pforzheimer, Vol. IV, pp. 787–8.

16. *Letters*, I, No. 381, p. 530.

17. *Peacock: Memoirs, Letters and Reviews*, pp. 88–9.

18. *Poetical Works*, p. 418.

19. A.H.Beaven, *J. & H.Smith*, 1899, pp. 136ff.

20. *The Diary of Benjamin Robert Haydon* ed. W.B.Pope, 1960, Vol. II, 23 January 1817.

21. *Peter Bell the Third, Poetical Works*, p. 359. Shelley's own footnote reads: 'See [Wordsworth's] description of the beautiful colours produced during the agonizing death of a number of trout . . . [*The Excursion*] contains curious evidence of the gradual hardening of a strong but circumscribed sensibility, of the perversion of a penetrating but panic-stricken understanding.'

22. *Haydon*, op. cit., 5 August 1822.

23. *The Autobiography of Benjamin Robert Haydon*, 1846.

24. John Keats to Leigh Hunt, 10 May 1817. *Letters of John Keats*, Robert Gittings (ed.), Oxford, 1970, p. 11.

25. John Keats to Benjamin Bailey, 8 October 1817. Gittings, op. cit., p. 27.

26. John Keats to George and Tom Keats, 23 January 1818. Gittings, op. cit., p. 56.

27. *The Collected Works of William Hazlitt*, A.B.Waller (ed.), Dent, 1903. 'On Paradox and Commonplace', Vol. VI, pp. 48–9.

28. Thornton Hunt in *Atlantic Monthly*, February 1863.

29. R.J.White, *Waterloo to Peterloo*, 1957, pp. 160–1.

30. *Mary*, No. 24, pp. 22–4.

31. This description of Cashman's execution was assembled from three contemporary newspaper reports by E.P.Thompson, *The Making of the English Working Class*, p. 664.

32. Samuel Bamford, *Passages in the Life of a Radical*, 1841.

33. *Prose*, pp. 161–2.

34. H.B.Forman, *The Vicissitudes of Queen Mab*, 1887.

Chapter 15   The Garden Days: Marlow 1817

1. Thornton Hunt in *Atlantic Monthly*, February 1863.

2. *Mary*, No. 28, p. 24.

3. *Letters*, I, No. 395, pp. 539–40.

4. Bod. MSS. Shelley Adds. e. 10.

5. *Poetical Works*, p. 551.

6. *Letters*, I, No. 398, pp. 542–3.

7. *Poetical Works*, p. 539.

8. Bod. MSS. Shelley e. 4. *Poetical Works*, p. 549.

9. *Letters*, I, No. 399, p. 543.

10. Elizabeth Kent, *Flora Domestica*, 1831, p. xix.

11. Mary's Note in *Poetical Works*, p. 157.

12. Dowden, *The Life of Percy Bysshe Shelley*, II, pp. 123–4. Dowden's information was

collected verbatim from Polly Rose in old age, and I have used it selectively, leaving out the more obvious Victorian filigree about Shelley's 'eyes like a deer', etc.

13. Miss Rose in a letter to Lady Shelley, Dowden, op. cit., II, p. 120.

14. ibid.

15. Dowden, op. cit., II, p. 123.

16. A.H.Beaven, *J. & H.Smith*, 1899, p. 171.

17. *Letters*, I, No. 405, p. 551.

18. *The Novels of Thomas Love Peacock*, David Garnett (ed.), 1970, Vol. 1, *Nightmare Abbey*, Ch. 2.

19. ibid.

20. *Letters*, II, No. 501, p. 98.

21. David Garnett (ed.), op. cit., *Nightmare Abbey*, Ch. 10.

22. *Letters*, I, No. 409, p. 553.

23. *Mary*, No. 44, p. 42.

24. *Letters*, I, No. 411, p. 557.

25. *Poetical Works*, p. 37.

26. *Letters*, I, No. 411, p. 557.

27. *Mary*, No. 35, p. 33.

28. *Mary*, No. 35, pp. 33–4.

29. ibid., No. 37, p. 37.

30. *Letters*, I, No. 415, pp. 560–1.

31. *Mary*, No. 39, p. 41

32. Ingpen, *Shelley in England*, pp. 523–6.

33. *Poetical Works*, pp. 178–9.

34. *Letters*, I, No. 417, p. 564.

35. *Poetical Works*, p. 886.

36. *Journal*, p. 85.

37. *Poetical Works*, pp. 34–5.

38. ibid., p. 32.

39. ibid., pp. 33–4.

40. *The Diary of Henry Crabbe Robinson*, ed. Thomas Sadler, 1869, Vol. II, pp. 67–8.

41. E.P.Thompson, *The Making of the English Working Class*, p. 727.

42. The Hammonds quoted in E.P.Thompson, op. cit., p. 730.

43. *Letters*, I, No. 420, p. 566.

44. *Prose*, p. 168.

45. ibid., p. 167.

46. ibid., pp. 166–7.

47. ibid., pp. 168–9.

48. *Letters*, I, No. 431, p. 575 n. 2.

49. *Letters*, I, No. 439, p. 586, n. 1.

50. ibid., No. 441, pp. 587–8.

51. ibid., No. 423, p. 568.

52. ibid., No. 426, p. 569.

53. ibid., No. 427, p. 571.

54. ibid., No. 432, pp. 577-8.

55. ibid., No. 433, pp. 579-80.

56. *Journal*, p. 87.

57. *Letters*, I, No. 435, p. 582.

58. *Peacock: Memoirs, Letters and Reviews*, p. 89.

59. *Letters*, I, No. 436, p. 584.

60. ibid., No. 429, pp. 572-3.

61. Bod. MS Shelley Adds. e. 19. There is also an earlier reference in the MS to 'William Godwin'; unlike the rest of the poem which appears in a separate notebook the first two cantos are written neatly in ink; Shelley later used much of the historical material as the basis for his 'Ode to Liberty' of 1820.

62. The poem is printed in *Poetical Works*, pp. 31-156, *Revolt of Islam* II, stanza 23.

63. ibid., II, stanza 43.

64. ibid., V, stanza 53.

65. ibid., VI, stanzas 16-17.

66. ibid., VI, stanzas 33-6; 38.

67. ibid., IX, stanzas 24-5.

68. ibid., X, stanzas 14-15.

69. ibid., X, stanzas 18-19.

70. ibid., X, stanzas 21-2.

71. *Poetical Works*, p. 887.

72. *The Revolt of Islam*, XII, stanza 5.

73. ibid., XII, stanza 13.

74. *The Purgatory of Suicides*, Bk II, stanza 7 in Thomas Cooper, *Poetical Works*, 1877.

75. See Toller: *Transfiguration*, 1919, and *Masses and Man*, 1920; Also Kaiser's trilogy, *Gas*, 1919-20. Toller in fact wrote one play actually about the English Luddites of 1812, *Die Maschinenstürmer* (*The Machine Wreckers*).

76. *Letters*, I, No. 448, p. 593.

77. ibid., No. 450, p. 594.

78. ibid., No. 453, p. 596.

79. *The Unextinguished Hearth*, p. 123.

80. *The Unextinguished Hearth*, p. 125.

81. ibid.

82. ibid., p. 128.

83. *Journal*, p. 91.

84. *Letters*, I, No. 436, p. 584.

85. ibid., No. 436, ibid.

86. ibid., No. 429, p. 573.

87. *Poetical Works*, p. 161.

88. ibid.

89. *Claire*, p. 80.

90. *Letters*, I, No. 454, p. 598.

91. Edmund Blunden, *Shelley: A Life Story*, 1946, p. 173.
92. *Claire*, p. 83.
93. ibid., p. 85.
94. Hogg to J.F.Newton in *New Shelley Letters*, p. 107.
95. Dowden, op. cit., II, p. 182.
96. Mary to Hogg, 3 October 1824, *New Shelley Letters*, p. 151.
97. *Poetical Works*, p. 552.
98. ibid., p. 550. 'Ozymandias' was first published in Hunt's *Examiner*, January 1818.
99. See N.I.White, *Shelley*, I, pp. 743–4 (notes) for discussion of this complicated deal. The documents are confusing and Dowden, Ingpen, Peck and White all believe the loan was only £2,000. But to me this seems inadequate in the light of Shelley's debts by 1822.
100. *Letters*, I, No. 455, p. 597 n. 3.
101. ibid., No. 455, pp. 597–8 n. 3.
102. ibid., which gives Godwin's Diary for February 1818.
103. *Claire*, p. 86.
104. *Letters*, I, No. 457, p. 599.
105. *Claire*, p. 87.
106. *Letters*, II, No. 459, p. 2.

Chapter 16   *The Platonist: Bagni di Lucca 1818*

1. *Letters*, II, No. 460, p. 4.
2. *Journal*, p. 93.
3. ibid., p. 94.
4. ibid.
5. ibid., pp. 94–5.
6. *Claire*, p. 88.
7. Dowden, *The Life of Percy Bysshe Shelley*, II, p. 190n.
8. *Claire*, p. 88.
9. *Letters*, II, No. 460, p. 4.
10. *Claire*, p. 89 n. 46.
11. *Letters*, II, No. 462, pp. 7–8.
12. ibid.
13. *Claire*, pp. 90–1, n. 48.
14. ibid., p. 91.
15. *Letters* II, No. 462, p. 9.
16. ibid., No. 461, p. 5.
17. Marchand, *Byron: A Biography*, II, p. 731.
18. Neither of Byron's letters about Claire and Allegra are extant, but their contents can be clearly inferred from Shelley's replies.
19. *Letters*, II, No. 463, pp. 10–11.

20. Marchand, op. cit., II, p. 730.

21. ibid., p. 772.

22. *Letters*, II, No. 464, p. 12.

23. ibid., No. 465, p. 16.

24. ibid., No. 468, p. 18.

24. Dowden, op. cit., II, p. 205; and Mary, No. 51, p. 50.

26. *Poetical Works*, pp. 552–3.

27. *Mary*, No. 51, p. 52.

28. *Journal*, p. 98.

29. *Letters*, II, No. 468, p. 18.

30. *Poetical Works*, p. 559.

31. *Journal*, p. 98.

32. Bod. MS Shelley Adds. e. 13, p. 2.

33. *Mary*, No. 73, p. 77.

34. *Claire*, Appendix C, p. 469.

35. *Letters*, II, No. 472, p. 26.

36. Claire's Diary is not extant for the period July 1818 to February 1819. It commences again in Rome on Sunday 7 March 1819. The Diary for 'April 23 to June' is held in MS by the Carl H. Pforzheimer Library; but the present editor, Donald H. Reiman, has advised me in answer to an inquiry about the personal contents of entries during this period, 'once the MSS have been published in *Shelley & His Circle*, they will be available to qualified scholars upon approval of application. It may, however, be helpful to you to know in advance that the portion of Claire Clairmont's Journal that remains unpublished contains no such revealing personal sidelights as that which you mention.' (Reiman to Holmes, 8 November 1971.)

37. *Mary*, No. 53, pp. 54–5.

38. *Letters*, II, No. 472, p. 25.

39. ibid., No. 470, p. 20.

40. ibid., No. 472, p. 25.

41. ibid., No. 471, p. 22.

42. ibid., No. 472, p. 25.

43. ibid., No. 472, p. 27.

44. ibid., No. 475, p. 29.

45. *Journal*, pp. 101–3.

46. 'Shelley's Translations from the Greek' by Benjamin Farrington, in *Dublin Magazine*, III, 1928.

47. ibid.

48. See the discussion of Plato's standing in England during the early nineteenth century in James A.Notopoulos, *The Platonism of Shelley*, Duke University Press, 1949, pp. 375–401.

49. *Mary*, No. 54, p. 56.

50. *Letters*, II, No. 475, p. 29.

51. For example, H.B.Forman's edition of Shelley's prose in 4 volumes, 1880; and the

authoritative Julian edition of 1926-30. Even D.L.Clark's edition of the prose, 1954-67, does not print *The Banquet*.

52. Edward Carpenter, *The Psychology of the Poet Shelley*, 1925; and Herbert Read, *The True Voice of Feeling*, 1947.

53. Bod. MSS Shelley Adds. d. 8, printed by Sir John C.E.Shelley-Rolls, Bart., and Roger Ingpen as *Plato's Banquet, Translated from the Greek* . . ., 1931. Also Notopoulos, op. cit.

54. Notopoulos, op. cit., p. 402.

55. 'A Defence of Poetry', in *Prose*, p. 280.

56. Notopoulos, op. cit., p. 411.

57. ibid., pp. 411-12.

58. ibid., pp. 407-8.

59. ibid., p. 412.

60. ibid.

61. Mary's Note, in *Poetical Works*, pp. 158-9.

62. Notopoulos, p. 422.

63. ibid., pp. 429-30.

64. His remarks on Agathon are in Bod. MS Shelley Adds. e. 16.

65. ibid.

66. Notopoulos, op. cit., pp. 441-2.

Chapter 17   An Evening with Count Maddalo: Venice

1. *Journal*, p. 104.

2. From Claire's letter to Byron, printed in *To Lord Byron*, eds. G.Paston and P. Quennell, 1939, p. 237. It also seems that Elise was upset by some of Byron's remarks regarding Shelley, Claire and Allegra.

3. *Letters*, II, No. 479, pp. 34-5.

4. ibid., No. 479, pp. 35-6.

5. ibid.

6. ibid., pp. 36-7.

7. ibid., pp. 37-8.

8. *Letters*, II, No. 483, p. 43.

9. Mary's Note in *Poetical Works*, p. 204.

10. *Journal*, p. 105.

11. *Letters*, II, No. 480, p. 38.

12. ibid., No. 481, pp. 39-40.

13. *Mary*, No. 55, p. 58.

14. For an excellent feminist critique of Shelley's mishandling of his children, see Ursula Orange, 'Shuttlecocks of Genius' in *Keats-Shelley Memorial Bulletin*, No. 195.

15. Mary's Note in *Poetical Works*, p. 204.

16. *Letters*, II, No. 482, pp. 40-41.

17. 'Mathilda' is discussed in Mrs Julian Marshall's *Life and Letters of Mary Shelley*, and has been edited by Elizabeth Nitchie, *Mathilda*, Chapel Hill, 1959 from Abinger MSS reels 6–7.

18. *Journal*, p. 105.

19. ibid., pp. 106–9.

20. *Letters*, II, No. 484, p. 44.

21. ibid., No. 483, p. 43.

22. ibid., No. 488, p. 58.

23. *Poetical Works*, p. 191.

24. ibid., p. 189.

25. ibid., p. 190.

26. ibid.

27. ibid., p .192.

28. ibid., p. 193.

29. ibid.

30. ibid., p. 194.

31. ibid., p. 190.

32. ibid., p. 195.

33. ibid., p. 199.

34. ibid., p. 201.

35. ibid., p. 202.

36. ibid., p. 203.

37. *Posthumous Poems*, 1824.

38. *Letters*, II, No. 540, p. 164.

Chapter 18   *The Tombs of Naples: 1818*

1. *Letters*, II, No. 485, p. 45.

2. ibid., pp. 45–7.

3. ibid., p. 48.

4. *Letters*, II, No. 486, pp. 50–2.

5. *Letters*, II, No. 487, p. 56.

6. *Journal*, p. 111.

7. *Letters*, II, No. 488, p. 59.

8. *Journal*, p. 111.

9. *Prose*, p. 226.

10. ibid., p. 224.

11. *Mary*, No. 59, p. 60.

12. *Letters*, II, No. 488, p. 60.

13. *Mary*, No. 59, p. 59.

14. *Mary*, No. 128, p. 148. Her letter to Mrs Hoppner of 10 August 1821.

15. *Letters*, II, No. 488, p. 60.

16. ibid., p. 61.

17. *Journal*, p. 113.

18. *Letters*, II, No. 491, p. 73.

19. *Poetical Works*, p. 561.

20. ibid., p. 559; p. 570.

21. ibid., pp. 564–9.

22. ibid., pp. 570–1.

23. *Letters*, II, No. 488, p. 54.

24. ibid., No. 489, pp. 67–8.

25. ibid., No. 490, p. 69.

26. ibid., No. 575, p. 211. Shelley to the Gisbornes in London 7 July 1820. The last sentence is a compounded quotation from *King Lear*, Act IV, Scene 6, which has a specifically sexual reference.

27. See *Mary*, to Maria Gisborne, 18 June 1820, No. 96, p. 108; *Letters*, II, to Claire, 18 February 1821, No. 609, p. 267; also *Mary*, to Mrs Hoppner, 10 August 1821, No. 128, p. 128.

28. These 3 documents first discovered and printed by N.I.White, *Shelley*, II, Appendix VII, pp. 546–50, with translations. White, who must take all the credit for this brilliant piece of research, discusses the implications in Chapter 20, and draws conclusions with which I do not agree.

29. *Journal*, p. 114.

30. ibid., p. 116.

31. Abinger MS (reel 5); and printed without the moon in *Journal*, p. 134.

32. Hoppner to Byron, *Lord Byron's Correspondence*, John Murray (ed.). Murray, 1922, II, pp. 179–83 (1922); and *Claire*, pp. 277–9, who speaks of Elise with a Miss Fairhill in March 1822.

33. *Lord Byron: Selected Prose*, ed. Peter Gunn, 1972, p. 354.

34. *Lord Byron's Correspondence*, II, pp. 179–83.

35. *Lord Byron: Selected Prose*, p. 355.

36. *Letters*, II, No. 488, p. 62.

37. *Mary*, No. 128, p. 148.

38. *Mary*, No. 127, p. 147.

39. *Journal*, p. 114.

40. *Mary*, No. 128, p. 148.

41. ibid.

42. *Letters*, II, No. 491, p. 76.

43. ibid.

44. *Letters*, II, No. 571, p. 208.

45. *Letters*, II, No. 553, p. 175.

46. *Mary*, No. 128, p. 148.

47. *Claire*, p. 274–83, February and March, 1822.

48. *Letters*, II, No. 491, p. 75.

49. ibid., p. 71.

50. *Poetical Works*, pp. 571–2. In the penultimate line, I have adopted the Harvard MS

Notebook reading, and that of the first printing of 1832. The Oxford edition gives, 'and Hell be thy guide'. Within 1819, the poem cannot be assigned with any certainty, and may belong to the autumn; but certain images, verbal echoes of the Neapolitan letters, and the generality of the political attack, convince me that it belongs early in the year.

51. *Letters*, II, No. 491, p. 75.
52. Charles MacFarlane, *Reminiscences of a Literary Life*, 1917, pp. 1–12.
53. *Letters*, II, No. 492, p. 80.
54. MacFarlane, op. cit., p. 9.
55. Letters, II. No. 492, pp. 80–81.
56. *Mary*, No. 63, p. 62.
57. *Letters*, II, No. 495, p. 84.

Appendix to Chapter 18

1. The Carl H.Pforzheimer Library have not yet published or made available the original MSS of eleven of Shelley's letters to Claire in 1820–2, but they have all except one been printed by F.L.Jones in his authoritative *Letters*, from previous transcripts, and it is doubtful if anything material will appear. However, we will see. Refer also to Chapter 16, Reference 36.
2. *Poetical Works*, pp. 285–6.

Chapter 19   A Roman Spring: 1819

1. *Journal*, p. 117.
2. *Mary*, No. 64, p. 64.
3. Dowden, *Life of Percy Bysshe Shelley*, II, p. 255.
4. *Claire*, p. 103.
5. *Mary*, No. 64, p. 64.
6. *Letters*, II, No. 498, p. 93.
7. *Claire*, p. 101.
8. *Letters*, II, No. 495, p. 87.
9. *With Shelley in Italy*, ed. Anna McMahan, 1908, pp. 101–2 n. 1.
10. *Poetical Works*, p. 205.
11. *Letters*, II, No. 495, p. 84–5.
12. ibid., No. 498, p. 94.
13. *Poetical Works*, p. 205.
14. ibid.
15. ibid., p. 218.
16. ibid.
17. ibid., p. 233.
18. ibid., p. 207.
19. ibid., p. 206.

20. ibid., p. 208.
21. ibid., p. 211.
22. ibid., p. 212.
23. ibid., p. 220.
24. ibid., p. 225.
25. ibid., p. 227.
26. ibid., p. 228.
27. ibid., p. 228.
28. ibid., p. 236.
29. ibid., p. 238.
30. ibid., p. 236.
31. ibid., pp. 237-8.
32. *Letters*, II, No. 495, p. 86.
33. ibid., p. 89.
34. *Poetical Works*, p. 239.
35. ibid., p. 239.
36. For a brilliant analysis of this revolutionary-democratic imagery running through out Shelley's poetry of the 1817-1821 period, see G.M.Matthews, 'A Volcano's Voice in Shelley' (1957), printed in *Shelley: Modern Judgements*, ed. R.B.Woodings, 1968.
37. *Poetical Works*, p. 242.
38. ibid., p. 249.
39. ibid., p. 260.

Chapter 20   The Palace of the Dark

1. *Mary*, No. 65, pp. 66-7.
2. *Mary*, No. 67, pp. 69-70.
3. *Letters*, II, No. 513, p. 116.
4. ibid., No. 498, pp. 93-4.
5. *Claire*, p. 109.
6. ibid., p. 110.
7. Medwin, *The Life of Percy Bysshe Shelley*, pp. 239-40.
8. *Mary*, No. 97, p. 111.
9. ibid., No. 141, p. 175 n. 2.
10. Mary's Note in *Poetical Works*, p. 335.
11. Murray MS.
12. ibid.
13. *Claire*, p. 111.
14. *Letters*, II, No. 497, p. 91.
15. *Claire*, pp. 111-12.
16. Preface to *The Cenci, Poetical Works*, p. 277.
17. ibid.
18. ibid., p. 278.

19. ibid., p. 276.
20. ibid., p. 278.
21. *Claire*, p. 112.
22. *Journal*, p. 121.
23. *Letters*, II, No. 499, p. 95.
24. *Mary*, No. 69, p. 71.
25. ibid., No. 73, p. 76.
26. *Letters*, II, No. 500, p. 97.

Chapter 21   The Hothouse: Livorno 1819

1. *Letters*, II, No. 501, p. 98.
2. *Mary*, No. 71, p. 73.
3. ibid., No. 72, pp. 74–5.
4. Murray MS.
5. *Poetical Works*, p. 582. The final line was first printed from Bod. MS Shelley Adds.
e. 12. p. 179 (rev.) by Judith Chernaik, *The Lyrics of Shelley*, 1972, p. 247.
6. ibid., p. 581.
7. *Mary*, No. 73, p. 76.
8. Mary's Note to *The Cenci, Poetical Works*, p. 336.
9. *Letters*, II, No. 511, p. 114.
10. ibid., No. 502, p. 100.
11. ibid., No. 501, p. 99.
12. See Chapter 15 for Scythrop at large in Marlow.
13. *Letters*, II, No. 502, p. 100.
14. ibid., No. 504, p. 101 n. 2.
15. ibid., No. 505, p. 104.
16. *Poetical Works*, p. 295.
17. ibid., pp. 320–1.
18. ibid., p. 299.
19. Preface to *The Cenci, Poetical Works*, p. 277.
20. *Measure for Measure*, Act III, scene 1. An account of these and some of the other more glaring plagiarisms was thoughtfully drawn up by Dr Leavis in his essay on Shelley in *Revaluation*, 1936. But his remarks *en passant* on *The Mask of Anarchy*, and *Peter Bell the Third* form one of the very few pieces of good modern English literary criticism of Shelley.
21. *Poetical Works*, p. 332.
22. ibid., p. 337.
23. *Letters*, II, No. 504, pp. 102–3.
24. ibid., No. 506, p. 106.
25. ibid., No. 509, p. 110.
26. ibid., No. 508, p. 108.
27. *Journal*, p. 122.

28. See Mrs Julian Marshall, *Life and Letters of Mary Shelley*.

29. *Letters*, II, No. 508, p. 109.

30. *Mary*, No. 76, p. 83.

31. Maria Gisborne to Mary Shelley in *Maria Gisborne and Edward E. Williams: Their Journals and Letters*, F.L. Jones (ed.), p. 54.

32. *Letters*, II, No. 511, p. 114.

33. *Gisborne*, p. 53.

34. *Letters*, II, No. 510, p. 111.

35. ibid., No. 499, p. 96.

36. ibid., No. 514, p. 118.

37. ibid., No. 511, p. 114.

Chapter 22 The West Wind: Florence 1819

1. *Letters*, II, No. 511, p. 115.

2. ibid., No. 513, p. 117.

3. *Poetical Works*, p. 298.

4. R.J. White, *Waterloo to Peterloo*, p. 191.

5. Bamford, *Autobiography*, Chs. 24–5.

6. R.J. White, p. 192.

7. For an authoritative discussion of the Home Office papers, see E.P. Thompson, *The Making of the English Working Class*, p. 750 n. 1.

8. R.J. White, p. 194.

9. From an eye-witness in *Three Accounts of Peterloo*, ed. F.A. Brutton, 1921.

10. Bamford, op. cit., p. 157.

11. E.P. Thompson, op. cit., p. 754.

12. *Letters*, II, No. 514, p. 119.

13. *Poetical Works*, p. 338.

14. ibid.

15. ibid., pp. 338–9.

16. ibid., pp. 339–40.

17. ibid., p. 340.

18. ibid., p. 342.

19. ibid., p. 343.

20. ibid., p. 344.

21. ibid.

22. *Letters*, II, No. 515, p. 120.

23. *Journal*, p. 124.

24. Mary's Note in *Poetical Works*, p. 345.

25. *Mary*, No. 75, p. 80.

26. *Mary*, No. 75, p. 81.

27. *Letters*, II, No. 517, p. 123.

28. ibid., No. 517, p. 122.

29. W.H.Wickwar, *The Struggle for the Freedom of the Press 1819–1822*, 1928. The whole passage on Burdett's trial is very instructive, pp. 115–28.

30. ibid.

31. Mary's Note in *Poetical Works*, p. 345.

32. *Maria Gisborne and Edward E.Williams: Their Journals and Letters*, p. 53.

33. *Letters*, II, No. 518, p. 124.

34. *Mary*, No. 76, p. 82.

35. *Letters*, II, No. 519, p. 126.

36. ibid., No. 518, p. 126.

37. *Journal*, p. 125–6.

38. *The Unextinguished Hearth*, pp. 133–42.

39. *Letters*, II, No. 519, p. 127.

40. *The Unextinguished Hearth*, p. 141.

41. ibid., p. 140.

42. ibid., p. 142.

43. Medwin, *The Life of Percy Bysshe Shelley*, p. 226.

44. *Letters*, II, No. 518, p. 126.

45. ibid., No. 519, p. 128.

46. This was almost certainly what is now the first of the three 'Bixby Notebooks' kept in the Huntington Library, California. Neville Rogers, in his fine examination of the Shelley notebooks in *Shelley at Work*, 1967, has labelled it 'Bixby-Huntington I'.

47. 'Bixby Huntington I', in Rogers, op. cit., p. 222.

48. ibid., p. 224.

49. *Journal*, p. 125.

50. Bod. MS Shelley Adds. e. 12, pp. 150–1. *Letters*, II, No. 522, p. 130.

51. *Poetical Works*, p. 577.

52. *Letters*, II, No. 522, p. 130 n. 1.

53. Bod. MS Shelley Adds. e. 12, p. 63. Illustrated on back of book-jacket.

54. Bod. MS Shelley Adds. e. 6, p. 137, rev.

55. Rogers, op. cit., p. 19. It is a quote from Euripides's *Hercules Furens*. Shelley had translated the *Cyclops* of Euripides earlier during the summer, and it was published in the *Examiner* for 10 October 1819.

56. *Letters*, II, No. 535, p. 160.

57. ibid., No. 524, p. 132.

58. ibid., No. 520, p. 129.

59. *Mary*, No. 78, p. 85.

60. *Letters*, II, No. 539, p. 164.

61. *Poetical Works*, p. 362.

62. ibid., p. 346.

63. ibid., p. 347.

64. *Poetical Works*, pp. 356–7.

65. ibid., pp. 350–2.

66. ibid., pp. 355–6.

67. Mary's note in *Poetical Works*, p. 363.

68. *Letters*, II, No. 526, p. 135.

69. ibid., No. 527, p. 136 n. 1.

70. ibid., II, No. 527, p. 143.

71. *The Shelley Correspondence in the Bodleian Library*, ed. R.H.Hill, 1926, pp. 21–30.

72. *Letters*, II, No. 527, p. 147.

73. *Journal*, p. 126.

74. *Letters*, II, No. 529, p. 151.

75. ibid., No. 528, p. 150.

Chapter 23   *From the Gallery: Florence 1820*

1. *Letters*, II, No. 529, p. 151.

2. ibid., No. 531, p. 155.

3. ibid., No. 532, p. 156.

4. ibid., No. 534, p. 159.

5. ibid., No. 523 p. 158.

6. ibid., No. 530, p. 153.

7. *Mary*, No. 79, p. 87.

8. ibid., No. 78, p. 85.

9. ibid.

10. ibid., No. 80, p. 87.

11. Bod. MS Shelley Adds. e. 6, p. 136 rev.

12. A fully integrated text of the 21 stanzas was first published in a small pamphlet in 1970, *England in 1819: Church, State and Poverty* by W.J.McTaggart, under the imprint of the Keats–Shelley Memorial Association. This edition contains a full discussion of all MS variants. My quotation starts from Bod. MS. and ends with Silsbee – Harrard MS.

13. *Mary*, No. 81, p. 88.

14. ibid., No. 81, p. 89. Grylls *Claire Clairmont*, p. 113.

15. Sophia Stacey's diary has not been published, but substantial extracts are given in *Shelley and his Friends in Italy* by Helena Rossetti Angeli, 1911.

16. *Claire*, p. 116.

17. H.R.Angeli, op. cit.

18. *Prose*, p. 346.

19. ibid.

20. ibid., p. 347. I have not unfortunately seen the holograph of this entry, but I suspect that the polite lacuna is an editor's – not Shelley's.

21. ibid., p. 351.

22. ibid., p. 351.

23. ibid., p. 348.

24. *Poetical Works*, pp. 580, 583, 610.

25. *Letters*, II, No. 544, p. 167.

26. *Poetical Works*, p. 627. But I have adopted the reading from the Stacey MS of 1820.

27. *Letters*, II, No. 539, pp. 163-4.
28. ibid., No. 542, p. 165.
29. ibid., No. 539, p. 164.
30. ibid., No. 543, p. 166.
31. *Poetical Works*, pp. 574-5. I have altered the endline punctuation, which is introduced by Mrs Shelley in 1839.
32. ibid., p. 583.

Chapter 24   *The Reformer: Pisa 1820*

1. *Prose*, pp. 196-214.
2. *Claire*, p. 117.
3. ibid., pp. 116-17.
4. ibid., p. 118.
5. *Letters*, II, No. 545, p. 169.
6. *Claire*, pp. 118-19.
7. Bod. MS Shelley Adds. e. 6, pp. 172-75, rev.
8. *Claire*, pp. 119 and 124-5; H.R.Angeli, *Shelley and his Friends in Italy*, pp. 115ff.
9. *Claire*, p. 119.
10. *Mary*, No. 85, pp. 96-7.
11. ibid., p. 95.
12. *Claire*, p. 122.
13. *Mary*, No. 85, p. 96.
14. *Claire*, p. 126.
15. ibid., pp. 127-9.
16. *Journal*, p. 129.
17. *Letters*, II, No. 554, p. 176.
18. ibid., No. 556, p. 179.
19. *Mary*, No. 87, p. 101.
20. ibid., No. 90, p. 103.
21. ibid., No. 86, p. 99.
22. *Claire*, p. 134.
23. *Letters*, II, No. 554, pp. 176-7.
24. ibid., No. 555, p. 178.
25. ibid., No. 557, p. 181.
26. ibid., No. 560, p. 187.
27. ibid., n. 6.
28. ibid., No. 557, p. 180.
29. *Mary*, No. 91, p. 104.
30. *Poetical Works*, pp. 594-5.
31. ibid., p. 599.
32. *Mary*, No. 92, p. 106; and *Journal*, p. 131.
33. *Letters*, II, No. 568, p. 201.

34. *Prose*, p. 239.

35. ibid., pp. 239–40.

36. ibid., pp. 230 and 231: see also 'A Defence of Poetry', *Prose*, p. 288, where Jesus Christ is consistently treated as a 'great Reformer', but the Catholic church as a vicious imperialism.

37. *Prose*, p. 240.

38. *Letters*, II, No. 564, p. 192.

39. *Prose*, p. 241.

40. ibid., pp. 244–5.

41. ibid., p. 242.

42. ibid., p. 249.

43. ibid., p. 250.

44. ibid., p. 251.

45. ibid.

46. ibid., p. 247.

47. ibid., p. 255.

48. ibid., p. 258.

49. ibid., p. 259.

50. ibid., p. 257.

51. ibid., p. 259.

52. ibid., p. 260.

53. *Letters*, II, No. 564, p. 193.

54. *Claire*, p. 146.

55. *Letters*, II, No. 568, p. 201.

56. But this was almost undoubtedly the result of pressure put on her by Sir Timothy Shelley during the preparation of the official edition of the *Prose* (1840). It was omitted from the later editions of the 1880s and was first published in a small monograph, *A Philosophical View of Reform*, ed. T.W.Rolleston, 1920.

57. *Letters*, II, No. 563, p. 191.

58. *Poetical Works*, pp. 338ff, 571, 572, 573, 574.

59. *Poetical Works*, p. 572–3.

60. *Letters*, II, No. 563, p. 191.

61. *The Unextinguished Hearth*, p. 181.

62. ibid., p. 167–97.

63. *Letters*, II, No. 577, p. 216.

64. ibid., No. 569, p. 201.

65. ibid., No. 566, p. 196.

66. *Mary*, No. 98, p. 112.

67. *Letters*, II, No. 568, p. 200.

68. *Claire*, p. 150 and p. 150 n. 2.

69. ibid., p. 151.

70. *Journal*, p. 134.

71. *Mary*, No. 96, p. 108.

72. *Letters*, II, No. 571, p. 207.
73. *Poetical Works*, p. 369.
74. ibid., p. 365.
75. *Letters*, II, No. 571, p. 208.
76. ibid., No. 573 and 574. p. 209.
77. *Journal*, p. 135.
78. *Claire*, pp. 153-4.
79. ibid., p. 154.
80. Byron to Hoppner, 22 April 1820, *Lord Byron: Selected Prose*, 1972, pp. 349-50.
81. *Letters*, II, No. 567, pp. 198-9.
82. ibid., No. 575, p. 210.
83. Probably in Shelley's letter to Peacock, *Letters*, II, No. 576, p. 213.
84. *Claire*, p. 156.
85. *Letters*, II, No. 576, p. 213.
86. ibid., p. 214.
87. *Claire*, pp. 156-7.
88. *Letters*, II, No. 578, p. 218.
89. ibid., No. 579, p. 221.
90. ibid., No. 578, pp. 218-20.
91. ibid., No. 580, p. 223.

Chapter 25   The Moons of Pisa: 1820

1. H.R.Angeli, *Shelley and his Friends in Italy*, pp. 150-3.
2. *Letters*, II, No. 580. p. 222.
3. *Claire*, p. 168.
4. *Letters*, II, No. 582, pp. 224-8.
5. ibid., No. 582A, p. 229.
6. *Maria Gisborne and Edward E. Williams: their Journals and Letters*, F.L.Jones (ed.), Monday 28 August 1820, pp. 47-8.
7. *Poetical Works*, p. 383.
8. ibid., p. 388.
9. ibid., p. 371.
10. J.O.Fuller, *Shelley*, Ch. 16, p. 323 n. 11.
11. ibid.
12. *Poetical Works*, pp. 379-80.
13. ibid., p. 387.
14. ibid., p. 386.
15. *Letters*, II, No. 570, p. 204.
16. ibid., p. 205 n. 3.
17. ibid., No. 583, pp. 230-2.
18. Southey to Shelley in *Letters*, II, No. 583, p. 232 n. 11.
19. *Poetical Works*, p. 410.

20. *Claire*, pp. 177-8.

21. *Poetical Works*, p. 409.

22. Dowden, *The Life of Percy Bysshe Shelley*, II, p. 345.

23. *Poetical Works*, p. 410; p. 908; and Wickwar, *The Struggle for the Freedom of the Press*.

24. *Poetical Works*, p. 727.

25. ibid., p. 614.

26. ibid., p. 621.

27. ibid.

28. *Letters*, II, No. 587, pp. 235-7.

29. ibid., No. 588, p. 237.

30. Medwin, *The Life of Percy Bysshe Shelley*, pp. 259-61.

31. *Letters*, II, No. 513, p. 117.

32. ibid., II, No. 589, pp. 239-40.

33. ibid., II, No. 589, pp. 239-40.

34. *Claire*, p. 179.

35. *Journal*, p. 139.

36. Mary to Maria Gisborne, 16 October 1820, in *Studies in Philology*, LII, 1955.

37. *Letters*, II, No. 575, p. 310.

38. *Claire*, Appendix C, p. 470.

39. ibid., p. 179.

40. ibid., p. 179.

41. ibid., p. 180.

42. Medwin, op. cit., pp. 233-4.

43. H.R.Angeli, op. cit., pp. 157-8.

44. *Journal*, p. 140.

45. Mary's Note in *Poetical Works*, p. 636.

Chapter 26   The Tuscan Set: 1821

1. *Letters*, II, No. 591, p. 242.

2. *Journal*, p. 140.

3. *Poetical Works*, p. 564.

4. *Letters*, II, No. 593, p. 246.

5. Medwin, *The Life of Percy Bysshe Shelley*, pp. 267-9.

6. But I have not seen the holograph as it is one of those still restricted by the Carl H.Pforzheimer Library. It has therefore to be borne in mind that this letter may have suffered from editorial omissions. See Appendix to Chapter 18, ref. 1.

7. *Letters*, II, No. 590, p. 241.

8. ibid., No. 591, pp. 241-3.

9. ibid., No. 592, p. 245.

10. Medwin, op. cit., p. 238.

11. ibid., p. 249.

12. *Poetical Works*, pp. 623–4.

13. Medwin, op. cit., pp. 250–1.

14. *Letters*, II, No. 395, p. 249.

15. *Claire*, p. 184.

16. Medwin, op. cit., p. 169.

17. *Journal*, p. 141.

18. *Claire*, p. 187.

19. For Professor Pacchiani, see Medwin, op. cit., pp. 273–8; *Mary*, No. 101, p. 117; and *Claire*, p. 188 n. 65.

20. *Claire*, Appendix C, p. 472.

21. Marchand, *Byron: A Biography*, II, p. 844.

22. *Mary*, No. 101, p. 117.

23. *Letters*, II, No. 599, p. 254 n. 1.

24. *Mary*, No. 101, p. 118.

25. *Journal*, pp. 141–2.

26. Medwin, op. cit., p. 279.

27. *Claire*, p. 196. Medwin, op. cit., pp. 269–70.

28. *Claire*, p. 196.

29. Bod. MS Shelley Adds. e. 9.

30. Medwin, op. cit., p. 270.

31. *Claire*, p. 198.

32. *Mary*, No. 107, p. 123.

33. ibid., No. 108, p. 126.

34. *Claire*, p. 195.

35. *Mary*, No. 109, p. 127.

36. ibid., No. 109, p. 129.

37. *Letters*, II, No. 599, pp. 254–5.

38. *Poetical Work*, p. 638.

39. Manuscript Notebook 'Bixby Huntington I', given by H.B. Forman in an annotation of Medwin, op. cit., p. 281.

40. *Letters*, II, Appendix I, pp. 447–9. These Italian letter fragments were first discovered among the Bod. MSS and printed by Neville Rogers, *Shelley at Work*, 1956.

41. See Maria Viviani della Rovvia, *Vita di Una Donna; l'Emily di Shelley*, Florence, 1936.

42. ibid., p. 84.

43. ibid., pp. 87–8.

44. *Mary*, No. 109, p. 129.

45. ibid., No. 110, p. 133.

46. Medwin, op. cit., pp. 283–4.

47. *Letters*, II, No. 601, p. 256.

48. ibid.

49. ibid.

50. *Poetical Works*, p. 420.

51. *Poetical Works*, p. 423.
52. ibid., p. 427.
53. ibid., p. 417.
54. ibid., p. 428.
55. ibid., p. 415.
56. ibid., pp. 424–5.
57. ibid., p. 425.
58. ibid., p. 411.
59. ibid., p. 418.
60. ibid., p. 419.
61. *Mary*, No. 135, p. 161.
62. *Poetical Works*, pp. 419–20.
63. ibid., p. 417
64. Thornton Hunt, article in *Atlantic Monthly*, February 1863.
65. *Poetical Works*, p. 105.
66. *Letters*, II, No. 606, p. 263.
67. ibid., No. 668, p. 363.
68. ibid., No. 715, p. 434.
69. *Journal*, p. 149.
70. ibid.
71. *Claire*, p. 216.
72. *Mary*, No. 116, p. 137.
73. *Letters*, II, No. 615, p. 276.
74. ibid., No. 618, p. 280.
75. ibid., No. 592, p. 245 n. 7.
76. ibid., No. 605, p. 261.
77. *Journal*, p. 148. The title given is that of the first edition 1595; Mary used the better known 'Defence of Poesy' from which Shelley took his own title.
78. Notebook, Bod. MS Shelley Adds. e. 8, pp. 71–7.
79. *Letters*, II, No. 614, p. 275.
80. Compare 'Essay on the Devil', *Prose*, p. 267, with *Prose*, p. 290.
81. *Letters*, II, No. 613, p. 273.
82 *Prose*, p. 280.
83. ibid., pp. 282–3.
84. ibid., p. 286.
85. ibid., p. 291.
86. ibid., p. 295.
87. ibid., p. 293.
88. *Letters*, II, No. 615, pp. 276.
89. ibid., No. 617, p. 278–9.
90. *Maria Gisborne and Edward E. Williams: their Journals and Letters*, F. L. Jones (ed.), pp. 70–1.
91. Mary's Note in *Poetical Works*, p. 663.

92. *Gisborne*, pp. 70–1.
93. *Letters*, II, No. 622, p. 285.
94. ibid., No. 623, p. 286.
95. ibid., No. 624, p. 288.
96. ibid., No. 621, p. 284.
97. See *Keats: the Critical Heritage*, ed. G.M.Matthews, 1971.
98. *Letters*, II, No. 597, p. 252.
99. *Lord Byron: Letters and Journals*, v, p. 266.
100. *Journal*, p. 152.
101. *Letters*, II, No. 620, pp. 281–2, n. 2.
102. ibid., No. 608, p. 264.
103. *Claire*, p. 223.
104. *Letters*, II, No. 624, p. 288.
105. *Claire*, p. 227.
106. Bod. MS Shelley Adds. e. 8, pp. 133–7 rev.
107. William Hazlitt in *Edinburgh Review*, July 1824.
108. *Poetical Works*, p. 653.
109. Bod. MS Shelley Adds. e. 8, pp. 42–3.
110. *Journal*, p. 153.
111. *Letters*, II, No. 626, p. 292.
112. *Poetical Works*, p. 656.
113. *Letters*, II, No. 626, p. 292.
114. *Mary*, No. 123, p. 144.
115. *Poetical Works*, p. 663.
116. Mary's Note in *Poetical Works*, p. 664.
117. *Poetical Works*, pp. 642–3.

Chapter 27   The Colony: 1821

1. *Letters*, II, No. 625, p. 291.
2. ibid., No. 626, p. 292.
3. *Mary*, No. 126, p. 145.
4. *Letters*, II, No. 630, p. 297.
5. *Journal*, p. 155.
6. *Letters*, II, No. 631, p. 297.
7. *Poetical Works*, p. 721.
8. ibid., p. 722.
9. *Letters*, II, No. 622, p. 348 n. 1.
10. *Verse and Prose from the Manuscripts of Percy Bysshe Shelley*, ed. by Shelley-Rolls and Ingpen, 1934, pp. 37–43.
11. *Letters*, II, No. 641, pp. 308–9.
12. *Poetical Works*, p. 433.
13. ibid., p. 435.

14. ibid., p. 441.

15. ibid., p. 663.

16. ibid., p. 444.

17. *Letters*, II, No. 639, p. 306.

18. ibid., No. 642, p. 310.

19. *Poetical Works*, p. 444.

20. Printed by Lewis M. Schwartz in 'Two New Reviews of "Queen Mab"' in *Keats-Shelley Journal*, 1970.

21. *The Unextinguished Hearth*, pp. 45–61.

22. *Letters*, II, No. 632, p. 298.

23. ibid., No. 633, pp. 300–1.

24. ibid., No. 634, p. 302.

25. ibid., Nos. 662 and 664.

26. *Claire*, p. 242.

27. ibid., p. 243.

28. ibid.

29. *Letters*, II, No. 650, p. 316.

30. *Journal*, p. 159.

31. *Claire*, p. 245.

32. *Letters*, II, No. 649, p. 315.

33. ibid., No. 647, p. 314.

34. ibid., No. 649, p. 316.

35. ibid., No. 650, p. 316.

36. ibid., No. 654, p. 331.

37. ibid., No. 651, p. 324.

38. ibid., No. 650, p. 317.

39. ibid., No. 656, p. 336.

40. ibid., No. 651, p. 323.

41. ibid., No. 609, p. 267

42. ibid., No. 650, p. 319.

43. *Mary*, No. 128, p. 149.

44. *Letters*, II, Nos. 655 and 656, pp. 332–9.

45. ibid., No. 661, p. 347.

46. ibid., No. 652, pp. 325–7.

47. ibid., No. 651, p. 323.

48. ibid., No. 651, p. 321.

49. ibid., No. 656, p. 335.

50. ibid., No. 651, p. 324.

51. ibid., No. 656, pp. 333–5.

52. *Letters*, I, No. 265, pp. 401–3.

53. *Letters*, II, No. 656, p. 339.

54. ibid., No. 673, p. 368 n. 1.

55. *Prose*, p. 274.

56. *Poetical Works*, p. 586.

57. *Claire*, p. 247.

58. *Letters*, II, No. 659, p. 343.

59. ibid., No. 660, p. 344.

60. ibid., No. 660, pp. 345–6 n. 3.

61. ibid., No. 663, p. 353.

62. ibid., No. 663, pp. 353–4.

63. ibid., No. 665, p. 356.

64. ibid., No. 661, p. 347.

65. ibid., No. 662, p. 351 n. 6.

66. ibid., No. 662, p. 350.

67. *Journal*, p. 160.

68. *Claire*, p. 248.

69. Edward Williams in his 'Journal' printed in *Maria Gisborne and Edward E. Williams: their Journals and Letters*, F. L. Jones (ed.), p. 103.

70. Claire, p. 249.

71. *Letters*, II, No. 665, p. 356.

72. *Claire*, pp. 249–51.

73. *Poetical Works*, p. 447.

74. ibid., p. 468.

75. ibid., p. 472.

76. ibid., p. 479.

77. ibid., p. 446.

78. ibid., p. 448.

79. *Poetical Works of Percy Bysshe Shelley*, Vol. IV, ed. H. B. Forman, 1892.

80. *Mary*, No. 129, p. 150.

81. *Letters*, II, No. 666, p. 358.

82. ibid., No. 668, pp. 362–3.

83. ibid., No. 667, pp. 361–2.

84. ibid., No. 667, p. 361 n. 5.

85. *Poetical Works*, p. 654. I have adopted the MS reading in Shelley's notebook, Bod. MS Shelley Adds. e. 9, p. 346–7 rev., for stanza 3, line 5. Shelley wrote the word 'East', and then uncertainly deleted it, with a single light stroke. But this word explains the context of the poem.

Chapter 28   The Byron Brigade: 1822

1. *Claire*, p. 253.

2. Williams in *Maria Gisborne and Edward E. Williams: Their Journals and Letters*, F. L. Jones (ed.), pp. 109–10. Henceforth given as Williams.

3. ibid., p. 116.

4. Medwin, *The Life of Percy Bysshe Shelley*, p. 329.

5. ibid.

6. *Letters*, II, No. 676, p. 374.

7. *Mary*, No. 129, p. 150.

8. ibid., No. 130, p. 153.

9. Williams, op. cit., p. 117.

10. *Letters*, II, No. 673, p. 368.

11. *Poetical Works*, p. 656

12. Williams, op. cit., p. 118.

13. Edward John Trelawny, 'Recollections of the Last Days of Shelley and Byron', in Humbert Wolfe, *The Life of Percy Bysshe Shelley*, II, p. 180.

14. Williams, op. cit., p. 120.

15. Medwin, op. cit., p. 335.

16. ibid., p. 331.

17. Tom Medwin, *Conversations with Lord Byron*, 1824; ed. E.J.Lovell, Jr, 1966, p. 80.

18. ibid., p. 38.

19. Williams, op. cit., p. 119.

20. *Letters*, II, No. 672, pp. 367–8, and 674.

21. ibid., No. 672, pp. 367–8.

22. ibid., No. 674, p. 371.

23. ibid., p. 370.

24. Williams, op. cit., p. 123.

25. *Letters*, II, No. 676, p. 373. Williams, op. cit., p. 123.

26. *Letters*, II, No. 677, p. 376.

27. *Poetical Works*, p. 753.

28. *Letters*, II, No. 697, p. 407.

29. *Poetical Works*, p. 758.

30. ibid., p. 767.

31. *Letters*, II, No. 697, p. 406.

32. ibid., No. 692, p. 401.

33. Medwin, op. cit., p. 325, who says it was £1,400; but there is no real evidence that such a large sum was involved. Medwin was inclined to muddle these things.

34. *Letters*, II, No. 678, p. 379.

35. Williams, op. cit., p. 126.

36. *Journal*, p. 165.

37. Trelawny, op. cit., p. 173.

38. ibid., p. 172.

39. ibid., p. 187.

40. Williams, op. cit., p. 125.

41. *Mary*, No. 132, pp. 155–6.

42. ibid.

43. Williams, op. cit., p. 131.

44. *Mary*, No. 132, p. 156.

45. *Letters*, II, No. 677, p. 375.

46. ibid., No. 683, pp. 387–8.
47. *Letters*, II, No. 681, pp. 384–6; and compare *Poetical Works*, p. 644.
48. Williams, op. cit., p. 127.
49. ibid., p. 128 n. 87.
50. *Poetical Works*, p. 671.
51. *Letters*, II, No. 678, p. 378; and 692, p. 400.
52. ibid., No. 682, p. 386.
53. *Claire*, p. 274.
54. BM. Ashley 4752.
55. *Mary*, No. 133, p. 157.
56. *Claire*, pp. 279–84.
57. Williams, op. cit., p. 133.
58. *Letters*, II, No. 687, pp. 391–2.
59. ibid., No. 689, p. 394.
60. ibid.
61. Williams, op. cit., p. 135.
62. ibid.
63. *Poetical Works*, p. 486.
64. *Letters*, II, No. 689, p. 394.
65. *Poetical Works*, pp. 506–7.
66. *Mary*, No. 136, p. 162.
67. ibid.
68. Captain Hay reported in Williams, op. cit., p. 138.
69. Williams, op. cit., p. 138.
70. *Mary*, No. 136, p. 162.
71. Evidence of the eyewitness Mr Crawfurd in Williams, op. cit., p. 139.
72. Williams, op. cit., p. 137.
73. ibid., p. 138.
74. *Letters*, II, Appendix 5, No. 2.
75. *Mary*, No. 121, p. 141.
76. *Letters*, II, No. 691, p. 399.
77. ibid., No. 695, p. 403.
78. ibid., No. 692, p. 400.
79. ibid.
80. ibid., No. 696, p. 404.
81. Williams, op. cit., p. 144.
82. ibid.
83. *Letters*, II, No. 697, pp. 408–9.
84. ibid., No. 698, p. 411.
85. ibid., No. 699, p. 412.
86. ibid., No. 696, p. 405.

Chapter 29   The Gulf of Spezia

1. Williams, in *Maria Gisborne and Edward E.Williams: their Journals and Letters*, p. 145.
2. ibid.
3. *Letters*, II, No. 701, p. 414.
4. Williams, op. cit., p. 145.
5. *Mary*, No. 139, p. 169.
6. *Letters*, II, No. 701, p. 413.
7. Williams, op. cit., p. 146.
8. ibid.
9. *Letters*, II, No. 703, p. 416.
10. ibid.
11. Williams, op. cit., p. 149.
12. ibid., p. 147.
13. ibid.
14. *Letters*, II, No. 705, p. 419.
15. Williams, op. cit., p. 149.
16. *Letters*, II, No. 707, p. 421.
17. *Mary*, No. 139, p. 171.
18. *Letters*, II, No. 708, p. 423.
19. ibid., p. 425 n. 3.
20. *Letters*, II, No. 711, p. 430.
21. ibid., No. 709, p. 427.
22. Bod. MS Shelley Adds. C. 4, F5.
23. *Shelley's 'The Triumph of Life'*, ed. Donald H.Reiman, University of Illinois Press, 1965, p. 160; compare *Poetical Works*, pp. 511–12.
24. Reiman, op. cit., pp. 138–40; compare *Poetical Works*, p. 508.
25. Reiman, op. cit., pp. 150–8; compare *Poetical Works*, pp. 510–11. Third and ninth stanzas from *Posthumous Poems* (1824).
26. Reiman, op. cit., p. 164; compare *Poetical Works*, p. 512.
27. Reiman, op. cit., pp. 191–2; compare *Poetical Works*, p. 517.
28. Reiman, op. cit., pp. 206–10; compare *Poetical Works*, pp. 519–20. Punctuation of last thirteen lines from *Posthumous Poems* (1824).
29. Bod. MS Shelley Adds. c. 4. F5, p. 52. This reading was first identified by G.M. Matthews in 'The Triumph of Life: A New Text', *Studia Neophilologica*, XXXII, 1960.
30. *Letters*, II, No. 710, p. 429.
31. *Mary*, No. 144, p. 179.
32. ibid., p. 179.
33. *Letters*, II, No. 715, p. 434.
34. *Mary*, No. 144, p. 181.
35. *Letters*, II, No. 714, p. 433.
36. ibid., No. 715, pp. 435–6.
37. ibid., No. 715A, p. 437.

38. Bod. MS Shelley Adds. C. 4. Folder 35–6. *Poetical Works*, p. 674.

39. *Mary*, No. 144, p. 181.

40. Bod. MS Shelley Adds. e. 18.

41. ibid., p. 118 rev.

42. ibid., p. 160 rev.

43. Williams, op. cit., p. 155.

44. ibid.

45. *Mary*, No. 144, p. 180.

46. *Letters*, II, No. 718, p. 440.

47. *Mary*, No. 144, p. 180.

48. Williams, op. cit., p. 155.

49. MS in Keats Shelley Memorial Association Collection, Rome. *Letters*, II, No. 719, pp. 442–3.

50. Williams, op. cit., p. 156.

51. *Mary*, No. 140, p. 172.

52. *Letters*, II, No. 720, p. 444.

53. Williams, op. cit., p. 162.

54. *Letters*, II, No. 720, p. 444.

55. ibid., No. 721, p. 445.

56. A report given to Taaffe and retold in conversation: *The Journal of Clarissa Trant* (1925), pp. 198–9, dating from 1826. There were, inevitably, numerous subsequent versions of the sinking which already had achieved a kind of mythic significance even before it occurred. The variations are discussed in the letters of Mary, Trelawny, Captain Roberts and in Dowden, *The Life of Percy Bysshe Shelley*, II, pp. 534–6. The main point of contention lies in whether the damage to the mainmasts and stern timbers was caused by manhandling during the salvage operation or by collision with a *felucca*. But Mary's original letter to Maria Gisborne of 15 August 1822 underwrites Taaffe's account: 'A Fishing boat saw them go down – It was about 4 in the afternoon – they saw the boy at mast head when baffling winds struck the sails they had looked away a moment & looking again the boat was gone.'

Index

meets Gisbornes, 423–4; rents Casa Bertini in Bagni di Lucca, 424; and expatriate life in Livorno, 424; drafts 'Tasso' scenes, 425; and reads 'Cenci Manuscript', 425–6; at Casa Bertini, 426–30; his love for waters of Italy, 427, 460; and landscapes and sky, 427–8, 443; goes riding to Lucca, 429–30; his translation of Plato's *Symposium*, 430–8; goes to Venice with Claire, 439–41; and meets Byron again, 441–2; invited to stay at Este, 442–4; begins work on *Prometheus Unbound*, 444; illness and death of Clara, 444–7; his views on Venice, 448–9; and writes 'Julian and Maddalo', 449–57; journeys south, 458–60; drafts 'The Colosseum' in Rome, 460–1; takes lodgings at 250 Riviera di Chiaia in Naples, 461–2; his illness, 462, 463, 464 & n.; and sightseeing, 462–3, 477; his period of crisis, 463–5, 474–5; Elena affair, 465–74, 481–4; renewed interest in politics, 475–6; and writes 'Lines Written During Castlereagh Administration', 476–7; and letter to Peacock on Neapolitan tombs, 477–8; his expedition to Paestum, 478–9; and leaves Naples, 479–80; in Rome (1819), 485–518: takes rooms at Palazzo Verospi, 485; and sightseeing, 485; visits Marianna Dioniga's salon, 486; and moonlight walks, 487; impressed by reliefs in Forum, 488, 503–4; and Baths of Caracalla, 489–90; writes *Prometheus Unbound* Acts I–III, 490–508; and its publication, 509–10 & n.; friendship with Aemilia Curran, 510–11; attacked by stranger in Post Office, 511; moves to Via Sestina, 511–12; Aemilia's portrait of, 512 & n., 516–17; his interest in Renaissance Rome, 512–13; and begins writing *The Cenci*, 513, 514–17; his illness, 513, 514; and illness and death of William, 517–18; leaves Rome, 518; and unhappy summer at Monte Nero, 519–20; uses tower of Villa Valsovano as his study, 521, 523, 528, 529; and continues work on *The Cenci*, 521, 523–5; his physical and spiritual recuperation, 521–3; and Mary's pregnancy, 526, 538–9, 550, 551, 556, 558; backs Reveley's

steamboat project, 527, 550; dedicates *The Cenci* to Hunt, 528; his reaction to news of Peterloo, 529–32; and writes *The Mask of Anarchy*, 532–40; moves to Florence, 541–2; visits Uffizi Gallery, 542; writes series of political poems, 542; and his open letter to *Examiner*, 542; and J. T. Coleridge's personal attack in *Quarterly* on, 543–6; writes 'Ode to the West Wind', 546–50; his business activities, 550–1; and writes *Peter Bell the Third*, 551–6; and his open letter to *Examiner* on Carlile, 556–8; birth of son Percy Florence, 560; and 'calderonizing' game, 560–1; Mary against his going to England, 562; writes ballad about mother and child, 562–4; his friendship with Sophia Stacey, 564–5, 568; and 'Notes on Sculpture in Florence', 565–8; begins writing *A Philosophical View of Reform*, 569; and his sonnet 'England in 1819', 569–70; his rheumatism, 571, 572; invites Tom Medwin to Italy, 572–3; moves to Pisa (1820), 572, 573–5; his friendship with Masons, 575, 576–7; and agricultural notes, 576; and his friendship with Andrea Vaccà, 577; ill again, 578; Elena affair, 578–9; and brush with Colonel Finch, 579; and letter to Sophia Stacey, 579; Cato Street conspiracy and, 580; and news of Republican insurrection in Madrid, 581; aimless violence expressed in his writing, 581–3; and his nervous attacks, 583; finishes *A Philosophical View of Reform*, 583–93; and his 'Popular Songs' not published, 593–4, 596; publication of *The Cenci*, 595; and Ollier contracts to publish *Prometheus* and collection of short poems, 595; Elena dies and Paolo's blackmail, 596; moves to Casa Ricci, Livorno, and consults del Rosso, 596–7; and Godwin's demands for money, 597, 598; Claire's anxiety over Allegra and, 598–9; and Byron's letter, 599; writes 'The Skylark' and 'The Cloud', 599–600; and Claire leaves, 600–1; invites Keats to Italy, 601; and news of insurrection in Naples, 601; moves to Casa Prinni in Bagni di Pisa, 601, 602–3; writes to Godwin about money, 603–4;

Index